REEDS

PRACTICAL Boat Owner®
BRITAIN'S BIGGEST SELLING YACHTING MAGAZINE   SAIL AND POWER

SMALL CRAFT ALMANAC 2006

EDITORS

Neville Featherstone & Peter Lambie

THE UNITED KINGDOM & IRELAND AND DENMARK TO GIBRALTAR

REEDS
Practical Boat Owner
BRITAIN'S BIGGEST SELLING YACHTING MAGAZINE SAIL AND POWER

SMALL CRAFT ALMANAC 2006

Editors: Neville Featherstone & Peter Lambie

The Editors would like to thank the many official bodies who have kindly provided essential information in the preparation of this Almanac. They include the UK Hydrographic Office, Trinity House, Northern Lighthouse Board, Irish Lights, HM Nautical Almanac Office, HM Stationery Office, HM Customs, Meteorological Office and the Maritime and Coastguard Agency.

Information from the Admiralty List of Lights, Admiralty Tide Tables and the Admiralty List of Radio Signals is reproduced with the permission of the UK Hydrographic Office and the Controller of HMSO. Extracts from the following are published by permission of the Controller of HM Stationery Office: International Code of Signals, 1969; Meteorological Office Weather Services for Shipping. Phases of the Moon and Sun/Moon rising and setting times are derived from the current editions of the Channel and Eastern Almanacs, and are included by permission of HM Nautical Almanac Office. UK and Foreign tidal predictions are supplied by the UK Hydrographic Office, Taunton TA1 2DN. Acknowledgment is also made to the following authorities for permission to use tidal predictions stated: Royal Danish Administration of Navigation and Hydrography, Farvandsvæsnet: Esbjerg. SHOM, France: Dunkerque, Dieppe, Le Havre, Cherbourg, St Malo, Brest, Pointe de Grave, Authorisation (No. 249/2005). Rijkswaterstaat, The Netherlands: Vlissingen, and Hoek van Holland. BSH, Hamburg and Rostock: Helgoland, Wilhelmshaven and Cuxhaven (BSH 8095·02/99-Z1102). Marina Institute Hidrográfico, Portugal: Lisboa, Authorisation (No. 3/2005). **Warning:** The UK Hydrographic Office has not verified the reproduced data and does not accept any liability for the accuracy of reproduction or any modifications made thereafter.

Corrections Any necessary corrections will be published on the website www.reedsalmanac.co.uk. Data in this almanac is corrected up to Edition 24/2005of the *Admiralty Notices to Mariners*.

Important note The information, charts, maps and diagrams in this Almanac should not be relied on for navigational purposes as this Almanac is intended as an aid to navigation only. The information contained within should be used in conjunction with official hydrographic data. Whilst every care has been taken in its compilation, this Almanac may contain inaccuracies and is no substitute for the relevant official hydrographic charts and data, which should always be consulted in advance of, and whilst, navigating in the area.

The publishers, editors and their agents accept no responsibility for any errors or omissions, or for any accidents or mishaps which may arise from its use.

Before using any waypoint or coordinate listed in this Almanac it must first be plotted on an appropriate official hydrographic chart to check its usefulness, accuracy and appropriateness for the prevailing weather and tidal conditions.

The decision to use and rely on any of the data in this Almanac is entirely at the discretion of, and is the sole responsibility of, the Captain of the vessel employing it.

Correspondence Letters on nautical matters should be addressed to: The Editor, Reeds PBO Small Craft Almanac, 38 Soho Square, London W1D 3HB.

Practical Boat Owner is published monthly by IPC Magazines Ltd, Kings Reach Tower, Stamford Street, London SE1 9LS. For subscription enquiries and overseas orders call 0845 676 7778 (fax: 01444 445599).

Almanac manager: Chris Stevens
Cartography & production: Jamie Russell, Chris Stevens

Adlard Coles Nautical
38 Soho Square, London W1D 3HB
Tel: +44 (0)207 758 0200 Fax: +44 (0)207 758 0222
www.reedsalmanac.co.uk

FOREWORD

This handy-size almanac is now in its 18th year and is more popular than ever with sailors and motorboaters alike. Together with up to date charts, pilot book and weather forecast for the area you are cruising, this one book provides all the information you need for successful passage planning.

As a quick reference to lights and shapes, how to send a distress call, flag signals and the meanings of buoys, the almanac is invaluable; make sure you always have it onboard.

For most skippers, the primary use of the almanac is, of course, the tide tables. This year, the tidal graphs have been redrawn, and the typeface of the tables is new, to make them even easier to read. Don't miss the tidal atlases. They are so essential for passage planning, and we have taken care to make them large enough to be user-friendly – no squinting or magnifying glass required.

As you flick though the almanac you will be amazed at how much information we've packed into its pages. There's a form on which to take down the shipping forecast, a simple guide to working out tidal heights, first aid advice, conversion tables, and much more.

Navigation marks, light characteristics, VHF channels for harbours and other important factors can be changed at any time. Please make sure you keep your almanac up to date by checking regularly on our free internet update service, at www.reedsalmanac.co.uk

We hope you find this year's edition a little brighter and more user friendly, thanks to the editors and designers at Reeds.

Wishing you happy cruising in 2006

Sarah Norbury

Sarah Norbury
Editor
Practical Boat Owner

CONTENTS

ABBREVIATIONS

AC, ACA	Admiralty chart, chart agent	Long	Longitude
AC, ⅅ	Shore power (electrical)	LT	Local time
ACN	Adlard Coles Nautical	Lt(s)	Light(s)
Al	Alternating lt	Lt F	Light float
ALL	Admiralty list of lights	Lt Ho	Lighthouse
ALRS	Admiralty list of radio signals	Lt V	Light vessel
ASD	Admiralty sailing directions (Pilot)	LW	Low water
ATT	Admiralty tide tables	M	Nautical mile(s)
ATT	Atterisage (landfall/SWM) buoy	m	Metre(s)
Bcn, Bn	Beacon	Météo	Météorologie/weather
Bkwtr	Breakwater	MF	Medium frequency
BST	British summer time (DST)	MHWN	Mean HW neaps
CD	Chart datum	MHWS	Mean HW springs
Cf	Compare, cross-refer to	MHz	Megahertz
CG	Coastguard	MLWN	Mean LW neaps
Ch	Channel (VHF)	MLWS	Mean LW springs
chan.	Channel (navigational)	MMSI	Maritime mobile service identity
CROSS	Centre régional opérationnel de	Mo	Morse
	surveillance et sauvetage (MRCC)	MRCC	Maritime rescue co-ordination
CRS	Coast radio station(s)		centre
DF	Direction finding	MRSC	Maritime rescue sub-centre
Dia	Diaphone (fog signal)	MSI	Maritime safety information
Dir Lt	Directional light	N	North
DSC	Digital selective calling	NCM	North cardinal mark (buoy/bcn)
DST	Daylight saving time	Oc	Occulting light
DZ	Danger zone (buoy)	PHM	Port-hand mark (buoy/bcn)
E	East	Pt(e), (a)	Point(e), Punta
ECM	East cardinal mark (buoy/beacon)	Q	Quick flashing
ED	European datum	R	Red. River
EPIRB	Emergency position indicating	Ra	Coast radar station
	radio beacon	Racon	Radar transponder beacon
F	Fixed light. Beaufort force	RCC	Rescue coordination centre
FFL	Fixed and flashing lt	RG	Emergency RDF station
Fl	Flashing light	R/T	Radiotelephony
FM	Frequency modulation	S	South
FV	Fishing vessel	s	second(s) of time
G	Green. Gravel	SAR	Search and rescue
GMDSS	Global maritime distress and	SCM	South cardinal mark (buoy/bcn)
	safety system	SHM	Starboard-hand mark (buoy/bcn)
H, Hrs, h	Hour(s)	Sig Stn	Signal station
H24	Continuous	SMS	Short message service (texting)
Hbr	Harbour	SNSM	Société nationale de sauvetage
Hd	Head, headland		en mer (French LB service)
HF	High frequency	SOG	Speed over the ground
HJ	Day service, sunrise to sunset	SOLAS	Safety of life at sea
ht	Height	SSB	Single sideband (radio)
HW	High water	SRR	SAR region
HX	No fixed hours	Stn	Station
Hz	Hertz	SWM	Safe water mark, landfall buoy
IALA	Int'l association of lt ho authorities	Tfc	Traffic
IDM	Isolated danger mark (buoy/bcn)	TSS	Traffic separation scheme
IMO	Int'l maritime organisation	UT	Universal time
Inmarsat	Int'l maritime satellite system	VHF	Very high frequency
IPTS	Int'l port traffic signals	VNF	Voie navigable de France (canals)
Is, I	Island, Islet	VTS	Vessel traffic service
Iso	Isophase light	W	West. White
ITZ	Inshore traffic zone	WCM	West cardinal mark (buoy/bcn)
Kn	Knot(s)	WGS	World geodetic system (datum)
Lanby	Large automatic navigational buoy	WIP	Work in progress
Lat	Latitude	WPT	Waypoint
LB	Lifeboat	Y	Yellow, orange, amber
Ldg	Leading (lt)		

GENERAL VOCABULARY. See also weather vocabulary in Chapter 2

ENGLISH	GERMAN	FRENCH	SPANISH	DUTCH
ASHORE				
Ashore	An Land	A terre	A tierra	Aan land
Airport	Flughafen	Aéroport	Aeropuerto	Vliegveld
Bank	Bank	Banque	Banco	Bank
Boathoist	Bootskran	Travelift	Travelift	Botenlift
Boatyard	Bootswerft	Chantier naval	Astilleros	Jachtwerf
Bureau de change	Wechselstelle	Bureau de change	Cambio	Geldwisselkantoor
Bus	Bus	Autobus	Autobús	Bus
Chandlery	Yachtausrüster	Shipchandler	Efectos navales	Scheepswinkel
Chemist	Apotheke	Pharmacie	Farmacia	Apotheek
Dentist	Zahnarzt	Dentiste	Dentista	Tandarts
Doctor	Arzt	Médecin	Médico	Dokter
Engineer	Motorenservice	Ingénieur/mécanique	Mecánico	Ingenieur
Ferry	Fähre	Ferry/transbordeur	Ferry	Veer/Pont
Garage	Autowerkstatt	Station service	Garage	Garage
Harbour	Hafen	Port	Puerto	Haven
Hospital	Krankenhaus	Hôpital	Hospital	Ziekenhuis
Mast crane	Mastenkran	Grue	Grúa	Masten kraan
Post office	Postamt	Bureau de poste/PTT	Correos	Postkantoor
Railway station	Bahnhof	Gare de chemin de fer	Estación de ferrocanil	Station
Sailmaker	Segelmacher	Voilier	Velero	Zeilmaker
Shops	Geschäfte	Boutiques	Tiendas	Winkels
Slip	Slip	Cale	Varadero	Helling
Supermarket	Supermarkt	Supermarché	Supermercado	Supermarkt
Taxi	Taxi	Taxi	Taxis	Taxi
Village	Ort	Village	Pueblo	Dorp
Yacht club	Yachtclub	Club nautique	Club náutico	Jacht club
NAVIGATION				
Abeam	Querab	A côté	Por el través	Naast
Ahead	Voraus	Avant	Avante	Voor
Astern	Achteraus	Arrière	Atrás	Achter
Bearing	Peilung	Cap	Maración	Peiling
Buoy	Tonne	Bouée	Boya	Boei
Binoculars	Fernglas	Jumelles	Prismáticos	Verrekijker
Channel	Kanal	Chenal	Canal	Kanaal
Chart	Seekarte	Carte	Carta náutica	Zeekaart
Compass	Kompass	Compas	Compás	Kompas
Compass course	Kompass Kurs	Cap du compas	Rumbo de aguja	Kompas koers
Current	Strömung	Courant	Coriente	Stroom
Dead reckoning	Koppelnavigation	Estime	Estimación	Gegist bestek
Degree	Grad	Degré	Grado	Graden
Deviation	Deviation	Déviation	Desvio	Deviatie
Distance	Entfernung	Distance	Distancia	Afstand
Downstream	Flußabwärts	En aval	Río abajo	Stroom afwaards
East	Ost	Est	Este	Oost
Ebb	Ebbe	Jusant	Marea menguante	Eb
Echosounder	Echolot	Sondeur	Sonda	Dieptemeter
Estimated position	Gegißte Position	Point estimé	Posición estimado	Gegiste positie
Fathom	Faden	Une brasse	Braza	Vadem
Feet	Fuß	Pieds	Pie	Voet
Flood	Flut	Flot	Flujo de marea	Vloed
Handbearing compass	Handpeilkompass	Compas de relèvement	Compás de marcaciones	Handpeil kompas

ENGLISH	GERMAN	FRENCH	SPANISH	DUTCH
Harbour guide	Hafenhandbuch	Guide du port	Guia del Puerto	Havengids
High water	Hochwasser	Peine mer	Altamer	Hoog water
Latitude	Geographische Breite	Latitude	Latitud	Breedte
Leading lights	Feuer in Linie	Alignement	Luz de enfilación	Geleide lichten
Leeway	Abdrift	Dérive	Hacia sotavento	Drift
Lighthouse	Leuchtturm	Phare	Faro	Vuurtoren
List of lights	Leuchtfeuer Verzeichnis	Liste des feux	Listude de Luces	Lichtenlijst
Log	Logge	Loch	Corredera	Log
Longitude	Geographische Länge	Longitude	Longitud	Lengte
Low water	Niedrigwasser	Basse mer	Bajamar	Laag water
Metre	Meter	Mètre	Metro	Meter
Minute	Minute	Minute	Minuto	Minuut
Nautical almanac	Nautischer Almanach	Almanach nautique	Almanaque náutico	Almanak
Nautical mile	Seemeile	Mille nautique	Milla marina	Zeemijl
Neap tide	Nipptide	Morte-eau	Marea muerta	Dood tij
North	Nord	Nord	Norte	Noord
Pilot	Lotse	Pilote	Práctico	Loods/Gids
Pilotage book	Handbuch	Instructions nautiques	Derrotero	Vaarwijzer
RDF	Funkpeiler	Radio gonio	Radio-gonió	Radio richtingzoeker
Radar	Radar	Radar	Radar	Radar
Radio receiver	Radio, Empfänger	Récepteur radio	Receptor de radio	Radio ontvanger
Radio transmitter	Sender	Emetteur radio	Radio-transmisor	Radio zender
River outlet	Flußmündung	Embouchure	Embocadura	Riviermond
South	Süd	Sud	Sud, Sur	Zuid
Spring tide	Springtide	Vive-eau	Marea viva	Springtij/ springvloed
Tide	Tide, Gezeit	Marée	Marea	Getijde
Tide tables	Tidenkalender	Annuaire des marées	Anuario de mareas	Getijdetafel
True course	Wahrer Kurs	Vrai cap	Rumbo	Ware Koers
Upstream	Flußaufwärts	En amont	Río arriba	Stroom opwaards
VHF	UKW	VHF	VHF	Marifoon
Variation	Mißweisung	Variation	Variación	Variatie
Waypoint	Wegpunkt	Point de rapport	Waypoint	Waypoint/Route punt
West	West	Ouest	Oeste	West

OFFICIALDOM

ENGLISH	GERMAN	FRENCH	SPANISH	DUTCH
Certificate of registry	Schiffszertifikat	Acte de franchisation	Doc de matrícuia	Zeebrief
Check in	Einklarieren	Enregistrement	Registrar	Check-in
Customs	Zoll	Douanes	Aduana	Douane
Declare	Verzollen	Déclarer	Declarar	Aangeven
Harbour master	Hafenmeister	Capitaine du port	Capitán del puerto	Havenmeester
Insurance	Versicherung	Assurance	Seguro	Verzekering
Insurance certificate	Versicherungspolice	Certificat d'assurance	Certificado deseguro	Verzekeringsbewijs
Passport	Paß	Passeport	Pasaporte	Paspoort
Police	Polizei	Police	Policía	Politie
Pratique	Verkehrserlaubnis	Pratique	Prático	Verlof tot ontscheping
Prohibited area	Sperrgebiet	Zone interdite	Zona de prohibida	Verboden gebied
Register	Register	Liste de passagers	Lista de tripulantes/rol	Register
Ship's log	Logbuch	Livre de bord	Cuaderno de bitácora	Logboek
Ship's papers	Schiffspapiere	Papiers de bateau	Documentos del barco	Scheepspapieren
Surveyor	Gutachter	Expert maritime	Inspector	Opzichter

CHAPTER 1 - NAVIGATION

CONTENTS

AREA 1 South West England - *Isles of Scilly to Anvil Point*

SELECTED LIGHTS, BUOYS & WAYPOINTS

Positions are referenced to WGS84

ISLES OF SCILLY

Bishop Rock ☆ Fl (2) 15s 44m **24M**; part obsc 204°-211°, obsc 211°-233° and 236°-259°; Gy ○ twr with helo platform; *Horn Mo (N) 90s; Racon T, 18M, 254°-215°*; 49°52'·37N 06°26'·74W.

Peninnis Hd ☆ Fl 20s 36m **17M**; 231°-117° but part obsc 048°-083° within 5M; W ○ twr on B frame, B cupola; 49°54'·28N 06°18'·22W.

Spanish Ledge ↨ Q (3) 10s; *Bell;* 49°53'·94N 06°18'·86W.

N Bartholomew ⚓ Fl R 5s; 49°54'·49N 06°19'·99W.

Spencers Ledge ↨ Q (6) + L Fl 15s; 49°54'·78N 06°22'·06W.

Steeple Rock ↨ Q (9) 15s; 49°55'·46N 06°24'·24W.

Round Island☆ Fl 10s 55m **18M**, shown during periods of reduced vis only; 021°-288°; *Horn (4) 60s; Racon M, 10M;* 49°58'·74N 06°19'·40W.

SCILLY TO LAND'S END

Seven Stones ⚓ Fl (3) 30s 12m **25M**; H24; *Horn (3) 60s; Racon O, 15M;* 50°03'·62N 06°04'·34W.

Wolf Rock ☆ Fl 15s 34m **16M**; H24; *Horn 30s; Racon T, 10M;* 49°56'·72N 05°48'·57W.

Longships ☆ Iso WR 10s 35m **W16M, R15**/13M; R189°-208°, R (unintens) 208°-307°, R307°-327°, W327°- 189°; Gy ○ twr with helicopter platform; *Horn 10s;* 50°04'·01N 05°44'·81W.

Runnel Stone ↨ Q (6) + L Fl 15s; *Whis;* 50°01'·19N 05°40'·36W.

Tater-du ☆ Fl (3) 15s 34m **20M**; 241°-074°; W ○ twr 50°03'·14N 05°34'·68W. Same twr FR 31m 13M, 060°-074° over Runnel Stone and in places 074°-077° within 4M; *Horn (2) 30s.*

NEWLYN and PENZANCE

S Pier ↙ Fl 5s 10m 9M; W ○ twr; 253°-336°; 50°06'·19N 05°32'·57W.

N Pier ↙ F WG 4m 2M; 238°-G-248°, W over hbr; 50°06'·19N 05°32'·62W.

Penzance S Pier ↙ Fl WR 5s 11m **W17M**, R12M; 159°-R-268°-W-344·5°-R-shore;   50°07'·07N 05°31'·68W.

Lizard ☆ Fl 3s 70m **26M**; H24; 250°-120°, partly visible 235°-250°; W 8-sided twr; *Horn 30s;* 49°57'·61N 05°12'·13W.

FALMOUTH

St Anthony Head ☆ Iso WR 15s 22m, **W16M**, R14M, H24; 295°-W-004°-R-022°-W-172°; W 8-sided twr; *Horn 30s;* 50°08'·47N 05°00'·96W.

Black Rock ↨ Q (3) 10s; 50°08'·68N 05°01'·74W.

The Governor ↨ VQ (3) 5s; 50°09'·15N 05°02'·40W.

MEVAGISSEY

Victoria Pier ↙ Fl (2) 10s 9m 12M; *Dia 30s;* 50°16'·15N 04°46'·93W.

FOWEY

Fowey ↙ L Fl WR 5s 28m W11M, R9M; 284°-R-295°-W-028°-R-054°; 50°19'·62N 04°38'·84W.

Whitehouse Pt ↙ Iso WRG 3s 11m W11M, R/G8M; 017°-G-022°- W-032°-R-037°; R col; 50°19'·98N 04°38'·24W.

POLPERRO

Spy House Pt ↙ Iso WR 6s 30m 7M; W288°-060°, R060°-288°; 50°19'·81N 04°30'·70W.

LOOE and EDDYSTONE

Banjo Pier ☆ Oc WR 3s 8m **W15M**, R12M; 207°-R267°- W-313°-R-332°; 50°21'·05N 04°27'·06W.

Eddystone ☆ Fl (2) 10s 41m **17M**; Gy twr, helicopter platform; *Horn 30s; Racon T, 10M,* 50°10'·85N 04°15'·94W. Same twr, Iso R 10s 28m 8M; 110·5°-130·5° over Hand Deeps.

PLYMOUTH

Draystone ⚓ Fl (2) R 5s; 50°18'·85N 04°11'·07W. Plymouth bkwtr W ↙ Fl WR 10s 19m W12M, R9M; 262°-W-208°-R-262°; W ○ twr. Same twr, Iso 4s 12m 10M; vis 033°-037°; *Horn 15s;* 50°20'·07N 04°09'·53W.

The Bridge Channel. No 1, ↨ QG 4m; 50°21'·03N 04°09'·53W. No 2, ↨ QR 4m.

Bkwtr E ↨ L Fl WR 10s 9m W8M, R6M; 190°-R-353°-W-001°-R-018°-W-190°; 50°20'·01N 04°08'·25W.

Ldg lts 349°. Front, Mallard Shoal ↨ Q WRG 5m W10M, R/G3M; 233°-G-043°- R-067°-G-087°-W-099°-R-108°; 50°21'·60N 04°08'·33W. Rear, 396m from front, Hoe ↨ Oc G 1·3s 11m 3M, 310°-040°; W ▽, Or bands.

QAB (Queen Anne's Battery) ldg lts ↙ 048·5°. Front, FR; Or/W bcn; 50°21'·84N 04°07'·84W. Rear, Dir Oc WRG 7.5s 14m 3M; 038°-G-047·2°-W-049·7°-R-060·5°.

Sutton Hbr lock; IPTS; 50°21'·98N 04°07'·96W.

PYH (Plymouth Yacht Haven), outer bkwtr, E end, 2 FG (vert); 50°21'·59N 04°07'·15W.

Mayflower marina, outer bkwtr, E end, 2 FR (vert).

RIVER YEALM

The Sand Bar ⚓ Fl R 5s; 50°18'·59N 04°04'·12W.

SALCOMBE

Sandhill Pt Dir ↙ 000°: Fl WRG 2s 27m W10M, R/G7M; 182·5°-G-357·5°-W-002·5°-R-182·5°; R/W ◊

9

on W mast; 50°13'·77N 03°46'·67W. 000° on with Pound Stone R/W ℓ, 230m S.

Start Pt ☆ Fl (3) 10s 62m **25M**; 184°-068°. Same twr; FR 55m 12M; 210°-255° over Skerries Bank; *Horn 60s;* 50°13'·33N 03°38'·54W.

DARTMOUTH

Kingswear Dir ⚡328°: Iso WRG 3s 9m 8M; 318°-G-325°-W-331°-R-340°; W ○ twr; 50°20'·81N 03°34'·10W.

Mewstone ℓ VQ (6) + L Fl 10s; 50°19'·92N 03°31'·89W.

West Rock ℓ Q (6) + L Fl 15s; 50°19'·86N 03°32'·47W.

Homestone ⌀ QR; 50°19'·60N 03°33'·56W.

Castle Ledge ⚓ Fl G 5s; 50°19'·99N 03°33'·12W.

BRIXHAM

Berry Head ☆ Fl (2) 15s 58m 14M; vis 100°-023°; W twr; 50°23'·97N 03°29'·01W. R lts on radio mast 5·7M NW, inland of Paignton.

Victoria bkwtr ⚡ Oc R 15s 9m 6M; W twr; 50°24'·33N 03°30'·78W.

Fairway Dir ⚡159°: Iso WRG 5s 4m 6M; 145°-G-157°-W-161°-R-173°; 50°23'·83N 03°30'·57W.

TORQUAY

⚓ QG (May-Sep); 50°27'·42N 03°31'·80W.

TEIGNMOUTH

Outfall ⌀ Fl Y 5, 288°/1·3M to hbr ent.
The Point ℓ Oc G 6s 3M & FG (vert); 50°32'·42N 03°30'·05W.

RIVER EXE

E Exe ℓ Q (3) 10s; 50°36'·00N 03°22'·38W.
Ldg lts 305°. Front, Iso 2s 6m 7M, 50°36'·99N 03°25'·34W. Rear, Q 12m 7M, 57m from front.
No. 10 ⌀ Fl R 3s; 50°36'·73N 03°24'·77W.
No. 12 Warren Pt ⌀ 50°36'·91N 03°25'·40W.

Straight Pt ⚡ Fl R 10s 34m 7M; 246°-071°; 50°36'·49N 03°21'·76W.

LYME REGIS

Outfall ℓ Q (6) + L Fl 15s; 50°43'·17N 02°55'·66W.
Ldg lts 284°: Front, Victoria Pier ⚡ Oc WR 8s 6m, W9M, R7M; 296°-R-116°-W-296°; 50°43'·19N 02°56'·17W. Rear, FG 8m 9M, 240m from front.

WEST BAY (BRIDPORT)

W pier root, Dir ⚡ F WRG 5m 4M; 165°-G-331°-W-341°-R-165°; 50°42'·62N 02°45'·89W.

W pier ⚡ Iso R 2s 5m 4M; 50°42'·51N 02°45'·83W.

E pier ⚡ Iso G 2s 5m 4M; 50°42'·53N 02°45'·80W.

PORTLAND

Portland Bill lt ho ⚡ Fl (4) 20s 43m **25M**. vis 221°-244° (gradual change from 1 Fl to 4 Fl); 244°-117° (shows 4 Fl); 117°-141° (gradual change from 4 Fl to 1 Fl). W ○ twr; *Dia 30s;* 50°30'·85N 02°27'·38W. Same twr, FR 19m 13M; 271°-291° over Shambles.

W Shambles ℓ Q (9) 15s; *Bell;* 50°29'·78N 02°24'·40W.

E Shambles ℓ Q (3) 10s; *Bell;* 50°30'·78N 02°20'·08W.

Portland hbr, outer bkwtr (N end) ⚡ QR 14m 5M; 013°-268°; 50°35'·11N 02°24'·87W.

NE Bkwtr (A Hd) ⚡ Fl 2·5s 22m **20M**; 50°35'·16N 02°25'·07W.

NE Bkwtr (B Hd) ⚡ Oc R 15s 11m 5M; 50°35'·65N 02°25'·88W.

WEYMOUTH TO ANVIL POINT

Weymouth ldg lts 239·6°: both FR 5/7m 7M; Front 50°36'·46N 02°26'·87W, R ♦ on W post; rear 17m from front, R ♦ on W mast.

N Pier hd ⚡ 2 FG (vert) 9m 6M; 50°36'·59N 02°26'·63W.

S Pier hd ⚡ Q 10m 9M; 50°36'·57N 02°26'·49W. IPTS 190m SW.

Lulworth Cove, E point 50°37'·00N 02°14'·78W.

Anvil Pt ☆ Fl 10s 45m **19M**; vis 237°-076° (H24); W ○ twr and dwelling; 50°35'·51N 01°57'·60W.

		1	2	3	4	5	6	7	8	9	10	11	12	13	14	15	16	17
1	Longships	**1**																
2	Scilly (Crow Rock)	22	**2**															
3	Penzance	15	35	**3**														
4	Lizard Point	23	42	16	**4**													
5	Falmouth	39	60	32	16	**5**												
6	Mevagissey	52	69	46	28	17	**6**											
7	Fowey	57	76	49	34	22	7	**7**										
8	Looe	63	80	57	39	29	16	11	**8**									
9	Plymouth (bkwtr)	70	92	64	49	39	25	22	11	**9**								
10	R. Yealm (ent)	72	89	66	49	39	28	23	16	4	**10**							
11	Salcombe	81	102	74	59	50	40	36	29	22	17	**11**						
12	Start Point	86	103	80	63	55	45	40	33	24	22	7	**12**					
13	Dartmouth	95	116	88	72	63	54	48	42	35	31	14	9	**13**				
14	Torbay	101	118	96	78	70	62	55	50	39	38	24	15	11	**14**			
15	Exmouth	113	131	107	90	82	73	67	61	51	49	33	27	24	12	**15**		
16	Lyme Regis	126	144	120	104	96	86	81	74	63	62	48	41	35	30	21	**16**	
17	Portland Bill	135	151	128	112	104	93	89	81	73	70	55	49	45	42	36	22	**17**

AREA 2 South Central England - *Anvil Point to Selsey Bill*

SELECTED LIGHTS, BUOYS & WAYPOINTS | Positions are referenced to WGS84

SWANAGE TO ISLE OF WIGHT

SWANAGE
Pier Hd ⚓ 2 FR (vert) 6m 3M; 50°36'·56N 01°56'·95W.
Peveril Ledge ⚓ QR; 50°36'·41N 01°56'·10W.

POOLE HARBOUR AND APPROACHES
Poole Bar (No.1) ⚓ QG; *Bell.*; 50°39·32N 01°55'·16W.

SWASH AND E LOOE CHANNELS
South Hook ⚓ 50°39'·70N 01°55'·20W.
No. 3 ⚓ Fl G 3s; 50°39'·76N 01°55'·49W.
Training Bank ⚓ 2 FR (vert); 50°39'·84N 01°55'·92W..
No. 12 (Chan) ⚓ Fl R 2s; 50°40'·45N 01°56'·26W.
No. 13 Swash ⚓ Q (9) 15s; 50°48'·88N 01°56'·70W.
East Looe ⚓ QR; 50°41'·34N 01°55'·94W.

South Deep. Marked by lit and unlit Bns from ent South of Brownsea Castle to Furzey Is.

BROWNSEA ROADS
N Haven ⚓ Q (9) 15s 5m; 50°41'·15N 01°57'·17W.
Brownsea ⚓ Q (3) 10s; 50°41'·16N 01°57'·41W.

MIDDLE SHIP AND N CHANNELS
No. 20 ⚓ Q (6) + L Fl 15s; *Bell*; 50°41'·38N 01°57'·10W.
Marked by PHM and SHM Lt Bys.
Aunt Betty ⚓ Q (3)10s; 50°41'·96N 01°57'·39W.
Diver ⚓ Q (9) 15s; 50°42'·28N 01°58'·34W.
Stakes ⚓ Q (6) + L Fl 15s; 50°42'·43N 01°59'·01W.

WAREHAM CHANNEL
Wareham Chan initially m'kd by ⚓'s and ⚓'s and then by stakes.

WESTERN APPROACHES TO SOLENT

NEEDLES AND NORTH CHANNELS
Needles Fairway ⚓ L Fl 10s; *Whis*; 50°38'·24N 01°38'·98W.
SW Shingles ⚓Fl R 2·5s;50°38'·24N 01°38'·98W.
Bridge ⚓ VQ (9) 10s; *Racon (T) 10M*; 50°39'·63N 01°36'·88W.

Needles 50°39'·73N 01°35'·50W; Oc (2) WRG 20s 24m **W17M**, R14M, R13M G14M; ○ Twr, R band and lantern; vis: shore-R-300°-W-083°-R (unintens)-212°-W-217°-G-224°. *Horn (2) 30s* H24. 01°33'·55W.

NE Shingles ⚓ Q (3) 10s; 50°41'·96N 01°33'·41W.

Hurst Point ☆ 50°42'·48N 01°33'·03W; Ldg Lts 042° Front. FL (4) WR 15s 23m W13M, R11M; W ○ Twr; vis:080°-W(unintens)-104°, 234°-W-244°-R-250°-W-053°. Same structure, Iso WRG 4s 19m **W21M**, **R18M**, **G17M**; vis: 038·8°-G-040·8°-W-041·8°-R- 043·8°; By day W7M, R5M, G5M.
N Head ⚓ Fl (3) G 10s; 50°42'·69N 01°35'·52W.

YARMOUTH/LYMINGTON
Sconce ⚓ Q; *Bell*; 50°42'·53N 01°31'·43W.
Black Rock ⚓ Fl G 5s; 50°42'·58N 01°30'·64W.
Y'mouth E F'wy ⚓ Fl R 2s. 50°42'·64N 01°29'·88W.
Pier Head, centre, ⚓ 2 FR (vert) 2M; G col. High intensity FW (occas); 50°42'·51N 01°29'·97W.
Jack in the Basket ⚓ Fl R 2s 9m; 50°44'·27N 01°30'·57W.
No. 1 ⚓ Fl G 2s 2m 3M; G △ on pile; 50°44'·41N 01°30'·48W.

SOLENT MARKS
Hamstead Ledge ⚓ Fl (2) G 5s; 50°43'·87N 01°26'18W.
Newtown River ⚓ Fl R 4s; 50°43'·75N 01°24'·91W.
W Lepe ⚓ Fl R 5s; 50°45'·24N 01°24'·09W.
Salt Mead ⚓ Fl (3) G 10s; 50°44'·51N 01°23'·04W.
Gurnard Ledge ⚓ Fl(4)G15s; 50°45'·51N 01°20'·59W.
E Lepe ⚓ Fl (2) R 5s; *Bell*; 50°46'·11N 01°20'·91W.
Lepe Spit ⚓ Q (6) + L Fl 15s; 50°46'·78N 01°20'·64W.
Beaulieu Millenium Dir lt 334°. ⚓ Oc Q WRG 4s 13m W4M, R3M, G3M; vis: 321°-G-331°-W-337°-R-347°; 50°47'·12N 01°21'·90W.
NE Gurnard ⚓ Fl (3) R 10s; 50°47'·06N 01°19'·42W.
W Bramble ⚓ VQ (9) 10s; *Bell*; *Racon (T) 3M.*; 50°47'·20N 01°18'·65W.
W Knoll ⚓ Fl Y 2·5s; 50°47'·43N 01°17'·84W.
Spanker⚓ (or) Fl Y 4s; 50°47'·11N01°18'·08W.
S Bramble ⚓ Fl G 2·5s; 50°46'·98N 01°17'·72W.

COWES
Gurnard ⚓ Q; 50°46'·22N 01°18'·84W.
Prince Consort ⚓ VQ; 50°46'·42N 01°17'·55W.
No. 1 ⚓ Fl G 3s; 50°46'·07N 01°18'·03W.
No. 2 ⚓ QR; 50°46'·07N 01°17'·87W.

SOUTHAMPTON WATER/RIVER HAMBLE
CALSHOT SPIT ⚓ Fl 5s 12m 11M; R hull, Lt Twr amidships; *Horn (2) 60s*; 50°48'·35N 01°17'·64W.
Calshot ⚓ VQ; *Bell* ; 50°48'·44N 01°17'·03W.
Black Jack ⚓ Fl (2) R 4s; 50°49'·13N 01°18'·09W.
Hook ⚓ QG; *Horn (1) 15s*; 50°49'·52N 01°18'·30W.
Bald Head ⚓ 50°49'·90N 01°18'·25W.
Hamble Pt ⚓ Q (6) + L Fl 15s; 50°50'·15N 01°18'·66W.
No. 1 ⚓ QG 2m 2M; 50°50'·34N 01°18'·65W.
No. 2 ⚓ Q (3) 10s 2m 2M; 50°50'·39N 01°18'·77W.
Greenland ⚓ IQ G 10s; 50°51'·11N 01°20'·38W.
Weston Shelf ⚓ Fl (3) G 15s; 50°52'·71N 01°23'·26W.
Hythe Pier Hd ⚓ 2 FR (vert) 12m 5M; 50°52'·49N 01°23'·61W.

SOUTHAMPTON/ITCHEN/TEST
Swinging Ground No. 1 ⚓ Oc G 4s; 50°53'·00N 01°23'·44W.
Queen Elizabeth II Terminal, S end ⚓ 4 FG (vert) 16m 3M; 50°53'·00N 01°23'·71W.
Gymp ⚓ QR; 50°53'·17N 01°24'·30W.

THE EAST SOLENT
NORTH CHANNEL/HILLHEAD
Hillhead ≈ Fl R 2·5s; 50°48'·07N 01°16'·00W.
Hillhead ⟂ Or Bn; 50°49'·06N 01°14'·78W.
E Bramble ⟨ VQ (3) 5s; 50°47'·23N 01°13'·64W.

EASTERN SOLENT MARKS/WOOTTON
W Ryde Middle ⟨ Q (9) 15s; 50°46'·48N 01°15'·79W.
Norris ≈ Fl (3) R 10s; 50°45'·97N 01°15'·51W.
N Ryde Middle ≈ Fl (4) R 20s; 50°46'·61N 01°14'·31W.
S Ryde Middle ▲ Fl G 5s; 50°46'·13N 01°14'·16W.
Peel Bank ≈ Fl (2) R 5s; 50°45'·49N 01°13'·35W.
SE Ryde Middle ⟨ VQ (6)+L Fl 10s; 50°45'·93N 01°12'·10W.
NE Ryde Middle ≈ Fl (2) R 10s; 50°46'·21N 01°11'·88W.
Wootton Bn ⟨ Q 1M; (NB); 50°44'·53N 01°12'·13W.
Mother Bank ≈ Fl R 3s; 50°45'·49N 01°11'·21W.
Browndown ▲ Fl G 15s; 50°46'·57N 01°10'·95W.

PORTSMOUTH AND APPROACHES
Horse Sand Ft ⚡ Iso G 2s 21m 8M; 50°45'·01N 01°04'·34W.
Horse Sand ▲ Fl G 2·5s; 50°45'·53N 01°05'·27W.
Outer Spit ⟨ Q (6) + L Fl 15s; 50°45'·58N 01°05'·50W.
Mary Rose ≈ Fl Y 5s; 50°45'·80N 01°06'·20W.
No. 1 Bar (NB) ▲ Fl (3) G 10s; 50°46'·77N 01°05'·81W.
No. 2 ≈ Fl (3) R 10s; 50°46'·69N 01°05'·97W.
No. 4 (NB) ≈ QR; 50°47'·01N 01°06'·36W.
BC Outer ⟨ Oc R 15s; 50°47'·32N 01°06'·68W.
Fort Blockhouse ⚡ Dir lt 320°; WRG 6m W13M, R5M, G5M; vis: 310°- Oc G-316°-Al WG(W phase incr with brg), 318·5°-Oc-321·5°-Al WR (R phase incr with brg), 324°-Oc R-330°. 2 FR (vert) 20m E; 50°47'·37N 01°06'·74W.
Ballast ⟨ Fl R 2·5s; 50°47'·62N 01°06'·83W.

EASTERN APPROACHES TO THE SOLENT
Outer Nab 1 ⟨ VQ (9) 10s; 50°38'·18N 00°56'·88W.
Outer Nab 2 ⟨ VQ (3) 5s; 50°38'·43N 00°57'·70W.

Nab Tower ☆ 50°40'·08N 00°57'·15W; Fl 10s 27m 16M, *Horn (2) 30s; Racon (T) 10M.*
N 2 ⟨ Fl Y 2·5s. 6M; 50°41'·03N 00°56'·74W.
N 1 ⟨ Fl Y (4)10s; 50°41'·26N 00°56'·52W.
N 7 ⟨ Fl Y 2·5s; 50°42'·35N 00°57'·20W.
New Grounds ⟨ VQ (3) 5s; 50°41'·84N 00°58'·49W.
Nab End ▲ Fl R 5s; *Whis*; 50°42'·63N 00°59'·49W.
Dean Tail ▲ Fl G 5s; 50°42'·99N 00°59'·17W.
Dean Tail S ⟨ Q (6)+L Fl 10s; 50°43'·04N 00°59'·57W.
Dean Tail N ⟨ Q; 50°43'·13N 00°59'·57W.
St Helens ≈ Fl (3) R 15s; 50°43'·36N 01°02'·41W.
Horse Elbow ▲ QG; 50°44'·26N 01°03'·88W.
Cambrian Wreck ⟨ 50°44'·43N 01°03'·43W.
Warner ⟨ QR; *Whis*; 50°43'·87N 01°03'·99W.
W Princessa ⟨ Q (9) 15s; 50°40'·16N 01°03'·65W.
Bembridge Ledge ⟨ Q (3) 10s; 50°41'·15N 01°02'·81W
St Helen's Fort ☆ (IOW) Fl (3) 10s 16m 8M; large ○ stone structure; 50°42'·30N 01°05'·05W.

SE COAST OF THE ISLE OF WIGHT
St Catherine's Point ☆ 50°34'·54N 01°17'·87W; Fl 5s 41m **27M**; vis: 257°-117°; FR 35m **17M** (same Twr) vis: 099°-116°.
Ventnor Haven W Bwtr ⚡ 2 FR (vert) 3M; 50°35'·50N 01°12'·30W.

LANGSTONE AND APPROACHES
Winner ⟨; 50°45'·10N 01°00'·10W.
Langstone F'wy ⟨ L Fl 10s; 50°46'·32N 01°01'·36W.

CHICHESTER ENTRANCE
West Pole ⟨ Fl WR 5s W7M, R5M; vis: 321°-W-081°-R-321°; 50°45'·71N 00°56'·50W.
Chichester Bar ▲ Fl (2) R 10s 14m 2M; Tide gauge; 50°45'·92N 00°56'·46W.
Eastoke ⟨ QR 2m 3M; 50°46'·66N 00°56'·16W.
West Winner ⟨ QG; Tide gauge. 50°46'·88N 00°55'·98W.

#		1	2	3	4	5	6	7	8	9	10	11	12	13	14	15	16	17	18
1	Portland Bill	1																	
2	Weymouth	8	2																
3	Swanage	22	22	3															
4	Poole Hbr ent	28	26	6	4														
5	Needles Lt Ho	35	34	14	14	5													
6	Lymington	42	40	20	24	6	6												
7	Yarmouth (IOW)	40	39	18	22	4	2	7											
8	Beaulieu R. ent	46	45	25	29	11	7	7	8										
9	Cowes	49	46	28	27	14	10	9	2	9									
10	Southampton	55	54	34	34	20	16	16	9	9	10								
11	R. Hamble (ent)	53	51	32	34	18	12	13	6	6	5	11							
12	Portsmouth	58	57	37	35	23	19	19	12	10	18	13	12						
13	Langstone Hbr	61	59	39	39	25	21	21	14	12	21	18	5	13					
14	Chichester Bar	63	62	42	42	28	23	24	17	15	23	18	8	5	14				
15	Bembridge	59	58	38	39	24	18	19	13	10	18	15	5	6	8	15			
16	Nab Tower	64	63	43	44	29	23	24	18	15	24	19	10	7	6	6	16		
17	St Catherine's Pt	45	44	25	25	12	19	21	27	15	36	29	20	20	19	17	15	17	
18	Littlehampton	79	79	60	61	46	44	45	38	36	45	42	31	28	25	28	22	35	18

AREA 3 South East England -*Selsey Bill to North Foreland*

SELECTED LIGHTS, BUOYS & WAYPOINTS | Positions are referenced to WGS84

SELSEY BILL TO NORTH FORELAND

SELSEY BILL AND THE OWERS
S Pullar ⟨ VQ (6) + L Fl 10s; 50°38'·84N 00°49'·29W.
Boulder ◣ Fl G 2·5s; 50°41'·56N 00°49'·09W.
Street ◿ QR; 50°41'·69N 00°48'·89W.
Mixon ⟨ Fl R 5s; 50°42'·35N 00°46'·21W.
Owers ⟨ Q (6) + L Fl 15s; *Whis; Racon (O) 10M.;*
50°38'·63N 00°41'·19W.
E'Boro Hd ⟨ Q (3) 10s *Bell;* 50°41'·54N 00°39'·09W

LITTLEHAMPTON/SHOREHAM
Littlehampton W Pier Hd ⟨ QR 7m 6M; 50°47'·88N
00°32'·46W.
Shoreham E Bkwtr Hd ⨍ Fl G 5s 8M; *Siren 120s;*
50°49'·54N 00°14'·80W.

BRIGHTON MARINA
W Bkwtr Hd ⨍ QR 10m 7M; W ◯ structure, R
bands; *Horn (2) 30s;* 50°48'·50N 00°06'·38W.
E Bkwtr Hd ⨍ QG 8m 7M and Fl (4) WR 20s 16m
W10M, R8M; W pillar, G bands; vis: 260°-R- 295°-
W-100°; 50°48'·47N 00°06'·37W.

NEWHAVEN TO DUNGENESS
Newhaven Bkwtr Hd ⨍ Oc (2) 10s 17m 12M;
50°46'·56N 00°03'·50E.
GREENWICH ⌒ 50°24'·54N 00°00'·10E; Fl 5s 12m
15M; Riding lt FW; R hull; *Racon (M) 10M; Horn 30s.*
Beachy Head ☆ 50°44'·03N 00°14'·49E; Fl (2) 20s
31m **20M;** W round twr, R band and lantern; vis:
248°-101°; (H24); *Horn 30s.*
Royal Sovereign ☆ Fl 20s 28m 12M; W ◯ twr, R
band on W cabin on col; *Horn (2) 30s;* 50°43'·45N
00°26'·09E.

SOVEREIGN HBR/RYE
Sovereign Hr Marina ⨍ Fl (3) 15s 12m 7M.;
50°47'·24N 00°19'·83E.
Rye Fairway, L Fl 10s; 50°54'·04N 00°48'·04E.

DUNGENESS - DOVER STRAIT
Dungeness ☆ 50°54'·81N 00°58'·56E; Fl 10s 40m
21M; B ◯ twr, W bands and lantern, floodlit; Part
obsc 078°-shore; (H24). F RG 37m 10M (same twr);
vis: 057°-R-073°-G-078°-196°-R-216°; *Horn (3) 60s;* FR
Lts shown between 2·4M and 5·2M WNW when
firing taking place. QR on radio mast 1·2M NW.
Folkestone Bkwtr Hd ⨍ 51°04'·56N 01°11'·69E; Fl
(2) 10s 14m **22M;** *Dia (4) 60s.* In fog Fl 2s; vis: 246°-
306°, intens 271·5°-280·5°.
VARNE ⌒ 51°01'·29N 01°23'·90E; Fl R 20s12m **19M;**
Racon (T)10M; Horn 30s.

DOVER TO NORTH FORELAND
Dover Admiralty Pier Extension Hd ⨍ 51°06'·69N
01°19'·66E; Fl 7·5s 21m **20M;** W twr; vis: 096°-
090°, obsc in The Downs by S Foreland inshore
of 226°; *Horn 10s;* Int Port Tfc sigs.
Knuckle ☆ 51°07'·04N 01°20'·49E; Fl (4) WR 10s
15m **W15M,** R13M; W twr; vis: 059°-R-239°-W-059°.
S GOODWIN ⌒ 51°07'·97N 01°28'·49E; Fl (2) 20s
12m **15M;** R hull; *Horn (2) 60s.*
SW Goodwin ⟨ Q (6) + L Fl 15s; 51°08'·50N
01°28'·88E.
E GOODWIN ⌒ 51°13'·26N 01°36'·37E; Fl 15s
12m **23M;** R hull with lt twr amidships; *Racon (T)*
10M; Horn 30s.
NE Goodwin ⟨ Q (3) 10s; *Racon (M) 10M.* 51°20'·31N
01°34'·16E.
Goodwin Fork ⟨ Q (6) + L Fl 15s; *Bell;* 51°14'·33N
01°26'·86E.
NW Goodwin ⟨ Q (9) 15s; *Bell;* 51°16'·57N 01°28'·57E.
Gull Stream ◿ QR; 51°18'·26N 01°29'·69E.

RAMSGATE/BROADSTAIRS
RA ⟨ Q(6) + L Fl 15s; 51°19'·60N 01°30'·13E.
E Brake ◿ Fl R 5s; 51°19'·47N 01°29'·20E.
Broadstairs Knoll ◿ Fl R 2·5s; 51°20'·88N 01°29'·48E.
North Foreland ☆ 51°22'·49N 01°26'·70E; Fl (5)
WR 20s 57m **W19M,** R16M, R15M; W 8-sided twr;
vis: shore-W-150°-R(**16M**)-181°-R(**15M**)-200°-W-
011°; H24.

		1															
1	Nab Tower	**1**															
2	Boulder Lt Buoy	5	**2**														
3	Owers Lt Buoy	11	8	**3**													
4	Littlehampton	19	13	12	**4**												
5	Shoreham	32	24	21	13	**5**											
6	Brighton	35	28	24	17	5	**6**										
7	Newhaven	40	34	29	24	12	7	**7**									
8	Beachy Head Lt	46	41	36	30	20	14	8	**8**								
9	Eastbourne	51	45	40	34	24	19	12	7	**9**							
10	Rye	72	67	62	56	46	41	34	25	23	**10**						
11	Dungeness Lt	76	71	66	60	50	44	38	30	26	9	**11**					
12	Folkestone	92	84	81	76	65	60	53	43	40	23	13	**12**				
13	Dover	97	89	86	81	70	65	58	48	45	28	18	5	**13**			
14	Ramsgate	112	104	101	96	85	80	73	63	60	43	33	20	15	**14**		
15	N Foreland Lt	115	107	104	99	88	83	76	66	63	46	36	23	18	3	**15**	
16	Sheerness	146	139	135	132	119	114	107	97	96	79	67	54	49	34	31	**16**
17	London Bridge	188	184	177	177	161	156	149	139	141	124	109	96	91	76	73	45	**17**

AREA 4 East England - *North Foreland to Berwick-upon-Tweed*

SELECTED LIGHTS, BUOYS & WAYPOINTS | Positions are referenced to WGS84

THAMES ESTUARY – SOUTHERN

(Direction of buoyage generally East to West)

IMPORTANT NOTE. Regular changes are made to Thames Estuary buoyage. Check Notices to Mariners for the latest information.

OUTER APPROACHES

Foxtrot 3 ⌐ 51°23'·85N 02°00'·51E; Fl 10s 12m **15M**; *Racon (T) 10M*; *Horn 10s*.
Drill Stone ⌊ Q (3) 10s Bell; 51°25'·88N 01°42'·89E.
NE Spit ⌊ VQ (3) 5s; 51°27'·93N 01°29'·89E.

N KENT COAST/THE SWALE

East Margate ⌐ Fl R 2·5s; 51°27'·03N 01°26'·40E.
Foreness Pt O'fall ⌐ Fl R 5s; 51°24'·61N 01°26'·02E.
SE Margate ⌊ Q (3) 10s; 51°24'·05N 01°20'·40E.
Hook Spit ⌐ QG; 51°24'·08N 01°12'·26E.
Spaniard ⌊ Q (3) 10s; 51°26'·23N 01°04'·00E.
Spile ⌐ Fl G 2·5s; 51°26'·43N 00°55'·70E.
Whitstable Street ⌊ Q; 51°23'·85N 01°01'·59E.
Pollard Spit ⌐ QR; 51°22'·98N 00° 58'·57E.
Queenboro Spit ⌊ Q (3) 10s; 51°25'·81N 00°43'·93E.

PRINCES CHANNEL /MEDWAY/SEA REACH

Outer Tongue ⌊ L Fl 10s; *Racon (T) 10M*; *Whis*; 51°30'·73N 01°26'·40E.
Princes Appr ⌊ Mo (A) 10s; 51°28'·60N 01°23'·60E.
E Redsand ⌐ Fl (2) R 5s; 51°29'·41N 01°04'·05E.
Sea Reach 1 ⌐ Fl Y 2·5s; *Racon (T) 10M*; 51°29'·45N 00°52'·57E.
Medway ⌊ Mo (A) 6s; 51°28'·83N 00°52'·81E.

FOULGER'S - FISHERMAN'S GATS

Long Sand Inner ⌐ Mo 'A' 15s; 51°38'·80N 01°25'·60E.
Long Sand Outer ⌐ L Fl 10s; 51°36'·00N 01°26'·30E.
Outer Fisherman ⌊ Q (3) 10s; 51°33'·89N 01°25'·01E.
Inner Fisherman ⌐ Q R; 51°36'·07N 01°19'·87E.

THAMES ESTUARY – NORTHERN

KENTISH KNOCK

Kentish Knock ⌊ Q (3) 10s; *Whis*; 51°38'·53N 01°40·39E.
S Knock ⌊ Q (6) + L Fl 15s; *Bell*; 51°34'·13N 01°34'·29E.

BLACK DEEP

No. 9 ⌊ Q (6) + L Fl 15s; 51°35'·13N 01°15'·09E.
No. 2 ⌐ Fl (4) R 15s; 51°45'·63N 01°32'·20E.
Sunk Hd Tr ⌊ Q; *Whis*; 51°46'·63N 01°30'·51E.
Black Deep ⌐ QR. 51°47'·10N 01°34'·68E.
Long Sand Hd ⌊ VQ; *Bell*; 51°47'·90N 01°39'·42E.

BARROW DEEP

SW Barrow ⌊ Q(6)+LFl15s; *Bell*; 51°32'·29N 01°00'·31E.
Barrow No. 9 ⌊ VQ (3) 5s; 51°35'·34N 01°10'·30E.
Barrow No. 5 ⌐ Fl G 10s; 51°40'·03N 01°16'·20E.
Barrow No. 3 ⌊ Q (3) 10s; *Racon (M)10M*; 51°42'·02N 01°20'·24E.

WEST SWIN AND MIDDLE DEEP

Blacktail Spit ⌐ Fl (3) G 10s; 51°31'·47N 00°56'·74E.
Maplin ⌊ Q (3) 10s; *Bell*; 51°34'·03N 01°02'·30E.
W Swin ⌐ QR; 51°33'·40N 01°01'·97E.
Maplin Edge ⌐ 51°35'·33N 01°03'·64E.
Maplin Bank ⌐ Fl (3) R 10s; 51°35'·50N 01°04'·70E.

EAST SWIN (KING'S) CHANNEL

NE Maplin ⌐ Fl G 5s; *Bell*; 51°37'·43N 01°04'·90E.
S Whitaker ⌐ Fl (2) G 10s; 51°40'·23N 01°09'·05E.
W Sunk ⌊ Q (9) 15s; 51°44'·33N 01°25'·80E.
Gunfleet Spit ⌊ Q (6) + L Fl 15s; *Bell*; 51°45'·33N 01°21'·70E.
Gunfleet Old Lt Ho 51°46'·09N 01°20'·39E.

WHITAKER CHANNEL AND RIVER CROUCH

Whitaker ⌊ Q (3) 10s; *Bell*; 51°41'·43N 01°10'·51E.
Swin Spitway ⌊ Iso 10s; *Bell*; 51°41'·95N 01°08'·35E.
Whitaker ⌊ 51°39'·64N 01°06'·16E.
Ridge ⌐ Fl R 10s; 51°40'·13N 01°04'·87E.
Sunken Buxey ⌊ Q; 51°39'·54N 01°00'·59E.
Outer Crouch ⌊ Q(6)+LFl15s; 51°38'·38N 00°58'·48E.

GOLDMER GAT/WALLET/COLNE BAR

NE Gunfleet ⌊ Q (3) 10s; 51°49'·93N 01°27'·79E.
Wallet No. 2 ⌐ Fl R 5s; 51°48'·88N 01°22'·99E.
Wallet No. 4 ⌐ Fl (4) R 10s; 51°46'·53N 01°17'·23E.
Wallet Spitway ⌐ L Fl 10s; *Bell*; 51°42'·86N 01°07'·30E.
Knoll ⌊ Q; 51°43'·88N 01°05'·07E.
N Eagle ⌊ Q; 51°44'·71N 01°04'·32E.
NW Knoll ⌐ Fl (2) R 5s; 51°44'·35N 01°02'·17E.
Colne Bar ⌐ Fl (2) G 5s; 51°44'·61N 01°02'·57E.
Bench Head ⌐ Fl (3) G 10s; 51°44'·69N 01°01'·10E.
Inner Bench Hd ⌐ Fl(2) R 5s; 51°45'·96N 01°01'·74E.
Brightlingsea Spit ⌊ Q (6) + L Fl 15s; 51°48'·08N 01°00'·70E.

RIVER BLACKWATER

The Nass ⌊ VQ (3) 5s 6m 2M; 51°45'·83N 00°54'·83E.
Thirslet ⌐ Fl (3) G 10s; 51°43'·73N 00°50'·39E. 00°57'·10E.

WALTON BACKWATERS

Naze Tower; 51°51'·87N 01°17'·29E.
Pye End ⌐ L Fl 10s; 51°55'·03N 01°17'·90E.
Crab Knoll No. 3 ⌐ Fl G 5s; 51°54'·41N 01°16'·41E.
Island Point ⌊ Q; 51°53'·36N 01°15'·36E.

HARWICH APPROACHES

(Direction of buoyage North to South)

MEDUSA CHAN/CORK SAND/ROUGHS

Medusa ⌐ Fl G 5s; 51°51'·23N 01°20'·35E.
Stone Banks ⌐ FlR 5s; 51°53'·19N 01°19'·23E.
S Cork ⌊ Q (6) + L Fl 15s; 51°51'·33N 01°24'·09E.

Roughs Tr SE ⟨ Q (3) 10s; 51°53'·64N 01°28'·94E.
Cork Sand Yacht Bn ⟨ VQ ; 51°55'·21N 01°25'·20E.

HARWICH CHANNEL

SUNK ⇌ Fl (2) 20s 12m **16M**; R hull with lt twr; *Racon (T)*; *Horn (2) 60s*; 51°51'·03N 01°34'·89E.
S Shipwash ⟨⟨ 2 By(s) Q (6) + L Fl 15s; 51°52'·71N 01°33'·97E.
Outer Tidal Bn ⟨ Mo (U) 15s 2m 3M; 51°52'·85N 01°32'·34E.
SW Shipwash ⟨ Q (9)15s; 51°54'·75N 01°34'·21E.
Haven ⟨ Mo (A) 5s; 51°55'·76N 01°35'·56E.
HA ⟨ Iso 5s; 51°56'·75N 01°30'·66E.
Harwich Chan No. 1 ⟨ Fl Y 2·5s; *Racon (T)10M*; 51°56'·13N 01°27'·06E.
S Bawdsey ⟨ Q (6) + L Fl 15s; *Whis*; 51°57'·23N 01°30'·22E.
Platters ⟨ Q (6) + L Fl 15s; 51°55'·64N 01°20'·97E.
Rolling Ground ⟨ QG; 51°55'·55N 01°19'·75E.
Inner Ridge ⟨ QR; 51°55'·38N 01°20'·20E.
Landguard ⟨ Q; 51°55'·45N 01°18'·84E.

HARWICH TO ORFORDNESS

OFFSHORE MARKS

E Shipwash ⟨ VQ (3) 5s; 51°57'·08N 01°37'·89E.
N Shipwash ⟨ Q 7M; *Racon (M) 10M*; *Bell*; 52°01'·73N 01°38'·27E.
S Galloper ⟨ Q (6) L Fl 15s; *Racon (T)10M*; *Whis*. 51°43'·98N 01°56'·39E.
Outer Gabbard ⟨ Q (3) 10s; *Racon (O)10M*; *Whis*; 51°57'·83N 02°04'·19E.

DEBEN/ORE/SUFFOLK COAST

Woodbridge Haven ⟨ Mo(A)15s; 51°58'·72N 01°24'·63E.
Cutler ⟨ QG; 51°58'·51N 01°27'·48E.
SW Whiting ⟨ Q (6) + L Fl 10s; 52°00'·96N 01°30'·69E.
Orford Haven ⟨ L Fl 10s; *Bell*. 52°01'·62N 01°28'·00E.
NE Whiting ⟨ Q (3) 10s; 52°03'·61N 01°33'·32E.
NE Bawdsey ⟨ Fl G 10s; 52°01'·73N 01°36'·09E.

ORFORDNESS TO #GT YARMOUTH

(Direction of buoyage is South to North)
Orford Ness ☆ 52°05'·03N 01°34'·46E; Fl 5s 28m **20M**; W ○ twr, R bands. F WRG 14m **W17M**, R13M, **G15M** (same twr). vis: R shore-210°, 038°-R-047°-G-shore; *Racon (T) 18M*. FR 13m 12M vis: 026°- 038° over Whiting Bank.
Aldeburgh Ridge ⟨ QR; 52°06'·72N 01°36'·95E.
Southwold ☆ 52°19'·63N 01°40'·89E; Fl (4) WR 20s 37m **W16M**, **R12M**, R14M; vis 204°-R (intens)-215°-W-001°.

LOWESTOFT/GT YARMOUTH APPROACHES

E Barnard ⟨ Q (3) 10s; 52°25'·14N 01°46'·38E .
Newcome Sand ⟨ QR; 52°26'·28N 01°46'·97E.
S Holm ⟨ VQ (6) + L Fl 10s; 52°27'·05N 01°47'·15E.

N Newcome ⟨ Fl (4) R 15s; 52°28'·39N 01°46'·37E.
Lowestoft ☆ 52°29'·22N 01°45'·35; Fl 15s 37m **23M**; W twr; part obscd 347°- shore;
E Newcome ⟨ Fl (2) R 5s; 52°28'·51N 01°49'·21E.
Corton ⟨ Q (3) 10s; *Whis*; 52°31'·13N 01°51'·39E.
E. Holm ⟨ Fl (3) R 10s; 52°30'·64N 01°49'·72E.
S Corton ⟨ Q (6) + L Fl 15s; *Bell*; 52°32'·47N 01°49'·36E.
Holm Sand ⟨ Q. 52°33'·36N 01°46'·85E.
W Corton ⟨ Q (9) 15s; 52°34'·59N 01°46'·62E.
Gorleston South Pier Hd ⟨ Fl R 3s 11m 11M; vis: 235°-340°; *Horn (3) 60s*; 52°34'·33N 01°44'·28E.

GREAT YARMOUTH TO THE WASH

(Direction of buoyage ⟳ South to North)

GT YARMOUTH/COCKLE GATWAY/OFFSHORE

SW Scroby ⟨ Fl G 2·5s; 52°35'·82N 01°46'·26E.
Scroby Sands Wind Farm, 30 turbines centred on 52°39'·00N 01°47'·00E. NW, NE, SW, SE extremities (F.R Lts) Fl Y 5s 5M Horn Mo (U) 30s.
N Scroby ⟨ VQ; 52°41'·39N 01°46'·47E.
Cockle ⟨ VQ (3) 5s; *Bell*; 52°44'·03N 01°43'·59E.
Winterton Church **Racon (T) 10M**; 52°42'·92N 01°41'·21E.
Cross Sand ⟨ L Fl 10s 6m 5M; *Racon (T)10M*; 52°37'·03N 01°59'·14E.
NE Cross Sand ⟨ VQ (3) 5s; 52°43'·03N 01° 53'·69E.
Smith's Knoll ⟨ Q (6) + L Fl 15s 7M; *Racon (T) 10M*; *Whis*; 52°43'·52N 02°17'·89E.
S Winterton Ridge ⟨ Q (6) + L Fl 15s; 52°47'·21N 02°03'·44E.
Newarp ⟨ L Fl 10s 7M; *Racon (O) 10M*; 52°48'·37N 01°55'·69E.
S Haisbro ⟨ Q (6) + L Fl 15s; *Bell*; 52°50'·82N 01°48'·29E.
N Haisbro ⟨ Q; *Racon (T) 10M*; *Bell*; 53°00'·22N 01°32'·29E.
Happisburgh ☆ Fl (3) 30s 41m 14M; 52°49'·21N 01°32'·18E.

N NORFOLK COAST/THE WASH

Cromer ☆ 52°55'·45N 01°19'·01E; Fl 5s 84m **21M**; W 8-sided twr; vis: 102°-307° H24; *Racon (O) 25M*.
E Sheringham ⟨ Q (3) 10s; 53°02'·21N 01°14'·84E.
Blakeney O'falls ⟨ Fl(2) R 5s; *Bell*; 53°03'·01N 01°01'·37E.
Wells Fairway ⟨ Q; 52°59'·67N 00°50'·36E.
S Race ⟨ Q (6) + L Fl 15s; *Bell*; 53°07'·81N 00°57'·34E.
S Inner Dowsing ⟨ Q (6) + L Fl 15s; *Bell*; 53°12'·12N 00°33'·69E.
Burnham Flats ⟨ Q (9) 15s; *Bell*; 53°07'·53N 00°34'·89E.
N Well ⟨ L Fl 10s; *Whis*; *Racon (T) 10M*; 53°03'·02N 00°27'·90E.
Roaring Middle ⟨ L Fl 10s 7m 8M; 52°58'·64N 00°21'·08E.
Sunk ⟨ Q (9) 15s; 52°56'·29N 00°23'·40E.

Boston Roads ⸱ L Fl 10s; 52°57'·66N 00°16'·04E.

THE WASH TO THE RIVER HUMBER

Dudgeon⸱ Q (9) 15s 7M; *Racon (O) 10M; Whis;* 53°16'·62N 01°16'·90E.
E Dudgeon ⸱ Q (3) 10s; *Bell;* 53°19'·72N 00°58'·69E.
N Outer Dowsing ⸱ Q; 53°33'·52N 00°59'·59E.

B.1D Platform Dowsing ⸱ 53°33'·68N 00°52'·63E; Fl (2) 10s 28m **22M**; Morse (U) R 15s 28m 3M; *Horn (2) 60s; Racon (T) 10M.*
Inner Dowsing ⸱ Q (3) 10s 7M, *Racon (T) 10M; Horn 60s;* 53°19'·10N 00°34'·80E.
Protector ⸱ Fl R 2·5s; 53°24'·84N 00°25'·12E.
Humber ⸱ L Fl 10s 7M; *Horn (2) 30s; Racon (T) 7M;* 53°38'·83N 00°20'·17E.

SPURN ⸱ Q (3) 10s 10m 8M; *Horn 20s; Racon (M) 5M;* 53°33'·56N 00°14'·20E.

RIVER HUMBER TO RIVER TYNE
BRIDLINGTON/FILEY

SW Smithic ⸱ Q (9) 15s; 54°02'·41N 00°09'·21W.
Flamborough Hd ☆ 54°06'·98N 00°04'·96W; Fl (4) 15s 65m **24M**; W○ twr; *Horn (2) 90s.*
Filey Brigg ⸱ Q (3) 10s; *Bell;* 54°12'·74N 00°14'·60W.

SCARBOROUGH/WHITBY

Scarborough Pier ⸱ Iso 5s 17m 9M; W○twr; vis: 219°-039° (tide sigs); *Dia 60s;* 54°16'·91N 00°23'·40W.
Whitby ⸱ Q; *Bell;* 54°30'·33N 00°36'·58W.
Whitby High ☆ 54°28'·67N 00°34'·10W; Ling Hill Fl WR 5s 73m **18M**, R16M; W 8-sided twr and dwellings; vis: 128°-R-143°-W- 319°.
Salt Scar ⸱ 54°38'·12N 01°00'·12W VQ; *Bell.*

TEES BAY/HARTLEPOOL/SUNDERLAND

Tees Fairway ⸱ Iso 4s 8m 8M; *Racon (B) unknown range; Horn (1) 5s;* 54°40'·94N 01°06'·48W.
Bkwtr Hd S Gare ☆ 54°38'·85N 01°08'·27W; Fl WR 12s 16m **W20M, R17M**; W○ twr; vis: 020°-W-274°-R-357°; Sig Stn; *Horn 30s.*
Longscar ⸱ Q (3) 10s; *Bell;* 54°40'·86N 01°09'·89W.
The Heugh ☆ 54°40'·09N 01°47'·98W; Fl (2) 10s 19m **19M** ; W twr.

Sunderland Roker Pier Hd ☆ 54°55'·28N 01°21'·15W; Fl 5s 25m **23M**; W□ twr, 3 R bands and cupola: vis: 211°- 357°; *Siren 20s.*

TYNE ENTRANCE/NORTH SHIELDS
Ent North Pier Hd ☆ 55°00'·88N 01°24'·18W; Fl (3) 10s 26m **26M**; Gy□twr, W lantern; *Horn 10s.*

RIVER TYNE TO BERWICK-ON-TWEED
BLYTH/COQUET ISLAND/ AMBLE

Blyth F'w'y ⸱ Fl G 3s; *Bell;* 55°06'·59N 01°28'·60W.
Blyth E Pier Hd ☆ 55°06'·98N 01°29'·37W; Fl (4) 10s 19m **21M**, W twr; same structure FR 13m 13M, vis:152°-249°; *Horn (3) 30s.*
Coquet ☆ 55°20'·03N 01°32'·39W; Fl (3) WR 30s 25m **W23M, R19M**; W□ twr, turreted parapet, lower half Gy; vis: 330°-R-140°-W-163°-R-180°-W-330°; sector boundaries are indeterminate and may appear as Alt WR; *Horn 30s.*
Amble N Pier Hd ⸱ Fl G 6s 12m 6M; 55°20'·39N 01°34'·25W.

BAMBURGH/FARNE ISLANDS

The Falls ⸱ Fl R 2·5s; 55°34'·61N 01°37'·12W.
Shoreston Outcars ⸱ QR; 55°35'·88N 01°39'·34W.
Bamburgh Black Rocks Point ☆ 55°36'·99N 01°43'·45W; Oc(2) WRG 8s 12m **W14M**, R11M, G11M; W bldg; vis: 122°-G-165°-W- 175°-R-191°-W- 238°-R- 275°-W- 289°-G-300°.
Inner Farne ⸱ Fl (2) WR 15s 27m W10M, R7M; W ○ twr; vis: 119°-R-280°-W -119°; 55°36'·92N 01°39'·35W.
Longstone ☆ **W side** 55°38'·62N 01°36'·65W; Fl 20s 23m **24M**; R twr, W band; *Horn (2) 60s.*
Swedman ⸱ Fl G 2·5s; 55°37'·65N 01°41'·63W.

HOLY ISLAND

Ridge ⸱ Q (3) 10s; 55°39'·70N 01°45'·97W.
Triton ⸱ QG; 55°39'·59N 01°46'·82W.
Plough Seat ⸱ QR; 55°40'·37N 01°44'·97W.
Goldstone ⸱ QG; 55°40'·25N 01°43'·64W.

BERWICK-ON-TWEED

Bkwtr Hd ⸱ Fl 5s 15m 6M; vis: 201°-009°, (obscured 155°-201°); W ○ twr, R cupola and base; FG (same twr) 8m 1M; vis 009°-G-155°; 55°45'·88N 01°59'·06W.

No.	Port													Port	No.
1	Ramsgate	1	11	31	61	78	91	107	126	189	205	205	232	Berwick-upon-Tweed	11
2	Sheerness	34	2	10	27	42	65	81	102	157	176	185	203	Amble	10
3	Gravesend	56	22	3	9	16	36	51	70	138	149	156	180	Sunderland	9
4	London Bridge	76	45	23	4	8	24	39	58	122	137	140	169	Hartlepool	8
5	Burnham-on-Crouch	44	34	53	76	5	7	16	35	88	114	121	143	Whitby	7
6	Brightlingsea	41	28	47	71	22	6	6	20	81	98	105	130	Scarborough	6
7	Harwich	40	50	65	83	31	24	7	5	58	83	87	114	Bridlington	5
8	River Deben (ent)	45	55	71	89	35	38	6	8	4	72	75	113	Hull	4
9	Southwold	62	80	95	113	58	63	30	23	9	3	34	83	Boston	3
10	Lowestoft	72	90	105	123	68	73	40	33	10	10	2	85	King's Lynn	2
11	Great Yarmouth	79	97	112	130	76	80	52	41	18	7	11	1	Great Yarmouth	1

AREA 5 E. Scotland - *Berwick-upon-Tweed to C Wrath & N Isles*

SELECTED LIGHTS, BUOYS & WAYPOINTS | Positions are referenced to WGS84

BERWICK-UPON-TWEED TO BASS ROCK
EYEMOUTH/ST ABB'S/DUNBAR

Blind Buss ↙ Q; 55°52'·80N 02°05'·25E.

Eyemouth E Bkwtr Hd ≮ Iso R 2s 8m 8M; 55°52'·50N 02°05'·29W.

St Abb's Hd ☆ 55°54'·96N 02°08'·29W; Fl 10s 68m **26M**; W twr; *Racon (T) 18M*.

Bass Rock, S side, ☆ Fl (3) 20s 46m 10M; W twr; vis: 241°-107°; 56°04'·61N 02°38'·48W.

FIRTH OF FORTH - SOUTH SHORE
SOUTH SIDE TO LEITH/PORT EDGAR

Fidra ☆ 56°04'·39N 02°47'·13W; Fl (4) 30s 34m **24M**; W twr; obsc by Bass Rk, Craig Leith & Lamb Is.

Wreck ⚓ Fl (2) R 10s; 56°04'·39N 02°52'·39W.

Inchkeith F'wy ⚓ Iso 2s; *Racon (T) 5M*; 56°03'·49N 03°00'·10W.

Narrow Deep ⚓ Fl (2) R 10s; 56°01'·46N 03°04'·59W.

Craigh Waugh ↙ Q; 56°00'·26N 03°04'·47W.

Leith Approach ⚓ Fl R 3s; 55°59'·95N 03°11'·51W.

Inch Garvie, NW ≮ L Fl 5s 9m 11M; 56°00'·10N 03°23'·37W.

Forth Rail Br. Centres of spans have W Lts and ends of cantilevers R Lts, defining N and S chans. Centre Piers; 2 Aero FR 47m 5M; 56°00'·33N 03°21'·79W.

Forth Road Br. N susp twr Iso G 4s 7m 6M on E and W sides. S susp twr Iso R 4s 7m 6M on E and W sides.

Port Edgar W Bkwtr Hd ≮ Fl R 4s 4m 8M; 55°59'·86N 03°24'·78W. W blockhouse

NORTH CHANNEL/MIDDLE BANK

Inchkeith ☆ 56°02'·01N 03°08'·17W; Fl 15s 67m **22M**; stone twr.

No. 7 ▲ QG; *Bell; Racon (T) 5M*; 56°02'·80N 03°10'·97W.

Oxcars ☆ Fl (2) WR 7s 16m W13M, R12M; W twr, R band; vis: 072°-W-087°-R-196°-W-313°-R-072°; 56°01'·36N 03°16'·84W.

FIRTH OF FORTH - N SHORE; ELIE TO FIFE NESS/RIVER TAY/ARBROATH

Thill Rock ⚓ Fl (4) R 10s; 56°10'·87N 02°49'·70W.

Elie Ness ☆ 56°11'·04N 02°48'·77W; Fl 6s 15m **18M**; W twr.

St Monans Bkwtr Hd ≮ Oc WRG 6s 5m W7M, R4M, G4M; vis: 282°-G-355°-W-026°-R-038°; 56°12'·20N 02°45'·94W.

Anstruther, W Pier Hd ≮ 2 FR (vert) 5m 4M; Gy mast; *Horn (3) 60s (occas)*; 56°13'·18N 02°41'·84W.

Isle of May ☆ 56°11'·12N 02°33'·46W(Summit); Fl (2) 15s 73m **22M**; □ twr on stone dwelling.

Fife Ness ☆ 56°16'·74N 02°35'·19W; Iso WR 10s 12m **W21M, R20M**; W bldg; vis: 143°-W-197°-R-217°-W-023°.

N Carr ↙ Q (3) 10s 3m 5M; 56°18'·05N 02°32'·94W.

Bell Rk ☆ 56°26'·08N 02°23'·21W; Fl 5s 28m **18M**; *Racon (M) 18M*.

Tay F'wy ⚓ L Fl 10s; *Bell*; 56°29'·24N 02°38'·26W.

Abertay N ↙ Q (3) 10s; *Racon (T) 8M*; 56°27'·39N 02°40'·36W.

Horse Shoe ↙ Q (6) + L Fl 15s; 56°27'·28N 02°50'·20W.

Tayport High Lt Ho ☆ 56°27'·17N 02°53'·96W; Dir lt 269°; Iso WRG3s 24m **W22M, R17M, G16M**; W twr; vis:267°-G-268°-W-270°-R-271°;56°27'·04N 02°56'·55W.

Arbroath E Pier S Elbow ≮ Fl G 3s 8m 5M; W twr; shows FR when hbr closed; *Siren (3) 60s (occas)*; 56°33'·25N 02°34'·97W.

MONTROSE TO RATTRAY HEAD
MONTROSE/JOHNSHAVEN/GOURDON HBR

Scurdie Ness ☆ 56°42'·10N 02°26'·24W; Fl (3) 20s 38m **23M**; W twr; *Racon (T) 14-16M*.

Montrose Ldg Lts 271·5°. Front, FR 11m 5M; W twin pillars, R bands; 56°42'·21N 02°27'·41W. Rear, 272m from front, FR 18m 5M; W twr, R cupola.

Annat Shoal ▲ QG 56°42'·37N 02°25'·19W.

Johnshaven, Ldg Lts 316°. Front, FR 5m; 56°47'·62N 02°20'·26W. Rear, 85m from front, FG 20m; shows R when unsafe to enter hbr.

Gourdon Hbr, Ldg Lts 358°. Front, FR 5m 5M; W twr; shows G when unsafe to enter; *Siren (2) 60s (occas)*; 56°49'·69N 02°17'·24W. Rear, 120m from front, FR 30m 5M; W twr.

Todhead ☆ Fl (4) 30s 41m **18M**; W twr; 56°53'·00N 02°12'·97W.

STONEHAVEN/ABERDEEN/PETERHEAD

Stonehaven Outer Pier Hd ≮ Iso WRG 4s 7m W11M, R7M, G8M; vis: 214°-G-246°-W-268°-R-280°; 56°57'·59N 02°12'·00W.

Girdle Ness ☆ Fl (2) 20s 56m **22M**; obsc by Greg Ness when brg more than about 020°; *Racon (G) 25M*; 57°08'·34N 02°02'·91W.

Aberdeen F'wy ⚓ Mo (A) 5s; *Racon (T) 7M*; 57°09'·31N 02°01'·95W.

Torry Ldg lts 235·7°. Front, FR or FG 14m 5M; FR entry safe, FG when entry dangerous; vis: 195°-279°; 57°08'·37N 02°04'·51W.Rear, FR 19m 5M.

Buchan Ness ☆ Fl 5s 40m **28M**; W twr, R bands; *Racon (O) 14-16M*; 57°28'·23N 01°46'·51W.

Cruden Skares ⚓ Fl R 10s; *Bell*; 57°23'·17N 01°50'·36W.

Peterhead Marina N Bkwtr Hd ≮ QG 5m 2M; vis: 185°-300°; 57°29'·81N 01°47'·49W.

Rattray Hd ☆ 57°36'·61N 01°49'·03W; Fl (3) 30s 28m **24M**; W twr; *Racon (M) 15M*.

RATTRAY HEAD TO INVERNESS

Rattray Hd ☆ 57°36'·61N 01°49'·03W Fl (3) 30s 28m **24M**; W twr; **Racon (M) 15M**; *Horn (2) 45s.*

FRASERBURGH/MACDUFF/BANFF

Fraserburgh, Balaclava Bkwtr Head ⚓ Fl (2) G 8s 26m 6M; dome on W twr; vis: 178°-326°; 57°41'·51N 01°59'·70W.

Kinnaird Hd ☆ 57°41'·87N 02°00'·26W Fl 5s 25m **22M**; vis: 092°-297°.

Macduff Pier Hd ⚓ Fl (2) WRG 6s 12m W9M, R7M; W twr; vis: shore-G-115°-W-174°-R-210°; 57°40'·25N 02°30'·02W.

Banff N Pier Hd ⚓ Fl 4s; 57°40'·22N 02°31'·27W.

WHITEHILLS/PORTSOY/FINDOCHTY

Whitehills Pier Hd ⚓ 57°40'·80N 02°34'·88W Fl WR 3s 7m W9M, R6M; W twr; vis: 132°-R-212°-W-245°.
Portsoy Pier Ldg Lts 160°, Front F 12m 5M; twr; 57°41'·17N 02°41'·49W. Rear FR 17m 5M; mast.
Findochty Middle Pier Ldg Lts 166°, Front FR 6m 3M; 57°41'·90N 02°54'·20W. Rear FR 10m 3M.

BUCKIE/LOSSIEMOUTH/HOPEMAN

West Muck ⚓ QR 5m 7M; tripod; 57°41'·06N 02°58'·01W.

N Pier 60m from Hd ☆ 57°40'·9N 02°57'·5W Oc R 10s 15m **15M** W twr.

BURGHEAD/FINDHORN/NAIRN

Lossiemouth S Pier Hd ⚓ Fl R 6s 11m 5M; *Siren 60s;* 57°43'·42N 03°16'·69W.

Covesea Skerries ☆ 57°43'·47N 03°20'·45W Fl WR 20s 49m **W24M, R20M**; W twr; vis: 076°-W-267°-R-282°.

Hopeman W Pier Hd ⚓ Oc G 4s 8m 4M; 57°42'·69N 03°26'·29W.

Burghead N Bkwtr Hd ⚓ Oc 8s 7m 5M; 57°42'·09N 03°30'·03W.

Findhorn Landfall ⚓ LF 10s 57°40'·33N 03°38'·65W.
Nairn W Pier Hd ⚓ QG 5m 1M; Gy post; 57°35'·60N 03°51'·63W.

INVERNESS FIRTH/CALEDONIAN CANAL

Navity Bk ⚓ Fl (3) G 15s; 57°38'·16N 04°01'·18W.
Riff Bank S ⚓ Q (6) + L Fl 15s; 57°36'·73N 04°00'·97W.
Craigmee ⚓ Fl R 6s 3m 4M; 57°35'·30N 04°05'·04W.

Chanonry ☆ 57°34'·44N 04°05'·57W Oc 6s 12m **15M**; W twr; vis: 148°-073°.

Kessock Bridge Centre , Or △; *Racon (K) 6M;* 57°29'·97N 04°13'·79W.

Clachnaharry, S Tr'ng Wall Hd ⚓ Iso G 4s 5m 2M; tfc sigs; 57°29'·43N 04°15'·86W.

INVERNESS TO DUNCANSBY HEAD

CROMARTY FIRTH

Fairway ⚓ L Fl 10s; *Racon (M) 5M;* 57°39'·96N 03°54'·19W.

Cromarty Bank ⚓ Fl (2) G 10s; 57°40'·66N 03°56'·78W.
Buss Bank ⚓ Fl R 3s 57°40'·97N 03°59'·54W.

The Ness ☆ 57°40'·98N 04°02'·20W Oc WR 10s 18m **W15M**, R11M; W twr; vis: 079°-R-088°-W-275°, obsc by N Sutor when brg less than 253°.
Three Kings ⚓ Q (3) 10s; 57°43'·73N 03°54'·25W.

DORNOCH FIRTH/LYBSTER/WICK

Tarbat Ness ☆ 57°51'·88N 03°46'·76W Fl (4) 30s 53m **24M**; W twr, R bands; *Racon (T) 14-16M.*

Lybster, S Pier Hd ⚓ Oc R 6s 10m 3M; 58°17'·79N 03°17'·41W.

Clyth Ness ☆ Fl (2) 30s 45m 14M; 58°18'·64N 03°12'·74W.

Wick S Pier Hd ⚓ Fl WRG 3s 12m W12M, R9M, G9M; W 8-sided twr; vis: 253°-G-270°-W-286°-R-329°; Bell (2) 10s (occas); 58°26'·34N 03°04'·73W.

Noss Hd ☆ 58°28'·71N 03°03'·09W Fl WR 20s 53m **W25M, R21M**; W twr; vis: shore-R-191°-W-shore.

DUNCANSBY HEAD TO CAPE WRATH

Duncansby Hd ☆ 58°38'·65N 03°01'·58W Fl 12s 67m **22M**; W twr; **Racon (T)**.

Pentland Skerries ☆ 58°41'·41N 02°55'·49W Fl (3) 30s 52m **23M**; W twr.

Lother Rock ⚓ Fl 2s 13m 6M; *Racon (M)10M*; 58°43'·79N 02°58'·69W.

Swona N Hd ⚓ Fl (3) 10s 16m 10M; 58°45'·11N 03°03'·10W.

Stroma ☆, Swilkie Point 58°41'·75N 03°07'·01W Fl (2) 20s 32m **26M**; W twr.

Dunnet Hd ☆ 58°40'·28N 03°22'·60W Fl (4) 30s 105m **23M**.

Scrabster Q. E. Pier Hd ⚓ Fl (2) 4s 8m 8M 58°36'·66N 03°32'·31W.

Strathy Pt ☆ 58°36'·04N 04°01'·12W Fl 20s 45m **26M**; W twr on W dwelling. F.R. on chy 100° 8·5M.

Sule Skerry ☆ 59°05'·09N 04°24'·38W Fl (2) 15s 34m **21M**; W twr; *Racon (T)*.

North Rona ☆ 59°07'·27N 05°48'·91W Fl (3) 20s 114m **24M**.

Sula Sgeir ⚓ Fl 15s 74m 11M; □ structure; 59°05'·61N 06°09'·57W.

Loch Eriboll, White Hd ⚓ Fl WR10s 18m W13M, R12M; W twr and bldg; vis: 030°-W-172°-R-191°-W-212°; 58°31'·01N 04°38'·90W.

Cape Wrath ☆ 58°37'·54N 04°59'·94W Fl (4) 30s 122m **22M**; W twr.

ORKNEY ISLANDS

Tor Ness ☆ 58°46'·78N 03°17'·86W Fl 5s 21m **17M**; W twr.

Cantick Hd (S Walls, SE end) ☆ 58°47'·23N 03°07'·88W Fl 20s 35m **18M**; W twr.

SCAPA FLOW AND APPROACHES
Ruff Reef, off Cantick Hd ≼ Fl 10s 10m 6M; 58°47'·43N 03°07'·80W.

Hoxa Hd ≼ Fl WR 3s 15m W9M, R6M; W twr; vis: 026°-W-163°-R-201°-W-215°; 58°49'·31N 03°02'·09W.

Stanger Hd ≼ Fl R 5s 25m 8M 58°48'·96N 03°04'·74W.

CLESTRAN SOUND/HOY SOUND
Peter Skerry ◣ Fl G 6s; 58°55'·25N 03°13'·51W.

Riddock Shoal ◿ Fl (2) R 12s; 58°55'·89N 03°15'·00W.

Graemsay Is Hoy Sound Low ☆ Ldg Lts 104°. **Front,** 58°56'·42N 03°18'·60W Iso 3s 17m **15M**; W twr; vis: 070°-255°. **High Rear,** 1·2M from front, Oc WR 8s 35m **W20M, R16M**; W twr; vis: 097°-R-112°-W-163°-R-178°-W-332°; obsc on Ldg line within 0·5M.

STROMNESS
Stromness ◿ QR; 58°57'·25N 03°17'·61W.

N Pier Hd ≼ Fl R 3s 8m 5M; 58°57'·75N 03°17'·71W.

AUSKERRY/KIRKWALL
Copinsay ☆ 58°53'·77N 02°40'·35W Fl (5) 30s 79m **21M**; W twr.

Auskerry ☆ 59°01'·51N 02°34'·34W Fl 20s 34m **20M**; W twr.

Scargun Shoal v Q (3) 10s; 59°00'·69N 02°58'·58W.

Kirkwall Pier N end ☆ 58°59'·29N 02°57'·72W Iso WRG 5s 8m **W15M**, R13M, G13M; W twr; vis: 153°-G-183°-W-192°-R-210°.

WIDE FIRTH
Linga Skerry ⌇ Q (3) 10s; 59°02'·39N 02°57'·56W.

Boray Skerries ⌇ Q (6) + L Fl 15s; 59°03'·65N 02°57'·66W.

Skertours ⌇ Q; 59°04'·11N 02°56'·72W.

Galt Skerry ⌇ Q; 59°05'·21N 02°54'·20W.

Brough of Birsay ☆ 59°08'·19N 03°20'·41W Fl (3) 25s 52m **18M**.

Papa Stronsay NE end, The Ness Fl(4)20s 8m 9M; W twr; 59°09'·34N 02°34'·93W

STRONSAY, PAPA SOUND
Quiabow ◣ Fl (2) G 12s; 59°09'·82N 02°36'·30W.

No. 1 ◣ Fl G 5s; (off Jacks Reef) 59°09'·16N 02°36'·51W.

Whitehall Pier Hd ≼ 2 FG (vert) 8m 4M; 50°08'·61N 02°35'·96W.

SANDAY ISLAND/NORTH RONALDSAY
Start Pt ☆ 59°16'·69N 02°22'·71W Fl (2) 20s 24m **18M**.

N Ronaldsay ☆ NE end, 59°23'·37N 02°23'·03W Fl 10s 43m **24M**; R twr, W bands; *Racon (T) 14-17M*; *Horn 60s.*

WESTRAY/PIEROWALL
Noup Head ☆ 59°19'·86N 03°04'·23W Fl 30s 79m **20M**; W twr; vis: about 335°-282° but partially obsc 240°-275°.

Pierowall E Pier Head ≼ Fl WRG 3s 7m W11M, R7M, G7M; vis: 254°-G-276°-W-291°-R-308°-G-215°; 59°19'·35N 02°58'·53W.

Papa Westray, Moclett Bay Pier Head ≼ Fl WRG 5s 7m W5M, R3M,G3M; vis: 306°-G-341°-W-040°-R-074°; 59°19'·60N 02°53'·52W.

SHETLAND ISLES
FAIR ISLE
Skadan South ☆, 59°30'·84N 01°39'·16W Fl (4) 30s 32m **22M**; W twr; vis: 260°-146°, obsc inshore 260°-282°; *Horn (2) 60s.*

Skroo ☆ N end 59°33'·13N 01°36'·58W Fl (2) 30s 80m **22M**; W twr; vis: 086·7°-358°.

MAINLAND, SOUTH
Sumburgh Head ☆ 59°51'·21N 01°16'·58W Fl (3) 30s 91m **23M**.

Pool of Virkie, Marina E Bkwtr Head ≼ 2 FG (vert) 6m 5M; 59°53'·01N 01°17'·16W.

BRESSAY/LERWICK
Bressay, Kirkabister Ness ☆ 60°07'·20N 01°07'·29W; Fl (2) 20s 32m **23M**.

Soldian Rock ⌇ Q (6) + L Fl 15s 60°12'·51N 01°04'·73W.

Gremista Marina S Hd ≼ Iso R 4s 3m 2M; 60°10'·20N 01°09'·61W.

Rova Hd ≼ 60°11'·46N 01°08'·60W Fl (3) WRG 18s 12m W12M, R9M, G9M; W twr; vis: 090°-R-182°-W-191°-G-213°-R-241°-W-261·5°-G-009°-R-040°. Same structure and synhcronised: Fl (3) WRG 18s 14m **W16M**, R13M, G13M; vis: 176·5°-R-182°-W-191°-G-196·5°.

1	Ramsgate	1			11	31	61	78	91	107	126	189	205	205	232	Berwick-upon-Tweed	11
2	Sheerness	34	2			10	27	42	65	81	102	157	176	185	203	Amble	10
3	Gravesend	56	22	3			9	16	36	51	70	138	149	156	180	Sunderland	9
4	London Bridge	76	45	23	4			8	24	39	58	122	137	140	169	Hartlepool	8
5	Burnham-on-Crouch	44	34	53	76	5			7	16	35	88	114	121	143	Whitby	7
6	Brightlingsea	41	28	47	71	22	6			6	20	81	98	105	130	Scarborough	6
7	Harwich	40	50	65	83	31	24	7			5	58	83	87	114	Bridlington	5
8	River Deben (ent)	45	55	71	89	35	38	6	8			4	72	75	113	Hull	4
9	Southwold	62	80	95	113	58	63	30	23	9			3	34	83	Boston	3
10	Lowestoft	72	90	105	123	68	73	40	33	10	10			2	85	King's Lynn	2
11	Great Yarmouth	79	97	112	130	76	80	52	41	18	7	11			1	Great Yarmouth	1

19

AREA 6 NW Scotland - *C. Wrath to Oban including The Western Isles*

SELECTED LIGHTS, BUOYS & WAYPOINTS | Positions are referenced to WGS84

CAPE WRATH TO LOCH TORRIDON

Cape Wrath ☆ 58°37'·54N 04°59'·99W Fl (4) 30s 122m **22M**; W twr.

LOCH INCHARD/LOCH LAXFORD

Bodha Ceann na Saile ⁅ Q; 58°27'·24N 05°04'·01W.
Kinlochbervie Dir lt 327° ☆. 58°27'·49N 05°03'·08W WRG 15m **16M**; vis: 326°-FG-326·5°-Al GW-326·75°-FW-327·25°-Al RW-327·5°-FR-328°.
Stoer Head ☆ 58°14'·43N 05°24'·07W Fl 15s 59m **24M**; W twr.

LOCH INVER/SUMMER ISLES/ULLAPOOL

Soyea I ⚲ Fl (2) 10s 34m 6M; 58°08'·56N 05°19'·67W.
Glas Leac ⚲ Fl WRG 3s 7m 5M; 58°08'·68N 05°16'·36W.
Rubha Cadail ⚲ Fl WRG 6s 11m W9M, R6M, G6M; W twr; vis: 311°-G-320°-W-325°-R-103°-W-111°-G-118°-W-127°-R-157°-W-199°; 57°55'·51N 05°13'·40W.
Ullapool Pt ⚲ QR; 57°53'·70N 05°10'·68W.
Cailleach Head ⚲ Fl (2) 12s 60m 9M; W twr; vis: 015°-236°; 57°55'·81N 05°24'·23W.

LOCH EWE/LOCH GAIRLOCH

Fairway ⚲ L Fl 10s; 57°51'·98N 05°40'·09W.
Rubha Reidh ☆ 57°51'·52N 05°48'·72W Fl (4) 15s 37m **24M**.
Glas Eilean ⚲Fl WRG 6s 9m W6M, R4M; vis: 080°-W-102°-R-296°-W-333°-G-080°; 57°42'·79N 05°42'·42W.
Gairloch Pier ⚲ QR 6m 2M. 57°42'·59N 05°41'·03W

OUTER HEBRIDES – EAST SIDE

LEWIS

Butt of Lewis ☆ 58°30'·89N 06°15'·84W Fl 5s 52m **25M**; R twr; vis: 056°-320°.
Tiumpan Head ☆ 58°15'·66N 06°08'·29W Fl (2) 15s 55m **25M**; W twr.
Reef Rock ⚲ QR; 58°11'·58N 06°21'·97W.
Arnish Point ☆ Fl WR 10s 17m W9M, R7M; W ○ twr; vis: 088°-W-198°-R-302°-W-013°; 58°11'·50N 06°22'·16W.
Rubh' Uisenis ⚲ Fl 5s 24m 11M; W twr; 57°56'·25N 06°28'·36W.
Shiants ⚲ QG; 57°54'·57N 06°25'·70W.
Sgeir Inoe ⚲ Fl G 6s; 57°50'·93N 06°33'·93W.
Scalpay, **Eilean Glas** ☆ 57°51'·41N 06°38'·55W Fl (3) 20s 43m **23M**; W twr, R bands; *Racon (T) 16-18M*.
Sgeir Bràigh Mor ⚲ Fl G 6s; 57°51'·51N 06°43'·84W.
Sgeir Graidach ⁅ Q (6) + L Fl 15s; 57°50'·36N 06°41'·37W.
Tarbert ⚲ Oc WRG 6s 10m 5M; 57°53'·82N 06°47'·93W

SOUND OF HARRIS/BERNERAY

Fairway ⚲ L Fl 10s; 57°40'·35N 07°02'·15W.

Cabbage ⚲ Fl (2) R 6s; *Racon (T) 5M (3cm)*; 57°42'·13N 07°03'·96W.
Bo Stainan ⁅ VQ(6) + LF 10s. 57°45'·76N 07°02'·40W
Trench ⚲ Q (3) G 10s; 57°41'·89N 07°09'·00W.

LOCH MADDY

Weaver's Pt ⚲ 57°36'·49N 07°06'·00W Fl 3s 24m 7M; W hut.
Glas Eilean Mòr ⚲ 57°35'·95N 07°06'·70W Fl (2) G 4s 8m 5M.

SOUTH UIST, LOCH CARNAN

Landfall ⁅ L Fl 10s; 57°22'·27N 07°11'·52W.
Ushenish ☆ (S Uist) 57°17'·89N 07°11'·58W Fl WR 20s 54m **W19M, R15M**; W twr; vis: 193°-W-356°-R-018°.

LOCH BOISDALE/BARRA/CASTLEBAY

MacKenzie Rk ⚲ Fl (3) R 15s 3m 4M; 57°08'·24N 07°13'·71W.
Calvay E End ⚲ Fl (2) WRG 10s 16m W7M, R4M, G4M; W twr; vis: 111°-W-190°-G-202°-W-286°-R-111°; 57°08'·53N 07°15'·38W.
Binch Rock ⁅ Q (6) + L Fl 15s; 57°01'·71N 07°17'·16W.
Bo Vich Chuan ⁅ Q (6) + L Fl 15s; *Racon (M) 5M*; 56°56'·15N 07°23'·31W.
Castle Bay S ⚲ Fl (2) R 8s; *Racon (T) 7M*; 56°56'·09N 07°27'·21W.
Barra Hd ☆ 56°47'·11N 07°39'·26W Fl 15s 208m **18M**; W twr; obsc by islands to NE.

OUTER HEBRIDES – WEST SIDE

Flannan I ☆, Eilean Mór 58°17'·32N 07°35'·23W Fl (2) 30s 101m **20M**; W twr; obsc in places by Is to W of Eilean Mór.
Haskeir I ☆ 57°41'·98N 07°41·36W Fl 20s 44m **23M**; W twr.

LOCH TORRIDON TO MULL

LITTLE MINCH/NORTH SKYE/RONA

Eugenie Rk ⁅ Q 6 + LF 15s; 57°46'·47N 06°27'·28W.
Eilean Trodday ⚲ Fl (2) WRG 10s 52m W12M, R9M, G9M; W Bn; vis: W062°-R088°-130°-W-322°-G-062°; 57°43'·64N 06°17'·89W.
Comet Rock ⚲ Fl R 6s; 57°44'·60N 06°20'·50W.
Rona NE Point £ 57°34'·68N 05°57'·56W Fl 12s 69m 19M; W twr; vis: 050°-358°.

CROWLIN ISLANDS/RAASAY

Sgeir Mhór ⚲Fl G 5s; 57°24'·57N 06°10'·53W.
Eilean Beag ⚲ Fl 6s 32m 6M; W Bn; 57°21'·21N 05°51'·42W.

Eyre Pt ⚓ Fl WR 3s 6m W9M, R6M; W twr; vis: 215°-W-266°-R- 288°-W-063°; 57°20'·01N 06°01'·29W.

KYLE AKIN AND KYLE OF LOCH ALSH

Carragh Rk ⚓ Fl (2) G 12s; *Racon (T) 5M*; 57°17'·18N 05°45'·36W.

Skye Br Centre ⚓ Oc 6s; 57°16'·57N 05°44'·58W.

String Rock ⚓ Fl R 6s; 57°16'·50N 05°42'·89W.

Sgeir-na-Caillich ⚓ Fl (2) R 6s 3m 4M; 57°15'·59N 05°38'·90W.

SOUND OF SLEAT

Kyle Rhea ⚓ Fl WRG 3s 7m W11M, R9M, G8M; W Bn; vis: shore-R-219-W-228°-G-338°-W-346°-R-shore; 57°14'·22N 05°39'·93W.

Ornsay, SE end ☆ 57°08'·59N 05°46'·88W Oc 8s 18m **15M**; W twr; vis: 157°-030°.

Pt. of Sleat ⚓ Fl 3s 20m9M; W twr; 57°01'·08N06°01'·08W.

MALLAIG

Sgeir Dhearg ⚓ QG; 57°00'·74N 05°49'·50W.

N Pier, E end ⚓ Iso WRG 4s 6m W9M, R6M, G6M; Gy twr; vis: 181°-G-185°-W-197°-R-201°. Fl G 3s 14m 6M; same structure; 57°00'·47N 05°49'·50W.

NW SKYE

Neist Point ☆ 57°25'·41N 06°47'·30W Fl 5s 43m **16M**; W twr.

WEST OF MULL AND SMALL ISLES

Hyskeir ☆ 56°58'·14N 06°40'·87W Fl (3) 30s 41m **24M**; W twr. *Racon(T) 14-17M*.

Bogha Ruadh⚓ Fl G 5s 4m 3M; 56°49'·56N 06°13'·05W.

Bo Faskadale ⚓ Fl (3) G 18s; 56°48'·18N 06°06'·37W.

Ardnamurchan ☆ 56°43'·63N 06°13'·58W Fl (2) 20s 55m **24M**; Gy twr; vis: 002°-217°; *Horn (2) 20s*.

TIREE

Roan Bogha ⚓ Q (6) + L Fl 15s 3m 5M; 56°32'·23N 06°40'·18W.

Placaid Bogha ⚓ Fl G 4s; 56°33'·22N 06°44'·06W.

Scarinish ☆, S side of ent 56°30'·01N 06°48'·27W Fl 3s 11m **16M**; W ☐ twr; vis: 210°-030°.

Skerryvore ☆ 56°19'·36N 07°06'·88W Fl 10s 46m **23M**; Gy twr; *Racon (M) 18M*; *Horn 60s*.

LOCH NA LÀTHAICH (LOCH LATHAICH)

Dubh Artach ☆ 56°07'·94N 06°38'·08W; Fl (2)30s 44m **20M**; Gy twr, R band.

SOUND OF MULL
LOCH SUNART/TOBERMORY/LOCH ALINE

Ardmore Pt ⚓ Fl (2) 10s 18m 13M; 56°39'·37N 06°07'·70W.

New Rks ⚓ Fl G 6s 56°39'·05N 06°03'·30W.

Rubha nan Gall ☆ 56°38'·33N 06°04'·00W Fl 3s 17m **15M**; W twr.

Avon Rock ⚓ Fl (4) R 12s; 56°30'·78N 05°46'·80W.

Yule Rocks ⚓ Fl R 15s; 56°30'·01N 05°43'·96W.

Glas Eileanan Gy Rks ⚓ Fl 3s 11m 6M; W ○ twr on W base; 56°29'·77N 05°42'·83W.

Craignure Ldg Lts 240·9°. Front, FR 10m; 56°28'·26N 05°42'·28W. Rear, 150m from front, FR 12m; vis: 225·8°-255·8°.

MULL TO OBAN

Lismore ☆, SW end 56°27'·34N 05°36'·45W Fl 10s 31m **17M**; W twr; vis: 237°-208°.

Lady's Rk ⚓ Fl 6s 12m 5M; 56°26'·92N 05°37'·05W.

Duart Pt ⚓ Fl (3) WR 18s 14m W5M, R3M; vis: 162°-W-261°-R-275°-W-353°-R-shore; 56°26'·84N 05°38'·77W.

DUNSTAFFNAGE BAY

Pier Hd ⚓ NE end, 2 FG (vert) 4m 2M; 56°27'·21N 05°26'·18W.

OBAN

N spit of Kerrera ⚓ Fl R 3s 9m 5M; W col, R bands; 56°25'·49N 05°29'·56W.

Dunollie ⚓ Fl (2) WRG 6s 7m W5M, G4M, R4M; vis:G351°-W009°-R047°-W120°-G138°-143°; 56°25'·37N 05°29'·05W.

Corran Ledge ⚓ VQ (9) 10s; 56°25'·19N 05°29'·11W.

Oban N Pier Mid ⚓ 2 FG (vert) 8m 5M; 56°24'·87N 05°28'·49W.

		1	2	3	4	5	6	7	8	9	10	11	12	13	14	15	16	17
1	Cape Wrath	1																
2	Ullapool	54	2															
3	Stornoway	53	45	3														
4	East Loch Tarbert	75	56	33	4													
5	Portree	83	57	53	42	5												
6	Kyle of Lochalsh	91	63	62	63	21	6											
7	Mallaig	112	82	83	84	42	21	7										
8	Eigg	123	98	97	75	54	35	14	8									
9	Castlebay (Barra)	133	105	92	69	97	76	59	46	9								
10	Tobermory	144	114	115	87	74	53	32	20	53	10							
11	Loch Aline	157	127	128	100	87	66	45	33	66	13	11						
12	Fort William	198	161	162	134	121	98	75	63	96	43	34	12					
13	Oban	169	138	139	111	100	77	56	44	77	24	13	29	13				
14	Loch Melfort	184	154	155	117	114	93	69	61	92	40	27	45	18	14			
15	Craobh Haven	184	155	155	117	114	92	70	60	93	40	27	50	21	5	15		
16	Crinan	187	157	158	129	112	95	74	63	97	42	30	54	25	14	9	16	
17	Mull of Kintyre	232	203	189	175	159	143	121	105	120	89	87	98	72	62	57	51	17

AREA 7 SW. Scotland - *Oban to Kirkudbright*

SELECTED LIGHTS, BUOYS & WAYPOINTS | Positions are referenced to WGS84

OBAN TO LOCH CRAIGNISH

Bogha Nuadh ◷ Q (6) + LFl 15s; 56°21'·69N 05°37'·88W.

Fladda ⚶ Fl (2) WRG 9s 13m W11M, R9M, G9M; W twr; vis: 169°-R-186°-W-337°-G-344°-W-356°-R-026°; 56°14'·89N 05°40'·83W.

Dubh Sgeir (Luing) ⚶ Fl WRG 6s 9m W6M, R4M. G4M; W twr; vis: W000°- R010°- W025°- G199°-000°; *Racon (M) 5M*; 56°14'·76N 05°40'·20W.

The Garvellachs, Eileach an Naoimh, SW end ⚶ Fl 6s 21m 9M; W Bn; vis: 240°-215°; 56°13'·04N 05°49'·06W.

LOCH MELFORT/CRAOBH HAVEN

Melfort Pier ⚶ Dir FR 6m 3M; (Private shown 1/4 to 31/10); 56°16'·14N 05°30'·19W.

Craobh Marina Bkwtr Hd ⚶ Iso WRG 5s 10m, W5M, R3M, G3M; vis:114°-G-162°-W-183°-R-200°; 56°12'·78N 05°33'·52W.

COLONSAY TO ISLAY

COLONSAY/SOUND OF ISLAY/PORT ELLEN

Scalasaig, Rubha Dubh ⚶ Fl (2) WR 10s 8m W8M, R6M; W bldg; vis: shore-R- 230°-W-337°-R-354°; 56°04'·01N 06°10'·90W.

Rhubh' a Mháil (Ruvaal) ☆ 55°56'·18N 06°07'·46W Fl (3) WR 15s 45m **W24M, R21M**; W twr; vis: 075°-R-180°-W-075°.

Black Rocks ▲ Fl G 6s; 55°47'·50N 06°04'·09W.

McArthur's Hd ⚶ Fl (2) WR 10s 39m W14M, R11M; W twr; W in Sound of Islay from NE coast, 159°-R-244°-W-E coast of Islay; 55°45'·84N 06°02'·90W.

Eilean a Chùirn ⚶ Fl (3) 18s 26m 8M; W Bn; obsc when brg more than 040°; 55°40'·12N 06°01'·22W.

Gigha Rocks ◷ Q (9) 15s; 55°39'·20N 05°43'·65W.

Otter Rk ◷ Q (6) + L Fl 15s; 55°33'·86N 06°07'·92W.

Port Ellen ◀ QG; 55°37'·00N 06°12'·27W.

Orsay Is, **Rhinns of Islay** ☆ 55°40'·40N 06°30'·84W Fl 5s 46m **24M**; W twr; vis: 256°-184°.

JURA TO MULL OF KINTYRE

SOUND OF JURA/CRAIGHOUSE/L.SWEEN/GIGHA

Reisa an t-Struith, S end of Is ⚶ Fl (2) 12s 12m 7M; W col; 56°07'·77N 05°38'·91W.

Ruadh Sgeir ⚶ Fl 6s 15m 9M; W ○ twr; 56°04'·32N 05°39'·77W.

Skervuile ⚶ Fl 15s 22m 9M; W twr; 55°52'·46N 05°49'·85W.

Eilean nan Gabhar ⚶ Fl 5s 7m 8M; framework twr; vis: 225°-010°; 55°50'·04N 05°56'·25W.

Sgeir Gigalum ▲ Fl G 6s 3m 4M; 55°39'·96N 05°42'·67W.

Cath Sgeir ◷ Q (9) 15s; 55°39'·66N 05°47'·50W.

Gigalum Rks ◷ Q (9) 15s; 55°39'·20N 05°43'·70W.

WEST LOCH TARBERT

Dunskeig Bay ⚶ Q (2) 10s 11m 8M; 55°45'·22N 05°35'·00W.

Eileen Tráighe (off S side) ⌐ Fl (2) R 5s 5m 3M; R post; 55°45'·37N 05°35'·75W.

Mull of Kintyre ☆ 55°18'·64N 05°48'·25W Fl (2) 20s 91m **24M**; W twr on W bldg; vis: 347°-178°; *Horn Mo (N) 90s.*

CRINAN CANAL/ARDRISHAIG

Crinan, E of lock ent ⚶ Fl WG 3s 8m 4M; W twr, R band; vis: shore-W-146°-G-shore; 56°05'·48N 05°33'·37W.

Ardrishaig Bkwtr Hd ⚶ L Fl WRG 6s 9m 4M; vis: 287°-G-339°-W-350°-R-035°; 56°00'·76N 05°26'·59W.

Sgeir Sgalag No. 49 ▲ Fl G 5s; 56°00'·36N 05°26'·30W.

LOCH FYNE TO SANDA ISLAND

EAST LOCH TARBERT

Madadh Maol ⚶ Fl R 2·5s 4m 3M; 55°52'·02N 05°24'·25W.

KILBRANNAN SOUND/CARRADALE BAY

Crubon Rk ◔ Fl (2) R 12s; 55°34'·48N 05°27'·07W.

Otterard Rk ◷ Q (3) 10s; 55°27'·07N 05°31'·11W.

CAMPBELTOWN LOCH

Davaar N Pt ☆ 55°25'·69N 05°32'·42W Fl (2) 10s 37m **23M**; W twr; vis: 073°-330°; *Horn (2) 20s.*

Methe Bk 'C' ◷ Fl (2) 6s; 55°25'·30N 05°34'·42W.

Arranman's Barrels ◔ Fl (2) R 12s; 55°19'·40N 05°32'·87W.

Sanda Island ☆ 55°16'·50N 05°35'·01W Fl 10s 50m **15M**; W twr.

Patersons Rk ◔ Fl (3) R 18s; 55°16'·90N 05°32'·48W.

KYLES OF BUTE TO RIVER CLYDE

KYLES OF BUTE/CALADH

Rubha Ban ◔ Fl R 4s; 55°54'·95N 05°12'·40W.

Burnt I No. 42 ◔ (S of Eilean Buidhe) Fl R 2s; 55°55'·76N 05°10'·39W.

Rubha á Bhodaich ▲ Fl G; 55°55'·38N 05°09'·59W.

Ardmaleish Pt No. 41 ◷ Q; 55°53'·02N 05°04'·70W.

FIRTH OF CLYDE

Ascog Patches No. 13 ◷ Fl (2) 10s 5m 5M; 55°49'·71N 05°00'·25W.

Toward Pt ☆ 55°51'·73N 04°58'·79W Fl 10s 21m **22M**; W twr.

Skelmorlie ◷ Iso 5s; 55°51'·65N 04°56'·34W.

WEMYSS/INVERKIP/HOLY LOCH

Kip ◂ QG; 55°54'·49N 04°52'·98W.
Warden Bank ◂ Fl G 2s; 55°54'·77N 04°54'·54W.
Cowal ◖ L Fl 10s; 55°56'·00N 04°54'·83W.
The Gantocks ◖ Fl R 6s 12m 6M; ○ twr;
55°56'·45N 04°55'·08W.
Cloch Point ⌁ Fl 3s 24m 8M; W○ twr, B band, W
dwellings; 55°56'·55N 04°52'·74W.
Holy Loch Marina 2 FR (vert) 4m 1M; 55°59'·00N
04°56'·80W.

LOCH LONG/LOCH GOIL/GOUROCK

Loch Long ◖ Oc 6s; 55°59'·15N 04°52'·42W.
Ashton ◖ Iso 5s; 55°58'·10N 04°50'·65W.
Whiteforeland ◖ L Fl 10s; 55°58'·11N 04°47'·28W.
Rosneath Patch ◖ Fl (2) 10s 5m 10M; 55°58'·52N
04°47'·45W.

ROSNEATH/RHU NARROWS/GARELOCH

Ldg Lts 356°. **Front, No. 7N** ◖ 56°00'·05N 04°45'·36W
Dir lt 356°. WRG 5m **W16M**, R13M, G13M; vis:
353°-Al WG- 355°- FW-357°-Al WR-000°-FR-002°.
Dir lt 115° WRG 5m **W16M**, R13M, G13M; vis:
111°-Al WG-114°-FW- 116°-Al WR-119°-FR-121°.
Row ◂ Fl G 5s; 55°59'·84N 04°45'·13W.
Cairndhu ◂ Fl G 2·5s; 56°00'·35N 04°46'·00W.
Rhu SE ◂ Fl G 3s; 56°00'·64N 04°47'·17W.
Rhu NE ◂ QG; 56°01'·02N 04°47'·58W.
Rhu Spit ◖ Fl 3s 6m 6M; 56°00'·84N 04°47'·34W.
8m 8M. are Fl G and Lts on N bank are Fl R.

CLYDE TO LOCH RYAN

LARGS/FAIRLIE

Approach ◖ L Fl 10s; 55°46'·40N 04°51'·85W.
Largs Marina S Bkwtr Hd ⌁ Oc G 10s 4m 4M;
55°46'·36N 04°51'·73W.
Fairlie Patch ◂ Fl G 1·5s; 55°45'·38N 04°52'·34W.

MILLPORT, GREAT CUMBRAE

The Eileans, W end ⌁ QG 5m 2M; 55°44'·89N
04°55'·59W.
Mountstuart ◖ L Fl 10s; 55°48'·00N 04°57'·57W.

Portachur ◂ Fl G 3s; 55°44'·35N 04°58'·52W.
Little Cumbrae Is, Cumbrae Elbow ⌁ Fl 6s 28m
14M; W twr; vis: 334°-193°; 55°43'·22N 04°58'·06W.

ARDROSSAN/TROON

Ardrossan N Bkwtr Hd ⌁ Fl R 5s 7m 5M; R gantry;
55°38'·53N 04°49'·64W.
W Crinan Rk ◄ Fl R 4s; 55°38'·47N 04°49'·89W.
Eagle Rock ◂ 55°38'·21N 04°49'·69W Fl G 5s.
Troon ◂ Fl G 4s; 55°33'·06N 04°41'·35W.
Lady I ◖ Fl 2s 19m 8M; W Bn; 55°31'·63N 04°44'·04W.

ARRAN/RANZA/LAMLASH

Hamilton Rk ◄ Fl R 6s; 55°32'·63N 05°04'·90W.
Pillar Rk Pt ☆ (Holy Island), 55°31'·04N
05°03'·67W Fl (2) 20s 38m **25M**; W □ twr.
Pladda ☆ 55°25'·50N 05°07'·12W Fl (3) 30s 40m
17M; W twr.

AYR/GIRVAN/LOCH RYAN

S. Nicholas ◂ 55°28'·12N 04°39'·44W Fl G 2s.
Turnberry Point ☆, near castle ruins 55°19'·56N
04°50'·71W Fl 15s 29m **24M**; W twr.
Ailsa Craig ☆ 55°15'·12N 05°06'·52W Fl 4s 18m
17M; W twr; vis: 145°-028°.
Girvan S Pier Hd °2 FG (vert) 8m 4M; W twr;
55°14'·72N 04°51'·90W.
Milleur Point ◖ Q; 55°01'·28N 05°05'·66W.
Cairn Pt ⌁ Fl (2) R 10s 14m 12M; W twr;
54°58'·46N 05°01'·85W.

LOCH RYAN TO KIRKUDBRIGHT

Corsewall Point ☆ 55°00'·41N 05°09'·58W Fl (5)
30s 34m **22M**; W twr; vis: 027°-257°.
Killantringan Black Head ☆ 54°51'·70N
05°08'·85W Fl (2) 15s 49m **25M**; W twr.
Crammag Hd ☆ 54°39'·90N 04°57'·92W Fl 10s
35m **18M**; W twr.
Mull of Galloway ☆, SE end 54°38'·08N
04°51'·45W Fl 20s 99m **28M**; W twr; vis: 182°-
105°.

KIRKCUDBRIGHT BAY

Hestan I, E end ⌁ Fl (2) 10s 42m 9M; 54°49'·95N
03°48'·53W.

1	Loch Craignish	1												
2	Crinan	5	2											
3	Ardrishaig	14	9	3										
6	East Loch Tarbert	24	19	10	4									
5	Campbeltown	55	50	39	31	5								
6	Lamlash	48	43	34	25	24	6							
7	Largs	48	43	34	24	39	17	7						
8	Kip Marina	53	48	39	28	50	25	10	8					
9	Greenock	59	54	45	36	53	31	16	6	9				
10	Rhu (Helensburgh)	62	57	48	37	59	33	19	9	4	10			
11	Troon	54	49	40	33	33	16	20	29	34	38	11		
12	Girvan	67	62	53	43	29	20	33	46	49	51	21	12	
13	Stranraer	89	84	75	65	34	39	56	69	65	74	44	23	13
14	Kirkcudbright	136	131	122	114	88	92	110	116	124	125	97	94	71	14

AREA 8 NW. England & Wales - *Kirkudbright and I.o.Man to Swansea*

SELECTED LIGHTS, BUOYS & WAYPOINTS | Positions are referenced to WGS84

SOLWAY FIRTH TO BARROW-IN-FURNESS
SILLOTH/MARYPORT
Two Feet Bk ⌀ Q (9) 15s; 54°42'·90N 03°47'·10W.
Solway ⚲ Fl G 4s; 54°46'·80N 03°30'·14W.
Maryport S Pier Hd ⚲.Fl 1·5s 10m 6M;54°43'·07N 03°30'·64W.
S Workington ⌀ VQ (6) + L Fl 10s; 54°37'·01N 03°38'·58W.
Whitehaven W Pier Hd ⚲ Fl G 5s 16m 13M; W ○ twr; 54°33'·17N 03°35'·92W.
Saint Bees Hd ☆ 54°30'·81N 03°38'·23W Fl (2) 20s 102m **18M**; W○ twr; obsc shore-340°.
Selker ⚲ Fl (3) G 10s; *Bell;* 54°16'·14N 03°29'·58W.
Barrow Wind Farm ⌀ VQ (6) + L Fl 10s; 53°58'·20N 03°17'·40W.
Lightning Knoll ⚲ L Fl 10s; *Bell;* 53°59'·83N 03°14'·28W.
Isle of Walney ☆ 54°02'·92N 03°10'·64W Fl 15s 21m **23M**; stone twr; obsc 122°-127° within 3M of shore.

ISLE OF MAN
Whitestone Bk ⌀ Q (9) 15s; 54°24'·58N 04°20'·41W.
Point of Ayre ☆ 54°24'·94N 04°22'·13W Fl (4) 20s 32m **19M**; W twr, two R bands, *Horn (3) 60s*, **Racon (M) 13-15M**.
Low Lt ⚲ 54°25'·03N 04°21'·86W Fl 3s 10m 8M; R twr, lower part W, on B Base; part obsc 335°-341°.
Thousla Rk ⚲ Fl R 3s 9m 4M; 54°03'·73N 04°48'·05W.
Calf of Man ☆ W Pt 54°03'·19N 04°49'·78W Fl 15s 93m **26M**; W 8-sided twr; vis 274°-190°; *Horn 45s*.
Chicken Rk ⚲ Fl 5s 38m 13M; twr; 54°02'·26N 04°50'·32W.
Douglas Head ☆ 54°08'·60N 04°27'·95W Fl 10s 32m **24M**; W twr; obsc brg more than 037°. FR Lts on radio masts 1 and 3M West.
Maughold Head ☆ 54°17'·72N 04°18'·58W Fl (3) 30s 65m **21M**.
Bahama ⌀ VQ (6) + L Fl 10s; 54°20'·01N 04°08'·57W.
King William Bank ⌀ Q (3) 10s; 54°26'·01N 04°00'·08W.

BARROW TO RIVERS MERSEY AND DEE
MORECAMBE/FLEETWOOD/RIVER RIBBLE
Morecambe ⌀ Q (9) 15s; *Whis;* 53°51'·99N 03°24'·10W.
Lune Deep ⌀ Q (6) + L Fl 15s; *Whis;* **Racon (T);** 53°55'·81N 03°11'·08W. 02°55'·80W.
R Lune ⌀ Q (9) 15s; 53°58'·63N 03°00'·03W. 53°58'·89N 02°52'·96W.
Gut ⚲ L Fl 10s; 53°41'·74N 03°08'·98W.
Jordan's Spit ⌀ Q (9) 15s; 53°35'·76N 03°19'·28W.

RIVER MERSEY APPROACHES
BAR ⚲ Fl 5s 10m 12M; *Horn (2) 20s;* **Racon (T) 10M;** 53°32'·01N 03°20'·98W.
Q1 ⚲ VQ; 53°31'·00N 03°16'·72W.
Formby ⚲ Iso 4s 11m 6M; R hull, W stripes; 53°31'·13N 03°13'·50W.
Crosby ⚲ Oc 5s 11m 8M; R hull, W stripes; 53°30'·72N 03°06'·29W.
Brazil ⚲ QG; G hull; 53°26'·84N 03°02'·24W.

RIVER DEE
HE1 ⌀ Q (9) 15s; 53°26'·33N 03°18'·08W.
Hilbre I ⚲ Fl R 3s 14m 5M; W twr; 53°22'·99N 03°13'·72W.
Salisbury Mid ⚲ Fl (3) R 10s; 53°21'·30N 03°16'·39W.
Dee ⌀ Q (6) + L Fl 15s; 53°21'·99N 03°18'·68W.

N AND NW WALES COAST
RIVER DEE TO CONWY
N Hoyle ⌀ VQ; 53°26'·68N 03°30'·58W.
S Hoyle Outer ⚲ Fl R 2·5s; 53°21'·47N 03°24'·70W.
Prestatyn ⚲ QG; 53°21'·51N 03°28'·51W.
N Rhyl ⌀ Q; 53°22'·76N 03°34'·58W.
N Hoyle Wind Farm (30 turbines, see 9.10.5) centred on 53°25'·00N 03°27'·00W. NW, NE, SW, SE extremities (F.R Lts) Fl Y 2.5s 5M Horn Mo (U) 30s.
W Constable ⌀ Q (9) 15s; **Racon (M) 10M;** 53°23'·14N 03°49'·26W.
Conwy F'wy ⚲ L Fl 10s; 53°17'·95N 03°55'·58W.
C2 ⚲ Fl (2) R 10s; 53°17'·64N 03°54'·69W.

MENAI STRIAT - N APPROACHES
Trwyn-Du ⚲ Fl 5s 19m 12M; W○ castellated twr, B bands; vis: 101°-023°; *Bell (1) 30s*, sounded continuously; 53°18'·77N 04°02'·44W.
Ten Feet Bank ⚲ QR; 53°19'·47N 04°02'·82W.

ANGLESEY
Point Lynas ☆ 53°24'·98N 04°17'·35W Oc 10s 39m **18M**; W castellated twr; vis: 109°-315°; *Horn 45s;* H24.
Archdeacon Rock ⌀ Q; 53°26'·71N 04°30'·87W.
The Skerries ☆ 53°25'·27N 04°36'·55W Fl (2) 15s 36m **20M**; W ○ twr, R band; **Racon (T) 25M.** Iso R 4s 26m 10M; same twr; vis: 233°-253°; *Horn (2) 60s.* H24 in periods of reduced visibility.
Langdon ⌀ Q (9) 15s; 53°22'·74N 04°38'·74W.
Holyhead Bkwtr Hd ⚲ Fl (3) G 10s 21m 14M; W □ twr, B band; Fl Y vis: 174°-226°; *Siren 20s;* 53°19'·86N 04°37'·16W.
Marina Bkwtr Hd ⚲ 2 FR (vert); 53°18'·40N 04°38'·63W.
South Stack ☆ 53°19'·31N 04°41'·98W Fl 10s 60m **24M**; (H24); W ○ twr; obsc to N by N Stack and part obsc in Penrhos bay; *Horn 30s.* Fog Det lt vis: 145°-325°.

MENAI STRAIT TO BARDSEY ISLAND
CAERNARFON APPROACHES
(Direction of buoyage ⌂ SW to NE)
C2 ⚓ Fl R 10s; 53°07'·07N 04°24'·52W.
Llanddwyn I ⚡Fl WR 2·5s 12m W7M, R4M; W twr; vis: 280°-R- 015°-W-120°; 53°08'·05N 04°24'·79W.
Mussel Bank ⚓ Fl (2) R 5s; 53°07'·27N 04°20'·81W.

LLEYN PENINSULA/BARDSEY ISLAND
Porth Dinllaen, Careg y Chwislen ⚲ 52°56'·99N 04°33'·51W.

Bardsey I ☆ 52°44'·97N 04°48'·02W Fl (5) 15s 39m **26M**; W ☐ twr, R bands; obsc by Bardsey Is 198°-250° and in Tremadoc B when brg less than 260°; *Horn Mo (N) 45s*; H24.

CARDIGAN BAY
St Tudwal's ⚡Fl WR 15s 46m W14, R10M; vis: 349°-W-169°-R- 221°-W-243°-R-259°-W-293°-R-349°; obsc by East I 211°-231°; 52°47'·92N 04°28'·30W.

PWLLHELI/PORTHMADOG/BARMOUTH/ABERDOVEY
Pwllheli App ⚲ Iso 2s; 52°53'·02N 04°23'·07W.
Porthmadog Fairway ⚓ L Fl 10s; 52°52'·97N 04°11'·18W.
Barmouth Outer ⚲ L Fl 10s; 52°42'·62N 04°04'·83W.
Sarn Badrig Causeway ⚲Q (9) 15s; *Bell;* 52°41'·19N 04°25'·36W.
Sarn-y-Bwch ⚲ VQ (9) 10s; 52°34'·81N 04°13'·58W.
Aberdovey Outer ⚓ Iso 4s; 52°32'·00N 04°05'·56W.
Patches ⚲ Q (9) 15s; 52°25'·83N 04°16'·41W.

ABERYSTWYTH/FISHGUARD
Aberystwyth S Bkwtr Hd ⚡ Fl (2) WG 10s 12m 10M; vis: 030°-G- 053°-W-210°; 52°24'·40N 04°05'·52W.
Fishguard N Bkwtr Hd ⚡Fl G 4·5s 18m 13M; *Bell (1) 8s;* 52°00'·76N 04°58'·23W. 89m 5M.

Strumble Head ☆ 52°01'·79N 05°04'·43W Fl (4) 15s 45m **26M**; vis: 038°-257°; (H24).

BISHOPS AND SMALLS
South Bishop ☆ 51°51'·14N 05°24'·74W Fl 5s 44m **16M**; W ○ twr; *Horn (3) 45s; Racon (O)10M*; (H24).

The Smalls ☆ 51°43'·27N 05°40'·19W Fl (3) 15s 36m **18M**; *Racon (T)* ; *Horn (2) 60s.* Same twr, Iso R 4s 33m 13M; vis: 253°-285° over Hats & Barrels Rk; both Lts shown H24 in periods of reduced visibility.

Skokholm I ☆, 51°41'·64N 05°17'·22W Fl WR 10s 54m **W18M, R15M**; vis: 301°-W-154°-R-301°; partially obsc 226°-258°.

W & S WALES - BRISTOL CHANNEL
MILFORD HAVEN
St Ann's Head ☆ 51°40'·87N 05°10'·42W Fl WR 5s 48m **W18M, R17M**, R14M; W 8-sided twr; vis: 233°-W-247°-R-285°-R(intens)-314°-R-332°-W131°, partially obscured between 124°-129°; *Horn (2) 60s.*
W Blockhouse Pt ⚲ Ldg Lts 022·5°. Front, F 54m 13M; B stripe on W twr; vis: 004·5°-040·5°; intens on lead. By day 10M; vis: 004·5°-040·5°; *Racon (Q) range unknown;* 51°41'·31N 05°09'·56W.
Watwick Point Common Rear ☆, 0·5M from front, F 80m **15M**; vis: 013·5°-031·5°. By day 10M; vis: 013·5°-031·5°; *Racon (Y).*
St Ann's ⚓ Fl R 2·5s; 51°40'·25N 05°10'·51W.
Sheep ⚲ QG; 51°40'·06N 05°08'·31W.
Dakotian ⚲ Q (3) 10s; 51°42'·15N 05°08'·29W.
Turbot Bk ⚲ VQ (9) 10s; 51°37'·41N 05°10'·08W.
St Gowan ⚲Q (6) + L Fl 15s, Whis, *Racon (T) 10M;* 51°31'·93N 04°59'·77W.

TENBY/CARMARTHEN BAY/BURRY INLET
Caldey I ⚡ Fl (3) WR 20s 65m W13M, R9M; vis: R173°- W212°- R088°-102°; 51°37'·90N 04°41'·08W.
Spaniel ⚲ 51°38'·06N 04°39'·75W.
Tenby Pier Hd ⚡FR 7m 7M; 51°40'·40N 04°41'·89W.
DZ7 ⚓ Fl Y 10s; 51°38'·09N 04°30'·12W.
DZ5 ⚓ Fl Y 2·5s; 51°36'·37N 04°24'·39W.
Burry Port ⚡51°40'·62N 04°15'·06W Fl 5s 7m **15M**.
W. Helwick (W HWK) ⚲ (9) 15s; *Racon (T) 10M; Whis;* 51°31'·40N 04°23'·65W Q.
E. Helwick ⚲ VQ (3) 5s; *Bell;* 51°31'·80N 04°12'·68W.

SWANSEA BAY
Ledge ⚲ VQ (6) + L Fl 10s; 51°29'·93N 03°58'·77W.
Mixon ⚓ Fl (2) R 5s; *Bell;* 51°33'·12N 03°58'·78W.

		1	2	3	4	5	6	7	8	9	10	11	12	13	14	15	16	17
1	Portpatrick	**1**																
2	Mull of Galloway	16	**2**															
3	Kirkcudbright	48	32	**3**														
4	Maryport	65	49	26	**4**													
5	Workington	63	47	25	6	**5**												
6	Ravenglass	70	54	40	30	23	**6**											
7	Point of Ayre	38	22	28	37	31	34	**7**										
8	Peel	41	26	46	55	49	52	18	**8**									
9	Douglas	60	42	46	50	44	39	19	30	**9**								
10	Glasson Dock	101	85	74	66	60	37	64	85	63	**10**							
11	Fleetwood	95	79	68	59	53	30	58	80	57	10	**11**						
12	Liverpool	118	102	97	89	83	60	80	86	70	52	46	**12**					
13	Conwy	111	95	95	92	86	58	72	72	59	62	56	46	**13**				
14	Beaumaris	109	93	94	95	89	72	71	73	58	66	60	49	12	**14**			
15	Caernarfon	117	103	104	105	99	82	81	73	68	76	70	59	22	10	**15**		
16	Holyhead	93	81	94	96	90	69	68	62	50	79	73	68	36	32	26	**16**	
17	Fishguard	171	158	175	175	169	160	153	140	134	153	147	136	100	88	78	89	**17**

AREA 9 S.Wales & SW. England - *Swansea to Padstow*

SELECTED LIGHTS, BUOYS & WAYPOINTS | Positions are referenced to WGS84

BRISTOL CHANNEL (NORTH SHORE)

SWANSEA BAY/PORT TALBOT/PORTHCAWL
Mixon ≈ Fl (2) R 5s; *Bell;* 51°33'·12N 03°58'·78W.
Grounds ↓ VQ (3) 5s; 51°32'·81N 03°53'·47W.
Mumbles ☆ 51°34'·01N 03°58'·27W Fl (4) 20s 35m **15M**; W twr; *Horn (3) 60s.*
SW Inner Green Grounds ↓ Q (6) + L Fl 15s; *Bell;* 51°34'·06N 03°57'·03W.
Cabenda ↓ VQ (6) + L Fl 10s; *Racon (Q);* 51°33'·36N 03°52'·23W.
P Talbot N Outer ≈ Fl R 5s; 51°33'·78N 03°51'·38W.
Kenfig ↓ VQ (3) 5s; 51°29'·44N 03°46'·06W.
W Scar ↓ Q (9) 15s, *Bell*, *Racon (T) 10M;* 51°28'·31N 03°55'·57W.
S Scar ↓ Q (6) + L Fl 15s; 51°27'·61N 03°51'·58W.
E Scar ↓ Q (3) 10s; *Bell;* 51°27'·98N 03°46'·76W.
Fairy ↓ Q (9) 15s; *Bell;* 51°27'·86N 03°42'·07W.
Tusker ≈ Fl (2) R 5s *Bell;* 51°26'·85N 03°40'·74W
W Nash ↓ VQ (9) 10s; *Bell;* 51°25'·99N 03°45'·95W.
East Nash ↓ Q (3) 10s; 51°24'·06N 03°34'·10W.
Nash ☆ 51°24'·03N 03°33'·06W Fl (2) WR 15s 56m **W21M, R16M**; vis: 280°-R-290°-W-100°-R-120°-W-128°.

BARRY/CARDIFF/PENARTH/NEWPORT DEEP
BREAKSEA ≈ Fl 15s 11m 12M; *Racon (T) 10M;* *Horn (2) 30s;* 51°19'·88N 03°19'·08W.
Merkur ≈ QR; 51°21'·88N 03°15'·95W.
Barry W Bkwtr Hd ↯ Fl 2·5s 12m 10M; 51°23'·46N 03°15'·52W.
Lavernock Spit ↓ VQ (6) + L Fl 10s; 51°23'·02N 03°10'·82W.
Mackenzie ≈ QR; 51°21'·75N 03°08'·24W.
Wolves ↓ VQ; 51°23'·13N 03°08'·88W.
Flat Holm ☆, SE Pt 51°22'·54N 03°07'·14W Fl (3) WR 10s 50m **W15M**, R12M; W○twr; vis: 106°-R-140°-W-151°-R-203°-W-106°; (H24).
Weston ≈ Fl (2) R 5s; 51°22'·60N 03°05'·75W.
Monkstone Rk ↯ Fl 5s 13m 12M; 51°24'·89N 03°06'·02W.
Ranie ≈ Fl (2) R 5s; 51°24'·23N 03°09'·39W.
S Cardiff ↓ Q (6) + L Fl 15s; *Bell;* 51°24'·18N 03°08'·57W.
Outer Wrach ↓ Q (9) 15s; 51°26'·20N 03°09'·46W.
N Cardiff ▲ QG; 51°26'·52N 03°07'·19W.
EW Grounds ↓ L Fl 10s 7M; *Bell; Racon (T) 7M;* 51°27'·12N 02°59'·95W.
Newport Deep ▲ Fl (3) G 10s; *Bell;* 51°29'·36N 02°59'·12W.
East Usk ☆ 51°32'·40N 02°58'·01W Fl (2) WRG 10s 11m W11M, R10M, G10M; vis: 284°-W-290° - obscured shore-324°-R- 017°-W-037°-G-115°-W-120°. Also Oc WRG 10s 10m W11M, R9M, G9M; vis: 018°-G-022°-W-024°-R-028°.

SEVERN ESTUARY

THE SHOOTS
Lower Shoots ↓ Q (9) 15s 6m 7M; 51°33'·85N 02°42'·05W.
2nd Severn Crossing, Centre span ↯ Q Bu 5M; *Racon (O) (3cm) range unknown;* 51°34'·45N 02°42'·03W.
Old Man's Hd ↓ VQ (9) W 10s 6m 7M; 51°34'·74N 02°41'·69W.
Lady Bench (Lts in line 234°) ↓ QR 6m 6M; 51°34'·85N 02°42'·20W. Rear, Oc R 5s 38m 3M.
Charston Rk ↯ Fl 3s 5m 8M; 51°35'·35N 02°41'·68W.
Chapel Rk ↯ Fl WRG 2·6s 6m 8M, vis: W213°-G284°-W049°-R051·5°-160°; 51°36'·44N 02°39'·21W.

SEVERN BRIDGE TO SHARPNESS
Aust ↯ 2 QG (vert) 11m 6M; 51°36'·16N 02°38'·00W.
West Tower ↯ 3 QR (hor) on upstream/downstream sides; *Siren (3) 30s;* obscured 040°-065°; 51°36'·73N 02°38'·80W.
Centre of span ↯ Q Bu, each side; 51°36'·59N 02°38'·43W.
Lyde Rock ↯ Q WR 5m 5M; vis: 148°-R-237°-W-336°-R-067°; 51°36'·89N 02°38'·67W.
COUNTS ↓ Q; 51°39'·48N 02°35'·84W .
LEDGES ↓ 51°39'·77N 02°34'·15W Fl (3) G 10s.
Bull Rock ↯ Fl 3s 6m 8M; 51°41'·80N 02°29'·89W.
Sharpness S Pier Hd ↯ 2 FG (vert) 6m 3M; *Siren 20s;* 51°42'·97N 02°29'·12W.

BRISTOL CHANNEL (SOUTH SHORE)

BRISTOL DEEP
N Elbow ▲ QG; *Bell;* 51°26'·97N 02°58'·65W.
S Mid Grounds ↓ VQ (6) + L Fl 10s; 51°27'·62N 02°58'·68W.
E Mid Grounds ≈ Fl R 5s; 51°28'·14N 02°53'·56W.
Clevedon ↓ VQ; 51°27'·39N 02°54'·93W.
Welsh Hook ↓ Q (6) + L Fl 15s; *Bell;* 51°28'·53N 02°51'·86W.
Avon ▲ Fl G 2·5s; 51°27'·92N 02°51'·73W.
Black Nore Point ☆ 51°29'·09N 02°48'·05W Fl (2) 10s 11m **17M**; obsc by Sand Pt when brg less than 049°; vis: 044°-243°.
Firefly ▲ Fl (2) G 5s; 51°29'·96N 02°45'·35W.
Portishead Point ☆ 51°29'·68N 02°46'·42W Q (3) 10s 9m **16M**; B twr, W base; vis: 060°-262°; *Horn 20s.*

AVONMOUTH/RIVER AVON
Royal Edward Dock N Pier Hd ↯ Fl 4s 15m 10M; vis: 060°-228·5°; 51°30'·49N 02°43'·09W.
Avonmouth S Pier Hd ↯ Oc RG 30s 9m 10M; vis: 294°-R-036°-G-194°; 51°30'·37N 02°43'·10W.

BRISTOL CHANNEL (SOUTH SHORE)
E Culver ⚡ Q (3) 10s; 51°18'·00N 03°15'·44W.
W Culver ⚡ VQ (9) 10s; 51°17'·37N 03°18'·68W.
Gore ⚬ Iso 5s; *Bell;* 51°13'·94N 03°09'·79W.

BURNHAM-ON-SEA/RIVER PARRETT
Lower Lt Ent ⚡ Fl 7·5s 7m 12M; vis: 074°-164°; 51°14'·89N 03°00'·36W.Dirlt076°.FWRG4mW12M, R10M, G10M; vis: 071°-G-075°-W-077°-R-081°.
Bridgewater Bar No. 1 ⚬ QR; 51°14'·53N 03°03'·75W.

WATCHET/MINEHEAD
Watchet W Bkwtr Hd ⚡ Oc G 3s 9m 9M; 51°11'·03N 03°19'·74W.
Minehead Bkwtr Hd ⚡ Fl (2) G 5s 4M; vis: 127°-262°; 51°12'·81N 03°28'·36W.
Lynmouth Foreland ☆ 51°14'·73N 03°47'·21W Fl (4) 15s 67m **18M;** W ○ twr; vis: 083°-275°; (H24).

LYNMOUTH/WATERMOUTH/ILFRACOMBE
Lynmouth Harbour Arm ⚡ 2 FG (vert) 6m 5M; 51°13'·92N 03°49'·84W.
Sand Ridge ⚓ Q G; 51°15'·01N 03°49'·77W.
Copperas Rock ▲ 51°13'·78N 04°00'·60W.
Watermouth ⚡ Oc WRG 5s 1m 3M; W △; vis: 149·5°-G-151·5°-W- 154·5°-R-156·5°; 51°12'·93N 04°04'·60W.
Lantern Hill ⚡ Fl G 2·5s 39m 6M; 51°12'·66N 04°06'·78W.
Horseshoe ⚡ Q; 51°15'·02N 04°12'·96W.
Bull Point ☆ 51°11'·94N 04°12'·09W Fl (3) 10s 54m **20M;** W ○ twr, obscd shore-056°. Same twr; FR 48m 12M; vis: 058°-096°.
Morte Stone ▲ 51°11'·30N 04°14'·95W.
Baggy Leap ▲ 51°08'·92N 04°16'·97W.

BIDEFORD, RIVERS TAW AND TORRIDGE
Bideford F'wy ⚡ L Fl 10s; *Bell;* 51°05'·25N 04°16'·25W.
Bideford Bar ⚓ Q G; 51°04'·96N 04°14'·83W.
Pulley ⚓ Fl G 10s; 51°04'·08N 04°12'·74W.
Instow ☆ Ldg Lts 118°. **Front,** 51°03'·62N 04°10'·67W Oc 6s 22m **15M;** vis: 104·5°-131·5°. **Rear,** 427m from front, Oc 10s 38m **15M;** vis: 104°-132°; (H24).

Crow Pt ⚡ Fl WR 2. 5s 8m W6M R5M; vis: 225°-R-232°-W-237°-R-358°-W-015°-R-045°; 51°03'·96N 04°11'·39W.

CLOVELLY/HARTLAND/LUNDY
Clovelly Hbr Quay Hd ⚡ 50°59'·92N 04°23'·83W Fl G 5s 5m 5M.
Lundy Near North Pt ☆ 51°12'·10N 04°40'·65W Fl 15s 48m **17M;** vis: 009°-285°.
Lundy South East Pt ☆ 51°09'·72N 04°39'·37W Fl 5s 53m **15M;** vis: 170°-073°; *Horn 25s.*
Jetty Head ⚡ Fl R 3s 8m 3M; 51°09'·80N 04°39'·20W.
Hartland Point ☆ 51°01'·29N 04°31'·59W Fl (6) 15s 37m **25M;** (H24); *Horn 60s.*

NORTH CORNWALL
PADSTOW/NEWQUAY
Stepper Point ⚡ L Fl 10s 12m 4M; 50°34'·12N 04°56'·72W.
Greenaway ⚬ Fl (2) R 10s; 50°33'·78N 04°56'·06W.
Bar ▲ Fl G 5s; 50°33'·46N 04°56'·12W.
Padstow N Quay Hd ⚡ 2 FG (vert) 6m 2M; 50°32'·50N 04°56'·16W.
Trevose Head ☆ 50°32'·94N 05°02'·13W Fl 7·5s 62m **21M;** *Horn (2) 30s.*
Newquay N Pier Hd ⚡ 2 FG (vert) 5m 2M; 50°25'·07N 05°05'·19W..

HAYLE/ST IVES
The Stones ⚡ Q; 50°15'·64N 05°25'·51W.
Godrevy I ⚡ Fl WR 10s 37m W12M, R9M; vis: 022°-W-101°-R-145°-W-272°; 50°14'·54N 05°24'·04W.
Hayle App ⚬ QR; 50°12'·26N 05°26'·30W.
St Ives App ▲ 50°12'·85N 05°28'·42W
East Pier Hd ⚡ 2 FG (vert) 8m 5M; 50°12'·80N 05°28'·61W.
West Pier Hd ⚡ 2 FR (vert) 5m 3M; 50°12'·77N 05°28'·73W.
Pendeen ☆ 50°09'·90N 05°40'·32W Fl (4) 15s 59m **16M;** vis: 042°-240°; in bay between Gurnard Hd and Pendeen it shows to coast; *Horn 20s.*

For Lts further W see Area 1 SW England - *Isles of Scilly to Anvil Point.*

1	Aberystwyth	1		12	64	66	122	164	192	224	254	286	299	318	361		Kilrush	12
2	Fishguard	40	2		11	13	69	111	139	171	201	233	246	265	308		Dingle	11
3	Milford Haven	84	48	3		10	56	102	131	165	188	227	242	252	295		Valentia	10
4	Tenby	107	71	28	4		9	42	70	102	132	164	177	196	239		Baltimore	9
5	Swansea	130	94	55	36	5		8	35	69	95	135	150	168	202		Kinsale	8
6	Cardiff	161	125	86	66	46	6		7	34	65	100	115	133	172		Youghal	7
7	Sharpness	192	156	117	106	75	33	7		6	32	69	84	102	139		Dunmore East	6
8	Avonmouth	175	139	100	89	58	20	18	8		5	34	47	66	108		Rosslare	5
9	Burnham-on-Sea	169	133	94	70	48	53	50	33	9		4	15	36	75		Arklow	4
10	Ilfracombe	128	92	53	35	25	44	74	57	45	10		3	21	63		Wicklow	3
11	Padstow	142	106	70	70	76	97	127	110	98	55	11		2	48		Dun Laoghaire	2
12	Longships	169	133	105	110	120	139	169	152	140	95	50	12		1		Carlingford Lough	1

AREA 10 Ireland - *South and Westwards from Rockabill to Inisheer*

SELECTED LIGHTS, BUOYS & WAYPOINTS | Positions are referenced to WGS84

LAMBAY ISLAND TO TUSKAR ROCK

MALAHIDE/LAMBAY ISLAND/HOWTH
Taylor Rks ⚓ Q; 53°30'·21N 06°01'·87W.
Rowan Rocks ⚓ Q (3) 10s; 53°23'·88N 06°03'·27W.
Howth E Pier Hd ⚡Fl (2) WR 7·5s 13m W12M, R9M; W twr; vis: W256°-R295°-256°; 53°23'·66N 06°04'·03W.
Baily ☆ 53°21'·70N 06°03'·14W Fl 15s 41m **26M**; twr.
Rosbeg E ⚓ Q (3) 10s; 53°21'·02N 06°03'·45W.
Rosbeg S ⚓ Q (6) + L Fl 15s; 53°20'·22N 06°04'·17W.
S Burford ⚓ VQ (6) + L Fl 10s; *Whis;* 53°18'·07N 06°01'·27W.

PORT OF DUBLIN/DUN LAOGHAIRE
Dublin Bay ⚓ Mo (A) 10s; *Racon (M);* 53°19'·92N 06°04'·64W.
Great S Wall Hd   Poolbeg ☆   Fl R 4s 20m 10M*(synchro with N.Bull);* R ○ twr; *Horn (2) 60s;* 53°20'·53N 06°09'·08W.
Dublin N Bank ☆ 53°20'·69N 06°10'·59W Oc G 8s 10m **16M**; G☐twr.
Dun Laoghaire E Bkwtr Hd ⚡ 53°18'·15N 06°07'·62W Fl (2) R 10s 16m **17M**; twr; R lantern; *Horn 30s (or Bell (1) 6s).*
Muglins ⚡Fl 5s 14m 11M; 53°16'·55N 06°04'·58W.
Bennett Bk ⚓ Q (6) + L Fl 15s; 53°20'·17N 05°55'·11W.
Kish Bank ☆ 53°18'·64N 05°55'·48W Fl (2) 20s 29m **22M**; W twr, R band; *Racon (T) 15M; Horn (2) 30s.*
S Codling ⚓ VQ (6) + L Fl 10s; 53°04'·74N 05°49'·76W.
S India ⚓ Q (6) + L Fl 15s; 53°00'·36N 05°53'·31W.
CODLING LANBY ⚓ 53°03'·02N 05°40'·76W Fl 4s 12m **15M**; tubular structure on By; *Racon (G)10M; Horn 20s.*

WICKLOW/ARKLOW
Wicklow E Pier Hd ⚡ Fl WR 5s 11m 6M; W twr, R base and cupola; vis: 136°-R-293°-W-136°; 52°58'·99N 06°02'·07W.
Wicklow Head ☆ 52°57'·95N 05°59'·89W Fl (3) 15s 37m **23M**; W twr.
N Arklow ⚓ Q; *Whis;* 52°53'·86N 05°55'·21W.
Arklow Bank Wind Farm from 52°48'·47N 05°56'·57W to 52°46'·47N 05°57'·11W, N and S Turbines Fl Y 5s14m 10M + Fl W Aero lts. AIS transmitters. Other turbines Fl Y 5s.
S Arklow ⚓ VQ (6) + L Fl 10s; 52°40'·82N 05°59'·21W.
ARKLOW LANBY ⚓ 52°39'·52N 05°58'·16W Fl (2) 12s 12m **15M**; *Racon (O)10M; Horn Mo (A) 30s.*
No. 2 Glassgorman ⚓ Fl (4) R 10s; 52°44'·52N 06°05'·36W.
S Blackwater ⚓ Q (6) + L Fl 15s; *Whis;* 52°22'·76N 06°12'·86W.

WEXFORD/ROSSLARE
S Long ⚓ VQ (6) + L Fl 10s; 52°14'·84N 06°15'·64W.

Splaugh ⚓ Fl R 6s; 52°14'·37N 06°16'·76W.
Tuskar ☆ 52°12'·17N 06°12'·42W Q (2) 7·5s 33m **24M**; W twr; *Horn (4) 45s, Racon (T) 18M.*

TUSKAR ROCK TO OLD HD OF KINSALE
S Rock ⚓ Q (6) + L Fl 15s; 52°10'·80N 06°12'·84W.
Barrels ⚓ Q (3) 10s; 52°08'·32N 06°22'·05W.

KILMORE/WATERFORD
St Patrick's Bridge ⚓ Fl R 6s; (Apr-Sep); 52°09'·30N 06°34'·71W
CONINGBEG ⚓ 52°02'·40N 06°39'·49W Fl (3) 30s 12m **24M**; R hull, and twr, *Racon (M) 13M; Horn (3) 60s.*
Hook Hd ☆ 52°07'·32N 06°55'·85W Fl 3s 46m **23M**; W twr, two B bands; *Racon (K) 10M vis 237°-177°; Horn (2) 45s.*
Waterford ⚓ Fl R 3s. Fl (3) R 10s; 52°08'·95N 06°57'·00W.
Dunmore East Pier Head ☆ 52°08'·93N 06°59'·37W Fl WR 8s 13m **W17M**, R13M; Gy twr, vis: W225°- R310°-004°.

DUNGARVAN
Helvick ⚓ Q (3) 10s; 52°03'·61N 07°32'·25W.
Mine Head ☆ 51°59'·52N 07°35'·25W Fl (4) 20s 87m **20M**; W twr, B band; vis: 228°-052°.

YOUGHAL/BALLYCOTTON
Youghal W side of ent ☆ 51°56'·57N 07°50'·53W Fl WR 2·5s 24m **W17M**, R13M; W twr; vis: W183°-R273°- W295°- R307°- W351°-003°.
Ballycotton ☆ 51°49'·52N 07° 59'·09W Fl WR 10s 59m **W21M**, **R17M**; B twr, within W walls, B lantern; vis: W238°- R048°-238°; *Horn (4) 90s.*

CORK
Cork ⚓ L Fl 10s; *Racon (T) 7M;* 51°42'·92N 08°15'·60W.
Fort Davis Ldg lts 354·1°. Front, 51°48'·82N 08°15'·80W Dir WRG 29m **17M**; vis: FG351·5°-AlWG352·25°-FW353°-AlWR355°-FR355·75°-356·5°. Rear, Dognose Quay, 203m from front, Oc 5s 37m 10M; Or 3, synch with front.
Roche's Point ☆ 51°47'·59N 08°15'·29W Fl WR 3s 30m **W20M**, **R16M**; vis: Rshore- W292°- R016°-033°, W(unintens) 033°- R159°- shore.

KINSALE/OYSTER HAVEN
Bulman ⚓ Q (6) + L Fl 15s; 51°40'·14N 08°29'·74W.
Charle's Fort ⚡ Fl WRG 5s 18m W9M, R6M, G7M; vis: G348°- W358°- R004°-168°; H24; 51°41'·74N 08°29'·97W.

OLD HEAD OF KINSALE TO MIZEN HEAD

Old Head of Kinsale ☆, S point 51°36'·28N 08°32'·03W Fl (2) 10s 72m **25M**; B twr, two W bands; *Horn (3) 45s.*

Galley Head ☆ summit 51°31'·80N 08°57'·19W Fl (5) 20s 53m **23M**; W twr; vis: 256°-065°.

Kowloon Br ⌇ Q (6)+LFl 15s; 51°27'·58N 09°13'·75W.

BALTIMORE/SCHULL/CROOKHAVEN

Barrack Pt ⚲ Fl (2) WR 6s 40m W6M, R3M; vis: R168°- W294°-038°; 51°28'·33N 09°23'·65W.

Fastnet ☆, W end 51°23'·35N 09°36'·19W Fl 5s 49m **27M**; Gy twr, *Horn (4) 60s,* **Racon (G) 18M.**

Mizen Head ☆ 51°27'·00N 09°49'·24W Iso 4s 55m **15M**; vis: 313°-133°.

MIZEN HEAD TO DINGLE BAY

Sheep's Hd ☆ 51°32'·60N 09°50'·95W Fl (3) WR 15s 83m **W18M, R15M**; W bldg; vis: 007°-R-017°-W-212°.

BANTRY BAY/KENMARE RIVER

Roancarrigmore ☆ 51°39'·19N 09°44'·83W Fl WR 3s 18m **W18M**, R14M; W☐twr, B band; vis: 312°-W-050°-R-122°-R(unintens)-242°-R-312°. Reserve lt W8M, R6M obsc 140°-220°.

Ardnakinna Pt ☆ 51°37'·11N 09°55'·08W Fl (2) WR 10s 62m **W17M**, R14M; W○twr; vis: 319°-R-348°-W-066°-R-shore.

Bull Rock ☆ 51°35'·51N 10°18'·08W Fl 15s 83m **21M**; W twr; vis: 220°-186°.

Skelligs Rock ☆ 51°46'·12N 10°32'·51W Fl (3) 15s 53m **19M**; W twr; vis: 262°-115°; part obsc within 6M 110°-115°.

VALENTIA/PORTMAGEE

Fort (Cromwell) Point ☆ 51°56'·02N 10°19'·27W Fl WR 2s 16m **W17M, R15M**; W twr; vis: 304°-R-351°,102°-W-304°; obsc from seaward by Doulus Head when brg more than 180°.

DINGLE BAY TO LOOP HEAD

DINGLE BAY/VENTRY/DINGLE/FENIT

Inishtearaght ☆, W end Blasket Islands 52°04'·55N 10°39'·68W Fl (2) 20s 84m **19M**; W twr; vis: 318°-221°; *Racon (O).*

Little Samphire Is ☆ 52°16'·26N 09°52'·91W Fl WRG 5s 17m **W16M**, R13M; G13M; Bu○twr; vis: 262°-R-275°, 280-R-090°-G-140°-W- 152°-R-172°.

SHANNON ESTUARY

Ballybunnion ⌇ VQ; *Racon (M) 6M*; 52°32'·52N 09°46'·93W.

Kilcredaune Hd ☆ Fl 6s 41m **15M**; W twr; 52°34'·79N 09°42'·58W; obsc 224°-247° by hill within 1M. twr; vis: 208°-092°; 52°36'·32N 09°31'·03W.

Loop Head ☆ 52°33'·68N 09°55'·96W Fl (4) 20s 84m **23M**.

Positions are referenced to WGS84

North and Westwards from Rockabill to Inisheer

LAMBAY ISLAND TO DONAGHADEE

Rockabill ☆ 53°35'·82N 06°00'·25W Fl WR 12s 45m **W22M, R18M**; W twr, B band; vis: 178°-W-329°-R-178°; *Horn (4) 60s.* H24 when horn is operating.

DROGHEDA/DUNDALK

Drogheda Port Appr Dir lt 53°43'·30N 06°14'·73W WRG 10m **W19M, R15M**, G15M; vis: 268°-FG- 269°-Al WG-269·5°-FW-270·5°-Al WR-271-FR-272°; H24.

Dundalk Pile Light ☆ 53°58'·56N 06°17'·70W Fl WR 15s 10m **W21M, R18M**; W Ho; vis: 124°-W-151°-R-284°-W-313°-R-124°. Fog Det lt VQ 7m, vis: when brg 358°; *Horn (3) 60s.*

CARLINGFORD LOUGH

Carlingford ⌖ L Fl 10s; 53°58'·76N 06°01'·06W.

Hellyhunter ⌇ Q (6) + L Fl 15s; *Racon;* 54°00'·35N 06°02'·10W.

Haulbowline ☆ 54°01'·19N 06°04'·74W Fl (3) 10s 32m **17M**; Gy twr; reserve lt 15M; Fog Det lt VQ 26m; vis: 330°. Turning lt ⚲ FR 21m 9M; same twr; vis: 196°-208°; *Horn 30s.*

DUNDRUM BAY

St John's Point ☆ 54°13'·61N 05°39'·30W Q (2) 7·5s 37m **25M**; B twr, Y bands; H24 when horn is operating. **Auxiliary Light** ☆ Fl WR 3s 14m **W15M**, R11M; same twr, vis: 064°-W-078°-R-shore; Fog Det lt VQ 14m vis: 270°; *Horn (2) 60s.*

STRANGFORD LOUGH/ARDS PENINSULA

Strangford ⌖ L Fl 10s; 54°18'·61N 05°28'·67W.

Bar Pladdy ⌇ Q (6) + L Fl 15s; 54°19'·34N 05°30'·51W.

Butter Pladdy ⌇ Q (3) 10s; 54°22'·45N 05°25'·74W.

SOUTH ROCK ⌐ 54°24'·49N 05°22'·02W Fl (3) R 30s 12m **20M**; R hull and lt twr, W Mast, *Horn (3) 45s, Racon (T) 13M.*

BALLYWATER/DONAGHADEE

Skulmartin ⌖ L Fl 10s; *Whis;* 54°31'·82N 05°24'·80W.

Donaghadee ☆, S Pier Hd 54°38'·70N 05°31'·86W Iso WR 4s 17m **W18M**, R14M; W twr; vis: shore-W-326°-R-shore; *Siren 12s.*

DONAGHADEE TO RATHLIN ISLAND

BELFAST LOUGH/BANGOR

Mew I ☆ NE end 54°41'·91N 05°30'·79W Fl (4) 30s 37m; B twr, W band; *Racon (O) 14M.*

S Briggs ⌖ 54°41'·19N 05°35'·72W Fl (2) R 10s.

BangorN Pier Hd ⚲ Iso R 12s 9m14M; 54°40'·03N 05°40'·34W.

Belfast Fairway ⌇ LFl10s; *Horn (1) 16s; Racon(G);* 54°41'·71N 05°46'·24W

29

CARRICKFERGUS/LARNE

Carrickfergus Marina E Bkwtr Hd ≰ QG 8m 3M; 54°42'·58N 05°48'·69W.

Black Hd ☆ 54°45'·99N 05°41'·33W Fl 3s 45m **27M**; W 8-sided twr.

N Hunter Rock ⨼ Q; 54°53'·04N 05°45'·13W.

Larne Chaine Twr ☆ Iso WR 5s 23m **16M**; Gy twr; vis: 230°-W-240°-240°-R-shore; 54°51'·27N 05°47'·90W.

East Maiden ≰ Fl (3) 20s 29m 24M; W twr, B band; *Racon (M) 11-21M.* Auxiliary lt Fl R 5s 15m 8M; 54°55'·74N 05°43'·65W; same twr; vis:142°-182° over Russel and Highland Rks.

RATHLIN ISLAND TO INISHTRAHULL
RATHLIN ISLAND

Altacarry Head Rathlin East ☆ 55°18'·06N 06°10'·30W Fl (4) 20s 74m **26M**; W twr, B band; vis: 110°-006° and 036°-058°; *Racon (G) 15-27M.*

Rathlin W 0·5M NE of Bull Pt ≰ 55°18'·05N 06°16'·82W Fl R 5s 62m **22M**; W twr, lantern at base; vis: 015°-225°; H24.

LOUGH FOYLE

Foyle ⨼ L Fl 10s; *Whis;* 55°15'·32N 06°52'·60W.

Inishowen ☆ 55°13'·56N 06°55'·75W Fl (2) WRG 10s 28m **W18M**, R14M, G14M; W twr, 2 B bands; vis: 197°-G-211°-W-249°-R-000°; *Horn (2) 30s.* Fog Det lt VQ 16m vis: 270°.

Inishtrahull ☆ 55°25'·86N 07°14'·62W Fl (3) 15s 59m **19M**; W twr; obscd 256°-261° within 3M; *Racon (T) 24M 060°-310°.*

INISHTRAHULL TO BLOODY FORELAND
L SWILLY/MULROY BAY/SHEEPHAVEN

Fanad Head ☆ 55°16'·57N 07°37'·91W Fl (5) WR 20s 39m **W18M**, R14M; W twr; vis 100°-R-110°-W-313°-R-345°-W-100°.

Limeburner ⨼ Q Fl; 55°18'·54N 07°48'·40W.

Tory Island ☆ 55°16'·36N 08°14'·97W Fl (4) 30s 40m **27M**; B twr, W band; vis: 302°-277°; *Racon (M) 12-23M*; H24.

Bloody Foreland ≰ Fl WG 7·5s 14m W6M, G4M; vis: 062°-W-232°-G-062°; 55°09'·51N 08°17'·03W.

BLOODY F'LD TO RATHLIN O'BIRNE

Aranmore, Rinrawros Pt ☆ 55°00'·90N 08°33'·66W Fl (2) 20s 71m **27M**; W twr; obsc by land about 234°-007° and about 013°. Auxiliary lt Fl R 3s 61m 13M, same twr; vis: 203°-234°.

Rathlin O'Birne, W side ☆ 54°39'·80N 08°49'·94W Fl WR 15s 35m **W18M**, R14M; W twr; vis: 195°-R-307°-W-195°; *Racon (O) 13M, vis 284°-203°.*

RATHLIN O'BIRNE TO EAGLE ISLAND

St John's Pt ≰ Fl 6s 30m 14M; W twr; 54°34'·16N 08°27'·64W.

Rotten I ☆ 54°36'·97N 08°26'·41W; Fl WR 4s 20m **W15M**, R11M; W twr; vis: W255°-R008°-W039°-208°.

SLIGO

Wheat Rk ⨼ Q (6) + LFl 15s; 54°18'·84N 08°39'·10W.

EAGLE ISLAND TO SLYNE HEAD

Eagle Is, W end ☆ 54°17'·02N 10°05'·56W Fl (3) 15s 67m **19M**; W twr.

Black Rk ☆ 54°04'·03N 10°19'·25W Fl WR 12s 86m **W20M**, R16M; W twr; vis: 276°-W-212°-R-276°.

BROAD HAVEN/BLACKSOD/CLEW BAYS

Gubacashel Pt ≰ Iso WR 4s 27m W17M, R12M; 110°-R-133°-W-355°-R-021° W twr; 54°16'·06N 09°53'·33W.

Blacksod ⨼ Q (3) 10s; 54°05'·89N 10°03'·01W.

Achillbeg I S Point ☆ 53°51'·51N 09°56'·85W Fl WR 5s 56m **W18M**, R18M, R15M; W ☐ twr on ☐ building; vis: 262°-R-281°-W-342°-R- 060°-W-092°-R(intens)-099°-W-118°.

Inishgort S Point ≰ L Fl 10s 11m 10M; W twr. Shown H24; 53°49'·61N 09°40'·25W.

Slyne Hd, North twr, Illaunamid ☆ 53°23'·99N 10°14'·06W; Fl (2) 15s 35m **19M**; B twr.

SLYNE HEAD TO BLACK HEAD
GALWAY BAY/INISHMORE

Eeragh, Rock Is ☆ 53°08'·10N 09°51'·39W Fl 15s 35m **23M**; W twr, two B bands; vis: 297°-262°.

Straw Is ☆ 53°07'·06N 09°37'·85W Fl (2) 5s 11m **15M**; W twr.

Black Hd ≰ Fl WR 5s 20m W11M, R8M, W ☐ twr; vis: 045°- R268°-276°; 53°09'·26N 09°15'·83W.

Inisheer ☆ 53°02'·78N 09°31'·58W Iso WR 12s 34m **W20M**, R16M; vis: 225°-W(partially vis >7M)-231°, 231°-W-245°-R-269°-W-115°; *Racon (K) 13M.*

See table on page 27 for distances anticlockwise between Kilrush and Carlingford Lough

1	Strangford Lough	**1**														
2	Bangor	34	**2**													
3	Carrickfergus	39	6	**3**												
4	Larne	45	16	16	**4**											
5	Carnlough	50	25	26	11	**5**										
6	Portrush	87	58	60	48	35	**6**									
7	Lough Foyle	92	72	73	55	47	11	**7**								
8	L Swilly (Fahan)	138	109	104	96	81	48	42	**8**							
9	Burtonport	153	130	130	116	108	74	68	49	**9**						
10	Killybegs	204	175	171	163	148	115	109	93	43	**10**					
11	Sligo	218	189	179	177	156	123	117	107	51	30	**11**				
12	Eagle Island	234	205	198	193	175	147	136	123	72	62	59	**12**			
13	Westport	295	266	249	240	226	193	187	168	120	108	100	57	**13**		
14	Galway	338	309	307	297	284	253	245	227	178	166	163	104	94	**14**	
15	Kilrush	364	335	332	323	309	276	270	251	203	191	183	142	119	76	**15**

AREA 11 West Denmark - *Skagen to Rømø*
SELECTED LIGHTS, BUOYS & WAYPOINTS

Positions are referenced to WGS84

SKAGEN
Skagen W ☆ Fl (3) WR 10s 31m **W17M**/R12M; 053°-W-248°-R-323°; W ○ twr; 57°44'·92N 10°35·66E.
Skagen ☆ Fl 4s 44m **23M**; Gy ○ twr; *Racon G, 20M;* 57°44'·11N 10°37'·76E.
Skagen No 1A ⚓ L Fl 10s; *Racon N;* 57°43'·42N 10°53'·51E.
Ldg lts 334·5°, both Iso R 4s 13/22m 8M. Front, 57°43'·06N 10°35'·45E; mast. Rear, 57°43'·2N 10°35'·4E; twr.
E bkwtr ⚓ Fl G 3s 8m 5M; G twr; *Horn (2) 30s;* 57°42'·88N 10°35'·66E.

HIRTSHALS
Hirtshals ☆ F Fl 30s 57m **F 18M; Fl 25M**; W ○ twr, approx 1M SSW of hbr ent; 57°35'·07N 09°56'·45E.
Ldg lts 166°, both 156°-176°. Front, Iso R 2s 10m 11M; R △ on twr; 57°35'·69N 09°57'·64E; marina ent is close N of this lt. Rear, Iso R 4s 18m 11M; R ▽ on twr; 330m from front.
Outer W mole ⚓ Fl G 3s 14m 6M; G mast; *Horn 15s;* 57°35'·97N 09°57'·36E.

HANSTHOLM
Hanstholm ☆ Fl (3) 20s 65m **26M**; shown by day in poor vis; W 8-sided twr; 57°06'·65N 08°35'·74E, approx 1M S of the hbr ent.
Hanstholm ⚓ LFl 10s; 57°08'·10N 08°34'·94E.
Ldg lts 142·6°, both Iso 2s 37/45m 13M; synch; 127·6°-157·6°; R △ on mast. Front, 57°07'·12N 08°36'·15E. Rear, 170m from front, R ▽ on mast.
W outer mole ⚓ Fl G 3s 11m 9M; 57°07'·54N 08°35'·46E. E outer mole ⚓ Fl R 3s 11m 9M; 57°07'·60N 08°35'·58E.

THYBORØN
Landfall ⚓ L Fl 10s; *Racon T, 10m;* 56°42'·55N 08°08'·70E.
Agger Tange ldg lts 082°: Front, Iso WRG 4s 8m W11M, R/G8M; 074·5°-G-079·5°-W-084·5°-R-089·5°; R △ on bcn; 56°42'·97N 08°14'·11E. Rear, Iso 4s 17m 11M; 075°-089°; synch; R ▽ on Gy twr.
Approach ☆ Fl (3) 10s 24m 12M; 56°42'·49N 08°12'·90E.
Langholm ldg lts 120°, both Iso 2s 7/13m 11M; synch; 113°-127°. Front, R △ on R hut, 56°42'·45N 08°14'·53E. Rear, R ▽ on Gy twr.
Yderhavn, N mole ⚓ Fl G 3s 6m 4M; G pedestal; 56°42'·02N 08°13'·52E.
S mole ⚓ Fl R 3s 6m 4M; 56°41'·97N 08°13'·53E.
Bovbjerg ☆ L Fl (2) 15s 62m **16M**; 56°30'·74N 08°07'·13E.

THORSMINDE HAVN (Positions approx)
Lt ho ⚓ F 30m 13M; 56°22'·34N 08°06'·99E.
Groyne, N ⚓ Fl 5s 8m 5M; 56°22'·46N 08°06'·82E.
N mole ⚓ Iso R 2s 9m 4M; 56°22'·36N 08°06'·62E.
S mole ⚓ Iso G 2s 9m 4M; 56°22'·26N 08°06'·92E.

HVIDE SANDE
Lyngvig ☆ Fl 5s 53m **22M**; 56°02'·95N 08°06'·17E.
N outer bkwtr ⚓ Fl R 3s 7m 8M; 55°59'·94N 08°06'·55E.
S mole ⚓ Fl G 5s 10m 6M; 55°59'·93N 08°06'·88E.
Lt ho ⚓ F 27m 14M; 56°00'·00N 08°07'·35E.

HORNS REV
Blåvands Huk ☆ Fl (3) 20s 55m **23M**; W □ twr; 55°33'·46N 08°04'·95E.

Horns Rev is encircled clockwise by:
Tuxen ⚓ Q; 55°34'·22N 07°41'·92E on the N side.
Vyl ⚓ Q (6) + L Fl 15s; 55°26'·22N 07°49'·99E.
No. 2 ⚓ L Fl 10s; 55°28'·74N 07°36'·49E, SW side.
Horns Rev W ⚓ Q (9) 15s; 55°34'·47N 07°26'·05E.

Slugen Channel (crosses Horns Rev ESE/WNW)
⚓ L Fl G 10s; 55°33'·99N 07°49'·38E.
⚓ Fl G 3s; 55°32'·26N 07°53'·65E.
⚓ Fl (2) R 5s; 55°31'·46N 07°52'·88E.
⚓ Fl (2) G 5s; 55°30'·52N 07°59'·20E.
⚓ Fl (3) R 10s; 55°29'·42N 08°02'·56E.

Wind farm in □ 2·7M x 2·5M, centred on 55°29'·22N 07°50'·21E: 80 turbines all R lts, the 12 perimeter turbines are lit Fl (3) Y 10s.
NE turbine, *Racon (U)*; 55°30'·28N 07°52'·63E & transformer platform, 2 Mo (U) 15s 15m 5M; 55°30'·52N 07°52'·53E.
SW turbine, *Racon (U)*; 55°28'·11N 07°48'·26E.
4 SPM buoys, Fl (5) Y 20s, mark recording stns.
Met mast (60m) ⚓ 2 Mo (U) 15s 8m 3M; 55°31'·32N 07°47'·33E.
2 Met masts, both 70m, ⚓ 2 Mo (U) 15s 12m 5M and Aero QR: 151B (55°29'·21N 07°54'·72E) and 151C (55°29'·24N 07°58'·52E).

APPROACHES TO ESBJERG
Grådyb ⚓ L Fl 10s; *Racon G, 10M;* 55°24'·63N 08°11'·59E.
Sædding Strand 053·8° triple ldg lts: valid up to Nos 7/8 buoys; H24: **Front** Iso 2s 13m **21M**; 052°-056°; R bldg; 55°29'·74N 08°23'·87E.
Middle Iso 4s 26m **21M**; 051°-057°; R twr, W bands; 55°29'·94N 08°24'·33E, 630m from front.
Rear F 37m **18M**; 052°-056°; R twr; 55°30'·18N 08°24'·92E, 0·75M from front.
No. 1 ⚓ Q; 55°25'·49N 08°13'·89E.
No. 2 ⚓ Fl (3) R 10s; 55°25'·62N 08°13'·73E.

31

No. 3 ⚓ Fl G 3s; 55°25'·93N 08°14'·84E.
No. 4 ⚓ Fl R 3s; 55°26'·02N 08°14'·72E.
Tide Gauge ⚟ Fl (5) Y 20s 8m 4M; 55°26'·05N 08°15'·93E.
No. 5 ⚓ Fl G 5s; 55°26'·32N 08°15'·83E.
No. 6 ⚓ Fl R 5s; 55°26'·44N 08°15'·70E.
No. 7 ⚟ Q; 55°26'·76N 08°16'·91E.
No. 8 ⚓ Fl (2) R 5s; 55°26'·89N 08°16'·81E.
Ldg lts 067°, valid up to Nos 9/10 buoys. Both FG 10/25m **16M**, H24. Front, Gy tripod; rear, Gy twr, 55°28'·76N 08°24'·70E.
No. 9 ⚓ Fl (2) G 10s; 55°27'·04N 08°18'·21E.
No.10 ⚓ Fl (2) R 10s; 55°27'·20N 08°18'·04E.
Ldg lts 049°, valid up to No 16 buoy/Jerg. Both FR 16/27m **16M**, H24. Front, W twr; rear, Gy twr, 55°29'·92N 08°23'·75E.
Konsumfiskerihavn, W mole ⚟ Fl R 3s 6m; 203°-119°; R twr; 55°28'·31N 08°25'·33E. Yacht hbr in SSE part of Basin II.
Aero ⚟ 3 x Fl 1·5s (vert, 82m apart) 251m 12M, H24; on chimney; 55°27'·27N 08°27'·32E.

FANØ
Slunden outer ldg lts 242°, both Iso 2s 5/8m 3M; 227°-257°. Front, twr; 55°27'·20N 08°24'·53E. Rear, twr, 106m from front.
Nordby ldg lts 214°, both FR 7/9m 4M; 123·7°-303·7°. Front , W mast;55°26'·94N 08°24'·44E. Rear, Gy twr, 84m from front. Kremer Sand ⚟ FG 5m 3M; G dolphin; 55°27'·3N 08°24'·9E.
Næs Søjord ⚟ FR 5m 3M; R pile; 55°27'·27N 08°24'·86E.
Nordby marina 55°26'·65N 08°24'·53E.

KNUDEDYB
G ⚟ 55°20'·50N 08°24'·28E.
K ⚟ 55°18'·92N 08°20'·06E.
No. 2 ⚓ 55°18'·82N 08°21'·33E.
No. 4 ⚓ 55°18'·81N 08°22'·21E.
No. 6 ⚓ 55°18'·38N 08°24'·63E.

No. 10 ⚓ 55°18'·68N 08°28'·50E.
Knoben ⚓ 55°18'·71N 08°30'·60E.

JUVRE DYB
No. 4 ⚓ 55°13'·76N 08°24'·73E.
No. 6 ⚓ 55°13'·41N 08°26'·60E.
No. 8 ⚓ 55°12'·69N 08°26'·83E.
No. 10 ⚓ 55°12'·55N 08°28'·72E.
Rejsby Stjært ⚟ 55°13'·15N 08°30'·55E.

OUTER APPROACH (Lister Tief) TO RØMØ
See overleaf for details of lights on Sylt.

Rode Klit Sand ⚟ Q (9) 15s, 55°11'·11N 08°04'·88E, (130°/9M to Lister Tief ⚟).
Lister Tief ⚟ Iso 8s, *Whis;* 55°05'·32N 08°16'·80E.
No. 1 ⚓ 55°05'·21N 08°18'·20E.
No. 3 ⚟ Fl G 4s; 55°04'·75E 08°18'·73E.
No. 2 ⚓ Fl (3) R 10s; 55°04'·23N 08°22'·32E.
No. 9 ⚟ Fl (2) G 9s; 55°03'·76N 08°23'·05E.
Lister Landtief No 5 ⚓ 55°03'·68N 08°24'·73E.
No. 4 ⚓ FL (2) R 5s; 55°03'·84N 08°25'·29E.
G1 ⚟ Fl Y 4s; 55°03'·27N 08°28'·32E.

RØMØ DYB and HAVN
No. 1 ⚓ Fl (2) G 10s; 55°03'·23N 08°30'·30E.
No. 10 ⚟ Fl (2) R 10s 5m 3M; R pole; 55°03'·50N 08°31'·10E.
No. 14 ⚟ Fl R 3s 6m 2M; R pole; 55°03'·85N 08°32'·55E.
No. 20 ⚟ Fl R 5s 5m 2M; R pole; 55°04'·79N 08°34'·13E.
No. 9 ⚓ 55°04'·79N 08°34'·63E.
No. 11 ⚓ 55°05'·17N 08°34'·69E.
Rømø Hbr:
S mole ⚟ Fl R 3s 7m 2M; Gy twr; 55°05'·19N 08°34'·31E.
N mole ⚟ Fl G 3s 7m 2M; Gy twr; 55°05'·23N 08°34'·30E.
Inner S mole ⚟ FR 4m 1M; 55°05'·2N 08°34'·2E.
Inner N mole ⚟ FG 4m 1M; 55°05'·3N 08°34'·2E.

		1	2	3	4	5	6	7	8	9	10	11	12	13	14	15	16	17	18
1	Skagen	**1**																	
2	Hirtshals	33	**2**																
3	Hanstholm	85	52	**3**															
4	Thyborøn	114	84	32	**4**														
5	Torsminde	141	108	56	24	**5**													
6	Hvide Sande	162	179	77	45	24	**6**												
7	Esbjerg	200	174	122	90	76	54	**7**											
8	Fanø	210	177	125	93	79	57	3	**8**										
9	Rømø	233	200	148	116	94	73	30	33	**9**									
10	Hörnum	248	215	163	131	108	86	70	73	29	**10**								
11	Husum	275	247	195	163	152	131	95	98	68	45	**11**							
12	Kiel/Holtenau	261	233	281	249	232	208	180	183	189	126	129	**12**						
13	Bremerhaven	306	285	233	201	185	163	127	129	107	83	82	123	**13**					
14	Wilhelmshaven	414	296	242	310	184	162	125	128	106	82	82	123	45	**14**				
15	Helgoland	259	238	186	154	141	119	83	85	63	39	47	104	44	43	**15**			
16	Cuxhaven	304	284	232	200	162	138	110	113	85	56	66	70	58	56	38	**16**		
17	Wangerooge	283	262	210	178	168	147	109	112	94	68	52	108	38	27	24	42	**17**	
18	Hamburg	338	317	265	233	216	192	163	167	139	99	113	90	81	110	88	54	61	**18**

AREA 12 Germany (North Sea coast) - *List to Emden*

SELECTED LIGHTS, BUOYS & WAYPOINTS

Positions are referenced to WGS84

SYLT

Lister Tief ⨼ Iso 8s; *Whis;* 55°05'·33N 08°16'·79E.
List West ⨍ Oc WRG 6s 19m W14M, R11M, G10M; 040°-R-133°-W-227°-R-266·4°-W-268°-G-285°- W-310°- W(unintens)-040°; W twr, R lantern; 55°03'·15N 08°24'·00E.
List Ost ⨍ Iso WRG 6s 22m W14M, R11M, G10M; 010·5°-W(unintens)-098°-W-262°-R-278°-W- 296°-R-323·3°-W-324·5°-G-350°-W-010·5°; W twr, R band; 55°02'·93N 08°26'·58E.
List Hafen, N mole ⨍ FG 8m 4M; 218°-038°; G mast; 55°01'·03N 08°26'·52E.
Kampen, Rote Kliff ☆ L Fl WR 10s 62m **W20M, R16M;** 193°-W-260°- W (unintens)-339°-W-165°- R-193°; W twr, B band; 54°56'·76N 08°20'·38E.
Hörnum ☆ Fl (2) 9s 48m **20M;** 54°45'·23N 08°17'·47E. Hbr, N pier ⨍ FG 6m 4M, 024°-260°.
Vortrapptief ⨼ Iso 4s; 54°34'·88N 08°12'·97E.

AMRUM ISLAND

Norddorf ☆ Oc WRG 6s 22m **W15M,** R12M, G11M; 031-W-097°-R-176·5°-W-178·5°-G-188°; W ○ twr, R lantern; 54°40'·13N 08°18'·46E.
Amrum ☆ Fl 7·5s 63m **23M;** R twr, W bands; 54°37'·84N 08°21'·23E.

FÖHR ISLAND

Nieblum Dir lt ☆ Oc (2) WRG 10s 11m **W19M, R/ G15M;** 028°-G-031°-W-032·5°-R-035·5°; R twr, W band; 54°41'·10N 08°29'·20E.

DAGEBÜLL

Dagebüll Iso WRG 8s 23m **W18M, R/G15M;** 042°- G-043°-W-044·5°- R-047°; G mast; 54°43'·82N 08°41'·43E. FW lts on N and S moles.

RIVER HEVER

Hever ⨼ Iso 4s; *Whis;* 54°20'·41N 08°18'·82E.
Westerheversand ☆ Oc (3) WRG 15s 41m **W21M, R17M, G16M;** 012·2°-W-069°-G-079·5°- W-080·5°-R-107°-W-233°-R-248°; 54°22'·37N 08°38'·36E.

RIVER EIDER

Eider ⨼ Iso 4s; 54°14'·54N 08°27'·61E.
St Peter ☆ L Fl (2) WR 15s 23m **W15M,** R12M; 271°-R-280·5°-W-035°-R-055°-W-068°-R-091°-W- 120°; R twr, B lantern; 54°17'·24N 08°39'·10E.

BÜSUM

Süderpiep ⨼ Iso 8s; *Whis;* 54°05'·82N 08°25'·70E.
Büsum ☆ Iso WR 6s 22m **W19M,** R12M; 248°- 317°-R-024°-W-148°; 54°07'·60N 08°51'·48E.
GB Light V 🔔 Iso 8s 12m **17M;** *Horn Mo (R) 30s;* **Racon T, 8M;** 54°10'·80N 07°27'·60E.

HELGOLAND

Helgoland ☆ Fl 5s 82m **28M;** brown □ twr, B lantern, W balcony; 54°10'·91N 07°52'·93E.
Vorhafen. Ostmole, S elbow ⨍ Oc WG 6s 5m W6M, G3M; 203°-W-250°-G-109°; G post; fog det lt; 54°10'·31N 07°53'·94E.
Düne. Ldg lts 020°. Front ⨍ Iso 4s 11m 8M; 54°10'·87N 07°54'·80E. Rear, Iso WRG 4s 17m W11M, R/G10M; synch; 010°-G-018·5°-W-021°-R- 030; 106°-G-125°-W-130°-R-144°.

RIVER ELBE APPROACHES

Elbe ⨼ Iso 10s; *Racon T, 8M;* 53°59'·95N 08°06'·49E. No.1 ⨼ QG; 53°59'·21N 08°13'·20E.
Neuwerk ☆, S side, L Fl (3) WRG 20s 38m **W16M,** R12M, G11M; 165·3°-G-215·3°-W-238·8°-R-321°; 343°-R-100°; 53°54'·92N 08°29'·73E.

CUXHAVEN/OTTERNDORF

Marina, F WR & F WG ⨍; 53°52'·43N 08°42'·49E.
Medem ⨍ Fl (3) 12s 6m 5M; B △, on B col; 53°50'·15N 08°53'·85E.

BRUNSBÜTTEL

Ldg lts 065·5°: both Iso 3s 24/46m **16/21M;** synch; R twrs, W bands. Front ☆ 53°53'·32N 09°08'·47E.
Alter Vorhafen ⨍ F WG 14m W10M, G6M; 266·3°-W-273·9°-G-088·8°; 53°53'·27N 09°08'·59E.

HAMBURG, WEDEL YACHT HAFEN

E ent ⨍ FG 5m 3M; 53°34'·25N 09°40'·79E.
City Sport Hafen ⨍ Iso Or 2s; 53°32'·52N 09°58'·81E.

RIVER WESER APPROACH CHANNELS

ALTE WESER

Schlüsseltonne ⨼ Iso 8s; 53°56'·25N 07°54'·76E.
Alte Weser ☆ F WRG 33m **W23M, R19M, G18M;** 288°-W-352°-R-003°-W-017°- G-045°-W-074°-G- 118°- W-123°- R-140°-G-175°-W-183°-R-196°-W- 238°; *Horn Mo (AL) 60s;* 53°51'·79N 08°07'·65E.

NEUE WESER

3/Jade 2 ⨳ Fl (2+1) G 15s; *Racon T, 8M;* 53°52'·40N 07°44'·00E.
Tegeler Plate ☆ Oc (3) WRG 12s 21m **W21M, R17M, G16M;** 329°-W-340°-R-014°-W-100°-G- 116°-W-119°-R-123°-G-144°-W-147°-R-264°; 53°47'·87N 08°11'·45E.

BREMERHAVEN

No. 61 ⨼ QG; 53°32'·26N 08°33'·93E (Km 66·0).
Vorhafen S pier hd ⨍ FG 15m 5M; 355°-265°; 53°32'·09N 08°34'·50E.

BREMEN

Hasenbüren Sporthafen ⚡2 FY (vert); 53°07'·51N 08°40'·03E.

RIVER JADE APPROACHES

Jade-Weser ∡ Oc 4s; *Racon T, 8M*; 53°58'·33N 07°38'·83E.
Mellumplate ☆ FW 28m **24M**; 116·1°-116·4°; R□ twr, W band; 53°46'·28N 08°05'·51E.

HOOKSIEL

No. 37/Hooksiel 1 ∡ IQ G 13s; 53°39'·37N 08°06'·58E.
Vorhafen ent ⚡ L Fl R 6s 9m 3M; 53°38'·63N 08°05'·25E.

WILHELMSHAVEN

Fluthafen N mole ⚡ F WG 9m, W6M, G3M; 216°-W-280°-G-010°-W-020°-G-130°; 53°30'·86N 08°09'·32E.

WANGEROOGE

Harle ∡ Iso 8s; 53°49'·24N 07°48'·92E.
Buhne W bkwtr ⚡ FR 3m 4M; 53°46'·33N 07°51'·93E.

SPIEKEROOG

Otzumer Balje ⚲ Iso 4s; 53°47'·98N 07°37'·12E.
Spiekeroog ⚡ FR 6m 4M; 53°45'·0N 07°41'·3E.

LANGEOOG

Accumer Ee ∡ Iso 8s; 53°46·81N 07°26·12E.
W mole ⚡ Oc WRG 6s 8m W7M, R5M, G4M; 064°-G-070°-W-074°-R-326°-W-330°-G-335°-R-064°; *Horn Mo (L) 30s*; 53°43'·42N 07°30'·13E .

NORDERNEY

Norderney N ∡ Q; 53°46'·06N 07°17'·12E.
Dovetief ∡ Iso 4s; 53°45'·25N 07°09'·13E.
Schluchter ∡ Iso 8s; 53°44'·45N 07°02'·23E,.
W mole ⚡ Oc (2) R 9s 13m 4M; 53°41'·9N 07°09'·9E.
Norderney ☆ Fl (3) 12s 59m **23M**; unintens 067°-077° and 270°-280°; R 8-sided twr; 53°42'·58N 07°13'·83E.

BENSERSIEL

E training wall head ⚡ Oc WRG 6s 6m W5M, R3M, G2M; 110°-G-119°-W-121°-R-110°; R post & platform; 53° 41'·80N 07°32'·84E.
Ldg lts 138°, both Iso 6s 12/18m 9M.
Inner hbr, W mole hd FG; E mole hd FR.

DORNUMER-ACCUMERSIEL

AB3 ∡ IQ G 13s; 53°41'·50N 07°29'·34E.
W bkwtr head, approx 53°41'·04N 07°29'·30E.

NESSMERSIEL

N mole ⚡ Oc 4s 6m 5M; G mast; 53°41'·9N 07°21'·7E.

NORDDEICH

W trng wall head ⚡ FG 8m 4M, 021°-327°; G framework twr; 53°38'·7N 07°09'·0E.
Outer ldg lts 144°, both B masts. Front, Iso WR 6s 6m W6M, R5M; 078°-R-122°-W-150°. Rear, Iso 6s 9m 6M; synch, 140m from front.

RIVER EMS APPROACHES

GW/EMS ⬟ Iso 8s 12m **17M**; *Horn Mo (R) 30s (H24)*; *Racon T, 8M*; 54°09'·96N 06°20'·72E.
Borkumriff ∡ Oc 4s; *Racon T, 8M*; 53°47'·44N 06°22'·05E.
Osterems ∡ Iso 4s; 53°41'·91N 06°36'·17E.
Riffgat ∡ Iso 8s; 53°38'·96N 06°27'·07E.
Westerems ∡ Iso 4s; *Racon T, 8M*; 53°36'·9N 06°19'·41E.
H1 ∡ 53°34'·91N 06°17'·97E.

BORKUM

Borkum Grosser ☆ Fl (2) 12s 63m **24M**; 53°35'·32N 06°39'·64E. Same twr, ⚡ F WRG 46m **W19M, R/G15M**; 107·4°-G-109°-W-111·2°- R-112·6°.
Fischerbalje ☆ Oc (2) WRG 16s 15m **W16M**, R12M, G11M; 260°-R-313°-G-014°-W-068°-R-123°; 53°33'·16N 06°42'·86E.

EMDEN

Outer hbr, W pier ⚡ FR 10m 4M; R 8-sided twr; *Horn Mo (ED) 30s*; 53°20'·06N 07°10'·49E.
E pier ⚡ FG 7m 5M; 53°20'·05N 07°10'·84E.

		1	2	3	4	5	6	7	8	9	10	11	12	13	14	15	16	17	18
1	Esbjerg	**1**																	
2	Hörnum Lt (Sylt)	47	**2**																
3	Husum	95	48	**3**															
4	Hamburg	163	112	113	**4**														
5	Kiel/Holtenau	179	128	129	90	**5**													
6	Brunsbüttel	126	75	76	37	53	**6**												
7	Cuxhaven	110	63	66	54	70	17	**7**											
8	Bremerhaven	127	80	82	81	131	78	58	**8**										
9	Wilhelmshaven	125	78	82	110	123	70	56	45	**9**									
10	Hooksiel	116	69	73	101	117	64	47	36	9	**10**								
11	Helgoland	83	38	47	88	104	51	38	44	43	35	**11**							
12	Wangerooge	109	60	52	61	108	55	42	38	27	19	24	**12**						
13	Langeoog	119	72	77	114	130	77	60	47	43	34	35	21	**13**					
14	Norderney	123	77	85	81	137	84	69	62	53	44	44	29	18	**14**				
15	Emden	165	129	137	174	190	137	120	115	106	97	85	80	63	47	**15**			
16	Borkum	133	97	105	104	163	110	95	88	80	71	67	55	46	31	32	**16**		
17	Delfzijl	155	119	127	159	173	120	105	100	89	83	81	65	56	41	10	22	**17**	
18	Den Helder	187	192	198	229	245	192	175	180	159	150	153	148	130	115	125	95	115	**18**

AREA 13 Netherlands & Belgium - *Delfzijl to Nieuwpoort*
SELECTED LIGHTS, BUOYS & WAYPOINTS

Positions are referenced to WGS84

DELFZIJL
W mole ⚓ FG; 53°19'·01N 07°00'·26E.
Ldg lts 203° both Iso 4s. Front, 53°18'·62N 07°00'·16E. Rear, 310m from front.

LAUWERSOOG
W mole head ⚓ FG 3M; *Horn (2) 30s;* 53°24'·68N 06°12'·00E.

KORNWERDERZAND SEALOCK
W mole ⚓ FG 9m 7M; *Horn Mo(N) 30s;* 53°04'·77N 05°20'·03E.

HARLINGEN
P9/BO44 ⚲ VQ; 53°10'·59N 05°23'·88E.
Pollendam ldg lts 112°, both Iso 6s 8/19m 13M (H24); B masts, W bands. Front, 53°10'·51N 05°24'·18E. Rear, 500m from front, vis 104·5°-119·5°.
N mole hd ⚓ FR 9m 4M; R/W pedestal; 53°10'·59N 05°24'·32E.

SCHIERMONNIKOOG TO AMELAND
WG (Westgat) ⚲ Iso 8s; *Racon N;* 53°31'·97N 06°11'·96E.
Schiermonnikoog ☆ Fl (4) 20s 43m **28M**; dark R ○ twr; 53°29'·19N 06°08'·76E. Same twr: FWR 29m **W15M**, R12M; W210°-221°, R221°-230°.

ZEEGAT VAN AMELAND
Ameland, W end ☆ Fl (3) 15s 57m **30M**; 53°26'·92N 05°37'·52E.

ZEEGAT VAN TERSCHELLING
Otto ⚲ VQ; 53°24'·65N 05°06'·31E.
TG ⚲ Q (9) 15s; 53°24'·17N 05°02'·31E.
ZS ⚲ Iso 4s; *Racon T;* 53°19'·71N 04°55'·86E.
ZS1 ⚲ VQ G; 53°19'·23N 04°57'·57E.
ZS5 ⚲ L Fl G 8s; 53°18'·50N 05°01'·10E.
ZS11-VS2 ⚲ Q (9) 15s; 53°18'·66N 05°05'·94E.

WEST TERSCHELLING
Brandaris Twr ☆ Fl 5s 54m **29M**, partly obscured by dunes on Vlieland and Terschelling; Y ☐ twr; 53°21'·61N 05°12'·85E.
W hbr mole ⚓ FR 5m 5M; R post, W bands; *Horn 15s;* 53°21'·25N 05°13'·09E.

VLIELAND
Vuurduin ☆ Iso 4s 54m **20M;** 53°17'·69N 05°03'·46E.
E mole hd ⚓ FG; 53°17'·68N 05°05'·51E.

EIERLANDSCHE GAT
Eierland ☆ Fl (2) 10s 52m **29M**; R ○ twr; 53°10'·93N 04°51'·30E, N tip of Texel.

OUDESCHILD
Dir ⚓ Oc 6s; intens 291°; 53°02'·40N 04°50'·94E; leads 291° into hbr between N mole head FG 6m; and S mole hd ⚓ FR 6m; *Horn (2) 30s* (sounded 0600-2300); 53°02'·33N 04°51'·17E.

DEN OEVER SEALOCK
LW ⚲ L Fl 10s; 52°59'·51N 04°55'·90E,.
Ldg lts 131°, both Oc 10s 6m 7M; 127°-137°. Front, 52°56'·32N 05°02'·98E. Rear, 280m SE.
Detached bkwtr N hd ⚓ L Fl R 10s 52°56'·76N 05°02'·29E.

APPROACHES TO ZEEGAT VAN TEXEL
NH ⚲ VQ; 53°00'·23N 04°35'·36E.
MR ⚲ Q (9) 15s; 52°56'·76N 04°33'·81E.
ZH ⚲ VQ (6) + L Fl 10s; 52°54'·65N 04°34'·71E.
TX1 ⚲ Fl G 5s; 52°48'·01N 04°15'·50E.
Vinca G ⚲ Q (9) 15s; *Racon D;* 52°45'·93N 04°12'·35E.

MOLENGAT (from the N)
MG ⚲ Mo (A) 8s; 53°03'·91N 04°39'·36E.
MG1 ⚲ Iso G 4s; 53°02'·89N 04°40'·84E.
S14-MG17 ⚲ VQ (6) + L Fl 10s; 52°58'·45N 04°43'·51E.

SCHULPENGAT (from the SSW)
Ldg lts 026·5°, both Oc 8s **18M** (by day 9M); vis 024·5°-028·5°. **Front** ☆, 53°00'·85N 04°44'·42E (on Texel). Rear, **Den Hoorn** ☆ ; church spire; 0·83M from front.
SG ⚲ Mo (A) 8s; *Racon Z;* 52°52'·90N 04°37'·90E.
Schilbolsnol ☆ F WRG 27m **W15M**, R12M, G11M; 338°-W-002°-G-035°-W(ldg sector)-038°-R-051°-W-068°; post; 53°00'·50N 04°45'·68E (on Texel).
Huisduinen ⚓ F WR 26m W14M, R11M; 070°-W-113°-R-158°-W-208°; ☐ twr; 52°57'·13N 04°43'·29E (2·5M WSW of Den Helder).
Kijkduin ☆ Fl (4) 20s 56m **30M**; vis 360°, except where obsc'd by dunes on Texel; brown twr; 52°57'·33N 04°43'·58E (mainland).

DEN HELDER
Ldg lts 191°, both Oc G 5s 15/24m 14M, synch. Front, vis 161°-221°; B ▽ on bldg; 52°57'·37N 04°47'·08E. Rear, vis 161°-247°; B ▽ on B lattice twr; 275m from front.
Marinehaven, W bkwtr head ⚓ QG 11m 8M; *Horn 20s;* 52°57'·95N 04°47'·07E (Harssens Is).
Ent W side, ⚓ Fl G 5s 9m 4M (H24); 180°-067°; 52°57'·78N 04°47'·08E.
Grote Kaap ⚓ Oc WRG 10s 30m W11M, R/G8M; 041°-G-088°-W-094°-R-131°; brown twr; 52°52'·85N 04°42'·88E.
Petten ⚲ VQ (9) 10s; 52°47'·33N 04°36'·68E.

IJMUIDEN

Mo (A) 8s; *Racon Y, 10M*; 52°28'·44N 04°23'·78E.
S bkwtr hd FG 14m 10M (in fog Fl 3s); *Horn (2) 30s;* W twr, G bands; 52°27'·82N 04°31'·94E.
N bkwtr hd FR 15m 10M; 52°28'·05N 04°32'·55E.
S bkwtr hd FG 14m 10M (in fog Fl 3s); *Horn (2) 30s;* W twr, G bands; 52°27'·82N 04°31'·94E.

AMSTERDAM

Sixhaven marina F & FR; 52°22'·99N 04°53'·69E.

SCHEVENINGEN

SCH Iso 4s; 52°07'·75N 04°14'·14E.
W mole FG 12m 9M; G twr, W bands; *Horn (3) 30s;* 52°06'·22N 04°15'·16E.

NOORD HINDER TSS

Garden City Q (9) 15s; 51°29'·12N 02°17'·92E.
Twin Fl (3) Y 9s; 51°32'·05N 02°22'·62E.
NHR-S Fl Y 10s; *Bell;* 51°51'·35N 02°28'·71E.
Birkenfels Q (9) 15s; 51°38'·96N 02°32'·03E.
Track Ferry Fl Y 5s; 51°33'·78N 02°36'·33E.
NHR-SE Fl G 5s; 51°45'·42N 02°39'·92E.
NHR-N L Fl 8s; *Racon K, 10M*; 52°10'·78N 03°04'·69E.

APPROACHES to HOEK VAN HOLLAND

Noord Hinder Fl (2) 10s; *Horn (2) 30s; Racon T, 12-15M;* 52°00'·04N 02° 51'·03E.
Goeree ☆ Fl (4) 20s 32m **28M**; R/W chequered twr on platform; helicopter platform; *Horn (4) 30s; Racon T, 12-15M;* 51°55'·42N 03°40'·03E.
Maas Center Iso 4s; *Racon M, 10M;* 52°01'12N 03°53'·44E.
Indusbank N VQ; 52°02'·88N 04°03'·55E.
MO Mo (A) 8s; 52°00'97N 03°58'·06E.
MVN VQ; 51°59'·59N 04°00'·19E.
MV Q (9) 15s; 51°57'·44N 03°58'·40E.
Westhoofd, 51°48'·78N 03°51'·82E, Fl (3) 15s 55m **30M**; R ☐ tr.

HOEK VAN HOLLAND

Nieuwe Waterweg ldg lts 107°: both Iso R 6s 29/43m **18M**; 099.5°-114.5°; R twr, W bands. Front, 51°58'·55N 04°07'·53E. Rear, 450m ESE.
Maasvlakte ☆ Fl (5) 20s 67m **28M**, H24; 340°-267°; W twr, B bands; 51°58'·20N 04°00'·85E, 1·5M SSW of Maas ent.
Nieuwe Zuiderdam FG 25m 10M [In fog Al Fl WG 6s; 330°-307°]; *Horn 10s*; G twr, W bands; 51°59'·13N 04°02'·47E.

ROTTERDAM

Maassluis FG & FR 6m; 51°54'·93N 04°14'·81E.
Vlaardingen FG & FR; 51°53'·99N 04°20'·95E.
Spuihaven, W ent FR; 51°53'·98N 04°23'·98E.
Veerhaven, E ent FG & FR; 51°54'·40N 04°28'·75E.

APPROACHES TO HARINGVLIET

Buitenbank , Iso 4s; 51°51'·14N 03°25'·69E.
West Schouwen ☆ Fl (2+1)15s 57m **30M**; Gy twr, R diagonals; 51°42'·53N 03°41'·48E
SG Iso 4s; 51°51'·93N 03°51'·40E.

STELLENDAM

N mole FG; *Horn (2) 15s;* 51°49'·87N 04°02'·01E.

HELIUSHAVEN/HELLEVOETSLUIS

Heliushaven E jetty 51°49'·23N 04°07'·28E, FG 7m 3M.
Hellevoetsluis 51°49'·18N 04°07'·66E, Iso WRG 10s 16m W11M, R8M, G7M; G266°-275°, W275°-294°, R294°-316°, W316°-036°, G036°-058°, W058°-095°, R095°-140°; W twr, R top.

OOSTERSCHELDE APPROACHES

Schouwenbank Mo (A) 8s; *Racon O, 10M;* 51°44'·94N 03°14'·32E.
Middelbank 51°40'·83N 03°18'·19E, Iso 8s.
Rabsbank Iso 4s; 51°38'·25N 03°09'·90E.
Westpit Iso 8s; 51°33'·65N 03°09'·92E.
SW Thornton Iso 8s; 51°30'·95N 02°50'·92E.

ROOMPOTSLUIS

Ldg lts 073·5°, both Oc G 5s; synch. Front, 51°37'·33N 03°40'·74E. Rear, 280m E.
N bkwtr 51°37'·30N 03°40'·09E, FR 7m; *Horn(2) 30s.*
Roompot marina, N mole FR; 51°35'·62N 03°43'·20E.
Kaloo Iso 8s; 51°35'·56N 03°23'·23E.
Westkapelle ☆, Common rear, Fl 3s 49m **28M**; partially obsc'd; ☐ twr; 51°31'·75N 03°26'·80E.
Molenhoofd Oc WRG 6s 10m; 306°-R-329°-W-349°-R-008°-G-034·5°-W-036·5°-G-144°-W-169°-R-198°; W mast R bands; 51°31'·58N 03°26'·03E.

OFFSHORE MARKS

West Hinder ☆ Fl (4) 30s 23m 13M; *Horn Mo (U) 30s; Racon W;* 51°23'·31N 02°26'·27E.
Oost-Dyck Q; 51°21'·39N 02°31'·11E.
Oostdyck radar twr ☆ Mo (U) 15s 15m 12M; *Horn Mo (U) 30s; Racon O.* R twr, 3 W bands, with red twr/helipad; 51°16'·49N 02°26'·83E.

SCHEUR CHANNEL

S1 Fl G 5s; 51°23'·15N 03°00'·12E.
MOW 0 ⊙ Fl (5) Y 20s; *Whis; Racon S, 10M;* 51°23'·67N 03°02'·75E.

WIELINGEN CHANNEL

W-Z Q (9) 15s; 51°22'·57N 03°10'·71E.
Nieuwe Sluis Oc WRG 10s 26m W14M, R11M, G10M; 055°-R-089°-W-093°-G-105°-R-134°-W-136·5°- G-156·5°-W-236·5°-G-243° -W-254°-R-292°-W-055°; B 8-sided twr, W bands; 51°24'·41N 03°31'·27E.

VLISSINGEN

Koopmanshaven, W mole root, ⚡ Iso WRG 3s 15m W12M, R10M, G9M; 253°-R-277°-W-284°-R-297°-W-306·5°-G-013°-W-024°-G-033°-W-035°-G-039°-W-055°-G-084·5°-R-092°-G-111°-W-114°; R pylon; 51°26'·37N 03°34'·52E.
E mole ⚡ FG 7m; W mast; 51°26'·32N 03°34'·66E.

BRESKENS

Yacht hbr, W mole ⚡ FG 7m; in fog FY; Gy post; 51°24'·04N 03°34'·06E. E mole ⚡ FR 6m; Gy mast; 51°23'·95N 03°34'·09E.

TERNEUZEN

W mole ⚡ OcWRG 5s 15m W9M, R7M, G6M; 090°-R-115°-W-120°-G-130°-W-245°-G-249°-W-279°-R-004°; B & W post; 51°20'·54N 03°49'·58E, close SW of ⚡ FG, W side of ent to marinas.

BELGIUM

ANTWERPEN

Royerssluis, ldg lts 091°, both FR. FR/FG, ent to Willemdok ⚓.
Linkeroever marina ⚓ F WR 9m W3M, R2M; shore-W-283°-R-shore; B ⊙, R lantern; 51°13'·91N 04°23'·70E. Marina ent, FR/FG.

ZEEBRUGGE

A2 ⚓ Iso 8s; 51°22'·42N 03°07'·05E.
Ldg lts 136°, both Oc 5s 22/45m 8M; 131°-141°; H24, synch; W cols, R bands. Front, 51°20'·71N 03°13'·11E. Rear, 890m SE.
W outer mole ⚡ Oc G 7s 31m 7M; G vert strip lts visible from seaward; 057°-267°; Horn (3) 30s; IPTS; 51°21'·73N 03°11'·17E.
Leopold II mole ☆ Oc WR 15s 22m, **W20M, R18M**; 068°-W-145°-R-212°-W-296°; IPTS; Horn (3+1) 90s; 51°20'·86N 03°12'·18E.

BLANKENBERGE

Lt ho ☆ Fl (2) 8s 30m **20M**; 065°-245°; W twr, B top; 51°18'·76N 03°06'·87E.

Ldg lts 134°, both FR 5/8m 3/10M; front, R cross (X) on mast.
E pier ⚡ FR 12m 11M; 290°-245°; W ◯ twr; Bell (2) 15s; 51°18'·91N 03°06'·56E.
W pier ⚡ FG 14m 11M; intens 065°-290°, unintens 290°-335°; W ◯ twr; 51°18'·89N 03°06'·43E.

OOSTENDE

A1 ⚓ Iso 8s; 51°22'·37N 02°53'·34E.
Ldg lts 128°: both Iso 4s (triple vert) 22/32m 4M; 051°-201°; X on framework twrs, R/W bands. Front, 51°14'·13N 02°55'·55E. Rear, 175m SE.
Oostende lt ho ☆ Fl (3) 10s 65m **27M**; obsc 069·5°-071°; Gy twr, 2 sinusoidal Bu bands; 51°14'·18N 02°55'·83E.
E pier ⚡ FR 15m 12M; 333°-243°; W ◯ twr; IPTS, plus QY when chan closed for ferry movement; Horn Mo(OE) 30s; 51°14'·39N 02°55'·14E.

NIEUWPOORT

Zuidstroom Bank ⚓ Fl R 5s; 51°12'·29N 02°47'·38E.
Weststroom Bank ⚓ Fl (4) R 20s; 51°11'·33N 02°43'·04E.
Lt ho ☆ Fl (2) R 14s 28m **16M**; R ◯ twr, W bands; 51°09'·28N 02°43'·80E, 2 ca E of E pier root.
E pier ⚡ FR 11m 10M; vis 025°-250° & 307°-347°; Horn Mo (K) 30s; W ◯ twr; 51°09'·42N 02°43'·08E.
W pier ⚡ FG 11m 9M; vis 025°-250° & 284°-324°; IPTS from root; Bell (2) 10s; W ◯ twr; 51°09'·35N 02°43'·00E.
Oostduinkerke ⚓ 51°09'·15N 02°39'·44E, Q.
Nieuwpoort Bank ⚓ 51°10'·17N 02°36'·09E, Q (9) 15s.
Den Oever wreck ⚓ 51°08'·10N 02°37'·45E.
Trapegeer ⚓ Fl G 10s; 51°08'·42N 02°34'·38E.
E12 ⚓ VQ (6) + L Fl 10s; 51°07'·88N 02°30'·70E.
E11 ⚓ Fl G 4s; 51°07'·25N 02°30'·65E.
For Passe de Zuydcoote, see overleaf.
Belgian/French border is between E12 and E11 buoys; see also AC 1873.

1	Delfzijl	1															
2	Terschelling	85	2														
3	Harlingen	102	19	3													
4	Den Oever	110	34	21	4												
5	Den Helder	115	39	30	11	5											
6	Amsterdam	159	83	81	62	51	6										
7	IJmuiden	146	70	68	49	38	13	7									
8	Scheveningen	171	95	93	74	63	38	25	8								
9	Rotterdam	205	129	127	108	97	72	59	34	9							
10	Hook of Holland	185	109	107	88	77	52	39	14	20	10						
11	Stellendam	201	125	123	104	93	68	55	30	36	16	11					
12	Roompotsluis	233	157	155	136	125	100	87	50	68	48	32	12				
13	Vlissingen	228	152	150	131	120	99	86	61	67	47	45	24	13			
14	Zeebrugge	239	163	161	142	131	106	93	68	74	54	50	28	16	14		
15	Blankenberge	244	168	166	147	136	111	98	73	79	59	55	33	21	5	15	
16	Oostende	239	163	161	142	131	110	106	81	87	67	72	40	29	13	9	16
17	Nieuwpoort	262	186	184	165	154	129	116	91	97	77	83	51	39	23	18	9	17

AREA 14, North France - *Dunkerque to Cap de la Hague*

SELECTED LIGHTS, BUOYS & WAYPOINTS

> Positions are referenced to WGS84

OFFSHORE MARKS

WH Zuid ⚹ Q (6) + L Fl 15s; 51°22'·78N 02°26'·25E.
Bergues N ⚹ Q; 51°19'·92N 02°24'·50E.
Oostdyck radar twr; ☆ Mo (U) 15s 15m 12M;
Horn Mo (U) 30s; Racon O; 51°16'·49N 02°26'·83E.
Bergues ⚹ Fl G 4s; 51°17'·15N 02°18'·62E.
Ruytingen N ⚹ 51°13'·10N 02°10'·28E, VQ.
Ruytingen SE ⚹ VQ (3) 15s; 51°09'·20N 02°08'·92E.
Sandettié SW ⚹ Q (9) 15s 5M; 51°09'·72N 01°45'·60E.
Sandettié ⚓ Fl 5s 12m **15M**; R hull; *Horn 30s;*
Racon T, 10M; 51°09'·34N 01°47'·10E.

PASSE DE ZUYDCOOTE

E12 ⚹ VQ (6) + L Fl 10s; 51°07'·90N 02°30'·59E.
E11 ⚹ Fl G 4s; 51°07'·24N 02°30'·61E.
E7 ⚹ Fl (3) G 12s; 51°05'·18N 02°28'·50E.

PASSE DE L'EST

E6 ⚹ QR; 51°04'·86N 02°27'·08E.
E2 ⚹ Fl (2) R 6s; 51°04'·32N 02°22'·31E.
⚹ Q (6) + L Fl 15s; 51°04'·29N 02°21'·72E.

DUNKERQUE PORT EST

Jetée Est ☆ Fl (2) R 10s 12m **16M**; in fog Fl (2)
10s; 51°03'·59N 02°21'·20E.
Dunkerque lt ho ☆ Fl (2) 10s 59m **26M**; 51°02'·93N
02°21'·86E.

GRAVELINES

W jetty ⚸ Fl (2) WG 6s 9m W8M, G6M; 317°-W-
327°-G-085°-W-244°; 51°00'·94N 02°05'·48E.

DUNKERQUE, WEST APPROACH

DW29 ⚹ Fl (3) G 12s; 51°03'·85N 02°20'·21E.
DW18 ⚹ Fl (3) R 12s; 51°03'·47N 02°10'·37E.
RCE ⚹ Iso G 4s; 51°02'·43N 01°53'·21E.
Dyck ⚹ Fl 3s; *Racon B*; 51°02'·99N 01°51'·78E.

CALAIS

Jetée Est ☆ Fl (2) R 6s 12m **17M**; Gy twr, R top;
Horn (2) 40s; 50°58'·40N 01°50'·46E.
Jetée Ouest ⚸ Iso G 3s 12m 9M; W twr, G top; *Bell
5s;* 50°58'·24N 01°50'·40E.
Calais ☆ Fl (4) 15s 59m **22M**; vis 073°-260°; W 8-
sided twr, B top; 50°57'·68N 01°51'·21E.

CALAIS, WESTERN APPROACH

CA3 ⚹ Fl G 4s; *Whis;* 50°56'·82N 01°41'·12E.
CA6 ⚹ VQ R; 50°58'·25N 01°45'·63E.
Sangatte ⚸ Oc WG 4s 13m W8M, G5M; 065°-G-
089°-W-152°-G-245°; 50°57'·19N 01°46'·47E.
CA8 ⚹ QR; 50°58'·38N 01°48'·65E.
CA10 ⚹ Fl (2) R 6s; 50°58'·63N 01°49'·92E.
Cap Gris-Nez ☆ Fl 5s 72m **29M**; 005°-232°; W twr,
B top; *Horn 60s;* 50°52'·09N 01°34'·94E.

DOVER STRAIT TSS, French side

Ruytingen SW ⚹ Fl (3) G 12s; 51°04'·98N 01°46'·83E.
ZC2 ⚹ Fl (2+1) Y 15s; 50°53'·53N 01°30'·88E.
ZC1 ⚹ Fl (4) Y 15s; 50°44'·99N 01°27'·21E.
Vergoyer N ⚹ VQ; *Racon C, 5-8M*; 50°39'·64N
01°22'·18E.
Vergoyer E ⚹ VQ (3) 5s; 50°35'·74N 01°19'·65E.
Bassurelle ⚹ Fl (4) R 15s 6M; *Racon B, 5-8m;*
50°32'·74N 00°57'·69E.
Vergoyer SW ⚹ VQ (9) 10s; 50°26'·98N 01°00'·00E.

BOULOGNE

⚹ VQ (6) + L Fl 10s 8m 6M; *Whis;* 50°45'·31N
01°31'·07E.
Digue Carnot (S) ☆ Fl (2+1) 15s 25m **19M**; W twr,
G top; *Horn (2+1) 60s;* 50°44'·44N 01°34'·05E.
Cap d'Alprech ☆ Fl (3) 15s 62m **23M**; W twr, B
top; 50°41'·90N 01°33'·75E, 2·5M S of hbr ent.

LE TOUQUET/ÉTAPLES

Le Touquet ☆ Fl (2) 10s 54m **25M**; Or twr, brown
band, W&G top; 50°31'·43N 01°35'·49E.
Pointe du Haut-Blanc ☆ Fl 5s 44m **23M**; W twr, R
bands, G top; 50°23'·89N 01°33'·62E.

ST VALÉRY-SUR-SOMME

ATSO ⚹ Mo (A) 12s; 50°14'·00N 01°28'·08E.
Trng wall hd, ⚹ Fl G 2.5s 2m 1M; 50°12'·25N
01°35'·85E.
Cayeux-sur-Mer ☆ Fl R 5s 32m **22M**; W twr, R
top; 50°11'·65N 01°30'·67E.

LE TRÉPORT

Ault ☆ Oc (3) WR 12s 95m **W15M**, R11M; 040°-
W-175°-R-220°; W twr, R top; 50°06'·28N 01°27'·23E.
Jetée Ouest ☆ Fl (2) G 10s 15m **20M**; W twr, G
top; *Horn (2) 30s;* 50°03'·87N 01°22'·13E.

DIEPPE

DI ⚹ VQ (3) 5s; 49°57'·05N 01°01'·25E.
Jetée Ouest ⚸ Iso G 4s 11m 8M; W twr, G top;
Horn 30s; 49°56'·27N 01°04'·95E.
Pte d'Ailly ☆ Fl (3) 20s 95m **31M**; W □ twr, G top;
Horn (3) 60s; 49°54'·96N 00°57'·49E.

SAINT VALÉRY-EN-CAUX

Jetée Est ⚸ Fl (2) R 6s 8m 4M; 49°52'·40N 00°42'·70E.

FÉCAMP

Jetée Nord ☆ Fl (2) 10s 15m **16M**; Gy twr, R top;
Horn (2) 30s; 49°45'·93N 00°21'·78E.
Jetée Sud ⚸ QG 14m 9M; Gy twr, G top;
49°45'·88N 00°21'·80E.
Cap d'Antifer ☆ Fl 20s 128m **29M**; 021°-222°;
Gy 8-sided twr, G top; 49°41'·01N 00°09'·90E.

LE HAVRE

Cap de la Hève ☆ Fl 5s 123m **24M**; 225°-196°; W 8-sided twr, R top; 49°30'·74N 00°04'·15E.

LHA ⌐ Mo (A) 12s 10m 9M; R&W; **Racon, 8-10M**; 49°31'·38N 00°09'·88W.

Digue Nord ☆ Fl R 5s 15m **21M**; IPTS; W ○ twr, R top; Horn 15s; 49°29'·19N 00°05'·44E.

CHENAL DE ROUEN/HONFLEUR

No. 2 ⌡ QR; **Racon T**; 49°27'·40N 00°01'·35E.

Ratier NW ⌡ Fl G 2·5s; 49°26'·85N 00°02'·50E.

No. 20 ⌡ QR; 49°25'·85N 00°13'·51E. Digue Ouest ⋠ QG 10m 6M; 49°25'·68N 00°13'·81E.

DEAUVILLE/TROUVILLE

Ratelets ⌡ Q (9) 15s; 49°25'·29N 00°01'·71E.

E jetty ⋠ Fl (4) WR 12s 8m W7M, R4M; 131°-W-175°-R-131°; 49°22'·22N 00°04'·33E.

DIVES-SUR-MER

DI ⌡ L Fl 10s; 49°19'·18N 00°05'·84W.

No. 1 ⊿ 49°18'·50N 00°05'·67W.

Dir lt 159·5°, Oc (2+1) WRG 12s 6m, W12M, R/G9M, 125°-G-157°-W-162°-R-194°; 49°17'·80N 00°05'·24W.

OUISTREHAM/CAEN

Ldg lts 185°, both Dir Oc (3+1) R 12s 10/30m **17M**. **Front**, 49°17'·09N 00°14'·80W.

Lt ho ☆ Oc WR 4s 37m **W17M**, R13M; 115°-R-151°-W-115°; 49°16'·85N 00°14'·80W.

COURSEULLES-SUR-MER

Courseulles ⌡ Iso 4s; 49°21'·28N 00°27'·69W.

W jetty ⋠ Iso WG 4s 7m; W9M, G6M; 135°-W-235°-G-135°; Horn 30s; 49°20'·41N 00°27'·37W.

Ver ☆ Fl (3)15s 42m **26M**; 49°20'·39N 00°31'·15W.

PORT-EN-BESSIN

W mole ⋠ Fl WG 4s 14m, W10M, G7M; G065°-114·5°, W114·5°-065°; 49°21'·17N 00°45'·39W.

GRANDCAMP

Ldg lts 146°, both Dir Q 9/12m **15M**, 144·5°-147·5°. **Front** ☆, 49°23'·42N 01°02'·92W.

Jetée Est ⋠ Oc (2) R 6s 9m 9M; Horn Mo(N) 30s; 49°23'·52N 01°02'·98W.

CARENTAN

C-I ⌡ Iso 4s; 49°25'·44N 01°07'·08W.

Trng wall ⌊ Fl (4) G 15s; 49°21'·94N 01°09'·96W.

Iles St-Marcouf ⋠ VQ (3) 5s 18m 8M; ☐ Gy twr, G top; 49°29'·86N 01°08'·82W.

ST VAAST-LA-HOUGUE

Le Gavendest ⌡ Q (6) + L Fl 15s; Whis; 49°34'·36N 01°13'·89W.

Jetty ⋠ Dir Oc (2) WRG 6s 12m W10M, R/G7M; 219°-R-237°-G-310°-W-350°-R-040°; Siren Mo (N) 30s; 49°35'·17N 01°15'·41W.

BARFLEUR

Ldg lts 219·5°, both Oc (3) 12s 7/13m 10M; synch. Front, W ☐ twr; 49°40'·18N 01°15'·61W. W jetty ⋠ Fl G 4s 8m 6M; 49°40'·32N 01°15'·57W.

Pte de Barfleur ☆ Fl (2) 10s 72m **29M**; Gy twr, B top; Horn (2) 60s; 49°41'·78N 01°15'·96W.

Les Équets ⌡ Q 8m 3M; 49°43'·62N 01°18'·36W.

La Pierre Noire ⌡ Q (9) 15s 8m 4M; 49°43'·53N 01°29'·09W.

CHERBOURG

La Truite ⌡ Fl (4) R 15s; 49°40'·33N 01°35'·50W.

Fort de l'Est ⋠ Iso G 4s 19m 9M; 49°40'·28N 01°35'·93W

Fort de l'Ouest ☆ Fl (3) WR 15s 19m **W24M, R20M**; 122°-W-355°-R-122°; Gy twr, R top; Horn (3) 60s; 49°40'·45N 01°38'·87W.

Fort de l'Ouest ☆ Fl (3) WR 15s 19m **W24M, R20M**; 122°-W-355°-R-122°; Gy twr, R top; Horn (3) 60s; 49°40'·45N 01°38'·87W.

Marina W mole ⋠ Fl (3) G 12s 7m 6M; G pylon; 49°38'·87N 01°37'·15W.

OMONVILLE-LA-ROGUE

L'Étonnard ⌿ 49°42'·32N 01°49'·85W.

Cap de la Hague ☆ Fl 5s 48m **23M**; Gy twr, W top; Horn 30s; 49°43'·31N 01° 57'·28W.

		1																	
1	Dunkerque	**1**																	
2	Calais	22	**2**																
3	Boulogne	42	20	**3**															
4	Étaples	51	32	12	**4**														
5	St Valéry-sur-Somme	69	50	30	19	**5**													
6	Dieppe	96	74	54	50	35	**6**												
7	St Valéry-en-Caux	103	81	61	58	45	16	**7**											
8	Fécamp	118	96	76	70	62	29	15	**8**										
9	Le Havre	143	121	101	90	85	54	38	25	**9**									
10	Honfleur	152	130	110	100	95	63	45	34	10	**10**								
11	Deauville/Trouville	150	128	108	100	95	61	44	32	10	8	**11**							
12	Dives-sur-Mer	151	129	108	117	97	67	55	39	17	13	7	**12**						
13	Ouistreham	160	138	115	110	103	68	58	39	24	19	14	8	**13**					
14	Courseulles	162	140	118	110	103	75	55	40	28	23	21	17	11	**14**				
15	Grandcamp-Maisy	190	168	135	130	125	94	80	64	50	45	43	38	35	25	**15**			
16	Carentan	192	170	145	140	132	105	88	72	62	56	56	51	46	37	13	**16**		
17	St Vaast	179	157	133	130	120	95	78	63	69	53	53	49	46	35	16	20	**17**	
18	Barfleur	170	148	128	124	120	94	77	64	56	62	56	53	46	39	21	26	10	**18**
19	Cherbourg	182	160	142	134	130	108	82	82	76	70	69	66	54	41	39	26	20	**19**

AREA 15 N Central France & Channel Is - *Cap de la Hague to St Quay*
SELECTED LIGHTS, BUOYS & WAYPOINTS | Positions are referenced to WGS84

DIELETTE
W bkwtr Dir lt 140°, Iso WRG 4s 12m W10M, R/
G7M; 070°-G-135°-W-145°-R-180°; 49°33'·17N
01°51'·84W.
E bkwtr ⚓ Fl R 4s 6m 2M; 49°33'·21N 01°51'·80W.

CARTERET
Cap de Carteret ☆ Fl (2+1) 15s 81m **26M**; Gy twr,
G top; 49°22'·40N 01°48'·44W.
W bkwtr ⚓ Oc R 4s 7m 7M; W post, R top;
49°22'·13N 01°47'·40W.

PORTBAIL
PB ⚓ 49°18'·39N 01°44'·76W.
Ldg lts 042°: Front, Q 14m 10M, 49°19'·74N
01°42'·51W. Rear, Oc 4s 20m 10M; stubby ch spire.

PASSAGE DE LA DÉROUTE
Les Trois-Grunes ⚓ Q (9) 15s, 49°21'·82N 01°55'·21W.
Le Sénéquet ⚓ Fl (3) WR 12s 18m W13M, R10M;
083·5°-R-116·5°-W-083·5°; 49°05'·47N 01°39'·75W.
NE Minquiers ⚓ VQ (3) 5s; *Bell;* 49°00'·84N
01°55'·31W.
S Minquiers ⚓ Q (6) + L Fl 15s; 48°53'·07N 02°10'·11W.

ÎLES CHAUSEY
L'Enseigne, W twr, B top; 48°53'·73N 01°50'·27W.
Grande Île ☆ Fl 5s 39m **23M**; Gy ☐ twr, G top;
Horn 30s; 48°52'·17N 01°49'·36W.
La Crabière Est ⚓ Oc WRG 4s 5m, W9M, R/G 6M;
079°-W-291°-G-329°-W-335°-R-079°; YB pylon;
48°52'·47N 01°49'·41W.

GRANVILLE
Pte du Roc ☆ Fl (4) 15s 49m **23M**; 48°50'·06N
01°36'·78W.
Le Loup ⚓ Fl (2) 6s 8m 11M; 48°49'·57N 01°36'·25W.
Marina S bkwtr ⚓ Fl (2) R 6s 12m 5M; W post, R
top; *Horn (2) 40s;* 48°49'·89N 01°35'·90W.

CANCALE
Pierre-de-Herpin ☆ Oc (2) 6s 20m **17M**; *Siren Mo
(N) 60s;* 48°43'·77N 01°48'·92W.
Jetty ⚓ Oc (3) G 12s 12m 7M; 48°40'·08N 01°51'·14W.

ST MALO, CHENAL DE LA PETITE PORTE
Outer ldg lts 129·7°: **Front, Le Grand Jardin** ☆ Fl
(2) R 10s 24m **15M**, 48°40'·20N 02°04'·97W. Rear,
La Balue ☆ FG 20m 22M; 48°38'·16N 02°01'·30W.
St Malo Fairway ⚓ Iso 4s; 48°41'·39N 02°07'·28W.
Inner ldg lts 128·6°, both Dir FG 20/69m **22/25M**;
H24. Front, **Les Bas Sablons** ☆; W☐ twr, B top;
48°38'·42N 02°01'·70W. Rear, **La Balue** ☆.

CHENAL DE LA GRANDE PORTE
Outer ldg lts 089·1°: **Front, Le Grand Jardin** ☆ (as

above). Rear, **Rochebonne** ☆ Dir FR 40m **24M**;
48°40'·32N 01°58'·61W. At Le Grand Jardin
continue on inner 128·6° ldg line (above).
Môle des Noires hd ⚓ Fl R 5s 11m 13M; W twr, R
top; *Horn (2) 20s;* 8°38'·52N 02°01'·91W.
Bas-Sablons marina ⚓ Fl G 4s 7m 5M; 48°38'·41N
02°01'·70W.

LA RANCE BARRAGE
La Jument ⚓ Fl G 4s 6m 4M; G twr, 48°37'·44N
02°01'·76W. Barrage lock, NW wall ⚓ Fl (2) G 6s
6m 5M, 191°-291°; 48°37'·06N 02°01'·73W.

ST CAST
Môle ⚓ Iso WG 4s 11m, W11M, G8M; 204°-W-
217°-G-233°-W-245°-G-204°; 48°38'·40N 02°14'·63W.
Cap Fréhel ☆ Fl (2) 10s 85m **29M**; Gy ☐ twr, G
lantern; *Horn (2) 60s;* 48°41'·04N 02°19'·15W.

ERQUY
S môle ⚓ Oc (2+1) WRG 12s 11m W11M, R/G8M;
055°-R-081°-W-094°-G-111°-W-120°-R-134°; W
twr; 48°38'·06N 02°28'·66W.

DAHOUET
La Petite Muette ⚓ Fl WRG 4s 10m W9M, R/G6M;
055°-G-114°-W-146°-R-196°; 48°34'·82N 02°34'·31W.

BAIE DE SAINT BRIEUC & LE LÉGUÉ
Grand Léjon ☆ Fl (5) WR 20s 17m **W18M**, R14M;
015°-R-058°-W-283°-R-350°-W-015°; R twr, W
bands; 48°44'·91N 02°39'·87W.
Le Rohein ⚓ VQ (9) WRG 10s 13m, W10M, R/
G7M; 072°-R-105°-W-180°-G-193°-W-237°-G-
282°-W-301°-G-330°-W-072°; Y twr, B band;
48°38'·80N 02°37'·77W.
Le Légué ⚓ Mo (A) 10s; *Whis;* 48°34'·32N 02°41'·16W.
Pte à l'Aigle ⚓ VQ G 13m 8M; 48°32'·12N 02°43'·12W.

BINIC
N môle ⚓ Oc (3) 12s 12m 11M; unintens 020°-
110°; W twr, G lantern; 48°36'·06N 02°48'·93W.

SAINT QUAY-PORTRIEUX
Herflux ⚓ Dir ⚓ 130°, Fl (2) WRG 6s 10m, W 8M,
R/G 6M; 115°-G-125°-W-135°-R-145°; 48°39'·06N
02°47'·95W.
Île Harbour ⚓ Oc (2) WRG 6s 16m, W10M, R/G
8M; 011°-R-133°-G-270°-R-306°-G-358°-W-011°;
48°39'·99N 02°48'·50W.
Marina, **NE mole elbow**, Dir lt 318·2°: Iso WRG 4s
16m **W15M**, R/G11M; W159°-179°, G179°-316°,
W316°-320·5°,   R320·5° -159°;   48°38'·99N
02°49'·09W.
NE môle hd ⚓ Fl (3) G 12s 10m 2M; 48°38'·84N
02°48'·92W.

CHANNEL ISLANDS

THE CASQUETS AND ALDERNEY
Casquets ☆ Fl (5) 30s 37m **24M**, H24; *Horn (2) 60s;* *Racon T, 25M;* 49°43'·32N 02°22'·62W.
Quenard Pt ☆ Fl (4) 15s 37m **23M**, H24; 085°-027°; *Horn 30s;* 49°43'·75N 02°09'·86W.
Braye, ldg lts 215°: both Q 8/17m 9/12M, synch; 210°-220°. Front, old pier, 49°43'·39N 02°11'·91W.
Admiralty bkwtr ≮ L Fl 10s; 49°43'·81N 02°11'·67W.

LITTLE RUSSEL CHANNEL
Platte Fougère ☆ Fl WR 10s 15m **16M**; 155°-W-085°-R-155°; W 8-sided twr, B band; *Horn 45s;* *Racon P;* 49°30'·82N 02°29'·14W.
Roustel ≮ Q 8m 7M; 49°29'·22N 02°28'·79W.
Platte ≮, Fl WR 3s 6m, W7M, R5M; 024°-R-219°-W-024°; G conical twr; 49°29'·08N 02°29'·57W.
Brehon ≮ Iso 4s 19m 9M; 49°28'·28N 02°29'·28W.

BIG RUSSEL
Noire Pute ≮ Fl (2) WR 15s 8m 6M; 220°-W-040°-R-220°; on 2m high rock; 49°28'·21N 02°25'·02W.
Lower Heads ¿ Q (6) + L Fl 15s; *Bell;* 49°25'·85N 02°28'·55W.

BEAUCETTE MARINA
Petite Canupe ¿ Q (6) + L Fl 15s; 49°30'·18N 02°29'·13W.
Ldg lts 276°, both FR. Front, 49°30'·19N 02°30'·23W.

ST PETER PORT
Outer ldg lts 220°: **Front**, Castle bkwtr, Al WR 10s 14m **16M**; 187°-007°; *Horn 15s;* 49°27'·31N 02°31'·44W. Rear, Oc 10s 61m 14M; 179°-269°.
White Rock pier ≮ Oc G 5s 11m 14M; tfc sigs; 49°27'·38N 02°31'·59W.
S Fairway ▲ QG; 49°27'·30N 02°31'·76W.

HERM
Hbr ldg lts 078°: White drums. ≮ 2F occas; 49°28'·30N 02°27'·02W.

SARK
Corbée du Nez ≮ Fl (4) WR 15s 14m 8M; 057°-W-230°-R-057°; W structure; 49°27'·08N 02°22'·17W.
Point Robert ☆ Fl 15s 65m **20M**; W 8-sided twr; *Horn (2) 30s;* 49°26'·19N 02°20'·75W.

JERSEY (West and South coasts)
Grosnez Point ☆ Fl (2) WR 15s 50m **W19M, R17M**; 081°-W-188°-R-241°; 49°15'·48N 02°14'·84W.
La Corbière ☆ Iso WR 10s 36m **W18M, R16M**; shore-W-294°-R-328°-W-148°-R-shore; W ○ twr; *Horn Mo (C) 60s;* 49°10'·85N 02°14'·92W.

WESTERN PASSAGE
Ldg lts 082°. Front Oc 5s 23m 14M; 034°-129°; 49°10'·15N 02°05'·09W. Rear, Oc R 5s 46m 12M.
Noirmont Pt ≮ Fl (4) 12s 18m 10M; B twr, W band; 49°09'·91N 02°10'·08W.

ST HELIER
Elizabeth marina: Dir ≮ 106°: F WRG 4m 1M; 096°-G-104°-W-108°-R-119°; 49°10'·76N 02°07'·12W.
Marina ent ≮ Oc G 4s 2M; 49°10'·69N 02°07'·21W.
Red & Green Passage, ldg lts 022·7° on dayglo R dolphins: Front, ≮ Oc G 5s 10m 11M; 49°10'·63N 02°06'·94W. Rear, ≮ Oc R 5s 18m 12M.
East Rock ▲ QG; 49°09'·95N 02°07'·29W.
Victoria pier hd, Port control twr; IPTS; 49°10'·57N 02°06'·88W.

JERSEY (South-East coast)
Demie de Pas ▲ Mo (D) WR 12s 11m, W14M, R10M; 130°-R-303°-W-130°; *Horn (3) 60s;* *Racon T, 10M;* B bn twr, Y top; 49°09'·00N 02°06'·15W.
Violet ¿ L Fl 10s; 49°07'·81N 01°57'·14W.

GOREY
Ldg lts 298°: Front, ≮ Oc RG 5s; 304°-R-353°-G-304°; 49°11'·80N 02°01'·34W. Rear, ≮ Oc R 5s 24m 8M.

ST CATHERINE BAY
Verclut bkwtr ≮ Fl 1·5s 18m 13M; 49°13'·34N 02°00'·64W. In line 315° with unlit turret, 49°13'·96N 02°01'·57W, on La Coupe Pt.

JERSEY (North coast)
Sorel Point ☆ L Fl WR 7·5s 50m **15M**; 095°-W-112°-R-173°-W-230°-R-269°-W-273°; 49°15'·60N 02°09'·54W.

1	Cherbourg	**1**															
2	Omonville	10	**2**														
3	Braye (Alderney)	25	15	**3**													
4	St Peter Port	44	34	23	**4**												
5	Creux (Sark)	37	29	22	10	**5**											
6	St Helier	64	51	46	29	24	**6**										
7	Carteret	41	29	28	31	23	26	**7**									
8	Portbail	49	33	32	35	27	25	5	**8**								
9	Iles Chausey	69	61	58	48	43	25	33	30	**9**							
10	Granville	75	67	66	55	50	30	38	35	9	**10**						
11	Dinan	102	91	85	66	64	50	62	59	29	35	**11**					
12	St Malo	90	79	73	54	52	38	50	47	17	23	12	**12**				
13	Dahouet	88	80	72	54	52	41	60	59	37	45	41	29	**13**			
14	Le Légué/St Brieuc	96	86	76	57	56	46	69	69	41	49	45	33	8	**14**		
15	Binic	95	84	75	56	55	46	70	70	43	51	45	33	10	8	**15**	
16	St Quay-Portrieux	88	80	73	56	51	46	64	64	47	54	47	35	11	7	4	**16**
17	Lézardrieux	88	80	68	48	38	47	68	71	53	54	61	49	33	32	30	21	**17**

AREA 16 N and S Brittany - *Paimpol to Pornichet*

SELECTED LIGHTS, BUOYS & WAYPOINTS

Positions are referenced to WGS84

OFFSHORE MARKS

Roches Douvres ☆ Fl 5s 60m **28M**; *Horn 60s*; 49°06'·28N 02°48'·89W.
Barnouic ⍭ VQ (3) 5s 7M; 49°01'·63N 02°48'·42W.

PAIMPOL

L'Ost Pic ⚓ Oc WR 4s 20m, W11M, R8M; 105°-W-116°-R-221°-W-253°-R-291°-W-329°; 48°46'·76N 02°56'·44W. **La Jument** ⚓ 48°47'·34N 02°57'·97W. Ldg lts 262·2°, both QR 5/12m 7/14M. Front, Kernoa jetty; W & R hut; 48°47'·09N 03°02'·44W.

ÎLE DE BRÉHAT

Kermouster Dir ⚓ 271°: Fl WRG 2s 16m, W 10M, R/G 8M; 267°-G-270°-W-272°- R-274°; W col; 48°49'·54N 03°05'·19W.
Rosédo ☆ Fl 5s 29m **20M**; 48°51'·45N 03°00'·30W.
Le Paon ⚓ F WRG 22m W11M, R/G8M; 033°-W-078°-G-181°-W-196°- R-307°-W-316°-R-348°; Y twr; 48°51'·93N 02°59'·17W.
La Horaine ⚓ Fl (3) 12s 13m 11M; Gy 8-sided twr on B hut; 48°53'·49N 02°55'·24W.

LÉZARDRIEUX

Ldg lts 224·7°: Front, **La Croix** ☆ Dir Oc 4s 15m **19M**; 48°50'·22N 03°03'·24W. Rear **Bodic** ☆ Dir Q 55m **22M**; intens 221°-229°; 2·1M from front.
Coatmer ldg lts 218·7°: Front, F RG 16m R/G9M; 200°-R-250°-G-053°; 48°48'·26N 03°05'·75W. Rear, FR 50m 9M; vis 197°-242°.
Les Perdrix ⚓ Fl (2) WG 6s 5m; 165°-G-197°-W-202·5°-G-040°; G twr; 48°47'·74N 03°05'·79W.

JAUDY (TRÉGUIER) RIVER

Les Héaux de Bréhat ☆ Oc (3) WRG 12s 48m, **W15M**, R/G11M; 227°-R-247°-W-270°-G-302°-W-227°; Gy ○ twr; 48°54'·50N 03°05'·18W.
Ldg lts 137°. Front, Oc 4s 12m 11M; 042°-232°; 48°51'·55N 03°07'·90W. Rear, Dir Oc R 4s 34m **15M**.
Basse Crublent ⍭ Fl (2) R 6s; *Whis*; 48°54'·29N 03°11'·18W.
Pierre à l'Anglais ⚓ 48°53'·21N 03°10'·47W.
La Corne ⚓ Fl (3) WRG 12s 14m W11M, R/G8M; 052°-W-059°-R-173°-G-213°-W-220°-R-052°; W twr, R base; 48°51'·34N 03°10'·63W.

PORT BLANC

Le Voleur Dir ⚓ 150·4°: Fl WRG 4s 17m, 14/11M; 140°-G-148°-W-152°-R-160°; 48°50'·20N 03°18'·52W.

PERROS-GUIREC

Passe de l'Est, ldg lts 224·5°. Front ☆ Dir Oc (4) 12s 28m **15M**; 48°47'·87N 03°26'·66W. Rear ☆, Dir Q 79m **21M**; intens 221°-228°.
Passe de l'Ouest. Kerjean ☆ Dir lt 143·6°, Oc (2+1)

WRG 12s 78m, **W15M**, R/G12M; 133·7°-G-143·2°-W-144·8°-R-154·3°; 48°47'·78N 03°23'·40W.
Jetée du Linkin ⚓ Fl (2) G 6s; 48°48'·20N 03°26'·31W.

PLOUMANAC'H and LES SEPT ÎLES

Men-Ruz ⚓ Oc WR 4s 26m W12M, R9M; 226°-W-242°-R-226°; pink ☐ twr; 48°50'·26N 03°29'·03W.
Île-aux-Moines ☆ Fl (3) 15s 59m **24M**; Gy twr and dwelling; 48°52'·73N 03°29'·43W.

TRÉBEURDEN

Ar Gouredec ⍭ VQ (6) + L Fl 10s; 48°46'·41N 03°36'·60W. NW bkwtr ⚓ Fl G 2·5s 8m 2M; IPTS; 48°46'·34N 03°35'·20W.

PRIMEL-TRÉGASTEL

Ldg lts 152°, both ⚓ FR 35/56m 6M, R vert stripe on W ☐. Front, 48°42'·45N 03°49'·20W.

BAIE DE MORLAIX

Chenal du Tréguier ldg lts 190·5°: Front, ⚓ Île Noire Oc (2) WRG 6s 15m, W11M, R/G8M; 051°-G-135°-R-211°-W-051°; 48°40'·34N 03°52'·56W.
Common rear, **La Lande** ☆ Fl 5s 85m **23M**; 48°38'·19N 03°53'·16W.
Grande Chenal ldg lts 176·4°: Front, **Île Louet** ☆ Oc (3) WG 12s 17m **W15M**, G10M; 305°-W-244°-G-305°; W ☐ twr, B top; 48°40'·40N 03°53'·34W.
Common rear, **La Lande** as above.

BLOSCON/ROSCOFF

Bloscon pier ⚓ Fl WG 4s 9m W10M, G7M; 200°-210°-G-200°; W twr, G top; 48°43'·21N 03°57'·69W.

CANAL DE L'ÎLE DE BATZ

Ar-Chaden ⍭ Q (6) + L Fl WR 15s 14m, W8M, R6M; 262°-R-289·5°-W-293°-R-326°- W-110°; YB twr; 48°43'·93N 03°58'·26W.
Men-Guen-Bras ⍭ Q WRG 14m, W9M, R/ G6M; 068°-W-073°-R-197°-W-257°-G-068°; BY twr; 48°43'·76N 03°58'·07W.
Jetty (LW landing) ⚓ Q 5m 1M; BY col; 48°43'·92N 03°58'·97W.
Basse Plate ⍭ 48°44'·25N 04°02'·54W.
Lt ho ☆ Fl (4) 25s 69m **23M**; 48°44'·71N 04°01'·63W. Same twr, aux lt, FR 65m 7M; 024°-059°.

L'ABER WRAC'H

Île-Vierge ☆ Fl 5s 77m **27M**; 337°-325°; Gy twr; 48°38'·33N 04°34'·06W.
Libenter ⍭ Q (9) 15s 6M; 48°37'·50N 04°38'·37W.
Outer ldg lts 100·1°: Front ⚓ QR 20m 7M; 48°36'·88N 04°34'·56W. Rear ⚓ Dir Q 55m 12M.
Dir ⚓ 128°, Oc (2) WRG 6s 5m W13M, R/G11M; 125·7°-G-127·2°-W-128·7°-R-130·2°; 48°35'·89N 04°33'·82W, root of W bkwtr .

L'ABER BENOÎT

Petite Fourche ⌐ 48°36'·98N 04°38'·75W.
Basse Paupian ⌐ 48°35'·31N 04°46'·28W.

CHENAUX DU FOUR ET DE LA HELLE

Le Four ☆ Fl (5) 15s 28m **18M**; Gy ○ twr; *Horn (3+2) 60s;* 48°31'·38N 04°48'·32W.
Ldg lts 158·5°. Front, **Kermorvan** ☆ Fl 5s 20m **22M**; W ☐ twr; *Horn 60s;* 48°21'·72N 04°47'·42W.
Rear, **Pte de St Mathieu** ☆ Fl 15s 56m **29M**; W twr, R top; 48°19'·79N 04°46'·27W.
Pte de Corsen ⌐ Dir Q WRG 33m W12M, R/G8M; 008°-R-012°-W-015°-G-021°; 48°24'·89N 04°47'·63W.
Grande Vinotière ⌐ L Fl R 10s; 48°21'·93N 04°48'·43W.
Les Vieux-Moines ⌐ Fl R 4s 16m 5M; 280°-133°; R 8-sided twr; 48°19'·33N 04°46'·63W.
Ldg lts 137·9°: Front, **Kermorvan** ☆ see above.
Rear, **Lochrist** ☆ Dir Oc (3) 12s 49m **22M**; 48°20'·55N 04°45'·82W.

BREST AND APPROACHES

Charles Martel ⌐ Fl (4) R 15s; *Whis;* 48°18'·85N 04°42'·19W.
Pte du Toulinguet ☆ Oc (3) WR 12s **W15M**, R11M; shore-W-028°-R-090°-W-shore; 48°16'·82N 04°37'·73W.
Pte du Petit-Minou ☆ Fl (2) WR 6s 32m **W19M, R15M**; Shore-R-252°-W-260°-R-307°-W-065·5°; 070·5°-W-shore; *Horn 60s;* 48°20'·19N 04°36'·87W.
Ldg lts 068°, both Dir Q 30/54m **23/22M. Front, Pte du Petit-Minou** (above). **Rear, Pte du Portzic** ☆, intens 065°-071°; 48°21'·49N 04°32'·06W.
Same twr, Oc (2) WR 12s 56m **W19M, R15M**; 219°-R-259°-W-338°-R-000°-W-065·5°-W-219°.
Moulin Blanc ⌐ Fl (3) R 12s; 48°22'·79N 04°25'·99W.

CAMARET

N môle ⌐ Iso WG 4s 7m W12M, G9M; 135°-W-182°-G-027°; 48°16'·85N 04°35'·32W.

MORGAT

Pte de Morgat ☆ Oc (4) WRG 12s 77m **W15M**, R11M, G10M; Shore-W-281°-G-301°-W-021°-R-043°; 48°13'·17N 04°29'·81W.

DOUARNENEZ TO RAZ DE SEIN

Île Tristan ⌐ Oc (3) WR 12s 35m, W13M, R10M; shore-W-138°-R-153°-W-shore; 48°06'·14N 04°20'·25W.
Port Rhu, Dir ⌐ 157°: Fl (5) WRG 20s 16m; 154°-G-156°-W-158°-R-160°; 48°05'·40N 04°19'·80W.

RAZ DE SEIN

Tévennec ⌐ Q WR 28m W9M R6M; 090°-W-345°-R-090°; 48°04'·28N 04°47'·73W. Same twr, Dir ⌐ Fl 4s 24m 12M; intens 324°-332° (Raz de Sein).
La Vieille ☆ Oc (2+1) WRG 12s 33m **W18M**, R13M, G14M; 290°-W-298°-R-325°-W-355°-G-017°- W-035°-G-105°-W-123°-R-158°-W-205°; Gy ☐ twr; *Horn (2+1) 60s;* 48°02'·43N 04°45'·43W.

La Plate ⌐ VQ (9) 10s 8M; 48°02'·35N 04°45'·61W.

AUDIERNE

Pointe de Lervily ⌐ Fl (3) WR 12s 20m W14M, R11M; 236°-W-269°-R-294°-W-087°-R-109°; W twr, R top; 48°00'·04N 04°33'·94W.
Kergadec Dir ⌐ 006°: Q WRG 43m 12/9M; 000°-G-005·3°-W-006·7°-R-017°; 48°00'·95N 04°32'·78W.

POINTE DE PENMARC'H

Eckmühl ☆ Fl 5s 60m **23M**; Gy 8-sided twr; *Horn 60s;* 47°47'·88N 04°22'·39W.   Spineg ⌐ Q (6) + L Fl 15s; *Whis;* 47°45'·18N 04°18'·92W.

LOCTUDY

Pte de Langoz ☆ Fl (4) WRG 12s 12m, **W15M**, R/G11M; 115°-W-257°-G-284°-W-295°-R-318°-W-328°-R-025°; 47°49'·87N 04°09'·59W.
Men Audierne ⌐ 47°50'·31N 04°09'·06W.
Groyne hd ⌐ Q 3m 10M; 47°50'·21N 04°10'·34W.

BENODET

Ldg lts 345·5°: Front Dir Oc (2+1) G 12s 11m **17M**; W ○ twr, G stripe; 47°52'·31N 04°06'·70W.
Rear ⌐ Oc (2+1) 12s 48m 11M; 338°-016°, synch.

PORT-LA-FORÊT

Linuen ⌐ Q (3) 10s; 47°50'·76N 03°57'·31W.
Cap Coz ⌐ Fl (2) WRG 6s 5m, 7/5M; shore-R-335°-G-340°-W-346°-R-shore; 47°53'·48N 03°58'·28W.

ÎLES DE GLÉNAN

Penfret ☆ Fl R 5s 36m **21M**; W ☐ twr, R top; 47°43'·26N 03°57'·17W. Same twr: auxiliary ⌐ Dir Q 34m 12M; 295°-315°.
La Pie ⌐ Fl (2) 6s 9m 3M; 47°43'·75N 03°59'·75W.

CONCARNEAU

Ldg lts 028·5°: Front, ⌐ Q 14m 13M; 006·5°-093°; 47°52'·15N 03°55'·08W. **Rear** ☆ Dir Q 87m **23M**; intens 026·5°-030·5°; spire, 1·34M from front.
Marina wavescreen ⌐ Fl (4) R 15s 3m 1M; 47°52'·20N 03°54'·72W.

ÎLE DE GROIX

Pen Men ☆ Fl (4) 25s 60m **29M**; 309°-275°; W ☐ twr, B top; 47°38'·86N 03°30'·54W.
Speerbrecker, ⌐ 47°39'·17N 03°26'·25W.
Port Tudy, N môle ⌐ Iso G 4s 12m 6M; W twr, G top; 47°38'·70N 03°26'·74W.

LORIENT

Passe de l'Ouest ldg lts 057°: both Dir Q 11/22m 13/**18M**. Front, 47°42'·13N 03°21'·83W
Les Trois Pierres ⌐ Q RG 11m R/G6M; 060°-G-196°-R-002°; B twr, W bands; 47°41'·53N 03°22'·47W.
A8 ⌐ Fl R 2·5s; 47°41'·90N 03°22'·52W.
Passe du Sud ldg lts 008·5°: both Dir QR 16/34m **17/16M**; 47°43'·76N 03°21'·74W.

La Citadelle ⚓ Oc G 4s 6m 6M; 012°-192°; 47°42'·59N 03°21'·94W.
Port Louis ☇ Iso G 4s 7m 6M; W twr, G top; 47°42'·71N 03°21'·20W.
Kernével marina, ent ☇ QR 1M; 47°43'·39N 03°22'·09W.
Ste Catherine marina ent ☇ QG 5m 3M; 47°43'·51N 03°21'·08W.
Pen-Mané marina, bkwtr elbow ☇ Fl (2) G 6s 4M; 47°44'·11N 03°20'·86W.
No. 8 ⚓ Fl R 2·5s; 47°44'·55N 03°20'·98W.

RIVIÈRE D'ÉTEL
W side ent ☇ Oc (2) WRG 6s 13m W9M, R/G6M; 022°-W-064°-R-123°-W-330°-G-022°; R twr; 47°38'·70N 03°12'·91W.
Conspic R/W radio mast, 47°39'·79N 03°12'·02W.

BELLE ÎLE
Pte des Poulains ☆ Fl 5s 34m **23M**; 023°-291°; W □ twr and dwelling; 47°23'·28N 03°15'·17W.
Sauzon, NW jetty ☇ Fl G 4s 8m 8M; 47°22'·51N 03°13'·10W.
Le Palais, N jetty ☇ Fl (2+1) G 12s 8m 7M; W twr, G top; 47°20'·82N 03°09'·08W.
Pte de Kerdonis ☆ Fl (3) R 15s 35m **15M**; 47°18'·59N 03°03'·61W.
Goulphar ☆ Fl (2) 10s 87m **27M**; Gy twr; 47°18'·65N 03°13'·63W.
La Teignouse ☆ Fl WR 4s 20m **W15M**, R11M; 033°-W-039°-R-033°; 47°27'·45N 03°02'·79W.

ÎLE DE HOUAT and ÎLE DE HOËDIC
Port St-Gildas N môle ☇ Fl (2) WG 6s 8m W9M, G6M; 168°-W-198°-G-210°-W-240°-G-168°; W twr, G top; 47°23'·57N 02°57'·34W.
Port de l'Argol bkwtr ☇ Fl WG 4s 10m W9M, G6M; 143°-W-163°-G-183°-W-194°-G-143°; W twr, G top; 47°20'·69N 02°52'·56W.

PORT HALIGUEN
Quiberon S ⚓ Q (6) + L Fl 15s; 47°28'·03N 03°02'·35W.
Quiberon N ⬗ 47°29'·63N 03°02'·59W.
E bkwtr hd ☇ Oc (2) WR 6s 10m, W11M, R8M; 233°-W-240·5°-R-299°-W-306°-R-233°; W twr, R top; 47°29'·30N 03°05'·99W.

LA TRINITÉ-SUR-MER
Ldg lts 347°: Front, ☇ Q WRG 11m W10M, R/G7M; 321°-G-345°-W-013·5°-R-080°; 47°34'·08N 03°00'·37W. **Rear**, Dir Q 21m **15M**; synch.
Marina pier ☇ Iso R 4s 8m 5M; 47°35'·27N 03°01'·47W.

GOLFE DU MORBIHAN
Pte de Port-Navalo ☆ Oc (3) WRG 12s 32m, W15M, R/G11M; 155°-W-220°; 317°-G-359°-W-015°-R-105°; 47°32'·87N 02°55'·11W.
Ldg marks 359°: Front, Grégan ⬗ Q (6) + L Fl 15s 3m 8M; 47°33'·90N 02°55'·05W. Rear, ch spire.

CROUESTY
Ldg lts 058°, Dir Q 10/27m **19M**: **Front**; 47°32'·54N 02°53'·94W. **Rear** ☆, grey lt ho.

VILAINE RIVER
Pte de Penlan ☆ Oc (2) WRG 6s 26m, **W15M**, R/G11M; 292·5°-R-025°-G-052°-W-060°-R-138°-G-180°; W twr, R bands; 47°30'·98N 02°30'·13W.

PIRIAC-SUR-MER
Grand Norven ⬗ Q; 47°23'·55N 02°32'·90W.
Inner mole ☇ Oc (2) WRG 6s 8m, W10M, R/G7M; 066°-R-148°-G-194°-W-201°-R-221°; 47°22'·93N 02°32'·72W. *Siren 120s (occas), 35m SW.*

LA TURBALLE
Jetée de Garlahy ☇ Fl (4) WR 12s 13m, W10M, R7M; 060°-R-315°-W-060°; W pylon, R top; 47°20'·70N 02°30'·93W.

LE CROISIC
Jetée du Tréhic ☇ Iso WG 4s 12m W14M, G11M; 042°-G-093°-W-137°-G-345°; Gy twr, G top; 47°18'·49N 02°31'·43W. F Bu fog det lt, 100m SE.

LE POULIGUEN
Basse Martineau ⚓ 47°15'·54N 02°24'·36W.
Petits Impairs ⚓ Fl (2) G 6s 6m 2M; 47°15'·98N 02°24'·61W.
SW jetty ☇ QR 13m 9M; 171°-081°; W col; 47°16'·39N 02°25'·40W.

PORNICHET (La Baule)
S bkwtr ☇ Iso WRG 4s 11m, W10M, R/G7M; 303°-G-081°-W-084°-R-180°; 47°15'·49N 02°21'·15W.

1	Lézardrieux	1		12	16	18	24	42	43	45	72	97	100	105	124	Pornic	12
2	Tréguier	22	2		11	12	24	39	40	41	66	87	90	95	113	St Nazaire	11
3	Perros-Guirec	28	21	3		10	13	30	30	34	55	78	80	85	106	La Baule/Pornichet	10
4	Trébeurden	40	32	17	4		9	18	22	27	48	73	75	79	100	Le Croisic	9
5	Morlaix	60	46	36	23	5		8	28	36	57	78	80	84	105	Arzal/Camoël	8
6	Roscoff	54	41	28	17	12	6		7	16	37	58	60	64	85	Crouesty	7
7	L'Aberwrac'h	84	72	60	49	48	32	7		6	26	47	48	54	74	Le Palais (Belle Ile)	6
8	Le Conquet	106	98	83	72	68	55	29	8		5	32	33	38	61	Lorient	5
9	Brest (marina)	114	107	92	83	79	67	42	18	9		4	4	12	37	Concarneau	4
10	Morgat	126	118	103	92	88	75	49	20	24	10		3	12	36	Port-la-Forêt	3
11	Douarnenez	131	123	108	97	93	80	54	25	29	11	11		2	30	Loctudy	2
12	Audierne	135	128	113	102	98	86	55	30	34	27	30	12		1	Audierne	1

AREA 17 South Biscay - *Pointe de Saint-Gildas to Hendaye*
SELECTED LIGHTS, BUOYS & WAYPOINTS | Positions are referenced to WGS84

Pte de Saint-Gildas ⚡ Q WRG 20m, W14M, R/G10M; 264°-R-308°-G-078°-W-088°-R-174°-W-180°-G-264°; col on W house; 47°08'·02N 02°14'·76W.

PORNIC
Appr buoy ⚲ L Fl 10s; 47°06'·45N 02°06'·64W.
Pte de Noëveillard ⚡ Oc (4) WRG 12s 22m W13M, R/G9M; Shore-G-051°-W-079°-R-shore; W ☐ twr, G top, W dwelling; 47°06'·62N 02°06'·92W.

ÎLE DE NOIRMOUTIER
Île du Pilier ☆ Fl (3) 20s 33m **29M**; Gy twr; 47°02'·55N 02°21'·61W. Same twr, ⚡ QR 10m 11M, 321°-034°.
Les Boeufs ⚡ VQ (9) 10s; 46°55'·04N 02°28'·02W.
L'Herbaudière, ldg lts 187·5°, both Q 5/21m 7M, Gy masts. Front, 47°01'·59N 02°17'·85W.
Martroger ⚓, Q WRG 11m W9M, R/G6M; 033°-G-055°-W-060°-R-095°-G-124°-W-153°-R-201°-W-240°-R-033°; 47°02'·60N 02°17'·12W.
W jetty ⚡ Oc (2+1) WG 12s 9m W10M, G7M; 187·5°-W-190°-G-187·5°; 47°01'·63N 02°17'·86W.
Noirmoutier-en-L'Île jetty ⚡ Oc (2) R 6s 6m 6M; W col, R top; 46°59'·27N 02°13'·14W.

ÎLE D'YEU
Petite Foule (main lt) ☆ Fl 5s 56m **24M**; W ☐ twr, G lantern; 46°43'·05N 02°22'·96W.

Port Joinville ldg lts 219°, both QR 11/16m 6M, 169°-269°: Front 46°43'·61N 02°20'·95W.
NW jetty ⚡ Oc (3) WG 12s 7m, W11M, G8M; Shore-G-150°-W-232°-G-279°-W-285°-G-shore; W 8-sided twr, G top; 46°43'·77N 02°20'·82W.
Pte des Corbeaux ☆ Fl (2+1) R 15s 25m **20M**; 083°-143° obsc by Île d'Yeu; 46°41'·42N 02°17'·11W.
Port de la Meule ⚡ Oc WRG 4s 9m, W9M, R/G6M; 007·5°-G-018°-W-027·5°-R-041·5°; Gy twr, R top; 46°41'·66N 02°20'·75W.

SAINT GILLES-CROIX-DE-VIE
Pte de Grosse Terre ☆ Fl (4) WR 12s 25m, **W18M, R15M**; 290°- R-339°-W-125°-R-145°; W truncated twr; 46°41'·54N 01°57'·92W.
Ldg lts 043·7°, Q 7/28m **15M**; 033·5°-053·5°: Front, 46°41'·85N 01°56'·67W.
Pilours ⚡ Q (6) + L Fl 15s; *Bell;* 46°40'·98N 01°58'·10W.
Jetée de la Garenne ⚡ Fl G 4s 8m 6M; 46°41'·45N 01°57'·26W.

LES SABLES D'OLONNE
Les Barges ⚡ Fl (2) R 10s 25m 13M; Gy twr; 46°29'·70N 01°50'·50W.
L'Armandèche ☆ Fl (2+1) 15s 42m **24M**; 295°-130°; W 6-sided twr, R top; 46°29'·40N 01°48'·29W.

Nouch Sud ⚡ Q (6) + L Fl 15s; 46°28'·55N 01°47'·42W.
SW Pass, ldg lts 032·5°, Iso 4s 12/33m **16M**, H24: **Front** ☆, 46°29'·42N 01°46'·37W.
SE Pass, ldg lts 320°: Front ⚡ QG 11m 8M; 46°29'·44N 01°47'·51W. Rear ⚡ Q 33m 13M.
Jetée St Nicolas (W jetty) ⚡ QR 16m 8M; 143°-094°; W twr, R top; 46°29'·23N 01°47'·52W.

BOURGENAY
Ldg lts 040°, QG 9/19m 7M. Front; 46°26'·37N 01°40'·61W. Rear, 010°-070°; 162m from front.
Landfall ⚡ L Fl 10s; 46°25'·28N 01°41'·91W.
Ent ⚡ Fl R 4s & ⚡ Iso G 4s; 46°26'·43N 01°40'·51W.

ÎLE-DE-RÉ
Les Baleineaux ⚡ Oc (2) 6s 23m 11M; pink twr, R top; 46°15'·81N 01°35'·22W.
Les Baleines ☆ Fl (4) 15s 53m **27M**; conspic Gy 8-sided twr, R lantern; 46°14'·64N 01°33'·69W.
Chanchardon ⚡ Fl WR 4s 15m W11M, R8M; 118°-R-290°-W-118°; 46°09'·73N 01°28'·44W.
Chauveau ☆ Oc (3) WR 12s 27m **W15M**, R11M; 057°-W-094°-R-104°-W-342°-R-057°; W ○ twr, R top; 46°08'·03N 01°16'·42W.
Pte de Sablanceaux ⚡ VQ (3) 5s 10m 5M; landing stage; 46°09'·76N 01°15'·17W.

ARS-EN-RÉ
Outer ldg lts 265·8°, ⚡ Iso 4s 5/13m 11/**15M**; synch: Front 46°14'·05N 01°28'·61W.
Le Fier d'Ars, inner ldg lts 232·5°: ⚡ Q 5/13m 9/11M; 46°12'·76N 01°30'·60W. Rear ⚡ Q 11M.

ST MARTIN DE RÉ
Rocha ⚡ Q; 46°14'·74N 01°20'·64W.
Lt ho, E of ent ⚡ Oc (2) WR 6s 18m W10M, R7M; Shore-W-245°-R-281°-W-shore; W twr, R top; 46°12'·44N 01°21'·89W.
W mole ⚡ Iso G 4s 10m 6M; 46°12'·49N 01°21'·89W.

LA ROCHELLE
Ldg lts 059°, both Dir Q 15/25m 13/14M; synch; by day Fl 4s. Front; 46°09'·35N 01°09'·16W.
Pte des Minimes ⚡ Fl (3) WG 12s 8m; W8M, G5M; 059°-W-213°; 313°-G-059°; 46°08'·33N 01°10'·68W.
Tour Richelieu ⚲ Fl R 4s 10m 9M; 46°08'·90N 01°10'·34W.
Marina ⚡ Fl (2)G 6s 9m 7M; 46°08'·82N 01°10'·15W.

LA CHARENTE
Ldg lts 115°, Dir QR 8/21m **19/20M**: Front ☆, 45°57'·96N 01°04'·38W.
Fort Boyard ⚡ Q (9) 15s; 45°59'·96N 01°12'·87W.
Île d'Aix ☆ Fl WR 5s 24m **W24M, R20M**; 103°-R-118°-W-103°; 46°00'·60N 01°10'·67W.

ÎLE D'OLÉRON

Chassiron ☆ Fl 10s **28M**; 46°02'·80N 01°24'·61W.
Antioche ↓ Q 20m 11M; 46°03'·94N 01°23'·71W.

ST DENIS

Dir ⚡205°, Iso WRG 4s 14m, W11M, R/G8M; 190°-
G-204°-W-206°-R-220°;46°01'·61N 01°21'·91W.
E jetty ⚡ Fl (2) WG 6s 6m, W9M, G6M; 205°-G-
277°-W-292°-G-165°; 46°02'·10N 01°22'·06W.

GIRONDE, PASSE DE L'OUEST

Pte de la Coubre ☆ Fl (2) 10s 64m **28M**;
45°41'·78N 01°13'·99W. Also, F RG 42m, R12M,
G10M; 030°-R-043°-G-060°-R-110°.
BXA ↓ Iso 4s 8m 7M; *Whis; Racon ;* 45°37'·53N
01°28'·69W.
Ldg lts 081·5° (not valid E of Nos 4 & 5 buoys).
Front ☆, Dir Iso 4s 21m **20M**; 45°39'·56N
01°08'·76W. Same structure, Q (2) 5s 10m 3M.
La Palmyre, common rear ☆ Dir Q 57m **27M**;
45°39'·71N 01°07'·24W. Same twr, Dir FR **17M**.

Cordouan ☆ Oc (2+1) WRG 12s 60m, **W22M, R/
G18M**; 014°-W-126°-G-178·5°-W-267°-R -294·5°-
R-014°; 45°35'·16N 01°10'·39W.

PASSE SUD (or DE GRAVE)

Ldg lts 063°: **Front**, Dir QG 22m **16M**; 45°33'·72N
01°05'·03W. **Rear**, Oc WRG 4s 26m, **W19M, R/
G15M**; 033°-W-233·5°-R-303°-W-312°-G-330°-
W-341°-025°.
G ↓*Whis;* 45°30'·32N 01°15'·56W.
G3 ↓45°32'·78N 01°07'·72W.
Ldg lts 041°, both Dir QR 33/61m **18M. Front, Le
Chay** ☆ intens 039·5°-042·5°; W twr, R top;
45°37'·30N 01°02'·40W. **Rear, St Pierre** ☆, intens
039°-043°; R water twr, 0·97M from front.
G5 ↓45°33'·97N 01°06'·39W.
G4 ↓45°34'·70N 01°05'·79W.
G6 ↓45°34'·99N 01°04'·80W.

ROYAN

R1 ↓ Iso G 4s; 45°36'·56N 01°01'·96W.
NE jetty ⚡Fl (3) G 12s 2m 5M; 45°37'·23N 01°01'·49W.

PORT-MÉDOC

N bkwtr ⚡ QG 4M; 45°33'·42N 01°03'·48W.
S bkwtr ⚡ QR 4M; 45°33'·37N 01°03'·44W.

PAUILLAC

Pauillac, NE elbow ⚡ Fl G 4s 7m 5M; 45°11'·96N
00°44'·61W.
Ent E side ⚡QG 7m 4M; 45°11'·86N 00°44'·60W.

BORDEAUX

Lock into Bassins Nos 1 & 2, 44°51'·74N 00°32'·94W.

ARCACHON, PASSE NORD

Cap Ferret ☆ Fl R 5s 53m **27M**; W ○ twr, R top;
44°38'·72N 01°14'·90W. Same twr, ⚡ Oc (3) 12s.
ATT-ARC ↓ L Fl 10s 8m 5M; 44°34'·61N 01°18'·74W.
Note: Buoys are moved as the channel shifts.
1N ↓ 44°33'·99N 01°17'·80W.
11 ↓ 44°37'·29N 01°14'·18W.
15 ↓ 44°39'·79N 01°12'·11W.
Marina ⚡QG 6m 6M; 44°39'·77N 01°09'·15W.

CAPBRETON

Digue Nord ⚡ Fl (2) R 6s 13m 12M; W ○ twr, R
top; *Horn 30s;* 43°39'·38N 01°27'·01W.
Estacade Sud ⚡ Fl (2) G 6s 9m 12M; 43°39'·25N
01°26'·89W.

ANGLET/BAYONNE

BA ↓ L Fl 10s; 43°32'·59N 01°32'·76W.
Outer S bkwtr ↓ Q (9) 15s 15m 6M; 43°31'·60N
01°31'·68W.
Anglet marina ent ⚡ Fl G 2s 5m 2M; 43°31'·57N
01°30'·51W.

ST JEAN DE LUZ

Inner ldg lts 150·7°, both Dir QG 18/27m **16M**;
intens 149·5°-152·2°. **Front, E jetty** ☆ W □ twr, R
stripe; 43°23'·25N 01°40'·15W. **Rear** ☆, W □ twr,
G stripe; at S corner of marina.

HENDAYE

Cabo Higuer ☆ Fl (2) 10s 63m **23M**; 43°23'·51N
01°47'·53W (in Spain).
W trng wall ⚡ Fl (3) G 9s 9m 5M; 43°22'·82N
01°47'·36W.

1	Port Joinville	1													
2	St Gilles-C-de-Vie	18	2												
3	Sables d'Olonne	31	16	3											
4	Bourgenay	40	25	9	4										
5	St Martin (I de Ré)	55	44	27	20	5									
6	La Rochelle	66	51	36	29	12	6								
7	Rochefort	84	75	61	54	36	26	7							
8	R La Seudre	89	71	58	52	33	24	30	8						
9	Port St Denis	59	48	33	30	21	13	26	22	9					
10	Port Bloc/Royan	97	85	71	60	56	52	68	27	42	10				
11	Bordeaux	152	140	126	115	111	107	123	82	97	55	11			
12	Cap Ferret	138	130	113	110	102	98	114	75	88	68	123	12		
13	Capbreton	192	186	169	166	165	156	172	131	145	124	179	58	13	
14	Anglet/Bayonne	200	195	181	178	177	168	184	143	157	132	187	70	12	14
15	Santander	212	210	204	204	206	202	218	184	192	180	235	133	106	103	15
16	Cabo Finisterre	377	395	393	394	406	407	423	399	397	401	456	376	370	373	274	16

AREA 18 N & NW Spain - *Fuenterrabia to Bayona*
SELECTED LIGHTS, BUOYS & WAYPOINTS

Positions are referenced to WGS84

FUENTERRABIA (See Hendaye, facing page)
Marina ent, ⚡ Fl (4) G 11s 9m 3m; 43°22'·59N 01°47'·51W. ⚡ Fl (4) R 11s 9m 1M, close SW.

PASAJES
⚡ Mo (A) 6s 11M; 43°21'·19N 01°56'·12W.
Senocozulúa Dir ⚡ 155·75°: Oc (2) WRG 12s 50m W6M, R/G3M; 129·5°-G-154·5°-W-157°-R-190°; W twr; *Racon M*; 43°19'·90N 01°55'·61W.

SAN SEBASTIÁN
Ldg lts 158°: Front ⚡ QR 10m 7M; 143°-173°; 43°18'·89N 01°59'·47W. Rear ⚡ Oc R 4s 16m 7M.
Igueldo ☆ Fl (2+1) 15s 132m **26M**; 43°19'·35N 02°00'·64W.

GUETARIA
I. de San Antón ☆ Fl (4) 15s 91m **21M**; 43°18'·62N 02°12'·09W.
N mole ⚡ Fl (3) G 9s 11m 5M; 43°18'·26N 02°11'·91W.

ZUMAYA
Lt ho ⚡ Oc (1+3) 12s 39m 12M; Port sigs; 43°18'·14N 02°15'·07W. Marina ent, ⚡ Fl (3) R 9s 6m 1M and ⚡ Fl (2+1) G 10s 6m 1M.

LEQUEITIO
Pta Amandarri ⚡ Fl G 4s 8m 5M; 43°21'·99N 02°29'·94W.
Cabo de Santa Catalina ☆ Fl (1+3) 20s 44m **17M**; *Horn Mo (L) 20s;* 43°22'·67N 02°30'·69W.

ELANCHOVE
Digue N ⚡ Fl G 3s 8m 4M.
Cabo Machichaco ☆ Fl 7s 120m **24M**; *Siren Mo (M) 60s;* 43°27'·30N 02°45'·19W.

BILBAO
Punta Galea ☆ Fl (3) 8s 82m **19M**; 011°-227°; *Siren Mo (G) 30s;* 43°22'·30N 03°02'·14W.
Pta Lucero bkwtr head ⚡ Fl G 5s 21m 10M; *Racon X, 20M;* 43°22'·67N 03°05'·04W.
Getxo marina bkwtr ⚡ QR 3m 2M, R col; 43°20'·23N 03°01'·02W.
Las Arenas marina (RCMA) ⚡ Oc G 4s 1m 1M; 43°19'·83N 03°00'·98W; and Oc R 4s 2m 1M.

CASTRO URDIALES
Castillo de Santa Ana ☆ Fl (4) 24s 47m **20M**; W twr; *Siren Mo (C) 60s;* 43°23'·06N 03°12'·89W.
N bkwtr ⚡ Fl G 3s 12m 6M; 43°22'·86N 03°12'·54W.

LAREDO and RIA DE SANTOÑA
Laredo N bkwtr ⚡ Fl (4) R 11s 9m 5M; 43°24'·89'N 03°25'·20W.

Santoña ldg lts 283·5°: Front, ⚡ Fl 2s 5m 8M; 43°26'·33N 03°27'·62W. Rear, ⚡ Oc (2) 5s 12m 11M.
C. Ajo ☆ Oc (3) 16s 69m **17M**; 43°30'·70N 03°35'·72W.

SANTANDER
Cabo Mayor ☆ Fl (2) 10s 89m **21M**; *Horn Mo (M) 40s;* 43°29'·37N 03°47'·51W.
Marina de Santander, ldg lts 235·6°: Front ⚡ Iso 2s 9m 2M; 43°25'·75N 03°48'·83W. Rear ⚡ Oc 5s.
Marina ent QR and QG.
Pta del Torco de Afuera ☆ Fl (1+2) 24s 33m **22M**; W twr; 43°26'·51N 04°02'·61W.

RIBADESELLA
Pta del Caballo ⚡ Fl (2) R 6s 10m 5M; 278·4°-212·9°; ○ twr; 43°28'·08N 05°03'·98W.
Marina trng wall ⚡ Q; approx 43°27'·83N 05°03'·70W.
Somos ☆ Fl (2+1) 12s 113m **25M**; twr; 43°28'·08N 05°03'·98W.
C. Lastres ☆ Fl (5) 25s 116m **23M**. W ○ twr; 43°32'·03N 05°18'·07W.

GIJÓN
Piedra Sacramento ⚡ Fl (2) G 6s 9m 5M; 8-sided twr; 43°32'·90N 05°40'·21W.
Marina, N bkwtr ⚡ Fl (2) R 6s 7m 3M; 43°32'·85N 05°40'·08W.
Cabo de Torres ☆ Fl (2) 10s 80m **18M**; 43°34'·29N 05°41'·97W.
Cabo Peñas ☆ Fl (3) 15s 115m **35M**; Gy 8-sided twr; *Siren Mo (P) 60s;* 43°39'·31N 05°50'·90W.

CUDILLERO
Pta Rebollera ☆ Oc (4) 16s 42m **16M**; W 8-sided twr; *Siren Mo (D) 30s;* 43°33'·96N 06°08'·68W.
Ent, N bkwtr ⚡ Fl (3) G 9s 3m 2M.
Cabo Vidio ☆ Fl 5s 99m **25M**; *Siren Mo (V) 60s;* 43°35'·60N 06°14'·79W.
Cabo Busto ☆ Fl (4) 20s 84m **25M**; 43°34'·13N 06°28'·23W.

LUARCA
Punta Altaya ⚡ Oc (3) 15s 63m 14M; W □ twr; *Siren Mo (L) 30s;* 43°33'·03N 06°31'·85W.
Ldg lts 170°, W cols, R bands: Front ⚡ Fl 5s 18m 2M; 43°32'·78N 06°32'·11W. Rear ⚡ Oc 4s 25m 2M.

RÍA DE RIBADEO
Pta de la Cruz ⚡ Fl (4) R 11s 16m 7M; 43°33'·40N 07°01'·75W.
Isla Pancha ☆ Fl (3+1) 20s 26m **21M**; *Siren Mo (R) 30s;* 43°33'·39N 07°02'·53W, W side of entrance.
1st ldg lts 140°, both R ◇s, W twrs. Front ⚡ Iso R

18m 5M; 43°32'·83N 07°01'·53W. Rear ⚡ Oc R 4s.
2nd ldg lts 205°. Front, ⚡ VQ R 8m 3M; R ◇, W twr;
43°32'·49N 07°02'·24W. Rear ⚡ Oc R 2s 18m 3M.
Yacht hbr, ⚡ Fl G 5s 9m 3M; 43°32'·45N 07°02'·16W.

RÍA DE VIVERO

Pta de Faro ⚡ Fl R 5s 18m 7M; 43°42'·74N 07°35'·03W.
Pta Socastro ⚡ Fl G 5s 18m 7M; 43°43'·08N
07°36'·42W. Marina ent ⚡ Fl (3) G 9s 7m 1M;
43°40'·22N 07°35'·62W.

Pta de la Estaca de Bares ☆ Fl (2) 7·5s 99m **25M**;
Siren Mo (B) 60s; 43°47'·21N 07°41'·14W.
Cabo Ortegal ☆ Oc 8s 122m **18M**; W ○ twr, R
band; 43°46'·22N 07°52'·30W,.

RÍA DE CEDEIRA

Piedras de Media Mar ⚡ Fl (2) 5s 12m 4M; W ○
twr; 43°39'·37N 08°04'·80W.
Bkwtr ⚡ Fl (2) R 7s 10m 4M; 43°39'·30N 08°04'·20W.
Cabo Prior ☆ Fl (1+2) 15s 105m **22M**; 055·5°-310°;
6-sided twr; 43°34'·05N 08°18'·87W.

RÍA DE FERROL

Cabo Prioriño Chico ☆ Fl 5s 34m **23M**; 225°-
129·5°; W 8-sided twr; 43°27'·52N 08°20'·40W.

RÍAs DE ARES & DE BETANZOS

Ares bkwtr ⚡ Fl (3) R 9s; 43°25'·35N 08°14'·27W.
Sada marina ⚡ Fl (4) G 11s; 43°21'·76N 08°14'·54W.

LA CORUÑA

Torre de Hércules ☆ Fl (4) 20s 104m **23M**; *Siren
Mo (L) 30s;* 43°23'·15N 08°24'·39W.
Ldg lts 108·5°: Front ⚡ Oc WR 4s 54m, W8M R3M;
000°-R-023°; 100·5°-R-105·5°-W-114·5°-R-153°;
Racon M, 18M; 020°-196°; 43°23'·00N 08°21'·28W.
Rear ⚡ Fl 4s 79m 8M; 357·5°-177·5°.
Ldg lts 182°: Front, ⚡ Iso WRG 2s 27m, W10M, R/
G7M; 146·4°-G-180°-W-184°-R-217·6°; *Racon X,
11-21M;* 43°20'·59N 08°22'·25W. Rear ⚡ Oc R 4s.
Darsena de la Marina ⚡ Fl G 5s 8m 2M; 43°21'·01N
08°23'·66W.

RÍA DE CORME Y LAGE

Pta Lage ☆ Fl (5) 20s 64m **20M**; 43°13'·88N
09°00'·83W. Lage, N mole ⚡ Fl G 3s 15m 4M;
43°13'·34N 08°59'·96W. Corme, mole ⚡ Fl (2) R 5s
12m 3M; 43°15'·64N 08°57'·83W.

C. Villano ☆ Fl (2) 15s 102m **28M**; *Siren Mo (V) 60s;
Racon M, 35M;* 43°09'·60N 09°12'·70W

1	Bilbao (ent)	1							
2	Santander	36	2						
3	Gijón	116	90	3					
4	Cabo Peñas	126	96	10	4				
5	Ría de Ribadeo	179	149	63	53	5			
6	Cabo Ortegal	214	184	98	88	40	6		
7	La Coruña	252	222	136	126	78	38	7	
8	Cabo Villano	284	254	168	158	110	70	43	8
9	Bayona	355	325	239	229	181	141	114	71	9

RÍA DE CAMARIÑAS

Ldg lts 081°: Front ⚡ Fl 5s 13m 9M; 43°07'·37N
09°11'·56W. Rear ⚡ Iso 4s 25m 11M.
Outer bkwtr ⚡ Fl R 5s 7m 3M; 43°07'·45N 09°10'·70W.
Cabo Toriñana ☆ Fl (2+1) 15s 63m **24M**; *Racon T,
35M (1.7M SE of ☆);* 43°03'·17N 09°18'·01W.
Cabo Finisterre ☆ Fl 5s 141m **23M**; *Racon O,
35M;* 42°52'·93N 09°16'·29W.

RÍA DE MUROS

Pta Queixal ⚡ Fl (2+1) 12s; 42°44'·36N 09°04'·75W.
Muros ⚡ Fl (4) R 13s 8m 4M; 42°46'·64N 09°03'·31W.
Portosin ⚡ Fl (3) G 9s 8m 5M; 42°45'·94N 08°56'·93W.
Pta Cabeiro ⚡ Oc WR 3s 35m 9/6M; 050°-R-054·5°-W-
058·5°-R-099·5°-W-189·5°; 42°44'·37N 08°59'·44W.

RÍA DE AROUSA (Selected lights only)

Isla Sálvora ☆ Fl (3+1) 20s 38m **21M**; 42°27'·82N
09°00'·80W. Same twr, ⚡ Fl (3) 20s; 126°-160°.
Santa Uxia ⚡ Fl (2) R 7s 7m 4M; 42°33'·58N
08°59'·24W. 50m SE, ⚡ Fl R 5s 8m 5M.
Isla Rúa ⚡ Fl (2+1) WR 21s 24m 13M; 121·5°-R-
211·5°-W-121·5°; *Racon K, 211°-121°, 10-20M;*
42°32'·95N 08°56'·38W.
Pobra do Caramiñal E bkwtr ⚡ Fl (3) G 9s 9m 5M;
W ○ twr, G band; 42°36'·28N 08°55'·87W.
Villagarcia, N mole ⚡ Iso 2s 2m 10M; 42°36'·11N
08°46'·33W. Marina ent, QG & QR, both 6m 3M.
Piedras Negras marina ⚡ Fl (4) WR 11s 5m, W4M
R3M; 305°-W-315°-R-305; 42°29'·85N 08°51'·51W.

RÍA DE PONTEVEDRA

Isla Ons ☆ Fl (4) 24s 125m **25M**; 8-sided twr;
42°22'·94N 08°56'·17W.
Sangenjo ⚡ QR 5m 4M; 42°23'·81N 08°48'·06W.
Combarro ⚡ Fl (2) R 8s 7m 3M; 42°25'·78N
08°42'·23W.
Aguete ⚡ Fl (4) G 11s 3M, 42°22'·66N 08°44'·21W.

RÍA DE VIGO

Ldg lts 129°: Front, ⚡ Fl 3s 36m 9M; 42°15'·15N
08°52'·37W. Rear ⚡ Oc 6s 53m 11M.
S Chan ldg lts 069·3°: **Front** ☆ Iso 2s 16m **18M**;
Horn Mo (V) 60s; Racon B, 22M; 42°11'·12N
08°48'·89W. **Rear** Oc 4s 48m **18M**.
Marina, QG/QR, 10m 5M, 42°14'·56N 08°43'·41W.

BAYONA

Las Serralleiras ⚡ Q (9) 15s 4M; 42°09'·23N 08°53'·35W.
Ldg lts 084°: Front ⚡ Fl 6s 8m 10M; 42°08'·24N
08°50'·09W. Rear ⚡ Oc 4s 18m 9M.
C. Silleiro ☆ Fl (2+1) 15s 84m **24M**; W 8-sided twr,
R bands; 42°06'·27N 08°53'·80W.

AREA 19 Portugal - *Viana do Castelo to Vila Real de Santo Antonio*
SELECTED LIGHTS, BUOYS & WAYPOINTS

Montedor £ Fl (2) 9·5s 102m 22M; R twr; *Horn Mo (S) 25s;* 41°45'·09N 08°52'·49W.

VIANA DO CASTELO
Outer mole ⚡ Fl R 3s 9M; *Horn 30s;* 41°40'·46N 08°50'·66W.

No. 2 ⚲ Fl R 3s; 41°40'·53N 08°50'·48W.

E mole ⚡ Fl G 3s 9M; 41°40'·67N 08°50'·25W.

No. 1 ⚭ Fl G 3s; 41°40'·68N 08°50'·29W.

No. 3 ⚭ Fl (2) G 3s; 41°40'·86N 08°50'·24W.

No. 4 ⚲ Fl (2+1) R 5s; 41°40'·89N 08°50'·36W.

Nos. 5-13 ⚭s are Fl G 3s. Nos. 6-14 ⚲s are Fl R 3s.

No. 13 ⚭ Fl G 3s; 41°41'·49N 08°49'·27W, SSE of marina ent.

No. 14 ⚲ Fl R 3s; 41°41'·56N 08°49'·33W, SSE of marina ent. Marina ent 41°41'·59N 08°49'·33W.

PÓVOA DE VARZIM
Molhe N ⚡ Fl R 3s 14m 12M; *Siren 40s;* 41°22'·29N 08°46'·23W. Molhe S ⚡ L Fl G 6s 4M.

LEIXÕES
Oil refinery ⚑ Fl (3) 15s 6M; *Horn (3) 30s;* 41°12'·10N 08°45'·07W.

Leça ☆ Fl (3) 14s 56m **28M**; W twr, B bands; 41°12'·08N 08°42'·73W.

Outer N mole ⚡ Fl WR 5s 23m W12M, R9M; 001°-R-180°-W-001°; *Horn 20s;* 41°10'·37N 08°42'·49W.

S mole ⚡ Fl G 4s 16m 7M; 328°-285°; *Horn 30s;* 41°10'·68N 08°42'·35W.

Marina ⚡ L Fl (2) R 12s 4m 2M; 41°11'·08N 08°42'·27W.

AVEIRO
Lt ho Aero ☆ Fl (4) 13s 65m **23M**; R/W twr; 40°38'·57N 08°44'·88W. Same twr ⚡ Fl G 4s 53m 9M, rear 085·4° ldg lt. Front 085·4° ldg lt Fl G 3s 16m 9M; 40°38'·54N 08°45'·48W.

Ldg lts 065·6°: Front ⚡ Oc R 3s 7m 9M; 40°38'·82N 08°44'·99W. Rear ⚡ Oc R 6s 8M, 440m from front.

Molhe N ⚡ Fl R 3s 11m 8M; W col, R bands; *Horn 15s;* 40°38'·61N 08°45'·81W.

Molhe S ⚡ Fl G 3s 16m 9M; front 085·4° ldg lt.

Molhe Central ⚡ L Fl G 5s; 40°38'·64N 08°44'·95W.

FIGUEIRA DA FOZ
Cabo Mondego ☆ Fl 5s 96m **28M**; W twr and house; *Horn 30s;* 40°11'·43N 08°54'·32W.

Ldg lts 081·5°, W cols, R bands: Front ⚡ Iso R 5s 6m 8M; 40°08'·83N 08°51'·23W. Rear, ⚡ Oc R 6s.

Molhe N ⚡ Fl R 6s 14m 9M; *Horn 35s;* 40°08'·74N 08°52'·50W.

Molhe S ⚡ Fl G 6s 13m 7M; 40°08'·59N 08°52'·41W.

Penedo da Saudade ☆ Fl (2) 15s 54m **30M**; □ twr, and house; 39°45'·84N 09°01'·89W.

NAZARÉ
Pontal da Nazaré ⚡ Oc 3s 49m 14M; twr & bldg; *Siren 35s;* 39°36'·25N 09°05'·18W.

Molhe S ⚡ L Fl G 5s 14m 8M; 39°35'·34N 09°04'·76W.

ILHA DA BERLENGA and PENICHE
Ilha da Berlenga ☆ Fl 10s 120m **27M**; W □ twr and houses; *Horn 28s;* 39°24'·90N 09°30'·63W.

Cabo Carvoeiro ☆ Fl (3) R 15s 56m **15M**; W □ twr; *Horn 35s;* 39°21'·61N 09°24'·51W.

Peniche molhe W ⚡ Fl R 3s 13m 9M; W twr, R bands; *Siren 120s;* 39°20'·85N 09°22'·56W.

C. da Roca ☆ Fl (4) 18s 164m **26M**; W twr and bldgs; 38°46'·88N 09°29'·90W.

Cabo Raso ☆ Fl (3) 9s 22m **15M**; 324°-189°; R twr; *Horn Mo (I) 60s;* 38°42'·56N 09°29'·15W.

CASCAIS
Ldg lts 284·7°: Front, ☆ Oc WR 6s 24m **W18M**, R14M; 233°-R-334°-W-098°; *Horn 10s;* 38°41'·42N 09°25'·27W. Rear, ☆ Iso WR 2s **W19M, R16M**; 326°-W-092°; 278°-R-292°; W twr. Marina S mole ⚡ Fl (3) R 4s 8m 6M; 38°41'·58N 09°24'·84W.

LISBOA
Triple ldg lts 047·1°: Front, ☆ Oc R 3s 30m **21M** H24; 38°41'·94N 09°15'·97W. Middle, ☆ Oc R 6s 81m **21M** H24; *Racon Q, 15M*. Rear, ☆ Iso 6s 153m **21M**; 38°43'·65N 09°13'·63W.

No. 1 ⚭ Fl G 2s; 38°39'·55N 09°18'·79W.

Forte Bugio ⚡ Fl G 5s 27m 9M; ○ twr on fortress; *Horn Mo (B) 30s;* 38°39'·62N 09°17'·93W.

No. 5 ⚭ Fl G 4s; 38°40'·43N 09°17'·66W.

No. 7 ⚭ Fl G 5s; 38°40'·64N 09°16'·90W.

No. 9 ⚭ Fl G 6s; 38°40'·63N 09°14'·49W.

Ponte 25 de Abril. The N (38°41'·64N 09°10'·69W) and S pillars are lit Fl (3) G 9s and Fl (3) R 9s.

Cabo Espichel ☆ Fl 4s 167m **26M**; W 6-sided twr; *Horn 31s;* 38°24'·94N 09°13'·05W.

SESIMBRA
Ldg lts 003·5°, L Fl R 5s 9/21m 7/6M: Front, 38°26'·56N 09°06'·16W. Rear 34m from front.

SETÚBAL
Ldg lts 039·7°, both Iso Y 6s 12/60m **22M**. Front, R structure, W stripes; 38°31'·08N 08°54'·01W.

No. 1 ⚭ Fl G 3s 5M; 38°26'·98N 08°58'·18W.

No. 2 ⚭ Fl (2) R 10s 13m 9M; *Racon B, 15M;* 38°27'·21N 08°58'·45W.

Forte de Outão ⚡ Oc R 6s 33m 12M; 38°29'·31N 08°56'·06W.

Pinheiro da Cruz ⚡ Fl 3s; 38°15'·46N 08°46'·34W.

SINES

Cabo de Sines ☆ Fl (2) 15s 55m **26M**; 37°57'·56N 08°52'·83W.
W mole ⚲ Fl 3s 20m 12M; 37°56'·48N 08°53'·33W.
Sines W ⚲ Fl R 3s 6M; 37°56'·12N 08°53'·25W.
Marina mole ⚲ Fl G 4s 4M; W twr, G bands; 37°57'·03N 08°52'·03W.
C. Sardão ☆ Fl (3) 15s 67m **23M**; 37°35'·94N 08°49'·02W.

CAPE ST VINCENT/SAGRES

Cabo de São Vicente ☆ Fl 5s 84m **32M**; *Horn Mo (I) 30s*; 37°01'·36N 08°59'·78W.
Ponta de Sagres ⚲ Iso R 2s 52m 11M; 36°59'·66N 08°56'·94W.
Baleeira mole ⚲ Fl WR 4s 12m, W14M, R11M; 254°-W-355°-R-254°; 37°00'·67N 08°55'·46W.

LAGOS

Pta da Piedade ☆ Fl 7s 50m **20M**; 37°04'·81N 08°40'·20W.
W mole ⚲ Fl (2) R 6s 5M; W col, R bands; 37°05'·85N 08°40'·02W.
E mole ⚲ Fl (2) G 6s 5M; W col, G bands; 37°05'·96N 08°39'·96W.
Alvor ent, ⚲ Fl R/G 4s; W twrs, R/G bands; 37°07'·13N 08°37'·14W.

PORTIMÃO

Ponta do Altar ☆ L Fl 5s 31m **16M**; 290°-170°; W twr and bldg; 37°06'·34N 08°31'·17W.
Ldg lts 020·9°: Front ⚲ Oc R 5s 18m 8M; 37°07'·35N 08°31'·31W. Rear ⚲ Oc R 7s 32m 8M; 87m from front.
E mole ⚲ Fl G 5s 9m 7M; 37°06'·50N 08°31'·59W.
W mole ⚲ Fl R 5s 9m 7M; 37°06'·52N 08°31'·77W.
No. 2 ⚲ Fl R 4s; 37°06'·96N 08°31'·53W.
Marina ent, S side ⚲ Fl R 6s 3M; 37°07'·10N 08°31'·58W.
N side ⚲ Fl G 6s 3M; 37°07'·14N 08°31'·58W.
N Mole ⚲ Iso R 4s 8m 3M; 37°07'·33N 08°31'·59W.
Pta de Alfanzina ☆ Fl (2) 15s 62m **29M**; 37°05'·22N 08°26'·59W.
Armação de Pera ⚲ Oc R 5s 24m 6M; 37°05'·92N 08°21'·21W.

ALBUFEIRA

Ponta da Baleeira ⚲ Oc 6s 30m 11M; 37°04'·84N 08°15'·85W.
N bkwtr ⚲, Fl (2) G 5s 9m 4M, approx 37°04'·90N 08°15'·52W.
S bkwtr ⚲, Fl (2) R 5s 9m 4M.
Praia da Albufeira, E end of bay, Olhos de Água ⚲ L Fl 5s 29m 7M; 37°05'·47N 08°11'·40W.

VILAMOURA

Vilamoura ☆, Fl 5s 17m **19M**; 37°04'·50N 08°07'·42W.
Marina, W mole ⚲ Fl R 4s 13m 5M; 37°04'·19N 08°07'·49W.
E mole ⚲ Fl G 4s 13m 5M; 37°04'·22N 08°07'·42W.

FARO, OLHÃO and TAVIRA

Ent from sea: E mole ⚲ Fl G 4s 9m 6M; 36°57'·79N 07°52'·14W.
W mole ⚲ Fl R 4s 9m 6M; 37°57'·84N 08°52'·26W, appr on 352°.
Access ldg lts 020·9°: Front, Barra Nova ⚲ Oc 4s 8m 6M; 37°58'·22N 07°52'·00W. Rear, **Cabo de Santa Maria** ☆ Fl (4) 17s 49m **25M**; W ○ twr; 36°58'·48N 07°51'·88W.
No. 6 ⚲ Fl R 6s; 36°58'·49N 07°52'·12W (NW to Faro; NE to Olhão).
No. 20 ⚲ Fl R 6s, 37°00'·13N 07°55'·11W (edge of AC 83 approx 2M before **Faro** proper).
No. 8 ⚲ Fl R 3s; 36°59'·90N 07°51'·07W, thence N & E to **Olhão**.
Tavira ldg lts 325·9°: Front, ⚲ Fl R 3s 6m 4M. Rear, Iso ⚲ R 6s 9m 5M. W mole ⚲ Fl R 2·5s 7m 7M; 37°06'·79N 07°37'·10W.

VILA REAL DE SANTO ANTONIO

Lt ho ☆ Fl 6·5s 51m **26M**; W twr, B bands; 37°11'·23N 07°25'·00W.
R. Guadiano, Bar buoys ⚲ Q (3) G 6s; 37°08'·90N 07°23'·44W.
⚲ Fl R 4s; 37°09'·14N 07°23'·82W.
W bkwtr ⚲ Fl R 5s 4M; 37°09'·75N 07°24'·03W.
E trng wall ⚲ Fl G 3s 4M; 37°09'·93N 07°23'·63W.
Marina, QR at S corner; QR/QG at ent; QR at N corner.

See also Area 20 Distance Table

		1										
1	Longships	**1**										
2	Ushant (Créac'h)	100	**2**									
3	La Coruña	418	338	**3**								
4	Cabo Villano	439	365	43	**4**							
5	Bayona	510	436	114	71	**5**						
6	Viana do Castelo	537	468	141	98	32	**6**					
7	Leixões (Pôrto)	565	491	169	126	63	33	**7**				
8	Nazaré	659	585	263	220	156	127	97	**8**			
9	Cabo Carvoeiro	670	596	274	231	171	143	114	22	**9**		
10	Cabo Raso	710	636	314	271	211	183	154	62	40	**10**	
11	Lisboa (bridge)	686	652	330	287	227	199	170	78	56	16	**11**
12	Cabo Espichel	692	658	336	293	233	205	176	84	62	22	23	**12**

AZORES – SELECTED LIGHTS

| Positions are referenced to WGS 84 |

ILHA DAS FLORES

Ponta do Albarnaz ⚟, Fl 5s 103m 22M, 035°-258°; W twr, R cupola. 39°31'·20N 31°14'·12W.
Ponta das Lajes ☆, Fl (3) 28s 98m **26M**, 263°-054°; W twr, R cupola. 39°22'·56N 31°10'·59W.
PORTO DAS LAJES, ldg lts 250·8°: Front, L Fl G 7s 17m 2M, 39°22'·74N 31°10'·24W; rear Oc G 4s. Bkwtr hd ⚟ Oc R 6s 2M. 39°22'·75N 31°09'·94W.

ILHA DO FAIAL

Ponta dos Cedros ⚟, Fl 7s 144m 12M; 38°38'·29N 28°43'·36W.
Ponta da Ribeirinha ⚟, Fl (3) 20s 131m 12M; post; 38°35'·73N 28°36'·15W, E end of island.

HORTA

Boa Viagem ⚟ Iso G 1·5s 12m 9M; appr brg 285°; B column on R cupola; 38°32'·28N 28°37'·49W.
Bkwtr hd ⚟ Fl R 3s 20m 11M; W structure. 38°32'·03N 28°37'·27W.
Ldg lts 194·9°: both Iso G 2s 13/15m 2M; Red X on W posts, R bands. Front 38°31'·67N 28°37'·51W.

ILHA TERCEIRA

Ponta da Sereta ☆ Fl (3) 15s 95m **21M**; W col, R top; 38°45'·97N 27°22'·45W, NW end of island.
Lajes ☆ Aero Al Fl WG 10s 132m **W28M, G23M**.
Praia da Vitoria, N mole Fl G 5s 11m 6M; G lantern, Gy post; 38°43'·56N 27°03'·04W.
S mole Fl R 3s 8m 6M; W twr, R bands; 38°43'·24N 27°02'·92W.
Ponta das Contendas ☆ Fl (4) WR 15s 190m **W23M, R20M**; 220°-W-020°-R-044°-W-072°-R-093°; W twr, R top; 38°38'·62N 27°05'·07W.
Monte Brasil, Oc WR 10s 21m 12M; 191°-R-295°-W-057°; W col, R bands; 38°38'·60N 27°13'·04W.

ANGRA DO HEROISMO

Ldg lts 340·9°: front, Fl R 4s 29m 7M, R mast; 38°39'·25N 27°13'·09W. Rear, Oc R 6s 54m 7M.
Marina ent, S side (Porto Pipas) ⚟ Fl G 3s 14m 6M.
N mole, ⚟ Fl (2) R 6s 8m 3M; 38°39'·12N 27°12'·95W.

ILHA DE SAO MIGUEL

Ponta da Ferraria ☆ Fl (3) 20s 106m **27M**; 339°-174°; W twr, R cupola. 37°51'·21N 25°51'·02W.
Airport ☆ Aero Al Fl WG 10s 83m **W28M, G23M**; 282°-124°; control twr; 37°44'·64N 25°42'·46W.
Santa Clara ☆ L Fl 5s 26m **15M**; 282°-102°; R lantern; 37°43'·99N 25°41'·15W.
Ponta Garça ☆ L Fl WR 5s 100m **W16M**, R13M; 240°-W-080-R-100°; 37°42'·85N 25°22'·18W.
Ponta do Arnel ☆ Aeromarine Fl 5s 65m **25M**; 157°-355°; W twr on ho; 37°49'·43N 25°08'·12W.

PONTA DELGADA

Bkwtr head ⚟ Oc R 3s 16m 5M; W twr, R bands. 37°44'·18N 25°39'·37W, SSE of marina.
Outer ldg lts 320·5°: Front, Iso G 5s 14m 7M; B lamp on Y ho; hard to see by day; 37°44'·54N 25°39'·56W. Rear, Oc G 5s 48m 7M; B lamp on R/W post; may be obsc'd by vegetation.
Marina mole hd ⚟ Oc G 3s 12m 10M; W twr, G bands. 37°44'·37N 25°39'·55W.
Baixa de São Pedro ↯ Q (6) + L Fl 15s 2M. 37°44'·27N 25°39'·72W.
Inner ldg lts 266·5°: both Oc R 6s 13/19m 9M. Front, W post, R bands; 37°44'·18N 25°40'·32W.
Ilhéus das Formigas ⚟ Fl (2) 12s 21m 9M; W twr. 37°16'·29N 24°46'·87W.

1	Falmouth	1										
2	Brest	136	2									
3	La Coruña	440	350	3								
4	Bayona	554	456	114	4							
5	Leixões (Pôrto)	617	526	176	63	5						
6	HORTA	1235	1202	966	927	937	6					
7	PONTA DELGADA	1183	1145	862	813	815	151	7				
8	Lisboa	780	658	327	227	163	904	771	8			
9	Cabo São Vicente	888	757	426	318	263	934	794	102	9		
10	Cádiz	1022	901	560	452	397	1068	928	236	134	10	
11	Europa Point	1087	960	618	506	455	1125	984	294	192	72	11
12	Casablanca	1114	978	637	525	474	1065	918	313	211	187	188	12

	1	131	152	190	282	320	Flores	1
		2	48	69	152	191	Horta	2
			3	44	138	185	Graciosa	3
				4	94	143	Terceira	4
					5	54	Ponta Delgada	5
						6	Sta Maria	6

DISTANCE TABLES
Approx distances in nautical miles are by the most direct route allowing for dangers and TSS.

AREA 20 SW Spain & Gibraltar - *Ayamonte to Europa Point*
SELECTED LIGHTS, BUOYS & WAYPOINTS

Positions are referenced to WGS84

AYAMONTE (E side of Rio Guadiana)
Bar buoys ⚓ Q (3) G 6s; 37°08'·90N 07°23'·44W.
⚓ Fl R 4s; 37°09'·14N 07°23'·82W.
W trng wall ⚡ Fl R 5s 4M; 37°09'·75N 07°24'·03W.
E trng wall ⚡ Fl G 3s 4M; 37°09'·93N 07°23'·63W.
Vila Real de Santo Antònio ☆ Fl 6·5s 51m **26M**;
W twr, B bands; 37°11'·23N 07°25'·00W (Portugal).

ISLA CANELA and ISLA CRISTINA
Appr ⚓ Fl 10s; 37°10'·51N 07°19'·49W.
W mole ⚡VQ (2) R 5s 9m 4M; 37°10'·83N 07°19'·58W.
Ldg lts 313°: Front ⚡ Q 8m 5M; 37°11'·50N
07°20'·40W approx. Rear ⚡ Fl 4s 13m 5M.
Both marina entrances are QR and QG.

RIO DE LAS PIEDRAS
No 1 Bar ⚓ L Fl 10s; 37°11'·64N 07°03'·00W. The
shifting chan is marked by lateral lt buoys.
El Rompido ☆ Fl (2) 10s 41m **24M**; W twr, B
bands; 37°13'·12N 07°07'·69W.

RIA DE HUELVA
⚓ VQ (6) + L Fl 10s; 37°09'·56N 06°57'·18W.
Punta Umbria, bkwtr hd ⚡ VQ (6) + L Fl 10s 8m
5M; 37°09'·75N 06°56'·92W.
Marina pier ⚡ Fl (2) G 10s 6m 3M; 37°10'·76N
06°57'·36W.
Dir ⚡ 339·2°, WRG 59m 8M; 337·5°- Fl G-338°-FG-
338·6°-OcG-339·1°-FW-339·3°-OcR-339·8°-FR-
340·4°-Fl R-340·9°; W twr; 37°08'·57N 06°50'·66W.
No. 1 ⚓ Fl G 5s; 37°06'·26N 06°49'·46W.
No. 2 ⚓ Fl R 5s; 37°06'·33N 06°49'·72W.
Bkwtr hd ⚡ Fl (3+1) WR 20s 29m, W12M, R9M;
165°-W-100°-R-125°; *Racon K, 12M;* 37°06'·47N
06°49'·93W.
No. 3 ⚓ Fl (2) G 10s; 37°06'·87N 06°49'·77W.
No. 5 ⚓ Fl (3) G 15s; 37°07'·38N 06°50'·03W.
No. 7 ⚓ Fl (4) G 20s; 37°07'·77N 06°50'·29W.

MAZAGÓN
Picacho lt ho ☆ Fl (2+4) 30s 52m **25M**; 37°08'·10N
06°49'·56W.
Marina, S pier ⚡ QG 7m 2M; 37°07'·91N 06°50'·03W.
⚓ Fl (2) 10s; 37°04'·22N 06°43'·67W.
La Higuera ☆ Fl (3) 20s 45m **20M**; 37°00'·47N
06°34'·16W.

CHIPIONA
Bajo Salmedina ⚡ Q (9) 15s 9m 5M; 36°44'·27N
06°28'·64W.
Pta de Chipiona ☆ Fl 10s 67m **25M**; 36°44'·26N
06°26'·53W.
Marina, No. 2 ⚓ Fl (2) R 7s; 36°45'·14N 06°25'·59W.
N bkwtr ⚡Fl (2) G 10s 6m 5M; 36°44'·96N 06°25'·70W.

RÍO GUADALQUIVIR
No. 1 ⚓ L Fl 10s; *Racon M, 10M;* 36°45'·74N
06°27'·03W.
Ldg lts 068·9°: Front ⚡ Q 28m 10M; 36°47'·84N
06°20'·24W. Rear, ⚡ Iso 4s 60m 10M.
No. 3 ⚓ Fl G 5s; 36°46'·16N 06°25'·36W.
Selected buoys in sequence as far as Bonanza:
No. 7 ⚓ Fl (3) G 10s; 36°46'·61N 06°24'·02W.
No. 8 ⚓ Fl (3) R 10s; 36°46'·67N 06°24'·12W.
No. 11 ⚓ Fl G 5s; 36°46'·96N 06°22'·90W.
No. 12 ⚓ Fl R 5s; 36°47'·05N 06°22'·94W.
No. 14 ⚓ Fl (2) R 6s; 36°47'·21N 06°22'·39W.
No.13 ⚓ Fl (2) G 6s; 36°47'·12N 06°22'·36W.
No.17 ⚓ Fl (4) G 12s; 36°47'·46N 06°21'·23W.
No. 20 ⚓ Fl R 5s; 36°47'·81N 06°20'·70W.
Bonanza lt ho Fl 5s 22m 6M; 36°48'·17N
06°20'·15W.

SEVILLA
No. 52 bcn ⚡ Fl (2+1) R 21s 9m 5M; 36°47'·81N
06°20'·71W.
Gelves marina Fl R 5s; 37°20'·51N 06°01'·31W;
and Fl G 3s.
Lock, 37°19'·89N 05°59'·64W, for city centre.
CN Sevilla pontoons, 37°22'·20N 05°59'·59W.

ROTA
Rota Aero ☆ Alt Fl WG 9s 79m **17M**; R/W
chequered water twr, conspic; 36°38'·13N
06°20'·84W.
Rota ⚡ Oc 4s 33m 13M; W lt ho, R band;
36°36'·96N 06°21'·44W.
Marina, S pier ⚡ Fl (3) R 10s 8m 9M; 36°36'·96N
06°21'·44W.

PUERTO SHERRY/PUERTO DE SANTA MARIA
Puerto Sherry marina, S bkwtr ⚡ Oc R 4s 4M;
36°34'·64N 06°15'·25W. N bkwtr ⚡ Oc G 5s 3M.
Santa María ldg lts 040°: Front ⚡ QG 16m 4M;
36°35'·77N 06°13'·36W. Rear ⚡ Iso G 4s 20m 4M.
W trng wall ⚡ Fl R 5s 10m 3M; 36°34'·34N
06°14'·96W.

CÁDIZ CITY and PUERTO AMERICA
⚓ L Fl 10s; 36°33'·99N 06°19'·80W.
No. 1 ⚓ Fl G 3s; 36°33'·12N 06°19'·07W.
No. 3 ⚓ Fl (2) G 4s; 36°33'·17N 06°18'·14W.
No. 5 ⚓ Fl (3) G 13s; 36°33'·03N 06°17'·38W.
San Felipe mole ⚡ Fl G 3s 10m 5M; G twr;
36°32'·56N 06°16'·77W.
Puerto America marina, NE bkwtr, ⚡ Fl (4) G 16s
1M.
RCN pier ⚡ FG; 36°32'·34N 06°17'·13W.

International Free Zone hbr: No. 1 ⚓ Fl (3) G 9s; 36°30'·66N 06°15'·45W.

Puerto Elcano marina 36°30'·08N 06°15'·45W.

Castillo de San Sebastián ☆ Fl (2) 10s 38m **25M**; *Horn Mo (N) 20s;* 36°31'·70N 06°18'·97W.

SANCTI PETRI
Punta del Arrecife ⚹ Q (9) 15s 7m 3M; 36°23'·66N 06°12'·99W.
Castle ⚹ Fl 3s 18m 9M; 36°22'·75N 06°13'·33W.
Outer ldg lts 050°: Front ⚹ Fl 5s 12m 6M. Rear ⚹ Oc (2) 6s 16m 6M.
No. 1 ⚓ Fl (3) G 9s; 36°22'·50N 06°12'·93W.
No. 2 ⚓ Fl (3) R 9s; 36°22'·46N 06°12'·81W.
No. 3 ⚓ Fl (4) G 11s; 36°22'·64N 06°12'·65W.
No. 4 ⚓ Fl (4) R 11s; 36°22'·66N 06°12'·71W.
Inner ldg lts 346·5°: Front ⚹ Fl 5s 11m 6M. Rear ⚹ Oc (2) 6s 21m.
⚓ Fl G 5s 8m 2M & ⚓ Fl R 5s; 36°23'·10N 06°12'·65W.
Cabo Roche ☆ Fl (4) 24s 44m **20M**; 36°17'·75N 06°08'·59W.
Cabo Trafalgar ☆ Fl (2+1) 15s 50m **22M**; 36°10'·95N 06°02'·12W.

BARBATE
Lt ho ⚹ Fl (2) WR 7s 22m, W10M, R7M; 281°-W-015°-R-095°; W twr, R bands; 36°11'·21N 05°55'·43W.
Ldg lts 297·5°, Q 3/8m 1M; 280·5°-310·5°; TE 2001.
SW mole ⚹ Fl R 4s 11m 5M; 36°10'·78N 05°55'·56W.
Marina ent, Fl (2+1) R 21s 2M (anti-oil boom) and Fl R 4s 2M.
⚓ Q; 36°10'·75N 05°55'·40W (1ca E of hbr ent) marks N end of a roughly △-shaped tunny net.
Torre de Gracia ⚹ Oc (2) 5s 74m 13M; 36°05'·38N 05°48'·69W.

TARIFA
Tarifa ☆ Fl (3) WR 10s 40m **W26M, R18M**; 113°-W-089°-R-113°; W twr; *Siren Mo (O) 60s; Racon C, 20M;* 36°00'·06N 05°36'·60W.
Outer SE mole ⚹ Fl G 5s 11m 5M; vis 249°-045°; G twr with statue; 36°00'·38N 05°36'·24W.

ALGECIRAS
Pta Carnero ☆ Fl (4) WR 20s 42m, **W16M**, R13M;

018°-W-325°-R-018°; *Siren Mo (K) 30s;* 36°04'·61N 05°25'·57W.
⚓ Q (3) 10s; 36°06'·73N 05°24'·76W.
Marina, outer S jetty ⚹ Q (3) R 9s 7m 3M; 36°07'·10N 05°26'·13W.

LA LÍNEA
⚓ Fl (3) G 6s; 36°09'·53N 05°22'·03W.
Dique de Abrigo ⚹ Fl (2) G 7s 8m 4M; 36°09'·51N 05°22'·05W.

GIBRALTAR
Aero ⚹ Mo (GB) R 10s 405m **30M**; 36°08'·57N 05°20'·60W.
Europa Pt ☆ Iso 10s 49m **19/15M**; vis 197°-042° & 067°-125°; W twr, R band; 36°06'·58N 05°20'·69W.
Also ⚹ FR 44m **15M**; 042°-067°; *Horn 20s.*
Same twr ⚹ Oc R 10s 49m **15M**; 042°-067°.
'A' Head ☆ Fl 2s 18m **15M**; *Horn 10s;* 36°08'·03N 05°21'·85W.
'B' head ⚹ QR 9m 5M; 36°08'·14N 05°21'·84W.
Queensway marina ⚹ 2 FR, 36°08'·04N 05°21'·41W; 2FG (vert).
Yacht reporting station; 36°08'·94N 05°21'·45W.

MOROCCO (WEST TO EAST)
Cap Spartel ☆ Fl (4) 20s 95m **30M**; Y☐ twr; *Dia (4) 90s;* 35°47'·47N 05°55'·43W.

TANGIER
Navaids are reported unreliable. They may be missing, unlit, off station or not as charted.
Monte Dirección (Le Charf) ☆ Oc (3) WRG 12s 88m **W16M**, R12M, G11M; 140°-G-174·5°-W-200°-R-225°; 35°45'·98N 05°47'·35W.
⚓ L Fl 10s; 35°47'·66N 05°47'·03W.
N pier ⚹ Fl (3) 12s 20m 14M; 35°47'·47N 05°47'·60W.
Jetée des Yachts ⚹ Iso G 4s 6m 6M; 35°47'·23N 05°48'·14W.
Pta Malabata ☆ Fl 5s 77m **22M**. W ☐ twr; 35°48'·99N 05°44'·92W.
Pte Círes ⚹ Fl (3) 10s 44m **18M**; 060°-330°; 35°54'·51N 05°28'·92W.

CEUTA (Spanish enclave)
Punta Almina ⚹ Fl (2) 10s 148m 22M; 35°53'·90N 05°16'·85W.
W pier ⚹ Fl G 5s 13m 10M; *Siren 15s; Racon O, 12M;* 35°53'·75N 05°18'·68W.
Marina ent ⚹ Fl (4) R 11s 8m 1M; 35°53'·45N 05°18'·90W.

1	Nazaré	1											
2	Cabo Carvoeiro	22	2										
3	Cabo Raso	62	40	3									
4	Lisboa (bridge)	78	56	16	4								
5	Cabo Espichel	84	62	22	23	5							
6	Sines	118	96	54	57	34	6						
7	Cabo São Vicente	169	147	104	108	85	57	7					
8	Lagos	189	167	124	128	105	77	20	8				
9	Vilamoura	212	190	147	151	128	100	43	27	9			
10	Cádiz	303	281	238	242	219	191	134	120	95	10		
11	Cabo Trafalgar	320	298	255	259	236	208	151	139	115	28	11	
12	Tarifa	344	322	279	283	260	232	175	163	139	52	24	12
13	Gibraltar	360	338	295	299	276	248	191	179	155	68	40	16	13

50°N 00°E/W. Times are UT - for DST add 1 hour in non-shaded areas

2006 Sunrise and Sunset Time

The times are based on **LAT 50°00'N LONG 0°00'W** - add 4 min for every degree West and subtract 4 min for every degree East

	Rise h m	Set h m	Rise h m	Set h m	Rise h m	Set h m	Rise h m	Set h m	Rise h m	Set h m	Rise h m	Set h m
	JANUARY		FEBRUARY		MARCH		APRIL		MAY		JUNE	
1	07 59	16 09	07 34	16 54	06 44	17 42	05 37	18 32	04 37	19 18	03 56	20 00
2	07 59	16 10	07 32	16 56	06 42	17 43	05 35	18 33	04 35	19 20	03 55	20 01
3	07 58	16 11	07 31	16 57	06 40	17 45	05 33	18 35	04 33	19 21	03 55	20 02
4	07 58	16 12	07 29	16 59	06 38	17 47	05 31	18 36	04 32	19 23	03 54	20 03
5	07 58	16 13	07 28	17 01	06 36	17 48	05 29	18 38	04 30	19 25	03 53	20 04
6	07 58	16 14	07 26	17 03	06 33	17 50	05 27	18 39	04 28	19 26	03 53	20 05
7	07 57	16 15	07 25	17 04	06 31	17 52	05 24	18 41	04 27	19 28	03 52	20 06
8	07 57	16 17	07 23	17 06	06 29	17 53	05 22	18 43	04 25	19 29	03 52	20 06
9	07 57	16 18	07 21	17 08	06 27	17 55	05 20	18 44	04 23	19 30	03 52	20 07
10	07 56	16 19	07 20	17 09	06 25	17 57	05 18	18 46	04 22	19 32	03 51	20 08
11	07 55	16 21	07 18	17 11	06 23	17 58	05 16	18 47	04 20	19 33	03 51	20 09
12	07 55	16 22	07 16	17 13	06 21	18 00	05 14	18 49	04 19	19 35	03 51	20 09
13	07 54	16 24	07 15	17 15	06 19	18 01	05 12	18 50	04 17	19 36	03 50	20 10
14	07 54	16 25	07 13	17 16	06 16	18 03	05 10	18 52	04 16	19 38	03 50	20 10
15	07 53	16 26	07 11	17 18	06 14	18 05	05 08	18 54	04 14	19 39	03 50	20 11
16	07 52	16 28	07 09	17 20	06 12	18 06	05 06	18 55	04 13	19 41	03 50	20 11
17	07 51	16 29	07 07	17 21	06 10	18 08	05 04	18 57	04 12	19 42	03 50	20 12
18	07 50	16 31	07 05	17 23	06 08	18 09	05 02	18 58	04 10	19 43	03 50	20 12
19	07 49	16 32	07 03	17 25	06 06	18 11	05 00	19 00	04 09	19 45	03 50	20 12
20	07 48	16 34	07 02	17 27	06 03	18 13	04 58	19 01	04 08	19 46	03 50	20 13
21	07 47	16 36	07 00	17 28	06 01	18 14	04 56	19 03	04 07	19 47	03 51	20 13
22	07 46	16 37	06 58	17 30	05 59	18 16	04 54	19 04	04 05	19 49	03 51	20 13
23	07 45	16 39	06 56	17 32	05 57	18 17	04 52	19 06	04 04	19 50	03 51	20 13
24	07 44	16 40	06 54	17 33	05 55	18 19	04 50	19 08	04 03	19 51	03 51	20 13
25	07 43	16 42	06 52	17 35	05 52	18 21	04 48	19 09	04 02	19 52	03 52	20 13
26	07 42	16 44	06 50	17 37	05 50	18 22	04 46	19 11	04 01	19 54	03 52	20 13
27	07 41	16 45	06 48	17 38	05 48	18 24	04 44	19 12	04 00	19 55	03 53	20 13
28	07 39	16 47	06 46	17 40	05 46	18 25	04 42	19 14	03 59	19 56	03 53	20 13
29	07 38	16 49			05 44	18 27	04 40	19 15	03 58	19 57	03 54	20 13
30	07 37	16 51			05 42	18 28	04 39	19 17	03 58	19 58	03 54	20 13
31	07 35	16 52			05 39	18 30			03 57	19 59		

	Rise h m	Set h m	Rise h m	Set h m	Rise h m	Set h m	Rise h m	Set h m	Rise h m	Set h m	Rise h m	Set h m
	JULY		AUGUST		SEPTEMBER		OCTOBER		NOVEMBER		DECEMBER	
1	03 55	20 13	04 29	19 43	05 15	18 44	06 00	17 39	06 49	16 37	07 36	16 01
2	03 55	20 12	04 30	19 41	05 16	18 42	06 01	17 37	06 51	16 36	07 38	16 01
3	03 56	20 12	04 32	19 40	05 18	18 40	06 03	17 35	06 53	16 34	07 39	16 00
4	03 57	20 11	04 33	19 38	05 19	18 38	06 04	17 32	06 54	16 32	07 40	16 00
5	03 58	20 11	04 35	19 36	05 21	18 36	06 06	17 30	06 56	16 31	07 42	15 59
6	03 58	20 10	04 36	19 35	05 22	18 34	06 07	17 28	06 58	16 29	07 43	15 59
7	03 59	20 10	04 38	19 33	05 24	18 32	06 09	17 26	06 59	16 27	07 44	15 59
8	04 00	20 09	04 39	19 31	05 25	18 29	06 10	17 24	07 01	16 26	07 45	15 58
9	04 01	20 09	04 40	19 30	05 27	18 27	06 12	17 22	07 03	16 24	07 46	15 58
10	04 02	20 08	04 42	19 28	05 28	18 25	06 14	17 20	07 04	16 23	07 47	15 58
11	04 03	20 07	04 43	19 26	05 29	18 23	06 15	17 18	07 06	16 22	07 48	15 58
12	04 04	20 07	04 45	19 24	05 31	18 21	06 17	17 15	07 08	16 20	07 49	15 58
13	04 05	20 06	04 46	19 22	05 32	18 18	06 18	17 13	07 09	16 19	07 50	15 58
14	04 06	20 05	04 48	19 21	05 34	18 16	06 20	17 11	07 11	16 17	07 51	15 58
15	04 07	20 04	04 49	19 19	05 35	18 14	06 21	17 09	07 12	16 16	07 52	15 58
16	04 08	20 03	04 51	19 17	05 37	18 12	06 23	17 07	07 14	16 15	07 53	15 58
17	04 09	20 02	04 52	19 15	05 38	18 10	06 25	17 05	07 16	16 14	07 53	15 59
18	04 11	20 01	04 54	19 13	05 40	18 07	06 26	17 03	07 17	16 13	07 54	15 59
19	04 12	20 00	04 55	19 11	05 41	18 05	06 28	17 01	07 19	16 11	07 55	15 59
20	04 13	19 59	04 57	19 09	05 43	18 03	06 30	16 59	07 20	16 10	07 55	16 00
21	04 14	19 58	04 58	19 07	05 44	18 01	06 31	16 57	07 22	16 09	07 56	16 00
22	04 16	19 57	05 00	19 05	05 46	17 59	06 33	16 55	07 23	16 08	07 56	16 01
23	04 17	19 55	05 01	19 03	05 47	17 56	06 34	16 54	07 25	16 07	07 57	16 01
24	04 18	19 54	05 03	19 01	05 49	17 54	06 36	16 52	07 27	16 06	07 57	16 02
25	04 19	19 53	05 04	18 59	05 50	17 52	06 38	16 50	07 28	16 05	07 58	16 03
26	04 21	19 51	05 06	18 57	05 52	17 50	06 39	16 48	07 29	16 05	07 58	16 03
27	04 22	19 50	05 07	18 55	05 54	17 48	06 41	16 46	07 31	16 04	07 58	16 04
28	04 23	19 49	05 09	18 53	05 55	17 45	06 43	16 44	07 32	16 03	07 58	16 05
29	04 25	19 47	05 10	18 51	05 57	17 43	06 44	16 42	07 34	16 02	07 58	16 06
30	04 26	19 46	05 12	18 49	05 58	17 41	06 46	16 41	07 35	16 02	07 59	16 06
31	04 28	19 44	05 13	18 47			06 48	16 39			07 59	16 07

50°N 00°E/W. Times are UT - for DST add 1 hour in non-shaded areas

2006 Moonrise and Moonset Time

The times are based on **LAT 50°00'N LONG 0°00'W** - add 4 min for every degree West and subtract 4 min for every degree East

	Rise h m	Set h m	Rise h m	Set h m	Rise h m	Set h m	Rise h m	Set h m	Rise h m	Set h m	Rise h m	Set h m
	JANUARY		FEBRUARY		MARCH		APRIL		MAY		JUNE	
1	09 40	17 34	09 08	21 04	07 26	19 59	06 38	23 14	06 22	** **	08 37	00 04
2	10 10	19 06	09 22	22 29	07 41	21 26	07 06	** **	07 20	00 24	09 50	00 23
3	10 32	20 36	09 37	23 52	07 56	22 53	07 43	00 34	08 28	01 08	11 00	00 38
4	10 48	22 02	09 53	** **	08 15	** **	08 34	01 42	09 41	01 40	12 09	00 51
5	11 03	23 25	10 12	01 15	08 38	00 18	09 35	02 34	10 54	02 02	13 17	01 02
6	11 17	** **	10 37	02 36	09 09	01 39	10 45	03 11	12 06	02 19	14 26	01 13
7	11 31	00 46	11 10	03 52	09 50	02 51	11 57	03 38	13 15	02 33	15 37	01 25
8	11 48	02 06	11 55	04 59	10 44	03 51	13 09	03 58	14 23	02 44	16 52	01 38
9	12 08	03 27	12 52	05 54	11 48	04 36	14 19	04 13	15 32	02 55	18 11	01 56
10	12 35	04 46	13 58	06 35	12 58	05 09	15 29	04 26	16 43	03 06	19 30	02 19
11	13 12	06 00	15 09	07 05	14 10	05 33	16 37	04 37	17 56	03 19	20 44	02 52
12	14 00	07 04	16 21	07 26	15 21	05 51	17 46	04 48	19 13	03 34	21 46	03 40
13	15 00	07 55	17 32	07 43	16 31	06 05	18 58	04 59	20 32	03 53	22 33	04 45
14	16 09	08 33	18 42	07 57	17 40	06 17	20 12	05 12	21 49	04 19	23 06	06 05
15	17 21	09 00	19 50	08 08	18 49	06 28	21 29	05 27	22 58	04 56	23 29	07 32
16	18 33	09 20	20 58	08 19	19 58	06 39	22 47	05 48	23 54	05 49	23 48	08 59
17	19 43	09 36	22 08	08 30	21 09	06 50	** **	06 17	** **	06 58	** **	10 25
18	20 52	09 49	23 20	08 42	22 24	07 04	00 01	06 58	00 34	08 20	00 03	11 48
19	22 00	10 00	** **	08 56	23 40	07 21	01 06	07 55	01 03	09 46	00 17	13 11
20	23 09	10 11	00 35	09 15	** **	07 43	01 56	09 08	01 24	11 12	00 31	14 34
21	** **	10 23	01 53	09 41	00 58	08 15	02 32	10 32	01 41	12 37	00 47	15 57
22	00 19	10 36	03 11	10 18	02 10	09 01	02 59	11 59	01 56	14 00	01 06	17 22
23	01 33	10 52	04 22	11 11	03 11	10 04	03 19	13 27	02 10	15 24	01 31	18 43
24	02 52	11 13	05 19	12 24	03 57	11 23	03 35	14 54	02 24	16 49	02 06	19 55
25	04 13	11 44	06 01	13 51	04 31	12 51	03 49	16 20	02 41	18 15	02 54	20 52
26	05 31	12 30	06 32	15 24	05 04	14 22	04 04	17 47	03 03	19 41	03 54	21 35
27	06 39	13 34	06 54	16 58	05 14	15 53	04 20	19 15	03 32	21 01	05 05	22 05
28	07 30	14 57	07 11	18 30	05 30	17 22	04 38	20 43	04 12	22 09	06 19	22 27
29	08 07	16 30			05 45	18 51	05 03	22 08	05 05	23 01	07 33	22 43
30	08 33	18 05			06 00	20 20	05 36	23 23	06 10	23 38	08 45	22 57
31	08 52	19 36			06 17	21 48			07 23	** **		

	Rise h m	Set h m	Rise h m	Set h m	Rise h m	Set h m	Rise h m	Set h m	Rise h m	Set h m	Rise h m	Set h m
	JULY		AUGUST		SEPTEMBER		OCTOBER		NOVEMBER		DECEMBER	
1	09 54	23 08	12 16	22 02	14 57	21 53	15 26	23 03	14 56	01 02	13 46	02 57
2	11 02	23 19	13 29	22 20	16 01	22 50	15 56	** **	15 11	02 28	14 04	04 24
3	12 10	23 30	14 45	22 43	16 52	** **	16 19	00 30	15 26	03 55	14 28	05 54
4	13 20	23 43	16 02	23 17	17 29	00 05	16 36	02 00	15 43	05 24	15 02	07 22
5	14 32	23 58	17 14	** **	17 56	01 31	16 52	03 30	16 04	06 55	15 48	08 43
6	15 48	** **	18 14	00 06	18 16	03 03	17 07	04 59	16 32	08 26	16 50	09 48
7	17 07	00 18	19 00	01 13	18 33	04 35	17 23	06 29	17 11	09 53	18 02	10 37
8	18 24	00 46	19 32	02 36	18 48	06 06	17 41	08 01	18 04	11 07	19 20	11 10
9	19 32	01 27	19 55	04 07	19 03	07 36	18 05	09 32	19 11	12 04	20 36	11 34
10	20 26	02 25	20 14	05 40	19 20	09 05	18 37	11 01	20 25	12 44	21 50	11 51
11	21 05	03 41	20 29	07 10	19 40	10 35	19 22	12 21	21 41	13 12	23 00	12 05
12	21 32	05 08	20 44	08 38	20 06	12 03	20 20	13 25	22 55	13 32	** **	12 17
13	21 53	06 39	20 59	10 05	20 42	13 25	21 28	14 12	** **	13 47	00 08	12 28
14	22 09	08 08	21 16	11 31	21 30	14 37	22 42	14 46	00 06	13 59	01 16	12 39
15	22 23	09 35	21 37	12 57	22 31	15 33	23 56	15 09	01 15	14 11	02 25	12 51
16	22 38	10 59	22 06	14 20	23 41	16 13	** **	15 27	02 22	14 21	03 35	13 06
17	22 53	12 22	22 45	15 38	** **	16 42	01 09	15 40	03 30	14 33	04 49	13 25
18	23 11	13 46	23 36	16 43	00 55	17 03	02 18	15 52	04 40	14 46	06 04	13 51
19	23 34	15 10	** **	17 34	02 08	17 19	03 27	16 03	05 52	15 02	07 18	14 28
20	** **	16 31	00 40	18 10	03 19	17 32	04 34	16 14	07 07	15 23	08 25	15 19
21	00 05	17 45	01 51	18 37	04 29	17 43	05 43	16 25	08 22	15 52	09 20	16 26
22	00 47	18 47	03 05	18 56	05 37	17 54	06 53	16 39	09 34	16 33	10 00	17 45
23	01 43	19 33	04 19	19 11	06 44	18 05	08 06	16 56	10 36	17 29	10 29	19 10
24	02 50	20 07	05 29	19 23	07 53	18 17	09 21	17 19	11 24	18 39	10 51	20 35
25	04 04	20 31	06 38	19 34	09 04	18 31	10 35	17 51	12 00	19 59	11 08	21 59
26	05 18	20 49	07 46	19 45	10 17	18 49	11 43	18 35	12 26	21 23	11 23	23 21
27	06 31	21 03	08 54	19 59	11 32	19 14	12 41	19 35	12 45	22 46	11 37	** **
28	07 41	21 15	10 03	20 09	12 45	19 49	13 25	20 48	13 02	** **	11 51	00 43
29	08 49	21 26	11 15	20 24	13 51	20 39	13 58	22 10	13 16	00 10	12 08	02 07
30	09 57	21 37	12 29	20 44	14 45	21 44	14 22	23 36	13 30	01 33	12 29	03 33
31	11 05	21 49	13 44	21 13			14 40	** **			12 58	04 59

55°N 00°E/W. Times are UT - for DST add 1 hour in non-shaded areas

2006 Sunrise and Sunset Time

The times are based on **LAT 55°00'N   LONG 0°** - add 4 min for every degree West and subtract 4 min for every degree East

	JANUARY Rise h m	JANUARY Set h m	FEBRUARY Rise h m	FEBRUARY Set h m	MARCH Rise h m	MARCH Set h m	APRIL Rise h m	APRIL Set h m	MAY Rise h m	MAY Set h m	JUNE Rise h m	JUNE Set h m
1	08 25	15 42	07 51	16 37	06 50	17 35	05 32	18 37	04 20	19 35	03 29	20 28
2	08 25	15 44	07 49	16 39	06 48	17 37	05 30	18 39	04 18	19 37	03 28	20 29
3	08 24	15 45	07 47	16 41	06 46	17 39	05 27	18 41	04 16	19 39	03 27	20 30
4	08 24	15 46	07 46	16 43	06 43	17 41	05 25	18 43	04 14	19 41	03 26	20 31
5	08 24	15 47	07 44	16 45	06 41	17 43	05 22	18 44	04 12	19 43	03 25	20 32
6	08 23	15 49	07 42	16 47	06 38	17 45	05 20	18 46	04 10	19 45	03 24	20 33
7	08 23	15 50	07 40	16 49	06 36	17 47	05 17	18 48	04 08	19 46	03 24	20 34
8	08 22	15 52	07 38	16 51	06 33	17 49	05 15	18 50	04 06	19 48	03 23	20 35
9	08 21	15 53	07 36	16 54	06 31	17 51	05 12	18 52	04 04	19 50	03 23	20 36
10	08 21	15 55	07 34	16 56	06 28	17 53	05 10	18 54	04 02	19 52	03 22	20 37
11	08 20	15 57	07 32	16 58	06 26	17 55	05 07	18 56	04 00	19 54	03 22	20 38
12	08 19	15 58	07 29	17 00	06 23	17 57	05 05	18 58	03 58	19 56	03 21	20 39
13	08 18	16 00	07 27	17 02	06 21	17 59	05 02	19 00	03 56	19 58	03 21	20 40
14	08 17	16 02	07 25	17 04	06 18	18 01	05 00	19 02	03 54	19 59	03 21	20 40
15	08 16	16 03	07 23	17 06	06 16	18 03	04 57	19 04	03 53	20 01	03 20	20 41
16	08 15	16 05	07 21	17 08	06 13	18 05	04 55	19 06	03 51	20 03	03 20	20 41
17	08 14	16 07	07 19	17 10	06 11	18 07	04 53	19 08	03 49	20 05	03 20	20 42
18	08 13	16 09	07 16	17 12	06 08	18 09	04 50	19 10	03 48	20 06	03 20	20 42
19	08 11	16 11	07 14	17 15	06 05	18 11	04 48	19 12	03 46	20 08	03 20	20 43
20	08 10	16 13	07 12	17 17	06 03	18 13	04 45	19 14	03 44	20 10	03 20	20 43
21	08 09	16 14	07 09	17 19	06 00	18 15	04 43	19 16	03 43	20 11	03 20	20 43
22	08 07	16 16	07 07	17 21	05 58	18 17	04 41	19 18	03 41	20 13	03 21	20 43
23	08 06	16 18	07 05	17 23	05 55	18 19	04 38	19 20	03 40	20 15	03 21	20 43
24	08 04	16 20	07 02	17 25	05 53	18 21	04 36	19 22	03 38	20 16	03 21	20 43
25	08 03	16 22	07 00	17 27	05 50	18 23	04 34	19 23	03 37	20 18	03 22	20 43
26	08 01	16 24	06 58	17 29	05 48	18 25	04 32	19 25	03 36	20 19	03 22	20 43
27	08 00	16 26	06 55	17 31	05 45	18 27	04 29	19 27	03 34	20 21	03 23	20 43
28	07 58	16 28	06 53	17 33	05 43	18 29	04 27	19 29	03 33	20 22	03 23	20 43
29	07 56	16 31			05 40	18 31	04 25	19 31	03 32	20 24	03 24	20 43
30	07 55	16 33			05 37	18 33	04 23	19 33	03 31	20 25	03 25	20 42
31	07 53	16 35			05 35	18 35			03 30	20 26		

	JULY Rise	JULY Set	AUGUST Rise	AUGUST Set	SEPTEMBER Rise	SEPTEMBER Set	OCTOBER Rise	OCTOBER Set	NOVEMBER Rise	NOVEMBER Set	DECEMBER Rise	DECEMBER Set
1	03 25	20 42	04 08	20 03	05 06	18 53	06 02	17 36	07 03	16 23	08 01	15 37
2	03 26	20 41	04 10	20 01	05 08	18 51	06 04	17 34	07 05	16 21	08 02	15 36
3	03 27	20 41	04 12	19 59	05 10	18 48	06 06	17 31	07 07	16 19	08 04	15 35
4	03 28	20 40	04 14	19 57	05 11	18 45	06 08	17 29	07 09	16 17	08 05	15 35
5	03 29	20 40	04 16	19 55	05 13	18 43	06 10	17 26	07 11	16 15	08 07	15 34
6	03 30	20 39	04 17	19 53	05 15	18 40	06 12	17 24	07 13	16 13	08 08	15 33
7	03 31	20 38	04 19	19 51	05 17	18 38	06 13	17 21	07 16	16 11	08 10	15 33
8	03 32	20 37	04 21	19 49	05 19	18 35	06 15	17 19	07 18	16 09	08 11	15 33
9	03 33	20 37	04 23	19 47	05 21	18 33	06 17	17 16	07 20	16 07	08 12	15 32
10	03 34	20 36	04 25	19 45	05 23	18 30	06 19	17 14	07 22	16 06	08 13	15 32
11	03 36	20 35	04 27	19 43	05 24	18 28	06 21	17 11	07 24	16 04	08 15	15 32
12	03 37	20 34	04 28	19 40	05 26	18 25	06 23	17 09	07 26	16 02	08 16	15 31
13	03 38	20 32	04 30	19 38	05 28	18 23	06 25	17 06	07 28	16 00	08 17	15 31
14	03 40	20 31	04 32	19 36	05 30	18 20	06 27	17 04	07 30	15 59	08 18	15 31
15	03 41	20 30	04 34	19 34	05 32	18 17	06 29	17 02	07 32	15 57	08 19	15 31
16	03 42	20 29	04 36	19 31	05 34	18 15	06 31	16 59	07 34	15 55	08 20	15 31
17	03 44	20 28	04 38	19 29	05 36	18 12	06 33	16 57	07 36	15 54	08 20	15 32
18	03 45	20 26	04 40	19 27	05 37	18 10	06 35	16 54	07 37	15 52	08 21	15 32
19	03 47	20 25	04 41	19 25	05 39	18 07	06 37	16 52	07 39	15 51	08 22	15 32
20	03 48	20 23	04 43	19 22	05 41	18 05	06 39	16 50	07 41	15 49	08 22	15 33
21	03 50	20 22	04 45	19 20	05 43	18 02	06 41	16 47	07 43	15 48	08 23	15 33
22	03 51	20 20	04 47	19 17	05 45	17 59	06 43	16 45	07 45	15 47	08 24	15 34
23	03 53	20 19	04 49	19 15	05 47	17 57	06 45	16 43	07 47	15 45	08 24	15 34
24	03 55	20 17	04 51	19 13	05 49	17 54	06 47	16 41	07 49	15 44	08 24	15 35
25	03 56	20 16	04 53	19 10	05 51	17 52	06 49	16 38	07 51	15 43	08 25	15 35
26	03 58	20 14	04 55	19 08	05 52	17 49	06 51	16 36	07 52	15 42	08 25	15 36
27	04 00	20 12	04 56	19 05	05 54	17 47	06 53	16 34	07 54	15 41	08 25	15 37
28	04 01	20 10	04 58	19 03	05 56	17 44	06 55	16 32	07 56	15 40	08 25	15 38
29	04 03	20 09	05 00	19 00	05 58	17 41	06 57	16 29	07 57	15 39	08 25	15 39
30	04 05	20 07	05 02	18 58	06 00	17 39	06 59	16 27	07 59	15 38	08 25	15 40
31	04 07	20 05	05 04	18 55			07 01	16 25			08 25	15 41

55°N 00°E/W. Times are UT - for DST add 1 hour in non-shaded areas

2006 Moonrise and Moonset Time

The times are based on **LAT 55°00'N LONG 0°** - add 4 min for every degree West and subtract 4 min for every degree East

	JANUARY Rise h m	Set h m	FEBRUARY Rise h m	Set h m	MARCH Rise h m	Set h m	APRIL Rise h m	Set h m	MAY Rise h m	Set h m	JUNE Rise h m	Set h m
1	10 13	17 02	09 12	21 03	07 27	20 01	06 13	23 47	05 39	00 06	08 12	00 31
2	10 34	18 44	09 20	22 35	07 35	21 37	06 32	** **	06 37	01 07	09 32	00 43
3	10 47	20 23	09 28	** **	07 43	23 11	07 03	01 14	07 51	01 46	10 49	00 51
4	10 57	21 56	09 37	00 06	07 54	** **	07 49	02 26	09 11	02 11	12 04	00 58
5	11 05	23 27	09 48	01 37	08 09	00 45	08 54	03 16	10 32	02 26	13 18	01 04
6	11 12	** **	10 06	03 06	08 32	02 15	10 10	03 47	11 50	02 36	14 33	01 09
7	11 20	00 55	10 32	04 30	09 07	03 34	11 30	04 06	13 06	02 44	15 51	01 15
8	11 29	02 22	11 12	05 42	10 00	04 35	12 49	04 19	14 21	02 50	17 13	01 23
9	11 43	03 51	12 09	06 36	11 08	05 16	14 07	04 28	15 35	02 55	18 40	01 33
10	12 02	05 18	13 21	07 12	12 26	05 42	15 22	04 34	16 52	03 01	20 08	01 49
11	12 32	06 39	14 40	07 35	13 46	05 59	16 37	04 40	18 12	03 07	21 28	02 14
12	13 17	07 47	15 59	07 50	15 04	06 10	17 52	04 45	19 37	03 15	22 30	02 56
13	14 20	08 36	17 17	08 00	16 21	06 18	19 10	04 51	21 04	03 27	23 09	04 02
14	15 35	09 08	18 33	08 07	17 36	06 24	20 31	04 58	22 29	03 45	23 34	05 29
15	16 54	09 28	19 47	08 13	18 50	06 29	21 56	05 07	23 43	04 15	23 49	07 05
16	18 14	09 41	21 02	08 19	20 06	06 35	23 22	05 25	** **	05 05	** **	08 42
17	19 31	09 51	22 17	08 24	21 24	06 40	** **	05 41	00 35	06 17	00 00	10 16
18	20 45	09 58	23 36	08 30	22 45	06 48	00 44	06 15	01 08	07 47	00 08	11 46
19	21 59	10 04	** **	08 38	** **	06 57	01 50	07 11	01 28	09 22	00 15	13 16
20	23 14	10 09	00 59	08 50	00 10	07 12	02 36	08 29	01 42	10 57	00 23	14 46
21	** **	10 15	02 25	09 07	01 36	07 36	03 04	10 01	01 51	12 29	00 32	16 18
22	00 31	10 22	03 51	09 36	02 54	08 16	03 22	11 38	01 59	14 00	00 44	17 51
23	01 52	10 31	05 06	10 26	03 55	09 20	03 34	13 14	02 06	15 31	01 01	19 20
24	03 19	10 45	06 01	11 42	04 35	10 46	03 43	14 49	02 14	17 04	01 28	20 37
25	04 48	11 08	06 35	13 18	05 00	12 24	03 50	16 22	02 24	18 39	02 11	21 34
26	06 14	11 46	06 56	15 02	05 15	14 04	03 58	17 57	02 38	20 13	03 13	22 11
27	07 23	12 51	07 09	16 45	05 26	15 44	04 07	19 33	02 58	21 41	04 29	22 34
28	08 08	14 20	07 19	18 25	05 35	17 21	04 18	21 10	03 31	22 52	05 51	22 49
29	08 36	16 03			05 42	18 57	04 34	22 44	04 22	23 41	07 13	22 59
30	08 52	17 47			05 50	20 34	04 59	** **	05 30	** **	08 31	23 06
31	09 04	19 27			06 00	22 11			06 50	00 12		

	JULY Rise h m	Set h m	AUGUST Rise h m	Set h m	SEPTEMBER Rise h m	Set h m	OCTOBER Rise h m	Set h m	NOVEMBER Rise h m	Set h m	DECEMBER Rise h m	Set h m
1	09 47	23 12	12 31	21 45	15 40	21 10	16 02	22 29	15 03	00 50	13 35	03 06
2	11 01	23 18	13 51	21 56	16 46	22 05	16 23	** **	15 11	02 24	13 46	04 41
3	12 15	23 23	15 16	22 11	17 32	23 25	16 37	00 05	15 19	03 59	14 01	06 19
4	13 31	23 30	16 41	22 37	18 01	** **	16 47	01 44	15 28	05 36	14 26	07 56
5	14 50	23 39	17 58	23 21	18 19	01 01	16 55	03 22	15 41	07 16	15 06	09 24
6	16 14	23 51	18 57	** **	18 31	02 43	17 03	04 59	16 00	08 56	16 07	10 31
7	17 41	** **	19 36	00 30	18 40	04 24	17 12	06 37	16 31	10 32	17 26	11 14
8	19 06	00 11	19 59	02 01	18 48	06 03	17 22	08 17	17 21	11 51	18 51	11 40
9	20 17	00 45	20 14	03 42	18 56	07 40	17 38	09 58	18 30	12 45	20 16	11 56
10	21 06	01 41	20 24	05 24	19 05	09 18	18 01	11 36	19 51	13 18	21 36	12 07
11	21 36	03 02	20 32	07 03	19 17	10 56	18 39	13 03	21 15	13 39	22 53	12 15
12	21 55	04 38	20 40	08 39	19 35	12 33	19 36	14 09	22 37	13 51	** **	12 21
13	22 07	06 18	20 48	10 13	20 02	14 04	20 50	14 52	23 55	14 00	00 07	12 27
14	22 16	07 56	20 58	11 47	20 46	15 21	22 12	15 18	** **	14 07	01 20	12 32
15	22 24	09 30	21 11	13 21	21 49	16 16	23 33	15 34	01 09	14 13	02 35	12 39
16	22 31	11 02	21 31	14 54	23 05	16 50	** **	15 44	02 23	14 18	03 52	12 47
17	22 40	12 33	22 03	16 18	** **	17 12	00 53	15 52	03 37	14 24	05 13	12 59
18	22 50	14 04	22 52	17 27	00 26	17 25	02 09	15 58	04 53	14 31	06 37	13 18
19	23 06	15 36	23 59	18 15	01 47	17 35	03 23	16 03	06 12	14 40	07 58	13 47
20	23 29	17 06	** **	18 45	03 06	17 42	04 37	16 08	07 34	14 54	09 09	14 35
21	** **	18 27	01 18	19 04	04 21	17 47	05 51	16 14	08 58	15 16	10 01	15 45
22	00 05	19 30	02 40	19 16	05 35	17 52	07 08	16 22	10 16	15 51	10 34	17 12
23	01 00	20 12	04 00	19 24	06 49	17 58	08 28	16 32	11 19	16 45	10 55	18 46
24	02 12	20 39	05 18	19 31	08 04	18 04	09 51	16 47	12 04	18 00	11 09	20 19
25	03 33	20 56	06 33	19 36	09 21	18 12	11 13	17 12	12 32	19 28	11 19	21 51
26	04 55	21 07	07 47	19 42	10 42	18 23	12 27	17 51	12 49	21 01	11 27	23 20
27	06 15	21 15	09 01	19 47	12 05	18 40	13 24	18 51	13 02	22 33	11 34	** **
28	07 32	21 21	10 16	19 54	13 25	19 08	14 03	20 11	13 11	** **	11 42	00 50
29	08 46	21 26	11 35	20 03	14 36	19 54	14 27	21 42	13 18	00 03	11 52	02 21
30	10 00	21 32	12 56	20 15	15 28	21 02	14 43	23 16	13 26	01 34	12 05	03 55
31	11 14	21 38	14 20	20 36			14 54	** **			12 25	05 31

SPEED, TIME AND DISTANCE (NAUTICAL MILES)

Speed in knots

Time in minutes	1	2	3	4	5	6	7	8	9	10	15	20
1	0·0	0·0	0·1	0·1	0·1	0·1	0·1	0·1	0·2	0·2	0·3	0·3
2	0·0	0·1	0·1	0·1	0·2	0·2	0·2	0·3	0·3	0·3	0·5	0·7
3	0·1	0·1	0·2	0·2	0·3	0·3	0·4	0·4	0·5	0·5	0·8	1·0
4	0·1	0·1	0·2	0·3	0·3	0·4	0·5	0·5	0·6	0·7	1·0	1·3
5	0·1	0·2	0·3	0·3	0·4	0·5	0·6	0·7	0·8	0·8	1·3	1·7
6	0·1	0·2	0·3	0·4	0·5	0·6	0·7	0·8	0·9	1·0	1·5	2·0
7	0·1	0·2	0·4	0·5	0·6	0·7	0·8	0·9	1·1	1·2	1·8	2·3
8	0·1	0·3	0·4	0·5	0·7	0·8	0·9	1·1	1·2	1·3	2·0	2·7
9	0·2	0·3	0·5	0·6	0·8	0·9	1·1	1·2	1·4	1·5	2·3	3·0
10	0·2	0·3	0·5	0·7	0·8	1·0	1·2	1·3	1·5	1·7	2·5	3·3
11	0·2	0·4	0·6	0·7	0·9	1·1	1·3	1·5	1·7	1·8	2·8	3·7
12	0·2	0·4	0·6	0·8	1·0	1·2	1·4	1·6	1·8	2·0	3·0	4·0
13	0·2	0·4	0·7	0·9	1·1	1·3	1·5	1·7	2·0	2·2	3·3	4·3
14	0·2	0·5	0·7	0·9	1·2	1·4	1·6	1·9	2·1	2·3	3·5	4·7
15	0·3	0·5	0·8	1·0	1·3	1·5	1·8	2·0	2·3	2·5	3·8	5·0
16	0·3	0·5	0·8	1·1	1·3	1·6	1·9	2·1	2·4	2·7	4·0	5·3
17	0·3	0·6	0·9	1·1	1·4	1·7	2·0	2·3	2·6	2·8	4·3	5·7
18	0·3	0·6	0·9	1·2	1·5	1·8	2·1	2·4	2·7	3·0	4·5	6·0
19	0·3	0·6	1·0	1·3	1·6	1·9	2·2	2·5	2·9	3·2	4·8	6·3
20	0·3	0·7	1·0	1·3	1·7	2·0	2·3	2·7	3·0	3·3	5·0	6·7
21	0·4	0·7	1·1	1·4	1·8	2·1	2·5	2·8	3·2	3·5	5·3	7·0
22	0·4	0·7	1·1	1·5	1·8	2·2	2·6	2·9	3·3	3·7	5·5	7·3
23	0·4	0·8	1·2	1·5	1·9	2·3	2·7	3·1	3·5	3·8	5·8	7·7
24	0·4	0·8	1·2	1·6	2·0	2·4	2·8	3·2	3·6	4·0	6·0	8·0
25	0·4	0·8	1·3	1·7	2·1	2·5	2·9	3·3	3·8	4·2	6·3	8·3
30	0·5	1·0	1·5	2·0	2·5	3·0	3·5	4·0	4·5	5·0	7·5	10·0
35	0·6	1·2	1·8	2·3	2·9	3·5	4·1	4·7	5·3	5·8	8·8	11·7
40	0·7	1·3	2·0	2·7	3·3	4·0	4·7	5·3	6·0	6·7	10·0	13·3
45	0·8	1·5	2·3	3·0	3·8	4·5	5·3	6·0	6·8	7·5	11·3	15·0
50	0·8	1·7	2·5	3·3	4·2	5·0	5·8	6·7	7·5	8·3	12·5	16·7

DISTANCE (NAUTICAL MILES) OFF RISING/DIPPING LIGHTS

Height of eye in feet

Height of light in metres	2	3	4	5	6	7	8	9	10	20	30	40	50
2	4·6	4·9	5·2	5·5	5·7	6·0	6·2	6·4	6·6	8·1	9·2	10·2	11·0
3	5·2	5·6	5·9	6·2	6·4	6·6	6·8	7·0	7·2	8·7	9·9	10·8	11·7
4	5·8	6·1	6·4	6·7	6·9	7·2	7·4	7·6	7·8	9·3	10·4	11·4	12·2
5	6·3	6·6	6·9	7·2	7·4	7·7	7·9	8·1	8·3	9·8	10·9	11·9	12·7
6	6·7	7·1	7·4	7·6	7·9	8·1	8·3	8·5	8·7	10·2	11·3	12·3	13·2
7	7·1	7·5	7·8	8·0	8·3	8·5	8·7	8·9	9·1	10·6	11·8	12·7	13·6
8	7·5	7·8	8·2	8·4	8·7	8·9	9·1	9·3	9·5	11·0	12·1	13·1	14·0
9	7·8	8·2	8·5	8·8	9·0	9·2	9·5	9·7	9·8	11·3	12·5	13·5	14·3
10	8·2	8·5	8·8	9·1	9·4	9·6	9·8	10·0	10·2	11·7	12·8	13·8	14·6
11	8·5	8·9	9·2	9·4	9·7	9·9	10·1	10·3	10·5	12·0	13·1	14·1	15·0
12	8·8	9·2	9·5	9·7	10·0	10·2	10·4	10·6	10·8	12·3	13·4	14·4	15·3
13	9·1	9·5	9·8	10·0	10·3	10·5	10·7	10·9	11·1	12·6	13·7	14·7	15·6
14	9·4	9·7	10·0	10·3	10·6	10·8	11·0	11·2	11·4	12·9	14·0	15·0	15·8
15	9·6	10·0	10·3	10·6	10·8	11·1	11·3	11·5	11·6	13·1	14·3	15·3	16·1
16	9·9	10·3	10·6	10·8	11·1	11·3	11·5	11·7	11·9	13·4	14·6	15·5	16·4
17	10·2	10·5	10·8	11·1	11·3	11·6	11·8	12·0	12·2	13·7	14·8	15·8	16·6
18	10·4	10·8	11·1	11·4	11·6	11·8	12·0	12·2	12·4	13·9	15·1	16·0	16·9
19	10·7	11·0	11·3	11·6	11·8	12·1	12·3	12·5	12·7	14·2	15·3	16·3	17·1
20	10·9	11·3	11·6	11·8	12·1	12·3	12·5	12·7	12·9	14·4	15·5	16·5	17·3
25	12·0	12·3	12·6	12·9	13·2	13·4	13·6	13·8	14·0	15·5	16·6	17·6	18·4
30	13·0	13·3	13·6	13·9	14·1	14·4	14·6	14·8	15·0	16·5	17·6	18·6	19·4
40	14·7	15·1	15·4	15·7	15·9	16·1	16·3	16·5	16·7	18·2	19·4	20·3	21·2
50	16·3	16·6	16·9	17·2	17·4	17·7	17·9	18·1	18·3	19·8	20·9	21·9	22·7
60	17·7	18·0	18·3	18·6	18·8	19·1	19·3	19·5	19·7	21·2	22·3	23·3	24·1

CONVERSION TABLE

Sq inches to sq millimetres *multiply by* **645.20**	**Sq millimetres to sq inches** *multiply by* **0.0016**
Inches to millimetres *multiply by* **25.40**	**Millimetres to inches** *multiply by* **0.0394**
Sq feet to square metres *multiply by* **0.093**	**Sq metres to sq feet** *multiply by* **10.7640**
Inches to centimetres *multiply by* **2.54**	**Centimetres to inches** *multiply by* **0.3937**
Feet to metres *multiply by* **0.305**	**Metres to feet** *multiply by* **3.2810**
Nautical miles to kilometres *multiply by* **1.852**	**Kilometres to nautical miles** *multiply by* **0.5400**
Statute miles to kilometres *multiply by* **1.609**	**Kilometres to statute miles** *multiply by* **0.6214**
Statute miles to nautical miles *multiply by* **0.8684**	**Nautical miles to statute miles** *multiply by* **1.1515**
HP to metric HP *multiply by* **1.014**	**Metric HP to HP** *multiply by* **0.9862**
Pounds per sq inch to **kg per sq centimetre** *multiply by* **0.0703**	**Kg per sq centimetre** **to pounds per sq inch** *multiply by* **14.2200**
HP to kilowatts *multiply by* **0.746**	**Kilowatts to HP** *multiply by* **1.341**
Cu inches to cu centimetres *multiply by* **16.39**	**Cu centimetres to cu inches** *multiply by* **0.0610**
Imperial gallons to litres *multiply by* **4.540**	**Litres to imperial gallons** *multiply by* **0.2200**
Pints to litres *multiply by* **0.5680**	**Litres to pints** *multiply by* **1.7600**
Pounds to kilogrammes *multiply by* **0.4536**	**Kilogrammes to pounds** *multiply by* **2.2050**

LIGHT CHARACTERISTICS

CLASS OF LIGHT	International abbreviations	National abbreviations	Illustration Period shown ├────┤
FIXED	F		
OCCULTING *(total duration of light longer than dark)*			
Single-occulting		Oc	Occ
Group-occulting	eg	Oc(2)	Gp Occ(2)
Composite group-occulting	eg	Oc(2+3)	Gp Occ(2+3)
ISOPHASE *(light and dark equal)*		Iso	
FLASHING *(total duration of light shorter than dark)*			
Single-flashing		Fl	
Long-flashing *(flash 2s or longer)*			L Fl
Group-flashing	eg	Fl(3)	Gp Fl(3)
Composite group-flashing	eg	Fl(2+1)	Gp Fl(2+1)
QUICK *(50 to 79, usually either 50 or 60, flashes per min.)*			
Continuous quick		Q	Qk Fl
Group quick	eg	Q(3)	Qk Fl(3)
Interrupted quick		IQ	Int Qk Fl
VERY QUICK *(80 to 159, usually either 100 or 120, flashes per min.)*			
Continuous very quick		VQ	V Qk Fl
Group very quick	eg	VQ(3)	V Qk Fl(3)
Interrupted very quick		IVQ	Int V Qk Fl
ULTRA QUICK *(160 or more, usually 240 to 300, flashes per min.)*			
Continuous ultra quick		UQ	
Interrupted ultra quick		IUQ	
MORSE CODE	eg	Mo(K)	
FIXED AND FLASHING		F Fl	
ALTERNATING	eg	Al. WR	Alt. WR

COLOUR	International abbreviations	NOMINAL RANGE in miles	International abbreviations
White	W *(may be omitted)*	Light with single range	eg 15M
Red	R	Light with two different ranges	eg 15/10M
Green	G	Light with three or more ranges	eg 15-7M
Blue	Bu		
Violet	Vi	**PERIOD** is given in seconds	eg 90s
Yellow	Y	**DISPOSITION** horizontally disposed	(hor)
Orange	Y		
Amber	Y	**ELEVATION** is given in metres (m) or feet (ft) above MHWS	

CHAPTER 2 - WEATHER

CONTENTS

Beaufort scale

Force	Wind speed (knots)	(km/h)	(m/sec)	Description	State of sea	Probable wave ht(m)
0	0–1	0–2	0–0·5	Calm	Like a mirror	0
1	1–3	2–6	0·5–1·5	Light airs	Ripples like scales are formed	0
2	4–6	7–11	2–3	Light breeze	Small wavelets, still short but more pronounced, not breaking	0·1
3	7–10	13–19	4–5	Gentle breeze	Large wavelets, crests begin to break; a few white horses	0·4
4	11–16	20–30	6–8	Moderate breeze	Small waves growing longer; fairly frequent white horses	1
5	17–21	31–39	8–11	Fresh breeze	Moderate waves, taking more pronounced form; many white horses, perhaps some spray	2
6	22–27	41–50	11–14	Strong breeze	Large waves forming; white foam crests more extensive; probably some spray	3
7	28–33	52–61	14–17	Near gale	Sea heaps up; white foam from breaking waves begins to blow in streaks	4
8	34–40	63–74	17–21	Gale	Moderately high waves of greater length; edge of crests break into spindrift; foam blown in well-marked streaks	5·5

Terminology used in forecasts
Pressure systems' speed of movement

Slowly	< 15 knots
Steadily	15–25 knots
Rather quickly	25–35 knots
Rapidly	35–45 knots
Very rapidly	> 45 knots

Visibility

Good	> 5 miles
Moderate	2–5 miles
Poor	1000 metres–2 miles
Fog	< 1000 metres

Barometric pressure tendency

Rising/falling slowly: Change of 0·1 to 1·5 hPa/mb in the preceding 3 hours.
Rising/falling: Change of 1·6 to 3·5 hPa/mb in the preceding 3 hours.
Rising/falling quickly: Change of 3·6 to 6 hPa/mb in the preceding 3 hours.
Rising/falling very rapidly: Change of > 6 hPa/mb in the preceding 3 hours.
Now rising/falling: Pressure has been falling (rising) or steady in the preceding 3 hours, but was definitely rising (falling) at the time of observation.

Gale warnings
A *Gale* warning means that winds of at least F8 (34-40kn) or gusts up to 43-51kn are expected somewhere within the area, but not necessarily over the whole area

Severe Gale means winds of at least F9 (41-47kn) or gusts reaching 52-60kn

Storm means winds of F10 (48-55kn) or gusts of 61-68kn

Violent Storm means winds of F11 (56-63kn) or gusts of 69+ kn

Hurricane Force means winds of F12 (64+ kn)

Gale warnings remain in force until amended or cancelled. If a gale persists for >24 hours the warning is re-issued.

Timing of gale warnings from time of issue

Imminent	<6 hrs
Soon	6–12 hrs
Later	>12 hrs

Strong wind warnings
Issued, if possible 6 hrs in advance, when winds F6 or more are expected up to 5M offshore; valid for 12 hrs.

MAP OF UK SHIPPING FORECAST AREAS

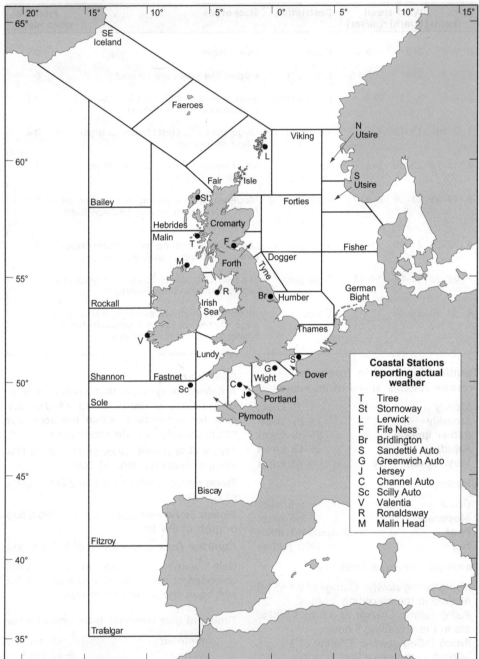

Coastal Stations reporting actual weather

T	Tiree
St	Stornoway
L	Lerwick
F	Fife Ness
Br	Bridlington
S	Sandettié Auto
G	Greenwich Auto
J	Jersey
C	Channel Auto
Sc	Scilly Auto
V	Valentia
R	Ronaldsway
M	Malin Head

SHIPPING FORECAST RECORD Time/Day/Date ....

GENERAL SYNOPSIS

at .... UT/BST

	System position	Present position at	Movement	Forecast	

Gales	SEA AREA FORECAST	Wind (At first)	(Later)	Weather	Visibility
	VIKING				
	NORTH UTSIRE				
	SOUTH UTSIRE				
	FORTIES				
	CROMARTY				
	FORTH				
	TYNE				
	DOGGER				
	FISHER				
	GERMAN BIGHT				
	HUMBER				
	THAMES				
	DOVER				
	WIGHT				
	PORTLAND				
	PLYMOUTH				
	BISCAY				
	FITZROY				
	TRAFALGAR				
	SOLE				
	LUNDY				
	FASTNET				
	IRISH SEA				
	SHANNON				
	ROCKALL				
	MALIN				
	HEBRIDES				
	BAILEY				
	FAIR ISLE				
	FAEROES				
	S E ICELAND				

COASTAL REPORTS BST at .... UTC	Wind Direction	Force	Weather	Visibility	Pressure	Change	COASTAL REPORTS	Wind Direction	Force	Weather	Visibility	Pressure	Change
Tiree (T)							Greenwich Lt V (G)						
Stornoway (St)							Jersey (J)						
Lerwick (L)							Channel auto (C)						
Fife Ness (F)							Scilly auto (Sc)						
Bridlington (Br)							Valentia (V)						
Sandettie auto (S)							Ronaldsway (R)						

SOURCES OF WEATHER INFORMATION IN THE UK

BBC Radio 4 Shipping forecasts
are broadcast at:

0048 LT[1]	LW, MW, FM
0536 LT[1]	LW, MW, FM
1201 LT	LW only
1754 LT	LW, FM (Sat/Sun)

[1] Includes weather reports from coastal stations

Frequencies

LW		198 kHz
MW	Tyneside	603 kHz
	London & N Ireland	720 kHz
	Redruth	756 kHz
	Plymouth & Enniskillen	774 kHz
	Aberdeen	1449 kHz
	Carlisle	1485 kHz
FM	England	92·4–94·6 MHz
	Scotland	91·3–96·1 MHz
		103·5–104·9 MHz
	Wales	92·8–96·1 MHz
		103·5–104·9 MHz
	N Ireland	93·2–96·0 MHz
		103·5–104·6 MHz
	Channel Islands	94·8 MHz

The Shipping forecast contains:

A summary of gale warnings in force at time of issue; a general synopsis of weather systems and their expected development over the next 24 hours; and a forecast of wind direction/force, weather and visibility in each sea area for the next 24 hours.

Gale warnings are also broadcast at the earliest juncture in Radio 4 programmes after receipt, as well as after the next news bulletin. Sea area **Trafalgar** is only included in the 0048 forecast.

Shipping forecasts cover large sea areas, and rarely include the detailed variations that may occur near land. The Inshore waters forecast can be more helpful to mariners on coastal passages.

Weather reports from coastal stations follow the 0048 and 0536 forecasts. They include wind direction and force, present weather, visibility, and sea-level pressure and tendency, if available. The stations are shown overleaf on the previous page.

BBC Radio 4 Inshore waters forecast

A forecast for inshore waters (up to 12M offshore) around the UK and N Ireland, valid until 1800, is broadcast after the 0048 and 0536 coastal station reports. It includes a general synopsis, forecasts of wind direction and force, visibility and weather for stretches of inshore waters. These are defined by well-known places and headlands from Cape Wrath clockwise via Orkney, Shetland, Duncansby Head, Berwick-upon-Tweed, Whitby, North Foreland, St Catherine's Point, Land's End, Colwyn Bay, Mull of Kintyre and Lough Foyle to Carlingford Lough, ie Northern Ireland.

Strong wind warnings are issued by the Met Office whenever winds of Force 6 or more are expected over coastal waters up to 5M offshore.

Reports of actual weather at the stations below are broadcast only after the 0048 Inshore waters forecast: Boulmer, *Bridlington*, Sheerness, St Catherine's Pt*, *Scilly**, Milford Haven, Aberporth, Valley, Liverpool (Crosby), *Ronaldsway*, Larne, Machrihanish*, Greenock, *Stornoway*, *Lerwick*, Wick*, Aberdeen and Leuchars. Asterisk* denotes an automatic station. Stations in italics also feature in the 0048 and 0536 shipping forecasts.

BBC general (land) forecasts

Land area forecasts may include an outlook period up to 48 hours beyond the shipping forecast, plus more details of frontal systems and weather along the coasts. The most comprehensive land area forecasts are broadcast by BBC Radio 4 on the frequencies above.

Land area forecasts – Wind strength

Wind descriptions used in land forecasts, with their Beaufort scale equivalents, are:

Calm	0	Fresh	5
Light	1–3	Strong	6–7
Moderate	4	Gale	8

Land area forecasts – Visibility

The following visibility definitions are used in land forecasts:

Mist	2000m–1000m
Fog	<1000m
Dense fog	< 50m

NAVTEX

Navtex uses a dedicated aerial, receiver and integral printer or LCD screen. The user programmes the receiver for the required station(s) and message categories. It automatically prints or displays MSI, ie weather, navigational and safety data.

Two frequencies are used: 518 kHz and *490 kHz*. 518 kHz messages are in English (occasionally in the national language as well), with excellent coverage of Europe. Interference between stations is avoided by time sharing and by limiting the range of transmitters to about 300M; see Fig. 5(4). Navtex information applies only to the geographic area for which each station is responsible.

490 kHz (for clarity shown in italics throughout this chapter) is used abroad for transmissions in the national language. In the UK it is used for inshore waters forecasts in English. Identification letters for 490 kHz stations differ from 518 kHz stations.

Weather information accounts for about 75% of all messages and Navtex is particularly valuable when out of range of other sources, otherwise occupied or if there is a language problem.

Messages

Each message is prefixed by a four-character group:

The first character is the code letter of the transmitting station (eg **E** for Niton).

The second character is the message category, see below.

The third and fourth are message serial numbers, running from 01 to 99 and then re-starting at 01.

The serial number 00 denotes urgent messages which are always printed.

Messages which are corrupt or have already been printed are rejected.

Weather messages, and certain other message types, are dated and timed.

Message categories

A*	Navigational warnings
B*	Meteorological warnings
C	Ice reports
D*	SAR info and piracy warnings
E	Weather forecasts
F	Pilot service
H	Loran-C
J	Satellite navigation
K	Other electronic navaids
L	Subfacts and Gunfacts (UK)
V	Amplifies Navwarnings initially sent under A; plus weekly oil/gas rig moves.
W-Y	Special service, trials
Z	No messages on hand at scheduled time

Missing category letters are unallocated.

*The receiver cannot reject these categories.

Navtex stations/areas – UK & W Europe

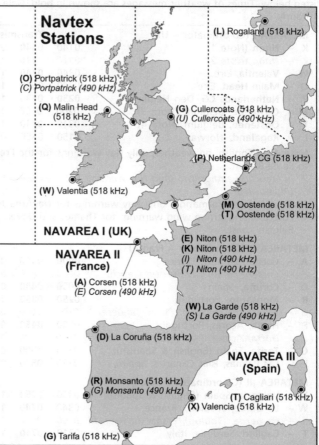

Navtex Stations

(L) Rogaland (518 kHz)

(O) Portpatrick (518 kHz)
(C) Portpatrick (490 kHz)

(Q) Malin Head (518 kHz)

(G) Cullercoats (518 kHz)
(U) Cullercoats (490 kHz)

(P) Netherlands CG (518 kHz)

(W) Valentia (518 kHz)

(M) Oostende (518 kHz)
(T) Oostende (518 kHz)

NAVAREA I (UK)

(E) Niton (518 kHz)
(K) Niton (518 kHz)
(I) Niton (490 kHz)
(T) Niton (490 kHz)

NAVAREA II (France)

(A) Corsen (518 kHz)
(E) Corsen (490 kHz)

(W) La Garde (518 kHz)
(S) La Garde (490 kHz)

(D) La Coruña (518 kHz)

NAVAREA III (Spain)

(R) Monsanto (518 kHz)
(G) Monsanto (490 kHz)

(T) Cagliari (518 kHz)
(X) Valencia (518 kHz)

(G) Tarifa (518 kHz)

WEATHER

UK 518 kHz stations

The times (UT) of weather messages are in bold; the times of an extended outlook (a further 2 or 3 days beyond the shipping forecast period) are in italics. The Sea Areas covered follow the sequence on page 70.

G –	**Cullercoats** Fair Isle clockwise to Thames, excluding N & S Utsire, Fisher and German Bight.	*0100*	0500	**0900**	1300	1700	**2100**	
O –	**Portpatrick** Lundy clockwise to SE Iceland.	0220	**0620**	1020	1420	**1820**	2220	
E –	**Niton** Thames clockwise to Fastnet, excluding Trafalgar.	*0040*	0440	**0840**	1240	1640	**2040**	

UK 490 kHz stations

These provide forecasts for the Inshore waters (12M offshore) of the UK, including Shetland, plus a national 3 day outlook for inshore waters. Times are UT.

U –	*Cullercoats*	*Cape Wrath to North Foreland*	*0720*	*1920*	
C –	*Portpatrick*	*St David's Head to Cape Wrath*	*0820*	*2020*	
I –	*Niton*	*The Wash to Colwyn Bay*	*0520*	*1720*	

Navtex coverage abroad

Selected Navtex stations in Metareas I to III, with their identity codes and transmission times, are listed below. Times of weather messages are shown in **bold**. Gale warnings are usually transmitted 4 hourly.

METAREA I (Co-ordinator – UK)	Transmission times (UT)					
K – **Niton** (Note 1)	0140	0540	0940	1340	1740	2140
T – Niton (Note 2)	*0310*	*0710*	*1110*	*1510*	*1910*	*2310*
W – **Valentia**, Eire	0340	**0740**	**1140**	1540	**1940**	2340
Q – **Malin Head**, Eire	0240	**0640**	**1040**	1440	**1840**	2240
P – **Netherlands CG**, Den Helder	**0230**	0630	1030	**1430**	1830	2230
M – **Oostende**, Belgium (Note 3)	**0200**	0600	1000	1400	1800	2200
T – **Oostende**, Belgium (Note 4)	**0310**	**0710**	1110	1510	**1910**	2310
L – **Rogaland**, Norway	**0150**	0550	0950	**1350**	1750	2150

Note 1 In English, no weather; only Nav warnings for the French coast from Cap Gris Nez to Île de Bréhat.
2 In French, weather info (and Nav warnings) for sea areas Humber to Ouessant (Plymouth).
3 No weather information, only Nav warnings for NavArea Juliett.
4 Forecasts and strong wind warnings for Thames and Dover, plus Nav info for the Belgian coast.

METAREA II (Co-ordinator – France)						
A – **Corsen**, Le Stiff, France	0000	0400	0800	**1200**	1600	2000
E – Corsen, Le Stiff, France (In French)	*0040*	*0440*	*0840*	*1240*	*1640*	*2040*
D – **Coruña**, Spain	0030	0430	**0830**	1230	1630	**2030**
R – **Monsanto**, Portugal	0250	0650	1050	1450	1850	2250
G – Monsanto, Portugal (In Portuguese)	*0100*	*0500*	*0900*	*1300*	*1700*	*2100*
F – **Horta**, Açores, Portugal	0050	0450	0850	**1250**	**1650**	2050
J – Horta, Açores, (In Portuguese)	*0130*	*0530*	*0930*	*1330*	*1730*	*2130*
G – **Tarifa**, Spain (English & Spanish)	0100	0500	0900	1300	1700	2100
I – **Las Palmas**, Islas Canarias, Spain	0120	0520	0920	**1320**	**1720**	2120

METAREA III (Co-ordinator – Spain)						
X – **Valencia**, Spain (English & Spanish)	0350	**0750**	1150	1550	**1950**	2350
W – **La Garde**, (Toulon), France	0340	0740	**1140**	1540	1940	**2340**
S – La Garde, (Toulon), France (In French)	*0300*	*0700*	*1100*	*1500*	*1900*	*2300*
T – **Cagliari**, Sardinia, Italy	0310	**0710**	1110	1510	**1910**	2310

WEATHER BY TELEPHONE

Marinecall offers 3 types of recorded forecasts as shown below. You can use Marinecall from any landline or mobile network within the UK (inc Channel Islands).

Actual weather
Current weather, updated hourly, gives hourly summaries for next 6 hours at over 160 locations around the UK. Dial **09068 969** + the required area number below.

5-day forecasts for Inshore waters
For UK inshore areas, call **09068 969** + the **Area number** shown below. For an inshore waters forecast covering the whole UK for 3 to 5 days ahead, dial **09068 969** 640.

Forecasts cover the waters out to 12M offshore for up to 5 days and include: General situation, strong wind or gale warnings in force, wind, weather, visibility, sea state, max air temp and mean sea temp. The local inshore forecast for Shetland is only available from Shetland CG on ☎ 01595 692976.

09068 calls cost 60p/min from a landline.

Offshore planning forecasts
For 2 to 5-day planning forecasts for offshore areas, updated by 0700, call **09068 969** + the number for the offshore area:

657 English Channel. **658** S North Sea. **659** Irish Sea. **660** Biscay. **661** NW Scotland **662** Northern North Sea

For further information contact:
Marinecall Customer Services, iTouch (UK) Ltd, Avalon House, 57-63 Scrutton Street, London EC2A 4PF.
☎ 0871 200 3985; ☒ 0870 600 4229.
www.marinecall.co.uk   marinecall@itouch.co.uk

WEATHER

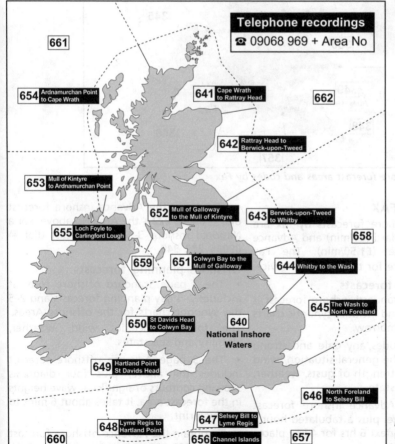

Inshore & offshore forecast areas by telephone

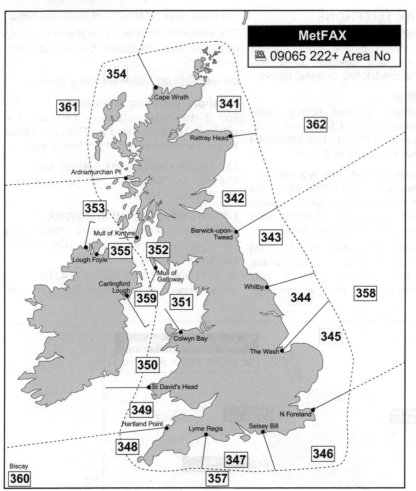

MetFAX
📠 09065 222+ Area No

Inshore and Offshore forecast areas and codes by Fax

WEATHER BY FAX

Inshore and offshore forecasts by fax are available at Standard (£1/min) and Advance levels of service (£1.50/min). The Fax numbers given are for the Advance service.

Inshore waters forecasts

• The 2 page Standard inshore forecast is for up to 48 hrs and includes synoptic charts for today and tomorrow.

The forecast includes any gale and strong wind warnings, the general situation, wind speed/direction, strength of gusts, weather, visibility and sea state.

• The 3 page Advance inshore forecast includes the above, plus a tabulated hourly forecast over the next 6 hrs for 4 key places in the Area.

• To obtain the Advance inshore forecast dial 📠 **09065 222** + the Area No above. For a National inshore 3–5 day forecast dial 📠 **09065 222 340**.

Offshore planning forecasts

• The 2 page Standard offshore forecast includes 2–5 day planning forecasts and 2–5 day synoptic charts for the offshore Areas.

The forecast includes wind, weather, visibility and sea states.

• The 3 page Advance offshore forecast includes the above, plus four diagrams showing contours of significant wave heights in the forecast area. It takes about 6 mins to receive/print.

• To obtain the Advance offshore forecast dial 📠 **09065 222** + Area Number required.

WEATHER BY MOBILE PHONE

Use your mobile to obtain forecasts by 3 different means:

- **SMS** (Short Message Service, or texting). A message includes: current weather and a forecast for 6 hrs later, at one of 161 coastal locations (below); updated hrly. Format: Location, date, time; max temp °C; mean wind direction/speed; visibility; % risk of precipitation. For example:

> Exmouth: 1/4/05
>
> 10am: 11c, WD 250d, WS 12kt, VIS 17.59km, RAIN 10%.
>
> 4pm: 12c, WD 290d, WS 14kt, VIS 13.50km, RAIN 12%.

To obtain this message, by return @ 25p per message, type **AC** and the location's name; then send it to 83141.

Or, for data received by 0900 daily @ £1.50 for 6 messages, type **AC Sub** and location's name; send it to 83141.

The message also contains an embedded Marinecall Tel No; press 'Dial' for a 2–5 day recorded forecast as in 5.8.2.

Coastal locations in Areas 1–11 (not N Ireland nor the Channel Islands) are listed alphabetically below.

Area 1, SW England

Anvil Point	Brixham
Darthaven marina	Dart marina
Exmouth	Falmouth
Fowey	Helford River
Lizard Point	Longships
Lyme Regis	Mayflower marina
Newton Ferrers, R Yealm	Penzance
Plymouth Yacht Haven	Portland Bill
Queen Anne's Battery	Salcombe
Start Point	Sutton Hbr marina
Torquay	Weymouth

Area 2, S England

Bembridge Harbour	Birdham Pool
Buckler's Hard, Beaulieu	Chichester marina
Christchurch	Cobbs Quay (Poole)
Cowes Yacht Haven	East Cowes marina
Emsworth marina	Gosport marina
Hamble Point	Haslar marina
Hythe marina	Island Hbr, R Medina
Lymington marina, Berthon	Lymington Yacht Haven
Mercury Yacht harbour	Needles Fairway buoy
Northney marina	Ocean Village marina
Poole Town Quay	Port Hamble marina
Port Solent marina	Ryde
St Catherines Point	Salterns marina
Shamrock Quay marina	Southsea marina
Sparkes Yacht harbour	Swanwick marina
(Moodys)	Town Quay
(Southampton)	Wootton Creek
Yarmouth, Isle of Wight	

Area 3, SE England

Beachy Head	Brighton
Dover	Dungeness
Littlehampton	Newhaven
North Foreland	Ramsgate
Rye	Selsey Bill
Shoreham	Sovereign Hbr,
	Eastbourne

Area 4, E England

Aldeburgh	Allington marina
Bradwell marina	Brightlingsea
Burnham Yacht Harbour	Chatham marina
Cuxton marina	Essex marina
Fox's marina	Gillingham marina
Great Yarmouth	Hoo marina
Ipswich marina	Landguard Pt (Harwich)
Lowestoft	Medway Bridge marina
Orford Ness	Port Medway
Queenborough	Shotley Point marina
Southend-on-sea	Southwold
Suffolk Yacht harbour	Tidemill Yacht harbour
Titchmarsh marina	Tollesbury
Whitstable	Woolverstone marina

Area 5, NE England

Amble	Berwick-upon-Tweed
Blyth	Boston
Bridlington	Cromer
Flamborough Head	Grimsby
Hartlepool	Holy Island
Hull	King's Lynn
Royal Quays marina, R Tyne	St Peter's marina, R Tyne
Spurn Head	Sunderland
Wells-next-the-Sea	Whitby

Area 6, SE Scotland

Aberdeen	Burntisland
Dundee	Eyemouth
Granton	Montrose
Peterhead	Port Edgar (Firth/ Forth)
Rattray Head	St Abbs Head
Stonehaven	

Area 7, NE Scotland

Duncansby Head	Lossiemouth
Whitehills	

Area 8, NW Scotland

Craobh marina	Iona
Oban	Tobermory

Area 9, SW Scotland

Ardrossan	Campbeltown
East Loch Tarbert	Lamlash
Mull of Kintyre	Portpatrick

Area 10, NW England

Beaumaris	Burrow Head
Caernarfon	Conwy
Glasson Dock	Holyhead
Liverpool	Maryport
Port Dinorwic	Preston
Whitehaven	Wyre Dock (Fleetwood)

Area 11, Wales–Land's End

Abersoch	Aberystwyth
Bardsey Island	Bristol Floating Hbr
Milford Dock (Haven)	Neyland (Milford Hvn)
Padstow	Penarth (Cardiff)
Portishead	Pwllheli
South Bishop (Lt ho)	Swansea

OTHER WEATHER SOURCES

Internet

www.metoffice.com (UK Met Office site) has 2 day and 3–5 day inshore forecasts, 2–5 day planning data, shipping forecasts, gale warnings, coastal reports, surface pressure charts and satellite images.

A pre-paid 'ticket' system (£10 for 20 tickets) pays for services used (MetWEB). To open a credit card account call ☎ 0845 300 0300 [+44 (0) 1344 855680 from abroad] or e-mail sales@metoffice.com

Other UK weather authorities and foreign Met Offices provide further information.

Press

Some national and regional papers include a synoptic chart which, in the absence of any other chart, can help to interpret the shipping forecast – unless the paper is already out of date when you buy it.

Television

Most TV forecasts show a synoptic chart and satellite pictures – a useful guide to the weather situation. In remote areas abroad a TV forecast in a bar, café or even shop window may be the best or only source of weather information.

In the UK Ceefax (BBC) gives the weather index on Ceefax page 400, weather warnings on page 405 and inshore waters forecasts on page 409.

Teletext (ITN) has general forecasts on page 151, shipping forecasts on page 157 and inshore waters forecasts on page 158. Antiope is the equivalent French system.

Broadcasts of shipping and inshore waters forecasts by HM Coastguard

Coastguard	Shipping f'cast areas	Inshore waters forecast areas	Broadcast times UT					
South Coast								
Falmouth	Plymouth, Lundy, Fastnet, Sole, FitzRoy	8 & 9	0140	0540	*0940*	1340	1740	*2140*
Brixham	Plymouth, Portland	8	0050	0450	*0850*	1250	1650	*2050*
Portland	Plymouth, Portland, Wight	7 & 8	0220	0620	*1020*	1420	1820	*2220*
Solent	Portland, Wight	6 & 7	0040	0440	*0840*	1240	1640	*2040*
Dover	Thames, Dover, Wight	5, 6 & 7	0105	0505	*0905*	1305	1707	*2105*
East Coast								
Thames	Thames, Dover	5	0010	0410	*0810*	1210	1610	*2010*
Yarmouth	Humber, Thames	5	0040	0440	*0840*	1240	1640	*2040*
Humber	Humber, Tyne, Dogger, German Bight	3 & 4	0340	*0740*	1140	1540	*1940*	2340
Forth	Forth, Tyne, Dogger, Forties	2	0205	0605	*1005*	1405	1805	*2205*
Aberdeen	Fair Is, Cromarty, Forth, Forties	1 & 2	0320	*0720*	1120	1520	*1920*	2320
Shetland	Faeroes, Fair Is, Viking	1 & 16	0105	0505	*0905*	1305	1705	*2105*
West Coast								
Stornoway	Fair Is, Faeroes, Bailey, Hebrides, Malin, Rockall	15	0110	0510	*0910*	1310	1710	*2110*
Clyde	Bailey, Hebrides, Rockall, Malin	13, 14 & 15	0020	0420	*0820*	1220	1620	*2020*
Belfast	Irish Sea, Malin	12	0305	*0705*	1105	1505	*1905*	2305
Liverpool	Irish Sea, Malin	11	0210	0610	*1010*	1410	1810	*2210*
Holyhead	Irish Sea	10	0235	*0635*	1035	1435	*1835*	2235
Milford Hvn	Lundy, Irish Sea, Fastnet	9 & 10	0335	*0735*	1135	1535	*1935*	2335
Swansea	Lundy, Irish Sea, Fastnet	9	0005	0405	*0805*	1205	1605	*2005*

CG transmitters and VHF channels

The VHF channels/positions of remote transmitters used for the broadcasts in 5.4.1 are listed below. Thus the relevant (clearest) channel can be pre-selected and/or verified by listening to the prior announcement on Ch 16.

Falmouth MRCC

Trevose Head	86	50°33'N	05°02'W
St Mary's	23	49°56'N	06°18'W
Lizard	86	49°58'N	05°12'W
Falmouth	23	50°09'N	05°06'W

Brixham MRSC

Fowey	86	50°20'N	04°38'W
Rame Head	10	50°19'N	04°13'W
Salcombe	84	50°15'N	03°45'W
East Prawle	73	50°13'N	03°42'W
Dartmouth	23	50°21'N	03°35'W
Berry Head	86	50°24'N	03°29'W
Teignmouth	10	50°34'N	03°32'W
Beer Head	84	50°41'N	03°05'W

Portland MRSC

Beer Head	86	50°41'N	03°05'W
Bincleaves	23	50°36'N	02°27'W
Grove Pt (Portland)	84	50°33'N	02°25'W
Hengistbury Head	23	50°43'N	01°46'W

Solent MRSC

Needles	86	50°39'N	01°35'W
Boniface (Ventnor, IoW)	23	50°36'N	01°12'W
Newhaven	86	50°47'N	00°03'E

Dover MRCC

Fairlight (Hastings)	23	50°52'N	00°39'E
Langdon Battery (Dover)	86	51°08'N	01°21'E
North Foreland	86	51°23'N	01°27'E

Thames MRSC

Shoeburyness	23	51°31'N	00°47'E
Bradwell (R Blackwater)	86	51°44'N	00°53'E
Walton/Naze	73	51°51'N	01°17'E
Bawdsey (R Deben)	84	52°00'N	01°25'E

Yarmouth MRCC

Lowestoft	86	52°29'N	01°46'E
Yarmouth	84	52°36'N	01°43'E
Trimingham	23	52°54'N	01°21'E
Langham	86	52°57'N	00°58'E
Guy's Head	84	52°48'N	00°13'E
Skegness	23	53°09'N	00°21'E

Humber MRSC

Easington	84	53°39'N	00°06'E
Flamborough Head	23	54°07'N	00°05'W
Whitby	84	54°29'N	00°36'W
Hartlepool	23	54°42'N	01°10'W
Cullercoats (Blyth)	84	55°04'N	01°28'W
Newton	23	55°31'N	01°37'W

Forth MRSC

St Abbs/Cross Law	86	55°54'N	02°12'W
Craigkelly	86	56°04'N	03°14'W
Fife Ness	23	56°17'N	02°35'W
Tay Law (Dundee)	86	56°28'N	02°59'W
Inverbervie	23	56°51'N	02°16'W

Aberdeen MRCC

Greg Ness	86	57°08'N	02°03'W
Peterhead	86	57°31'N	01°46'W
Windyheads Hill	23	57°39'N	02°14'W
Banff	23	57°38'N	02°31'W
Foyers (Loch Ness)	86	57°14'N	04°31'W
Rosemarkie	86	57°38'N	04°05'W
Thrumster (Wick)	84	58°24'N	03°07'W
Noss Head (Wick)	84	58°29'N	03°03'W
Dunnet Hd (Thurso)	84	58°40'N	03°22'W
Ben Tongue	23	58°30'N	04°24'W
Durness (L Eriboll)	23	58°34'N	04°44'W

Shetland MRSC

Wideford Hill	23	58°59'N	03°01'W
Fitful Head	10	59°54'N	01°23'W
Shetland MRSC	84	60°10'N	01°08'W
Collafirth	73	60°32'N	01°23'W
Saxa Vord (Unst)	23	60°42'N	00°51'W

Stornoway MRSC

Butt of Lewis	10	58°28'N	06°14'W
Portnaguran	84	58°15'N	06°10'W
Forsneval	73	58°13'N	07°00'W
Melvaig (Loch Ewe)	67	57°50'N	05°47'W
Rodel (S Harris)	10	57°45'N	06°57'W
Clettreval (N Uist)	73	57°37'N	07°26'W
Skriag (Portree)	67	57°23'N	06°15'W
Drumfearn (Skye)	84	57°12'N	05°48'W
Barra	10	57°01'N	07°30'W
Arisaig	73	56°55'N	06°50'W

Clyde MRCC

Glengorm (N Mull)	23	56°38'N	06°08'W
Tiree	73	56°31'N	06°57'W
Torosay (E Mull)	10	56°27'N	05°43'W
Clyde MRCC	23	55°58'N	04°48'W
South Knapdale	23	55°55'N	05°28'W
Kilchiaran (W Islay)	84	55°46'N	06°27'W
Lawhill (Ardrossan)	86	55°42'N	04°50'W
Rhu Staffnish	10	55°22'N	05°32'W

Belfast MRSC

Navar	73	54°28'N	07°54'W
Limvady (L Foyle)	84	55°06'N	06°53'W
West Torr	73	55°12'N	06°06'W
Black Mountain	86	54°35'N	06°01'W
Orlock Point	84	54°40'N	05°35'W
Slievemartin	73	54°06'N	06°10'W

Liverpool MRSC

Caldbeck (Carlisle)	10	54°46'N	03°07'W
Snaefell (IoM)	86	54°16'N	04°28'W
Langthwaite	73	54°02'N	02°46'W
Moel-y-Parc	23	53°13'N	04°28'W

Holyhead MRSC

Great Ormes Head	84	53°20′N	03°51′W
Holyhead MRSC	10	53°19′N	04°38′W
Mynydd Rhiw	73	52°50′N	04°38′W

Milford Haven MRSC

Blaenplwyf	84	52°22′N	04°06′W
Dinas Hd	86	52°00′N	04°54′W
St Ann's Head	84	51°40′N	05°11′W
Tenby (Monkstone)	86	51°42′N	04°41′W

Swansea MRCC

Mumbles	84	51°34′N	03°59′W
St Hillary (Barry)	86	51°27′N	03°25′W
Severn Bridges	84	51°36′N	02°38′W
Combe Martin	86	51°12′N	04°03′W
Hartland Point	84	51°01′N	04°31′W

Inshore waters forecasts: Area boundaries used by the Coastguard

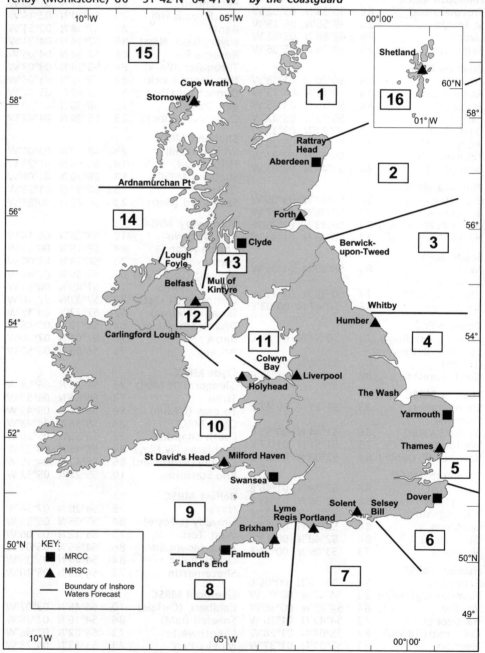

CHANNEL ISLANDS

Jersey Meteorological department

From the CI and UK call ☎ 0900 665 0022 for the Channel Islands recorded shipping forecast. From France call ☎ +44 1534 492256. For Guernsey only, call ☎ 06969 8800; it is chargeable. For more detailed info call ☎ +44 1534 745550, 🖷 746351.

Forecasts include: general situation, 24hr forecast for wind, weather, vis, sea state, swell, sea temperature, plus 2 & 4 day outlooks and St Helier tide times/heights. The area is bounded by 50°N, 03°W and the mainland from Cap de la Hague to Ile de Bréhat.

Weather broadcasts and bulletins

BBC Radio Guernsey 93·2 MHz, 1116 kHz
Bulletins for the waters around Guernsey, Herm and Sark are broadcast Mon-Fri at 0630, 0730 and 0830 LT; Sat/Sun at 0730 and 0830 LT. They contain forecast, synopsis, coastal forecast, storm warnings and wind strength.

In the summer coastal reports are included from: Portland, Chan lt V, Alderney, Guernsey, Jersey, Cherbourg, Cap de la Hague and Dinard.

BBC Radio Jersey 1026 kHz, 88·8 MHz.
Storm warnings on receipt. Wind info for Jersey waters: Mon-Fri 0725, 0825, 1325, 1725 LT; Sat/Sun 0825.

Shipping forecast for local waters: Mon-Fri @ H+00 (0600-1900, after the news) and 0625 & 1825 LT; Sat/Sun @ H+00 (0700-1300, after the news) and 0725 LT.

Jersey Radio Ch 25, 82. Gale warnings at 0307, 0907, 1507 and 2107 UT. Gale warnings, synopsis, 24h forecast, outlook for next 24 hrs, plus reports from observation stations, are broadcast on request and at 0645*, 0745*, 0845*, 1245, 1845, 2245 UT; *broadcast 1 hr earlier when DST in force

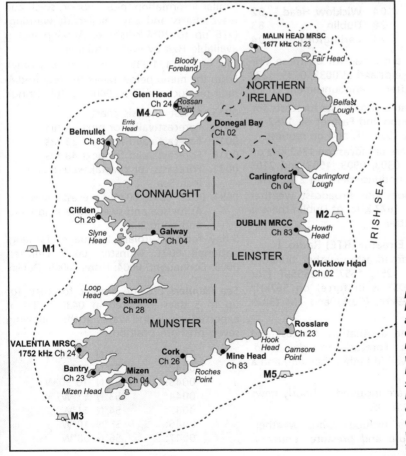

Provinces, headlands, sea areas and coastal stations referred to in weather broadcasts are shown here. Forecasts for coastal waters cover areas within 30M of the shore.

IRELAND

Met Éireann (Irish Met Office) is at Glasnevin Hill, Dublin 9, Ireland. ☎ 1 806 4250, 🖷 1 806 4250, www.met.ie. General forecasting division: ☎ 1 806 4255, 🖷 1 806 4275 (H24, charges may apply).

Coast radio stations

CRS and their VHF channels are listed below (anti-clockwise from Malin Head) and shown overleaf. Weather bulletins for 30M offshore and the Irish Sea are broadcast on VHF at 0103, 0403, 0703, 1003, 1303, 1603, 1903 and 2203UT after an announcement on Ch 16. Broadcasts are made 1 hour earlier when DST is in force. Bulletins include gale warnings, synopsis and a 24-hour forecast.

Malin Head	23	Bantry	23
Glen Head	24	Mizen Head	04
Donegal Bay	02	Cork	26
Belmullet	83	Mine Head	83
Clifden	26	Rosslare	23
Galway	04	Wicklow Head	02
Shannon	28	Dublin	83
Valentia	24	Carlingford	04

Gale warnings are broadcast on these VHF channels on receipt and at 0033, 0633, 1233 and 1833 UT, after an announcement Ch 16.

MF Valentia Radio broadcasts forecasts for sea areas Shannon and Fastnet on 1752 kHz at 0833 & 2033 UT, and on request.

Gale warnings are broadcast on 1752 kHz on receipt and at 0303, 0903, 1503 and 2103 (UT) after an announcement on 2182 kHz.

Malin Head does not broadcast weather information on 1677 kHz. At Dublin there is no MF transmitter.

Radio Telefís Éireann (RTE) Radio 1

RTE Radio 1 broadcasts weather bulletins daily at 0602, 1255, 1657 & 2355LT (1hr earlier when DST is in force) on 567kHz (Tullamore), 729kHz (Cork) and FM (88·2-95·2MHz).

Bulletins contain a situation, forecast and coastal reports. Forecasts include: wind, weather, vis, swell (if higher than 4m) and a 24 hrs outlook.

Gale warnings are included in hourly news bulletins on FM & MF.

Coastal reports include wind, weather, visibility, pressure and pressure tendency.

The change over the last 3 hrs is described as:

Steady	=	0–0·4hPa
Rising/falling slowly	=	0·5–1·9
Rising/falling	=	2·0–3·4
Rising/falling rapidly	=	3·5–5·9
Rising/falling very rapidly	=	> 6·0

Weather by telephone

The latest sea area forecast and gale warnings are available H24 from Weatherdial as recorded messages. Dial ☎ 1550 123 855 (only within Eire) plus the suffixes below:

850	Munster
851	Leinster
852	Connaught
853	Ulster
854	Dublin (plus winds in Dublin Bay and HW times)
855	Coastal waters and Irish Sea.

Weather by fax

Similar information, plus isobaric, swell and wave charts and any small craft warnings (>F6 up to 10M offshore; Apr-Sep inc) is available H24 by Weatherdial Fax.

Dial 🖷 1550 131 838 (from within Eire only). From the menu below select the required 4-digit product code (see 0400 for full listing):

0015: Latest analysis chart
0016: Forecast valid for next 24 hrs
0017: Forecast valid for next 36 hrs
0018: Forecast valid for next 48 hrs
0021: Forecasts for coastal waters and Irish Sea
0031, 0032, 0033, 0034: Forecast (days 1-4) for sea and swell wave heights and periods

5-day forecasts (plain language, farming/national) 0001: Munster. 0002: Leinster. 0003: Connaught. 0004: Ulster. 0005: Dublin.

Sea Planners provide graphic forecasts for up to 5 days (updated at 0430 daily) of expected winds and waves at the following seven offshore positions:

0041:	53°N	05°30'W
0042:	51°N	06°W
0043:	51°N	10°30'W
0044:	53°N	11°W
0045:	54°N	11°W
0046:	55°N	10°W
0047:	56°N	08°W

DENMARK

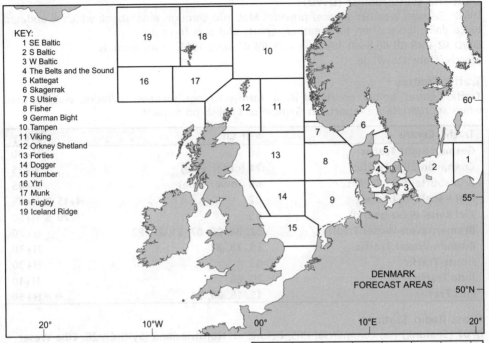

KEY:
1 SE Baltic
2 S Baltic
3 W Baltic
4 The Belts and the Sound
5 Kattegat
6 Skagerrak
7 S Utsire
8 Fisher
9 German Bight
10 Tampen
11 Viking
12 Orkney Shetland
13 Forties
14 Dogger
15 Humber
16 Ytri
17 Munk
18 Fugloy
19 Iceland Ridge

DENMARK FORECAST AREAS

Gale warnings & forecasts are broadcast on receipt, or on request, in Danish/English by remote CRS, callsign *Lyngby Radio*:

CRS	Chan/Freq	Areas
Skagen	04, 1758 kHz	4, 5, 6
Hirtshals	66	4, 5, 6, 8
Hanstholm	01	6, 8
Bovbjerg	02	6, 8, 9
Blåvand	23, 1734 kHz	8, 9

Forecast areas: see above. Skagen and Blåvand CRS broadcast on MF gale warnings for all areas on receipt.

Danmarks Radio broadcasts

Kalundborg (55°44'N 11°E) broadcasts on AM 243 and 1062 kHz at 0445, 0745, 1045, 1645 and 2145 UT:

Gale warnings, weather situation, outlook and coastal reports for areas 1–19.

A 5 day outlook for areas 2–9 and 13–15 and a 7 day outlook for Jutland & the Islands is broadcast only at 1045 & 1645.

Strong wind warnings (up to F6, 12m/sec) for Areas 2–5 & Limfjorden, plus the area south of Esbjerg (1 May – 31 Oct), are broadcast on every Hour by:

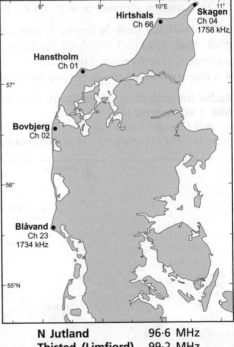

N Jutland	96·6 MHz
Thisted (Limfjord)	99·2 MHz
W Jutland	92·9 MHz
SW Jutland	92·3 MHz
S Jutland	97·2 MHz

77

GERMANY

Deutsche Wetterdienst (DWD)

DWD (German weather service) provides Met info through a databank which is updated twice daily; more often for weather reports and text forecasts.

DWD ☎ + 49 (0) 40 6690 1851. 🖷 + 49 (0) 40 6690 1946. www.dwd.de seeschifffahrt@dwd.de.

Traffic Centres

Traffic Centres, below, broadcast local storm warnings, weather bulletins, visibility (and when appropriate ice reports) in German or **English** on request.

Traffic Centre	VHF Ch	Every
German Bight Traffic	80	**H+00**
Cuxhaven-Elbe Traffic	71 (outer Elbe)	**H+35**
Brunsbüttel-Elbe Traffic	68 (lower Elbe)	**H+05**
Kiel Kanal II (E-bound)	02	**H+15 & H+45**
Kiel Kanal III (W-bound)	03	**H+20 & H+50**
Bremerhaven-Weser Traffic	02, 04, 05, 07, 21, 22, 82	**H+20**
Bremen-Weser Traffic	19, 78, 81	**H+30**
Hunte Traffic	63	**H+30**
Jade Traffic	20, 63	**H+10**
Ems Traffic	15, 18, 20, 21	**H+50**

Coast Radio Stations

DP07 (Seefunk) has commercial CRS, below, at: **Nordfriesland (Sylt)** Ch 26. **Elbe-Weser** Ch 24. **Hamburg** (Control centre) Ch 83. **Bremen** Ch 25. **Borkum** Ch 28.

DP07 broadcasts (only in German): gale and strong wind warnings on receipt. At 0745[A], 0945, 1245, 1645 and 1945[A] UT for Fisher, German Bight and Humber, DP07 broadcasts: a synopsis, 12hr forecast, 24hrs outlook and coastal station reports. [A]summer only. Also a 4–5 day outlook for the North Sea (and Baltic) at 0945 and 1645.

Radio broadcasting: Nord Deutscher Rundfunk (NDR)

NDR 1 Welle Nord (FM)

A wind forecast for the German Bight, valid for the next 12 to 30 hrs, is broadcast in the news bulletins by: **Sylt** 90·9 MHz; **Helgoland** 88·9 MHz; **Cuxhaven** 98·4 MHz; **Hamburg** 89·5

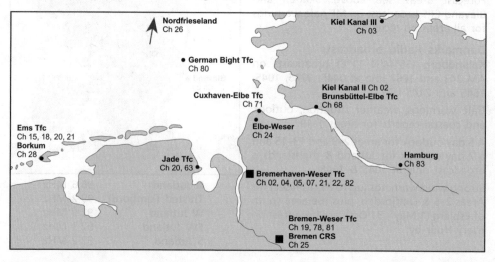

& 90·3 MHz; **Flensburg** 89·6 MHz; **Heide** 90·5 MHz; **Kiel** 91·3 MHz.

NDR 4 Info (AM)
Synopsis, forecast and coastal station reports for the North Sea (and Baltic) are broadcast at 0005, 0830 and 2205 UT on 972 (Hamburg) & 702 (Flensburg) kHz.

Radio Bremen (MW and FM)
A wind forecast, valid for the next 12hrs, for the North Sea (and Baltic) is broadcast in German on receipt by: **Bremerhaven** 936 kHz; 89·3, 92·1, 95·4 & 100·8 MHz; and by **Bremen** 88·3, 93·8, 96·7 & 101·2 MHz.

Telephone forecasts (Marineweather)
For wind forecast and outlook (1 April – 30 Sept) call 0190 1160 (only within Germany) plus two digits for the following areas:

45	North Frisian Islands and Helgoland
46	R Elbe, Cuxhaven to Hamburg
47	Weser , Jade Bay and Helgoland
48	East Frisians and Ems Estuary
53	For pleasure craft

For year-round weather synopsis, forecast and outlook, call 0190 1169 plus two digits:

20	General information
21	North Sea and Baltic
22	German Bight, Fisher and SW North Sea
31	Reports for North Sea and Baltic

For the latest wind warnings (greater than F6) and storm warnings for individual areas of the North Sea coasts, call +49 40 66901209 (H24). If no warning is in force, a wind forecast for the German Bight, west and southern Baltic is given.

NETHERLANDS
Coastguard VHF weather broadcasts
Forecasts for Dutch coastal waters (up to 30M offshore) and inland waters (IJsselmeer, Markermeer, Oosterschelde) are broadcast in **English** and Dutch at 0805, 1305, 1905, 2305 LT on the VHF channels shown below, **without** prior announcement on Ch 16 or DSC 70.

Westkapelle	23	**Hoorn**	83
Woensdrecht	83	**Wezep**	23
Renesse	83	**Kornwerderzand**	23

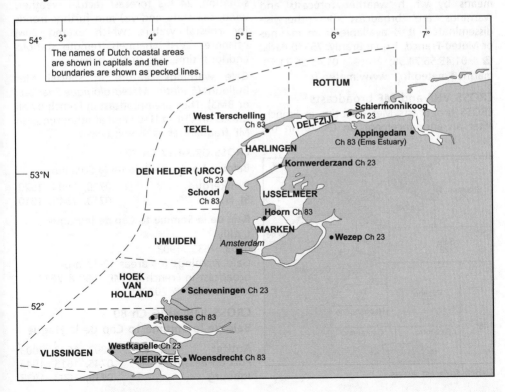

The names of Dutch coastal areas are shown in capitals and their boundaries are shown as pecked lines.

Scheveningen	23	West Terschelling	83
Schoorl	83	Schiermonnikoog	23
Den Helder	23	Appingedam	83

Gale warnings are broadcast on receipt and at 0333, 0733, 1133, 1533, 1933, 2333 UT.

MF weather broadcasts

Forecasts for areas Dover, Thames, Humber, German Bight, Dogger, Fisher, Forties and Viking are broadcast by Scheveningen in **English** at 0940 & 2140 UT on 3673 kHz. Gale warnings for these areas are broadcast in **English** on receipt and at 0333, 0733, 1133, 1533, 1933 and 2333 UT.

Radio Noord-Holland (FM)

Coastal forecasts for northern areas, gale warnings and wind strength are broadcast in Dutch, Mon-Fri at 0730, 0838, 1005, 1230 and 1705LT; Sat/Sun 1005, by: **Haarlem** 97.6 MHz and **Wieringermeer** 93.9 MHz.

Omroep Zeeland (FM)

Coastal forecasts for southern areas, synopsis, gale warnings and wind strength are broadcast in Dutch, Mon-Fri at 0715, 0915, 1215 and 1715LT; Sat/Sun 1015, by:

Philippine 97.8 MHz and **Goes** 101.9 MHz.

BELGIUM

Coast radio stations

Oostende Radio broadcasts in **English** and Dutch on VHF Ch 27 and 2761 kHz: Strong wind warnings on receipt and at 0820 and 1720 UT, together with a forecast for sea areas Thames and Dover.

Antwerpen Radio broadcasts in **English** and Dutch on VHF Ch 24 for the Schelde estuary: Gale warnings on receipt and at every odd H+05. Also strong wind warnings (F6+) on receipt and at every H+03 and H+48.

FRANCE

Le Guide Marine is a useful, free annual booklet which summarises the various means by which weather forecasts and warnings are broadcast or otherwise disseminated. It is available from marinas or Météo-France, 1 quai Branly, 75340 Paris. ☎ 01.45.56.74.36; 📠 01.45.56.71.70. marine@meteo.fr www.meteo.fr

CROSS VHF and MF broadcasts

CROSS broadcasts Met bulletins in French, after an announcement on Ch 16. In the

English Channel broadcasts can be given in English, on request Ch 16. Broadcasts include: Any gale warnings, general situation, 24 hrs forecast (actual weather, wind, sea state and vis) and further trends for coastal waters, which extend 20M offshore. VHF channels, remote stations and local times are shown below.

Gale warnings feature in Special Met Bulletins (*Bulletins Météorologique Spéciaux* or BMS). They are broadcast in French by all CROSS on VHF at H+03 and at other times on MF frequencies as shown below.

CROSS GRIS-NEZ Ch 79
Belgian border to Baie de la Somme

Dunkerque	0720, 1603, 1920
St Frieux	0710, 1545, 1910

Baie de la Somme to Cap de la Hague
L'Ailly
0703, 1533, 1903
Gale warnings for areas 12-13 are broadcast in French on MF 1650 & 2677 kHz at 0833 & 2033LT

CROSS JOBOURG Ch 80
Baie de la Somme to Cap de la Hague

Antifer	0803, 1633, 2003
Port-en-Bessin	0745, 1615, 1945
Jobourg	0733, 1603, 1933

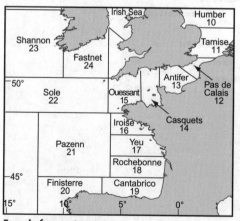

French forecast areas

CROSS Jobourg continued

Cap de la Hague to Pointe de Penmarc'h

Jobourg	0715, 1545, 1915
Granville	0703, 1533, 1903

Gale warnings for areas 13-14 in **English** on receipt and at H+20 and H+50. No gale warnings on MF.

CROSS CORSEN Ch 79

Cap de la Hague to Pte de Penmarc'h
(Times in bold = 1 May to 30 Sep only).

Cap Fréhel	0545, 0803, **1203**, 1633, 2003
Bodic	0533, 0745, **1145**, 1615, 1945
Ile de Batz	0515, 0733, **1133**, 1603, 1933
Le Stiff	0503, 0715, **1115**, 1545, 1915

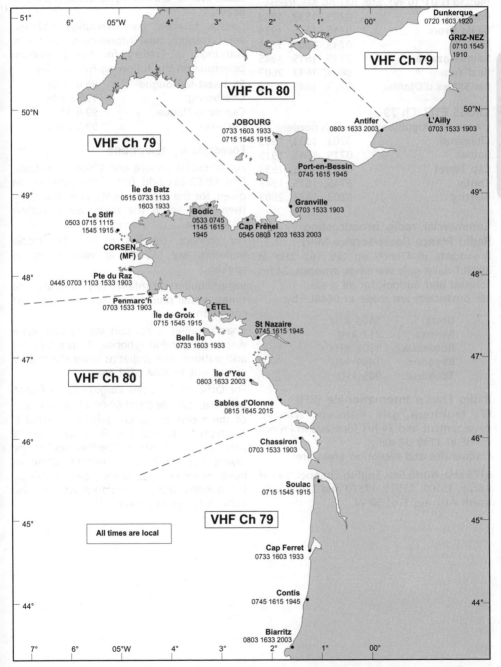

All times are local

Dunkerque 0720 1603 1920
GRIZ-NEZ 0710 1545 1910
L'Ailly 0703 1533 1903
Antifer 0803 1633 2003
JOBOURG 0733 1603 1933 / 0715 1545 1915
Port-en-Bessin 0745 1615 1945
Granville 0703 1533 1903
Île de Batz 0515 0733 1133 1603 1933
Le Stiff 0503 0715 1115 1545 1915
Bodic 0533 0745 1145 1615 1945
Cap Fréhel 0545 0803 1203 1633 2003
CORSEN (MF)
Pte du Raz 0445 0703 1103 1533 1903
Penmarc'h 0703 1533 1903
Île de Groix 0715 1545 1915
ÉTEL
Belle Île 0733 1603 1933
St Nazaire 0745 1615 1945
Île d'Yeu 0803 1633 2003
Sables d'Olonne 0815 1645 2015
Chassiron 0703 1533 1903
Soulac 0715 1545 1915
Cap Ferret 0733 1603 1933
Contis 0745 1615 1945
Biarritz 0803 1633 2003

VHF Ch 79 (×4)
VHF Ch 80 (×2)

Pte du Raz   0445, 0703, **1103**, 1533, 1903
Corsen broadcasts gale warnings for areas 13-22 in French at 0815 and 2015LT on MF 1650 & 2677 kHz.

CROSS ÉTEL Ch 80
Pte de Penmarc'h to l'Anse de l'Aiguillon (46° 15'N 01°10'W). Étel has no MF freqs

Penmarc'h	0703, 1533, 1903
Ile de Groix	0715, 1545, 1915
Belle Ile	0733, 1603, 1933
Saint-Nazaire	0745, 1615, 1945
Ile d'Yeu	0803, 1633, 2003
Les Sables d'Olonne	0815, 1645, 2015

CROSS ÉTEL Ch 79
L'Anse de l'Aiguillon to Spanish border

Chassiron	0703, 1533, 1903
Soulac	0715, 1545, 1915
Cap Ferret	0733, 1603, 1933
Contis	0745, 1615, 1945
Biarritz	0803, 1633, 2003

Commercial radio broadcasting
Radio France (Inter-Service-Mer)
Broadcasts in French on LW 162 kHz at 2003LT daily: gale warnings, synopsis, 24 hrs forecast and outlook for all areas.
MF broadcasts are made at 0640LT by:

Brest	1404 kHz
Rennes	711 kHz
Bordeaux	1206 kHz
Bayonne	1494 kHz
Toulouse	945 kHz

Radio France Internationale (RFI)
RFI broadcasts gale warnings, synopsis, development and 24 hrs forecasts in French on HF at 1130 UT daily.
Frequencies and reception areas are:

6175 kHz: North Sea, English Channel, Bay of Biscay. 15300, 15515, 17570 and 21645 kHz: North Atlantic, E of 50°W.

See opposite for the High Seas forecast areas in the Eastern Atlantic.
Engineering bulletins giving any changes in frequency are transmitted between H+53 and H+00.

Local radio (FM)
Radio France Cherbourg broadcasts daily at 0829 LT:
Coastal forecast, gale warnings, visibility, wind strength, tidal information, small craft warnings, in French, for the Cherbourg peninsula on the following frequencies:

St Vaast-la-Hougue	85·0 MHz
Cherbourg	100·7 MHz
Cap de la Hague	99·8 MHz
Carteret	99·9 MHz

Forecasts by telephone
For recorded Inshore and Coastal forecasts. Dial 08·92·68·02·dd (dd is the number, as given, for the *département*); press the * key then 1 to access the main menu. Follow instructions ...

For Inshore (*rivage*) or Coastal (*côte*) bulletins, say "STOP" as your choice is spoken.

Inshore bulletins contain 7 day forecasts, tide times, actual reports, sea temperature, surf conditions, etc.

Coastal bulletins contain strong wind/gale warnings, general synopsis, 24 hrs forecast and outlook. Five bulletins cover the N & W coasts, out to 20M offshore.

For Offshore bulletins (*large*), out to 200M offshore, dial ☎ 08·92·68·08·77. Select one of three offshore areas (English Channel & southern North Sea, Bay of Biscay or the N part of the western Mediterranean) by saying "STOP" as it is named. Offshore bulletins contain strong wind/gale warnings, the general synopsis and forecast, and the outlook for up to 7 days.

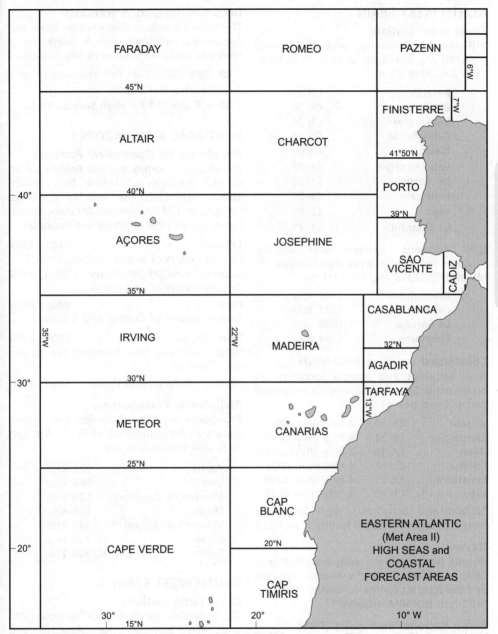

Forecast areas for the Eastern Atlantic and Coastal/Offshore Areas off France, Spain, Portugal and North West Africa

NORTH WEST SPAIN

Coast radio stations

VHF weather warnings and 48h coastal forecasts are broadcast in Spanish at 0840, 1240 and 2010 UT by:

Pasajes	Ch 27
Bilbao	Ch 26
Santander	Ch 24
Cabo Peñas	Ch 26
Navia	Ch 60
Cabo Ortegal	Ch 02
La Coruña	Ch 26
Finisterre	Ch 22
Vigo	Ch 65
La Guardia	Ch 21

Gale warnings, synopsis and 24h/48h forecasts for Atlantic areas are broadcast on MF at 0703, 1303 and 1903 UT by:

Machichaco	1707 kHz
Cabo Peñas	1677 kHz
La Coruña	1698 kHz
Finisterre	1764 kHz

Coastguard weather broadcasts

Gale warnings and coastal forecasts are broadcast in Spanish and English on receipt and as listed below:

Bilbao*	Ch 10	4 hrly from 0033
Santander	Ch 74	4 hrly from 0245
Gijón	Ch 10	2 hrly (0215-2215)
Coruña	Ch 10	4 hrly from 0005
Finisterre	Ch 11	4 hrly from 0233
Vigo	Ch 10	4 hrly from 0015

*Bilbao also broadcasts High Seas gale warnings and forecasts 4 hourly from 0233.

Navtex

Coruna Navtex (D) transmits on 518 kHz at 0830 and 2030 UT: gale warnings, synopsis and the forecast for the following 18-36 hrs, valid out to 450M offshore.

Radio Nacional de España (MW)

Broadcasts storm warnings, synopsis and 12h or 18h forecasts for Cantábrico and Galicia at 1100, 1400, 1800 & 2200 LT in Spanish. Stations/frequencies are:

San Sebastián	774 kHz
Bilbao	639 kHz
Santander	855 kHz
Oviedo	729 kHz
La Coruña	639 kHz

Recorded telephone forecasts

This service is only available within Spain and for vessels equipped with Autolink. For a recorded weather bulletin in Spanish, call:

☎ 906 365 372 for the coasts of Cantábrico and Galicia.

☎ 906 365 374 for High Seas bulletins.

PORTUGAL & THE AZORES

Broadcasts by Radionaval Portugal

Broadcasts in Portuguese and **English** are on Ch 11 at the times (UT) below. They contain: Storm, gale and poor visibility warnings; synopsis and 24 hrs forecasts for three coastal zones out to 20M offshore; see opposite:

Leixões   0705, 1905
Coastal waters of N and Central zones.
Alges (also on MF 2657 kHz)   0905, 2105
Coastal waters of all 3 zones.
Faro   0805, 2005
Coastal waters of Central and S Zones.

Horta (Azores, LT)   0900, 2100
Waters off Faial, Pico, Graciosa, São Jorge and Terceira

Waters off Corvo and Flores   1000, 1900

Radiofusão Portuguesa

Broadcasts weather bulletins for coastal waters in Portuguese at 1100 UT. Stations (N-S) and frequencies are:

Porto	720 kHz
Viseu	666 kHz
Montemer (Coimbra)	630 kHz
Lisboa 1	666 kHz
Miranda do Douro	630 kHz
Elvas	720 kHz
Faro	97·6 MHz, 720 kHz

SOUTH WEST SPAIN

Coast radio stations

CRS broadcast gale warnings, synopsis, 24h and 48h forecasts for Atlantic and Mediterranean areas, in Spanish, at the times (UT) and on the VHF and MF frequencies shown below:

Chipiona	1656 kHz	0733	1233	1933
Cadiz	Ch 26	0833	1133	2003
Tarifa	Ch 81	0833	1133	2003
	1704 kHz	0733	1233	1933
Malaga	Ch 26	0833	1133	2003
Cabo Gata	Ch 27	0833	1133	2003

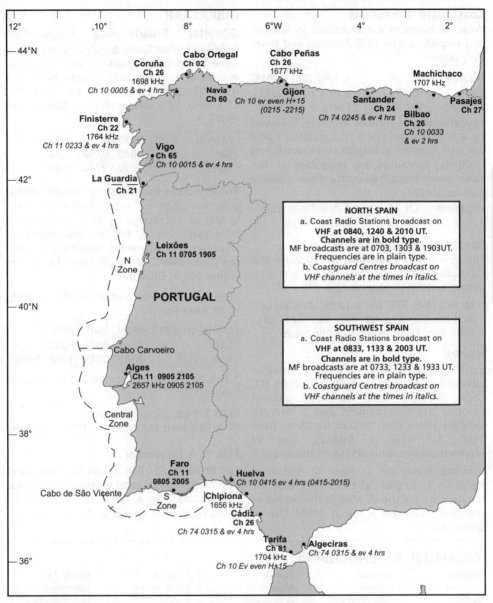

12°   10°   8°   6°W   4°   2°

44°N

Coruña
Ch 26
1698 kHz
Ch 10 0005 & ev 4 hrs

Cabo Ortegal
Ch 02

Cabo Peñas
Ch 26
1677 kHz

Machichaco
1707 kHz

Navia
Ch 60

Gijon
*Ch 10 ev even H+15
(0215 -2215)*

Santander
Ch 24
Ch 74 0245 & ev 4 hrs

Bilbao
Ch 26
*Ch 10 0033
& ev 2 hrs*

Pasajes
Ch 27

Finisterre
Ch 22
1764 kHz
Ch 11 0233 & ev 4 hrs

Vigo
Ch 65
Ch 10 0015 & ev 4 hrs

42°

La Guardia
Ch 21

N
Zone

Leixões
Ch 11 0705 1905

PORTUGAL

40°N

Cabo Carvoeiro

Alges
Ch 11 0905 2105
2657 kHz 0905 2105

Central
Zone

38°

Faro
Ch 11
0805 2005

Huelva
Ch 10 0415 ev 4 hrs (0415-2015)

Cabo de São Vicente

S
Zone

Chipiona
1656 kHz

Cádiz
Ch 26
Ch 74 0315 & ev 4 hrs

Tarifa
Ch 81
1704 kHz
Ch 10 Ev even H+15

Algeciras
Ch 74 0315 & ev 4 hrs

36°

> **NORTH SPAIN**
> a. Coast Radio Stations broadcast on
> **VHF at 0840, 1240 & 2010 UT.**
> **Channels are in bold type.**
> MF broadcasts are at 0703, 1303 & 1903UT.
> Frequencies are in plain type.
> b. *Coastguard Centres broadcast on*
> *VHF channels at the times in italics.*

> **SOUTHWEST SPAIN**
> a. Coast Radio Stations broadcast on
> **VHF at 0833, 1133 & 2003 UT.**
> **Channels are in bold type.**
> MF broadcasts are at 0733, 1233 & 1933 UT.
> Frequencies are in plain type.
> b. *Coastguard Centres broadcast on*
> *VHF channels at the times in italics.*

WEATHER

Spain and Portugal: MSI broadcasts by CRS and MRCCs/MRSCs (all times UT)

Coastguard broadcasts

Weather bulletins are broadcast in Spanish and **English** on the VHF channels and times (UT) below:

Huelva	Ch 10	4 hrly (0415-2015)
Cadiz	Ch 74	4 hrly from 0315
Tarifa	Ch 10, 67	Every even H+15.

Actual wind and visibility at Tarifa, followed by a forecast for Strait of Gibraltar, Cádiz Bay and Alborán, in **English** and Spanish. Fog (visibility) warnings are broadcast at the same times, more frequently when visibility falls below 2M.

Algeciras	Ch 74	4 hrly from 0315 and at 0515.

Recorded telephone forecasts

The service is only available within Spain and for Autolink-equipped vessels. For a coastal waters bulletin in Spanish call:

☎ 906 365 373 for Atlantic Andalucia and the Canaries. ☎ 906 365 374 for High Seas bulletin for Atlantic areas.

Navtex

Tarifa (G, 518 kHz) transmits weather bulletins in English at 0900 and 2100 UT. These include: Gale warnings, general synopsis and development and a forecast, valid for 18 hrs from 0900 or for 36 hrs from 2100, for the N Atlantic and W Mediterranean within 450M of the coast.

Valencia (Cabo de la Nao: X, 518 kHz) transmits in English at 0750 and 1950 UT similar data for the W Med within 450M of the coast. Valencia is about 300M ENE of Gibraltar.

GIBRALTAR

Gibraltar Broadcasting Corporation (GBC)

Gibraltar Radio broadcasts in English: General synopsis, situation, wind direction and force, visibility and sea state, radius 5M from Gibraltar. Frequencies are 1458 kHz, 91·3 MHz, 92·6 MHz and 100·5 MHz. Times (UT):

Mon-Fri:	0530, 0630, 0730, 1030, 1230
Sat:	0530, 0630, 0730, 1030
Sun:	0630, 0730, 1030

British Forces Broadcasting Service (BFBS)

Gale warnings for the Gibraltar area are broadcast on receipt by BFBS 1 and 2. All broadcasts are in English and comprise: Shipping forecast, wind, weather, visbility, sea state, swell, HW & LW times for waters within 5M of Gibraltar.

BFBS 1 frequencies and times (Local): 93·5, 97·8* MHz FM.

Mon-Fri:	0745, 0845, 1005, 1605
Sat:	0845, 0945, 1202
Sun:	0845, 0945, 1202, 1602

* This frequency is reported to have greater range.

BFBS 2 frequencies and time:
89·4, 99·5 MHz FM. Mon-Fri: 1200 Local time

Talk to a forecaster

Call ☎ 08700 767 818 to talk to a forecaster in Gibraltar about local weather in the Med or Canaries. Pay a flat rate of £17·00 by credit card, for a typical 5-10 mins briefing.

WEATHER VOCABULARY

English	German	French	Spanish	Dutch
Air mass	Luftmasse	Masse d'air	Massa de aire	Luchtmassa
Anticyclone	Antizyklonisch	Anticyclone	Anticiclón	Hogedrukgebied
Area	Gebiet	Zone	Zona	Gebied
Backing wind	Rückdrehender Wind	Vent reculant	Rolar el viento	Krimpende wind
Barometer	Barometer	Baromètre	Barómetro	Barometer
Breeze	Brise	Brise	Brisa	Bries
Calm	Flaute	Calme	Calma	Kalmte
Centre	Zentrum	Centre	Centro	Centum
Clouds	Wolken	Nuages	Nube	Wolken
Cold	Kalt	Froid	Frio	Koud
Cold front	Kaltfront	Front froid	Frente frio	Kou front
Cyclonic	Zyklonisch	Cyclonique	Ciclonica	Cycloonachtig
Decrease	Abnahme	Affaiblissement	Disminución	Afnemen
Deep	Tief	Profond	Profundo	Diep
Deepening	Vertiefend	Approfondissant	Ahondamiento	Verdiepend
Depression	Sturmtief	Dépression	Depresión	Depressie

English	German	French	Spanish	Dutch
Direction	Richtung	Direction	Direción	Richting
Dispersing	Auflösend	Se dispersant	Disipación	Oplossend
Disturbance	Störung	Perturbation	Perturbación	Verstoving
Drizzle	Niesel	Bruine	Lioviena	Motregen
East	Ost	Est	Este	Oosten
Extending	Ausdehnung	S'étendant	Extension	Uitstrekkend
Extensive	Ausgedehnt	Etendu	General	Uitgebreid
Falling	Fallend	Descendant	Bajando	Dalen
Filling	Auffüllend	Secomblant	Relleno	Vullend
Fog	Nebel	Brouillard	Niebla	Nevel
Fog bank	Nebelbank	Ligne de brouillard	Banco de niebla	Mist bank
Forecast	Vorhersage	Prévision	Previsión	Vooruitzicht
Frequent	Häufig	Fréquent	Frecuenta	Veelvuldig
Fresh	Frisch	Frais	Fresco	Fris
Front	Front	Front	Frente	Front
Gale	Sturm	Coup de vent	Temporal	Storm
Gale warning	Sturmwarnung	Avis de coup de vent	Aviso de temporal	Stormwaarschuwing
Good	Gut	Bon	Bueno	Goed
Gradient	Druckunterschied	Gradient	Gradiente	Gradiatie
Gust, squall	Bö	Rafalle	Ráfaga	Windvlaag
Hail	Hagel	Grêle	Granizo	Hagel
Haze	Diesig	Brume	Calina	Nevel
Heavy	Schwer	Abondant	Abunante	Zwaar
High	Hoch	Anticyclone	Alta presión	Hoog
Increasing	Zunehmend	Augmentant	Aumentar	Toenemend
Isobar	Isobar	Isobare	Isobara	Isobar
Isolated	Vereinzelt	Isolé	Aislado	Verspreid
Lightning	Blitze	Eclair de foudre	Relampago	Bliksem
Local	Örtlich	Locale	Local	Plaatselijk
Low	Tief	Dépression	Baja presión	Laag
Mist	Dunst	Brume légere	Nablina	Mist
Moderate	Mäßig	Modéré	Moderado	Matig
Moderating	Abnehmend	Se modérant	Medianente	Matigend
Moving	Bewegend	Se déplacant	Movimiento	Bewegend
North	Nord	Nord	Septentrional	Noorden
Occluded	Okklusion	Couvert	Okklusie	Bewolkt
Poor	Schlecht	Mauvais	Mal	Slecht
Precipitation	Niederschlag	Précipitation	Precipitación	Neerslag
Pressure	Druck	Pression	Presión	Druk
Rain	Regen	Pluie	lluvia	Regen
Ridge	Hochdruckbrücke	Crête	Cresta	Rug
Rising	Ansteigend	Montant	Subiendo	Stijgen
Rough	Rauh	Agitée	Bravo o alborotado	Ruw
Sea	See	Mer	Mar	Zee
Seaway	Seegang	Haute mer	Alta mar	Zee
Scattered	Vereinzelt	Sporadiques	Difuso	Verspreid
Shower	Schauer	Averse	Aguacero	Bui
Slight	Leicht	Un peu	Leicht	Licht
Slow	Langsam	Lent	Lent	Langzaam
Snow	Schnee	Neige	Nieve	Sneeuw
South	Süd	Sud	Sur	Zuiden
Storm	Sturm	Tempête	Temporal	Storm
Sun	Sonne	Soleil	Sol	Zon
Swell	Schwell	Houle	Mar de fondo	Deining
Thunder	Donner	Tonnerre	Tormenta	Donder
Thunderstorm	Gewitter	Orage	Tronada	Onweer
Trough	Trog, Tiefausläufer	Creux	Seno	Trog
Variable	Umlaufend	Variable	Variable	Veranderlijk
Veering	Rechtdrehend	Virement de vent	Dextrogiro	Ruimende wind
Warm front	Warmfront	Front chaud	Frente calido	Warm front
Weather	Wetter	Temps	Tiempo	Weer
Wind	Wind	Vent	Viento	Wind
Weather report	Wetterbericht	Météo	Previsión	Weer bericht meteorologica

WEATHER

CHAPTER 3 - COMMUNICATIONS

CONTENTS

RADIO OPERATION

Avoiding interference
Before transmitting, first listen on the VHF channel. If occupied, wait for a break before transmitting, or choose another channel. If you cause interference you must comply immediately with any request from a Coastguard or Coast radio station to stop transmitting. The request will state how long to desist.

Control of communications
Ship-to-Shore: Except in the case of distress, urgency or safety, communications between ship and shore-based stations are controlled by the latter.

Intership: The ship *called* controls communication. If you call another ship, then it has control. If you are called by a ship, you assume control. If a shore-based station breaks in, both ships must comply with instructions given. A shore-based station has better aerials and equipment and so its transmission and reception ranges are greater.

Radio confidentiality
Inevitably you will overhear private conversations on VHF. It is illegal to reproduce them, pass them on or use them for any purpose.

Voice technique
There are two considerations when speaking:

What to say, ie *voice Procedure*

How to say it, ie *voice Technique*

Clear R/T speech is vital. If a message cannot be understood by the receiving operator it is useless.

Anyone can become a good operator by following a few simple rules:

The voice should be pitched at a higher level than for normal conversation. Avoid dropping the voice pitch at the end of a word or phrase. Hold the microphone a few inches in front of the mouth and speak directly into it at a normal level. Speak clearly so that there can be no confusion. Emphasise words with weak syllables; 'Tower', if badly pronounced, could sound like 'tar'. People with strong regional or foreign accents must try to use as understandable a pronunciation as possible.

Messages which have to be written down at the receiving station should be spoken slowly. This gives time for it to be written down by the receiving operator. If the transmitting operator himself writes it down all should be well.

Remember, the average reading speed is 250 words a minute, whilst average writing speed is only 20.

Difficult words may be spelled phonetically. Operators precede this with 'I spell'. If the word is pronounceable include it before and after it has been spelt.

For example, if an operator sends the message 'I will berth on the yacht *Coila*' he would transmit: 'I will berth on the yacht *Coila* – I spell – Charlie Oscar India Lima Alfa – *Coila*'.

When asked for your international callsign, (if it is MGLA4) transmit: 'My callsign is Mike Golf Lima Alfa Four.'

The phonetic alphabet
The syllables to emphasise are underlined

Letter	Morse	Phonetic	Spoken as
A	• –	Alfa	AL-fah
B	– • • •	Bravo	BRAH-voh
C	– • – •	Charlie	CHAR-lee
D	– • •	Delta	DELL-tah
E	•	Echo	ECK-oh
F	• • – •	Foxtrot	FOKS-trot
G	– – •	Golf	GOLF
H	• • • •	Hotel	hoh-TELL
I	• •	India	IN-dee-ah
J	• – – –	Juliett	JEW-lee-ett
K	– • –	Kilo	KEY-loh
L	• – • •	Lima	LEE-mah
M	– –	Mike	MIKE
N	– •	November	no-VEM-ber
O	– – –	Oscar	OSS-car
P	• – – •	Papa	pa-PAH
Q	– – • –	Quebec	keh-BECK
R	• – •	Romeo	ROW-me-oh
S	• • •	Sierra	see-AIR-rah
T	–	Tango	TANG-go
U	• • –	Uniform	OO-nee-form
V	• • • –	Victor	VIK-tah
W	• – –	Whiskey	WISS-key
X	– • • –	X-Ray	ECKS-ray
Y	– • – –	Yankee	YANG-key
Z	– – • •	Zulu	ZOO-loo

Phonetic numerals
When numerals are transmitted, the following pronunciations make them easier to understand.

No	Morse	Spoken	No	Morse	Spoken
1	• – – – –	WUN	6	– • • • •	SIX
2	• • – – –	TOO	7	– – • • •	SEV-EN
3	• • • – –	TREE	8	– – – • •	AIT
4	• • • • –	FOW-ER	9	– – – – •	NIN-ER
5	• • • • •	FIFE	0	– – – – –	ZERO

Numerals are transmitted digit by digit except that multiples of thousands may be spoken as follows:

Numeral	Spoken as
44	FOW-ER FOW-ER
90	NIN-ER ZERO
136	WUN TREE SIX
500	FIFE ZERO ZERO
1478	WUN FOW-ER SEV-EN AIT
7000	SEV-EN THOU-SAND

Punctuation

Punctuation marks should be used only where their omission would cause confusion.

Mark	Word	Spoken as
.	Decimal	DAY-SEE-MAL
,	Comma	COMMA
.	Stop	STOP

Procedure words or 'prowords'

These are used to shorten transmissions

All after: Used after proword 'say again' to request repetition of a portion of a message

All before: Used after proword 'say again' to request repetition of a portion of message

Correct: Reply to repetition of message that was preceded by prowords 'read back for check' when it has been correctly repeated. Often said twice

Correction: Spoken during the transmission of a message means an error has been made in this transmission. Cancel the last word or group of words. The correct word or group follows

In figures: Following numeral or group of numerals to be written as figures

In letters: Following numeral or group of numerals to be written as figures as spoken

I say again: I am repeating transmission or portion indicated

I spell: I shall spell the next word or group of letters phonetically

Out: This is the end of working to you

Over: Invitation to reply

Read back: If receiving station is doubtful about accuracy of whole or part of message it may repeat it back to the sending station, preceding the repetition with prowords 'I read back'

Say again: Repeat your message or portion referred to ie 'Say again all after', 'Say again address', etc

Station calling: Used when a station is uncertain of the calling station's identification

This is: This transmission is from the station whose callsign or name immediately follows

Wait: If a called station is unable to accept traffic immediately, it will reply **'WAIT.......MINUTES'**. If probable delay exceeds 10 minutes the reason will be given

Word after or Word before: Used after the proword 'say again' to request repetition

Wrong: Reply to repetition of message preceded by prowords 'read back' when it has been incorrectly repeated

Calls, calling and callsigns

Shore-based stations normally identify themselves by using their geographical name followed by the words Coastguard or Radio, eg Solent Coastguard, Dublin Radio etc. Vessels usually identify themselves by the name on their licence but the International callsign assigned to the ship may be used in certain cases. If two yachts bear the same name or where some confusion may result, you should give your International callsign when starting communications, and thereafter use your ship's name as callsign.

'All ships' broadcast

Information to be received or used by all who intercept it, eg gale warnings, navigational warnings, weather forecasts etc, is generally broadcast by Coastguard Radio and addressed 'All stations'. No reply is needed.

Establishing communication with a shore-based station

The initial call is usually made on a working channel. Channel 16 should not be used except for distress, urgency or very briefly to establish a working channel.

- Switch to one of the station's working channels, pausing to check no-one is transmitting
- Are you close enough to try low power (1 watt) first? Possible at ranges up to 10 miles. Otherwise use high power (25 watts) with more battery drain.
- The callsign of calling station up to three times only, and prowords 'This is'
- Indication of number of R/T calls you have to make
- Proword 'Over'

Small faults can drastically reduce your transmitting range. Possibly the aerial for the channel chosen has been optimised for areas east of the station and you are to the west. If approaching the station wait 15 minutes and call again. If the range is opening, either try again in hope, or try another station within range.

Every time you call at high power, you are decreasing battery state and the range your VHF will achieve. Continued calling also clutters up the channel and denies access to other users.

RADIO DATA

SHORT, MEDIUM and LONG RANGE RADIO COMMUNICATIONS

A suitable radio receiver on board will provide weather forecasts and time signals at scheduled times on a number of frequencies in various wavebands. With a maritime receiver you are not limited to the familiar BBC and commercial broadcasts. HM Coastguard transmit navigation warnings, storm warnings and weather messages for shipping in their respective sea areas.

Short range radiotelephony (RT) transmits and receives on VHF channels in the marine VHF (Very High Frequency) band. The equipment and procedures are simple, but range is normally limited to about 20 miles from ship to shore, rather less from ship to ship. Interconnection with national telephone systems is possible on certain VHF/RT channels when a yacht is within range of a Coast Radio Station, although there are now no such stations on the mainland of the UK, France or the Netherlands. Mobile telephones are now by far the most common form of ship to shore communication.

Medium range two-way communication operate in the marine MF (medium frequency) RT band, the 2MHz 'trawler band'. Single sideband techniques are employed on these medium frequencies and SSB equipment is essential. The effective range depends on the power of the transmitter and the sensitivity of the associated receiver; in general this might be up to 200 miles from certain (but not all) Coast Radio Stations.

Each channel in the VHF/RT band and each frequency in the MF/RT band has its specific purpose and may not be used at random for general conversation. Calling on the wrong channel merely wastes time and causes annoyance to other users.

THE MARINE VHF BAND

VHF is used by most vessels, Coast Radio Stations, Coastguard centres and other rescue services. Its range is slightly better than the line of sight between the transmitting and receiving aerials. It pays to fit a good aerial, as high as possible.

In the Marine VHF/RT band the individual frequencies are separated from their neighbours by exactly 25kHz 'elbow-room' to eliminate mutual interference. For convenience each working frequency is given a channel number; the numbers do not run consecutively because the channels were originally spaced 50kHz apart.

But it has since become possible to fit another channel in between each original one and so make fuller use of the waveband. Marine VHF frequencies are in the band 156·00–174·00 MHz. Channels 29 to 59 are allocated to other purposes. Thus 55 channels are available, plus some with special purposes (see below).

Of the 55 channels available in the Marine VHF/RT band, small craft are unlikely to need more than a selected dozen, some of which may vary with the area in which a boat operates.

The simplest and earliest VHF/RT transmitter-receivers operated only in the 'simplex' mode, ie transmit and receive on the same channel, so that only one person can talk at a time. The channel numbers are 06 (mandatory), 08 to 17, 67 to 74 and 77.

All other channels are for 'duplex' working, ie transmit and receive on different frequencies, so that conversation is normal.

For full duplex operation a more elaborate and expensive transmitter-receiver with either twin aerials or a special filter is needed, but it can interconnect with the shore telephone system so as to converse with subscribers who have no knowledge of radio procedures.

More common among yachtsmens' VHF/RTs, however, are the semi-duplex operating sets which, although involving simplex procedures, allow you to communicate with stations operating duplex systems and to link with shore telephones via Coast Radio Stations.

VHF Channel Grouping

Channels are grouped for three main purposes, but some can be used for more than one purpose. They are listed below in their preferred order of usage:

- **Public correspondence** (ie used to access the shore telephone system via Coast Radio Stations): Ch 26, 27, 25, 24, 23, 28, 04, 01, 03, 02, 07, 05, 84, 87, 86, 83, 85, 88, 61, 64, 65, 62, 66, 63, 60, 82, 78, 81. All channels are duplex.

- **Inter-ship:** Ch 06, 08, 10, 13, 09, 72, 73, 67, 69, 77, 15, 17. These are all simplex channels. It is as well to know them, so that if another vessel calls you, you can swiftly nominate a working channel from within this group.

- **Port Operations:**
Simplex: Ch 12, 14, 11, 13, 09, 68, 71, 74, 69, 73, 17, 15.

Duplex: Ch 20, 22, 18, 19, 21, 05, 07, 02, 03, 01, 04, 78, 82, 79, 81, 80, 60, 63, 66, 62, 65, 64, 61, 84.

Special purposes. The following channels have one specific purpose only:

Ch 0 (156·00 MHz): SAR ops, not available to yachts.

Ch's 10 (156·500 MHz), 23 (161·750 MHz), 73 (156·675 MHz), 84 (161·825 MHz) and 86 (161·925 MHz): for MSI broadcasts by HMCG.

Ch 13 (156·650 MHz): Intership safety of navigation (sometimes referred to as bridge-to-bridge); a possible channel for calling a merchant ship if no contact on Ch 16.

Ch 16 (156·80 MHz): Distress, Safety and calling. *See Chapter 4 for Distress and Safety.* Ch 16 will be monitored by ships, CG centres (and, in some areas, any remaining Coast Radio Stations) for Distress and Safety until at least 2005, in parallel with DSC Ch 70. Yachts should monitor Ch 16. After an initial call, the stations concerned **must** switch to a working channel, except for Safety matters.

Ch 67 (156·375 MHz): the Small Craft Safety channel in the UK, accessed via Ch 16.

Ch 70 (156·525 MHz): exclusively for digital selective calling for Distress and Safety purposes.

Ch 80 (157·025 MHz): the primary working channel between yachts and UK marinas.

Ch M (157·85 MHz): the secondary working channel between yachts and UK marinas; previously known as Ch 37.

Ch M2 (161·425 MHz): for race control, with Ch M as stand-by. YCs may apply to use Ch M2.

MEDIUM RANGE MF/RT

The limited line-of-sight range of VHF/RT makes a longer-range system desirable for small craft which need to maintain contact with shore stations when offshore or in a coastal area to which VHF cover does not extend.

Single sideband MF/RT provides such contact all around the waters of the UK and Western Europe. A receiver alone gives the ability to hear weather bulletins, storm and navigation warnings for local sea areas broadcast from Coast Radio Stations in the 1.6 to 4.0MHz maritime band, ie on frequencies between 1605 and 4200 kHz. Not all radio stations are equipped to deal with this traffic but there are sufficient stations adequately spaced around the coast to cover all UK coastal waters.

Unlike VHF and HF, MF transmissions tend to follow the curvature of the earth, which makes them suitable for direction-finding equipment. For this reason, and because of their good range, the marine Distress radiotelephone frequency is in the MF band (2182 kHz).

TRAFFIC LISTS

Coast stations wishing to contact a vessel at sea will first attempt to do so by a direct call on Channel 16 which will be heard if the vessel is within range and a loudspeaker watch is kept. Failing this, the vessel's name will be added to the Traffic List broadcast at (usually) two hour intervals at the times and on the frequencies (channels) shown elsewhere in Coast Radio Stations section, pages 110 - 112. Unless you monitor that frequency at the appropriate time you may never know that there is incoming traffic awaiting attention. When such a call is received, the response is to call the station concerned on the working channel.

SILENCE PERIODS

Although there is no official silence period for VHF, it is generally advised that no transmission be made during the silence periods which are enforced for the 2182kHz distress frequency. The periods are the three minutes immediately after the whole and half hours, ie H to H+03 and H+30 to H+33.

LONG RANGE HF RADIO

HF radiotelephones use frequencies in the 4, 8, 12, 16 and 22 MHz bands (short wave) that are chosen to suit propagation conditions. HF is more expensive than MF and requires more power, but can provide worldwide coverage. A good installation and skilled operating techniques are essential for satisfactory results.

HF waves travel upwards and bounce off the ionosphere back to earth. Reception is better at night when the ionosphere is denser. The directional properties of HF transmissions are poor, so there is no HF Distress frequency.

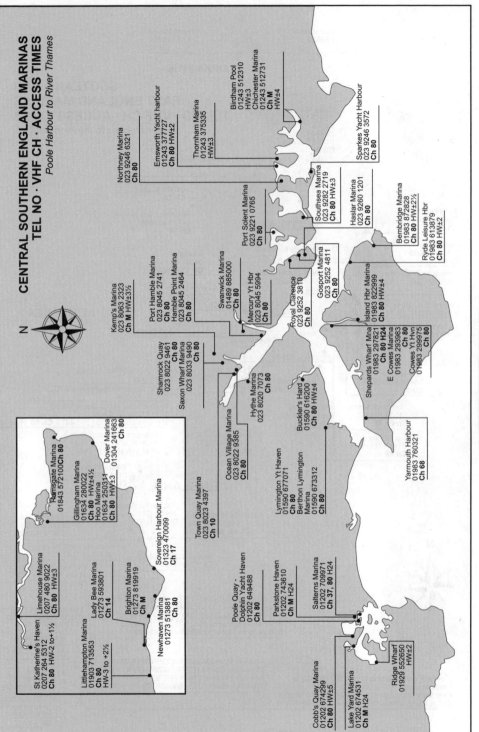

CENTRAL SOUTHERN ENGLAND MARINAS
TEL NO · VHF CH · ACCESS TIMES
Poole Harbour to River Thames

Northney Marina
023 9246 6321
Ch 80

Emsworth Yacht harbour
01243 377727
Ch 80 HW±2

Thornham Marina
01243 375335
HW±3

Birdham Pool
01243 512310
HW±3
Chichester Marina
01243 512731
Ch M
HW±4

Sparkes Yacht Harbour
023 9246 3572
Ch 80

Port Solent Marina
023 9221 0765
Ch 80

Southsea Marina
023 9282 2719
Ch 80 HW±3

Haslar Marina
023 9260 1201
Ch 80

Bembridge Marina
01983 872828
Ch 80 HW±2½
Ryde Leisure Hbr
01983 613879
Ch 80 HW±2

Kemp's Marina
023 8063 2323
Ch M HW±3½

Port Hamble Marina
023 8045 2741
Ch 80
Hamble Point Marina
023 8045 2464
Ch 80

Swanwick Marina
01489 885000
Ch 80

Mercury Yt Hbr
023 8045 5994
Ch 80

Royal Clarence
023 9252 3810
Ch 80

Gosport Marina
023 9252 4811
Ch 80

Island Hbr Marina
01983 822999
Ch 80 HW±4

Shepards Wharf Mna
01983 297821
Ch 80 H24
E Cowes Marina
01983 293983
Cowes Yt Hvn
01983 299975
Ch 80

Shamrock Quay
023 8022 9461
Ch 80
Saxon Wharf Marina
023 8033 9490
Ch 80

Ocean Village Marina
023 8022 9385
Ch 80

Hythe Marina
023 8020 7073
Ch 80

Buckler's Hard
01590 616200
Ch 80 HW±4

Yarmouth Harbour
01983 760321
Ch 68

Town Quay Marina
023 8023 4397
Ch 10

Lymington Yt Haven
01590 677071
Ch 80
Berthon Lymington
Marina
01590 673312
Ch 80

St Katherine's Haven
0207 264 5312
Ch 80 HW-2 to+1½

Limehouse Marina
0207 480 9022
Ch 80 HW±3

Ramsgate Marina
01843 572100**Ch 80**

Gillingham Marina
01634 280022
Ch 80 HW±4½
Hoo Marina
01634 250311
Ch 80 HW±3

Dover Marina
01304 241663
Ch 80

Littlehampton Marina
01903 713553
Ch 80
HW-3 to +2½

Lady Bee Marina
01273 593801
Ch 14

Brighton Marina
01273 819919
Ch M

Sovereign Harbour Marina
01323 470099
Ch 17

Newhaven Marina
01273 513881
Ch 80

Poole Quay -
Dolphin Yacht Haven
01202 649488
Ch 80

Parkstone Haven
01202 743610
Ch M H24

Salterns Marina
01202 709971
Ch 37, 80 H24

Cobb's Quay Marina
01202 674299
Ch 80 HW±5

Lake Yard Marina
01202 674531
Ch M H24

Ridge Wharf
01929 552650
HW±2

COMMUNICATIONS

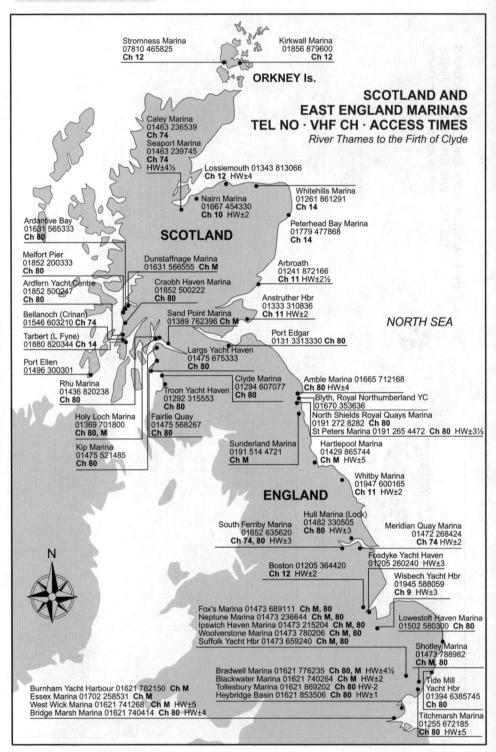

Stromness Marina
07810 465825
Ch 12

Kirkwall Marina
01856 879600
Ch 12

ORKNEY Is.

SCOTLAND AND
EAST ENGLAND MARINAS
TEL NO · VHF CH · ACCESS TIMES
River Thames to the Firth of Clyde

Caley Marina
01463 236539
Ch 74
Seaport Marina
01463 239745
Ch 74
HW±4½

Lossiemouth 01343 813066
Ch 12 HW±4

Whitehills Marina
01261 861291
Ch 14

Nairn Marina
01667 454330
Ch 10 HW±2

Peterhead Bay Marina
01779 477868
Ch 14

SCOTLAND

Melfort Pier
01852 200333
Ch 80

Dunstaffnage Marina
01631 566555 **Ch M**

Craobh Haven Marina
01852 500222
Ch 80

Ardfern Yacht Centre
01852 500247
Ch 80

Arbroath
01241 872166
Ch 11 HW±2½

Anstruther Hbr
01333 310836
Ch 11 HW±2

Ardantive Bay
01631 565333
Ch 80

Bellanoch (Crinan)
01546 603210 **Ch 74**

Sand Point Marina
01389 762396 **Ch M**

NORTH SEA

Port Edgar
0131 3313330 **Ch 80**

Tarbert (L Fyne)
01880 820344 **Ch 14**

Largs Yacht Haven
01475 675333
Ch 80

Port Ellen
01496 300301

Rhu Marina
01436 820238
Ch 80

Troon Yacht Haven
01292 315553
Ch 80

Clyde Marina
01294 607077
Ch 80

Amble Marina 01665 712168
Ch 80 HW±4

Blyth, Royal Northumberland YC
01670 353636

North Shields Royal Quays Marina
0191 272 8282 **Ch 80**
St Peters Marina 0191 265 4472 **Ch 80** HW±3½

Holy Loch Marina
01369 701800
Ch 80, M

Fairlie Quay
01475 568267
Ch 80

Hartlepool Marina
01429 865744
Ch M HW±5

Kip Marina
01475 521485
Ch 80

Sunderland Marina
0191 514 4721
Ch M

Whitby Marina
01947 600165
Ch 11 HW±2

ENGLAND

Hull Marina (Lock)
01482 330505
Ch 80 HW±3

South Ferriby Marina
01652 635620
Ch 74, 80 HW±3

Meridian Quay Marina
01472 268424
Ch 74 HW±2

Fosdyke Yacht Haven
01205 260240 HW±3

Boston 01205 364420
Ch 12 HW±2

Wisbech Yacht Hbr
01945 588059
Ch 9 HW±3

Fox's Marina 01473 689111 **Ch M, 80**
Neptune Marina 01473 236644 **Ch M, 80**
Ipswich Haven Marina 01473 215204 **Ch M, 80**
Woolverstone Marina 01473 780206 **Ch M, 80**
Suffolk Yacht Hbr 01473 659240 **Ch M, 80**

Lowestoft Haven Marina
01502 580300 **Ch 80**

Shotley Marina
01473 788982
Ch M, 80

Bradwell Marina 01621 776235 **Ch 80, M** HW±4½
Blackwater Marina 01621 740264 **Ch M** HW±2
Tollesbury Marina 01621 869202 **Ch 80** HW-2
Heybridge Basin 01621 853506 **Ch 80** HW±1

Tide Mill
Yacht Hbr
01394 6385745
Ch 80

Burnham Yacht Harbour 01621 782150 **Ch M**
Essex Marina 01702 258531 **Ch M**
West Wick Marina 01621 741268 **Ch M** HW±5
Bridge Marsh Marina 01621 740414 **Ch 80** HW±4

Titchmarsh Marina
01255 672185
Ch 80 HW±5

N

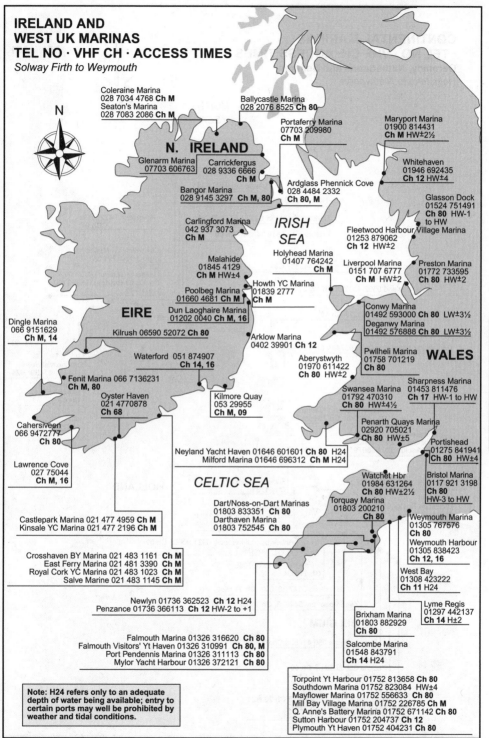

IRELAND AND WEST UK MARINAS
TEL NO · VHF CH · ACCESS TIMES
Solway Firth to Weymouth

N

Coleraine Marina
028 7034 4768 **Ch M**
Seaton's Marina
028 7083 2086 **Ch M**

Ballycastle Marina
028 2076 8525 **Ch 80**

Portaferry Marina
07703 209980
Ch M

Maryport Marina
01900 814431
Ch M HW±2½

N. IRELAND

Glenarm Marina
07703 606763

Carrickfergus
028 9336 6666
Ch M

Whitehaven
01946 692435
Ch 12 HW±4

Bangor Marina
028 9145 3297 **Ch M, 80**

Ardglass Phennick Cove
028 4484 2332
Ch 80, M

Glasson Dock
01524 751491
Ch 80 HW-1
to HW

Carlingford Marina
042 937 3073
Ch M

IRISH SEA

Fleetwood Harbour Village Marina
01253 879062
Ch 12 HW±2

Holyhead Marina
01407 764242
Ch M

Liverpool Marina
0151 707 6777
Ch M HW±2

Preston Marina
01772 733595
Ch 80 HW±2

Malahide
01845 4129
Ch M HW±4

Howth YC Marina
01839 2777
Ch M

Conwy Marina
01492 593000 **Ch 80** LW±3½
Deganwy Marina
01492 576888 **Ch 80** LW±3½

Poolbeg Marina
01660 4681 **Ch M**

EIRE

Dun Laoghaire Marina
01202 0040 **Ch M, 16**

Pwllheli Marina
01758 701219
Ch 80

WALES

Dingle Marina
066 9151629
Ch M, 14

Kilrush 06590 52072 **Ch 80**

Arklow Marina
0402 39901 **Ch 12**

Aberystwyth
01970 611422
Ch 80 HW±2

Waterford   051 874907
Ch 14, 16

Swansea Marina
01792 470310
Ch 80 HW±4½

Sharpness Marina
01453 811476
Ch 17 HW-1 to HW

Fenit Marina 066 7136231
Ch M, 80

Oyster Haven
021 4770878
Ch 68

Kilmore Quay
053 29955
Ch M, 09

Penarth Quays Marina
02920 705021
Ch 80 HW±5

Cahersiveen
066 9472777
Ch 80

Portishead
01275 841941
Ch 80 HW±4

Lawrence Cove
027 75044
Ch M, 16

Neyland Yacht Haven 01646 601601 **Ch 80** H24
Milford Marina 01646 696312 **Ch M** H24

CELTIC SEA

Watchet Hbr
01984 631264
Ch 80 HW±2½

Bristol Marina
0117 921 3198
Ch 80
HW-3 to HW

Castlepark Marina 021 477 4959 **Ch M**
Kinsale YC Marina 021 477 2196 **Ch M**

Dart/Noss-on-Dart Marinas
01803 833351 **Ch 80**
Darthaven Marina
01803 752545 **Ch 80**

Torquay Marina
01803 200210
Ch 80

Weymouth Marina
01305 767576
Ch 80

Crosshaven BY Marina 021 483 1161 **Ch M**
East Ferry Marina 021 481 3390 **Ch M**
Royal Cork YC Marina 021 483 1023 **Ch M**
Salve Marine 021 483 1145 **Ch M**

Weymouth Harbour
01305 838423
Ch 12, 16

West Bay
01308 423222
Ch 11 H24

Newlyn 01736 362523 **Ch 12** H24
Penzance 01736 366113 **Ch 12** HW-2 to +1

Lyme Regis
01297 442137
Ch 14 H±2

Brixham Marina
01803 882929
Ch 80

Falmouth Marina 01326 316620 **Ch 80**
Falmouth Visitors' Yt Haven 01326 310991 **Ch 80, M**
Port Pendennis Marina 01326 311113 **Ch 80**
Mylor Yacht Harbour 01326 372121 **Ch 80**

Salcombe Marina
01548 843791
Ch 14 H24

Torpoint Yt Harbour 01752 813658 **Ch 80**
Southdown Marina 01752 823084 HW±4
Mayflower Marina 01752 556633 **Ch 80**
Mill Bay Village Marina 01752 226785 **Ch M**
Q. Anne's Battery Marina 01752 671142 **Ch 80**
Sutton Harbour 01752 204737 **Ch 12**
Plymouth Yt Haven 01752 404231 **Ch 80**

Note: H24 refers only to an adequate
depth of water being available; entry to
certain ports may well be prohibited by
weather and tidal conditions.

COMMUNICATIONS

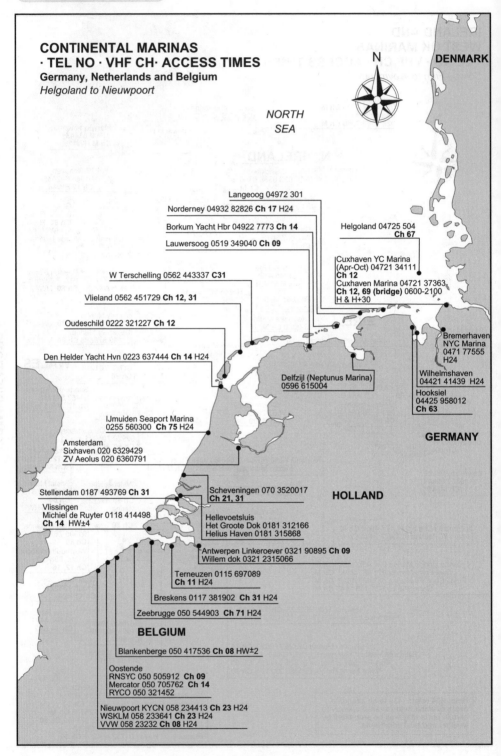

CONTINENTAL MARINAS
· TEL NO · VHF CH· ACCESS TIMES
Germany, Netherlands and Belgium
Helgoland to Nieuwpoort

N

DENMARK

NORTH SEA

Langeoog 04972 301

Norderney 04932 82826 **Ch 17** H24

Borkum Yacht Hbr 04922 7773 **Ch 14**

Lauwersoog 0519 349040 **Ch 09**

Helgoland 04725 504 **Ch 67**

Cuxhaven YC Marina (Apr-Oct) 04721 34111 **Ch 12**
Cuxhaven Marina 04721 37363 **Ch 12, 69 (bridge)** 0600-2100 H & H+30

W Terschelling 0562 443337 **C31**

Vlieland 0562 451729 **Ch 12, 31**

Oudeschild 0222 321227 **Ch 12**

Den Helder Yacht Hvn 0223 637444 **Ch 14** H24

Delfzijl (Neptunus Marina) 0596 615004

Bremerhaven NYC Marina 0471 77555 H24

Wilhelmshaven 04421 41439 H24

Hooksiel 04425 958012 **Ch 63**

IJmuiden Seaport Marina 0255 560300 **Ch 75** H24

Amsterdam Sixhaven 020 6329429 ZV Aeolus 020 6360791

GERMANY

Stellendam 0187 493769 **Ch 31**

Scheveningen 070 3520017 **Ch 21, 31**

HOLLAND

Vlissingen Michiel de Ruyter 0118 414498 **Ch 14** HW±4

Hellevoetsluis Het Groote Dok 0181 312166 Helius Haven 0181 315868

Antwerpen Linkeroever 0321 90895 **Ch 09** Willem dok 0321 2315066

Terneuzen 0115 697089 **Ch 11** H24

Breskens 0117 381902 **Ch 31** H24

Zeebrugge 050 544903 **Ch 71** H24

BELGIUM

Blankenberge 050 417536 **Ch 08** HW±2

Oostende RNSYC 050 505912 **Ch 09** Mercator 050 705762 **Ch 14** RYCO 050 321452

Nieuwpoort KYCN 058 234413 **Ch 23** H24 WSKLM 058 233641 **Ch 23** H24 VVW 058 23232 **Ch 08** H24

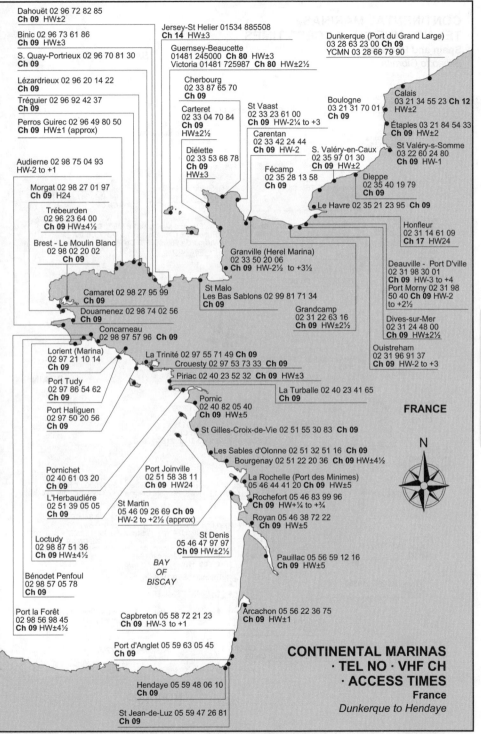

CONTINENTAL MARINAS
· TEL NO · VHF CH
· ACCESS TIMES
France
Dunkerque to Hendaye

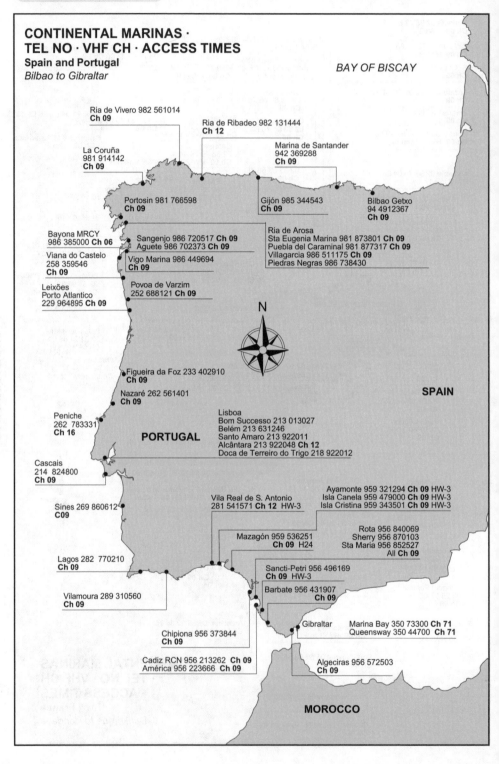

CONTINENTAL MARINAS ·
TEL NO · VHF CH · ACCESS TIMES
Spain and Portugal
Bilbao to Gibraltar

BAY OF BISCAY

Ria de Vivero 982 561014
Ch 09

Ria de Ribadeo 982 131444
Ch 12

La Coruña
981 914142
Ch 09

Marina de Santander
942 369288
Ch 09

Portosin 981 766598
Ch 09

Gijón 985 344543
Ch 09

Bilbao Getxo
94 4912367
Ch 09

Bayona MRCY
986 385000 **Ch 06**

Sangenjo 986 720517 **Ch 09**
Aguete 986 702373 **Ch 09**

Ria de Arosa
Sta Eugenia Marina 981 873801 **Ch 09**
Puebla del Caraminal 981 877317 **Ch 09**
Villagarcia 986 511175 **Ch 09**
Piedras Negras 986 738430

Viana do Castelo
258 359546
Ch 09

Vigo Marina 986 449694

Leixões
Porto Atlantico
229 964895 **Ch 09**

Povoa de Varzim
252 688121 **Ch 09**

N

Figueira da Foz 233 402910
Ch 09

Nazaré 262 561401
Ch 09

SPAIN

Peniche
262 783331
Ch 16

PORTUGAL

Lisboa
Bom Successo 213 013027
Belém 213 631246
Santo Amaro 213 922011
Alcântara 213 922048 **Ch 12**
Doca de Terreiro do Trigo 218 922012

Cascais
214 824800
Ch 09

Ayamonte 959 321294 **Ch 09** HW-3
Isla Canela 959 479000 **Ch 09** HW-3
Isla Cristina 959 343501 **Ch 09** HW-3

Sines 269 860612
C09

Vila Real de S. Antonio
281 541571 **Ch 12** HW-3

Rota 956 840069
Sherry 956 870103
Sta Maria 956 852527
All **Ch 09**

Mazagón 959 536251
Ch 09 H24

Lagos 282 770210
Ch 09

Sancti-Petri 956 496169
Ch 09 HW-3

Vilamoura 289 310560
Ch 09

Barbate 956 431907
Ch 09

Gibraltar

Marina Bay 350 73300 **Ch 71**
Queensway 350 44700 **Ch 71**

Chipiona 956 373844
Ch 09

Algeciras 956 572503
Ch 09

Cadiz RCN 956 213262 **Ch 09**
América 956 223666 **Ch 09**

MOROCCO

PORT RADIO STATIONS

The following listings are derived from ALRS (Admiralty List of Radio Signals). They are therefore biassed towards 'Big Ships'. However if read in conjunction with Marina R/T details which appear on pages 93–98, the most complete picture will emerge. (It is hoped to combine the two listings in a later edition).

Annotations: Ch 16 is almost universally guarded; it is therefore omitted. *Call on a working channel if essential. In many larger ports it is sensible to monitor the primary port channel (in bold) before changing to a marina channel.* Times are local, unless marked **UT. H24** = continuous watch. **HJ** = day only. **HO** = Office hours. **HX** = no specific hours.

ENGLAND – SOUTH COAST

ST MARY'S HARBOUR, Isles of Scilly: Ch 14, 69 (Pilots). Summer 0800-1700 daily.
NEWLYN HARBOUR:
Hbr office: Ch 09 12
Mon-Fri: 0800-1700, Sat: 0800-1200
PENZANCE hbr radio:
Hbr office: Ch 09 12 Mon-Fri: 0830-1730 and on all tides HW −2 to +1.
FALMOUTH hbr radio:
Ch 12 14 (Mon-Fri 0800-1700). Harbour Launch *Killigrew*: **Ch 12**
Truro Hbr office: Call *Carrick One* **Ch 12**
MEVAGISSEY:
Hbr office: Ch 14
Summer: 0900-2100, Winter: 0900-1700
CHARLESTOWN:
Hbr office: Ch 14 HW −2 to +1, only when a vessel is expected.
PAR PORT RADIO:
Hbr office: Ch 12 HO. Pilots HW ±2.
FOWEY Hbr Radio:
(0900-1700) **Hbr Patrol: Ch 12** (0900-2000).
Water Taxi: Ch 06.
LOOE: Ch 16 Occas.
PLYMOUTH:
Movement Control: *Long Room Port Control* **Ch 14** H24.
Sutton Hbr Lock: Ch 12 H24.
Cattewater Hbr: Ch 14 (Mon-Fri 0900-1700).
SALCOMBE:
Salcombe Hbr or launch: Ch 14 May to mid-Sep: 7/7, 0600-2200; otherwise: M-F 0900-1600
Salcombe Hbr Taxi **Ch 12**. Fuel barge: **Ch 06**
Egremont (ICC Floating HQ): **Ch M**
DARTMOUTH:
Dart Nav Ch 11 M-F: 0900-1700 ±1, Sat: 0900-1200.
Fuel barge: **Ch 06**. Water taxi: **Ch 08**.
TORBAY HARBOURS:
Call *Brixham Port* or *Torquay Port* **Ch 14** May-

Sep: 0800-1800; Oct-Apr: Mon-Fri: 0900-1700.
TEIGNMOUTH Hbr Radio:
Ch 12 Mon-Fri 0830-1700; Sat 0900-1200 and when vessel due.
EXETER:
Port of Exeter Ch 12 Mon-Fri: 0730-1730 and when vessel expected. **Exmouth Dock Ch 14.**
Retreat Boatyard: Ch M HW±2
LYME REGIS Harbour Radio:
Ch 14. Summer: 0800-2000, Winter: 1000-1500. Access HW±2½.
BRIDPORT Radio:
Ch 11
PORTLAND Harbour Radio:
Ch 74 (H24)
WEYMOUTH Harbour Radio:
Hbr Office & Town Bridge: Ch 12 Mon-Fri: 0800-2000 (summer & when vessel is due).
Marina Ch 80. Fuel: Ch 60
POOLE:
Harbour Control & Bridge Ch 14 (H24)
Poole Bay Fuels: Ch M Mon-Fri: 0900-1730, weekends in season 0830-1800
YARMOUTH (IoW):
Hbr office & Yar Bridge: Ch 68 H24. **Water taxi: Ch 15**
NEWPORT (IoW):
Hr Mr: 69 0800-1600
COWES:
Hbr Office & Chain Ferry Ch 69
Mon-Fri: 0800-1700 and by arrangement
Water Taxi: Ch 77
RYDE:
Hbr office: Ch 80
Summer 0800-2000 Winter HX. Access HW±2
BEMBRIDGE:
Harbour launch **Ch M**
SOUTHAMPTON:
Monitor Port operations Ch 12 14
VTS Broadcasts Ch 12 Every H 0600-2200, 1 Jun-30 Sep
HAMBLE:
Hbr Radio: Ch 68 Apr-Sep daily: 0600-2200, Oct-Mar 0700-1830
Water Taxi: Call *Blue Star Boats* **Ch 77** 06
PORTSMOUTH:
Monitor Ch 11. Call *QHM* **Ch 11** if essential
PORTSMOUTH COMMERCIAL HARBOUR:
Call *Portsmouth Hbr Radio* **Ch 11** 14 (H24)
LANGSTONE:
Hbr office: Ch 12. Summer: daily 0830-1700; Winter: Mon-Fri 0830-1700; Sat-Sun 0830-1300
CHICHESTER:
Hbr office: Ch 14. 1 Apr - 30 Sep: M-Fri: 0900-1300, 1400-1700. Sat: 0900-1300. 1 Oct - 31 March: 0900-1300, 1400-1700
Water taxi Ch 08 0900-1800, mobile 07970 378350
LITTLEHAMPTON:
Hbr office (Town Quay) & Bridge: Ch 71 HX

Arun Yacht Club: Ch M Access HW±3
SHOREHAM:
Shoreham Hbr Radio: **Ch 14** (H24) and lock
BRIGHTON:
Call *Brighton Control*: **Ch M 80.** Inner hbr only, access 0800-1800 via lock
NEWHAVEN:
Newhaven Radio Ch 12; ditto Swing bridge
EASTBOURNE:
Sovereign Hbr, inc Lock/berthing: **Ch 17**
RYE:
Hbr radio: Ch 14 0900-1700 or when ship due
FOLKESTONE:
Call **Port Control: Ch 15** for clearance to enter
DOVER:
Call **Port Control Ch 74** for clearance to enter
DOVER STRAIT:
Channel Navigation Information Service CNIS:
Dover Coastguard **Ch 11 67 80**
Ch 11 bcsts Info H+40 plus extra bcst when visibility <2M; ditto Gris Nez Traffic **Ch 79** at H+10, plus additional bcst every H+25 when visibility <2M
RAMSGATE:
Port Control Ch 14

ENGLAND – EAST COAST

MEDWAY:
Monitor **Medway Radio Ch 74**
Kingsferry Bridge (W Swale): Ch 10 H24
Whitstable
Hbr Radio: Ch 09 12, Mon-Fri: 0830-1700 and –3HW+1
PORT OF LONDON:
LONDON VTS: Ch 69 (from seaward approaches to Sea Reach No 4 buoy)
LONDON VTS: Ch 68
Sea Reach No 4 Lt buoy to Crayford Ness
LONDON VTS: Ch 14, 22
Above Crayford Ness
Thames Barrier:
All VHF-equipped vessels intending to navigate in the Thames Barrier Control Zone must report to **LONDON VTS** on **Ch 14**
RIVER THAMES:
Patrol Launches: Call *Thames Patrol* **Ch 06 12 14 16 68**
King George V Dock Lock: Call *KG Control* **Ch 13**
West India Dock Lock: Ch 13
Greenwich Yacht Club: Ch M
Thames Lock (Brentford): Ch 74
Summer 0800-1800 Winter 0800-1630
Cadogan Pier: Ch 14 0900-1700
RIVER ROACH:
Havengore Bridge: Ch 72 HJ, Access HW±2
BURNHAM-ON-CROUCH:
HM Launch Ch 80 0900-1700
RIVER BLACKWATER:
River Bailiff: Ch 16 0900-1700

Heybridge Lock: Ch 80 –2HW+1
RIVER COLNE, BRIGHTLINGSEA:
Hbr Radio: Ch 68 0800-2000
RIVERS STOUR AND ORWELL:
HARWICH VTS: Ch 71 11 14 16 H24
SUNK VTS Ch 14 H24
Harwich International Port Ch 13
Ipswich Port Radio: Ch 68 H24
RIVER DEBEN:
Hbr office: Ch 08
SOUTHWOLD:
Port Radio: Ch 09 12;
LOWESTOFT:
Hbr Control: Ch 11 14
Royal Norfolk & Suffolk YC: Ch 80
Access HW±4
Mutford Lock and Road Bridge: Ch 09 14
GREAT YARMOUTH:
Yarmouth Radio: Ch 12 H24
Haven Bridge Breydon Bridge: Ch 12
WELLS-NEXT-THE-SEA:
Wells Hbr Radio: Ch 12
HJ and HW–3 when vessel expected
WISBECH:
Ch 09 HW–3 when vessel expected
Sutton Bridge: Ch 09
KING'S LYNN:
Call *KLCB* **Ch 14** 11
Mon-Fri: 0800-1730 and –4HW+1
BOSTON:
Pot Control: Ch 11 12
Grand Sluice: Ch 74 only when lock operates
Denver Sluice: Ch 73 when vessel expected
RIVER HUMBER:
VTS Area 1: Ch 14 (from sea to Clee Ness Lt F)
VTS Area 2: Ch 12 (up-river to Garleston on R Trent and Goole on R Ouse). MSI broadcasts on Ch 12 & 14 every 2hrs from 0103
Grimsby Docks: Ch 74; 18 79 H24
South Ferriby sluice: Ch 74 80
Mon-Fri: 0930-1700; Sat, Sun & Holidays: 1030-1700. Access HW±3
RIVER TRENT TO NEAR NEWARK
Burton-upon-Stather, Flixborough, Grove, Keadby, Gunness, Gainsborough: All Ch 17.
Locks at Keadby, West Stockwith, Torksey and Cromwell: All Ch 74
RIVER OUSE TO NABURN
Blacktoft Jetty: Ch 14
Goole Docks: Ch 14 H24
Goole Railway Bridge: Ch 09
Howdendyke: Ch 09
Boothferry bridge: Ch 09
Selby lock: Ch 74 HJ
Selby railway and Toll bridges: Ch 09 contact 10 mins in advance
Naburn Lock: Ch 74
BRIDLINGTON:
Hbr office: Ch 12 HX. Access HW±3

SCARBOROUGH:
Scarborough Lt Ho **Ch 12** H24. Access HW±3
WHITBY:
HM & Bridge: **Ch 11**, 12 H24. Access HW±2
TEES and HARTLEPOOL:
Tees Port control: **Ch** 08, 11, 12, **14, 22**
R. Tees Barrage: **Ch M** H24
SEAHAM:
Hbr office: **Ch 12** Mon-Fri: 0800-1800
Access HW −2½ to +1½
SUNDERLAND:
Hbr Radio: **Ch 14** (H24)
TYNE, PORT OF:
Tyne Hbr Radio: **Ch 11 12** 14, inc Info service
Harbour Launch: **Ch** 06 08 11 12 14
BLYTH:
Port control: **Ch 11 12**
WARKWORTH HARBOUR (Amble):
Hbr office: **Ch 14** (Mon-Fri 0900-1700)
BERWICK-UPON-TWEED:
Hbr office: **Ch 12** Mon-Fri 0800-1700

SCOTLAND

Eyemouth:
Ch 12 office hours
FORTH PORTS:
Call *Forth Navigation* **Ch 71**; 12, 20 on request
Leith: **Ch 12**
Granton, Royal Forth YC: Call *Boswell* **Ch M**
Access HW±4
Grangemouth Docks: Ch 14
Forth & Clyde Canal:
Call *Carron Sea Lock* **Ch 74**
Methil Docks: **Ch 14** Access −3HW+1
Anstruther: **Ch 11** Access HW±2
PERTH:
Perth Harbour **Ch 09**
DUNDEE:
Dundee Harbour Radio **Ch 12**
Royal Tay YC: Ch M
ARBROATH:
Arbroath Port Control **Ch 11**
MONTROSE:
Montrose Port Control **Ch 12**
STONEHAVEN:
Stonehaven **Ch 11**
ABERDEEN:
Aberdeen Port Control **Ch** 06 11 **12** 13
PETERHEAD:
Peterhead Hbrs **Ch 14** for cl'nce to enter/exit
FRASERBURGH: Ch 12 H24
MACDUFF: Ch 12 H24
BANFF: Ch 14 HX, access HW±4
WHITEHILLS: *Whitehills Hbr Radio* **Ch 14**
BUCKIE: Ch 12 (Ch 16 is H24)
LOSSIEMOUTH:
Ch 12 0700-1700 & 1hr before vessel is due
HOPEMAN and BURGHEAD:
Burghead Radio **Ch 14** HX or when vessel due

INVERNESS:
Inverness Hbr Office: Ch 12
M-Fri: 0900-1700 and when vessel expected
Clachnaharry Sea Lock **Ch 74** HW±4 in HO
CROMARTY FIRTH, inc Invergordon: Ch 11
HELMSDALE: Ch 13
WICK: Ch 14 HX
SCRABSTER:
Port: **Ch 12** H24. Call on entry and exit.
ORKNEY HARBOURS NAVIGATION SERVICE:
Orkney Harbour Radio **Ch 09 11** 12
Kirkwall: Ch 12
M-Fri: 0900-1700 and when vessel expected
Stromness Harbour: Ch 12 M-Fri: 0900-1700
Pierowall (Westray Pier): Ch 14 when vessel
is expected
SHETLAND
Lerwick Hbr: Ch 11 12
Scalloway Hbr Radio: Ch 09 12
Mon-Fri: 0600-1800, Sat: 0600-1230
Sullom Voe VTS: Ch 14 for traffic info, weather
and radar assistance on request
Balta Sound Harbour: Ch 16 20 HO
OUTER HEBRIDES
STORNOWAY: Hbr office Ch 12 H24
Loch Maddy, N Uist: Ch 12 HX
St Kilda: Call *Kilda Radio* **Ch 16 12 73** HJ
MAINLAND
Kinlochbervie: Ch 14 HX
Lochinver: Ch 09 HX
ULLAPOOL: Ch 14 12 H24 fishing season,
otherwise HO
Gairloch Harbour: Ch 16 0900-1400; 1900-2300
ISLE OF SKYE
Uig: Ch 08 HX. **Portree Harbour: Ch 12** HX
Skye Bridge Crossing: Ch 12
KYLE OF LOCH ALSH: Ch 11
Mallaig: Ch 09 HO
Tiree, Gott Bay Pier, : Ch 31 HX
Isle of Coll, Arinagour Pier: Ch 31
Loch Sunart, Salen Jetty: Ch 16 (Occas)
ISLAND OF MULL
Tobermory: Ch 12 M HJ
Craignure Pier: Ch 31 HX
Corpach/Caledonian Canal: Ch 16 74
Summer: 0800-1730; Spring/Autumn: 0830-
1730; Winter: 0900-1600
OBAN:
Port **Ch 12** 0900-1700. **Oban Bay**, monitor **16**
CRINAN CANAL: Ch 74
May-Sep: 0830-1900; other months call 01546
603210 for information.
Tarbert, Loch Fyne: Ch 14
CAMPBELTOWN: Ch 12 13 Mon-Fri: 0900-1700
ROTHESAY, Bute: Ch 12
May-Sep: 0600-2100; Oct-Apr: 0600-1900
ARDROSSAN:
Hbr office: Ch 12 14

CLYDEPORT:
Clydeport Estuary Radio: Ch 12 H24
QHM Faslane: Ch 73 13
Greenock Control: Ch 73
IRVINE: Ch 12
Port & Bridge: Ch 12 HX, Mon-Fri: 0800-1600
TROON: Ch 14
Seacat, daily Arr: 0930, 2030; Dep 1015, 2100
AYR: Ch 14 H24
GIRVAN: Ch 12 Mon-Fri: 0900-1700
STRANRAER: Ch 14 (H24) Monitor for ferries
KIRKCUDBRIGHT: Ch 12 0800-1700
Access HW±3

ENGLAND W COAST & WALES

Silloth Docks: Ch 12 Access −2½HW+1
MARYPORT: Ch 12 Access −HW±2½
WORKINGTON:
Hbr Radio: Ch 11 14 Access −2½HW+2
WHITEHAVEN: Ch 12 Access HW±3
ISLE OF MAN
Douglas Hbr Control and Info: Ch 12 H24.
Note: if unable to contact other IoM hbrs
below, call Douglas
Castletown: Ch 12 0830-1700
Port St Mary: Ch 12 HJ and when vessel due
Peel: Ch 12 HJ and when vessel expected
Ramsey: Ch 12 HO and when vessel due
MAINLAND
Barrow Port Control: Ch 12
Heysham Port: Ch 14 74
Glasson Dock Ch 69 Access −1½HW through lock
FLEETWOOD:
Fleetwood Dock Radio: Ch 12 0900-1700
Access HW±2 through lock
PRESTON: Call *Riversway* **Ch 16, 14** Access −
HW±2
LIVERPOOL:
Call *Mersey Radio* **Ch 12** for port operations
Information broadcasts: Ch 09 at 3h and 2h
before HW. **Radar assistance Ch 18**
Brunswick Dock: Ch M for Liverpool marina
Canning Dock: Ch M 0900-1700. Access −2HW
through lock to Albert Dock
CONWY:
Ch 12 14 Summer: 0900-1700 daily; Winter
same times Mon-Fri. Access HW±3
MENAI STRAIT
Beaumaris & Menai Bridge: Ch 69
Mon-Fri: 0800-1700
Caernarfon: Call *Caernarfon Hbr* **Ch 14**
Mon-Fri: 0900-1700 Sat: 0900-1200
HOLYHEAD
Port Control: Ch 14 H24
PWLLHELI
Hbr office **Ch 12** 0900-1715.
PORTHMADOG
Call *Portmadog Hbr* **Ch 12 14** 0900-1700, and
when vessel expected. Access HW±1½

BARMOUTH
Call *Barmouth Hbr* **Ch 12** May-Sept: 0900-1700
- available later for HW; Oct-April: 0900-1600
weekdays only
ABERDOVEY: Call *Aberdovet Hbr* **Ch 12** 0900-
1700 Access HW±3
ABERYSTWYTH: Ch 14 Access HW±3
ABERAERON: Ch 14 Served by **New Quay**
Harbourmaster. 0900-1700. Access HW±3
FISHGUARD: Hbr office: Ch 14
MILFORD HAVEN
Port Control & Patrol launch: Ch 12, monitor
continuously whilst under way
Milford Docks: Call *Pierhead* **Ch 14** 09 12
Locking approx HW±3; freeflow HW −2 to HW
Tenby: Ch 80 Access HW±2½
Saundersfoot: Ch 11 Summer: 0800-2100,
Winter: Mon-Fri: 0800-1800. Access HW±2
SWANSEA BAY
Docks Radio: Ch 14 H24
Tawe Lock for marina: **Ch 18**
River Neath: Ch 77 H24 **Port Talbot: Ch 12** H24
BARRY: *Barry Radio* **Ch 11** Access −4HW+3
CARDIFF
Cardiff Radio **Ch 14. Barrage control: Ch 18**
NEWPORT: Port: Ch 09 69 71 Access HW±4
SHARPNESS
Call *Sharpness Radio* **Ch 13** for locking in
Canal operations: Ch 74 Access −5HW+1
BRISTOL
Avonmouth Sig Stn *Bristol VTS*: **Ch 12** 09 11
for mandatory reporting to VTS
City Docks Radio: **Ch 11 14** (on low power)
Access −3HW+1
Bristol Floating Hbr: **Ch 73** HO; Access −
3HW+1 through lock
Prince Street Bridge and Netham Lock: Ch 73
BURNHAM-ON-SEA/BRIDGWATER
Hbr office: Ch 08 Access −3HW when vessel
is expected
ILFRACOMBE:
Hbr office: Ch 12 Apr-Oct: 0815-1700, when
manned; Nov-Mar: HX. Access HW±2
APPLEDORE-BIDEFORD:
Call Port/PV *'Two Rivers'* **Ch 12** Access −2HW
BUDE:
Hbr office: Ch 12 When vessel expected
PADSTOW:
Ch 12 M-Fri: 0800-1700 and HW±2
ST IVES: Ch 12, 16 (Occas) HX

IRELAND

SHANNON ESTUARY: Call *Shannon Estuary*
Radio **Ch 12 13** (HO)
GALWAY: Ch 12 Access −2½HW+1
ROSSAVEEL: Ch 12 14 Office Hours
KINSALE: Ch 14. HO and when vessel expected
BANTRY: Ch 06 11 12 14 H24

CASTLETOWN BEARHAVEN: Ch 14
DINGLE: Ch 11 M
LIMERICK: Ch 12 13
Office hours & when vessel expected
FENIT: Ch 14 M HX
ROSSLARE: Hbr office: Ch 06 12 14 H24
CORK: Call *Cork Hbr Radio* Ch 12 14 16 H24
WATERFORD & NEW ROSS: Ch 12 14 16 HJ &
when vessel expected
YOUGHAL: Ch 14 Access HW±3
ARKLOW: Port: Ch 12
WICKLOW: Port: Ch 14 12
DUN LAOGHAIRE: Hbr office: Ch 14
DUBLIN:
Port Radio: Ch 12 13
Lifting Bridge: Call Eastlink Ch 12 13
HOWTH:
Hr Mr: Ch 13 Mon-Fri: 0700-2300
Sat/Sun: HX
CARLINGFORDFORD LOUGH
Warrenpoint: Ch 12 H24
Greenore: Ch 16 HJ
STRANGFORD HARBOUR:
Ch 12 14 M
Ardglass Harbour: Ch 14 12
Mon-Fri 0900-1700
Killyleagh: Ch 12 HX
Kilkeel: Ch 12 14 Mon-Fri: 0900-2000
DUNDALK: Ch 14 Mon-Fri: 0900-1700
DROGHEDA: Ch 11 Mon-Fri: 0800-1700. HX
BELFAST:
VTS: Ch 12
Portavogie: Ch 12 14 Mon-Fri 0900-1700
LARNE:
Port Control: Ch 14 11 16
COLERAINE:
Ch 12 Mon-Fri 0900-1700
Portrush: Ch 12 Mon-Fri 0900-1700; Sat-Sun
0900-1700, Jun-Sep only

LONDONDERRY: Hbr radio: Ch 14 12
KILLYBEGS: Ch 14 16
SLIGO:
Hr Mr: Ch 12 14
0900-1700 and when vessel expected
Burton Port: Ch 14 06 12

DENMARK

Skagen: Ch 12 13 H24
Hirtshals Havn: Ch 12 13 HX
Torup Strand: Ch 12 13 HX
Hanstholm Havn: Ch 12 13 HX
THYBORØN: Ch 12 13 HX.
Thisted (Limfjorden): Ch 12 13 HX.
Torsminde: Ch 12 13 0300-1300, 1400-2400.
Hvide Sande: Ch 12 13 HX.
Esbjerg Hbr Control: Ch 12 13 14 H24.
Rømø Havn: Ch 10 12 13 HX.

GERMANY

HELGOLAND:
Port: Ch 67
May-Aug: Mon-Thu: 0700-1200, 1300-2000.
Fri-Sat: 0700-2000. Sun: 0700-1200.
Sep-Apr: Mon-Thu: 0700-1200, 1300-1600.
Fri: 0700-1200.
List Port: Ch 11 0800-1200 1600-1800
Hornum: 67; M-Th 0700-1600, Fri 0700-1230.
Wyk Port: Ch 11
Pellworm Port: Ch 11 0700-1700
Husum Port: Ch 11. Access −4HW+2.
Information bcsts: Ch 11 every H+00.
Eider Lock: Ch 14
Büsum Port: Ch 11
INNER DEUTSCHE BUCHT
(GERMAN BIGHT):
VTS: Eastern part: Ch 80
VTS: Western part: Ch 79
BRUNSBÜTTEL ELBE PORT: Ch 12
NORD-OSTSEE KANAL (KIEL CANAL):
VTS Canal 1 Ch 13
VTS Canal 2 Ch 02
VTS Canal 3 Ch 03
VTS Canal 4 Ch 12
Brieholz: Ch 73
Ostermoor: Ch 73
Friedrichskoog: Ch 10 Access HW±2
RIVER ELBE:
Cuxhaven Elbe Port: Ch 12 HX
Cuxhaven Lock: Ch 69
VTS: Ch 71
Brunsbüttel Elbe Traffic: Ch 68
Oste Bridge (flood barrage): Ch 69
Apr-Sep the bridge is opened on request
Ch 69. Oct-Mar request through Ch 03 or 16
Belum Radar or Ch 21 Cuxhaven Radar
Oste Bridge Geversdorf: Ch 69; The bridge
opens on request for small craft Apr-Sep: 0730-
1930 and every H+00 and H+30
Oberndorf Bridge: Ch 69 Oct-Mar H24,
Apr-Sep 1930-0730. The bridge is opened on
request by telephone 04772 86 10 11.
Stör Lock: Ch 09 Bridge opens on request.
Glückstadt Lock: Ch 11 0700-1600 & thru HW.
Stadersand Elbe Port: Ch 12
Este Lock: Ch 10
Este Bridge: Ch 10 Opened on request
HAMBURG:
VTS: Ch 74 13 14
Port Traffic: Ch 74 13 14
Elbe Port: Ch 12
Rethe Bridge: Ch 13
Kattwyk Bridge: Ch 13
Harburg Lock: Ch 13
Tiefstack Lock: Ch 11
DIE WESER AND DIE HUNTE:
Bremerhaven Weser Tfc: Ch 02 04 05 07 21 22 82
Bremen Weser Traffic: Ch 19 78 81

Hunte Traffic:
VTS: Ch 63
Info in German: Ch 02 04 05 07 21 22 82 every H+20 by Bremerhaven Weser Traffic
Info in German: Ch 19 78 81 H+30 by Bremen Weser Traffic
Info in German: Ch 63 H+30 by Hunte Traffic
BREMERHAVEN:
Port: Ch 12
Fischereihafen Lock: Ch 69 70
Bremerhaven Nord Lock: 69 70
Bremerhaven Weser:
Port: Ch 14
Brake Lock: Ch 10
Elsfleth-Ohrt Railway Bridge: Ch 73 – 2h before sunrise to 2h after sunset
Hunte Lock: Ch 73
Hunte lifting bridge: Ch 73 – 2h before sunrise to 2h after sunset
Oldenburg:
Railway Bridge: Ch 73
H24 except Sun and public holidays 0030-0630
Lock: Ch 20 Mon-Sat: 0500-2100
Sun: 0900-1200
Cäcilien Bridge: Ch 73
Oslebshausen Lock: Ch 12
BREMEN:
Port: Ch 03
Lock: Ch 20 Mon-Sat: 0600-2200, Sun: Oct-Apr 0800-1100 May-Sep: 0800-1400 1730-1930
DIE JADE:
VTS: Ch 63 20
Info bcsts (in German): Ch 20 63 every H+10
WILHEMSHAVEN:
Port: Ch 11. Lock: Ch 13
Bridges: Ch 11
VAREL Lock: Ch 13 HW±2
Wangerooge: Ch 17 0700-1700
Harlesiel: lock Ch 17 0700-2100
Bensersiel: Ch 17 Oct-Mar Mon-Fri: 0700-1230 1330-1700, Apr-Sep Mon-Fri: 0700-1900 Sat & Sun: 0700-1100 1300-1700
Langeoog: Ch 17 0700-1700
Norderney: Ch 17 Mon: 0700-1200 1230-1730, Tues: 0900-1200 1230-1900, Wed-Sun: 0700-1200 1230-1900
Norddeich: Ch 17
Mon: 0730-1900, Tue-Fri: 0700-1300 1330-1900, Sat & Sun: 0800-1200 1230-1730
BORKUM:
Port: Ch 14 All year Mon-Fri: 0700-2200, Sep-Apr Sat & Sun: 0700-1700, May-Aug Sat: 0800-1200 1500-2100 Sun: 0700-1100 1400-2000
DIE EMS VTS: Call Ems Traffic **Ch 15 18 20 21** Ems Traffic broadcasts every H+50 on Ch 15 18 20 and 21 in German. All vessels must keep a continuous watch on the appropriate channel

Emden Locks: Ch 13
Oldersum Lock: Ch 13 May-Sep Mon-Fri 0700-2000 Sat & Sun 0800-2000, Oct-Apr Mon-Thu 0700-1530 Fri 0700-1400
Leer Bridge: Ch 15
Leer Lock: Ch 13 16
Weener Bridge: Ch 15
Weener Lock: Ch 13 1 Apr- 31 Oct only: Mon-Thu 0700-1600 Fri: 0700-sunset Sat & Sun: sunrise-sunset
Papenburg Lock: Ch 13

NETHERLANDS
VTS DELFZIJL/EEMSHAVEN
Delfzijl Radar: Ch 03
Eemshaven Radar: Ch 01
Port Control: Ch 66
Intership: Ch 10
DELFZIJL:
Hbr office: Ch 14 Radar assistance given when visibility falls below 2000m
Info broadcasts: Ch 66 Every even H+10
Locks: Ch 11 Mon-Sat: H24, Sun & holidays on request
Weiwerder Bridge: Ch 11
Heemskes and Handelshaven Bridges: Ch 14 Mon-Sat: 0600-1400
Farmsumerhaven: Ch 14
EEMSHAVEN:
Hbr office: Ch 14. Radar: Ch 01 19
LAUWERSOOG:
Havendienst, Ch 09. Mon 0000-1700; Tue-Wed 0800-1700; Thur-Sat 0700-1500.
Terschelling: Call Brandaris VTS **Ch 02** All vessels must keep a listening watch **Ch 02**
Harlingen: Ch 11 Mon 0000-Sat 2200
DEN HELDER: VTS Tfc Centre Ch 12
Port Control: Ch 14
Moormanbrug Bridge: Ch 18
Koopvaarders Lock: Ch 22
IJsselmeer
Den Oever Lock: Ch 20
Kornwerderzand: locks Ch 18
AMSTERDAM:
Port Control: Ch 04 68
Port Information: Ch 14
Beverwijk: Ch 71
Wilhelminasluis: Ch 20
Westerkeersluis: Ch 22
Haarlem: Ch 18
Oranjesluisen: Ch 18
Enkhuizen or Krabbersgat: Ch 22
Lock operates weekdays 0300-2300, Sun and holidays 0800-2000
IJMUIDEN:
Traffic Centre: Ch 07 West of IJmuiden lt buoy
Port Control: Ch 61 From IJmuiden Lt buoy to the North Sea Locks
NORDZEE KANAAL:
VTS: Ch 68

From Ijmuiden Lt By to the IJmuiden Sluices
Noordzee sluizen: Call Sluis IJmuiden **Ch 22**
Noordzee kanaal: Ch 03 From IJmuiden Sluices
to km 11·2
Zijkanaal C Sluice: Call Sluis IJmuiden **Ch 18**
SCHEVENINGEN:
Traffic Centre: Ch 21
Port: Ch 14
MAAS APPROACH: Ch 01. Oude Maas: Ch 62
HOEK VAN HOLLAND ROADS:
VTS: To cross the mouth of the Maas, Call *Maas Entrance* **Ch 03**; report vessel's name, position and course. Follow a track close W of a line joining buoys MV, MVN and Indusbank N. Whilst crossing, maintain continuous listening watch and a very sharp lookout.
NIEUWE WATERWEG:
HCC Central Traffic Control **Ch 11 14 19** See VTS Chart No 4. Report to and keep a continuous listening watch on the appropriate Tfc Centre
Bridges and locks in the Rotterdam area:
Botlekbrug: Ch 18
Koninginnebrug: Ch 18
Spijkenisserbrug: Ch 18
Brienenoordbrug: Ch 20
Sluis Weurt: Ch 18
Prins Bernhardsluis: Ch 18
Sluis S. Andries: Ch 20
Maassluis (Buitehaven ent): Ch 80
Manderssluis: Ch 20
DORDRECHT:
Tfc Control: Dordrecht **Ch 79,** Heerjansdam **Ch 04**
Port: Ch 74
General nautical information: Ch 71
Bruggen Dordrecht: Ch 19
Alblasserdamse brug: Ch 22
Papendrechtse brug: Ch 19
Merwedesluis en Verkeersbrug: Ch 18
Algera sluis en Stuw: Ch 22
Julianasluis: Ch 18
Grote Sluis Vianen: Ch 22
Andel Wilhelminasluis: Ch 22
Dordrecht Railway and Rd Bridge: Ch 71
Broombrug/Wijnhavn: Ch 74
OOSTERSCHELDE:
Call Roompotsluis **Ch 18** Lock operating hours: Mon and Thu, 0000-2200; Tue and Sun, 0600-0000; Wed H24; Fri and Sat: 0600-2200.
Roompot Harbour: Ch 31
Ouddorp Coastguard: Ch 25
Wemeldinge Bridge and Locks: Ch 68
Zeelandbrug Bridge: Ch 18
Krammer Locks: Ch 22
Kreekraksluizen: Ch 20 Vessels should report to the locks as follows: S bound, after Tholen Hr; N bound, after Bath bridge
Haringvliet-Sluizen: Ch 20 Operating times Mon-Fri 0000-2200; 1 Nov - 1 April Sat 0800-2200 Sun 0800-1000, 1600-1800; 1 April - 1 Nov Sat & Sun 0800-2000

WESTERSCHELDE:
VTS: See VTS Chart No 3. Reporting, in English or Dutch, is compulsory for all In- and Out-bound vessels, but not yachts. All vessels, including those at anchor, must keep a continuous listening watch on the VHF channel for the appropriate Traffic Area. The boundaries of each Traffic Area are marked by buoys. In emergency call the relevant Traffic Centre: **Ch 67.**
STEENBANK TRAFFIC AREA:
VTS Tfc Centre: Ch 64
VLISSINGEN TRAFFIC AREA:
VTS Tfc Centre: Ch 14. Info: Ch 14 every H+50
TERNEUZEN TRAFFIC AREA:
VTS Tfc Centre: Ch 03. Info: Ch 11 every H+00
GENT/TERNEUZEN TRAFFIC AREA:
VTS Tfc Centre: Ch 11
HANSWEERT TRAFFIC AREA:
VTS Tfc Centre: Ch 65
VLISSINGEN:
Call Flushing Port Control **Ch 09**
Locks & Bridge: Ch 18
TERNEUZEN:
Hr office: Ch 11
Locks: Ch 69
Westsluis and Middensluis: Ch 06
Oostsluis: Ch 18
Gent: Ch 05 11
Hansweert Locks: Ch 22

BELGIUM

ANTWERPEN TRAFFIC AREA:
VTS: Tfc Centre: Ch 12. Info: Ch 12 every H+30
ANTWERPEN:
Calling and safety: Ch 74
VTS Centre: Ch 18
Bridges: Ch 62
Boudewijnsluis & Van Cauwelaertsluis: Ch 08 71
Royerssluis Ch 74
Kattendijksluis: Ch 22
Kallosluis: Ch 08 74
Zandvlietsluis and Berendrechtsluis: Ch 06 79
Winthamsluis: Ch 68
ZEEBRUGGE TRAFFIC AREA:
VTS Tfc Centre: Ch 69. Info: Ch 69 every H+10
ZEEBRUGGE:
Port Control: Ch 71 H24. **Locks: Ch 68**
WANDELAAR TRAFFIC AREA:
VTS Tfc Centre: Ch 65
OOSTENDE:
Port Control: Ch 09 H24. **Lock: Ch 14**
NIEUWPOORT:
Hbr office: Ch 09 H24

NORTH FRANCE

DUNKERQUE PORT
Port: Ch 73 H24

CALAIS:
Port: Call Calais Port Traffic **Ch 12** H24
Ecluse Carnot: Ch 12 HX
BOULOGNE:
Call Control Tower, Boulogne Port **Ch 12**
Le Touquet: Ch 09; 77 Access HW−2 to +1
Étaples-Sur-Mer: Ch 09 Access HW±2
Le Treport: Ch 12 72 Access HW±3
DIEPPE:
Port: **Ch 12** HO
ST VALÉRY-EN-CAUX: lock Ch 09 Day: HW±26,
Night: HW±½ (Bridge opens H & H+30 during
these periods)
Fécamp: Ch 10 12 Access HW−3 to +1
Antifer Port: Ch 22 H24.
LE HAVRE:
Port Operations: Ch 67 69
Control Tower: Ch 12 20
Tancarville Port: Ch 16 H24. **Lock: Ch 18** HX
LA SEINE:
VTS: Ch 73, 15 (Estuary), **68** (River)
Radar Ch 13 73 82
HONFLEUR: Port: Ch 17 73 HX
Locks and Bridges: Ch 17 H24
Port Jérome: Call PR **Ch 73** H24
ROUEN:
Port: **Ch 73** 68 H24
ROUEN TO PARIS – LOCKS:
Poses-Amfreville: Ch 18
Notre-Dame-de-la-Garenne: Ch 22
Mericourt: Ch 18
Andrésy: Ch 22
Bougival: Ch 22
Chatou: Ch 18
Suresnes: Ch 22
Paris-Arsenal: Ch 09
Deauville-Trouville: Ch 09 0800-1730.
**OUISTREHAM-CAEN: Ouistreham: Ch 74. Lock:
Ch 12** Access HW−2 to +3. **Canal:** Monitor **Ch
68** H24. **Port de Caen Ch 74.**
Courseulles-sur-Mer: Ch 09 HW±3
Port-en-Bessin Lock & Bridge: Ch 18 HW±2
CHERBOURG:
Call Vigie du Homet **Ch 12** H24. Marina **Ch 09**.
Lock: Ch 06 Access HW±¾
GRANVILLE:
Hbr office: Ch 12 HW±1½
ST MALO:
Hbr office: Ch 12 H24. Marinas **Ch 09**.
Rance barrage lock: Ch 13. Chatelier lock Ch 14
DAHOUËT: Marina: Ch 09
LE LÉGUÉ – SAINT BRIEUC:
Call Légué Port **Ch 12** Approx HW−2 to +1½.
Paimpol Port/lock Ch 09 HW±2.
Pontrieux Lock: Ch 12 Access HW−2 to +1.
ROSCOFF-BLOSCON:
Port: **Ch 12**
0830-1200, 1330-1800

CHANNEL ISLANDS

BRAYE, Alderney Radio:
Port: Ch 12 74
Apr & Sep daily: 0800-1700. May-Aug: 0800-
2000 daily. Oct-Mar: Mon-Fri: 0800-1700.
Outside these hours, call St Peter Port Radio.
GUERNSEY:
St Peter Port: Ch 12 H24. Access HW±3
St Sampson: Ch 12 H24 via St Peter Port
Port Control.
JERSEY:
St Helier: Ch 14 H24. Access HW±3
(Note: Do not use Ch M in St Helier)
Gorey: Ch 74 HW±3.

WEST FRANCE

LE CONQUET:
Port: Ch 08 Season 0830-1200 1330-1800;
BREST:
Port de Commerce: Ch 12. Naval Port: Ch 74
CAMARET: Ch 09 Season 0730-2200; out of
season: 0830-1200 1330-1730
DOUARNENEZ:
Hbr office: Ch 12 0800-1200 1330-1730
SAINT GUÉNOLE: Ch 12 HJ
LE GUILVINEC:
Port: Ch 12 HX
LOCTUDY:
Hbr office: Ch 12 Mon-Fri: 0630-1200 1400-
1900; Sat: 0800-1200
CONCARNEAU: Port Ch 12
LORIENT:
Hbr office: Call Vigie Port Louis **Ch 12**
SAINT-NAZAIRE:
PORT: Ch 06 12 14 67 69
Loire VTS: Saint–Nazaire Port Control **Ch 12**
DONGES: Port: Ch 12 69 H24
Nantes: Ch 12 06 14 67 69
Les Sables d'Olonne:
Lock: Ch 12 HM Mon-Fri: 0800-1800
LA ROCHELLE
Port: Ch 12 H24
ROCHEFORT:
Hbr office: Ch 12 0800-1200, 1400-1800LT
Tonnay-Charente: Ch 12 HX
LA GIRONDE:
VTS: Ch 12 Compulsory from BXA Lt buoy to
Bordeaux, except for leisure craft which
should monitor. **Radar: Ch 12.** Height of water
between Le Verdon and Bordeaux is broadcast
automatically **Ch 17** every 5 mins.
PAUILLAC:
Hbr office: Ch 12 0800-1200, 1400-1800.
BLAYE:
Port: Ch 12 0800-1200, 1400-1800.
Ambès: Ch 12 H24
BORDEAUX:
Hbr office: Ch 12 H24
Bayonne: Ch 12 H24

N & NW SPAIN

BILBAO:
Bilbao Traffic: Ch 10
Signal Station: Ch 12 13 HX
SANTANDER:
Port: Ch 14
PUERTO DE SAN CIPRIÁN: Ch 14
FERROL: Ch 14 (H24) 10 11 12 13
LA CORUÑA:
Port: Ch 12 13 HX
CORCUBIÓN: Ch 14 when vessel is expected
FINISTERRE TRAFFIC:
VTS: Ch 11 74 H24
VILLAGARCIA DE AROUSA:
Port: Ch 12 H24
VIGO:
VTS: Call Vigo Traffic **Ch 10** H24
Port: Call Vigo Prácticos **Ch 14** HX

PORTUGAL (Marinas Ch 09)

VIANA DO CASTELO:
Ch 11 Mon-Fri 0900-1200, 1400-1700.
PÓVOA DE VARZIM:
Ch 11 Mon-Fri 0900-1200, 1400-1700.
Vila Do Conde: Ch 11 Mon-Fri 0900-1200, 1400-1700.
Leixões: Ch 12 11 13 19 60
Marina: Ch 62
Radar Station: Ch 12, H24.
Douro: Ch 11 Mon-Fri 0900-1200, 1400-1700.
Aveiro: Ch 11 Mon-Fri 0900-1200, 1400-1700.
Figueira da Foz: Ch 11 Mon-Fri 0900-1200, 1400-1700.
Nazaré: Ch 11 Mon-Fri 0900-1200, 1400-1700.
Peniche: Ch 11
LISBOA: Call *Lisboa Port Control* **Ch 74**
Doca de Alcântara: Ch 12 05
Sesimbra: Ch 11
Mon-Fri 0900-1200, 1400-1700.

Setúbal: Ch 11 H24
Sines: Ch 12 14
Lagos: Ch 11 Mon-Fri 0900-1200, 1400-1700.
Portimão: Ch 11 H24.
Vilamoura: Ch 62 H24
Faro: Ch 11
OLHÃO: Ch 11
VILA REAL DE SANTO ANTÓNIO: Ch 11
Mon-Fri 0900-1200, 1400-1700.

SW SPAIN

EL ROMPIDO: Marina: Ch 09 HX
PUNTA UMBRÍA: Club: Ch 09 HX
RÍO GUADALQUIVIR:
Call Sevilla **Ch 12**
CÁDIZ:
Call Cádiz Trafico **Ch 74** H24
Rota: Ch 09

STRAIT OF GIBRALTAR

TARIFA:
VTS: Call Tarifa Traffic **Ch 10**
Information (on request): Ch 67
Urgent messages will be bcst at any time on Ch 10 and Ch 16. Routine messages will be bcst every even H+15 on Ch 10
ALGECIRAS:
Port: Call Algeciras Prácticos **Ch 09 12** HX

GIBRALTAR

Gibraltar Bay Ch 12 Yachts to monitor this working channel whilst under way.
Commercial Port: Ch 06 13 14
Queen's Harbour Master: Ch 08 Mon-Thu: 0800-1630; Fri: 0800-1600.
Marinas: Queensway Quay and Sheppards Ch 71. Marina Bay Ch 73.

NOTES
_____
_____
_____
_____
_____
_____
_____
_____
_____
_____
_____
_____
_____
_____
_____

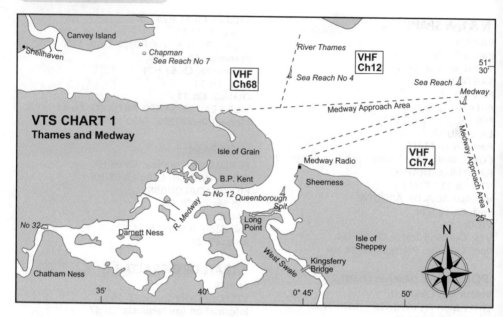

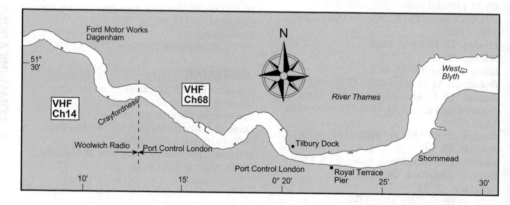

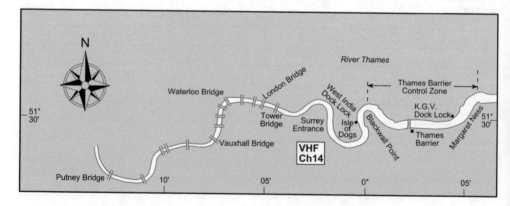

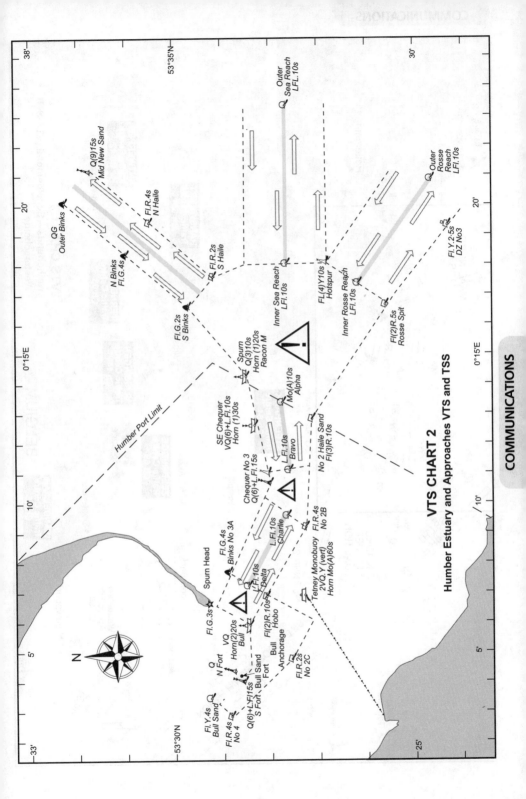

VTS CHART 2

Humber Estuary and Approaches VTS and TSS

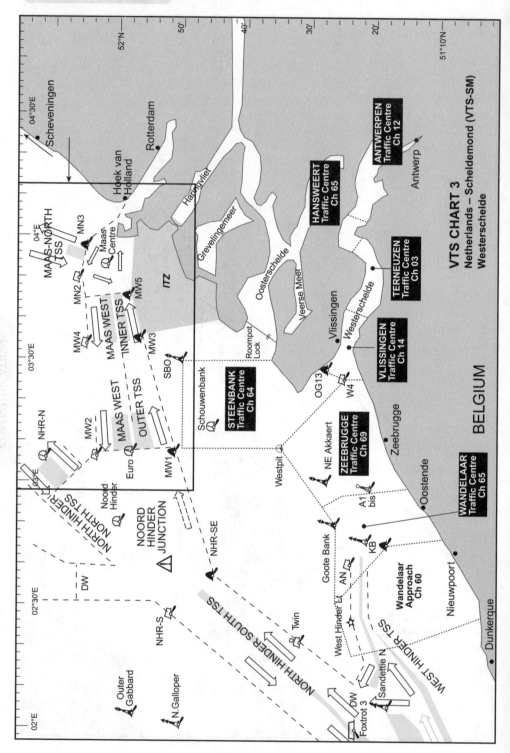

VTS CHART 3
Netherlands – Scheldemond (VTS-SM)
Westerschelde

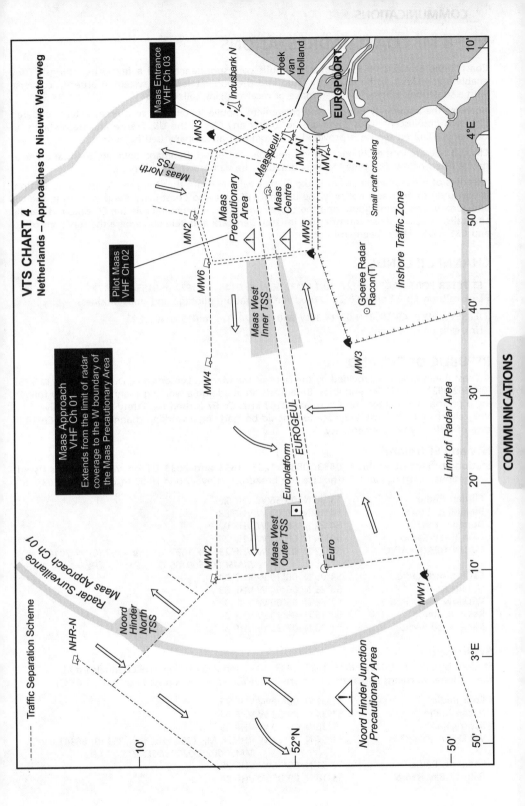

VTS CHART 4
Netherlands – Approaches to Nieuwe Waterweg

Maas Entrance
VHF Ch 03

Indusbank N

Hoek van Holland

EUROPOORT

Maas North TSS

MN3

Maasgeul

Pilot Maas
VHF Ch 02

Maas Precautionary Area

MN2

Maas Centre

MV-N

MV-Z

Small craft crossing

MW5

MW6

Maas West Inner TSS

Goeree Radar Racon(T)

Inshore Traffic Zone

Maas Approach
VHF Ch 01
Extends from the limit of radar coverage to the W boundary of the Maas Precautionary Area

MW4

MW3

Limit of Radar Area

Europlatform
EUROGEUL

Maas West Outer TSS

Euro

Traffic Separation Scheme

Radar Surveillance
Maas Approach Ch 01

NHR-N

Noord Hinder North TSS

MW2

Noord Hinder Junction Precautionary Area

MW1

------- Traffic Separation Scheme

50'

10'

3°E

52°N

4°E

50'

40'

30'

20'

10'

10'

COMMUNICATIONS

111

VHF & MF COAST RADIO STATIONS

Coast Radio Stations* (CRS) deal with public correspondence (and a few other things). They enable a yachtsman to be linked by radio into the public telephone system in order to converse with a subscriber ashore, ie he can make or receive a Link call.

However the immensely popular and convenient mobile 'phone has to a great extent rendered Link calls obsolescent. Thus there are no longer any CRS in the UK, France and Netherlands. In Germany a limited service is provided by a commercial company (see below).

CRS still operate in the Channel Islands, Republic of Ireland, Denmark, Belgium, Spain and Portugal, as listed below. But they too may gradually be withdrawn from service.

*Readers of the Admiralty List of Radio Signals will be aware that the term 'Coast Radio Station' is now used to embrace, not only the original CRS, but also Coastguard Centres, both in the UK and abroad. This is ambiguous and therefore confusing. As a general rule the CG does **not** handle Link calls, except in those countries (eg Ireland, Denmark and Belgium) where the functions of CG and CRS have always been co-located.

CHANNEL ISLANDS

ST PETER PORT RADIO 49°27'·00N 02°32'00W ☎ 01481 720672 m 01534 714177
Link calls on **Ch 62** only. Ch 20 is used for navigation, pilotage and ships' business

JERSEY RADIO 49°10'·85N 02°14'30W ☎ 01534 741121 m 01534 499089
Link calls on **Ch 25** only

REPUBLIC OF IRELAND

A Coast Radio service is provided by the Dept of the Marine, Leeson Lane, Dublin 2, Eire. ☎ +353 (0)1 662 0922; ext 670 for enquiries. Broadcasts are made on a working channel/frequency following a prior announcement on Ch 16 and 2182 kHz. Ch 67 is used for Safety messages only.
VHF calls to an Irish Coast Radio Station should be made on a working channel. Only use Ch 16 in case of difficulty or in emergency.

NW and SE Ireland

Stations broadcast at 0033, 0433, 0833, 1233, 1633 and 2033 UT on VHF Channels listed. Navigational warnings and Traffic Lists are broadcast at every odd H+03 (except 0303 0703).

Clifden Radio	53°30'N 09°56'W VHF 26	
Belmullet Radio	54°16'N 10°03'W VHF 83	
Donegal Bay	54°22'N 08°31'W VHF 02	
Glen Head Radio	54°44'N 08°43'W VHF 24	
MALIN HEAD RADIO	55°22'N 07°21'W VHF 23 MF 1677 kHz, ☎ +353 (0) 77 70103	
	MMSI 002500100 DSC: 2187·5 kHz	
Carlingford Radio	54°05'N 06°19'W VHF 04	
Dublin Radio	53°23'N 06°04'W VHF 83	
Wicklow Head Radio	52°58'N 06°00'W VHF 02	
Rosslare Radio	52°15'N 06°20'W VHF 23	
Mine Head Radio	52°00'N 07°35'W VHF 83	

SW Ireland

Stations broadcast at 0233, 0633, 1033, 1433, 1833 and 2233 UT on VHF Channels listed. Navigational warnings and Traffic Lists are broadcast at every odd H+33 (not 0133 0533).

Cork Radio	51°51'N 08°29'W VHF 26	
Mizen Radio	51°34'N 09°33'W VHF 04	
Bantry Radio	51°38'N 10°00'W VHF 23	
VALENTIA RADIO	51°56'N 10°21'W VHF 24 MF 1752 kHz, ☎ + 353 (0) 66947 6109	
	MMSI 002500200, DSC: 2187·5 kHz	
Shannon Radio	52°31'N 09°36'W VHF 28	
Galway Bay Radio	53°18'N 09°07'W VHF 04	

DENMARK

All VHF/MF Coast Radio Stations are remotely controlled from Lyngby Radio (55°50N 11°25'E) (MMSI 002191000). Call on working frequencies to help keep Ch 16 clear. The callsign for all stations is Lyngby Radio. Traffic lists are broadcast on all VHF channels every odd H+05. All MF stations, except Skagen, keep watch H24 on 2182 kHz. The stations listed below monitor Ch 16 H24 and Ch 70 DSC. Blåvand, Skagen and Lyngby also monitor MF 2187·5 kHz DSC. MF DSC Public correspondence facilities are available from Blåvand and Skagen on 1624·5 and 2177 kHz.

VHF AND MF			
Lyngby	55°50'N 11°25'E	VHF Ch 07, 85	MF 1704, 2170·5 kHz
Blåvand	55°33'N 08°07'E	VHF Ch 23	MF 1734, 1767, 2593
Bovbjerg	56°32'N 08°10'E	VHF Ch 02	MF 1734, 1767, 2593
Hanstholm	57°07'N 08°39'E	VHF Ch 01	
Hirtshals	57°31'N 09°57'E	VHF Ch 66	
Skagen	57°44'N 10°35'E	VHF Ch 04	MF 1758

GERMANY

Coast Radio Stations: DPO7 – Seefunk (Hamburg) *(MMSI 002113100)*

Hamburg	53°33'N 09°58'E	VHF Ch 83	DSC Ch 70 & 16
Borkum	53°35'N 06°40'E	VHF Ch 28	DSC Ch 70 & 16
Bremen	53°05'N 08°48'E	VHF Ch 25	DSC Ch 70 & 16
Elbe Weser	53°50'N 08°39'E	VHF Ch 01, 24	DSC Ch 70 & 16
Nordfriesland	54°31'N 08°41'E	VHF Ch 26	DSC Ch 70 & 16

Traffic Lists: 0745, 0945, 1245, 1645, 1945 and every H & H+30 on request Ch 16

NORTH & NORTHWEST SPAIN

Call on the working channel as listed below, using the callsign of the remotely controlled station; Ch 16 is not continuously guarded. Stations are remotely controlled by Bilbao and Coruna Communications Centres.

Traffic lists are broadcast only on MF, every odd H+33, 0333-2333, except 2133. All times UT.

Pasajes 43°17'N 01°55'W *VHF 27*

Machichaco Radio 43°27'N 02°45'W   *No VHF*
MF: Transmits 1707, 2182 kHz (H24);
receives on 2132, 2045, 2048, 2182 (H24).
Traffic lists:1707 kHz; every odd H+33
Navigation warnings:1707 kHz Urgent warnings on receipt, after next silence period and at 0703 1903 in English and Spanish

Bilbao 43°22'N 03°02'W *VHF 26*. Controls Pasajes to Navia

Santander 43°25'N 03°36'W *VHF 24*

Cabo Peñas 43°26'N 05°35'W   *VHF 23, MF 1677 kHz*
Navigation warnings: 1677 kHz. Urgent warnings on receipt, after next silence period and at 0703 1903 in English and Spanish

Navia 43°25'N 06°50'W *VHF 60*

Cabo Ortegal 43°35'N 07°47'W *VHF 02*
Navigation warnings: *VHF 02* at 0840 and 2010

Coruña 43°22'N 08°27'W *VHF 26, MF 1698 kHz*
Navigation warnings: *VHF 26* at 0840 and 2010; *1698 kHz* at 0703, 1903

Finisterre 42°54'N 09°16'W *VHF 22, MF 1764 kHz*
Navigation warnings: *VHF 22* at 0840 and 2010; *1764 kHz* at 0703, 1903

Vigo 42°10'N 08°41'W *VHF 65*. Nav warnings: *VHF 20* at 0840 and 2010

La Guardia 41°53'N 08°52'W *VHF 21*. Nav warnings: *VHF 82* at 0840 and 2010

PORTUGAL

Stations are remotely controlled from Lisboa. All monitor Ch 16 H24

Arga Radio	41°48'N 08°41'W	*VHF 25 28*
Arestal Radio	40°46'N 08°21'W	*VHF 24 26*
Montejunto Radio	39°10'N 09°03'W	*VHF 25 26*
LISBOA RADIO	38°33'N 09°11'W	*VHF 23 26. MF: Transmits on 2182, 2578, 2640, 2691, 2781, 3607, 2778, 2693 kHz. Receives on 2182 (kHz) (H24)*
		Traffic lists: 2693 kHz every even H+05, after announcement on 2182 kHz
Atalaia Radio	38°10'N 08°38'W	*VHF 24 25*
Picos Radio	37°50'N 08°35'W	*VHF 23 28*
Estoi Radio	37°10'N 07°50'W	*VHF 24 28*

SOUTH WEST SPAIN

Stations are remotely controlled from Malaga. Initially call Ch 16 H24 using station callsign

Chipiona Radio	36°41'N 06°25'W	*No VHF. MF: Transmits 1656, 2182 kHz (H24); receives on 2081 2182*
		Traffic lists: 1656 kHz every odd H+33 (except 0133 & 2133). Navigation warnings: 1656 kHz. Urgent warnings on receipt, and at 0733 1933, *in Spanish*
Cádiz Radio	36°21'N 06°17'W	*VHF 83*
		Navigation warnings: *Ch 26* on receipt, after next silence period, and at 0833, 2003, *in Spanish*
Tarifa Radio	36°03'N 05°33'W	*VHF 81; MF 1704 kHz: Transmits kHz 1704, 2182, (H24). Receives 2129, 2182 (H24), 2045, 2048, 2610, 3290 (Autolink)*
		Traffic lists: *1704 kHz*. Navigation warnings: *VHF 81* at 0833 and 2003. *1704 kHz* on receipt, at 0733 1933, *in Spanish*

NOTES

SOUND SIGNALS
MANOEUVRING AND WARNING SIGNALS (Rule 34)

Short blast ● = about 1 second. Long blast ▬▬ = about 5 seconds

●	I am altering course to **Starboard**
● ●	I am altering course to **Port**
● ● ●	My engines are going **Astern**
● ● ● ● ●	I do not understand your intentions/actions

In a narrow channel

▬▬ ▬▬ ●	I intend to overtake you on your **Starboard** side
▬▬ ▬▬ ● ●	I intend to overtake you on your **Port** side
▬▬ ● ▬▬ ●	In response to the above two signals - **Agreed**

Nearing a bend in the channel or an area where other vessels may be hidden by obstructions

▬▬	Warns of a vessel's presence
▬▬	Acknowledgement by any approaching vessel

VESSELS IN RESTRICTED VISIBILITY (Rule 35)

▬▬	Power vessel underway: every 2 mins
▬▬ ▬▬	Power vessel underway but stopped: every 2 mins
▬▬ ● ●	Vessels not under command, restricted in their ability to manoeuvre, constrained by draught, sailing, fishing or towing: every 2 mins
▬▬ ● ● ●	Last vessel in tow: immediately after tug's signal
♫ 5 seconds	At anchor: bell, every minute
♫ 5 seconds + ⊙ 5 seconds	At anchor over 100m: bell forward, gong aft, every minute
● ▬▬ ●	At ⚓, as well as above, to warn an approaching vessel

Yachts under 12m are not obliged to sound the fog signals listed above, but if they do not, they *must* make some efficient noise every two minutes

SHAPES

▼	Sailing vessel under sail *and* power. **Rule 25**	◆	Towing vessel - length of tow over 200m. **Rule 24**
●	Vessel at anchor. **Rule 30**	●◆●	Vessel restricted in her ability to manoeuvre. **Rule 27**
▼▲	Vessel fishing or trawling. **Rule 26**	●●	Vessel not under command. **Rule 27**
▼▲ + ▲	Vessel fishing with outlying gear over 150m long.	▮	Vessel constrained by her draught **Rule 28**

CHAPTER 4 - SAFETY

CONTENTS

THINK ABOUT SAFETY – IN FOG

This is the second article in a series about safety at sea, intended for owners of leisure craft, sail or power.

It is evident that on occasion well-equipped commercial vessels substantially exceed what may be deemed a safe speed in fog (Rules 6 and 19b). Small craft owners should beware of high speed when deciding what avoiding action to take in fog. For example crossing ahead of a large ship, which even in good visibility can be worrying, in fog becomes foolhardy, because a small craft's radar (and its owner) may not be able to resolve the large ship's course/speed with acceptable accuracy.

Thus the yachtsman is always the loser – unless he has analysed the problem, studied various solutions and gained a sound working knowledge of Rule 19 of the Collision Regulations. He should then buy a radar and learn to use it efficiently in all visibilities and sea states. Eventually he should be able to recognise potentially dangerous situations, as seen on the radar, and take the correct avoiding action.

TRAINING. First read the manufacturer's handbook, then attend a radar course of at least two days. Next get to sea, ideally with a knowledgeable mentor onboard, and apply what you have learned to your own radar set. Thereafter use the radar in good visibility so as to relate the blips on the screen to the ships that you see with the naked eye. It helps to have a chum on visual watch in the cockpit with whom to compare notes. Next start to track individual contacts, assessing their course and deciding whether a risk of collision exists. Ultimately you should be able to track say three contacts simultaneously, as in real life. This requires a careful record at regular intervals of each ship's bearing and distance from which to determine those passing clear and those likely to pose a threat. Concentrate on the latter and decide how best to remove your craft from danger asap.

KNOWLEDGE. What you decide largely depends on your understanding of Rule 19 (Conduct of vessels in restricted visibility). This rule is complex in that:

(a) It differs markedly from Rules 11-18 (Conduct of vessels in sight of one another) which clearly distinguish between stand-on and give-way vessels.

(b) It contains no such distinction; every vessel should keep clear of others.

(c) Rule 19d (i) & (ii) state what avoiding actions should *not* be taken, leaving the mariner to infer what more positive options are open to him. These boil down to:

- Alter starboard to avoid a vessel forward of the beam
- Alter away from a vessel abeam or abaft the beam

Make a note or sketch of these; envisage their application to various situations.

DEFINITIONS OF DISTRESS, URGENCY AND SAFETY

Yachts at sea should always monitor VHF Channel 16. Otherwise a distress call from another nearby craft may be missed; likewise broadcasts of navigation and weather warnings. Transfer asap from Channel 16 to a working channel.

MAYDAY, the distress call, requests immediate assistance for a ship or person in grave and imminent danger. This includes a man overboard, if he is not immediately recovered. Yachts hearing a MAYDAY must give what assistance they can, provided it does not endanger their own yacht or crew.

PAN-PAN, the urgency prefix, is used when the safety of a ship or person is at risk, or medical advice is urgently required (see PAN-PAN MEDICO overleaf).

SECURITE, the safety prefix, is used by coast stations before navigation or weather warnings. Or ships at sea might use it to report hazards, eg a buoy adrift.

HOW TO MAKE A DISTRESS CALL

- Switch on the VHF Radio
- Select Channel 16
- Select **HIGH POWER (25W)**
- Switch off DUAL WATCH
- Holding down the button on microphone or handset, say slowly and clearly:
- **MAYDAY, MAYDAY, MAYDAY**
- This is.....................................(Say your boat's name 3 times)
- MAYDAY...........(Say the boat's name once only)
- My position is...................

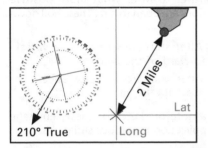

210° True | Lat | Long | 2 Miles

Give your position either as:

Lat and Long (from the GPS); or as

Bearing and distance <u>from</u> a known landmark or feature:

For example 'My position is 2 miles SSW of Portland Bill'

Say if you are not sure of position– do not guess!

- **_Tell them what is wrong:_** For example, the boat is sinking; how many people (including you) on board; if you have fired flares; if you are abandoning ship, etc. If there is time, repeat your position
- **I require immediate assistance**. Over - This means: please reply
- Release the microphone button and listen
- Only if you can't hear clearly, adjust the _VOLUME_ and/or _SQUELCH_

   If there is no reply, check the radio switches and repeat the message

MAYDAY RELAY

- **If you hear a MAYDAY CALL, write it down**
- If practicable, give assistance

- If the MAYDAY is not answered, pass it on like this:
- Select VHF Channel 16
- Select HIGH POWER (25W)
- Switch off DUAL WATCH

- Then, holding down the button on microphone or handset, say slowly and clearly:
MAYDAY RELAY, MAYDAY RELAY, MAYDAY RELAY
- This is.......................(say your boat's name 3 times)
- **State the MAYDAY message, exactly as you wrote it down**
- **Over** - This means: please reply
- Release the button and listen

HELICOPTER RESCUE

- **COMMUNICATE ON CHANNEL 16**
- Use flares or smoke when helicopter is seen or heard
- Pilot may ask you to drop sails and motor an **EXACT COURSE**
- You may be asked to stream tender astern with casualty in
- Brief crew early (too noisy when helicopter is close)
- **HELM MUST KEEP ON COURSE** and not be distracted
- Weighted line lowered
- Let it touch boat or water first (to earth any static charge)
- Take in slack line only
- **PULL IN AS DIRECTED**
- **DO NOT SECURE IT TO THE BOAT**
- **DO AS YOU ARE TOLD**

Note: The text and sketch relate to a Hi-line transfer, one of several techniques which may be used

MEDICAL HELP

- CH 16, High power, Dual watch off
- **PAN PAN** .... (repeat 3 times)
- **ALL STATIONS** .... (repeat 3 times)
- **This is** ....(repeat 3 times)
- **Over**

Next message should contain:
> Yacht's name, callsign, nationality
> Yacht's position and nearest harbour
> Patient's details, symptoms and advice wanted
> The medication you have on board

MEDICAL ADVICE BY RADIO

European countries covered by this Almanac will give free medical advice on request. Messages are usually sent via Coastguard or Coast Radio Stations of the country concerned.

Medical Advice (UK) can be obtained by contacting the nearest CG Centre on VHF 16, VHF DSC, or MF DSC, requesting medical advice. In a particularily urgent situation, broadcast an urgency alert using the pro-words 'PAN PAN'.

Priority is given to Medical Advice requests. A Medilink service doctor will be connected by telephone - VHF(usually Ch's 23,84,86) or MF link to the vessel. As this call is being placed the CG will request relevant additional information. The doctor will advise of suitable action and this call may be monitored by the CG. for operational reasons. If evacuation is necessary, then the CG is bound to act upon it. A Medilink service call (free of charge) will always precede a request for medical evacuation.

REPUBLIC OF IRELAND Call nearest Coast Radio Station by name. Procedures are similar to UK.

DENMARK Call 'Radiomedical Lyngby': English, Danish, Norwegian, Swedish, French or German are spoken.

GERMANY Call nearest Coast Radio Station using 'Funkarzt. . . (name of station)'. English or German are spoken.

NETHERLANDS Call 'Netherlands Coastguard, Radio medical advice'. English and Dutch are spoken. Expect transfer to working Ch 23 or 83 for duty doctor.

BELGIUM Call 'Radiomedical Ostend': English, French, Dutch or German are spoken.

FRANCE Call nearest CROSS, eg 'Radiomedical CROSS Jobourg' with PAN-PAN prefix. French, English or International Code of Signals. SAMU (Urgent Medical Aid Service) in Toulouse may be contacted by the CROSS to advise on treatment and/or possible evacuation. CROSS Etel specialises in providing medical advice.

SPAIN Call 'Medrad ... (any Coast Radio Station)': Spanish.

PORTUGAL Call 'Radiomedical Lisboa': English, French, Portuguese are spoken.

FIRST AID

First ensure your own safety and that of the vessel.

GETTING HELP

Recognising signs of serious injury is not usually difficult, but it is always better to ask advice if not sure. This is available by making a **PAN-PAN** call by R/T or VHF radio, which will normally be processed by a Coast Radio Station and/or the Coastguard. You will be connected to a local doctor or hospital for advice and, if assistance is required, it will be co-ordinated by the Coastguard (see LH column).

FIRST STEPS

A - AIRWAY - NOT BREATHING: Know how to achieve and maintain an airway in all unconscious patients, by:

- Clearing any seaweed, excess saliva, vomit, false teeth, etc from mouth and nose.
- Lifting the chin to prevent choking by tongue and soft palate falling back.

B - BREATHING - Sealing mouth with own mouth and pinching nose, then blow slowly and gently until the casualty's chest rises. Ten inflations should improve colour, then continue after 2-4 seconds another 10 ventilations, then re-assess. You can use mouth to nose ventilation if the casualty's mouth cannot be opened enough to breath into. The best position for maintaining spontaneous breathing after restarting is in the semi-prone or coma position. The casualty is rolled carefully on his side keeping head and neck in line.

C - CIRCULATION - HEART NOT BEATING: You can revive an unconscious or possibly near dead patient by external cardiac massage, if there is no pulse. The best place to find a pulse is in the neck beside the Trachea (Windpipe).

The patient must be lying on a firm surface. First ventilate 1–2 breaths. Then apply cardiac massage by pressure over the lower third of the sternum (breastbone). The heel of one hand should be placed two fingers width above the lower extremity of the sternum, and the heel of the other hand placed on top, with the fingers interlocked, keeping the elbows straight. Press down firmly on the sternum using just enough force to depress it (4.5cm), then release keeping hands in place. Continue by pressing firmly over the sternum with both hands, one on top of the other, with intermittent mouth to mouth respiration. The rate should be 80 compresses per minute, and the ratio of breaths to pressure should be 2:15. This should be continued until either colour improves, breathing starts or a pulse becomes palpable in the neck. Then place the patient in the recovery position.

BLEEDING: Know how to deal with severe haemorrhage.

EXTERNAL BLEEDING:

- Remove any loose foreign bodies from wounds.
- Press a folded handkerchief or soft pad directly on to wound, adding more padding if this becomes soaked.
- If possible raise bleeding part.
- If pressure is used to control bleeding check colour and temperature of parts distal to pressure pad to ensure adequate blood supply, releasing pressure frequently.

INTERNAL BLEEDING: Apparent when blood appears from the mouth or rectum, or suspected when a person collapses with pallor, sweating and a fast pulse.

All that can be done is to place the victim in the semi-prone position and prevent heat loss by covering with a blanket or sleeping bag. Supervision is necessary. *ADVICE SHOULD BE SOUGHT AS SOON AS POSSIBLE BY RADIO* (Make VHF **PAN-PAN** call).

LIVES CAN BE SAVED in all cases of injury by attending to the **A**IRWAY, **B**REATHING, **C**IRCULATION AND **C**ONSCIOUS LEVEL of injured crew and doing this in an organised method. Using a check list prevents less important factors taking precedent. Always keep checking on anyone who has had an injury or been in the water.

GENERAL MEDICAL INFO

ARREST of heart's action can be caused by near drowning, by blood loss and by illness such as heart attack. It is not hard to recognise as the victim is obviously near death and a pulse cannot be found.

Refer to resuscitation above and perform external cardiac massage with patient on a firm surface such as deck or cabin sole, and with mouth to mouth resuscitation in a ratio of roughly 2 breaths to 15 chest pressings. Start with 2 breaths of expired air.

BREATHING: In conscious patients, problems can be caused by pain from injured ribs or chest infection. Help is given by pain killing tablets and/or antibiotics. Crew members with asthma will usually have their own medication and should be kept propped up. Keep checking. In an unconscious patient the airway must be cleared, the jaw tipped up and mouth to mouth breathing started if necessary, or if the patient is able to breath by himself he must be placed in the semi-prone position and carefully watched

in case the airway gets blocked by his tongue or by vomit or saliva.

CIRCULATION: Problems of central (the heart/pump) and peripheral (blood vessels/distribution) should be tackled as follows:

- Central: Failure of heart's action - dealt with by External Cardiac Massage (see above)
- Peripheral: Attempt to stop haemorrhage by method described above (see Bleeding)

BROKEN BONES: Principles are immobilisation and observation of circulation to the part beyond the probable fracture.

Skull: suspect fracture in severe blows to the head, especially if the patient is unconscious.

Priorities are (a) airway clearance and maintenance and cardiac massage if required (b) pressure if scalp bleeding is severe (c) monitoring of conscious or unconscious state (d) remember the possibility of neck injuries, keep neck and shoulders in line.

Spine: possible in falls from a height. Priority is always airway clearance and maintenance. *DO NOT USE EXCESSIVE CHIN TILT*, but if possible try to roll or lift patient from danger with head and back in a straight line – for example on a board large enough to stretch from head to buttocks with a rolled towel around the neck to minimise movement. The head should be held steady at all times in line with body in horizontal and vertical planes. *THIS IS ESSENTIAL TO PROTECT THE SPINAL CORD.*

Ribs: are often fractured in crush injuries and falls and do not take precedent over skull or spine injuries. If they appear to be the only injury then pain relief is essential to allow free movement of the chest for efficient breathing. Consider internal bleeding if patient becomes pale, clammy and collapsed. Possible internal damage if he becomes breathless.

Upper limbs: can be splinted to the trunk whether the fracture is closed or if bone is protruding. The bone should be immobilised at the joint above and below the fracture and padding should be inserted below any bandage or strapping. This should not be too tight and the part of the limb beyond should be checked regularly for changes in colour and temperature and for swelling which can restrict the blood flow. If this happens the bindings must be loosened. If the bone is protruding, cut clothing away and if possible cover with sterile gauze. Pain killers and, in the case of open fracture, antibiotics should be given as soon as possible.

Lower limbs: immobilise at point above and below fracture if possible. Check circulation in limb. Give pain relief or antibiotic cover for open fractures. The other limb, or an oar, is a suitable splint. Strapping should be added and distal circulation monitored.

BURNS: Best treatment is immediate immersion of affected part in clean, cold sea water for at least 10 minutes. Severe burns will swell a lot so any tight clothing or jewellery should be cut open or removed. The swelling around the burn is fluid from the body, which is then lost from the circulation so the victim can be shocked and dehydrated and fluid replacement is essential.

Burned tissue is easily infected and should not be handled, removed or blisters pricked. If clothing is stuck it should be left. Sunburn is a form of burn and can result in severe dehydration and shock.

BRUISES can cause a lot of pain under a finger or toenail. These can be treated safely by flaming the end of a piece of wire (such as a paper clip) and burning through the nail, just enough to release the blood.

COLD INJURY: Hypothermia should be suspected after any accidental immersion. Treat, whether apparent or not, by gradual re-warming. Shelter, dry clothes, gentle warmth from another person or handwarm heat source in a sleeping bag will help. *RESUSCITATION MAY BE REQUIRED.* Continual observation is essential.

CHOKING can be relieved by a sharp blow to the back preferably in the head down position. Alternatively grasp the victim from behind and pull clasped hands into the upper abdomen.

COLLAPSE can complicate injuries involving loss of blood, pain and loss of fluid. If the patient is unconscious then airway clearance, resuscitation and treatment of blood loss, followed by maintenance in the semi-prone position is paramount. Heat loss must be prevented but no active heating should be used. If the patient is conscious, loosen tight clothes and elevate the lower limbs. Fluids should be given (if conscious) frequently in small amounts.

CUTS: If deep, remove any foreign body and treat bleeding with compression. Clean and dry cut. Bring the edges together using Steristrips (or adhesive tape) to hold them closed, starting in mid-cut and working to ends. Reinforce middle strips to prevent bursting.

DROWNING: Try all the resuscitation techniques in the introduction, according to need.

A - Airway: clearance and maintenance

B - Breathing: by mouth to mouth or mouth to nose

C - Circulation: External Cardiac Massage may be required.

If successful, monitor level of consciousness and check airway. Maintain semi-prone position and keep under observation.

Hypothermia: usually complicates cold water immersion. Remove wet clothes and put patient in a dry sleeping bag with either a handwarm hot water bottle or a warm dry person. Look after patient out of wind, chill and rain and warm the cabin if possible. It can help to raise lower limbs and wrap towel round abdomen. Remember to watch for deterioration during warming.

DIARRHOEA should be treated by oral fluids only; no solid food for 24/48 hours.

EYE INJURIES - Foreign body(ies):

- Try to flush out with plenty of clean water.
- Try pulling upper lid over lower then releasing to remove foreign body from under upper lid.
- Raise upper, then lower lid, asking casualty to look all around. The upper lid can be turned back on itself over a matchstick. The speck can usually be seen and removed with a Q-tip or clean handkerchief.

If the foreign body cannot be removed it may have penetrated the eye and no further attempts should be made to remove it. The eye should be covered and both eyes rested. If pain persists after the speck is removed there may be a concealed abrasion and the eyes should be rested and Chloromycetin eye drops or a solution of 1 teaspoonful salt to 1 pint of boiled cooled water inserted.

Lost contact lenses can sometimes be lodged under upper lid in upper outer part of eye. It is possible to see them by turning back the lid and massaging them back into position through the lid.

FISH HOOKS can penetrate the skin and may have to be pushed right through until the barb can be cut off with pliers and the hook withdrawn.

HEART ATTACK: Though often hard to be sure, the following treatment should at least do no harm. If the patient is conscious, make them comfortable in the half-sitting position and give the strongest available pain killers. If the patient becomes semi-conscious place them in the recovery position, and observe carefully for maintenance of clear airway, and commence resuscitation should it be necessary.

HYPOTHERMIA nearly always complicates cold water immersion and should be considered even when not apparent. If conscious the victim may be confused and appear drunk, seeming lethargic and remote from what is going on. Shivering fits may or may not occur and poor colour, vomiting or faintness can develop. The treatment is mentioned under Cold Injury above and consists of gradual rewarming by removal from wet and cold, replacement of wet clothing and if conscious rewarming in a warm sleeping bag. Priority must be given to attention to airway and the semi-prone position if the victim is unconscious.

INTERNAL INJURIES may occur in any of the accidents which cause broken bones and bleeding and should be suspected when the patient seems unduly distressed, collapsed or blood appears from the body openings. The abdomen may appear rigid.

The priorities are airway clearance and maintenance and the adoption of the semi-prone position with careful observation to ensure prompt treatment of respiratory or cardiac arrest. The victim should be covered to prevent heat loss.

JOINTS can be strained and sprained on decks and winches. The treatment is rest and time, but supporting crepe bandages can be comforting.

SEASICKNESS is best avoided by starting treatment such as Stugeron or your favourite at least 12 hours before sailing. All these drugs may cause drowsiness. Alcohol must be avoided and hangovers predispose to seasickness.

ALL SEASICK CREW ON DECK SHOULD WEAR A HARNESS and should not be allowed to vomit over the side. Oral rehydration with very small amounts of rehydration fluids should be started, and fresh air and the ability to see the horizon can help. The danger of cold should not be ignored. Stemetil anti-sickness suppositories can be useful.

SWALLOWING: Accidentally swallowed objects can usually be left to nature. Dangerous objects such as watch batteries and open safety pins should be treated as emergencies.

STINGS from jellyfish are treated by oral antihistamines.

TOOTHACHE: Caused by abscess and accompanied by swelling can be treated with antibiotics and painkillers. You can buy dental kits over the counter.

VOMITING: Attempts should be made at rehydration using small amounts of fluid, preferably oral rehydration packs.

The information in the above list should give a casualty the best possibility of recovering until help arrives.

FIRST AID KIT

*Asterisked items require a prescription from a General Practitioner, who will have his/her own preferences and opinion on the need for a prescription. The following are mainly for guidance:

ANALGESICS – for pain relief
Paracetamol (Panadol) tabs 500mg. Dose; 2 tabs 4-6 hours for medium to moderate pain.

*Dihydrocodeine tabs. Dose: 1 tab 4-6 hourly for moderate to severe pain. Cause constipation with long term use. Can be used at night for cough or in the treatment of diarrhoea. Pharmacists will discuss other over the counter painkillers which are used for moderate pain.

ANTACIDS – for heartburn and indigestion. Gaviscon tabs. Dose; 2 tabs chewed and swallowed 3/4 times daily.

ANTIBIOTICS – for infections.
*Amoxycillin capsules 250mg. Dose: 2 caps three times daily. Check for allergy, otherwise safe.
*Erythromycin tablets 250mg for infection if allergic to Penicillin. Dose: 1 tab four times daily.

DIARRHOEALS – Imodium capsules after each loose stool. Up to 6 per day in conjunction with oral rehydration and avoiding solid food.

ANTIEMETICS – for seasickness. Prevention - Stugeron or other proprietory preparation.
*Stemetil suppositories along with oral rehydration in severe cases.

ANTIHISTAMINES – for stings, bites and hay fever. Newer Antihistamine - Loratadine, 1 tablet daily is less likely to cause drowsiness.
Piriton tablets 4mg - cause drowsiness

ANTISEPTICS – Savlon, TCP, Dettol etc.

DRESSINGS – Melolin Sterile Squares 10cm x 10cm. Put shiny side to wound, can be cut up and secured with Elastoplast or Micropore Tape. Crepe bandages - assorted widths for dressings, sprains or for securing splints. Steristrips for wound closure.

EYE DROPS – for sticky, gritty or red eyes.
*Chloromycetin drop.

ORAL REHYDRATION – for vomiting and diarrhoea. Rehidrat or Diarolyte Powders in sachets with instructions. Start with small amounts then give freely to replace lost fluid in vomiting, diarrhoea, burns and sunburn.

UK EMERGENCY VHF DIRECTION FINDING SERVICE

Remotely controlled H24 by a Coastguard Centre (MRCC) or (MRSC), this equipment is for emergency use only. It is not a free navigational service and should only be used 'one stage down' from real distress. It is in all yachtsmen's interests not to abuse the service.

After contact on Ch 16, invariably Ch 67 is used for the DF procedure; this may be a count from 1-10. Note that the bearing obtained is in °True from the station to the vessel.

VHF-DF stations are marked on charts by a dot and magenta circle, suffixed 'RG'.

STATION	CONTROLLED BY MRCC/MRSC	POSITION	
Barra	Stornoway	57°00'·81N	07°30'·42W
Bawdsey	Thames	51°59'·60N	01°25'·00E
Berry Head	Brixham	50°23'·97N	03°29'·05W
Boniface	Solent	50°36'·21N	01°12'·03W
Compass Head	Shetland	59°52'·05N	01°16'·30W
Crosslaw	Forth	55°54'·48N	02°12'·31W
Cullercoats	Humber	55°04'·00N	01°28'·00W
Dunnet Head	Aberdeen	58°40'·31N	03°22'·52W
Easington	Humber	53°39'·13N	00°05'·90E
East Prawle	Brixham	50°13'·10N	03°42'·50W
Fairlight	Dover	50°52'·19N	00°38'·74E
Fife Ness	Forth	56°16'·70N	02°35'·30W
Flamborough	Humber	54°07'·08N	00°05'·21W
Great Ormes Head	Holyhead	53°19'·96N	03°51'·25W
Grove Point	Portland	50°32'·93N	02°25'·20W
Hartland Pt	Swansea	51°01'·22N	04°31'·40W
Hartlepool	Humber	54°41'·79N	01°10'·57W
Hengistbury Head	Portland	50°42'·95N	01°45'·64W
Inverbervie	Forth	56°51'·10N	02°15'·65W
Kilchiaran	Clyde	55°45'·90N	06°27'·19W
Lands End	Falmouth	50°08'·13N	05°38'·19W
Landgon Battery	Dover	51°07'·97N	01°20'·59E
Law Hill	Clyde	55°41'·76N	04°50'·46W
Lizard	Falmouth	49°57'·60N	05°12'·06W
Lowestoft	Yarmouth	52°28'·60N	01°42'·20E
Newhaven	Solent	50°46'·93N	00°03'·01E
Newton	Humber	55°31'·01N	01°37'·10W
North Foreland	Dover	51°22'·53N	01°26'·72E
Noss Head	Aberdeen	58°28'·80N	03°03'·00W
Rame Head	Brixham	50°19'·03N	04°13'·20W
Rhiw	Holyhead	52°50'·00N	04°37'·82W
Rodel	Stornoway	57°44'·90N	06°57'·41W
St Ann's Head	Milford Haven	51°40'·97N	05°10'·52W
St Mary's, Isles of Scilly	Falmouth	49°55'·73N	06°18'·25W
Sandwick	Stornoway	58°12'·65N	06°21'·27W
Selsey	Solent	50°43'·80N	00°48'·22W
Shoeburyness	Thames	51°31'·38N	00°46'·50E
Skegness	Yarmouth	53°09'·00N	00°21'·00E
Snaefell	Liverpool	54°15'·84N	04°27'·66W
Tiree	Clyde	56°30'·62N	06°57'·68W
Trevose Head	Falmouth	50°32'·91N	05°01'·99W
Trimingham	Yarmouth	52°54'·57N	01°20'·60E
Tynemouth	Humber	55°01'·07N	01°24'·99W
Walney Island	Liverpool	54°06'·61N	03°16'·00W
Whitby	Humber	54°29'·40N	00°36'·30W
Wideford Hill	Shetland	58°59'·29N	03°01'·40W
Windyhead	Aberdeen	57°38'·90N	02°14'·50W
CHANNEL ISLANDS			
Guernsey	Ship transmits on Ch 16 (Distress only)	49°26'·27N	02°35'·77W
Jersey	or Ch 67 (Guernsey) or Ch 82 (Jersey)	49°10'·85N	02°14'·30W
NORTHERN IRELAND			
Orlock Head	Belfast	54°40'·41N	05°34'·97W
West Torr	Belfast	55°11'·70N	06°05'·20W

VHF EMERGENCY DIRECTION FINDING SERVICES

N

United Kingdom	Ch 16 (Distress only) Ch 67
Guernsey	Ch 16 (Distress) Ch 67
Jersey	Ch 16 (Distress) Ch 82
France	Ch 16 11 67

Compass Head
Wideford Hill
Dunnett Head
Noss Head
Sandwick
Rodel
Windyhead
Barra
Inverbervie
Tiree
Fife Ness
Kilchiaran
Crosslaw
Law Hill
Newton
Cullercoats
Tynemouth
West Torr
Hartlepool
Orlock Head
Whitby
Snaefell
Flamborough
Walney Island
Easington
Great Ormes Head
Skegness
Rhiw
Trimingham
Lowestoft
St Ann's Head
Bawdsey
Shoeburyness
North Foreland
Langdon Battery
Dunkerque
Fairlight
Hartland
Selsey Bill
Hengistbury Head
Gris-Nez
Trevose Head
Grove Point
Boniface
Newhaven
Boulogne
Ramé Head
Berry Head
Land's End
E Prawle
Levy
Ault
St Mary's
Lizard
Homet
Barfleur
Dieppe
Jobourg
Saint-Vaast
Fécamp
La Hague
La Hève
Guernsey
Carteret
Roches-Douvres
Villerville
Ploumanach
Jersey
Port-en-Bessin
Batz
Bréhat
Le Roc
Brignogan
Grouin
Créach
Saint-Cast
Saint-Mathieu
Toulinguet
Cap de la Chèvre
S-Quay-Portrieux
Pointe du Raz
Beg-Meil
Penmarc'h
Étel
Beg Melen
Saint-Julien
Port Louis
Piriac
Le Talut
Chemoulin
Taillefer
Saint-Sauveur
Les Baleines
Chassiron
La Coubre
Pointe de Grave
Cap Ferret
Messanges
Socoa

SAFETY

HM COASTGUARD - CONTACT DETAILS OF MRCCs and MRSCs

EASTERN REGION

PORTLAND COASTGUARD (MRSC)
50°36'N 02°27'W. DSC MMSI 002320012
Custom House Quay, Weymouth DT4 8BE.
☎ 01305 760439. ◳ 01305 760452.
Area: Topsham to Chewton Bunney
(50°44'N 01°42'W).

SOLENT COASTGUARD (MRSC)
50°48'N 01°12'W. DSC MMSI 002320011
44A Marine Parade West, Lee-on-Solent,
PO13 9NR.
☎ 02392 552100. ◳ 02392 551763.
Area: Chewton Bunney to Beachy Head.
Make routine initial calls on Ch 67 (H24) to
avoid congestion on Ch 16.

DOVER COASTGUARD (MRCC)
50°08'N 01°20'E. DSC MMSI 002320010
Langdon Battery, Dover CT15 5NA.
☎ 01304 210008. ◳ 01304 210302.
Area: Beachy Head to Reculver Towers
(51°23'N 01°12'E). Operates Channel
Navigation Information Service.

THAMES COASTGUARD (MRSC)
51°51'N 01°17'E. MMSI 002320009
East Terrace, Walton-on-the-Naze CO14
8PY.
☎ 01255 675518. ◳ 01255 675249.
Area: Reculver Towers to Southwold.

LONDON COASTGUARD
51°30'N 00°03'E. MMSI 002320063
Thames Barrier Navigation Centre, Unit 28,
34 Bowater Rd, Woolwich, London SE18 5TF.
☎ 0208 312 7382. ◳ 0208 312 7679.
Area: River Thames from Shell Haven Pt (N
bank) & Egypt Bay (S bank) up-river to
Teddington Lock.

YARMOUTH COASTGUARD (MRCC)
52°37'N 01°43'E. MMSI 002320008
Haven Bridge House, North Quay,
Great Yarmouth NR30 1HZ.
☎ 01493 851338. ◳ 01493 852307.
Area: Southwold to Haile Sand Fort.

†HUMBER COASTGUARD (MRSC)
54°06'N 00°11'W. MMSI 002320007
Lime Kiln Lane, Bridlington, N Humberside
YO15 2LX.
☎ 01262 672317. ◳ 01262 606915.
Area: Haile Sand Fort to the Scottish
border.

SCOTLAND & NORTHERN IRELAND

FORTH COASTGUARD (MRSC)
56°17'N 02°35'W. MMSI 002320005
Fifeness, Crail, Fife KY10 3XN.
☎ 01333 450666. ◳ 01333 450725.
Area: English border to Doonies Pt
(57°01'N 02°10'W).

†ABERDEEN COASTGUARD (MRCC)
57°08'N 02°05'W. MMSI 002320004
Marine House, Blaikies Quay, Aberdeen
AB11 5PB.
☎ 01224 592334. ◳ 01224 575920.
Area: Doonies Pt to Cape Wrath, incl
Pentland Firth.

†SHETLAND COASTGUARD (MRSC)
60°09'N 01°08'W. MMSI 002320001
Knab Road, Lerwick ZE1 0AX.
☎ 01595 692976. ◳ 01595 694810.
Area: Orkney, Fair Isle and Shetland.

†*STORNOWAY COASTGUARD (MRSC)
58°12'N 06°22'W. MMSI 002320024
Battery Pt, Stornoway, Isle of Lewis H51 2RT.
☎ 01851 702013. ◳ 01851 704387.
Area: Cape Wrath to Ardnamurchan Pt,
Western Isles and St Kilda.

†*CLYDE COASTGUARD (MRCC)
55°58'N 04°48'W. MMSI 002320022
Navy Bldgs, Eldon St, Greenock PA16 7QY.
☎ 01475 729988. ◳ 01475 786955.
Area: Ardnamurchan Pt to Mull of
Galloway inc islands.

*BELFAST COASTGUARD (MRSC)
54°40'N 05°40'W. MMSI 002320021
Bregenz House, Quay St, Bangor, Co Down
BT20 5ED.
☎ 02891 463933. ◳ 02891 465886.
Area: Carlingford Lough to Lough Foyle.

WESTERN REGION

LIVERPOOL COASTGUARD (MRSC)
53°30'N 03°03'W. MMSI 002320019
Hall Rd West, Crosby, Liverpool L23 8SY.
☎ 0151 9313341. ◳ 0151 9313347
Area: Mull of Galloway to Queensferry
(near Chester).

†HOLYHEAD COASTGUARD (MRSC)
53°19'N 04°38'W. MMSI 002320018
Prince of Wales Rd, Holyhead, Anglesey
LL65 1ET.

☎ 01407 762051. 🖷 01407 764373
Area: Queensferry to Friog (1·6M S of
Barmouth).

†MILFORD HAVEN COASTGUARD (MRSC)
51°42'N 05°03'W. MMSI 002320017
Gorsewood Drive, Hakin, Milford Haven,
SA73 2HD.
☎ 01646 690909. 🖷 01646 692176.
Area: Friog to River Towy (11M N of
Worms Head).

SWANSEA COASTGUARD (MRCC)
51°34'N 03°58'W. MMSI 002320016
Tutt Head, Mumbles, Swansea SA3 4EX.
☎ 01792 366534. 🖷 01792 369005.
Area: River Towy to Marsland Mouth (near
Bude).

†*FALMOUTH COASTGUARD (MRCC)
50°09'N 05°03'W. MMSI 002320014
Pendennis Point, Castle Drive, Falmouth
TR11 4WZ.
☎ 01326 317575. 🖷 01326 318342.
Area: Marsland Mouth (near Bude) to
Dodman Point.

*BRIXHAM COASTGUARD (MRSC)
50°24'N 03°31'W. DSC MMSI 002320013
King's Quay, Brixham TQ5 9TW.
☎ 01803 882704. 🖷 01803 882780.
Area: Dodman Point to Topsham (R. Exe).

NOTES: †Monitors DSC MF 2187.5 kHz.
*Broadcasts Gunfacts/Subfacts.

THE CHANNEL ISLANDS
There is no Coastguard in the Channel Islands.
The HMs at St Peter Port and St Helier direct
SAR operations within the Northern and
Southern areas respectively.

The two Coast radio stations, St Peter Port
Radio and Jersey Radio, provide
communications on VHF, MF and DSC.

Close liaison is maintained with adjacent
French SAR authorities and a distress situation
may be controlled by the Channel Islands or
France, whichever is more appropriate. For
example a British yacht in difficulty in French
waters may be handled by St Peter Port or
Jersey so as to avoid language problems; and
vice versa for a French yacht.

ST PETER PORT RADIO (CRS)
49°27'·00N 02°32'00W. DSC MMSI
002320064. ☎ 01481 720672. 🖷 714177
Area: The Channel Islands Northern area.

JERSEY RADIO (CRS)
49°10'·85N 02°14'30W. DSC MMSI
002320060. ☎: 01534 741121. 🖷: 499089.
Area: The Channel Islands southern area.

SEARCH AND RESCUE ABROAD
THE IRISH REPUBLIC
The Irish CG co-ordinates SAR operations
around the coast of Eire via Dublin MRCC,
Malin Head and Valentia MRSCs and remote
sites. It may liaise with the UK and France
during any rescue operation within 100M of
the Irish coast. It is part of the Dept of Marine,
Leeson Lane, Dublin 2. ☎ (01) 6620922;
🖷 (01) 6620795. The Irish EPIRB Registry is co-
located; ☎ (01) 6199280; 🖷 (01) 6621571.

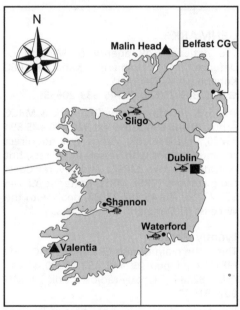

Irish Coastguard centres

The MRCC/MRSCs are co-located with the
Coast radio stations of the same name and
manned by the same staff. All stations keep
watch H24 on VHF Ch 16 and DSC Ch 70. If
ashore dial 999 or 112 in an emergency and
ask for Marine Rescue.

Details of the MRCC/MRSCs are as follows:
DUBLIN (MRCC)
53°20'N 06°15W. DSC MMSI 002500300
(+2187·5 kHz).
☎ +353 1 662 0922/3; 🖷 +353 1 662 0795.
Area: Carlingford Lough to Youghal.

SAFETY

VALENTIA (MRSC)
51°56'N 10°21'W.DSC MMSI 002500200 (+2187·5 kHz).
☎ +353 669 476 109; 🖷 +353 669 476 289.
Area: Youghal to Slyne Head.

MALIN HEAD (MRSC)
55°22'N 07°20W. DSC MMSI 002500100 (+2187·5 kHz).
☎ +353 77 70103; 🖷 +353 77 70221.
Area: Slyne Head to Lough Foyle.

SAR resources
The Irish CG provides some 50 units around the coast and is on call H24. The RNLI maintains 4 stations around the coast and operates 42 lifeboats; six community-run inshore rescue boats are also available.

Sikorsky S-61 helicopters, based at Dublin, Waterford, Shannon and Sligo, can respond within 15 to 45 minutes and operate to a radius of 200M. They are equipped with infrared search equipment and can uplift 30 survivors.

Military and civilian aircraft and vessels, together with the Garda and lighthouse service, can also be called upon.

Some stations provide specialist cliff climbing services. They are manned by volunteers, who are trained in first aid and equipped with inflatables, breeches buoys, cliff ladders etc. Their ☎ numbers (the Leader's residence) are given, where appropriate, under each port.

DENMARK
The national SAR agency is: Ministry of Defence, 42 Holmens Kanal,DK-1060 København K, Denmark.
☎ +45 339 23320; 🖷 +45 333 20655.

The SAR coordinator for Denmark is MRCC Århus, ☎ +45 894 33099 ext 3203; 🖷 +45 894 33230; mrcc@sok.dk. Århus has no direct communications with vessels in distress, but operates via two MRSCs and several Coast radio stations (CRS). MRSC Kattegat, ☎ +45 992 22255; 🖷 +45 992 22838, deals with the W coast of Denmark.

Lyngby Radio
This is the main Danish CRS and is DSC VHF/MF/HF equipped (☎ +45 452 89800; 🖷 +45 458 82485, lyngby-radio@tdc.dk MMSI 002191000).

It operates through remote sites at Skagen, Hirtshals, Hantsholm, Bovbjerg and Blavand, all of which guard Ch 16 H24 and use callsign *Lyngby Radio*. Their VHF and MF frequencies are shown in the chartlet opposite.

There are at least 12 lifeboats stationed at the major harbours along the west coast. They are designed to double up as Pilot boats.

Firing practice areas
There are 4 such areas on the W coast as in the chartlet and listed below. Firing times are broadcast daily by Danmarks Radio 1 after the weather at 1645UT. Times can also be obtained from the Range office Ch 16 or ☎.

Ⓐ Tranum & Blokhus ☎ 982 35088 or call *Tranum*.

Ⓑ Nymindegab ☎ 752 89355 or call *Nymindegab*.

Ⓒ Oksbøl ☎ 765 41213 or call *Oksbøl*.

Ⓓ Rømø E ☎ 747 55219; Rømø W ☎ 745 41340 – or call *Fly Rømø*.

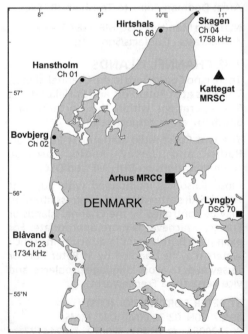

Danish Coastguard centres

GERMANY

The national SAR agency is: *Deutsche Gesellschaft zur Rettung Schiffbrüchiger* (DGzRS), the German Sea Rescue Service. Werderstrasse 2, Hermann-Helms-Haus, D-28199 Bremen. mail@mrcc-bremen.de. ☎ 421 537 070; 🖷 421 537 0714.

DGzRS is responsible for coordinating SAR operations, supported by ships and SAR helicopters of the German Navy.

Bremen MRCC (☎ 421 536870; 🖷 421 5368714; MMSI 002111240), using callsign *Bremen Rescue Radio,* maintains an H24 watch on Ch 16 and DSC Ch 70 via remote Coast radio stations at:

Sylt, Nordfriesland, Eiderstedt, Helgoland, Elbe-Weser, Hamburg and Norddeich.

There are 21 offshore lifeboats, LOA 23–

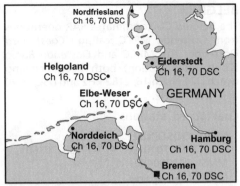

German Coastguard stations

44m, and 21 smaller <10m lifeboats, based at List, Amrum, Helgoland, Cuxhaven, Bremerhaven, Wilhelmshaven, Langeoog, Norderney and Borkum. There are also many inshore lifeboats.

Netherlands Coastguard stations

The JRCC keeps a listening watch H24 on DSC Ch 70, and MF DSC 2187·5 kHz (but not on 2182 kHz); MMSI 002442000.

Coastguard Operations can be contacted H24 via:

In emergency:
☎ + 31 9000 111 or dial 112.

Operational telephone number:
☎ + 31 223 542300. 🖷 + 31 223 658358; ccc@kustwacht.nl If using a mobile phone, call 9000 111, especially if the International emergency number 112 is subject to delays.

Admin/info (HO)
☎+ 31 223 658300. 🖷+31 223 658303. info@kustwacht.nl PO Box 10000, 1780 CA Den Helder.

THE NETHERLANDS

The national SAR agency is: SAR Commission, Directorate Transport Safety (DGG), PO Box 20904, 2500 EX The Hague, Netherlands.

The Netherlands CG at Den Helder, co-located with the Navy HQ, coordinates SAR operations as the Dutch JRCC for A1 and A2 Sea Areas. (JRCC = Joint Rescue Coordination Centre – marine & aeronautical.) Callsign is *Netherlands Coastguard*, but *Den Helder Rescue* during SAR operations.

Remote CG stations are shown above. Working channels are VHF 23 and 83.

BELGIUM

The Belgian CG coordinates SAR operations from Oostende MRCC, callsign *Coastguard Oostende*. The MRCC and *Oostende Radio* (Coast radio rtation) both keep listening watch H24 on Ch 16, 2182 kHz and DSC Ch 70 and 2187·5 kHz.

Coastguard stations

MRCC OOSTENDE
☎ +32 59 701000; 📠 +32 59 703605.
MMSI 002050480.

MRSC Nieuwpoort
☎ +32 58 230000; 📠 +32 58 231575.

MRSC Zeebrugge
☎ +32 50 550801; 📠 +32 50 547400.

RCC Brussels (COSPAS/SARSAT agency)
☎ +32 2 7200338; 📠 +32 2 7524201.

Coast Radio Stations

OOSTENDE Radio
☎ 59 702438; 📠 59 701339.
Ch 16, DSC Ch 70 and MF DSC 2187·5 kHz.
MMSI 002050480.

Antwerpen Radio (remotely controlled by Oostende CRS) MMSI 002050485. Ch 16, DSC Ch 70.

Resources

Offshore and inshore lifeboats are based at Nieuwpoort, Oostende and Zeebrugge.

The Belgian Air Force provides helicopters from Koksijde near the French border. The Belgian Navy also participates in SAR operations as required.

FRANCE – CROSS

Four CROSS (Centres Régionaux Opérationnels de Surveillance et de Sauvetage, ie an MRCC) provide a permanent, H24, all weather operational presence along the N and W coasts and liaise with foreign CGs.

CROSS' main functions include:

- Co-ordinating SAR operations.
- Navigational surveillance.
- Broadcasting navigational warnings.
- Broadcasting weather information.
- Anti-pollution control.
- Marine and fishery surveillance.

CROSS locations and areas of responsibility

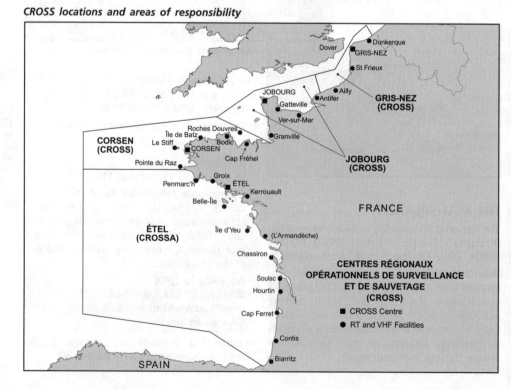

All centres keep watch on VHF Ch 16 as well as Ch 70 (DSC)and co-ordinate SAR on Ch 15, 67, 68, 73. They also broadcast gale warnings, weather forecasts and local navigational warnings.

CROSSA Étel specialises in medical advice and responds to alerts from Cospas/Sarsat satellites.

CROSS can be contacted by R/T, by ☎, through Coast Radio Stations, via the National Gendarmerie or Affaires Maritimes, or via a Semaphore station. Call *Semaphore* stations on Ch 16 (working Ch 10) or by ☎ as listed later in this section.

CROSS also monitor TSS in the Dover Strait, off Casquets and off Ouessant using, for example, the callsign *Corsen Traffic*.

For medical advice call CROSS which will contact a doctor or SAMU (Service d'Aide Médicale Urgente). In harbour/marina SAMU responds faster to a medical emergency than calling a doctor. Simply dial 15.

CROSS stations (Emergency ☎ 1616).

CROSS Gris-Nez
50°52'N 01°35'E   MMSI 002275100
☎ 03 21 87 21 87; 🖷 03 21 87 78 55
Belgian border to Cap d'Antifer.

NavWarnings Ch 79 at every H+10 via Dunkerque, Saint-Frieux and L'Ailly.

CROSS Jobourg
49°41'N 01°54'W   MMSI 002275200
☎ 02 33 52 72 13; 🖷 02 33 52 71 72
Cap de la Hague to Mont St Michel

NavWarnings Ch 80 every H+20 and H+50 via Antifer, Ver-sur-Mer, Gatteville, Jobourg, Granville and Roche Douvres.

CROSS Corsen
48°24'N 04°47'W   MMSI 002275300
☎ 02 98 89 31 31; 🖷 02 98 89 65 75
Mont St Michel to Pointe de Penmarc'h.

NavWarnings Ch 79 every H+10 and H+40 via Cap Fréhel, Bodic, Ile de Batz, Le Stiff and Pte du Raz.

CROSS Étel
47°39'N 03°12'W   MMSI 002275000
☎ 02 97 55 35 35; 🖷 02 97 55 49 34
Pte de Penmarc'h to the Spanish border

NavWarnings Ch 79 for Landes range activity via Chassiron 1903; Soulac 1915; Cap Ferret 1933; Contis 1945; and Biarritz 2003.

Semaphore stations keep visual, radar and radio watch (Ch 16); are equipped with VHF DF; relay emergency calls to CROSS; show gale warning signals, repeat forecasts and offer local weather reports. Hours sunrise-sunset, but * H24.

* Dunkerque	03·28·66·86·18
Boulogne	03·21·31·32·10
Ault	03·22·60·47·33
Dieppe	02·35·84·23·82
* Fécamp	02·35·28·00·91
* La Hève	02·35·46·07·81
* Le Havre	02·35·21·74·39
Villerville	02·31·88·11·13
* Port-en-Bessin	02·31·21·81·51
St-Vaast	02·33·54·44·50
* Barfleur	02·33·54·04·37
Lévy	02·33·54·31·17
* Le Homet	02·33·92·60·08
La Hague	02·33·52·71·07
Carteret	02·33·53·85·08
Barneville Le Roc	02·33·50·05·85
St-Cast	02·96·41·85·30
* St Quay-Portrieux	02·96.70.42.18
Bréhat	02·96·20·00·12

* Ploumanac'h	02·96·91·46·51
Batz	02·98·61·76·06
* Brignogan	02·98·83·50·84
* Ouessant Stiff	02·98·48·81·50
* St-Mathieu	02·98·89·01·59
* Portzic (Ch 08)	02·98·22·21·47
Toulinguet	02·98·27·90·02
Cap-de-la-Chèvre	02·98·27·09·55
* Pointe-du-Raz	02·98·70·66·57
* Penmarc'h	02·98·58·61·00
Beg Meil	02·98·94·98·92
* Port-Louis	02·97·82·52·10
Étel Mât Fenoux	02·97·55·35·35
Beg Melen (Groix)	02·97·86·80·13
Talut (Belle-Île)	02·97·31·85·07
St-Julien	02·97·50·09·35
Piriac-sur-Mer	02·40·23·59·87
* Chemoulin	02·40·91·99·00
St-Sauveur (Yeu)	02·51·58·31·01
Les Baleines (Ré)	05·46·29·42·06
Chassiron (Oléron)	05·46·47·85·43
* Pointe-de-Grave	05·56·09·60·03
Cap Ferret	05·56·60·60·03
Messanges	05·58·48·94·10
* Socoa	05·59·47·18·54

EMERGENCY VHF DF SERVICE

A yacht in emergency can call CROSS on VHF Ch 16, 11 or 67 to obtain a true bearing of the yacht *from* the DF station. These monitor Ch 16 and other continuously scanned frequencies, which include Ch 1-29, 36, 39, 48, 50, 52, 55, 56 and 60-88. The Semaphore stations overleaf are also equipped with VHF DF.

HJ = Day service only.

VHF DF stations, are listed below geographically from NE to W then S:

Station	Lat/Long	Hrs
Dunkerque	51°03'.40N 02°20'.40E	H24
*Gris-Nez	50°52'.20N 01°35'.01E	H24
Boulogne	50°44'.00N 01°36'.00E	HJ
Ault	50°06'.50N 01°27'.50E	HJ
Dieppe	49°56'.00N 01°05'.20E	HJ
Fécamp	49°46'.10N 00°22'.20E	H24
La Hève	49°30'.60N 00°04'.20E	H24
Villerville	49°23'.20N 00°06'.50E	HJ
Port-en-Bessin	49°21'.10N 00°46'.30W	H24
Saint-Vaast	49°34'.50N 01°16'.50W	HJ
Barfleur	49°41'.90N 01°15'.90W	H24
Levy	49°41'.70N 01°28'.20W	HJ
†Homet	49°39'.50N 01°37'.90W	H24
*Jobourg	49°41'.50N 01°54'.50W	H24
La Hague	49°43'.60N 01°56'.30W	HJ
Carteret	49°22'.40N 01°48'.30W	HJ
Le Roc	48°50'.10N 01°36'.90W	HJ
Grouin/Cancale	48°42'.60N 01°50'.60W	HJ
Saint-Cast	48°38'.60N 02°14'.70W	HJ
St-Quay-Port'x	48°39'.30N 02°49'.50W	H24
Bréhat	48°51'.30N 03°00'.10W	HJ
Ploumanac'h	48°49'.50N 03°28'.20W	H24
Batz	48°44'.80N 04°00'.60W	HJ
Brignogan	48°40'.60N 04°19'.70W	H24
Creac'h (Ushant)	48°27'.60N 05°07'.70W	HJ

*Creac'h	48°27'.60N 05°07'.80W	H24
†Saint-Mathieu	48°19'.80N 04°46'.20W	H24
Toulinguet	48°16'.80N 04°37'.50W	HJ
Cap de la Chèvre	48°10'.20N 04°33'.00W	HJ
Pointe du Raz	48°02'.30N 04°43'.80W	H24
Penmarc'h	47°47'.90N 04°22'.40W	H24
Beg-Meil	47°51'.30N 03°58'.40W	HJ
Beg Melen	47°39'.20N 03°30'.10W	HJ
†Port-Louis	47°42'.60N 03°21'.80W	H24
*Etel	47°39'.80N 03°12'.00W	H24
Saint-Julien	47°29'.70N 03°07'.50W	HJ
Taillefer	47°21'.80N 03°09'.00W	HJ
Le Talut	47°17'.70N 03°13'.00W	HJ
Piriac	47°22'.50N 02°33'.40W	HJ
Chemoulin	47°14'.10N 02°17'.80W	H24
Saint-Sauveur	46°41'.70N 02°18'.80W	HJ
Les Baleines	46°14'.60N 01°33'.70W	HJ
Chassiron	46°02'.80N 01°24'.50W	HJ
La Coubre	45°41'.90N 01°13'.40W	H24
Pointe de Grave	45°34'.30N 01°03'.90W	HJ
Cap Ferret	44°37'.50N 01°15'.00W	HJ
Messanges	43°48'.80N 01°23'.90W	HJ
Socoa	43°23'.30N 01°41'.10W	H24

Lifeboats

The lifeboat service Société National de Sauvetage en Mer (SNSM) comes under CROSS, but ashore it is best to contact local lifeboat stations direct. A hefty charge may be levied if a SNSM lifeboat attends a vessel not in distress.

Navigation warnings

Long-range warnings are broadcast by SafetyNet for Navarea II, which includes the W coast of France. The N coast is in Navarea I.

Avurnavs (AVis URgents aux NAVigateurs) are regional, coastal and local warnings issued by Cherbourg and Brest and broadcast by Niton and Brest Navtex and on MF. Warnings are prefixed by 'Sécurité Avurnav'.

SPAIN

The Society for Maritime Rescue and Safety (Sociedad de Salvamento y Seguridad Maritima – SASEMAR) is the national agency for SAR operations (and the prevention of pollution); akin to MCA in the UK.

MRCC Madrid coordinates SAR operations via 3 MRCCs (Bilbao, Gijon and Finisterre) on the N coast and Tarifa MRCC on the SW coast – as listed below.

All Centres monitor (H24) VHF Ch 16, MF 2182 kHz and DSC Ch 70, 2187·5 kHz. They also broadcast weather as shown in Chapter 2 and Nav warnings; but do *not* handle commercial link calls.

North and North West Spain

In N and NW Spain CG Centres do not keep continuous watch on Ch 16, so call on a working channel.

Spanish & Portuguese Coastguard Radio Stations

MADRID MRCC
MMSI 002241008 ☎ 91 7559 132/3;
🖷 9l 5261440.

Bilbao MRCC
43°21'N 03°02'W   MMSI 002240996
☎ 944 839411; 🖷 944 83 9161.

Santander MRSC
43°28'N 03°43'W   MMSI 002241009
☎ 942 213 030; 🖷 942 213 638.

Gijón MRCC
43°34'N 05°42'W   MMSI 002240997
☎ 985 326050; 🖷 985 320908.

Finisterre MRCC
42°42'N 08°59'W   MMSI 002240993
☎ 981 767320; 🖷 981 767740.

Coruña MRSC
43°22'N 08°23'W   MMSI 002241022
☎ 981 209541; 🖷 981 209518.

Vigo MRSC
42°10'N 08°41'W   MMSI 002240998
☎ 986 222230; 🖷 986 228957.

PORTUGAL
The Portuguese Navy coordinates SAR in two regions, Lisboa and Santa Maria (Azores) via MRCCs at Lisboa, Ponta Delgada (Azores) and one planned at Horta (Azores). A network of CRS maintains an H24 listening watch on all distress frequencies.

The Naval HQ (Estado Maior da Armada, 3 Divisao) is at: Praca do Comercio, 1188 Lisboa Codex, Portugal.
☎ 21 346 8965. 🖷 21 347 9591.

MAINLAND
Lisboa MRCC
38°41'N 09°19'W   MMSI 002630100
☎ 21 4401919; 🖷 21 4401954.
mrcclisboa@netc.pt
Planned DSC Ch 70; 2187·5 kHz

Remotely controlled MF DSC stations are planned (2005) at:
Apulia 41°28'N 08°45'W. MMSI 002630200.
Sagres 37°00'N 08°56'W. MMSI 002630400.

AZORES
Ponta Delgada MRCC
37°44'N 25°40'W   MMSI 002040100
☎ 296 281777; 🖷 296 281999
mrccdelgada@mail.telepac.pt
Planned DSC Ch 70; 2187·5 kHz.

SOUTH-WEST SPAIN
Tarifa MRCC coordinates SAR in SW Spain and the Gibraltar Strait.

Tarifa MRCC
36°01'N 05°35'W   MMSI 002240994
☎ 956 684740; 🖷 956 680 606.

Huelva MRSC
37°13'N 07°07'W   MMSI 002241012
☎ 959 243000; 🖷 959 242103.

Cadiz MRSC
36°32'N 06°18'W   MMSI 002241011
☎ 956 214253; 🖷 956 226091.

Algeciras MRSC (controlled by Malaga MRCC)
36°08'N 05°26'W   MMSI 002241001
☎ 956 580930; 🖷 956 585402.

NAVAL EXERCISE AREAS

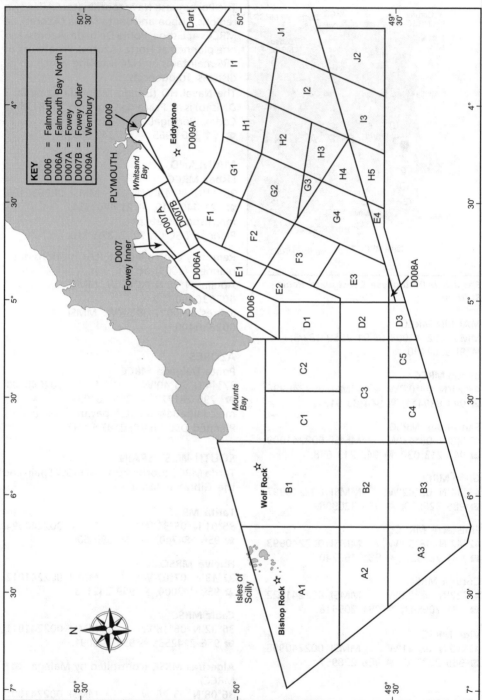

KEY

D006 = Falmouth
D006A = Falmouth Bay North
D007A = Fowey
D007B = Fowey Outer
D009A = Wembury

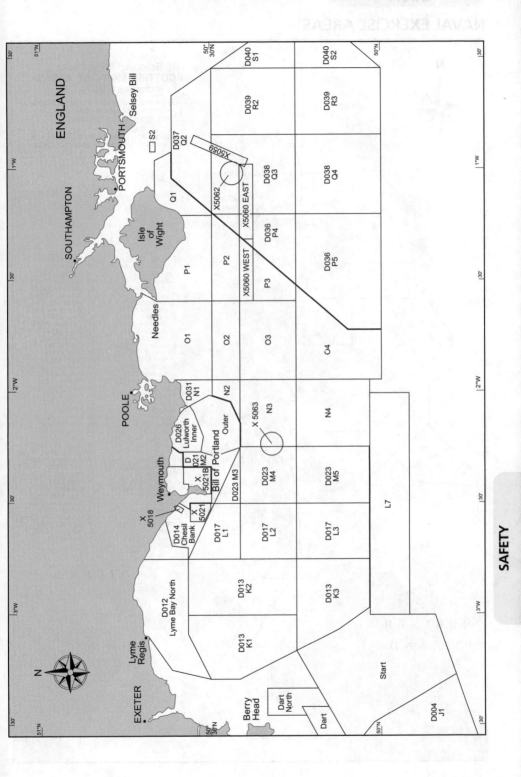

NAVAL EXERCISE AREAS

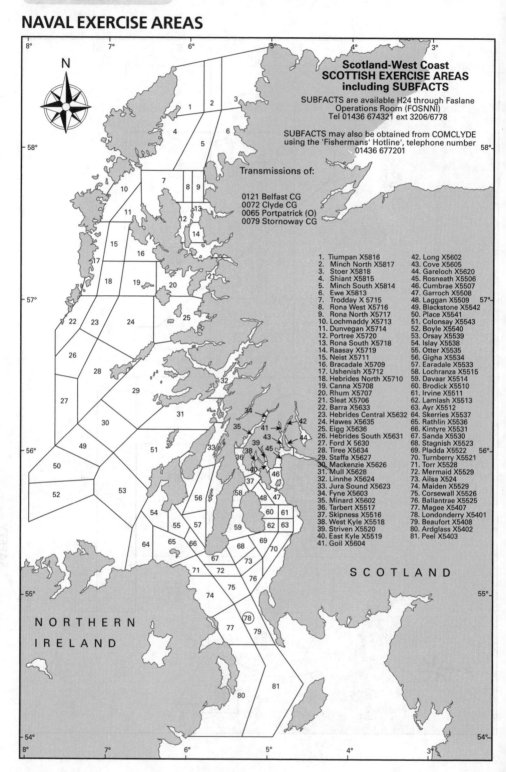

Scotland-West Coast
SCOTTISH EXERCISE AREAS
including SUBFACTS

SUBFACTS are available H24 through Faslane
Operations Room (FOSNNI)
Tel 01436 674321 ext 3206/6778

SUBFACTS may also be obtained from COMCLYDE
using the 'Fishermans' Hotline', telephone number
01436 677201

Transmissions of:

0121 Belfast CG
0072 Clyde CG
0065 Portpatrick (O)
0079 Stornoway CG

1. Tiumpan X5816
2. Minch North X5817
3. Stoer X5818
4. Shiant X5815
5. Minch South X5814
6. Ewe X5813
7. Trodday X 5715
8. Rona West X5716
9. Rona North X5717
10. Lochmaddy X5713
11. Dunvegan X5714
12. Portree X5720
13. Rona South X5718
14. Raasay X5719
15. Neist X5711
16. Bracadale X5709
17. Ushenish X5712
18. Hebrides North X5710
19. Canna X5708
20. Rhum X5707
21. Sleat X5706
22. Barra X5633
23. Hebrides Central X5632
24. Hawes X5635
25. Eigg X5636
26. Hebrides South X5631
27. Ford X 5630
28. Tiree X5634
29. Staffa X5627
30. Mackenzie X5626
31. Mull X5628
32. Linnhe X5624
33. Jura Sound X5623
34. Fyne X5603
35. Minard X5602
36. Tarbert X5517
37. Skipness X5516
38. West Kyle X5518
39. Striven X5520
40. East Kyle X5519
41. Goil X5604

42. Long X5602
43. Cove X5605
44. Gareloch X5620
45. Rosneath X5506
46. Cumbrae X5507
47. Garroch X5508
48. Laggan X5509
49. Blackstone X5542
50. Place X5541
51. Colonsay X5543
52. Boyle X5540
53. Orsay X5539
54. Islay X5538
55. Otter X5535
56. Gigha X5534
57. Earadale X5533
58. Lochranza X5515
59. Davaar X5514
60. Brodick X5510
61. Irvine X5511
62. Lamlash X5513
63. Ayr X5512
64. Skerries X5537
65. Rathlin X5536
66. Kintyre X5531
67. Sanda X5530
68. Stagnish X5523
69. Pladda X5522
70. Turnberry X5521
71. Torr X5528
72. Mermaid X5529
73. Ailsa X524
74. Maiden X5529
75. Corsewall X5526
76. Ballantrae X5525
77. Magee X5407
78. Londonderry X5401
79. Beaufort X5408
80. Ardglass X5402
81. Peel X5403

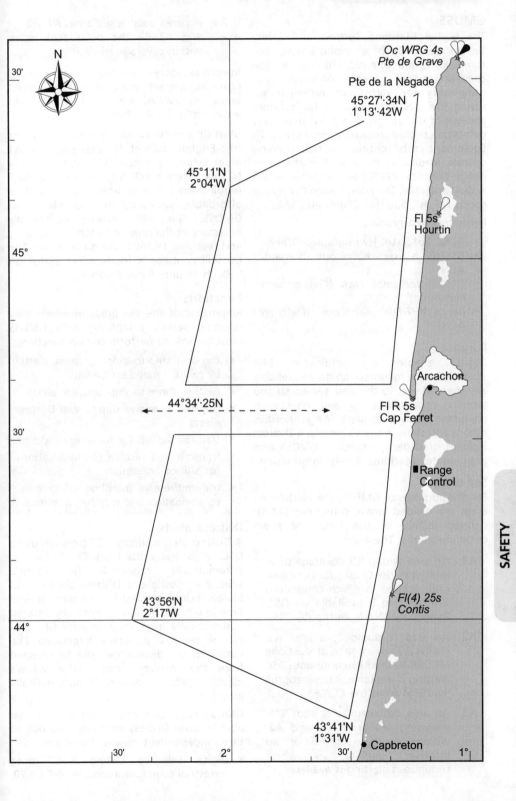

Oc WRG 4s
Pte de Grave

Pte de la Négade
45°27'·34N
1°13'·42W

45°11'N
2°04'W

Fl 5s
Hourtin

44°34'·25N

Arcachon

Fl R 5s
Cap Ferret

Range
Control

43°56'N
2°17'W

Fl(4) 25s
Contis

43°41'N
1°31'W

Capbreton

SAFETY

137

GMDSS

The Global Maritime Distress and Safety System (GMDSS) is a sophisticated, but complex, semi-automatic, third-generation communications system. Although not compulsory for yachts, its potential for saving life, particularly when far offshore and out of VHF range, is so great that every yachtsman should consider it most seriously. Equipment costs continue to fall. Training courses, leading to the award of the Short Range Certificate (SRC) of Competence, are widely available. The Long Range Certificate covers MF, HF, SatCom, EPIRBs and SART.

Recommended reading:

- *ALRS, Vol 5* (UK Hydrographic Office)
- *GMDSS: a user's handbook* (Bréhaut/ACN)
- *GMDSS for small craft* (Clemmetsen/Fernhurst)
- *Reeds VHF/DSC Handbook* (Fletcher/ACN)

Purpose

GMDSS enables a coordinated SAR operation to be mounted rapidly and reliably anywhere at sea. To this end, terrestrial and satellite communications and navigation equipment is used to alert SAR authorities ashore and ships in the vicinity to a Distress incident or Urgency situation. GMDSS also promulgates Maritime Safety Information.

Sea areas

For the purposes of GMDSS, the world's sea areas are divided into 4 categories (A1-4), defined mainly by the range of radio communications. These are:

A1 An area within R/T coverage of at least one VHF Coastguard or Coast radio station in which continuous VHF alerting is available via DSC. Range: 20–50M from the CG/CRS.

A2 An area, excluding sea area A1, within R/T coverage of at least one MF CG/CRS in which continuous DSC alerting is available. Range: approx 50–250M from the CG/CRS.

A3 An area between 70°N and 70°S, excluding sea areas A1 and A2, within coverage of HF or an Inmarsat satellite in which continuous alerting is available.

A4 An area outside sea areas A1, A2 and A3, ie the polar regions, within coverage of HF.

In each category of sea area certain types of radio equipment must be carried. In A1 areas VHF DSC; A2 areas MF or HF DSC; A3 areas SatCom; A4 MF/HF.

Most UK yachtsmen will operate in A1 areas (the English Channel, for example, is an A1 area) where a simple VHF radio and a Navtex receiver will initially meet GMDSS requirements. As equipment becomes more affordable, yachtsmen may decide to fit GMDSS. This will become increasingly necessary as the present system for sending and receiving Distress calls is run down. The CG will continue a loudspeaker watch on VHF Ch 16 until further notice.

Functions

Regardless of the sea areas in which they operate, vessels complying with GMDSS must be able to perform certain functions:

- transmit ship-to-shore Distress alerts by two independent means
- receive shore-to-ship Distress alerts
- transmit & receive ship-to-ship Distress alerts
- transmit signals for locating incidents
- transmit and receive communications for SAR co-ordination
- transmit/receive maritime safety info, eg navigation and weather warnings

Distress alerts

A Distress alert is simply a Distress call using DSC. It is transmitted on Ch 70 and is automatically repeated five times. Whenever possible, a Distress alert should always include the last known position and time in UT. The position is normally entered automatically from an interfaced GPS, but can be entered manually if required. The nature of the distress can also be selected from the receiver's menu. The vessel's identity (MMSI number) is automatically included.

GMDSS requires participating ships to be able to send Distress alerts by two out of three independent means. These are:

- Digital Selective Calling (DSC) using terrestrial communications, ie VHF Ch 70,

MF 2187·5 kHz, or HF distress and alerting frequencies in the 4, 6, 8,12 and 16 MHz bands.

- Emergency Position Indicating Radio Beacons (EPIRBs), either float-free or manually released, using the Cospas/Sarsat satellites on 406 MHz with homing on 121·5 MHz; or those using Inmarsat satellites in the 1·6 GHz band. Both types transmit Distress messages which include the position and identification of the vessel in distress. See below for further details of EPIRBs.

- Inmarsat, via ship terminals.

Digital Selective Calling

DSC is an essential component of GMDSS. It is so called because information is sent by a burst of digital code; selective because it can be addressed to a specific DSC-equipped vessel or to a selected group of vessels.

In all DSC messages every vessel and relevant shore station has a 9-digit identification number, or MMSI (Maritime Mobile Service Identity), which is in effect an automatic, electronic callsign.

DSC is used to transmit Distress alerts from ships, to receive Distress acknowledgements from ships or shore stations; to send Urgency and Safety alerts; to relay Distress alerts; and for routine calling & answering. A thorough working knowledge is needed.

Using the procedures and switches applicable to your particular VHF/DSC radio, a VHF/DSC Distress alert might be sent as follows:

- Momentarily press the (red, guarded) Distress button. The set automatically switches to Ch 70 (DSC Distress chan) and transmits a basic Distress alert with position & time. It then reverts to Ch I6.

- If time permits, select from the DSC menu the nature of the distress, eg Collision. Then press the Distress button for 5 seconds to send a full Distress alert.

A CG/CRS automatically sends a Distress acknowledgement on Ch 70, before replying on Ch 16. Ships in range should reply directly on Ch 16.

If a Distress acknowledgement is not received from a CG/CRS, the Distress alert will automatically be repeated every four minutes.

- When a DSC Distress acknowledgement has been received, or after about 15 seconds, the vessel in distress should transmit a MAYDAY message by voice on Ch 16, adding its MMSI.

NB: If a Distress alert is inadvertently transmitted, an All stations DSC message cancelling the false alert (by date and time) must be sent at once.

Maritime Safety Information (MSI)

MSI consists of the vital navigational, weather and safety messages which traditionally were sent to vessels at sea by CRS in Morse, but by R/T on VHF and MF in more recent years – and now by GMDSS. For navigation and weather warnings see this and chapter 2 respectively.

GMDSS transmits MSI in English by two independent but complementary means, Navtex and SafetyNet.

- Navtex on MF (518 kHz and 490 kHz) which can be received out to about 300 miles offshore, see Chapter 2.

- SafetyNet uses Inmarsat-C satellites to cover beyond MF range. Enhanced Group Calling (EGC) is a part of SafetyNet which enables MSI to be sent to selected groups of users in any of the four oceans.

SATELLITES FOR SAR

Inmarsat (International Maritime Satellite system) and COSPAS/SARSAT (joint Russian-American system) provide satellite alerts and communications for SAR.

Inmarsat

Near-global communications are provided by four Inmarsat geostationary satellites, each positioned 1900M above the four oceans (Pacific, Indian, East Atlantic & West Atlantic). The polar regions, ie N of about 70°N and S of 70°S, are not covered. Inmarsat-E enables distress alerting in the L-band 1.6 GHz frequency. From pressing the red button in a yacht to reception at an MRCC usually takes less than 2 minutes. From 1 Feb 2009 the 121·5 MHz service will be discontinued.

COSPAS/SARSAT (C/S)

These Russian/US C/S satellites were specifically designed for SAR operations. They not only detect a 406 MHz Distress alert transmitted by an EPIRB, but also locate it with a high degree of accuracy. There are 10 ground receiving stations in 9 countries worldwide.

There are four geostationary satellites (GEOSAR) in a 24 hr orbit at 2000M above the equator, ie apparently fixed in relation to the earth. Four more low earth orbit (LEOSAR) satellites, about 450M high, pass over both poles every 100 minutes.

These 8 satellites give global coverage and receive both 406 and 121.5 MHz signals. But coverage is not quite continuous due to possible delays in detection by the LEOSAR system; waiting time is greater in equatorial regions.

LEOSAR satellites calculate an EPIRB's position by Doppler effect. GEOSAR satellites cannot do this since there is no Doppler shift between beacon and satellite. However this problem is solved by newer (and dearer) EPIRBs which have a built-in GPS receiver to provide location directly and with continuous updating.

EPIRBS

These are best categorised by their frequencies, ie:

- 406 MHz, as specifically designed to be processed by C/S. They emit a powerful and frequency-stable signal which ensures proven success in detection and location. C/S has established its own beacon specification and issues type approvals.

- 1·6 GHz, as used exclusively with Inmarsat satellites. L-band EPIRBs, known as Inmarsat-E, provide global distress alerting (as an alternative to 406 MHz EPIRBs in the C/S system). Inmarsat-E EPIRBs can also be equipped with an optional 121·5 MHz locator beacon for homing purposes and/or a Search and Rescue Radar Transponder (SART).

- 121·5 MHz (civilian aeronautical distress). These simple, inexpensive beacons are mainly used in conjunction with 406 MHz beacons for homing purposes. However their outdated technology was never designed to be detected by satellites. As a result from 1 Feb 2009 they will no longer be used at sea for satellite alerting.

If you own a basic 121·5 MHz beacon, do not throw it away; it can still be detected at long range by overflying airliners/Nimrods and at short range by homing lifeboats and helicopters.

- 243·0 MHz (military aeronautical distress). These too will be phased out from 1 Feb 2009 since their limitations are similar to 121·5 MHz beacons.

EPIRBs can be hand-held or float-free. Hand-held are popular in small craft because of their smaller size and portability. Many have lanyards for securing them to a liferaft or person in the water; these must not be secured to the yacht.

Float-free must be correctly installed so that they can indeed float free without snagging on a sinking vessel.

Most modern EPIRBs have a built-in GPS and a 48 hrs battery life. Costs range from £500 to £1200 for float-free, built-in GPS models. Inmarsat-E beacons cost about £1500.

Accuracy

All frequencies can be detected by C/S satellites. The processed positions are automatically passed to a Mission Control Centre (MCC) for assessment of any SAR action required; the UK MCC is co-located with the ARCC at Kinloss, NE Scotland.

C/S location accuracy is normally better than 5 km on 406 MHz, but no better than 20 km on 121·5 and 243·0 MHz. Dedicated SAR aircraft can home on 121·5 MHz and 243·0 MHz, but not on 406 MHz. Typically a helicopter at 1000 feet can receive homing signals from about 30M range whilst fixed-wing aircraft at higher altitudes can home from about 60M.

Best results will invariably be obtained from those 406 MHz EPIRBs with a built-in GPS receiver which transmits continuously updated positions.

CHAPTER 5 - TIDES

CONTENTS

DOVER RANGES & TIMES OF HW 2006

January

Day	HW	Range	HW
1	1135	5.5	
2	0001	5.7	1225
3	0049	5.6	1314
4	0138	5.6	1406
5	0228	5.3	1500
6	0321	4.9	1558
7	0417	4.4	1659
8	0518	4.3	1807
9	0627	3.8	1917
10	0739	3.7	2023
11	0847	3.8	2121
12	0945	4.2	2211
13	1034	4.5	2253
14	1115	4.8	2332
15	1152	4.7	
16	0008	4.9	1227
17	0043	4.9	1259
18	0115	4.8	1329
19	0142	4.7	1355
20	0208	4.5	1422
21	0238	4.2	1454
22	0317	3.9	1537
23	0406	3.4	1634
24	0513	3.4	1802
25	0638	3.1	1929
26	0754	3.6	2035
27	0858	4.2	2131
28	0954	4.9	2222
29	1046	5.5	2310
30	1134	5.9	2355
31	1219	6.1	

February

Day	HW	Range	HW
1	0039	6.3	1303
2	0123	6.3	1347
3	0207	6.0	1432
4	0252	5.5	1519
5	0340	4.8	1612
6	0435	4.2	1715
7	0541	3.3	1831
8	0706	3.0	1957
9	0837	3.1	2110
10	0944	3.8	2202
11	1030	4.4	2242
12	1107	4.8	2318
13	1138	5.0	2351
14	1207	4.9	
15	0021	5.2	1235
16	0048	5.2	1300
17	0111	5.1	1321
18	0133	5.0	1344
19	0201	4.9	1414
20	0236	4.4	1453
21	0319	3.8	1542
22	0418	3.3	1655
23	0602	2.8	1908
24	0744	3.2	2024
25	0854	4.1	2123
26	0951	5.0	2214
27	1040	5.7	2259
28	1124	6.3	2341

March

Day	HW	Range	HW
1	1205	6.4	
2	0021	6.7	1244
3	0102	6.6	1323
4	0142	6.2	1403
5	0223	5.6	1447
6	0308	4.6	1536
7	0400	3.6	1637
8	0507	2.9	1753
9	0634	2.5	1929
10	0831	2.8	2053
11	0933	3.6	2144
12	1014	4.4	2222
13	1046	4.8	2255
14	1114	5.1	2325
15	1140	5.2	2352
16	1206	5.1	
17	0017	5.3	1229
18	0039	5.4	1249
19	0102	5.3	1313
20	0130	5.1	1345
21	0205	4.6	1425
22	0249	3.8	1515
23	0349	3.0	1633
24	0559	2.7	1852
25	0735	3.2	2008
26	0843	4.2	2107
27	0938	5.2	2156
28	1024	5.9	2239
29	1106	6.4	2320
30	1144	6.4	
31	0000	6.9	1221

April

Day	HW	Range	HW
1	0039	6.5	1259
2	0117	6.0	1338
3	0157	5.3	1421
4	0241	4.4	1510
5	0334	3.4	1609
6	0441	2.7	1721
7	0603	2.4	1848
8	0800	2.8	2017
9	0902	3.6	2110
10	0941	4.2	2149
11	1011	4.7	2221
12	1038	5.0	2250
13	1105	5.2	2317
14	1132	5.3	2342
15	1157	5.2	
16	0008	5.4	1222
17	0036	5.3	1251
18	0108	5.0	1327
19	0147	4.5	1411
20	0237	3.8	1510
21	0352	3.2	1647
22	0554	3.0	1829
23	0717	3.7	1942
24	0822	4.5	2041
25	0915	5.2	2130
26	1001	5.8	2215
27	1042	6.2	2257
28	1121	6.3	2337
29	1159	6.2	
30	0017	6.0	1238

May

Day	HW	Range	HW
1	0056	5.6	1318
2	0137	5.0	1402
3	0223	4.2	1450
4	0315	3.5	1545
5	0417	2.9	1647
6	0528	2.4	1759
7	0651	2.8	1917
8	0803	3.3	2018
9	0848	3.9	2101
10	0923	4.4	2136
11	0955	4.7	2207
12	1027	5.0	2238
13	1058	5.1	2310
14	1129	5.2	2343
15	1202	5.2	
16	0018	5.2	1240
17	0059	5.0	1324
18	0146	4.6	1416
19	0246	4.1	1522
20	0407	3.8	1637
21	0533	3.6	1755
22	0648	4.0	1907
23	0752	4.5	2008
24	0846	5.0	2101
25	0934	5.4	2150
26	1018	5.6	2236
27	1100	5.7	2319
28	1141	5.5	
29	0001	5.4	1223
30	0043	5.2	1304
31	0124	4.7	1347

June

Day	HW	Range	HW
1	0208	4.3	1431
2	0255	3.8	1518
3	0347	3.4	1609
4	0445	2.9	1706
5	0549	3.0	1808
6	0652	3.2	1909
7	0747	3.5	2001
8	0832	4.0	2044
9	0913	4.4	2125
10	0952	4.7	2205
11	1031	5.0	2246
12	1111	5.2	2328
13	1153	5.3	
14	0013	5.3	1239
15	0100	5.2	1326
16	0152	5.0	1418
17	0249	4.8	1514
18	0352	4.6	1613
19	0458	4.2	1716
20	0606	4.3	1823
21	0713	4.2	1931
22	0815	4.4	2034
23	0910	4.6	2131
24	1001	4.8	2223
25	1047	5.0	2311
26	1130	5.1	2353
27	1211	5.2	
28	0033	5.0	1251
29	0112	4.8	1330
30	0150	4.6	1407

July

Day	HW	Range	HW
1	0228	4.3	1444
2	0307	4.0	1522
3	0350	3.7	1604
4	0441	3.2	1656
5	0542	3.2	1757
6	0647	3.2	1902
7	0746	3.5	2001
8	0839	3.9	2055
9	0928	4.4	2145
10	1015	4.9	2234
11	1101	5.3	2322
12	1147	5.5	
13	0009	5.7	1232
14	0056	5.7	1318
15	0143	5.7	1405
16	0231	5.6	1453
17	0323	5.2	1544
18	0418	4.6	1639
19	0521	4.0	1743
20	0632	3.7	1856
21	0747	3.6	2015
22	0856	3.8	2126
23	0953	4.2	2222
24	1040	4.6	2307
25	1120	4.9	2345
26	1157	5.2	
27	0020	5.1	1234
28	0053	5.0	1308
29	0125	4.9	1339
30	0153	4.7	1406
31	0219	4.5	1432

August

Day	HW	Range	HW
1	0246	4.2	1504
2	0321	3.8	1547
3	0411	3.2	1647
4	0535	2.9	1813
5	0710	3.0	1934
6	0818	3.6	2040
7	0915	4.2	2137
8	1004	5.0	2227
9	1050	5.5	2313
10	1134	5.9	2357
11	1216	6.4	
12	0039	6.3	1259
13	0122	6.3	1342
14	0205	6.0	1427
15	0251	5.4	1514
16	0342	4.5	1606
17	0443	3.7	1709
18	0557	3.1	1829
19	0726	3.0	2011
20	0849	3.4	2128
21	0946	4.0	2218
22	1028	4.6	2257
23	1104	5.0	2329
24	1138	5.2	2358
25	1210	5.5	
26	0026	5.2	1240
27	0053	5.1	1305
28	0115	5.0	1326
29	0134	4.8	1348
30	0158	4.6	1418
31	0232	4.0	1457

September

Day	HW	Range	HW
1	0317	3.3	1551
2	0424	2.6	1740
3	0647	2.7	1921
4	0802	3.4	2030
5	0900	4.3	2126
6	0948	5.2	2214
7	1032	5.9	2257
8	1114	6.3	2337
9	1155	6.8	
10	0016	6.6	1235
11	0055	6.4	1316
12	0136	6.0	1359
13	0221	5.2	1445
14	0312	4.3	1538
15	0414	3.3	1645
16	0529	2.7	1809
17	0703	2.6	2011
18	0834	3.3	2117
19	0926	4.1	2200
20	1005	4.7	2234
21	1039	5.1	2302
22	1111	5.3	2328
23	1140	5.3	2354
24	1206	5.3	
25	0018	5.2	1229
26	0038	5.1	1248
27	0057	5.0	1312
28	0124	4.6	1343
29	0200	4.1	1423
30	0246	3.3	1517

October

Day	HW	Range	HW
1	0356	2.7	1735
2	0625	2.7	1906
3	0739	3.5	2013
4	0837	4.4	2107
5	0925	5.4	2152
6	1008	6.0	2234
7	1049	6.4	2312
8	1129	6.5	2350
9	1209	6.7	
10	0029	6.2	1250
11	0111	5.7	1330
12	0156	4.9	1420
13	0248	4.0	1516
14	0350	3.1	1624
15	0500	2.7	1745
16	0626	2.6	1941
17	0757	3.2	2045
18	0852	3.9	2126
19	0931	4.5	2158
20	1005	4.9	2226
21	1036	5.1	2252
22	1104	5.2	2319
23	1129	5.2	2343
24	1153	5.2	
25	0006	5.1	1218
26	0031	5.0	1247
27	0103	4.6	1322
28	0144	4.1	1407
29	0236	3.5	1511
30	0401	3.0	1719
31	0553	3.1	1842

November

Day	HW	Range	HW
1	0707	3.7	1946
2	0806	4.5	2040
3	0856	5.2	2126
4	0941	5.8	2208
5	1024	6.1	2248
6	1106	6.3	2328
7	1148	6.2	
8	0010	5.8	1230
9	0053	5.3	1314
10	0139	4.7	1403
11	0229	4.0	1458
12	0325	3.3	1600
13	0427	3.1	1710
14	0537	2.7	1832
15	0655	3.0	1946
16	0759	3.5	2034
17	0845	4.0	2111
18	0922	4.4	2144
19	0955	4.7	2215
20	1025	4.9	2245
21	1056	5.1	2315
22	1127	5.1	2346
23	1200	5.0	
24	0019	4.9	1237
25	0059	4.7	1319
26	0145	4.3	1410
27	0242	4.0	1517
28	0352	3.7	1645
29	0510	3.8	1804
30	0623	3.9	1910

December

Day	HW	Range	HW
1	0728	4.4	2008
2	0825	4.8	2059
3	0916	5.2	2146
4	1004	5.5	2231
5	1051	5.6	2316
6	1136	5.5	2359
7	1220	5.2	
8	0042	5.1	1304
9	0126	4.7	1349
10	0211	4.2	1436
11	0257	3.8	1527
12	0347	3.3	1624
13	0443	3.3	1726
14	0544	3.0	1831
15	0649	3.1	1930
16	0746	3.4	2019
17	0833	3.8	2102
18	0914	4.2	2142
19	0953	4.6	2220
20	1033	4.9	2257
21	1113	5.1	2336
22	1153	5.1	
23	0016	5.2	1236
24	0059	5.1	1320
25	0144	5.0	1408
26	0234	4.9	1502
27	0328	4.6	1603
28	0429	4.6	1711
29	0535	4.2	1824
30	0647	4.0	1933
31	0756	4.1	2037

BREST TIDAL COEFFICIENTS 2006

Date	Jan am	Jan pm	Feb am	Feb pm	Mar am	Mar pm	Apr am	Apr pm	May am	May pm	June am	June pm	July am	July pm	Aug am	Aug pm	Sept am	Sept pm	Oct am	Oct pm	Nov am	Nov pm	Dec am	Dec pm
1	91	92	107	105	114	116	105	98	83	76	59	54	60	57	54	50	37	33	30	31	49	57	63	68
2	93	94	102	98	115	113	91	82	69	62	50	46	53	50	45	41	30	30	36		65	73	73	78
3	93	91	92	85	108	102	73	64	54	48	43	40	47	44	38	35	34		43	52	81	88	82	86
4	88	85	77	69	95	87	55	46	42	37	39	38	41	40	34		40	49	62	72	94	99	88	90
5	80	76	61	53	77	68	38	32	33	32	39		39		35	39	58	67	81	91	103	105	91	91
6	71	66	46	40	58	49	28	28	33		41	43	40	41	43	50	77	86	98	105	105	104	90	88
7	60	56	37		40	33	31		35	39	46	50	44	47	57	64	94	101	110	113	102	98	85	82
8	53		36	39	29		35	42	44	49	53	57	51	56	72	79	107	111	114	114	93	87	78	74
9	50	49	42	48	28	32	48	54	54	58	61	65	61	66	86	92	114	115	111	107	80	73	69	65
10	50	52	53	58	37	44	60	65	63	67	69	72	71	76	98	102	113	110	101	94	66	58	60	55
11	54	58	63	68	50	57	70	74	71	75	75	78	80	84	105	106	105	99	86	77	51	45	51	47
12	61	64	72	76	62	68	78	81	77	80	80	81	87	90	106	105	91	82	68	58	40	36	43	40
13	67	70	79	81	73	77	84	86	82	83	82	82	92	93	102	97	73	63	49	41	34	35	38	37
14	73	75	83	84	80	83	87	88	84	82	82	81	93	92	91	84	54	44	35	31	36		38	
15	76	77	84	84	86	87	88	87	83	81	79	77	90	87	76	68	37	32	31		40	43	39	41
16	77	77	83	82	88	89	85	83	79	76	75	73	84	79	60	52	31		33	38	48	52	44	47
17	77	76	80	77	88	87	80	76	72	68	70	67	74	69	45	40	34	39	44	49	56	60	51	55
18	74	72	74	70	85	83	71	66	64	60	65	63	64	58	38		46	52	55	61	64	68	59	63
19	70	67	66	61	79	75	60	54	56	53	61	60	54		39	42	58	64	66	70	71	74	67	70
20	63	60	56	50	71	65	48	43	51	51	60		51	50	47	53	70	74	74	77	76	78	73	76
21	56	52	45	40	59	53	40	39	53		61	62	50	52	59	64	78	81	80	82	79	80	78	80
22	48	44	36	33	47	40	42		56	60	64	66	55	58	69	73	83	85	83	84	80	79	81	81
23	41	38	34		36	33	47	54	64	69	68	70	62	65	77	80	86	87	84	84	78	68	81	81
24	37		39	46	34		63	71	74	79	73	75	69	72	82	84	86	85	83	81	74	71	80	78
25	38	40	54	64	40	48	79	86	83	86	76	77	75	77	84	85	84	82	79	76	67	64	76	73
26	45	50	74	83	58	68	93	98	88	90	78	78	79	79	84	83	79	76	72	68	60	57	70	67
27	57	64	92	100	78	87	102	104	90	90	78	77	80	79	81	79	71	67	63	58	54	51	64	61
28	72	79	106	111	96	103	105	105	88	86	76	74	79	77	76	73	62	56	52	47	50	50	59	57
29	86	93			109	112	103	99	84	80	72	69	75	73	69	64	50	44	42	38	52		56	
30	98	102			115	115	95	89	76	72	66	63	70	66	59	54	38	33	37	38	55	59	57	58
31	105	107			113	110			68	63			63	59	48	43			43				60	63

These tidal coefficients indicate at a glance the magnitude of the tide on any particular day by assigning a non-dimensional coefficient to the twice-daily range of tide. The coefficient is based on a scale of 45 for mean neap (morte eau) and 95 for mean spring (vive eau) ranges at Brest. The coefficient is 70 for an average tide. A very small neap tide may have a coefficient of only 20, whilst a very big spring tide might be as high as 120. The ratio of the coefficients of different tides equals the ratio of their ranges; the range, for example, of the largest spring tide (120) is six times that of the smallest neap tide (20). The table above is for Brest, but holds good elsewhere along the Channel and Atlantic coasts of France.

French translations of common tidal terms are as follows:

HW	Pleine mer (PM)	MHWS	Pleine mer moyenne de VE
LW	Basse mer (BM)	MHWN	Pleine mer moyenne de ME
Springs	Vive eau (VE)	MLWN	Basse mer moyenne de ME
Neaps	Morte eau (ME)	MLWS	Basse mer moyenne de VE

TIDES

TIDAL CALCULATIONS

Find the height at a given time (STANDARD PORT)

1. On Standard Curve diagram, plot heights of HW and LW occuring either side of required time and join by sloping line.
2. Enter HW Time and sufficient others to bracket required time.
3. From required time, proceed vertically to curves, using heights plotted in (1) to help interpolation between Spring and Neaps. Do NOT extrapolate.
4. Proceed horizontally to sloping line, thence vertically to Height scale.
5. Read off height.

EXAMPLE:

Find the height of tide at ULLAPOOL at 1900 on 6th January

From tables	JANUARY	
ULLAPOOL	**6** 0420	4.6
	1033	1.6
	1641	4.6
	F 2308	1.2

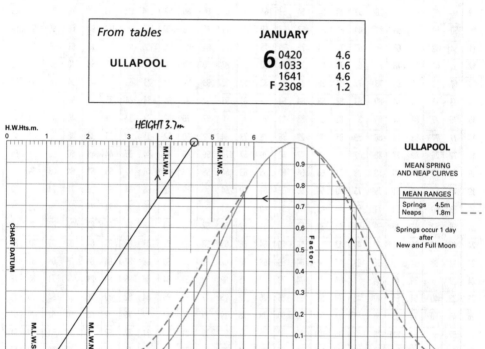

ULLAPOOL

MEAN SPRING AND NEAP CURVES

MEAN RANGES

Springs 4.5m
Neaps 1.8m

Springs occur 1 day after New and Full Moon

Find the time for a given height (STANDARD PORT)

1. On Standard Curve diagram, plot heights of HW and LW occurring either side of required event and join by sloping line.
2. Enter HW time and those for half-tidal cycle covering required event.
3. From required height, proceed vertically to sloping line, thence horizontally to curves, using heights plotted in (1) to assist interpolation between Spring and Neaps. Do NOT extrapolate.
4. Proceed vertically to Time scale.
5. Read off time.

EXAMPLE:
Find the time at which the afternoon tide at ULLAPOOL falls to 3.7m on 6 January

From tables	JANUARY	
ULLAPOOL	**6** 0420	4.6
	1033	1.6
	1641	4.6
	F 2308	1.2

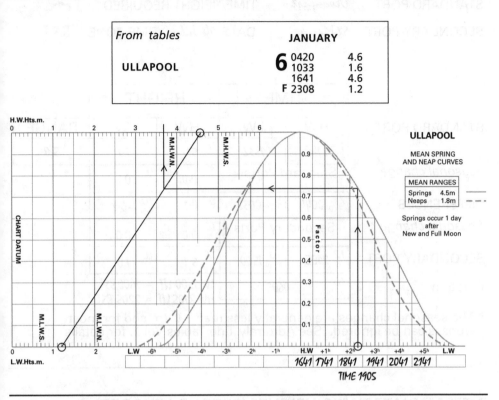

Find the time and height of HW and LW at a Secondary Port

EXAMPLE:
Find the time and height of the afternoon HW and LW at ST MARY's (Isles of Scilly) on 14th July (BST)
Note: *The data used in this example do not refer to the year of these tables.*

From tables	JULY	
PLYMOUTH (DEVONPORT)	**14** 0309	1.0
	0927	5.3
	1532	1.1
	SA 2149	5.0

From tables			High Water		Low Water		MHWS	MHWN	MLWN	MLWS
Location	Lat	Long								
			0000	0600	0000	0600				
DEVONPORT	50°22'N	4°11'W	and	and	and	and	5.5	4.4	2.2	0.8
Standard port			1200	1800	1200	1800				
St Mary's, *Scilly*	49° 55'N	6°19'W	–0035	–0100	–0040	–0025	+0.2	–0.1	–0.2	–0.1

TIDAL PREDICTION FORM (NP 204)

STANDARD PORT ...*Devonport*...   TIME/HEIGHT REQUIRED ....*pm*........

SECONDARY PORT ...*St Mary's*...   DATE *14 July* ... TIME ZONE ... *B.S.T*

	TIME		HEIGHT		
STANDARD PORT	HW	LW	HW	LW	RANGE
	1 2149	2 1532	3 5·0	4 1·1	5 3·9
Seasonal change	Standard Ports -		6 0·0	6 0·0	
DIFFERENCES	7* -0044	8 -0032	9 0·1	10 -0·1	
Seasonal change *	Secondary Ports +		11 0·0	11 0·0	
SECONDARY PORT	12 2105	13 1500	14 5·1	15 1·0	
Duration	16 0605		LW 1500 UT = 1600 BST HW 2105 UT = 2205 BST		

* The seasonal changes are generally less than ± 0.1m and for most purposes can be ignored. See Admiraly Tide Tables Vol 1. for details

---

INTERMEDIATE TIMES/HEIGHTS (SECONDARY PORT)

These are the same as the appropriate calculations for a Standard Port except that the Standard Curve diagram for the Standard Port must be entered with HW and LW heights and times for the Secondary Port obtained on Form N.P. 204. When interpolating between the Spring and Neap curves the Range at the Standard Port must be used.

EXAMPLE:

Find the height of the tide at PADSTOW at 1100 on 28th February. Find the time at which the morning tide at PADSTOW falls to 4.9m on 28th February.

Notes:
The data in these examples do not refer to the year of these tables.

From tables	FEBRUARY	
MILFORD HAVEN	**28** 0315	1.1
	0922	6.6
	1538	1.3
	TU 2145	6.3

From tables Location	Lat	Long	High Water		Low Water		MHWS	MHWN	MLWN	MLWS
MILFORD HAVEN Standard port	51°42'N	5°03'W	0100 and 1300	0700 and 1900	0100 and 1300	0700 and 1900	7.0	5.2	2.5	0.7
River Camel										
Padstow	50°33'N	4°56'W	–0055	–0050	–0040	–0050	+0.3	+0.4	+0.1	+0.1
Wadebridge	50°31'N	4°50'W	–0052	–0052	+0235	+0245	–3.8	–3.8	–2.5	–0.4

TIDAL PREDICTION FORM (NP 204)

STANDARD PORT ....*Milford Haven*.... TIME/HEIGHT REQUIRED.... *1100 : 4.9*

SECONDARY PORT ....*Padstow*.... DATE *28 Feb* TIME ZONE *UT*

	TIME		HEIGHT		
STANDARD PORT	HW	LW	HW	LW	RANGE
	¹ 0922	² 1538	³ 6·6	⁴ 1·3	⁵ 5·3
Seasonal change	Standard Ports +		⁶ 0·0	⁶ 0·0	
DIFFERENCES	⁷* -0052	⁸ –	⁹ +0·3	¹⁰ +0·1	
Seasonal change *	Secondary Ports -		¹¹ 0·0	¹¹ 0·0	
SECONDARY PORT	¹² 0830	¹³ –	¹⁴ 6·9	¹⁵ 1·4	
Duration	¹⁶ –				

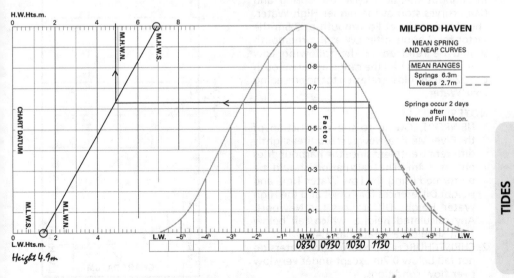

MILFORD HAVEN

MEAN SPRING AND NEAP CURVES

MEAN RANGES
Springs 6.3m
Neaps 2.7m

Springs occur 2 days after New and Full Moon.

H.W.Hts.m.

CHART DATUM

M.H.W.N. M.H.W.S.

M.L.W.S. M.L.W.N.

Factor

L.W. –5ʰ –4ʰ –3ʰ –2ʰ –1ʰ H.W. +1ʰ +2ʰ +3ʰ +4ʰ +5ʰ L.W.

L.W.Hts.m.

0830 | 0930 | 1030 | 1130

Height 4.9m

TIDES

SPECIAL INSTRUCTIONS FOR PLACES BETWEEN BOURNEMOUTH AND SELSEY BILL

• Owing to the rapid change of tidal characteristics and distortion of the tidal curve in this area, curves are shown for individual ports. It is a characteristic of the tide here that Low Water is more sharply defined than High Water and these curves have therefore been drawn with their times relative to that of Low Water.

• Apart from differences caused by referring the times to Low Water the procedure for obtaining intermediate heights at places whose curves are shown is identical to that used for normal Secondary Ports.

• The **height** differences for ports between Bournemouth and Yarmouth always refer to the higher High Water, i.e. that which is shown as reaching a factor of 1.0 on the curves. Note that the **time** differences, which are not required for this calculation, also refer to the higher High Water.

• The tide at ports between Bournemouth and Christchurch shows considerable change of shape and duration between Springs and Neaps and it is not practical to define the tide with only two curves. A third curve has therefore been drawn for the range at Portsmouth at which the two High Waters are equal at the port concerned – this range being marked on the body of the graph. Interpolation here should be between this 'critical' curve and either the Spring or Neap curve as appropriate.

Note that while the critical curve extends throughout the tidal cycle the Spring and Neap curves stop at the higher High Water. Thus for a range at Portsmouth of 3.5m the factor for 7 hours after LW at Bournemouth should be referred to the following Low Water, whereas had the range at Portsmouth been 2.5, it should be referred to the preceding Low Water.

NOTES

1. NEWPORT. Owing to the constriction of the River Medina, Newport requires slightly different treatment since the harbour dries out at 1.4m. The calculation should be performed using the Low Water Time and Height Differences for Cowes and the High Water Height Differences for Newport. Any calculated heights which fall below 1.4m should be treated as 1.4m

2. CHRISTCHURCH (Tuckton). Low Waters do not fall below 0.7m except under very low river flow conditions.

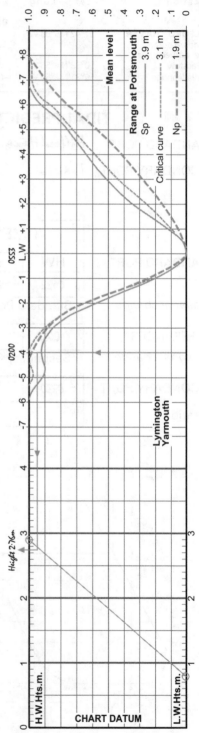

To find the Height of tide at a given time at any Secondary Port between Bournemouth and Selsey Bill

1. Complete top section of N.P. 204 (as below). Omit HW time column (Boxes 1,7,12)
2. On Standard Curve diagram (previous page), plot Secondary Port HW and LW heights and join by sloping line.
3. From the time required, using Secondary Port LW time, proceed vertically to curve, interpolating as necessary using Range at Portsmouth. Do NOT extrapolate.
4. Proceed horizontally to sloping line, thence vertically to Height Scale.
5. Read off height.

EXAMPLE:

Find the height of tide at LYMINGTON at 0200 UT on 18th November

From tables		NOVEMBER	
PORTSMOUTH	**18**	0110	4.6
		0613	1.1
		1318	4.6
		SA 1833	1.0

From tables Location	Lat	Long	High Water		Low Water		MHWS	MHWN	MLWN	MLWS
			0000	0600	0500	1100				
PORTSMOUTH	50°48'N	1°07'W	and	and	and	and	4.7	3.8	1.9	0.8
Standard port			1200	1800	1700	2300				
Lymington	50°46'N	1°32'W	–0110	+0005	–0020	–0020	–1.7	–1.2	–0.5	–0.1

STANDARD PORT ...... *Portsmouth* ...... TIME/HEIGHT REQUIRED *0200*

SECONDARY PORT ...... *Lymington* ...... DATE *18 Nov* TIME ZONE ...... *UT*

	TIME		HEIGHT		
STANDARD PORT	HW	LW	HW	LW	RANGE
	1 –	2 0613	3 4·6	4 1·1	5 3·5
Seasonal change	Standard Ports -		6 0·0	6 0·0	
DIFFERENCES	7* –	8 –0020	9 –1·7	10 –0·2	
*Seasonal change ***	Secondary Ports +		11 0·0	11 0·0	
SECONDARY PORT	12 –	13 0553	14 2·9	15 0·9	
Duration	16 –				

* The Seasonal changes are generally less than ± 0.1m and for most purposes can be ignored. See Admiralty Tide Tables Vol 1 for full details.

TIDES

TIDAL CURVES -
BOURNEMOUTH TO FRESHWATER

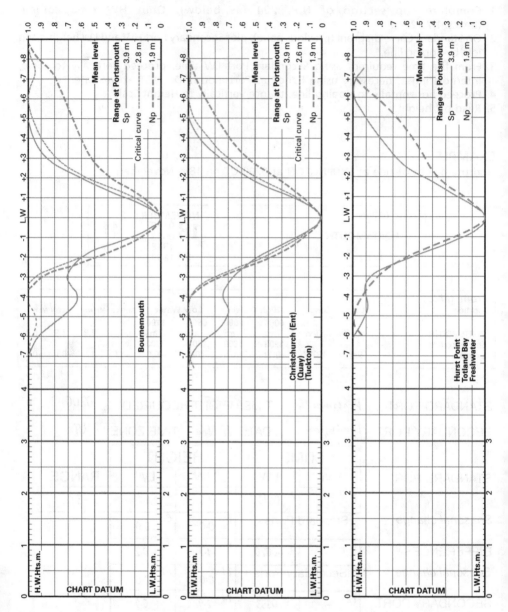

Note: The curves for Lymington and Yarmouth are on page 148, together with a worked example.

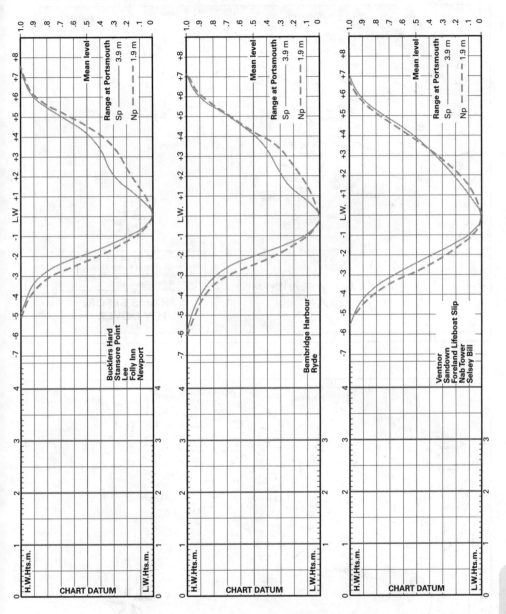

Mean level

Range at Portsmouth
Sp ——— 3.9 m
Np ——— 1.9 m

Bucklers Hard
Stansore Point
Lee
Folly Inn
Newport

Bembridge Harbour
Ryde

Ventnor
Sandown
Foreland Lifeboat Slip
Nab Tower
Selsey Bill

H.W.Hts.m.
CHART DATUM
L.W.Hts.m.

TIDES

151

ENGLISH CHANNEL AND SOUTH BRITTANY

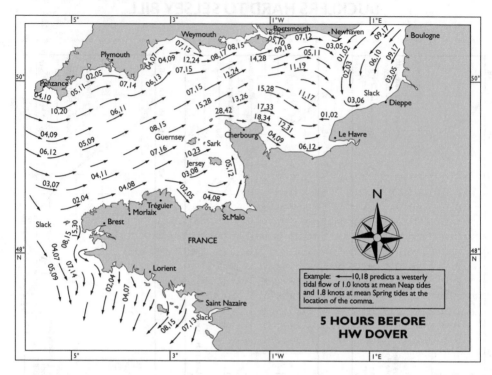

Example: ←—10,18 predicts a westerly tidal flow of 1.0 knots at mean Neap tides and 1.8 knots at mean Spring tides at the location of the comma.

5 HOURS BEFORE HW DOVER

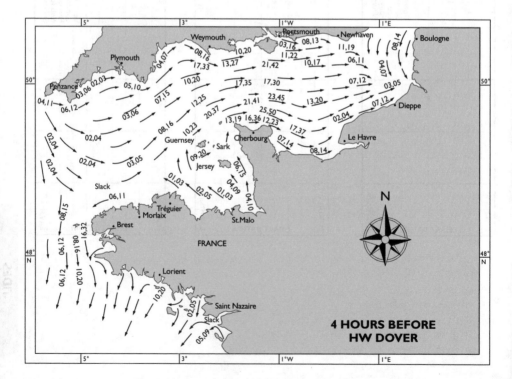

4 HOURS BEFORE HW DOVER

ENGLISH CHANNEL AND SOUTH BRITTANY

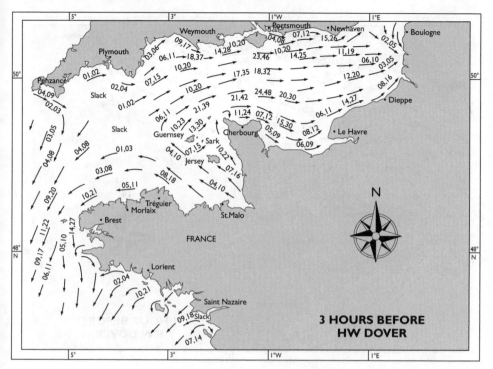

3 HOURS BEFORE HW DOVER

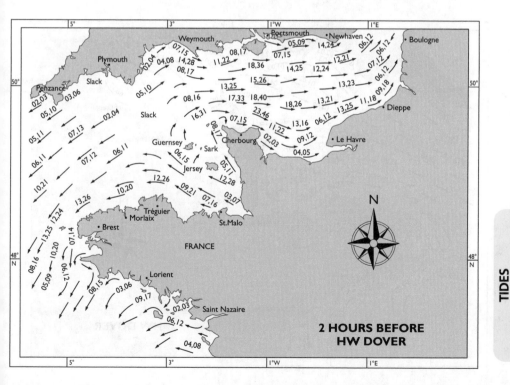

2 HOURS BEFORE HW DOVER

ENGLISH CHANNEL AND SOUTH BRITTANY

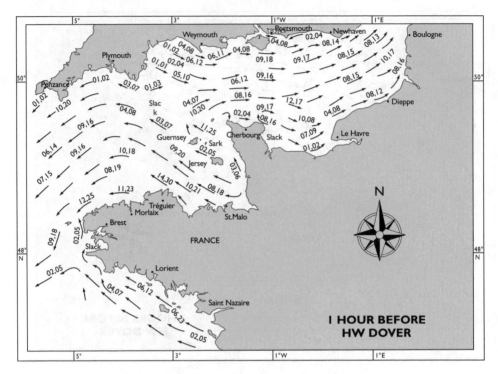

I HOUR BEFORE HW DOVER

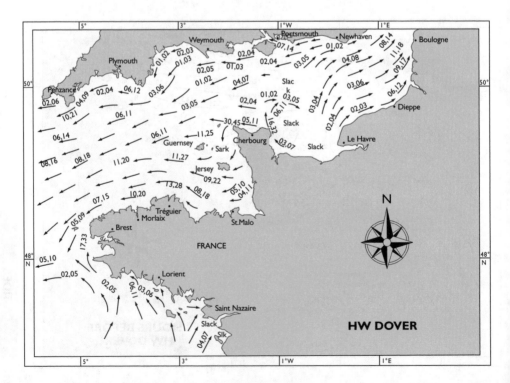

HW DOVER

ENGLISH CHANNEL AND SOUTH BRITTANY

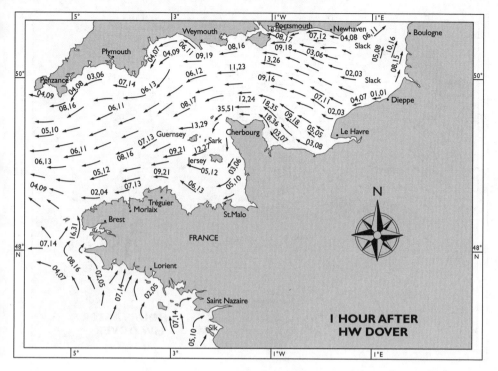

1 HOUR AFTER HW DOVER

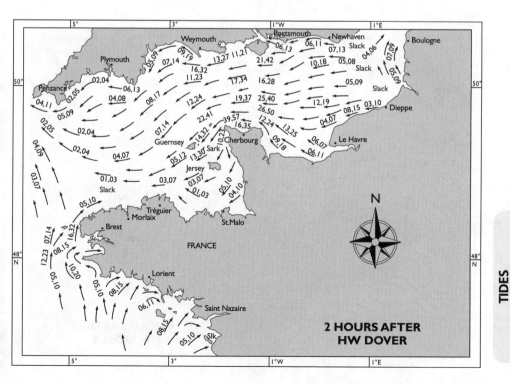

2 HOURS AFTER HW DOVER

ENGLISH CHANNEL AND SOUTH BRITTANY

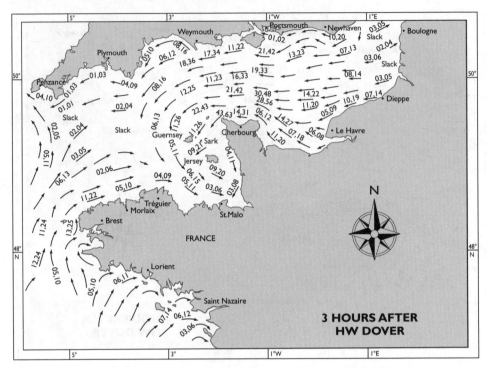

3 HOURS AFTER
HW DOVER

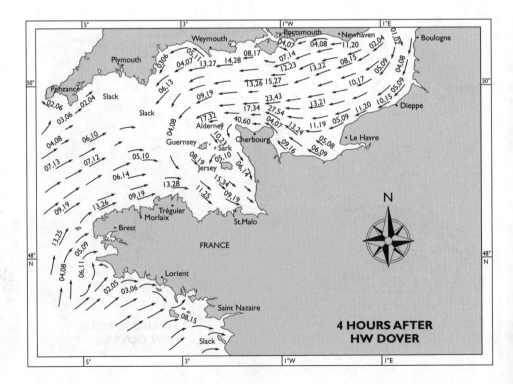

4 HOURS AFTER
HW DOVER

ENGLISH CHANNEL AND SOUTH BRITTANY

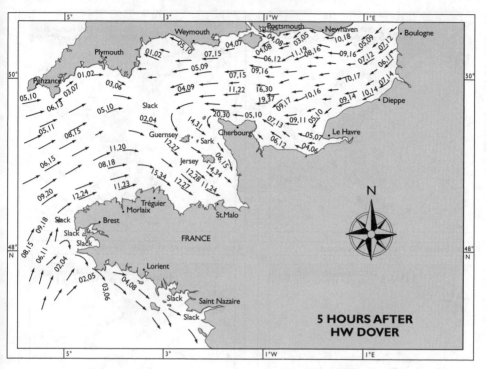

5 HOURS AFTER HW DOVER

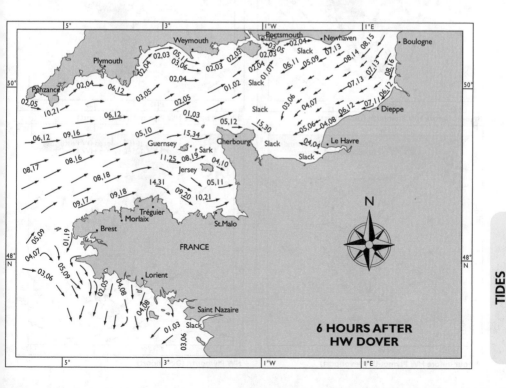

6 HOURS AFTER HW DOVER

PORTLAND

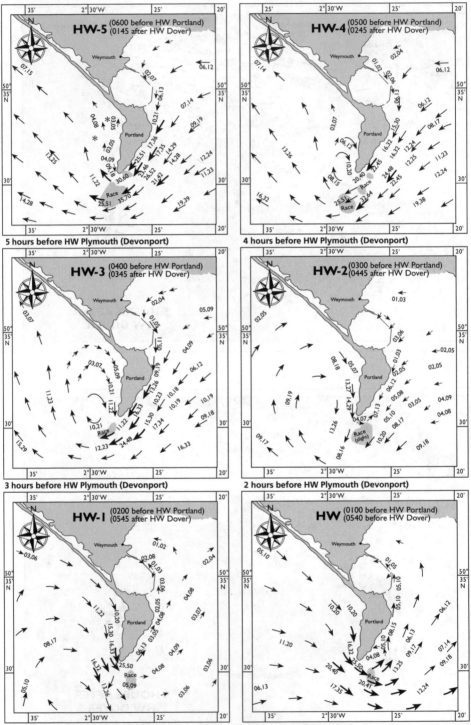

5 hours before HW Plymouth (Devonport)

4 hours before HW Plymouth (Devonport)

3 hours before HW Plymouth (Devonport)

2 hours before HW Plymouth (Devonport)

1 hour before HW Plymouth (Devonport)

HW Plymouth (Devonport)

PORTLAND

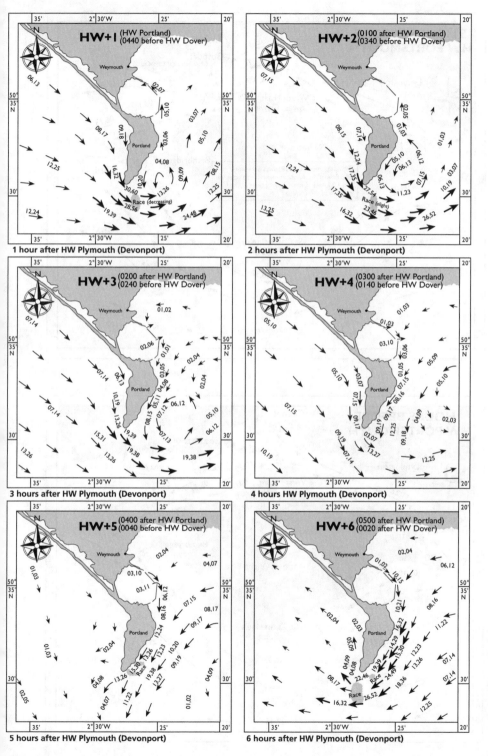

TIDES

ISLE OF WIGHT

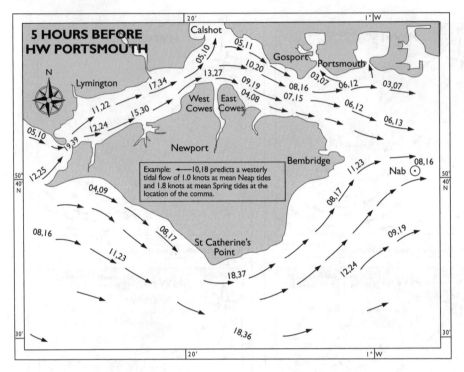

5 HOURS BEFORE HW PORTSMOUTH

Example: ◄—10,18 predicts a westerly tidal flow of 1.0 knots at mean Neap tides and 1.8 knots at mean Spring tides at the location of the comma.

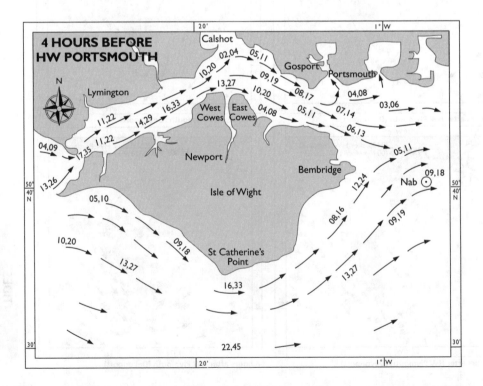

4 HOURS BEFORE HW PORTSMOUTH

ISLE OF WIGHT

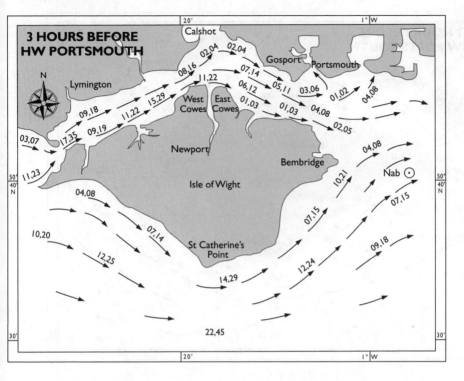

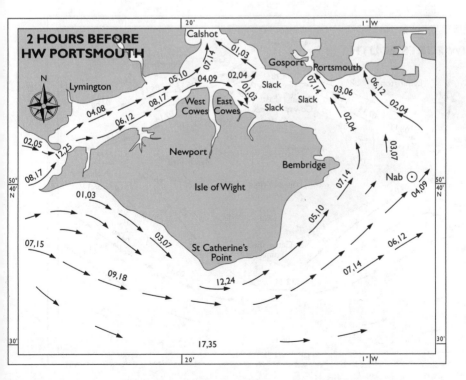

ISLE OF WIGHT

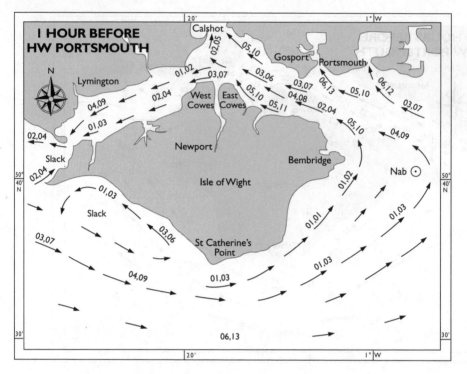

I HOUR BEFORE HW PORTSMOUTH

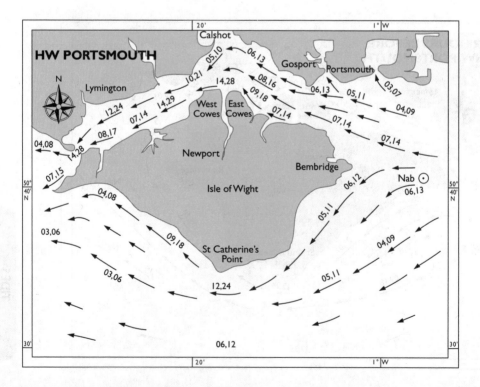

HW PORTSMOUTH

ISLE OF WIGHT

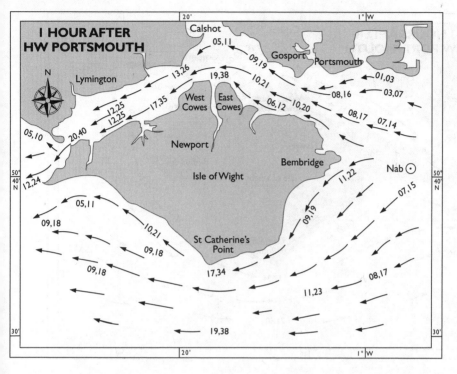

1 HOUR AFTER HW PORTSMOUTH

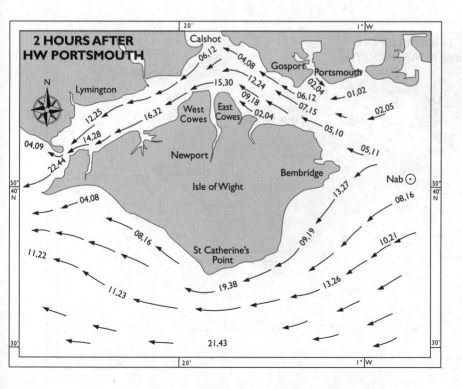

2 HOURS AFTER HW PORTSMOUTH

ISLE OF WIGHT

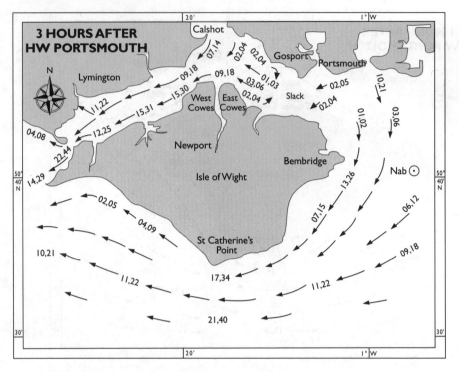

3 HOURS AFTER HW PORTSMOUTH

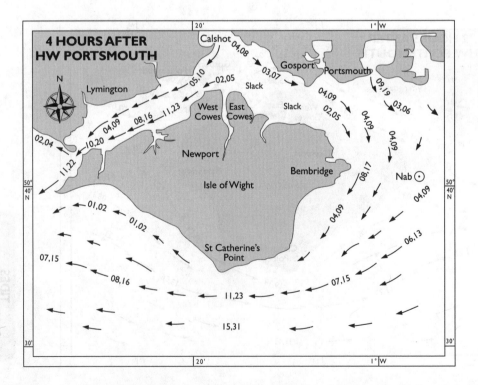

4 HOURS AFTER HW PORTSMOUTH

ISLE OF WIGHT

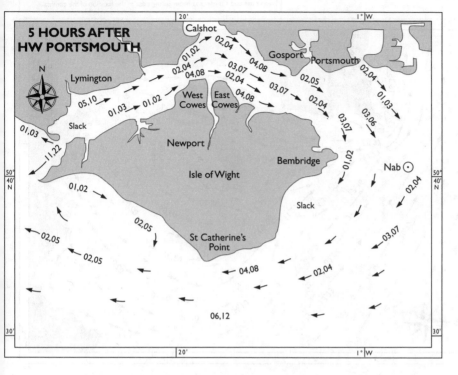

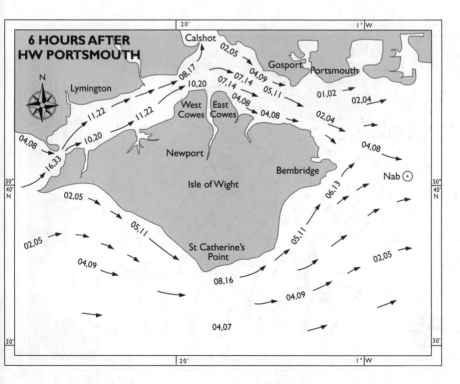

CHANNEL ISLANDS

Example: ←10,18 predicts a westerly tidal flow of 1.0 knots at mean Neap tides and 1.8 knots at mean Spring tides at the location of the comma.

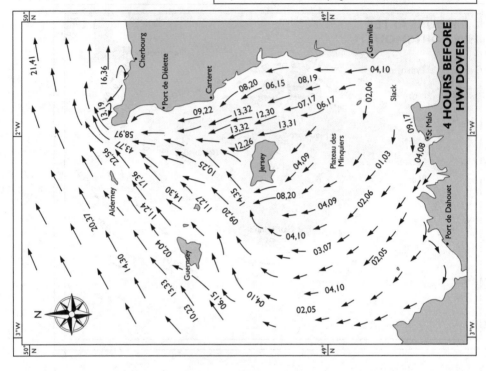

4 HOURS BEFORE HW DOVER

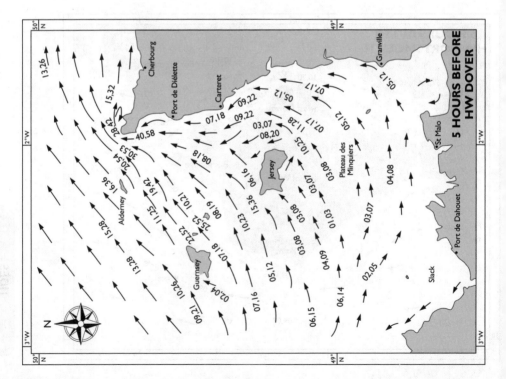

5 HOURS BEFORE HW DOVER

CHANNEL ISLANDS

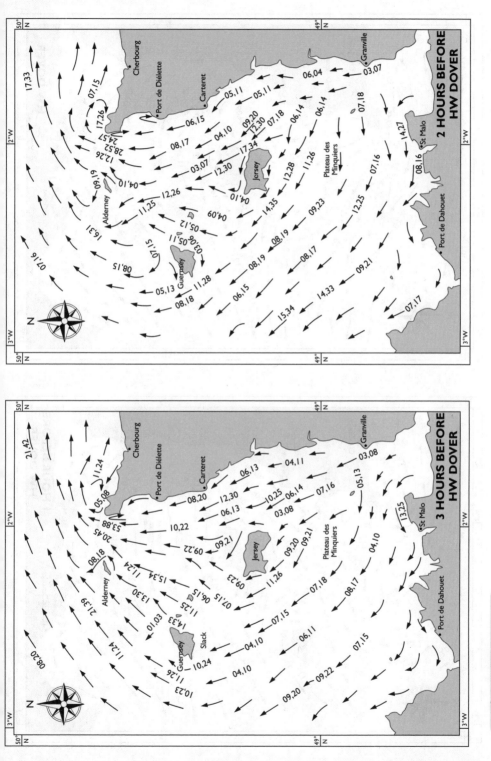

CHANNEL ISLANDS

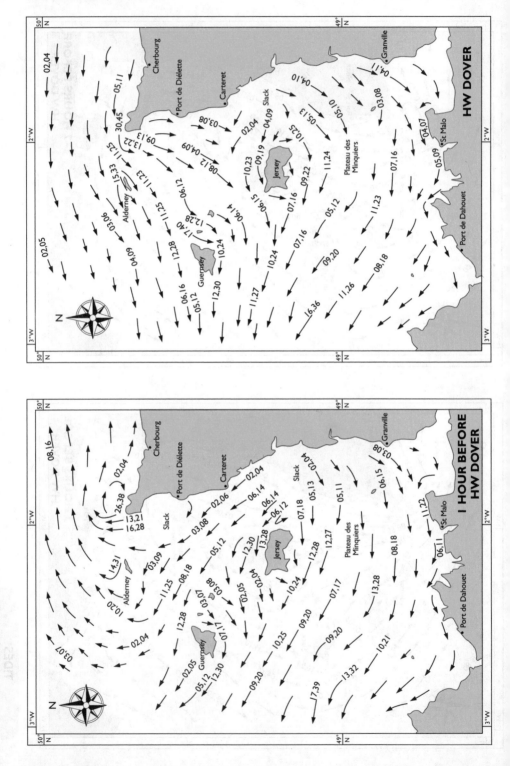

CHANNEL ISLANDS

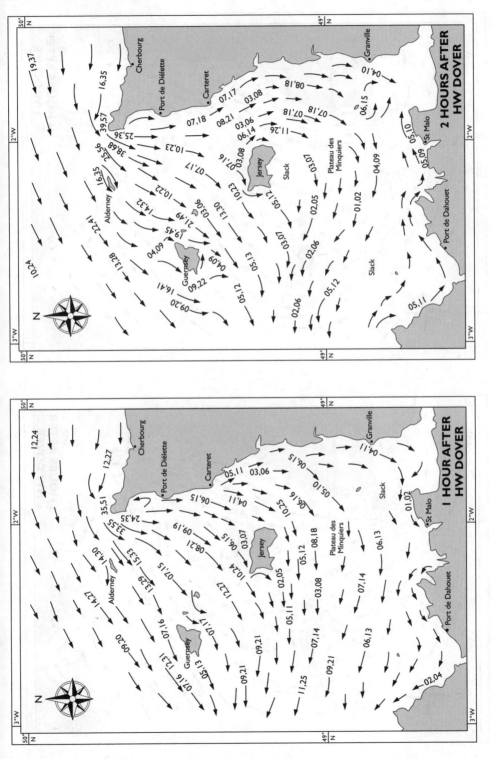

2 HOURS AFTER HW DOVER

1 HOUR AFTER HW DOVER

CHANNEL ISLANDS

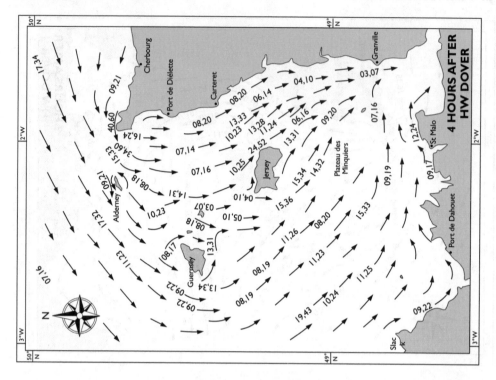

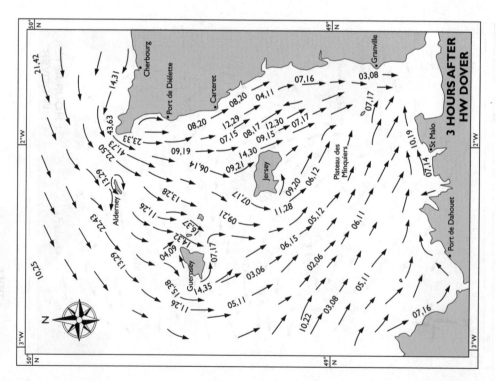

CHANNEL ISLANDS

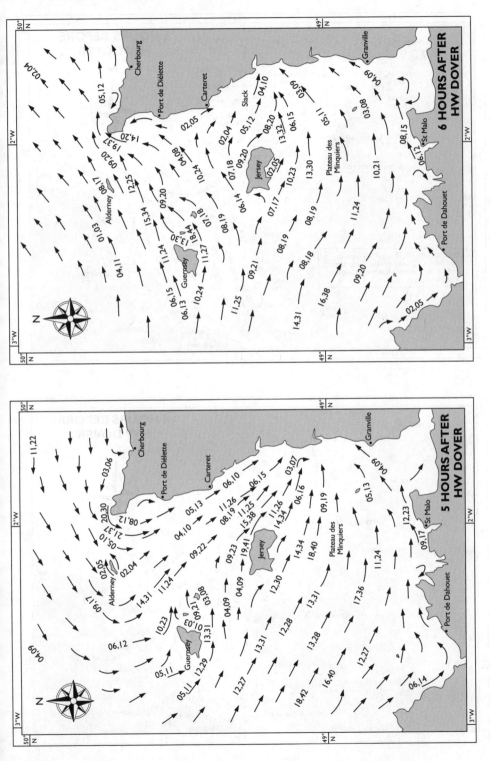

6 HOURS AFTER HW DOVER

5 HOURS AFTER HW DOVER

NORTH SEA

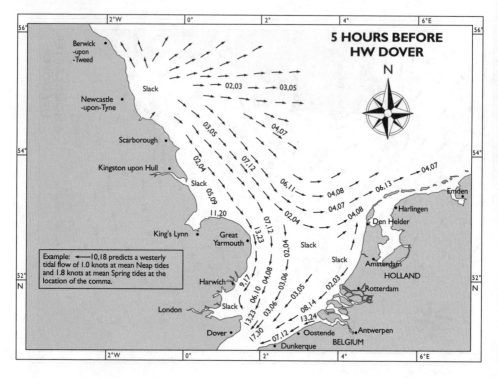

5 HOURS BEFORE HW DOVER

Example: ◄—10,18 predicts a westerly tidal flow of 1.0 knots at mean Neap tides and 1.8 knots at mean Spring tides at the location of the comma.

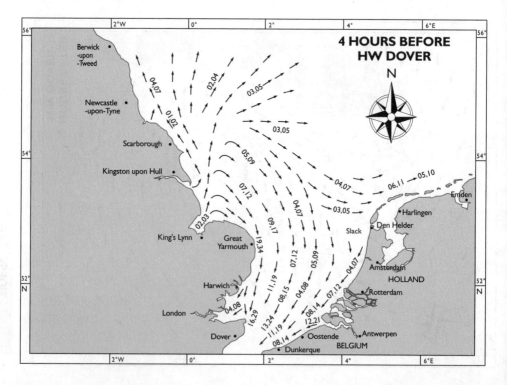

4 HOURS BEFORE HW DOVER

NORTH SEA

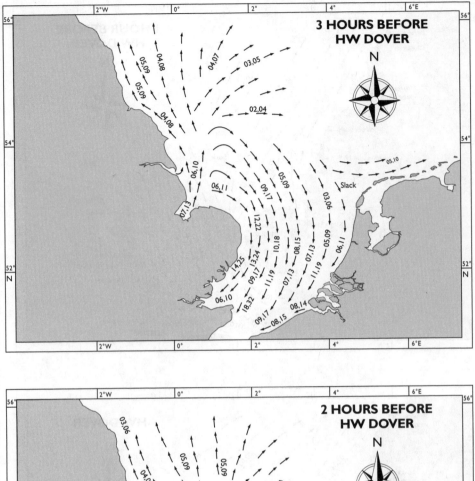

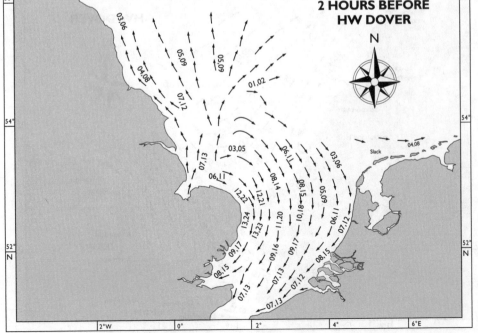

NORTH SEA

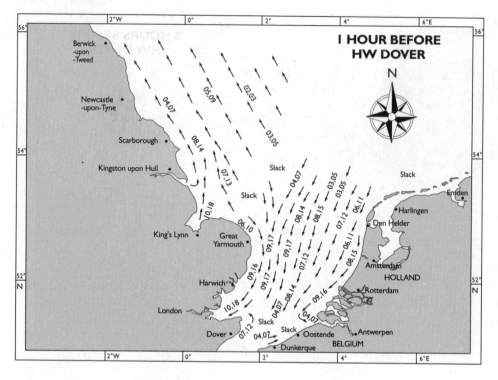

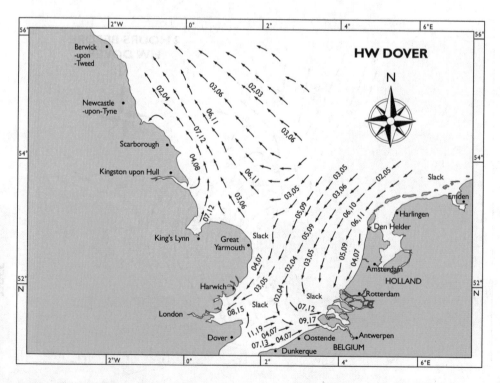

NORTH SEA

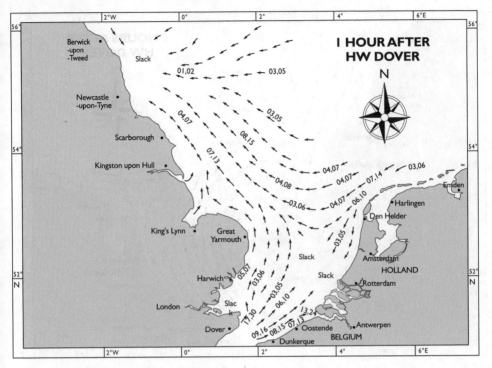

I HOUR AFTER HW DOVER

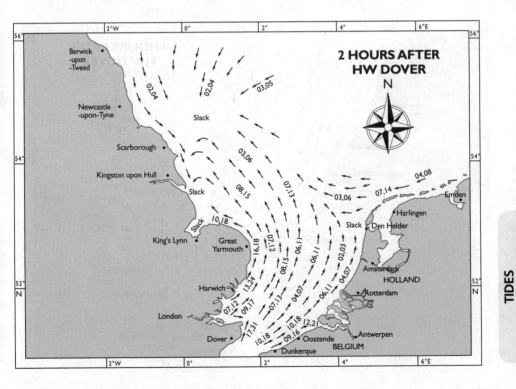

2 HOURS AFTER HW DOVER

NORTH SEA

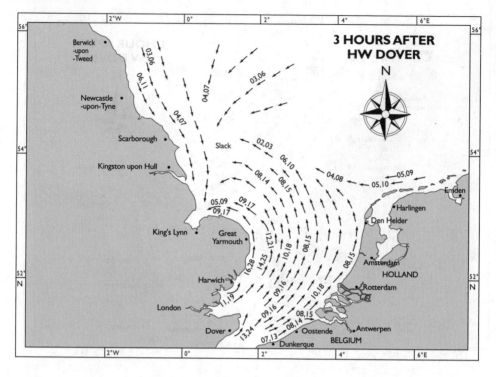

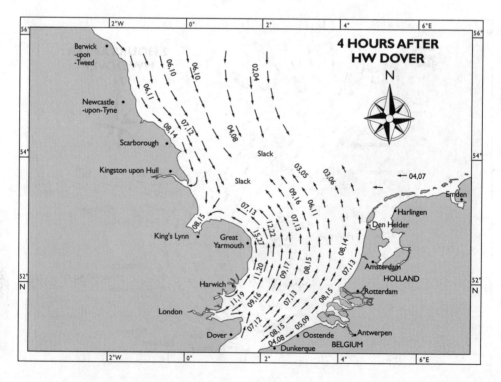

NORTH SEA

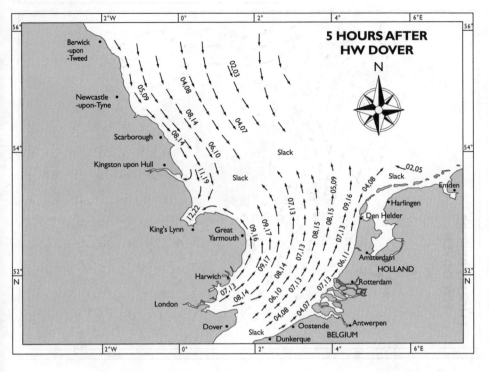

5 HOURS AFTER
HW DOVER

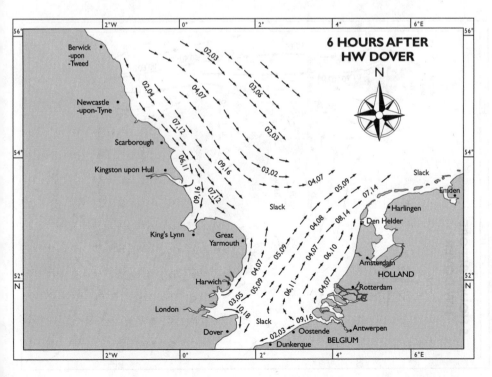

6 HOURS AFTER
HW DOVER

SCOTLAND

Example: ←—10,18 predicts a westerly tidal flow of 1.0 knots at mean Neap tides and 1.8 knots at mean Spring tides at the location of the comma.

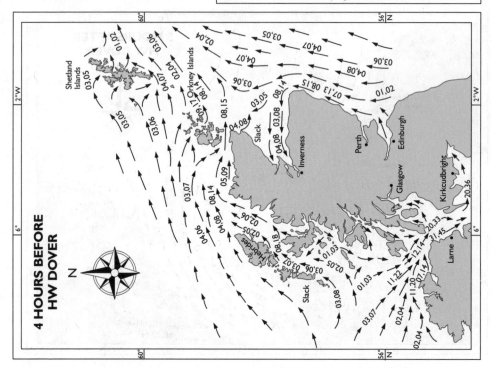

4 HOURS BEFORE HW DOVER

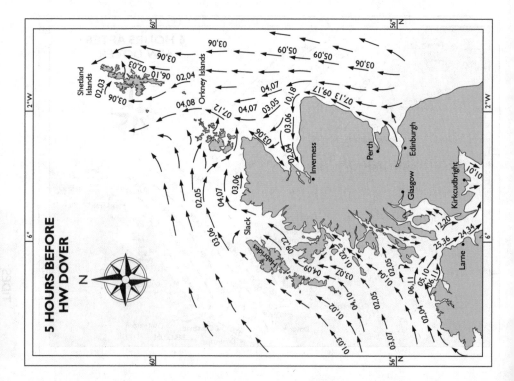

5 HOURS BEFORE HW DOVER

SCOTLAND

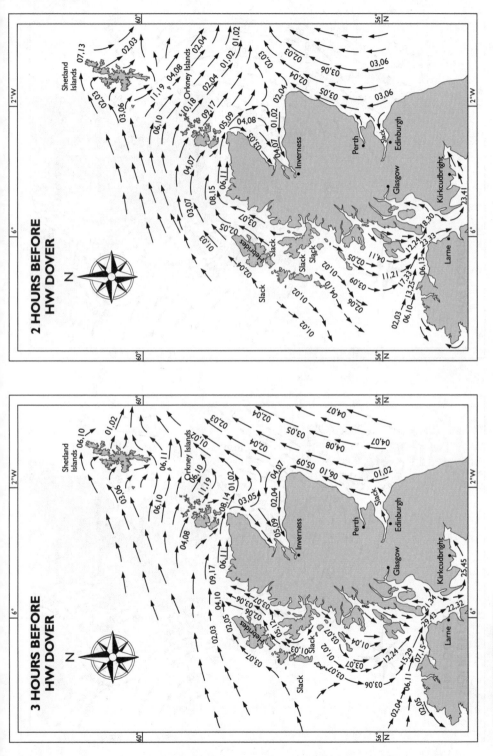

SCOTLAND

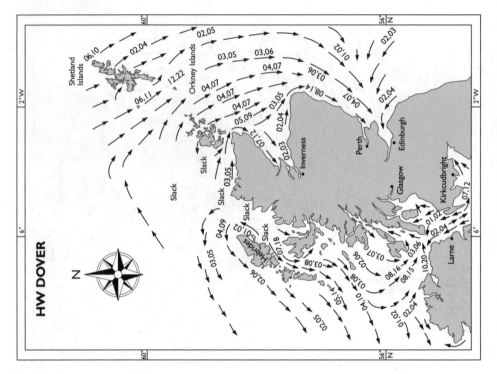

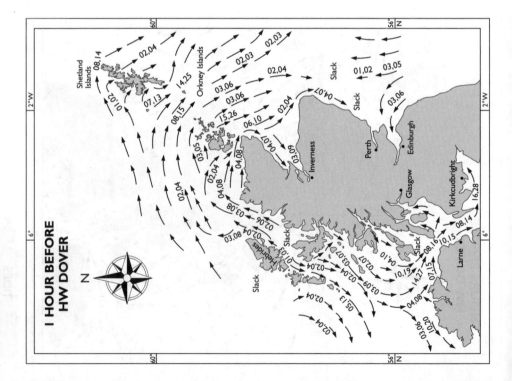

SCOTLAND

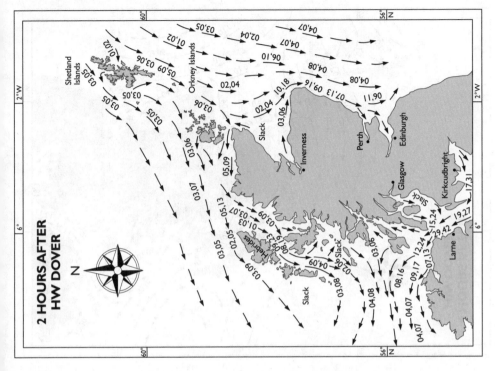

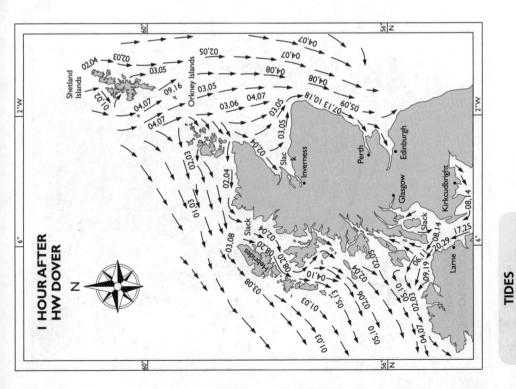

SCOTLAND

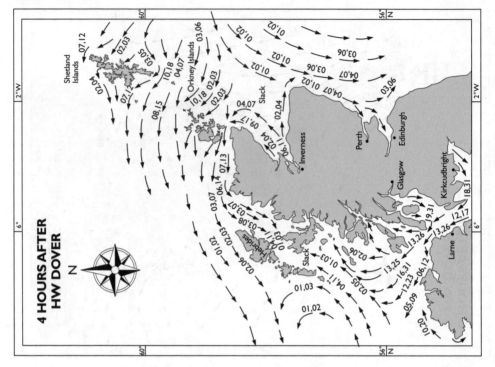

4 HOURS AFTER HW DOVER

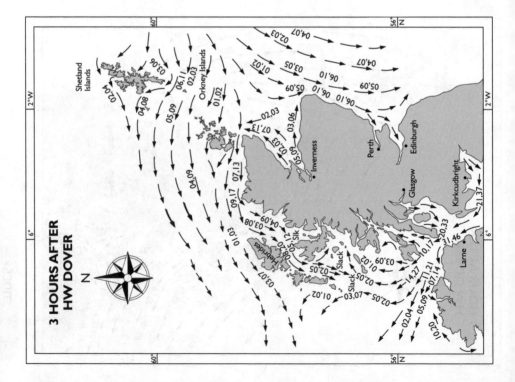

3 HOURS AFTER HW DOVER

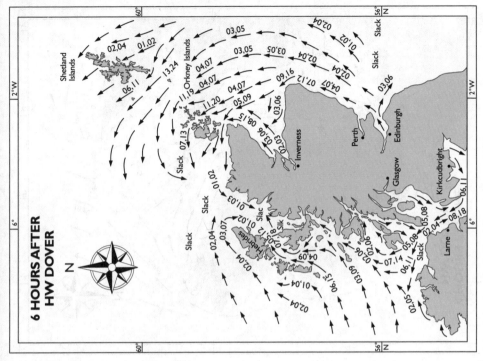

6 HOURS AFTER HW DOVER

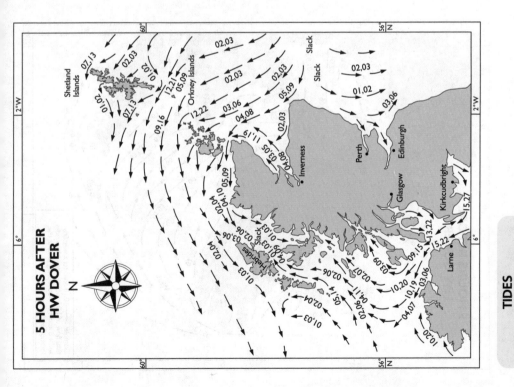

5 HOURS AFTER HW DOVER

WEST UK AND IRELAND

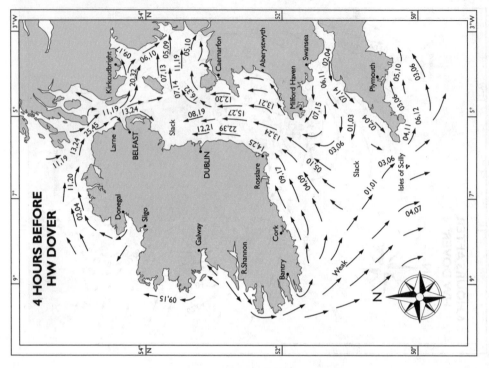

4 HOURS BEFORE HW DOVER

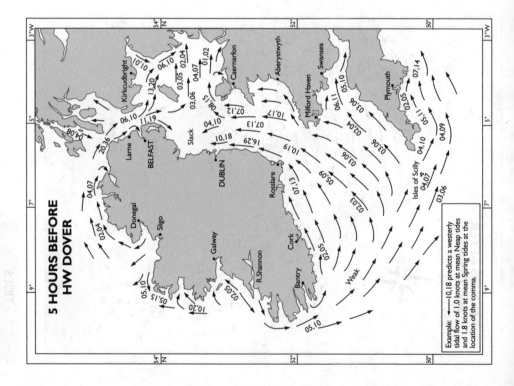

5 HOURS BEFORE HW DOVER

Example: ——10,18 predicts a westerly tidal flow of 1.0 knots at mean Neap tides and 1.8 knots at mean Spring tides at the location of the comma.

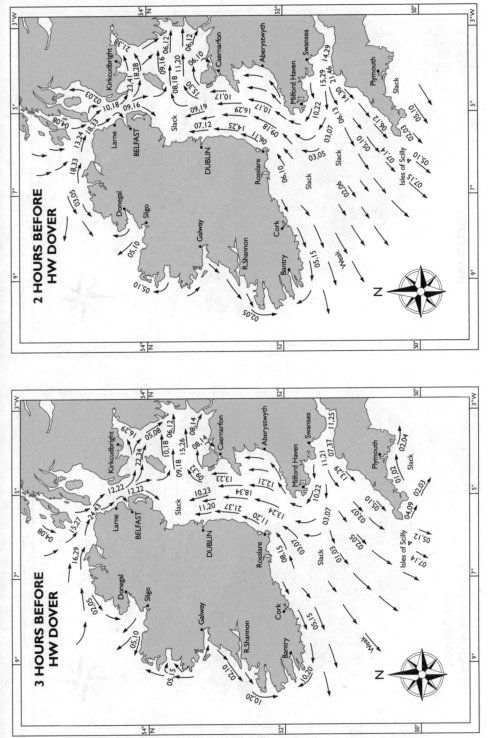

WEST UK AND IRELAND

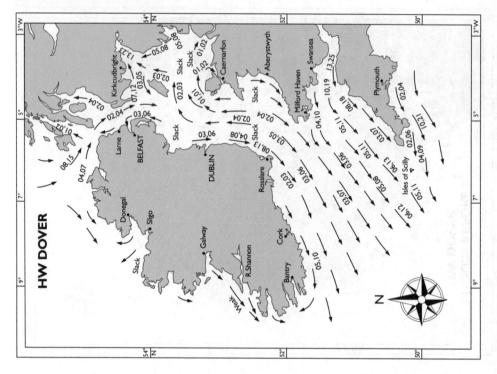

HW DOVER

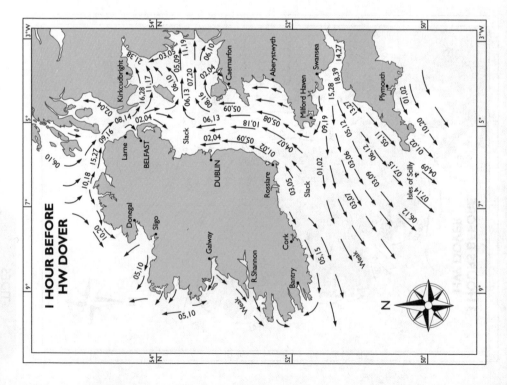

1 HOUR BEFORE HW DOVER

WEST UK AND IRELAND

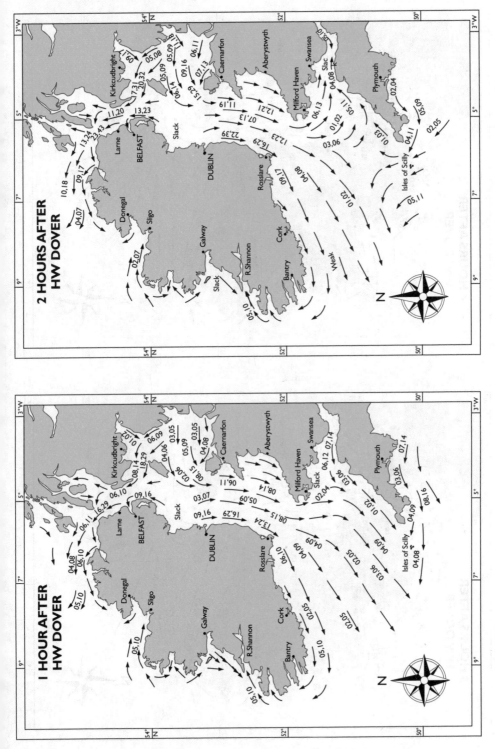

WEST UK AND IRELAND

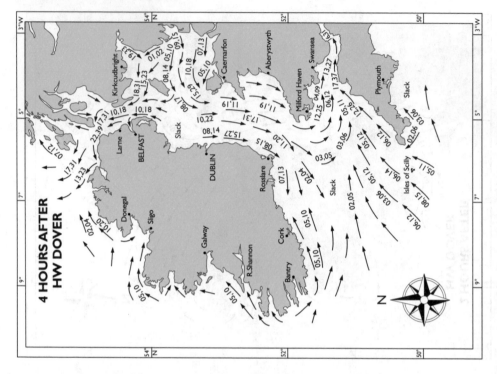

4 HOURS AFTER HW DOVER

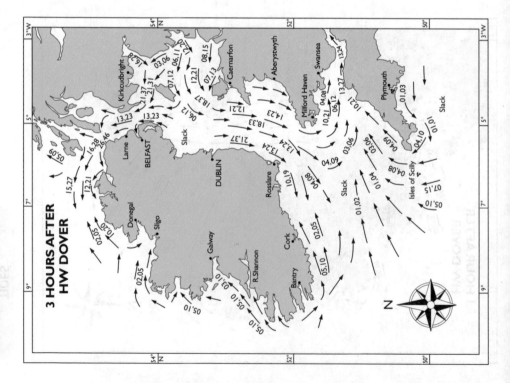

3 HOURS AFTER HW DOVER

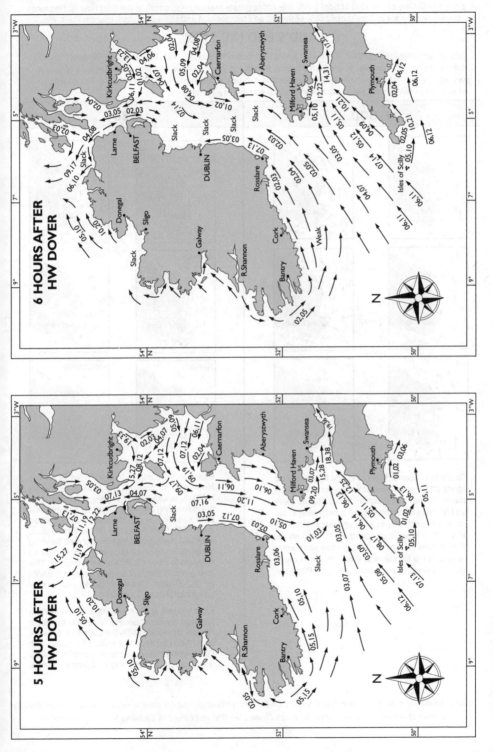

TIDAL GATES - SOUTHERN ENGLAND

A guide to the time of tide turn at tidal gates, the approximate maximum strength of the tidal flow (spring rates shown - neaps are approximately 60% of these), and the position and timing of races, counter tides, etc.

LAND'S END (AC 1148)

Tidal streams set hard north/south round Land's End, and east/west around Gwennap and Pendeen. But the inshore currents run counter to the tidal streams. By staying close inshore, this tidal gate favours a N-bound passage. With careful timing nearly 9½hrs of fair tide can be carried, from HWD−3 to HWD+5. The chartlets, referenced to HW Dover, depict both tidal streams and inshore currents.

FLOOD	EBB

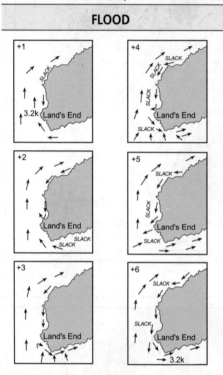

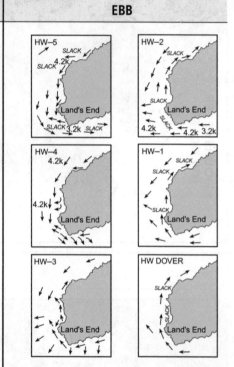

Example N-bound: At HWD+1 the N-going flood starts off Gwennap and does not turn NE along the N Cornish coast until HWD+3. But as early as HWD−3 an inshore current is beginning to set north. Utilise this by arriving off Runnel Stone at HWD−2 and then keeping within ¼M of the shore. If abeam the Brisons at HWD, the tide and current should serve for the next 6 or 7 hours to make good St Ives, or even Newquay and Padstow.

Example S-bound: If S-bound from St Ives to Newlyn, aim to reach the Runnel Stone by HWD+5, ie with 2hrs of E-going tide in hand for the remaining 9M to Newlyn. To achieve this 20M passage, leave St Ives 5 hours earlier, ie at HWD. Buck a foul tide for the first 3 hours, then use the S-going inshore current, keeping as close inshore as is prudent, only moving seaward to clear the Wra and the Brisons. This timing would also suit a passage from S Wales or the Bristol Channel, going inshore of Longships if conditions allow.

From Ireland, ie Cork or further W, the inshore passage would not benefit. But aim to be off the Runnel Stone at HWD+5 if bound for Newlyn; or at HWD+3 if bound for Helford/Falmouth, with the W-going stream slackening and 5hrs of fair tide to cover the remaining 20M past the Lizard.

With acknowledgements to the Royal Cruising Club Pilotage Foundation for their kind permission to use the tidal stream chartlets and text written by Hugh Davies, as first published in Yachting Monthly *magazine.*

TIDAL GATES - SOUTHERN ENGLAND

A guide to the time of tide turn at tidal gates, the approximate maximum strength of the tidal flow (spring rates shown - neaps are approximately 60% of these), and the position and timing of races, counter tides, etc.

FLOOD	EBB

THE LIZARD (AC 777, 2345)

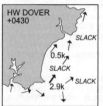

Drying rocks lie approx 5 cables S of the Lizard lt ho and extend westwards. 49°57'N is about as far N as yachts may safely pass inshore of the Race, which extends 2-3M to seaward of these rocks. Race conditions may also exist SE of the Lizard with short, heavy seas in westerlies. If passing S of the Race, route via 49°55'N 05°13'W to clear the worst of the Race.

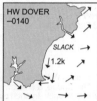

Inshore the E-going Channel flood, 2kn max @ springs, begins at HW Dover +0145; and outside the Race at approx HWD +0300.	Inshore the W-going Channel ebb, 3kn max @ springs, begins at HW Dover –0345; and outside the Race at HWD –0240.

START POINT (AC 1634)

Start Pt, and to a lesser extent Prawle Pt (3.3M WSW), can be slow to round when W-bound with a fair tide against a W'ly wind raising a bad sea. Drying rocks extend 3 cables SSE of the lt ho and a Race may extend up to 1.7M ESE and 1.0M S of the lt ho. It is safe to pass between the Race and the rocks, but in bad weather wiser to go outside the Race. The Skerries Bank (least depth 2.1m) lies 8 cables NE of Start Pt. On both the flood and the ebb back eddies form between Start Pt and Hallsands, 1M NW.

The NE-going Channel flood, 3.1kn max @ springs, begins at HW Dover +0430.	The SW-going Channel ebb, 2.2kn max @ springs, begins at HW Dover –0140, but an hour earlier it is possible to round Start Pt close inshore using the back eddy.

PORTLAND (AC 2255)

A dangerous Race forms between 200 metres and 2 miles south of Portland Bill. The Race shifts westward on the W-going stream and eastward on the E-going stream. In the latter case it is not advisable to pass between the Race and the Shambles Bank. Study carefully the hourly tidal stream chartlets on pp.184-185 or in NP 257. The Race may be avoided either by passing to seaward of it, ie 3-5M south of the Bill and east of the Shambles; or by using the inshore passage – if conditions suit.

Seaward of the Race.

E-bound: The Channel flood sets east from HW Dover +6 to HWD –1.	W-bound: The ebb sets west from HW Dover to HWD +5½.

The inshore passage, (a narrow stretch of relatively smooth water between the Bill and the Race), should be started, in either direction, from a position 2M north of the Bill, keeping close inshore to the Portland peninsula. It should not be used at night (due to pot floats), nor in winds >F4/5, nor at springs especially with wind against tide.

If E-bound via the inshore passage, slackish water or a fair stream occurs around the Bill from HW Portland –3 to +1. The passage across Lyme Bay should be specifically timed to meet this critical window.	W-bound, similar conditions occur from HW Portland +4 to –6. The W-bound timing is easy if you have started from Weymouth, Portland harbour or Lulworth Cove.

ST ALBAN'S HEAD (AC 2610)

A sometimes vicious Race forms over St Alban's Ledge, a rocky dorsal ridge (least depth 8.5m) which extends approx 4M SW from St Alban's Head. Three yellow naval target buoys (DZ A, B and C) straddle the middle and outer sections, but are only occasionally used. In settled weather and at neaps the Race may be barely perceptible in which case it can be crossed with impunity. Avoid it either by keeping to seaward via 50°31'.40N 02°07'.80W; or by using the narrow inshore passage at the foot of St Alban's Head.

Based on a position 1M S of St Alban's Head, the tidal stream windows are:

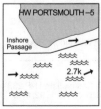

ESE-going stream starts at HW Portsmouth +0530. Spring rates are the same, max 4kn. Along the W side of St Alban's Head the stream runs almost continuously SE due to a back eddy.

WNW-going stream starts at HW Portsmouth. Overfalls extend 2.5M further SW than on the E-going stream and are more dangerous to small craft. Slack water lasts barely half an hour.

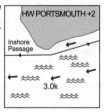

The inshore passage lies as close to the foot of St Alban's Head as feels comfortable. It may be hard to see the width of clear water in the inshore passage until committed to it, but except in onshore gales when it is better to stay offshore, the passage will be swiftly made with only a few, if any, overfalls. The NCI station on the Head (☎ 01929 439220) may advise on conditions.

TIDAL GATES - SOUTHERN ENGLAND

A guide to the time of tide turn at tidal gates, the approximate maximum strength of the tidal flow (spring rates shown - neaps are approximately 60% of these), and the position and timing of races, counter tides, etc.

FLOOD	EBB

THE NEEDLES CHANNEL (AC 2035)

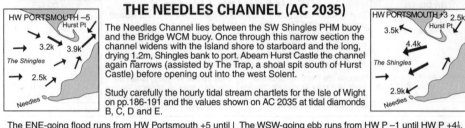

The Needles Channel lies between the SW Shingles PHM buoy and the Bridge WCM buoy. Once through this narrow section the channel widens with the Island shore to starboard and the long, drying 1.2m, Shingles bank to port. Abeam Hurst Castle the channel again narrows (assisted by The Trap, a shoal spit south of Hurst Castle) before opening out into the west Solent.

Study carefully the hourly tidal stream chartlets for the Isle of Wight on pp.186-191 and the values shown on AC 2035 at tidal diamonds B, C, D and E.

The ENE-going flood runs from HW Portsmouth +5 until HW P −1½, at springs reaching 3.1kn at The Bridge and 3.9kn at Hurst.

The WSW-going ebb runs from HW P −1 until HW P +4½, reaching 4.4kn at Hurst and 3.4kn at The Bridge, both spring rates. The ebb sets strongly WSW across the Shingles which with adequate rise is routinely crossed by racing yachts; but cruisers should stay clear even in calm conditions when any swell causes the sea to break heavily.

Prevailing W/SW winds, even if only F4, against the ebb raise dangerous breaking seas in the Needles Channel and at The Bridge, a shallow ridge extending 9 cables west from the Needles light. Worst conditions are often found just after LW slack. In such conditions it is safer to go via the North Channel to Hurst. In W/SW gales avoid the Needles altogether by sheltering at Poole or going east-about via Nab Tower.

ON PASSAGE UP CHANNEL

The following 3 tidal gates (The Looe, Beachy Head and Dungeness) are components in the tidal conveyor belt which, if stepped onto at the outset, can enable a fastish yacht to carry a fair tide for 88M from Selsey Bill to Dover. Go through the Looe at slackish water, HW Portsmouth +4½ (HW Dover +5). Based on a mean SOG of 7 knots, Beachy Head will be passed at HW D −1, Dungeness at HW D +3 and Dover at HW +5½, only bucking the first of the ebb in the last hour. A faster boat could make Ramsgate. The down-Channel passage is less rewarding and many yachts will pause at Brighton.

THE LOOE (AC 2045, 1652)

This channel is little shorter than the detour south of the Owers, but is much used by yachts on passage from/to points east of the Solent. Although adequately lit, it is best not attempted at night due to many lobster floats; nor in onshore gales as searoom is limited by extensive shoals on which the sea breaks.

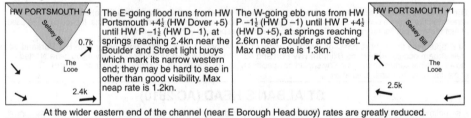

The E-going flood runs from HW Portsmouth +4½ (HW Dover +5) until HW P −1½ (HW D −1), at springs reaching 2.4kn near the Boulder and Street light buoys which mark its narrow western end; they may be hard to see in other than good visibility. Max neap rate is 1.2kn.

The W-going ebb runs from HW P −1½ (HW D −1) until HW P +4½ (HW D +5), at springs reaching 2.6kn near Boulder and Street. Max neap rate is 1.3kn.

At the wider eastern end of the channel (near E Borough Head buoy) rates are greatly reduced.

BEACHY HEAD (AC 1652, 536)

Stay at least 5 cables to seaward of the towering chalk cliffs to avoid isolated boulders and rocky, part-drying ridges such as Head Ledge. The lt ho stands on a drying rock ledge. Close inshore many fishing floats are a trap for the unwary. In bad weather stay 2M offshore to avoid overfalls caused by a ridge of uneven ground which extends 1M SSE from Beachy Head.

2M south of Beachy Head the E-going flood starts at HW Dover +0530, max spring rate 2.6kn.

The W-going ebb starts at HW Dover +0030, max spring rate 2.0kn.

Between 5M and 7M east of Beachy Head avoid breakers and eddies caused by the Horse of Willingdon, Royal Sovereign and other shoals.

DUNGENESS (AC 536, 1892)

Tidal stream atlases: Dungeness is on the east and west edges respectively of NP 250 (English Channel) and NP 233 (Dover Strait). The nearest tidal stream diamond (2.2M SE of Dungeness) is 'H' on AC 536 and 'B' on AC 1892; their positions and values are the same.

The NE-going flood starts at HW Dover −0100, max spring rate 1.9kn.

The SW-going ebb starts at HW Dover +0430, max spring rate 2.1kn.

TIDAL GATES - NORTH EAST SCOTLAND

A guide to the time of tide turn at tidal gates, and in straits and estuaries, showing the approximate strength of the tidal flow (spring rates shown - neaps are approximately 60% of these), and the position and timing of races, counter tides etc.

FLOOD	EBB

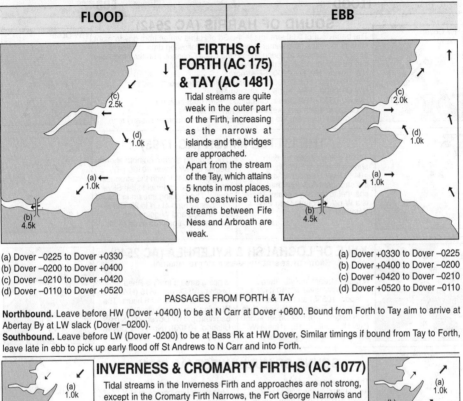

FIRTHS of FORTH (AC 175) & TAY (AC 1481)

Tidal streams are quite weak in the outer part of the Firth, increasing as the narrows at islands and the bridges are approached.

Apart from the stream of the Tay, which attains 5 knots in most places, the coastwise tidal streams between Fife Ness and Arbroath are weak.

(a) Dover –0225 to Dover +0330	(a) Dover +0330 to Dover –0225
(b) Dover –0200 to Dover +0400	(b) Dover +0400 to Dover –0200
(c) Dover –0210 to Dover +0420	(c) Dover +0420 to Dover –0210
(d) Dover –0110 to Dover +0520	(d) Dover +0520 to Dover –0110

PASSAGES FROM FORTH & TAY

Northbound. Leave before HW (Dover +0400) to be at N Carr at Dover +0600. Bound from Forth to Tay aim to arrive at Abertay By at LW slack (Dover –0200).

Southbound. Leave before LW (Dover -0200) to be at Bass Rk at HW Dover. Similar timings if bound from Tay to Forth, leave late in ebb to pick up early flood off St Andrews to N Carr and into Forth.

INVERNESS & CROMARTY FIRTHS (AC 1077)

Tidal streams in the Inverness Firth and approaches are not strong, except in the Cromarty Firth Narrows, the Fort George Narrows and the Kessock Road, including off the entrance to the Caledonian Canal.

(a) Dover –0555 to Dover +0030	(a) Dover +0030 to Dover –0555
(b) Dover –0400 to Dover +0115	(b) Dover +0115 to Dover –0400
(c) Dover –0400 to Dover –0220	(c) Dover +0115 to Dover –0440
(d) Dover –0430 to Dover +0100	(d) Dover –0130 to Dover +0545

PENTLAND FIRTH & ORKNEYS (AC 1954)

The tide flows strongly around and through the Orkney Islands. The Pentland Firth is a dangerous area for all craft, tidal flows reach 12 knots between Duncansby Head and S Ronaldsay. W of Dunnet Hd & Hoy is less violent. There is little tide within Scapa Flow.

(a) Dover –0500 to Dover +0100	(a) Dover +0115 to Dover –0535
(b) Dover +0500 to Dover –0110	(b) Dover –0110 to Dover +0050
(c) Dover –0530 to Dover +0040	(c) Dover +0040 to Dover –0530

SHETLAND ISLANDS (AC 219)

The tidal flow around the Shetland Islands rotates as the cycle progresses. When the flood begins, at –0400 HW Dover, the tidal flow is to the E, at HW Dover it is S, at Dover +0300 it is W, and at –0600 Dover it is N.

(a) Dover –0410 to Dover +0020	(a) Dover +0050 to Dover –0410
(b) Dover –0400 to Dover +0030	(b) Dover +0130 to Dover –0500
(c) Dover –0530 to Dover +0100	(c) Dover +0100 to Dover –0530
(d) Dover –0400 to Dover –0200	(d) Dover +0200 to Dover +0500

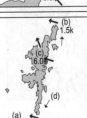

TIDES

TIDAL GATES - NORTH WEST SCOTLAND

A guide to the time of tide turn at tidal gates, the approximate maximum strength of the tidal flow (spring rates shown - neaps are approximately 60% of these), and the position and timing of races, counter tides, etc.

FLOOD	EBB

SOUND OF HARRIS (AC 2642)

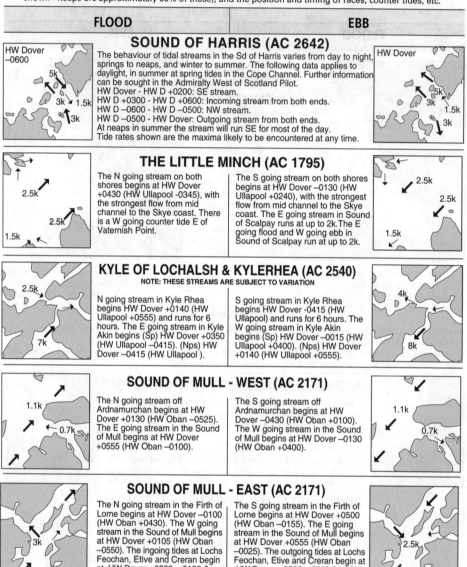

HW Dover −0600

The behaviour of tidal streams in the Sd of Harris varies from day to night, springs to neaps, and winter to summer. The following data applies to daylight, in summer at spring tides in the Cope Channel. Further information can be sought in the Admiralty West of Scotland Pilot.
HW Dover - HW D +0200: SE stream.
HW D +0300 - HW D +0600: Incoming stream from both ends.
HW D −0600 - HW D −0500: NW stream.
HW D −0500 - HW Dover: Outgoing stream from both ends.
At neaps in summer the stream will run SE for most of the day.
Tide rates shown are the maxima likely to be encountered at any time.

HW Dover

THE LITTLE MINCH (AC 1795)

The N going stream on both shores begins at HW Dover +0430 (HW Ullapool -0345), with the strongest flow from mid channel to the Skye coast. There is a W going counter tide E of Vaternish Point.

The S going stream on both shores begins at HW Dover −0130 (HW Ullapool +0240), with the strongest flow from mid channel to the Skye coast. The E going stream in Sound of Scalpay runs at up to 2k. The E going flood and W going ebb in Sound of Scalpay run at up to 2k.

KYLE OF LOCHALSH & KYLERHEA (AC 2540)

NOTE: THESE STREAMS ARE SUBJECT TO VARIATION

N going stream in Kyle Rhea begins HW Dover +0140 (HW Ullapool +0555) and runs for 6 hours. The E going stream in Kyle Akin begins (Sp) HW Dover +0350 (HW Ullapool −0415). (Nps) HW Dover −0415 (HW Ullapool).

S going stream in Kyle Rhea begins HW Dover -0015 (HW Ullapool) and runs for 6 hours. The W going stream in Kyle Akin begins (Sp) HW Dover −0015 (HW Ullapool +0400). (Nps) HW Dover +0140 (HW Ullapool +0555).

SOUND OF MULL - WEST (AC 2171)

The N going stream off Ardnamurchan begins at HW Dover +0130 (HW Oban −0525). The E going stream in the Sound of Mull begins at HW Dover +0555 (HW Oban −0100).

The S going stream off Ardnamurchan begins at HW Dover −0430 (HW Oban +0100). The W going stream in the Sound of Mull begins at HW Dover −0130 (HW Oban +0400).

SOUND OF MULL - EAST (AC 2171)

The N going stream in the Firth of Lorne begins at HW Dover −0100 (HW Oban +0430). The W going stream in the Sound of Mull begins at HW Dover +0105 (HW Oban −0550). The ingoing tides at Lochs Feochan, Etive and Creran begin at HW Dover +0300, −0100 & +0030.

The S going stream in the Firth of Lorne begins at HW Dover +0500 (HW Oban −0155). The E going stream in the Sound of Mull begins at HW Dover +0555 (HW Oban −0025). The outgoing tides at Lochs Feochan, Etive and Creran begin at HW Dover −0500, −0520 & −0505.

SOUND OF LUING & DORUS MOR (AC 2343)

The N or W going stream begins as follows:
Dorus Mor: HW Dover −0200 (HW Oban +0330). Springs: 8 knots.
Corryvreckan: HW D −0120 (HW O +0410). Sp: 8.5 knots.
Cuan Sound: HW D −0110 (HW O +0420). Sp: 6 knots.
Sound of Jura: HW D −0130 (HW O +0400). Sp: 4 knots.
Sound of Luing: HW D −0100 (HW O +0430). Sp: 7 knots.
The S or E going stream begins as follows:
Dorus Mor: HW Dover +0440 (HW Oban −0215). Springs: 8 knots.
Corryvreckan: HW D +0445 (HW O −0210). Sp: 8.5 knots.
Cuan Sound: HW D +0455 (HW O −0200). Sp: 6 knots.
Sound of Jura: HW D +0450 (HW O −0205). Sp: 4 knots.
Sound of Luing: HW D +0500 (HW O −0155). Sp: 7 knots.

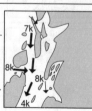

TIDAL GATES - SOUTH WEST SCOTLAND

A guide to the time of tide turn at tidal gates, the approximate maximum strength of the tidal flow (spring rates shown - neaps are approximately 60% of these), and the position and timing of races, counter tides, etc.

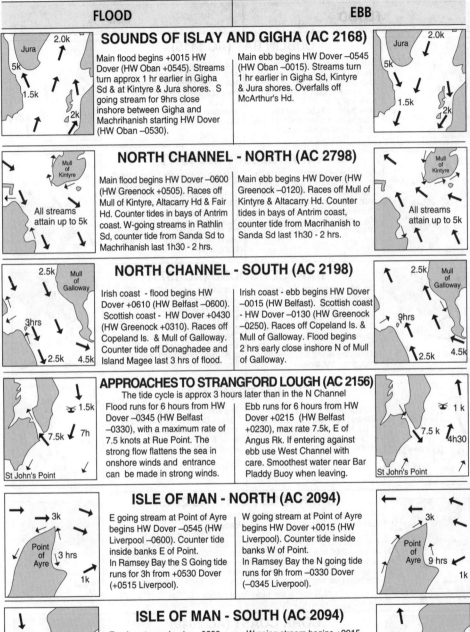

FLOOD	EBB

SOUNDS OF ISLAY AND GIGHA (AC 2168)

FLOOD: Main flood begins +0015 HW Dover (HW Oban +0545). Streams turn approx 1 hr earlier in Gigha Sd & at Kintyre & Jura shores. S going stream for 9hrs close inshore between Gigha and Machrihanish starting HW Dover (HW Oban −0530).

EBB: Main ebb begins HW Dover −0545 (HW Oban −0015). Streams turn 1 hr earlier in Gigha Sd, Kintyre & Jura shores. Overfalls off McArthur's Hd.

NORTH CHANNEL - NORTH (AC 2798)

FLOOD: Main flood begins HW Dover −0600 (HW Greenock +0505). Races off Mull of Kintyre, Altacarry Hd & Fair Hd. Counter tides in bays of Antrim coast. W-going streams in Rathlin Sd, counter tide from Sanda Sd to Machrihanish last 1h30 - 2 hrs.

EBB: Main ebb begins HW Dover (HW Greenock −0120). Races off Mull of Kintyre & Altacarry Hd. Counter tides in bays of Antrim coast, counter tide from Macrihanish to Sanda Sd last 1h30 - 2 hrs.

NORTH CHANNEL - SOUTH (AC 2198)

FLOOD: Irish coast - flood begins HW Dover +0610 (HW Belfast −0600). Scottish coast - HW Dover +0430 (HW Greenock +0310). Races off Copeland Is. & Mull of Galloway. Counter tide off Donaghadee and Island Magee last 3 hrs of flood.

EBB: Irish coast - ebb begins HW Dover −0015 (HW Belfast). Scottish coast - HW Dover −0130 (HW Greenock −0250). Races off Copeland Is. & Mull of Galloway. Flood begins 2 hrs early close inshore N of Mull of Galloway.

APPROACHES TO STRANGFORD LOUGH (AC 2156)

The tide cycle is approx 3 hours later than in the N Channel

FLOOD: Flood runs for 6 hours from HW Dover −0345 (HW Belfast −0330), with a maximum rate of 7.5 knots at Rue Point. The strong flow flattens the sea in onshore winds and entrance can be made in strong winds.

EBB: Ebb runs for 6 hours from HW Dover +0215 (HW Belfast +0230), max rate 7.5k, E of Angus Rk. If entering against ebb use West Channel with care. Smoothest water near Bar Pladdy Buoy when leaving.

ISLE OF MAN - NORTH (AC 2094)

FLOOD: E going stream at Point of Ayre begins HW Dover −0545 (HW Liverpool −0600). Counter tide inside banks E of Point. In Ramsey Bay the S Going tide runs for 3h from +0530 Dover (+0515 Liverpool).

EBB: W going stream at Point of Ayre begins HW Dover +0015 (HW Liverpool). Counter tide inside banks W of Point. In Ramsey Bay the N going tide runs for 9h from −0330 Dover (−0345 Liverpool).

ISLE OF MAN - SOUTH (AC 2094)

FLOOD: E going stream begins −0600 Dover (Liverpool +0610). Overfalls and race E of Chicken Rock. Calf Sound: The E going stream begins earlier, at approximately Dover +0400 (Liverpool +0345).

EBB: W going stream begins +0015 Dover (HW Liverpool). Overfalls and race N of Chicken Rock. Calf Sound: The W going stream begins earlier, at approximately −0130 Dover (−0145 Liverpool). Note: all times may vary due to weather conditions.

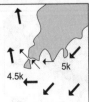

TIDAL GATES - IRISH SEA

A guide to the time of tide turn at tidal gates, the approximate strength of the tidal flow (spring rates shown — neaps are approximately 60% of these), and the position and timing of races, counter tides, etc.

FLOOD	EBB

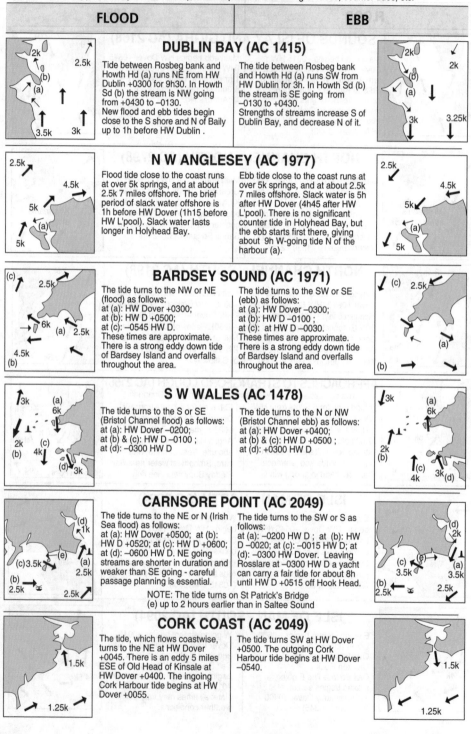

DUBLIN BAY (AC 1415)

FLOOD: Tide between Rosbeg bank and Howth Hd (a) runs NE from HW Dublin +0300 for 9h30. In Howth Sd (b) the stream is NW going from +0430 to –0130. New flood and ebb tides begin close to the S shore and N of Baily up to 1h before HW Dublin .

EBB: The tide between Rosbeg bank and Howth Hd (a) runs SW from HW Dublin for 3h. In Howth Sd (b) the stream is SE going from –0130 to +0430. Strengths of streams increase S of Dublin Bay, and decrease N of it.

N W ANGLESEY (AC 1977)

FLOOD: Flood tide close to the coast runs at over 5k springs, and at about 2.5k 7 miles offshore. The brief period of slack water offshore is 1h before HW Dover (1h15 before HW L'pool). Slack water lasts longer in Holyhead Bay.

EBB: Ebb tide close to the coast runs at over 5k springs, and at about 2.5k 7 miles offshore. Slack water is 5h after HW Dover (4h45 after HW L'pool). There is no significant counter tide in Holyhead Bay, but the ebb starts first there, giving about 9h W-going tide N of the harbour (a).

BARDSEY SOUND (AC 1971)

FLOOD: The tide turns to the NW or NE (flood) as follows:
at (a): HW Dover +0300;
at (b): HW D +0500;
at (c): –0545 HW D.
These times are approximate. There is a strong eddy down tide of Bardsey Island and overfalls throughout the area.

EBB: The tide turns to the SW or SE (ebb) as follows:
at (a): HW Dover –0300;
at (b): HW D –0100 ;
at (c): at HW D –0030.
These times are approximate. There is a strong eddy down tide of Bardsey Island and overfalls throughout the area.

S W WALES (AC 1478)

FLOOD: The tide turns to the S or SE (Bristol Channel flood) as follows:
at (a): HW Dover –0200;
at (b) & (c): HW D –0100 ;
at (d): –0300 HW D

EBB: The tide turns to the N or NW (Bristol Channel ebb) as follows:
at (a): HW Dover +0400;
at (b) & (c): HW D +0500 ;
at (d): +0300 HW D

CARNSORE POINT (AC 2049)

FLOOD: The tide turns to the NE or N (Irish Sea flood) as follows:
at (a): HW Dover +0500; at (b): HW D +0520; at (c): HW D +0600; at (d): –0600 HW D. NE going streams are shorter in duration and weaker than SE going - careful passage planning is essential.

EBB: The tide turns to the SW or S as follows:
at (a): –0200 HW D ; at (b): HW D –0020; at (c): –0015 HW D; at (d): –0300 HW Dover. Leaving Rosslare at –0300 HW D a yacht can carry a fair tide for about 8h until HW D +0515 off Hook Head.

NOTE: The tide turns on St Patrick's Bridge (e) up to 2 hours earlier than in Saltee Sound

CORK COAST (AC 2049)

FLOOD: The tide, which flows coastwise, turns to the NE at HW Dover +0045. There is an eddy 5 miles ESE of Old Head of Kinsale at HW Dover +0400. The ingoing Cork Harbour tide begins at HW Dover +0055.

EBB: The tide turns SW at HW Dover +0500. The outgoing Cork Harbour tide begins at HW Dover –0540.

MENAI STRAIT (AC 1464) – TIDAL GATES

FLOOD

(T) : turning   → : < 2k   ➡ : 2-4k   ⫸ : 4k +

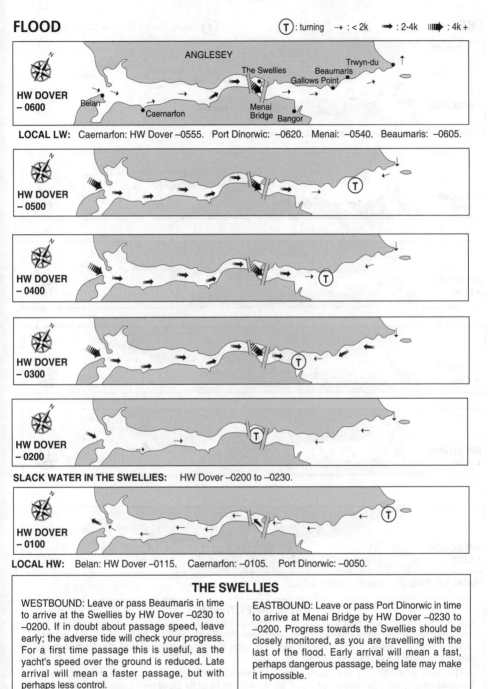

HW DOVER – 0600

LOCAL LW: Caernarfon: HW Dover –0555.   Port Dinorwic: –0620.   Menai: –0540.   Beaumaris: –0605.

HW DOVER – 0500

HW DOVER – 0400

HW DOVER – 0300

HW DOVER – 0200

SLACK WATER IN THE SWELLIES: HW Dover –0200 to –0230.

HW DOVER – 0100

LOCAL HW: Belan: HW Dover –0115.   Caernarfon: –0105.   Port Dinorwic: –0050.

THE SWELLIES

WESTBOUND: Leave or pass Beaumaris in time to arrive at the Swellies by HW Dover –0230 to –0200. If in doubt about passage speed, leave early; the adverse tide will check your progress. For a first time passage this is useful, as the yacht's speed over the ground is reduced. Late arrival will mean a faster passage, but with perhaps less control.

EASTBOUND: Leave or pass Port Dinorwic in time to arrive at Menai Bridge by HW Dover –0230 to –0200. Progress towards the Swellies should be closely monitored, as you are travelling with the last of the flood. Early arrival will mean a fast, perhaps dangerous passage, being late may make it impossible.

MENAI STRAIT (AC 1464) – TIDAL GATES *contd*

EBB

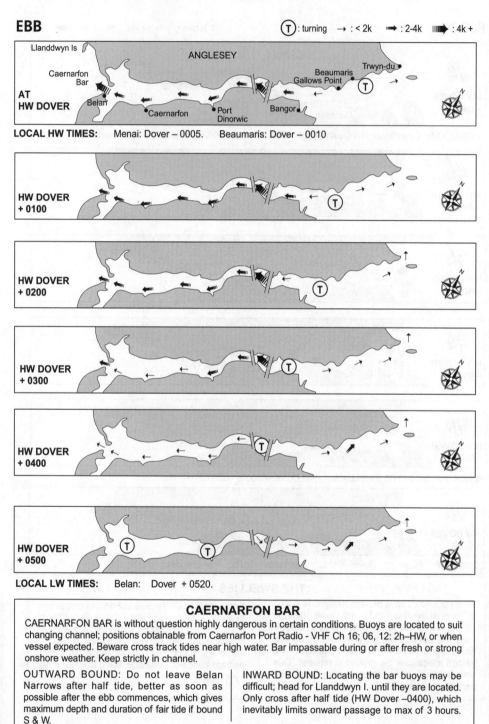

LOCAL HW TIMES: Menai: Dover – 0005. Beaumaris: Dover – 0010

LOCAL LW TIMES: Belan: Dover + 0520.

CAERNARFON BAR

CAERNARFON BAR is without question highly dangerous in certain conditions. Buoys are located to suit changing channel; positions obtainable from Caernarfon Port Radio - VHF Ch 16; 06, 12: 2h–HW, or when vessel expected. Beware cross track tides near high water. Bar impassable during or after fresh or strong onshore weather. Keep strictly in channel.

OUTWARD BOUND: Do not leave Belan Narrows after half tide, better as soon as possible after the ebb commences, which gives maximum depth and duration of fair tide if bound S & W.	**INWARD BOUND:** Locating the bar buoys may be difficult; head for Llanddwyn I. until they are located. Only cross after half tide (HW Dover –0400), which inevitably limits onward passage to max of 3 hours.

SECONDARY PORTS: TIME & HEIGHT DIFFERENCES
SOUTH COAST OF ENGLAND *Time Zone UT*

Location	Lat	Long	High Water		Low Water		MHWS	MHWN	MLWN	MLWS
			0000	0600	0000	0600				
PLYMOUTH (DEVONPORT)	50 22N	4 11W	and	and	and	and	5.5	4.4	2.2	0.8
Standard port			1200	1800	1200	1800				
Isles of Scilly, St Mary's	49 55N	6 19W	−0035	−0100	−0040	−0025	+0.2	−0.1	−0.2	−0.1
Penzance & Newlyn	50 06N	5 33W	−0040	−0110	−0035	−0025	+0.1	0.0	−0.2	0.0
Porthleven	50 05N	5 19W	−0045	−0105	−0030	−0025	0.0	−0.1	−0.2	0.0
Lizard Point	49 57N	5 12W	−0045	−0100	−0030	−0030	−0.2	−0.2	−0.3	−0.2
Coverack	50 01N	5 05W	−0030	−0050	−0020	−0015	−0.2	−0.2	−0.3	−0.2
Helford River Entrance	50 05N	5 05W	−0030	−0035	−0015	−0010	−0.2	−0.2	−0.3	−0.2
FALMOUTH	50 09N	5 03W	*standard port (no secondaries)*							
Truro	50 16N	5 03W	−0020	−0025	*dries*	*dries*	−2.0	−2.0	*dries*	
Mevagissey	50 16N	4 47W	−0015	−0020	−0010	−0005	−0.1	−0.1	−0.2	−0.1
Par	50 21N	4 42W	−0010	−0015	−0010	−0005	−0.4	−0.4	−0.4	−0.2
Fowey	50 20N	4 38W	−0010	−0015	−0010	−0005	−0.1	−0.1	−0.2	−0.2
Lostwithiel	50 24N	4 40W	+0005	−0010	*dries*	*dries*	−4.1	−4.1	*dries*	
Looe	50 21N	4 27W	−0010	−0010	−0005	−0005	−0.1	−0.2	−0.2	−0.2
Whitsand Bay	50 20N	4 15W	0000	0000	0000	0000	0.0	+0.1	−0.1	+0.2
River Tamar										
Saltash	50 24N	4 12W	0000	+0010	0000	−0005	+0.1	+0.1	+0.1	+0.1
Cargreen	50 26N	4 12W	0000	+0010	+0020	+0020	0.0	0.0	−0.1	0.0
Cotehele Quay	50 29N	4 13W	0000	+0020	+0045	+0045	−0.9	−0.9	−0.8	−0.4
Lopwell, R Tavy	50 28N	4 09W	*no data*	*no data*	*dries*	*dries*	−2.6	−2.7	*dries*	
Jupiter Point	50 23N	4 14W	+0010	+0005	0000	−0005	0.0	0.0	+0.1	0.0
St Germans	50 23N	4 18W	0000	0000	+0020	+0020	−0.3	−0.1	0.0	+0.2
Turnchapel	50 22N	4 07W	0000	0000	+0010	−0015	0.0	+0.1	+0.2	+0.1
Bovisand Pier	50 20N	4 08W	0000	−0020	0000	−0010	−0.2	−0.1	0.0	+0.1
River Yealm Entrance	50 18N	4 04W	+0006	+0006	+0002	+0002	−0.1	−0.1	−0.1	−0.1
			0100	0600	0100	0600				
PLYMOUTH (DEVONPORT)	50 22N	4 11W	and	and	and	and	5.5	4.4	2.2	0.8
Standard port			1300	1800	1300	1800				
Salcombe	50 13N	3 47W	0000	+0010	+0005	−0005	−0.2	−0.3	−0.1	−0.1
Start Point	50 13N	3 39W	+0015	+0015	+0005	+0010	−0.1	−0.2	+0.1	+0.2
River Dart										
DARTMOUTH	50 21N	3 34W	*standard port (no secondaries)*							
Greenway Quay	50 23N	3 35W	+0030	+0045	+0025	+0005	−0.6	−0.6	−0.2	−0.2
Totnes	50 26N	3 41W	+0030	+0040	+0115	+0030	−2.0	−2.1	*dries*	
Torquay	50 28N	3 31W	+0025	+0045	+0010	0000	−0.6	−0.7	−0.2	−0.1
Teignmouth Approaches	50 33N	3 29W	+0020	+0050	+0025	0000	−0.9	−0.8	−0.2	−0.1
Teignmouth New Quay	50 33N	3 30W	+0025	+0055	+0040	+0005	−0.8	−0.8	−0.2	+0.1
Exmouth Approaches	50 36N	3 23W	+0030	+0050	+0015	+0005	−0.9	−1.0	−0.5	−0.3
River Exe										
Exmouth Dock	50 37N	3 25W	+0035	+0055	+0050	+0020	−1.5	−1.6	−0.9	−0.6
Starcross	50 38N	3 27W	+0040	+0110	+0035	+0025	−1.4	−1.5	−0.8	−0.1
Topsham	50 41N	3 28W	+0045	+0105	*no data*	*no data*	−1.5	−1.6	*no data*	
Lyme Regis	50 43N	2 56W	+0040	+0100	+0005	−0005	−1.2	−1.3	−0.5	−0.2
Bridport West Bay	50 42N	2 45W	+0025	+0040	0000	0000	−1.4	−1.4	−0.6	−0.2
Chesil Beach	50 37N	2 33W	+0040	+0055	−0005	+0010	−1.6	−1.5	−0.5	0.0
Chesil Cove	50 34N	2 28W	+0035	+0050	−0010	+0005	−1.5	−1.6	−0.5	−0.2
			0100	0700	0100	0700				
PORTLAND	50 34N	2 26W	and	and	and	and	2.1	1.4	0.8	0.1
Standard port			1300	1900	1300	1900				
Lulworth Cove	50 37N	2 15W	+0005	+0015	−0005	0000	+0.1	+0.1	+0.2	+0.1
Mupe Bay	50 37N	2 13W	+0005	+0015	−0005	0000	+0.1	+0.1	+0.2	+0.1
			0000	0600	0500	1100				
PORTSMOUTH	50 48N	1 07W	and	and	and	and	4.7	3.8	1.9	0.8
standard port			1200	1800	1700	2300				
Swanage	50 37N	1 57W	−0250	+0105	−0105	−0105	−2.7	−2.2	−0.7	−0.3
Poole Harbour Entrance	50 41N	1 57W	−0230	+0115	−0045	−0020	−2.5	−2.1	−0.6	−0.2
POOLE, TOWN QUAY	50 43N	1 59W	*standard port*							
Pottery Pier	50 42N	1 59W	−0150	+0200	−0010	0000	−2.7	−2.1	−0.6	0.0
Wareham *River Frome*	50 41N	2 06W	−0140	+0205	+0110	+0035	−2.5	−2.1	−0.7	+0.1
Cleavel Point	50 40N	2 00W	−0220	+0130	−0025	−0015	−2.6	−2.3	−0.7	−0.3
Bournemouth	50 43N	1 52W	−0240	+0055	−0050	−0030	−2.7	−2.2	−0.8	−0.3
Christchurch *Entrance*	50 43N	1 45W	−0230	+0030	−0035	−0035	−2.9	−2.4	−1.2	−0.2
Christchurch *Quay*	50 44N	1 46W	−0210	+0100	+0105	+0055	−2.9	−2.4	−1.0	0.0
Christchurch *Tuckton*	50 44N	1 47W	−0205	+0110	+0110	+0105	−3.0	−2.5	−1.0	+0.1

TIDES

TIDES

Location	Lat	Long	High Water		Low Water		MHWS	MHWN	MLWN	MLWS
Hurst Point	50 42N	1 33W	−0115	−0005	−0030	−0025	−2.0	−1.5	−0.5	−0.1
Lymington	50 46N	1 32W	−0110	+0005	−0020	−0020	−1.7	−1.2	−0.5	−0.1
Bucklers Hard	50 48N	1 25W	−0040	−0010	+0010	−0010	−1.0	−0.8	−0.2	−0.3
Stansore Point	50 47N	1 21W	−0050	−0010	−0005	−0010	−0.8	−0.5	−0.3	−0.1
Isle of Wight										
Yarmouth	50 42N	1 30W	−0105	+0005	−0025	−0030	−1.7	−1.2	−0.3	0.0
Totland Bay	50 41N	1 33W	−0130	−0045	−0035	−0045	−2.2	−1.7	−0.4	−0.1
Freshwater	50 40N	1 31W	−0210	+0025	−0040	−0020	−2.1	−1.5	−0.4	0.0
Ventnor	50 36N	1 12W	−0025	−0030	−0025	−0030	−0.8	−0.6	−0.2	+0.2
Sandown	50 39N	1 09W	0000	+0005	+0010	+0025	−0.6	−0.5	−0.2	0.0
Foreland *Lifeboat Slip*	50 41N	1 04W	−0005	0000	+0005	+0010	+0.1	+0.1	0.0	+0.1
Bembridge Harbour	50 42N	1 06W	+0020	0000	+0100	+0020	−1.5	−1.4	−1.3	−1.0
Ryde	50 44N	1 07W	−0010	+0010	−0005	−0010	−0.2	−0.1	0.0	+0.1
Medina River										
Cowes	50 46N	1 18W	−0015	+0015	0000	−0020	−0.5	−0.3	−0.1	0.0
Folly Inn	50 44N	1 17W	−0015	+0015	0000	−0020	−0.6	−0.4	−0.1	+0.2
Newport	50 42N	1 17W	no data	no data	no data	no data	−0.6	−0.4	+0.1	+0.8
			0400	**1100**	**0000**	**0600**				
SOUTHAMPTON	50 54N	1 24W	and	and	and	and	**4.5**	**3.7**	**1.8**	**0.5**
standard port			**1600**	**2300**	**1200**	**1800**				
Calshot Castle	50 49N	1 18W	0000	+0025	0000	0000	0.0	0.0	+0.2	+0.3
Redbridge	50 55N	1 28W	−0020	+0005	0000	−0005	−0.1	−0.1	−0.1	−0.1
River Hamble										
Warsash	50 51N	1 18W	+0020	+0010	+0010	0000	0.0	+0.1	+0.1	+0.3
Bursledon	50 53N	1 18W	+0020	+0020	+0010	+0010	+0.1	+0.1	+0.2	+0.2
			0500	**1000**	**0000**	**0600**				
PORTSMOUTH	50 48N	1 07W	and	and	and	and	**4.7**	**3.8**	**1.9**	**0.8**
standard port			**1700**	**2200**	**1200**	**1800**				
Lee–on–the–Solent	50 48N	1 12W	−0005	+0005	−0015	−0010	−0.2	−0.1	+0.1	+0.2
Chichester Harbour										
Entrance	50 47N	0 56W	−0010	+0005	+0015	+0020	+0.2	+0.2	0.0	+0.1
Northney	50 50N	0 58W	+0010	+0015	+0015	+0025	+0.2	0.0	−0.2	−0.3
Bosham	50 50N	0 52W	0000	+0010	no data	no data	+0.2	+0.1	no data	
Itchenor	50 48N	0 52W	−0005	+0005	+0005	+0025	+0.1	0.0	−0.2	−0.2
Dell Quay	50 49N	0 49W	+0005	+0015	no data	no data	+0.2	+0.1	no data	
Selsey Bill	50 43N	0 47W	+0010	−0010	+0035	+0020	+0.5	+0.2	−0.2	−0.2
Nab Tower	50 40N	0 57W	+0015	0000	+0015	+0015	−0.2	0.0	+0.2	0.0
			0500	**1000**	**0000**	**0600**				
SHOREHAM	50 50N	0 15W	and	and	and	and	**6.3**	**4.8**	**1.9**	**0.6**
standard port			**1700**	**2200**	**1200**	**1800**				
Pagham	50 46N	0 43W	+0015	0000	−0015	−0025	−0.7	−0.5	−0.1	−0.1
Bognor Regis	50 47N	0 40W	+0010	−0005	−0005	−0020	−0.6	−0.5	−0.2	−0.1
River Arun										
Littlehampton *Entrance*	50 48N	0 32W	+0010	0000	−0005	−0010	−0.4	−0.4	−0.2	−0.2
Littlehampton *UMA wharf*	50 48N	0 33W	+0015	+0005	0000	+0045	−0.7	−0.7	−0.3	+0.2
Arundel	50 51N	0 33W	no data	+0120	no data	no data	−3.1	−2.8	no data	
Worthing	50 48N	0 22W	+0010	0000	−0005	−0010	−0.1	−0.2	0.0	0.0
Brighton	50 49N	0 08W	0000	−0005	0000	0000	+0.3	+0.2	+0.1	0.0
Newhaven	50 47N	0 04E	−0015	−0010	0000	0000	+0.2	+0.1	−0.1	−0.2
Eastbourne	50 46N	0 17E	−0010	−0005	+0015	+0020	+1.1	+0.6	+0.2	+0.1
			0000	**0600**	**0100**	**0700**				
DOVER	51 07N	1 19E	and	and	and	and	**6.8**	**5.3**	**2.1**	**0.8**
standard port			**1200**	**1800**	**1300**	**1900**				
Hastings	50 51N	0 35E	0000	−0010	−0030	−0030	+0.8	+0.5	+0.1	−0.1
Rye *Approaches*	50 55N	0 47E	+0005	−0010	no data	no data	+1.0	+0.7	no data	
Rye *Harbour*	50 56N	0 46E	+0005	−0010	dries	dries	−1.4	−1.7	dries	
Dungeness	50 54N	0 58E	−0010	−0015	−0020	−0010	+1.0	+0.6	+0.4	+0.1
Folkestone	51 05N	1 12E	−0020	−0005	−0010	−0010	+0.4	+0.4	0.0	−0.1
Deal	51 13N	1 25E	+0010	+0020	+0010	+0005	−0.6	−0.3	0.0	0.0
Richborough	51 18N	1 21E	+0015	+0015	+0030	+0030	−3.4	−2.6	−1.7	−0.7
Ramsgate	51 20N	1 25E	+0030	+0030	+0017	+0007	−1.6	−1.3	−0.7	−0.2

EAST COAST ENGLAND *Time Zone UT*

Location	Lat	Long	High Water		Low Water		MHWS	MHWN	MLWN	MLWS
			0200	**0800**	**0200**	**0700**				
SHEERNESS	51 27N	0 45E	and	and	and	and	**5.8**	**4.7**	**1.5**	**0.6**
standard port			**1400**	**2000**	**1400**	**1900**				
Margate	51 23N	1 23E	−0050	−0040	−0020	−0050	−0.9	−0.9	−0.1	0.0
Herne Bay	51 23N	1 07E	−0025	−0015	0000	−0025	−0.5	−0.5	−0.1	−0.1
Whitstable	51 22N	1 02E	−0008	−0011	+0005	0000	−0.3	−0.3	0.0	−0.1

Location	Lat	Long	High Water		Low Water		MHWS	MHWN	MLWN	MLWS
River Swale										
Grovehurst Jetty	51 22N	0 46E	−0007	0000	0000	+0016	0.0	0.0	0.0	−0.1
Faversham	51 19N	0 54E	*no data*	*no data*	*no data*	*no data*	−0.2	−0.2	*no data*	
River Medway										
Bee Ness	51 25N	0 39E	+0002	+0002	0000	+0005	+0.2	+0.1	0.0	0.0
Bartlett Creek	51 23N	0 38E	+0016	+0008	*no data*	*no data*	+0.1	0.0	*no data*	
Darnett Ness	51 24N	0 36E	+0004	+0004	0000	+0010	+0.2	+0.1	0.0	−0.1
Chatham *Lock approaches*	51 24N	0 33E	+0010	+0012	+0012	+0018	+0.3	+0.1	−0.1	−0.2
Upnor	51 25N	0 32E	+0015	+0015	+0015	+0025	+0.2	+0.2	−0.1	−0.1
Rochester *Strood Pier*	51 24N	0 30E	+0018	+0018	+0018	+0028	+0.2	+0.2	−0.2	−0.3
Wouldham	51 21N	0 27E	+0030	+0025	+0035	+0120	−0.2	−0.3	−1.0	−0.3
New Hythe	51 19N	0 28E	+0035	+0035	+0220	+0240	−1.6	−1.7	−1.2	−0.3
Allington Lock	51 17N	0 30E	+0050	+0035	*no data*	*no data*	−2.1	−2.2	−1.3	−0.4
River Thames										
Southend–on–Sea	51 31N	0 43E	−0005	0000	0000	+0005	0.0	0.0	−0.1	−0.1
Coryton	51 30N	0 31E	+0005	+0010	+0010	+0015	+0.4	+0.3	+0.1	−0.1
			0300	0900	0400	1100				
LONDON BRIDGE	51 30N	0 05W	and	and	and	and	7.1	5.9	1.3	0.5
standard port			1500	2100	1600	2300				
Albert Bridge	51 29N	0 10W	+0025	+0020	+0105	+0110	−0.9	−0.8	−0.7	−0.4
Hammersmith Bridge	51 29N	0 14W	+0040	+0035	+0205	+0155	−1.4	−1.3	−1.0	−0.5
Kew Bridge	51 29N	0 17W	+0055	+0050	+0255	+0235	−1.8	−1.8	−1.2	−0.5
Richmond Lock	51 28N	0 19W	+0105	+0055	+0325	+0305	−2.2	−2.2	−1.3	−0.5
			0200	0700	0100	0700				
SHEERNESS	51 27N	0 45E	and	and	and	and	5.8	4.7	1.5	0.6
standard port			1400	1900	1300	1900				
Thames Estuary Shivering Sand	51 30N	1 05E	−0025	−0019	−0008	−0026	−0.6	−0.6	−0.1	−0.1
			0000	0600	0500	1100				
WALTON–ON–THE–NAZE	51 51N	1 17E	and	and	and	and	4.2	3.4	1.1	0.4
standard port			1200	1800	1700	2300				
Whitaker Beacon	51 40N	1 06E	+0022	+0024	+0033	+0027	+0.6	+0.5	+0.2	+0.1
Holliwell Point	51 38N	0 56E	+0034	+0037	+0100	+0037	+1.1	+0.9	+0.3	+0.1
River Roach Rochford	51 35N	0 43E	+0050	+0040	*dries*	*dries*	−0.8	−1.1		*dries*
River Crouch										
BURNHAM–ON–CROUCH	51 37N	0 48E	*standard port - see full predictions page 263*							
North Fambridge	51 38N	0 41E	+0115	+0050	+0130	+0100	+1.1	+0.8	0.0	−0.1
Hullbridge	51 38N	0 38E	+0115	+0050	+0135	+0105	+1.1	+0.8	0.0	−0.1
Battlesbridge	51 37N	0 34E	+0120	+0110	*dries*	*dries*	−1.8	−2.0		*dries*
River Blackwater										
Bradwell Waterside	51 45N	0 53E	+0035	+0023	+0047	+0004	+1.0	+0.8	+0.2	0.0
Osea Island	51 43N	0 46E	+0057	+0045	+0050	+0007	+1.1	+0.9	+0.1	0.0
Maldon	51 44N	0 42E	+0107	+0055	*no data*	*no data*	−1.3	−1.1		*no data*
West Mersea	51 47N	0 54E	+0035	+0015	+0055	+0010	+0.9	+0.4	+0.1	+0.1
River Colne										
Brightlingsea	51 48N	1 00E	+0025	+0021	+0046	+0004	+0.8	+0.4	+0.1	0.0
Colchester	51 53N	0 56E	+0035	+0025	*dries*	*dries*	0.0	−0.3		*dries*
Clacton–on–Sea	51 47N	1 09E	+0012	+0010	+0025	+0008	+0.3	+0.1	+0.1	+0.1
Bramble Creek	51 53N	1 14E	+0010	−0007	−0005	+0010	+0.3	+0.3	+0.3	+0.3
Sunk Head	51 46N	1 30E	0000	+0002	−0002	+0002	−0.3	−0.3	−0.1	−0.1
Harwich	51 57N	1 17E	+0007	+0002	−0010	−0012	−0.2	0.0	0.0	0.0
Wrabness	51 57N	1 10E	+0017	+0015	−0010	−0012	−0.1	0.0	0.0	0.0
Mistley	51 57N	1 05E	+0032	+0027	−0010	−0012	0.0	0.0	−0.1	−0.1
Pin Mill	52 00N	1 17E	+0012	+0015	−0008	−0012	−0.1	0.0	0.0	0.0
Ipswich	52 03N	1 10E	+0022	+0027	0000	−0012	0.0	0.0	−0.1	−0.1
			0100	0700	0100	0700				
WALTON–ON–THE–NAZE	51 51N	1 17E	and	and	and	and	4.2	3.4	1.1	0.4
standard port			1300	1900	1300	1900				
Felixstowe Pier	51 57N	1 21E	−0005	−0007	−0018	−0020	−0.5	−0.4	0.0	0.0
River Deben										
Woodbridge Haven	51 59N	1 24E	0000	−0005	−0020	−0025	−0.5	−0.5	−0.1	+0.1
Woodbridge	52 05N	1 19E	+0045	+0025	+0025	−0020	−0.2	−0.3	−0.2	0.0
Bawdsey	52 00N	1 26E	−0016	−0020	−0030	−0032	−0.8	−0.6	−0.1	−0.1
Orford Haven										
Bar	52 02N	1 28E	−0026	−0030	−0036	−0038	−1.0	−0.8	−0.1	0.0
Orford Quay	52 05N	1 32E	+0040	+0040	+0055	+0055	−1.4	−1.1	0.0	+0.2
Slaughden Quay	52 08N	1 36E	+0105	+0105	+0125	+0125	−1.3	−0.8	−0.1	+0.2
Iken Cliffs	52 09N	1 31E	+0130	+0130	+0155	+0155	−1.3	−1.0	0.0	+0.2

Location	Lat	Long	High Water		Low Water		MHWS	MHWN	MLWN	MLWS
			0300	0900	0200	0800				
LOWESTOFT	52 28N	1 45E	and	and	and	and	2.4	2.1	1.0	0.5
standard port			1500	2100	1400	2000				
Orford Ness	52 05N	1 35E	+0135	+0135	+0135	+0125	+0.4	+0.6	−0.1	0.0
Aldeburgh	52 09N	1 36E	+0130	+0130	+0115	+0120	+0.3	+0.2	−0.1	−0.2
Minsmere Sluice	52 14N	1 38E	+0110	+0110	+0110	+0110	0.0	−0.1	−0.2	−0.2
Southwold	52 19N	1 40E	+0105	+0105	+0055	+0055	0.0	0.0	−0.1	0.0
Great Yarmouth										
Gorleston–on–Sea	52 34N	1 44E	−0035	−0035	−0030	−0030	0.0	0.0	0.0	0.0
Britannia Pier	52 36N	1 45E	−0105	−0100	−0040	−0055	+0.1	+0.1	0.0	0.0
Caister–on–Sea	52 39N	1 44E	−0120	−0120	−0100	−0100	0.0	−0.1	0.0	0.0
Winterton–on–Sea	52 43N	1 42E	−0225	−0215	−0135	−0135	+0.8	+0.5	+0.2	+0.1
			0100	0700	0100	0700				
IMMINGHAM	53 38N	0 11E	and	and	and	and	7.3	5.8	2.6	0.9
standard port			1300	1900	1300	1900				
Cromer	52 56N	1 18E	+0050	+0030	+0050	+0130	−2.1	−1.7	−0.5	−0.1
Blakeney Bar	52 59N	0 59E	+0035	+0025	+0030	+0040	−1.6	−1.3	no data	
Blakeney	52 57N	1 01E	+0115	+0055	no data	no data	−3.9	−3.8	no data	
Wells Bar	52 59N	0 49E	+0020	+0020	+0020	+0020	−1.3	−1.0	no data	
Wells	52 57N	0 51E	+0035	+0045	+0340	+0310	−3.8	−3.8	not below CD	
Burnham *Overy Staithe*	52 58N	0 48E	+0045	+0055	no data	no data	−5.0	−4.9	no data	
The Wash										
Hunstanton	52 56N	0 29E	+0010	+0020	+0105	+0025	+0.1	−0.2	−0.1	0.0
West Stones	52 50N	0 21E	+0025	+0025	+0115	+0040	−0.3	−0.4	−0.3	+0.2
King's Lynn	52 45N	0 24E	+0030	+0030	+0305	+0140	−0.5	−0.8	−0.8	+0.1
Wisbech Cut	52 48N	0 13E	+0020	+0025	+0200	+0030	−0.3	−0.7	−0.4	no data
Lawyer's Creek	52 53N	0 05E	+0010	+0020	no data	no data	−0.3	−0.6	no data	
Tabs Head	52 56N	0 05E	0000	+0005	+0125	+0020	+0.2	−0.2	−0.2	−0.2
Boston	52 58N	0 01W	0000	+0010	+0140	+0050	−0.5	−1.0	−0.9	−0.5
Skegness	53 09N	0 21E	+0010	+0015	+0030	+0020	−0.4	−0.5	−0.1	0.0
Inner Dowsing Light Tower	53 20N	0 34E	0000	0000	+0010	+0010	−0.9	−0.7	−0.1	+0.3
River Humber										
Bull Sand Fort	53 34N	0 04E	−0020	−0030	−0035	−0015	−0.4	−0.3	+0.1	+0.2
Grimsby	53 35N	0 04W	−0012	−0012	−0015	−0015	−0.2	−0.1	0.0	+0.2
Hull *King George Dock*	53 44N	0 16W	+0010	+0010	+0021	+0017	+0.3	+0.2	−0.1	−0.2
Hull *Albert Dock*	53 44N	0 21W	+0019	+0019	+0033	+0027	+0.3	+0.1	−0.1	−0.2
Humber Bridge	53 43N	0 27W	+0027	+0022	+0049	+0039	−0.1	−0.4	−0.7	−0.6
River Trent										
Burton Stather	53 39N	0 42W	+0105	+0045	+0335	+0305	−2.1	−2.3	−2.3	*dries*
Flixborough Wharf	53 37N	0 42W	+0120	+0100	+0400	+0340	−2.3	−2.6	*dries*	
Keadby	53 36N	0 44W	+0135	+0120	+0425	+0410	−2.5	−2.8	*dries*	
Owston Ferry	53 29N	0 46W	+0155	+0145	*dries*	*dries*	−3.5	−3.9	*dries*	
River Ouse										
Blacktoft	53 42N	0 43W	+0100	+0055	+0325	+0255	−1.6	−1.8	−2.2	−1.1
Goole	53 42N	0 52W	+0130	+0115	+0355	+0350	−1.6	−2.1	−1.9	−0.6
			0200	0800	0100	0800				
R. TYNE, N. SHIELDS	55 01N	1 26W	and	and	and	and	5. 0	3.9	1.8	0.7
standard port			1400	2000	1300	2000				
Bridlington	54 05N	0 11W	+0119	+0109	+0109	+0104	+1.1	+0.8	+0.5	+0.4
Filey Bay	54 13N	0 16W	+0101	+0101	+0101	+0048	+0.8	+1.0	+0.6	+0.3
Scarborough	54 17N	0 23W	+0059	+0059	+0044	+0044	+0.7	+0.7	+0.5	+0.2
Whitby	54 29N	0 37W	+0034	+0049	+0034	+0019	+0.6	+0.4	+0.1	+0.1
Middlesborough	54 35N	1 13W	+0019	+0021	+0014	+0011	+0.6	+0.6	+0.3	+0.1
Hartlepool	54 41N	1 11W	+0015	+0015	+0008	+0008	+0.4	+0.3	0.0	+0.1
Seaham	54 50N	1 19W	+0004	+0004	−0001	−0001	+0.2	+0.2	+0.2	0.0
Sunderland	54 55N	1 21W	+0002	−0002	−0002	−0002	+0.2	+0.3	+0.2	+0.1
Newcastle–upon–Tyne	54 58N	1 36W	+0003	+0003	+0008	+0008	+0.3	+0.2	+0.1	+0.1
Blyth	55 07N	1 29W	+0005	−0007	−0001	+0009	0.0	0.0	−0.1	+0.1
Coquet Island	55 20N	1 32W	−0010	−0010	−0020	−0020	+0.1	+0.1	0.0	+0.1
Amble	55 20N	1 34W	−0013	−0013	−0016	−0020	0.0	0.0	+0.1	+0.1
North Sunderland	55 34N	1 38W	−0048	−0044	−0058	−0102	−0.2	−0.2	−0.2	0.0
Holy Island	55 40N	1 47W	−0043	−0039	−0105	−0110	−0.2	−0.2	−0.3	−0.1
Berwick	55 47N	2 00W	−0053	−0053	−0109	−0109	−0.3	−0.1	−0.5	−0.1

SCOTLAND *Time Zone UT*

Location	Lat	Long	High Water		Low Water		MHWS	MHWN	MLWN	MLWS
			0300	0900	0300	0900				
LEITH	55 59N	3 11W	and	and	and	and	5.6	4.4	2.0	0.8
standard port			1500	2100	1500	2100				
Eyemouth	55 52N	2 05W	−0003	+0008	+0011	+0005	−0.5	−0.4	−0.1	0.0
Dunbar	56 00N	2 31W	−0003	+0003	+0003	−0003	−0.3	−0.3	0.0	+0.1
Fidra	56 04N	2 47W	−0001	0000	−0002	+0001	−0.2	−0.2	0.0	0.0

Location	Lat	Long	High Water		Low Water		MHWS	MHWN	MLWN	MLWS
Cockenzie	55 58N	2 57W	−0007	−0015	−0013	−0005	−0.2	0.0	no data	
Granton	55 59N	3 13W	0000	0000	0000	0000	0.0	0.0	0.0	0.0
Grangemouth	56 02N	3 41W	+0025	+0010	−0052	−0015	−0.1	−0.2	−0.3	−0.3
Kincardine	56 04N	3 43W	+0015	+0030	−0030	−0030	0.0	−0.2	−0.5	−0.3
Alloa	56 07N	3 48W	+0040	+0040	+0025	+0025	−0.2	−0.5	no data	−0.7
Stirling	56 07N	3 56W	+0100	+0100	no data		−2.9	−3.1	−2.3	−0.7
Firth of Forth										
Burntisland	56 03N	3 14W	+0013	+0004	−0002	+0007	+0.1	0.0	+0.1	+0.2
Kirkcaldy	56 09N	3 09W	+0005	0000	−0004	−0001	−0.3	−0.3	−0.2	−0.2
Methil	56 11N	3 00W	−0005	−0001	−0001	−0001	−0.1	−0.1	−0.1	−0.1
Anstruther Easter	56 13N	2 42W	−0018	−0012	−0006	−0008	−0.3	−0.2	0.0	0.0
ABERDEEN	57 09N	2 05W	0000 and 1200	0600 and 1800	0100 and 1300	0700 and 1900	4.3	3.4	1.6	0.6
standard port										
River Tay										
Bar	56 27N	2 38W	+0100	+0100	+0050	+0110	+0.9	+0.8	+0.3	+0.1
Dundee	56 27N	2 58W	+0140	+0120	+0055	+0145	+1.1	+0.9	+0.3	+0.1
Newburgh	56 21N	3 14W	+0215	+0200	+0250	+0335	−0.2	−0.4	−1.1	−0.5
Perth	56 24N	3 27W	+0220	+0225	+0510	+0530	−0.9	−1.4	−1.2	−0.3
Arbroath	56 33N	2 35W	+0056	+0037	+0034	+0055	+0.7	+0.7	+0.2	+0.1
Montrose	56 42N	2 27W	+0055	+0055	+0030	+0040	+0.5	+0.4	+0.2	0.0
Stonehaven	56 58N	2 12W	+0013	+0008	+0013	+0009	+0.2	+0.2	+0.1	0.0
Peterhead	57 30N	1 46W	−0035	−0045	−0035	−0040	−0.5	−0.3	−0.1	−0.1
Fraserburgh	57 41N	2 00W	−0105	−0115	−0120	−0110	−0.6	−0.5	−0.2	0.0
ABERDEEN	57 09N	2 05W	0200 and 1400	0900 and 2100	0400 and 1600	0900 and 2100	4.3	3.4	1.6	0.6
standard port										
Banff	57 40N	2 31W	−0100	−0150	−0150	−0050	−0.4	−0.2	−0.1	+0.2
Whitehills	57 41N	2 35W	−0122	−0137	−0117	−0127	−0.4	−0.3	+0.1	+0.1
Buckie	57 40N	2 58W	−0130	−0145	−0125	−0140	−0.2	−0.2	0.0	+0.1
Lossiemouth	57 43N	3 18W	−0125	−0200	−0130	−0130	−0.2	−0.2	0.0	0.0
Burghead	57 42N	3 29W	−0120	−0150	−0135	−0120	−0.2	−0.2	0.0	0.0
Nairn	57 36N	3 52W	−0120	−0150	−0135	−0130	0.0	−0.1	0.0	+0.1
McDermott Base	57 36N	3 59W	−0110	−0140	−0120	−0115	−0.1	−0.1	+0.1	+0.3
ABERDEEN	57 09N	2 05W	0300 and 1500	1000 and 2200	0000 and 1200	0700 and 1900	4.3	3.4	1.6	0.6
standard port										
Inverness Firth										
Fortrose	57 35N	4 08W	−0125	−0125	−0125	−0125	0.0	0.0	no data	
Inverness	57 30N	4 15W	−0050	−0150	−0200	−0150	+0.5	+0.3	+0.2	+0.1
Cromarty Firth										
Cromarty	57 42N	4 03W	−0120	−0155	−0155	−0120	0.0	0.0	+0.1	+0.2
Invergordon	57 41N	4 10W	−0105	−0200	−0200	−0110	+0.1	+0.1	+0.1	+0.1
Dingwall	57 36N	4 25W	−0045	−0145	no data	no data	+0.1	+0.2	no data	
ABERDEEN	57 09N	2 05W	0300 and 1500	0800 and 2000	0200 and 1400	0800 and 2000	4.3	3.4	1.6	0.6
standard port										
Dornoch Firth										
Portmahomack	57 50N	3 50W	−0120	−0210	−0140	−0110	−0.2	−0.1	+0.1	+0.1
Meikle Ferry	57 51N	4 08W	−0100	−0140	−0120	−0055	+0.1	0.0	−0.1	0.0
Golspie	57 58N	3 59W	−0130	−0215	−0155	−0130	−0.3	−0.3	−0.1	0.0
WICK	58 26N	3 05W	0000 and 1200	0700 and 1900	0200 and 1400	0700 and 1900	3.5	2.8	1.4	0.7
standard port										
Helmsdale	58 07N	3 39W	+0025	+0015	+0035	+0030	+0.4	+0.3	+0.1	0.0
Duncansby Head	58 39N	3 02W	−0115	−0115	−0110	−0110	−0.4	−0.4	no data	
Orkney Islands										
Muckle Skerry	58 41N	2 55W	−0025	−0025	−0020	−0020	−0.9	−0.8	−0.4	−0.3
Burray Ness	58 51N	2 52W	+0005	+0005	+0015	+0015	−0.2	−0.3	−0.1	−0.1
Deer Sound	58 58N	2 50W	−0040	−0040	−0035	−0035	−0.3	−0.3	−0.1	−0.1
Kirkwall	58 59N	2 58W	−0042	−0042	−0041	−0041	−0.5	−0.4	−0.1	−0.1
Loth	59 12N	2 42W	−0052	−0052	−0058	−0058	−0.1	0.0	+0.3	+0.4
Kettletoft Pier	59 14N	2 36W	−0025	−0025	−0015	−0015	0.0	0.0	+0.2	+0.2
Rapness	59 15N	2 52W	−0205	−0205	−0205	−0205	+0.1	0.0	+0.2	0.0
Pierowall	59 19N	2 58W	−0150	−0150	−0145	−0145	+0.2	0.0	0.0	−0.1
Tingwall	59 05N	3 02W	−0200	−0125	−0145	−0125	−0.4	−0.4	−0.1	−0.1

Location	Lat	Long	High Water		Low Water		MHWS	MHWN	MLWN	MLWS
Stromness	58 58N	3 18W	−0225	−0135	−0205	−0205	+0.1	−0.1	0.0	0.0
St Mary's	58 54N	2 55W	−0140	−0140	−0140	−0140	−0.2	−0.2	0.0	−0.1
Widewall Bay	58 49N	3 01W	−0155	−0155	−0150	−0150	+0.1	−0.1	−0.1	−0.3
Bur Wick	58 44N	2 58W	−0100	−0100	−0150	−0150	−0.1	−0.1	+0.2	+0.1
LERWICK	60 09N	1 08W	0000 and 1200	0600 and 1800	0100 and 1300	0800 and 2000	2.1	1.7	0.9	0.5
standard port										
Fair Isle	59 32N	1 36W	−0006	−0015	−0031	−0037	+0.1	0.0	+0.1	+0.1
Shetland Islands										
Sumburgh *Grutness Voe*	59 53N	1 17W	+0006	+0008	+0004	−0002	−0.3	−0.3	−0.2	−0.1
Dury Voe	60 21N	1 10W	−0015	−0015	−0010	−0010	0.0	−0.1	0.0	−0.2
Out Skerries	60 25N	0 45W	−0025	−0025	−0010	−0010	+0.1	0.0	0.0	−0.1
Toft Pier	60 28N	1 12W	−0105	−0100	−0125	−0115	+0.2	+0.1	−0.1	−0.1
Burra Voe *Yell Sound*	60 30N	1 03W	−0025	−0025	−0025	−0025	+0.2	+0.1	0.0	−0.1
Mid Yell	60 36N	1 03W	−0030	−0020	−0035	−0025	+0.3	+0.2	+0.2	+0.1
Balta Sound	60 45N	0 50W	−0055	−0055	−0045	−0045	+0.2	+0.1	0.0	−0.1
Burra Firth	60 48N	0 52W	−0110	−0110	−0115	−0115	+0.4	+0.2	0.0	0.0
Bluemull Sound	60 42N	1 00W	−0135	−0135	−0155	−0155	+0.5	+0.2	+0.1	0.0
Sullom Voe	60 27N	1 18W	−0135	−0125	−0135	−0120	0.0	0.0	−0.2	−0.2
Hillswick	60 29N	1 29W	−0220	−0220	−0200	−0200	−0.1	−0.1	−0.1	−0.1
Scalloway	60 08N	1 16W	−0150	−0150	−0150	−0150	−0.5	−0.4	−0.3	0.0
Bay of Quendale	59 54N	1 20W	−0025	−0025	−0030	−0030	−0.4	−0.3	0.0	+0.1
Foula	60 07N	2 03W	−0140	−0130	−0140	−0120	−0.1	−0.1	0.0	0.0
WICK	58 26N	3 05W	0200 and 1400	0700 and 1900	0100 and 1300	0700 and 1900	3.5	2.8	1.4	0.7
Standard port										
Stroma	58 40N	3 08W	−0115	−0115	−0110	−0110	−0.4	−0.5	−0.1	−0.2
Gills Bay	58 38N	3 10W	−0150	−0150	−0202	−0202	+0.7	+0.7	+0.6	+0.3
Scrabster	58 37N	3 33W	−0255	−0225	−0240	−0230	+1.5	+1.2	+0.8	+0.3
Sule Skerry	59 05N	4 24W	−0320	−0255	−0315	−0250	+0.4	+0.3	+0.2	+0.1
Loch Eriboll *Portnancon*	58 30N	4 42W	−0340	−0255	−0315	−0255	+1.6	+1.3	+0.8	+0.4
Kyle of Durness	58 36N	4 47W	−0350	−0350	−0315	−0315	+1.1	+0.7	+0.4	−0.1
Rona	59 08N	5 49W	−0410	−0345	−0330	−0340	−0.1	−0.2	−0.2	−0.1
STORNOWAY	58 12N	6 23W	0100 and 1300	0700 and 1900	0300 and 1500	0900 and 2100	4.8	3.7	2.0	0.7
standard port										
Outer Hebrides										
Loch Shell	58 00N	6 25W	−0013	0000	0000	−0017	0.0	−0.1	−0.1	0.0
E. Loch Tarbert	57 54N	6 48W	−0025	−0010	−0010	−0020	+0.2	0.0	+0.1	+0.1
Loch Maddy	57 36N	7 06W	−0044	−0014	−0016	−0030	0.0	−0.1	−0.1	0.0
Loch Carnan	57 22N	7 16W	−0050	−0010	−0020	−0040	−0.3	−0.5	−0.1	−0.1
Loch Skiport	57 20N	7 16W	−0100	−0025	−0024	−0024	−0.2	−0.4	−0.3	−0.2
Loch Boisdale	57 09N	7 16W	−0055	−0030	−0020	−0040	−0.7	−0.7	−0.3	−0.2
Barra *North Bay*	57 00N	7 24W	−0103	−0031	−0034	−0048	−0.6	−0.5	−0.2	−0.1
Castle Bay	56 57N	7 29W	−0115	−0040	−0045	−0100	−0.5	−0.6	−0.3	−0.1
Barra Head	56 47N	7 38W	−0115	−0040	−0045	−0055	−0.8	−0.7	−0.2	+0.1
Shillay	57 31N	7 41W	−0103	−0043	−0047	−0107	−0.6	−0.7	−0.7	−0.3
Balivanich	57 29N	7 23W	−0103	−0017	−0031	−0045	−0.7	−0.6	−0.5	−0.2
Scolpaig	57 39N	7 29W	−0033	−0033	−0040	−0040	−1.0	−0.9	−0.5	0.0
Leverburgh	57 46N	7 01W	−0025	−0025	−0015	−0025	−0.2	−0.2	−0.1	−0.1
W. Loch Tarbert	57 55N	6 55W	−0015	−0015	−0046	−0046	−1.1	−0.9	−0.5	0.0
Little Bernera	58 16N	6 52W	−0021	−0011	−0017	−0027	−0.5	−0.6	−0.4	−0.2
Carloway	58 17N	6 47W	−0040	+0020	−0035	−0015	−0.6	−0.5	−0.4	−0.1
St Kilda Village Bay	57 48N	8 34W	−0040	−0040	−0045	−0045	−1.4	−1.2	−0.8	−0.3
Flannan Isles	58 16N	7 36W	−0026	−0016	−0016	−0026	−0.9	−0.7	−0.6	−0.2
Rockall	57 36N	13 41W	−0055	−0055	−0105	−0105	−1.8	−1.5	−0.9	−0.2
ULLAPOOL	57 54N	5 10W	0000 and 1200	0600 and 1800	0300 and 1500	0900 and 2100	5.2	3.9	2.1	0.7
standard port										
Loch Bervie	58 27N	5 03W	+0030	+0010	+0010	+0020	−0.3	−0.3	−0.2	0.0
Loch Laxford	58 24N	5 05W	+0015	+0015	+0005	+0005	−0.3	−0.4	−0.2	0.0
Eddrachillis Bay										
Badcall Bay	58 19N	5 08W	+0005	+0005	+0005	+0005	−0.7	−0.5	−0.5	+0.2
Loch Nedd	58 14N	5 10W	0000	0000	0000	0000	−0.3	−0.2	−0.2	0.0
Loch Inver	58 09N	5 18W	−0005	−0005	−0005	−0005	−0.2	0.0	0.0	+0.1
Summer Isles Tanera Mor	58 01N	5 24W	−0005	−0005	−0010	−0010	−0.1	+0.1	0.0	+0.1

Location	Lat	Long	High Water		Low Water		MHWS	MHWN	MLWN	MLWS
Loch Ewe Mellon Charles	57 51N	5 38W	−0010	−0010	−0010	−0010	−0.1	−0.1	−0.1	0.0
Loch Gairloch Gairloch	57 43N	5 41W	−0020	−0020	−0010	−0010	0.0	+0.1	−0.3	−0.1
Loch Torridon Shieldaig	57 31N	5 39W	−0020	−0020	−0015	−0015	+0.4	+0.3	+0.1	0.0
Inner Sound Applecross	57 26N	5 49W	−0010	−0015	−0010	−0010	0.0	0.0	0.0	+0.1
Loch Carron Plockton	57 20N	5 39W	+0005	−0025	−0005	−0010	+0.5	+0.5	+0.5	+0.2
Rona Loch a' Bhraige	57 35N	5 58W	−0020	0000	−0010	0000	−0.1	−0.1	−0.1	−0.2
Skye										
Broadford Bay	57 15N	5 54W	−0015	−0015	−0010	−0015	+0.2	+0.1	+0.1	0.0
Portree	57 24N	6 11W	−0025	−0025	−0025	−0025	+0.1	−0.2	−0.2	0.0
Loch Snizort (Uig Bay)	57 35N	6 22W	−0045	−0020	−0005	−0025	+0.1	−0.4	−0.2	0.0
Loch Dunvegan	57 27N	6 38W	−0105	−0030	−0020	−0040	0.0	−0.1	0.0	0.0
Loch Harport	57 20N	6 25W	−0115	−0035	−0020	−0100	−0.1	−0.1	0.0	+0.1
Soay Camus nan Gall	57 09N	6 13W	−0055	−0025	−0025	−0045	−0.4	−0.2	no data	
Loch Alsh										
Kyle of Lochalsh	57 17N	5 43W	−0040	−0020	−0005	−0025	+0.1	0.0	0.0	−0.1
Dornie Bridge	57 17N	5 31W	−0040	−0010	−0005	−0020	+0.1	−0.1	0.0	0.0
Kyle Rhea Glenelg Bay	57 13N	5 38W	−0105	−0035	−0035	−0055	−0.4	−0.4	−0.9	−0.1
Loch Hourn	57 06N	5 34W	−0125	−0050	−0040	−0110	−0.2	−0.1	−0.1	+0.1

Location	Lat	Long	High Water		Low Water		MHWS	MHWN	MLWN	MLWS
OBAN	56 25N	5 29W	0000 and 1200	0600 and 1800	0100 and 1300	0700 and 1900	4.0	2.9	1.8	0.7
standard port										
Loch Nevis										
Inverie Bay	57 02N	5 41W	+0030	+0020	+0035	+0020	+1.0	+0.9	+0.2	0.0
Mallaig	57 00N	5 50W	+0017	+0017	+0017	+0017	+1.0	+0.7	+0.3	+0.1
Eigg Bay of Laig	56 55N	6 10W	+0015	+0030	+0040	+0005	+0.7	+0.6	− 0.2	− 0.2
Loch Moidart	56 47N	5 53W	+0015	+0015	+0040	+0020	+0.8	+0.6	− 0.2	−0.2
Coll Loch Eatharna	56 37N	6 31W	+0025	+0010	+0015	+0025	+0.4	+0.3	no data	
Tiree Gott Bay	56 31N	6 48W	0000	+0010	+0005	+0010	0.0	+0.1	0.0	0.0

Location	Lat	Long	High Water		Low Water		MHWS	MHWN	MLWN	MLWS
OBAN	56 25N	5 29W	0100 and 1300	0700 and 1900	0100 and 1300	0800 and 2000	4.0	2.9	1.8	0.7
standard port										
Mull										
Carsaig Bay	56 19N	5 59W	−0015	−0005	−0030	+0020	+0.1	+0.2	0.0	−0.1
Iona	56 19N	6 23W	−0010	−0005	−0020	+0015	0.0	+0.1	−0.3	−0.2
Bunessan	56 19N	6 14W	−0015	−0015	−0010	−0015	+0.3	+0.1	0.0	−0.1
Ulva Sound	56 29N	6 08W	−0010	−0015	0000	−0005	+0.4	+0.3	0.0	−0.1
Loch Sunart Salen	56 42N	5 47W	−0015	+0015	+0010	+0005	+0.6	+0.5	−0.1	−0.1
Sound of Mull										
Tobermory	56 37N	6 04W	+0025	+0010	+0015	+0025	+0.4	+0.4	0.0	0.0
Salen	56 31N	5 57W	+0045	+0015	+0020	+0030	+0.2	+0.2	−0.1	0.0
Loch Aline	56 32N	5 46W	+0012	+0012	no data	no data	+0.5	+0.3	no data	
Craignure	56 28N	5 42W	+0030	+0005	+0010	+0015	0.0	+0.1	−0.1	−0.1
Loch Linnhe										
Corran	56 43N	5 14W	+0007	+0007	+0004	+0004	+0.4	+0.4	−0.1	0.0
Corpach	56 50N	5 07W	0000	+0020	+0040	0000	0.0	0.0	−0.2	−0.2
Loch Eil Head	56 51N	5 20W	+0025	+0045	+0105	+0025	no data		no data	
Loch Leven Head	56 43N	5 00W	+0045	+0045	+0045	+0045	no data		no data	
Loch Linnhe Port Appin	56 33N	5 25W	−0005	−0005	−0030	0000	+0.2	+0.2	+0.1	+0.1
Loch Creran										
Barcaldine Pier	56 32N	5 19W	+0010	+0020	+0040	+0015	+0.1	+0.1	0.0	+0.1
Loch Creran Head	56 33N	5 16W	+0015	+0025	+0120	+0020	−0.3	−0.3	−0.4	−0.3
Loch Etive										
Dunstaffnage Bay	56 27N	5 26W	+0005	0000	0000	+0005	+0.1	+0.1	+0.1	+0.1
Connel	56 27N	5 24W	+0020	+0005	+0010	+0015	−0.3	−0.2	−0.1	+0.1
Bonawe	56 27N	5 13W	+0150	+0205	+0240	+0210	−2.0	−1.7	−1.3	−0.5
Seil Sound	56 18N	5 35W	−0035	−0015	−0040	−0015	−1.3	−0.9	−0.7	−0.3
Colonsay Scalasaig	56 04N	6 10W	−0020	−0005	−0015	+0005	−0.1	−0.2	−0.2	−0.2
Jura Glengarrisdale Bay	56 06N	5 47W	−0020	0000	−0010	0000	−0.4	−0.2	0.0	−0.2
Islay										
Rubha A'Mhail	55 56N	6 07W	−0020	0000	+0005	−0015	−0.3	−0.1	−0.3	−0.1
Ardnave Point	55 52N	6 20W	−0035	+0010	0000	−0025	−0.4	−0.2	−0.3	−0.1
Orsay	55 41N	6 31W	−0110	−0110	−0040	−0040	−1.4	−0.6	−0.5	−0.2
Bruichladdich	55 48N	6 22W	−0105	−0035	−0110	−0110	−1.8	−1.3	−0.4	+0.1
Port Ellen	55 38N	6 11W	−0530	−0050	−0045	−0530	−3.1	−2.1	−1.3	−0.4
Port Askaig	55 51N	6 06W	−0110	−0030	−0020	−0020	−1.9	−1.4	−0.8	−0.3
Sound of Jura										
Craighouse	55 50N	5 57W	−0230	−0250	−0150	−0230	−3.0	−2.4	−1.3	−0.6
Loch Melfort	56 15N	5 29W	−0055	−0025	−0040	−0035	−1.2	−0.8	−0.5	−0.1

Location	Lat	Long	High Water		Low Water		MHWS	MHWN	MLWN	MLWS
Loch Beag	56 09N	5 36W	−0110	−0045	−0035	−0045	−1.6	−1.2	−0.8	−0.4
Carsaig Bay	56 02N	5 38W	−0105	−0040	−0050	−0050	−2.1	−1.6	−1.0	−0.4
Sound of Gigha	55 41N	5 44W	−0450	−0210	−0130	−0410	−2.5	−1.6	−1.0	−0.1
Machrihanish	55 25N	5 45W	−0520	−0350	−0340	−0540	Mean range 0.5 metres			
			0000	**0600**	**0000**	**0600**				
GREENOCK	55 57N	4 46W	and	and	and	and	**3.4**	**2.8**	**1.0**	**0.3**
standard port			**1200**	**1800**	**1200**	**1800**				
Firth of Clyde										
Southend, Kintyre	55 19N	5 38W	−0030	−0010	+0005	+0035	−1.3	−1.2	−0.5	−0.2
Campbeltown	55 25N	5 36W	−0025	−0005	−0015	+0005	−0.5	−0.3	+0.1	+0.2
Carradale	55 36N	5 28W	−0015	−0005	−0005	+0005	−0.3	−0.2	+0.1	+0.1
Loch Ranza	55 43N	5 18W	−0015	−0005	−0010	−0005	−0.4	−0.3	−0.1	0.0
Loch Fyne										
East Loch Tarbert	55 52N	5 24W	−0005	−0005	0000	−0005	+0.2	+0.1	0.0	0.0
Inveraray	56 14N	5 04W	+0011	+0011	+0034	+0034	−0.1	+0.1	−0.5	−0.2
Kyles of Bute										
Rubha a'Bhodaich	55 55N	5 09W	−0020	−0010	−0007	−0007	−0.2	−0.1	+0.2	+0.2
Tighnabruich	55 55N	5 13W	+0007	−0010	−0002	−0015	0.0	+0.2	+0.4	+0.5
Firth of Clyde – continued										
Millport	55 45N	4 56W	−0005	−0025	−0025	−0005	0.0	−0.1	0.0	+0.1
Rothesay Bay	55 51N	5 03W	−0020	−0015	−0010	−0002	+0.2	+0.2	+0.2	+0.2
Wemyss Bay	55 53N	4 53W	−0005	−0005	−0005	−0005	0.0	0.0	+0.1	+0.1
Loch Long										
Coulport	56 03N	4 53W	−0011	−0011	−0008	−0008	0.0	0.0	0.0	0.0
Lochgoilhead	56 10N	4 54W	+0015	0000	−0005	−0005	−0.2	−0.3	−0.3	−0.3
Arrochar	56 12N	4 45W	−0005	−0005	−0005	−0005	0.0	0.0	−0.1	−0.1
Gareloch										
Rosneath	56 01N	4 47W	−0005	−0005	−0005	−0005	0.0	−0.1	0.0	0.0
Faslane	56 04N	4 49W	−0010	−0010	−0010	−0010	0.0	0.0	−0.1	−0.2
Garelochhead	56 05N	4 50W	0000	0000	0000	0000	0.0	0.0	0.0	−0.1
River Clyde										
Helensburgh	56 00N	4 44W	0000	0000	0000	0000	0.0	0.0	0.0	0.0
Port Glasgow	55 56N	4 41W	+0010	+0005	+0010	+0020	+0.2	+0.1	0.0	0.0
Bowling	55 56N	4 29W	+0020	+0010	+0030	+0055	+0.6	+0.5	+0.3	+0.1
Clydebank *Rothesay Dock*	55 54N	4 24W	+0025	+0015	+0035	+0100	+1.0	+0.8	+0.5	+0.4
Glasgow	55 51N	4 16W	+0025	+0015	+0035	+0105	+1.3	+1.2	+0.6	+0.4
Firth of Clyde – continued										
Brodick Bay	55 35N	5 08W	0000	0000	+0005	+0005	−0.2	−0.2	0.0	0.0
Lamlash	55 32N	5 07W	−0016	−0036	−0024	−0004	−0.2	−0.2	no data	
Ardrossan	55 38N	4 49W	−0020	−0010	−0010	−0010	−0.2	−0.2	+0.1	+0.1
Irvine	55 36N	4 41W	−0020	−0020	−0030	−0010	−0.3	−0.3	−0.1	0.0
Troon	55 33N	4 41W	−0025	−0025	−0020	−0020	−0.2	−0.2	0.0	0.0
Ayr	55 28N	4 39W	−0025	−0025	−0030	−0015	−0.4	−0.3	+0.1	+0.1
Girvan	55 15N	4 52W	−0025	−0040	−0035	−0010	−0.3	−0.3	−0.1	0.0
Loch Ryan Stranraer	54 55N	5 03W	−0030	−0025	−0010	−0010	−0.2	−0.1	0.0	+0.1

WEST COAST ENGLAND *Time Zone UT*

Location	Lat	Long	High Water		Low Water		MHWS	MHWN	MLWN	MLWS
			0000	**0600**	**0200**	**0800**				
LIVERPOOL	53 24N	3 01W	and	and	and	and	**9.3**	**7.4**	**2.9**	**0.9**
standard port			**1200**	**1800**	**1400**	**2000**				
Portpatrick	54 50N	5 07W	+0018	+0026	0000	−0035	−5.5	−4.4	−2.0	−0.6
Luce Bay										
Drummore	54 41N	4 53W	+0030	+0040	+0015	+0020	−3.4	−2.5	−0.9	−0.3
Port William	54 46N	4 35W	+0030	+0030	+0025	0000	−2.9	−2.2	−0.8	no data
Wigtown Bay										
Isle of Whithorn	54 42N	4 22W	+0020	+0025	+0025	+0005	−2.4	−2.0	−0.8	−0.2
Garlieston	54 47N	4 22W	+0025	+0035	+0030	+0005	−2.3	−1.7	−0.5	no data
Solway Firth										
Kirkcudbright Bay	54 48N	4 04W	+0015	+0015	+0010	0000	−1.8	−1.5	−0.5	−0.1
Hestan Islet	54 50N	3 48W	+0025	+0025	+0020	+0025	−1.0	−1.1	−0.5	0.0
Southerness Point	54 52N	3 36W	+0030	+0030	+0030	+0010	−0.7	−0.7	no data	
Annan Waterfoot	54 58N	3 16W	+0050	+0105	+0220	+0310	−2.2	−2.6	−2.7	
Torduff Point	54 58N	3 09W	+0105	+0140	+0520	+0410	−4.1	−4.9		
Redkirk	54 59N	3 06W	+0110	+0215	+0715	+0445	−5.5	−6.2		
Silloth	54 52N	3 24W	+0030	+0040	+0045	+0055	−0.1	−0.3	−0.6	−0.1
Maryport	54 43N	3 30W	+0017	+0032	+0020	+0005	−0.7	−0.8	−0.4	0.0
Workington	54 39N	3 34W	+0020	+0020	+0020	+0010	−1.2	−1.1	−0.3	0.0
Whitehaven	54 33N	3 36W	+0005	+0015	+0010	+0005	−1.3	−1.1	−0.5	+0.1
Tarn Point	54 17N	3 25W	+0005	+0005	+0010	0000	−1.0	−1.0	−0.4	0.0
Duddon Bar	54 09N	3 20W	+0003	+0003	+0008	+0002	−0.8	−0.8	−0.3	0.0

Location	Lat	Long	High Water		Low Water		MHWS	MHWN	MLWN	MLWS
			0000 and 1200	0600 and 1800	0200 and 1400	0700 and 1900				
LIVERPOOL	53 24N	3 01W					9.3	7.4	2.9	0.9
standard port										
Barrow–in–Furness	54 06N	3 12W	+0015	+0015	+0015	+0015	0.0	−0.3	+0.1	+0.2
Ulverston	54 11N	3 04W	+0020	+0040	no data	no data	0.0	−0.1	no data	
Arnside	54 12N	2 51W	+0100	+0135	no data	no data	+0.5	+0.2	no data	
Morecambe	54 04N	2 52W	+0005	+0010	+0030	+0015	+0.2	0.0	0.0	+0.2
Heysham	54 02N	2 55W	+0005	+0005	+0015	0000	+0.1	0.0	0.0	+0.2
River Lune Glasson Dock	54 00N	2 51W	+0020	+0030	+0220	+0240	−2.7	−3.0	no data	
Lancaster	54 03N	2 49W	+0110	+0030	dries	dries	−5.0	−4.9	dries	
River Wyre										
Wyre Lighthouse	53 57N	3 02W	−0010	−0010	+0005	0000	−0.1	−0.1	no data	
Fleetwood	53 56N	3 00W	−0008	−0008	−0003	−0003	−0.1	−0.1	+0.1	+0.3
Blackpool	53 49N	3 04W	−0015	−0005	−0005	−0015	−0.4	−0.4	−0.1	+0.1
River Ribble Preston	53 46N	2 45W	+0010	+0010	+0335	+0310	−4.0	−4.1	−2.8	−0.8
Liverpool Bay										
Southport	53 39N	3 01W	−0020	−0010	no data	no data	−0.3	−0.3	no data	
Formby	53 32N	3 07W	−0015	−0010	−0020	−0020	−0.3	−0.1	0.0	+0.1
River Mersey										
Gladstone Dock	53 27N	3 01W	−0003	−0003	−0003	−0003	−0.1	−0.1	0.0	−0.1
Eastham	53 19N	2 57W	+0010	+0010	+0009	+0009	+0.3	+0.1	−0.1	−0.3
Hale Head	53 19N	2 48W	+0030	+0025	no data	no data	−2.4	−2.5	no data	
Widnes	53 21N	2 44W	+0040	+0045	+0400	+0345	−4.2	−4.4	−2.5	−0.3
Fiddler's Ferry	53 22N	2 39W	+0100	+0115	+0540	+0450	−5.9	−6.3	−2.4	−0.4
River Dee										
Hilbre Island	53 23N	3 13W	−0015	−0012	−0010	−0015	−0.3	−0.2	+0.2	+0.4
Mostyn Docks	53 19N	3 16W	−0020	−0015	−0020	−0020	−0.8	−0.7	no data	
Connah's Quay	53 13N	3 03W	0000	+0015	+0355	+0340	−4.6	−4.4	dries	
Chester	53 12N	2 54W	+0105	+0105	+0500	+0500	−5.3	−5.4	dries	
Isle of Man										
Peel	54 14N	4 42W	+0005	+0005	−0015	−0025	−4.1	−3.1	−1.4	−0.5
Ramsey	54 19N	4 22W	+0005	+0015	−0005	−0015	−1.9	−1.5	−0.6	0.0
Douglas	54 09N	4 28W	+0005	+0015	−0015	−0025	−2.4	−2.0	−0.5	−0.1
Port St Mary	54 04N	4 44W	+0005	+0015	−0010	−0030	−3.4	−2.6	−1.3	−0.4
Calf Sound	54 04N	4 48W	+0005	+0005	−0015	−0025	−3.2	−2.6	−0.9	−0.3
Port Erin	54 05N	4 46W	−0005	+0015	−0010	−0050	−4.1	−3.2	−1.3	−0.5

WALES *Time Zone UT*

Location	Lat	Long	High Water		Low Water		MHWS	MHWN	MLWN	MLWS
Colwyn Bay	53 18N	3 43W	−0020	−0020	no data	no data	−1.5	−1.3	no data	
Llandudno	53 20N	3 50W	−0020	−0020	−0035	−0040	−1.7	−1.4	−0.7	−0.3
			0000 and 1200	0600 and 1800	0500 and 1700	1100 and 2300				
HOLYHEAD	53 19N	4 37W					5.6	4.4	2.0	0.7
standard port										
Conwy	53 17N	3 50W	+0025	+0035	+0120	+0105	+2.3	+1.8	+0.6	+0.4
Menai Strait										
Beaumaris	53 16N	4 05W	+0025	+0010	+0055	+0035	+2.0	+1.6	+0.5	+0.1
Menai Bridge	53 13N	4 09W	+0030	+0010	+0100	+0035	+1.7	+1.4	+0.3	0.0
Port Dinorwic	53 11N	4 13W	−0015	−0025	+0030	0000	0.0	0.0	0.0	+0.1
Caernarfon	53 09N	4 16W	−0030	−0030	+0015	−0005	−0.4	−0.4	−0.1	−0.1
Fort Belan	53 07N	4 20W	−0040	−0015	−0025	−0005	−1.0	−0.9	−0.2	−0.1
Trwyn Dinmor	53 19N	4 03W	+0025	+0015	+0050	+0035	+1.9	+1.5	+0.5	+0.2
Moelfre	53 20N	4 14W	+0025	+0020	+0050	+0035	+1.9	+1.4	+0.5	+0.2
Amlwch	53 25N	4 20W	+0020	+0010	+0035	+0025	+1.6	+ 1.3	+0.5	+0.2
Cemaes Bay	53 25N	4 27W	+0020	+0025	+0040	+0035	+1.0	+0.7	+0.3	+0.1
Trearddur Bay	53 16N	4 37W	−0045	−0025	−0015	−0015	−0.4	−0.4	0.0	+0.1
Porth Trecastell	53 12N	4 30W	−0045	−0025	−0005	−0015	−0.6	−0.6	0.0	0.0
Llanddwyn Island	53 08N	4 25W	−0115	−0055	−0030	−0020	−0.7	−0.5	−0.1	0.0
Trefor	53 00N	4 25W	−0115	−0100	−0030	−0020	−0.8	−0.9	−0.2	−0.1
Porth Dinllaen	52 57N	4 34W	−0120	−0105	−0035	−0025	−1.0	−1.0	−0.2	−0.2
Porth Ysgaden	52 54N	4 39W	−0125	−0110	−0040	−0035	−1.1	−1.0	−0.1	−0.1
Bardsey Island	52 46N	4 47W	−0220	−0240	−0145	−0140	−1.2	−1.2	−0.5	−0.1
			0100 and 1300	0800 and 2000	0100 and 1300	0700 and 1900				
MILFORD HAVEN	51 42N	5 03W					7.0	5.2	2.5	0.7
standard port										
Cardigan Bay										
Aberdaron	52 48N	4 43W	+0210	+0200	+0240	+0310	−2.4	−1.9	−0.6	−0.2
St Tudwal's Roads	52 49N	4 29W	+0155	+0145	+0240	+0310	−2.2	−1.9	−0.7	−0.2
Pwllheli	52 53N	4 24W	+0210	+0150	+0245	+0320	−2.0	− 1.8	−0.6	−0.2
Criccieth	52 55N	4 14W	+0210	+0155	+0255	+0320	−2.0	−1.8	−0.7	−0.3
Porthmadog	52 55N	4 08W	+0235	+0210	no data	no data	−1.9	−1.8	no data	

Location	Lat	Long	High Water		Low Water		MHWS	MHWN	MLWN	MLWS
Barmouth	52 43N	4 03W	+0215	+0205	+0310	+0320	−2.0	−1.7	−0.7	0.0
Aberdovey	52 32N	4 03W	+0215	+0200	+0230	+0305	−2.0	−1.7	−0.5	0.0
Aberystwyth	52 24N	4 05W	+0145	+0130	+0210	+0245	−2.0	−1.7	−0.7	0.0
New Quay	52 13N	4 21W	+0150	+0125	+0155	+0230	−2.1	−1.8	−0.6	−0.1
Aberporth	52 08N	4 33W	+0135	+0120	+0150	+0220	−2.1	−1.8	−0.6	−0.1
Port Cardigan	52 07N	4 42W	+0140	+0120	+0220	+0130	−2.3	−1.8	−0.5	0.0
Cardigan *Town*	52 05N	4 40W	+0220	+0150	no data	no data	−2.2	−1.6	no data	
Fishguard	52 00N	4 58W	+0115	+0100	+0110	+0135	−2.2	−1.8	−0.5	+0.1
Porthgain	51 57N	5 11W	+0055	+0045	+0045	+0100	−2.5	−1.8	−0.6	0.0
Ramsey Sound	51 53N	5 19W	+0030	+0030	+0030	+0030	−1.9	−1.3	−0.3	0.0
Solva	51 52N	5 12W	+0015	+0010	+0035	+0015	−1.5	−1.0	−0.2	0.0
Little Haven	51 46N	5 06W	+0010	+0010	+0025	+0015	−1.1	−0.8	−0.2	0.0
Martin's Haven	51 44N	5 15W	+0010	+0010	+0015	+0015	−0.8	−0.5	+0.1	+0.1
Skomer Island	51 44N	5 17W	−0005	−0005	+0005	+0005	−0.4	−0.1	0.0	0.0
Dale Roads	51 42N	5 09W	−0005	−0005	−0008	−0008	0.0	0.0	0.0	−0.1
Cleddau River										
Neyland	51 42N	4 57W	+0002	+0010	0000	0000	0.0	0.0	0.0	0.0
Black Tar	51 45N	4 54W	+0010	+0020	+0005	0000	+0.1	+0.1	0.0	−0.1
Haverfordwest	51 48N	4 58W	+0010	+0025	dries	dries	−4.8	−4.9	dries	
Stackpole Quay	51 37N	4 54W	−0005	+0025	−0010	−0010	+0.9	+0.7	+0.2	+0.3
Tenby	51 40N	4 42W	−0015	−0010	−0015	−0020	+1.4	+1.1	+0.5	+0.2
Towy River										
Ferryside	51 46N	4 22W	0000	−0010	+0220	0000	−0.3	−0.7	−1.7	−0.6
Carmarthen	51 51N	4 18W	+0010	0000	dries	dries	−4.4	−4.8	dries	
Burry Inlet										
Burry Port	51 41N	4 15W	+0003	+0003	+0007	+0007	+1.6	+1.4	+0.5	+0.4
Llanelli	51 40N	4 10W	−0003	−0003	+0150	+0020	+0.8	+0.6	no data	
Mumbles	51 34N	3 58W	+0005	+0010	−0020	−0015	+2.3	+1.7	+0.6	+0.2
River Neath Entrance	51 37N	3 51W	+0002	+0011	dries	dries	+2.7	+2.2	dries	
Port Talbot	51 35N	3 49W	+0003	+0005	−0010	−0003	+2.6	+2.2	+1.0	+0.5
Porthcawl	51 28N	3 42W	+0005	+0010	−0010	−0005	+2.9	+2.3	+0.8	+0.3
BRISTOL, AVONMOUTH *standard port*	51 30N	2 44W	0600 and 1800	1100 and 2300	0300 and 1500	0800 and 2000	13.2	9.8	3.8	1.0
Barry	51 23N	3 16W	−0030	−0015	−0125	−0030	−1.8	−1.3	+0.2	0.0
Flat Holm	51 23N	3 07W	−0015	−0015	−0045	−0045	−1.3	−1.1	−0.2	+0.2
Steep Holm	51 20N	3 06W	−0020	−0020	−0050	−0050	−1.6	−1.2	−0.2	−0.2
Cardiff	51 27N	3 09W	−0015	−0015	−0100	−0030	−1.0	−0.6	+0.1	0.0
Newport	51 33N	2 59W	−0020	−0010	0000	−0020	−1.1	−1.0	−0.6	−0.7
River Wye Chepstow	51 39N	2 40W	+0020	+0020	no data	no data	no data		no data	
BRISTOL, AVONMOUTH *standard port*	51 30N	2 44W	0000 and 1200	0600 and 1800	0000 and 1200	0700 and 1900	13.2	9.8	3.8	1.0

WEST COAST ENGLAND *Time Zone UT*

Location	Lat	Long	High Water		Low Water		MHWS	MHWN	MLWN	MLWS
River Severn										
Sudbrook	51 35N	2 43W	+0010	+0010	+0025	+0015	+0.2	+0.1	−0.1	+0.1
Beachley *Aust*	51 36N	2 38W	+0010	+0015	+0040	+0025	−0.2	−0.2	−0.5	−0.3
Inward Rocks	51 39N	2 37W	+0020	+0020	+0105	+0045	−1.0	−1.1	−1.4	−0.6
Narlwood Rocks	51 39N	2 36W	+0025	+0025	+0120	+0100	−1.9	−2.0	−2.3	−0.8
White House	51 40N	2 33W	+0025	+0025	+0145	+0120	−3.0	−3.1	−3.6	−1.0
Berkeley	51 42N	2 30W	+0030	+0045	+0245	+0220	−3.8	−3.9	−3.4	−0.5
Sharpness Dock	51 43N	2 29W	+0035	+0050	+0305	+0245	−3.9	−4.2	−3.3	−0.4
Wellhouse Rock	51 44N	2 29W	+0040	+0055	+0320	+0305	−4.1	−4.4	−3.1	−0.2
Epney	51 42N	2 24W	+0130	no data	no data	no data	−9.4	no data	no data	
Minsterworth	51 50N	2 23W	+0140	no data	no data	no data	−10.1	no data	no data	
Llanthony	51 51N	2 21W	+0215	no data	no data	no data	−10.7	no data	no data	
BRISTOL, AVONMOUTH *standard port*	51 30N	2 44W	0200 and 1400	0800 and 2000	0300 and 1500	0800 and 2000	13.2	9.8	3.8	1.0
River Avon										
Shirehampton	51 29N	2 41W	0000	0000	+0035	+0010	−0.7	−0.7	−0.8	0.0
Sea Mills	51 29N	2 39W	+0005	+0005	+0105	+0030	−1.4	−1.5	−1.7	−0.1
Cumberland Basin *Entrance*	51 27N	2 37W	+0010	+0010	dries	dries	−2.9	−3.0	dries	
Portishead	51 30N	2 45W	−0002	0000	no data	no data	−0.1	−0.1	no data	
Clevedon	51 27N	2 52W	−0010	−0020	−0025	−0015	−0.4	−0.2	+0.2	0.0
St Thomas Head	51 24N	2 56W	0000	0000	−0030	−0030	−0.4	−0.2	+0.1	+0.1
English & Welsh Grounds	51 28N	2 59W	−0008	−0008	−0030	−0030	−0.5	−0.8	−0.3	0.0
Weston–super–Mare	51 21N	2 59W	−0020	−0030	−0130	−0030	−1.2	−1.0	−0.8	−0.2
River Parrett										
Burnham-on-Sea	51 14N	3 00W	−0020	−0025	−0030	0000	−2.3	−1.9	−1.4	−1.1
Bridgwater	51 08N	3 00W	−0015	−0030	+0305	+0455	−8.6	−8.1	dries	

Location	Lat	Long	High Water		Low Water		MHWS	MHWN	MLWN	MLWS
Hinkley Point	51 13N	3 08W	−0020	−0025	−0100	−0040	−1.7	−1.4	−0.2	−0.2
Watchet	51 11N	3 20W	−0035	−0050	−0145	−0040	−1.9	−1.5	+0.1	+0.1
Minehead	51 13N	3 28W	−0037	−0052	−0155	−0045	−2.6	−1.9	−0.2	0.0
Porlock Bay	51 13N	3 38W	−0045	−0055	−0205	−0050	−3.0	−2.2	−0.1	−0.1
Lynmouth	51 14N	3 49W	−0055	−0115	no data	no data	−3.6	−2.7	no data	

Location	Lat	Long	High Water		Low Water		MHWS	MHWN	MLWN	MLWS
			0100	0700	0100	0700				
MILFORD HAVEN	51 42N	5 03W	and	and	and	and	7.0	5.2	2.5	0.7
standard port			1300	1900	1300	1900				
Ilfracombe	51 13N	4 07W	−0016	−0016	−0041	−0031	+2.3	+1.8	+0.6	+0.3
Rivers Taw & Torridge										
Appledore	51 03N	4 12W	−0020	−0025	+0015	−0045	+0.5	0.0	−0.9	−0.5
Yelland Marsh	51 04N	4 10W	−0010	−0015	+0100	−0015	+0.1	−0.4	−1.2	−0.6
Fremington	51 05N	4 07W	−0010	−0015	+0030	−0030	−1.1	−1.8	−2.2	−0.5
Barnstaple	51 05N	4 04W	0000	−0015	−0155	−0245	−2.9	−3.8	−2.2	−0.4
Bideford	51 01N	4 12W	−0020	−0025	0000	0000	−1.1	−1.6	−2.5	−0.7
Clovelly	51 00N	4 24W	−0030	−0030	−0020	−0040	+1.3	+1.1	+0.2	+0.2
Lundy	51 10N	4 40W	−0025	−0025	−0020	−0035	+1.0	+0.7	+0.2	0.0
Bude	50 50N	4 33W	−0040	−0040	−0035	−0045	+0.7	+0.6	no data	
Boscastle	50 41N	4 42W	−0045	−0010	−0110	−0100	+0.3	+0.4	+0.2	+0.2
Port Isaac	50 35N	4 50W	−0100	−0100	−0100	−0100	+0.5	+0.6	0.0	+0.2
River Camel										
Padstow	50 33N	4 56W	−0055	−0050	−0040	−0050	+0.3	+0.4	+0.1	+0.1
Wadebridge	50 31N	4 50W	−0052	−0052	+0235	+0245	−3.8	−3.8	−2.5	−0.4
Newquay	50 25N	5 05W	−0100	−0110	−0105	−0050	0.0	+0.1	0.0	−0.1
Perranporth	50 21N	5 09W	−0100	−0110	−0110	−0050	−0.1	0.0	0.0	+0.1
St Ives	50 13N	5 28W	−0050	−0115	−0105	−0040	−0.4	−0.3	−0.1	+0.1
Cape Cornwall	50 08N	5 42 W	−0130	−0145	−0120	−0120	−1.0	−0.9	−0.5	−0.1
Sennen Cove	50 04N	5 42W	−0130	−0145	−0125	−0125	−0.9	−0.4	no data	

IRELAND *Time Zone UT*

Location	Lat	Long	High Water		Low Water		MHWS	MHWN	MLWN	MLWS
			0000	0700	0000	0500				
DUBLIN, NORTH WALL	53 21N	6 13W	and	and	and	and	4.1	3.4	1.5	0.7
standard port			1200	1900	1200	1700				
Courtown	52 39N	6 13W	−0328	−0242	−0158	−0138	−2.8	−2.4	−0.5	0.0
Arklow	52 47N	6 08W	−0315	−0201	−0140	−0134	−2.7	−2.2	−0.6	−0.1
Wicklow	52 59N	6 02W	−0019	−0019	−0024	−0026	−1.4	−1.1	−0.4	0.0
Greystones	53 09N	6 04W	−0008	−0008	−0008	−0008	−0.5	−0.4	no data	
Dun Laoghaire	53 18N	6 08W	−0006	−0001	−0002	−0003	0.0	0.0	0.0	+0.1
Dublin Bar	53 21N	6 09W	−0006	−0001	−0002	−0003	0.0	0.0	0.0	+0.1
Howth	53 23N	6 04W	−0007	−0005	+0001	+0005	0.0	−0.1	−0.2	−0.2
Malahide	53 27N	6 09W	+0002	+0003	+0009	+0009	+0.1	−0.2	−0.4	−0.2
Balbriggan	53 37N	6 11W	−0021	−0015	+0010	+0002	+0.3	+0.2	no data	
River Boyne Bar	53 43N	6 14W	−0005	0000	+0020	+0030	+0.4	+0.3	−0.1	−0.2
Dunany Point	53 52N	6 14W	−0028	−0018	−0008	−0006	+0.7	+0.9	no data	
Dundalk Soldiers Point	54 00N	6 21W	−0010	−0010	0000	+0045	+1.0	+0.8	+0.1	−0.1

NORTHERN IRELAND *Time Zone UT*

Location	Lat	Long	High Water		Low Water		MHWS	MHWN	MLWN	MLWS
Carlingford Lough										
Cranfield Point	54 01N	6 03W	−0027	−0011	+0005	−0010	+0.7	+0.9	+0.3	+0.2
Warrenpoint	54 06N	6 15W	−0020	−0010	+0025	+0035	+1.0	+0.7	+0.2	+0.0
Newry *Victoria Lock*	54 09N	6 19W	+0005	+0015	+0045	dries	+1.2	+0.9	+0.1	dries

Location	Lat	Long	High Water		Low Water		MHWS	MHWN	MLWN	MLWS
			0100	0700	0000	0600				
BELFAST	54 36N	5 55W	and	and	and	and	3.5	3.0	1.1	0.4
standard port			1300	1900	1200	1800				
Kilkeel	54 03N	5 59W	+0040	+0030	+0010	+0010	+1.2	+1.1	+0.4	+0.4
Newcastle	54 12N	5 53W	+0025	+0035	+0020	+0040	+1.6	+1.1	+0.4	+0.1
Killough Harbour	54 15N	5 38W	0000	+0020	no data	no data	+1.8	+1.6	no data	
Ardglass	54 16N	5 36W	+0010	+0015	+0005	+0010	+1.7	+1.2	+0.6	+0.3
Strangford Lough										
Killard Point	54 19N	5 31W	+0011	+0021	+0005	+0025	+1.0	+0.8	+0.1	+0.1
Strangford	54 22N	5 33W	+0147	+0157	+0148	+0208	+0.1	+0.1	−0.2	0.0
Quoile Barrier	54 22N	5 41W	+0150	+0200	+0150	+0300	+0.2	+0.2	−0.3	−0.1
Killyleagh	54 24N	5 39W	+0157	+0207	+0211	+0231	+0.3	+0.3	no data	
South Rock	54 24N	5 25W	+0023	+0023	+0025	+0025	+1.0	+0.8	+0.1	+0.1
Portavogie	54 28N	5 26W	+0010	+0020	+0010	+0020	+1.2	+0.9	+0.3	+0.2
Donaghadee	54 38N	5 32W	+0020	+0020	+0023	+0023	+0.5	+0.4	0.0	+0.1
Carrickfergus	54 43N	5 48W	+0005	+0005	+0005	+0005	−0.3	−0.3	−0.2	−0.1
Larne	54 51N	5 47W	+0005	0000	+0010	−0005	−0.7	−0.5	−0.3	0.0
Red Bay	55 04N	6 03W	+0022	−0010	+0007	−0017	−1.9	−1.5	−0.8	−0.2
Cushendun	55 08N	6 02W	+0010	−0030	0000	−0025	−1.7	−1.5	−0.6	−0.2
Portrush	55 12N	6 40W	−0433	−0433	−0433	−0433	−1.6	−1.6	−0.3	0.0
Coleraine	55 08N	6 40W	−0403	−0403	−0403	−0403	−1.3	−1.2	−0.2	0.0

TIDES

Location	Lat	Long	High Water		Low Water		MHWS	MHWN	MLWN	MLWS
			0200	0900	0200	0800				
GALWAY	53 16N	9 03W	and	and	and	and	5.1	3.9	2.0	0.6
standard port			1400	2100	1400	2000				
Londonderry	55 00N	7 19W	+0254	+0319	+0322	+0321	−2.4	−1.8	−0.8	−0.1

IRELAND *Time Zone UT*

Location	Lat	Long	High Water		Low Water		MHWS	MHWN	MLWN	MLWS
Inishtrahull	55 26N	7 14W	+0100	+0100	+0115	+0200	−1.8	−1.4	−0.4	−0.2
Portmore	55 22N	7 20W	+0120	+0120	+0135	+0135	−1.3	−1.1	−0.4	−0.1
Trawbreaga Bay	55 19N	7 23W	+0115	+0059	+0109	+0125	−1.1	−0.8	*no data*	
Lough Swilly										
Rathmullan	55 05N	7 31W	+0125	+0050	+0126	+0118	−0.8	−0.7	−0.1	−0.1
Fanad Head	55 16N	7 38W	+0115	+0040	+0125	+0120	−1.1	−0.9	−0.5	−0.1
Mulroy Bay										
Bar	55 15N	7 46W	+0108	+0052	+0102	+0118	−1.2	−1.0	*no data*	
Fanny's Bay	55 12N	7 49W	+0145	+0129	+0151	+0207	−2.2	−1.7	*no data*	
Seamount Bay	55 11N	7 44W	+0210	+0154	+0226	+0242	−3.1	−2.3	*no data*	
Cranford Bay	55 09N	7 42W	+0329	+0313	+0351	+0407	−3.7	−2.8	*no data*	
Sheephaven										
Downies Bay	55 11N	7 50W	+0057	+0043	+0053	+0107	−1.1	−0.9	*no data*	
Inishbofin Bay	55 10N	8 10W	+0040	+0026	+0032	+0046	−1.2	−0.9	*no data*	

Location	Lat	Long	High Water		Low Water		MHWS	MHWN	MLWN	MLWS
			0600	1100	0000	0700				
GALWAY	53 16N	9 03W	and	and	and	and	5.1	3.9	2.0	0.6
standard port			1800	2300	1200	1900				
Gweedore Harbour	55 04N	8 19W	+0048	+0100	+0055	+0107	−1.3	−1.0	−0.5	−0.1
Burtonport	54 59N	8 26W	+0042	+0055	+0115	+0055	−1.2	−1.0	−0.6	−0.1
Loughros More Bay	54 47N	8 30W	+0042	+0054	+0046	+0058	−1.1	−0.9	*no data*	
Donegal Bay										
Killybegs	54 38N	8 26W	+0040	+0050	+0055	+0035	−1.0	−0.9	−0.5	0.0
Donegal Hbr *Salt Hill Quay*	54 38N	8 13W	+0038	+0050	+0052	+0104	−1.2	−0.9	*no data*	
Mullaghmore	54 28N	8 27W	+0036	+0048	+0047	+0059	−1.4	−1.0	−0.4	−0.2
Sligo Harbour *Oyster Island*	54 18N	8 34W	+0043	+0055	+0042	+0054	−1.0	−0.9	−0.5	−0.1
Ballysadare Bay *Culleenamore*	54 16N	8 36W	+0059	+0111	+0111	+0123	−1.2	−0.9	*no data*	
Killala Bay *Inishcrone*	54 13N	9 06W	+0035	+0055	+0030	+0050	−1.3	−1.2	−0.7	−0.2
Broadhaven	54 16N	9 53W	+0040	+0050	+0040	+0050	−1.4	−1.1	−0.4	−0.1
Blacksod Bay										
Blacksod Quay	54 06N	10 03W	+0025	+0035	+0040	+0040	−1.2	−1.0	−0.6	−0.2
Bull's Mouth	54 02N	9 55W	+0101	+0057	+0109	+0105	−1.5	− 1.0	−0.6	−0.1
Clare Island	53 48N	9 57W	+0019	+0013	+0029	+0023	−1.0	−0.7	−0.4	−0.1
Westport Bay										
Inishraher	53 48N	9 38W	+0030	+0012	+0058	+0026	−0.6	−0.5	−0.3	−0.1
Killary Harbour	53 38N	9 53W	+0021	+0015	+0035	+0029	−1.0	−0.8	−0.4	−0.1
Inishbofin Bofin Harbour	53 37N	10 13W	+0013	+0009	+0021	+0017	−1.0	−0.8	−0.4	−0.1
Clifden Bay	53 29N	10 04W	+0005	+0005	+0016	+0016	−0.7	−0.5	*no data*	
Slyne Head	53 24N	10 14W	+0002	+0002	+0010	+0010	−0.7	−0.5	*no data*	
Roundstone Bay	53 23N	9 55W	+0003	+0003	+0008	+0008	−0.7	−0.5	−0.3	−0.1
Kilkieran Cove	53 20N	9 44W	+0005	+0005	+0016	+0016	−0.3	−0.2	−0.1	0.0
Aran Islands Killeany Bay	53 07N	9 39W	−0008	−0008	+0003	+0003	−0.4	−0.3	−0.2	−0.1
Liscannor	52 56N	9 23W	−0003	−0007	+0006	+0002	−0.4	−0.3	*no data*	
Seafield Point	52 48N	9 30W	−0006	−0014	+0004	−0004	−0.5	−0.4	*no data*	
Kilrush	52 38N	9 30W	−0006	+0027	+0057	−0016	−0.1	−0.2	−0.3	−0.1
Limerick Dock	52 40N	8 38W	+0135	+0141	+0141	+0219	+1.0	+0.7	−0.8	−0.2

Location	Lat	Long	High Water		Low Water		MHWS	MHWN	MLWN	MLWS
			0500	1100	0500	1100				
COBH	51 51N	8 18 W	and	and	and	and	4.1	3.2	1.3	0.4
standard port			1700	2300	1700	2300				
Tralee Bay Fenit Pier	52 16N	9 52W	−0057	−0017	−0029	−0109	+0.5	+0.2	+0.3	+0.1
Smerwick Harbour	52 12N	10 24W	−0107	−0027	−0041	−0121	−0.3	−0.4	*no data*	
Dingle Harbour	52 07N	10 15W	−0111	−0041	−0049	−0119	−0.1	0.0	+0.3	+0.4
Castlemaine Hbr										
Cromane Point	52 09N	9 54W	−0026	−0006	−0017	−0037	+0.4	+0.2	+0.4	+0.2
Valentia Harbour										
Knights Town	51 56N	10 18W	−0118	−0038	−0056	−0136	−0.6	−0.4	−0.1	0.0
Ballinskelligs Bay										
Castle	51 49N	10 16W	−0119	−0039	−0054	−0134	−0.5	−0.5	−0.1	0.0
Kenmare River										
West Cove	51 46N	10 03W	−0113	−0033	−0049	−0129	−0.6	−0.5	−0.1	0.0
Dunkerron Harbour	51 52N	9 38W	−0117	−0027	−0050	−0140	−0.2	−0.3	+0.1	0.0
Coulagh Bay										
Ballycrovane Hbr	51 43N	9 57W	−0116	−0036	−0053	−0133	−0.6	−0.5	−0.1	0.0

Location	Lat	Long	High Water		Low Water		MHWS	MHWN	MLWN	MLWS
Black Ball Harbour	51 36N	10 02W	−0115	−0035	−0047	−0127	−0.7	−0.6	−0.1	+0.1
Bantry Bay										
Castletown Bearhaven	51 39N	9 54W	−0048	−0012	−0025	−0101	−0.9	−0.6	−0.1	0.0
Bantry	51 41N	9 28W	−0045	−0025	−0040	−0105	−0.9	−0.8	−0.2	0.0
Dunmanus Bay										
Dunbeacon Harbour	51 37N	9 33W	−0057	−0025	−0032	−0104	−0.8	−0.7	−0.3	−0.1
Dunmanus Harbour	51 32N	9 40W	−0107	−0031	−0044	−0120	−0.7	−0.6	−0.2	0.0
Crookhaven	51 28N	9 43W	−0057	−0033	−0048	−0112	−0.8	−0.6	−0.4	−0.1
Schull	51 31N	9 32W	−0040	−0015	−0015	−0110	−0.9	−0.6	−0.2	0.0
Baltimore	51 29N	9 23W	−0025	−0005	−0010	−0050	−0.6	−0.3	+0.1	+0.2
Castletownshend	51 32N	9 10W	−0020	−0030	−0020	−0050	−0.4	−0.2	+0.1	+0.3
Clonakilty Bay	51 35N	8 50W	−0033	−0011	−0019	−0041	−0.3	−0.2	*no data*	
Courtmacsherry	51 38N	8 42W	−0029	−0007	+0005	−0017	−0.4	−0.3	−0.2	−0.1
Kinsale	51 42N	8 31W	−0019	−0005	−0009	−0023	−0.2	0.0	+0.1	+0.2
Roberts Cove	51 45N	8 19W	−0005	−0005	−0005	−0005	−0.1	0.0	0.0	+0.1
Cork Harbour										
Ringaskiddy	51 50N	8 19W	+0005	+0020	+0007	+0013	+0.1	+0.1	+0.1	+0.1
Marino Point	51 53N	8 20W	0000	+0010	0000	+0010	+0.1	+0.1	0.0	0.0
Cork City	51 54N	8 27W	+0005	+0010	+0020	+0010	+0.4	+0.4	+0.3	+0.2
Ballycotton	51 50N	8 01W	−0011	+0001	+0003	−0009	0.0	0.0	−0.1	0.0
Youghal	51 57N	7 51W	0000	+0010	+0010	0000	−0.2	−0.1	−0.1	−0.1
Dungarvan Harbour	52 05N	7 34W	+0004	+0012	+0007	−0001	+0.1	+0.1	−0.2	0.0
Waterford Harbour										
Dunmore East	52 09N	6 59W	+0008	+0003	0000	0000	+0.1	0.0	+0.1	+0.2
Cheekpoint	52 16N	7 00W	+0022	+0020	+0020	+0020	+0.3	+0.2	+0.2	+0.1
Kilmokea Point	52 17N	7 00W	+0026	+0022	+0020	+0020	+0.2	+0.1	+0.1	+0.1
Waterford	52 16N	7 07W	+0057	+0057	+0046	+0046	+0.4	+0.3	−0.1	+0.1
New Ross	52 24N	6 57W	+0100	+0030	+0055	+0130	+0.3	+0.4	+0.3	+0.4
Baginbun Head	52 10N	6 50W	+0003	+0003	−0008	−0008	−0.2	−0.1	+0.2	+0.2
Great Saltee	52 07N	6 38W	+0019	+0009	−0004	+0006	−0.3	−0.4	*no data*	
Carnsore Point	52 10N	6 22W	+0029	+0019	−0002	+0008	−1.1	−1.0	*no data*	
Rosslare Harbour	52 15N	6 21W	+0045	+0035	+0015	−0005	−2.2	−1.8	−0.5	−0.1
Wexford Harbour	52 20N	6 27W	+0126	+0126	+0118	+0108	−2.1	−1.7	−0.3	+0.1

DENMARK *Time Zone −0100*

			0300	0700	0100	0800				
ESBJERG	55 28N	8 27E	and	and	and	and	**1.9**	**1.5**	**0.5**	**0.1**
Standard port			1500	1900	1300	2000				
Hirtshals	57 36N	9 58E	+0055	+0320	+0340	+0100	−1.6	−1.3	−0.4	−0.1
Hanstholm	57 08N	8 36E	+0100	+0340	+0340	+0130	−1.6	−1.2	−0.4	−0.1
Thyborøn	56 42N	8 13E	+0120	+0230	+0410	+0210	−1.5	−1.2	−0.4	−0.1
Torsminde	56 22N	8 07E	+0045	+0050	+0040	+0010	−1.3	−1.0	−0.4	−0.1
Hvide Sande	56 00N	8 07E	0000	+0010	−0015	−0025	−1.1	−0.8	−0.3	−0.1
Blavandshuk	55 33N	8 05E	−0120	−0110	−0050	−0100	−0.1	−0.1	−0.2	−0.1
Gradyb Bar	55 26N	8 15E	−0130	−0115	*no data*	*no data*	−0.4	−0.3	−0.2	−0.1
Rømø Havn	55 05N	8 34E	−0040	−0005	0000	−0020	0.0	+0.1	−0.2	−0.2
Hojer	54 58N	8 40E	−0020	+0015	*no data*	*no data*	+0.5	+0.6	−0.1	−0.1

GERMANY *Time Zone −0100*

			0100	0600	0100	0800				
HELGOLAND	54 11N	7 53E	and	and	and	and	**2.7**	**2.4**	**0.4**	**0.0**
Standard port			1300	1800	1300	2000				
Lister Tief, List	55 01N	8 27E	+0252	+0240	+0201	+0210	−0.8	−0.6	−0.2	0.0
Hörnum	54 45N	8 18E	+0223	+0218	+0131	+0137	−0.5	−0.4	−0.2	0.0
Amrum–Hafen	54 38N	8 23E	+0138	+0137	+0128	+0134	+0.1	+0.2	−0.1	0.0
Dagebüll	54 44N	8 41E	+0226	+0217	+0211	+0225	+0.5	+0.5	−0.1	0.0
Suderoogsand	54 25N	8 30E	+0116	+0102	+0038	+0122	+0.5	+0.4	+0.1	0.0
Hever, Husum	54 28N	9 01E	+0205	+0152	+0118	+0200	+1.2	+1.1	+0.1	0.0
Suederhoeft	54 16N	8 42E	+0103	+0056	+0051	+0112	+0.7	+0.6	−0.1	0.0
Eidersperrwerk	54 16N	8 51E	+0120	+0115	+0130	+0155	+0.7	+0.6	−0.1	0.0
Linnenplate	54 13N	8 40E	+0047	+0046	+0034	+0046	+0.7	+0.6	0.0	−0.1
Büsum	54 07N	8 52E	+0054	+0049	−0001	+0027	+0.9	+0.8	+0.1	+0.1

			0200	0800	0200	0900				
CUXHAVEN	53 52N	8 43E	and	and	and	and	**3.3**	**2.9**	**0.4**	**0.1**
Standard port			1400	2000	1400	2100				
River Elbe										
Großer Vogelsand	54 00N	8 29E	−0044	−0046	−0101	−0103	0.0	0.0	+0.1	0.0
Scharhörn	53 58N	8 28E	−0045	−0047	−0101	−0103	+0.1	+0.1	+0.1	0.0
Otterndorf	53 50N	8 52E	+0025	+0025	+0022	+0022	−0.1	−0.1	0.0	0.0
Brunsbüttel	53 53N	9 08E	+0057	+0105	+0121	+0112	−0.2	−0.2	−0.1	0.0

Location	Lat	Long	High Water		Low Water		MHWS	MHWN	MLWN	MLWS
Glückstadt	53 47N	9 25E	+0205	+0214	+0220	+0213	−0.3	−0.2	−0.2	0.0
Stadersand	53 38N	9 32E	+0241	+0245	+0300	+0254	−0.1	0.0	−0.2	0.0
Schulau	53 34N	9 42E	+0304	+0315	+0337	+0321	+0.1	+0.2	−0.3	−0.1
Seemannshoeft	53 32N	9 53E	+0324	+0332	+0403	+0347	+0.2	+0.3	−0.4	−0.2
Hamburg	53 33N	9 58E	+0338	+0346	+0422	+0406	+0.3	+0.4	−0.4	−0.3
Harburg	53 28N	10 00E	+0344	+0350	+0430	+0416	+0.4	+0.4	−0.4	−0.3
			0200	0800	0200	0900				
WILHELMSHAVEN	53 31N	8 09E	and	and	and	and	4.3	3.8	0.6	0.0
Standard port			1400	2000	1400	2100				
River Weser										
Alter Weser Lt Hse	53 32N	8 08E	−0055	−0048	−0015	−0029	−1.1	−0.9	−0.2	−0.1
Bremerhaven	53 33N	8 34E	+0029	+0046	+0033	+0038	−0.2	−0.1	−0.2	0.0
Nordenham	53 28N	8 29E	+0051	+0109	+0055	+0058	−0.2	−0.1	−0.4	−0.2
Brake	53 19N	8 29E	+0120	+0119	+0143	+0155	−0.3	−0.2	−0.4	−0.2
Elsfleth	53 16N	8 29E	+0137	+0137	+0206	+0216	−0.2	−0.1	−0.3	−0.2
Vegesack	53 10N	8 37E	+0208	+0204	+0250	+0254	−0.2	−0.2	−0.5	−0.2
Bremen	53 07N	8 43E	+0216	+0211	+0311	+0314	−0.1	−0.1	−0.6	−0.3
River Jade										
Wangerooge East	53 46N	7 59E	−0058	−0053	−0024	−0034	−0.9	−0.9	−0.1	0.0
Wangerooge West	53 47N	7 52E	−0101	−0058	−0035	−0045	−1.1	−1.0	−0.2	0.0
Schillig	53 42N	8 03E	−0031	−0025	−0006	−0014	−0.7	−0.6	0.0	0.0
Hooksiel	53 39N	8 05E	−0023	−0022	−0008	−0012	−0.5	−0.4	0.0	0.0
			0200	0700	0200	0800				
HELGOLAND	54 11N	7 53E	and	and	and	and	2.7	2.4	0.4	0.0
Standard port			1400	1900	1400	2000				
East Frisian Islands and coast										
Spiekeroog	53 45N	7 41E	+0003	−0003	−0031	−0012	+0.4	+0.3	0.0	0.0
Neuharlingersiel	53 42N	7 42E	+0014	+0008	−0024	−0013	+0.5	+0.4	0.0	−0.1
Langeoog	53 43N	7 30E	+0003	−0001	−0034	−0018	+0.4	+0.2	0.0	0.0
Norderney (Riffgat)	53 42N	7 09E	−0024	−0030	−0056	−0045	+0.1	0.0	0.0	0.0
Norddeich Hafen	53 37N	7 10E	−0018	−0017	−0029	−0012	+0.1	+0.1	0.0	−0.1
Juist	53 40N	7 00E	−0026	−0032	−0019	−0008	+0.2	+0.1	0.0	0.0
River Ems										
Memmert	53 38N	6 54E	−0032	−0038	−0114	−0103	+0.1	+0.1	0.0	0.0
Borkum (Fischerbalje)	53 33N	6 45E	−0048	−0052	−0124	−0105	0.0	0.0	0.0	0.0
Emshorn	53 30N	6 50E	−0037	−0041	−0108	−0047	+0.1	+0.1	0.0	0.0
Knock	53 20N	7 02E	+0018	+0005	−0028	+0004	+0.6	+0.6	0.0	0.0
Emden	53 20N	7 11E	+0041	+0028	−0011	+0022	+0.8	+0.8	0.0	0.0

NETHERLANDS *Time Zone −0100*

Location	Lat	Long	High Water		Low Water		MHWS	MHWN	MLWN	MLWS
			0200	0700	0200	0800				
HELGOLAND	54 11N	7 53E	and	and	and	and	2.7	2.4	0.4	0.0
Standard port			1400	1900	1400	2000				
Nieuwe Statenzijl	53 14N	7 13E	+0101	+0045	+0026	+0026	+1.0	+0.8	+0.9	+0.6
Delfzijl	53 20N	6 56E	+0020	−0005	−0040	0000	+0.8	+0.8	+0.2	+0.2
Eemshaven	53 26N	6 52E	−0025	−0045	−0115	−0045	+0.5	+0.4	+0.3	+0.3
Schiermonnikoog	53 28N	6 12E	−0120	−0130	−0240	−0220	+0.1	+0.1	+0.3	+0.3
Waddenzee										
Lauwersoog	53 25N	6 12E	−0130	−0145	−0235	−0220	+0.1	+0.1	+0.2	+0.2
Nes	53 26N	5 47E	−0135	−0150	−0245	−0225	+0.1	0.0	+0.2	+0.2
West Terschelling	53 22N	5 13E	−0220	−0250	−0335	−0310	−0.4	−0.4	+0.1	+0.2
Vlieland−Haven	53 18N	5 06E	−0250	−0320	−0355	−0330	−0.4	−0.4	+0.1	+0.2
Harlingen	53 10N	5 25E	−0155	−0245	−0210	−0130	−0.5	−0.5	−0.1	+0.2
Kornwerderzand	53 04N	5 20E	−0210	−0315	−0300	−0215	−0.5	−0.5	−0.1	+0.2
Den Oever	52 56N	5 02E	−0245	−0410	−0400	−0305	−0.8	−0.7	0.0	+0.2
Oudeschild	53 02N	4 51E	−0310	−0420	−0445	−0400	−1.0	−0.8	0.0	+0.2
Den Helder	52 58N	4 45E	−0410	−0520	−0520	−0430	−1.0	−0.8	0.0	+0.2
Noordwinning (Platform K13−A)	53 13N	3 13E	−0420	−0430	−0520	−0530	−1.1	−1.1	+0.1	+0.1
			0300	0900	0400	1000				
VLISSINGEN	51 27N	3 36E	and	and	and	and	4.7	3.8	0.8	0.2
Standard port			1500	2100	1600	2200				
IJmuiden	52 28N	4 35E	+0145	+0140	+0305	+0325	−2.6	−2.1	−0.5	0.0
Scheveningen	52 06N	4 16E	+0105	+0100	+0220	+0245	−2.6	−2.1	−0.6	0.0
Europlatform	52 00N	3 17E	+0005	−0005	−0030	−0055	−2.6	−2.1	−0.5	0.0

Location	Lat	Long	High Water		Low Water		MHWS	MHWN	MLWN	MLWS
Nieuwe Waterweg										
HOEK VAN HOLLAND			*standard port*							
Maassluis	51 55N	4 15E	+0155	+0115	+0100	+0310	−2.7	−2.1	−0.6	0.0
Nieuwe Maas, Vlaardingen	51 54N	4 21E	+0150	+0120	+0130	+0330	−2.6	−2.1	−0.6	0.0
Lek										
Krimpen Aan de Lek	51 53N	4 38E	+0225	+0200	+0325	+0445	−3.1	−2.5	−0.7	0.0
Schoonhoven	51 57N	4 51E	+0415	+0315	+0435	+0545	−3.1	−2.3	−0.4	+0.2
Oude Maas										
Spijkenisse	51 52N	4 20E	+0145	+0120	+0145	+0310	−2.9	−2.3	−0.6	0.0
Goidschalxoord	51 50N	4 27E	+0200	+0140	+0240	+0410	−3.3	−2.7	−0.7	0.0
Merwede										
Dordrecht	51 49N	4 39E	+0220	+0210	+0420	+0510	−3.7	−3.0	−0.7	−0.1
Werkendam	51 49N	4 53E	+0425	+0410	+0550	+0650	−4.0	−3.2	−0.5	+0.1
Moerdijk	51 42N	4 36E	+0525	+0450	+0520	+0605	−4.2	−3.3	−0.6	+0.1
Haringvlietsluizen	51 50N	4 02E	+0015	+0015	+0015	−0020	−1.7	−1.6	−0.4	+0.1
Brouwershavensche Gat	51 45N	3 49E	0000	+0010	0000	−0030	−1.5	−1.3	−0.3	+0.1
Ooster Schelde										
Roompot Buiten	51 37N	3 40E	−0015	+0005	+0005	−0020	−1.1	−0.9	−0.2	+0.1
Stavenisse	51 36N	4 01E	+0150	+0120	+0055	+0115	−1.2	−0.8	−0.4	+0.1
Bergse Diepsluis (West)	51 30N	4 12E	+0145	+0125	+0105	+0115	−0.6	−0.3	−0.2	+0.1
Zijpe, Philipsdam (West)	51 40N	4 11E	+0215	+0125	+0100	+0110	−1.1	−0.7	−0.4	0.0
Walcheren, Westkapelle	51 31N	3 27E	−0025	−0015	−0010	−0025	−0.5	−0.5	−0.1	+0.1
Westerschelde										
Terneuzen	51 20N	3 50E	+0020	+0020	+0020	+0030	+0.4	+0.4	0.0	+0.1
Hansweert	51 27N	4 00E	+0100	+0050	+0040	+0100	+0.6	+0.7	0.0	+0.1
Bath	51 24N	4 13E	+0125	+0115	+0115	+0140	+1.0	+1.0	0.0	+0.1

BELGIUM *Time Zone −0100*

Location	Lat	Long	High Water		Low Water		MHWS	MHWN	MLWN	MLWS
Antwerpen	51 21N	4 14E	+0128	+0116	+0121	+0144	+1.2	+1.0	+0.1	+0.1
Zeebrugge	51 21N	3 12E	−0035	−0015	−0020	−0035	+0.2	+0.2	+0.4	+0.2
Blankenberge	51 19N	3 07E	−0040	−0040	−0040	−0040	−0.3	0.0	+0.3	+0.2
Oostende	51 14N	2 56E	−0055	−0040	−0030	−0045	+0.5	+0.5	+0.4	+0.2
Nieuwpoort	51 09N	2 43E	−0110	−0050	−0035	−0045	+0.7	+0.6	+0.5	+0.2

FRANCE *Time Zone −0100*

Location	Lat	Long	High Water		Low Water		MHWS	MHWN	MLWN	MLWS
			0200	0800	0200	0900				
DUNKERQUE	51 03N	2 22E	and	and	and	and	6.0	5.0	1.5	0.6
Standard port			1400	2000	1400	2100				
Gravelines	51 01N	2 06E	−0005	−0015	−0005	+0005	+0.3	+0.1	−0.1	−0.1
Sandettie Bank	51 09N	1 47E	−0015	−0025	−0020	−0005	+0.1	−0.1	−0.1	−0.1
Calais	51 58N	1 51E	−0020	−0030	−0015	−0005	+1.2	+0.9	+0.6	+0.3
Wissant	50 53N	1 40E	−0035	−0050	−0030	−0010	+1.9	+1.5	+0.8	+0.4

			0100	0600	0100	0700				
DIEPPE	49 56N	1 05E	and	and	and	and	9.3	7.4	2.5	0.8
Standard port			1300	1800	1300	1900				
Boulogne	50 44N	1 35E	+0014	+0027	+0035	+0033	−0.4	−0.2	+0.1	+0.3
Le Touquet, Étaples	50 31N	1 35E	+0007	+0017	+0032	+0032	+0.2	+0.3	+0.4	+0.4
Berck	50 24N	1 34E	+0007	+0017	+0028	+0028	+0.5	+0.5	+0.4	+0.4
La Somme										
Le Hourdel	50 13N	1 34E	+0020	+0020	no data	no data	+0.8	+0.6	no data	
St Valéry	50 11N	1 37E	+0035	+0035	no data	no data	+0.9	+0.7	no data	
Cayeux	50 11N	1 29E	0000	+0005	+0015	+0010	+0.4	+0.5	+0.5	+0.5
Le Tréport	50 04N	1 22E	+0005	0000	+0007	+0007	+0.1	+0.1	0.0	+0.1
St Valéry–en–Caux	49 52N	0 42E	−0005	−0005	−0015	−0020	−0.5	−0.4	−0.1	−0.1
Fécamp	49 46N	0 22E	−0015	−0010	−0030	−0040	−1.0	−0.6	+0.3	+0.4
Etretat	49 42N	0 12E	−0020	−0020	−0045	−0050	−1.2	−0.8	+0.3	+0.4

			0000	0500	0000	0700				
LE HAVRE	49 29N	0 07E	and	and	and	and	7.9	6.6	2.8	1.2
Standard port			1200	1700	1200	1900				
Antifer (Le Havre)	49 39N	0 09E	+0025	+0015	+0005	−0007	+0.1	0.0	0.0	0.0
La Seine										
Honfleur	49 25N	0 14E	−0135	−0135	+0015	+0040	+0.1	+0.1	+0.1	+0.3
Tancarville	49 28N	0 28E	−0105	−0100	+0105	+0140	−0.1	−0.1	0.0	+1.0
Quilleboeuf	49 28N	0 32E	−0045	−0050	+0120	+0200	0.0	0.0	+0.2	+1.4
Vatteville	49 29N	0 40E	+0005	−0020	+0225	+0250	0.0	−0.1	+0.8	+2.3
Caudebec	49 32N	0 44E	+0020	−0015	+0230	+0300	−0.3	−0.2	+0.9	+2.4
Heurteauville	49 27N	0 49E	+0110	+0025	+0310	+0330	−0.5	−0.2	+1.1	+2.7

TIDES

213

Location	Lat	Long	High Water		Low Water		MHWS	MHWN	MLWN	MLWS
Duclair	49 29N	0 53E	+0225	+0150	+0355	+0410	−0.4	−0.3	+1.4	+3.3
Rouen	49 27N	1 06E	+0440	+0415	+0525	+0525	−0.2	−0.1	+1.6	+3.6
Trouville	49 22N	0 05E	−0100	−0010	0000	+0005	+0.4	+0.3	+0.3	+0.1
Dives	49 18N	0 05W	−0100	−0010	0000	0000	+0.3	+0.2	+0.2	+0.1
Ouistreham	49 17N	0 15W	−0045	−0010	−0005	0000	−0.3	−0.3	−0.2	−0.3
Courseulles–sur–Mer	49 20N	0 27W	−0045	−0015	−0020	−0025	−0.5	−0.5	−0.1	−0.1
Arromanches	49 21N	0 37W	−0055	−0025	−0027	−0035	−0.6	−0.6	−0.2	−0.2
Port–en–Bessin	49 21N	0 45W	−0055	−0030	−0030	−0035	−0.7	−0.7	−0.2	−0.1
Alpha–Baie de Seine	49 49N	0 20W	+0030	+0020	−0005	−0020	−1.0	−0.9	−0.4	−0.2
			0300	1000	0400	1000				
CHERBOURG	49 39N	1 38W	and	and	and	and	6.4	5.0	2.5	1.1
Standard port			1500	2200	1600	2200				
Rade de la Capelle	49 25N	1 05W	+0115	+0050	+0130	+0117	+0.8	+0.9	+0.1	+0.1
Iles Saint Marcouf	49 30N	1 08W	+0118	+0052	+0125	+0110	+0.6	+0.7	+0.1	+0.1
St Vaast–la–Hougue	49 34N	1 16W	+0120	+0050	+0120	+0115	+0.3	+0.5	0.0	−0.1
Barfleur	49 40N	1 15W	+0110	+0055	+0052	+0052	+0.1	+0.3	0.0	0.0
Omonville	49 42N	1 50W	−0010	−0010	−0015	−0015	−0.1	−0.1	0.0	0.0
Goury	49 43N	1 57W	−0100	−0040	−0105	−0120	+1.7	+1.6	+1.0	+0.3

CHANNEL ISLANDS *Time Zone UT*

			0300	0900	0200	0900				
ST HELIER	49 11N	2 07W	and	and	and	and	11.0	8.1	4.0	1.4
Standard port			1500	2100	1400	2100				
Alderney, Braye	49 43N	2 12W	+0050	+0040	+0025	+0105	−4.8	−3.4	−1.5	−0.5
Sark, Maseline Pier	49 26N	2 21W	+0005	+0015	+0005	+0010	−2.1	−1.5	−0.6	−0.3
Guernsey, St PETER PORT	49 27N	2 31W	*standard port (no secondaries)*							
Jersey										
St Catherine Bay	49 13N	2 01W	0000	+0010	+0010	+0010	0.0	−0.1	0.0	+0.1
Bouley Bay	49 14N	2 05W	+0002	+0002	+0004	+0004	−0.3	−0.3	−0.1	−0.1
Les Ecrehou	49 17N	1 56W	+0005	+0009	+0011	+0009	−0.2	+0.1	−0.2	0.0
Les Minquiers	48 57N	2 08W	−0014	−0018	−0001	−0008	+0.5	+0.6	+0.1	+0.1

FRANCE *Time Zone −0100*

			0100	0800	0300	0800				
ST MALO	48 38N	2 02W	and	and	and	and	12.2	9.3	4.2	1.5
Standard port			1300	2000	1500	2000				
Iles Chausey	48 52N	1 49W	+0005	+0005	+0015	+0015	+0.8	+0.7	+0.6	+0.4
Diélette	49 33N	1 52W	+0045	+0035	+0020	+0035	−2.5	−1.9	−0.7	−0.3
Carteret	49 22N	1 47W	+0030	+0020	+0015	+0030	−1.6	−1.2	−0.5	−0.2
Portbail	49 18N	1 45W	+0030	+0025	+0025	+0030	−0.8	−0.6	−0.2	−0.1
St Germain sur Ay	49 14N	1 36W	+0025	+0025	+0035	+0035	−0.7	−0.5	0.0	+0.1
Le Sénéquet	49 05N	1 40W	+0015	+0015	+0023	+0023	−0.3	−0.3	+0.1	+0.1
Regnéville sur Mer	49 01N	1 33W	+0010	+0010	+0030	+0020	+0.4	+0.3	+0.2	0.0
Granville	48 50N	1 36W	+0005	+0005	+0020	+0010	+0.7	+0.5	+0.3	+0.1
Cancale	48 40N	1 51W	−0002	−0002	+0010	+0010	+0.8	+0.6	+0.3	+0.1
Ile des Hebihens	48 37N	2 11W	−0002	−0002	−0005	−0005	−0.2	−0.2	−0.1	−0.1
St Cast	48 38N	2 15W	−0002	−0002	−0005	−0005	−0.2	−0.2	−0.1	−0.1
Erquy	48 38N	2 28W	−0010	−0005	−0023	−0017	−0.6	−0.5	0.0	0.0
Dahouët	48 35N	2 34W	−0010	−0010	−0025	−0020	−0.9	−0.7	−0.2	−0.2
Le Légué (Buoy)	48 34N	2 41W	−0010	−0005	−0020	−0015	−0.8	−0.5	−0.2	−0.1
Binic	48 36N	2 49W	−0008	−0008	−0030	−0015	−0.8	−0.7	−0.2	−0.2
St Quay-Portrieux	48 38N	2 49W	−0010	−0005	−0025	−0020	−0.9	−0.7	−0.2	−0.1
Paimpol	48 47N	3 02W	−0010	−0005	−0035	−0025	−1.4	−1.0	−0.4	−0.2
Ile de Bréhat	48 51N	3 00W	−0015	−0010	−0045	−0035	−1.9	−1.4	−0.6	−0.3
Les Héaux de Bréhat	48 55N	3 05W	−0020	−0015	−0055	−0035	−2.4	−1.7	−0.7	−0.3
Lézardrieux	48 47N	3 06W	−0020	−0015	−0055	−0045	−1.7	−1.3	−0.5	−0.2
Port–Béni	48 51N	3 10W	−0025	−0025	−0105	−0050	−2.4	−1.7	−0.6	−0.2
Tréguier	48 47N	3 13W	−0020	−0020	−0100	−0045	−2.3	−1.6	−0.6	−0.2
Perros–Guirec	48 49N	3 28W	−0040	−0045	−0120	−0105	−2.9	−2.0	−0.8	−0.3
Ploumanac'h	48 50N	3 29W	−0035	−0040	−0120	−0100	−2.9	−2.0	−0.7	−0.2
			0000	0600	0000	0600				
BREST	48 23N	4 30W	and	and	and	and	6.9	5.4	2.6	1.0
Standard port			1200	1800	1200	1800				
Trébeurden	48 46N	3 35W	+0100	+0110	+0120	+0100	+2.3	+1.9	+0.9	+0.4
Locquirec	48 42N	3 38W	+0058	+0108	+0120	+0100	+2.2	+1.8	+0.8	+0.3
Anse de Primel	48 43N	3 50W	+0100	+0110	+0120	+0100	+2.1	+1.7	+0.8	+0.3

Location	Lat	Long	High Water		Low Water		MHWS	MHWN	MLWN	MLWS
Chateau du Taureau (Morlaix)	48 41N	3 53W	+0055	+0105	+0115	+0055	+2.0	+1.7	+0.8	+0.3
Roscoff	48 43N	3 58W	+0055	+0105	+0115	+0055	+1.9	+1.6	+0.8	+0.3
Ile de Batz	48 44N	4 00W	+0045	+0100	+0105	+0055	+2.0	+1.6	+0.9	+0.4
Brignogan	48 40N	4 19W	+0040	+0045	+0058	+0038	+1.5	+1.2	+0.6	+0.2
L'Aber Vrac'h, Ile Cézon	48 36N	4 34W	+0030	+0030	+0040	+0035	+0.8	+0.7	+0.2	0.0
Aber Benoit	48 35N	4 37W	+0022	+0025	+0035	+0020	+0.9	+0.7	+0.3	+0.1
Portsall	48 34N	4 43W	+0015	+0020	+0025	+0015	+0.6	+0.5	+0.1	0.0
L'Aber Ildut	48 28N	4 45W	+0010	+0010	+0023	+0010	+0.4	+0.3	0.0	0.0
Ouessant, Baie de Lampaul	48 27N	5 06W	+0005	+0005	−0005	−0003	0.0	−0.1	−0.1	0.0
Molene	48 24N	4 58W	+0012	+0012	+0017	+0017	+0.4	+0.3	+0.2	+0.1
Le Conquet	48 22N	4 47W	−0005	0000	+0007	+0007	−0.1	−0.1	−0.1	0.0
Le Trez Hir	48 21N	4 42W	−0010	−0005	−0008	−0008	−0.3	−0.3	−0.1	0.0
Camaret	48 17N	4 35W	−0010	−0010	−0013	−0013	−0.3	−0.3	−0.1	0.0
Morgat	48 13N	4 30W	−0008	−0008	−0020	−0010	−0.4	−0.4	−0.2	0.0
Douarnenez	48 06N	4 19W	−0010	−0015	−0018	−0008	−0.5	−0.5	−0.3	−0.1
Ile de Sein	48 02N	4 51W	−0005	−0005	−0010	−0005	−0.7	−0.6	−0.2	−0.1
Audierne	48 01N	4 33W	−0035	−0030	−0035	−0030	−1.7	−1.3	−0.6	−0.2
Le Guilvinec	47 48N	4 17W	−0010	−0025	−0025	−0015	−1.8	−1.4	−0.6	−0.1
Lesconil	47 48N	4 13W	−0008	−0028	−0028	−0018	−1.9	−1.4	−0.6	−0.1
Pont l'Abbe River, Loctudy	47 50N	4 10W	−0010	−0030	−0030	−0020	−2.0	−1.6	−0.7	−0.3
Odet River										
Bénodet	47 53N	4 07W	0000	−0020	−0023	−0013	−1.8	−1.4	−0.6	−0.2
Corniguel	47 58N	4 06W	+0015	+0010	−0015	−0010	−2.0	−1.6	−1.0	−0.7
Concarneau	47 52N	3 55W	−0010	−0030	−0030	−0020	−1.9	−1.5	−0.7	−0.2
Iles de Glenan, Ile de Penfret	47 44N	3 57W	−0005	−0030	−0028	−0018	−1.9	−1.5	−0.7	−0.2
Port Louis	47 42N	3 21W	+0004	−0021	−0022	−0012	−1.8	−1.4	−0.6	−0.1
Lorient	47 45N	3 21W	+0003	−0022	−0020	−0010	−1.8	−1.4	−0.6	−0.2
Hennebont	47 48N	3 17W	+0015	−0017	+0005	+0003	−1.9	−1.5	−0.8	−0.2
Ile de Groix, Port Tudy	47 39N	3 27W	0000	−0025	−0025	−0015	−1.8	−1.4	−0.6	−0.1
Port d'Etel	47 39N	3 12W	+0020	−0010	+0030	+0010	−2.0	−1.3	−0.4	+0.5
Port–Haliguen	47 29N	3 06W	+0015	−0020	−0015	−0010	−1.7	−1.3	−0.6	−0.3
Port Maria	47 29N	3 08W	+0010	−0025	−0025	−0015	−1.6	−1.3	−0.6	−0.1
Belle–Ile, Le Palais	47 21N	3 09W	+0007	−0028	−0025	−0020	−1.8	−1.4	−0.7	−0.3
Crac'h River, La Trinité	47 35N	3 01W	+0020	−0020	−0015	−0005	−1.5	−1.1	−0.5	−0.2
Golfe du Morbihan										
Port–Navalo	47 33N	2 55W	+0030	−0005	−0010	−0005	−2.0	−1.5	−0.8	−0.3
Auray	47 40N	2 59W	+0055	0000	+0020	+0005	−2.0	−1.4	−0.8	−0.2
Arradon	47 37N	2 50W	+0155	+0145	+0145	+0130	−3.7	−2.7	−1.6	−0.5
Vannes	47 39N	2 46W	+0220	+0200	+0200	+0125	−3.6	−2.7	−1.6	−0.5
St Armel (Le Passage)	47 36N	2 43W	+0205	+0200	+0210	+0140	−3.5	−2.5	−1.5	−0.5
Le Logeo	47 33N	2 51W	+0155	+0140	+0145	+0125	−3.7	−2.7	−1.6	−0.5
Port du Crouesty	47 32N	2 54W	+0013	−0022	−0017	−0012	−1.6	−1.2	−0.6	−0.3
Ile de Houat	47 24N	2 57W	+0010	−0025	−0020	−0015	−1.7	−1.3	−0.6	−0.2
Ile de Hoedic	47 20N	2 52W	+0010	−0035	−0027	−0022	−1.8	−1.4	−0.7	−0.3
Pénerf	47 31N	2 37W	+0020	−0025	−0015	−0015	−1.5	−1.1	−0.6	−0.3
Tréhiguier	47 30N	2 27W	+0035	−0020	−0005	−0010	−1.4	−1.0	−0.5	−0.3
Le Croisic	47 18N	2 31W	+0015	−0040	−0020	−0015	−1.5	−1.1	−0.6	−0.3
Le Pouliguen	47 17N	2 25W	+0020	−0025	−0020	−0025	−1.5	−1.1	−0.6	−0.3
Le Grand–Charpentier	47 13N	2 19W	+0015	−0045	−0025	−0020	−1.5	−1.1	−0.6	−0.3
Pornichet	47 16N	2 21W	+0020	−0045	−0022	−0022	−1.4	−1.0	−0.5	−0.2
La Loire										
St Nazaire	47 16N	2 12W	+0030	−0040	−0010	−0010	−1.1	−0.8	−0.4	−0.2
Donges	47 18N	2 05W	+0035	−0035	+0005	+0005	−1.0	−0.7	−0.5	−0.4
Cordemais	47 17N	1 54W	+0055	−0005	+0105	+0030	−0.7	−0.5	−0.7	−0.4
Le Pellerin	47 12N	1 46W	+0110	+0010	+0145	+0100	−0.7	−0.5	−0.9	−0.4
Nantes (Chantenay)	47 12N	1 35W	+0135	+0055	+0215	+0125	−0.6	−0.3	−0.8	−0.1
			0500	1100	0500	1100				
BREST	48 23N	4 30W	and	and	and	and	6.9	5.4	2.6	1.0
Standard port			1700	2300	1700	2300				
Pointe de Saint–Gildas	47 08N	2 15W	−0045	+0025	−0020	−0020	−1.3	−1.0	−0.5	−0.2
Pornic	47 06N	2 07W	−0050	+0030	−0010	−0010	−1.1	−0.8	−0.4	−0.2
Ile de Noirmoutier, L'Herbaudière	47 02N	2 18W	−0047	+0023	−0020	−0020	−1.4	−1.0	−0.5	−0.2
Fromentine	46 54N	2 10W	−0050	+0020	+0020	+0010	−1.6	−1.2	−0.7	−0.0
Ile de Yeu, Port Joinville	46 44N	2 21W	−0040	+0015	−0030	−0035	−1.9	−1.4	−0.7	−0.3
St Gilles–Croix–de–Vie	46 41N	1 56W	−0030	+0015	−0032	−0032	−1.8	−1.3	−0.6	−0.3
Les Sables d'Olonne	46 30N	1 48W	−0030	+0015	−0035	−0035	−1.7	−1.3	−0.6	−0.3

Location	Lat	Long	High Water		Low Water		MHWS	MHWN	MLWN	MLWS
			0000	0600	0500	1200				
POINTE DE GRAVE	45 34N	1 04W	and	and	and	and	**5.4**	**4.4**	**2.1**	**1.0**
Standard port			1200	1800	1700	2400				
Ile de Ré, St Martin	46 12N	1 22W	+0015	−0030	−0025	−0020	+0.6	+0.5	+0.3	−0.1
La Pallice	46 10N	1 13W	+0015	−0030	−0025	−0020	+0.6	+0.5	+0.3	−0.1
La Rochelle	46 09N	1 09W	+0015	−0030	−0025	−0020	+0.6	+0.5	+0.3	−0.1
Ile d'Aix	46 01N	1 10W	+0015	−0040	−0030	−0025	+0.7	+0.5	+0.3	−0.1
La Charente, Rochefort	45 57N	0 58W	+0035	−0010	+0030	+0125	+1.1	+0.9	+0.1	−0.2
Le Chapus	45 51N	1 11W	+0015	−0040	−0025	−0015	+0.6	+0.6	+0.4	+0.2
La Cayenne	45 47N	1 08W	+0030	−0015	−0010	−0005	+0.2	+0.2	+0.3	0.0
Pointe de Gatseau	45 48N	1 14W	+0005	−0005	−0015	−0025	−0.1	−0.1	+0.2	+0.2
Cordouan	45 35N	1 10W	−0010	−0010	−0015	−0025	−0.5	−0.4	−0.1	−0.2
La Gironde										
Royan	45 37N	1 01W	0000	−0005	−0005	−0005	−0.3	−0.2	0.0	0.0
Richard	45 27N	0 56W	+0018	+0018	+0028	+0033	−0.1	−0.1	−0.4	−0.5
Lamena	45 20N	0 48W	+0035	+0045	+0100	+0125	+0.2	+0.1	−0.5	−0.3
Pauillac	45 12N	0 45W	+0100	+0100	+0135	+0205	+0.1	0.0	−1.0	−0.5
La Reuille	45 03N	0 36W	+0135	+0145	+0230	+0305	−0.2	−0.3	−1.3	−0.7
La Garonne										
Le Marquis	45 00N	0 33W	+0145	+0150	+0247	+0322	−0.3	−0.4	− 1.5	−0.9
Bordeaux	44 52N	0 33W	+0200	+0225	+0330	+0405	−0.1	−0.2	−1.7	−1.0
La Dordogne, Libourne	44 55N	0 15W	+0250	+0305	+0525	+0540	−0.7	−0.9	−2.0	−0.4
Bassin d' Arcachon										
Cap Ferret	44 37N	1 15W	−0015	+0005	−0005	+0015	−1.4	−1.2	−0.8	−0.5
Arcachon (Eyrac)	44 40N	1 10W	+0010	+0025	0000	+0020	−1.1	−1.0	−0.8	−0.6
L'Adour, Boucau	43 31N	1 31W	−0030	−0035	−0025	−0040	−1.2	−1.1	−0.4	−0.3
St Jean de Luz, Socoa	43 23N	1 40W	−0040	−0045	−0030	−0045	−1.1	−1.1	−0.6	−0.4

Spain *Time Zone −0100*

Location	Lat	Long	High Water		Low Water		MHWS	MHWN	MLWN	MLWS
Pasajes	43 20N	1 56W	−0050	−0030	−0015	−0045	−1.2	−1.3	−0.5	−0.5
San Sebastian	43 19N	1 59W	−0110	−0030	−0020	−0040	−1.2	−1.2	−0.5	−0.4
Guetaria	43 18N	2 12W	−0110	−0030	−0020	−0040	−1.0	−1.0	−0.5	−0.4
Lequeitio	43 22N	2 30W	−0115	−0035	−0025	−0045	−1.2	−1.2	−0.5	−0.4
Bermeo	43 25N	2 43W	−0055	−0015	−0005	−0025	−0.8	−0.7	−0.5	−0.4
Abra de Bilbao	43 21N	3 02W	−0125	−0045	−0035	−0055	−1.2	−1.2	−0.5	−0.4
Portugalete (Bilbao)	43 20N	3 02W	−0100	−0020	−0010	−0030	−0.7	−1.2	−0.2	−0.6
Castro Urdiales	43 23N	3 13W	−0040	−0120	−0020	−0110	−1.4	−1.5	−0.6	−0.6
Ria de Santona	43 26N	3 28W	−0005	−0045	+0015	−0035	−0.7	−1.2	−0.3	−0.7
Santander	43 28N	3 47W	−0020	−0100	0000	−0050	−0.7	−1.2	−0.3	−0.7
Ria de Suances	43 27N	4 03W	0000	−0030	+0020	−0020	−1.5	−1.5	−0.6	−0.6
San Vicente de la Barquera	43 23N	4 24W	−0020	−0100	0000	−0050	−1.5	−1.5	−0.6	−0.6
Ria de Tina Mayor	43 24N	4 31W	−0020	−0100	0000	−0050	−1.4	−1.5	−0.6	−0.6
Ribadesella	43 28N	5 04W	+0005	−0020	+0020	−0020	−1.4	−1.3	−0.6	−0.4
Gijon	43 34N	5 42W	−0005	−0030	+0010	−0030	−1.0	−1.4	−0.4	−0.7
Luanco	43 37N	5 47W	−0010	−0035	+0005	−0035	−1.4	−1.3	−0.6	−0.4
Aviles	43 35N	5 56W	−0100	−0040	−0015	−0050	−1.2	−1.6	−0.5	−0.7
San Esteban de Pravia	43 34N	6 05W	−0005	−0030	+0010	−0030	−1.4	−1.3	−0.6	−0.4
Luarca	43 33N	6 32W	+0010	−0015	+0025	−0015	−1.2	−1.1	−0.5	−0.3
Ribadeo	43 33N	7 02W	+0010	−0015	+0025	−0015	−1.3	−1.5	−0.7	−0.8
Burela	43 39N	7 21W	+0010	−0015	+0025	−0015	−1.5	−1.5	−0.7	−0.6
Ria de Vivero	43 43N	7 36W	+0010	−0015	+0025	−0015	−1.4	−1.3	−0.6	−0.4
Santa Marta de Ortigueira	43 41N	7 51W	−0020	0000	+0020	−0010	−1.3	−1.2	−0.6	−0.4
El Ferrol del Caudillo	43 28N	8 16W	−0045	−0100	−0010	−0105	−1.6	−1.4	−0.7	−0.4
La Coruna	43 22N	8 24W	−0110	−0050	−0030	−0100	−1.6	−1.6	−0.6	−0.5
Ria de Corme	43 16N	8 58W	−0025	−0005	+0015	−0015	−1.7	−1.6	−0.6	−0.5
Ria de Camarinas	43 08N	9 11W	−0115	−0055	0000	−0105	−1.6	−1.6	−0.6	−0.5

Location	Lat	Long	High Water		Low Water		MHWS	MHWN	MLWN	MLWS
			0500	1000	0300	0800				
LISBOA	38 42N	9 07W	and	and	and	and	**3.8**	**3.0**	**1.5**	**0.6**
Standard port			1700	2200	1500	2000				
Corcubion	42 57N	9 12W	+0055	+0110	+0120	+0135	−0.5	−0.4	−0.3	−0.1
Muros	42 46N	9 03W	+0050	+0105	+0115	+0130	−0.3	−0.3	−0.2	−0.1
Ria de Arosa, Villagarcia	42 37N	8 47W	+0040	+0100	+0110	+0120	−0.3	−0.2	−0.2	−0.1
Ria de Pontevedra, Marin	42 24N	8 42W	+0050	+0110	+0120	+0130	−0.5	−0.4	−0.3	−0.1
Vigo	42 15N	8 43W	+0040	+0100	+0105	+0125	−0.4	−0.3	−0.2	−0.1
Bayona	42 07N	8 51W	+0035	+0050	+0100	+0115	−0.3	−0.3	−0.2	−0.1
La Guardia	41 54N	8 53W	+0040	+0055	+0105	+0120	−0.5	−0.4	−0.3	−0.2

Location	Lat	Long	High Water		Low Water		MHWS	MHWN	MLWN	MLWS
LISBOA *Standard port*	38 42N	9 07W	0400 and 1600	0900 and 2100	0400 and 1600	0900 and 2100	3.8	3.0	1.5	0.6

PORTUGAL *Time Zone UT*

Location	Lat	Long	High Water		Low Water		MHWS	MHWN	MLWN	MLWS
Viana do Castelo	41 41N	8 50W	−0020	0000	+0010	+0015	−0.4	−0.4	−0.1	0.0
Esposende	41 32N	8 47W	−0020	0000	+0010	+0015	−0.6	−0.5	−0.2	−0.1
Povoa de Varzim	41 22N	8 46W	−0020	0000	+0010	+0015	−0.3	−0.3	−0.1	−0.1
Porto de Leixoes	41 11N	8 42W	−0025	−0010	0000	+0010	−0.4	−0.4	−0.1	0.0
Rio Douro										
Entrance	41 09N	8 40W	−0010	+0005	+0015	+0025	−0.6	−0.5	−0.2	−0.1
Oporto (Porto)	41 08N	8 37W	+0002	+0002	+0040	+0040	−0.5	−0.4	−0.2	0.0
Porto de Aveiro	40 39N	8 45W	+0005	+0010	+0010	+0015	−0.6	−0.4	−0.1	0.0
Figueira da Foz	40 09N	8 51W	−0015	0000	+0010	+0020	−0.4	−0.4	−0.1	0.0
Nazare (Pederneira)	39 35N	9 04W	−0030	−0015	−0005	+0005	−0.5	−0.4	−0.1	0.0
Peniche	39 21N	9 22W	−0035	−0015	−0005	0000	−0.4	−0.3	−0.1	0.0
Ericeira	38 58N	9 25W	−0040	−0025	−0010	−0010	−0.4	−0.3	−0.1	0.0
River Tagus (Rio Tejo)										
Cascais	38 42N	9 25W	−0040	−0025	−0015	−0010	−0.3	−0.3	0.0	+0.1
Paco de Arcos	38 41N	9 18W	−0020	−0030	−0005	−0005	−0.4	−0.4	−0.2	−0.1
Pedroucos	38 42N	9 13W	−0010	−0015	0000	0000	−0.2	−0.1	−0.1	−0.1
Alfeite	38 40N	9 09W	+0005	0000	0000	+0005	0.0	0.0	−0.1	−0.1
Alcochete	38 45N	8 58W	+0010	+0010	+0010	+0010	+0.5	+0.4	+0.1	0.0
Vila Franca de Xira	38 57N	8 59W	+0045	+0040	+0100	+0140	+0.3	+0.2	−0.2	+0.3
Sesimbra	38 26N	9 07W	−0045	−0030	−0020	−0010	−0.4	−0.4	−0.1	0.0
Setubal	38 30N	8 54W	−0020	−0015	−0005	+0005	−0.4	−0.4	−0.1	−0.1
Porto de Sines	37 57N	8 53W	−0050	−0030	−0020	−0010	−0.4	−0.4	−0.1	0.0
Milfontes	37 43N	8 47W	−0040	−0030	no data	no data	−0.1	−0.1	0.0	+0.1
Arrifana	37 17N	8 52W	−0030	−0020	no data	no data	−0.1	0.0	−0.1	+0.1
Enseada de Belixe	37 01N	8 58W	−0050	−0030	−0020	−0015	+0.3	+0.2	+0.2	+0.2
Lagos	37 06N	8 40W	−0100	−0040	−0030	−0025	−0.4	−0.4	−0.1	0.0
Portimao	37 07N	8 32W	−0100	−0040	−0030	−0025	−0.5	−0.4	−0.1	+0.1
Ponta do Altar	37 06N	8 31W	−0100	−0040	−0030	−0025	−0.3	−0.3	−0.1	0.0
Enseada de Albufeira	37 05N	8 15W	−0035	+0015	−0005	0000	−0.2	−0.2	0.0	+0.1
Porto de Faro-Olhao	36 59N	7 52W	−0050	−0030	−0015	+0005	−0.4	−0.4	−0.1	0.0
Rio Guadiana										
Vila Real de Santo António	37 12N	7 25W	−0050	−0015	−0010	0000	−0.4	−0.4	−0.1	+0.1

Location	Lat	Long	High Water		Low Water		MHWS	MHWN	MLWN	MLWS
LISBOA *Standard port*	38 42N	9 07W	0500 and 1700	1000 and 2200	0500 and 1700	1100 and 2300	3.8	3.0	1.5	0.6

SPAIN *Time Zone −0100*

Location	Lat	Long	High Water		Low Water		MHWS	MHWN	MLWN	MLWS
Ayamonte	37 13N	7 25W	+0005	+0015	+0025	+0045	−0.7	−0.6	−0.1	−0.2
Ria de Huelva										
Bar	37 08N	6 52W	0000	+0015	+0035	+0030	−0.1	−0.6	−0.1	−0.4
Huelva, Muelle de Fabrica	37 15N	6 58W	+0010	+0025	+0045	+0040	−0.3	−0.3	−0.3	−0.1
Rio Guadalquivir										
Bar	36 45N	6 26W	−0005	+0005	+0020	+0030	−0.6	−0.5	−0.2	−0.1
Bonanza	36 48N	6 20W	+0025	+0040	+0100	+0120	−0.8	−0.6	−0.4	−0.1
Corta de los Jerónimos	37 08N	6 06W	+0210	+0230	+0255	+0345	−1.2	−0.9	−0.5	−0.1
Sevilla	37 23N	6 00W	+0400	+0430	+0510	+0545	−1.7	−1.2	−0.6	−0.1
Rota	36 37N	6 21W	−0010	+0010	+0025	+0015	−0.7	−0.6	−0.3	−0.1
Puerto de Santa Maria	36 36N	6 13W	+0006	+0006	+0027	+0027	−0.6	−0.4	−0.4	−0.1
Cadiz										
Puerto Cadiz	36 32N	6 17W	0000	+0020	+0040	+0025	−0.5	−0.5	−0.3	0.0
La Carraca	36 30N	6 11W	+0020	+0050	+0100	+0040	−0.5	−0.4	−0.1	0.0
Cabo Trafalgar	36 11N	6 02W	−0003	−0003	+0026	+0026	−1.4	−1.1	−0.6	−0.1
Barbate	36 11N	5 56W	+0016	+0016	+0045	+0045	−1.9	−1.5	−0.5	+0.1
Punta Camarinal	36 05N	5 48W	−0007	−0007	+0013	+0013	−1.7	−1.4	−0.7	−0.2

GIBRALTAR *Time Zone −0100*

Location	Lat	Long	High Water		Low Water		MHWS	MHWN	MLWN	MLWS
GIBRALTAR *Standard port*	36 08N	5 21W	0000 and 1200	0700 and 1900	0100 and 1300	0600 and 1800	1.0	0.7	0.3	0.1
Tarifa	36 00N	5 36W	−0038	−0038	−0042	−0042	+0.4	+0.3	+0.3	+0.2
Punta Carnero	36 04N	5 26W	−0010	−0010	0000	0000	0.0	+0.1	+0.1	+0.1
Algeciras	36 07N	5 27W	−0010	−0010	−0010	−0010	+0.1	+0.2	+0.1	+0.1

TIDES

217

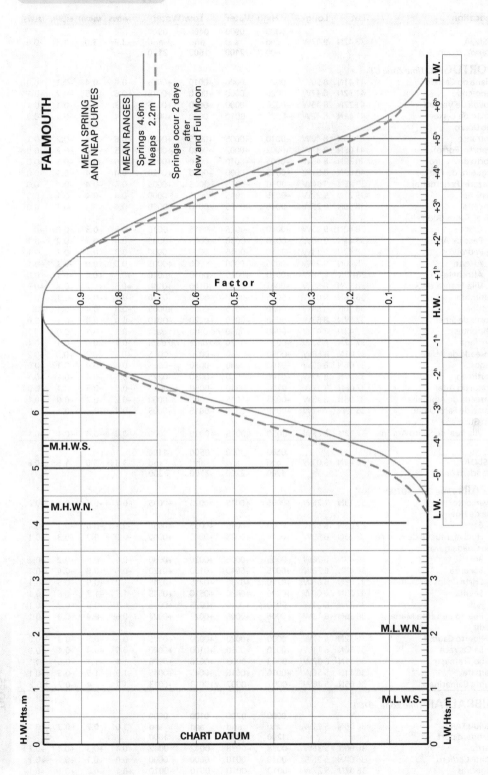

FALMOUTH

MEAN SPRING
AND NEAP CURVES

MEAN RANGES
Springs 4.6m
Neaps 2.2m

Springs occur 2 days
after
New and Full Moon

Factor

0.9 0.8 0.7 0.6 0.5 0.4 0.3 0.2 0.1

H.W.Hts.m

M.H.W.S.

M.H.W.N.

CHART DATUM

L.W.Hts.m

M.L.W.N.

M.L.W.S.

TIME ZONE (UT)
For Summer Time add ONE hour in **non-shaded areas**

ENGLAND – FALMOUTH   2006

LAT 50°09'N   LONG 5°03'W

TIMES AND HEIGHTS OF HIGH AND LOW WATERS

JANUARY

Day	Time	m	Time	m	Time	m	Time	m
1 SU	0003	1.1	0550	5.4	1232	0.9	1819	5.2
2 M	0052	1.0	0638	5.5	1320	0.8	1909	5.2
3 TU	0139	0.9	0727	5.5	1407	0.8	1958	5.2
4 W	0224	1.0	0815	5.5	1453	0.9	2046	5.1
5 TH	0308	1.1	0902	5.3	1537	1.1	2133	4.9
6 F	0352	1.3	0949	5.1	1624	1.3	2223 ☽	4.7
7 SA	0440	1.5	1042	4.9	1716	1.5	2321	4.5
8 SU	0538	1.8	1146	4.6	1819	1.8		
9 M	0026	4.4	0650	1.9	1256	4.5	1932	1.9
10 TU	0134	4.4	0808	2.0	1404	4.4	2044	1.9
11 W	0236	4.5	0919	1.8	1505	4.5	2146	1.7
12 TH	0331	4.7	1017	1.6	1557	4.7	2238	1.5
13 F	0418	4.9	1106	1.5	1641	4.8	2323	1.4
14 SA	0458	5.1	1149	1.3	1720 ○	4.9		
15 SU	0003	1.3	0533	5.2	1229	1.2	1757	4.9
16 M	0041	1.3	0610	5.2	1305	1.2	1833	4.9
17 TU	0114	1.3	0646	5.1	1337	1.3	1909	4.8
18 W	0144	1.4	0723	5.1	1406	1.4	1945	4.7
19 TH	0212	1.5	0758	5.0	1433	1.5	2020	4.6
20 F	0238	1.5	0832	4.8	1500	1.5	2053	4.5
21 SA	0305	1.6	0904	4.7	1529	1.6	2127	4.4
22 SU	0338	1.7	0940	4.5	1605	1.8	2209	4.3
23 M	0422	1.9	1027	4.4	1657	2.0	2306	4.2
24 TU	0529	2.1	1134	4.3	1819	2.1		
25 W	0018	4.2	0704	2.1	1252	4.3	1945	2.0
26 TH	0139	4.4	0825	1.9	1415	4.4	2058	1.8
27 F	0253	4.6	0935	1.6	1528	4.6	2203	1.5
28 SA	0356	4.9	1037	1.3	1627	4.9	2302	1.2
29 SU	0448	5.2	1133	0.9	1718	5.1	2355	0.8
30 M	0537	5.5	1224	0.6	1809	5.3		
31 TU	0044	0.6	0628	5.6	1312	0.4	1859	5.4

FEBRUARY

Day	Time	m	Time	m	Time	m	Time	m
1 W	0130	0.5	0716	5.7	1356	0.3	1945	5.4
2 TH	0212	0.5	0801	5.7	1437	0.4	2027	5.3
3 F	0251	0.6	0843	5.5	1516	0.7	2107	5.1
4 SA	0329	0.9	0924	5.2	1553	1.1	2146	4.8
5 SU	0407	1.3	1005	4.8	1633	1.5	2228 ☽	4.5
6 M	0452	1.7	1054	4.4	1721	1.9	2329	4.2
7 TU	0552	2.1	1211	4.1	1831	2.2		
8 W	0053	4.1	0726	2.3	1337	4.0	2016	2.3
9 TH	0210	4.2	0908	2.1	1448	4.2	2136	2.0
10 F	0313	4.5	1010	1.7	1545	4.6	2229	1.6
11 SA	0401	4.8	1057	1.5	1629	4.6	2312	1.4
12 SU	0442	5.0	1138	1.2	1706	4.8	2351	1.2
13 M	0518	5.1	1216	1.1	1742 ○	4.9		
14 TU	0027	1.1	0554	5.2	1250	1.0	1817	4.9
15 W	0058	1.1	0630	5.2	1319	1.0	1850	4.9
16 TH	0125	1.1	0704	5.1	1344	1.1	1922	4.9
17 F	0149	1.1	0735	5.0	1406	1.2	1951	4.8
18 SA	0211	1.2	0803	4.9	1428	1.3	2017	4.7
19 SU	0234	1.4	0827	4.8	1452	1.4	2041	4.6
20 M	0303	1.5	0853	4.6	1523	1.6	2114	4.4
21 TU	0341	1.7	0938	4.4	1606	1.8	2214	4.2
22 W	0436	2.0	1051	4.1	1715	2.1	2336	4.1
23 TH	0621	2.2	1220	4.1	1915	2.2		
24 F	0108	4.2	0806	2.0	1400	4.2	2043	1.9
25 SA	0236	4.6	0923	1.5	1517	4.6	2152	1.5
26 SU	0340	5.0	1025	1.1	1615	4.9	2249	1.0
27 M	0433	5.3	1119	0.6	1704	5.2	2340	0.6
28 TU	0520	5.6	1208	0.3	1752 ●	5.4		

MARCH

Day	Time	m	Time	m	Time	m	Time	m
1 W	0027	0.4	0608	5.7	1254	0.2	1837	5.5
2 TH	0111	0.2	0655	5.8	1336	0.2	1920	5.5
3 F	0151	0.2	0738	5.7	1414	0.2	2000	5.4
4 SA	0228	0.4	0818	5.5	1449	0.6	2035	5.2
5 SU	0302	0.8	0854	5.1	1522	1.0	2106	4.9
6 M	0337	1.3	0926	4.7	1556	1.5	2135 ☽	4.5
7 TU	0416	1.7	1001	4.3	1639	2.0	2219	4.2
8 W	0511	2.2	1111	3.9	1743	2.4		
9 TH	0006	4.0	0644	2.4	1316	3.8	1948	2.5
10 F	0146	4.1	0858	2.2	1431	4.0	2121	2.1
11 SA	0250	4.4	0953	1.7	1526	4.3	2210	1.4
12 SU	0340	4.7	1036	1.4	1608	4.6	2251	1.4
13 M	0420	4.9	1115	1.1	1645	4.8	2328	1.1
14 TU	0456	5.1	1150	0.9	1718 ○	5.0		
15 W	0002	1.0	0530	5.2	1223	0.8	1752	5.0
16 TH	0032	0.9	0605	5.2	1250	0.8	1824	5.0
17 F	0058	0.9	0638	5.1	1314	0.9	1853	5.0
18 SA	0121	1.0	0708	5.1	1337	1.0	1920	4.9
19 SU	0144	1.1	0733	4.9	1359	1.1	1944	4.8
20 M	0208	1.2	0757	4.8	1424	1.3	2008	4.7
21 TU	0238	1.4	0827	4.6	1455	1.5	2046	4.5
22 W	0316	1.6	0919	4.3	1537	1.8	2148	4.3
23 TH	0413	2.0	1033	4.1	1648	2.2	2311	4.2
24 F	0607	2.2	1208	4.0	1902	2.2		
25 SA	0051	4.3	0755	1.9	1354	4.2	2030	1.8
26 SU	0220	4.6	0908	1.4	1503	4.6	2135	1.4
27 M	0320	5.0	1007	0.9	1556	5.0	2230	0.9
28 TU	0411	5.4	1058	0.5	1642	5.3	2319	0.5
29 W	0459	5.6	1145	0.2	1726 ●	5.4		
30 TH	0004	0.3	0544	5.7	1229	0.2	1810	5.5
31 F	0047	0.2	0630	5.7	1310	0.2	1851	5.5

APRIL

Day	Time	m	Time	m	Time	m	Time	m
1 SA	0126	0.3	0712	5.5	1347	0.4	1928	5.4
2 SU	0203	0.5	0750	5.3	1422	0.7	2000	5.2
3 M	0237	0.9	0822	4.9	1454	1.2	2027	4.9
4 TU	0311	1.4	0851	4.5	1527	1.6	2055	4.6
5 W	0349	1.7	0925	4.2	1608	2.1	2138 ☽	4.2
6 TH	0443	2.2	1024	3.8	1711	2.4	2252	4.0
7 F	0609	2.4	1250	3.7	1855	2.5		
8 SA	0114	4.0	0823	2.2	1401	4.0	2043	2.2
9 SU	0218	4.3	0918	1.8	1454	4.3	2134	1.7
10 M	0307	4.6	1001	1.5	1537	4.6	2215	1.5
11 TU	0348	4.8	1039	1.2	1614	4.8	2253	1.2
12 W	0426	5.0	1114	1.0	1648	5.0	2327	1.0
13 TH	0502	5.1	1146	0.9	1721	5.1	2358 ○	0.9
14 F	0536	5.1	1216	0.9	1754	5.1		
15 SA	0027	0.9	0610	5.1	1244	0.9	1825	5.1
16 SU	0055	0.9	0641	5.0	1310	0.9	1852	5.0
17 M	0122	1.0	0711	4.9	1337	1.1	1920	5.0
18 TU	0151	1.2	0741	4.8	1406	1.4	1954	4.8
19 W	0225	1.4	0822	4.5	1442	1.5	2039	4.6
20 TH	0309	1.6	0918	4.3	1531	1.9	2140	4.4
21 F	0415	1.9	1028	4.1	1652	2.2	2258	4.3
22 SA	0603	2.0	1203	4.1	1847	2.1		
23 SU	0035	4.4	0736	1.7	1336	4.3	2008	1.7
24 M	0156	4.7	0843	1.3	1438	4.7	2109	1.3
25 TU	0255	5.0	0940	0.9	1529	5.0	2203	0.9
26 W	0346	5.3	1031	0.6	1616	5.2	2252	0.6
27 TH	0434	5.4	1118	0.4	1700	5.4	2338 ●	0.5
28 F	0518	5.5	1202	0.4	1742	5.4		
29 SA	0021	0.4	0603	5.4	1243	0.5	1822	5.4
30 SU	0101	0.5	0645	5.3	1321	0.7	1858	5.3

Chart Datum: 2·91 metres below Ordnance Datum (Newlyn)

TIME ZONE (UT)
For Summer Time add ONE hour in **non-shaded areas**

ENGLAND – FALMOUTH

LAT 50°09'N   LONG 5°03'W

TIMES AND HEIGHTS OF HIGH AND LOW WATERS

2006

MAY

Day	Time m	Time m	Day	Time m	Time m
1 M	0139 0.8	0723 5.0	**16** TU	0109 1.0	0659 4.9
	1356 1.0	1928 5.1		1326 1.2	1910 5.0
2 TU	0215 1.1	0756 4.7	**17** W	0146 1.2	0739 4.8
	1430 1.4	1957 4.9		1403 1.4	1951 4.9
3 W	0251 1.5	0827 4.4	**18** TH	0229 1.3	0826 4.6
	1505 1.7	2030 4.6		1447 1.5	2039 4.8
4 TH	0331 1.8	0906 4.2	**19** F	0320 1.5	0921 4.4
	1547 2.0	2115 4.4		1541 1.7	2137 4.7
5 F	0422 2.1	1003 3.9	**20** SA	0424 1.6	1026 4.3
	☽ 1646 2.3	2218 4.1		☽ 1654 1.9	2246 4.6
6 SA	0533 2.2	1157 3.8	**21** SU	0545 1.7	1148 4.3
	1805 2.4			1820 1.8	
7 SU	0011 4.1	0704 2.1	**22** M	0010 4.6	0704 1.5
	1313 4.0	1931 2.2		1303 4.5	1934 1.6
8 M	0128 4.2	0816 1.9	**23** TU	0124 4.7	0810 1.3
	1407 4.2	2035 1.9		1405 4.7	2036 1.4
9 TU	0219 4.5	0905 1.6	**24** W	0224 4.9	0908 1.1
	1452 4.5	2123 1.6		1458 4.9	2133 1.2
10 W	0305 4.7	0948 1.4	**25** TH	0318 5.1	1001 0.9
	1533 4.7	2205 1.4		1548 5.1	2225 1.0
11 TH	0348 4.8	1027 1.2	**26** F	0409 5.1	1051 0.8
	1612 4.9	2245 1.2		1634 5.2	2313 0.8
12 F	0429 4.9	1105 1.1	**27** SA	0456 5.2	1137 0.8
	1649 5.0	2322 1.1		1715 5.3	● 2358 0.8
13 SA	0507 5.0	1141 1.0	**28** SU	0539 5.1	1220 0.9
	1724 5.1	○ 2358 1.0		1755 5.2	
14 SU	0545 5.0	1216 1.0	**29** M	0041 0.9	0623 5.0
	1759 5.1			1300 1.0	1832 5.2
15 M	0033 1.0	0622 5.0	**30** TU	0121 1.0	0702 4.8
	1251 1.1	1834 5.1		1337 1.2	1906 5.0
			31 W	0159 1.2	0738 4.6
				1413 1.5	1939 4.9

JUNE

Day	Time m	Time m	Day	Time m	Time m
1 TH	0237 1.5	0815 4.4	**16** F	0236 1.1	0831 4.8
	1450 1.6	2017 4.7		1454 1.3	2041 5.1
2 F	0316 1.6	0855 4.3	**17** SA	0324 1.2	0922 4.7
	1530 1.9	2100 4.5		1543 1.4	2133 5.0
3 SA	0400 1.8	0944 4.1	**18** SU	0417 1.3	1016 4.6
	☽ 1617 2.0	2152 4.4		☽ 1638 1.5	2230 4.8
4 SU	0453 2.0	1046 4.0	**19** M	0517 1.5	1120 4.5
	1716 2.1	2257 4.3		1743 1.6	2339 4.7
5 M	0555 2.0	1158 4.1	**20** TU	0623 1.5	1225 4.5
	1823 2.1			1852 1.6	
6 TU	0010 4.3	0658 1.9	**21** W	0048 4.6	0730 1.5
	1302 4.2	1925 2.0		1329 4.5	2000 1.6
7 W	0116 4.3	0755 1.7	**22** TH	0153 4.6	0835 1.5
	1356 4.4	2021 1.8		1428 4.7	2104 1.5
8 TH	0213 4.5	0848 1.6	**23** F	0253 4.7	0935 1.4
	1445 4.5	2113 1.6		1523 4.8	2202 1.4
9 F	0304 4.6	0938 1.5	**24** SA	0349 4.8	1030 1.3
	1533 4.7	2202 1.5		1612 5.0	2255 1.2
10 SA	0354 4.7	1025 1.3	**25** SU	0439 4.9	1119 1.2
	1618 4.9	2249 1.3		1656 5.1	● 2343 1.1
11 SU	0441 4.8	1111 1.2	**26** M	0522 4.9	1204 1.2
	1700 5.0	○ 2334 1.1		1736 5.1	
12 M	0524 4.9	1156 1.1	**27** TU	0028 1.1	0604 4.8
	1742 5.1			1246 1.2	1815 5.1
13 TU	0019 1.0	0609 4.9	**28** W	0109 1.1	0645 4.8
	1240 1.1	1824 5.2		1324 1.3	1850 5.0
14 W	0104 1.0	0655 4.9	**29** TH	0148 1.2	0723 4.7
	1324 1.1	1907 5.2		1400 1.4	1927 4.9
15 TH	0149 1.0	0742 4.9	**30** F	0223 1.4	0800 4.6
	1408 1.2	1953 5.2		1434 1.5	2004 4.8

JULY

Day	Time m	Time m	Day	Time m	Time m
1 SA	0257 1.5	0838 4.5	**16** SU	0314 0.8	0908 5.0
	1507 1.6	2042 4.7		1530 1.0	2119 5.2
2 SU	0330 1.6	0918 4.4	**17** M	0357 1.0	0953 4.8
	1541 1.7	2124 4.6		1613 1.3	◐ 2206 5.0
3 M	0407 1.7	1000 4.3	**18** TU	0443 1.3	1043 4.6
	1621 1.9	☽ 2208 4.4		1703 1.6	2301 4.7
4 TU	0451 1.8	1050 4.2	**19** W	0537 1.5	1145 4.4
	1713 2.0	2300 4.3		1807 1.8	
5 W	0548 1.9	1149 4.2	**20** TH	0011 4.4	0646 1.8
	1819 2.1			1255 4.3	1924 1.9
6 TH	0002 4.3	0653 1.9	**21** F	0127 4.3	0805 1.8
	1252 4.2	1926 2.0		1403 4.4	2044 1.8
7 F	0111 4.3	0756 1.8	**22** SA	0236 4.4	0919 1.7
	1356 4.4	2029 1.8		1505 4.6	2152 1.6
8 SA	0220 4.4	0857 1.7	**23** SU	0336 4.5	1019 1.5
	1456 4.6	2128 1.6		1557 4.8	2247 1.5
9 SU	0323 4.5	0955 1.5	**24** M	0426 4.7	1109 1.4
	1551 4.8	2225 1.4		1641 5.0	2335 1.2
10 M	0419 4.7	1051 1.3	**25** TU	0509 4.8	1153 1.2
	1641 5.0	2319 1.2		1720 5.1	●
11 TU	0510 4.9	1143 1.1	**26** W	0018 1.1	0548 4.8
	1727 5.2	○		1234 1.2	1757 5.1
12 W	0010 0.9	0559 5.0	**27** TH	0057 1.1	0627 4.8
	1233 1.0	1815 5.3		1310 1.2	1834 5.1
13 TH	0100 0.8	0649 5.1	**28** F	0132 1.1	0703 4.8
	1320 0.9	1902 5.4		1343 1.2	1909 5.1
14 F	0147 0.7	0737 5.1	**29** SA	0203 1.2	0737 4.7
	1405 0.8	1949 5.4		1411 1.3	1944 5.0
15 SA	0231 0.7	0824 5.1	**30** SU	0229 1.3	0810 4.7
	1448 0.9	2034 5.4		1436 1.4	2017 4.8
			31 M	0253 1.4	0843 4.6
				1500 1.5	2049 4.7

AUGUST

Day	Time m	Time m	Day	Time m	Time m
1 TU	0317 1.5	0917 4.4	**16** W	0408 1.3	1005 4.7
	1526 1.7	2121 4.5		1628 1.5	◐ 2222 4.5
2 W	0347 1.7	0953 4.3	**17** TH	0454 1.7	1100 4.4
	1601 1.9	◐ 2201 4.4		1725 2.0	2334 4.2
3 TH	0428 1.9	1043 4.2	**18** F	0600 2.1	1223 4.2
	1657 2.1	2259 4.2		1854 2.2	
4 F	0540 2.1	1151 4.1	**19** SA	0109 4.0	0747 2.3
	1833 2.2			1346 4.2	2042 2.1
5 SA	0016 4.1	0714 2.1	**20** SU	0227 4.1	0915 2.0
	1311 4.2	1957 2.0		1453 4.5	2148 1.5
6 SU	0146 4.2	0830 1.9	**21** M	0328 4.4	1011 1.6
	1429 4.5	2107 1.7		1545 4.8	2238 1.5
7 M	0303 4.5	0937 1.6	**22** TU	0414 4.6	1057 1.4
	1531 4.8	2210 1.4		1627 5.0	2321 1.2
8 TU	0403 4.7	1036 1.3	**23** W	0453 4.8	1137 1.2
	1624 5.1	2306 1.0		1703 5.1	
9 W	0455 5.0	1130 1.0	**24** TH	0000 1.0	0527 4.9
	1711 5.4	○ 2358 0.7		1215 1.0	1736 5.2
10 TH	0544 5.2	1221 0.7	**25** F	0036 0.9	0602 5.0
	1759 5.6			1248 1.0	1812 5.2
11 F	0047 0.4	0633 5.3	**26** SA	0107 1.0	0635 5.0
	1307 0.5	1847 5.7		1317 1.1	1844 5.1
12 SA	0132 0.3	0719 5.3	**27** SU	0133 1.0	0707 4.9
	1350 0.5	1932 5.7		1340 1.2	1916 5.1
13 SU	0214 0.4	0803 5.3	**28** M	0154 1.2	0736 4.8
	1429 0.5	2016 5.5		1401 1.3	1945 4.9
14 M	0253 0.5	0843 5.2	**29** TU	0214 1.3	0804 4.7
	1507 0.8	2056 5.3		1420 1.4	2010 4.8
15 TU	0330 0.9	0923 5.0	**30** W	0234 1.5	0831 4.6
	1545 1.2	2136 4.9		1444 1.5	2036 4.6
			31 TH	0301 1.6	0903 4.6
				1517 1.8	☽ 2114 4.4

Chart Datum: 2·91 metres below Ordnance Datum (Newlyn)

TIME ZONE (UT)
For Summer Time add ONE hour in **non-shaded areas**

ENGLAND – FALMOUTH

LAT 50°09'N   LONG 5°03'W

TIMES AND HEIGHTS OF HIGH AND LOW WATERS

2006

SEPTEMBER

Day	Time	m	Time	m	Day	Time	m	Time	m
1 F	0338	1.9	1605	2.1	16 SA	0522	2.4	1833	2.5
	0954	4.3	2219	4.1		1152	4.1		
2 SA	0435	2.2	1744	2.3	17 SU	0059	3.9	1331	4.2
	1107	4.1	2344	4.0		0742	2.5	2037	2.2
3 SU	0644	2.3	1938	2.1	18 M	0216	4.1	1436	4.4
	1238	4.2				0903	2.1	2132	1.8
4 M	0129	4.2	1411	4.5	19 TU	0312	4.6	1524	4.8
	0815	2.0	2054	1.7		0951	1.7	2216	1.5
5 TU	0251	4.5	1513	4.9	20 W	0354	4.7	1604	5.0
	0923	1.6	2155	1.3		1033	1.4	2255	1.2
6 W	0349	4.9	1605	5.3	21 TH	0430	4.9	1640	5.2
	1021	1.2	2249	0.8		1111	1.2	2332	1.0
7 TH	0437	5.1	1652	5.6	22 F	0502	5.0	1711	5.3
	1113	0.8	○ 2339	0.5		1146	1.0		
8 F	0522	5.4	1737	5.7	23 SA	0004	0.9	1218	1.0
	1200	0.5				0532	5.1	1744	5.3
9 SA	0025	0.3	1245	0.3	24 SU	0033	0.9	1244	1.0
	0608	5.5	1824	5.8		0604	5.1	1816	5.2
10 SU	0109	0.2	1327	0.3	25 M	0057	1.0	1307	1.1
	0653	5.5	1909	5.7		0635	5.1	1846	5.1
11 M	0149	0.3	1405	0.5	26 TU	0118	1.1	1328	1.2
	0734	5.5	1951	5.5		0704	5.0	1913	5.0
12 TU	0226	0.6	1441	0.8	27 W	0139	1.3	1349	1.4
	0813	5.3	2029	5.2		0728	4.9	1936	4.8
13 W	0301	1.0	1517	1.3	28 TH	0201	1.5	1416	1.7
	0849	5.0	2105	4.8		0754	4.8	2004	4.6
14 TH	0336	1.5	1557	1.7	29 F	0229	1.6	1450	1.8
	0924	4.7	☽ 2143	4.4		0829	4.6	2051	4.4
15 F	0418	2.0	1652	2.2	30 SA	0307	1.9	1539	2.1
	1009	4.3	2251	4.0		0926	4.4	☽ 2200	4.1

OCTOBER

Day	Time	m	Time	m	Day	Time	m	Time	m
1 SU	0405	2.3	1724	2.4	16 M	0035	3.9	1301	4.2
	1041	4.2	2328	4.0		0658	2.6	2005	2.3
2 M	0626	2.4	1924	2.1	17 TU	0147	4.1	1404	4.4
	1214	4.3				0828	2.3	2058	1.9
3 TU	0119	4.2	1350	4.6	18 W	0240	4.4	1452	4.7
	0800	2.0	2037	1.6		0916	1.8	2141	1.5
4 W	0234	4.6	1451	5.0	19 TH	0321	4.7	1532	4.9
	0905	1.5	2134	1.2		0958	1.5	2219	1.3
5 TH	0326	5.0	1542	5.4	20 F	0357	4.9	1608	5.1
	0959	1.1	2226	0.7		1036	1.3	2255	1.1
6 F	0413	5.3	1629	5.6	21 SA	0432	5.1	1642	5.2
	1049	0.6	2314	0.4		1110	1.2	2327	1.1
7 SA	0457	5.5	1713	5.7	22 SU	0503	5.2	1715	5.2
	1135	0.5	○ 2359	0.1		1142	1.1	● 2356	1.1
8 SU	0541	5.6	1758	5.7	23 M	0534	5.2	1748	5.2
	1220	0.4				1211	1.0		
9 M	0042	0.3	1301	0.4	24 TU	0023	1.1	1237	1.2
	0624	5.6	1843	5.6		0606	5.2	1820	5.1
10 TU	0122	0.5	1340	0.6	25 W	0048	1.2	1303	1.3
	0706	5.5	1924	5.4		0635	5.1	1848	5.0
11 W	0159	0.8	1417	1.0	26 TH	0114	1.3	1330	1.4
	0742	5.3	2002	5.1		0704	5.0	1918	4.8
12 TH	0233	1.3	1454	1.4	27 F	0141	1.5	1401	1.5
	0817	5.0	2036	4.7		0734	4.9	1954	4.6
13 F	0309	1.7	1534	1.8	28 SA	0214	1.7	1441	1.8
	0849	4.7	2113	4.3		0817	4.7	2046	4.4
14 SA	0351	2.1	1628	2.3	29 SU	0257	2.0	1537	2.1
	0931	4.4	2214	3.9		0913	4.5	☽ 2152	4.2
15 SU	0453	2.5	1801	2.5	30 M	0403	2.3	1716	2.2
	1053	4.1				1024	4.4	2314	4.2
					31 TU	0602	2.3	1859	2.0
						1151	4.5		

NOVEMBER

Day	Time	m	Time	m	Day	Time	m	Time	m
1 W	0054	4.3	1319	4.7	16 TH	0150	4.3	1404	4.6
	0732	2.0	2009	1.5		0820	2.1	2049	1.8
2 TH	0204	4.7	1422	5.1	17 F	0236	4.6	1449	4.7
	0836	1.5	2106	1.2		0900	1.8	2131	1.5
3 F	0258	5.0	1514	5.3	18 SA	0316	4.8	1531	4.9
	0931	1.2	2158	0.9		0951	1.5	2210	1.4
4 SA	0346	5.3	1604	5.5	19 SU	0356	5.0	1611	5.0
	1022	0.9	2246	0.7		1029	1.4	2246	1.3
5 SU	0432	5.5	1650	5.6	20 M	0433	5.1	1649	5.1
	1110	0.7	○ 2333	0.6		1106	1.3	● 2321	1.3
6 M	0515	5.5	1735	5.5	21 TU	0509	5.2	1725	5.1
	1155	0.6				1140	1.2	2354	1.2
7 TU	0016	0.7	1238	0.7	22 W	0543	5.2	1801	5.1
	0558	5.5	1820	5.4		1215	1.2		
8 W	0057	0.8	1319	0.9	23 TH	0028	1.3	1249	1.3
	0639	5.5	1902	5.2		0617	5.2	1836	5.0
9 TH	0135	1.1	1358	1.2	24 F	0102	1.4	1325	1.4
	0717	5.3	1940	4.9		0651	5.1	1914	4.9
10 F	0212	1.5	1437	1.5	25 SA	0137	1.5	1404	1.5
	0752	5.1	2018	4.6		0730	5.0	1957	4.7
11 SA	0250	1.7	1518	1.8	26 SU	0217	1.6	1449	1.6
	0827	4.8	2057	4.3		0816	4.9	2047	4.6
12 SU	0332	2.1	1608	2.2	27 M	0304	1.8	1545	1.8
	0909	4.5	☽ 2152	4.1		0908	4.8	2145	4.4
13 M	0427	2.4	1717	2.4	28 TU	0405	2.0	1656	1.9
	1010	4.3	2338	4.0		1010	4.7	2256	4.4
14 TU	0544	2.5	1849	2.3	29 W	0526	2.1	1819	1.8
	1156	4.2				1123	4.7		
15 W	0056	4.1	1310	4.4	30 TH	0014	4.4	1240	4.7
	0717	2.4	2000	2.1		0650	1.9	1931	1.6

DECEMBER

Day	Time	m	Time	m	Day	Time	m	Time	m
1 F	0125	4.6	1347	4.9	16 SA	0134	4.4	1353	4.5
	0800	1.7	2033	1.5		0802	2.1	2029	1.9
2 SA	0224	4.9	1446	5.1	17 SU	0227	4.5	1448	4.6
	0900	1.5	2129	1.2		0857	1.9	2120	1.7
3 SU	0318	5.1	1541	5.2	18 M	0317	4.7	1539	4.7
	0956	1.3	2221	1.1		0947	1.7	2208	1.5
4 M	0408	5.3	1631	5.3	19 TU	0404	4.9	1625	4.9
	1047	1.1	2310	1.0		1034	1.5	2252	1.5
5 TU	0454	5.4	1717	5.3	20 W	0446	5.1	1708	5.0
	1136	1.0	○ 2356	1.0		1118	1.4	● 2335	1.3
6 W	0537	5.4	1802	5.2	21 TH	0526	5.2	1750	5.0
	1222	1.0				1201	1.2		
7 TH	0040	1.1	1305	1.1	22 F	0017	1.3	1244	1.2
	0620	5.4	1845	5.0		0607	5.2	1833	5.0
8 F	0120	1.3	1346	1.3	23 SA	0100	1.2	1326	1.1
	0700	5.3	1926	4.9		0649	5.3	1916	5.0
9 SA	0159	1.5	1425	1.5	24 SU	0141	1.3	1409	1.2
	0736	5.1	2005	4.7		0731	5.3	2000	4.9
10 SU	0237	1.6	1504	1.6	25 M	0223	1.3	1453	1.3
	0813	4.9	2044	4.5		0816	5.2	2046	4.7
11 M	0315	1.8	1545	1.9	26 TU	0306	1.4	1539	1.4
	0854	4.7	2128	4.3		0902	5.1	2134	4.7
12 TU	0358	2.1	1632	2.0	27 W	0354	1.5	1630	1.5
	0940	4.6	☽ 2220	4.2		0952	5.0	☽ 2228	4.6
13 W	0449	2.2	1728	2.2	28 TH	0449	1.7	1731	1.6
	1036	4.4	2326	4.2		1051	4.8	2333	4.5
14 TH	0552	2.3	1832	2.2	29 F	0558	1.8	1843	1.7
	1145	4.3				1159	4.7		
15 F	0033	4.2	1253	4.4	30 SA	0043	4.5	1312	4.6
	0700	2.2	1934	2.0		0716	1.9	1956	1.7
					31 SU	0152	4.6	1421	4.7
						0830	1.7	2104	1.6

Chart Datum: 2·91 metres below Ordnance Datum (Newlyn)

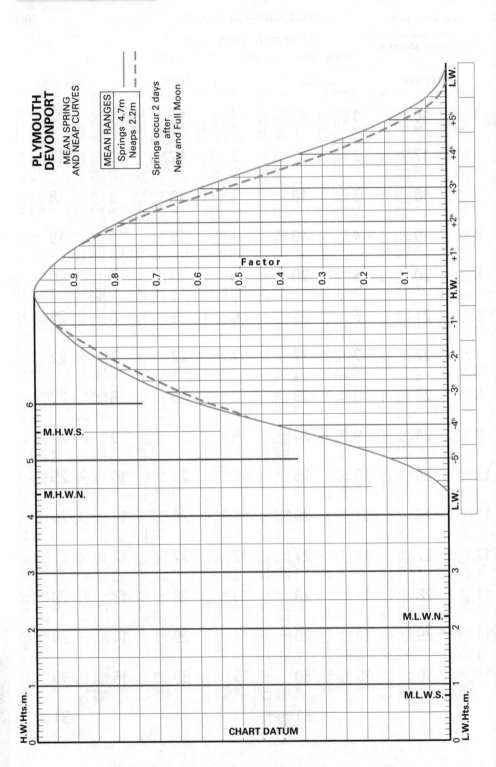

PLYMOUTH DEVONPORT

MEAN SPRING AND NEAP CURVES

MEAN RANGES
Springs 4.7m
Neaps 2.2m

Springs occur 2 days after New and Full Moon

ENGLAND – PLYMOUTH

LAT 50°22'N   LONG 4°11'W

TIMES AND HEIGHTS OF HIGH AND LOW WATERS

2006

JANUARY

Day	Time m	Time m	Time m	Time m		Day	Time m	Time m	Time m	Time m
1 SU	0013 1.1	0624 5.5	1242 0.9	1852 5.3		**16** M	0051 1.3	0644 5.3	1315 1.2	1906 5.0
2 M	0102 1.0	0711 5.6	1330 0.8	1941 5.3		**17** TU	0124 1.3	0719 5.2	1347 1.3	1941 4.9
3 TU	0149 0.9	0759 5.6	1417 0.8	2029 5.3		**18** W	0154 1.4	0755 5.2	1416 1.4	2016 4.8
4 W	0234 1.0	0845 5.6	1503 0.9	2115 5.2		**19** TH	0222 1.5	0829 5.1	1443 1.5	2050 4.7
5 TH	0318 1.1	0931 5.4	1547 1.1	2201 5.0		**20** F	0248 1.6	0902 4.9	1510 1.6	2122 4.6
6 F	0402 1.3	1017 5.2	1634 1.3	◐ 2250 4.8		**21** SA	0315 1.7	0933 4.8	1539 1.7	2155 4.5
7 SA	0450 1.6	1109 5.0	1726 1.6	2346 4.6		**22** SU	0348 1.8	1008 4.6	1615 1.9	◑ 2236 4.4
8 SU	0548 1.9	1211 4.7	1829 1.9			**23** M	0432 2.0	1054 4.5	1707 2.1	2332 4.3
9 M	0053 4.5	0700 2.0	1323 4.6	1942 2.0		**24** TU	0539 2.2	1159 4.4	1829 2.2	
10 TU	0202 4.5	0818 2.1	1433 4.5	2054 2.0		**25** W	0045 4.3	0714 2.2	1319 4.4	1955 2.1
11 W	0306 4.6	0929 1.9	1536 4.6	2156 1.8		**26** TH	0207 4.5	0835 2.0	1445 4.5	2108 1.9
12 TH	0403 4.8	1027 1.7	1630 4.8	2248 1.6		**27** F	0324 4.7	0945 1.7	1600 4.7	2213 1.6
13 F	0451 5.0	1116 1.5	1715 4.9	2333 1.4		**28** SA	0428 5.0	1047 1.3	1700 5.0	2312 1.2
14 SA ○	0532 5.2	1159 1.3	1755 5.0			**29** SU ●	0522 5.3	1143 0.9	1753 5.2	
15 SU	0013 1.3	0608 5.3	1239 1.2	1831 5.0		**30** M	0005 0.9	0612 5.6	1234 0.6	1843 5.4
						31 TU	0054 0.6	0701 5.7	1322 0.4	1931 5.5

FEBRUARY

Day	Time m	Time m	Time m	Time m		Day	Time m	Time m	Time m	Time m
1 W	0140 0.5	0748 5.8	1406 0.3	2016 5.5		**16** TH	0135 1.1	0736 5.2	1354 1.1	1954 5.0
2 TH	0222 0.5	0832 5.8	1447 0.4	2057 5.4		**17** F	0159 1.1	0807 5.1	1416 1.2	2022 4.9
3 F	0301 0.6	0913 5.6	1526 0.7	2136 5.2		**18** SA	0221 1.2	0834 5.0	1438 1.3	2047 4.8
4 SA	0339 0.9	0952 5.3	1603 1.1	2214 4.9		**19** SU	0244 1.4	0857 4.9	1502 1.4	2111 4.7
5 SU ◐	0417 1.3	1032 4.9	1643 1.5	2255 4.6		**20** M	0313 1.5	0922 4.7	1533 1.7	2143 4.5
6 M	0502 1.8	1120 4.5	1731 2.0	2354 4.3		**21** TU	0351 1.8	1006 4.5	1616 1.9	2241 4.3
7 TU	0602 2.2	1237 4.2	1841 2.3			**22** W	0446 2.1	1117 4.2	1725 2.2	
8 W	0120 4.2	0736 2.4	1405 4.1	2026 2.4		**23** TH	0001 4.2	0631 2.3	1247 4.2	1925 2.3
9 TH	0239 4.3	0918 2.2	1519 4.3	2146 2.1		**24** F	0136 4.3	0816 2.1	1429 4.3	2053 2.0
10 F	0344 4.6	1020 1.8	1617 4.5	2239 1.7		**25** SA	0306 4.7	0933 1.6	1549 4.7	2202 1.5
11 SA	0434 4.9	1107 1.5	1702 4.7	2322 1.4		**26** SU	0412 5.1	1035 1.1	1648 5.0	2259 1.0
12 SU	0516 5.1	1148 1.2	1740 4.9			**27** M	0506 5.4	1129 0.6	1738 5.3	2350 0.6
13 M ○	0001 1.2	0553 5.2	1226 1.1	1816 5.0		**28** TU ●	0555 5.7	1218 0.3	1826 5.5	
14 TU ○	0037 1.1	0628 5.3	1300 1.0	1850 5.0						
15 W	0108 1.1	0703 5.3	1329 1.0	1923 5.0						

MARCH

Day	Time m	Time m	Time m	Time m		Day	Time m	Time m	Time m	Time m
1 W	0037 0.4	0642 5.8	1304 0.1	1910 5.6		**16** TH	0042 0.9	0639 5.3	1300 0.8	1857 5.1
2 TH	0121 0.2	0728 5.9	1346 0.1	1952 5.6		**17** F	0108 0.9	0711 5.2	1324 0.9	1926 5.1
3 F	0201 0.2	0810 5.8	1424 0.2	2031 5.5		**18** SA	0131 1.0	0740 5.2	1347 1.0	1952 5.0
4 SA	0238 0.4	0848 5.6	1459 0.6	2105 5.3		**19** SU	0154 1.1	0805 5.0	1409 1.1	2015 4.9
5 SU	0312 0.8	0923 5.2	1532 1.0	2135 5.0		**20** M	0218 1.2	0828 4.9	1434 1.3	2039 4.8
6 M	0347 1.3	0954 4.8	1606 1.6	◐ 2203 4.6		**21** TU	0248 1.6	0857 4.7	1505 1.6	2115 4.6
7 TU	0426 1.8	1029 4.4	1649 2.1	2246 4.3		**22** W	0326 1.7	0947 4.4	1547 1.9	◑ 2216 4.4
8 W	0521 2.3	1137 4.0	1753 2.5			**23** TH	0423 2.1	1100 4.2	1658 2.3	2337 4.3
9 TH	0032 4.1	0654 2.5	1344 3.9	1958 2.6		**24** F	0617 2.3	1234 4.1	1912 2.3	
10 F	0215 4.2	0908 2.3	1501 4.1	2131 2.2		**25** SA	0118 4.4	0805 2.0	1423 4.3	2040 1.9
11 SA	0321 4.5	1003 1.8	1558 4.4	2220 1.8		**26** SU	0250 4.7	0918 1.4	1534 4.7	2145 1.4
12 SU	0412 4.8	1046 1.4	1641 4.7	2301 1.4		**27** M	0352 5.1	1017 0.9	1628 5.1	2240 0.9
13 M	0453 5.0	1125 1.1	1719 4.9	2338 1.1		**28** TU	0444 5.5	1108 0.5	1716 5.4	2329 0.5
14 TU ○	0530 5.2	1200 0.9	1753 5.1			**29** W	0533 5.7	1155 0.2	1801 5.5	
15 W	0012 1.0	0605 5.3	1233 0.8	1826 5.1		**30** TH	0014 0.3	0618 5.8	1239 0.1	1844 5.6
						31 F	0057 0.2	0703 5.8	1320 0.1	1924 5.6

APRIL

Day	Time m	Time m	Time m	Time m		Day	Time m	Time m	Time m	Time m
1 SA	0136 0.3	0744 5.6	1357 0.4	2000 5.5		**16** SU	0105 0.9	0714 5.1	1320 1.0	1925 5.1
2 SU	0213 0.5	0821 5.4	1432 0.7	2031 5.3		**17** M	0132 1.0	0743 5.0	1347 1.1	1952 5.1
3 M	0247 0.9	0852 5.0	1504 1.2	2057 5.0		**18** TU	0201 1.2	0813 4.9	1416 1.4	2025 4.9
4 TU	0321 1.4	0920 4.6	1537 1.7	2124 4.7		**19** W	0235 1.4	0852 4.6	1452 1.6	2109 4.7
5 W ◐	0359 1.8	0953 4.3	1618 2.2	2206 4.3		**20** TH	0319 1.7	0946 4.4	1541 2.0	2208 4.5
6 TH	0453 2.3	1051 3.9	1721 2.5	2318 4.1		**21** F	0425 2.0	1055 4.2	1702 2.3	◑ 2324 4.4
7 F	0619 2.5	1317 3.8	1905 2.6			**22** SA	0613 2.1	1229 4.2	1857 2.2	
8 SA	0142 4.1	0833 2.3	1430 4.1	2053 2.3		**23** SU	0102 4.5	0746 1.8	1404 4.4	2018 1.8
9 SU	0248 4.4	0928 1.9	1525 4.4	2144 1.8		**24** M	0225 4.8	0853 1.3	1508 4.8	2119 1.3
10 M	0338 4.7	1011 1.5	1609 4.7	2225 1.5		**25** TU	0326 5.1	0950 0.9	1601 5.1	2213 0.9
11 TU	0420 4.9	1049 1.2	1647 4.9	2303 1.2		**26** W	0418 5.4	1041 0.6	1649 5.3	2302 0.6
12 W	0459 5.1	1124 1.0	1722 5.1	2337 1.0		**27** TH	0507 5.5	1128 0.4	1734 5.5	● 2348 0.5
13 TH	0536 5.2	1156 0.9	1756 5.2			**28** F	0553 5.6	1212 0.4	1816 5.5	
14 F	0008 0.9	0611 5.2	1226 0.9	1828 5.2		**29** SA	0031 0.4	0637 5.5	1253 0.5	1855 5.5
15 SA	0037 0.9	0644 5.2	1254 0.9	1858 5.2		**30** SU	0111 0.5	0718 5.4	1331 0.7	1930 5.4

Chart Datum: 3·22 metres below Ordnance Datum (Newlyn)

TIDES

TIME ZONE (UT)
For Summer Time add ONE hour in **non-shaded areas**

ENGLAND – PLYMOUTH

2006

LAT 50°22′N   LONG 4°11′W

TIMES AND HEIGHTS OF HIGH AND LOW WATERS

MAY

Time	m		Time	m
1 0149	0.8		**16** 0119	1.0
0755	5.1		0731	5.0
M 1406	1.0		TU 1336	1.2
2000	5.2		1942	5.1
2 0225	1.1		**17** 0156	1.2
0827	4.8		0811	4.9
TU 1440	1.4		W 1413	1.4
2028	5.0		2022	5.0
3 0301	1.5		**18** 0239	1.3
0857	4.5		0856	4.7
W 1515	1.8		TH 1457	1.6
2100	4.7		2109	4.9
4 0341	1.9		**19** 0330	1.6
0935	4.3		0949	4.5
TH 1557	2.1		F 1551	1.8
2144	4.5		2205	4.8
5 0432	2.2		**20** 0434	1.7
1030	4.0		1053	4.4
F 1656	2.4		SA 1704	2.0
☽ 2245	4.2		◑ 2313	4.7
6 0543	2.3		**21** 0555	1.8
1223	3.9		1213	4.4
SA 1815	2.5		SU 1830	1.9
7 0037	4.2		**22** 0036	4.7
0714	2.2		0714	1.6
SU 1341	4.1		M 1331	4.6
1941	2.3		1944	1.7
8 0156	4.3		**23** 0152	4.8
0826	2.0		0820	1.3
M 1436	4.3		TU 1434	4.8
2045	2.0		2046	1.4
9 0249	4.6		**24** 0254	5.0
0915	1.7		0918	1.1
TU 1523	4.6		W 1529	5.0
2133	1.7		2143	1.2
10 0336	4.8		**25** 0350	5.2
0958	1.4		1011	0.9
W 1605	4.8		TH 1620	5.2
2215	1.4		2235	1.0
11 0420	4.9		**26** 0442	5.2
1037	1.2		1101	0.8
TH 1645	5.0		F 1707	5.3
2255	1.2		2323	0.8
12 0502	5.0		**27** 0530	5.3
1115	1.1		1147	0.8
F 1723	5.1		SA 1750	5.4
2332	1.1		●	
13 0541	5.1		**28** 0008	0.8
1151	1.0		0614	5.2
SA 1759	5.2		SU 1230	0.9
○			1829	5.3
14 0008	1.0		**29** 0051	0.9
0619	5.1		0656	5.1
SU 1226	1.0		M 1310	1.0
1833	5.2		1905	5.3
15 0043	1.0		**30** 0131	1.0
0655	5.1		0734	4.9
M 1301	1.1		TU 1347	1.2
1907	5.2		1938	5.1
			31 0209	1.2
			0810	4.7
			W 1423	1.5
			2011	5.0

JUNE

Time	m		Time	m
1 0247	1.5		**16** 0246	1.1
0845	4.5		0901	4.9
TH 1500	1.7		F 1504	1.3
2047	4.8		2111	5.2
2 0326	1.7		**17** 0334	1.2
0924	4.4		0950	4.8
F 1540	2.0		SA 1553	1.4
2129	4.6		2201	5.1
3 0410	1.9		**18** 0427	1.3
1012	4.2		1043	4.7
SA 1627	2.1		SU 1648	1.6
◐ 2220	4.5		◑ 2257	4.9
4 0503	2.1		**19** 0527	1.5
1113	4.1		1145	4.6
SU 1726	2.2		M 1753	1.7
2323	4.4			
5 0605	2.1		**20** 0004	4.8
1224	4.2		0633	1.5
M 1833	2.2		TU 1252	4.6
			1902	1.7
6 0036	4.4		**21** 0115	4.7
0708	2.0		0740	1.5
TU 1329	4.3		W 1357	4.6
1935	2.1		2010	1.7
7 0144	4.4		**22** 0222	4.7
0805	1.8		0845	1.5
W 1425	4.5		TH 1458	4.8
2031	1.9		2114	1.5
8 0242	4.6		**23** 0324	4.8
0858	1.7		0945	1.4
TH 1516	4.6		F 1555	4.9
2123	1.7		2212	1.4
9 0335	4.7		**24** 0421	4.9
0948	1.5		1040	1.3
F 1605	4.8		SA 1645	5.1
2212	1.5		2305	1.2
10 0426	4.8		**25** 0512	5.0
1035	1.3		1129	1.2
SA 1651	5.0		SU 1730	5.2
2259	1.3		● 2353	1.1
11 0514	4.9		**26** 0557	5.0
1121	1.2		1214	1.2
SU 1734	5.1		M 1811	5.2
○ 2344	1.1			
12 0559	5.0		**27** 0038	1.1
1206	1.1		0638	4.9
M 1816	5.2		TU 1256	1.2
			1848	5.2
13 0029	1.0		**28** 0119	1.1
0643	5.0		0718	4.9
TU 1250	1.1		W 1334	1.3
1857	5.3		1923	5.1
14 0114	1.0		**29** 0158	1.2
0728	5.0		0755	4.8
W 1334	1.1		TH 1410	1.4
1939	5.3		1959	5.0
15 0159	1.0		**30** 0233	1.4
0814	5.0		0831	4.7
TH 1418	1.2		F 1444	1.5
2024	5.3		2035	4.9

JULY

Time	m		Time	m
1 0307	1.5		**16** 0324	0.8
0908	4.6		0937	5.1
SA 1517	1.7		SU 1540	1.0
2112	4.8		2147	5.3
2 0340	1.7		**17** 0407	1.0
0946	4.5		1021	4.9
SU 1551	1.8		M 1623	1.3
2152	4.7		◑ 2233	5.1
3 0417	1.8		**18** 0453	1.3
1028	4.4		1110	4.7
M 1631	2.0		TU 1713	1.6
◐ 2235	4.5		2327	4.8
4 0501	1.9		**19** 0547	1.6
1116	4.3		1210	4.5
TU 1723	2.1		W 1817	1.9
2326	4.4			
5 0558	2.0		**20** 0037	4.5
1214	4.3		0656	1.9
W 1829	2.2		TH 1322	4.4
			1934	2.0
6 0028	4.4		**21** 0155	4.4
0703	2.0		0815	1.9
TH 1319	4.3		F 1432	4.5
1936	2.1		2054	1.9
7 0139	4.4		**22** 0306	4.5
0806	1.9		0929	1.8
F 1425	4.5		SA 1536	4.7
2039	1.9		2202	1.7
8 0250	4.5		**23** 0408	4.6
0907	1.8		1029	1.6
SA 1527	4.7		SU 1630	4.9
2138	1.7		2257	1.5
9 0355	4.6		**24** 0459	4.8
1005	1.5		1119	1.4
SU 1623	4.9		M 1715	5.1
2235	1.4		2345	1.2
10 0452	4.8		**25** 0543	4.9
1101	1.3		1203	1.2
M 1714	5.1		TU 1755	5.2
● 2329	1.2			
11 0544	5.0		**26** 0028	1.1
1153	1.1		0622	4.9
TU 1802	5.3		W 1244	1.2
○			1831	5.2
12 0020	0.9		**27** 0107	1.1
0633	5.1		0700	4.9
W 1243	1.0		TH 1320	1.2
1848	5.4		1907	5.2
13 0110	0.8		**28** 0142	1.1
0722	5.2		0735	4.9
TH 1330	0.9		F 1353	1.2
1934	5.5		1941	5.2
14 0157	0.7		**29** 0213	1.2
0809	5.2		0809	4.8
F 1415	0.8		SA 1421	1.3
2020	5.5		2015	5.1
15 0241	0.7		**30** 0239	1.3
0854	5.2		0841	4.8
SA 1458	0.9		SU 1446	1.4
2104	5.3		2047	4.9
			31 0303	1.4
			0913	4.7
			M 1510	1.6
			2118	4.8

AUGUST

Time	m		Time	m
1 0327	1.6		**16** 0418	1.3
0945	4.5		1032	4.8
TU 1536	1.8		W 1638	1.6
2149	4.6		◑ 2249	4.6
2 0357	1.8		**17** 0504	1.8
1021	4.4		1126	4.5
W 1611	2.0		TH 1735	2.1
◐ 2229	4.5		2359	4.3
3 0438	2.0		**18** 0610	2.2
1110	4.3		1250	4.3
TH 1707	2.2		F 1904	2.3
2325	4.3			
4 0550	2.2		**19** 0137	4.1
1217	4.2		0757	2.4
F 1843	2.3		SA 1415	4.3
			2052	2.2
5 0042	4.2		**20** 0257	4.2
0724	2.2		0925	2.1
SA 1339	4.3		SU 1524	4.6
2007	2.1		2158	1.8
6 0214	4.3		**21** 0400	4.5
0840	2.0		1021	1.7
SU 1459	4.6		M 1617	4.9
2117	1.8		2248	1.5
7 0334	4.6		**22** 0447	4.7
0947	1.7		1107	1.4
M 1603	4.9		TU 1700	5.1
2220	1.4		2331	1.2
8 0436	4.8		**23** 0527	4.9
1046	1.3		1147	1.2
TU 1657	5.2		W 1737	5.2
2316	1.0		●	
9 0529	5.1		**24** 0010	1.0
1140	1.0		0602	5.0
W 1746	5.5		TH 1225	1.0
○			1811	5.2
10 0008	0.7		**25** 0046	0.9
0618	5.3		0636	5.1
TH 1231	0.7		F 1258	1.0
1833	5.7		1845	5.3
11 0057	0.4		**26** 0117	1.0
0706	5.4		0708	5.1
F 1317	0.5		SA 1327	1.1
1920	5.8		1917	5.3
12 0142	0.3		**27** 0143	1.0
0751	5.4		0739	5.0
SA 1400	0.5		SU 1350	1.2
2004	5.8		1948	5.2
13 0224	0.4		**28** 0204	1.2
0834	5.4		0808	4.9
SU 1439	0.5		M 1411	1.3
2046	5.6		2016	5.0
14 0303	0.5		**29** 0224	1.3
0913	5.3		0835	4.8
M 1517	0.8		TU 1430	1.4
2125	5.4		2041	4.9
15 0340	0.9		**30** 0244	1.5
0951	5.0		0901	4.7
TU 1555	1.2		W 1454	1.6
2204	5.0		2106	4.7
			31 0311	1.7
			0932	4.5
			TH 1527	1.9
			◐ 2143	4.5

Chart Datum: 3·22 metres below Ordnance Datum (Newlyn)

TIME ZONE (UT)
For Summer Time add ONE hour in **non-shaded areas**

SEPTEMBER

Time	m	Time	m
1 0348 2.0 1022 4.4 F 1615 2.2 2246 4.2		**16** 0532 2.5 1218 4.2 SA 1843 2.6	
2 0445 2.3 1133 4.2 SA 1754 2.4		**17** 0126 4.0 0752 2.6 SU 1359 4.3 2047 2.3	
3 0009 4.1 0654 2.4 SU 1305 4.3 1948 2.2		**18** 0246 4.2 0810 2.1 M 1506 4.5 2142 1.9	
4 0157 4.3 0825 2.1 M 1440 4.6 2104 1.8		**19** 0343 4.5 1001 1.8 TU 1556 4.9 2226 1.5	
5 0322 4.6 0933 1.7 TU 1545 5.0 2205 1.3		**20** 0426 4.8 1043 1.4 W 1637 5.1 2305 1.2	
6 0421 5.0 1031 1.2 W 1638 5.4 2259 0.8		**21** 0503 5.0 1121 1.2 TH 1713 5.3 2342 1.0	
7 0510 5.2 1123 0.8 TH 1726 5.7 ○ 2349 0.5		**22** 0536 5.1 1156 1.0 F 1746 5.4	
8 0557 5.5 1210 0.5 F 1812 5.8		**23** 0014 0.9 0607 5.2 SA 1228 1.0 1818 5.4	
9 0035 0.3 0642 5.6 SA 1255 0.3 1857 5.9		**24** 0043 0.9 0638 5.2 SU 1254 1.0 1849 5.3	
10 0119 0.2 0726 5.6 SU 1337 0.3 1941 5.8		**25** 0107 1.0 0708 5.2 M 1317 1.1 1919 5.2	
11 0159 0.3 0806 5.6 M 1415 0.5 2022 5.6		**26** 0128 1.1 0736 5.1 TU 1338 1.2 1945 5.1	
12 0238 0.6 0844 5.4 TU 1451 0.8 2059 5.3		**27** 0149 1.2 0800 5.0 W 1359 1.4 2008 4.9	
13 0311 1.0 0918 5.1 W 1527 1.3 2134 4.9		**28** 0211 1.5 0825 4.9 TH 1426 1.6 2035 4.7	
14 0346 1.5 0952 4.8 TH 1607 1.8 ◐ 2211 4.5		**29** 0239 1.7 0859 4.7 F 1500 1.9 2120 4.5	
15 0428 2.1 1036 4.4 F 1702 2.3 2317 4.1		**30** 0317 2.0 0954 4.5 SA 1549 2.2 ◑ 2228 4.2	

OCTOBER

Time	m	Time	m
1 0415 2.4 1108 4.3 SU 1734 2.5 2353 4.1		**16** 0102 4.0 0708 2.7 M 1328 4.3 2015 2.4	
2 0636 2.5 1240 4.4 M 1934 2.2		**17** 0216 4.2 0838 2.4 TU 1433 4.5 2108 2.0	
3 0147 4.3 0810 2.1 TU 1419 4.7 2047 1.7		**18** 0310 4.5 0926 1.9 W 1523 4.8 2151 1.6	
4 0304 4.7 0915 1.6 W 1522 5.1 2144 1.2		**19** 0353 4.8 1008 1.6 TH 1604 5.0 2229 1.3	
5 0358 5.1 1009 1.1 TH 1614 5.5 2236 0.7		**20** 0430 5.0 1046 1.3 F 1641 5.2 2305 1.1	
6 0446 5.4 1059 0.7 F 1702 5.7 2324 0.4		**21** 0505 5.2 1120 1.2 SA 1716 5.3 2337 1.1	
7 0531 5.6 1145 0.5 SA 1748 5.8 ○		**22** 0537 5.3 1152 1.1 SU 1750 5.3 ●	
8 0009 0.3 0615 5.7 SU 1230 0.4 1832 5.8		**23** 0006 1.1 0609 5.3 M 1221 1.1 1822 5.3	
9 0052 0.3 0657 5.7 M 1311 0.4 1916 5.7		**24** 0033 1.1 0640 5.3 TU 1247 1.2 1853 5.2	
10 0132 0.5 0738 5.6 TU 1350 0.6 1956 5.5		**25** 0058 1.2 0708 5.2 W 1313 1.3 1921 5.1	
11 0209 0.8 0814 5.4 W 1427 1.0 2033 5.2		**26** 0124 1.3 0736 5.1 TH 1340 1.4 1950 4.9	
12 0243 1.3 0847 5.1 TH 1504 1.4 2106 4.8		**27** 0151 1.5 0806 5.0 F 1411 1.6 2025 4.7	
13 0319 1.8 0918 4.8 F 1544 1.9 2142 4.4		**28** 0224 1.8 0847 4.8 SA 1451 1.9 2115 4.5	
14 0401 2.2 0959 4.5 SA 1638 2.4 ◑ 2241 4.0		**29** 0307 2.1 0942 4.6 SU 1547 2.2 ◐ 2220 4.3	
15 0503 2.6 1119 4.2 SU 1811 2.6		**30** 0413 2.4 1051 4.5 M 1726 2.3 2340 4.3	
		31 0612 2.4 1217 4.6 TU 1909 2.1	

NOVEMBER

Time	m	Time	m
1 0121 4.4 0742 2.1 W 1347 4.8 2019 1.6		**16** 0219 4.4 0830 2.2 TH 1433 4.7 2059 1.9	
2 0233 4.8 0846 1.6 TH 1452 5.2 2116 1.2		**17** 0306 4.7 0918 1.9 F 1520 4.8 2141 1.6	
3 0329 5.1 0941 1.2 F 1546 5.4 2208 0.9		**18** 0348 4.9 1001 1.6 SA 1603 5.0 2220 1.4	
4 0418 5.4 1032 0.9 SA 1637 5.6 2256 0.7		**19** 0428 5.1 1039 1.4 SU 1644 5.1 2256 1.3	
5 0505 5.6 1120 0.7 SU 1724 5.7 ○ 2343 0.6		**20** 0506 5.2 1116 1.3 M 1723 5.2 ● 2331 1.3	
6 0550 5.6 1205 0.6 M 1810 5.6		**21** 0543 5.3 1150 1.2 TU 1800 5.2	
7 0026 0.7 0632 5.6 TU 1248 0.7 1853 5.5		**22** 0004 1.2 0617 5.3 W 1225 1.2 1835 5.2	
8 0107 0.8 0712 5.6 W 1329 0.9 1934 5.3		**23** 0038 1.3 0650 5.3 TH 1259 1.3 1909 5.1	
9 0145 1.1 0749 5.4 TH 1408 1.2 2012 5.0		**24** 0112 1.4 0724 5.2 F 1335 1.4 1946 5.0	
10 0222 1.5 0823 5.2 F 1447 1.5 2048 4.7		**25** 0147 1.5 0802 5.1 SA 1414 1.5 2028 4.8	
11 0300 1.8 0857 4.9 SA 1528 1.9 2126 4.4		**26** 0227 1.7 0846 5.0 SU 1459 1.7 2116 4.7	
12 0342 2.2 0938 4.6 SU 1618 2.3 ◑ 2220 4.2		**27** 0314 1.9 0937 4.9 M 1555 1.9 2213 4.5	
13 0437 2.5 1037 4.4 M 1727 2.5		**28** 0415 2.1 1037 4.8 TU 1706 2.0 ◐ 2322 4.3	
14 0003 4.1 0554 2.6 TU 1222 4.3 1859 2.4		**29** 0536 2.2 1148 4.8 W 1829 1.9	
15 0123 4.2 0727 2.5 W 1338 4.5 2010 2.2		**30** 0040 4.5 0700 2.0 TH 1307 4.8 1941 1.7	

DECEMBER

Time	m	Time	m
1 0153 4.7 0810 1.8 F 1416 5.0 2043 1.5		**16** 0202 4.5 0812 2.2 SA 1422 4.6 2039 2.0	
2 0254 5.0 0910 1.5 SA 1517 5.2 2139 1.2		**17** 0257 4.6 0907 2.0 SU 1519 4.7 2130 1.8	
3 0350 5.2 1006 1.3 SU 1613 5.3 2231 1.1		**18** 0349 4.8 0957 1.8 M 1611 4.8 2218 1.6	
4 0441 5.4 1057 1.1 M 1704 5.4 2320 1.0		**19** 0437 5.0 1044 1.5 TU 1658 5.0 2302 1.5	
5 0528 5.5 1146 1.0 TU 1752 5.4 ○		**20** 0520 5.2 1128 1.4 W 1742 5.1 ● 2345 1.3	
6 0006 1.0 0612 5.5 W 1232 1.0 1836 5.3		**21** 0601 5.2 1211 1.2 TH 1824 5.1	
7 0050 1.1 0653 5.5 TH 1315 1.1 1918 5.1		**22** 0027 1.3 0641 5.3 F 1254 1.2 1906 5.1	
8 0130 1.3 0732 5.4 F 1356 1.3 1958 5.0		**23** 0110 1.2 0722 5.4 SA 1336 1.1 1948 5.1	
9 0209 1.5 0808 5.2 SA 1435 1.5 2036 4.8		**24** 0151 1.3 0803 5.4 SU 1419 1.2 2031 5.0	
10 0247 1.7 0844 5.0 SU 1514 1.7 2114 4.6		**25** 0233 1.3 0846 5.3 M 1503 1.3 2115 4.9	
11 0325 1.9 0923 4.8 M 1555 2.0 2156 4.4		**26** 0316 1.4 0931 5.2 TU 1549 1.4 2202 4.8	
12 0408 2.2 1008 4.7 TU 1642 2.1 ◑ 2247 4.3		**27** 0404 1.6 1020 5.1 W 1640 1.6 ◐ 2255 4.7	
13 0459 2.3 1103 4.5 W 1738 2.3 2351 4.3		**28** 0459 1.8 1117 4.9 TH 1741 1.7 2358 4.6	
14 0602 2.4 1210 4.4 TH 1842 2.3		**29** 0608 1.9 1225 4.8 F 1853 1.9	
15 0100 4.3 0710 2.3 F 1320 4.5 1944 2.1		**30** 0110 4.6 0726 2.0 SA 1340 4.7 2006 1.8	
		31 0221 4.7 0840 1.8 SU 1451 4.8 2114 1.7	

TIDES

Chart Datum: 3·22 metres below Ordnance Datum (Newlyn)

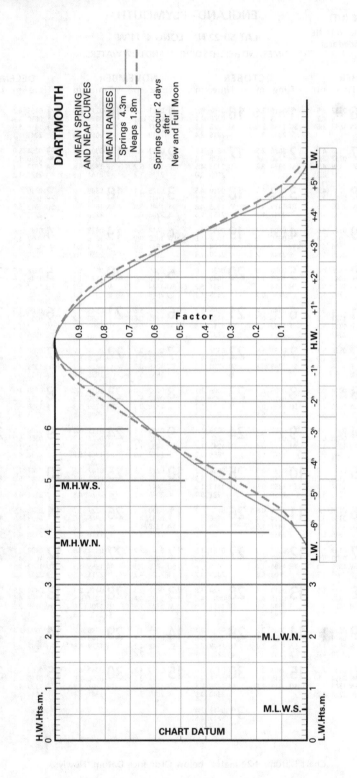

DARTMOUTH

MEAN SPRING
AND NEAP CURVES

MEAN RANGES
Springs 4.3m
Neaps 1.8m

Springs occur 2 days
after
New and Full Moon

ENGLAND - DARTMOUTH

LAT 50°21'N LONG 3°34'W

TIMES AND HEIGHTS OF HIGH AND LOW WATERS

2006

JANUARY

Day	Time m	Time m	Time m	Time m
1 SU	0012 0.9	0649 4.9	1242 0.7	1916 4.7
16 M	0051 1.1	0708 4.7	1315 1.0	1930 4.4
2 M	0102 0.8	0735 5.0	1329 0.6	2004 4.7
17 TU	0124 1.1	0742 4.6	1346 1.1	2004 4.3
3 TU	0148 0.7	0821 5.0	1416 0.6	2051 4.7
18 W	0153 1.2	0817 4.6	1415 1.2	2038 4.2
4 W	0232 0.8	0906 5.0	1501 0.7	2135 4.6
19 TH	0221 1.3	0851 4.5	1441 1.3	2111 4.1
5 TH	0316 0.9	0951 4.8	1544 0.9	2220 4.4
20 F	0246 1.4	0923 4.3	1508 1.4	2142 4.0
6 F	0359 1.1	1036 4.6	1630 1.1	☽ 2308 4.2
21 SA	0313 1.5	0953 4.2	1536 1.5	2214 3.9
7 SA	0446 1.4	1127 4.4	1722 1.4	
22 SU	0345 1.6	1027 4.0	1612 1.7	2254 3.8
8 SU	0002 4.0	0543 1.7	1227 4.1	1824 1.7
23 M	0428 1.8	1112 3.9	1703 1.9	2349 3.7
9 M	0108 3.9	0656 1.8	1339 4.0	1938 1.8
24 TU	0534 2.0	1215 3.8	1824 2.0	
10 TU	0219 3.9	0814 1.9	1451 3.9	2051 1.8
25 W	0100 3.7	0710 2.0	1335 3.8	1951 1.9
11 W	0325 4.0	0926 1.7	1556 4.0	2154 1.6
26 TH	0224 3.9	0832 1.8	1504 3.9	2105 1.7
12 TH	0424 4.2	1025 1.5	1652 4.2	2247 1.4
27 F	0344 4.1	0943 1.5	1621 4.1	2211 1.3
13 F	0514 4.4	1115 1.3	1739 4.3	2332 1.3
28 SA	0450 4.4	1046 1.1	1723 4.4	2311 1.0
14 SA	0556 4.6	1158 1.1	1820 4.4 ○	
29 SU	0546 4.7	1142 0.7	1818 4.6 ●	
15 SU	0012 1.1	0633 4.7	1239 1.0	1855 4.4
30 M	0004 0.7	0637 5.0	1234 0.4	1907 4.8
31 TU	0054 0.4	0725 5.1	1322 0.2	1954 4.9

FEBRUARY

Day	Time m	Time m	Time m	Time m
1 W	0139 0.3	0810 5.2	1405 0.1	2038 4.9
16 TH	0134 0.9	0759 4.6	1353 0.9	2016 4.4
2 TH	0221 0.3	0853 5.2	1445 0.2	2118 4.8
17 F	0158 0.9	0829 4.5	1415 1.0	2044 4.3
3 F	0259 0.4	0934 5.0	1524 0.5	2156 4.6
18 SA	0220 1.0	0855 4.4	1436 1.1	2108 4.2
4 SA	0336 0.7	1011 4.7	1600 0.9	2233 4.3
19 SU	0242 1.2	0918 4.3	1500 1.2	2132 4.1
5 SU	0414 1.1	1050 4.3	1639 1.3	☽ 2313 4.0
20 M	0311 1.3	0942 4.1	1530 1.5	2203 3.9
6 M	0458 1.6	1137 3.9	1726 1.8	
21 TU	0348 1.6	1025 3.9	1613 1.7	2259 3.7
7 TU	0010 3.7	0557 2.0	1252 3.6	1837 2.1
22 W	0442 1.9	1134 3.6	1721 2.0	
8 W	0136 3.6	0732 2.2	1422 3.5	2022 2.2
23 TH	0017 3.6	0627 2.1	1302 3.6	1921 2.1
9 TH	0257 3.7	0915 2.0	1539 3.7	2144 1.9
24 F	0152 3.7	0812 1.9	1447 3.7	2050 1.8
10 F	0404 4.0	1018 1.6	1639 3.9	2238 1.5
25 SA	0325 4.1	0931 1.4	1610 4.1	2200 1.3
11 SA	0456 4.3	1106 1.3	1725 4.1	2321 1.2
26 SU	0433 4.5	1034 0.9	1711 4.4	2258 0.8
12 SU	0540 4.5	1147 1.0	1804 4.3	
27 M	0529 4.8	1128 0.4	1802 4.7	2349 0.4
13 M	0000 1.0	0618 4.6	1225 0.9	1841 4.4 ○
28 TU	0620 5.1	1217 0.1	1851 4.9 ●	
14 TU	0037 0.9	0653 4.7	1300 0.8	1914 4.4
15 W	0108 0.9	0727 4.7	1329 0.8	1946 4.4

MARCH

Day	Time m	Time m	Time m	Time m
1 W	0037 0.2	0706 5.2	1304 -0.1	1934 5.0
16 TH	0042 0.7	0703 4.7	1300 0.6	1921 4.5
2 TH	0121 0.0	0751 5.3	1345 -0.1	2014 5.0
17 F	0108 0.7	0735 4.6	1324 0.7	1949 4.5
3 F	0200 0.0	0832 5.2	1423 0.0	2052 4.9
18 SA	0130 0.8	0803 4.6	1346 0.8	2014 4.4
4 SA	0236 0.2	0909 5.0	1457 0.2	2126 4.7
19 SU	0153 0.9	0827 4.4	1408 0.9	2037 4.3
5 SU	0310 0.6	0943 4.6	1529 0.8	2155 4.4
20 M	0217 1.0	0850 4.3	1432 1.1	2100 4.2
6 M	0344 1.1	1013 4.2	1603 1.4	☽ 2222 4.0
21 TU	0246 1.2	0918 4.1	1503 1.4	2135 4.0
7 TU	0423 1.6	1048 3.8	1645 1.9	2304 3.7
22 W	0324 1.5	1006 3.8	1544 1.7	☽ 2235 3.8
8 W	0517 2.1	1154 3.4	1748 2.3	
23 TH	0420 1.9	1118 3.6	1654 2.1	2354 3.7
9 TH	0047 3.5	0650 2.3	1400 3.3	1954 2.4
24 F	0612 2.1	1249 3.5	1908 2.1	
10 F	0233 3.6	0905 2.1	1520 3.5	2129 2.0
25 SA	0134 3.8	0801 1.8	1441 3.7	2037 1.7
11 SA	0341 3.8	1001 1.6	1619 3.8	2218 1.6
26 SU	0309 4.1	0915 1.2	1554 4.1	2143 1.2
12 SU	0433 4.2	1045 1.2	1703 4.1	2300 1.2
27 M	0413 4.5	1015 0.7	1650 4.5	2239 0.7
13 M	0516 4.4	1124 0.9	1743 4.3	2337 0.9
28 TU	0506 4.9	1107 0.3	1740 4.8	2328 0.3
14 TU	0554 4.6	1159 0.7	1818 4.5	
29 W	0557 5.1	1154 0.0	1826 4.9 ●	
15 W	0011 0.8	0630 4.7	1233 0.6	1851 4.5
30 TH	0013 0.1	0643 5.2	1239 -0.1	1908 5.0
31 F	0057 0.0	0727 5.2	1320 -0.1	1947 5.0

APRIL

Day	Time m	Time m	Time m	Time m
1 SA	0135 0.1	0807 5.0	1356 0.2	2022 4.9
16 SU	0105 0.7	0738 4.5	1320 0.8	1948 4.5
2 SU	0212 0.3	0843 4.8	1430 0.5	2052 4.7
17 M	0131 0.8	0806 4.4	1346 0.9	2014 4.5
3 M	0245 0.7	0913 4.4	1502 1.0	2118 4.4
18 TU	0200 1.0	0835 4.3	1415 1.2	2047 4.3
4 TU	0319 1.2	0940 4.0	1534 1.5	2144 4.1
19 W	0233 1.2	0913 4.0	1450 1.4	2130 4.1
5 W	0356 1.6	1012 3.7	1615 2.0	☽ 2225 3.7
20 TH	0317 1.5	1005 3.8	1538 1.8	2227 3.9
6 TH	0449 2.1	1109 3.3	1717 2.3	2335 3.5
21 F	0422 1.8	1113 3.6	1658 2.1	☽ 2341 3.8
7 F	0614 2.3	1333 3.2	1901 2.4	
22 SA	0608 1.9	1245 3.6	1853 2.0	
8 SA	0158 3.5	0830 2.1	1448 3.5	2050 2.1
23 SU	0117 3.9	0742 1.6	1421 3.8	2014 1.6
9 SU	0307 3.8	0925 1.7	1545 3.8	2142 1.6
24 M	0243 4.2	0850 1.1	1527 4.2	2116 1.1
10 M	0358 4.1	1009 1.3	1630 4.1	2223 1.3
25 TU	0346 4.5	0948 0.7	1622 4.5	2211 0.7
11 TU	0442 4.3	1048 1.0	1710 4.3	2302 1.0
26 W	0440 4.8	1040 0.4	1712 4.7	2301 0.4
12 W	0522 4.5	1123 0.8	1746 4.5	2336 0.8
27 TH	0530 4.9	1127 0.2	1758 4.9	● 2347 0.3
13 TH	0600 4.6	1155 0.7	1821 4.6 ○	
28 F	0618 5.0	1211 0.2	1841 4.9	
14 F	0007 0.7	0636 4.6	1225 0.7	1853 4.6
29 SA	0031 0.2	0701 4.9	1253 0.3	1919 4.9
15 SA	0037 0.7	0708 4.6	1254 0.7	1922 4.6
30 SU	0111 0.3	0741 4.8	1330 0.5	1953 4.8

TIDES

Chart Datum: 2·62 metres below Ordnance Datum (Newlyn)

ENGLAND - DARTMOUTH

2006

LAT 50°21'N   LONG 3°34'W

TIMES AND HEIGHTS OF HIGH AND LOW WATERS

TIME ZONE (UT)
For Summer Time add ONE hour in **non-shaded areas**

MAY

Day	Time m	Day	Time m
1 M	0148 0.6 / 0817 4.5 / 1405 0.8 / 2022 4.6	**16** TU	0119 0.8 / 0754 4.4 / 1335 1.0 / 2005 4.5
2 TU	0224 0.9 / 0849 4.2 / 1438 1.2 / 2050 4.4	**17** W	0155 1.0 / 0833 4.3 / 1412 1.2 / 2044 4.4
3 W	0259 1.3 / 0918 3.9 / 1513 1.6 / 2121 4.1	**18** TH	0237 1.1 / 0917 4.1 / 1455 1.4 / 2130 4.3
4 TH	0338 1.7 / 0955 3.7 / 1554 1.9 / 2204 3.9	**19** F	0327 1.4 / 1008 3.9 / 1548 1.6 / 2224 4.2
5 F	0428 2.0 / 1048 3.4 / 1652 2.2 / ☾ 2303 3.6	**20** SA	0430 1.5 / 1111 3.8 / 1700 1.8 / ◑ 2331 4.1
6 SA	0538 2.1 / 1239 3.3 / 1810 2.3	**21** SU	0550 1.6 / 1229 3.8 / 1826 1.7
7 SU	0052 3.6 / 0710 2.0 / 1357 3.5 / 1937 2.1	**22** M	0051 4.1 / 0710 1.4 / 1347 4.0 / 1940 1.5
8 M	0213 3.7 / 0822 1.8 / 1454 3.7 / 2042 1.8	**23** TU	0209 4.2 / 0816 1.1 / 1452 4.2 / 2043 1.2
9 TU	0308 4.0 / 0912 1.5 / 1543 4.0 / 2131 1.5	**24** W	0313 4.4 / 0915 0.9 / 1549 4.4 / 2141 1.0
10 W	0356 4.2 / 0956 1.2 / 1626 4.2 / 2213 1.2	**25** TH	0411 4.6 / 1009 0.7 / 1642 4.6 / 2234 0.8
11 TH	0442 4.3 / 1036 1.0 / 1708 4.4 / 2254 1.0	**26** F	0504 4.6 / 1100 0.6 / 1730 4.7 / 2322 0.6
12 F	0525 4.4 / 1114 0.9 / 1747 4.5 / 2331 0.9	**27** SA	0554 4.7 / 1146 0.6 / 1815 4.8 / ●
13 SA	0605 4.5 / 1150 0.8 / 1824 4.6 / ○	**28** SU	0007 0.6 / 0639 4.6 / 1230 0.7 / 1854 4.7
14 SU	0007 0.8 / 0644 4.5 / 1225 0.8 / 1857 4.6	**29** M	0051 0.7 / 0720 4.5 / 1310 0.8 / 1929 4.7
15 M	0043 0.8 / 0719 4.5 / 1301 0.9 / 1931 4.6	**30** TU	0130 0.8 / 0757 4.3 / 1346 1.0 / 2001 4.5
		31 W	0208 1.0 / 0832 4.1 / 1422 1.3 / 2033 4.4

JUNE

Day	Time m	Day	Time m
1 TH	0245 1.3 / 0906 3.9 / 1458 1.5 / 2108 4.2	**16** F	0244 0.9 / 0922 4.3 / 1502 1.1 / 2132 4.6
2 F	0324 1.5 / 0944 3.8 / 1537 1.8 / 2149 4.0	**17** SA	0331 1.0 / 1009 4.2 / 1550 1.2 / 2220 4.5
3 SA	0407 1.7 / 1031 3.6 / 1624 1.9 / ◑ 2239 3.9	**18** SU	0424 1.1 / 1101 4.1 / 1644 1.4 / ◑ 2315 4.3
4 SU	0459 1.9 / 1131 3.5 / 1722 2.0 / 2340 3.8	**19** M	0523 1.3 / 1201 4.0 / 1748 1.5
5 M	0600 1.9 / 1240 3.6 / 1829 2.0	**20** TU	0020 4.2 / 0629 1.3 / 1307 4.0 / 1858 1.5
6 TU	0051 3.8 / 0704 1.8 / 1345 3.7 / 1931 1.9	**21** W	0131 4.1 / 0736 1.3 / 1414 4.0 / 2006 1.5
7 W	0200 3.8 / 0801 1.6 / 1443 3.9 / 2028 1.7	**22** TH	0240 4.1 / 0842 1.3 / 1517 4.2 / 2111 1.3
8 TH	0300 4.0 / 0855 1.5 / 1536 4.0 / 2120 1.5	**23** F	0344 4.2 / 0943 1.2 / 1616 4.3 / 2210 1.2
9 F	0355 4.1 / 0946 1.3 / 1626 4.2 / 2210 1.3	**24** SA	0443 4.3 / 1039 1.1 / 1708 4.5 / 2304 1.0
10 SA	0448 4.2 / 1034 1.1 / 1714 4.4 / 2258 1.1	**25** SU	0535 4.4 / 1128 1.0 / 1754 4.6 / ● 2352 0.9
11 SU	0537 4.3 / 1120 1.0 / 1758 4.5 / ○ 2343 0.9	**26** M	0622 4.4 / 1213 1.0 / 1836 4.6
12 M	0624 4.4 / 1205 0.9 / 1841 4.6	**27** TU	0038 0.9 / 0702 4.3 / 1256 1.0 / 1912 4.6
13 TU	0028 0.8 / 0707 4.4 / 1250 0.9 / 1921 4.7	**28** W	0119 0.9 / 0741 4.3 / 1333 1.1 / 1946 4.5
14 W	0114 0.8 / 0751 4.4 / 1333 0.9 / 2002 4.7	**29** TH	0157 1.0 / 0817 4.2 / 1409 1.2 / 2021 4.4
15 TH	0158 0.8 / 0836 4.4 / 1417 1.0 / 2046 4.7	**30** F	0231 1.2 / 0852 4.1 / 1442 1.3 / 2056 4.3

JULY

Day	Time m	Day	Time m
1 SA	0305 1.3 / 0929 4.0 / 1515 1.5 / 2133 4.2	**16** SU	0322 0.6 / 0957 4.5 / 1537 0.8 / 2206 4.7
2 SU	0337 1.5 / 1005 3.9 / 1548 1.6 / 2211 4.1	**17** M	0404 0.8 / 1040 4.3 / 1620 1.1 / ◐ 2251 4.5
3 M	0414 1.6 / 1047 3.8 / 1627 1.8 / ◑ 2253 3.9	**18** TU	0449 1.1 / 1128 4.1 / 1709 1.4 / 2344 4.2
4 TU	0457 1.7 / 1133 3.7 / 1719 1.9 / 2343 3.8	**19** W	0542 1.4 / 1226 3.9 / 1812 1.7
5 W	0553 1.8 / 1230 3.7 / 1824 2.0	**20** TH	0052 3.9 / 0652 1.7 / 1338 3.8 / 1930 1.8
6 TH	0044 3.8 / 0659 1.8 / 1335 3.7 / 1932 1.9	**21** F	0212 3.8 / 0811 1.7 / 1450 3.9 / 2051 1.7
7 F	0155 3.8 / 0802 1.7 / 1443 3.9 / 2036 1.7	**22** SA	0325 3.9 / 0926 1.6 / 1556 4.1 / 2200 1.5
8 SA	0309 3.9 / 0904 1.6 / 1547 4.1 / 2136 1.5	**23** SU	0429 4.0 / 1027 1.4 / 1652 4.3 / 2256 1.3
9 SU	0416 4.0 / 1003 1.3 / 1645 4.3 / 2234 1.2	**24** M	0522 4.2 / 1118 1.2 / 1739 4.5 / 2344 1.0
10 M	0515 4.2 / 1100 1.1 / 1737 4.5 / 2328 1.0	**25** TU	0607 4.3 / 1202 1.0 / 1820 4.7 / ●
11 TU	0608 4.4 / 1152 0.9 / 1827 4.7 / ○	**26** W	0027 0.9 / 0647 4.3 / 1244 1.0 / 1855 4.6
12 W	0019 0.7 / 0657 4.5 / 1243 0.8 / 1912 4.8	**27** TH	0107 0.9 / 0724 4.3 / 1320 1.0 / 1931 4.6
13 TH	0110 0.6 / 0745 4.6 / 1329 0.7 / 1957 4.9	**28** F	0141 0.9 / 0758 4.3 / 1352 1.0 / 2004 4.6
14 F	0156 0.5 / 0831 4.6 / 1414 0.6 / 2042 4.9	**29** SA	0212 1.0 / 0831 4.2 / 1420 1.1 / 2037 4.5
15 SA	0239 0.5 / 0915 4.6 / 1456 0.7 / 2125 4.9	**30** SU	0237 1.1 / 0902 4.2 / 1444 1.2 / 2108 4.3
		31 M	0301 1.2 / 0934 4.1 / 1508 1.4 / 2138 4.2

AUGUST

Day	Time m	Day	Time m
1 TU	0325 1.4 / 1004 3.9 / 1533 1.6 / 2208 4.0	**16** W	0415 1.1 / 1050 4.2 / 1634 1.4 / ◐ 2307 4.0
2 W	0354 1.6 / 1040 3.8 / 1608 1.8 / ◐ 2248 3.9	**17** TH	0500 1.6 / 1143 3.9 / 1730 1.9
3 TH	0434 1.8 / 1128 3.7 / 1703 2.0 / 2342 3.7	**18** F	0015 3.7 / 0605 2.0 / 1305 3.7 / 1900 2.1
4 F	0545 2.0 / 1233 3.6 / 1839 2.1	**19** SA	0153 3.5 / 0753 2.2 / 1433 3.7 / 2049 2.0
5 SA	0057 3.6 / 0720 2.0 / 1355 3.7 / 2003 1.9	**20** SU	0316 3.6 / 0922 1.9 / 1544 4.0 / 2156 1.6
6 SU	0231 3.7 / 0837 1.8 / 1518 4.0 / 2114 1.6	**21** M	0421 3.9 / 1019 1.5 / 1639 4.3 / 2247 1.3
7 M	0354 4.0 / 0945 1.5 / 1624 4.3 / 2218 1.2	**22** TU	0510 4.1 / 1106 1.2 / 1723 4.5 / 2330 1.0
8 TU	0458 4.2 / 1045 1.1 / 1720 4.6 / 2315 0.8	**23** W	0551 4.3 / 1146 1.0 / 1801 4.6 / ●
9 W	0553 4.5 / 1139 0.8 / 1811 4.9 / ○	**24** TH	0009 0.8 / 0627 4.4 / 1224 0.8 / 1836 4.7
10 TH	0007 0.5 / 0643 4.7 / 1231 0.5 / 1857 5.1	**25** F	0046 0.7 / 0700 4.5 / 1258 0.7 / 1909 4.7
11 F	0057 0.2 / 0730 4.8 / 1317 0.3 / 1943 5.2	**26** SA	0117 0.8 / 0732 4.5 / 1327 0.9 / 1940 4.7
12 SA	0141 0.1 / 0813 4.8 / 1359 0.3 / 2026 5.2	**27** SU	0142 0.8 / 0802 4.4 / 1349 1.0 / 2010 4.6
13 SU	0223 0.2 / 0855 4.8 / 1437 0.3 / 2107 5.0	**28** M	0203 1.0 / 0830 4.3 / 1410 1.1 / 2038 4.4
14 M	0301 0.3 / 0934 4.7 / 1515 0.6 / 2145 4.8	**29** TU	0223 1.2 / 0856 4.2 / 1428 1.2 / 2102 4.3
15 TU	0337 0.7 / 1010 4.5 / 1552 1.0 / 2223 4.4	**30** W	0242 1.3 / 0922 4.0 / 1452 1.4 / 2127 4.1
		31 TH	0309 1.5 / 0952 3.9 / 1525 1.7 / ◐ 2203 3.9

Chart Datum: 2·62 metres below Ordnance Datum (Newlyn)

ENGLAND - DARTMOUTH 2006

LAT 50°21'N LONG 3°34'W

TIMES AND HEIGHTS OF HIGH AND LOW WATERS

SEPTEMBER

Time	m		Time	m
1 0345	1.8	**16** 0527	2.3
1041	3.8	1234	3.6
F 1612	2.0	SA 1839	2.4
2304	3.6		
2 0441	2.1	**17** 0142	3.4
1150	3.6	0748	2.4
SA 1749	2.2	SU 1416	3.7
		2044	2.1
3 0025	3.5	**18** 0305	3.6
0650	2.2	0910	2.0
SU 1320	3.7	M 1525	3.9
1944	2.0	2140	1.7
4 0214	3.7	**19** 0403	3.9
0821	1.9	0959	1.6
M 1458	4.0	TU 1617	4.3
2101	1.6	2224	1.3
5 0342	4.0	**20** 0448	4.2
0931	1.5	1042	1.2
TU 1606	4.4	W 1659	4.5
2203	1.1	2304	1.0
6 0443	4.4	**21** 0526	4.4
1030	1.0	1120	1.0
W 1700	4.8	TH 1736	4.7
2258	0.6	2341	0.8
7 0533	4.6	**22** 0600	4.5
1122	0.6	1155	0.8
TH 1750	5.1	F 1811	4.8
○ 2348	0.3		
8 0622	4.9	**23** 0013	0.7
1209	0.3	0632	4.6
F 1837	5.2	SA 1227	0.8
		1843	4.8
9 0035	0.1	**24** 0043	0.7
0706	5.0	0702	4.6
SA 1255	0.1	SU 1254	0.8
1921	5.3	1913	4.7
10 0119	0.0	**25** 0107	0.8
0749	5.0	0732	4.6
SU 1336	0.1	M 1317	0.9
2004	5.2	1942	4.6
11 0158	0.1	**26** 0128	0.9
0828	5.0	0759	4.6
M 1414	0.3	TU 1337	1.0
2044	5.0	2007	4.5
12 0234	0.4	**27** 0148	1.1
0905	4.8	0822	4.4
TU 1449	0.6	W 1358	1.2
2120	4.7	2030	4.3
13 0309	0.8	**28** 0210	1.3
0938	4.5	0847	4.3
W 1525	1.1	TH 1425	1.4
2154	4.3	2056	4.1
14 0343	1.3	**29** 0237	1.5
1011	4.2	0920	4.1
TH 1604	1.6	F 1458	1.7
◗ 2230	3.9	2140	3.9
15 0425	1.9	**30** 0315	1.8
1054	3.8	1013	3.9
F 1658	2.1	SA 1546	2.0
2334	3.5	◖ 2247	3.6

OCTOBER

Time	m		Time	m
1 0412	2.2	**16** 0117	3.4
1126	3.7	0704	2.5
SU 1729	2.3	M 1344	3.7
		2011	2.2
2 0009	3.5	**17** 0234	3.6
0632	2.3	0835	2.2
M 1255	3.8	TU 1451	3.9
1930	2.0	2105	1.8
3 0204	3.7	**18** 0329	3.9
0806	1.9	0923	1.7
TU 1437	4.1	W 1543	4.2
2044	1.5	2149	1.4
4 0323	4.1	**19** 0414	4.2
0912	1.4	1006	1.4
W 1542	4.5	TH 1625	4.4
2142	1.0	2227	1.1
5 0419	4.5	**20** 0452	4.4
1007	0.9	1045	1.1
TH 1635	4.9	F 1703	4.6
2235	0.5	2304	0.9
6 0509	4.8	**21** 0528	4.6
1058	0.5	1119	1.0
F 1725	5.1	SA 1740	4.7
2323	0.2	2336	0.9
7 0555	5.0	**22** 0601	4.7
1144	0.3	1151	0.9
SA 1813	5.2	SU 1815	4.7
○		●	
8 0008	0.1	**23** 0005	0.9
0640	5.1	0634	4.7
SU 1230	0.2	M 1220	0.9
1856	5.2	1847	4.7
9 0052	0.1	**24** 0033	0.9
0721	5.1	0704	4.7
M 1311	0.2	TU 1247	1.0
1939	5.1	1917	4.6
10 0131	0.3	**25** 0058	1.0
0801	5.0	0732	4.6
TU 1349	0.4	W 1313	1.1
2018	4.9	1944	4.5
11 0208	0.6	**26** 0124	1.1
0836	4.8	0759	4.5
W 1426	0.8	TH 1339	1.2
2054	4.6	2012	4.3
12 0241	1.1	**27** 0150	1.3
0908	4.5	0828	4.4
TH 1502	1.2	F 1410	1.4
2127	4.2	2047	4.1
13 0317	1.6	**28** 0223	1.6
0938	4.2	0908	4.2
F 1541	1.7	SA 1449	1.7
2202	3.8	2135	3.9
14 0358	2.0	**29** 0305	1.9
1018	3.9	1002	4.0
SA 1634	2.0	SU 1544	2.0
◗ 2259	3.4	◗ 2239	3.7
15 0459	2.4	**30** 0410	2.2
1136	3.6	1109	3.9
SU 1806	2.4	M 1722	2.1
		2357	3.7
		31 0607	2.2
		1233	4.0
		TU 1905	1.9

NOVEMBER

Time	m		Time	m
1 0137	3.8	**16** 0237	3.8
0738	1.9	0827	2.0
W 1404	4.2	TH 1451	4.1
2015	1.4	2056	1.7
2 0251	4.2	**17** 0325	4.1
0843	1.4	0915	1.7
TH 1511	4.6	F 1540	4.2
2113	1.0	2139	1.4
3 0349	4.5	**18** 0409	4.3
0939	1.0	0959	1.4
F 1607	4.8	SA 1624	4.4
2206	0.7	2218	1.2
4 0440	4.8	**19** 0450	4.5
1031	0.7	1038	1.2
SA 1659	5.0	SU 1706	4.5
2255	0.5	2255	1.1
5 0528	5.0	**20** 0529	4.6
1119	0.5	1115	1.1
SU 1748	5.1	M 1747	4.6
○ 2342	0.4	● 2330	1.1
6 0615	5.0	**21** 0607	4.7
1204	0.4	1149	0.9
M 1835	5.0	TU 1825	4.6
7 0025	0.5	**22** 0003	1.0
0656	5.0	0642	4.7
TU 1248	0.5	W 1224	1.0
1917	4.9	1859	4.6
8 0107	0.6	**23** 0038	1.1
0736	5.0	0714	4.7
W 1329	0.7	TH 1259	1.1
1957	4.7	1933	4.5
9 0144	0.9	**24** 0112	1.2
0811	4.9	0747	4.6
TH 1407	1.0	F 1334	1.2
2034	4.4	2008	4.4
10 0221	1.3	**25** 0146	1.3
0845	4.6	0824	4.5
F 1445	1.3	SA 1413	1.3
2109	4.1	2050	4.2
11 0258	1.6	**26** 0226	1.5
0918	4.3	0907	4.4
SA 1526	1.7	SU 1457	1.5
2146	3.8	2136	4.1
12 0339	2.0	**27** 0312	1.7
0958	4.0	0957	4.3
SU 1615	2.1	M 1552	1.7
◖ 2239	3.6	2232	3.9
13 0433	2.3	**28** 0412	1.9
1055	3.8	1055	4.2
M 1723	2.3	TU 1702	1.8
		◖ 2339	3.9
14 0019	3.5	**29** 0531	2.0
0549	2.4	1204	4.2
TU 1238	3.7	W 1824	1.7
1855	2.2		
15 0139	3.6	**30** 0055	3.9
0723	2.3	0656	1.8
W 1354	3.9	TH 1322	4.2
2006	2.0	1937	1.5

DECEMBER

Time	m		Time	m
1 0210	4.1	**16** 0219	3.9
0806	1.6	0808	2.0
F 1434	4.4	SA 1440	4.0
2040	1.3	2036	1.8
2 0313	4.4	**17** 0316	4.0
0907	1.3	0904	1.8
SA 1537	4.6	SU 1539	4.1
2137	1.0	2128	1.6
3 0411	4.6	**18** 0410	4.2
1004	1.1	0955	1.6
SU 1634	4.7	M 1632	4.2
2230	0.9	2216	1.4
4 0503	4.8	**19** 0459	4.4
1056	0.9	1043	1.3
M 1727	4.8	TU 1721	4.4
2319	0.8	2301	1.3
5 0552	4.8	**20** 0544	4.6
1145	0.8	1127	1.2
TU 1817	4.8	W 1806	4.5
○		● 2344	1.1
6 0005	0.8	**21** 0626	4.7
0637	4.9	1210	1.0
W 1232	0.8	TH 1849	4.5
1900	4.7		
7 0050	0.9	**22** 0026	1.1
0717	4.9	0705	4.7
TH 1315	0.9	F 1254	1.0
1941	4.5	1930	4.5
8 0129	1.1	**23** 0110	1.0
0755	4.8	0745	4.8
F 1355	1.1	SA 1335	0.9
2020	4.4	2010	4.5
9 0208	1.3	**24** 0150	1.1
0830	4.6	0825	4.8
SA 1433	1.3	SU 1418	1.0
2057	4.2	2052	4.4
10 0245	1.5	**25** 0231	1.1
0905	4.4	0907	4.7
SU 1512	1.5	M 1501	1.1
2135	4.0	2135	4.3
11 0323	1.7	**26** 0314	1.2
0943	4.2	0951	4.6
M 1552	1.8	TU 1546	1.2
2215	3.8	2221	4.2
12 0405	2.0	**27** 0401	1.4
1027	4.1	1039	4.5
TU 1638	1.9	W 1636	1.4
◖ 2305	3.7	◖ 2313	4.1
13 0455	2.1	**28** 0455	1.6
1121	3.9	1134	4.3
W 1733	2.1	TH 1736	1.5
14 0007	3.7	**29** 0014	4.0
0557	2.2	0603	1.7
TH 1226	3.8	F 1241	4.2
1838	2.1	1849	1.6
15 0115	3.7	**30** 0125	4.0
0706	2.1	0722	1.6
F 1336	3.9	SA 1356	4.1
1940	1.9	2002	1.6
		31 0239	4.1
		0837	1.6
		SU 1510	4.2
		2111	1.5

Chart Datum: 2·62 metres below Ordnance Datum (Newlyn)

TIDES

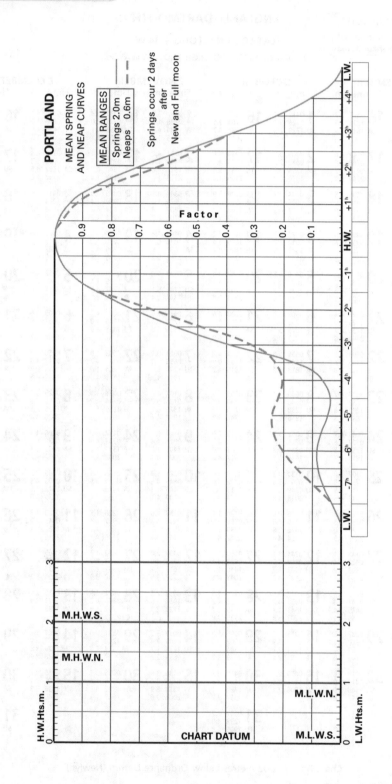

PORTLAND

MEAN SPRING
AND NEAP CURVES

MEAN RANGES
Springs 2.0m
Neaps 0.6m

Springs occur 2 days
after
New and Full moon

Factor

0.9 0.8 0.7 0.6 0.5 0.4 0.3 0.2 0.1

L.W. +4ʰ +3ʰ +2ʰ +1ʰ H.W. -1ʰ -2ʰ -3ʰ -4ʰ -5ʰ -6ʰ -7ʰ L.W.

H.W.Hts.m.

M.H.W.S.

M.H.W.N.

CHART DATUM

M.L.W.N.

M.L.W.S.

L.W.Hts.m.

ENGLAND – PORTLAND

LAT 50°34'N   LONG 2°26'W

TIMES AND HEIGHTS OF HIGH AND LOW WATERS

Note - Double LWs occur at Portland. The predictions are for the first LW. The second LW occurs from 3 to 4 Hrs later and may, at Springs, on occasions be lower than the first.

JANUARY

Day	Time m	Time m	Time m	Time m
1 SU	0721 2.2	1223 0.3	1950 2.0	
16 M	0038 0.4	0742 2.0	1307 0.4	2012 1.8
2 M	0041 0.3	0808 2.2	1312 0.3	2037 2.0
17 TU	0115 0.3	0813 2.0	1343 0.3	2042 1.7
3 TU	0129 0.3	0853 2.2	1400 0.2	2122 1.9
18 W	0149 0.3	0844 1.9	1414 0.3	2111 1.7
4 W	0215 0.3	0937 2.1	1448 0.3	2205 1.9
19 TH	0216 0.4	0913 1.8	1438 0.3	2140 1.6
5 TH	0301 0.4	1021 2.0	1538 0.3	2248 1.8
20 F	0238 0.4	0941 1.7	1457 0.4	2206 1.5
6 F	0349 0.5	1105 1.9	1630 0.4	◑ 2333 1.7
21 SA	0300 0.5	1007 1.6	1522 0.4	2235 1.4
7 SA	0440 0.6	1153 1.7	1727 0.5	
22 SU	0330 0.5	1037 1.5	1558 0.5	◐ 2312 1.4
8 SU	0026 1.6	0540 0.7	1249 1.6	1828 0.6
23 M	0414 0.6	1119 1.4	1651 0.5	
9 M	0130 1.5	0651 0.8	1357 1.5	1934 0.6
24 TU	0010 1.3	0519 0.7	1223 1.3	1804 0.6
10 TU	0246 1.5	0811 0.8	1515 1.5	2041 0.6
25 W	0137 1.4	0649 0.7	1357 1.3	1930 0.6
11 W	0357 1.6	0925 0.7	1625 1.5	2141 0.6
26 TH	0312 1.5	0824 0.7	1538 1.4	2053 0.6
12 TH	0455 1.7	1021 0.7	1724 1.6	2232 0.6
27 F	0426 1.7	0940 0.6	1655 1.6	2201 0.4
13 F	0544 1.8	1107 0.6	1815 1.7	2317 0.5
28 SA	0528 1.9	1039 0.4	1800 1.8	2258 0.3
14 SA	0629 1.9	1149 0.5	1900 1.7	○ 2359 0.4
29 SU	0624 2.1	1131 0.3	1857 1.9	2349 0.2
15 SU	0708 2.0	1228 0.4	1939 1.8	
30 M	0716 2.2	1219 0.1	1947 2.0	
31 TU	0036 0.1	0804 2.3	1305 0.1	2032 2.1

FEBRUARY

Day	Time m	Time m	Time m	Time m
1 W	0121 0.0	0847 2.4	1350 0.0	2112 2.1
16 TH	0131 0.1	0832 2.0	1351 0.1	2056 1.8
2 TH	0203 0.0	0927 2.3	1433 0.0	2149 2.0
17 F	0158 0.2	0900 1.9	1413 0.2	2120 1.7
3 F	0243 0.1	1004 2.1	1515 0.1	2223 1.9
18 SA	0218 0.2	0925 1.8	1430 0.2	2141 1.6
4 SA	0323 0.2	1039 1.9	1557 0.3	2257 1.7
19 SU	0238 0.3	0947 1.6	1451 0.3	2202 1.5
5 SU	0403 0.4	1115 1.7	1641 0.4	◐ 2335 1.5
20 M	0301 0.3	1010 1.5	1519 0.3	2229 1.4
6 M	0450 0.6	1156 1.5	1733 0.6	
21 TU	0333 0.4	1042 1.4	1558 0.5	2312 1.4
7 TU	0023 1.4	0554 0.8	1253 1.3	1843 0.7
22 W	0424 0.6	1135 1.3	1702 0.6	
8 W	0138 1.4	0736 0.8	1436 1.3	2014 0.8
23 TH	0026 1.3	0600 0.7	1308 1.2	1859 0.7
9 TH	0327 1.4	0926 0.8	1617 1.4	2129 0.7
24 F	0222 1.4	0815 0.7	1517 1.3	2047 0.6
10 F	0440 1.6	1019 0.7	1720 1.4	2220 0.6
25 SA	0404 1.6	0939 0.5	1650 1.5	2156 0.5
11 SA	0533 1.7	1058 0.5	1809 1.6	2302 0.5
26 SU	0515 1.8	1034 0.3	1754 1.8	2250 0.3
12 SU	0617 1.9	1134 0.4	1852 1.7	2342 0.4
27 M	0612 2.1	1122 0.1	1846 2.0	2337 0.1
13 M	0657 2.0	1211 0.3	1929 1.8	○
28 TU	0703 2.3	1206 -0.1	1933 2.1	●
14 TU	0021 0.2	0731 2.0	1248 0.2	2000 1.9
15 W	0058 0.1	0803 2.0	1322 0.1	2029 1.9

MARCH

Day	Time m	Time m	Time m	Time m
1 W	0021 -0.1	0747 2.4	1250 -0.2	2013 2.2
16 TH	0031 0.1	0740 2.1	1253 0.0	2005 2.0
2 TH	0103 -0.1	0828 2.4	1331 -0.2	2050 2.1
17 F	0104 0.1	0811 2.0	1321 0.0	2032 1.9
3 F	0143 -0.1	0906 2.3	1410 -0.1	2124 2.1
18 SA	0131 0.1	0839 1.9	1343 0.1	2056 1.8
4 SA	0220 0.0	0940 2.1	1447 0.0	2155 1.9
19 SU	0153 0.1	0903 1.8	1403 0.2	2115 1.7
5 SU	0255 0.1	1011 1.9	1522 0.2	2223 1.7
20 M	0214 0.2	0925 1.7	1424 0.2	2135 1.6
6 M	0330 0.3	1041 1.6	1557 0.4	◑ 2253 1.5
21 TU	0237 0.3	0949 1.5	1449 0.3	2201 1.5
7 TU	0409 0.6	1116 1.4	1637 0.6	2333 1.4
22 W	0308 0.4	1021 1.4	1524 0.5	◐ 2241 1.4
8 W	0508 0.8	1207 1.2	1748 0.8	
23 TH	0358 0.6	1118 1.3	1624 0.7	2355 1.4
9 TH	0036 1.3	0722 0.9	1424 1.1	1947 0.9
24 F	0554 0.7	1256 1.2	1858 0.8	
10 F	0302 1.3	0926 0.8	1617 1.2	2111 0.8
25 SA	0154 1.4	0814 0.7	1513 1.3	2040 0.6
11 SA	0422 1.5	1004 0.6	1708 1.4	2158 0.6
26 SU	0343 1.6	0926 0.5	1637 1.6	2142 0.4
12 SU	0511 1.7	1035 0.5	1750 1.6	2238 0.5
27 M	0453 1.9	1016 0.2	1734 1.8	2232 0.2
13 M	0554 1.8	1108 0.3	1828 1.7	2316 0.3
28 TU	0549 2.1	1102 0.0	1823 2.0	2317 0.1
14 TU	0632 1.9	1144 0.2	1904 1.9	○ 2355 0.2
29 W	0639 2.3	1145 -0.1	1907 2.2	●
15 W	0708 2.0	1219 0.1	1936 1.9	
30 TH	0000 -0.1	0723 2.4	1227 -0.2	1947 2.3
31 F	0041 -0.1	0804 2.4	1307 -0.2	2024 2.2

APRIL

Day	Time m	Time m	Time m	Time m
1 SA	0119 -0.1	0841 2.3	1344 -0.1	2057 2.1
16 SU	0101 0.1	0814 1.9	1313 0.1	2030 1.9
2 SU	0155 0.0	0914 2.0	1418 0.1	2126 1.9
17 M	0127 0.2	0841 1.8	1339 0.2	2052 1.8
3 M	0229 0.2	0944 1.8	1450 0.3	2152 1.7
18 TU	0154 0.3	0906 1.7	1405 0.3	2116 1.7
4 TU	0303 0.4	1012 1.5	1520 0.5	2218 1.6
19 W	0223 0.3	0936 1.5	1436 0.4	2147 1.6
5 W	0342 0.6	1046 1.3	1550 0.7	◑ 2253 1.4
20 TH	0303 0.5	1018 1.4	1518 0.6	2232 1.5
6 TH	0442 0.8	1139 1.1	1654 0.9	2353 1.3
21 F	0408 0.6	1122 1.3	1643 0.8	◐ 2349 1.4
7 F	0653 0.8	1429 1.1	1906 0.9	
22 SA	0604 0.7	1304 1.3	1851 0.8	
8 SA	0152 1.3	0855 0.7	1553 1.3	2033 0.8
23 SU	0141 1.5	0751 0.6	1455 1.4	2017 0.7
9 SU	0342 1.5	0928 0.6	1636 1.4	2123 0.7
24 M	0315 1.7	0858 0.4	1607 1.7	2117 0.5
10 M	0431 1.6	0959 0.4	1715 1.6	2204 0.5
25 TU	0422 1.9	0949 0.2	1703 1.9	2207 0.3
11 TU	0514 1.8	1033 0.3	1752 1.8	2244 0.3
26 W	0519 2.0	1035 0.1	1752 2.0	2252 0.2
12 W	0555 1.9	1109 0.2	1828 1.9	2323 0.2
27 TH	0610 2.2	1119 0.0	1837 2.2	● 2335 0.1
13 TH	0633 2.0	1144 0.1	1902 2.0	○ 2359 0.1
28 F	0657 2.2	1201 -0.1	1919 2.2	
14 F	0710 2.0	1217 0.1	1934 2.0	
29 SA	0017 0.0	0738 2.2	1241 0.0	1957 2.2
15 SA	0032 0.1	0743 2.0	1247 0.1	2004 2.0
30 SU	0056 0.1	0817 2.1	1319 0.1	2031 2.1

Chart Datum: 0·93 metres below Ordnance Datum (Newlyn)

TIDES

TIME ZONE (UT)
For Summer Time add ONE hour in **non-shaded areas**

2006

ENGLAND – PORTLAND

LAT 50°34'N   LONG 2°26'W

TIMES AND HEIGHTS OF HIGH AND LOW WATERS

Note - Double LWs occur at Portland. The predictions are for the first LW. The second LW occurs from 3 to 4 Hrs later and may, at Springs, on occasions be lower than the first.

MAY

Day	Time	m	Time	m	Time	m	Time	m
1 M	0133	0.2	0852	1.9	1353	0.2	2100	1.9
2 TU	0210	0.3	0922	1.7	1426	0.4	2125	1.8
3 W	0247	0.5	0951	1.5	1457	0.6	2151	1.6
4 TH	0328	0.6	1027	1.3	1530	0.8	2224	1.5
5 F	0426	0.7	1121	1.2	1627	0.9	◐ 2318	1.4
6 SA	0558	0.8	1259	1.2	1814	0.9		
7 SU	0041	1.3	0731	0.7	1454	1.3	1939	0.8
8 M	0218	1.4	0829	0.6	1544	1.4	2038	0.7
9 TU	0328	1.5	0911	0.5	1625	1.5	2125	0.6
10 W	0421	1.7	0950	0.3	1705	1.7	2207	0.4
11 TH	0509	1.8	1027	0.3	1745	1.9	2246	0.3
12 F	0554	1.9	1104	0.2	1825	2.0	2323	0.3
13 SA	0637	1.9	1139	0.2	1902	2.0	○ 2358	0.2
14 SU	0717	1.9	1213	0.2	1938	2.0		
15 M	0032	0.2	0753	1.9	1248	0.2	2010	2.0
16 TU	0107	0.3	0826	1.8	1324	0.3	2040	1.9
17 W	0144	0.3	0900	1.7	1402	0.4	2112	1.8
18 TH	0226	0.4	0938	1.6	1446	0.5	2151	1.7
19 F	0317	0.5	1027	1.5	1541	0.6	2243	1.6
20 SA	0425	0.5	1133	1.5	1657	0.7	◑ 2354	1.6
21 SU	0549	0.6	1257	1.5	1823	0.7		
22 M	0121	1.6	0712	0.5	1420	1.6	1940	0.7
23 TU	0240	1.7	0819	0.4	1528	1.7	2044	0.5
24 W	0347	1.8	0916	0.3	1627	1.8	2138	0.4
25 TH	0447	1.9	1006	0.2	1720	2.0	2227	0.3
26 F	0542	2.0	1054	0.2	1809	2.1	2313	0.3
27 SA	0632	2.0	1138	0.2	1854	2.1	● 2358	0.3
28 SU	0718	2.0	1220	0.2	1935	2.1		
29 M	0040	0.3	0800	1.9	1300	0.3	2011	2.0
30 TU	0120	0.3	0837	1.8	1338	0.4	2042	1.9
31 W	0200	0.4	0910	1.7	1413	0.5	2109	1.8

JUNE

Day	Time	m	Time	m	Time	m	Time	m
1 TH	0238	0.5	0940	1.5	1447	0.6	2136	1.7
2 F	0318	0.5	1015	1.4	1522	0.7	2209	1.6
3 SA	0402	0.6	1100	1.3	1603	0.8	◐ 2251	1.5
4 SU	0458	0.7	1159	1.3	1709	0.8	2349	1.4
5 M	0609	0.7	1311	1.3	1832	0.8		
6 TU	0102	1.4	0716	0.6	1424	1.4	1941	0.8
7 W	0218	1.4	0810	0.5	1524	1.5	2036	0.7
8 TH	0325	1.5	0857	0.5	1616	1.6	2124	0.6
9 F	0424	1.6	0941	0.4	1705	1.8	2207	0.5
10 SA	0517	1.7	1023	0.3	1751	1.9	2250	0.4
11 SU	0608	1.8	1107	0.3	1836	2.0	○ 2332	0.4
12 M	0656	1.9	1151	0.3	1919	2.0		
13 TU	0015	0.3	0741	1.9	1236	0.3	2000	2.0
14 W	0059	0.3	0824	1.9	1321	0.3	2041	2.0
15 TH	0144	0.3	0907	1.8	1406	0.4	2122	2.0
16 F	0232	0.3	0950	1.8	1454	0.4	2205	1.9
17 SA	0323	0.4	1037	1.7	1545	0.5	2253	1.8
18 SU	0419	0.4	1129	1.6	1642	0.6	◑ 2347	1.7
19 M	0521	0.4	1229	1.6	1746	0.6		
20 TU	0049	1.6	0628	0.5	1336	1.6	1854	0.7
21 W	0159	1.6	0736	0.5	1445	1.6	2004	0.6
22 TH	0310	1.6	0842	0.5	1552	1.7	2110	0.6
23 F	0418	1.7	0941	0.4	1652	1.8	2209	0.5
24 SA	0520	1.7	1035	0.4	1747	1.9	2301	0.5
25 SU	0616	1.8	1124	0.4	1836	2.0	● 2348	0.4
26 M	0706	1.8	1208	0.4	1920	2.0		
27 TU	0031	0.4	0751	1.8	1249	0.4	1959	2.0
28 W	0112	0.3	0829	1.8	1327	0.4	2032	2.0
29 TH	0151	0.3	0902	1.7	1403	0.4	2100	1.9
30 F	0227	0.4	0930	1.6	1437	0.5	2127	1.8

JULY

Day	Time	m	Time	m	Time	m	Time	m
1 SA	0301	0.4	0959	1.5	1507	0.5	2156	1.7
2 SU	0331	0.5	1032	1.4	1534	0.6	2227	1.6
3 M	0359	0.5	1111	1.4	1607	0.7	◐ 2303	1.5
4 TU	0435	0.5	1200	1.3	1656	0.7	2351	1.4
5 W	0528	0.6	1304	1.3	1806	0.8		
6 TH	0059	1.3	0636	0.6	1419	1.4	1924	0.7
7 F	0223	1.4	0748	0.6	1529	1.5	2034	0.7
8 SA	0341	1.5	0855	0.5	1630	1.7	2135	0.6
9 SU	0447	1.6	0955	0.5	1725	1.8	2229	0.5
10 M	0548	1.7	1050	0.4	1818	2.0	2319	0.4
11 TU	0644	1.8	1141	0.3	1908	2.1	○	
12 W	0008	0.3	0736	1.9	1230	0.2	1956	2.0
13 TH	0055	0.2	0824	2.0	1316	0.2	2041	2.2
14 F	0141	0.2	0908	2.0	1401	0.2	2124	2.2
15 SA	0227	0.1	0948	1.9	1446	0.2	2204	2.1
16 SU	0312	0.2	1027	1.9	1530	0.3	2243	1.9
17 M	0400	0.3	1107	1.7	1616	0.4	◐ 2325	1.8
18 TU	0450	0.4	1152	1.6	1708	0.5		
19 W	0012	1.6	0547	0.5	1247	1.5	1810	0.7
20 TH	0112	1.5	0654	0.6	1400	1.5	1928	0.7
21 F	0234	1.4	0814	0.6	1524	1.5	2057	0.7
22 SA	0401	1.5	0929	0.6	1637	1.6	2206	0.7
23 SU	0512	1.5	1026	0.6	1736	1.8	2257	0.6
24 M	0611	1.6	1113	0.5	1826	1.9	2339	0.5
25 TU	0700	1.7	1154	0.4	1910	2.0	●	
26 W	0019	0.4	0741	1.8	1233	0.3	1947	2.0
27 TH	0057	0.3	0817	1.8	1311	0.3	2019	2.0
28 F	0133	0.2	0846	1.8	1346	0.3	2046	2.0
29 SA	0207	0.2	0911	1.8	1418	0.3	2112	1.9
30 SU	0236	0.3	0936	1.7	1444	0.4	2137	1.8
31 M	0257	0.3	1001	1.6	1502	0.4	2202	1.6

AUGUST

Day	Time	m	Time	m	Time	m	Time	m
1 TU	0314	0.4	1027	1.5	1524	0.5	2225	1.5
2 W	0340	0.4	1057	1.4	1556	0.6	2256	1.4
3 TH	0420	0.5	1142	1.3	1649	0.7	2344	1.3
4 F	0520	0.6	1255	1.3	1812	0.8		
5 SA	0104	1.3	0649	0.7	1437	1.4	1957	0.8
6 SU	0301	1.3	0829	0.6	1601	1.6	2121	0.7
7 M	0430	1.5	0944	0.5	1706	1.8	2221	0.5
8 TU	0538	1.7	1041	0.4	1804	2.0	2311	0.3
9 W	0636	1.9	1131	0.2	1857	2.2	○ 2358	0.2
10 TH	0727	2.0	1218	0.1	1946	2.3		
11 F	0043	0.0	0812	2.1	1303	0.0	2029	2.4
12 SA	0128	0.0	0852	2.2	1345	0.0	2108	2.3
13 SU	0210	0.0	0929	2.1	1426	0.1	2145	2.2
14 M	0252	0.0	1003	2.0	1506	0.2	2220	2.0
15 TU	0333	0.2	1037	1.8	1547	0.4	2256	1.8
16 W	0417	0.4	1115	1.6	1632	0.6	◑ 2335	1.6
17 TH	0507	0.6	1202	1.5	1733	0.7		
18 F	0029	1.4	0616	0.7	1316	1.4	1909	0.9
19 SA	0216	1.3	0803	0.8	1513	1.4	2110	0.8
20 SU	0408	1.4	0926	0.8	1631	1.6	2207	0.7
21 M	0513	1.5	1015	0.7	1725	1.7	2246	0.6
22 TU	0601	1.6	1055	0.6	1811	1.9	2321	0.4
23 W	0643	1.8	1132	0.4	1851	2.0	● 2356	0.3
24 TH	0720	1.9	1209	0.3	1926	2.1		
25 F	0031	0.2	0752	1.9	1246	0.2	1955	2.1
26 SA	0107	0.1	0819	1.9	1321	0.2	2022	2.0
27 SU	0139	0.1	0843	1.9	1351	0.2	2048	2.0
28 M	0204	0.2	0906	1.9	1414	0.3	2112	1.8
29 TU	0221	0.3	0928	1.7	1429	0.4	2133	1.7
30 W	0236	0.3	0947	1.6	1447	0.4	2153	1.5
31 TH	0256	0.3	1011	1.5	1512	0.5	◑ 2219	1.4

Chart Datum: 0·93 metres below Ordnance Datum (Newlyn)

TIME ZONE (UT)
For Summer Time add ONE hour in **non-shaded areas**

ENGLAND – PORTLAND

LAT 50°34'N   LONG 2°26'W

TIMES AND HEIGHTS OF HIGH AND LOW WATERS

Note - Double LWs occur at Portland. The predictions are for the first LW. The second LW occurs from 3 to 4 Hrs later and may, at Springs, on occasions be lower than the first.

2006

SEPTEMBER

Day	Time m	Day	Time m
1 F	0327 0.5 / 1048 1.4 / 1554 0.7 / 2301 1.3	**16** SA	0537 0.9 / 1231 1.4 / 1936 0.9
2 SA	0417 0.7 / 1152 1.3 / 1724 0.8	**17** SU	0247 1.2 / 0759 1.0 / 1510 1.4 / 2114 0.8
3 SU	0022 1.2 / 0614 0.8 / 1345 1.4 / 1952 0.8	**18** M	0414 1.4 / 0912 0.9 / 1615 1.6 / 2152 0.7
4 M	0243 1.3 / 0826 0.7 / 1538 1.6 / 2115 0.6	**19** TU	0458 1.5 / 0952 0.7 / 1700 1.8 / 2220 0.5
5 TU	0423 1.5 / 0936 0.6 / 1649 1.8 / 2209 0.4	**20** W	0536 1.7 / 1026 0.6 / 1740 1.9 / 2250 0.4
6 W	0526 1.8 / 1028 0.4 / 1746 2.1 / 2256 0.2	**21** TH	0612 1.8 / 1102 0.5 / 1817 2.0 / 2323 0.3
7 TH	0619 2.0 / 1114 0.2 / 1837 2.3 / ○ 2340 0.0	**22** F	0646 1.9 / 1138 0.3 / 1851 2.1 / 2358 0.2
8 F	0706 2.2 / 1158 0.0 / 1923 2.4	**23** SA	0717 1.9 / 1215 0.2 / 1922 2.1
9 SA	0023 -0.1 / 0747 2.3 / 1241 0.0 / 2005 2.5	**24** SU	0032 0.1 / 0744 2.0 / 1249 0.2 / 1951 2.1
10 SU	0105 -0.1 / 0826 2.3 / 1322 0.0 / 2044 2.4	**25** M	0103 0.1 / 0810 2.0 / 1319 0.2 / 2018 2.0
11 M	0146 -0.1 / 0901 2.2 / 1401 0.1 / 2119 2.2	**26** TU	0126 0.2 / 0834 1.9 / 1340 0.3 / 2043 1.8
12 TU	0224 0.1 / 0934 2.1 / 1438 0.2 / 2153 2.0	**27** W	0144 0.3 / 0855 1.8 / 1357 0.4 / 2105 1.7
13 W	0301 0.3 / 1005 1.9 / 1516 0.4 / 2226 1.7	**28** TH	0200 0.4 / 0914 1.7 / 1415 0.5 / 2126 1.6
14 TH	0339 0.5 / 1038 1.9 / 1600 0.6 / ◑ 2302 1.5	**29** F	0220 0.5 / 0937 1.6 / 1441 0.6 / 2154 1.4
15 F	0423 0.7 / 1119 1.5 / 1705 0.8 / 2356 1.3	**30** SA	0248 0.6 / 1012 1.5 / 1523 0.7 / ◐ 2241 1.3

OCTOBER

Day	Time m	Day	Time m
1 SU	0333 0.8 / 1117 1.4 / 1718 0.8	**16** M	0250 1.2 / 0706 1.1 / 1435 1.4 / 2043 0.8
2 M	0012 1.3 / 0614 0.9 / 1313 1.4 / 1947 0.6	**17** TU	0348 1.4 / 0835 1.0 / 1536 1.6 / 2113 0.7
3 TU	0244 1.4 / 0815 0.8 / 1514 1.6 / 2056 0.6	**18** W	0424 1.6 / 0915 0.8 / 1618 1.7 / 2139 0.5
4 W	0408 1.6 / 0917 0.6 / 1623 1.9 / 2146 0.4	**19** TH	0458 1.7 / 0950 0.6 / 1656 1.9 / 2210 0.4
5 TH	0503 1.9 / 1006 0.4 / 1718 2.1 / 2231 0.2	**20** F	0531 1.9 / 1026 0.5 / 1732 1.9 / 2245 0.2
6 F	0551 2.1 / 1051 0.2 / 1808 2.3 / 2315 0.0	**21** SA	0604 2.0 / 1104 0.4 / 1808 2.0 / 2320 0.2
7 SA	0636 2.2 / 1134 0.1 / 1854 2.4 / ○ 2357 -0.1	**22** SU	0636 2.1 / 1140 0.3 / 1844 2.0 / ● 2353 0.2
8 SU	0717 2.3 / 1215 0.0 / 1937 2.4	**23** M	0708 2.1 / 1214 0.3 / 1918 2.0
9 M	0038 -0.1 / 0756 2.3 / 1256 0.1 / 2016 2.3	**24** TU	0023 0.2 / 0737 2.1 / 1243 0.3 / 1949 2.0
10 TU	0117 0.0 / 0832 2.3 / 1334 0.2 / 2053 2.1	**25** W	0049 0.3 / 0804 2.0 / 1308 0.4 / 2017 1.9
11 W	0154 0.2 / 0904 2.1 / 1412 0.3 / 2126 1.9	**26** TH	0113 0.4 / 0828 1.9 / 1332 0.4 / 2042 1.7
12 TH	0228 0.4 / 0934 1.9 / 1450 0.5 / 2158 1.6	**27** F	0136 0.5 / 0851 1.8 / 1358 0.5 / 2109 1.6
13 F	0302 0.6 / 1003 1.7 / 1536 0.7 / 2234 1.4	**28** SA	0201 0.6 / 0918 1.7 / 1432 0.7 / 2145 1.5
14 SA	0340 0.8 / 1039 1.6 / 1614 0.9 / ◑ 2334 1.2	**29** SU	0235 0.7 / 0957 1.6 / 1529 0.7 / ◐ 2242 1.4
15 SU	0453 1.0 / 1142 1.4 / 1929 0.9	**30** M	0332 0.9 / 1104 1.5 / 1729 0.8
		31 TU	0016 1.3 / 0604 0.9 / 1253 1.5 / 1916 0.7

NOVEMBER

Day	Time m	Day	Time m
1 W	0222 1.5 / 0745 0.8 / 1440 1.7 / 2023 0.5	**16** TH	0333 1.5 / 0821 0.9 / 1511 1.6 / 2047 0.6
2 TH	0335 1.7 / 0847 0.7 / 1548 1.9 / 2115 0.4	**17** F	0408 1.7 / 0907 0.7 / 1558 1.7 / 2125 0.5
3 F	0430 1.9 / 0938 0.5 / 1645 2.0 / 2202 0.2	**18** SA	0443 1.8 / 0949 0.6 / 1643 1.8 / 2203 0.4
4 SA	0518 2.1 / 1024 0.3 / 1736 2.2 / 2246 0.1	**19** SU	0520 1.9 / 1028 0.5 / 1726 1.9 / 2239 0.3
5 SU	0604 2.2 / 1108 0.2 / 1825 2.2 / ○ 2329 0.1	**20** M	0558 2.0 / 1105 0.4 / 1809 1.9 / ● 2314 0.3
6 M	0648 2.3 / 1150 0.2 / 1910 2.2	**21** TU	0635 2.1 / 1140 0.4 / 1849 1.9 / 2348 0.3
7 TU	0011 0.1 / 0728 2.3 / 1232 0.2 / 1952 2.2	**22** W	0711 2.1 / 1213 0.4 / 1927 1.9
8 W	0051 0.2 / 0805 2.2 / 1313 0.3 / 2031 2.0	**23** TH	0021 0.4 / 0743 2.1 / 1246 0.4 / 2001 1.8
9 TH	0128 0.4 / 0839 2.1 / 1353 0.4 / 2106 1.8	**24** F	0056 0.4 / 0814 2.0 / 1321 0.5 / 2033 1.8
10 F	0203 0.5 / 0908 1.9 / 1434 0.6 / 2139 1.6	**25** SA	0131 0.5 / 0845 1.9 / 1400 0.5 / 2109 1.7
11 SA	0238 0.7 / 0936 1.8 / 1522 0.7 / 2216 1.4	**26** SU	0209 0.6 / 0920 1.8 / 1447 0.6 / 2152 1.6
12 SU	0316 0.9 / 1009 1.6 / 1624 0.8 / ◐ 2310 1.3	**27** M	0256 0.7 / 1005 1.7 / 1549 0.6 / 2249 1.5
13 M	0412 1.0 / 1100 1.5 / 1750 0.9 ◐	**28** TU	0402 0.8 / 1106 1.6 / 1709 0.7
14 TU	0129 1.2 / 0550 1.1 / 1221 1.4 / 1914 0.8	**29** W	0005 1.5 / 0531 0.8 / 1229 1.6 / 1830 0.6
15 W	0251 1.4 / 0720 1.0 / 1408 1.5 / 2007 0.7	**30** TH	0134 1.4 / 0656 0.8 / 1356 1.7 / 1939 0.5

DECEMBER

Day	Time m	Day	Time m
1 F	0250 1.7 / 0806 0.7 / 1509 1.8 / 2038 0.4	**16** SA	0258 1.5 / 0816 0.8 / 1454 1.5 / 2033 0.6
2 SA	0352 1.8 / 0905 0.6 / 1611 1.9 / 2131 0.4	**17** SU	0352 1.6 / 0907 0.7 / 1556 1.6 / 2117 0.5
3 SU	0446 2.0 / 0958 0.5 / 1708 2.0 / 2220 0.3	**18** M	0440 1.8 / 0952 0.6 / 1651 1.7 / 2200 0.5
4 M	0537 2.1 / 1047 0.4 / 1801 2.0 / 2307 0.3	**19** TU	0526 1.9 / 1034 0.5 / 1742 1.8 / 2243 0.4
5 TU	0624 2.2 / 1134 0.4 / 1851 2.0 / ○ 2352 0.3	**20** W	0610 2.0 / 1115 0.5 / 1830 1.8 / ● 2326 0.4
6 W	0708 2.2 / 1219 0.4 / 1937 2.0	**21** TH	0654 2.1 / 1156 0.4 / 1916 1.9
7 TH	0034 0.4 / 0748 2.2 / 1302 0.4 / 2019 1.9	**22** F	0010 0.4 / 0735 2.1 / 1239 0.4 / 1959 1.9
8 F	0114 0.4 / 0824 2.1 / 1344 0.4 / 2057 1.8	**23** SA	0053 0.4 / 0815 2.1 / 1321 0.4 / 2040 1.8
9 SA	0152 0.5 / 0855 2.0 / 1425 0.5 / 2130 1.6	**24** SU	0136 0.4 / 0854 2.0 / 1405 0.4 / 2120 1.8
10 SU	0228 0.6 / 0924 1.8 / 1507 0.6 / 2202 1.5	**25** M	0220 0.4 / 0933 1.9 / 1452 0.4 / 2200 1.7
11 M	0303 0.7 / 0954 1.7 / 1553 0.7 / 2241 1.4	**26** TU	0305 0.5 / 1015 1.9 / 1543 0.4 / 2245 1.6
12 TU	0341 0.8 / 1032 1.6 / 1645 0.7 / ◐ 2331 1.3	**27** W	0355 0.6 / 1103 1.8 / 1640 0.5 / ◐ 2337 1.5
13 W	0434 0.9 / 1122 1.5 / 1748 0.7	**28** TH	0454 0.6 / 1158 1.7 / 1744 0.5
14 TH	0036 1.3 / 0556 0.9 / 1229 1.4 / 1850 0.7	**29** F	0039 1.5 / 0602 0.7 / 1305 1.6 / 1851 0.5
15 F	0151 1.4 / 0714 0.9 / 1343 1.4 / 1945 0.6	**30** SA	0153 1.6 / 0717 0.7 / 1423 1.6 / 1959 0.6
		31 SU	0310 1.6 / 0833 0.7 / 1540 1.6 / 2104 0.5

Chart Datum: 0·93 metres below Ordnance Datum (Newlyn)

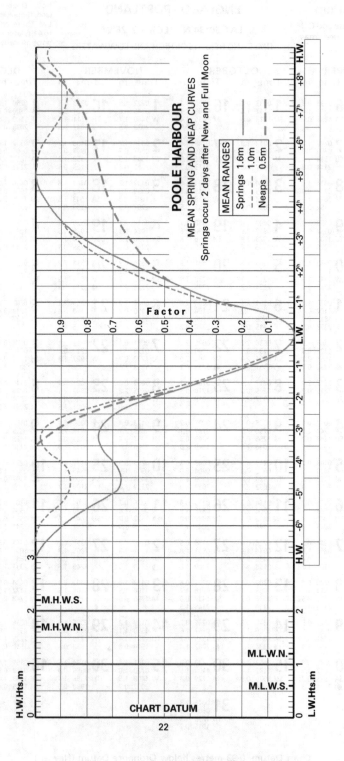

POOLE HARBOUR

MEAN SPRING AND NEAP CURVES

Springs occur 2 days after New and Full Moon

MEAN RANGES	
Springs 1.6m	
Neaps 1.0m	
0.5m	

Factor

H.W.Hts.m

L.W.Hts.m

M.H.W.S.

M.H.W.N.

M.L.W.N.

M.L.W.S.

CHART DATUM

H.W.

L.W.

H.W.

ENGLAND – POOLE HARBOUR

LAT 50°42′N   LONG 1°59′W

TIMES AND HEIGHTS OF HIGH AND LOW WATERS

Note – HW times are not shown because they cannot be predicted with reasonable accuracy. Approximate times can be gained using LW times and the Tidal Curves at the start of this section.

JANUARY

Date	Time — m	Date	Time — m
1 SU	0448 0.7 / 2.2 / 1718 0.6	16 M	0529 2.1 / 0.9 / 1750 0.7
2 M	0537 0.7 / 2.3 / 2.2 / 1806 0.6	17 TU	0604 2.0 / 0.9 / 1823 0.8
3 TU	0626 0.7 / 2.3 / 2.2 / 1854 0.6	18 W	0636 2.0 / 1853 0.8
4 W	0716 0.7 / 2.2 / 2.1 / 1943 0.6	19 TH	0706 2.0 / 1.9 / 1923 0.8
5 TH	0808 0.8 / 2.2 / 2.0 / 2033 0.7	20 F	0737 2.0 / 1.9 / 1953 0.9
6 F	0901 0.9 / 2.1 / 2.0 / ◑ 2125 0.8	21 SA	0811 1.9 / 1.8 / 2029 1.0
7 SA	0959 1.0 / 2.0 / 1.9 / 2222 0.9	22 SU	0853 1.9 / 1.8 / ◑ 2114 1.0
8 SU	1103 1.0 / 2.0 / 1.8 / 2326 1.0	23 M	0945 1.8 / 2212 1.2
9 M	1214 1.1 / 1.9 / 1.8	24 TU	1055 1.8 / 1.3 / 2328 1.3
10 TU	0037 1.1 / 1.9 / 1323 1.1 / 1.8	25 W	1220 1.8 / 1.7
11 W	0144 1.1 / 1.9 / 1423 1.0 / 1.9	26 TH	0052 1.2 / 1339 1.1 / 1.8
12 TH	0242 1.0 / 2.0 / 1514 0.9 / 2.0	27 F	0204 1.1 / 1440 0.9 / 2.0
13 F	0330 1.0 / 2.0 / 1558 0.9 / 2.0	28 SA	0302 0.9 / 2.1 / 1533 0.7 / 2.1
14 SA	0413 0.9 / 2.0 / ○ 1639 0.8 / 2.0	29 SU	0354 0.8 / 2.1 / ● 1623 / 2.2
15 SU	0453 0.9 / 2.0 / 1716 0.8	30 M	0443 0.7 / 2.2 / 1711 0.4
		31 TU	0530 0.6 / 2.3 / 1757 0.4

FEBRUARY

Date	Time — m	Date	Time — m
1 W	0616 0.5 / 2.3 / 1842 0.4	16 TH	0613 2.1 / 0.7 / 1828 0.7
2 TH	0701 0.5 / 2.3 / 1925 0.4	17 F	0638 2.1 / 0.8 / 1853 0.7
3 F	0746 0.6 / 2.3 / 2008 0.6	18 SA	0704 2.0 / 0.8 / 1920 0.8
4 SA	0831 0.7 / 2.1 / 2052 0.7	19 SU	0734 2.0 / 0.9 / 1952 0.9
5 SU	0920 0.8 / 2.0 / ◑ 2141 0.9	20 M	0811 1.9 / 0.9 / 2032 1.0
6 M	1018 0.9 / 1.9 / 2244 1.1	21 TU	0857 1.8 / 1.1 / 2126 1.2
7 TU	1134 1.2 / 1.8	22 W	1004 1.7 / 1.2 / 2249 1.3
8 W	0005 1.3 / 1.7 / 1259 1.2 / 1.6	23 TH	1148 1.3 / 1.6
9 TH	0129 1.3 / 1.8 / 1410 1.2 / 1.8	24 F	0039 1.3 / 1.8 / 1328 1.1 / 1.8
10 F	0234 1.2 / 1.9 / 1502 1.0 / 1.9	25 SA	0159 1.1 / 1.9 / 1432 0.9 / 2.0
11 SA	0322 1.0 / 2.0 / 1545 0.9 / 2.0	26 SU	0256 0.9 / 2.0 / 1524 0.7 / 2.1
12 SU	0402 0.9 / 2.0 / 1622 0.8 / 2.0	27 M	0346 0.7 / 2.1 / 1611 0.5 / 2.3
13 M	0438 0.8 / 2.1 / ○ 1658 0.7	28 TU	0432 0.5 / 2.3 / ● 1656 0.4 / 2.3
14 TU	0512 0.8 / 2.1 / 1731 0.7		
15 W	0544 0.7 / 2.1 / 1801 0.7		

MARCH

Date	Time — m	Date	Time — m
1 W	0516 0.4 / 2.3 / 1740 0.3	16 TH	0518 0.7 / 2.1 / 1734 0.6
2 TH	0559 0.4 / 2.4 / 1821 0.3	17 F	0545 0.7 / 2.1 / 1800 0.6
3 F	0640 0.4 / 2.4 / 1901 0.4	18 SA	0610 0.7 / 2.1 / 1825 0.7
4 SA	0720 0.5 / 2.3 / 1939 0.6	19 SU	0635 0.7 / 2.1 / 1852 0.7
5 SU	0759 0.7 / 2.1 / 2018 0.8	20 M	0705 0.8 / 2.0 / 1924 0.8
6 M	0841 0.8 / 2.0 / ◑ 2104 1.0	21 TU	0742 0.9 / 1.9 / 2005 1.0
7 TU	0934 1.0 / 1.8 / 2206 1.2	22 W	0828 1.0 / 1.8 / ◑ 2101 1.2
8 W	1056 1.3 / 1.6 / 2340 1.4	23 TH	0938 1.2 / 1.7 / 2234 1.3
9 TH	1235 1.3 / 1.5	24 F	1134 1.2 / 1.6
10 F	0116 1.3 / 1.6 / 1352 1.2 / 1.8	25 SA	0031 1.3 / 1.7 / 1313 1.0 / 1.8
11 SA	0222 1.2 / 1.8 / 1443 1.0 / 1.9	26 SU	0147 1.0 / 1.9 / 1415 0.8 / 2.0
12 SU	0306 1.0 / 1.9 / 1522 0.9 / 2.0	27 M	0241 0.8 / 2.0 / 1504 0.6 / 2.2
13 M	0342 0.8 / 1.9 / 1557 0.7 / 2.0	28 TU	0328 0.6 / 2.1 / 1550 0.4 / 2.3
14 TU	0416 0.7 / 2.0 / ○ 1631 0.6 / 2.1	29 W	0412 0.4 / 2.3 / ● 1634 0.3 / 2.4
15 W	0448 0.7 / 2.0 / 1704 0.6	30 TH	0455 0.3 / 2.3 / 1716 0.3
		31 F	0536 0.3 / 2.4 / 1755 0.3

APRIL

Date	Time — m	Date	Time — m
1 SA	0615 0.4 / 2.3 / 1833 0.4	16 SU	0542 0.7 / 2.1 / 1759 0.7
2 SU	0652 0.5 / 2.3 / 1910 0.6	17 M	0612 0.7 / 2.1 / 1830 0.8
3 M	0730 0.7 / 2.1 / 1949 0.8	18 TU	0646 0.7 / 2.0 / 1908 0.9
4 TU	0810 0.9 / 2.0 / 2034 1.0	19 W	0727 0.9 / 2.0 / 1954 1.0
5 W	0900 1.1 / 1.8 / ◑ 2137 1.3	20 TH	0820 1.0 / 1.9 / 2058 1.2
6 TH	1020 1.3 / 1.6 / 2312 1.4	21 F	0936 1.1 / 1.8 / ◑ 2230 1.3
7 F	1200 1.3 / 1.5	22 SA	1117 1.1 / 1.7
8 SA	0048 1.3 / 1.6 / 1318 1.2 / 1.8	23 SU	0007 1.2 / 1.8 / 1244 1.0 / 1.9
9 SU	0152 1.2 / 1.7 / 1408 1.0 / 1.9	24 M	0119 1.0 / 1.9 / 1346 0.8 / 2.1
10 M	0235 1.0 / 1.8 / 1447 0.9 / 2.0	25 TU	0214 0.8 / 2.0 / 1436 0.6 / 2.2
11 TU	0310 0.9 / 1.9 / 1523 0.8 / 2.0	26 W	0302 0.6 / 2.1 / 1522 0.5 / 2.3
12 W	0344 0.8 / 1.9 / 1557 0.7 / 2.1	27 TH	0347 0.5 / 2.2 / ● 1606 0.4 / 2.3
13 TH	0416 0.7 / 2.0 / ○ 1631 0.7 / 2.1	28 F	0430 0.4 / 2.3 / 1649 0.4 / 2.3
14 F	0447 0.7 / 2.0 / 1702 0.7	29 SA	0512 0.5 / 2.3 / 1730 0.5
15 SA	0515 0.6 / 2.0 / 1730 0.7	30 SU	0551 0.5 / 2.3 / 1808 0.6

Chart Datum: 1·40 metres below Ordnance Datum (Newlyn)

TIDES

TIME ZONE (UT)
For Summer Time add ONE hour in **non-shaded areas**

2006

ENGLAND – POOLE HARBOUR

LAT 50°42'N   LONG 1°59'W

TIMES AND HEIGHTS OF HIGH AND LOW WATERS

Note - HW times are not shown because they cannot be predicted with reasonable accuracy. Approximate times can be gained using LW times and the Tidal Curves at the start of this section.

MAY

Day	Time	m	Day	Time	m
1 M	0629 / 1846	2.2 0.6 / 2.1 0.7	16 TU	0557 / 1818	2.1 0.7 / 2.1 0.8
2 TU	0707 / 1926	2.1 0.7 / 2.0 0.9	17 W	0639 / 1903	2.0 0.7 / 2.0 0.9
3 W	0748 / 2013	1.9 0.9 / 1.9 1.1	18 TH	0727 / 1956	2.0 0.8 / 2.0 1.0
4 TH	0837 / 2112	1.8 1.0 / 1.8 1.3	19 F	0824 / 2100	1.9 0.9 / 1.9 1.0
5 F ◑	0944 / 2231	1.6 1.2 / 1.7 1.3	20 SA ◑	0933 / 2213	1.8 1.0 / 1.9 1.1
6 SA	1107 / 2354	1.5 1.3 / 1.7 1.3	21 SU	1050 / 2331	1.8 1.0 / 1.9 1.0
7 SU	1222	1.5 1.2 1.8	22 M	1203	1.8 0.9 2.0
8 M	0101 / 1318	1.2 1.6 / 1.1 1.9	23 TU	0041 / 1308	0.9 1.9 / 0.8 2.1
9 TU	0148 / 1401	1.1 1.8 / 1.0 1.9	24 W	0141 / 1403	0.8 2.1 / 0.7 2.1
10 W	0228 / 1441	0.9 1.8 / 0.9 2.0	25 TH	0233 / 1453	0.7 2.0 / 0.7 2.2
11 TH	0304 / 1518	0.8 1.9 / 0.8 2.0	26 F	0322 / 1540	0.6 2.1 / 0.6 2.2
12 F	0339 / 1554	0.8 2.0 / 0.8 2.1	27 SA ●	0408 / 1625	0.6 2.1 / 0.6 2.2
13 SA ○	0413 / 1628	0.7 2.0 / 0.7 2.1	28 SU	0452 / 1708	0.6 2.1 / 0.7
14 SU	0447 / 1703	0.7 2.1 / 0.7	29 M	0533 / 1749	2.2 0.6 / 2.1 0.7
15 M	0520 / 1739	2.1 0.7 / 2.1 0.8	30 TU	0612 / 1829	2.1 0.7 / 2.1 0.8
			31 W	0651 / 1909	2.0 0.8 / 2.0 0.9

JUNE

Day	Time	m	Day	Time	m
1 TH	0731 / 1953	1.9 0.9 / 1.9 1.0	16 F	0728 / 1954	2.0 0.7 / 2.1 0.8
2 F	0815 / 2042	1.8 1.0 / 1.9 1.2	17 SA	0821 / 2050	2.0 0.7 / 2.0 0.9
3 SA ◑	0906 / 2140	1.7 1.1 / 1.8 1.3	18 SU ◑	0918 / 2150	1.9 0.8 / 2.0 0.9
4 SU	1005 / 2245	1.6 1.2 / 1.8 1.3	19 M	1018 / 2254	1.9 0.8 / 2.0 0.9
5 M	1109 / 2350	1.6 1.2 / 1.8 1.3	20 TU	1122	1.9 0.9 2.0
6 TU	1211	1.6 1.2 1.8	21 W	0002 / 1229	0.9 / 0.9 2.0
7 W	0048 / 1305	1.2 1.7 / 1.1 1.9	22 TH	0108 / 1332	0.9 1.9 / 0.9 2.0
8 TH	0137 / 1352	1.0 1.8 / 1.0 1.9	23 F	0209 / 1430	0.9 1.9 / 0.9 2.1
9 F	0221 / 1436	0.9 1.9 / 0.9 2.0	24 SA	0303 / 1522	0.8 2.0 / 0.8 2.1
10 SA	0303 / 1519	0.9 1.9 / 0.9 2.0	25 SU ●	0352 / 1610	0.7 2.0 / 0.8 2.1
11 SU ○	0343 / 1601	0.8 1.9 / 0.8 2.0	26 M	0438 / 1654	0.7 2.1 / 0.8 2.1
12 M	0425 / 1644	0.7 2.0 / 0.8 2.1	27 TU	0520 / 1735	0.7 2.1 / 0.8
13 TU	0507 / 1728	0.7 2.1 / 0.8	28 W	0558 / 1814	2.0 0.7 / 2.1 0.8
14 W	0551 / 1813	2.1 0.7 / 2.0 0.8	29 TH	0635 / 1852	2.0 0.8 / 2.0 0.9
15 TH	0638 / 1902	2.1 0.7 / 2.1 0.8	30 F	0711 / 1929	1.9 0.8 / 2.0 0.9

JULY

Day	Time	m	Day	Time	m
1 SA	0747 / 2008	1.9 0.9 / 1.9 1.0	16 SU	0806 / 2030	2.1 0.6 / 2.1 0.7
2 SU	0824 / 2048	1.8 0.9 / 1.9 1.1	17 M ◑	0854 / 2122	2.0 0.7 / 2.1 0.8
3 M ◑	0905 / 2134	1.8 1.0 / 1.8 1.2	18 TU	0946 / 2220	1.9 0.8 / 2.0 0.9
4 TU	0953 / 2229	1.7 1.1 / 1.8 1.2	19 W	1046 / 2327	1.8 0.9 / 1.9 1.0
5 W	1051 / 2333	1.7 1.2 / 1.8 1.2	20 TH	1156	1.8 0.9 1.9
6 TH	1157	1.6 1.2 1.8	21 F	0042 / 1311	1.0 1.8 / 1.1 1.9
7 F	0041 / 1304	1.2 1.7 / 1.2 1.9	22 SA	0154 / 1417	1.0 1.8 / 1.1 1.9
8 SA	0142 / 1402	1.0 1.8 / 1.1 1.9	23 SU	0253 / 1513	0.9 1.9 / 1.0 2.0
9 SU	0235 / 1455	0.9 1.9 / 1.0 2.0	24 M	0342 / 1600	0.8 2.0 / 0.9 2.0
10 M ●	0324 / 1544	0.8 2.0 / 0.9 2.1	25 TU	0425 / 1642	0.8 2.0 / 0.8 2.0
11 TU ○	0412 / 1632	0.7 2.1 / 0.8 2.1	26 W	0504 / 1720	0.7 2.1 / 0.8
12 W	0459 / 1720	0.6 2.1 / 0.7	27 TH	0540 / 1756	0.7 2.0 / 0.8
13 TH	0545 / 1807	0.6 2.1 / 0.7	28 F	0614 / 1829	2.0 0.7 / 2.1 0.8
14 F	0632 / 1854	2.1 0.5 / 2.2 0.6	29 SA	0646 / 1900	2.0 0.7 / 2.0 0.8
15 SA	0719 / 1941	2.1 0.5 / 2.2 0.7	30 SU	0715 / 1930	1.9 0.8 / 2.0 0.9
			31 M	0743 / 2001	1.9 0.8 / 2.0 0.9

AUGUST

Day	Time	m	Day	Time	m
1 TU	0815 / 2038	1.8 0.9 / 1.9	16 W ◑	0914 / 2146	1.9 0.9 / 1.0
2 W ◑	0854 / 2123	1.8 1.0 / 1.2	17 TH	1013 / 2257	1.8 1.1 / 1.2
3 TH	0946 / 2225	1.7 1.2 / 1.3	18 F	1132	1.6 1.3 1.7
4 F	1058 / 2351	1.6 1.3 / 1.3	19 SA	0026 / 1302	1.2 1.6 / 1.6 1.8
5 SA	1229	1.6 1.3 1.8	20 SU	0146 / 1413	1.2 1.8 / 1.2 1.8
6 SU	0118 / 1345	1.2 1.8 / 1.2 1.9	21 M	0245 / 1506	1.0 1.9 / 1.0 2.0
7 M	0221 / 1444	1.0 1.9 / 1.0 2.0	22 TU	0329 / 1547	0.9 2.0 / 0.9 2.0
8 TU	0313 / 1534	0.8 2.0 / 0.8 2.1	23 W ●	0407 / 1624	0.8 2.1 / 0.8 2.0
9 W ○	0401 / 1622	0.6 2.1 / 0.7 2.1	24 TH	0443 / 1659	0.7 2.1 / 0.8 2.0
10 TH	0447 / 1708	0.5 2.3 / 0.6	25 F	0516 / 1731	0.6 2.0 / 0.7
11 F	0532 / 1752	2.2 0.4 / 2.3 0.5	26 SA	0547 / 1801	2.0 0.6 / 2.1 0.7
12 SA	0616 / 1837	2.3 0.4 / 2.3 0.5	27 SU	0616 / 1828	2.0 0.7 / 2.1 0.8
13 SU	0700 / 1920	2.2 0.4 / 2.3 0.5	28 M	0641 / 1853	2.0 0.8 / 2.0 0.8
14 M	0742 / 2005	2.1 0.5 / 2.2 0.6	29 TU	0706 / 1921	2.0 0.8 / 2.0 0.8
15 TU	0826 / 2051	2.1 0.7 / 2.1 0.8	30 W	0734 / 1954	1.9 0.9 / 1.9 1.0
			31 TH ◑	0810 / 2037	1.8 1.0 / 1.8 1.1

Chart Datum: 1·40 metres below Ordnance Datum (Newlyn)

ENGLAND – POOLE HARBOUR

LAT 50°42'N   LONG 1°59'W

TIMES AND HEIGHTS OF HIGH AND LOW WATERS

TIME ZONE (UT)
For Summer Time add ONE hour in **non-shaded areas**

2006

Note - HW times are not shown because they cannot be predicted with reasonable accuracy. Approximate times can be gained using LW times and the Tidal Curves at the start of this section.

Moon phase symbols: ● new · ○ full · ◐ last quarter · ◑ first quarter.
Each day lists, in chronological order, the tidal readings ("time m" for Low Waters; "m" only for High Waters, whose times are not shown).

SEPTEMBER

Day				
1 F	1.7	0900 1.2	1.8	2138 1.3
2 SA	1.6	1018 1.4	1.7	2318 1.3
3 SU	1.6	1215 1.4	1.7	
4 M	0105 1.2	1337 1.2	1.9	
5 TU	0209 1.0	1432 1.0	2.0	
6 W	0259 0.7	1520 0.8	2.1	
7 TH ○	0344 0.6	2.3	1604 0.6	2.3
8 F	0428 0.4	2.3	1648 0.5	2.3
9 SA	0511 0.3	2.4	1731 0.4	
10 SU	2.3	0553 0.3	2.4	1813 0.4
11 M	2.3	0634 0.4	2.3	1854 0.5
12 TU	0714 0.6	2.2	1935 0.7	
13 W	0756 0.7	2.1	2019 0.8	
14 TH ◐	0842 1.0	1.9	2113 1.0	1.9
15 F	0946 1.2	1.8	2230 1.3	1.8
16 SA	1.6	1116 1.4	1.6	
17 SU	0010 1.3	1.7	1254 1.4	1.7
18 M	0134 1.2	1.8	1403 1.2	1.8
19 TU	0227 1.0	2.0	1448 1.0	1.9
20 W	0307 0.9	2.1	1524 0.9	2.0
21 TH	0341 0.8	2.1	1558 0.8	2.1
22 F ●	0414 0.7	2.1	1630 0.7	2.1
23 SA	0446 0.6	2.1	1701 0.7	2.1
24 SU	0517 0.7	2.1	1730 0.7	
25 M	2.1	0544 0.7	2.1	1755 0.7
26 TU	2.1	0608 0.8	2.1	1820 0.8
27 W	2.0	0633 0.8	2.0	1847 0.9
28 TH	2.0	0703 0.9	2.0	1921 1.0
29 F	0740 1.1	1.9	2004 1.1	
30 SA ◑	0832 1.3	1.8	2109 1.3	

OCTOBER

Day				
1 SU	1.7	1000 1.4	2258 1.3	
2 M	1.7	1201 1.4	1.7	
3 TU	0044 1.2	1.8	1318 1.2	1.9
4 W	0147 0.9	2.0	1411 0.9	2.0
5 TH	0235 0.7	2.2	1457 0.7	2.2
6 F	0320 0.6	2.3	1541 0.6	2.3
7 SA ○	0403 0.4	2.4	1624 0.4	2.3
8 SU	0445 0.4	2.4	1706 0.4	2.1
9 M	2.4	0526 0.4	2.4	1747 0.4
10 TU	2.3	0607 0.5	2.3	1828 0.6
11 W	2.3	0647 0.7	2.2	1908 0.7
12 TH	2.1	0729 0.8	2.0	1952 0.9
13 F	2.1	0817 1.1	1.9	2045 1.1
14 SA ◐	0923 1.3	1.8	2201 1.3	1.7
15 SU	1.7	1053 1.4	2338 1.3	
16 M	1.7	1227 1.4	1.6	
17 TU	0100 1.3	1.9	1333 1.3	1.8
18 W	0153 1.1	2.0	1416 1.1	1.9
19 TH	0232 0.9	2.1	1452 0.9	2.0
20 F	0306 0.8	2.1	1525 0.8	2.0
21 SA	0339 0.8	2.1	1557 0.8	2.1
22 SU ●	0412 0.7	2.1	1629 0.7	2.1
23 M	0444 0.7	2.1	1658 0.7	2.1
24 TU	0512 0.8	2.1	1725 0.8	
25 W	2.1	0539 0.8	2.1	1753 0.8
26 TH	2.1	0608 0.9	2.1	1824 0.9
27 F	2.0	0643 1.0	2.0	1903 1.0
28 SA	1.9	0726 1.1	1.9	1951 1.1
29 SU ◑	0824 1.3	1.9	2100 1.2	
30 M	0950 1.4	1.8	2234 1.2	
31 TU	1.8	1128 1.3	1.8	

NOVEMBER

Day				
1 W	0004 1.1	1.9	1243 1.1	1.9
2 TH	0111 0.9	2.1	1340 0.9	2.0
3 F	0203 0.8	2.2	1428 0.8	2.1
4 SA	0250 0.6	2.3	1514 0.6	2.3
5 SU ○	0335 0.6	2.4	1559 0.6	2.3
6 M	0419 0.5	2.4	1643 0.5	2.1
7 TU	0502 0.6	2.4	1726 0.6	
8 W	2.3	0543 0.7	2.3	1807 0.6
9 TH	2.2	0625 0.8	2.1	1848 0.8
10 F	2.1	0709 0.9	2.0	1932 0.9
11 SA	2.0	0757 1.1	1.9	2023 1.1
12 SU ◐	1.9	0858 1.3	1.7	2126 1.2
13 M	1013 1.4	1.6	2243 1.3	
14 TU	1135 1.4	1.6	2359 1.3	
15 W	1242 1.3	1.7		
16 TH	0058 1.2	1.9	1331 1.2	1.8
17 F	0144 1.0	2.0	1411 1.0	1.9
18 SA	0224 1.0	2.0	1447 0.9	2.0
19 SU	0301 0.9	2.1	1523 0.9	2.0
20 M ●	0337 0.9	2.3	1557 0.8	2.1
21 TU	0411 0.8	2.1	1630 0.8	2.1
22 W	0445 0.8	2.1	1702 0.8	
23 TH	2.1	0518 0.9	2.1	1737 0.8
24 F	2.1	0554 0.9	2.1	1815 0.8
25 SA	2.1	0636 1.0	2.0	1859 0.9
26 SU	2.0	0724 1.0	2.0	1951 0.9
27 M	1.9	0823 1.2	1.9	2053 1.0
28 TU ◑	1.9	0932 1.2	1.8	2204 1.0
29 W	1047 1.2	1.8	2317 1.0	
30 TH	1200 1.1	1.9		

DECEMBER

Day				
1 F	0025 0.9	2.1	1304 1.0	2.0
2 SA	0126 0.9	2.1	1400 0.8	2.1
3 SU	0220 0.8	2.1	1451 0.8	2.1
4 M	0311 0.7	2.3	1540 0.7	2.2
5 TU ○	0358 0.7	2.3	1627 0.7	2.2
6 W	0444 0.7	2.3	1712 0.7	
7 TH	2.2	0528 0.8	2.2	1754 0.7
8 F	2.1	0611 0.8	2.1	1835 0.8
9 SA	2.1	0653 0.9	2.0	1917 0.9
10 SU	2.0	0738 1.0	1.9	2000 1.0
11 M	1.9	0826 1.2	1.8	2047 1.1
12 TU ◐	1.9	0921 1.3	1.7	2141 1.2
13 W	1.8	1023 1.3	1.6	2241 1.2
14 TH	1129 1.3	1.6	2345 1.2	
15 F	1.8	1230 1.3	1.6	
16 SA	0044 1.2	1.9	1323 1.1	1.8
17 SU	0136 1.2	1.9	1408 1.1	1.9
18 M	0223 1.0	2.0	1450 1.0	1.9
19 TU	0305 1.0	2.1	1531 0.9	2.0
20 W ●	0346 0.9	2.1	1610 0.8	2.1
21 TH	0426 0.9	2.1	1650 0.8	2.1
22 F	0507 0.8	2.1	1731 0.7	
23 SA	2.1	0549 0.8	2.1	1813 0.7
24 SU	2.1	0633 0.8	2.1	1859 0.7
25 M	2.1	0721 0.7	2.0	1947 0.7
26 TU	2.1	0812 0.8	2.0	2038 0.8
27 W ◑	1.9	0908 1.0	2.0	2134 0.9
28 TH	2.0	1010 1.0	1.9	2235 1.0
29 F	1118 1.0	1.9	2343 1.0	
30 SA	1229 1.0	2.0		
31 SU	0054 1.0	2.0	1338 1.0	1.9

Chart Datum: 1·40 metres below Ordnance Datum (Newlyn)

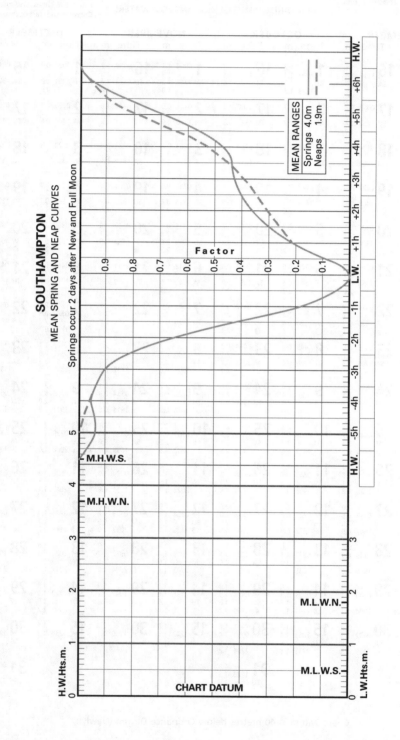

SOUTHAMPTON

MEAN SPRING AND NEAP CURVES

Springs occur 2 days after New and Full Moon

MEAN RANGES
Springs 4.0m
Neaps 1.9m

Factor

0.9 0.8 0.7 0.6 0.5 0.4 0.3 0.2 0.1

H.W. +6h +5h +4h +3h +2h +1h L.W. -1h -2h -3h -4h -5h

M.H.W.S.

M.H.W.N.

M.L.W.N.

M.L.W.S.

H.W.Hts.m.

L.W.Hts.m.

CHART DATUM

H.W.

TIME ZONE (UT)
For Summer Time add ONE hour in **non-shaded areas**

ENGLAND–SOUTHAMPTON

LAT 50°54′N   LONG 1°24′W

TIMES AND HEIGHTS OF HIGH AND LOW WATERS

Note - Double HWs occur at Southampton. The predictions are for the first HW.

2006

JANUARY

Time	m	Time	m
1 SU 0455 / 1119 / 1724 / 2348	0.9 / 4.7 / 0.7 / 4.6	**16** M 0536 / 1154 / 1755	1.1 / 4.3 / 0.9
2 M 0544 / 1206 / 1811	0.8 / 4.7 / 0.6	**17** TU 0017 / 0610 / 1228 / 1827	4.3 / 1.1 / 4.3 / 0.9
3 TU 0035 / 0632 / 1254 / 1858	4.6 / 0.8 / 4.6 / 0.6	**18** W 0051 / 0643 / 1301 / 1856	4.3 / 1.1 / 4.3 / 1.0
4 W 0125 / 0721 / 1343 / 1946	4.6 / 0.9 / 4.5 / 0.7	**19** TH 0124 / 0713 / 1335 / 1925	4.3 / 1.2 / 4.2 / 1.1
5 TH 0216 / 0811 / 1433 / 2035	4.5 / 1.0 / 4.4 / 0.9	**20** F 0159 / 0743 / 1409 / 1955	4.2 / 1.3 / 4.1 / 1.3
6 F 0309 / 0903 / 1527 / ◗ 2128	4.4 / 1.2 / 4.2 / 1.1	**21** SA 0235 / 0817 / 1445 / 2030	4.1 / 1.5 / 3.9 / 1.5
7 SA 0406 / 1001 / 1625 / 2226	4.2 / 1.4 / 4.0 / 1.4	**22** SU 0315 / 0857 / 1528 / ◑ 2115	4.0 / 1.7 / 3.8 / 1.7
8 SU 0508 / 1104 / 1731 / 2331	4.1 / 1.6 / 3.9 / 1.6	**23** M 0403 / 0951 / 1623 / 2215	3.8 / 1.8 / 3.7 / 1.9
9 M 0615 / 1214 / 1844	4.0 / 1.7 / 3.8	**24** TU 0505 / 1102 / 1736 / 2335	3.8 / 1.9 / 3.6 / 2.0
10 TU 0040 / 0723 / 1323 / 1954	1.6 / 4.0 / 1.6 / 3.9	**25** W 0620 / 1226 / 1900	3.8 / 1.9 / 3.7
11 W 0146 / 0825 / 1424 / 2056	1.6 / 4.1 / 1.5 / 4.0	**26** TH 0058 / 0735 / 1341 / 2013	1.9 / 3.9 / 1.6 / 3.9
12 TH 0243 / 0919 / 1516 / 2147	1.5 / 4.2 / 1.3 / 4.1	**27** F 0208 / 0839 / 1444 / 2113	1.6 / 4.1 / 1.3 / 4.1
13 F 0333 / 1004 / 1601 / 2230	1.4 / 4.3 / 1.2 / 4.2	**28** SA 0307 / 0934 / 1539 / 2204	1.3 / 4.4 / 1.0 / 4.4
14 SA 0417 / 1044 / 1642 / ○ 2308	1.2 / 4.3 / 1.0 / 4.3	**29** SU 0400 / 1023 / 1629 / 2252	1.0 / 4.6 / 0.6 / 4.6
15 SU 0458 / 1120 / 1720 / 2343	1.1 / 4.4 / 0.9 / 4.3	**30** M 0449 / 1109 / 1717 / 2338	0.7 / 4.7 / 0.4 / 4.7
		31 TU 0537 / 1155 / 1803	0.5 / 4.8 / 0.2

FEBRUARY

Time	m	Time	m
1 W 0023 / 0622 / 1240 / 1846	4.8 / 0.4 / 4.8 / 0.2	**16** TH 0024 / 0620 / 1235 / 1833	4.4 / 0.8 / 4.3 / 0.7
2 TH 0108 / 0706 / 1324 / 1928	4.7 / 0.5 / 4.7 / 0.3	**17** F 0054 / 0645 / 1305 / 1857	4.3 / 0.9 / 4.3 / 0.9
3 F 0152 / 0749 / 1408 / 2009	4.6 / 0.6 / 4.5 / 0.6	**18** SA 0124 / 0710 / 1335 / 1921	4.3 / 1.0 / 4.2 / 1.0
4 SA 0237 / 0832 / 1453 / 2052	4.5 / 0.9 / 4.3 / 0.9	**19** SU 0155 / 0738 / 1406 / 1951	4.2 / 1.2 / 4.1 / 1.2
5 SU 0325 / 0919 / 1543 / ◗ 2140	4.2 / 1.2 / 4.0 / 1.3	**20** M 0228 / 0812 / 1442 / 2028	4.0 / 1.4 / 3.9 / 1.5
6 M 0419 / 1015 / 1644 / 2242	4.0 / 1.6 / 3.7 / 1.7	**21** TU 0308 / 0857 / 1530 / 2120	3.9 / 1.6 / 3.7 / 1.8
7 TU 0527 / 1131 / 1806	3.8 / 1.8 / 3.6	**22** W 0405 / 1003 / 1643 / 2241	3.7 / 1.9 / 3.6 / 2.0
8 W 0006 / 0653 / 1300 / 1940	1.9 / 3.7 / 1.9 / 3.6	**23** TH 0530 / 1144 / 1824	3.6 / 2.0 / 3.6
9 TH 0132 / 0814 / 1414 / 2052	1.9 / 3.8 / 1.7 / 3.8	**24** F 0031 / 0706 / 1322 / 1955	2.0 / 3.7 / 1.7 / 3.8
10 F 0238 / 0912 / 1508 / 2143	1.7 / 4.0 / 1.5 / 4.0	**25** SA 0155 / 0823 / 1432 / 2059	1.7 / 4.0 / 1.3 / 4.1
11 SA 0327 / 0957 / 1551 / 2222	1.5 / 4.1 / 1.2 / 4.2	**26** SU 0257 / 0920 / 1527 / 2151	1.2 / 4.3 / 0.8 / 4.4
12 SU 0407 / 1033 / 1628 / 2256	1.2 / 4.3 / 0.9 / 4.3	**27** M 0350 / 1009 / 1617 / 2236	0.8 / 4.6 / 0.4 / 4.6
13 M 0445 / 1106 / 1704 / ○ 2326	1.0 / 4.3 / 0.8 / 4.3	**28** TU 0438 / 1054 / 1703 / ● 2320	0.5 / 4.7 / 0.1 / 4.8
14 TU 0519 / 1135 / 1737 / 2355	0.9 / 4.3 / 0.7 / 4.4		
15 W 0552 / 1205 / 1807	0.8 / 4.3 / 0.7		

MARCH

Time	m	Time	m
1 W 0523 / 1136 / 1746	0.2 / 4.8 / 0.0	**16** TH 0525 / 1136 / 1739 / 2353	0.6 / 4.3 / 0.6 / 4.4
2 TH 0002 / 0605 / 1219 / 1826	4.9 / 0.1 / 4.8 / 0.0	**17** F 0552 / 1205 / 1805	0.6 / 4.3 / 0.7
3 F 0044 / 0645 / 1300 / 1904	4.8 / 0.2 / 4.7 / 0.1	**18** SA 0021 / 0617 / 1235 / 1828	4.4 / 0.7 / 4.3 / 0.8
4 SA 0124 / 0723 / 1341 / 1941	4.7 / 0.4 / 4.5 / 0.5	**19** SU 0051 / 0641 / 1305 / 1853	4.3 / 0.8 / 4.2 / 1.0
5 SU 0205 / 0801 / 1423 / 2018	4.5 / 0.7 / 4.3 / 0.9	**20** M 0121 / 0709 / 1337 / 1922	4.2 / 1.0 / 4.1 / 1.2
6 M 0248 / 0842 / 1508 / ◗ 2100	4.2 / 1.2 / 4.0 / 1.4	**21** TU 0155 / 0743 / 1414 / 2000	4.1 / 1.2 / 4.0 / 1.5
7 TU 0336 / 0932 / 1606 / 2159	3.9 / 1.6 / 3.6 / 1.9	**22** W 0235 / 0828 / 1504 / ◑ 2053	3.9 / 1.5 / 3.8 / 1.8
8 W 0442 / 1049 / 1736 / 2338	3.6 / 2.0 / 3.4 / 2.2	**23** TH 0333 / 0935 / 1621 / 2219	3.7 / 1.8 / 3.6 / 2.0
9 TH 0624 / 1238 / 1930	3.5 / 2.0 / 3.5	**24** F 0503 / 1122 / 1807	3.6 / 1.9 / 3.6
10 F 0124 / 0759 / 1359 / 2041	2.1 / 3.6 / 1.8 / 3.8	**25** SA 0017 / 0646 / 1304 / 1938	2.0 / 3.7 / 1.6 / 3.9
11 SA 0228 / 0857 / 1450 / 2126	1.8 / 3.8 / 1.5 / 4.0	**26** SU 0141 / 0804 / 1413 / 2041	1.6 / 4.0 / 1.2 / 4.2
12 SU 0311 / 0938 / 1528 / 2202	1.5 / 4.0 / 1.2 / 4.2	**27** M 0241 / 0901 / 1507 / 2130	1.1 / 4.3 / 0.7 / 4.5
13 M 0347 / 1012 / 1604 / 2232	1.2 / 4.2 / 0.9 / 4.3	**28** TU 0331 / 0948 / 1555 / 2214	0.7 / 4.6 / 0.3 / 4.7
14 TU 0421 / 1041 / 1638 / ○ 2259	0.9 / 4.3 / 0.7 / 4.3	**29** W 0418 / 1032 / 1640 / ● 2256	0.3 / 4.7 / 0.1 / 4.8
15 W 0454 / 1109 / 1710 / 2325	0.7 / 4.3 / 0.6 / 4.4	**30** TH 0501 / 1114 / 1722 / 2337	0.1 / 4.8 / 0.0 / 4.9
		31 F 0542 / 1154 / 1801	0.0 / 4.8 / 0.0

APRIL

Time	m	Time	m
1 SA 0017 / 0620 / 1235 / 1838	4.8 / 0.1 / 4.7 / 0.3	**16** SU 0550 / 1208 / 1802	0.7 / 4.3 / 0.8
2 SU 0057 / 0657 / 1316 / 1913	4.6 / 0.4 / 4.5 / 0.6	**17** M 0023 / 0618 / 1242 / 1832	4.4 / 0.8 / 4.3 / 1.0
3 M 0136 / 0733 / 1357 / 1949	4.4 / 0.8 / 4.2 / 1.1	**18** TU 0058 / 0650 / 1319 / 1906	4.3 / 1.0 / 4.2 / 1.2
4 TU 0217 / 0811 / 1443 / 2030	4.1 / 1.2 / 3.9 / 1.6	**19** W 0136 / 0730 / 1403 / 1950	4.2 / 1.2 / 4.0 / 1.5
5 W 0303 / 0858 / 1542 / ◗ 2129	3.8 / 1.6 / 3.6 / 2.0	**20** TH 0222 / 0820 / 1501 / 2051	4.0 / 1.5 / 3.9 / 1.8
6 TH 0406 / 1011 / 1711 / 2311	3.5 / 2.0 / 3.4 / 2.3	**21** F 0327 / 0932 / 1621 / ◑ 2222	3.8 / 1.7 / 3.7 / 1.9
7 F 0545 / 1159 / 1859	3.4 / 2.1 / 3.5	**22** SA 0455 / 1110 / 1756	3.7 / 1.7 / 3.8
8 SA 0055 / 0723 / 1320 / 2007	2.2 / 3.5 / 1.9 / 3.8	**23** SU 0001 / 0627 / 1238 / 1915	1.8 / 3.8 / 1.5 / 4.0
9 SU 0156 / 0823 / 1411 / 2052	1.9 / 3.7 / 1.6 / 4.0	**24** M 0116 / 0739 / 1344 / 2015	1.5 / 4.0 / 1.1 / 4.3
10 M 0238 / 0905 / 1451 / 2126	1.5 / 3.9 / 1.3 / 4.2	**25** TU 0214 / 0835 / 1438 / 2104	1.1 / 4.3 / 0.7 / 4.5
11 TU 0314 / 0938 / 1528 / 2156	1.2 / 4.1 / 1.0 / 4.3	**26** W 0305 / 0923 / 1526 / 2149	0.7 / 4.5 / 0.4 / 4.7
12 W 0348 / 1008 / 1602 / 2224	0.9 / 4.2 / 0.8 / 4.3	**27** TH 0351 / 1008 / 1612 / ● 2231	0.4 / 4.6 / 0.3 / 4.8
13 TH 0421 / 1037 / 1635 / ○ 2251	0.8 / 4.2 / 0.7 / 4.4	**28** F 0435 / 1050 / 1654 / 2312	0.3 / 4.6 / 0.3 / 4.7
14 F 0452 / 1106 / 1706 / 2320	0.7 / 4.3 / 0.7 / 4.4	**29** SA 0517 / 1132 / 1735 / 2352	0.3 / 4.6 / 0.4 / 4.6
15 SA 0522 / 1136 / 1735 / 2351	0.6 / 4.3 / 0.7 / 4.4	**30** SU 0556 / 1213 / 1813	0.4 / 4.5 / 0.6

Chart Datum: 2·74 metres below Ordnance Datum (Newlyn)

TIDES

239

TIME ZONE (UT)
For Summer Time add ONE hour in **non-shaded areas**

2006

ENGLAND–SOUTHAMPTON

LAT 50°54′N   LONG 1°24′W

TIMES AND HEIGHTS OF HIGH AND LOW WATERS

Note - Double HWs occur at Southampton. The predictions are for the first HW.

MAY

Time	m		Time	m
1 0032 0633 M 1256 1850	4.5 0.6 4.3 0.9	**16**	0004 0603 TU 1230 1821	4.4 0.8 4.3 1.1
2 0112 0710 TU 1339 1928	4.3 0.9 4.1 1.3	**17**	0045 0643 W 1314 1904	4.3 0.9 4.2 1.3
3 0154 0748 W 1426 2011	4.0 1.2 3.9 1.7	**18**	0130 0729 TH 1405 1955	4.2 1.1 4.1 1.5
4 0240 0834 TH 1523 2109	3.8 1.6 3.7 2.0	**19**	0224 0824 F 1506 2059	4.1 1.3 4.0 1.6
5 0338 0936 F 1635 2232	3.6 1.8 3.6 2.2	**20**	0328 0933 SA 1618 2216	3.9 1.5 4.0 1.7
6 0455 1100 SA 1800 2358	3.4 2.0 3.6 2.1	**21**	0444 1051 SU 1736 2335	3.9 1.5 4.1 1.6
7 0620 1218 SU 1909	3.5 1.9 3.8	**22**	0601 1204 M 1845	3.9 1.3 4.1
8 0102 0727 M 1316 1959	1.9 3.6 1.7 3.9	**23**	0043 0708 TU 1308 1944	1.4 3.8 1.1 4.3
9 0149 0816 TU 1402 2039	1.6 3.8 1.4 4.1	**24**	0142 0806 W 1404 2036	1.1 4.2 0.9 4.5
10 0230 0855 W 1443 2113	1.4 3.9 1.2 4.2	**25**	0235 0858 TH 1456 2123	0.9 4.3 0.8 4.5
11 0307 0930 TH 1521 2146	1.1 4.2 1.0 4.3	**26**	0324 0945 F 1544 2208	0.7 4.4 0.7 4.6
12 0343 1003 F 1558 2218	0.9 4.2 0.9 4.4	**27**	0411 1031 SA 1630 2251	0.6 4.4 0.7 4.5
13 0418 1037 SA 1634 2251	0.8 4.3 0.9 4.4	**28**	0455 1115 SU 1713 2332	0.6 4.4 0.8 4.4
14 0453 1112 SU 1708 2327	0.7 4.3 1.0 4.4	**29**	0536 1158 M 1755	0.7 4.3 0.9
15 0527 1150 M 1744	0.7 4.3 1.0	**30**	0013 0615 TU 1242 1834	4.3 0.8 4.3 1.1
		31	0055 0653 W 1325 1914	4.2 1.0 4.1 1.4

JUNE

Time	m		Time	m
1 0136 0731 TH 1410 1956	4.0 1.2 4.0 1.6	**16**	0129 0730 F 1404 1958	4.3 0.9 4.3 1.2
2 0220 0812 F 1458 2045	3.9 1.4 3.9 1.8	**17**	0221 0823 SA 1500 2054	4.2 1.0 4.2 1.3
3 0308 0900 SA 1552 2143	3.7 1.6 3.8 2.0	**18**	0319 0920 SU 1601 2156	4.1 1.3 4.2 1.4
4 0404 0959 SU 1652 2249	3.6 1.8 3.8 2.0	**19**	0421 1022 M 1705 2301	4.0 1.2 4.1 1.4
5 0508 1105 M 1755 2354	3.5 1.9 3.8 1.9	**20**	0527 1126 TU 1810	4.0 1.3 4.1
6 0616 1209 TU 1854	3.6 1.8 3.9	**21**	0006 0634 W 1231 1912	1.4 4.0 1.3 4.2
7 0050 0716 W 1306 1944	1.8 3.7 1.7 4.0	**22**	0110 0738 TH 1333 2010	1.3 4.0 1.3 4.2
8 0139 0808 TH 1355 2029	1.6 3.8 1.5 4.1	**23**	0209 0838 F 1431 2104	1.2 4.1 1.2 4.3
9 0224 0853 F 1441 2110	1.3 4.0 1.3 4.2	**24**	0304 0932 SA 1525 2153	1.1 4.2 1.2 4.3
10 0307 0934 SA 1525 2150	1.1 4.0 1.2 4.3	**25**	0354 1021 SU 1614 2238	1.0 4.2 1.1 4.3
11 0349 1015 SU 1607 2230	1.0 4.2 1.1 4.4	**26**	0440 1107 M 1700 2321	0.9 4.3 1.1 4.3
12 0431 1056 M 1650 2311	0.9 4.3 1.0 4.4	**27**	0523 1149 TU 1743	0.9 4.3 1.1
13 0513 1139 TU 1734 2354	0.8 4.3 1.0 4.4	**28**	0001 0602 W 1229 1823	4.3 0.9 4.3 1.2
14 0557 1224 W 1819	0.8 4.4 1.0	**29**	0040 0639 TH 1308 1900	4.2 0.9 4.3 1.3
15 0040 0642 TH 1312 1906	4.4 0.8 4.3 1.1	**30**	0117 0713 F 1346 1937	4.1 1.1 4.2 1.4

JULY

Time	m		Time	m
1 0155 0748 SA 1425 2013	4.0 1.2 4.1 1.5	**16**	0207 0809 SU 1440 2036	4.4 0.7 4.4 1.0
2 0235 0823 SU 1506 2053	3.9 1.4 4.0 1.7	**17**	0256 0857 M 1532 2127	4.3 0.9 4.3 1.2
3 0317 0904 M 1551 2140	3.8 1.6 3.9 1.8	**18**	0350 0949 TU 1628 2224	4.1 1.1 4.2 1.4
4 0406 0954 TU 1643 2237	3.7 1.7 3.8 1.9	**19**	0451 1048 W 1732 2330	3.9 1.4 4.0 1.6
5 0504 1055 W 1742 2341	3.6 1.8 3.8 1.9	**20**	0601 1157 TH 1843	3.8 1.6 4.0
6 0611 1203 TH 1846	3.6 1.9 3.8	**21**	0044 0718 F 1312 1954	1.7 3.8 1.7 4.0
7 0046 0719 F 1309 1946	1.8 3.7 1.8 3.9	**22**	0155 0830 SA 1420 2056	1.6 3.9 1.6 4.1
8 0146 0819 SA 1408 2040	1.6 3.9 1.6 4.1	**23**	0256 0930 SU 1518 2148	1.4 4.0 1.5 4.2
9 0239 0912 SU 1501 2129	1.4 4.0 1.4 4.3	**24**	0347 1019 M 1607 2232	1.2 4.2 1.3 4.3
10 0329 0959 M 1551 2215	1.1 4.2 1.2 4.4	**25**	0431 1101 TU 1651 2311	1.0 4.2 1.2 4.3
11 0418 1045 TU 1640 2300	0.9 4.4 1.0 4.5	**26**	0511 1144 W 1731 2346	0.9 4.3 1.1 4.3
12 0505 1130 W 1727 2346	0.7 4.5 0.9 4.5	**27**	0548 1211 TH 1807	0.9 4.3 1.0
13 0552 1216 TH 1814	0.6 4.6 0.8	**28**	0019 0621 F 1244 1840	4.3 0.8 4.3 1.0
14 0032 0637 F 1303 1901	4.6 0.5 4.5 0.8	**29**	0052 0651 SA 1316 1910	4.2 0.9 4.3 1.1
15 0119 0723 SA 1351 1948	4.5 0.6 4.5 0.9	**30**	0125 0719 SU 1349 1938	4.1 1.0 4.2 1.3
		31	0158 0746 M 1422 2007	4.0 1.2 4.1 1.4

AUGUST

Time	m		Time	m
1 0232 0817 TU 1458 2042	3.9 1.4 4.0 1.6	**16**	0317 0914 W 1551 2148	4.1 1.2 4.0 1.5
2 0311 0855 W 1540 2127	3.8 1.7 3.9 1.8	**17**	0415 1011 TH 1656 2258	3.9 1.6 3.9 1.8
3 0359 0946 TH 1635 2231	3.7 1.9 3.7 2.0	**18**	0534 1131 F 1821	3.6 2.0 3.7
4 0507 1059 F 1748 2355	3.6 2.1 3.7 2.0	**19**	0030 0712 SA 1306 1949	1.8 3.6 2.0 3.8
5 0632 1229 SA 1909	3.6 2.1 3.8	**20**	0154 0832 SU 1422 2054	1.8 3.8 1.9 4.0
6 0116 0753 SU 1346 2018	1.8 3.8 1.9 4.0	**21**	0253 0928 M 1515 2142	1.6 4.0 1.7 4.2
7 0222 0855 M 1447 2113	1.5 4.0 1.5 4.2	**22**	0338 1010 TU 1557 2221	1.3 4.2 1.4 4.3
8 0317 0946 TU 1540 2202	1.1 4.3 1.2 4.4	**23**	0416 1046 W 1635 2254	1.0 4.3 1.1 4.4
9 0408 1032 W 1630 2247	0.8 4.5 0.9 4.6	**24**	0451 1117 TH 1710 2323	0.8 4.4 1.0 4.3
10 0455 1116 TH 1717 2331	0.5 4.6 0.6 4.7	**25**	0525 1145 F 1743 2352	0.7 4.4 0.9 4.3
11 0540 1200 F 1802	0.3 4.7 0.5	**26**	0556 1213 SA 1813	0.7 4.4 0.9
12 0015 0624 SA 1244 1845	4.8 0.2 4.8 0.5	**27**	0021 0623 SU 1241 1838	4.3 0.8 4.3 1.0
13 0059 0706 SU 1328 1928	4.7 0.3 4.7 0.6	**28**	0051 0647 M 1311 1902	4.2 0.9 4.3 1.1
14 0143 0747 M 1412 2010	4.5 0.5 4.6 0.8	**29**	0121 0710 TU 1341 1926	4.2 1.1 4.2 1.3
15 0228 0828 TU 1459 2055	4.4 0.8 4.4 1.1	**30**	0152 0736 W 1412 1956	4.1 1.3 4.1 1.5
		31	0226 0810 TH 1449 2037	3.9 1.6 3.9 1.8

Chart Datum: 2·74 metres below Ordnance Datum (Newlyn)

TIME ZONE (UT)
For Summer Time add ONE hour in **non-shaded areas**

ENGLAND–SOUTHAMPTON

LAT 50°54'N   LONG 1°24'W

TIMES AND HEIGHTS OF HIGH AND LOW WATERS

Note - Double HWs occur at Southampton. The predictions are for the first HW.

2006

SEPTEMBER

Time m	Time m
1 0310 3.8 / 0856 1.9 / F 1541 3.8 / 2136 2.0	**16** 0518 3.6 / 1116 2.2 / SA 1805 3.6
2 0418 3.6 / 1010 2.2 / SA 1701 3.6 / 2314 2.1	**17** 0020 2.1 / 0709 3.6 / SU 1305 2.2 / 1940 3.7
3 0558 3.6 / 1203 2.2 / SU 1840 3.7	**18** 0144 1.9 / 0822 3.9 / M 1413 1.9 / 2040 4.0
4 0057 1.9 / 0732 3.8 / M 1332 1.9 / 1959 4.0	**19** 0235 1.6 / 0910 4.1 / TU 1457 1.6 / 2122 4.2
5 0208 1.5 / 0837 4.1 / TU 1434 1.5 / 2056 4.3	**20** 0314 1.3 / 0947 4.3 / W 1533 1.3 / 2157 4.3
6 0303 1.1 / 0927 4.4 / W 1526 1.1 / 2144 4.5	**21** 0348 1.0 / 1018 4.4 / TH 1607 1.1 / 2226 4.4
7 0351 0.6 / 1012 4.6 / TH 1613 0.7 / ○ 2227 4.7	**22** 0422 0.8 / 1046 4.4 / F 1640 0.9 / ○ 2254 4.4
8 0437 0.3 / 1055 4.8 / F 1659 0.4 / 2310 4.9	**23** 0454 0.7 / 1112 4.4 / SA 1711 0.8 / 2321 4.4
9 0520 0.1 / 1137 4.9 / SA 1742 0.1 / 2352 4.9	**24** 0524 0.7 / 1138 4.4 / SU 1740 0.8 / 2349 4.4
10 0602 0.1 / 1218 4.9 / SU 1823 0.3	**25** 0551 0.8 / 1206 4.4 / M 1805 0.9
11 0034 4.8 / 0641 0.2 / M 1301 4.8 / 1903 0.5	**26** 0018 4.3 / 0614 1.0 / TU 1235 4.4 / 1828 1.1
12 0117 4.7 / 0720 0.5 / TU 1343 4.6 / 1942 0.8	**27** 0049 4.3 / 0638 1.2 / W 1305 4.3 / 1854 1.2
13 0200 4.4 / 0759 0.9 / W 1427 4.3 / 2024 1.2	**28** 0120 4.2 / 0705 1.4 / TH 1337 4.2 / 1925 1.5
14 0248 4.1 / 0843 1.4 / TH 1518 4.0 / ◑ 2115 1.6	**29** 0156 4.0 / 0740 1.7 / F 1416 4.0 / 2006 1.7
15 0348 3.8 / 0941 1.9 / F 1625 3.7 / 2231 2.0	**30** 0242 3.9 / 0829 2.0 / SA 1510 3.8 / ◑ 2108 2.0

OCTOBER

Time m	Time m
1 0356 3.7 / 0949 2.2 / SU 1635 3.7 / 2251 2.1	**16** 0640 3.7 / 1237 2.2 / M 1907 3.7
2 0539 3.7 / 1147 2.2 / M 1818 3.8	**17** 0105 2.0 / 0748 3.9 / TU 1339 2.0 / 2006 3.9
3 0036 1.9 / 0711 3.9 / TU 1313 1.9 / 1936 4.0	**18** 0156 1.7 / 0834 4.2 / W 1422 1.7 / 2048 4.1
4 0145 1.4 / 0814 4.2 / W 1413 1.4 / 2033 4.4	**19** 0235 1.4 / 0910 4.3 / TH 1458 1.4 / 2122 4.2
5 0238 1.0 / 0903 4.6 / TH 1503 1.0 / 2120 4.6	**20** 0310 1.2 / 0941 4.4 / F 1532 1.1 / 2153 4.3
6 0326 0.6 / 0947 4.8 / F 1550 0.6 / 2203 4.8	**21** 0344 1.0 / 1009 4.5 / SA 1605 1.0 / 2221 4.4
7 0411 0.3 / 1029 4.9 / SA 1634 0.4 / ○ 2246 4.9	**22** 0418 0.9 / 1036 4.5 / SU 1637 0.9 / ● 2249 4.4
8 0454 0.2 / 1110 5.0 / SU 1717 0.3 / 2327 4.9	**23** 0449 0.9 / 1104 4.5 / M 1707 0.9 / 2319 4.4
9 0535 0.2 / 1152 4.9 / M 1758 0.3	**24** 0519 0.9 / 1134 4.5 / TU 1735 0.9 / 2351 4.4
10 0009 4.8 / 0615 0.4 / TU 1233 4.8 / 1837 0.6	**25** 0546 1.1 / 1206 4.4 / W 1802 1.1
11 0052 4.6 / 0653 0.7 / W 1315 4.6 / 1916 0.9	**26** 0024 4.4 / 0614 1.2 / TH 1240 4.4 / 1832 1.2
12 0137 4.4 / 0733 1.2 / TH 1400 4.3 / 1957 1.3	**27** 0101 4.3 / 0647 1.5 / F 1317 4.2 / 1909 1.4
13 0226 4.1 / 0818 1.6 / F 1450 4.0 / 2048 1.7	**28** 0142 4.1 / 0728 1.7 / SA 1401 4.1 / 1955 1.7
14 0329 3.8 / 0919 2.1 / SA 1558 3.7 / ◑ 2202 2.1	**29** 0236 4.0 / 0824 2.0 / SU 1500 3.9 / ◑ 2101 1.9
15 0459 3.6 / 1057 2.3 / SU 1735 3.6 / 2346 2.1	**30** 0351 3.8 / 0946 2.1 / M 1622 3.8 / 2234 1.9
	31 0522 3.9 / 1125 2.0 / TU 1752 3.9

NOVEMBER

Time m	Time m
1 0005 1.7 / 0642 4.1 / W 1243 1.7 / 1906 4.1	**16** 0100 1.8 / 0742 4.1 / TH 1333 1.8 / 2000 3.9
2 0112 1.4 / 0743 4.4 / TH 1343 1.3 / 2004 4.4	**17** 0146 1.6 / 0824 4.2 / F 1414 1.5 / 2041 4.1
3 0207 1.0 / 0834 4.6 / F 1434 1.0 / 2053 4.6	**18** 0227 1.4 / 0855 4.3 / SA 1452 1.3 / 2117 4.2
4 0256 0.7 / 0920 4.8 / SA 1522 0.7 / 2139 4.7	**19** 0305 1.1 / 0932 4.4 / SU 1528 1.1 / 2150 4.3
5 0342 0.5 / 1003 4.9 / SU 1608 0.5 / ○ 2222 4.8	**20** 0342 1.1 / 1004 4.5 / M 1604 1.0 / ● 2223 4.4
6 0426 0.4 / 1046 4.9 / M 1652 0.5 / 2306 4.8	**21** 0417 1.1 / 1037 4.5 / TU 1638 1.0 / 2257 4.4
7 0509 0.5 / 1128 4.8 / TU 1734 0.5 / 2350 4.7	**22** 0452 1.1 / 1111 4.5 / W 1712 1.0 / 2333 4.4
8 0551 0.7 / 1210 4.7 / W 1815 0.7	**23** 0526 1.2 / 1147 4.5 / TH 1746 1.0
9 0034 4.5 / 0631 1.0 / TH 1254 4.5 / 1855 1.0	**24** 0011 4.4 / 0601 1.3 / F 1226 4.4 / 1823 1.1
10 0120 4.3 / 0713 1.3 / F 1339 4.2 / 1936 1.3	**25** 0053 4.3 / 0641 1.4 / SA 1308 4.3 / 1905 1.3
11 0211 4.1 / 0759 1.7 / SA 1428 4.1 / 2024 1.7	**26** 0139 4.2 / 0727 1.6 / SU 1356 4.2 / 1954 1.4
12 0309 3.9 / 0857 2.0 / SU 1527 3.8 / ◐ 2126 1.9	**27** 0234 4.1 / 0824 1.7 / M 1454 4.1 / 2056 1.6
13 0420 3.8 / 1015 2.2 / M 1641 3.6 / 2246 2.0	**28** 0340 4.0 / 0935 1.8 / TU 1603 4.0 / ◐ 2209 1.6
14 0540 3.8 / 1138 2.2 / TU 1802 3.6	**29** 0454 4.1 / 1052 1.8 / W 1718 4.0 / 2324 1.6
15 0002 2.0 / 0649 3.9 / W 1244 2.0 / 1909 3.8	**30** 0605 4.2 / 1204 1.6 / TH 1829 4.1

DECEMBER

Time m	Time m
1 0032 1.4 / 0708 4.3 / F 1307 1.4 / 1931 4.2	**16** 0049 1.9 / 0728 4.0 / SA 1325 1.8 / 1954 3.9
2 0131 1.2 / 0804 4.5 / SA 1404 1.2 / 2027 4.4	**17** 0142 1.7 / 0817 4.1 / SU 1413 1.6 / 2042 4.1
3 0225 1.0 / 0855 4.6 / SU 1456 1.0 / 2117 4.5	**18** 0229 1.6 / 0900 4.3 / M 1456 1.4 / 2124 4.2
4 0316 0.9 / 0942 4.7 / M 1546 0.8 / 2205 4.6	**19** 0312 1.4 / 0939 4.4 / TU 1538 1.2 / 2204 4.3
5 0404 0.8 / 1028 4.7 / TU 1632 0.7 / ○ 2252 4.6	**20** 0353 1.3 / 1018 4.5 / W 1618 1.0 / ● 2242 4.4
6 0450 0.9 / 1112 4.6 / W 1717 0.8 / 2337 4.5	**21** 0434 1.2 / 1057 4.5 / TH 1658 0.9 / 2322 4.4
7 0534 1.0 / 1155 4.5 / TH 1759 0.8	**22** 0514 1.1 / 1137 4.5 / F 1738 0.9
8 0022 4.5 / 0616 1.1 / F 1239 4.4 / 1839 1.0	**23** 0003 4.5 / 0555 1.1 / SA 1219 4.5 / 1819 0.9
9 0107 4.3 / 0659 1.3 / SA 1321 4.3 / 1919 1.2	**24** 0047 4.4 / 0639 1.1 / SU 1302 4.4 / 1903 0.9
10 0153 4.2 / 0742 1.5 / SU 1405 4.1 / 2000 1.4	**25** 0133 4.4 / 0725 1.2 / M 1349 4.4 / 1950 1.0
11 0240 4.1 / 0828 1.7 / M 1452 3.9 / 2046 1.6	**26** 0223 4.3 / 0815 1.3 / TU 1439 4.3 / 2040 1.2
12 0331 4.0 / 0921 1.9 / TU 1544 3.8 / ◐ 2139 1.8	**27** 0317 4.2 / 0911 1.4 / W 1535 4.1 / ◐ 2137 1.3
13 0428 3.9 / 1024 2.0 / W 1644 3.7 / 2243 1.9	**28** 0417 4.2 / 1013 1.5 / TH 1638 4.0 / 2241 1.4
14 0530 3.8 / 1130 2.0 / TH 1751 3.6 / 2349 1.9	**29** 0523 4.1 / 1121 1.6 / F 1747 4.0 / 2349 1.5
15 0633 3.9 / 1231 1.9 / F 1858 3.7	**30** 0631 4.2 / 1231 1.6 / SA 1858 4.0
	31 0058 1.5 / 0736 4.2 / SU 1338 1.4 / 2005 4.1

Chart Datum: 2·74 metres below Ordnance Datum (Newlyn)

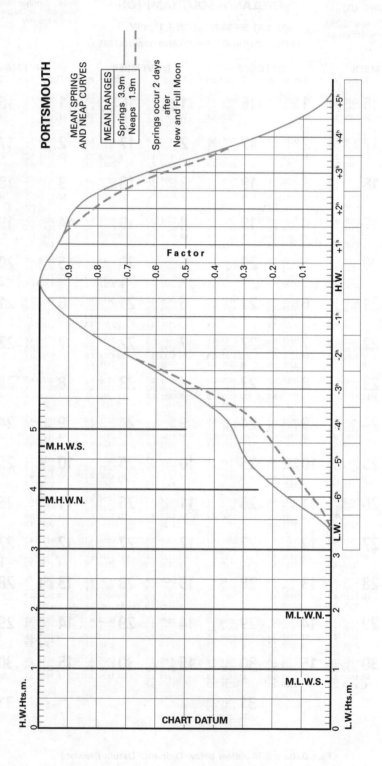

PORTSMOUTH

MEAN SPRING
AND NEAP CURVES

MEAN RANGES	
Springs	3.9m
Neaps	1.9m

Springs occur 2 days
after
New and Full Moon

TIME ZONE (UT)
For Summer Time add ONE hour in **non-shaded areas**

LAT 50°48'N   LONG 1°07'W

TIMES AND HEIGHTS OF HIGH AND LOW WATERS

JANUARY

Time m	Time m
1 0503 1.0 / 1151 4.7 / SU 1733 0.8	**16** 0019 4.5 / 0544 1.3 / M 1223 4.4 / 1805 1.0
2 0026 4.8 / 0552 1.0 / M 1239 4.7 / 1821 0.7	**17** 0052 4.4 / 0619 1.3 / TU 1256 4.4 / 1838 1.1
3 0116 4.8 / 0641 1.0 / TU 1327 4.7 / 1909 0.7	**18** 0126 4.4 / 0651 1.3 / W 1330 4.3 / 1908 1.1
4 0206 4.7 / 0731 1.0 / W 1417 4.6 / 1958 0.8	**19** 0159 4.4 / 0721 1.4 / TH 1404 4.2 / 1938 1.2
5 0257 4.7 / 0823 1.1 / TH 1508 4.4 / 2048 0.9	**20** 0234 4.3 / 0752 1.5 / F 1438 4.1 / 2008 1.3
6 0349 4.6 / 0916 1.3 / F 1601 4.3 / ☾ 2140 1.1	**21** 0309 4.2 / 0826 1.6 / SA 1513 4.0 / 2044 1.5
7 0442 4.4 / 1014 1.5 / SA 1656 4.1 / 2237 1.4	**22** 0348 4.1 / 0908 1.7 / SU 1555 3.9 / ☽ 2129 1.6
8 0540 4.3 / 1118 1.6 / SU 1759 4.0 / 2341 1.6	**23** 0434 4.0 / 1000 1.9 / M 1648 3.8 / 2227 1.8
9 0644 4.2 / 1229 1.7 / M 1912 3.9	**24** 0535 3.9 / 1110 2.0 / TU 1801 3.7 / 2343 2.0
10 0052 1.7 / 0751 4.2 / TU 1338 1.7 / 2025 3.9	**25** 0652 3.9 / 1235 1.9 / W 1929 3.8
11 0159 1.7 / 0853 4.2 / W 1438 1.6 / 2129 4.1	**26** 0107 1.9 / 0806 4.1 / TH 1354 1.7 / 2044 4.0
12 0257 1.6 / 0947 4.3 / TH 1529 1.4 / 2221 4.2	**27** 0219 1.7 / 0908 4.3 / F 1455 1.4 / 2145 4.3
13 0345 1.5 / 1033 4.4 / F 1613 1.3 / 2306 4.4	**28** 0317 1.4 / 1003 4.5 / SA 1548 1.0 / 2239 4.5
14 0428 1.4 / 1113 4.4 / SA 1654 1.1 / ○ 2344 4.4	**29** 0409 1.1 / 1053 4.6 / ● 2329 4.7
15 0508 1.3 / 1148 4.4 / SU 1731 1.1	**30** 0458 0.9 / 1142 4.7 / M 1726 0.5
	31 0017 4.8 / 0545 0.7 / TU 1230 4.8 / 1812 0.4

FEBRUARY

Time m	Time m
1 0104 4.9 / 0631 0.6 / W 1317 4.8 / 1857 0.4	**16** 0101 4.5 / 0628 1.0 / TH 1310 4.4 / 1843 0.9
2 0150 4.9 / 0716 0.6 / TH 1403 4.7 / 1940 0.5	**17** 0131 4.5 / 0653 1.1 / F 1340 4.3 / 1908 1.0
3 0234 4.8 / 0801 0.8 / F 1448 4.6 / 2023 0.7	**18** 0200 4.4 / 0719 1.1 / SA 1410 4.3 / 1935 1.1
4 0318 4.6 / 0846 1.0 / SA 1533 4.4 / 2107 1.0	**19** 0230 4.3 / 0749 1.3 / SU 1441 4.2 / 2007 1.3
5 0403 4.4 / 0935 1.3 / SU 1620 4.1 / ☽ 2156 1.4	**20** 0302 4.2 / 0826 1.4 / M 1518 4.0 / 2047 1.5
6 0452 4.1 / 1033 1.6 / M 1716 3.9 / 2259 1.7	**21** 0342 4.0 / 0912 1.7 / TU 1607 3.8 / 2141 1.8
7 0554 3.9 / 1149 1.9 / TU 1834 3.7	**22** 0440 3.8 / 1019 1.9 / W 1722 3.7 / 2304 2.1
8 0020 2.0 / 0717 3.8 / W 1314 1.9 / 2011 3.7	**23** 0606 3.7 / 1203 2.0 / TH 1901 3.7
9 0144 2.0 / 0838 3.9 / TH 1425 1.8 / 2123 3.9	**24** 0054 2.0 / 0738 3.9 / F 1343 1.7 / 2028 4.0
10 0249 1.8 / 0938 4.1 / F 1517 1.5 / 2214 4.2	**25** 0214 1.7 / 0851 4.1 / SA 1447 1.3 / 2133 4.3
11 0337 1.6 / 1024 4.2 / SA 1600 1.3 / 2255 4.3	**26** 0311 1.3 / 0948 4.4 / SU 1539 0.9 / 2225 4.6
12 0417 1.3 / 1102 4.3 / SU 1637 1.1 / 2330 4.4	**27** 0401 0.9 / 1039 4.6 / M 1626 0.6 / 2313 4.8
13 0453 1.2 / 1135 4.4 / M 1713 0.9 / ○	**28** 0447 0.6 / 1127 4.8 / TU 1711 0.4 / ● 2359 4.9
14 0002 4.5 / 0527 1.1 / TU 1207 4.4 / 1746 0.9	
15 0032 4.5 / 0559 1.0 / W 1239 4.4 / 1816 0.9	

MARCH

Time m	Time m
1 0531 0.4 / 1213 4.8 / W 1755 0.2	**16** 0003 4.5 / 0533 0.9 / TH 1215 4.4 / 1749 0.8
2 0043 5.0 / 0614 0.4 / TH 1259 4.9 / 1836 0.3	**17** 0032 4.5 / 0600 0.9 / F 1245 4.4 / 1815 0.8
3 0125 5.0 / 0655 0.4 / F 1342 4.8 / 1916 0.4	**18** 0100 4.5 / 0625 0.9 / SA 1315 4.4 / 1840 0.9
4 0205 4.8 / 0735 0.6 / SA 1424 4.6 / 1954 0.7	**19** 0128 4.5 / 0650 1.0 / SU 1345 4.4 / 1907 1.0
5 0244 4.6 / 0814 0.9 / SU 1505 4.4 / 2033 1.1	**20** 0157 4.4 / 0720 1.1 / M 1417 4.3 / 1939 1.2
6 0324 4.3 / 0856 1.2 / M 1549 4.1 / ☽ 2119 1.5	**21** 0229 4.2 / 0757 1.3 / TU 1455 4.1 / 2020 1.5
7 0407 4.0 / 0949 1.6 / TU 1642 3.8 / 2221 1.9	**22** 0309 4.0 / 0843 1.6 / W 1548 3.9 / ☽ 2116 1.9
8 0505 3.7 / 1111 2.0 / W 1804 3.6 / 2355 2.2	**23** 0410 3.8 / 0953 1.9 / TH 1706 3.7 / 2249 2.1
9 0644 3.5 / 1250 2.0 / TH 2000 3.7	**24** 0538 3.7 / 1149 1.9 / F 1845 3.8
10 0131 2.1 / 0825 3.7 / F 1407 1.8 / 2108 3.9	**25** 0046 2.0 / 0716 3.8 / SA 1328 1.6 / 2012 4.0
11 0237 1.8 / 0923 3.9 / SA 1458 1.5 / 2155 4.2	**26** 0202 1.6 / 0832 4.1 / SU 1430 1.2 / 2113 4.4
12 0321 1.5 / 1006 4.1 / SU 1537 1.3 / 2233 4.3	**27** 0256 1.2 / 0929 4.4 / M 1519 0.8 / 2204 4.7
13 0357 1.2 / 1042 4.2 / M 1612 1.0 / 2306 4.4	**28** 0343 0.8 / 1019 4.6 / TU 1605 0.5 / 2250 4.8
14 0431 1.0 / 1114 4.3 / TU 1646 0.9 / ○ 2335 4.5	**29** 0427 0.5 / 1106 4.8 / W 1649 0.3 / ● 2335 5.0
15 0503 0.9 / 1144 4.4 / W 1719 0.8	**30** 0510 0.3 / 1152 4.8 / TH 1731 0.3
	31 0017 5.0 / 0551 0.3 / F 1236 4.9 / 1810 0.3

APRIL

Time m	Time m
1 0058 4.9 / 0630 0.4 / SA 1318 4.8 / 1848 0.5	**16** 0031 4.5 / 0557 0.9 / SU 1252 4.5 / 1814 1.0
2 0136 4.8 / 0707 0.6 / SU 1359 4.6 / 1925 0.8	**17** 0102 4.5 / 0627 0.9 / M 1326 4.4 / 1845 1.1
3 0213 4.6 / 0745 0.9 / M 1440 4.4 / 2004 1.2	**18** 0134 4.4 / 0701 1.1 / TU 1403 4.3 / 1923 1.3
4 0250 4.3 / 0825 1.3 / TU 1524 4.1 / 2049 1.6	**19** 0210 4.3 / 0742 1.3 / W 1448 4.2 / 2009 1.6
5 0332 3.9 / 0915 1.7 / W 1618 3.8 / ☽ 2152 2.0	**20** 0256 4.1 / 0835 1.5 / TH 1546 4.0 / 2113 1.8
6 0428 3.6 / 1035 2.0 / TH 1739 3.6 / 2327 2.2	**21** 0400 3.9 / 0951 1.7 / F 1702 3.9 / ☽ 2245 2.0
7 0602 3.5 / 1215 2.0 / F 1930 3.7	**22** 0523 3.8 / 1132 1.7 / SA 1830 3.9
8 0103 2.1 / 0754 3.6 / SA 1333 1.9 / 2036 3.9	**23** 0022 1.8 / 0652 3.9 / SU 1259 1.5 / 1946 4.2
9 0207 1.8 / 0852 3.8 / SU 1423 1.6 / 2121 4.2	**24** 0134 1.5 / 0805 4.1 / M 1401 1.2 / 2046 4.5
10 0250 1.5 / 0934 4.0 / M 1502 1.3 / 2158 4.5	**25** 0229 1.1 / 0903 4.4 / TU 1451 0.8 / 2137 4.7
11 0325 1.3 / 1009 4.1 / TU 1538 1.1 / 2230 4.4	**26** 0317 0.8 / 0954 4.6 / W 1537 0.6 / 2224 4.8
12 0359 1.1 / 1042 4.2 / W 1612 0.9 / 2300 4.5	**27** 0402 0.6 / 1042 4.7 / TH 1621 0.5 / ● 2308 4.9
13 0431 0.9 / 1113 4.3 / TH 1646 0.9 / ○ 2330 4.5	**28** 0445 0.5 / 1129 4.8 / F 1704 0.5 / 2351 4.9
14 0502 0.9 / 1146 4.4 / F 1717 0.9	**29** 0527 0.5 / 1213 4.8 / SA 1745 0.6
15 0000 4.5 / 0530 0.8 / SA 1219 4.4 / 1745 0.9	**30** 0031 4.8 / 0606 0.6 / SU 1257 4.7 / 1823 0.8

Chart Datum: 2·73 metres below Ordnance Datum (Newlyn)

TIDES

ENGLAND – PORTSMOUTH

2006

TIME ZONE (UT)
For Summer Time add ONE hour in **non-shaded areas**

LAT 50°48′N   LONG 1°07′W

TIMES AND HEIGHTS OF HIGH AND LOW WATERS

MAY

Day	Time	m	Time	m	Time	m	Time	m
1 M	0110	4.7	0644	0.7	1338	4.6	1901	1.0
16 TU	0042	4.5	0612	0.9	1313	4.5	1833	1.1
2 TU	0147	4.5	0722	1.0	1420	4.4	1941	1.3
17 W	0121	4.4	0654	1.0	1357	4.4	1918	1.3
3 W	0225	4.2	0803	1.3	1505	4.1	2028	1.7
18 TH	0204	4.3	0742	1.2	1447	4.3	2011	1.5
4 TH	0307	4.0	0852	1.6	1558	3.9	2127	2.0
19 F	0255	4.2	0839	1.3	1546	4.2	2115	1.6
5 F ◑	0401	3.7	0959	1.9	1706	3.8	2246	2.1
20 SA ◐	0357	4.0	0948	1.5	1654	4.1	2228	1.7
6 SA	0513	3.5	1122	2.0	1830	3.8		
21 SU	0508	4.0	1105	1.5	1807	4.2	2346	1.6
7 SU	0009	2.1	0646	3.5	1237	1.9	1939	3.9
22 M	0624	4.0	1218	1.4	1915	4.3		
8 M	0116	1.9	0756	3.7	1333	1.7	2029	4.1
23 TU	0056	1.4	0733	4.1	1323	1.2	2014	4.5
9 TU	0203	1.7	0843	3.9	1416	1.5	2109	4.2
24 W	0156	1.2	0834	4.3	1418	1.0	2108	4.6
10 W	0243	1.4	0924	4.0	1456	1.3	2145	4.3
25 TH	0248	1.0	0929	4.4	1508	0.9	2158	4.7
11 TH	0319	1.2	1001	4.2	1533	1.1	2220	4.4
26 F	0337	0.8	1021	4.5	1555	0.8	2245	4.7
12 F	0354	1.1	1039	4.3	1609	1.1	2256	4.5
27 SA ●	0423	0.8	1109	4.6	1640	0.8	2329	4.7
13 SA ○	0428	1.0	1116	4.4	1643	1.0	2331	4.5
28 SU	0507	0.7	1156	4.6	1723	0.9		
14 SU	0502	0.9	1154	4.5	1718	1.0		
29 M	0010	4.7	0548	0.8	1240	4.6	1804	1.0
15 M	0006	4.5	0535	0.9	1233	4.5	1754	1.1
30 TU	0049	4.6	0627	0.9	1322	4.5	1844	1.2
31 W	0126	4.4	0706	1.1	1403	4.4	1924	1.4

JUNE

Day	Time	m	Time	m	Time	m	Time	m
1 TH	0205	4.2	0746	1.3	1446	4.2	2008	1.6
16 F	0201	4.4	0743	0.9	1444	4.5	2009	1.2
2 F	0246	4.0	0830	1.5	1533	4.1	2057	1.8
17 SA	0252	4.3	0836	1.0	1538	4.4	2105	1.3
3 SA ◑	0333	3.8	0921	1.7	1624	3.9	2155	2.0
18 SU ◐	0348	4.2	0933	1.1	1636	4.4	2205	1.4
4 SU	0427	3.7	1020	1.8	1721	3.9	2300	2.0
19 M	0448	4.1	1033	1.2	1736	4.3	2309	1.4
5 M	0529	3.6	1124	1.8	1821	3.9		
20 TU	0552	4.1	1137	1.3	1839	4.3		
6 TU	0005	2.0	0635	3.7	1226	1.8	1919	4.0
21 W	0017	1.4	0700	4.1	1244	1.4	1941	4.3
7 W	0103	1.8	0737	3.8	1320	1.7	2011	4.1
22 TH	0123	1.4	0807	4.1	1347	1.3	2041	4.4
8 TH	0152	1.6	0832	3.9	1407	1.5	2058	4.2
23 F	0224	1.3	0910	4.2	1445	1.3	2136	4.5
9 F	0236	1.4	0921	4.1	1451	1.4	2142	4.3
24 SA	0318	1.2	1006	4.3	1537	1.2	2227	4.5
10 SA	0318	1.3	1007	4.2	1534	1.3	2224	4.4
25 SU ●	0407	1.0	1058	4.4	1625	1.2	2312	4.5
11 SU ○	0358	1.1	1051	4.4	1616	1.2	2306	4.5
26 M	0453	1.0	1144	4.5	1709	1.2	2353	4.5
12 M	0440	1.0	1135	4.5	1659	1.1	2347	4.5
27 TU	0535	1.0	1227	4.5	1750	1.2		
13 TU	0522	0.9	1219	4.5	1743	1.1		
28 W	0032	4.4	0613	1.0	1307	4.5	1829	1.2
14 W	0029	4.6	0606	0.9	1305	4.6	1828	1.1
29 TH	0109	4.3	0650	1.1	1345	4.4	1907	1.3
15 TH	0113	4.5	0653	0.9	1353	4.6	1917	1.1
30 F	0145	4.2	0726	1.2	1423	4.3	1944	1.4

JULY

Day	Time	m	Time	m	Time	m	Time	m
1 SA	0223	4.1	0802	1.3	1501	4.2	2023	1.6
16 SU	0241	4.5	0821	0.7	1519	4.6	2045	1.0
2 SU	0302	4.0	0839	1.4	1541	4.1	2103	1.7
17 M ◑	0330	4.4	0909	0.9	1608	4.5	2137	1.2
3 M	0344	3.9	0920	1.6	1624	4.0	2149	1.8
18 TU	0421	4.2	1001	1.2	1700	4.4	2235	1.4
4 TU	0431	3.8	1008	1.7	1713	4.0	2244	1.9
19 W	0519	4.0	1101	1.4	1800	4.2	2342	1.6
5 W	0526	3.7	1106	1.8	1810	3.9	2348	1.9
20 TH	0628	3.9	1211	1.6	1909	4.1		
6 TH	0633	3.7	1212	1.9	1914	4.0		
21 F	0057	1.6	0748	3.9	1326	1.7	2021	4.1
7 F	0056	1.8	0744	3.8	1319	1.8	2015	4.1
22 SA	0209	1.6	0902	4.0	1432	1.7	2124	4.2
8 SA	0157	1.6	0847	4.0	1417	1.7	2110	4.2
23 SU	0308	1.4	1002	4.2	1528	1.5	2217	4.3
9 SU	0250	1.4	0943	4.2	1510	1.5	2200	4.4
24 M ●	0357	1.2	1052	4.3	1615	1.4	2301	4.4
10 M ○	0339	1.2	1034	4.4	1559	1.3	2247	4.5
25 TU	0440	1.1	1135	4.4	1657	1.2	2340	4.4
11 TU	0427	1.0	1122	4.5	1647	1.1	2332	4.6
26 W	0519	1.0	1213	4.5	1735	1.2		
12 W	0514	0.8	1209	4.6	1735	1.0		
27 TH	0015	4.4	0555	0.9	1248	4.5	1811	1.1
13 TH	0018	4.6	0600	0.7	1257	4.7	1822	0.9
28 F	0049	4.3	0629	0.9	1321	4.5	1844	1.2
14 F	0105	4.6	0647	0.6	1344	4.7	1909	0.8
29 SA	0122	4.3	0701	1.0	1353	4.4	1915	1.2
15 SA	0153	4.6	0734	0.6	1432	4.7	1956	0.9
30 SU	0155	4.2	0730	1.1	1425	4.4	1945	1.3
31 M	0229	4.1	0758	1.2	1458	4.3	2016	1.4

AUGUST

Day	Time	m	Time	m	Time	m	Time	m
1 TU	0303	4.0	0830	1.4	1532	4.2	2053	1.6
16 W ◑	0352	4.2	0929	1.3	1622	4.3	2201	1.5
2 W ◐	0340	3.9	0909	1.6	1612	4.0	2138	1.8
17 TH	0447	4.0	1028	1.7	1719	4.0	2312	1.8
3 TH	0428	3.8	1001	1.9	1703	3.9	2240	2.0
18 F	0602	3.7	1147	2.0	1841	3.8		
4 F	0536	3.7	1113	2.0	1816	3.8		
19 SA	0041	1.9	0743	3.7	1317	2.0	2013	3.9
5 SA	0006	2.0	0704	3.7	1244	2.0	1937	3.9
20 SU	0201	1.8	0902	4.0	1428	1.9	2119	4.1
6 SU	0133	1.8	0824	3.9	1400	1.8	2045	4.1
21 M	0300	1.5	0957	4.2	1521	1.6	2208	4.2
7 M	0236	1.5	0927	4.2	1459	1.5	2141	4.3
22 TU	0344	1.3	1041	4.4	1602	1.4	2248	4.4
8 TU	0328	1.1	1019	4.4	1549	1.2	2230	4.5
23 W ●	0422	1.1	1118	4.5	1639	1.2	2323	4.4
9 W ○	0416	0.8	1108	4.6	1637	0.9	2317	4.6
24 TH	0458	0.9	1151	4.5	1714	1.1	2355	4.4
10 TH	0502	0.6	1154	4.8	1723	0.7		
25 F	0531	0.8	1221	4.5	1746	1.0		
11 F	0004	4.7	0547	0.4	1240	4.9	1807	0.6
26 SA	0024	4.4	0602	0.8	1250	4.5	1816	1.0
12 SA	0050	4.8	0631	0.4	1325	4.9	1852	0.6
27 SU	0055	4.4	0631	0.9	1319	4.5	1843	1.1
13 SU	0135	4.7	0715	0.4	1408	4.9	1935	0.6
28 M	0125	4.4	0656	1.0	1348	4.4	1908	1.2
14 M	0220	4.6	0757	0.6	1451	4.7	2020	0.8
29 TU	0155	4.3	0721	1.2	1417	4.4	1936	1.3
15 TU	0305	4.5	0841	0.9	1535	4.5	2106	1.1
30 W	0226	4.2	0749	1.4	1447	4.2	2009	1.5
31 TH ◑	0300	4.0	0825	1.6	1522	4.0	2052	1.7

Chart Datum: 2·73 metres below Ordnance Datum (Newlyn)

TIME ZONE (UT)
For Summer Time add ONE hour in **non-shaded areas**

ENGLAND – PORTSMOUTH

LAT 50°48′N   LONG 1°07′W

TIMES AND HEIGHTS OF HIGH AND LOW WATERS

SEPTEMBER

Day	Time	m	Time	m	Day	Time	m	Time	m
1 F	0345 0915 F 1613 2153	3.8 1.9 3.9 2.1			16 SA	0544 1131 SA 1822	3.7 2.2 3.7		
2 SA	0456 1033 SA 1730 2333	3.7 2.2 3.8 2.1			17 SU	0025 0739 SU 1309 2006	2.1 3.8 2.2 3.8		
3 SU	0636 1230 SU 1907	3.7 2.2 3.8			18 M	0149 0850 M 1418 2106	1.9 4.0 1.9 4.0		
4 M	0120 0807 M 1352 2026	1.9 3.9 1.9 4.1			19 TU	0242 0938 TU 1503 2150	1.6 4.3 1.6 4.2		
5 TU	0224 0911 TU 1447 2123	1.5 4.2 1.5 4.4			20 W	0322 1017 W 1539 2227	1.3 4.5 1.3 4.4		
6 W	0314 1001 W 1535 2212	1.0 4.5 1.1 4.6			21 TH	0356 1051 TH 1613 2258	1.1 4.6 1.1 4.4		
7 TH	0359 1047 TH 1619 O 2258	0.7 4.8 0.8 4.8			22 F	0429 1121 F 1645 ● 2327	0.9 4.6 1.0 4.5		
8 F	0443 1132 F 1703 2343	0.4 4.9 0.6 4.9			23 SA	0501 1149 SA 1716 2356	0.8 4.6 1.0 4.5		
9 SA	0526 1215 SA 1746	0.3 5.0 0.5			24 SU	0532 1216 SU 1745	0.9 4.6 1.0		
10 SU	0028 0608 SU 1258 1828	4.9 0.3 5.0 0.5			25 M	0025 0559 M 1245 1810	4.5 0.9 4.5 1.0		
11 M	0112 0649 M 1340 1909	4.9 0.4 4.9 0.6			26 TU	0056 0623 TU 1313 1835	4.5 1.1 4.5 1.1		
12 TU	0155 0729 TU 1420 1950	4.7 0.7 4.7 0.9			27 W	0125 0648 W 1341 1902	4.4 1.2 4.4 1.3		
13 W	0238 0811 W 1501 2034	4.5 1.0 4.5 1.2			28 TH	0156 0718 TH 1411 1936	4.3 1.4 4.3 1.5		
14 TH	0324 0857 TH 1546 (2128	4.2 1.5 4.2 1.6			29 F	0232 0755 F 1448 2019	4.1 1.7 4.1 1.7		
15 F	0420 1001 F 1644 2245	3.9 1.9 3.9 2.0			30 SA	0321 0847 SA 1542 (2124	3.9 2.0 3.9 2.0		

OCTOBER

Day	Time	m	Time	m	Day	Time	m	Time	m
1 SU	0436 1015 SU 1703 2313	3.8 2.3 3.7 2.1			16 M	0712 1242 M 1939	3.8 2.2 3.7		
2 M	0614 1216 M 1841	3.8 2.2 3.8			17 TU	0115 0818 TU 1348 2036	2.0 4.1 2.0 4.0		
3 TU	0059 0744 TU 1333 2001	1.9 4.0 1.8 4.1			18 W	0208 0904 W 1431 2119	1.7 4.3 1.7 4.2		
4 W	0202 0846 W 1426 2059	1.4 4.4 1.4 4.4			19 TH	0247 0942 TH 1507 2154	1.4 4.5 1.4 4.3		
5 TH	0250 0935 TH 1512 2148	1.0 4.7 1.0 4.7			20 F	0321 1014 F 1540 2225	1.2 4.5 1.2 4.4		
6 F	0335 1020 F 1556 2234	0.7 4.9 0.7 4.8			21 SA	0354 1044 SA 1612 2255	1.1 4.6 1.1 4.5		
7 SA	0418 1104 SA 1644 O 2320	0.5 5.0 0.5 4.9			22 SU	0427 1113 SU 1644 ● 2326	1.0 4.6 1.0 4.5		
8 SU	0500 1148 SU 1721	0.4 5.1 0.5			23 M	0459 1142 M 1713 2357	1.0 4.6 1.0 4.6		
9 M	0004 0541 M 1231 1802	5.0 0.4 5.0 0.5			24 TU	0527 1213 TU 1740	1.1 4.6 1.1		
10 TU	0049 0622 TU 1312 1843	4.9 0.6 4.9 0.7			25 W	0029 0554 W 1243 1808	4.6 1.2 4.5 1.2		
11 W	0132 0702 W 1352 1923	4.8 0.9 4.7 1.0			26 TH	0103 0623 TH 1314 1839	4.5 1.3 4.5 1.3		
12 TH	0215 0744 TH 1432 2007	4.5 1.2 4.4 1.3			27 F	0138 0658 F 1348 1918	4.4 1.5 4.3 1.5		
13 F	0302 0832 F 1517 2100	4.2 1.7 4.1 1.7			28 SA	0219 0741 SA 1430 2006	4.2 1.7 4.1 1.7		
14 SA	0400 0938 SA 1616 (2216	3.9 2.1 3.8 2.0			29 SU	0313 0839 SU 1528 (2115	4.1 2.0 4.0 1.9		
15 SU	0526 1108 SU 1756 2353	3.8 2.3 3.6 2.1			30 M	0426 1005 M 1644 2249	3.9 2.2 3.9 1.9		
					31 TU	0552 1143 TU 1811	4.0 2.1 3.9		

NOVEMBER

Day	Time	m	Time	m	Day	Time	m	Time	m
1 W	0019 0711 W 1258 1928	1.7 4.2 1.8 4.1			16 TH	0113 0812 TH 1346 2030	1.8 4.2 1.8 4.0		
2 TH	0126 0813 TH 1355 2029	1.4 4.5 1.4 4.4			17 F	0159 0853 F 1426 2110	1.6 4.3 1.6 4.1		
3 F	0218 0905 F 1443 2121	1.1 4.7 1.1 4.6			18 SA	0239 0929 SA 1502 2146	1.5 4.4 1.4 4.3		
4 SA	0305 0952 SA 1529 2210	0.8 4.9 0.8 4.8			19 SU	0316 1004 SU 1538 2222	1.3 4.5 1.3 4.4		
5 SU	0350 1038 SU 1614 O 2258	0.7 5.0 0.7 4.9			20 M	0352 1038 M 1612 ● 2258	1.3 4.6 1.2 4.5		
6 M	0434 1122 M 1658 2344	0.6 5.0 0.6 4.9			21 TU	0426 1112 TU 1645 2334	1.2 4.6 1.1 4.5		
7 TU	0517 1205 TU 1741	0.7 5.0 0.7			22 W	0500 1146 W 1717	1.2 4.6 1.1		
8 W	0029 0558 W 1248 1822	4.7 0.9 4.8 0.8			23 TH	0010 0533 TH 1222 1752	4.6 1.3 4.6 1.1		
9 TH	0114 0640 TH 1328 1903	4.7 1.1 4.6 1.1			24 F	0048 0609 F 1258 1830	4.6 1.3 4.5 1.2		
10 F	0159 0724 F 1409 1947	4.5 1.4 4.4 1.4			25 SA	0129 0651 SA 1338 1914	4.5 1.5 4.4 1.3		
11 SA	0246 0812 SA 1455 2038	4.3 1.7 4.1 1.7			26 SU	0216 0739 SU 1424 2006	4.4 1.6 4.3 1.4		
12 SU	0342 0913 SU 1549 (2141	4.1 2.0 3.8 1.9			27 M	0310 0838 M 1520 2108	4.3 1.8 4.1 1.6		
13 M	0451 1028 M 1702 2258	3.9 2.2 3.7 2.0			28 TU	0414 0947 TU 1626 (2219	4.2 1.8 4.0 1.6		
14 TU	0613 1150 TU 1833	3.9 2.2 3.7			29 W	0524 1102 W 1738 2332	4.2 1.8 4.0 1.6		
15 W	0014 0722 W 1257 1941	2.0 4.0 2.0 3.8			30 TH	0634 1215 TH 1851	4.3 1.7 4.1		

DECEMBER

Day	Time	m	Time	m	Day	Time	m	Time	m
1 F	0040 0738 F 1319 1956	1.4 4.5 1.5 4.3			16 SA	0059 0752 SA 1338 2015	1.9 4.1 1.9 3.9		
2 SA	0141 0834 SA 1415 2056	1.3 4.6 1.2 4.5			17 SU	0151 0841 SU 1423 2106	1.8 4.2 1.7 4.1		
3 SU	0235 0927 SU 1506 2150	1.1 4.8 1.1 4.6			18 M	0238 0926 M 1505 2152	1.6 4.4 1.5 4.2		
4 M	0326 1016 M 1555 2242	1.0 4.8 0.9 4.7			19 TU	0320 1008 TU 1546 2235	1.5 4.5 1.3 4.4		
5 TU	0413 1103 TU 1642 O 2331	1.0 4.9 0.9 4.7			20 W	0401 1048 W 1625 ● 2316	1.4 4.5 1.2 4.5		
6 W	0459 1147 W 1727	1.0 4.8 0.9			21 TH	0441 1128 TH 1705 2358	1.3 4.6 1.1 4.6		
7 TH	0017 0543 TH 1230 1809	4.7 1.1 4.7 1.0			22 F	0522 1207 F 1746	1.2 4.6 1.0		
8 F	0102 0626 F 1311 1850	4.6 1.2 4.6 1.1			23 SA	0040 0604 SA 1249 1828	4.6 1.2 4.6 1.0		
9 SA	0146 0708 SA 1352 1932	4.5 1.4 4.4 1.3			24 SU	0124 0648 SU 1332 1914	4.6 1.2 4.5 1.0		
10 SU	0230 0753 SU 1434 2015	4.4 1.6 4.2 1.5			25 M	0211 0736 M 1419 2002	4.6 1.3 4.4 1.0		
11 M	0316 0841 M 1519 2102	4.2 1.8 4.0 1.7			26 TU	0300 0827 TU 1509 2053	4.5 1.4 4.3 1.1		
12 TU	0406 0936 TU 1609 (2156	4.0 2.0 3.8 1.8			27 W	0354 0923 W 1604 (2149	4.4 1.5 4.2 1.3		
13 W	0500 1038 W 1706 2256	4.0 2.1 3.7 1.9			28 TH	0451 1025 TH 1704 2250	4.3 1.6 4.1 1.4		
14 TH	0558 1144 TH 1810	4.0 2.1 3.7			29 F	0554 1133 F 1812 2358	4.3 1.6 4.1 1.5		
15 F	0000 0657 F 1245 1916	1.9 4.0 2.0 3.7			30 SA	0701 1244 SA 1926	4.3 1.6 4.1		
					31 SU	0109 0806 SU 1353 2037	1.5 4.4 1.5 4.2		

Chart Datum: 2·73 metres below Ordnance Datum (Newlyn)

TIDES

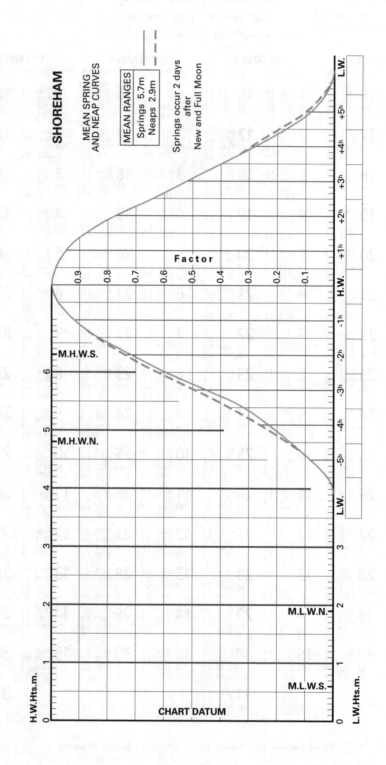

SHOREHAM

MEAN SPRING
AND NEAP CURVES

MEAN RANGES
Springs 5.7m
Neaps 2.9m

Springs occur 2 days
after
New and Full Moon

ENGLAND – SHOREHAM

LAT 50°50′N   LONG 0°15′W

TIMES AND HEIGHTS OF HIGH AND LOW WATERS

TIME ZONE (UT)
For Summer Time add ONE hour in **non-shaded areas**

JANUARY

Day	Time m	Time m	Time m	Time m		Day	Time m	Time m	Time m	Time m
1 SU	0541 1.0	1146 6.3	1808 0.7			16 M	0020 5.9	0620 1.2	1226 5.8	1839 1.0
2 M	0020 6.3	0629 0.9	1235 6.3	1855 0.6		17 TU	0054 5.9	0654 1.2	1257 5.8	1913 1.1
3 TU	0109 6.3	0717 0.9	1324 6.2	1944 0.7		18 W	0124 5.9	0727 1.2	1327 5.7	1946 1.1
4 W	0158 6.3	0807 0.9	1413 6.1	2034 0.8		19 TH	0152 5.8	0800 1.3	1356 5.6	2018 1.2
5 TH	0247 6.2	0859 1.0	1504 5.9	2126 0.9		20 F	0219 5.8	0833 1.4	1427 5.5	2050 1.4
6 F	0338 6.0	0954 1.2	1558 5.7	(2221 1.1		21 SA	0251 5.5	0908 1.6	1503 5.3	2124 1.6
7 SA	0433 5.7	1053 1.4	1656 5.4	2320 1.4		22 SU	0329 5.3	0949 1.7	1547 5.1	2207 1.8
8 SU	0532 5.5	1158 1.6	1801 5.1			23 M	0418 5.1	1042 1.9	1642 4.9	2304 2.0
9 M	0026 1.6	0638 5.3	1307 1.7	1914 5.0		24 TU	0522 4.9	1152 2.0	1801 4.7	
10 TU	0135 1.7	0748 5.3	1412 1.6	2026 5.1		25 W	0021 2.1	0647 4.9	1312 2.0	1929 4.8
11 W	0238 1.7	0853 5.4	1510 1.5	2128 5.3		26 TH	0145 2.0	0802 5.1	1426 1.7	2039 5.2
12 TH	0334 1.5	0947 5.5	1601 1.3	2220 5.5		27 F	0256 1.7	0904 5.5	1528 1.3	2139 5.6
13 F	0422 1.4	1034 5.7	1646 1.2	2304 5.7		28 SA	0353 1.3	0959 5.9	1620 1.0	2233 6.0
14 SA	0505 1.3	1115 5.8	1727 1.1	○ 2343 5.8		29 SU	0444 1.0	1050 6.2	1709 0.7	● 2324 6.3
15 SU	0544 1.2	1152 5.8	1804 1.0			30 M	0532 0.8	1140 6.4	1757 0.5	
						31 TU	0013 6.5	0618 0.6	1228 6.5	1843 0.3

FEBRUARY

Day	Time m	Time m	Time m	Time m		Day	Time m	Time m	Time m	Time m
1 W	0100 6.6	0705 0.5	1314 6.5	1929 0.3		16 TH	0058 6.0	0703 1.0	1302 5.9	1920 0.9
2 TH	0144 6.6	0751 0.5	1359 6.4	2015 0.4		17 F	0121 5.9	0732 1.0	1328 5.8	1946 1.0
3 F	0227 6.5	0837 0.7	1442 6.2	2059 0.6		18 SA	0145 5.9	0758 1.1	1356 5.7	2011 1.1
4 SA	0309 6.2	0923 0.9	1526 5.8	2145 1.0		19 SU	0214 5.8	0826 1.2	1428 5.6	2041 1.3
5 SU	0353 5.8	1013 1.3	1615 5.4	(2235 1.4		20 M	0249 5.6	0902 1.4	1506 5.4	2121 1.6
6 M	0445 5.4	1111 1.7	1715 5.0	2339 1.8		21 TU	0331 5.3	0950 1.7	1555 5.0	2216 1.9
7 TU	0549 5.0	1228 1.9	1830 4.7			22 W	0427 4.9	1058 2.0	1706 4.7	2335 2.2
8 W	0104 2.1	0708 4.8	1350 2.0	2005 4.7		23 TH	0600 4.7	1233 2.1	1902 4.7	
9 TH	0222 2.0	0837 4.9	1456 1.8	2120 5.0		24 F	0120 2.1	0741 4.9	1408 1.8	2025 5.0
10 F	0322 1.8	0939 5.2	1549 1.5	2212 5.4		25 SA	0244 1.7	0851 5.3	1515 1.3	2129 5.6
11 SA	0410 1.5	1026 5.5	1632 1.2	2254 5.7		26 SU	0342 1.3	0949 5.8	1607 0.9	2223 6.1
12 SU	0451 1.3	1105 5.7	1711 1.0	2330 5.9		27 M	0431 0.8	1040 6.2	1654 0.5	2312 6.5
13 M	0527 1.1	1139 5.8	1746 0.9	○		28 TU	0517 0.5	1128 6.5	1739 0.3	● 2357 6.7
14 TU	0003 6.0	0601 1.0	1210 5.9	1818 0.9						
15 W	0033 6.0	0633 1.0	1237 5.9	1850 0.9						

MARCH

Day	Time m	Time m	Time m	Time m		Day	Time m	Time m	Time m	Time m
1 W	0602 0.3	1214 6.7	1824 0.1			16 TH	0004 6.0	0606 0.9	1211 5.9	1822 0.8
2 TH	0041 6.8	0645 0.2	1258 6.7	1907 0.1		17 F	0027 6.0	0636 0.8	1235 5.9	1850 0.8
3 F	0122 6.8	0728 0.3	1338 6.5	1948 0.3		18 SA	0050 6.0	0702 0.9	1301 5.9	1915 0.9
4 SA	0200 6.6	0810 0.5	1417 6.3	2029 0.6		19 SU	0116 6.0	0727 0.9	1329 5.9	1940 1.0
5 SU	0238 6.2	0850 0.8	1457 5.9	2109 1.0		20 M	0145 5.9	0756 1.0	1401 5.7	2013 1.2
6 M	0317 5.8	0932 1.2	1541 5.4	(2153 1.5		21 TU	0218 5.6	0833 1.3	1439 5.5	2054 1.5
7 TU	0404 5.2	1023 1.7	1639 4.9	2252 2.0		22 W	0300 5.3	0922 1.6	1529 5.1	(2152 1.9
8 W	0508 4.7	1140 2.1	1755 4.5			23 TH	0357 4.9	1032 1.9	1645 4.7	2318 2.2
9 TH	0034 2.3	0632 4.4	1328 2.2	1946 4.5		24 F	0539 4.6	1212 2.0	1848 4.7	
10 F	0205 2.2	0823 4.6	1438 1.9	2106 4.9		25 SA	0109 2.1	0725 4.8	1353 1.7	2011 5.1
11 SA	0306 1.9	0926 5.0	1530 1.6	2154 5.3		26 SU	0230 1.6	0838 5.3	1458 1.2	2114 5.7
12 SU	0352 1.5	1009 5.4	1610 1.2	2233 5.7		27 M	0325 1.1	0935 5.8	1548 0.7	2205 6.2
13 M	0429 1.2	1045 5.6	1646 1.0	2307 5.9		28 TU	0412 0.6	1024 6.2	1633 0.4	2251 6.6
14 TU	0503 1.0	1117 5.8	1719 0.9	○ 2337 6.0		29 W	0456 0.4	1110 6.5	1717 0.4	● 2335 6.8
15 W	0535 0.9	1145 5.9	1752 0.8			30 TH	0539 0.2	1154 6.6	1759 0.2	
						31 F	0017 6.8	0621 0.2	1236 6.6	1841 0.2

APRIL

Day	Time m	Time m	Time m	Time m		Day	Time m	Time m	Time m	Time m
1 SA	0056 6.7	0702 0.3	1316 6.5	1921 0.4		16 SU	0021 6.0	0636 0.8	1238 5.9	1849 0.9
2 SU	0133 6.5	0742 0.5	1354 6.2	2000 0.7		17 M	0051 6.0	0705 0.9	1310 5.9	1920 1.0
3 M	0209 6.1	0820 0.9	1432 5.8	2039 1.1		18 TU	0123 5.8	0739 1.0	1345 5.7	1958 1.2
4 TU	0246 5.6	0900 1.2	1516 5.3	2122 1.6		19 W	0201 5.6	0820 1.2	1428 5.4	2045 1.5
5 W	0331 5.1	0948 1.7	1613 4.8	(2218 2.1		20 TH	0247 5.3	0914 1.5	1524 5.1	2148 1.8
6 TH	0435 4.6	1056 2.1	1726 4.5	2352 2.4		21 F	0351 4.9	1026 1.8	1651 4.8	(2314 2.0
7 F	0557 4.3	1252 2.2	1904 4.5			22 SA	0534 4.7	1200 1.8	1831 4.9	
8 SA	0136 2.3	0747 4.4	1406 2.0	2031 4.8		23 SU	0052 1.9	0705 4.9	1329 1.5	1949 5.3
9 SU	0237 1.9	0854 4.8	1457 1.6	2120 5.3		24 M	0206 1.4	0816 5.3	1431 1.1	2049 5.8
10 M	0321 1.5	0937 5.2	1538 1.3	2158 5.6		25 TU	0300 1.0	0912 5.8	1522 0.7	2140 6.2
11 TU	0358 1.2	1013 5.5	1613 1.1	2231 5.8		26 W	0347 0.6	1001 6.1	1607 0.5	2226 6.5
12 W	0432 1.0	1044 5.7	1647 0.9	2301 5.9		27 TH	0431 0.4	1047 6.3	1651 0.4	● 2309 6.6
13 TH	0504 0.9	1112 5.8	1720 0.9	○ 2328 6.0		28 F	0515 0.3	1132 6.4	1734 0.4	2351 6.6
14 F	0537 0.8	1139 5.9	1754 0.9			29 SA	0557 0.4	1214 6.4	1817 0.5	
15 SA	0608 0.8	1208 5.9	1822 0.9			30 SU	0031 6.4	0638 0.5	1255 6.2	1857 0.7

Chart Datum: 3·27 metres below Ordnance Datum (Newlyn)

TIDES

TIME ZONE (UT)
For Summer Time add ONE hour in **non-shaded areas**

ENGLAND – SHOREHAM

2006

LAT 50°50′N LONG 0°15′W

TIMES AND HEIGHTS OF HIGH AND LOW WATERS

MAY

Day	Time m	Time m	Time m	Time m		Day	Time m	Time m	Time m	Time m
1 M	0108 6.2	0718 0.7	1334 6.0	1936 0.9		16 TU	0034 5.9	0652 0.9	1259 5.9	1911 1.1
2 TU	0145 5.9	0757 1.0	1415 5.7	2016 1.3		17 W	0113 5.8	0733 1.0	1342 5.7	1955 1.2
3 W	0224 5.5	0837 1.3	1459 5.3	2100 1.6		18 TH	0157 5.6	0820 1.1	1431 5.5	2047 1.4
4 TH	0309 5.0	0924 1.7	1552 5.0	2154 2.0		19 F	0249 5.4	0916 1.3	1532 5.3	2150 1.6
5 F	0409 4.7	1024 2.0	1656 4.7	2306 2.2		20 SA	0356 5.1	1023 1.5	1646 5.2	2305 1.7
6 SA	0520 4.4	1145 2.1	1807 4.7			21 SU	0517 5.0	1141 1.5	1804 5.2	
7 SU	0041 2.2	0636 4.4	1312 2.0	1923 4.8		22 M	0024 1.6	0635 5.1	1256 1.4	1915 5.5
8 M	0149 2.0	0752 4.7	1409 1.8	2024 5.1		23 TU	0133 1.3	0744 5.4	1359 1.1	2017 5.7
9 TU	0237 1.7	0844 5.0	1454 1.5	2107 5.4		24 W	0230 1.0	0843 5.6	1452 0.9	2110 6.0
10 W	0317 1.4	0924 5.3	1533 1.3	2143 5.6		25 TH	0320 0.8	0936 5.9	1541 0.8	2159 6.1
11 TH	0354 1.2	0959 5.5	1611 1.1	2217 5.8		26 F	0407 0.7	1024 6.0	1628 0.7	2245 6.2
12 F	0430 1.0	1034 5.7	1647 1.0	2250 5.9		27 SA	0453 0.6	1111 6.1	1714 0.7	2328 6.2
13 SA	0506 0.9	1109 5.8	1722 1.0	2323 5.9		28 SU	0537 0.7	1155 6.1	1757 0.8	
14 SU	0541 0.9	1145 5.9	1757 1.0	2358 6.0		29 M	0009 6.1	0619 0.7	1238 6.0	1839 1.0
15 M	0616 0.9	1221 5.9	1832 1.0			30 TU	0049 5.9	0700 0.9	1319 5.9	1919 1.1
						31 W	0128 5.7	0740 1.1	1400 5.7	1959 1.3

JUNE

Day	Time m	Time m	Time m	Time m		Day	Time m	Time m	Time m	Time m
1 TH	0207 5.4	0820 1.3	1442 5.5	2042 1.6		16 F	0157 5.8	0820 0.9	1433 5.9	2046 1.1
2 F	0250 5.1	0903 1.5	1528 5.2	2130 1.8		17 SA	0249 5.7	0913 1.0	1527 5.7	2143 1.2
3 SA	0339 4.9	0953 1.7	1619 5.0	2224 1.9		18 SU	0347 5.5	1011 1.1	1626 5.6	2245 1.3
4 SU	0436 4.7	1049 1.9	1715 4.9	2327 2.0		19 M	0450 5.3	1114 1.2	1729 5.5	2351 1.4
5 M	0538 4.6	1152 1.9	1814 4.9			20 TU	0557 5.2	1220 1.3	1834 5.5	
6 TU	0033 2.0	0639 4.7	1258 1.9	1912 5.0		21 W	0057 1.3	0706 5.2	1325 1.3	1940 5.5
7 W	0135 1.8	0737 4.8	1356 1.7	2005 5.2		22 TH	0200 1.3	0813 5.3	1425 1.3	2041 5.6
8 TH	0227 1.6	0829 5.1	1447 1.6	2052 5.4		23 F	0257 1.1	0913 5.5	1521 1.2	2136 5.7
9 F	0313 1.4	0916 5.3	1532 1.4	2136 5.6		24 SA	0349 1.0	1008 5.6	1612 1.1	2226 5.8
10 SA	0355 1.2	1000 5.5	1615 1.3	2217 5.8		25 SU	0438 1.0	1057 5.8	1659 1.1	2312 5.9
11 SU	0437 1.0	1043 5.7	1656 1.1	2259 5.9		26 M	0523 0.9	1143 5.8	1744 1.1	2355 5.8
12 M	0518 0.9	1127 5.9	1738 1.1	2341 6.0		27 TU	0606 0.9	1225 5.9	1825 1.1	
13 TU	0601 0.9	1210 5.9	1821 1.0			28 W	0034 5.8	0645 1.0	1305 5.9	1904 1.2
14 W	0024 6.0	0644 0.8	1256 6.0	1906 1.0		29 TH	0112 5.7	0723 1.1	1343 5.8	1942 1.4
15 TH	0109 5.9	0730 0.8	1343 5.9	1954 1.0		30 F	0149 5.5	0800 1.2	1419 5.6	2019 1.4

JULY

Day	Time m	Time m	Time m	Time m		Day	Time m	Time m	Time m	Time m
1 SA	0224 5.4	0838 1.3	1455 5.5	2059 1.5		16 SU	0237 6.0	0857 0.7	1509 6.1	2124 0.9
2 SU	0300 5.2	0918 1.5	1532 5.3	2142 1.7		17 M	0326 5.8	0948 0.9	1557 5.9	2217 1.1
3 M	0341 5.0	1002 1.6	1613 5.1	2231 1.8		18 TU	0419 5.5	1042 1.1	1651 5.6	2317 1.3
4 TU	0430 4.8	1050 1.8	1704 5.0	2325 1.9		19 W	0518 5.2	1143 1.4	1752 5.3	
5 W	0531 4.7	1147 1.9	1806 4.9			20 TH	0024 1.6	0627 5.0	1254 1.6	1902 5.2
6 TH	0026 1.9	0638 4.7	1251 2.0	1909 5.0		21 F	0136 1.6	0747 5.0	1406 1.7	2019 5.2
7 F	0131 1.8	0743 4.9	1357 1.9	2009 5.1		22 SA	0241 1.5	0901 5.1	1508 1.6	2125 5.3
8 SA	0232 1.6	0841 5.1	1458 1.7	2103 5.4		23 SU	0338 1.4	1001 5.4	1602 1.4	2218 5.5
9 SU	0326 1.4	0935 5.4	1550 1.4	2154 5.7		24 M	0427 1.2	1050 5.6	1649 1.3	2304 5.7
10 M	0415 1.1	1025 5.7	1638 1.2	2242 5.9		25 TU	0511 1.0	1133 5.8	1731 1.2	2344 5.8
11 TU	0502 0.9	1114 5.9	1725 1.0	2329 6.0		26 W	0550 1.0	1212 5.9	1809 1.1	
12 W	0548 0.7	1202 6.1	1811 0.9			27 TH	0021 5.8	0627 1.0	1248 6.0	1845 1.1
13 TH	0016 6.1	0634 0.6	1250 6.2	1857 0.8		28 F	0054 5.8	0701 1.0	1320 5.9	1918 1.1
14 F	0103 6.2	0721 0.6	1336 6.3	1945 0.7		29 SA	0124 5.7	0735 1.2	1349 5.8	1951 1.2
15 SA	0150 6.1	0809 0.6	1422 6.3	2033 0.8		30 SU	0152 5.6	0807 1.1	1415 5.7	2024 1.3
						31 M	0219 5.5	0839 1.3	1441 5.6	2058 1.4

AUGUST

Day	Time m	Time m	Time m	Time m		Day	Time m	Time m	Time m	Time m
1 TU	0251 5.3	0911 1.5	1514 5.4	2135 1.6		16 W	0347 5.6	1006 1.3	1615 5.6	2240 1.5
2 W	0329 5.1	0949 1.7	1556 5.2	2221 1.8		17 TH	0444 5.1	1106 1.7	1716 5.1	2352 1.9
3 TH	0419 4.9	1040 2.0	1652 4.9	2324 2.0		18 F	0557 4.8	1229 2.0	1833 4.8	
4 F	0530 4.6	1151 2.1	1814 4.8			19 SA	0119 2.0	0734 4.7	1354 2.1	2010 4.8
5 SA	0042 2.0	0704 4.7	1317 2.1	1936 4.9		20 SU	0232 1.8	0859 5.0	1500 1.8	2122 5.1
6 SU	0202 1.8	0817 5.0	1435 1.9	2042 5.2		21 M	0329 1.5	0955 5.3	1552 1.5	2211 5.5
7 M	0308 1.5	0919 5.4	1535 1.5	2138 5.6		22 TU	0414 1.2	1039 5.7	1634 1.3	2252 5.7
8 TU	0400 1.1	1012 5.8	1624 1.2	2229 6.0		23 W	0454 1.0	1117 5.9	1712 1.1	2329 5.9
9 W	0447 0.8	1102 6.2	1710 0.9	2317 6.2		24 TH	0529 0.9	1151 6.1	1747 1.0	
10 TH	0533 0.5	1149 6.4	1756 0.6			25 F	0001 5.9	0602 0.9	1223 6.1	1819 1.0
11 F	0004 6.4	0618 0.4	1235 6.6	1841 0.5		26 SA	0030 5.9	0634 0.9	1251 6.1	1850 1.0
12 SA	0050 6.5	0703 0.3	1319 6.6	1926 0.5		27 SU	0054 5.9	0705 1.0	1313 6.0	1920 1.1
13 SU	0134 6.4	0748 0.6	1401 6.6	2011 0.6		28 M	0117 5.8	0733 1.0	1334 5.9	1947 1.2
14 M	0216 6.3	0832 0.5	1443 6.4	2057 0.8		29 TU	0143 5.7	0758 1.2	1400 5.8	2014 1.3
15 TU	0259 6.0	0917 0.8	1526 6.0	2145 1.1		30 W	0212 5.6	0826 1.4	1431 5.6	2046 1.5
						31 TH	0247 5.3	0902 1.6	1509 5.3	2130 1.8

Chart Datum: 3·27 metres below Ordnance Datum (Newlyn)

TIME ZONE (UT)
For Summer Time add ONE hour in **non-shaded areas**

ENGLAND – SHOREHAM

LAT 50°50'N   LONG 0°15'W

TIMES AND HEIGHTS OF HIGH AND LOW WATERS

2006

SEPTEMBER

Time	m	Time	m
1 0331 / 0953 / F 1601 / 2233	5.0 / 2.0 / 4.9 / 2.1	**16** 0534 / 1208 / SA 1810	4.6 / 2.3 / 4.6
2 0438 / 1108 / SA 1726	4.6 / 2.3 / 4.6	**17** 0103 / 0724 / SU 1342 / 2003	2.2 / 4.6 / 2.3 / 4.7
3 0003 / 0637 / SU 1251 / 1914	2.2 / 4.6 / 2.3 / 4.8	**18** 0218 / 0847 / M 1447 / 2109	2.0 / 5.0 / 1.9 / 5.1
4 0143 / 0801 / M 1421 / 2027	2.0 / 4.9 / 1.9 / 5.2	**19** 0312 / 0936 / TU 1534 / 2153	1.6 / 5.4 / 1.6 / 5.5
5 0253 / 0905 / TU 1520 / 2125	1.5 / 5.5 / 1.4 / 5.7	**20** 0353 / 1015 / W 1612 / 2230	1.3 / 5.8 / 1.3 / 5.8
6 0344 / 0957 / W 1607 / 2214	1.0 / 6.0 / 1.0 / 6.1	**21** 0429 / 1051 / TH 1646 / 2304	1.1 / 6.1 / 1.1 / 5.9
7 0431 / 1044 / TH 1651 / O 2301	0.6 / 6.4 / 0.6 / 6.5	**22** 0502 / 1122 / F 1719 / 2333	0.9 / 6.1 / 1.0 / 6.0
8 0512 / 1129 / F 1735 / 2346	0.4 / 6.7 / 0.4 / 6.6	**23** 0534 / 1151 / SA 1750 / 2358	0.9 / 6.1 / 0.9 / 6.0
9 0555 / 1213 / SA 1819	0.2 / 6.8 / 0.3	**24** 0605 / 1214 / SU 1821	0.9 / 6.1 / 1.0
10 0029 / 0638 / SU 1255 / 1902	6.7 / 0.2 / 6.8 / 0.4	**25** 0022 / 0634 / M 1236 / 1848	6.0 / 1.0 / 6.0 / 1.0
11 0112 / 0721 / M 1335 / 1944	6.6 / 0.4 / 6.7 / 0.5	**26** 0046 / 0700 / TU 1300 / 1914	5.9 / 1.1 / 6.0 / 1.1
12 0152 / 0803 / TU 1414 / 2027	6.4 / 0.6 / 6.4 / 0.8	**27** 0113 / 0724 / W 1327 / 1940	5.9 / 1.2 / 5.8 / 1.3
13 0233 / 0846 / W 1455 / 2111	6.0 / 1.0 / 5.9 / 1.2	**28** 0142 / 0754 / TH 1358 / 2014	5.7 / 1.4 / 5.6 / 1.5
14 0319 / 0932 / TH 1542 / ◑ 2203	5.5 / 1.5 / 5.4 / 1.7	**29** 0216 / 0833 / F 1436 / 2100	5.6 / 1.7 / 5.3 / 1.8
15 0417 / 1032 / F 1646 / 2319	5.0 / 2.0 / 4.9 / 2.1	**30** 0302 / 0928 / SA 1528 / ◑ 2206	5.1 / 2.0 / 4.9 / 2.1

OCTOBER

Time	m	Time	m
1 0412 / 1048 / SU 1702 / 2338	4.7 / 2.3 / 4.6 / 2.2	**16** 0033 / 0649 / M 1316 / 1930	2.3 / 4.7 / 2.3 / 4.6
2 0619 / 1234 / M 1856	4.7 / 2.3 / 4.8	**17** 0147 / 0811 / TU 1418 / 2036	2.1 / 5.0 / 2.0 / 5.0
3 0122 / 0742 / TU 1402 / 2009	2.0 / 5.1 / 1.9 / 5.3	**18** 0240 / 0901 / W 1504 / 2121	1.7 / 5.4 / 1.6 / 5.4
4 0231 / 0845 / W 1458 / 2105	1.5 / 5.7 / 1.4 / 5.8	**19** 0322 / 0941 / TH 1541 / 2158	1.4 / 5.7 / 1.3 / 5.7
5 0321 / 0935 / TH 1544 / 2154	1.0 / 6.2 / 0.9 / 6.2	**20** 0357 / 1015 / F 1615 / 2230	1.2 / 5.9 / 1.1 / 5.8
6 0405 / 1021 / F 1628 / 2240	0.6 / 6.6 / 0.5 / 6.5	**21** 0431 / 1045 / SA 1648 / 2258	1.1 / 6.0 / 1.0 / 5.9
7 0448 / 1104 / SA 1710 / O 2324	0.4 / 6.8 / 0.3 / 6.7	**22** 0503 / 1112 / SU 1720 / ● 2325	1.0 / 6.1 / 1.0 / 6.0
8 0530 / 1147 / SU 1753	0.3 / 6.9 / 0.3	**23** 0535 / 1138 / M 1751 / 2352	1.0 / 6.1 / 1.0 / 6.0
9 0007 / 0612 / M 1228 / 1836	6.7 / 0.3 / 6.8 / 0.4	**24** 0605 / 1204 / TU 1821	1.1 / 6.0 / 1.0
10 0049 / 0655 / TU 1308 / 1918	6.6 / 0.5 / 6.6 / 0.6	**25** 0020 / 0633 / W 1233 / 1849	6.0 / 1.1 / 6.0 / 1.1
11 0129 / 0736 / W 1347 / 2000	6.3 / 0.8 / 6.2 / 0.9	**26** 0051 / 0701 / TH 1303 / 1920	5.9 / 1.3 / 5.8 / 1.2
12 0211 / 0819 / TH 1427 / 2043	6.0 / 1.2 / 5.8 / 1.4	**27** 0123 / 0736 / F 1338 / 1958	5.8 / 1.4 / 5.6 / 1.5
13 0258 / 0906 / F 1516 / 2134	5.5 / 1.7 / 5.3 / 1.8	**28** 0202 / 0820 / SA 1420 / 2048	5.5 / 1.7 / 5.3 / 1.7
14 0357 / 1005 / SA 1621 / ◑ 2245	5.0 / 2.1 / 4.8 / 2.2	**29** 0253 / 0919 / SU 1518 / ◑ 2154	5.2 / 2.0 / 5.0 / 2.0
15 0511 / 1138 / SU 1743	4.7 / 2.4 / 4.5	**30** 0410 / 1037 / M 1653 / 2319	4.9 / 2.2 / 4.8 / 2.1
		31 0555 / 1210 / TU 1830	4.9 / 2.1 / 4.9

NOVEMBER

Time	m	Time	m
1 0050 / 0713 / W 1331 / 1941	1.8 / 5.3 / 1.7 / 5.3	**16** 0152 / 0807 / TH 1420 / 2031	1.9 / 5.2 / 1.8 / 5.1
2 0159 / 0815 / TH 1429 / 2039	1.4 / 5.7 / 1.3 / 5.8	**17** 0239 / 0852 / F 1502 / 2112	1.7 / 5.5 / 1.5 / 5.4
3 0251 / 0907 / F 1517 / 2129	1.0 / 6.2 / 0.9 / 6.2	**18** 0320 / 0929 / SA 1540 / 2147	1.5 / 5.7 / 1.3 / 5.6
4 0338 / 0953 / SA 1602 / 2216	0.7 / 6.5 / 0.6 / 6.4	**19** 0357 / 1002 / SU 1616 / 2220	1.3 / 5.8 / 1.2 / 5.8
5 0422 / 1038 / SU 1646 / O 2301	0.6 / 6.6 / 0.5 / 6.5	**20** 0433 / 1034 / M 1651 / ● 2254	1.2 / 5.9 / 1.1 / 5.9
6 0506 / 1121 / M 1730 / 2345	0.5 / 6.7 / 0.5 / 6.5	**21** 0508 / 1106 / TU 1726 / 2328	1.2 / 6.0 / 1.1 / 6.0
7 0550 / 1203 / TU 1814	0.6 / 6.6 / 0.6	**22** 0541 / 1139 / W 1800	1.2 / 6.0 / 1.1
8 0029 / 0633 / W 1244 / 1857	6.4 / 0.8 / 6.4 / 0.8	**23** 0002 / 0614 / TH 1214 / 1834	6.0 / 1.2 / 6.0 / 1.1
9 0112 / 0716 / TH 1325 / 1939	6.2 / 1.0 / 6.0 / 1.1	**24** 0039 / 0650 / F 1251 / 1911	5.9 / 1.3 / 5.9 / 1.2
10 0155 / 0759 / F 1408 / 2023	5.9 / 1.4 / 5.7 / 1.4	**25** 0117 / 0730 / SA 1331 / 1954	5.8 / 1.4 / 5.7 / 1.3
11 0243 / 0846 / SA 1456 / 2112	5.6 / 1.7 / 5.2 / 1.7	**26** 0202 / 0817 / SU 1418 / 2044	5.7 / 1.5 / 5.5 / 1.5
12 0337 / 0941 / SU 1556 / ◑ 2211	5.2 / 2.0 / 4.9 / 2.0	**27** 0255 / 0914 / M 1516 / 2144	5.5 / 1.7 / 5.3 / 1.6
13 0440 / 1052 / M 1704 / 2330	4.9 / 2.3 / 4.6 / 2.2	**28** 0402 / 1022 / TU 1631 / ◑ 2255	5.3 / 1.8 / 5.1 / 1.7
14 0550 / 1212 / TU 1821	4.8 / 2.3 / 4.6	**29** 0520 / 1138 / W 1752	5.3 / 1.8 / 5.1
15 0052 / 0706 / W 1330 / 1937	2.1 / 5.0 / 2.1 / 4.8	**30** 0011 / 0633 / TH 1252 / 1903	1.6 / 5.4 / 1.6 / 5.3

DECEMBER

Time	m	Time	m
1 0120 / 0738 / F 1354 / 2006	1.4 / 5.7 / 1.3 / 5.6	**16** 0139 / 0748 / SA 1413 / 2014	2.0 / 5.1 / 1.8 / 5.0
2 0219 / 0835 / SA 1449 / 2102	1.2 / 6.0 / 1.1 / 5.9	**17** 0234 / 0838 / SU 1501 / 2103	1.8 / 5.3 / 1.6 / 5.3
3 0312 / 0926 / SU 1539 / 2154	1.0 / 6.2 / 0.9 / 6.1	**18** 0322 / 0922 / M 1545 / 2147	1.6 / 5.6 / 1.4 / 5.5
4 0401 / 1015 / M 1627 / 2243	0.9 / 6.3 / 0.8 / 6.2	**19** 0404 / 1003 / TU 1626 / 2229	1.5 / 5.8 / 1.2 / 5.7
5 0449 / 1101 / TU 1714 / O 2330	0.9 / 6.3 / 0.7 / 6.2	**20** 0444 / 1043 / W 1706 / ● 2310	1.3 / 5.9 / 1.1 / 5.9
6 0535 / 1145 / W 1759	0.9 / 6.3 / 0.8	**21** 0524 / 1122 / TH 1746 / 2351	1.2 / 6.0 / 1.0 / 6.0
7 0016 / 0619 / TH 1229 / 1843	6.2 / 1.0 / 6.1 / 0.9	**22** 0603 / 1203 / F 1826	1.2 / 6.0 / 1.0
8 0100 / 0702 / F 1310 / 1925	6.1 / 1.2 / 5.9 / 1.1	**23** 0032 / 0643 / SA 1245 / 1907	6.0 / 1.1 / 6.0 / 0.9
9 0143 / 0744 / SA 1352 / 2007	5.9 / 1.3 / 5.7 / 1.3	**24** 0115 / 0726 / SU 1328 / 1950	6.0 / 1.1 / 6.0 / 1.0
10 0226 / 0827 / SU 1436 / 2050	5.7 / 1.6 / 5.4 / 1.5	**25** 0200 / 0812 / M 1414 / 2038	6.0 / 1.2 / 5.8 / 1.0
11 0311 / 0913 / M 1523 / 2136	5.5 / 1.8 / 5.1 / 1.7	**26** 0248 / 0903 / TU 1505 / 2129	5.9 / 1.3 / 5.7 / 1.2
12 0400 / 1005 / TU 1617 / ◑ 2229	5.2 / 2.0 / 4.9 / 1.9	**27** 0341 / 1000 / W 1602 / ◑ 2227	5.7 / 1.4 / 5.5 / 1.3
13 0454 / 1104 / W 1716 / 2329	5.1 / 2.1 / 4.7 / 2.0	**28** 0440 / 1103 / TH 1707 / 2331	5.6 / 1.5 / 5.3 / 1.5
14 0553 / 1209 / TH 1818	5.0 / 2.1 / 4.7	**29** 0547 / 1212 / F 1818	5.6 / 1.6 / 5.2
15 0034 / 0651 / F 1316 / 1918	2.1 / 5.0 / 2.0 / 4.8	**30** 0041 / 0656 / SA 1322 / 1931	1.5 / 5.5 / 1.5 / 5.3
		31 0150 / 0805 / SU 1426 / 2040	1.5 / 5.5 / 1.4 / 5.4

Chart Datum: 3·27 metres below Ordnance Datum (Newlyn)

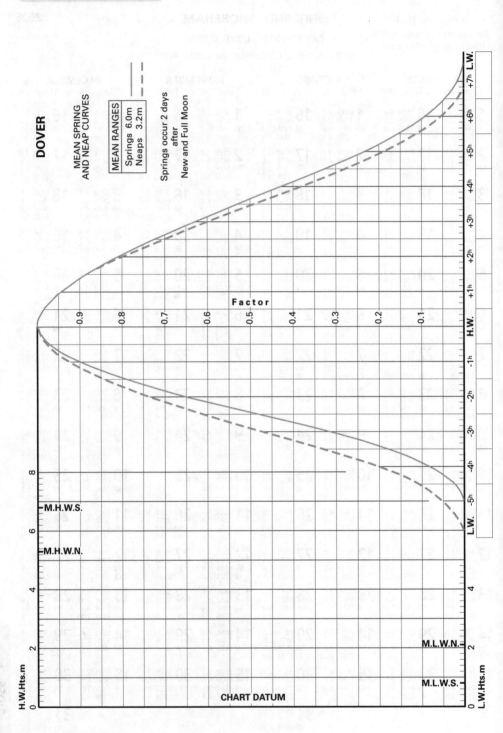

TIME ZONE (UT)
For Summer Time add ONE hour in **non-shaded areas**

ENGLAND – DOVER

LAT 51°07'N   LONG 1°19'E

TIMES AND HEIGHTS OF HIGH AND LOW WATERS

JANUARY

Day	Time m	Time m	Time m	Time m
1 SU	0643 1.1	1135 6.6	1909 1.1	
2 M	0001 6.7	0733 1.0	1225 6.6	1957 1.0
3 TU	0049 6.7	0824 0.9	1314 6.5	2046 1.1
4 W	0138 6.7	0914 0.9	1406 6.4	2132 1.1
5 TH	0228 6.6	1002 1.0	1500 6.2	2218 1.3
6 F	0321 6.4	1050 1.1	1558 6.0	2306 1.5
7 SA	0417 6.2	1141 1.4	1659 5.7	2358 1.7
8 SU	0518 5.9	1236 1.6	1807 5.5	
9 M	0058 1.9	0627 5.7	1338 1.8	1917 5.5
10 TU	0205 2.0	0739 5.7	1445 1.9	2023 5.5
11 W	0316 2.0	0847 5.7	1556 1.8	2121 5.7
12 TH	0423 1.8	0945 5.9	1658 1.7	2211 5.9
13 F	0518 1.6	1034 6.0	1746 1.6	2253 6.2
14 SA	0604 1.4	1115 6.1	1826 1.5	○ 2332 6.3
15 SU	0644 1.3	1152 6.2	1900 1.5	
16 M	0008 6.4	0718 1.3	1227 6.2	1931 1.5
17 TU	0043 6.4	0751 1.3	1259 6.1	2000 1.5
18 W	0115 6.4	0822 1.3	1329 6.0	2030 1.5
19 TH	0142 6.3	0854 1.4	1355 5.9	2102 1.5
20 F	0208 6.2	0927 1.5	1422 5.9	2135 1.6
21 SA	0238 6.1	1001 1.6	1454 5.7	2211 1.8
22 SU	0317 5.9	1040 1.8	1537 5.6	◑ 2252 2.1
23 M	0406 5.7	1127 2.0	1634 5.3	2346 2.3
24 TU	0513 5.5	1232 2.1	1802 5.2	
25 W	0105 2.4	0638 5.4	1358 2.1	1929 5.3
26 TH	0236 2.2	0754 5.6	1514 1.9	2035 5.6
27 F	0346 1.9	0858 5.9	1618 1.6	2131 6.0
28 SA	0447 1.5	0954 6.1	1717 1.3	2222 6.3
29 SU	0544 1.1	1046 6.5	1813 1.0	● 2310 6.6
30 M	0639 0.8	1134 6.7	1907 0.9	2355 6.8
31 TU	0733 0.6	1219 6.8	1956 0.7	

FEBRUARY

Day	Time m	Time m	Time m	Time m
1 W	0039 7.0	0821 0.5	1303 6.7	2039 0.7
2 TH	0123 7.0	0905 0.5	1347 6.7	2118 0.7
3 F	0207 6.9	0945 0.6	1432 6.4	2155 0.9
4 SA	0252 6.7	1024 0.8	1519 6.3	2233 1.2
5 SU	0340 6.4	1105 1.3	1612 5.8	◑ 2317 1.6
6 M	0435 5.9	1153 1.7	1715 5.4	
7 TU	0012 2.0	0541 5.5	1256 2.1	1831 5.2
8 W	0125 2.3	0706 5.3	1410 2.3	1957 5.2
9 TH	0246 2.3	0837 5.3	1531 2.2	2110 5.4
10 F	0407 2.0	0944 5.6	1647 1.9	2202 5.8
11 SA	0510 1.7	1030 5.9	1738 1.6	2242 6.1
12 SU	0557 1.4	1107 6.1	1818 1.5	2318 6.3
13 M	0635 1.3	1138 6.2	1851 1.4	○ 2351 6.4
14 TU	0707 1.2	1207 6.2	1918 1.3	
15 W	0021 6.5	0734 1.1	1235 6.2	1943 1.3
16 TH	0048 6.4	0802 1.1	1300 6.2	2009 1.2
17 F	0111 6.4	0830 1.1	1321 6.2	2038 1.3
18 SA	0133 6.4	0859 1.2	1344 6.2	2107 1.4
19 SU	0201 6.4	0928 1.3	1414 6.1	2138 1.5
20 M	0236 6.2	1001 1.6	1453 5.9	2213 1.8
21 TU	0319 5.9	1042 1.9	1542 5.6	2301 2.1
22 W	0418 5.5	1140 2.2	1655 5.1	
23 TH	0014 2.4	0602 5.2	1317 2.3	1908 5.1
24 F	0204 2.3	0744 5.2	1452 2.1	2024 5.4
25 SA	0325 1.9	0854 5.8	1602 1.7	2123 5.8
26 SU	0432 1.4	0951 6.2	1706 1.2	2214 6.4
27 M	0533 1.0	1040 6.5	1804 0.9	2259 6.8
28 TU	0631 0.6	1124 6.8	1856 0.6	● 2341 7.0

MARCH

Day	Time m	Time m	Time m	Time m
1 W	0721 0.3	1205 6.9	1941 0.5	
2 TH	0021 7.1	0805 0.2	1244 6.9	2019 0.4
3 F	0102 7.2	0844 0.3	1323 6.8	2053 0.5
4 SA	0142 7.0	0919 0.5	1403 6.6	2127 0.8
5 SU	0223 6.8	0953 0.8	1447 6.3	2201 1.2
6 M	0308 6.3	1029 1.3	1536 5.8	◑ 2239 1.7
7 TU	0400 5.8	1113 1.9	1637 5.4	2332 2.2
8 W	0507 5.3	1217 2.4	1753 5.0	
9 TH	0053 2.5	0634 5.0	1343 2.5	1929 5.0
10 F	0224 2.4	0831 5.1	1511 2.4	2053 5.3
11 SA	0353 2.1	0933 5.5	1629 2.0	2144 5.7
12 SU	0455 1.6	1014 5.8	1719 1.6	2222 6.1
13 M	0539 1.3	1046 6.0	1758 1.4	2255 6.3
14 TU	0614 1.2	1114 6.2	1829 1.3	○ 2325 6.4
15 W	0642 1.1	1140 6.3	1854 1.2	2352 6.4
16 TH	0708 1.0	1206 6.3	1918 1.2	
17 F	0017 6.4	0735 1.0	1229 6.3	1944 1.1
18 SA	0039 6.5	0802 1.0	1249 6.3	2012 1.1
19 SU	0102 6.5	0830 1.1	1313 6.4	2040 1.2
20 M	0130 6.5	0859 1.3	1345 6.3	2111 1.4
21 TU	0205 6.3	0931 1.5	1425 6.1	2147 1.7
22 W	0249 5.9	1013 1.9	1515 5.6	◑ 2236 2.1
23 TH	0349 5.4	1111 2.2	1633 5.1	2351 2.4
24 F	0559 5.1	1254 2.4	1852 5.1	
25 SA	0145 2.3	0735 5.3	1434 2.1	2008 5.5
26 SU	0307 1.8	0843 5.8	1545 1.6	2107 6.0
27 M	0414 1.3	0938 6.2	1648 1.2	2156 6.5
28 TU	0517 0.8	1024 6.6	1744 0.8	2239 6.8
29 W	0612 0.5	1106 6.8	1833 0.6	● 2320 7.1
30 TH	0700 0.3	1144 6.9	1915 0.5	
31 F	0000 7.1	0741 0.2	1221 6.9	1952 0.5

APRIL

Day	Time m	Time m	Time m	Time m
1 SA	0039 7.1	0817 0.4	1259 6.8	2026 0.6
2 SU	0117 6.9	0850 0.6	1338 6.6	2059 0.9
3 M	0157 6.6	0922 1.0	1421 6.3	2132 1.3
4 TU	0241 6.2	0956 1.5	1510 5.8	2208 1.7
5 W	0334 5.7	1036 2.1	1609 5.4	◑ 2259 2.2
6 TH	0441 5.2	1142 2.5	1721 5.1	
7 F	0026 2.5	0603 4.9	1316 2.6	1848 5.0
8 SA	0158 2.4	0800 5.0	1439 2.4	2017 5.3
9 SU	0317 2.0	0902 5.4	1547 2.0	2110 5.7
10 M	0416 1.7	0941 5.7	1639 1.7	2149 6.0
11 TU	0459 1.4	1011 6.0	1719 1.4	2221 6.2
12 W	0535 1.2	1038 6.1	1752 1.3	2250 6.3
13 TH	0605 1.1	1105 6.2	1820 1.2	○ 2317 6.4
14 F	0635 1.0	1132 6.3	1848 1.1	2342 6.4
15 SA	0706 1.0	1157 6.3	1918 1.1	
16 SU	0008 6.4	0736 1.0	1222 6.4	1948 1.1
17 M	0036 6.5	0806 1.1	1251 6.4	2019 1.2
18 TU	0108 6.4	0837 1.3	1327 6.3	2053 1.4
19 W	0147 6.2	0913 1.5	1411 6.0	2134 1.7
20 TH	0237 5.8	0959 1.9	1510 5.6	2229 2.0
21 F	0352 5.4	1102 2.2	1647 5.3	◑ 2350 2.2
22 SA	0554 5.3	1244 2.3	1829 5.3	
23 SU	0129 2.0	0717 5.5	1412 1.9	1942 5.7
24 M	0244 1.6	0822 5.9	1519 1.5	2041 6.1
25 TU	0349 1.2	0915 6.2	1619 1.2	2130 6.5
26 W	0451 0.8	1001 6.5	1714 0.9	2215 6.8
27 TH	0546 0.6	1042 6.7	1803 0.7	● 2257 6.9
28 F	0633 0.5	1121 6.7	1846 0.6	2337 6.9
29 SA	0714 0.5	1159 6.7	1925 0.7	
30 SU	0017 6.9	0750 0.7	1238 6.6	2001 0.8

Chart Datum: 3·67 metres below Ordnance Datum (Newlyn)

TIDES

TIME ZONE (UT)
For Summer Time add ONE hour in **non-shaded areas**

ENGLAND – DOVER

LAT 51°07′N   LONG 1°19′E

TIMES AND HEIGHTS OF HIGH AND LOW WATERS

2006

MAY

Day	Time	m	Day	Time	m
1 M	0056	6.7	16 TU	0018	6.4
	0824	0.9		0750	1.2
	1318	6.5		1240	6.4
	2035	1.1		2008	1.2
2 TU	0137	6.4	17 W	0059	6.3
	0857	1.3		0827	1.3
	1402	6.2		1324	6.3
	2110	1.4		2048	1.4
3 W	0223	6.0	18 TH	0146	6.1
	0929	1.7		0909	1.5
	1450	5.9		1416	6.1
	2147	1.8		2136	1.5
4 TH	0315	5.6	19 F	0246	5.8
	1007	2.1		1000	1.7
	1545	5.6		1522	5.8
	2237	2.1		2235	1.7
5 F ☾	0417	5.2	20 SA ☾	0407	5.6
	1107	2.4		1106	1.9
	1647	5.3		1637	5.7
	2354	2.4		2350	1.8
6 SA	0528	5.0	21 SU	0533	5.5
	1235	2.6		1227	1.9
	1759	5.2		1755	5.7
7 SU	0114	2.3	22 M	0106	1.7
	0651	5.0		0648	5.6
	1351	2.4		1340	1.6
	1917	5.3		1907	5.8
8 M	0221	2.1	23 TU	0214	1.4
	0803	5.3		0752	5.8
	1452	2.1		1444	1.5
	2018	5.5		2008	6.1
9 TU	0315	1.8	24 W	0316	1.2
	0848	5.5		0846	6.1
	1544	1.8		1544	1.3
	2101	5.8		2101	6.3
10 W	0402	1.5	25 TH	0419	1.0
	0923	5.8		0934	6.3
	1628	1.6		1642	1.1
	2136	6.0		2150	6.5
11 TH	0444	1.4	26 F	0517	0.9
	0955	6.0		1017	6.5
	1707	1.4		1734	1.0
	2207	6.2		2236	6.6
12 F	0524	1.2	27 SA ●	0607	0.9
	1027	6.1		1100	6.5
	1744	1.3		1821	0.9
	2238	6.3		2319	6.6
13 SA ○	0602	1.1	28 SU	0650	0.9
	1058	6.2		1141	6.5
	1820	1.2		1903	1.0
	2310	6.3			
14 SU	0639	1.1	29 M	0001	6.5
	1129	6.3		0728	1.1
	1856	1.2		1223	6.5
	2343	6.4		1941	1.1
15 M	0715	1.1	30 TU	0043	6.4
	1202	6.4		0804	1.2
	1931	1.2		1304	6.4
				2019	1.3
			31 W	0124	6.2
				0838	1.5
				1347	6.2
				2056	1.5

JUNE

Day	Time	m	Day	Time	m
1 TH	0208	5.9	16 F	0152	6.2
	0911	1.7		0915	1.3
	1431	6.0		1418	6.3
	2134	1.7		2144	1.2
2 F	0255	5.7	17 SA	0249	6.1
	0948	2.0		1005	1.4
	1518	5.8		1514	6.2
	2217	1.9		2238	1.3
3 SA ☾	0347	5.4	18 SU	0352	5.9
	1032	2.2		1100	1.5
	1609	5.6		1613	6.1
	2311	2.1		2335	1.4
4 SU	0445	5.2	19 M	0458	5.8
	1131	2.3		1158	1.6
	1706	5.4		1716	6.0
5 M	0013	2.1	20 TU	0035	1.4
	0549	5.1		0610	5.7
	1241	2.3		1301	1.7
	1808	5.3		1823	5.9
6 TU	0116	2.1	21 W	0137	1.5
	0652	5.2		0713	5.7
	1345	2.2		1404	1.7
	1909	5.4		1931	5.9
7 W	0213	1.9	22 TH	0240	1.5
	0747	5.4		0815	5.8
	1443	2.1		1508	1.6
	2001	5.6		2034	6.0
8 TH	0307	1.7	23 F	0346	1.4
	0832	5.6		0910	6.0
	1537	1.8		1612	1.5
	2044	5.8		2131	6.1
9 F	0358	1.5	24 SA	0451	1.4
	0913	5.8		1001	6.1
	1626	1.6		1711	1.4
	2125	6.0		2223	6.2
10 SA	0447	1.4	25 SU ●	0546	1.3
	0952	6.0		1047	6.2
	1712	1.4		1802	1.2
	2205	6.2		2311	6.3
11 SU ○	0534	1.3	26 M	0632	1.3
	1031	6.2		1130	6.3
	1756	1.3		1847	1.2
	2246	6.3		2353	6.3
12 M	0618	1.2	27 TU	0713	1.3
	1111	6.3		1211	6.4
	1839	1.2		1929	1.2
	2328	6.4			
13 TU	0701	1.3	28 W	0033	6.2
	1153	6.4		0750	1.4
	1922	1.1		1251	6.4
				2007	1.3
14 W	0013	6.4	29 TH	0112	6.1
	0743	1.2		0824	1.5
	1239	6.4		1330	6.3
	2006	1.1		2043	1.4
15 TH	0100	6.3	30 F	0150	6.0
	0828	1.2		0855	1.6
	1326	6.4		1407	6.2
	2053	1.1		2117	1.5

JULY

Day	Time	m	Day	Time	m
1 SA	0228	5.8	16 SU	0231	6.4
	0925	1.7		0955	1.0
	1444	6.0		1453	6.6
	2151	1.6		2223	0.9
2 SU	0307	5.6	17 M	0323	6.2
	0959	1.8		1038	1.2
	1522	5.8		1544	6.4
	2228	1.7		2309	1.1
3 M ☾	0350	5.5	18 TU	0418	6.0
	1038	2.0		1124	1.5
	1604	5.7		1639	6.1
	2312	1.9		2359	1.4
4 TU	0441	5.3	19 W	0521	5.7
	1126	2.1		1219	1.7
	1656	5.5		1743	5.8
5 W	0005	2.0	20 TH	0058	1.7
	0542	5.2		0632	5.5
	1227	2.3		1325	2.0
	1757	5.4		1856	5.6
6 TH	0110	2.0	21 F	0206	1.9
	0647	5.2		0747	5.5
	1341	2.3		1438	2.0
	1902	5.4		2015	5.6
7 F	0218	2.0	22 SA	0320	1.9
	0746	5.4		0856	5.6
	1451	2.1		1552	1.9
	2001	5.6		2126	5.8
8 SA	0321	1.8	23 SU	0436	1.8
	0839	5.6		0953	5.8
	1552	1.8		1659	1.6
	2055	5.8		2222	6.0
9 SU	0418	1.6	24 M	0536	1.6
	0928	5.9		1040	6.1
	1646	1.6		1754	1.4
	2145	6.1		2307	6.1
10 M	0512	1.4	25 TU ●	0623	1.5
	1015	6.1		1120	6.3
	1737	1.3		1840	1.3
	2234	6.3		2345	6.2
11 TU ○	0602	1.2	26 W	0703	1.4
	1101	6.4		1157	6.4
	1826	1.1		1919	1.2
	2322	6.4			
12 W	0652	1.1	27 TH	0020	6.2
	1147	6.5		0737	1.4
	1929	1.2		1234	6.5
				1953	1.2
13 TH	0009	6.5	28 F	0053	6.2
	0741	1.0		0806	1.4
	1232	6.7		1308	6.4
	2006	0.8		2023	1.2
14 F	0056	6.5	29 SA	0125	6.1
	0829	1.0		0831	1.4
	1318	6.7		1339	6.3
	2054	0.8		2050	1.3
15 SA	0143	6.5	30 SU	0153	6.0
	0913	1.0		0856	1.5
	1405	6.7		1406	6.2
	2139	0.8		2118	1.4
			31 M	0219	5.9
				0925	1.6
				1432	6.1
				2149	1.5

AUGUST

Day	Time	m	Day	Time	m
1 TU	0246	5.8	16 W ☾	0342	6.0
	0958	1.7		1050	1.5
	1504	5.9		1606	6.1
	2224	1.7		2323	1.6
2 W	0321	5.6	17 TH	0443	5.6
	1036	1.9		1142	1.9
	1547	5.7		1709	5.7
	2306	1.9			
3 TH	0411	5.4	18 F	0023	2.1
	1124	2.2		0557	5.3
	1647	5.4		1254	2.3
				1829	5.3
4 F	0003	2.2	19 SA	0140	2.3
	0535	5.1		0726	5.2
	1233	2.4		1418	2.3
	1813	5.3		2011	5.3
5 SA	0130	2.3	20 SU	0309	2.2
	0710	5.2		0849	5.4
	1411	2.4		1548	2.1
	1934	5.4		2128	5.6
6 SU	0252	2.1	21 M	0435	2.0
	0818	5.5		0946	5.8
	1525	2.0		1658	1.7
	2040	5.7		2218	5.9
7 M	0357	1.8	22 TU	0530	1.7
	0915	5.8		1028	6.1
	1626	1.6		1748	1.4
	2137	6.0		2257	6.1
8 TU	0454	1.4	23 W ●	0612	1.5
	1004	6.2		1104	6.4
	1721	1.3		1829	1.2
	2227	6.4		2329	6.2
9 W ○	0549	1.2	24 TH	0648	1.4
	1050	6.5		1138	6.5
	1815	1.0		1903	1.1
	2313	6.6		2358	6.3
10 TH	0643	1.0	25 F	0717	1.3
	1134	6.8		1210	6.6
	1908	0.7		1930	1.1
	2357	6.7			
11 F	0732	0.8	26 SA	0026	6.3
	1216	7.0		0739	1.3
	1957	0.6		1240	6.5
				1953	1.2
12 SA	0039	6.8	27 SU	0053	6.2
	0816	0.7		0759	1.3
	1259	7.0		1305	6.5
	2041	0.5		2017	1.2
13 SU	0122	6.7	28 M	0115	6.2
	0855	0.7		0824	1.3
	1342	7.0		1326	6.4
	2120	0.5		2044	1.3
14 M	0205	6.6	29 TU	0134	6.1
	0931	0.8		0852	1.4
	1427	6.9		1348	6.3
	2158	0.8		2112	1.4
15 TU	0251	6.4	30 W	0158	6.1
	1008	1.1		0922	1.6
	1514	6.6		1418	6.2
	2237	1.1		2143	1.6
			31 TH ☾	0232	5.9
				0956	1.9
				1457	5.9
				2221	2.0

Chart Datum: 3·67 metres below Ordnance Datum (Newlyn)

TIME ZONE (UT)
For Summer Time add ONE hour in **non-shaded areas**

ENGLAND – DOVER

LAT 51°07′N   LONG 1°19′E

TIMES AND HEIGHTS OF HIGH AND LOW WATERS

2006

SEPTEMBER

Time	m	Time	m
1 0317	5.6	**16** 0529	5.2
1039	2.2	1230	2.5
F 1551	5.5	SA 1809	5.1
2312	2.3		
2 0424	5.1	**17** 0122	2.6
1142	2.5	0703	5.1
SA 1740	5.1	SU 1408	2.5
		2011	5.2
3 0040	2.5	**18** 0304	2.4
0647	5.1	0834	5.4
SU 1338	2.5	M 1544	2.1
1921	5.3	2117	5.6
4 0229	2.3	**19** 0419	2.0
0802	5.4	0926	5.9
M 1503	2.1	TU 1643	1.6
2030	5.7	2200	5.9
5 0339	1.9	**20** 0507	1.7
0900	5.9	1005	6.2
TU 1607	1.6	W 1727	1.3
2126	6.1	2234	6.2
6 0438	1.4	**21** 0546	1.4
0948	6.4	1039	6.4
W 1704	1.1	TH 1804	1.2
2214	6.5	2302	6.3
7 0533	1.1	**22** 0619	1.3
1032	6.8	1111	6.6
TH 1759	0.8	F 1833	1.1
○ 2257	6.8	● 2328	6.4
8 0624	0.8	**23** 0644	1.3
1114	7.0	1140	6.6
F 1851	0.5	SA 1856	1.1
2337	6.9	2354	6.4
9 0710	0.7	**24** 0704	1.3
1155	7.2	1206	6.5
SA 1936	0.4	SU 1919	1.2
10 0016	7.0	**25** 0018	6.3
0751	0.6	0727	1.3
SU 1235	7.2	M 1229	6.5
2016	0.4	1944	1.2
11 0055	6.9	**26** 0038	6.3
0827	0.7	0754	1.3
M 1316	7.1	TU 1248	6.4
2053	0.6	2012	1.3
12 0136	6.7	**27** 0057	6.3
0902	0.8	0822	1.4
TU 1359	6.9	W 1312	6.4
2128	0.9	2040	1.4
13 0221	6.4	**28** 0124	6.3
0938	1.2	0852	1.6
W 1445	6.5	TH 1343	6.2
2205	1.4	2111	1.7
14 0312	6.0	**29** 0200	6.1
1018	1.6	0927	1.9
TH 1538	6.0	F 1423	5.9
2249	1.9	2150	2.0
15 0414	5.6	**30** 0246	5.7
1109	2.2	1012	2.2
F 1645	5.5	SA 1517	5.5
2352	2.4	◐ 2241	2.4

OCTOBER

Time	m	Time	m
1 0356	5.2	**16** 0059	2.8
1116	2.5	0626	5.2
SU 1735	5.1	M 1347	2.5
		1941	5.2
2 0005	2.6	**17** 0231	2.5
0625	5.1	0757	5.4
M 1312	2.5	TU 1509	2.1
1906	5.3	2045	5.5
3 0207	2.4	**18** 0338	2.1
0739	5.5	0852	5.8
TU 1440	2.0	W 1605	1.7
2013	5.8	2126	5.8
4 0317	1.9	**19** 0426	1.8
0837	6.0	0931	6.1
W 1544	1.5	TH 1648	1.4
2107	6.2	2158	6.1
5 0415	1.4	**20** 0506	1.5
0925	6.3	1005	6.3
TH 1641	1.0	F 1722	1.3
2152	6.6	2226	6.2
6 0508	1.1	**21** 0539	1.4
1008	6.9	1036	6.4
F 1736	0.7	SA 1751	1.2
2234	6.9	2252	6.3
7 0557	0.8	**22** 0605	1.4
1049	7.1	1104	6.5
SA 1825	0.5	SU 1817	1.2
○ 2312	7.0	● 2319	6.4
8 0642	0.7	**23** 0631	1.3
1129	7.2	1129	6.5
SU 1909	0.5	M 1846	1.2
2350	7.0	2343	6.4
9 0722	0.7	**24** 0659	1.3
1209	7.2	1153	6.4
M 1948	0.5	TU 1916	1.2
10 0029	6.9	**25** 0006	6.4
0759	0.8	0729	1.3
TU 1250	7.1	W 1218	6.4
2024	0.8	1945	1.3
11 0111	6.7	**26** 0031	6.4
0835	1.0	0759	1.4
W 1333	6.8	TH 1247	6.4
2059	1.1	2016	1.5
12 0156	6.4	**27** 0103	6.3
0912	1.4	0832	1.6
TH 1420	6.3	F 1322	6.2
2136	1.6	2050	1.7
13 0248	6.0	**28** 0144	6.1
0953	1.8	0910	1.8
F 1516	5.8	SA 1407	5.9
2219	2.1	2132	2.0
14 0350	5.6	**29** 0236	5.8
1046	2.3	0959	2.1
SA 1624	5.4	SU 1511	5.5
◐ 2325	2.6	◐ 2226	2.3
15 0500	5.3	**30** 0401	5.4
1210	2.6	1107	2.3
SU 1745	5.1	M 1719	5.3
		2349	2.5
		31 0553	5.4
		1248	2.3
		TU 1842	5.5

NOVEMBER

Time	m	Time	m
1 0135	2.3	**16** 0238	2.3
0707	5.7	0759	5.6
W 1410	1.9	TH 1503	1.9
1946	5.8	2034	5.6
2 0245	1.9	**17** 0331	2.0
0806	6.1	0845	5.9
TH 1513	1.4	F 1549	1.7
2040	6.2	2111	5.8
3 0343	1.5	**18** 0415	1.8
0856	6.5	0922	6.1
F 1612	1.1	SA 1630	1.5
2126	6.5	2144	6.0
4 0437	1.1	**19** 0454	1.6
0941	6.8	0955	6.2
SA 1707	0.8	SU 1707	1.4
2208	6.7	2215	6.2
5 0528	0.9	**20** 0528	1.5
1024	7.0	1025	6.3
SU 1758	0.7	M 1743	1.3
○ 2248	6.3	● 2245	6.2
6 0614	0.8	**21** 0602	1.4
1106	7.1	1056	6.4
M 1842	0.7	TU 1818	1.3
2328	6.9	2315	6.4
7 0656	0.8	**22** 0636	1.3
1148	7.0	1127	6.4
TU 1923	0.8	W 1854	1.3
		2346	6.4
8 0010	6.8	**23** 0711	1.3
0736	0.9	1200	6.4
W 1230	6.8	TH 1928	1.4
2000	1.1		
9 0053	6.6	**24** 0019	6.4
0815	1.2	0747	1.4
TH 1314	6.5	F 1237	6.3
2037	1.4	2003	1.5
10 0139	6.4	**25** 0059	6.3
0854	1.5	0825	1.5
F 1403	6.2	SA 1319	6.1
2114	1.8	2042	1.6
11 0229	6.1	**26** 0145	6.2
0937	1.8	0908	1.7
SA 1458	5.8	SU 1410	5.9
2157	2.2	2126	1.8
12 0325	5.8	**27** 0242	6.0
1029	2.2	0959	1.8
SU 1600	5.4	M 1517	5.7
◑ 2255	2.5	2221	2.0
13 0427	5.5	**28** 0352	5.8
1140	2.4	1104	1.9
M 1710	5.2	TU 1645	5.6
		◑ 2332	2.1
14 0016	2.7	**29** 0510	5.7
0537	5.3	1219	1.9
TU 1258	2.4	W 1804	5.6
1832	5.1		
15 0133	2.6	**30** 0052	2.1
0655	5.4	0623	5.8
W 1406	2.2	TH 1331	1.7
1946	5.3	1910	5.8

DECEMBER

Time	m	Time	m
1 0202	1.9	**16** 0221	2.3
0728	6.1	0746	5.5
F 1435	1.5	SA 1447	2.0
2008	6.0	2019	5.5
2 0304	1.6	**17** 0319	2.1
0825	6.3	0833	5.7
SA 1537	1.3	SU 1540	1.8
2059	6.2	2102	5.7
3 0404	1.4	**18** 0410	1.9
0916	6.5	0914	5.9
SU 1638	1.1	M 1629	1.6
2146	6.4	2142	5.9
4 0501	1.2	**19** 0456	1.6
1004	6.6	0953	6.1
M 1733	1.0	TU 1714	1.4
2231	6.5	2220	6.1
5 0552	1.1	**20** 0538	1.4
1051	6.7	1051	6.3
TU 1822	1.0	W 1757	1.3
○ 2316	6.6	● 2257	6.2
6 0638	1.1	**21** 0619	1.3
1136	6.6	1113	6.3
W 1905	1.1	TH 1839	1.3
2359	6.6	2336	6.4
7 0722	1.1	**22** 0700	1.2
1220	6.5	1153	6.4
TH 1945	1.3	F 1920	1.3
8 0042	6.6	**23** 0016	6.5
0804	1.2	0742	1.2
F 1304	6.3	SA 1236	6.4
2023	1.5	2000	1.3
9 0126	6.4	**24** 0059	6.5
0845	1.4	0826	1.2
SA 1349	6.1	SU 1320	6.3
2101	1.7	2043	1.4
10 0211	6.2	**25** 0144	6.5
0926	1.6	0912	1.3
SU 1436	5.8	M 1408	6.2
2139	2.0	2128	1.4
11 0257	6.0	**26** 0234	6.4
1009	1.9	1000	1.3
M 1527	5.6	TU 1502	6.1
2219	2.2	2215	1.5
12 0347	5.7	**27** 0328	6.3
1056	2.0	1051	1.4
TU 1624	5.3	W 1603	5.9
◑ 2308	2.4	◑ 2308	1.7
13 0443	5.5	**28** 0429	6.1
1150	2.2	1147	1.5
W 1726	5.2	TH 1711	5.7
14 0009	2.5	**29** 0008	1.8
0544	5.4	0535	5.9
TH 1250	2.2	F 1249	1.6
1831	5.2	1824	5.6
15 0118	2.4	**30** 0116	1.9
0649	5.4	0647	5.9
F 1350	2.1	SA 1355	1.7
1930	5.3	1933	5.7
		31 0225	1.9
		0756	5.9
		SU 1503	1.7
		2037	5.8

Chart Datum: 3·67 metres below Ordnance Datum (Newlyn)

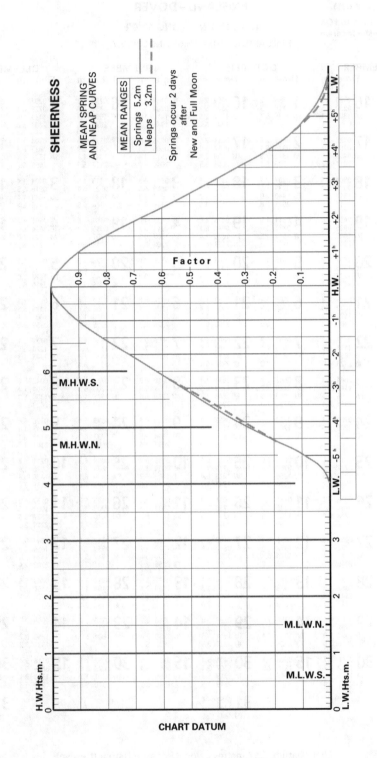

SHEERNESS

MEAN SPRING
AND NEAP CURVES

MEAN RANGES
Springs 5.2m
Neaps 3.2m

Springs occur 2 days
after
New and Full Moon

Factor

0.9
0.8
0.7
0.6
0.5
0.4
0.3
0.2
0.1

H.W.Hts.m.

L.W.Hts.m.

M.H.W.S.

M.H.W.N.

M.L.W.N.

M.L.W.S.

CHART DATUM

L.W.

+5ʰ
+4ʰ
+3ʰ
+2ʰ
+1ʰ
H.W.
-1ʰ
-2ʰ
-3ʰ
-4ʰ
-5ʰ
L.W.

TIME ZONE (UT)
For Summer Time add ONE hour in **non-shaded areas**

ENGLAND – SHEERNESS

LAT 51°27'N   LONG 0°45'E

TIMES AND HEIGHTS OF HIGH AND LOW WATERS

JANUARY

Time	m	Time	m
1 0052 / 0712 SU 1319 / 1929	5.5 / 0.7 / 5.8 / 0.8	**16** 0133 / 0751 M 1358 / 1944	5.3 / 0.8 / 5.4 / 1.1
2 0138 / 0804 M 1407 / 2015	5.6 / 0.6 / 5.8 / 0.8	**17** 0205 / 0824 TU 1431 / 2015	5.3 / 0.8 / 5.3 / 1.1
3 0223 / 0855 TU 1456 / 2101	5.6 / 0.4 / 5.8 / 0.8	**18** 0236 / 0854 W 1504 / 2046	5.3 / 0.8 / 5.3 / 1.1
4 0309 / 0944 W 1546 / 2146	5.6 / 0.4 / 5.8 / 0.9	**19** 0307 / 0924 TH 1536 / 2117	5.3 / 0.8 / 5.2 / 1.1
5 0356 / 1032 TH 1636 / 2231	5.5 / 0.5 / 5.6 / 1.1	**20** 0339 / 0954 F 1610 / 2150	5.2 / 0.9 / 5.1 / 1.2
6 0445 / 1120 F 1729 / 2318 ◐	5.4 / 0.6 / 5.4 / 1.2	**21** 0412 / 1026 SA 1647 / 2224	5.1 / 1.0 / 5.0 / 1.3
7 0538 / 1210 SA 1826	5.3 / 0.8 / 5.2	**22** 0449 / 1100 SU 1728 / 2303 ◑	5.0 / 1.1 / 4.8 / 1.5
8 0012 / 0636 SU 1307 / 1928	1.3 / 5.1 / 1.0 / 5.0	**23** 0533 / 1142 M 1819 / 2355	4.8 / 1.3 / 4.7 / 1.6
9 0115 / 0743 M 1411 / 2033	1.4 / 5.0 / 1.1 / 4.9	**24** 0633 / 1241 TU 1926	4.7 / 1.4 / 4.6
10 0226 / 0853 TU 1518 / 2139	1.4 / 4.9 / 1.2 / 4.9	**25** 0109 / 0750 W 1413 / 2041	1.7 / 4.6 / 1.5 / 4.7
11 0337 / 1002 W 1621 / 2239	1.4 / 5.0 / 1.3 / 5.0	**26** 0247 / 0912 TH 1538 / 2153	1.6 / 4.7 / 1.4 / 4.9
12 0445 / 1103 TH 1715 / 2332	1.2 / 5.1 / 1.1 / 5.1	**27** 0406 / 1024 F 1643 / 2256	1.4 / 5.0 / 1.2 / 5.1
13 0543 / 1156 F 1759	1.0 / 5.2 / 1.2	**28** 0512 / 1126 SA 1741 / 2352	1.1 / 5.4 / 1.0 / 5.4
14 0017 / 0632 SA 1242 / 1837 ○	5.2 / 0.9 / 5.3 / 1.1	**29** 0613 / 1220 SU 1833	0.8 / 5.7 / 0.8
15 0058 / 0714 SU 1322 / 1911	5.3 / 0.8 / 5.4 / 1.1	**30** 0041 / 0709 M 1311 / 1921	5.5 / 0.5 / 5.9 / 0.7
		31 0127 / 0801 TU 1359 / 2007	5.7 / 0.3 / 6.0 / 0.6

FEBRUARY

Time	m	Time	m
1 0211 / 0848 W 1444 / 2050	5.8 / 0.1 / 6.0 / 0.6	**16** 0215 / 0834 TH 1438 / 2028	5.5 / 0.6 / 5.5 / 0.9
2 0254 / 0932 TH 1529 / 2130	5.9 / 0.1 / 5.9 / 0.7	**17** 0244 / 0902 F 1508 / 2057	5.5 / 0.6 / 5.4 / 0.9
3 0336 / 1012 F 1613 / 2208	5.8 / 0.2 / 5.7 / 0.8	**18** 0312 / 0929 SA 1538 / 2123	5.4 / 0.7 / 5.3 / 1.0
4 0419 / 1049 SA 1658 / 2245	5.7 / 0.5 / 5.4 / 1.0	**19** 0342 / 0954 SU 1610 / 2148	5.3 / 0.9 / 5.2 / 1.1
5 0505 / 1126 SU 1747 ◑ 2329	5.5 / 0.8 / 5.1 / 1.2	**20** 0415 / 1017 M 1646 / 2219	5.2 / 1.0 / 5.0 / 1.2
6 0557 / 1210 M 1843	5.2 / 1.1 / 4.8	**21** 0455 / 1049 TU 1732 / 2305	5.0 / 1.2 / 4.8 / 1.4
7 0026 / 0703 TU 1315 / 1951	1.4 / 4.8 / 1.4 / 4.6	**22** 0549 / 1144 W 1835	4.8 / 1.4 / 4.6
8 0146 / 0824 W 1439 / 2109	1.5 / 4.7 / 1.6 / 4.6	**23** 0016 / 0707 TH 1324 / 2000	1.6 / 4.6 / 1.6 / 4.5
9 0317 / 0948 TH 1559 / 2222	1.5 / 4.7 / 1.5 / 4.7	**24** 0213 / 0843 F 1513 / 2127	1.6 / 4.6 / 1.5 / 4.7
10 0439 / 1056 F 1703 / 2319	1.2 / 4.9 / 1.4 / 5.0	**25** 0348 / 1008 SA 1627 / 2239	1.3 / 5.0 / 1.2 / 5.0
11 0540 / 1149 SA 1749	1.0 / 5.2 / 1.3	**26** 0503 / 1114 SU 1728 / 2336	0.9 / 5.4 / 0.9 / 5.4
12 0005 / 0625 SU 1232 / 1826	5.1 / 0.8 / 5.3 / 1.2	**27** 0606 / 1208 M 1821	0.6 / 5.8 / 0.7
13 0044 / 0702 M 1308 / 1857 ○	5.3 / 0.8 / 5.4 / 1.1	**28** 0025 / 0659 TU 1257 ● 1907	5.6 / 0.3 / 6.0 / 0.6
14 0117 / 0734 TU 1339 / 1927	5.3 / 0.7 / 5.4 / 1.0		
15 0147 / 0804 W 1409 / 1957	5.4 / 0.6 / 5.4 / 0.9		

MARCH

Time	m	Time	m
1 0109 / 0746 W 1341 / 1950	5.8 / 0.1 / 6.1 / 0.5	**16** 0120 / 0736 TH 1340 / 1935	5.5 / 0.6 / 5.5 / 0.8
2 0151 / 0830 TH 1423 / 2031	6.0 / 0.0 / 6.1 / 0.5	**17** 0148 / 0806 F 1409 / 2006	5.5 / 0.5 / 5.6 / 0.8
3 0231 / 0909 F 1504 / 2108	6.0 / 0.0 / 6.0 / 0.5	**18** 0217 / 0835 SA 1437 / 2035	5.5 / 0.6 / 5.5 / 0.8
4 0311 / 0943 SA 1544 / 2142	6.0 / 0.2 / 5.7 / 0.7	**19** 0245 / 0902 SU 1507 / 2100	5.5 / 0.7 / 5.4 / 0.9
5 0351 / 1014 SU 1624 / 2215	5.8 / 0.5 / 5.4 / 0.8	**20** 0316 / 0924 M 1539 / 2123	5.4 / 0.9 / 5.3 / 1.0
6 0433 / 1043 M 1707 / 2254 ◑	5.5 / 0.9 / 5.1 / 1.1	**21** 0350 / 0945 TU 1615 / 2153	5.3 / 1.0 / 5.1 / 1.1
7 0523 / 1123 TU 1758 / 2347	5.1 / 1.2 / 4.7 / 1.3	**22** 0432 / 1020 W 1700 ◑ 2242	5.1 / 1.2 / 4.8 / 1.3
8 0629 / 1225 W 1908	4.7 / 1.6 / 4.4	**23** 0529 / 1121 TH 1803 / 2358	4.8 / 1.5 / 4.6 / 1.5
9 0113 / 0757 TH 1405 / 2038	1.6 / 4.5 / 1.8 / 4.3	**24** 0648 / 1305 F 1932	4.6 / 1.7 / 4.4
10 0302 / 0931 F 1538 / 2159	1.5 / 4.6 / 1.7 / 4.5	**25** 0200 / 0827 SA 1453 / 2105	1.5 / 4.7 / 1.7 / 4.6
11 0425 / 1040 SA 1644 / 2258	1.2 / 4.9 / 1.5 / 4.9	**26** 0335 / 0952 SU 1607 / 2217	1.1 / 5.1 / 1.2 / 5.0
12 0522 / 1130 SU 1730 / 2342	1.0 / 5.2 / 1.3 / 5.1	**27** 0449 / 1057 M 1708 / 2314	0.7 / 5.5 / 0.9 / 5.4
13 0603 / 1209 M 1805	0.8 / 5.4 / 1.1	**28** 0550 / 1149 TU 1759	0.4 / 5.8 / 0.7
14 0019 / 0636 TU 1243 / 1835 ○	5.3 / 0.7 / 5.6 / 1.0	**29** 0001 / 0639 W 1235 ● 1844	5.7 / 0.2 / 6.0 / 0.6
15 0051 / 0707 W 1312 / 1905	5.4 / 0.6 / 5.5 / 0.9	**30** 0044 / 0723 TH 1317 / 1927	5.9 / 0.1 / 6.1 / 0.4
		31 0125 / 0803 F 1357 / 2006	6.0 / 0.1 / 6.0 / 0.4

APRIL

Time	m	Time	m
1 0205 / 0839 SA 1436 / 2043	6.1 / 0.2 / 5.9 / 0.5	**16** 0150 / 0807 SU 1409 / 2014	5.5 / 0.7 / 5.6 / 0.8
2 0245 / 0911 SU 1514 / 2118	6.0 / 0.4 / 5.7 / 0.6	**17** 0222 / 0836 M 1441 / 2044	5.5 / 0.8 / 5.5 / 0.9
3 0326 / 0940 M 1551 / 2152	5.8 / 0.7 / 5.4 / 0.8	**18** 0257 / 0903 TU 1515 / 2113	5.4 / 0.9 / 5.3 / 1.0
4 0408 / 1009 TU 1631 / 2228	5.4 / 1.1 / 5.0 / 1.0	**19** 0336 / 0933 W 1554 / 2151	5.3 / 1.0 / 5.1 / 1.1
5 0458 / 1048 W 1719 / 2318 ◑	5.0 / 1.4 / 4.7 / 1.3	**20** 0423 / 1016 TH 1643 ◑ 2246	5.1 / 1.3 / 4.9 / 1.2
6 0602 / 1147 TH 1827	4.6 / 1.8 / 4.3	**21** 0524 / 1123 F 1749 ◑	4.9 / 1.5 / 4.6
7 0045 / 0727 F 1328 / 1958	1.6 / 4.4 / 2.0 / 4.2	**22** 0007 / 0643 SA 1259 / 1914	1.3 / 4.8 / 1.6 / 4.6
8 0236 / 0859 SA 1502 / 2122	1.5 / 4.5 / 1.8 / 4.5	**23** 0153 / 0813 SU 1428 / 2040	1.2 / 4.9 / 1.5 / 4.8
9 0350 / 1008 SU 1607 / 2222	1.4 / 4.8 / 1.6 / 4.8	**24** 0317 / 0931 M 1538 / 2149	0.9 / 5.2 / 1.2 / 5.1
10 0444 / 1057 M 1654 / 2307	1.0 / 5.1 / 1.3 / 5.1	**25** 0426 / 1032 TU 1638 / 2245	0.6 / 5.5 / 1.0 / 5.4
11 0526 / 1135 TU 1732 / 2344	0.8 / 5.3 / 1.1 / 5.3	**26** 0523 / 1124 W 1730 / 2333	0.4 / 5.8 / 0.7 / 5.7
12 0601 / 1208 W 1805	0.7 / 5.4 / 1.0	**27** 0612 / 1209 TH 1817 ●	0.3 / 5.9 / 0.5
13 0017 / 0633 TH 1239 / 1837 ○	5.4 / 0.7 / 5.5 / 0.9	**28** 0017 / 0653 F 1251 / 1900	5.9 / 0.3 / 5.9 / 0.5
14 0048 / 0704 F 1308 / 1909	5.5 / 0.7 / 5.6 / 0.8	**29** 0100 / 0732 SA 1331 / 1942	6.0 / 0.3 / 5.9 / 0.5
15 0119 / 0736 SA 1338 / 1942	5.6 / 0.6 / 5.6 / 0.8	**30** 0142 / 0808 SU 1409 / 2022	6.0 / 0.4 / 5.8 / 0.5

Chart Datum: 2·90 metres below Ordnance Datum (Newlyn)

TIDES

TIME ZONE (UT)
For Summer Time add ONE hour in **non-shaded areas**

ENGLAND – SHEERNESS   2006

LAT 51°27′N   LONG 0°45′E

TIMES AND HEIGHTS OF HIGH AND LOW WATERS

MAY		JUNE		JULY		AUGUST	
Time m	Time m	Time m	Time m	Time m	Time m	Time m	Time m

MAY

1 0224 5.8 / 0841 0.7 / M 1447 5.6 / 2100 0.7
16 0206 5.5 / 0817 0.9 / TU 1423 5.5 / 2037 0.8

2 0306 5.6 / 0912 1.0 / TU 1524 5.3 / 2135 0.9
17 0247 5.5 / 0854 1.0 / W 1502 5.3 / 2118 0.9

3 0351 5.3 / 0943 1.2 / W 1603 5.0 / 2212 1.1
18 0332 5.4 / 0934 1.1 / TH 1546 5.2 / 2205 0.9

4 0439 5.0 / 1021 1.5 / TH 1649 4.7 / 2259 1.3
19 0424 5.2 / 1023 1.3 / F 1639 5.0 / 2303 1.0

5 0538 4.7 / 1114 1.8 / F 1750 4.4 ☽
20 0526 5.1 / 1126 1.4 / SA 1743 4.9 ◐

6 0012 1.4 / 0648 4.5 / SA 1235 2.0 / 1908 4.3
21 0017 1.0 / 0637 5.0 / SU 1242 1.5 / 1856 4.9

7 0149 1.4 / 0805 4.5 / SU 1407 1.9 / 2026 4.4
22 0137 0.9 / 0752 5.1 / M 1356 1.4 / 2010 5.0

8 0258 1.3 / 0914 4.7 / M 1513 1.7 / 2130 4.7
23 0248 0.8 / 0902 5.3 / TU 1502 1.2 / 2116 5.2

9 0352 1.1 / 1007 4.9 / TU 1605 1.4 / 2220 5.0
24 0353 0.7 / 1003 5.4 / W 1602 1.1 / 2214 5.4

10 0438 0.9 / 1050 5.2 / W 1649 1.2 / 2302 5.2
25 0451 0.6 / 1056 5.6 / TH 1658 0.9 / 2306 5.5

11 0518 0.8 / 1127 5.3 / TH 1728 1.1 / 2339 5.3
26 0540 0.6 / 1143 5.6 / F 1750 0.8 / 2354 5.7

12 0555 0.8 / 1202 5.4 / F 1806 1.0
27 0624 0.6 / 1227 5.6 / SA 1838 0.7 ●

13 0015 5.4 / 0630 0.8 / SA 1237 5.5 / 1843 0.9 ○
28 0040 5.7 / 0703 0.7 / SU 1309 5.6 / 1924 0.6

14 0052 5.5 / 0706 0.8 / SU 1312 5.6 / 1921 0.8
29 0126 5.8 / 0742 0.8 / M 1349 5.6 / 2008 0.6

15 0128 5.5 / 0742 0.8 / M 1347 5.5 / 1959 0.8
30 0210 5.6 / 0817 0.9 / TU 1428 5.4 / 2049 0.7

31 0254 5.4 / 0851 1.1 / W 1506 5.2 / 2126 0.9

JUNE

1 0337 5.2 / 0923 1.3 / TH 1544 5.0 / 2202 1.0
16 0332 5.6 / 0936 1.0 / F 1544 5.4 / 2218 0.6

2 0422 5.0 / 0959 1.5 / F 1626 4.9 / 2242 1.1
17 0424 5.5 / 1024 1.1 / SA 1635 5.3 / 2310 0.7

3 0510 4.8 / 1044 1.6 / SA 1715 4.7 / 2332 1.3 ◐
18 0519 5.4 / 1117 1.2 / SU 1730 5.2 ◐

4 0603 4.7 / 1140 1.8 / SU 1814 4.6
19 0007 0.7 / 0619 5.3 / M 1215 1.3 / 1831 5.1

5 0037 1.3 / 0702 4.6 / M 1249 1.8 / 1919 4.5
20 0108 0.8 / 0724 5.2 / TU 1318 1.3 / 1937 5.1

6 0148 1.3 / 0804 4.6 / TU 1402 1.8 / 2024 4.6
21 0212 0.8 / 0829 5.2 / W 1424 1.3 / 2044 5.2

7 0250 1.2 / 0903 4.8 / W 1506 1.6 / 2123 4.8
22 0316 0.9 / 0932 5.2 / TH 1529 1.2 / 2147 5.2

8 0344 1.1 / 0957 5.0 / TH 1600 1.4 / 2215 5.0
23 0418 0.9 / 1030 5.3 / F 1633 1.1 / 2247 5.3

9 0433 1.0 / 1044 5.2 / F 1650 1.2 / 2302 5.2
24 0513 1.0 / 1123 5.3 / SA 1732 0.9 / 2342 5.4

10 0518 1.0 / 1128 5.3 / SA 1736 1.1 / 2347 5.3
25 0600 1.0 / 1211 5.4 / SU 1826 0.8 ●

11 0601 0.9 / 1210 5.4 / SU 1821 1.0 ○
26 0032 5.5 / 0643 1.0 / M 1256 5.4 / 1915 0.7

12 0030 5.4 / 0642 0.9 / M 1252 5.5 / 1906 0.8
27 0119 5.5 / 0723 1.0 / TU 1337 5.4 / 2000 0.7

13 0114 5.5 / 0724 0.9 / TU 1332 5.5 / 1952 0.7
28 0202 5.5 / 0800 1.1 / W 1415 5.3 / 2040 0.7

14 0158 5.6 / 0807 0.9 / W 1414 5.5 / 2039 0.7
29 0243 5.4 / 0834 1.2 / TH 1451 5.3 / 2116 0.8

15 0243 5.6 / 0851 0.9 / TH 1457 5.4 / 2128 0.6
30 0321 5.3 / 0905 1.2 / F 1526 5.2 / 2148 0.9

JULY

1 0359 5.2 / 0938 1.3 / SA 1602 5.1 / 2219 1.0
16 0412 5.7 / 1012 0.9 / SU 1619 5.6 / 2256 0.4

2 0437 5.0 / 1014 1.4 / SU 1640 5.0 / 2255 1.1
17 0500 5.6 / 1054 1.0 / M 1707 5.5 / 2340 0.6 ◐

3 0518 4.9 / 1055 1.5 / M 1723 4.8 / 2337 1.2 ◐
18 0552 5.3 / 1141 1.2 / TU 1800 5.3

4 0603 4.7 / 1143 1.6 / TU 1813 4.7
19 0029 0.8 / 0650 5.1 / W 1238 1.3 / 1902 5.1

5 0029 1.3 / 0657 4.7 / W 1243 1.7 / 1914 4.6
20 0129 1.1 / 0754 5.0 / TH 1347 1.4 / 2014 5.0

6 0134 1.4 / 0759 4.7 / TH 1356 1.7 / 2023 4.6
21 0240 1.2 / 0903 4.9 / F 1504 1.4 / 2129 5.0

7 0247 1.4 / 0904 4.8 / F 1511 1.6 / 2130 4.8
22 0352 1.3 / 1011 5.0 / SA 1621 1.2 / 2239 5.1

8 0352 1.3 / 1005 5.0 / SA 1615 1.4 / 2230 5.0
23 0456 1.3 / 1111 5.1 / SU 1729 1.0 / 2339 5.2

9 0448 1.1 / 1100 5.2 / SU 1712 1.2 / 2325 5.2
24 0549 1.2 / 1202 5.2 / M 1824 0.9

10 0539 1.0 / 1150 5.3 / M 1805 1.0
25 0029 5.4 / 0632 1.2 / TU 1247 5.3 / 1909 0.8 ●

11 0016 5.5 / 0626 0.9 / TU 1238 5.5 / 1857 0.8 ○
26 0112 5.4 / 0709 1.1 / W 1325 5.4 / 1949 0.7

12 0104 5.6 / 0713 0.9 / W 1322 5.6 / 1949 0.6
27 0150 5.5 / 0743 1.1 / TH 1400 5.4 / 2024 0.7

13 0151 5.8 / 0800 0.8 / TH 1406 5.6 / 2039 0.4
28 0225 5.4 / 0815 1.1 / F 1432 5.4 / 2055 0.7

14 0238 5.7 / 0845 0.8 / F 1450 5.7 / 2127 0.3
29 0258 5.4 / 0845 1.1 / SA 1502 5.4 / 2124 0.7

15 0325 5.8 / 0929 0.8 / SA 1534 5.7 / 2212 0.3
30 0329 5.3 / 0914 1.1 / SU 1533 5.3 / 2151 0.8

31 0401 5.2 / 0944 1.2 / M 1604 5.2 / 2219 0.9

AUGUST

1 0435 5.1 / 1016 1.3 / TU 1638 5.1 / 2251 1.1
16 0519 5.3 / 1107 1.1 / W 1728 5.4 / 2344 1.0 ◑

2 0512 4.9 / 1052 1.5 / W 1719 4.9 / 2329 1.3
17 0612 5.0 / 1159 1.3 / TH 1830 5.0

3 0558 4.8 / 1139 1.7 / TH 1811 4.7
18 0043 1.4 / 0718 4.7 / F 1316 1.5 / 1950 4.8

4 0023 1.5 / 0658 4.6 / F 1247 1.8 / 1924 4.5
19 0209 1.6 / 0837 4.6 / SA 1451 1.5 / 2118 4.8

5 0149 1.6 / 0813 4.6 / SA 1425 1.7 / 2048 4.6
20 0336 1.6 / 0956 4.8 / SU 1620 1.3 / 2235 5.0

6 0317 1.5 / 0930 4.8 / SU 1548 1.5 / 2204 4.9
21 0448 1.5 / 1100 5.0 / M 1727 1.0 / 2332 5.3

7 0424 1.3 / 1036 5.1 / M 1654 1.2 / 2308 5.3
22 0539 1.3 / 1149 5.3 / TU 1815 0.7

8 0521 1.1 / 1133 5.3 / TU 1754 0.9
23 0017 5.4 / 0618 1.2 / W 1231 5.4 / ● 1853 0.7

9 0003 5.6 / 0613 0.9 / W 1223 5.6 / ○ 1849 0.6
24 0056 5.5 / 0650 1.1 / TH 1306 5.5 / 1927 0.7

10 0052 5.8 / 0701 0.8 / TH 1308 5.7 / 1940 0.3
25 0129 5.5 / 0721 1.1 / F 1336 5.5 / 1957 0.7

11 0138 6.0 / 0747 0.7 / F 1351 5.9 / 2027 0.4
26 0159 5.5 / 0750 1.0 / SA 1405 5.5 / 2025 0.6

12 0223 6.1 / 0831 0.6 / SA 1432 5.9 / 2111 0.1
27 0228 5.5 / 0820 1.0 / SU 1433 5.5 / 2053 0.7

13 0306 6.0 / 0911 0.7 / SU 1513 5.9 / 2152 0.2
28 0256 5.5 / 0848 1.0 / M 1501 5.5 / 2120 0.8

14 0349 5.9 / 0949 0.8 / M 1554 5.8 / 2229 0.4
29 0325 5.4 / 0915 1.1 / TU 1530 5.4 / 2144 1.0

15 0432 5.6 / 1026 0.9 / TU 1638 5.6 / 2304 0.7
30 0355 5.2 / 0940 1.3 / W 1602 5.2 / 2208 1.1

31 0429 5.1 / 1008 1.4 / TH 1639 5.0 / ◑ 2238 1.3

Chart Datum: 2·90 metres below Ordnance Datum (Newlyn)

TIME ZONE (UT)
For Summer Time add ONE hour in **non-shaded areas**

ENGLAND – SHEERNESS

LAT 51°27′N   LONG 0°45′E

TIMES AND HEIGHTS OF HIGH AND LOW WATERS

2006

SEPTEMBER

Time	m		Time	m
1 0511	4.9		**16** 0003	1.7
1049	1.6		0642	4.6
F 1729	4.8		SA 1253	1.6
2327	1.6		1930	4.6
2 0608	4.6		**17** 0141	1.9
1155	1.7		0810	4.5
SA 1840	4.6		SU 1444	1.5
			2105	4.7
3 0056	1.8		**18** 0318	1.8
0728	4.5		0935	4.7
SU 1348	1.8		M 1609	1.2
2014	4.6		2219	5.0
4 0249	1.7		**19** 0428	1.6
0859	4.7		1038	5.0
M 1526	1.5		TU 1707	1.0
2143	4.9		2312	5.3
5 0403	1.4		**20** 0516	1.4
1014	5.0		1125	5.3
TU 1639	1.1		W 1750	0.8
2251	5.4		2354	5.5
6 0503	1.1		**21** 0552	1.2
1112	5.4		1204	5.4
W 1741	0.7		TH 1825	0.8
2345	5.8			
7 0555	0.9		**22** 0029	5.6
1201	5.7		0623	1.1
TH 1834	0.4		F 1237	5.5
O			● 1854	0.7
8 0033	6.0		**23** 0100	5.6
0642	0.7		0652	1.0
F 1245	5.9		SA 1306	5.6
1921	0.2		1923	0.7
9 0117	6.1		**24** 0127	5.6
0726	0.6		0722	0.9
SA 1326	6.1		SU 1334	5.6
2005	0.1		1951	0.7
10 0159	6.1		**25** 0154	5.6
0808	0.6		0752	0.9
SU 1406	6.1		M 1402	5.6
2046	0.1		2020	0.7
11 0240	6.1		**26** 0222	5.6
0847	0.6		0821	1.0
M 1446	6.1		TU 1431	5.5
2122	0.3		2047	0.9
12 0320	5.9		**27** 0251	5.5
0923	0.7		0848	1.1
TU 1527	5.9		W 1501	5.4
2155	0.6		2111	1.0
13 0400	5.6		**28** 0321	5.4
0958	0.9		0912	1.2
W 1610	5.7		TH 1534	5.3
2226	0.9		2133	1.2
14 0444	5.2		**29** 0355	5.2
1037	1.1		0939	1.3
TH 1700	5.3		F 1614	5.1
◑ 2304	1.3		2203	1.4
15 0534	4.9		**30** 0437	4.9
1129	1.4		1022	1.5
F 1804	4.9		SA 1705	4.9
			◐ 2256	1.7

OCTOBER

Time	m		Time	m
1 0534	4.7		**16** 0104	2.1
1131	1.7		0735	4.4
SU 1817	4.7		M 1420	1.5
			2033	4.6
2 0028	1.9		**17** 0240	2.0
0655	4.5		0858	4.6
M 1326	1.7		TU 1534	1.3
1951	4.7		2146	4.9
3 0220	1.7		**18** 0348	1.7
0830	4.7		1002	4.9
TU 1505	1.3		W 1629	1.0
2120	5.0		2238	5.2
4 0335	1.4		**19** 0437	1.5
0946	5.1		1049	5.2
W 1617	0.9		TH 1711	0.9
2227	5.3		2320	5.4
5 0436	1.1		**20** 0515	1.3
1044	5.5		1128	5.4
TH 1718	0.6		F 1745	0.8
2321	5.8		2354	5.5
6 0528	0.9		**21** 0549	1.1
1132	5.8		1201	5.5
F 1810	0.4		SA 1816	0.8
7 0007	6.0		**22** 0023	5.6
0615	0.7		0620	1.0
SA 1216	6.0		SU 1232	5.6
O 1854	0.3		● 1846	0.8
8 0051	6.1		**23** 0052	5.6
0659	0.6		0652	1.0
SU 1258	6.1		M 1303	5.6
1936	0.2		1916	0.8
9 0132	6.1		**24** 0121	5.6
0741	0.6		0724	0.9
M 1339	6.2		TU 1334	5.6
2015	0.3		1947	0.8
10 0211	6.0		**25** 0151	5.6
0821	0.6		0756	1.0
TU 1421	6.1		W 1406	5.5
2050	0.5		2016	1.0
11 0251	5.8		**26** 0222	5.5
0859	0.6		0826	1.0
W 1504	5.9		TH 1439	5.5
2122	0.8		2044	1.1
12 0330	5.2		**27** 0255	5.4
0936	0.9		0856	1.1
TH 1549	5.6		F 1517	5.3
2153	1.2		2113	1.3
13 0412	5.2		**28** 0332	5.2
1015	1.2		0931	1.2
F 1640	5.2		SA 1601	5.2
2232	1.6		2152	1.4
14 0502	4.8		**29** 0417	5.0
1107	1.4		1019	1.4
SA 1744	4.8		SU 1656	5.0
◑ 2329	1.9		◐ 2249	1.6
15 0609	4.5		**30** 0515	4.8
1233	1.6		1130	1.5
SU 1905	4.6		M 1807	4.8
			31 0013	1.8
			0632	4.7
			TU 1310	1.4
			1931	4.9

NOVEMBER

Time	m		Time	m
1 0146	1.7		**16** 0250	1.8
0758	4.8		0908	4.7
W 1437	1.2		TH 1534	1.2
2051	5.2		2148	4.9
2 0259	1.4		**17** 0345	1.6
0911	5.1		1001	5.0
TH 1546	0.9		F 1620	1.1
2157	5.5		2233	5.1
3 0400	1.2		**18** 0430	1.4
1010	5.5		1045	5.2
F 1646	0.6		SA 1700	1.0
2251	5.7		2311	5.3
4 0454	1.0		**19** 0510	1.2
1101	5.7		1123	5.3
SA 1738	0.5		SU 1736	0.9
2339	5.9		2346	5.4
5 0544	0.8		**20** 0548	1.1
1147	5.9		1159	5.4
SU 1824	0.5		M 1811	0.9
O			●	
6 0023	5.9		**21** 0019	5.5
0631	0.7		0623	1.0
M 1232	6.0		TU 1235	5.5
1905	0.5		1844	0.9
7 0105	5.9		**22** 0054	5.6
0716	0.6		0700	1.0
TU 1317	6.0		W 1311	5.5
1944	0.6		1919	0.9
8 0146	5.8		**23** 0128	5.5
0800	0.6		0737	0.9
W 1401	5.9		TH 1348	5.5
2020	0.6		1954	1.0
9 0226	5.6		**24** 0203	5.5
0842	0.8		0815	0.9
TH 1447	5.7		F 1427	5.5
2055	1.1		2029	1.1
10 0307	5.4		**25** 0240	5.4
0922	0.9		0854	1.0
F 1534	5.4		SA 1509	5.4
2128	1.4		2107	1.2
11 0349	5.1		**26** 0320	5.3
1002	1.1		0937	1.0
SA 1624	5.1		SU 1557	5.3
2206	1.6		2151	1.3
12 0436	4.8		**27** 0408	5.1
1050	1.4		1028	1.1
SU 1722	4.8		M 1652	5.2
◐ 2256	1.9		2246	1.5
13 0535	4.6		**28** 0504	5.0
1200	1.5		1131	1.2
M 1828	4.6		TU 1756	5.2
			◐ 2352	1.6
14 0008	2.1		**29** 0610	4.9
0647	4.5		1246	1.1
TU 1330	1.4		W 1907	5.0
1941	4.6			
15 0139	2.0		**30** 0106	1.5
0802	4.5		0722	5.0
W 1439	1.4		TH 1400	1.0
2051	4.7		2018	5.1

DECEMBER

Time	m		Time	m
1 0216	1.4		**16** 0240	1.8
0833	5.1		0900	4.7
F 1508	0.9		SA 1522	1.3
2123	5.3		2135	4.8
2 0320	1.3		**17** 0340	1.6
0935	5.3		0956	4.9
SA 1610	0.8		SU 1613	1.2
2221	5.5		2225	5.0
3 0420	1.1		**18** 0431	1.4
1032	5.5		1046	5.1
SU 1705	0.8		M 1659	1.1
2312	5.6		2311	5.2
4 0517	0.9		**19** 0517	1.2
1125	5.7		1131	5.2
M 1754	0.8		TU 1741	1.1
			2353	5.4
5 0000	5.6		**20** 0601	1.1
0610	0.8		1214	5.4
TU 1215	5.7		W 1821	1.0
O 1838	0.8			
6 0045	5.6		**21** 0033	5.4
0700	0.7		0643	0.9
W 1303	5.8		TH 1256	5.5
1920	0.9		1900	1.0
7 0128	5.6		**22** 0113	5.5
0748	0.7		0727	0.8
TH 1351	5.7		F 1338	5.6
1959	1.0		1940	0.9
8 0210	5.5		**23** 0152	5.5
0833	0.7		0813	0.7
F 1437	5.6		SA 1421	5.6
2035	1.2		2022	0.9
9 0251	5.3		**24** 0233	5.5
0914	0.9		0859	0.7
SA 1522	5.4		SU 1506	5.6
2109	1.3		2105	1.0
10 0331	5.1		**25** 0315	5.4
0953	1.0		0945	0.7
SU 1607	5.2		M 1553	5.5
2144	1.5		2148	1.1
11 0413	5.0		**26** 0400	5.4
1030	1.2		1031	0.7
M 1653	4.9		TU 1643	5.4
2224	1.7		2234	1.2
12 0459	4.8		**27** 0449	5.3
1114	1.3		1119	0.8
TU 1743	4.7		W 1737	5.2
◐ 2313	1.8		◐ 2325	1.3
13 0552	4.7		**28** 0544	5.2
1210	1.2		1213	0.9
W 1838	4.6		TH 1837	5.1
14 0014	1.9		**29** 0023	1.4
0652	4.6		0645	5.1
TH 1318	1.2		F 1315	1.0
1938	4.6		1942	5.0
15 0128	1.9		**30** 0131	1.4
0757	4.6		0755	5.1
F 1424	1.4		SA 1425	1.1
2039	4.7		2049	5.0
			31 0243	1.4
			0906	5.0
			SU 1535	1.1
			2154	5.1

Chart Datum: 2·90 metres below Ordnance Datum (Newlyn)

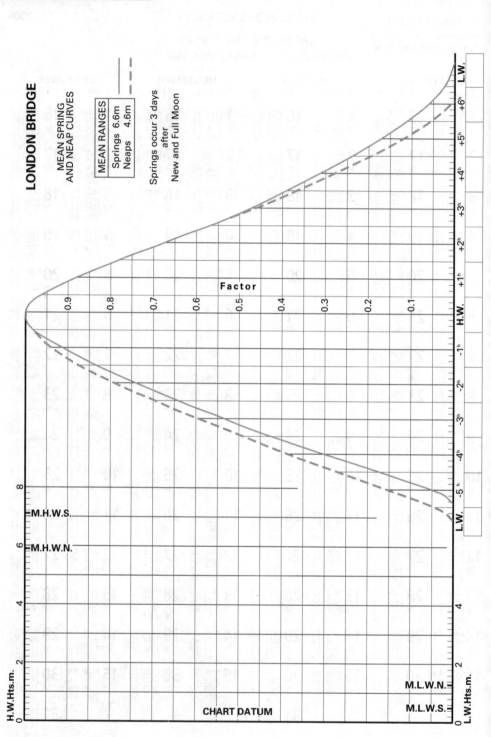

LONDON BRIDGE

MEAN SPRING
AND NEAP CURVES

MEAN RANGES	
Springs	6.6m
Neaps	4.6m

Springs occur 3 days
after
New and Full Moon

TIME ZONE (UT)
For Summer Time add ONE hour in **non-shaded areas**

ENGLAND – LONDON BRIDGE

2006

LAT 51°30'N   LONG 0°05'W

TIMES AND HEIGHTS OF HIGH AND LOW WATERS

JANUARY

Day	Time m	Time m	Time m	Time m		Day	Time m	Time m	Time m	Time m
1 SU	0212 6.9	0854 0.7	1439 7.1	2111 0.8		**16** M	0251 6.5	0937 0.8	1519 6.6	2137 1.3
2 M	0258 6.9	0948 0.6	1529 7.1	2158 0.8		**17** TU	0322 6.4	1013 0.9	1552 6.5	2203 1.3
3 TU	0345 6.8	1039 0.5	1619 7.1	2242 0.9		**18** W	0351 6.4	1041 0.9	1623 6.5	2220 1.3
4 W	0431 6.8	1126 0.5	1708 7.0	2325 1.0		**19** TH	0421 6.4	1101 1.1	1655 6.5	2246 1.2
5 TH	0511 6.7	1210 0.5	1758 6.9			**20** F	0454 6.4	1122 1.0	1730 6.5	2318 1.1
6 F	0007 1.0	0605 6.6	1253 0.6	1850 6.6 ◐		**21** SA	0530 6.3	1151 1.0	1809 6.4	2355 1.1
7 SA	0052 1.2	0658 6.5	1337 0.8	1946 6.4		**22** SU	0610 6.2	1227 1.1	1852 6.2	
8 SU	0141 1.3	0757 6.3	1427 1.0	2047 6.1		**23** M	0037 1.3	0657 6.0	1312 1.3	1942 6.0
9 M	0237 1.5	0901 6.2	1525 1.3	2149 6.0		**24** TU	0130 1.5	0756 5.8	1414 1.5	2042 5.8
10 TU	0342 1.6	1007 6.1	1636 1.4	2251 6.0		**25** W	0242 1.7	0905 5.7	1536 1.6	2153 5.7
11 W	0500 1.6	1113 6.1	1747 1.4	2350 6.1		**26** TH	0407 1.7	1022 5.8	1659 1.5	2309 5.9
12 TH	0618 1.3	1213 6.3	1845 1.3			**27** F	0526 1.5	1139 6.1	1814 1.3	
13 F	0043 6.3	0717 1.1	1308 6.5	1935 1.2		**28** SA	0015 6.3	0645 1.1	1244 6.5	1917 1.0
14 SA	0132 6.4	0809 0.9	1357 6.6	2020 1.1 ○		**29** SU	0110 6.6	0754 0.7	1339 6.9	2013 0.8 ●
15 SU	0214 6.5	0855 0.8	1441 6.6	2102 1.2		**30** M	0159 6.9	0852 0.6	1429 7.2	2105 0.7
						31 TU	0246 7.0	0945 0.2	1518 7.3	2152 0.6

FEBRUARY

Day	Time m	Time m	Time m	Time m		Day	Time m	Time m	Time m	Time m
1 W	0331 7.1	1032 0.1	1605 7.3	2235 0.6		**16** TH	0333 6.4	1024 1.0	1558 6.5	2207 1.3
2 TH	0415 7.1	1114 0.1	1651 7.3	2314 0.7		**17** F	0400 6.4	1042 1.0	1627 6.4	2226 1.2
3 F	0458 7.1	1151 0.2	1735 7.1	2350 0.7		**18** SA	0428 6.5	1055 1.0	1659 6.4	2254 1.0
4 SA	0540 7.0	1223 0.5	1819 6.8			**19** SU	0501 6.5	1118 0.9	1735 6.6	2326 0.9
5 SU	0024 0.9	0623 6.8	1255 0.7	1905 6.4 ◐		**20** M	0540 6.5	1149 0.9	1815 6.4	
6 M	0102 1.1	0711 6.4	1334 1.1	1956 6.0		**21** TU	0002 1.0	0625 6.3	1227 1.1	1902 6.1
7 TU	0148 1.4	0812 6.0	1424 1.5	2101 5.6		**22** W	0047 1.3	0721 5.9	1320 1.4	1959 5.7
8 W	0247 1.7	0932 5.7	1529 1.8	2215 5.4		**23** TH	0151 1.6	0828 5.6	1440 1.8	2109 5.5
9 TH	0359 1.8	1052 5.7	1701 1.9	2326 5.6		**24** F	0327 1.8	0947 5.6	1628 1.8	2236 5.6
10 F	0606 1.6	1200 6.0	1827 1.7			**25** SA	0510 1.6	1122 5.9	1802 1.5	2356 5.9
11 SA	0026 6.0	0708 1.2	1256 6.3	1920 1.3		**26** SU	0648 1.1	1232 6.5	1909 1.0	
12 SU	0116 6.3	0756 0.8	1344 6.6	2006 1.1		**27** M	0054 6.6	0748 0.5	1326 7.0	2002 0.7
13 M	0159 6.5	0839 0.7	1425 6.7	2047 1.1 ○		**28** TU	0143 6.9	0841 0.2	1414 7.3	2051 0.5 ●
14 TU	0235 6.5	0919 0.7	1500 6.7	2124 1.1						
15 W	0306 6.5	0955 0.8	1530 6.6	2152 1.3						

MARCH

Day	Time m	Time m	Time m	Time m		Day	Time m	Time m	Time m	Time m
1 W	0227 7.2	0929 0.0	1500 7.5	2136 0.4		**16** TH	0241 6.5	0928 0.8	1501 6.6	2130 1.2
2 TH	0310 7.3	1012 -0.1	1543 7.4	2217 0.4		**17** F	0308 6.4	0957 0.7	1529 6.5	2149 1.2
3 F	0351 7.3	1050 0.0	1625 7.3	2254 0.5		**18** SA	0334 6.4	1016 0.7	1557 6.6	2207 1.1
4 SA	0431 7.3	1122 0.2	1705 7.1	2325 0.6		**19** SU	0403 6.5	1029 0.8	1629 6.6	2232 0.9
5 SU	0511 7.1	1148 0.5	1743 6.8	2354 0.7		**20** M	0437 6.6	1051 0.9	1705 6.6	2302 0.8
6 M	0551 6.9	1215 0.8	1821 6.3			**21** TU	0517 6.5	1122 0.9	1745 6.4	2337 0.9
7 TU	0026 1.0	0634 6.4	1250 1.2	1901 5.9		**22** W	0603 6.3	1201 1.1	1832 6.0 ◐	
8 W	0109 1.3	0730 5.9	1339 1.7	1955 5.4		**23** TH	0021 1.2	0659 6.0	1253 1.5	1928 5.7
9 TH	0210 1.7	0901 5.4	1447 2.1	2139 5.1		**24** F	0123 1.6	0806 5.6	1409 1.9	2038 5.4
10 F	0324 1.9	1033 5.5	1616 2.2	2300 5.4		**25** SA	0304 1.8	0930 5.5	1610 1.9	2212 5.5
11 SA	0552 1.7	1141 5.9	1807 1.8			**26** SU	0515 1.5	1111 5.9	1748 1.5	2336 6.0
12 SU	0002 5.9	0647 1.1	1235 6.3	1859 1.3		**27** M	0635 0.8	1217 6.7	1850 0.9	
13 M	0053 6.5	0731 0.7	1321 6.7	1943 1.0		**28** TU	0032 6.6	0729 0.3	1308 7.1	1940 0.6
14 TU	0134 6.6	0812 0.6	1359 6.8	2024 0.9 ○		**29** W	0119 7.0	0817 0.0	1353 7.4	2027 0.3 ●
15 W	0211 6.6	0852 0.6	1432 6.7	2101 1.0		**30** TH	0202 7.3	0902 -0.1	1436 7.5	2112 0.3
						31 F	0244 7.4	0943 0.0	1517 7.4	2153 0.3

APRIL

Day	Time m	Time m	Time m	Time m		Day	Time m	Time m	Time m	Time m
1 SA	0325 7.4	1019 0.1	1556 7.2	2229 0.4		**16** SU	0310 6.4	0946 1.0	1531 6.5	2150 1.0
2 SU	0405 7.3	1050 0.4	1634 6.9	2301 0.5		**17** M	0343 6.5	1007 1.0	1605 6.6	2218 0.9
3 M	0445 7.1	1115 0.6	1709 6.6	2328 0.7		**18** TU	0421 6.6	1034 0.9	1642 6.5	2250 0.8
4 TU	0527 6.7	1142 0.9	1744 6.3	2359 0.9		**19** W	0503 6.5	1108 1.0	1724 6.3	2327 0.9
5 W	0612 6.3	1216 1.3	1823 5.8 ◐			**20** TH	0552 6.3	1150 1.2	1811 6.0	
6 TH	0042 1.3	0708 5.7	1306 1.7	1912 5.4		**21** F	0014 1.2	0649 6.0	1246 1.5	1909 5.7
7 F	0146 1.6	0838 5.4	1416 2.1	2100 5.1		**22** SA	0123 1.5	0759 5.7	1403 1.9	2022 5.5
8 SA	0301 1.8	1006 5.5	1541 2.2	2227 5.4		**23** SU	0307 1.6	0926 5.7	1553 1.8	2153 5.7
9 SU	0505 1.6	1110 5.9	1729 1.8	2329 5.8		**24** M	0459 1.2	1051 6.2	1719 1.4	2307 6.2
10 M	0610 1.1	1203 6.3	1826 1.4			**25** TU	0607 0.6	1152 6.7	1821 0.9	
11 TU	0019 6.2	0654 0.7	1248 6.6	1910 1.1		**26** W	0004 6.7	0659 0.2	1242 7.1	1912 0.5
12 W	0102 6.5	0736 0.6	1326 6.7	1950 1.0		**27** TH	0052 7.1	0746 0.0	1327 7.3	2000 0.3 ●
13 TH	0138 6.5	0815 0.7	1359 6.7	2026 1.0		**28** F	0136 7.3	0830 0.0	1410 7.3	2045 0.3
14 F	0211 6.5	0851 0.8	1429 6.6	2058 1.1 ●		**29** SA	0219 7.3	0911 0.2	1450 7.2	2127 0.3
15 SA	0240 6.4	0922 1.0	1459 6.5	2125 1.1		**30** SU	0302 7.2	0948 0.4	1529 7.0	2206 0.4

Chart Datum: 2·90 metres below Ordnance Datum (Newlyn)

TIME ZONE (UT)
For Summer Time add ONE hour in **non-shaded areas**

ENGLAND – LONDON BRIDGE

LAT 51°30′N   LONG 0°05′W

TIMES AND HEIGHTS OF HIGH AND LOW WATERS

2006

MAY

Time	m		Time	m
1 M 0345 / 1020 / 1606 / 2240	7.1 / 0.6 / 6.7 / 0.6		**16** TU 0330 / 0953 / 1548 / 2214	6.6 / 0.9 / 6.6 / 0.8
2 TU 0427 / 1049 / 1642 / 2311	6.9 / 0.9 / 6.5 / 0.8		**17** W 0413 / 1028 / 1629 / 2253	6.6 / 1.0 / 6.5 / 0.8
3 W 0511 / 1118 / 1718 / 2344	6.5 / 1.1 / 6.2 / 1.0		**18** TH 0459 / 1107 / 1713 / 2336	6.5 / 1.0 / 6.3 / 0.9
4 TH 0558 / 1153 / 1758	6.2 / 1.4 / 5.9		**19** F 0551 / 1153 / 1803	6.4 / 1.2 / 6.1
5 F 0027 / 0652 / 1240 / ◑1848	1.2 / 5.8 / 1.7 / 5.6		**20** SA 0029 / 0649 / 1249 / ◐1901	1.0 / 6.1 / 1.5 / 5.9
6 SA 0126 / 0804 / 1343 / 2007	1.5 / 5.5 / 2.0 / 5.3		**21** SU 0137 / 0757 / 1400 / 2013	1.2 / 6.0 / 1.6 / 5.8
7 SU 0234 / 0922 / 1456 / 2139	1.6 / 5.5 / 2.1 / 5.4		**22** M 0300 / 0913 / 1524 / 2129	1.2 / 6.1 / 1.6 / 6.0
8 M 0346 / 1026 / 1613 / 2243	1.5 / 5.8 / 1.9 / 5.7		**23** TU 0424 / 1022 / 1642 / 2235	1.0 / 6.3 / 1.3 / 6.3
9 TU 0504 / 1120 / 1726 / 2336	1.2 / 6.1 / 1.6 / 6.0		**24** W 0531 / 1122 / 1746 / 2333	0.7 / 6.7 / 1.0 / 6.7
10 W 0603 / 1205 / 1820	1.0 / 6.4 / 1.3		**25** TH 0626 / 1214 / 1842	0.4 / 6.9 / 0.7
11 TH 0021 / 0649 / 1246 / 1904	6.3 / 0.8 / 6.5 / 1.1		**26** F 0025 / 0714 / 1302 / 1933	6.9 / 0.3 / 7.0 / 0.5
12 F 0101 / 0731 / 1323 / 1944	6.4 / 0.8 / 6.6 / 1.0		**27** SA 0114 / 0759 / 1346 / ●2021	7.0 / 0.4 / 7.2 / 0.4
13 SA 0138 / 0810 / 1358 / ○2023	6.4 / 0.8 / 6.6 / 1.0		**28** SU 0200 / 0842 / 1428 / 2106	7.1 / 0.5 / 7.2 / 0.5
14 SU 0214 / 0846 / 1434 / 2100	6.5 / 0.9 / 6.6 / 0.9		**29** M 0246 / 0922 / 1509 / 2149	7.0 / 0.7 / 6.7 / 0.6
15 M 0250 / 0920 / 1510 / 2138	6.5 / 0.9 / 6.6 / 0.9		**30** TU 0332 / 0958 / 1547 / 2227	6.8 / 0.9 / 6.5 / 0.7
			31 W 0416 / 1030 / 1623 / 2301	6.6 / 1.1 / 6.4 / 0.8

JUNE

Time	m		Time	m
1 TH 0459 / 1101 / 1700 / 2335	6.4 / 1.2 / 6.4 / 1.0		**16** F 0457 / 1111 / 1709 / 2350	6.7 / 1.0 / 6.5 / 0.6
2 F 0542 / 1133 / 1740	6.2 / 1.4 / 6.1		**17** SA 0548 / 1157 / 1758	6.6 / 1.1 / 6.4
3 SA 0012 / 0627 / 1214 / ◑1825	1.1 / 6.0 / 1.6 / 5.9		**18** SU 0039 / 0643 / 1247 / ◐1852	0.7 / 6.5 / 1.2 / 6.3
4 SU 0059 / 0719 / 1304 / 1920	1.4 / 5.8 / 1.7 / 5.7		**19** M 0132 / 0743 / 1344 / 1953	0.8 / 6.3 / 1.3 / 6.2
5 M 0154 / 0817 / 1403 / 2027	1.3 / 5.7 / 1.8 / 5.5		**20** TU 0232 / 0847 / 1447 / 2058	0.9 / 6.3 / 1.4 / 6.2
6 TU 0253 / 0920 / 1508 / 2137	1.3 / 5.7 / 1.8 / 5.6		**21** W 0339 / 0951 / 1556 / 2202	0.9 / 6.3 / 1.4 / 6.3
7 W 0355 / 1020 / 1612 / 2240	1.3 / 5.9 / 1.7 / 5.8		**22** TH 0448 / 1051 / 1707 / 2304	0.9 / 6.4 / 1.2 / 6.4
8 TH 0457 / 1115 / 1714 / 2334	1.2 / 6.1 / 1.5 / 6.0		**23** F 0550 / 1147 / 1813	0.9 / 6.5 / 1.0
9 F 0555 / 1203 / 1812	1.0 / 6.3 / 1.2		**24** SA 0003 / 0644 / 1240 / 1911	6.5 / 0.8 / 6.6 / 0.8
10 SA 0023 / 0646 / 1249 / 1904	6.2 / 0.9 / 6.5 / 1.0		**25** SU 0058 / 0734 / 1328 / ●2004	6.7 / 0.8 / 6.7 / 0.7
11 SU 0108 / 0733 / 1331 / ○1954	6.4 / 0.8 / 6.6 / 0.9		**26** M 0149 / 0820 / 1413 / 2054	6.7 / 0.8 / 6.6 / 0.6
12 M 0152 / 0818 / 1413 / 2043	6.6 / 0.8 / 6.7 / 0.8		**27** TU 0237 / 0903 / 1456 / 2139	6.7 / 0.9 / 6.6 / 0.6
13 TU 0236 / 0901 / 1456 / 2131	6.7 / 0.8 / 6.7 / 0.7		**28** W 0323 / 0943 / 1534 / 2219	6.7 / 1.1 / 6.5 / 0.7
14 W 0321 / 0945 / 1539 / 2218	6.8 / 0.9 / 6.6 / 0.6		**29** TH 0404 / 1018 / 1609 / 2254	6.6 / 1.2 / 6.4 / 0.8
15 TH 0408 / 1027 / 1623 / 2304	6.8 / 0.9 / 6.6 / 0.6		**30** F 0442 / 1047 / 1643 / 2324	6.5 / 1.3 / 6.3 / 0.9

JULY

Time	m		Time	m
1 SA 0518 / 1114 / 1718 / 2352	6.3 / 1.3 / 6.3 / 1.0		**16** SU 0535 / 1150 / 1743	6.9 / 0.8 / 6.8
2 SU 0555 / 1145 / 1756	6.2 / 1.4 / 6.2		**17** M 0028 / 0624 / 1232 / ◑1829	0.4 / 6.7 / 0.9 / 6.7
3 M 0023 / 0635 / 1224 / ◑1839	1.0 / 6.1 / 1.4 / 6.0		**18** TU 0108 / 0716 / 1317 / 1921	0.6 / 6.5 / 1.1 / 6.5
4 TU 0104 / 0721 / 1311 / 1929	1.1 / 5.9 / 1.5 / 5.8		**19** W 0151 / 0814 / 1407 / 2021	0.8 / 6.2 / 1.3 / 6.3
5 W 0156 / 0814 / 1409 / 2028	1.2 / 5.8 / 1.7 / 5.7		**20** TH 0244 / 0916 / 1506 / 2128	1.1 / 6.0 / 1.5 / 6.0
6 TH 0257 / 0915 / 1516 / 2134	1.3 / 5.8 / 1.7 / 5.6		**21** F 0351 / 1020 / 1618 / 2240	1.4 / 5.9 / 1.6 / 6.0
7 F 0403 / 1020 / 1624 / 2244	1.3 / 5.8 / 1.6 / 5.8		**22** SA 0513 / 1123 / 1751 / 2348	1.5 / 6.0 / 1.5 / 6.1
8 SA 0509 / 1123 / 1730 / 2348	1.2 / 6.1 / 1.4 / 6.1		**23** SU 0622 / 1222 / 1901	1.3 / 6.2 / 1.1
9 SU 0611 / 1219 / 1835	1.0 / 6.4 / 1.1		**24** M 0048 / 0717 / 1316 / 1956	6.4 / 1.1 / 6.4 / 0.8
10 M 0044 / 0707 / 1310 / ●1936	6.4 / 0.8 / 6.6 / 0.8		**25** TU 0141 / 0805 / 1402 / ●2044	6.6 / 1.0 / 6.6 / 0.6
11 TU 0135 / 0800 / 1357 / ○2035	6.7 / 0.7 / 6.8 / 0.6		**26** W 0228 / 0850 / 1444 / 2128	6.8 / 1.0 / 6.6 / 0.5
12 W 0224 / 0851 / 1443 / 2129	6.9 / 0.7 / 6.8 / 0.5		**27** TH 0310 / 0931 / 1520 / 2207	6.7 / 1.0 / 6.6 / 0.6
13 TH 0312 / 0940 / 1529 / 2220	7.0 / 0.8 / 6.9 / 0.4		**28** F 0346 / 1007 / 1551 / 2240	6.6 / 1.1 / 6.5 / 0.7
14 F 0400 / 1026 / 1609 / 2306	7.1 / 0.8 / 6.8 / 0.3		**29** SA 0418 / 1034 / 1620 / 2306	6.5 / 1.3 / 6.5 / 0.9
15 SA 0447 / 1109 / 1658 / 2348	7.0 / 0.8 / 6.8 / 0.3		**30** SU 0448 / 1052 / 1650 / 2324	6.5 / 1.3 / 6.4 / 0.9
			31 M 0520 / 1117 / 1723 / 2343	6.4 / 1.1 / 6.4 / 0.9

AUGUST

Time	m		Time	m
1 TU 0555 / 1147 / 1800	6.3 / 1.2 / 6.3		**16** W 0032 / 0640 / 1245 / ◐1844	0.6 / 6.4 / 1.0 / 6.6
2 W 0013 / 0635 / 1226 / ◑1842	1.0 / 6.2 / 1.3 / 6.1		**17** TH 0107 / 0731 / 1328 / 1941	1.0 / 6.0 / 1.3 / 6.1
3 TH 0053 / 0723 / 1315 / 1935	1.2 / 5.9 / 1.5 / 5.8		**18** F 0155 / 0835 / 1425 / 2057	1.4 / 5.6 / 1.6 / 5.7
4 F 0151 / 0820 / 1424 / 2039	1.4 / 5.7 / 1.7 / 5.6		**19** SA 0300 / 0951 / 1536 / 2224	1.8 / 5.5 / 1.8 / 5.6
5 SA 0312 / 0928 / 1544 / 2154	1.6 / 5.6 / 1.7 / 5.6		**20** SU 0433 / 1103 / 1746 / 2337	1.9 / 5.6 / 1.7 / 5.9
6 SU 0432 / 1045 / 1700 / 2317	1.5 / 5.8 / 1.5 / 5.9		**21** M 0608 / 1206 / 1852	1.6 / 6.0 / 1.3
7 M 0546 / 1155 / 1819	1.3 / 6.1 / 1.2		**22** TU 0037 / 0702 / 1259 / 1941	6.4 / 1.2 / 6.4 / 0.7
8 TU 0026 / 0651 / 1252 / 1931	6.4 / 1.0 / 6.6 / 0.8		**23** W 0127 / 0749 / 1344 / ●2025	6.7 / 0.9 / 6.7 / 0.4
9 W 0121 / 0749 / 1341 / ○2030	6.8 / 0.7 / 6.9 / 0.4		**24** TH 0211 / 0832 / 1424 / 2106	6.9 / 0.8 / 6.8 / 0.3
10 TH 0210 / 0841 / 1427 / 2122	7.1 / 0.6 / 7.0 / 0.2		**25** F 0248 / 0912 / 1458 / 2143	6.9 / 0.9 / 6.7 / 0.5
11 F 0257 / 0930 / 1511 / 2209	7.3 / 0.6 / 7.1 / 0.1		**26** SA 0320 / 0948 / 1526 / 2216	6.7 / 1.1 / 6.5 / 0.7
12 SA 0342 / 1015 / 1553 / 2252	7.3 / 0.6 / 7.1 / 0.1		**27** SU 0347 / 1014 / 1552 / 2240	6.6 / 1.2 / 6.5 / 1.0
13 SU 0427 / 1056 / 1635 / 2330	7.2 / 0.6 / 7.1 / 0.2		**28** M 0414 / 1027 / 1619 / 2251	6.5 / 1.3 / 6.5 / 1.0
14 M 0511 / 1133 / 1717	7.1 / 0.7 / 7.1		**29** TU 0443 / 1045 / 1649 / 2304	6.5 / 1.2 / 6.5 / 1.0
15 TU 0002 / 0554 / 1208 / 1758	0.4 / 6.8 / 0.8 / 6.9		**30** W 0516 / 1113 / 1724 / 2330	6.5 / 1.1 / 6.4 / 0.9
			31 TH 0554 / 1147 / 1806 / ◐	6.4 / 1.1 / 6.2

Chart Datum: 2·90 metres below Ordnance Datum (Newlyn)

TIME ZONE (UT)
For Summer Time add ONE hour in **non-shaded areas**

ENGLAND – LONDON BRIDGE

LAT 51°30′N   LONG 0°05′W

TIMES AND HEIGHTS OF HIGH AND LOW WATERS

SEPTEMBER

Day	Time m (1–15)	Day	Time m (16–30)
1 F	0004 1.1 / 0638 6.0 / 1230 1.4 / 1857 5.9	16 SA	0115 1.7 / 0744 5.4 / 1356 1.7 / 2038 5.5
2 SA	0052 1.4 / 0733 5.7 / 1331 1.7 / 2000 5.6	17 SU	0225 2.1 / 0925 5.2 / 1512 1.9 / 2209 5.5
3 SU	0210 1.8 / 0841 5.5 / 1508 1.9 / 2116 5.5	18 M	0403 2.2 / 1040 5.5 / 1732 1.6 / 2319 5.9
4 M	0359 1.9 / 1007 5.5 / 1639 1.7 / 2253 5.7	19 TU	0547 1.8 / 1142 6.0 / 1829 1.0
5 TU	0529 1.5 / 1133 6.0 / 1816 1.2	20 W	0015 6.5 / 0639 1.2 / 1234 6.5 / 1913 0.6
6 W	0010 6.4 / 0639 1.1 / 1232 6.5 / 1921 0.6	21 TH	0103 6.8 / 0724 0.9 / 1317 6.8 / 1955 0.4
7 TH	0104 6.9 / 0734 0.7 / 1319 6.9 / ○ 2014 0.2	22 F	0144 7.0 / 0806 0.8 / 1356 6.8 / 2035 0.4
8 F	0150 7.3 / 0823 0.5 / 1403 7.2 / 2102 0.0	23 SA	0218 6.9 / 0845 0.8 / 1429 6.7 / 2112 0.6
9 SA	0235 7.5 / 0910 0.4 / 1445 7.3 / 2147 0.0	24 SU	0248 6.7 / 0920 1.0 / 1457 6.5 / 2144 0.9
10 SU	0318 7.4 / 0954 0.4 / 1526 7.3 / 2227 0.1	25 M	0313 6.6 / 0945 1.2 / 1522 6.4 / 2207 1.1
11 M	0400 7.3 / 1034 0.5 / 1607 7.3 / 2301 0.3	26 TU	0339 6.5 / 0959 1.4 / 1548 6.4 / 2215 1.1
12 TU	0440 7.1 / 1109 0.6 / 1648 7.2 / 2328 0.5	27 W	0408 6.6 / 1019 1.2 / 1620 6.5 / 2232 1.0
13 W	0520 6.8 / 1141 0.8 / 1730 6.9 / 2354 0.8	28 TH	0441 6.6 / 1046 1.1 / 1657 6.5 / 2259 1.0
14 TH	0600 6.3 / 1214 1.2 / 1815 6.5 / ◐	29 F	0519 6.4 / 1119 1.1 / 1740 6.3 / 2335 1.3
15 F	0027 1.2 / 0642 5.9 / 1257 1.3 / 1910 6.0	30 SA	0603 6.1 / 1200 1.3 / 1833 6.0 / ◐

OCTOBER

Day	Time m (1–15)	Day	Time m (16–31)
1 SU	0021 1.5 / 0657 5.7 / 1259 1.6 / 1936 5.7	16 M	0156 2.2 / 0854 5.2 / 1454 1.8 / 2143 5.6
2 M	0131 1.9 / 0805 5.4 / 1440 1.8 / 2052 5.5	17 TU	0327 2.3 / 1009 5.5 / 1650 1.5 / 2248 5.9
3 TU	0329 2.1 / 0933 5.5 / 1627 1.6 / 2233 5.8	18 W	0509 1.9 / 1108 6.0 / 1750 1.1 / 2343 6.4
4 W	0509 1.7 / 1104 6.0 / 1800 1.0 / 2348 6.5	19 TH	0606 1.4 / 1159 6.4 / 1836 0.7
5 TH	0617 1.1 / 1203 6.6 / 1858 0.5	20 F	0029 6.7 / 0651 1.0 / 1243 6.6 / 1917 0.6
6 F	0040 7.0 / 0710 0.7 / 1251 7.0 / 1948 0.1	21 SA	0109 6.8 / 0732 0.9 / 1322 6.7 / 1957 0.6
7 SA	0126 7.4 / 0758 0.4 / 1335 7.3 / ○ 2034 0.0	22 SU	0143 6.8 / 0810 0.9 / 1355 6.6 / ● 2034 0.8
8 SU	0208 7.5 / 0844 0.4 / 1417 7.4 / 2117 0.1	23 M	0213 6.7 / 0843 1.1 / 1425 6.5 / 2106 1.0
9 M	0250 7.4 / 0928 0.4 / 1459 7.4 / 2155 0.2	24 TU	0240 6.6 / 0910 1.2 / 1454 6.4 / 2129 1.1
10 TU	0330 7.2 / 1008 0.5 / 1541 7.3 / 2228 0.4	25 W	0309 6.6 / 0934 1.2 / 1524 6.5 / 2147 1.1
11 W	0410 7.0 / 1045 0.6 / 1624 7.1 / 2256 0.7	26 TH	0340 6.6 / 1000 1.1 / 1600 6.5 / 2210 1.1
12 TH	0447 6.7 / 1117 0.8 / 1708 6.8 / 2324 1.0	27 F	0415 6.5 / 1030 1.0 / 1640 6.5 / 2242 1.0
13 F	0525 6.3 / 1151 1.1 / 1755 6.4 / 2357 1.4	28 SA	0454 6.4 / 1106 1.1 / 1726 6.4 / 2321 1.2
14 SA	0604 5.9 / 1236 1.4 / 1854 5.9 / ◐	29 SU	0539 6.2 / 1151 1.3 / 1820 6.1 / ◐
15 SU	0045 1.8 / 0659 5.6 / 1337 1.7 / 2021 5.5	30 M	0010 1.5 / 0633 5.8 / 1253 1.5 / 1922 5.8
		31 TU	0118 1.9 / 0741 5.6 / 1427 1.6 / 2039 5.7

NOVEMBER

Day	Time m (1–15)	Day	Time m (16–30)
1 W	0259 2.0 / 0908 5.7 / 1608 1.4 / 2208 6.0	16 TH	0353 2.0 / 1023 5.8 / 1646 1.3 / 2258 6.1
2 TH	0436 1.7 / 1029 6.1 / 1728 0.9 / 2317 6.5	17 F	0507 1.7 / 1116 6.1 / 1743 1.1 / 2346 6.3
3 F	0545 1.2 / 1130 6.6 / 1827 0.5	18 SA	0602 1.4 / 1203 6.3 / 1830 0.9
4 SA	0011 7.0 / 0640 0.8 / 1221 7.0 / 1916 0.3	19 SU	0028 6.5 / 0645 1.2 / 1244 6.4 / 1912 0.9
5 SU	0058 7.3 / 0730 0.5 / 1307 7.3 / ○ 2002 0.2	20 M	0105 6.6 / 0725 1.1 / 1322 6.5 / ● 1951 0.9
6 M	0142 7.4 / 0817 0.4 / 1352 7.4 / 2045 0.3	21 TU	0139 6.6 / 0802 1.1 / 1357 6.5 / 2026 1.0
7 TU	0224 7.3 / 0903 0.4 / 1437 7.3 / 2125 0.5	22 W	0213 6.6 / 0838 1.2 / 1432 6.5 / 2057 1.1
8 W	0304 7.1 / 0946 0.5 / 1522 7.2 / 2200 0.7	23 TH	0247 6.6 / 0914 1.0 / 1509 6.6 / 2128 1.1
9 TH	0344 6.8 / 1025 0.7 / 1608 7.0 / 2232 1.0	24 F	0322 6.6 / 0951 1.0 / 1550 6.6 / 2201 1.1
10 F	0422 6.5 / 1102 0.9 / 1655 6.7 / 2302 1.2	25 SA	0400 6.6 / 1029 1.0 / 1633 6.6 / 2238 1.1
11 SA	0500 6.2 / 1139 1.1 / 1743 6.3 / 2337 1.5	26 SU	0441 6.4 / 1111 1.0 / 1721 6.5 / 2320 1.2
12 SU	0541 5.9 / 1223 1.3 / 1838 5.9 / ◐	27 M	0527 6.3 / 1159 1.1 / 1814 6.3
13 M	0021 1.8 / 0632 5.6 / 1318 1.5 / 1946 5.7	28 TU	0009 1.4 / 0619 6.1 / 1259 1.2 / ◐ 1913 6.1
14 TU	0121 2.1 / 0800 5.4 / 1422 1.6 / 2059 5.6	29 W	0111 1.6 / 0724 5.9 / 1411 1.3 / 2023 6.0
15 W	0235 2.2 / 0921 5.5 / 1533 1.5 / 2203 5.8	30 TH	0227 1.7 / 0840 6.0 / 1532 1.2 / 2137 6.1

DECEMBER

Day	Time m (1–15)	Day	Time m (16–31)
1 F	0352 1.6 / 0953 6.2 / 1649 1.0 / 2244 6.4	16 SA	0341 1.9 / 1016 5.7 / 1629 1.4 / 2249 5.9
2 SA	0506 1.3 / 1057 6.5 / 1752 0.8 / 2341 6.7	17 SU	0445 1.7 / 1114 5.9 / 1729 1.3 / 2341 6.1
3 SU	0609 1.0 / 1153 6.8 / 1845 0.6	18 M	0545 1.4 / 1205 6.1 / 1823 1.1
4 M	0032 6.9 / 0704 0.8 / 1245 7.0 / 1933 0.6	19 TU	0028 6.4 / 0638 1.2 / 1251 6.4 / 1911 1.0
5 TU	0119 7.0 / 0755 0.6 / 1334 7.1 / ○ 2019 0.6	20 W	0111 6.5 / 0755 0.8 / 1334 6.5 / ● 1955 1.0
6 W	0203 6.9 / 0844 0.6 / 1423 7.1 / 2102 0.8	21 TH	0152 6.7 / 0816 0.9 / 1416 6.7 / 2037 1.0
7 TH	0246 6.8 / 0931 0.6 / 1511 6.9 / 2141 1.0	22 F	0232 6.7 / 0905 0.9 / 1459 6.8 / 2119 1.0
8 F	0327 6.6 / 1015 0.8 / 1558 6.8 / 2217 1.1	23 SA	0312 6.7 / 0953 0.8 / 1544 6.8 / 2200 1.0
9 SA	0406 6.4 / 1055 0.9 / 1643 6.6 / 2250 1.3	24 SU	0353 6.6 / 1038 0.8 / 1629 6.8 / 2240 1.1
10 SU	0444 6.3 / 1131 1.0 / 1727 6.4 / 2321 1.5	25 M	0435 6.6 / 1131 0.8 / 1716 6.7 / 2322 1.1
11 M	0523 6.1 / 1207 1.2 / 1811 6.2 / 2356 1.6	26 TU	0520 6.5 / 1205 0.8 / 1805 6.6
12 TU	0606 6.0 / 1248 1.3 / 1857 5.9 / ◐	27 W	0007 1.2 / 0607 6.4 / 1252 0.9 / ◐ 1858 6.4
13 W	0039 1.8 / 0657 5.8 / 1337 1.4 / 1949 5.8	28 TH	0056 1.3 / 0702 6.3 / 1343 1.0 / 1957 6.2
14 TH	0133 1.9 / 0800 5.6 / 1431 1.5 / 2048 5.7	29 F	0153 1.4 / 0807 6.2 / 1442 1.2 / 2102 6.1
15 F	0236 2.0 / 0911 5.6 / 1529 1.5 / 2150 5.7	30 SA	0300 1.6 / 0916 6.1 / 1554 1.3 / 2209 6.1
		31 SU	0418 1.6 / 1025 6.2 / 1712 1.3 / 2312 6.2

Chart Datum: 2·90 metres below Ordnance Datum (Newlyn)

TIDES

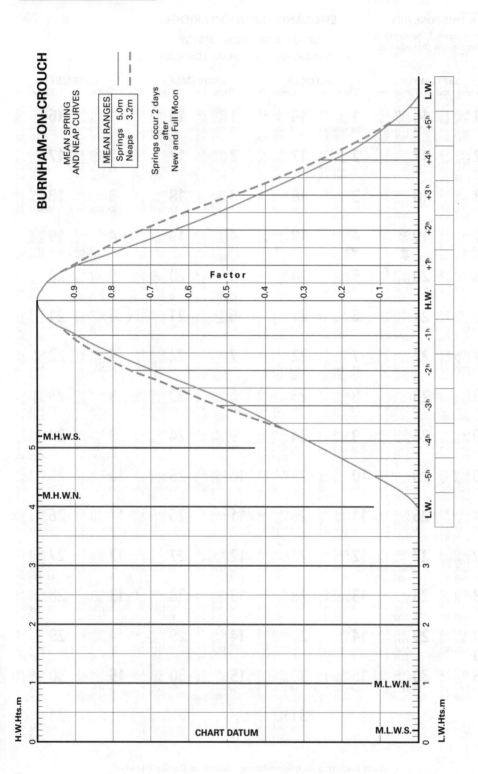

BURNHAM-ON-CROUCH

MEAN SPRING
AND NEAP CURVES

MEAN RANGES
Springs 5.0m
Neaps   3.2m

Springs occur 2 days
after
New and Full Moon

Factor

H.W.Hts.m

CHART DATUM

L.W.Hts.m

M.H.W.S.

M.H.W.N.

M.L.W.N.

M.L.W.S.

TIME ZONE (UT)
For Summer Time add ONE hour in **non-shaded areas**

ENGLAND – BURNHAM-ON-CROUCH

LAT 51°37'N LONG 0°48'E

TIMES AND HEIGHTS OF HIGH AND LOW WATERS

JANUARY

Day	Time m	Day	Time m
1 SU	0046 4.9 / 0721 0.3 / 1312 5.2 / 1938 0.5	**16** M	0129 4.8 / 0805 0.4 / 1352 4.8 / 1958 0.9
2 M	0132 5.0 / 0809 0.2 / 1400 5.2 / 2019 0.5	**17** TU	0200 4.8 / 0837 0.4 / 1422 4.7 / 2026 0.8
3 TU	0216 5.1 / 0856 0.1 / 1447 5.2 / 2059 0.7	**18** W	0228 4.7 / 0905 0.4 / 1451 4.7 / 2053 0.8
4 W	0301 5.1 / 0940 0.1 / 1534 5.1 / 2141 0.7	**19** TH	0257 4.7 / 0931 0.4 / 1521 4.7 / 2122 0.8
5 TH	0347 5.0 / 1026 0.1 / 1623 5.1 / 2224 0.8	**20** F	0328 4.7 / 1002 0.5 / 1554 4.6 / 2155 0.9
6 F	0433 4.8 / 1115 0.2 / 1714 4.8 / 2313 0.9	**21** SA	0403 4.7 / 1036 0.5 / 1632 4.6 / 2234 1.0
7 SA	0524 4.7 / 1211 0.4 / 1809 4.6	**22** SU	0443 4.5 / 1117 0.7 / 1718 4.3 / 2320 1.1
8 SU	0011 1.0 / 0622 4.6 / 1320 0.5 / 1912 4.3	**23** M	0532 4.3 / 1211 0.8 / 1810 4.2
9 M	0125 1.1 / 0730 4.5 / 1433 0.8 / 2020 4.3	**24** TU	0022 1.2 / 0631 4.2 / 1322 0.9 / 1917 4.1
10 TU	0245 1.0 / 0840 4.5 / 1541 0.8 / 2127 4.3	**25** W	0139 1.2 / 0747 4.2 / 1439 1.0 / 2033 4.1
11 W	0358 0.9 / 0950 4.5 / 1642 0.8 / 2227 4.5	**26** TH	0259 1.1 / 0904 4.3 / 1554 0.9 / 2145 4.3
12 TH	0505 0.8 / 1051 4.6 / 1734 0.8 / 2321 4.6	**27** F	0417 1.0 / 1014 4.6 / 1701 0.8 / 2247 4.6
13 F	0602 0.5 / 1147 4.7 / 1819 0.8	**28** SA	0528 0.7 / 1117 4.8 / 1758 0.7 / 2343 4.8
14 SA	0009 4.7 / 0649 0.4 / 1236 4.8 / 1854 0.8	**29** SU	0627 0.4 / 1213 5.1 / 1845 0.5
15 SU	0052 4.7 / 0729 0.4 / 1317 4.8 / 1927 0.8	**30** M	0035 5.0 / 0716 0.2 / 1304 5.3 / 1926 0.5
		31 TU	0121 5.1 / 0800 0.0 / 1351 5.5 / 2005 0.4

FEBRUARY

Day	Time m	Day	Time m
1 W	0205 5.2 / 0843 -0.1 / 1435 5.5 / 2044 0.4	**16** TH	0208 4.8 / 0838 0.4 / 1427 4.8 / 2030 0.7
2 TH	0247 5.3 / 0924 -0.1 / 1518 5.4 / 2123 0.4	**17** F	0234 4.8 / 0903 0.3 / 1453 4.8 / 2058 0.7
3 F	0328 5.3 / 1004 0.0 / 1601 5.2 / 2202 0.5	**18** SA	0301 4.8 / 0930 0.4 / 1524 4.8 / 2129 0.7
4 SA	0409 5.2 / 1044 0.1 / 1644 5.0 / 2244 0.7	**19** SU	0333 4.8 / 0958 0.4 / 1559 4.7 / 2202 0.7
5 SU	0453 5.0 / 1128 0.4 / 1730 4.6 / 2330 0.8	**20** M	0409 4.7 / 1032 0.5 / 1639 4.6 / 2241 0.8
6 M	0543 4.7 / 1222 0.8 / 1824 4.2	**21** TU	0451 4.5 / 1115 0.8 / 1728 4.2 / 2333 1.0
7 TU	0034 1.0 / 0647 4.3 / 1335 1.0 / 1935 4.0	**22** W	0547 4.2 / 1224 1.0 / 1828 4.0
8 W	0200 1.1 / 0812 4.1 / 1502 1.0 / 2057 4.0	**23** TH	0052 1.2 / 0702 4.1 / 1358 1.1 / 1951 3.8
9 TH	0339 1.0 / 0938 4.2 / 1621 1.1 / 2210 4.2	**24** F	0227 1.1 / 0838 4.1 / 1533 1.1 / 2121 4.1
10 F	0456 0.8 / 1045 4.5 / 1718 1.0 / 2306 4.5	**25** SA	0407 0.9 / 1005 4.5 / 1646 0.9 / 2233 4.5
11 SA	0554 0.5 / 1139 4.7 / 1804 0.9 / 2355 4.7	**26** SU	0522 0.5 / 1108 4.8 / 1743 0.7 / 2328 4.8
12 SU	0638 0.4 / 1223 4.8 / 1840 0.9	**27** M	0618 0.2 / 1201 5.2 / 1829 0.5
13 M	0037 4.8 / 0715 0.3 / 1303 4.8 / 1912 0.8	**28** TU	0018 5.1 / 0703 0.0 / 1251 5.5 / 1909 0.4
14 TU	0112 4.8 / 0746 0.3 / 1334 4.8 / 1939 0.8		
15 W	0142 4.8 / 0813 0.3 / 1402 4.8 / 2004 0.8		

MARCH

Day	Time m	Day	Time m
1 W	0104 5.3 / 0745 -0.3 / 1334 5.5 / 1946 0.3	**16** TH	0116 4.8 / 0743 0.3 / 1335 4.8 / 1940 0.7
2 TH	0146 5.5 / 0824 -0.3 / 1416 5.5 / 2025 0.3	**17** F	0143 4.8 / 0808 0.3 / 1359 4.8 / 2007 0.5
3 F	0226 5.5 / 0901 -0.3 / 1456 5.3 / 2102 0.2	**18** SA	0209 4.8 / 0834 0.3 / 1426 4.8 / 2036 0.5
4 SA	0304 5.5 / 0937 0.0 / 1534 5.2 / 2139 0.3	**19** SU	0236 5.0 / 0901 0.3 / 1457 4.8 / 2107 0.4
5 SU	0343 5.3 / 1012 0.2 / 1612 5.0 / 2217 0.4	**20** M	0308 5.0 / 0929 0.4 / 1531 4.8 / 2139 0.5
6 M	0424 5.1 / 1050 0.5 / 1652 4.6 / 2300 0.7	**21** TU	0344 4.8 / 1000 0.5 / 1610 4.6 / 2217 0.7
7 TU	0510 4.6 / 1136 0.9 / 1737 4.1 / 2355 0.9	**22** W	0427 4.6 / 1043 0.9 / 1656 4.2 / 2309 0.9
8 W	0610 4.2 / 1245 1.2 / 1841 3.8	**23** TH	0523 4.2 / 1147 1.1 / 1756 4.0
9 TH	0127 1.1 / 0746 4.0 / 1423 1.5 / 2022 3.7	**24** F	0027 1.1 / 0638 4.0 / 1332 1.2 / 1920 3.8
10 F	0322 1.0 / 0922 4.1 / 1555 1.3 / 2146 4.0	**25** SA	0216 1.0 / 0827 4.1 / 1515 1.1 / 2100 4.0
11 SA	0439 0.8 / 1028 4.5 / 1657 1.1 / 2244 4.3	**26** SU	0400 0.8 / 0954 4.5 / 1627 0.9 / 2212 4.5
12 SU	0532 0.5 / 1118 4.7 / 1742 1.0 / 2330 4.7	**27** M	0506 0.3 / 1052 5.0 / 1721 0.7 / 2306 4.8
13 M	0616 0.4 / 1200 4.8 / 1820 0.8	**28** TU	0559 0.0 / 1143 5.2 / 1808 0.4 / 2354 5.1
14 TU	0011 4.8 / 0649 0.3 / 1238 5.0 / 1850 0.8	**29** W	0642 -0.1 / 1229 5.5 / 1848 0.3
15 W	0047 4.8 / 0718 0.3 / 1309 4.8 / 1916 0.7	**30** TH	0040 5.3 / 0722 -0.3 / 1312 5.5 / 1926 0.2
		31 F	0122 5.5 / 0800 -0.3 / 1353 5.3 / 2003 0.2

APRIL

Day	Time m	Day	Time m
1 SA	0202 5.5 / 0835 -0.1 / 1431 5.2 / 2042 0.2	**16** SU	0144 4.8 / 0808 0.4 / 1401 4.8 / 2017 0.4
2 SU	0241 5.5 / 0909 0.1 / 1507 5.1 / 2119 0.2	**17** M	0216 4.8 / 0838 0.4 / 1435 4.8 / 2052 0.4
3 M	0320 5.2 / 0943 0.3 / 1543 4.8 / 2156 0.3	**18** TU	0251 4.8 / 0909 0.5 / 1510 4.7 / 2127 0.4
4 TU	0401 5.0 / 1019 0.7 / 1619 4.5 / 2238 0.5	**19** W	0330 4.8 / 0944 0.7 / 1551 4.6 / 2208 0.5
5 W	0447 4.6 / 1104 1.0 / 1701 4.2 / 2334 0.9	**20** TH	0417 4.6 / 1030 0.9 / 1638 4.2 / 2303 0.8
6 TH	0547 4.1 / 1209 1.3 / 1800 3.8	**21** F	0517 4.2 / 1135 1.2 / 1740 4.0
7 F	0106 1.0 / 0717 3.8 / 1345 1.6 / 1940 3.7	**22** SA	0024 0.9 / 0633 4.1 / 1313 1.3 / 1901 3.8
8 SA	0252 1.0 / 0851 4.1 / 1519 1.5 / 2107 4.0	**23** SU	0211 0.8 / 0812 4.2 / 1449 1.1 / 2031 4.1
9 SU	0405 0.8 / 0956 4.3 / 1622 1.2 / 2208 4.3	**24** M	0339 0.5 / 0929 4.6 / 1558 0.9 / 2140 4.5
10 M	0457 0.5 / 1045 4.7 / 1709 1.0 / 2254 4.6	**25** TU	0442 0.2 / 1026 5.0 / 1652 0.7 / 2235 4.8
11 TU	0539 0.4 / 1126 4.8 / 1747 0.8 / 2334 4.7	**26** W	0532 0.0 / 1117 5.2 / 1740 0.4 / 2324 5.1
12 W	0614 0.3 / 1204 4.8 / 1821 0.7	**27** TH	0619 -0.1 / 1202 5.2 / 1824 0.3
13 TH	0011 4.7 / 0642 0.4 / 1236 4.8 / 1848 0.7	**28** F	0012 5.2 / 0657 -0.1 / 1247 5.2 / 1905 0.2
14 F	0044 4.7 / 0710 0.4 / 1304 4.8 / 1916 0.5	**29** SA	0057 5.2 / 0733 0.0 / 1329 5.1 / 1945 0.2
15 SA	0113 4.7 / 0739 0.4 / 1332 4.8 / 1946 0.5	**30** SU	0140 5.2 / 0810 0.2 / 1407 5.1 / 2025 0.2

Chart Datum: 2·35 metres below Ordnance Datum (Newlyn)

TIDES

TIDES

TIME ZONE (UT)
For Summer Time add ONE hour in **non-shaded areas**

ENGLAND – BURNHAM-ON-CROUCH 2006

LAT 51°37'N LONG 0°48'E

TIMES AND HEIGHTS OF HIGH AND LOW WATERS

MAY

No.	Day	Time m	Time m	Time m	Time m
1	M	0221 5.2	0844 0.3	1443 4.8	2104 0.2
2	TU	0301 5.1	0919 0.5	1520 4.7	2143 0.3
3	W	0344 4.8	0955 0.8	1556 4.5	2226 0.5
4	TH	0430 4.5	1038 1.1	1638 4.2	2321 0.8
5 ☾	F	0525 4.2	1136 1.3	1734 4.0	
6	SA	0038 0.9	0637 4.0	1300 1.5	1850 3.8
7	SU	0203 0.9	0801 4.1	1427 1.5	2011 4.0
8	M	0314 0.8	0907 4.2	1535 1.2	2115 4.2
9	TU	0407 0.5	1000 4.5	1625 1.0	2206 4.5
10	W	0451 0.5	1042 4.7	1706 0.9	2248 4.6
11	TH	0528 0.4	1121 4.8	1742 0.8	2329 4.7
12	F	0605 0.4	1156 4.8	1818 0.7	
13 ○	SA	0008 4.7	0640 0.4	1231 4.8	1851 0.5
14	SU	0046 4.7	0714 0.4	1306 4.8	1928 0.5
15	M	0123 4.8	0748 0.5	1342 4.8	2005 0.4
16	TU	0202 4.8	0824 0.5	1419 4.7	2044 0.4
17	W	0242 4.8	0900 0.7	1459 4.7	2125 0.4
18	TH	0327 4.8	0940 0.8	1542 4.6	2211 0.4
19	F	0417 4.6	1027 1.0	1632 4.3	2307 0.5
20 ○	SA	0517 4.5	1128 1.1	1733 4.2	
21	SU	0022 0.7	0626 4.3	1248 1.2	1843 4.2
22	M	0151 0.5	0745 4.5	1411 1.1	1958 4.3
23	TU	0309 0.3	0855 4.6	1522 0.9	2103 4.6
24	W	0411 0.2	0954 4.8	1621 0.7	2202 4.8
25	TH	0504 0.1	1046 5.0	1713 0.5	2254 5.0
26	F	0552 0.1	1135 5.0	1803 0.4	2347 5.1
27 ●	SA	0634 0.2	1223 5.0	1849 0.3	
28	SU	0037 5.1	0712 0.3	1307 5.0	1932 0.3
29	M	0123 5.0	0748 0.4	1348 4.8	2014 0.3
30	TU	0207 5.0	0825 0.5	1426 4.8	2056 0.3
31	W	0249 4.8	0900 0.8	1502 4.7	2135 0.4

JUNE

No.	Day	Time m	Time m	Time m	Time m
1	TH	0330 4.7	0935 0.9	1539 4.6	2215 0.5
2	F	0412 4.5	1013 1.1	1618 4.5	2301 0.7
3 ○	SA	0458 4.3	1101 1.2	1705 4.2	2354 0.8
4	SU	0551 4.1	1201 1.3	1802 4.1	
5	M	0059 0.8	0653 4.1	1315 1.3	1907 4.1
6	TU	0205 0.8	0801 4.2	1425 1.3	2012 4.2
7	W	0303 0.7	0900 4.3	1524 1.1	2109 4.3
8	TH	0355 0.7	0950 4.5	1614 1.0	2202 4.5
9	F	0442 0.5	1036 4.6	1701 0.9	2249 4.6
10	SA	0529 0.5	1120 4.7	1747 0.8	2335 4.7
11 ○	SU	0615 0.5	1204 4.8	1833 0.7	
12	M	0022 4.8	0655 0.5	1247 4.8	1916 0.5
13	TU	0107 4.8	0734 0.5	1330 4.8	1959 0.4
14	W	0153 5.0	0814 0.7	1411 4.8	2042 0.4
15	TH	0237 5.0	0854 0.7	1454 4.8	2126 0.2
16	F	0325 5.0	0934 0.8	1539 4.7	2212 0.2
17	SA	0414 4.8	1019 0.9	1627 4.7	2302 0.3
18 ○	SU	0508 4.7	1111 1.0	1721 4.6	
19	M	0003 0.3	0607 4.6	1212 1.0	1819 4.6
20	TU	0115 0.4	0712 4.6	1327 1.0	1923 4.5
21	W	0229 0.4	0818 4.6	1441 1.0	2030 4.6
22	TH	0337 0.4	0922 4.6	1550 0.8	2134 4.7
23	F	0436 0.4	1020 4.7	1652 0.7	2235 4.7
24	SA	0528 0.4	1114 4.7	1749 0.5	2332 4.8
25 ●	SU	0616 0.5	1207 4.8	1841 0.4	
26	M	0026 4.8	0655 0.7	1254 4.8	1926 0.3
27	TU	0114 4.8	0732 0.7	1335 4.8	2008 0.3
28	W	0157 4.8	0808 0.8	1413 4.8	2047 0.3
29	TH	0236 4.8	0842 0.9	1447 4.7	2122 0.4
30	F	0312 4.7	0914 0.9	1520 4.7	2155 0.4

JULY

No.	Day	Time m	Time m	Time m	Time m
1	SA	0348 4.6	0946 1.0	1553 4.6	2229 0.5
2	SU	0424 4.5	1022 1.1	1631 4.5	2307 0.7
3 ○	M	0504 4.3	1106 1.2	1716 4.3	2353 0.8
4	TU	0550 4.2	1200 1.2	1807 4.2	
5	W	0053 0.8	0646 4.2	1307 1.3	1908 4.2
6	TH	0156 0.9	0750 4.2	1416 1.2	2014 4.2
7	F	0301 0.8	0856 4.3	1523 1.1	2118 4.3
8	SA	0402 0.8	0956 4.5	1626 1.0	2217 4.5
9	SU	0459 0.8	1050 4.7	1726 0.8	2312 4.7
10	M	0554 0.7	1143 4.8	1822 0.7	
11 ○	TU	0006 4.8	0640 0.7	1231 4.8	1908 0.4
12	W	0057 5.1	0721 0.7	1318 5.0	1953 0.3
13	TH	0144 5.2	0802 0.7	1402 5.1	2037 0.1
14	F	0230 5.2	0842 0.7	1445 5.1	2119 0.1
15	SA	0315 5.2	0922 0.7	1528 5.1	2201 0.0
16	SU	0401 5.2	1003 0.7	1611 5.1	2245 0.1
17 ☽	M	0449 5.0	1047 0.8	1656 5.0	2331 0.3
18	TU	0540 4.7	1137 0.9	1748 4.7	
19	W	0032 0.4	0635 4.6	1242 1.0	1849 4.6
20	TH	0142 0.7	0741 4.3	1401 1.1	2001 4.5
21	F	0301 0.8	0853 4.3	1526 1.0	2116 4.5
22	SA	0412 0.9	1002 4.3	1643 0.9	2226 4.6
23	SU	0512 0.9	1102 4.6	1746 0.7	2328 4.7
24	M	0602 0.9	1155 4.7	1837 0.4	
25 ●	TU	0021 4.8	0642 0.9	1243 4.8	1919 0.3
26	W	0106 4.8	0718 0.9	1323 5.0	1957 0.3
27	TH	0146 4.8	0755 0.9	1357 5.0	2030 0.3
28	F	0219 4.8	0822 0.9	1427 4.8	2059 0.4
29	SA	0249 4.7	0850 0.9	1455 4.8	2126 0.4
30	SU	0317 4.7	0918 0.9	1523 4.8	2152 0.4
31	M	0347 4.7	0949 0.9	1554 4.7	2223 0.5

AUGUST

No.	Day	Time m	Time m	Time m	Time m
1	TU	0421 4.6	1024 1.0	1631 4.6	2301 0.7
2	W	0501 4.5	1107 1.1	1715 4.5	2348 0.9
3	TH	0550 4.3	1204 1.2	1809 4.2	
4	F	0056 1.0	0650 4.2	1320 1.3	1920 4.1
5	SA	0213 1.1	0806 4.1	1440 1.3	2040 4.2
6	SU	0329 1.0	0924 4.3	1602 1.1	2155 4.5
7	M	0438 0.9	1030 4.6	1713 0.8	2258 4.7
8	TU	0536 0.8	1126 4.8	1812 0.5	2353 5.1
9 ○	W	0625 0.7	1216 5.1	1858 0.3	
10	TH	0045 5.2	0706 0.5	1303 5.2	1941 0.1
11	F	0131 5.3	0746 0.5	1346 5.3	2022 0.0
12	SA	0215 5.5	0824 0.5	1427 5.3	2101 -0.1
13	SU	0257 5.5	0903 0.5	1506 5.5	2139 0.0
14	M	0339 5.3	0941 0.5	1547 5.3	2218 0.1
15	TU	0422 5.1	1022 0.7	1629 5.2	2258 0.3
16 ☽	W	0507 4.8	1107 0.8	1717 4.8	2345 0.7
17	TH	0558 4.5	1205 1.0	1815 4.5	
18	F	0055 1.0	0702 4.1	1328 1.1	1937 4.2
19	SA	0224 1.2	0827 4.1	1514 1.1	2108 4.2
20	SU	0353 1.2	0947 4.2	1639 0.9	2223 4.5
21	M	0458 1.1	1049 4.6	1740 0.7	2321 4.7
22	TU	0547 1.0	1140 4.8	1826 0.5	
23 ●	W	0009 5.0	0626 0.9	1224 5.0	1903 0.3
24	TH	0050 5.0	0659 0.9	1303 5.1	1934 0.3
25	F	0126 5.0	0730 0.9	1334 5.0	2003 0.4
26	SA	0155 4.8	0758 0.9	1401 5.0	2028 0.4
27	SU	0219 4.8	0823 0.8	1425 5.0	2053 0.4
28	M	0243 4.8	0850 0.8	1451 5.0	2117 0.4
29	TU	0310 4.8	0919 0.8	1520 4.8	2143 0.5
30	W	0343 4.8	0952 0.8	1553 4.8	2215 0.7
31 ☽	TH	0421 4.7	1030 1.0	1632 4.6	2254 0.9

Chart Datum: 2·35 metres below Ordnance Datum (Newlyn)

TIME ZONE (UT)
For Summer Time add ONE hour in **non-shaded areas**

ENGLAND – BURNHAM-ON-CROUCH

LAT 51°37'N   LONG 0°48'E

TIMES AND HEIGHTS OF HIGH AND LOW WATERS

SEPTEMBER

Time	m	Time	m
1 0506	4.3	**16** 0015	1.3
1120	1.2	0624	4.0
F 1723	4.3	SA 1309	1.2
2355	1.1	1919	4.1
2 0604	4.1	**17** 0153	1.6
1237	1.3	0759	4.0
SA 1833	4.1	SU 1502	1.1
		2057	4.2
3 0130	1.3	**18** 0330	1.5
0721	4.0	0826	4.1
SU 1410	1.3	M 1621	0.9
2011	4.1	2208	4.5
4 0303	1.2	**19** 0436	1.3
0856	4.2	1025	4.6
M 1547	1.1	TU 1717	0.5
2142	4.5	2300	4.8
5 0419	1.0	**20** 0523	1.1
1010	4.5	1113	4.8
TU 1700	0.7	W 1801	0.4
2245	4.8	2343	5.1
6 0515	0.9	**21** 0602	0.9
1105	4.8	1155	5.1
W 1755	0.5	TH 1836	0.3
2338	5.2		
7 0604	0.7	**22** 0022	5.1
1153	5.2	0636	0.9
TH 1840	0.1	F 1232	5.1
○		● 1904	0.4
8 0025	5.5	**23** 0056	5.0
0645	0.5	0704	0.8
F 1240	5.3	SA 1304	5.0
1920	0.4	1931	0.4
9 0110	5.6	**24** 0124	5.0
0723	0.4	0730	0.8
SA 1322	5.5	SU 1331	5.0
2000	-0.1	1955	0.5
10 0153	5.6	**25** 0147	4.8
0802	0.4	0757	0.8
SU 1402	5.6	M 1356	4.8
2037	-0.1	2019	0.5
11 0233	5.5	**26** 0211	4.8
0842	0.4	0825	0.7
M 1441	5.6	TU 1421	5.0
2113	0.0	2045	0.5
12 0312	5.2	**27** 0238	5.0
0920	0.4	0856	0.7
TU 1521	5.5	W 1452	5.0
2148	0.2	2111	0.5
13 0352	5.1	**28** 0311	4.8
0959	0.5	0928	0.8
W 1602	5.2	TH 1526	4.8
2226	0.5	2141	0.7
14 0432	4.7	**29** 0348	4.7
1044	0.8	1005	0.9
TH 1644	4.8	F 1605	4.6
◐ 2310	0.9	2218	1.0
15 0520	4.3	**30** 0431	4.5
1139	1.0	1055	1.1
F 1749	4.3	SA 1656	4.3
		◑ 2315	1.2

OCTOBER

Time	m	Time	m
1 0528	4.1	**16** 0119	1.7
1209	1.2	0720	4.0
SU 1807	4.1	M 1432	1.0
		2027	4.1
2 0055	1.5	**17** 0252	1.6
0646	4.0	0844	4.2
M 1352	1.2	TU 1546	0.8
1950	4.1	2135	4.5
3 0236	1.3	**18** 0358	1.3
0826	4.1	0947	4.5
TU 1529	0.9	W 1640	0.5
2123	4.5	2224	4.7
4 0352	1.1	**19** 0448	1.1
0941	4.6	1035	4.8
W 1637	0.5	TH 1722	0.4
2223	5.0	2307	5.0
5 0449	0.9	**20** 0528	0.9
1035	4.8	1117	5.0
TH 1730	0.2	F 1759	0.4
2312	5.2	2345	5.0
6 0537	0.7	**21** 0604	0.9
1123	5.2	1153	5.0
F 1817	0.0	SA 1829	0.4
2359	5.5		
7 0621	0.4	**22** 0018	5.0
1209	5.5	0635	0.6
SA 1856	-0.1	SU 1227	5.0
○		● 1856	0.5
8 0044	5.5	**23** 0048	5.0
0701	0.4	0703	0.8
SU 1254	5.5	M 1258	4.8
1934	0.0	1923	0.5
9 0126	5.5	**24** 0113	4.8
0741	0.4	0728	0.8
M 1336	5.6	TU 1328	4.8
2011	0.0	1951	0.5
10 0206	5.3	**25** 0142	5.0
0821	0.3	0804	0.7
TU 1417	5.5	W 1358	4.8
2046	0.2	2020	0.7
11 0245	5.2	**26** 0213	5.0
0901	0.4	0838	0.7
W 1459	5.3	TH 1432	5.0
2121	0.4	2049	0.7
12 0324	5.0	**27** 0247	4.8
0942	0.4	0913	0.7
TH 1541	5.1	F 1509	4.8
2158	0.8	2121	0.8
13 0403	4.7	**28** 0325	4.7
1027	0.7	0953	0.8
F 1629	4.7	SA 1552	4.6
2242	1.1	2202	1.0
14 0448	4.3	**29** 0409	4.5
1126	0.9	1045	0.9
SA 1718	4.3	SU 1646	4.3
◑ 2343	1.5	◐ 2259	1.2
15 0550	4.1	**30** 0506	4.2
1254	1.1	1154	1.0
SU 1855	4.1	M 1756	4.0
		31 0024	1.5
		0621	4.1
		TU 1330	1.0
		1928	4.2

NOVEMBER

Time	m	Time	m
1 0200	1.3	**16** 0309	1.3
0750	4.2	0854	4.3
W 1500	0.8	TH 1549	0.8
2051	4.6	2138	4.6
2 0316	1.1	**17** 0403	1.2
0902	4.6	0947	4.6
TH 1607	0.4	F 1634	0.7
2151	5.0	2222	4.7
3 0416	0.9	**18** 0446	1.0
1000	5.0	1032	4.7
F 1700	0.2	SA 1713	0.5
2242	5.2	2302	4.8
4 0506	0.7	**19** 0525	0.9
1050	5.2	1112	4.8
SA 1748	0.1	SU 1749	0.5
2330	5.3	2338	4.8
5 0555	0.4	**20** 0602	0.8
1140	5.3	1151	4.8
SU 1831	0.1	M 1824	0.7
○		●	
6 0016	5.3	**21** 0012	4.8
0639	0.4	0636	0.8
M 1227	5.3	TU 1228	4.8
1909	0.1	1857	0.7
7 0100	5.2	**22** 0046	4.8
0722	0.3	0712	0.7
TU 1313	5.3	W 1305	4.8
1946	0.3	1931	0.7
8 0142	5.2	**23** 0120	4.8
0805	0.3	0749	0.7
W 1357	5.3	TH 1342	4.8
2024	0.4	2003	0.7
9 0221	5.1	**24** 0156	4.8
0848	0.3	0828	0.5
TH 1441	5.2	F 1420	5.0
2100	0.7	2038	0.8
10 0300	4.8	**25** 0233	4.8
0931	0.4	0908	0.5
F 1527	5.0	SA 1501	4.8
2137	0.9	2114	0.9
11 0340	4.7	**26** 0313	4.7
1018	0.7	0951	0.5
SA 1613	4.7	SU 1548	4.7
2219	1.2	2155	1.0
12 0424	4.5	**27** 0358	4.6
1113	0.8	1040	0.7
SU 1708	4.3	M 1640	4.6
◐ 2313	1.5	2247	1.1
13 0519	4.2	**28** 0453	4.3
1224	0.9	1141	0.7
M 1816	4.1	TU 1744	4.3
		◑ 2351	1.2
14 0032	1.7	**29** 0558	4.3
0630	4.1	1259	0.7
TU 1343	0.9	W 1856	4.3
1936	4.1		
15 0158	1.6	**30** 0114	1.2
0749	4.1	0712	4.3
W 1453	0.9	TH 1420	0.5
2044	4.3	2011	4.5

DECEMBER

Time	m	Time	m
1 0232	1.1	**16** 0258	1.2
0822	4.6	0849	4.5
F 1530	0.4	SA 1535	0.8
2116	4.7	2129	4.3
2 0338	0.9	**17** 0353	1.1
0925	4.8	0944	4.5
SA 1628	0.3	SU 1625	0.8
2211	5.0	2217	4.6
3 0437	0.7	**18** 0442	1.0
1021	5.0	1034	4.6
SU 1721	0.3	M 1712	0.8
2303	5.0	2301	4.7
4 0532	0.5	**19** 0529	0.9
1115	5.1	1121	4.7
M 1809	0.3	TU 1757	0.7
2352	5.1	2344	4.8
5 0624	0.4	**20** 0616	0.7
1209	5.2	1206	4.8
TU 1850	0.4	W 1837	0.7
○			
6 0040	5.0	**21** 0025	4.8
0711	0.3	0658	0.7
W 1259	5.2	TH 1250	4.8
1929	0.5	1916	0.7
7 0124	5.0	**22** 0106	4.8
0756	0.3	0740	0.5
TH 1346	5.1	F 1332	5.0
2006	0.7	1952	0.7
8 0205	4.8	**23** 0146	4.8
0841	0.3	0822	0.4
F 1430	5.0	SA 1414	5.0
2042	0.8	2029	0.6
9 0244	4.8	**24** 0226	4.8
0923	0.4	0904	0.3
SA 1512	4.8	SU 1456	5.0
2119	1.0	2107	0.6
10 0322	4.7	**25** 0306	4.8
1005	0.5	0945	0.3
SU 1554	4.7	M 1541	5.0
2155	1.1	2146	0.8
11 0401	4.6	**26** 0350	4.8
1049	0.7	1029	0.3
M 1638	4.5	TU 1630	4.8
2237	1.3	2231	0.9
12 0445	4.3	**27** 0437	4.7
1138	0.8	1118	0.4
TU 1727	4.3	W 1723	4.6
◐ 2329	1.5	◑ 2322	1.0
13 0537	4.2	**28** 0531	4.6
1237	0.9	1218	0.5
W 1824	4.1	TH 1822	4.6
14 0039	1.5	**29** 0026	1.0
0638	4.2	0633	4.5
TH 1339	0.9	F 1331	0.6
1932	4.1	1931	4.3
15 0152	1.5	**30** 0143	1.0
0747	4.2	0745	4.5
F 1439	0.9	SA 1449	0.7
2035	4.2	2039	4.5
		31 0302	1.0
		0856	4.6
		SU 1600	0.7
		2144	4.5

Chart Datum: 2·35 metres below Ordnance Datum (Newlyn)

TIDES

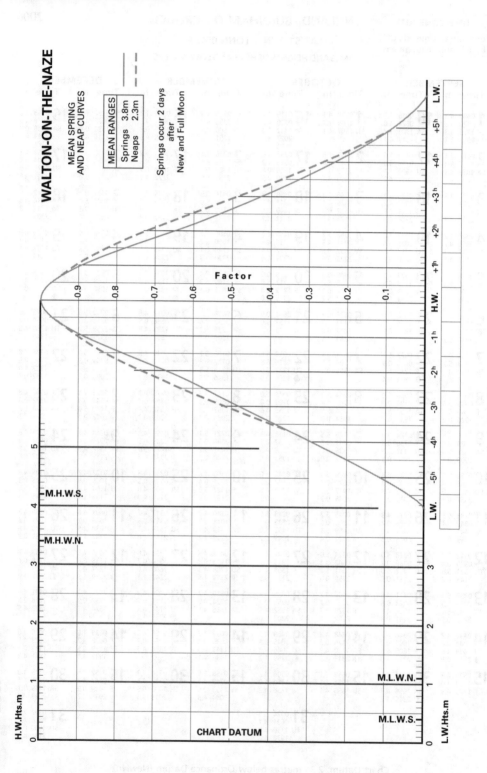

WALTON-ON-THE-NAZE

MEAN SPRING
AND NEAP CURVES

MEAN RANGES
Springs 3.8m
Neaps 2.3m

Springs occur 2 days
after
New and Full Moon

ENGLAND – WALTON-ON-THE-NAZE

LAT 51°51′N LONG 1°17′E

TIMES AND HEIGHTS OF HIGH AND LOW WATERS

2006

TIME ZONE (UT)
For Summer Time add ONE hour in **non-shaded areas**

JANUARY

#	Time m	#	Time m
1 SU	0611 0.5 / 1223 4.2 / 1829 0.7	**16** M	0040 3.9 / 0658 0.6 / 1304 3.9 / 1850 1.0
2 M	0043 4.0 / 0702 0.4 / 1313 4.2 / 1913 0.7	**17** TU	0113 3.9 / 0732 0.6 / 1336 3.8 / 1920 0.9
3 TU	0130 4.1 / 0752 0.3 / 1402 4.2 / 1956 0.8	**18** W	0142 3.8 / 0802 0.6 / 1406 3.8 / 1949 0.9
4 W	0217 4.1 / 0840 0.3 / 1451 4.2 / 2041 0.8	**19** TH	0212 3.8 / 0831 0.6 / 1437 3.8 / 2021 0.9
5 TH	0304 4.0 / 0930 0.3 / 1542 4.1 / 2128 0.9	**20** F	0245 3.8 / 0904 0.7 / 1512 3.7 / 2057 1.0
6 F	0353 3.9 / 1022 0.4 / 1635 3.9 / ◐ 2220 1.0	**21** SA	0321 3.8 / 0941 0.7 / 1552 3.7 / 2139 1.1
7 SA	0446 3.8 / 1120 0.6 / 1733 3.7 / 2320 1.1	**22** ◔	0403 3.6 / 1025 0.8 / 1639 3.5 / 2228 1.2
8 SU	0546 3.7 / 1224 0.7 / 1835 3.5	**23** M	0454 3.5 / 1120 0.9 / 1734 3.4 / 2330 1.3
9 M	0029 1.2 / 0652 3.6 / 1332 0.9 / 1941 3.5	**24** TU	0556 3.4 / 1226 1.0 / 1840 3.3
10 TU	0143 1.1 / 0800 3.6 / 1436 0.9 / 2045 3.5	**25** W	0042 1.3 / 0709 3.4 / 1338 1.1 / 1953 3.3
11 W	0252 1.0 / 0907 3.6 / 1533 0.9 / 2143 3.6	**26** TH	0156 1.2 / 0823 3.5 / 1448 1.0 / 2102 3.5
12 TH	0354 0.9 / 1006 3.7 / 1622 0.9 / 2234 3.7	**27** F	0309 1.1 / 0930 3.7 / 1551 0.9 / 2202 3.7
13 F	0448 0.7 / 1059 3.8 / 1704 0.9 / 2320 3.8	**28** SA	0416 0.8 / 1030 3.9 / 1644 0.8 / 2255 3.9
14 SA	0536 0.6 / 1146 3.9 / 1742 0.9 / ○	**29** SU	0513 0.6 / 1124 4.1 / 1732 0.7 / ● 2345 4.0
15 SU	0002 3.8 / 0619 0.6 / 1228 3.9 / 1817 0.9	**30** M	0605 0.4 / 1214 4.3 / 1816 0.7
		31 TU	0032 4.1 / 0653 0.2 / 1303 4.4 / 1858 0.6

FEBRUARY

#	Time m	#	Time m
1 W	0118 4.2 / 0739 0.1 / 1349 4.4 / 1940 0.6	**16** TH	0121 3.9 / 0733 0.6 / 1341 4.0 / 1925 0.8
2 TH	0202 4.3 / 0823 0.1 / 1434 4.3 / 2022 0.6	**17** F	0148 3.9 / 0800 0.5 / 1408 3.9 / 1955 0.8
3 F	0245 4.3 / 0906 0.2 / 1519 4.2 / 2104 0.7	**18** SA	0217 3.9 / 0829 0.6 / 1440 3.9 / 2028 0.8
4 SA	0327 4.2 / 0949 0.5 / 1604 4.0 / 2149 0.8	**19** SU	0250 3.9 / 0900 0.6 / 1517 3.8 / 2104 0.8
5 SU	0413 4.0 / 1036 0.6 / 1652 3.7 / ◐ 2239 0.9	**20** M	0327 3.8 / 0936 0.7 / 1559 3.7 / 2146 0.9
6 M	0505 3.8 / 1130 0.9 / 1748 3.4 / 2341 1.1	**21** TU	0411 3.6 / 1023 0.9 / 1650 3.4 / 2242 1.1
7 TU	0611 3.5 / 1238 1.1 / 1857 3.2	**22** W	0509 3.4 / 1132 1.1 / 1753 3.2 / 2358 1.3
8 W	0102 1.2 / 0733 3.3 / 1359 1.3 / 2016 3.2	**23** TH	0626 3.3 / 1300 1.2 / 1913 3.1
9 TH	0234 1.1 / 0855 3.4 / 1513 1.2 / 2126 3.4	**24** F	0127 1.2 / 0758 3.3 / 1428 1.2 / 2039 3.3
10 F	0346 0.9 / 1000 3.6 / 1607 1.1 / 2220 3.6	**25** SA	0300 1.0 / 0921 3.6 / 1537 1.0 / 2148 3.6
11 SA	0440 0.7 / 1051 3.8 / 1650 1.0 / 2307 3.8	**26** SU	0410 0.7 / 1022 3.9 / 1630 0.8 / 2241 3.9
12 SU	0525 0.6 / 1134 3.9 / 1727 1.0 / 2347 3.9	**27** M	0503 0.4 / 1113 4.2 / 1715 0.7 / 2329 4.1
13 M	0604 0.5 / 1213 3.9 / 1801 0.9 / ○	**28** TU	0551 0.2 / 1201 4.4 / 1758 0.6 / ●
14 TU	0023 3.9 / 0637 0.5 / 1246 3.9 / 1830 0.9		
15 W	0054 3.9 / 0706 0.5 / 1315 3.9 / 1857 0.9		

MARCH

#	Time m	#	Time m
1 W	0014 4.3 / 0636 0.0 / 1246 4.4 / 1838 0.5	**16** TH	0027 3.9 / 0634 0.5 / 1247 3.9 / 1831 0.8
2 TH	0058 4.4 / 0718 0.0 / 1329 4.4 / 1919 0.5	**17** F	0055 3.9 / 0701 0.5 / 1312 3.9 / 1900 0.7
3 F	0140 4.4 / 0758 0.0 / 1411 4.3 / 1959 0.4	**18** SA	0122 3.9 / 0729 0.5 / 1340 3.9 / 1931 0.7
4 SA	0220 4.4 / 0837 0.2 / 1451 4.2 / 2039 0.5	**19** SU	0151 4.0 / 0758 0.5 / 1412 3.9 / 2004 0.6
5 SU	0300 4.3 / 0915 0.4 / 1531 4.0 / 2120 0.6	**20** M	0224 4.0 / 0828 0.6 / 1448 3.9 / 2039 0.7
6 M	0343 4.1 / 0956 0.7 / 1612 3.7 / 2206 0.8	**21** TU	0301 3.9 / 0902 0.7 / 1528 3.7 / 2120 0.8
7 TU	0431 3.7 / 1045 1.0 / 1659 3.3 / 2305 1.0	**22** ◔	0346 3.7 / 0948 1.0 / 1617 3.4 / 2216 1.0
8 W	0534 3.4 / 1152 1.3 / 1806 3.1	**23** TH	0444 3.4 / 1057 1.2 / 1719 3.2 / 2335 1.2
9 TH	0031 1.2 / 0708 3.2 / 1323 1.5 / 1943 3.0	**24** F	0603 3.2 / 1236 1.3 / 1843 3.1
10 F	0218 1.1 / 0840 3.3 / 1449 1.4 / 2103 3.2	**25** SA	0117 1.1 / 0747 3.3 / 1411 1.2 / 2019 3.2
11 SA	0330 0.9 / 0944 3.6 / 1547 1.2 / 2159 3.5	**26** SU	0253 0.9 / 0911 3.6 / 1519 1.0 / 2128 3.6
12 SU	0420 0.7 / 1031 3.8 / 1629 1.1 / 2243 3.8	**27** M	0355 0.5 / 1007 4.0 / 1609 0.8 / 2220 3.9
13 M	0501 0.6 / 1112 3.9 / 1705 0.9 / 2322 3.9	**28** TU	0445 0.2 / 1055 4.2 / 1653 0.6 / 2306 4.1
14 TU	0536 0.5 / 1148 4.0 / 1737 0.7 / ○ 2357 3.9	**29** W	0529 0.1 / 1140 4.4 / 1735 0.5 / ● 2350 4.3
15 W	0607 0.5 / 1220 3.9 / 1805 0.7	**30** TH	0612 0.0 / 1223 4.4 / 1816 0.4
		31 F	0033 4.4 / 0652 0.0 / 1305 4.3 / 1856 0.4

APRIL

#	Time m	#	Time m
1 SA	0115 4.4 / 0730 0.1 / 1345 4.2 / 1937 0.4	**16** SU	0056 3.9 / 0701 0.6 / 1314 3.9 / 1911 0.6
2 SU	0156 4.4 / 0807 0.3 / 1423 4.1 / 2017 0.4	**17** M	0130 3.9 / 0733 0.6 / 1349 3.9 / 1948 0.6
3 M	0236 4.2 / 0844 0.5 / 1500 3.9 / 2058 0.5	**18** TU	0206 3.9 / 0807 0.7 / 1426 3.8 / 2026 0.6
4 TU	0319 4.0 / 0923 0.8 / 1538 3.6 / 2143 0.7	**19** W	0247 3.9 / 0845 0.8 / 1508 3.7 / 2111 0.7
5 W	0407 3.7 / 1011 1.1 / 1622 3.4 / ◐ 2243 1.0	**20** TH	0336 3.7 / 0934 1.0 / 1558 3.4 / 2210 0.9
6 TH	0509 3.3 / 1118 1.4 / 1723 3.1	**21** F	0438 3.4 / 1044 1.3 / 1702 3.2 / ◔ 2332 1.0
7 F	0011 1.1 / 0640 3.1 / 1248 1.6 / 1902 3.0	**22** SA	0558 3.3 / 1218 1.4 / 1825 3.1
8 SA	0150 1.1 / 0810 3.3 / 1415 1.5 / 2026 3.2	**23** SU	0112 0.9 / 0733 3.4 / 1347 1.2 / 1951 3.3
9 SU	0258 0.9 / 0913 3.6 / 1514 1.3 / 2124 3.5	**24** M	0234 0.7 / 0847 3.7 / 1452 1.0 / 2057 3.6
10 M	0347 0.7 / 1000 3.8 / 1558 1.1 / 2209 3.7	**25** TU	0333 0.4 / 0942 4.0 / 1542 0.8 / 2150 3.9
11 TU	0426 0.6 / 1039 3.9 / 1634 0.9 / 2247 3.8	**26** W	0420 0.2 / 1030 4.2 / 1627 0.6 / 2237 4.1
12 W	0459 0.5 / 1115 3.9 / 1706 0.8 / 2322 3.8	**27** TH	0504 0.1 / 1114 4.2 / 1710 0.5 / 2323 4.2
13 TH	0529 0.6 / 1146 3.9 / 1735 0.8 / ○ 2354 3.8	**28** F	0545 0.1 / 1157 4.2 / 1754 0.4
14 F	0559 0.6 / 1214 3.9 / 1805 0.7	**29** SA	0007 4.2 / 0624 0.2 / 1240 4.1 / 1836 0.4
15 SA	0024 3.8 / 0630 0.6 / 1243 3.9 / 1837 0.7	**30** SU	0052 4.2 / 0703 0.4 / 1320 4.1 / 1919 0.4

Chart Datum: 2·16 metres below Ordnance Datum (Newlyn)

TIME ZONE (UT)
For Summer Time add ONE hour in **non-shaded areas**

ENGLAND – WALTON-ON-THE-NAZE   2006

LAT 51°51'N   LONG 1°17'E

TIMES AND HEIGHTS OF HIGH AND LOW WATERS

MAY

Time	m		Time	m
1 M 0135 / 0740 / 1358 / 2001	4.2 / 0.5 / 3.9 / 0.4		**16** TU 0115 / 0718 / 1333 / 1940	3.9 / 0.7 / 3.8 / 0.6
2 TU 0217 / 0818 / 1436 / 2044	4.1 / 0.7 / 3.8 / 0.5		**17** W 0157 / 0757 / 1414 / 2024	3.9 / 0.8 / 3.8 / 0.6
3 W 0301 / 0857 / 1514 / 2130	3.9 / 0.9 / 3.6 / 0.7		**18** TH 0243 / 0840 / 1459 / 2114	3.9 / 0.9 / 3.7 / 0.6
4 TH 0350 / 0943 / 1558 / 2229	3.6 / 1.2 / 3.4 / 0.9		**19** F 0336 / 0931 / 1552 / 2214	3.7 / 1.1 / 3.5 / 0.7
5 ◐ SA 0447 / 1045 / 1656 / 2345	3.4 / 1.4 / 3.2 / 1.0		**20** SA 0438 / 1036 / 1655 / 2330 ○	3.6 / 1.2 / 3.4 / 0.8
6 SA 0602 / 1206 / 1814	3.2 / 1.5 / 3.1		**21** SU 0551 / 1154 / 1808	3.5 / 1.3 / 3.4
7 SU 0105 / 0722 / 1327 / 1932	1.0 / 3.3 / 1.5 / 3.2		**22** M 0053 / 0707 / 1312 / 1919	0.7 / 3.6 / 1.2 / 3.5
8 M 0210 / 0826 / 1430 / 2033	0.9 / 3.4 / 1.3 / 3.4		**23** TU 0206 / 0814 / 1418 / 2022	0.5 / 3.7 / 1.0 / 3.7
9 TU 0300 / 0916 / 1517 / 2122	0.7 / 3.6 / 1.1 / 3.6		**24** W 0304 / 0911 / 1513 / 2118	0.4 / 3.9 / 0.8 / 3.9
10 W 0341 / 0957 / 1555 / 2203	0.7 / 3.8 / 1.0 / 3.7		**25** TH 0353 / 1001 / 1602 / 2209	0.3 / 4.0 / 0.7 / 4.0
11 TH 0416 / 1034 / 1629 / 2242	0.6 / 3.9 / 0.9 / 3.8		**26** F 0438 / 1048 / 1649 / 2259	0.3 / 4.0 / 0.6 / 4.1
12 F 0451 / 1108 / 1703 / 2319	0.6 / 3.9 / 0.8 / 3.8		**27** ● SA 0520 / 1134 / 1736 / 2347	0.4 / 4.0 / 0.5 / 4.1
13 ○ SA 0527 / 1142 / 1739 / 2356	0.6 / 3.9 / 0.7 / 3.8		**28** SU 0601 / 1218 / 1823	0.5 / 4.0 / 0.5
14 SU 0603 / 1217 / 1818	0.6 / 3.9 / 0.7		**29** M 0034 / 0640 / 1300 / 1908	4.0 / 0.6 / 3.9 / 0.5
15 M 0034 / 0640 / 1254 / 1858	3.9 / 0.7 / 3.9 / 0.6		**30** TU 0120 / 0719 / 1340 / 1952	4.0 / 0.7 / 3.9 / 0.5
			31 W 0204 / 0757 / 1418 / 2035	3.9 / 0.9 / 3.8 / 0.6

JUNE

Time	m		Time	m
1 TH 0247 / 0835 / 1456 / 2118	3.8 / 1.0 / 3.7 / 0.7		**16** F 0241 / 0834 / 1456 / 2115	4.0 / 0.9 / 3.8 / 0.4
2 F 0331 / 0916 / 1537 / 2207	3.6 / 1.2 / 3.6 / 0.8		**17** SA 0333 / 0923 / 1546 / 2209	3.9 / 1.0 / 3.8 / 0.5
3 ◐ SA 0419 / 1007 / 1626 / 2304	3.5 / 1.3 / 3.4 / 0.9		**18** ○ SU 0429 / 1018 / 1642 / 2312	3.5 / 1.1 / 3.7 / 0.5
4 SU 0514 / 1110 / 1725	3.3 / 1.4 / 3.3		**19** M 0531 / 1121 / 1743	3.7 / 1.1 / 3.7
5 M 0005 / 0617 / 1220 / 1830	0.9 / 3.3 / 1.4 / 3.3		**20** TU 0020 / 0635 / 1231 / 1846	0.6 / 3.7 / 1.1 / 3.6
6 TU 0106 / 0722 / 1325 / 1933	0.9 / 3.4 / 1.4 / 3.4		**21** W 0129 / 0739 / 1340 / 1950	0.6 / 3.7 / 1.1 / 3.7
7 W 0200 / 0819 / 1420 / 2028	0.8 / 3.5 / 1.2 / 3.5		**22** TH 0232 / 0840 / 1444 / 2051	0.6 / 3.7 / 0.9 / 3.8
8 TH 0249 / 0907 / 1507 / 2118	0.8 / 3.6 / 1.1 / 3.6		**23** F 0327 / 0936 / 1542 / 2150	0.6 / 3.8 / 0.8 / 3.8
9 F 0333 / 0951 / 1551 / 2204	0.7 / 3.7 / 1.0 / 3.7		**24** SA 0416 / 1028 / 1636 / 2245	0.6 / 3.8 / 0.7 / 3.9
10 SA 0417 / 1033 / 1634 / 2248	0.7 / 3.8 / 0.9 / 3.8		**25** ● SU 0501 / 1118 / 1728 / 2337	0.7 / 3.9 / 0.6 / 3.9
11 ○ SU 0500 / 1115 / 1719 / 2333	0.7 / 3.9 / 0.8 / 3.9		**26** M 0543 / 1204 / 1816	0.8 / 3.9 / 0.5
12 M 0543 / 1157 / 1805	0.8 / 3.9 / 0.7		**27** TU 0025 / 0623 / 1247 / 1901	3.9 / 0.8 / 3.9 / 0.5
13 TU 0018 / 0625 / 1239 / 1851	3.9 / 0.7 / 3.9 / 0.6		**28** W 0110 / 0701 / 1326 / 1943	3.9 / 0.9 / 3.9 / 0.5
14 W 0105 / 0707 / 1324 / 1938	4.0 / 0.8 / 3.9 / 0.5		**29** TH 0151 / 0737 / 1402 / 2021	3.9 / 0.9 / 3.8 / 0.6
15 TH 0152 / 0750 / 1409 / 2025	4.0 / 0.8 / 3.9 / 0.4		**30** F 0228 / 0812 / 1436 / 2057	3.8 / 1.0 / 3.8 / 0.6

JULY

Time	m		Time	m
1 SA 0305 / 0847 / 1511 / 2133	3.7 / 1.1 / 3.7 / 0.7		**16** SU 0319 / 0905 / 1529 / 2150	4.2 / 0.8 / 4.1 / 0.3
2 ◖ SU 0343 / 0926 / 1551 / 2214	3.6 / 1.2 / 3.6 / 0.8		**17** M 0409 / 0953 / 1617 / 2240 ◖	4.0 / 0.9 / 4.0 / 0.5
3 ◐ M 0425 / 1013 / 1637 / 2303	3.5 / 1.3 / 3.5 / 0.9		**18** TU 0502 / 1046 / 1711 / 2339	3.8 / 1.0 / 3.8 / 0.6
4 TU 0513 / 1109 / 1731 / 2359	3.4 / 1.3 / 3.4 / 0.9		**19** W 0600 / 1149 / 1813	3.7 / 1.1 / 3.7
5 W 0610 / 1212 / 1831	3.4 / 1.4 / 3.4		**20** TH 0045 / 0703 / 1303 / 1922	0.8 / 3.5 / 1.2 / 3.6
6 TH 0058 / 0712 / 1317 / 1935	1.0 / 3.4 / 1.3 / 3.4		**21** F 0158 / 0812 / 1422 / 2034	0.7 / 3.5 / 1.1 / 3.6
7 F 0158 / 0815 / 1419 / 2036	0.9 / 3.5 / 1.2 / 3.5		**22** SA 0305 / 0918 / 1534 / 2142	1.0 / 3.6 / 1.0 / 3.7
8 SA 0255 / 0913 / 1518 / 2133	0.9 / 3.6 / 1.1 / 3.6		**23** SU 0401 / 1016 / 1633 / 2241	1.0 / 3.7 / 0.8 / 3.8
9 SU 0349 / 1005 / 1614 / 2226	0.9 / 3.8 / 0.9 / 3.8		**24** M 0448 / 1107 / 1724 / 2332	1.0 / 3.8 / 0.6 / 3.9
10 M 0440 / 1055 / 1707 / 2317	0.8 / 3.9 / 0.8 / 3.9		**25** ● TU 0529 / 1153 / 1809	1.0 / 3.9 / 0.5
11 ○ TU 0527 / 1142 / 1757	0.8 / 3.9 / 0.7		**26** W 0017 / 0607 / 1234 / 1849	3.9 / 1.0 / 4.0 / 0.5
12 W 0007 / 0611 / 1229 / 1845	4.1 / 0.8 / 4.0 / 0.5		**27** TH 0058 / 0643 / 1310 / 1925	3.9 / 1.0 / 4.0 / 0.5
13 TH 0056 / 0655 / 1315 / 1932	4.2 / 0.8 / 4.1 / 0.3		**28** F 0133 / 0716 / 1341 / 1956	3.9 / 1.0 / 3.9 / 0.6
14 F 0144 / 0738 / 1400 / 2017	4.2 / 0.8 / 4.1 / 0.3		**29** SA 0204 / 0746 / 1410 / 2025	3.8 / 1.0 / 3.9 / 0.6
15 SA 0231 / 0821 / 1444 / 2103	4.2 / 0.8 / 4.1 / 0.2		**30** SU 0233 / 0816 / 1439 / 2054	3.8 / 1.0 / 3.9 / 0.6
			31 M 0304 / 0850 / 1512 / 2127	3.8 / 1.0 / 3.8 / 0.7

AUGUST

Time	m		Time	m
1 TU 0340 / 0928 / 1551 / 2207	3.7 / 1.1 / 3.7 / 0.8		**16** W 0428 / 1014 / 1638 / 2255 ◖	3.9 / 0.9 / 3.9 / 0.8
2 ◖ W 0422 / 1014 / 1636 / 2258	3.6 / 1.2 / 3.6 / 1.0		**17** TH 0521 / 1114 / 1739	3.6 / 1.1 / 3.6
3 TH 0513 / 1113 / 1733	3.5 / 1.3 / 3.4		**18** F 0001 / 0626 / 1232 / 1859	1.1 / 3.3 / 1.2 / 3.4
4 F 0002 / 0614 / 1224 / 1843	1.1 / 3.4 / 1.4 / 3.3		**19** SA 0124 / 0747 / 1410 / 2027	1.3 / 3.3 / 1.2 / 3.4
5 SA 0114 / 0727 / 1339 / 2000	1.2 / 3.3 / 1.4 / 3.4		**20** SU 0247 / 0904 / 1530 / 2139	1.3 / 3.4 / 1.0 / 3.6
6 SU 0224 / 0842 / 1455 / 2112	1.1 / 3.5 / 1.2 / 3.6		**21** M 0348 / 1004 / 1627 / 2234	1.2 / 3.7 / 0.8 / 3.8
7 M 0329 / 0945 / 1602 / 2212	1.0 / 3.7 / 0.9 / 3.8		**22** TU 0434 / 1052 / 1712 / 2320	1.1 / 3.9 / 0.6 / 4.0
8 TU 0423 / 1039 / 1657 / 2305	0.9 / 3.9 / 0.7 / 4.1		**23** ● W 0512 / 1135 / 1751	1.0 / 4.0 / 0.5
9 W 0511 / 1127 / 1746 / 2355	0.8 / 4.1 / 0.5 / 4.2		**24** TH 0000 / 0547 / 1213 / 1825	4.2 / 1.0 / 4.1 / 0.5
10 ○ TH 0555 / 1213 / 1832	0.7 / 4.2 / 0.3		**25** F 0037 / 0620 / 1246 / 1856	4.0 / 1.0 / 4.0 / 0.6
11 F 0042 / 0637 / 1258 / 1916	4.3 / 0.7 / 4.3 / 0.2		**26** SA 0107 / 0650 / 1314 / 1923	3.9 / 1.0 / 4.0 / 0.6
12 SA 0128 / 0718 / 1341 / 1958	4.4 / 0.7 / 4.3 / 0.1		**27** SU 0133 / 0717 / 1339 / 1949	3.9 / 0.9 / 4.0 / 0.6
13 SU 0212 / 0800 / 1422 / 2039	4.4 / 0.6 / 4.4 / 0.2		**28** M 0158 / 0746 / 1406 / 2015	3.9 / 0.9 / 4.0 / 0.6
14 M 0256 / 0842 / 1504 / 2121	4.3 / 0.7 / 4.3 / 0.3		**29** TU 0226 / 0818 / 1436 / 2044	3.9 / 0.9 / 3.9 / 0.6
15 TU 0341 / 0926 / 1548 / 2204	4.1 / 0.8 / 4.2 / 0.5		**30** W 0300 / 0853 / 1511 / 2118	3.9 / 1.0 / 3.9 / 0.8
			31 TH 0340 / 0934 / 1552 / 2200 ◐	3.8 / 1.1 / 3.8 / 1.0

Chart Datum: 2·16 metres below Ordnance Datum (Newlyn)

TIME ZONE (UT)
For Summer Time add ONE hour in **non-shaded areas**

LAT 51°51'N   LONG 1°17'E

TIMES AND HEIGHTS OF HIGH AND LOW WATERS

SEPTEMBER

Day	Time m	Time m		Day	Time m	Time m
1 F	0427 3.5 / 1028 1.3	1645 3.5 / 2305 1.2		**16** SA	0548 3.2 / 1214 1.3	1842 3.3
2 SA	0527 3.3 / 1144 1.4	1758 3.3		**17** SU	0055 1.6 / 0720 3.2	1359 1.2 / 2016 3.4
3 SU	0034 1.4 / 0644 3.2	1311 1.4 / 1932 3.3		**18** M	0225 1.5 / 0842 3.4	1513 1.0 / 2124 3.6
4 M	0200 1.3 / 0815 3.5	1441 1.2 / 2059 3.6		**19** TU	0327 1.4 / 0941 3.7	1606 0.7 / 2214 3.9
5 TU	0311 1.1 / 0926 3.6	1550 0.8 / 2200 3.9		**20** W	0411 1.2 / 1027 3.9	1647 0.6 / 2255 4.1
6 W	0404 1.0 / 1019 3.9	1641 0.5 / 2250 4.2		**21** TH	0448 1.0 / 1107 4.1	1722 0.5 / 2333 4.1
7 TH	0450 0.8 / 1105 4.2	1727 0.4 / ○ 2336 4.4		**22** F	0522 1.0 / 1143 4.1	1753 0.6 ●
8 F	0532 0.7 / 1150 4.3	1810 0.2		**23** SA	0006 4.0 / 0552 0.9	1215 4.0 / 1821 0.6
9 SA	0021 4.5 / 0613 0.6	1233 4.4 / 1852 0.1		**24** SU	0035 4.0 / 0620 0.9	1242 4.0 / 1847 0.7
10 SU	0105 4.5 / 0655 0.6	1315 4.5 / 1932 0.1		**25** M	0059 3.9 / 0649 0.9	1308 3.9 / 1913 0.7
11 M	0147 4.4 / 0737 0.6	1356 4.5 / 2011 0.2		**26** TU	0124 3.9 / 0719 0.8	1335 4.0 / 1941 0.7
12 TU	0228 4.3 / 0819 0.6	1437 4.4 / 2049 0.4		**27** W	0153 4.0 / 0752 0.8	1407 4.0 / 2009 0.7
13 W	0310 4.1 / 0901 0.7	1520 4.2 / 2130 0.7		**28** TH	0227 3.9 / 0827 0.9	1442 3.9 / 2041 0.9
14 TH	0352 3.8 / 0949 0.9	1609 4.1 / ◐ 2217 1.0		**29** F	0305 3.8 / 0907 1.0	1523 3.7 / 2121 1.1
15 F	0441 3.5 / 1048 1.1	1712 3.5 / 2323 1.4		**30** SA	0351 3.6 / 1001 1.2	1617 3.5 / ◑ 2223 1.3

OCTOBER

Day	Time m	Time m		Day	Time m	Time m
1 SU	0450 3.3 / 1118 1.3	1731 3.3		**16** M	0023 1.7 / 0643 3.2	1331 1.1 / 1947 3.3
2 M	0001 1.5 / 0610 3.2	1254 1.3 / 1912 3.3		**17** TU	0150 1.6 / 0804 3.4	1440 0.9 / 2052 3.6
3 TU	0135 1.4 / 0746 3.3	1424 1.0 / 2041 3.6		**18** W	0252 1.4 / 0904 3.6	1531 0.7 / 2140 3.8
4 W	0246 1.2 / 0858 3.6	1528 0.7 / 2139 4.0		**19** TH	0338 1.2 / 0950 3.9	1610 0.6 / 2221 4.0
5 TH	0339 1.0 / 0950 4.0	1618 0.4 / 2226 4.2		**20** F	0416 1.0 / 1030 4.0	1645 0.6 / 2257 4.0
6 F	0424 0.8 / 1036 4.2	1702 0.2 / 2311 4.4		**21** SA	0450 1.0 / 1105 4.0	1715 0.6 / 2329 4.0
7 SA	0506 0.6 / 1120 4.4	1744 0.1 / ○ 2354 4.4		**22** SU	0521 0.9 / 1138 4.0	1744 0.7 / ● 2358 4.0
8 SU	0549 0.6 / 1204 4.4	1825 0.2		**23** M	0551 0.9 / 1208 3.9	1813 0.9
9 M	0037 4.4 / 0632 0.5	1248 4.5 / 1904 0.2		**24** TU	0024 3.9 / 0622 0.8	1239 3.9 / 1843 0.7
10 TU	0119 4.3 / 0715 0.5	1331 4.4 / 1942 0.4		**25** W	0054 4.0 / 0657 0.8	1311 3.9 / 1914 0.4
11 W	0200 4.2 / 0758 0.5	1414 4.3 / 2020 0.6		**26** TH	0126 4.0 / 0733 0.8	1346 4.0 / 1945 0.4
12 TH	0240 4.0 / 0843 0.6	1458 4.1 / 2100 0.9		**27** F	0202 3.9 / 0811 0.8	1425 3.9 / 2020 0.9
13 F	0321 3.8 / 0931 0.8	1548 3.8 / 2147 1.2		**28** SA	0241 3.8 / 0855 0.9	1510 3.7 / 2104 1.1
14 SA	0408 3.5 / 1034 1.0	1606 3.5 / ◐ 2252 1.5		**29** SU	0327 3.6 / 0950 1.0	1606 3.5 / ◑ 2205 1.3
15 SU	0513 3.3 / 1200 1.2	1819 3.3		**30** M	0427 3.4 / 1104 1.1	1719 3.4 / 2332 1.5
				31 TU	0545 3.3 / 1234 1.1	1850 3.4

NOVEMBER

Day	Time m	Time m		Day	Time m	Time m
1 W	0102 1.4 / 0712 3.4	1357 0.9 / 2010 3.7		**16** TH	0206 1.4 / 0813 3.5	1443 0.9 / 2055 3.7
2 TH	0212 1.2 / 0821 3.7	1500 0.6 / 2108 4.0		**17** F	0256 1.3 / 0904 3.7	1525 0.8 / 2138 3.8
3 F	0308 1.0 / 0916 4.0	1550 0.4 / 2157 4.2		**18** SA	0337 1.1 / 0947 3.8	1602 0.7 / 2216 3.9
4 SA	0355 0.8 / 1005 4.2	1635 0.3 / 2243 4.3		**19** SU	0413 1.0 / 1026 3.9	1636 0.7 / 2250 3.9
5 SU	0441 0.6 / 1052 4.3	1717 0.3 / ○ 2327 4.3		**20** M	0448 0.9 / 1103 3.9	1710 0.8 / ● 2323 3.9
6 M	0526 0.6 / 1138 4.3	1758 0.3		**21** TU	0523 0.9 / 1139 3.9	1745 0.8 / 2356 3.9
7 TU	0010 4.2 / 0612 0.5	1224 4.3 / 1838 0.5		**22** W	0601 0.8 / 1216 3.9	1821 0.8
8 W	0054 4.2 / 0658 0.5	1310 4.3 / 1918 0.6		**23** TH	0031 3.9 / 0641 0.8	1254 3.8 / 1856 0.8
9 TH	0135 4.1 / 0744 0.5	1356 4.2 / 1957 0.8		**24** F	0108 3.9 / 0722 0.7	1334 3.7 / 1933 0.9
10 F	0216 3.9 / 0831 0.6	1443 4.0 / 2037 1.0		**25** SA	0147 3.9 / 0806 0.7	1417 3.9 / 2012 1.0
11 SA	0257 3.8 / 0921 0.8	1532 3.8 / 2122 1.3		**26** SU	0229 3.8 / 0852 0.7	1505 3.8 / 2057 1.1
12 SU	0343 3.6 / 1020 0.9	1629 3.5 / ◑ 2220 1.5		**27** M	0316 3.7 / 0945 0.8	1600 3.7 / 2152 1.2
13 M	0440 3.4 / 1132 1.0	1740 3.3 / 2339 1.7		**28** TU	0413 3.5 / 1050 0.8	1706 3.5 / ◑ 2301 1.3
14 TU	0555 3.3 / 1246 1.0	1858 3.3		**29** W	0521 3.5 / 1205 0.8	1820 3.5
15 W	0100 1.6 / 0711 3.3	1351 1.0 / 2004 3.5		**30** TH	0019 1.3 / 0635 3.5	1320 0.7 / 1932 3.6

DECEMBER

Day	Time m	Time m		Day	Time m	Time m
1 F	0131 1.2 / 0743 3.7	1425 0.6 / 2034 3.8		**16** SA	0155 1.3 / 0809 3.5	1430 0.9 / 2047 3.5
2 SA	0233 1.0 / 0843 3.9	1520 0.5 / 2127 4.0		**17** SU	0247 1.2 / 0901 3.6	1517 0.9 / 2133 3.7
3 SU	0328 0.8 / 0937 4.0	1609 0.5 / 2217 4.0		**18** M	0333 1.1 / 0949 3.7	1601 0.9 / 2215 3.8
4 M	0420 0.7 / 1029 4.1	1654 0.5 / 2304 4.1		**19** TU	0417 1.0 / 1034 3.8	1643 0.8 / 2256 3.9
5 TU	0510 0.6 / 1120 4.2	1737 0.6 / 2350 4.0		**20** W	0501 0.8 / 1117 3.9	1724 0.8 / ● 2336 3.9
6 W	0600 0.5 / 1209 4.2	1819 0.7		**21** TH	0546 0.8 / 1200 3.9	1805 0.8
7 TH	0035 4.0 / 0648 0.5	1258 4.1 / 1859 0.8		**22** F	0017 3.9 / 0631 0.7	1243 4.0 / 1844 0.8
8 F	0118 3.9 / 0736 0.5	1344 4.0 / 1938 0.9		**23** SA	0058 3.9 / 0716 0.6	1327 4.0 / 1924 0.9
9 SA	0159 3.9 / 0822 0.6	1428 3.9 / 2017 1.1		**24** SU	0140 3.9 / 0801 0.5	1411 4.0 / 2004 0.9
10 SU	0238 3.8 / 0908 0.7	1512 3.8 / 2057 1.2		**25** M	0222 3.9 / 0846 0.5	1458 4.0 / 2047 0.9
11 M	0319 3.7 / 0955 0.8	1558 3.6 / 2142 1.4		**26** TU	0307 3.9 / 0933 0.5	1549 3.9 / 2135 1.0
12 TU	0405 3.5 / 1047 0.9	1649 3.4 / ◑ 2238 1.5		**27** W	0357 3.8 / 1026 0.6	1644 3.7 / ◑ 2230 1.1
13 W	0459 3.4 / 1144 1.0	1748 3.3 / 2346 1.5		**28** TH	0453 3.7 / 1126 0.7	1746 3.6 / 2334 1.1
14 TH	0603 3.4 / 1242 1.0	1854 3.3		**29** F	0558 3.6 / 1235 0.7	1853 3.5
15 F	0054 1.5 / 0709 3.4	1338 1.0 / 1955 3.4		**30** SA	0046 1.1 / 0707 3.6	1347 0.6 / 1959 3.6
				31 SU	0159 1.1 / 0815 3.7	1453 0.8 / 2101 3.6

Chart Datum: 2·16 metres below Ordnance Datum (Newlyn)

TIDES

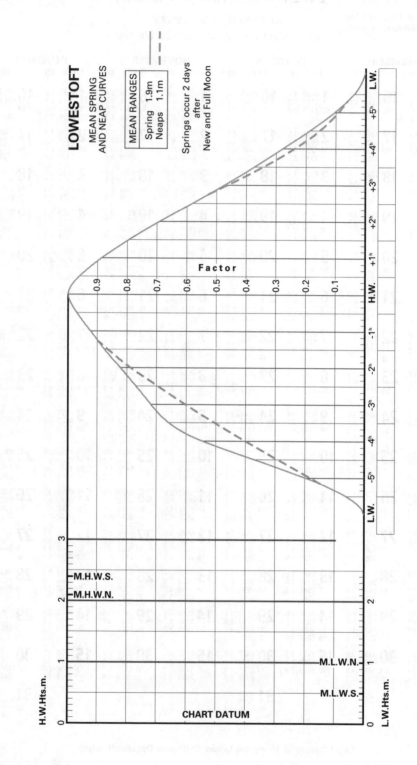

LOWESTOFT

MEAN SPRING
AND NEAP CURVES

MEAN RANGES

Spring 1.9m
Neaps 1.1m

Springs occur 2 days
after
New and Full Moon

TIME ZONE (UT)
For Summer Time add ONE hour in **non-shaded areas**

ENGLAND – LOWESTOFT

LAT 52°28'N   LONG 1°45'E

TIMES AND HEIGHTS OF HIGH AND LOW WATERS

2006

JANUARY

Day	Time	m	Time	m		Day	Time	m	Time	m
1 SU	0357 1006 1610 2215	0.6 2.5 0.8 2.5				**16** M	0447 1100 1635 2244	0.6 2.2 1.0 2.5		
2 M	0450 1058 1656 2300	0.5 2.5 0.8 2.6				**17** TU	0522 1133 1703 2318	0.6 2.2 1.0 2.5		
3 TU	0541 1149 1742 2346	0.4 2.4 0.9 2.6				**18** W	0556 1205 1733 2353	0.6 2.2 1.0 2.5		
4 W	0631 1240 1826	0.3 2.4 0.9				**19** TH	0628 1236 1806	0.6 2.1 1.0		
5 TH	0032 0721 1335 1910	2.6 0.4 2.2 1.0				**20** F	0030 0701 1311 1842	2.4 0.7 2.1 1.0		
6 F	0121 0813 1440 ◑1958	2.6 0.4 2.1 1.1				**21** SA	0109 0737 1349 1923	2.4 0.7 2.0 1.1		
7 SA	0212 0910 1558 2052	2.5 0.5 2.1 1.2				**22** SU	0150 0818 1436 ◑2010	2.3 0.8 2.0 1.2		
8 SU	0312 1013 1702 2203	2.4 0.7 2.1 1.2				**23** M	0237 0909 1545 2107	2.2 0.9 2.0 1.3		
9 M	0428 1119 1758 2328	2.3 0.8 2.1 1.2				**24** TU	0336 1018 1710 2227	2.2 1.0 2.0 1.3		
10 TU	0542 1220 1851	2.3 0.9 2.2				**25** W	0458 1134 1809 2358	2.1 1.0 2.1 1.2		
11 W	0043 0652 1318 1939	1.1 2.3 0.9 2.3				**26** TH	0612 1235 1900	2.2 0.9 2.2		
12 TH	0148 0800 1408 2022	0.9 2.3 1.0 2.3				**27** F	0103 0715 1329 1946	1.0 2.2 0.9 2.2		
13 F	0242 0856 1453 2100	0.8 2.3 1.0 2.4				**28** SA	0201 0816 1422 2031	0.8 2.3 0.8 2.3		
14 SA	0328 0942 1531 ○2136	0.7 2.3 1.0 2.4				**29** SU	0257 0911 1512 2116	0.6 2.4 0.8 2.5		
15 SU	0409 1023 1605 2211	0.6 2.3 1.0 2.5				**30** M	0351 1001 1601 2200	0.4 2.5 0.7 2.6		
						31 TU	0441 1048 1646 2245	0.2 2.5 0.7 2.7		

FEBRUARY

Day	Time	m	Time	m		Day	Time	m	Time	m
1 W	0528 1133 1728 2329	0.1 2.4 0.7 2.7				**16** TH	0527 1131 1712 2329	0.5 2.2 0.8 2.5		
2 TH	0614 1218 1807	0.1 2.3 0.8				**17** F	0556 1200 1742	0.5 2.2 0.8		
3 F	0013 0657 1304 1846	2.7 0.2 2.2 0.8				**18** SA	0003 0625 1233 1815	2.5 0.6 2.1 0.9		
4 SA	0058 0742 1353 1929	2.6 0.4 2.1 0.9				**19** SU	0038 0656 1308 1851	2.4 0.7 2.1 0.9		
5 SU	0147 0830 1454 ◑2018	2.5 0.6 2.0 1.0				**20** M	0115 0731 1349 1934	2.3 0.8 2.1 1.0		
6 M	0246 0930 1612 2124	2.4 0.8 2.0 1.1				**21** TU	0200 0816 1441 2028	2.2 0.9 2.0 1.1		
7 TU	0411 1048 1719 2307	2.2 1.0 2.0 1.1				**22** W	0258 0918 1556 2144	2.1 1.0 2.0 1.2		
8 W	0539 1204 1822	2.1 1.1 2.1				**23** TH	0429 1058 1723 2335	2.1 1.1 2.0 1.1		
9 TH	0036 0706 1312 1922	1.0 2.1 1.1 2.2				**24** F	0600 1215 1826	2.1 1.1 2.1		
10 F	0145 0812 1406 2009	0.9 2.2 1.1 2.2				**25** SA	0046 0713 1316 1920	0.9 2.2 1.0 2.2		
11 SA	0235 0858 1448 2047	0.7 2.2 1.1 2.3				**26** SU	0148 0814 1410 2009	0.7 2.3 1.0 2.3		
12 SU	0316 0935 1522 2120	0.6 2.2 1.0 2.4				**27** M	0245 0903 1500 2055	0.4 2.4 0.8 2.5		
13 M	0352 1007 1551 ○2151	0.5 2.2 0.9 2.4				**28** TU	0336 0947 1545 ●2140	0.2 2.5 0.7 2.6		
14 TU	0426 1036 1617 2223	0.5 2.2 0.9 2.5								
15 W	0457 1104 1643 2255	0.5 2.2 0.8 2.5								

MARCH

Day	Time	m	Time	m		Day	Time	m	Time	m
1 W	0423 1029 1627 2224	0.1 2.5 0.6 2.7				**16** TH	0424 1031 1619 2229	0.5 2.3 0.7 2.5		
2 TH	0507 1109 1706 2307	0.0 2.4 0.6 2.8				**17** F	0453 1058 1648 2302	0.5 2.3 0.7 2.5		
3 F	0548 1150 1744 2351	0.1 2.3 0.6 2.7				**18** SA	0521 1128 1719 2336	0.5 2.2 0.7 2.4		
4 SA	0628 1231 1823	0.3 2.2 0.6				**19** SU	0550 1200 1752	0.6 2.2 0.8		
5 SU	0036 0707 1313 1905	2.6 0.5 2.1 0.7				**20** M	0011 0620 1236 1826	2.3 0.7 2.2 0.8		
6 M	0126 0750 1400 ◑1954	2.4 0.8 2.1 0.9				**21** TU	0050 0655 1316 1909	2.3 0.8 2.1 0.9		
7 TU	0230 0842 1504 2101	2.2 1.0 2.0 1.0				**22** W	0137 0740 1406 ◑2005	2.2 1.0 2.1 1.0		
8 W	0407 1013 1627 2255	2.1 1.2 2.0 1.0				**23** TH	0241 0842 1511 2127	2.1 1.1 2.0 1.0		
9 TH	0539 1154 1741	2.1 1.3 2.0				**24** F	0424 1027 1634 2319	2.1 1.2 2.0 0.9		
10 F	0021 0706 1304 1852	0.9 2.1 1.2 2.1				**25** SA	0559 1157 1749	2.1 1.1 2.1		
11 SA	0124 0802 1353 1944	0.8 2.2 1.1 2.2				**26** SU	0029 0708 1259 1849	0.7 2.3 1.0 2.2		
12 SU	0211 0841 1430 2022	0.7 2.2 1.1 2.2				**27** M	0129 0802 1352 1941	0.5 2.3 0.9 2.3		
13 M	0249 0913 1500 2053	0.6 2.2 1.0 2.3				**28** TU	0225 0845 1439 2029	0.3 2.4 0.8 2.5		
14 TU	0323 0941 1527 ○2124	0.5 2.2 0.9 2.4				**29** W	0314 0925 1523 ●2115	0.2 2.4 0.6 2.6		
15 W	0355 1006 1552 2155	0.5 2.2 0.8 2.5				**30** TH	0358 1003 1604 2201	0.1 2.4 0.5 2.7		
						31 F	0439 1042 1643 2246	0.1 2.4 0.5 2.7		

APRIL

Day	Time	m	Time	m		Day	Time	m	Time	m
1 SA	0519 1121 1723 2331	0.2 2.3 0.5 2.6				**16** SU	0449 1059 1659 2312	0.6 2.3 0.7 2.4		
2 SU	0556 1200 1803	0.4 2.3 0.5				**17** M	0520 1133 1734 2350	0.6 2.3 0.7 2.3		
3 M	0018 0633 1240 1847	2.5 0.7 2.2 0.6				**18** TU	0554 1210 1813	0.7 2.3 0.7		
4 TU	0112 0713 1323 1938	2.3 0.9 2.1 0.8				**19** W	0034 0632 1253 1900	2.2 0.9 2.2 0.8		
5 W	0225 0800 1416 ◑2047	2.1 1.2 2.1 0.9				**20** TH	0128 0721 1344 2001	2.2 1.0 2.1 0.8		
6 TH	0400 0919 1530 2235	2.0 1.4 2.0 0.9				**21** F	0240 0825 1446 ◑2131	2.1 1.2 2.1 0.8		
7 F	0522 1128 1649 2348	2.1 1.4 2.0 0.8				**22** SA	0430 1000 1558 2301	2.1 1.3 2.1 0.7		
8 SA	0639 1233 1759	2.1 1.3 2.0				**23** SU	0550 1129 1712	2.2 1.2 2.1		
9 SU	0046 0733 1322 1858	0.7 2.2 1.2 2.1				**24** M	0006 0651 1231 1815	0.6 2.3 1.1 2.2		
10 M	0133 0811 1358 1941	0.7 2.2 1.1 2.2				**25** TU	0104 0739 1324 1911	0.4 2.3 0.9 2.4		
11 TU	0212 0843 1428 2017	0.6 2.2 1.0 2.3				**26** W	0158 0821 1412 2002	0.3 2.4 0.8 2.5		
12 W	0246 0909 1455 2051	0.5 2.2 0.9 2.4				**27** TH	0246 0859 1457 ●2051	0.2 2.4 0.6 2.6		
13 TH	0317 0933 1522 ○2125	0.5 2.3 0.8 2.4				**28** F	0330 0937 1541 2140	0.2 2.4 0.5 2.6		
14 F	0348 0959 1553 2200	0.5 2.3 0.7 2.4				**29** SA	0411 1016 1624 2228	0.3 2.4 0.5 2.6		
15 SA	0418 1027 1625 2235	0.5 2.3 0.7 2.4				**30** SU	0450 1055 1706 2316	0.4 2.4 0.5 2.5		

Chart Datum: 1·50 metres below Ordnance Datum (Newlyn)

ENGLAND – LOWESTOFT

2006

TIME ZONE (UT)
For Summer Time add ONE hour in **non-shaded areas**

LAT 52°28'N   LONG 1°45'E

TIMES AND HEIGHTS OF HIGH AND LOW WATERS

MAY

Day	Time m	Day	Time m
1 M	0528 0.6 / 1134 2.3 / 1749 0.5	**16** TU	0459 0.7 / 1112 2.4 / 1727 0.6 / 2339 2.3
2 TU	0008 2.3 / 0604 0.8 / 1214 2.3 / 1834 0.6	**17** W	0538 0.8 / 1152 2.3 / 1813 0.6
3 W	0105 2.2 / 0642 1.0 / 1255 2.2 / 1926 0.7	**18** TH	0030 2.2 / 0622 0.9 / 1238 2.3 / 1905 0.7
4 TH	0218 2.1 / 0725 1.2 / 1344 2.2 / 2033 0.8	**19** F	0129 2.2 / 0713 1.1 / 1330 2.2 / 2010 0.7
5 F	0338 2.0 / 0821 1.4 / 1442 2.1 / ☽ 2157 0.8	**20** SA	0242 2.1 / 0813 1.2 / 1427 2.2 / 2125 0.6
6 SA	0448 2.0 / 1028 1.4 / 1552 2.1 / 2305 0.8	**21** SU	0419 2.1 / 0927 1.2 / 1530 2.2 / 2237 0.5
7 SU	0555 2.1 / 1143 1.4 / 1700 2.1	**22** M	0528 2.2 / 1047 1.2 / 1639 2.2 / 2339 0.5
8 M	0000 0.7 / 0651 2.1 / 1234 1.3 / 1758 2.1	**23** TU	0624 2.2 / 1153 1.1 / 1745 2.3
9 TU	0047 0.7 / 0733 2.2 / 1313 1.2 / 1849 2.2	**24** W	0036 0.4 / 0712 2.3 / 1252 1.0 / 1844 2.4
10 W	0127 0.7 / 0806 2.2 / 1346 1.0 / 1934 2.2	**25** TH	0130 0.4 / 0755 2.3 / 1346 0.8 / 1940 2.5
11 TH	0203 0.6 / 0833 2.2 / 1418 0.9 / 2015 2.3	**26** F	0210 0.5 / 0835 2.4 / 1436 0.7 / 2033 2.5
12 F	0237 0.6 / 0859 2.3 / 1451 0.8 / 2054 2.3	**27** SA	0304 0.5 / 0914 2.4 / 1524 0.6 / 2126 2.5
13 SA	0311 0.6 / 0928 2.3 / 1527 0.7 / ○ 2133 2.3	**28** SU	0347 0.6 / 0954 2.4 / 1611 0.5 / 2218 2.4
14 SU	0346 0.6 / 1000 2.4 / 1605 0.7 / 2213 2.3	**29** M	0427 0.7 / 1034 2.4 / 1656 0.5 / 2310 2.3
15 M	0422 0.6 / 1034 2.4 / 1645 0.6 / 2255 2.3	**30** TU	0505 0.8 / 1113 2.4 / 1741 0.5
		31 W	0002 2.2 / 0540 1.0 / 1153 2.4 / 1825 0.6

JUNE

Day	Time m	Day	Time m
1 TH	0055 2.1 / 0616 1.1 / 1233 2.3 / 1913 0.6	**16** F	0028 2.3 / 0616 0.9 / 1227 2.4 / 1909 0.5
2 F	0154 2.1 / 0654 1.2 / 1316 2.3 / 2005 0.7	**17** SA	0124 2.2 / 0704 1.0 / 1315 2.4 / 2004 0.5
3 SA	0259 2.0 / 0737 1.3 / 1404 2.2 / ☽ 2105 0.7	**18** SU	0227 2.2 / 0755 1.1 / 1406 2.4 / ☽ 2104 0.5
4 SU	0402 2.0 / 0828 1.4 / 1457 2.2 / 2208 0.8	**19** M	0350 2.1 / 0852 1.2 / 1502 2.4 / 2207 0.5
5 M	0501 2.0 / 0933 1.4 / 1557 2.1 / 2306 0.8	**20** TU	0457 2.1 / 1000 1.2 / 1609 2.3 / 2309 0.5
6 TU	0555 2.0 / 1109 1.4 / 1702 2.1 / 2355 0.8	**21** W	0554 2.2 / 1115 1.1 / 1721 2.3
7 W	0642 2.1 / 1211 1.3 / 1801 2.1	**22** TH	0009 0.6 / 0644 2.2 / 1225 1.0 / 1826 2.3
8 TH	0039 0.8 / 0720 2.2 / 1258 1.1 / 1853 2.2	**23** F	0106 0.7 / 0731 2.3 / 1328 0.9 / 1928 2.3
9 F	0120 0.7 / 0754 2.2 / 1340 1.0 / 1942 2.2	**24** SA	0158 0.7 / 0815 2.3 / 1425 0.8 / 2029 2.3
10 SA	0200 0.7 / 0827 2.3 / 1423 0.9 / 2028 2.3	**25** SU	0246 0.8 / 0856 2.4 / 1517 0.6 / ● 2126 2.3
11 SU	0240 0.7 / 0901 2.3 / 1506 0.8 / ○ 2113 2.3	**26** M	0330 0.8 / 0937 2.4 / 1605 0.5 / 2217 2.3
12 M	0321 0.7 / 0937 2.4 / 1551 0.7 / 2159 2.3	**27** TU	0411 0.9 / 1017 2.5 / 1649 0.5 / 2305 2.3
13 TU	0403 0.7 / 1015 2.4 / 1638 0.6 / 2247 2.3	**28** W	0448 0.9 / 1056 2.5 / 1731 0.5 / 2349 2.2
14 W	0446 0.8 / 1057 2.4 / 1726 0.6 / 2337 2.3	**29** TH	0522 0.9 / 1133 2.4 / 1811 0.5
15 TH	0531 0.8 / 1140 2.4 / 1817 0.5	**30** F	0031 2.2 / 0552 1.0 / 1210 2.4 / 1850 0.6

JULY

Day	Time m	Day	Time m
1 SA	0113 2.1 / 0625 1.1 / 1248 2.4 / 1929 0.6	**16** SU	0104 2.3 / 0647 0.9 / 1255 2.6 / 1943 0.3
2 SU	0155 2.0 / 0701 1.1 / 1329 2.4 / 2009 0.7	**17** M	0156 2.2 / 0730 1.0 / 1343 2.6 / ☽ 2034 0.4
3 M	0243 2.0 / 0743 1.2 / 1414 2.3 / ☽ 2055 0.8	**18** TU	0301 2.1 / 0819 1.0 / 1436 2.5 / 2131 0.6
4 TU	0347 2.0 / 0832 1.3 / 1504 2.2 / 2151 0.9	**19** W	0418 2.1 / 0919 1.1 / 1545 2.4 / 2238 0.7
5 W	0449 2.0 / 0932 1.3 / 1606 2.2 / 2254 0.9	**20** TH	0520 2.1 / 1042 1.1 / 1707 2.3 / 2346 0.9
6 TH	0543 2.1 / 1055 1.3 / 1718 2.1 / 2352 0.9	**21** F	0617 2.2 / 1209 1.0 / 1823 2.2
7 F	0631 2.1 / 1213 1.2 / 1820 2.1	**22** SA	0050 0.9 / 0711 2.2 / 1323 0.9 / 1938 2.2
8 SA	0043 0.9 / 0716 2.2 / 1310 1.1 / 1917 2.2	**23** SU	0149 1.0 / 0800 2.3 / 1424 0.8 / 2041 2.3
9 SU	0130 0.9 / 0757 2.3 / 1401 0.9 / 2011 2.2	**24** M	0240 1.0 / 0843 2.4 / 1514 0.6 / 2130 2.3
10 M	0217 0.8 / 0837 2.3 / 1451 0.8 / 2103 2.3	**25** TU	0322 1.0 / 0923 2.4 / 1557 0.5 / ● 2212 2.3
11 TU	0304 0.8 / 0918 2.4 / 1542 0.6 / ○ 2153 2.4	**26** W	0359 1.0 / 1000 2.5 / 1636 0.5 / 2250 2.3
12 W	0351 0.8 / 0959 2.5 / 1632 0.5 / 2242 2.4	**27** TH	0431 1.0 / 1035 2.5 / 1713 0.5 / 2325 2.2
13 TH	0438 0.8 / 1042 2.6 / 1721 0.3 / 2329 2.4	**28** F	0500 0.9 / 1109 2.5 / 1746 0.5 / 2357 2.2
14 F	0522 0.8 / 1126 2.6 / 1809 0.3	**29** SA	0528 0.9 / 1143 2.5 / 1818 0.6
15 SA	0016 2.4 / 0605 0.8 / 1210 2.6 / 1855 0.3	**30** SU	0028 2.2 / 0557 1.0 / 1218 2.5 / 1849 0.6
		31 M	0100 2.1 / 0630 1.0 / 1255 2.4 / 1922 0.7

AUGUST

Day	Time m	Day	Time m
1 TU	0136 2.1 / 0708 1.1 / 1335 2.4 / 1958 0.8	**16** W	0212 2.1 / 0752 0.9 / 1414 2.5 / ☽ 2051 0.8
2 W	0218 2.1 / 0752 1.2 / 1420 2.3 / ☽ 2043 0.9	**17** TH	0321 2.1 / 0852 1.0 / 1533 2.3 / 2204 1.0
3 TH	0315 2.0 / 0845 1.3 / 1517 2.2 / 2144 1.0	**18** F	0439 2.1 / 1026 1.1 / 1708 2.2 / 2331 1.1
4 F	0439 2.0 / 0958 1.3 / 1637 2.1 / 2305 1.1	**19** SA	0545 2.2 / 1205 1.0 / 1836 2.2
5 SA	0544 2.1 / 1137 1.2 / 1756 2.1	**20** SU	0046 1.2 / 0649 2.2 / 1320 0.9 / 1952 2.3
6 SU	0013 1.1 / 0638 2.2 / 1246 1.1 / 1902 2.2	**21** M	0147 1.2 / 0745 2.3 / 1415 0.7 / 2041 2.3
7 M	0109 1.0 / 0728 2.3 / 1343 0.9 / 2004 2.3	**22** TU	0232 1.1 / 0827 2.4 / 1459 0.6 / 2119 2.3
8 TU	0200 0.9 / 0813 2.4 / 1437 0.7 / 2057 2.4	**23** W	0309 1.1 / 0903 2.5 / 1537 0.5 / ● 2153 2.3
9 W	0251 0.9 / 0857 2.5 / 1530 0.5 / ○ 2143 2.5	**24** TH	0340 1.0 / 0936 2.5 / 1612 0.5 / 2224 2.3
10 TH	0339 0.8 / 0939 2.6 / 1619 0.3 / 2227 2.5	**25** F	0408 0.9 / 1008 2.6 / 1644 0.5 / 2252 2.2
11 F	0423 0.7 / 1022 2.7 / 1705 0.2 / 2310 2.5	**26** SA	0434 0.9 / 1041 2.6 / 1714 0.5 / 2320 2.1
12 SA	0505 0.7 / 1105 2.8 / 1749 0.1 / 2352 2.4	**27** SU	0501 0.9 / 1114 2.6 / 1742 0.6 / 2348 2.1
13 SU	0545 0.7 / 1148 2.8 / 1831 0.2	**28** M	0529 0.9 / 1148 2.5 / 1809 0.6
14 M	0035 2.3 / 0624 0.8 / 1232 2.7 / 1913 0.4	**29** TU	0018 2.1 / 0600 0.9 / 1223 2.5 / 1838 0.7
15 TU	0121 2.3 / 0705 0.9 / 1319 2.6 / 1958 0.6	**30** W	0053 2.2 / 0636 1.0 / 1300 2.4 / 1911 0.8
		31 TH	0133 2.2 / 0718 1.1 / 1344 2.3 / ☽ 1952 0.7

Chart Datum: 1·50 metres below Ordnance Datum (Newlyn)

TIME ZONE (UT)
For Summer Time add ONE hour in **non-shaded areas**

ENGLAND – LOWESTOFT

LAT 52°28'N   LONG 1°45'E

TIMES AND HEIGHTS OF HIGH AND LOW WATERS

SEPTEMBER

Time	m		Time	m
1 0221 0809 F 1440 2047	2.1 1.2 2.2 1.1	**16**	0351 1022 SA 1709 2319	2.1 1.0 2.2 1.4
2 0326 0920 SA 1604 2215	2.1 1.3 2.2 1.2	**17**	0507 1152 SU 1837	2.2 0.9 2.2
3 0452 1111 SU 1743 2348	2.1 1.2 2.2 1.2	**18**	0034 0616 M 1259 1940	1.3 2.2 0.8 2.3
4 0600 1224 M 1856	2.2 1.0 2.3	**19**	0130 0717 TU 1350 2022	1.3 2.3 0.7 2.3
5 0050 0655 TU 1324 1954	1.1 2.3 0.8 2.4	**20**	0210 0759 W 1431 2056	1.2 2.4 0.6 2.3
6 0143 0744 W 1419 2042	1.0 2.4 0.6 2.5	**21**	0243 0833 TH 1506 2125	1.1 2.5 0.6 2.3
7 0233 0829 TH 1510 ○ 2124	0.9 2.6 0.4 2.5	**22**	0312 0905 F 1538 2152	1.0 2.5 0.6 2.4
8 0318 0913 F 1557 2204	0.8 2.7 0.2 2.6	**23**	0338 0937 SA 1608 2217	0.9 2.6 0.5 2.4
9 0401 0957 SA 1640 2244	0.7 2.8 0.1 2.5	**24**	0405 1010 SU 1636 2243	0.9 2.6 0.6 2.4
10 0442 1041 SU 1722 2324	0.7 2.8 0.1 2.5	**25**	0433 1044 M 1703 2312	0.8 2.6 0.6 2.4
11 0521 1125 M 1802	0.7 2.9 0.3	**26**	0503 1118 TU 1731 2343	0.9 2.5 0.7 2.4
12 0004 0601 TU 1211 1841	2.4 0.7 2.8 0.5	**27**	0535 1153 W 1800	0.9 2.4 0.8
13 0047 0643 W 1300 1923	2.3 0.8 2.6 0.8	**28**	0018 0610 TH 1232 1834	2.3 1.0 2.3 0.9
14 0133 0733 TH 1402 ◑ 2012	2.2 0.9 2.4 1.0	**29**	0058 0652 F 1317 1916	2.3 1.0 2.3 1.1
15 0231 0837 F 1536 2126	2.2 1.0 2.2 1.3	**30**	0145 0745 SA 1417 ◑ 2012	2.2 1.1 2.2 1.2

OCTOBER

Time	m		Time	m
1 0245 0900 SU 1549 2133	2.2 1.1 2.1 1.3	**16**	0422 1122 M 1812	2.2 0.9 2.2
2 0359 1049 M 1734 2320	2.2 1.1 2.2 1.3	**17**	0001 0530 TU 1222 1910	1.4 2.2 0.8 2.3
3 0517 1201 TU 1842	2.2 0.9 2.3	**18**	0055 0630 W 1311 1952	1.3 2.3 0.7 2.3
4 0025 0618 W 1259 1934	1.2 2.3 0.7 2.4	**19**	0136 0717 TH 1352 2025	1.2 2.4 0.7 2.3
5 0118 0710 TH 1353 2018	1.1 2.5 0.5 2.5	**20**	0209 0755 F 1428 2053	1.1 2.4 0.7 2.4
6 0206 0758 F 1443 2058	0.9 2.6 0.3 2.5	**21**	0238 0833 SA 1459 2118	1.0 2.5 0.6 2.4
7 0252 0845 SA 1529 ○ 2137	0.8 2.8 0.2 2.6	**22**	0306 0905 SU 1529 ● 2142	0.9 2.5 0.6 2.4
8 0335 0931 SU 1612 2216	0.7 2.9 0.2 2.6	**23**	0335 0940 M 1558 2210	0.9 2.5 0.7 2.4
9 0417 1017 M 1652 2255	0.6 2.9 0.3 2.5	**24**	0407 1016 TU 1628 2240	0.8 2.5 0.7 2.5
10 0459 1104 TU 1732 2336	0.6 2.8 0.5 2.5	**25**	0441 1052 W 1659 2314	0.8 2.4 0.8 2.4
11 0542 1153 W 1811	0.6 2.7 0.7	**26**	0516 1130 TH 1732 2350	0.9 2.4 0.9 2.4
12 0017 0628 TH 1248 1851	2.4 0.7 2.5 1.0	**27**	0554 1212 F 1809	0.9 2.3 1.0
13 0102 0720 F 1359 1938	2.3 0.8 2.3 1.2	**28**	0031 0639 SA 1303 1854	2.3 1.0 2.2 1.1
14 0156 0828 SA 1533 ◑ 2045	2.3 0.9 2.2 1.4	**29**	0120 0736 SU 1407 1951	2.3 1.0 2.2 1.3
15 0305 1005 SU 1655 2249	2.3 0.9 2.2 1.5	**30**	0218 0855 M 1543 2106	2.2 1.0 2.2 1.4
		31	0323 1025 TU 1717 2240	2.2 0.9 2.2 1.3

NOVEMBER

Time	m		Time	m
1 0434 1132 W 1817 2349	2.3 0.7 2.3 1.2	**16**	0005 0534 TH 1226 1914	1.4 2.3 0.8 2.2
2 0540 1229 TH 1908	2.4 0.6 2.4	**17**	0051 0626 F 1308 1950	1.3 2.3 0.8 2.3
3 0044 0636 F 1323 1950	1.1 2.5 0.5 2.5	**18**	0128 0712 SA 1345 2018	1.2 2.4 0.8 2.3
4 0136 0729 SA 1413 2030	1.0 2.6 0.4 2.5	**19**	0201 0755 SU 1419 2043	1.1 2.4 0.8 2.4
5 0224 0819 SU 1500 ○ 2110	0.8 2.7 0.4 2.5	**20**	0234 0835 M 1451 ● 2110	1.0 2.4 0.8 2.4
6 0311 0909 M 1543 2149	0.7 2.8 0.4 2.6	**21**	0309 0914 TU 1524 2140	0.9 2.4 0.8 2.5
7 0358 0959 TU 1625 2230	0.6 2.8 0.5 2.5	**22**	0346 0953 W 1559 2214	0.8 2.4 0.8 2.5
8 0443 1051 W 1706 2311	0.6 2.6 0.7 2.5	**23**	0425 1034 TH 1636 2250	0.8 2.4 0.8 2.5
9 0530 1144 TH 1745 2353	0.6 2.5 0.9 2.5	**24**	0506 1117 F 1714 2330	0.8 2.4 0.9 2.5
10 0618 1243 F 1825	0.7 2.3 1.1	**25**	0551 1204 SA 1756	0.7 2.3 1.0
11 0037 0711 SA 1352 1909	2.4 0.7 2.2 1.3	**26**	0013 0640 SU 1258 1843	2.4 0.8 2.3 1.1
12 0127 0814 SU 1512 ◑ 2001	2.3 0.8 2.2 1.5	**27**	0102 0738 M 1359 1936	2.4 0.8 2.2 1.2
13 0224 0930 M 1624 2126	2.3 0.9 2.1 1.5	**28**	0155 0845 TU 1520 ◑ 2039	2.4 0.8 2.2 1.3
14 0329 1040 TU 1730 2306	2.3 0.8 2.2 1.5	**29**	0252 0956 W 1648 2151	2.4 0.7 2.2 1.3
15 0435 1137 W 1828	2.2 0.8 2.2	**30**	0355 1101 TH 1747 2305	2.4 0.6 2.3 1.3

DECEMBER

Time	m		Time	m
1 0505 1159 F 1838	2.4 0.6 2.3	**16**	0539 1222 SA 1904	2.2 0.9 2.2
2 0009 0608 SA 1255 1923	1.1 2.5 0.6 2.4	**17**	0040 0634 SU 1303 1939	1.3 2.2 0.9 2.3
3 0108 0705 SU 1346 2005	1.0 2.6 0.6 2.4	**18**	0124 0725 M 1342 2011	1.1 2.3 0.9 2.3
4 0203 0801 M 1435 2046	0.9 2.6 0.6 2.4	**19**	0206 0812 TU 1420 2043	1.0 2.3 0.9 2.4
5 0256 0857 TU 1521 ○ 2128	0.7 2.6 0.7 2.5	**20**	0248 0857 W 1459 ● 2117	0.9 2.3 0.9 2.4
6 0347 0952 W 1605 2210	0.6 2.6 0.8 2.5	**21**	0332 0941 TH 1540 2155	0.8 2.3 0.8 2.5
7 0436 1046 TH 1646 2252	0.6 2.5 0.9 2.5	**22**	0417 1026 F 1622 2234	0.7 2.4 0.9 2.5
8 0523 1140 F 1725 2334	0.6 2.4 1.0 2.5	**23**	0504 1113 SA 1705 2316	0.6 2.4 0.9 2.5
9 0610 1233 SA 1803	0.6 2.3 1.1	**24**	0552 1200 SU 1749	0.6 2.3 0.9
10 0015 0657 SU 1329 1840	2.5 0.6 2.2 1.2	**25**	0000 0640 M 1249 1832	2.5 0.6 2.3 1.0
11 0059 0747 M 1430 1920	2.4 0.7 2.1 1.3	**26**	0045 0730 TU 1341 1919	2.5 0.6 2.2 1.1
12 0144 0841 TU 1536 ◑ 2005	2.4 0.8 2.1 1.4	**27**	0132 0823 W 1442 ◑ 2009	2.5 0.6 2.1 1.1
13 0234 0942 W 1637 2059	2.3 0.9 2.1 1.5	**28**	0223 0922 TH 1605 2107	2.5 0.6 2.1 1.2
14 0331 1042 TH 1733 2222	2.3 0.9 2.1 1.5	**29**	0321 1026 F 1713 2218	2.4 0.7 2.1 1.2
15 0436 1136 F 1822 2348	2.2 0.9 2.1 1.4	**30**	0436 1131 SA 1808 2339	2.4 0.7 2.2 1.1
		31	0549 1231 SU 1858	2.4 0.8 2.3

Chart Datum: 1·50 metres below Ordnance Datum (Newlyn)

TIDES

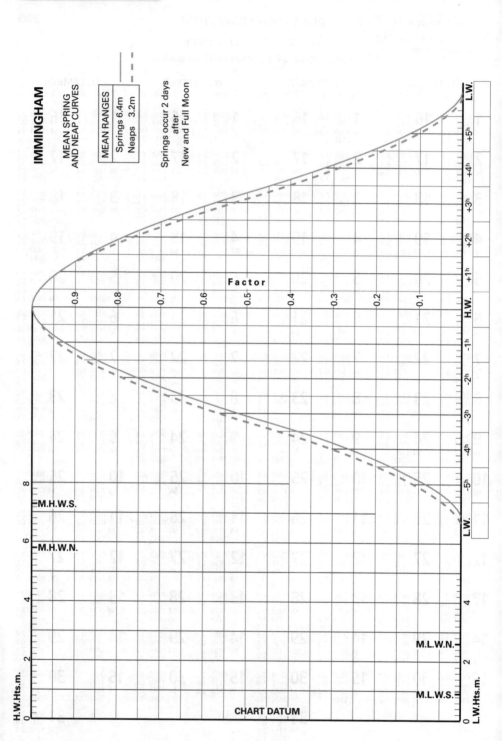

IMMINGHAM

MEAN SPRING
AND NEAP CURVES

MEAN RANGES	
Springs	6.4m
Neaps	3.2m

Springs occur 2 days
after
New and Full Moon

TIME ZONE (UT)
For Summer Time add ONE hour in **non-shaded areas**

ENGLAND – IMMINGHAM

LAT 53°38'N   LONG 0°11'W

TIMES AND HEIGHTS OF HIGH AND LOW WATERS

2006

JANUARY

Day	Time	m	Time	m		Day	Time	m	Time	m
1 SU	0029	1.2	0631	7.1		**16** M	0116	1.4	0713	6.6
	1247	1.4	1843	7.3			1315	1.8	1914	7.0
2 M	0120	1.0	0722	7.1		**17** TU	0152	1.4	0747	6.6
	1334	1.4	1927	7.4			1346	1.9	1946	6.9
3 TU	0210	0.9	0813	7.1		**18** W	0223	1.5	0818	6.5
	1420	1.5	2012	7.4			1415	1.9	2017	6.8
4 W	0258	0.9	0903	6.9		**19** TH	0253	1.6	0849	6.4
	1505	1.6	2059	7.3			1444	2.0	2048	6.7
5 TH	0347	1.0	0954	6.7		**20** F	0322	1.7	0920	6.3
	1552	1.8	2148	7.1			1515	2.1	2120 ◑	6.5
6 F	0436	1.2	1048	6.5		**21** SA	0354	1.9	0955	6.1
◑	1640	2.0	2241	6.9			1549	2.3	2156	6.3
7 SA	0528	1.5	1146	6.2		**22** SU	0430	2.1	1036	5.9
	1739	2.3	2342	6.6			1631	2.5	2240	6.1
8 SU	0625	1.9	1247	6.0		**23** M	0519	2.3	1128	5.7
	1839	2.5					1727	2.7	2338	5.9
9 M	0051	6.3	0729	2.1		**24** TU	0625	2.5	1240	5.6
	1351	5.9	1954	2.6			1842	2.8		
10 TU	0203	6.2	0836	2.3		**25** W	0056	5.8	0740	2.5
	1453	6.0	2107	2.4			1405	5.7	2003	2.7
11 W	0313	6.2	0937	2.2		**26** TH	0227	5.9	0853	2.4
	1551	6.1	2210	2.2			1514	6.0	2120	2.4
12 TH	0416	6.3	1030	2.2		**27** F	0341	6.2	0958	2.1
	1640	6.4	2304	1.9			1612	6.4	2228	1.9
13 F	0510	6.4	1117	2.0		**28** SA	0443	6.6	1055	1.8
	1723	6.6	2352	1.6			1702	6.8	2329	1.4
14 SA	0556	6.5	1200	1.9		**29** SU	0539	6.9	1148	1.5
○	1802	6.8				●	1748	7.1		
15 SU	0036	1.5	0637	6.6		**30** M	0023	1.0	0630	7.2
	1239	1.9	1839	6.9			1238	1.3	1833	7.4
						31 TU	0114	0.6	0718	7.3
							1325	1.1	1917	7.6

FEBRUARY

Day	Time	m	Time	m		Day	Time	m	Time	m
1 W	0201	0.4	0803	7.3		**16** TH	0202	1.3	0751	6.7
	1408	1.1	2000	7.7			1356	1.6	1953	7.0
2 TH	0245	0.4	0845	7.2		**17** F	0229	1.4	0817	6.6
	1450	1.1	2042	7.7			1421	1.7	2020	6.9
3 F	0326	0.6	0926	7.0		**18** SA	0253	1.5	0845	6.5
	1530	1.3	2125	7.4			1447	1.7	2048	6.8
4 SA	0406	1.0	1008	6.6		**19** SU	0316	1.7	0914	6.4
	1609	1.7	2211	7.0			1516	1.9	2120	6.6
5 SU	0447	1.5	1055	6.2		**20** M	0344	1.9	0948	6.1
	1653	2.1	2304 ◑	6.5			1551	2.1	2159	6.3
6 M	0534	2.1	1152	5.8		**21** TU	0422	2.2	1031	5.8
	1747	2.5					1640	2.5	2252	5.9
7 TU	0013	6.0	0635	2.6		**22** W	0524	2.6	1133	5.5
	1303	5.6	1906	2.8			1755	2.7		
8 W	0137	5.7	0800	2.8		**23** TH	0009	5.6	0655	2.8
	1418	5.6	2051	2.7			1316	5.4	1930	2.7
9 TH	0301	5.7	0919	2.8		**24** F	0211	5.6	0827	2.7
	1527	5.8	2202	2.4			1449	5.8	2103	2.4
10 F	0415	5.9	1018	2.5		**25** SA	0337	6.0	0943	2.3
	1624	6.2	2255	2.0			1554	6.3	2222	1.8
11 SA	0509	6.2	1105	2.2		**26** SU	0440	6.5	1045	1.8
	1709	6.5	2341	1.6			1646	6.8	2321	1.2
12 SU	0550	6.4	1147	2.0		**27** M	0533	7.0	1136	1.4
	1747	6.8					1733	7.3		
13 M	0021	1.4	0624	6.6		**28** TU	0012	0.7	0619	7.3
○	1224	1.8	1822	6.9		●	1224	1.1	1816	7.6
14 TU	0059	1.3	0654	6.6						
	1300	1.7	1854	7.0						
15 W	0133	1.3	0723	6.7						
	1330	1.6	1924	7.0						

MARCH

Day	Time	m	Time	m		Day	Time	m	Time	m
1 W	0059	0.3	0701	7.5		**16** TH	0104	1.2	0653	6.8
	1308	0.8	1858	7.8			1306	1.5	1856	7.0
2 TH	0142	0.2	0741	7.5		**17** F	0134	1.2	0719	6.8
	1349	0.7	1939	7.9			1332	1.5	1925	7.0
3 F	0222	0.3	0818	7.3		**18** SA	0200	1.3	0746	6.8
	1428	0.8	2020	7.8			1357	1.5	1953	6.9
4 SA	0258	0.6	0853	7.1		**19** SU	0223	1.4	0812	6.7
	1504	1.1	2101	7.4			1423	1.5	2022	6.8
5 SU	0333	1.1	0929	6.7		**20** M	0246	1.6	0841	6.5
	1539	1.5	2143	6.9			1452	1.7	2054	6.6
6 M	0407	1.7	1007	6.2		**21** TU	0314	1.8	0914	6.3
◑	1617	2.0	2233 ◑	6.3			1527	1.9	2135	6.3
7 TU	0446	2.3	1057	5.7		**22** W	0352	2.2	0957	6.0
	1706	2.5	2344	5.7		◑	1616	2.3	2229	5.9
8 W	0542	2.9	1217	5.4		**23** TH	0453	2.7	1058	5.6
	1824	2.9					1735	2.6	2357	5.5
9 TH	0121	5.4	0720	3.2		**24** F	0629	2.9	1241	5.5
	1347	5.4	2041	2.8			1916	2.6		
10 F	0251	5.5	0903	3.0		**25** SA	0211	5.6	0809	2.8
	1503	5.8	2148	2.3			1426	5.8	2055	2.1
11 SA	0405	5.8	1001	2.5		**26** SU	0329	6.1	0928	2.3
	1602	6.1	2237	1.9			1532	6.3	2208	1.5
12 SU	0454	6.2	1046	2.2		**27** M	0427	6.6	1027	1.8
	1647	6.4	2318	1.5			1624	6.9	2302	0.9
13 M	0529	6.4	1126	1.9		**28** TU	0515	7.1	1116	1.3
	1724	6.7	2356	1.3			1710	7.4	2350	0.5
14 TU	0600	6.6	1203	1.7		**29** W	0558	7.3	1202	0.9
○	1757	6.9				●	1753	7.7		
15 W	0031	1.2	0627	6.7		**30** TH	0034	0.2	0636	7.5
	1237	1.6	1827	6.9			1245	0.7	1835	7.8
						31 F	0115	0.2	0712	7.4
							1326	0.6	1917	7.8

APRIL

Day	Time	m	Time	m		Day	Time	m	Time	m
1 SA	0153	0.4	0747	7.3		**16** SU	0130	1.3	0717	6.8
	1404	0.8	1957	7.6			1335	1.4	1930	6.9
2 SU	0228	0.8	0821	7.0		**17** M	0157	1.4	0746	6.8
	1440	1.0	2038	7.2			1405	1.5	2004	6.8
3 M	0301	1.3	0855	6.7		**18** TU	0226	1.6	0818	6.6
	1515	1.5	2121	6.7			1439	1.5	2041	6.5
4 TU	0333	1.9	0931	6.2		**19** W	0259	1.9	0855	6.4
	1552	1.9	2212	6.0			1521	1.8	2128	6.2
5 W	0411	2.5	1016	5.8		**20** TH	0344	2.3	0941	6.1
	1641	2.4	2327 ◑	5.5			1617	2.1	2231	5.8
6 TH	0505	3.0	1135	5.4		**21** F	0448	2.7	1047	5.8
	1759	2.8				◑	1737	2.3		
7 F	0103	5.2	0634	3.3		**22** SA	0016	5.6	0617	2.9
	1315	5.3	2011	2.7			1226	5.7	1909	2.2
8 SA	0225	5.4	0831	3.2		**23** SU	0159	5.8	0748	2.7
	1430	5.6	2116	2.3			1357	6.0	2035	1.8
9 SU	0332	5.7	0931	2.7		**24** M	0308	6.2	0901	2.2
	1529	6.0	2203	1.9			1502	6.5	2140	1.3
10 M	0419	6.1	1016	2.3		**25** TU	0403	6.7	0959	1.7
	1615	6.3	2243	1.6			1556	6.9	2234	0.9
11 TU	0456	6.4	1055	1.9		**26** W	0449	7.0	1050	1.3
	1651	6.6	2320	1.4			1644	7.3	2321	0.6
12 W	0526	6.6	1132	1.7		**27** TH	0530	7.2	1136	1.0
	1724	6.7	2356	1.2		●	1729	7.5		
13 TH	0553	6.9	1205	1.5		**28** F	0005	0.5	0607	7.3
○	1755	6.8					1221	0.8	1813	7.6
14 F	0029	1.2	0620	6.8		**29** SA	0047	0.6	0644	7.3
	1237	1.5	1826	6.9			1303	0.8	1856	7.5
15 SA	0101	1.2	0648	6.8		**30** SU	0125	0.8	0719	7.1
	1306	1.4	1858	6.9			1343	0.9	1939	7.2

Chart Datum: 3·90 metres below Ordnance Datum (Newlyn)

TIME ZONE (UT)
For Summer Time add ONE hour in **non-shaded areas**

ENGLAND – IMMINGHAM 2006

LAT 53°38'N   LONG 0°11'W

TIMES AND HEIGHTS OF HIGH AND LOW WATERS

MAY

Day	Time	m	Day	Time	m
1 M	0201 / 0754 / 2023	1.2 / 6.9 / 6.9	**16** TU	0139 / 0729 / 1357 / 1957	1.5 / 6.8 / 1.4 / 6.7
2 TU	0235 / 0829 / 1459 / 2108	1.6 / 6.6 / 1.4 / 6.4	**17** W	0216 / 0807 / 1439 / 2043	1.6 / 6.7 / 1.5 / 6.5
3 W	0309 / 0906 / 1539 / 2159	2.1 / 6.3 / 1.9 / 5.9	**18** TH	0257 / 0849 / 1528 / 2137	1.9 / 6.6 / 1.6 / 6.2
4 TH	0348 / 0951 / 1629 / 2307	2.5 / 5.9 / 2.3 / 5.5	**19** F	0346 / 0941 / 1628 / 2246	2.2 / 6.3 / 1.8 / 6.0
5 F ○	0438 / 1058 / 1737	2.9 / 5.6 / 2.5	**20** SA ○	0449 / 1046 / 1739	2.4 / 6.1 / 1.8
6 SA	0028 / 0550 / 1227 / 1905	5.3 / 3.2 / 5.5 / 2.6	**21** SU	0013 / 0602 / 1207 / 1853	5.9 / 2.5 / 6.1 / 1.8
7 SU	0141 / 0722 / 1342 / 2020	5.4 / 3.1 / 5.6 / 2.3	**22** M	0130 / 0718 / 1324 / 2004	6.0 / 2.4 / 6.3 / 1.6
8 M	0242 / 0838 / 1442 / 2112	5.6 / 2.8 / 5.8 / 2.0	**23** TU	0235 / 0827 / 1429 / 2106	6.3 / 2.1 / 6.5 / 1.3
9 TU	0332 / 0931 / 1530 / 2157	5.9 / 2.5 / 6.1 / 1.8	**24** W	0331 / 0928 / 1527 / 2202	6.5 / 1.8 / 6.8 / 1.1
10 W	0412 / 1014 / 1609 / 2237	6.2 / 2.1 / 6.4 / 1.6	**25** TH	0419 / 1022 / 1619 / 2251	6.8 / 1.5 / 7.0 / 1.0
11 TH	0445 / 1053 / 1646 / 2316	6.4 / 1.9 / 6.5 / 1.4	**26** F	0502 / 1112 / 1709 / 2337	6.9 / 1.2 / 7.1 / 1.0
12 F	0516 / 1130 / 1722 / 2353	6.6 / 1.7 / 6.7 / 1.3	**27** SA ●	0542 / 1200 / 1757	7.0 / 1.1 / 7.1
13 SA ○	0548 / 1206 / 1759	6.8 / 1.5 / 6.8	**28** SU	0021 / 0620 / 1245 / 1843	1.1 / 7.0 / 1.1 / 6.9
14 SU	0029 / 0621 / 1242 / 1836	1.3 / 6.8 / 1.4 / 6.8	**29** M	0102 / 0658 / 1329 / 1929	1.3 / 6.9 / 1.1 / 6.8
15 M	0104 / 0655 / 1319 / 1916	1.4 / 6.9 / 1.4 / 6.8	**30** TU	0140 / 0736 / 1410 / 2013	1.5 / 6.8 / 1.3 / 6.6
			31 W	0216 / 0813 / 1450 / 2057	1.8 / 6.6 / 1.5 / 6.3

JUNE

Day	Time	m	Day	Time	m
1 TH	0252 / 0851 / 1530 / 2143	2.1 / 6.4 / 1.8 / 6.0	**16** F	0257 / 0849 / 1535 / 2142	1.7 / 6.9 / 1.2 / 6.5
2 F	0329 / 0933 / 1615 / 2234	2.4 / 6.2 / 2.0 / 5.7	**17** SA	0345 / 0939 / 1629 / 2242	1.9 / 6.8 / 1.3 / 6.3
3 SA ◑	0413 / 1023 / 1706 / 2332	2.7 / 5.9 / 2.2 / 5.5	**18** SU ◑	0439 / 1036 / 1726 / 2347	2.0 / 6.6 / 1.4 / 6.2
4 SU	0506 / 1125 / 1804	2.9 / 5.7 / 2.3	**19** M	0538 / 1140 / 1826	2.2 / 6.5 / 1.5
5 M	0034 / 0609 / 1233 / 1905	5.5 / 3.0 / 5.7 / 2.3	**20** TU	0052 / 0643 / 1249 / 1929	6.1 / 2.3 / 6.4 / 1.6
6 TU	0135 / 0717 / 1336 / 2005	5.6 / 2.9 / 5.7 / 2.2	**21** W	0155 / 0751 / 1356 / 2032	6.1 / 2.2 / 6.4 / 1.6
7 W	0231 / 0824 / 1432 / 2100	5.7 / 2.7 / 5.9 / 2.0	**22** TH	0255 / 0858 / 1501 / 2132	6.2 / 2.1 / 6.5 / 1.6
8 TH	0319 / 0921 / 1523 / 2150	6.0 / 2.4 / 6.1 / 1.8	**23** F	0350 / 0959 / 1601 / 2226	6.4 / 1.8 / 6.6 / 1.6
9 F	0402 / 1010 / 1609 / 2236	6.2 / 2.1 / 6.3 / 1.7	**24** SA	0438 / 1055 / 1657 / 2316	6.5 / 1.6 / 6.6 / 1.6
10 SA	0442 / 1055 / 1654 / 2320	6.5 / 1.8 / 6.5 / 1.5	**25** SU ●	0522 / 1147 / 1749	6.7 / 1.4 / 6.7
11 SU ○	0521 / 1140 / 1739	6.7 / 1.6 / 6.7	**26** M	0002 / 0604 / 1235 / 1837	1.6 / 6.8 / 1.3 / 6.7
12 M	0003 / 0600 / 1224 / 1823	1.5 / 6.8 / 1.4 / 6.8	**27** TU	0046 / 0644 / 1321 / 1922	1.7 / 6.8 / 1.3 / 6.6
13 TU	0045 / 0640 / 1310 / 1910	1.5 / 6.9 / 1.3 / 6.8	**28** W	0126 / 0722 / 1403 / 2003	1.8 / 6.8 / 1.3 / 6.5
14 W	0128 / 0720 / 1357 / 1958	1.5 / 7.0 / 1.2 / 6.8	**29** TH	0202 / 0759 / 1441 / 2041	1.9 / 6.8 / 1.4 / 6.4
15 TH	0211 / 0803 / 1445 / 2049	1.6 / 7.0 / 1.2 / 6.6	**30** F	0236 / 0835 / 1516 / 2117	2.0 / 6.6 / 1.6 / 6.2

JULY

Day	Time	m	Day	Time	m
1 SA	0309 / 0910 / 1551 / 2153	2.1 / 6.5 / 1.8 / 6.0	**16** SU	0333 / 0926 / 1613 / 2218	1.5 / 7.2 / 0.9 / 6.7
2 SU	0344 / 0948 / 1629 / 2233	2.3 / 6.3 / 1.9 / 5.9	**17** M ◑	0418 / 1015 / 1700 / 2310	1.7 / 7.0 / 1.2 / 6.4
3 M	0423 / 1032 / 1712 / 2321	2.5 / 6.1 / 2.1 / 5.7	**18** TU	0507 / 1110 / 1752	1.9 / 6.7 / 1.6
4 TU	0510 / 1124 / 1804	2.7 / 5.9 / 2.3	**19** W	0009 / 0604 / 1215 / 1851	6.1 / 2.2 / 6.4 / 2.0
5 W	0018 / 0608 / 1226 / 1902	5.6 / 2.8 / 5.7 / 2.4	**20** TH	0113 / 0715 / 1328 / 2000	5.9 / 2.4 / 6.1 / 2.2
6 TH	0124 / 0715 / 1335 / 2005	5.6 / 2.8 / 5.7 / 2.3	**21** F	0220 / 0835 / 1443 / 2110	5.9 / 2.4 / 6.0 / 2.3
7 F	0228 / 0824 / 1441 / 2106	5.8 / 2.6 / 5.9 / 2.2	**22** SA	0324 / 0947 / 1555 / 2211	6.0 / 2.2 / 6.1 / 2.2
8 SA	0325 / 0929 / 1541 / 2203	6.1 / 2.3 / 6.1 / 2.0	**23** SU	0421 / 1047 / 1658 / 2303	6.2 / 1.9 / 6.3 / 2.1
9 SU	0415 / 1028 / 1636 / 2255	6.3 / 2.0 / 6.4 / 1.8	**24** M	0509 / 1149 / 1749 / 2350	6.5 / 1.5 / 6.5 / 1.9
10 M ●	0501 / 1122 / 1728 / 2344	6.6 / 1.6 / 6.6 / 1.6	**25** TU	0551 / 1226 / 1833	6.7 / 1.3 / 6.6
11 TU ○	0545 / 1215 / 1818	6.9 / 1.3 / 6.8	**26** W	0033 / 0629 / 1310 / 1910	1.8 / 6.9 / 1.2 / 6.6
12 W	0032 / 0628 / 1306 / 1908	1.5 / 7.1 / 1.0 / 7.0	**27** TH	0112 / 0706 / 1348 / 1944	1.7 / 6.9 / 1.2 / 6.6
13 TH	0120 / 0712 / 1355 / 1956	1.4 / 7.2 / 0.8 / 7.0	**28** F	0146 / 0740 / 1422 / 2015	1.7 / 6.9 / 1.3 / 6.5
14 F	0205 / 0756 / 1442 / 2044	1.3 / 7.3 / 0.7 / 7.0	**29** SA	0217 / 0812 / 1452 / 2044	1.8 / 6.9 / 1.4 / 6.5
15 SA	0249 / 0840 / 1528 / 2130	1.4 / 7.3 / 0.7 / 6.9	**30** SU	0244 / 0843 / 1520 / 2113	1.9 / 6.7 / 1.6 / 6.3
			31 M	0312 / 0913 / 1549 / 2144	2.0 / 6.6 / 1.8 / 6.2

AUGUST

Day	Time	m	Day	Time	m
1 TU	0342 / 0947 / 1621 / 2221	2.2 / 6.3 / 2.0 / 6.0	**16** W ◑	0434 / 1040 / 1711 / 2323	1.9 / 6.7 / 1.9 / 6.0
2 W ◑	0419 / 1027 / 1702 / 2307	2.4 / 6.1 / 2.3 / 5.7	**17** TH	0526 / 1146 / 1809	2.3 / 6.1 / 2.5
3 TH	0508 / 1120 / 1801	2.7 / 5.8 / 2.5	**18** F	0033 / 0642 / 1310 / 1933	5.7 / 2.7 / 5.8 / 2.8
4 F	0015 / 0617 / 1238 / 1915	5.5 / 2.8 / 5.6 / 2.6	**19** SA	0151 / 0827 / 1437 / 2058	5.6 / 2.7 / 5.7 / 2.8
5 SA	0142 / 0739 / 1410 / 2031	5.6 / 2.8 / 5.7 / 2.6	**20** SU	0305 / 0944 / 1559 / 2202	5.8 / 2.3 / 5.9 / 2.6
6 SU	0255 / 0859 / 1525 / 2139	5.8 / 2.5 / 6.0 / 2.3	**21** M	0407 / 1040 / 1658 / 2252	6.2 / 1.9 / 6.2 / 2.2
7 M	0354 / 1012 / 1627 / 2239	6.2 / 2.1 / 6.4 / 2.0	**22** TU	0454 / 1127 / 1741 / 2335	6.5 / 1.5 / 6.5 / 2.0
8 TU	0444 / 1113 / 1722 / 2331	6.6 / 1.5 / 6.7 / 1.6	**23** W ●	0534 / 1209 / 1816	6.8 / 1.3 / 6.6
9 W ○	0530 / 1207 / 1812	7.0 / 1.1 / 7.0	**24** TH	0014 / 0609 / 1248 / 1846	1.7 / 7.0 / 1.2 / 6.7
10 TH	0020 / 0614 / 1257 / 1858	1.4 / 7.3 / 0.7 / 7.2	**25** F	0051 / 0642 / 1323 / 1915	1.6 / 7.1 / 1.2 / 6.7
11 F	0107 / 0657 / 1343 / 1942	1.1 / 7.6 / 0.4 / 7.3	**26** SA	0123 / 0714 / 1354 / 1942	1.6 / 7.1 / 1.2 / 6.7
12 SA	0150 / 0739 / 1426 / 2024	1.0 / 7.7 / 0.4 / 7.3	**27** SU	0151 / 0743 / 1421 / 2008	1.6 / 7.0 / 1.2 / 6.7
13 SU	0231 / 0821 / 1507 / 2104	1.0 / 7.7 / 0.5 / 7.1	**28** M	0215 / 0811 / 1445 / 2034	1.7 / 6.9 / 1.5 / 6.6
14 M	0311 / 0904 / 1546 / 2145	1.2 / 7.5 / 0.8 / 6.8	**29** TU	0239 / 0839 / 1508 / 2101	1.8 / 6.7 / 1.7 / 6.4
15 TU	0351 / 0949 / 1626 / 2229	1.5 / 7.2 / 1.3 / 6.4	**30** W	0306 / 0908 / 1532 / 2132	2.0 / 6.5 / 2.0 / 6.2
			31 TH ◑	0338 / 0944 / 1606 / 2212	2.2 / 6.2 / 2.3 / 5.9

Chart Datum: 3·90 metres below Ordnance Datum (Newlyn)

TIME ZONE (UT)
For Summer Time add ONE hour in **non-shaded areas**

LAT 53°38'N LONG 0°11'W

TIMES AND HEIGHTS OF HIGH AND LOW WATERS

SEPTEMBER

	Time	m		Time	m
1 F	0422 / 1033 / 1701 / 2309	2.5 / 5.8 / 2.7 / 5.6	**16** SA	0618 / 1300 / 1908	2.9 / 5.5 / 3.3
2 SA	0533 / 1151 / 1830	2.9 / 5.5 / 2.9	**17** SU	0125 / 0822 / 1430 / 2045	5.5 / 2.7 / 5.6 / 3.1
3 SU	0057 / 0707 / 1355 / 2004	5.4 / 2.9 / 5.6 / 2.9	**18** M	0243 / 0930 / 1548 / 2144	5.8 / 2.3 / 5.9 / 2.7
4 M	0230 / 0842 / 1517 / 2123	5.7 / 2.5 / 6.0 / 2.5	**19** TU	0344 / 1020 / 1639 / 2230	6.2 / 1.8 / 6.3 / 2.3
5 TU	0333 / 1003 / 1618 / 2224	6.2 / 1.9 / 6.5 / 2.0	**20** W	0430 / 1102 / 1715 / 2310	6.6 / 1.5 / 6.6 / 1.9
6 W	0424 / 1100 / 1710 / 2315	6.8 / 1.3 / 6.9 / 1.6	**21** TH	0508 / 1140 / 1746 / 2348	6.9 / 1.3 / 6.7 / 1.7
7 TH ○	0509 / 1150 / 1755	7.2 / 0.8 / 7.3	**22** F ●	0542 / 1216 / 1814	7.0 / 1.2 / 6.8
8 F	0001 / 0552 / 1236 / 1837	1.2 / 7.6 / 0.4 / 7.4	**23** SA	0022 / 0613 / 1249 / 1840	1.6 / 7.1 / 1.2 / 6.9
9 SA	0046 / 0634 / 1319 / 1917	0.9 / 7.9 / 0.3 / 7.5	**24** SU	0054 / 0643 / 1320 / 1906	1.5 / 7.2 / 1.3 / 6.9
10 SU	0127 / 0715 / 1400 / 1954	0.8 / 8.0 / 0.3 / 7.4	**25** M	0121 / 0712 / 1346 / 1932	1.6 / 7.0 / 1.4 / 6.8
11 M	0207 / 0757 / 1438 / 2031	0.8 / 7.9 / 0.6 / 7.2	**26** TU	0146 / 0740 / 1410 / 1958	1.6 / 6.9 / 1.6 / 6.8
12 TU	0246 / 0839 / 1514 / 2108	1.1 / 7.6 / 1.0 / 6.9	**27** W	0210 / 0808 / 1432 / 2025	1.7 / 6.8 / 1.8 / 6.6
13 W	0323 / 0923 / 1549 / 2148	1.4 / 7.1 / 1.6 / 6.4	**28** TH	0238 / 0839 / 1457 / 2056	1.9 / 6.5 / 2.0 / 6.4
14 TH ◑	0403 / 1014 / 1629 / 2238	1.9 / 6.5 / 2.3 / 5.9	**29** F	0311 / 0916 / 1532 / 2135	2.1 / 6.2 / 2.4 / 6.0
15 F	0453 / 1125 / 1725 / 2355	2.5 / 5.8 / 2.9 / 5.6	**30** SA ◐	0356 / 1007 / 1626 / 2231	2.5 / 5.8 / 2.8 / 5.7

OCTOBER

	Time	m		Time	m
1 SU	0510 / 1135 / 1756	2.8 / 5.5 / 3.1	**16** M	0053 / 0753 / 1403 / 2010	5.6 / 2.7 / 5.5 / 3.2
2 M	0013 / 0648 / 1345 / 1939	5.5 / 2.8 / 5.6 / 3.0	**17** TU	0209 / 0857 / 1511 / 2111	5.8 / 2.3 / 5.9 / 2.8
3 TU	0201 / 0827 / 1501 / 2101	5.8 / 2.4 / 6.1 / 2.6	**18** W	0309 / 0945 / 1601 / 2158	6.2 / 1.9 / 6.2 / 2.4
4 W	0305 / 0941 / 1559 / 2200	6.3 / 1.7 / 6.6 / 2.0	**19** TH	0357 / 1026 / 1638 / 2238	6.5 / 1.6 / 6.5 / 2.0
5 TH	0357 / 1036 / 1648 / 2250	6.9 / 1.1 / 7.0 / 1.5	**20** F	0435 / 1103 / 1710 / 2315	6.8 / 1.4 / 6.7 / 1.8
6 F	0443 / 1123 / 1730 / 2335	7.4 / 0.7 / 7.4 / 1.1	**21** SA	0509 / 1138 / 1738 / 2349	6.9 / 1.3 / 6.8 / 1.6
7 SA ○	0526 / 1207 / 1809	7.7 / 0.4 / 7.5	**22** SU ●	0540 / 1211 / 1805	7.0 / 1.3 / 6.9
8 SU	0019 / 0608 / 1250 / 1846	0.9 / 7.9 / 0.4 / 7.5	**23** M	0021 / 0611 / 1243 / 1833	1.6 / 7.0 / 1.4 / 7.0
9 M	0102 / 0651 / 1330 / 1923	0.8 / 8.0 / 0.5 / 7.4	**24** TU	0051 / 0643 / 1312 / 1901	1.6 / 7.0 / 1.5 / 6.9
10 TU	0142 / 0733 / 1407 / 1959	0.8 / 7.8 / 0.9 / 7.2	**25** W	0119 / 0715 / 1339 / 1930	1.6 / 6.9 / 1.6 / 6.9
11 W	0221 / 0817 / 1442 / 2035	1.1 / 7.4 / 1.4 / 6.9	**26** TH	0148 / 0747 / 1406 / 2000	1.7 / 6.7 / 1.8 / 6.7
12 TH	0259 / 0903 / 1517 / 2114	1.5 / 6.9 / 1.9 / 6.5	**27** F	0220 / 0823 / 1437 / 2034	1.8 / 6.5 / 2.1 / 6.5
13 F	0340 / 0956 / 1555 / 2202	2.0 / 6.2 / 2.5 / 6.0	**28** SA	0259 / 0906 / 1517 / 2116	2.0 / 6.2 / 2.4 / 6.2
14 SA	0432 / 1112 / 1649 / 2318	2.5 / 5.7 / 3.1 / 5.6	**29** SU ◐	0350 / 1004 / 1614 / 2215	2.3 / 5.9 / 2.8 / 5.9
15 SU	0559 / 1243 / 1824	2.8 / 5.4 / 3.4	**30** M	0503 / 1137 / 1735 / 2343	2.5 / 5.6 / 3.0 / 5.8
			31 TU	0632 / 1321 / 1908	2.4 / 5.8 / 2.9

NOVEMBER

	Time	m		Time	m
1 W	0120 / 0758 / 1433 / 2025	6.0 / 2.1 / 6.2 / 2.5	**16** TH	0221 / 0855 / 1511 / 2112	6.0 / 2.2 / 6.0 / 2.7
2 TH	0229 / 0907 / 1530 / 2127	6.5 / 1.6 / 6.6 / 2.0	**17** F	0312 / 0939 / 1554 / 2157	6.3 / 1.9 / 6.3 / 2.3
3 F	0324 / 1002 / 1618 / 2219	6.9 / 1.2 / 7.0 / 1.6	**18** SA	0355 / 1019 / 1630 / 2236	6.5 / 1.7 / 6.5 / 2.0
4 SA	0414 / 1051 / 1701 / 2307	7.3 / 0.9 / 7.2 / 1.2	**19** SU	0432 / 1057 / 1702 / 2313	6.6 / 1.6 / 6.7 / 1.8
5 SU ○	0500 / 1136 / 1740 / 2353	7.6 / 0.7 / 7.4 / 1.0	**20** M ●	0508 / 1133 / 1733 / 2349	6.8 / 1.5 / 6.9 / 1.7
6 M	0546 / 1219 / 1818	7.7 / 0.8 / 7.4	**21** TU	0544 / 1209 / 1806	6.8 / 1.5 / 6.9
7 TU	0038 / 0630 / 1301 / 1856	0.9 / 7.6 / 0.9 / 7.3	**22** W	0023 / 0620 / 1243 / 1838	1.6 / 6.9 / 1.6 / 7.0
8 W	0121 / 0716 / 1339 / 1934	1.0 / 7.4 / 1.2 / 7.2	**23** TH	0059 / 0658 / 1316 / 1912	1.6 / 6.8 / 1.7 / 6.9
9 TH	0203 / 0802 / 1416 / 2012	1.2 / 7.1 / 1.7 / 6.9	**24** F	0135 / 0738 / 1351 / 1946	1.6 / 6.7 / 1.8 / 6.9
10 F	0244 / 0850 / 1452 / 2052	1.5 / 6.6 / 2.1 / 6.6	**25** SA	0215 / 0821 / 1429 / 2025	1.7 / 6.6 / 2.0 / 6.7
11 SA	0327 / 0944 / 1531 / 2138	1.9 / 6.2 / 2.6 / 6.2	**26** SU	0259 / 0909 / 1513 / 2110	1.8 / 6.3 / 2.3 / 6.5
12 SU ◑	0418 / 1050 / 1620 / 2240	2.3 / 5.7 / 3.0 / 5.9	**27** M	0352 / 1008 / 1608 / 2207	1.9 / 6.1 / 2.5 / 6.4
13 M	0526 / 1206 / 1728	2.6 / 5.5 / 3.3	**28** TU ◐	0456 / 1123 / 1714 / 2317	2.0 / 5.9 / 2.7 / 6.2
14 TU	0003 / 0652 / 1316 / 1857	5.7 / 2.6 / 5.5 / 3.3	**29** W	0608 / 1243 / 1830	2.2 / 6.0 / 2.7
15 W	0118 / 0802 / 1418 / 2016	5.8 / 2.4 / 5.7 / 3.0	**30** TH	0036 / 0720 / 1353 / 1943	6.3 / 1.9 / 6.1 / 2.5

DECEMBER

	Time	m		Time	m
1 F	0148 / 0827 / 1453 / 2050	6.5 / 1.7 / 6.4 / 2.2	**16** SA	0212 / 0838 / 1500 / 2059	5.9 / 2.3 / 5.9 / 2.7
2 SA	0250 / 0927 / 1545 / 2149	6.8 / 1.5 / 6.7 / 1.8	**17** SU	0307 / 0930 / 1546 / 2152	6.1 / 2.1 / 6.2 / 2.4
3 SU	0347 / 1020 / 1632 / 2243	7.0 / 1.3 / 6.9 / 1.5	**18** M	0356 / 1016 / 1627 / 2238	6.3 / 1.9 / 6.5 / 2.1
4 M	0440 / 1109 / 1715 / 2333	7.2 / 1.2 / 7.1 / 1.3	**19** TU	0440 / 1059 / 1706 / 2321	6.5 / 1.8 / 6.7 / 1.8
5 TU ○	0530 / 1154 / 1757	7.2 / 1.3 / 7.1	**20** W ●	0524 / 1141 / 1744	6.7 / 1.7 / 6.9
6 W	0021 / 0619 / 1238 / 1837	1.2 / 7.2 / 1.4 / 7.1	**21** TH	0004 / 0606 / 1222 / 1822	1.6 / 6.8 / 1.7 / 7.0
7 TH	0108 / 0707 / 1320 / 1917	1.2 / 7.1 / 1.6 / 7.1	**22** F	0048 / 0650 / 1302 / 1900	1.5 / 6.8 / 1.7 / 7.1
8 F	0153 / 0754 / 1359 / 1957	1.3 / 6.8 / 1.8 / 7.0	**23** SA	0132 / 0735 / 1343 / 1939	1.4 / 6.8 / 1.7 / 7.1
9 SA	0236 / 0841 / 1436 / 2036	1.5 / 6.6 / 2.1 / 6.8	**24** SU	0216 / 0820 / 1425 / 2020	1.3 / 6.8 / 1.8 / 7.1
10 SU	0317 / 0927 / 1512 / 2117	1.7 / 6.3 / 2.4 / 6.5	**25** M	0302 / 0907 / 1509 / 2105	1.3 / 6.6 / 1.9 / 7.0
11 M	0359 / 1015 / 1552 / 2203	2.0 / 6.0 / 2.6 / 6.2	**26** TU	0349 / 0958 / 1556 / 2154	1.4 / 6.5 / 2.0 / 6.9
12 TU ◑	0446 / 1108 / 1639 / 2258	2.2 / 5.7 / 2.9 / 6.0	**27** W ◐	0440 / 1054 / 1649 / 2250	1.5 / 6.3 / 2.2 / 6.7
13 W	0539 / 1207 / 1737	2.4 / 5.6 / 3.0	**28** TH	0536 / 1158 / 1750 / 2355	1.7 / 6.1 / 2.4 / 6.5
14 TH	0003 / 0638 / 1308 / 1844	5.8 / 2.5 / 5.6 / 3.1	**29** F	0639 / 1305 / 1900	1.9 / 6.0 / 2.5
15 F	0110 / 0740 / 1406 / 1955	5.8 / 2.4 / 5.7 / 2.9	**30** SA	0107 / 0747 / 1411 / 2014	6.4 / 2.0 / 6.1 / 2.4
			31 SU	0220 / 0854 / 1513 / 2125	6.4 / 2.0 / 6.2 / 2.2

Chart Datum: 3·90 metres below Ordnance Datum (Newlyn)

TIDES

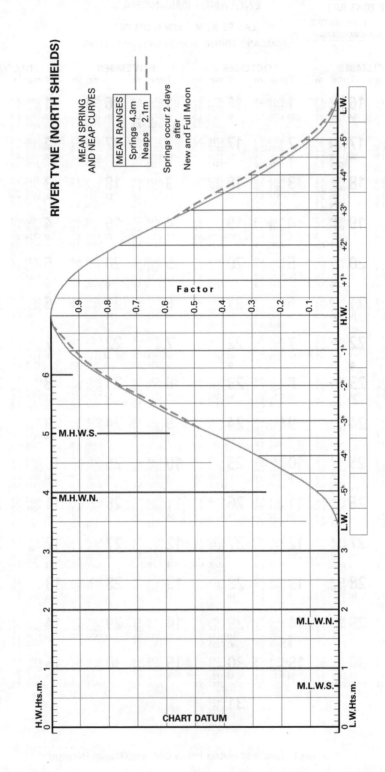

RIVER TYNE (NORTH SHIELDS)

MEAN SPRING AND NEAP CURVES

MEAN RANGES
Springs 4.3m
Neaps 2.1m

Springs occur 2 days after New and Full Moon

ENGLAND – NORTH SHIELDS

LAT 55°01′N   LONG 1°26′W

TIMES AND HEIGHTS OF HIGH AND LOW WATERS

TIME ZONE (UT)
For Summer Time add ONE hour in **non-shaded areas**

JANUARY

Time m	Time m
1 SU 0356 5.0 / 1012 1.1 / 1607 5.1 / 2243 0.7	**16** M 0438 4.7 / 1038 1.4 / 1641 4.9 / 2312 1.0
2 M 0446 5.1 / 1058 1.1 / 1652 5.2 / 2332 0.6	**17** TU 0512 4.6 / 1109 1.4 / 1714 4.9 / 2345 1.0
3 TU 0536 5.0 / 1144 1.1 / 1738 5.2	**18** W 0546 4.6 / 1140 1.4 / 1747 4.8
4 W 0021 0.6 / 0627 4.9 / 1231 1.3 / 1827 5.1	**19** TH 0017 1.1 / 0620 4.5 / 1211 1.5 / 1821 4.7
5 TH 0112 0.7 / 0720 4.7 / 1319 1.4 / 1919 5.0	**20** F 0052 1.2 / 0656 4.3 / 1245 1.6 / 1857 4.6
6 F 0204 0.9 / 0815 4.5 / 1411 1.6 / ● 2016 4.8	**21** SA 0128 1.3 / 0735 4.2 / 1321 1.8 / 1937 4.4
7 SA 0300 1.1 / 0915 4.3 / 1510 1.8 / 2119 4.6	**22** SU 0209 1.5 / 0819 4.1 / 1405 1.9 / ○ 2024 4.3
8 SU 0403 1.4 / 1019 4.2 / 1620 1.9 / 2229 4.4	**23** M 0258 1.7 / 0912 4.0 / 1503 2.1 / 2123 4.1
9 M 0511 1.5 / 1125 4.2 / 1736 1.9 / 2342 4.4	**24** TU 0400 1.8 / 1016 3.9 / 1620 2.2 / 2236 4.0
10 TU 0620 1.6 / 1229 4.2 / 1848 1.8	**25** W 0516 1.9 / 1129 4.0 / 1749 2.1 / 2357 4.1
11 W 0051 4.4 / 0720 1.7 / 1326 4.4 / 1949 1.6	**26** TH 0632 1.8 / 1238 4.2 / 1905 1.8
12 TH 0151 4.4 / 0811 1.6 / 1415 4.5 / 2040 1.4	**27** F 0109 4.3 / 0735 1.6 / 1336 4.4 / 2005 1.4
13 F 0241 4.5 / 0854 1.6 / 1457 4.7 / 2124 1.2	**28** SA 0210 4.6 / 0829 1.3 / 1426 4.7 / 2058 1.0
14 SA 0325 4.6 / 0932 1.5 / 1534 4.8 / ○ 2203 1.1	**29** SU 0302 4.9 / 0918 1.1 / ● 2147 0.6
15 SU 0403 4.6 / 1046 1.4 / 1609 4.9 / 2239 1.0	**30** M 0350 5.1 / 1003 0.9 / 1555 5.2 / 2235 0.3
	31 TU 0436 5.2 / 1047 0.8 / 1638 5.4 / 2321 0.2

FEBRUARY

Time m	Time m
1 W 0522 5.2 / 1129 0.8 / 1722 5.4	**16** TH 0518 4.7 / 1116 1.1 / 1721 4.9 / 2348 0.9
2 TH 0005 0.2 / 0607 5.0 / 1210 0.9 / 1807 5.4	**17** F 0548 4.6 / 1144 1.2 / 1751 4.8
3 F 0050 0.4 / 0652 4.8 / 1252 1.1 / 1854 5.2	**18** SA 0018 1.0 / 0618 4.5 / 1214 1.3 / 1822 4.7
4 SA 0134 0.7 / 0740 4.6 / 1336 1.3 / 1945 4.9	**19** SU 0049 1.2 / 0651 4.4 / 1245 1.5 / 1857 4.5
5 SU 0221 1.1 / 0832 4.3 / 1428 1.6 / ● 2044 4.5	**20** M 0123 1.4 / 0729 4.2 / 1323 1.7 / 1940 4.3
6 M 0317 1.5 / 0933 4.1 / 1536 1.9 / 2155 4.2	**21** TU 0205 1.6 / 0817 4.0 / 1413 1.9 / 2037 4.1
7 TU 0429 1.9 / 1045 3.9 / 1706 2.0 / 2320 4.0	**22** W 0305 1.9 / 0921 3.9 / 1530 2.1 / 2158 3.9
8 W 0555 2.0 / 1204 4.0 / 1837 1.9	**23** TH 0434 2.1 / 1046 3.8 / 1716 2.0 / 2337 3.9
9 TH 0044 4.0 / 0710 2.0 / 1313 4.2 / 1945 1.6	**24** F 0612 1.9 / 1212 4.0 / 1849 1.7
10 F 0150 4.2 / 0808 1.8 / 1406 4.4 / 2035 1.4	**25** SA 0100 4.2 / 0723 1.7 / 1319 4.3 / 1953 1.4
11 SA 0238 4.4 / 0847 1.7 / 1448 4.6 / 2115 1.2	**26** SU 0201 4.6 / 0817 1.3 / 1410 4.7 / 2046 0.7
12 SU 0316 4.5 / 0921 1.5 / 1523 4.7 / 2149 1.0	**27** M 0250 4.9 / 0904 1.0 / 1455 5.1 / 2133 0.3
13 M 0349 4.6 / 0952 1.3 / 1556 4.8 / ○ 2221 0.9	**28** TU 0335 5.2 / 0947 0.8 / 1537 5.4 / ● 2218 0.1
14 TU 0420 4.7 / 1021 1.2 / 1623 4.9 / 2250 0.8	
15 W 0449 4.7 / 1049 1.2 / 1652 4.9 / 2319 0.8	

MARCH

Time m	Time m
1 W 0417 5.3 / 1027 0.6 / 1618 5.5 / 2300 0.0	**16** TH 0420 4.7 / 1024 1.0 / 1625 4.9 / 2249 0.7
2 TH 0459 5.2 / 1107 0.6 / 1700 5.6 / 2341 0.1	**17** F 0447 4.7 / 1051 1.0 / 1653 4.9 / 2317 0.8
3 F 0540 5.1 / 1145 0.6 / 1744 5.4	**18** SA 0515 4.7 / 1118 1.0 / 1722 4.8 / 2345 0.9
4 SA 0021 0.4 / 0620 4.9 / 1225 0.8 / 1828 5.2	**19** SU 0544 4.6 / 1147 1.1 / 1753 4.7
5 SU 0101 0.8 / 0703 4.6 / 1306 1.1 / 1918 4.8	**20** M 0014 1.1 / 0615 4.5 / 1219 1.3 / 1829 4.5
6 M 0143 1.3 / 0751 4.3 / 1355 1.5 / ● 2015 4.4	**21** TU 0047 1.4 / 0653 4.3 / 1258 1.5 / 1915 4.3
7 TU 0233 1.8 / 0849 4.0 / 1502 1.8 / 2128 4.0	**22** W 0129 1.6 / 0742 4.1 / 1351 1.7 / 2018 4.0
8 W 0347 2.1 / 1005 3.8 / 1641 2.0 / 2302 3.8	**23** TH 0233 2.0 / 0849 3.9 / 1513 1.9 / 2146 3.9
9 TH 0534 2.3 / 1137 3.8 / 1825 1.9	**24** F 0414 2.1 / 1018 3.8 / 1703 1.8 / 2328 3.9
10 F 0035 3.9 / 0658 2.1 / 1255 4.0 / 1931 1.6	**25** SA 0557 2.0 / 1149 4.0 / 1832 1.4
11 SA 0138 4.1 / 0751 1.9 / 1348 4.3 / 2017 1.3	**26** SU 0046 4.3 / 0705 1.6 / 1256 4.4 / 1934 1.0
12 SU 0221 4.3 / 0829 1.6 / 1428 4.5 / 2053 1.1	**27** M 0143 4.6 / 0757 1.3 / 1347 4.8 / 2025 0.5
13 M 0255 4.5 / 0900 1.4 / 1501 4.7 / 2124 0.9	**28** TU 0230 4.9 / 0841 0.9 / 1432 5.1 / 2111 0.2
14 TU 0325 4.6 / 0929 1.2 / 1530 4.8 / ○ 2153 0.8	**29** W 0312 5.1 / 0923 0.7 / 1513 5.4 / ● 2153 0.0
15 W 0353 4.7 / 0957 1.1 / 1557 4.9 / 2221 0.7	**30** TH 0352 5.2 / 1003 0.5 / 1555 5.5 / 2234 0.1
	31 F 0431 5.2 / 1042 0.5 / 1637 5.5 / 2313 0.2

APRIL

Time m	Time m
1 SA 0510 5.0 / 1121 0.6 / 1721 5.3 / 2351 0.6	**16** SU 0445 4.7 / 1056 0.9 / 1658 4.8 / 2317 0.9
2 SU 0549 4.8 / 1201 0.8 / 1807 5.0	**17** M 0516 4.7 / 1128 1.0 / 1734 4.6 / 2349 1.1
3 M 0028 1.0 / 0630 4.6 / 1244 1.0 / 1857 4.6	**18** TU 0551 4.6 / 1205 1.2 / 1817 4.5
4 TU 0108 1.5 / 0716 4.3 / 1334 1.4 / 1954 4.2	**19** W 0026 1.4 / 0632 4.4 / 1251 1.3 / 1910 4.2
5 W 0156 1.9 / 0811 4.0 / 1439 1.7 / ● 2105 3.8	**20** TH 0115 1.7 / 0726 4.2 / 1352 1.5 / 2019 4.0
6 TH 0308 2.3 / 0925 3.8 / 1613 1.9 / 2235 3.7	**21** F 0226 2.0 / 0835 4.0 / 1515 1.6 / ○ 2144 3.9
7 F 0459 2.4 / 1058 3.7 / 1752 1.8	**22** SA 0402 2.0 / 1000 4.0 / 1649 1.5 / 2313 4.1
8 SA 0005 3.8 / 0626 2.2 / 1219 3.9 / 1857 1.6	**23** SU 0531 1.9 / 1122 4.1 / 1807 1.2
9 SU 0106 4.0 / 0717 1.9 / 1314 4.1 / 1941 1.3	**24** M 0023 4.3 / 0636 1.6 / 1227 4.5 / 1907 0.8
10 M 0148 4.2 / 0755 1.7 / 1354 4.4 / 2017 1.1	**25** TU 0118 4.6 / 0728 1.2 / 1320 4.8 / 1958 0.5
11 TU 0222 4.4 / 0828 1.4 / 1428 4.6 / 2048 0.9	**26** W 0203 4.9 / 0814 0.9 / 1405 5.1 / 2044 0.3
12 W 0252 4.6 / 0858 1.2 / 1458 4.7 / 2119 0.8	**27** TH 0245 5.0 / 0857 0.7 / 1449 5.3 / ● 2126 0.3
13 TH 0320 4.7 / 0927 1.1 / 1526 4.8 / 2148 0.7	**28** F 0325 5.1 / 0939 0.6 / 1533 5.3 / 2207 0.4
14 F 0347 4.7 / 0956 1.0 / 1555 4.9 / 2217 0.7	**29** SA 0404 5.1 / 1021 0.5 / 1618 5.2 / 2246 0.6
15 SA 0415 4.8 / 1025 0.9 / 1626 4.8 / 2247 0.8	**30** SU 0443 5.0 / 1102 0.6 / 1703 5.0 / 2323 0.9

Chart Datum: 2·60 metres below Ordnance Datum (Newlyn)

TIDES

TIME ZONE (UT)
For Summer Time add ONE hour in **non-shaded areas**

ENGLAND – NORTH SHIELDS 2006

LAT 55°01'N LONG 1°26'W

TIMES AND HEIGHTS OF HIGH AND LOW WATERS

MAY

Day	Time	m	Day	Time	m
1 M	0523	4.8	16 TU	0456	4.7
	1145	0.8		1119	0.9
	1751	4.7		1727	4.6
				2336	1.2
2 TU	0001	1.3	17 W	0537	4.6
	0604	4.6		1204	1.0
	1229	1.0		1816	4.5
	1840	4.4			
3 W	0041	1.6	18 TH	0021	1.4
	0649	4.4		0624	4.5
	1319	1.3		1256	1.1
	1935	4.1		1913	4.3
4 TH	0127	2.0	19 F	0116	1.6
	0741	4.1		0719	4.4
	1418	1.6		1358	1.2
	2038	3.8		2019	4.2
5 F	0230	2.2	20 SA	0223	1.8
	0845	3.9		0824	4.3
	1531	1.7		1510	1.2
	◑ 2152	3.7		◐ 2132	4.1
6 SA	0358	2.3	21 SU	0340	1.9
	1003	3.8		0938	4.2
	1652	1.7		1625	1.2
	2309	3.7		2246	4.2
7 SU	0524	2.2	22 M	0455	1.8
	1120	3.9		1050	4.4
	1759	1.6		1735	1.0
				2351	4.3
8 M	0012	3.9	23 TU	0600	1.6
	0624	2.0		1155	4.5
	1221	4.0		1836	0.9
	1849	1.4			
9 TU	0100	4.1	24 W	0047	4.5
	0709	1.8		0656	1.3
	1307	4.1		1251	4.7
	1930	1.2		1929	0.7
10 W	0138	4.3	25 TH	0135	4.7
	0747	1.5		0747	1.1
	1346	4.4		1342	4.9
	2007	1.1		2017	0.7
11 TH	0212	4.4	26 F	0220	4.8
	0822	1.3		0835	0.9
	1420	4.6		1430	5.0
	2041	1.0		2101	0.7
12 F	0244	4.6	27 SA	0301	4.9
	0856	1.2		0921	0.8
	1454	4.7		● 1518	5.0
	2114	0.9		2143	0.8
13 SA	0315	4.7	28 SU	0342	4.9
	0929	1.0		1006	0.7
	1528	4.7		1605	4.9
	○ 2147	0.9		2224	1.0
14 SU	0347	4.8	29 M	0422	4.9
	1003	1.0		1050	0.7
	1604	4.8		1651	4.8
	2221	0.9		2302	1.2
15 M	0420	4.8	30 TU	0503	4.8
	1040	0.9		1133	0.9
	1643	4.7		1738	4.6
	2257	1.0		2340	1.4
			31 W	0544	4.6
				1216	1.0
				1824	4.4

JUNE

Day	Time	m	Day	Time	m
1 TH	0019	1.6	16 F	0019	1.3
	0626	4.5		0616	4.8
	1301	1.2		1257	0.8
	1912	4.2		1908	4.6
2 F	0101	1.8	17 SA	0110	1.4
	0713	4.3		0709	4.7
	1350	1.4		1352	0.8
	2004	4.0		2006	4.4
3 SA	0150	2.0	18 SU	0206	1.5
	0805	4.1		0807	4.6
	1444	1.5		1451	0.9
	◑ 2100	3.8		◐ 2108	4.3
4 SU	0251	2.1	19 M	0307	1.6
	0905	4.0		0910	4.5
	1544	1.6		1555	1.0
	2201	3.8		2212	4.3
5 M	0402	2.2	20 TU	0414	1.7
	1009	4.0		1017	4.5
	1647	1.6		1700	1.1
	2303	3.8		2316	4.3
6 TU	0511	2.1	21 W	0522	1.6
	1112	4.0		1124	4.5
	1746	1.5		1804	1.1
	2359	4.0			
7 W	0611	1.9	22 TH	0016	4.3
	1209	4.1		0627	1.5
	1838	1.4		1229	4.5
				1903	1.1
8 TH	0047	4.1	23 F	0111	4.5
	0700	1.7		0727	1.3
	1259	4.2		1328	4.6
	1923	1.3		1957	1.2
9 F	0130	4.3	24 SA	0201	4.6
	0745	1.5		0822	1.1
	1344	4.4		1422	4.7
	2004	1.2		2045	1.2
10 SA	0209	4.5	25 SU	0246	4.7
	0826	1.3		0912	1.0
	1426	4.5		1512	4.7
	2044	1.1		● 2128	1.2
11 SU	0247	4.6	26 M	0328	4.8
	0906	1.1		0958	0.9
	1508	4.6		1558	4.7
	○ 2124	1.1		2209	1.2
12 M	0324	4.7	27 TU	0408	4.8
	0948	1.0		1041	0.8
	1551	4.7		1642	4.6
	2205	1.0		2246	1.3
13 TU	0403	4.8	28 W	0447	4.8
	1031	0.8		1121	0.9
	1636	4.8		1723	4.6
	2247	1.1		2322	1.4
14 W	0444	4.8	29 TH	0525	4.7
	1117	0.8		1159	0.9
	1724	4.7		1803	4.4
	2331	1.2		2357	1.5
15 TH	0529	4.8	30 F	0603	4.6
	1205	0.7		1237	1.0
	1814	4.7		1843	4.3

JULY

Day	Time	m	Day	Time	m
1 SA	0032	1.6	16 SU	0052	1.1
	0642	4.5		0650	5.1
	1316	1.2		1333	0.6
	1924	4.2		1941	4.6
2 SU	0111	1.7	17 M	0139	1.3
	0725	4.4		0742	4.9
	1357	1.3		1423	0.8
	2008	4.0		◐ 2036	4.4
3 M	0154	1.9	18 TU	0232	1.5
	0812	4.2		0840	4.7
	1444	1.5		1520	1.1
	◑ 2058	3.9		2135	4.2
4 TU	0246	2.0	19 W	0335	1.6
	0904	4.1		0946	4.5
	1537	1.6		1624	1.4
	2153	3.9		2241	4.1
5 W	0349	2.1	20 TH	0450	1.7
	1003	4.0		1100	4.3
	1638	1.7		1737	1.5
	2253	3.9		2349	4.2
6 TH	0501	2.1	21 F	0610	1.7
	1108	4.0		1216	4.3
	1741	1.7		1848	1.6
	2353	4.0			
7 F	0611	1.9	22 SA	0054	4.3
	1213	4.1		0720	1.5
	1841	1.6		1326	4.3
				1948	1.6
8 SA	0049	4.2	23 SU	0151	4.4
	0710	1.7		0819	1.3
	1313	4.2		1423	4.5
	1934	1.5		2037	1.5
9 SU	0139	4.4	24 M	0238	4.6
	0802	1.5		0908	1.1
	1406	4.4		1510	4.6
	2023	1.3		2119	1.4
10 M	0224	4.6	25 TU	0319	4.7
	0851	1.2		0951	0.9
	1454	4.6		1551	4.6
	● 2109	1.2		● 2156	1.3
11 TU	0307	4.8	26 W	0356	4.8
	0937	0.9		1028	0.8
	1541	4.8		1627	4.6
	○ 2154	1.0		2230	1.3
12 W	0349	5.0	27 TH	0430	4.9
	1024	0.6		1102	0.8
	1628	4.9		1702	4.6
	2238	1.0		2301	1.3
13 TH	0432	5.1	28 F	0503	4.9
	1111	0.4		1135	0.8
	1715	5.0		1735	4.6
	2323	1.0		2331	1.3
14 F	0516	5.1	29 SA	0535	4.8
	1157	0.4		1206	0.9
	1802	4.9		1808	4.5
15 SA	0007	1.0	30 SU	0001	1.4
	0602	5.1		0609	4.7
	1245	0.4		1239	1.0
	1851	4.8		1842	4.4
			31 M	0034	1.5
				0645	4.6
				1313	1.2
				1920	4.2

AUGUST

Day	Time	m	Day	Time	m
1 TU	0108	1.6	16 W	0159	1.4
	0724	4.4		0812	4.7
	1351	1.4		1443	1.4
	2001	4.1		◑ 2058	4.2
2 W	0149	1.8	17 TH	0303	1.7
	0808	4.2		0921	4.3
	1436	1.6		1551	1.8
	2050	4.0		2208	4.0
3 TH	0242	2.0	18 F	0428	1.8
	0903	4.0		1046	4.1
	1533	1.8		1718	2.0
	2150	3.9		2329	4.0
4 F	0354	2.1	19 SA	0604	1.8
	1013	3.9		1215	4.1
	1647	1.9		1842	2.0
	2301	3.9			
5 SA	0524	2.1	20 SU	0044	4.2
	1135	3.9		0720	1.5
	1807	1.9		1328	4.2
				1944	1.8
6 SU	0014	4.0	21 M	0143	4.4
	0644	1.8		0815	1.3
	1252	4.1		1420	4.4
	1914	1.7		2029	1.6
7 M	0116	4.3	22 TU	0228	4.6
	0746	1.5		0858	1.1
	1352	4.4		1500	4.6
	2008	1.4		2106	1.5
8 TU	0206	4.6	23 W	0305	4.7
	0837	1.1		0934	0.9
	1443	4.7		1534	4.7
	2056	1.2		● 2138	1.3
9 W	0250	4.9	24 TH	0337	4.9
	0925	0.7		1006	0.8
	1529	5.0		1605	4.7
	2140	0.9		2207	1.2
10 TH	0332	5.2	25 F	0407	5.0
	1011	0.3		1035	0.7
	1613	5.2		1634	4.7
	2223	0.8		2235	1.1
11 F	0414	5.4	26 SA	0436	5.0
	1055	0.1		1104	0.7
	1656	5.2		1703	4.7
	2304	0.7		2303	1.1
12 SA	0456	5.5	27 SU	0505	5.0
	1139	0.1		1132	0.8
	1740	5.1		1732	4.7
	2345	0.8		2330	1.2
13 SU	0540	5.4	28 M	0535	4.9
	1222	0.2		1201	1.0
	1824	5.0		1803	4.6
				2359	1.3
14 M	0026	0.9	29 TU	0607	4.7
	0626	5.3		1231	1.2
	1305	0.5		1835	4.4
	1910	4.7			
15 TU	0110	1.1	30 W	0031	1.5
	0715	5.0		0642	4.5
	1351	0.9		1304	1.4
	2000	4.5		1911	4.3
			31 TH	0108	1.7
				0724	4.3
				1344	1.7
				◑ 1957	4.1

Chart Datum: 2·60 metres below Ordnance Datum (Newlyn)

ENGLAND – NORTH SHIELDS

LAT 55°01′N LONG 1°26′W

TIMES AND HEIGHTS OF HIGH AND LOW WATERS

2006

SEPTEMBER

Day	Time m		Day	Time m	
1 F	0156 1.9 / 0819 4.1 / 1439 2.0 / 2058 3.9		**16** SA	0416 1.9 / 1036 3.9 / 1704 2.3 / 2308 4.0	
2 SA	0309 2.1 / 0936 3.9 / 1604 2.2 / 2218 3.9		**17** SU	0559 1.8 / 1210 4.0 / 1833 2.2	
3 SU	0452 2.1 / 1113 3.9 / 1744 2.1 / 2345 4.0		**18** M	0028 4.2 / 0709 1.5 / 1317 4.2 / 1929 1.9	
4 M	0625 1.8 / 1237 4.2 / 1858 1.8		**19** TU	0126 4.4 / 0758 1.3 / 1402 4.4 / 2010 1.7	
5 TU	0053 4.3 / 0729 1.3 / 1338 4.5 / 1952 1.5		**20** W	0207 4.6 / 0835 1.1 / 1437 4.6 / 2042 1.5	
6 W	0145 4.7 / 0820 0.9 / 1426 4.9 / 2037 1.1		**21** TH	0241 4.8 / 0906 0.9 / 1508 4.7 / 2111 1.3	
7 TH	0229 5.1 / 0906 0.4 / 1509 5.1 / ○ 2119 0.8		**22** F	0311 4.9 / 0935 0.8 / 1535 4.8 / ● 2139 1.2	
8 F	0310 5.4 / 0949 0.1 / 1550 5.3 / 2200 0.7		**23** SA	0339 5.0 / 1003 0.8 / 1602 4.8 / 2207 1.1	
9 SA	0350 5.6 / 1032 0.0 / 1631 5.3 / 2240 0.6		**24** SU	0406 5.0 / 1030 0.8 / 1629 4.8 / 2234 1.1	
10 SU	0432 5.7 / 1111 0.2 / 1711 5.2 / 2320 0.6		**25** M	0435 5.0 / 1058 0.9 / 1657 4.8 / 2302 1.1	
11 M	0515 5.6 / 1154 0.3 / 1753 5.1		**26** TU	0504 4.9 / 1126 1.0 / 1726 4.7 / 2331 1.3	
12 TU	0000 0.8 / 0601 5.3 / 1235 0.7 / 1836 4.8		**27** W	0536 4.8 / 1155 1.2 / 1757 4.6	
13 W	0044 1.1 / 0651 5.0 / 1318 1.2 / 1924 4.5		**28** TH	0003 1.4 / 0611 4.6 / 1227 1.5 / 1833 4.4	
14 TH	0134 1.4 / 0750 4.5 / 1408 1.7 / ◑ 2022 4.2		**29** F	0041 1.6 / 0656 4.3 / 1306 1.8 / 1920 4.2	
15 F	0240 1.7 / 0903 4.1 / 1520 2.1 / 2137 4.0		**30** SA	0132 1.9 / 0756 4.1 / 1405 2.1 / ◑ 2023 4.0	

OCTOBER

Day	Time m		Day	Time m	
1 SU	0249 2.0 / 0919 3.9 / 1539 2.3 / 2148 3.9		**16** M	0531 1.8 / 1142 3.9 / 1802 2.3 / 2355 4.1	
2 M	0433 2.0 / 1058 4.0 / 1724 2.2 / 2317 4.1		**17** TU	0637 1.6 / 1245 4.2 / 1857 2.1	
3 TU	0603 1.6 / 1218 4.3 / 1835 1.8		**18** W	0052 4.4 / 0723 1.4 / 1329 4.4 / 1936 1.8	
4 W	0026 4.4 / 0705 1.2 / 1315 4.7 / 1927 1.5		**19** TH	0134 4.6 / 0759 1.2 / 1404 4.5 / 2009 1.6	
5 TH	0118 4.8 / 0755 0.7 / 1402 5.0 / 2012 1.1		**20** F	0209 4.7 / 0830 1.1 / 1434 4.7 / 2040 1.4	
6 F	0202 5.2 / 0840 0.4 / 1443 5.2 / 2053 0.8		**21** SA	0240 4.9 / 0900 1.0 / 1503 4.8 / 2109 1.2	
7 SA	0244 5.5 / 0923 0.2 / 1523 5.4 / ○ 2134 0.6		**22** SU	0309 5.0 / 0929 0.9 / 1530 4.9 / ● 2139 1.2	
8 SU	0325 5.7 / 1005 0.1 / 1602 5.4 / 2215 0.6		**23** M	0338 5.0 / 0958 0.9 / 1558 4.9 / 2208 1.1	
9 M	0408 5.7 / 1045 0.3 / 1642 5.3 / 2256 0.6		**24** TU	0409 4.9 / 1027 1.0 / 1627 4.9 / 2238 1.2	
10 TU	0453 5.5 / 1125 0.6 / 1723 5.1 / 2338 0.8		**25** W	0441 4.9 / 1057 1.2 / 1657 4.8 / 2311 1.2	
11 W	0541 5.2 / 1205 1.0 / 1806 4.8		**26** TH	0516 4.7 / 1128 1.3 / 1730 4.7 / 2347 1.4	
12 TH	0024 1.1 / 0633 4.8 / 1247 1.5 / 1854 4.5		**27** F	0556 4.5 / 1203 1.6 / 1810 4.5	
13 F	0117 1.4 / 0733 4.4 / 1338 2.0 / 1951 4.3		**28** SA	0030 1.5 / 0646 4.3 / 1248 1.9 / 1859 4.4	
14 SA	0224 1.7 / 0846 4.0 / 1450 2.3 / ◑ 2105 4.0		**29** SU	0127 1.7 / 0750 4.1 / 1351 2.2 / ◑ 2003 4.2	
15 SU	0356 1.9 / 1014 3.9 / 1635 2.5 / ◑ 2235 4.0		**30** M	0243 1.8 / 0909 4.0 / 1520 2.2 / 2123 4.1	
			31 TU	0412 1.7 / 1036 4.1 / 1652 2.1 / 2245 4.3	

NOVEMBER

Day	Time m		Day	Time m	
1 W	0532 1.4 / 1149 4.4 / 1801 2.0 / 2352 4.6		**16** TH	0001 4.2 / 0632 1.6 / 1242 4.2 / 1851 2.0	
2 TH	0634 1.1 / 1245 4.7 / 1856 1.5		**17** F	0050 4.4 / 0714 1.4 / 1322 4.4 / 1930 1.8	
3 F	0047 4.9 / 0726 0.8 / 1333 4.9 / 1943 1.2		**18** SA	0130 4.6 / 0750 1.3 / 1357 4.6 / 2006 1.6	
4 SA	0135 5.2 / 0812 0.5 / 1416 5.1 / 2027 0.9		**19** SU	0206 4.7 / 0824 1.2 / 1430 4.7 / 2041 1.4	
5 SU	0220 5.4 / 0857 0.5 / 1457 5.2 / ○ 2111 0.8		**20** M	0241 4.8 / 0858 1.1 / 1501 4.8 / ● 2114 1.3	
6 M	0305 5.5 / 0939 0.5 / 1537 5.3 / 2155 0.7		**21** TU	0315 4.8 / 0930 1.1 / 1532 4.9 / 2148 1.2	
7 TU	0350 5.5 / 1020 0.7 / 1617 5.2 / 2239 0.7		**22** W	0350 4.8 / 1003 1.2 / 1603 4.9 / 2223 1.2	
8 W	0438 5.3 / 1101 1.0 / 1659 5.1 / 2324 0.9		**23** TH	0427 4.8 / 1037 1.3 / 1638 4.9 / 2301 1.2	
9 TH	0528 5.0 / 1141 1.3 / 1742 4.9		**24** F	0507 4.7 / 1114 1.4 / 1715 4.8 / 2343 1.2	
10 F	0012 1.1 / 0620 4.7 / 1224 1.7 / 1829 4.6		**25** SA	0552 4.6 / 1155 1.6 / 1758 4.7	
11 SA	0104 1.4 / 0717 4.3 / 1311 2.1 / 1923 4.4		**26** SU	0030 1.3 / 0643 4.5 / 1243 1.8 / 1848 4.6	
12 SU	0204 1.6 / 0820 4.1 / 1413 2.3 / ◑ 2027 4.2		**27** M	0127 1.4 / 0743 4.3 / 1342 1.9 / 1947 4.5	
13 M	0316 1.8 / 0932 3.9 / 1534 2.5 / 2143 4.1		**28** TU	0232 1.5 / 0851 4.2 / 1453 2.0 / ◑ 2055 4.4	
14 TU	0434 1.8 / 1047 3.9 / 1700 2.4 / 2259 4.1		**29** W	0343 1.4 / 1004 4.3 / 1609 2.0 / 2207 4.5	
15 W	0541 1.7 / 1152 4.0 / 1804 2.2		**30** TH	0454 1.3 / 1112 4.4 / 1719 1.8 / 2315 4.6	

DECEMBER

Day	Time m		Day	Time m	
1 F	0559 1.2 / 1212 4.6 / 1820 1.6		**16** SA	0620 1.7 / 1232 4.2 / 1846 2.0	
2 SA	0016 4.8 / 0655 1.0 / 1305 4.7 / 1915 1.4		**17** SU	0046 4.3 / 0708 1.6 / 1318 4.3 / 1933 1.8	
3 SU	0111 5.0 / 0747 0.9 / 1352 4.9 / 2007 1.2		**18** M	0134 4.4 / 0752 1.5 / 1358 4.5 / 2015 1.6	
4 M	0203 5.1 / 0835 0.9 / 1436 5.0 / 2056 0.9		**19** TU	0217 4.5 / 0831 1.4 / 1436 4.7 / 2055 1.4	
5 TU	0253 5.2 / 0920 1.0 / 1519 5.1 / ○ 2144 0.9		**20** W	0258 4.7 / 0910 1.3 / 1512 4.8 / ● 2135 1.2	
6 W	0342 5.1 / 1003 1.1 / 1601 5.1 / 2231 0.8		**21** TH	0338 4.8 / 0948 1.3 / 1548 4.9 / 2215 1.1	
7 TH	0431 5.0 / 1044 1.3 / 1643 5.0 / 2317 0.9		**22** F	0419 4.8 / 1027 1.3 / 1625 5.0 / 2257 1.0	
8 F	0519 4.8 / 1125 1.5 / 1725 4.9		**23** SA	0502 4.8 / 1108 1.3 / 1706 5.0 / 2341 0.9	
9 SA	0002 1.0 / 0606 4.6 / 1204 1.7 / 1808 4.7		**24** SU	0547 4.8 / 1151 1.4 / 1749 5.0	
10 SU	0048 1.2 / 0654 4.4 / 1245 1.9 / 1854 4.6		**25** M	0028 0.9 / 0635 4.7 / 1236 1.5 / 1835 4.9	
11 M	0135 1.4 / 0744 4.2 / 1330 2.1 / 1945 4.4		**26** TU	0118 1.0 / 0727 4.6 / 1325 1.6 / 1927 4.8	
12 TU	0225 1.6 / 0838 4.0 / 1425 2.2 / ◑ 2042 4.2		**27** W	0211 1.1 / 0824 4.4 / 1420 1.7 / ◑ 2024 4.7	
13 W	0322 1.7 / 0937 3.9 / 1531 2.3 / 2145 4.1		**28** TH	0309 1.2 / 0926 4.3 / 1523 1.8 / 2129 4.6	
14 TH	0424 1.8 / 1040 3.9 / 1644 2.3 / 2250 4.1		**29** F	0414 1.3 / 1032 4.3 / 1634 1.8 / 2239 4.5	
15 F	0525 1.8 / 1139 4.0 / 1750 2.2 / 2352 4.2		**30** SA	0522 1.4 / 1138 4.3 / 1748 1.8 / 2350 4.6	
			31 SU	0630 1.4 / 1240 4.4 / 1857 1.6	

Chart Datum: 2·60 metres below Ordnance Datum (Newlyn)

TIDES

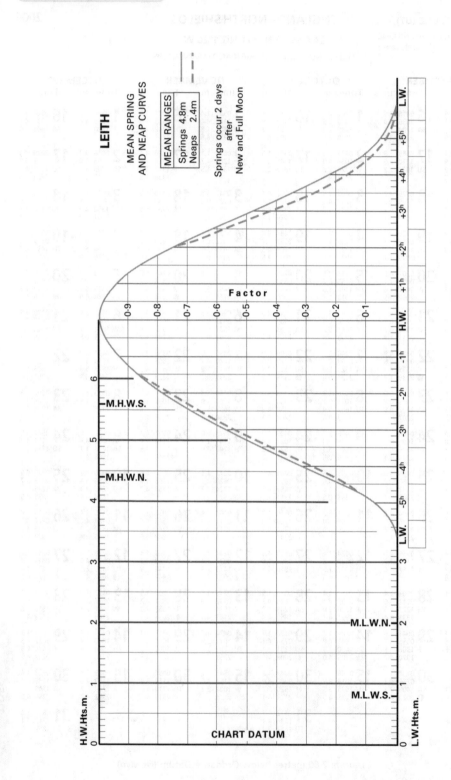

LEITH

MEAN SPRING
AND NEAP CURVES

MEAN RANGES
Springs 4.8m
Neaps 2.4m

Springs occur 2 days
after
New and Full Moon

Factor

0·9 0·8 0·7 0·6 0·5 0·4 0·3 0·2 0·1

M.H.W.S.

M.H.W.N.

M.L.W.N.

M.L.W.S.

CHART DATUM

H.W.Hts.m.

L.W.Hts.m.

L.W.

H.W.

L.W.

SCOTLAND – LEITH

LAT 55°59'N   LONG 3°11'W

TIMES AND HEIGHTS OF HIGH AND LOW WATERS

2006

JANUARY

Time	m		Time	m
1 SU 0306 / 0904 / 1517 / 2134	5.6 / 1.1 / 5.5 / 0.7		**16** M 0346 / 0918 / 1558 / 2158	5.1 / 1.4 / 5.1 / 1.0
2 M 0353 / 0952 / 1602 / 2225	5.7 / 1.1 / 5.6 / 0.6		**17** TU 0419 / 0949 / 1630 / 2227	5.1 / 1.4 / 5.2 / 1.1
3 TU 0440 / 1039 / 1648 / 2314	5.6 / 1.1 / 5.6 / 0.6		**18** W 0453 / 1018 / 1703 / 2256	5.0 / 1.4 / 5.1 / 1.1
4 W 0529 / 1125 / 1737	5.5 / 1.3 / 5.5		**19** TH 0528 / 1048 / 1738 / 2327	4.9 / 1.5 / 5.0 / 1.3
5 TH 0003 / 0621 / 1210 / 1828	0.7 / 5.3 / 1.5 / 5.4		**20** F 0606 / 1117 / 1814 / 2359	4.8 / 1.7 / 4.9 / 1.4
6 F 0052 / 0716 / 1257 / 1926 ☽	1.0 / 5.1 / 1.7 / 5.2		**21** SA 0646 / 1148 / 1854	4.6 / 1.8 / 4.7
7 SA 0145 / 0817 / 1353 / 2032	1.3 / 4.8 / 1.9 / 5.0		**22** SU 0035 / 0730 / 1228 / 1939 ☽	1.6 / 4.5 / 2.0 / 4.6
8 SU 0246 / 0921 / 1502 / 2141	1.6 / 4.7 / 2.0 / 4.8		**23** M 0121 / 0822 / 1325 / 2038	1.8 / 4.4 / 2.2 / 4.4
9 M 0359 / 1025 / 1618 / 2250	1.8 / 4.6 / 2.0 / 4.7		**24** TU 0223 / 0922 / 1453 / 2151	2.0 / 4.3 / 2.4 / 4.3
10 TU 0511 / 1130 / 1730 / 2357	1.8 / 4.6 / 1.9 / 4.8		**25** W 0353 / 1030 / 1638 / 2307	2.1 / 4.4 / 2.2 / 4.4
11 W 0612 / 1231 / 1835	1.8 / 4.8 / 1.7		**26** TH 0522 / 1138 / 1753	2.0 / 4.6 / 1.9
12 TH 0058 / 0701 / 1324 / 1929	4.8 / 1.8 / 4.9 / 1.4		**27** F 0017 / 0625 / 1242 / 1853	4.7 / 1.7 / 4.8 / 1.5
13 F 0150 / 0740 / 1409 / 2014	4.9 / 1.7 / 5.1 / 1.3		**28** SA 0118 / 0720 / 1335 / 1948	5.1 / 1.5 / 5.1 / 1.1
14 SA 0233 / 0815 / 1448 / 2053 ○	5.1 / 1.6 / 5.2 / 1.1		**29** SU 0209 / 0810 / 1421 / 2041	5.4 / 1.2 / 5.4 / 0.7
15 SU 0311 / 0847 / 1524 / 2127	5.1 / 1.5 / 5.2 / 1.1		**30** M 0255 / 0857 / 1504 / 2130	5.7 / 0.9 / 5.7 / 0.3
			31 TU 0340 / 0942 / 1548 / 2217	5.8 / 0.8 / 5.9 / 0.2

FEBRUARY

Time	m		Time	m
1 W 0424 / 1025 / 1632 / 2300	5.8 / 0.8 / 5.9 / 0.2		**16** TH 0426 / 1000 / 1637 / 2232	5.1 / 1.1 / 5.3 / 0.9
2 TH 0510 / 1105 / 1717 / 2341	5.7 / 0.9 / 5.8 / 0.4		**17** F 0458 / 1024 / 1708 / 2257	5.0 / 1.2 / 5.2 / 1.0
3 F 0557 / 1141 / 1805	5.4 / 1.1 / 5.6		**18** SA 0532 / 1044 / 1740 / 2318	4.9 / 1.3 / 5.0 / 1.2
4 SA 0019 / 0645 / 1216 / 1856	0.8 / 5.1 / 1.3 / 5.3		**19** SU 0608 / 1107 / 1815 / 2341	4.8 / 1.5 / 4.8 / 1.4
5 SU 0056 / 0739 / 1259 / 1956	1.2 / 4.8 / 1.7 / 4.9		**20** M 0647 / 1138 / 1858	4.6 / 1.7 / 4.6
6 M 0140 / 0840 / 1406 / 2107	1.7 / 4.5 / 2.0 / 4.6		**21** TU 0015 / 0733 / 1224 / 1952	1.7 / 4.4 / 2.0 / 4.4
7 TU 0257 / 0947 / 1548 / 2224	2.1 / 4.3 / 2.1 / 4.4		**22** W 0111 / 0832 / 1340 / 2108	2.0 / 4.3 / 2.2 / 4.3
8 W 0442 / 1102 / 1725 / 2346	2.3 / 4.3 / 2.0 / 4.4		**23** TH 0259 / 0949 / 1607 / 2239	2.3 / 4.2 / 2.2 / 4.3
9 TH 0605 / 1217 / 1841	2.2 / 4.5 / 1.8		**24** F 0508 / 1111 / 1743	2.2 / 4.4 / 1.9
10 F 0056 / 0658 / 1316 / 1932	4.6 / 2.0 / 4.8 / 1.5		**25** SA 0000 / 0615 / 1223 / 1847	4.6 / 1.8 / 4.7 / 1.4
11 SA 0147 / 0735 / 1401 / 2011	4.8 / 1.8 / 5.0 / 1.3		**26** SU 0104 / 0709 / 1318 / 1941	5.1 / 1.4 / 5.1 / 0.8
12 SU 0226 / 0806 / 1437 / 2044	5.0 / 1.6 / 5.1 / 1.1		**27** M 0154 / 0757 / 1403 / 2030	5.5 / 1.0 / 5.5 / 0.4
13 M 0258 / 0834 / 1509 / 2112 ○	5.1 / 1.4 / 5.2 / 0.9		**28** TU 0238 / 0841 / 1445 / 2115 ●	5.8 / 0.7 / 5.9 / 0.1
14 TU 0327 / 0903 / 1539 / 2139	5.1 / 1.1 / 5.3 / 0.8			
15 W 0356 / 0932 / 1608 / 2206	5.1 / 1.1 / 5.3 / 0.8			

MARCH

Time	m		Time	m
1 W 0320 / 0923 / 1527 / 2158	5.9 / 0.5 / 6.0 / -0.1		**16** TH 0328 / 0909 / 1541 / 2138	5.2 / 1.0 / 5.3 / 0.7
2 TH 0402 / 1003 / 1610 / 2238	5.9 / 0.5 / 6.1 / 0.0		**17** F 0356 / 0936 / 1610 / 2204	5.2 / 0.9 / 5.3 / 0.8
3 F 0445 / 1040 / 1654 / 2314	5.7 / 0.6 / 5.9 / 0.4		**18** SA 0427 / 0958 / 1641 / 2224	5.1 / 1.0 / 5.2 / 0.9
4 SA 0528 / 1113 / 1740 / 2344	5.4 / 0.8 / 5.6 / 0.8		**19** SU 0500 / 1016 / 1714 / 2240	5.0 / 1.1 / 5.1 / 1.1
5 SU 0614 / 1142 / 1830	5.1 / 1.2 / 5.2		**20** M 0535 / 1038 / 1751 / 2301	4.9 / 1.3 / 4.9 / 1.4
6 M 0010 / 0703 / 1221 / 1928 ☽	1.4 / 4.7 / 1.6 / 4.8		**21** TU 0614 / 1110 / 1836 / 2335	4.7 / 1.5 / 4.7 / 1.7
7 TU 0048 / 0802 / 1325 / 2039	1.9 / 4.4 / 2.0 / 4.4		**22** W 0700 / 1157 / 1933 ☽	4.5 / 1.8 / 4.4
8 W 0200 / 0912 / 1532 / 2159	2.4 / 4.2 / 2.2 / 4.2		**23** TH 0033 / 0758 / 1320 / 2049	2.1 / 4.3 / 2.1 / 4.3
9 TH 0422 / 1032 / 1725 / 2331	2.5 / 4.2 / 2.0 / 4.2		**24** F 0300 / 0920 / 1602 / 2221	2.4 / 4.2 / 2.1 / 4.4
10 F 0554 / 1157 / 1832	2.3 / 4.4 / 1.7		**25** SA 0454 / 1048 / 1731 / 2342	2.2 / 4.4 / 1.6 / 4.7
11 SA 0044 / 0644 / 1258 / 1917	4.5 / 2.1 / 4.7 / 1.5		**26** SU 0557 / 1200 / 1832	1.8 / 4.8 / 1.1
12 SU 0131 / 0717 / 1340 / 1951	4.7 / 1.8 / 4.9 / 1.2		**27** M 0043 / 0647 / 1254 / 1923	5.1 / 1.3 / 5.2 / 0.6
13 M 0206 / 0745 / 1415 / 2020	4.9 / 1.5 / 5.1 / 1.0		**28** TU 0132 / 0733 / 1339 / 2009	5.5 / 0.9 / 5.6 / 0.3
14 TU 0235 / 0812 / 1445 / 2046	5.0 / 1.3 / 5.2 / 0.8		**29** W 0214 / 0816 / 1421 / 2052 ●	5.7 / 0.6 / 5.9 / 0.0
15 W 0301 / 0841 / 1513 / 2112	5.1 / 1.1 / 5.3 / 0.7		**30** TH 0255 / 0858 / 1504 / 2133	5.8 / 0.4 / 6.0 / 0.0
			31 F 0336 / 0939 / 1548 / 2210	5.8 / 0.4 / 6.0 / 0.2

APRIL

Time	m		Time	m
1 SA 0418 / 1016 / 1633 / 2244	5.6 / 0.5 / 5.8 / 0.6		**16** SU 0358 / 0937 / 1617 / 2155	5.2 / 1.0 / 5.2 / 1.0
2 SU 0501 / 1050 / 1720 / 2310	5.4 / 0.8 / 5.5 / 1.1		**17** M 0432 / 0959 / 1655 / 2215	5.1 / 1.1 / 5.1 / 1.2
3 M 0545 / 1121 / 1810 / 2332	5.0 / 1.1 / 5.0 / 1.6		**18** TU 0509 / 1026 / 1737 / 2242	5.0 / 1.2 / 4.9 / 1.5
4 TU 0633 / 1159 / 1907	4.7 / 1.5 / 4.6		**19** W 0551 / 1104 / 1826 / 2324	4.8 / 1.4 / 4.7 / 1.8
5 W 0010 / 0730 / 1302 / 2013 ☽	2.1 / 4.4 / 1.9 / 4.3		**20** TH 0640 / 1204 / 1925	4.6 / 1.7 / 4.5
6 TH 0123 / 0840 / 1517 / 2128	2.5 / 4.2 / 2.1 / 4.1		**21** F 0046 / 0741 / 1348 / 2040 ☽	2.2 / 4.4 / 1.9 / 4.4
7 F 0349 / 0958 / 1657 / 2255	2.6 / 4.1 / 2.0 / 4.1		**22** SA 0301 / 0902 / 1550 / 2203	2.3 / 4.4 / 1.7 / 4.5
8 SA 0512 / 1119 / 1757	2.4 / 4.3 / 1.7		**23** SU 0426 / 1025 / 1706 / 2317	2.0 / 4.6 / 1.4 / 4.8
9 SU 0011 / 0602 / 1222 / 1840	4.4 / 2.1 / 4.6 / 1.5		**24** M 0526 / 1132 / 1805	1.7 / 4.9 / 1.0
10 M 0058 / 0639 / 1306 / 1914	4.6 / 1.8 / 4.8 / 1.2		**25** TU 0016 / 0616 / 1226 / 1856	5.1 / 1.3 / 5.3 / 0.6
11 TU 0132 / 0710 / 1341 / 1943	4.8 / 1.5 / 5.0 / 1.0		**26** W 0105 / 0703 / 1313 / 1942	5.4 / 1.0 / 5.6 / 0.4
12 W 0201 / 0741 / 1412 / 2010	5.0 / 1.3 / 5.2 / 0.9		**27** TH 0148 / 0748 / 1357 / 2025 ●	5.6 / 0.7 / 5.8 / 0.3
13 TH 0228 / 0811 / 1441 / 2038 ○	5.1 / 1.1 / 5.2 / 0.8		**28** F 0229 / 0833 / 1442 / 2105	5.6 / 0.5 / 5.8 / 0.4
14 F 0256 / 0842 / 1512 / 2106	5.2 / 0.9 / 5.3 / 0.7		**29** SA 0311 / 0916 / 1528 / 2143	5.6 / 0.5 / 5.7 / 0.6
15 SA 0326 / 0911 / 1543 / 2133	5.2 / 0.9 / 5.3 / 0.8		**30** SU 0354 / 0957 / 1615 / 2216	5.5 / 0.6 / 5.5 / 0.9

Chart Datum: 2·90 metres below Ordnance Datum (Newlyn)

TIDES

SCOTLAND – LEITH

LAT 55°59′N   LONG 3°11′W

TIMES AND HEIGHTS OF HIGH AND LOW WATERS

2006

TIME ZONE (UT)
For Summer Time add ONE hour in **non-shaded areas**

MAY

Time	m		Time	m
1 M 0437	5.3		**16** TU 0411	5.2
1035	0.8		1000	1.0
1703	5.2		1642	5.1
2243	1.3		2216	1.3
2 TU 0521	5.0		**17** W 0452	5.1
1110	1.1		1042	1.1
1753	4.9		1728	5.0
2307	1.7		2258	1.6
3 W 0609	4.7		**18** TH 0537	4.9
1148	1.5		1133	1.3
1846	4.6		1820	4.9
2347	2.1		2357	1.8
4 TH 0704	4.5		**19** F 0629	4.8
1243	1.8		1238	1.4
1944	4.3		1919	4.7
5 F 0051	2.4		**20** SA 0113	2.0
0807	4.3		0729	4.7
1424	2.0		1358	1.5
◐ 2047	4.1		◑ 2027	4.7
6 SA 0242	2.5		**21** SU 0236	2.0
0916	4.2		0843	4.7
1602	1.9		1522	1.4
2155	4.1		2140	4.7
7 SU 0410	2.4		**22** M 0348	1.9
1024	4.3		0957	4.8
1701	1.8		1632	1.2
2306	4.3		2247	4.8
8 M 0505	2.2		**23** TU 0448	1.7
1127	4.5		1102	5.0
1746	1.6		1731	1.0
			2346	5.0
9 TU 0002	4.5		**24** W 0542	1.4
0549	1.9		1158	5.2
1217	4.7		1825	0.9
1824	1.4			
10 W 0043	4.7		**25** TH 0037	5.2
0628	1.6		0633	1.1
1257	4.8		1250	5.4
1857	1.2		1913	0.8
11 TH 0118	4.9		**26** F 0124	5.3
0704	1.4		0724	0.9
1334	5.0		1339	5.5
1929	1.0		1957	0.8
12 F 0151	5.0		**27** SA 0208	5.4
0739	1.2		0813	0.7
1409	5.1		1427	5.5
2002	1.0		● 2039	0.8
13 SA 0224	5.1		**28** SU 0251	5.4
0813	1.0		0900	0.7
1445	5.2		1515	5.4
○ 2034	0.9		2118	1.0
14 SU 0258	5.2		**29** M 0335	5.3
0848	1.0		0944	0.7
1521	5.2		1602	5.3
2107	1.0		2153	1.2
15 M 0334	5.2		**30** TU 0418	5.2
0923	0.9		1024	0.9
1600	5.2		1648	5.1
2141	1.1		2223	1.5
			31 W 0502	5.0
			1101	1.1
			1734	4.9
			2252	1.7

JUNE

Time	m		Time	m
1 TH 0547	4.8		**16** F 0527	5.2
1136	1.3		1146	0.9
1820	4.7		1810	5.2
2329	1.9			
2 F 0635	4.6		**17** SA 0003	1.5
1218	1.6		0617	5.1
1909	4.5		1241	1.0
			1905	5.0
3 SA 0018	2.1		**18** SU 0059	1.7
0728	4.5		0713	5.0
1312	1.8		1339	1.1
◐ 2000	4.3		◑ 2006	4.9
4 SU 0123	2.3		**19** M 0159	1.8
0825	4.4		0818	4.9
1424	1.9		1444	1.2
2055	4.2		2111	4.8
5 M 0243	2.3		**20** TU 0305	1.8
0923	4.3		0926	4.9
1540	1.8		1551	1.3
2151	4.2		2215	4.8
6 TU 0357	2.2		**21** W 0410	1.7
1020	4.4		1033	4.9
1639	1.7		1656	1.3
2247	4.4		2316	4.8
7 W 0455	2.0		**22** TH 0512	1.6
1115	4.5		1135	5.0
1727	1.6		1755	1.3
2341	4.5			
8 TH 0543	1.8		**23** F 0013	4.9
1207	4.6		0612	1.4
1810	1.4		1235	5.0
			1849	1.3
9 F 0030	4.7		**24** SA 0106	5.0
0627	1.6		0710	1.2
1255	4.8		1329	5.1
1850	1.3		1936	1.3
10 SA 0114	4.9		**25** SU 0154	5.1
0708	1.4		0803	1.0
1340	5.0		1419	5.2
1930	1.2		● 2019	1.3
11 SU 0156	5.0		**26** M 0239	5.2
0750	1.2		0851	0.9
1423	5.1		1506	5.2
○ 2010	1.1		2059	1.3
12 M 0235	5.2		**27** TU 0322	5.2
0833	1.0		0934	0.8
1505	5.2		1550	5.1
2053	1.1		2134	1.4
13 TU 0315	5.2		**28** W 0403	5.2
0918	0.9		1012	0.9
1548	5.3		1631	5.1
2137	1.1		2205	1.4
14 W 0356	5.3		**29** TH 0443	5.1
1005	0.8		1046	1.0
1632	5.3		1711	4.9
2224	1.2		2235	1.5
15 TH 0440	5.3		**30** F 0522	5.0
1055	0.8		1116	1.1
1720	5.3		1750	4.8
2313	1.4		2307	1.6

JULY

Time	m		Time	m
1 SA 0602	4.9		**16** SU 0600	5.5
1148	1.3		1222	0.7
1830	4.6		1843	5.2
2344	1.8			
2 SU 0645	4.7		**17** M 0029	1.3
1226	1.5		0650	5.3
1914	4.5		1309	0.9
			◐ 1938	5.0
3 M 0027	2.0		**18** TU 0117	1.6
0731	4.6		0748	5.1
1312	1.6		1400	1.3
◐ 2001	4.4		2038	4.7
4 TU 0122	2.1		**19** W 0218	1.8
0822	4.5		0856	4.9
1407	1.8		1505	1.6
2053	4.3		2143	4.6
5 W 0230	2.2		**20** TH 0335	1.9
0919	4.4		1008	4.7
1514	1.9		1624	1.8
2149	4.3		2249	4.6
6 TH 0349	2.2		**21** F 0455	1.8
1019	4.4		1121	4.7
1627	1.9		1738	1.8
2248	4.4		2356	4.7
7 F 0459	2.1		**22** SA 0608	1.6
1121	4.4		1230	4.8
1729	1.8		1839	1.7
2347	4.6			
8 SA 0556	1.8		**23** SU 0057	4.9
1222	4.6		0711	1.3
1822	1.6		1329	4.9
			1927	1.6
9 SU 0043	4.8		**24** M 0148	5.0
0646	1.5		0802	1.1
1317	4.9		1417	5.0
1910	1.4		2008	1.5
10 M 0133	5.0		**25** TU 0232	5.2
0735	1.2		0845	1.0
1406	5.1		1458	5.1
1957	1.3		● 2043	1.4
11 TU 0218	5.2		**26** W 0311	5.2
0824	0.9		0922	0.9
1451	5.4		1535	5.1
○ 2044	1.1		2115	1.3
12 W 0301	5.4		**27** TH 0347	5.3
0914	0.7		0954	0.8
1535	5.5		1609	5.1
2132	1.0		2144	1.3
13 TH 0343	5.5		**28** F 0420	5.3
1004	0.5		1022	0.9
1620	5.6		1642	5.0
2218	1.0		2212	1.3
14 F 0427	5.6		**29** SA 0454	5.2
1051	0.4		1049	0.9
1705	5.6		1716	5.0
2303	1.0		2240	1.4
15 SA 0512	5.6		**30** SU 0528	5.1
1137	0.5		1116	1.1
1753	5.4		1752	4.8
2346	1.1		2308	1.5
			31 M 0603	4.9
			1146	1.3
			1831	4.7
			2338	1.7

AUGUST

Time	m		Time	m
1 TU 0642	4.8		**16** W 0037	1.5
1219	1.5		0722	5.1
1913	4.6		1314	1.5
			○ 2005	4.7
2 W 0014	1.9		**17** TH 0138	1.8
0726	4.6		0832	4.7
1301	1.6		1420	2.0
◐ 2001	4.4		2113	4.5
3 TH 0105	2.1		**18** F 0314	2.0
0821	4.4		0950	4.5
1358	2.0		1606	2.2
2058	4.3		2227	4.4
4 F 0228	2.3		**19** SA 0458	1.9
0929	4.3		1113	4.5
1526	2.2		1738	2.2
2203	4.3		2345	4.6
5 SA 0418	2.3		**20** SU 0618	1.7
1043	4.3		1231	4.6
1701	2.1		1839	2.0
2312	4.4			
6 SU 0536	2.0		**21** M 0050	4.8
1155	4.5		0714	1.4
1805	1.8		1327	4.9
			1921	1.8
7 M 0018	4.7		**22** TU 0139	5.0
0634	1.6		0756	1.1
1259	4.9		1409	5.0
1858	1.6		1954	1.6
8 TU 0115	5.0		**23** W 0219	5.2
0727	1.2		0831	1.0
1350	5.3		1443	5.1
1946	1.3		● 2023	1.4
9 W 0201	5.3		**24** TH 0253	5.3
0817	0.7		0901	0.9
1435	5.6		1514	5.2
○ 2033	1.0		2051	1.3
10 TH 0243	5.6		**25** F 0323	5.4
0906	0.4		0928	0.8
1518	5.8		1542	5.2
2118	0.8		2119	1.1
11 F 0324	5.8		**26** SA 0353	5.4
0951	0.1		0953	0.8
1600	5.8		1611	5.2
2201	0.7		2146	1.1
12 SA 0407	6.0		**27** SU 0422	5.3
1035	0.1		1018	0.8
1644	5.8		1643	5.1
2241	0.7		2211	1.2
13 SU 0450	5.9		**28** M 0454	5.2
1116	0.2		1041	1.0
1729	5.6		1716	5.0
2320	0.9		2233	1.2
14 M 0536	5.6		**29** TU 0527	5.1
1155	0.6		1103	1.2
1816	5.3		1752	4.9
2356	1.1		2255	1.5
15 TU 0626	5.5		**30** W 0604	4.9
1232	1.0		1125	1.5
1907	5.0		1831	4.7
			2323	1.7
			31 TH 0646	4.6
			1155	1.8
			1916	4.5
			◑	

Chart Datum: 2·90 metres below Ordnance Datum (Newlyn)

TIME ZONE (UT)
For Summer Time add ONE hour in **non-shaded areas**

SCOTLAND – LEITH

LAT 55°59′N   LONG 3°11′W

TIMES AND HEIGHTS OF HIGH AND LOW WATERS

2006

SEPTEMBER

Time	m		Time	m
1 0005	2.0	**16** 0312	2.1
0738	4.4	0934	4.3
F 1246	2.1	SA 1559	2.5
2011	4.3	2207	4.4
2 0118	2.3	**17** 0502	2.0
0849	4.2	1102	4.4
SA 1436	2.4	SU 1730	2.4
2124	4.3	2328	4.5
3 0349	2.3	**18** 0610	1.7
1013	4.3	1220	4.6
SU 1645	2.3	M 1823	2.1
2243	4.4		
4 0523	2.0	**19** 0032	4.8
1134	4.6	0658	1.4
M 1752	2.0	TU 1311	4.9
2356	4.7	1859	1.9
5 0623	1.5	**20** 0118	5.1
1239	5.0	0734	1.2
TU 1843	1.6	W 1348	5.0
		1928	1.6
6 0052	5.1	**21** 0155	5.3
0715	1.0	0803	1.0
W 1330	5.4	TH 1418	5.2
1929	1.2	1954	1.3
7 0138	5.5	**22** 0226	5.4
0802	0.5	0829	0.9
TH 1413	5.8	F 1445	5.2
○ 2012	0.8	2022	1.2
8 0219	5.9	**23** 0254	5.4
0847	0.1	0854	0.8
F 1454	5.9	SA 1511	5.3
2055	0.6	2051	1.1
9 0300	6.1	**24** 0322	5.4
0930	0.0	0919	0.8
SA 1535	6.0	SU 1539	5.3
2136	0.5	2118	1.0
10 0342	6.2	**25** 0352	5.4
1011	0.0	0944	0.9
SU 1618	5.9	M 1610	5.2
2216	0.5	2142	1.1
11 0427	6.1	**26** 0424	5.3
1049	0.3	1005	1.0
M 1701	5.6	TU 1642	5.1
2253	0.7	2203	1.3
12 0513	5.8	**27** 0458	5.1
1124	0.7	1022	1.3
TU 1747	5.3	W 1717	5.0
2327	1.1	2224	1.4
13 0604	5.4	**28** 0536	4.9
1154	1.3	1042	1.5
W 1837	5.0	TH 1755	4.8
		2253	1.7
14 0007	1.5	**29** 0620	4.7
0701	5.0	1112	1.9
TH 1232	1.9	F 1840	4.6
◐ 1936	4.6	2336	1.9
15 0112	1.9	**30** 0715	4.5
0813	4.6	1201	2.2
F 1343	2.4	SA 1937	4.4
2048	4.4	◑	

OCTOBER

Time	m		Time	m
1 0055	2.2	**16** 0438	2.0
0825	4.3	1032	4.3
SU 1425	2.5	M 1651	2.5
2052	4.3	2255	4.5
2 0334	2.2	**17** 0538	1.7
0950	4.4	1147	4.5
M 1625	2.3	TU 1743	2.2
2217	4.5	2358	4.8
3 0505	1.8	**18** 0623	1.5
1111	4.7	1238	4.8
TU 1728	2.0	W 1820	1.9
2329	4.9		
4 0603	1.3	**19** 0044	5.0
1214	5.2	0657	1.3
W 1818	1.5	TH 1315	5.0
		1851	1.7
5 0025	5.3	**20** 0121	5.2
0652	0.8	0725	1.2
TH 1304	5.5	F 1345	5.1
1902	1.1	1921	1.4
6 0111	5.7	**21** 0153	5.3
0738	0.4	0751	1.0
F 1347	5.8	SA 1412	5.2
1945	0.8	1952	1.2
7 0153	6.0	**22** 0223	5.4
0821	0.2	0817	0.9
SA 1427	6.0	SU 1439	5.3
○ 2028	0.6	● 2022	1.1
8 0235	6.2	**23** 0254	5.4
0903	0.1	0845	0.9
SU 1509	6.0	M 1508	5.3
2110	0.5	2052	1.1
9 0319	6.2	**24** 0326	5.3
0943	0.1	0911	1.0
M 1551	5.8	TU 1540	5.3
2152	0.5	2120	1.1
10 0405	6.0	**25** 0400	5.2
1021	0.6	0935	1.2
TU 1635	5.6	W 1613	5.2
2231	0.8	2145	1.3
11 0454	5.7	**26** 0437	5.1
1053	1.1	0956	1.4
W 1721	5.3	TH 1649	5.1
2309	1.1	2211	1.4
12 0546	5.3	**27** 0518	5.0
1120	1.6	1021	1.7
TH 1811	5.0	F 1729	4.9
2352	1.5	2246	1.6
13 0646	4.8	**28** 0605	4.8
1157	2.1	1057	2.0
F 1911	4.6	SA 1816	4.7
		2339	1.9
14 0058	1.9	**29** 0701	4.6
0755	4.5	1201	2.3
SA 1311	2.6	SU 1914	4.6
2024	4.4	◐	
15 0304	2.1	**30** 0112	2.0
0910	4.3	0808	4.5
SU 1530	2.7	M 1345	2.5
2139	4.4 ◑	2027	4.5
		31 0310	2.0
		0927	4.6
		TU 1550	2.3
		2149	4.7

NOVEMBER

Time	m		Time	m
1 0433	1.6	**16** 0531	1.7
1042	4.8	1144	4.6
W 1654	1.9	TH 1730	2.1
2258	5.0	2358	4.8
2 0532	1.2	**17** 0609	1.6
1144	5.2	1228	4.8
TH 1745	1.6	F 1810	1.9
2354	5.3		
3 0623	0.9	**18** 0040	5.0
1234	5.5	0641	1.4
F 1832	1.2	SA 1304	4.9
		1847	1.6
4 0042	5.7	**19** 0118	5.1
0709	0.6	0712	1.3
SA 1320	5.7	SU 1336	5.1
1917	0.9	1922	1.4
5 0128	5.9	**20** 0154	5.2
0754	0.5	0743	1.2
SU 1402	5.8	M 1408	5.2
○ 2003	0.7	● 1957	1.3
6 0214	6.0	**21** 0229	5.2
0836	0.5	0814	1.2
M 1444	5.8	TU 1442	5.3
2050	0.6	2031	1.2
7 0301	6.0	**22** 0306	5.3
0917	0.7	0847	1.2
TU 1528	5.7	W 1516	5.3
2135	0.7	2106	1.2
8 0349	5.8	**23** 0343	5.2
0955	1.0	0920	1.3
W 1613	5.6	TH 1552	5.3
2218	0.9	2142	1.2
9 0440	5.5	**24** 0423	5.2
1029	1.4	0953	1.5
TH 1659	5.3	F 1630	5.2
2300	1.2	2221	1.3
10 0532	5.2	**25** 0506	5.1
1057	1.8	1031	1.7
F 1749	5.0	SA 1712	5.1
2344	1.5	2307	1.4
11 0628	4.8	**26** 0554	5.0
1134	2.2	1119	1.9
SA 1847	4.7	SU 1800	5.0
12 0041	1.8	**27** 0004	1.6
0728	4.5	0647	4.9
SU 1233	2.5	M 1226	2.1
◐ 1953	4.5	1855	4.9
13 0215	2.0	**28** 0114	1.6
0832	4.4	0749	4.8
M 1414	2.7	TU 1346	2.2
2100	4.5	◑ 2000	4.8
14 0343	2.0	**29** 0233	1.6
0939	4.3	0859	4.7
TU 1546	2.6	W 1504	2.2
2205	4.5	2114	4.9
15 0444	1.9	**30** 0349	1.5
1046	4.4	1008	4.9
W 1644	2.4	TH 1611	2.0
2306	4.6	2223	5.0

DECEMBER

Time	m		Time	m
1 0453	1.3	**16** 0511	1.9
1111	5.0	1123	4.5
F 1709	1.7	SA 1728	2.1
2323	5.2	2352	4.6
2 0550	1.2	**17** 0557	1.7
1205	5.2	1215	4.7
SA 1803	1.4	SU 1815	1.9
3 0018	5.4	**18** 0042	4.8
0641	1.0	0637	1.6
SU 1255	5.4	M 1301	4.9
1855	1.2	1857	1.7
4 0110	5.6	**19** 0128	4.9
0729	1.0	0715	1.5
M 1341	5.5	TU 1343	5.1
1947	0.9	1937	1.4
5 0201	5.6	**20** 0210	5.1
0815	1.0	0754	1.4
TU 1427	5.6	W 1422	5.2
○ 2038	0.8	● 2017	1.3
6 0250	5.6	**21** 0251	5.2
0858	1.1	0833	1.3
W 1512	5.5	TH 1500	5.3
2126	0.8	2059	1.1
7 0339	5.5	**22** 0331	5.3
0938	1.3	0915	1.3
TH 1557	5.4	F 1538	5.4
2211	0.9	2143	1.0
8 0428	5.3	**23** 0412	5.4
1013	1.5	0957	1.3
F 1643	5.3	SA 1617	5.4
2253	1.1	2229	1.0
9 0516	5.1	**24** 0455	5.3
1042	1.8	1041	1.4
SA 1729	5.1	SU 1700	5.4
2331	1.3	2316	1.0
10 0603	4.9	**25** 0541	5.3
1114	2.0	1126	1.5
SU 1819	4.9	M 1745	5.3
11 0009	1.6	**26** 0004	1.1
0652	4.6	0630	5.1
M 1156	2.2	TU 1213	1.7
1911	4.7	1834	5.2
12 0054	1.8	**27** 0054	1.2
0742	4.5	0724	5.0
TU 1251	2.3	W 1306	1.8
◐ 2007	4.6	◑ 1930	5.1
13 0155	2.0	**28** 0150	1.4
0836	4.3	0816	4.8
W 1402	2.5	TH 1410	2.0
2104	4.5	2035	5.0
14 0311	2.0	**29** 0257	1.5
0931	4.3	0932	4.7
TH 1525	2.5	F 1522	2.0
2200	4.5	2148	4.9
15 0418	2.0	**30** 0410	1.6
1028	4.4	1037	4.8
F 1633	2.3	SA 1635	1.9
2257	4.5	2257	4.9
		31 0520	1.6
		1140	4.9
		SU 1742	1.7

Chart Datum: 2·90 metres below Ordnance Datum (Newlyn)

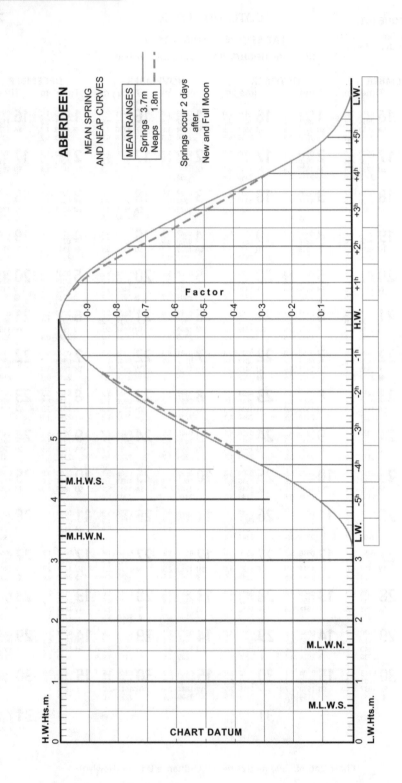

ABERDEEN

MEAN SPRING
AND NEAP CURVES

MEAN RANGES
Springs 3.7m
Neaps 1.8m

Springs occur 2 days
after
New and Full Moon

SCOTLAND – ABERDEEN

LAT 57°09′N   LONG 2°05′W

TIMES AND HEIGHTS OF HIGH AND LOW WATERS

2006

Chart Datum: 2·25 metres below Ordnance Datum (Newlyn)

JANUARY

Day	Time m	Time m	Time m	Time m	Day	Time m	Time m	Time m	Time m
1 SU	0151 4.3	0748 1.0	1359 4.4	2017 0.7	16 M	0234 3.9	0817 1.3	1434 4.2	2048 0.9
2 M	0240 4.3	0833 1.0	1444 4.4	2105 0.6	17 TU	0307 3.9	0848 1.3	1507 4.1	2121 0.9
3 TU	0331 4.3	0920 1.1	1530 4.4	2155 0.6	18 W	0341 3.9	0919 1.3	1539 4.1	2154 1.0
4 W	0422 4.2	1007 1.2	1620 4.4	2247 0.6	19 TH	0415 3.8	0951 1.4	1614 4.0	2228 1.1
5 TH	0515 4.0	1056 1.3	1712 4.2	2341 0.8	20 F	0451 3.7	1024 1.5	1651 3.9	2305 1.2
6 F ◐	0609 3.8	1151 1.5	1809 4.1		21 SA	0531 3.6	1102 1.6	1732 3.8	2346 1.4
7 SA	0038 1.0	0708 3.7	1252 1.6	1912 3.9	22 SU ◑	0617 3.5	1147 1.8	1821 3.6	
8 SU	0140 1.2	0812 3.6	1359 1.7	2022 3.8	23 M	0037 1.5	0710 3.4	1247 1.9	1921 3.5
9 M	0248 1.4	0920 3.6	1515 1.7	2137 3.7	24 TU	0139 1.7	0814 3.4	1404 2.0	2034 3.4
10 TU	0400 1.5	1024 3.6	1629 1.6	2247 3.7	25 W	0252 1.7	0925 3.4	1527 1.9	2153 3.5
11 W	0501 1.5	1120 3.8	1729 1.4	2346 3.8	26 TH	0407 1.6	1032 3.6	1642 1.6	2305 3.7
12 TH	0551 1.5	1208 3.9	1818 1.3		27 F	0512 1.5	1129 3.8	1742 1.3	
13 F	0036 3.9	0632 1.4	1250 4.0	1900 1.1	28 SA	0003 3.9	0605 1.3	1218 4.0	1833 0.9
14 SA ○	0120 3.9	0710 1.4	1327 4.1	1939 1.0	29 SU ●	0056 4.2	0653 1.1	1303 4.3	1921 0.6
15 SU	0158 3.9	0744 1.3	1401 4.1	2015 0.9	30 M	0144 4.3	0738 0.9	1347 4.5	2008 0.4
					31 TU	0230 4.4	0822 0.8	1431 4.6	2053 0.2

FEBRUARY

Day	Time m	Time m	Time m	Time m	Day	Time m	Time m	Time m	Time m
1 W	0315 4.4	0904 0.8	1515 4.6	2139 0.2	16 TH	0311 3.9	0854 1.1	1513 4.2	2124 0.8
2 TH	0400 4.3	0946 0.9	1600 4.6	2224 0.4	17 F	0340 3.9	0922 1.1	1544 4.1	2153 0.9
3 F	0446 4.1	1029 1.0	1647 4.4	2310 0.7	18 SA	0412 3.8	0951 1.2	1616 4.0	2224 1.1
4 SA	0534 3.9	1115 1.2	1739 4.2	2359 1.0	19 SU	0446 3.7	1023 1.3	1653 3.8	2259 1.2
5 SU ◐	0626 3.6	1209 1.5	1838 3.9		20 M	0525 3.6	1102 1.5	1737 3.7	2342 1.5
6 M	0055 1.4	0727 3.5	1317 1.7	1950 3.6	21 TU	0615 3.4	1154 1.7	1836 3.5	
7 TU	0205 1.7	0840 3.4	1445 1.8	2117 3.4	22 W	0044 1.7	0721 3.3	1313 1.8	1957 3.3
8 W	0337 1.8	0959 3.4	1607 1.6	2242 3.5	23 TH	0211 1.8	0842 3.3	1455 1.8	2131 3.4
9 TH	0452 1.8	1107 3.6	1724 1.5	2346 3.6	24 F	0348 1.8	1004 3.4	1627 1.5	2254 3.6
10 F	0543 1.7	1158 3.7	1811 1.3		25 SA	0501 1.5	1110 3.7	1730 1.1	2354 3.9
11 SA	0033 3.7	0623 1.5	1240 3.9	1850 1.1	26 SU	0554 1.2	1201 4.0	1821 0.7	
12 SU	0111 3.8	0657 1.4	1314 4.0	1924 0.9	27 M	0043 4.2	0639 1.0	1247 4.3	1906 0.4
13 M	0143 3.9	0729 1.2	1345 4.2	1956 0.8	28 TU ●	0128 4.4	0721 0.7	1329 4.5	1950 0.1
14 TU	0213 3.9	0758 1.1	1415 4.2	2026 0.8					
15 W	0242 4.0	0826 1.1	1444 4.2	2055 0.7					

MARCH

Day	Time m	Time m	Time m	Time m	Day	Time m	Time m	Time m	Time m
1 W	0210 4.5	0802 0.6	1411 4.7	2033 0.0	16 TH	0212 4.0	0800 0.9	1417 4.2	2024 0.7
2 TH	0251 4.4	0841 0.5	1453 4.7	2114 0.1	17 F	0239 4.0	0827 0.9	1446 4.1	2051 0.7
3 F	0332 4.3	0920 0.6	1536 4.6	2155 0.4	18 SA	0307 3.9	0854 0.9	1516 4.1	2119 0.8
4 SA	0413 4.1	1001 0.8	1622 4.4	2236 0.7	19 SU	0337 3.9	0923 1.0	1549 4.0	2148 1.0
5 SU	0456 3.9	1044 1.0	1712 4.1	2320 1.2	20 M	0410 3.8	0955 1.1	1627 3.8	2222 1.2
6 M	0545 3.6	1136 1.3	1811 3.7		21 TU	0448 3.6	1034 1.3	1713 3.6	2306 1.5
7 TU	0013 1.6	0644 3.4	1245 1.6	1925 3.4	22 W ◑	0537 3.5	1129 1.5	1817 3.4	
8 W	0126 1.9	0800 3.2	1423 1.8	2101 3.2	23 TH	0012 1.7	0645 3.3	1253 1.7	1944 3.3
9 TH	0319 2.0	0931 3.3	1609 1.6	2234 3.3	24 F	0152 1.9	0812 3.2	1441 1.6	2120 3.4
10 F	0440 1.9	1047 3.4	1710 1.4	2334 3.5	25 SA	0335 1.8	0939 3.4	1612 1.3	2241 3.6
11 SA	0528 1.7	1139 3.6	1753 1.2		26 SU	0444 1.5	1048 3.7	1712 0.9	2337 3.9
12 SU	0016 3.6	0604 1.5	1218 3.8	1827 1.0	27 M	0535 1.2	1139 4.0	1801 0.5	
13 M	0049 3.8	0636 1.3	1251 3.9	1859 0.8	28 TU	0023 4.2	0618 0.9	1224 4.3	1844 0.2
14 TU ○	0118 3.9	0705 1.1	1321 4.1	1929 0.7	29 W ●	0104 4.3	0658 0.6	1306 4.5	1927 0.1
15 W	0145 3.9	0733 1.0	1349 4.1	1957 0.7	30 TH	0144 4.4	0738 0.5	1348 4.7	2007 0.1
					31 F	0223 4.4	0817 0.4	1430 4.6	2046 0.3

APRIL

Day	Time m	Time m	Time m	Time m	Day	Time m	Time m	Time m	Time m
1 SA	0301 4.3	0856 0.5	1514 4.5	2125 0.6	16 SU	0237 4.0	0831 0.8	1454 4.0	2051 0.9
2 SU	0341 4.1	0937 0.7	1600 4.2	2204 0.9	17 M	0309 3.9	0903 0.9	1530 3.9	2123 1.0
3 M	0423 3.9	1021 0.9	1652 3.9	2246 1.3	18 TU	0345 3.8	0940 1.0	1613 3.8	2202 1.3
4 TU	0510 3.6	1113 1.2	1752 3.5	2337 1.7	19 W	0426 3.7	1026 1.2	1706 3.6	2252 1.5
5 W ◐	0608 3.4	1221 1.5	1905 3.2		20 TH	0518 3.5	1128 1.3	1816 3.4	
6 TH	0051 2.0	0722 3.2	1356 1.7	2034 3.1	21 F ◑	0005 1.7	0628 3.4	1254 1.4	1939 3.3
7 F	0242 2.1	0851 3.2	1539 1.6	2205 3.2	22 SA	0142 1.8	0752 3.3	1428 1.3	2105 3.4
8 SA	0408 1.9	1010 3.3	1638 1.4	2303 3.4	23 SU	0311 1.7	0912 3.5	1547 1.0	2218 3.7
9 SU	0456 1.7	1104 3.5	1720 1.2	2343 3.5	24 M	0416 1.4	1019 3.7	1646 0.7	2312 3.9
10 M	0533 1.5	1144 3.7	1755 1.0		25 TU	0507 1.1	1112 4.0	1735 0.5	2357 4.1
11 TU	0015 3.7	0605 1.3	1218 3.8	1826 0.8	26 W	0552 0.9	1158 4.3	1820 0.3	
12 W	0044 3.8	0635 1.1	1249 4.0	1855 0.7	27 TH ●	0037 4.2	0634 0.7	1243 4.4	1901 0.3
13 TH ○	0112 3.9	0704 1.0	1319 4.0	1924 0.7	28 F	0117 4.3	0715 0.5	1326 4.5	1941 0.4
14 F	0139 4.0	0732 0.9	1349 4.1	1952 0.7	29 SA	0156 4.2	0756 0.5	1411 4.4	2020 0.5
15 SA	0208 4.0	0801 0.8	1420 4.1	2021 0.8	30 SU	0235 4.2	0838 0.6	1457 4.2	2059 0.8

TIDES

TIME ZONE (UT)
For Summer Time add ONE hour in **non-shaded areas**

SCOTLAND – ABERDEEN
LAT 57°09'N   LONG 2°05'W
TIMES AND HEIGHTS OF HIGH AND LOW WATERS

2006

MAY

Day	Time m	Time m		Day	Time m	Time m
1	0315 4.0 / 0920 0.7	M 1545 4.0 / 2138 1.1		16	0249 4.0 / 0854 0.9	TU 1522 3.9 / 2112 1.1
2	0357 3.8 / 1006 0.9	TU 1637 3.7 / 2220 1.5		17	0329 3.9 / 0939 0.9	W 1611 3.8 / 2158 1.3
3	0443 3.6 / 1057 1.2	W 1735 3.4 / 2309 1.7		18	0415 3.8 / 1031 1.0	TH 1708 3.6 / 2253 1.5
4	0538 3.4 / 1159 1.4	TH 1838 3.2		19	0511 3.7 / 1135 1.1	F 1815 3.5
5	0014 2.0 / 0643 3.3	F 1315 1.5 / ◖ 1948 3.1		20	0002 1.6 / 0617 3.6	SA 1249 1.1 / ◗ 1926 3.5
6	0140 2.0 / 0756 3.2	SA 1438 1.5 / 2106 3.1		21	0121 1.6 / 0729 3.6	SU 1405 1.0 / 2039 3.5
7	0307 1.9 / 0912 3.3	SU 1545 1.4 / 2209 3.3		22	0235 1.6 / 0841 3.6	M 1514 0.9 / 2146 3.6
8	0407 1.8 / 1013 3.4	M 1633 1.2 / 2255 3.4		23	0340 1.4 / 0947 3.8	TU 1615 0.8 / 2242 3.8
9	0451 1.6 / 1059 3.5	TU 1712 1.1 / 2332 3.6		24	0436 1.2 / 1045 4.0	W 1708 0.7 / 2329 3.9
10	0527 1.4 / 1138 3.7	W 1747 1.0		25	0526 1.0 / 1136 4.1	TH 1755 0.6
11	0005 3.7 / 0600 1.2	TH 1214 3.8 / 1818 0.9		26	0012 4.0 / 0613 0.8	F 1225 4.2 / 1838 0.7
12	0037 3.8 / 0633 1.0	F 1248 3.9 / 1850 0.8		27	0054 4.1 / 0658 0.7	SA 1312 4.2 / ● 1920 0.7
13	0108 3.9 / 0705 1.0	SA 1323 4.0 / ○ 1923 0.8		28	0134 4.1 / 0742 0.6	SU 1359 4.1 / 2000 0.9
14	0140 4.0 / 0739 0.9	SU 1400 4.0 / 1957 0.9		29	0215 4.1 / 0826 0.7	M 1446 4.0 / 2040 1.1
15	0213 4.0 / 0815 0.8	M 1439 4.0 / 2033 1.0		30	0256 4.0 / 0909 0.8	TU 1534 3.8 / 2119 1.3
				31	0337 3.9 / 0953 0.9	W 1622 3.7 / 2159 1.5

JUNE

Day	Time m	Time m		Day	Time m	Time m
1	0421 3.7 / 1039 1.0	TH 1712 3.5 / 2243 1.6		16	0409 4.0 / 1032 0.7	F 1704 3.8 / 2248 1.3
2	0510 3.6 / 1130 1.2	F 1803 3.3 / 2334 1.8		17	0502 3.9 / 1129 0.8	SA 1801 3.7 / 2346 1.4
3	0603 3.5 / 1226 1.3	SA 1857 3.2		18	0600 3.9 / 1230 0.8	SU 1902 3.6
4	0036 1.9 / 0700 3.4	SU 1328 1.4 / 1955 3.2		19	0049 1.5 / 0702 3.8	M 1334 0.9 / 2005 3.6
5	0146 1.9 / 0802 3.3	M 1430 1.4 / 2057 3.2		20	0156 1.5 / 0809 3.8	TU 1438 1.0 / 2110 3.6
6	0253 1.8 / 0906 3.3	TU 1528 1.4 / 2154 3.3		21	0302 1.4 / 0917 3.8	W 1543 1.0 / 2211 3.7
7	0352 1.7 / 1004 3.4	W 1619 1.3 / 2242 3.5		22	0408 1.3 / 1023 3.8	TH 1644 1.0 / 2305 3.8
8	0442 1.5 / 1054 3.5	TH 1703 1.2 / 2324 3.6		23	0509 1.2 / 1123 3.9	F 1737 1.0 / 2354 3.9
9	0524 1.4 / 1139 3.7	F 1743 1.1		24	0602 1.0 / 1217 3.9	SA 1825 1.1
10	0003 3.8 / 0604 1.2	SA 1222 3.8 / 1821 1.0		25	0039 4.0 / 0650 0.9	SU 1307 3.9 / ● 1907 1.1
11	0040 3.9 / 0643 1.0	SU 1303 3.9 / ○ 1901 1.0		26	0122 4.0 / 0735 0.8	M 1354 3.9 / 1947 1.1
12	0117 4.0 / 0724 0.9	M 1346 4.0 / 1941 1.0		27	0202 4.0 / 0817 0.7	TU 1438 3.9 / 2025 1.2
13	0156 4.0 / 0807 0.8	TU 1431 4.0 / 2024 1.0		28	0241 4.0 / 0857 0.8	W 1520 3.8 / 2101 1.3
14	0237 4.1 / 0852 0.7	W 1518 4.0 / 2109 1.1		29	0319 4.0 / 0936 0.8	TH 1600 3.7 / 2137 1.3
15	0320 4.1 / 0940 0.7	TH 1609 3.9 / 2156 1.2		30	0358 3.9 / 1015 0.9	F 1640 3.6 / 2213 1.4

JULY

Day	Time m	Time m		Day	Time m	Time m
1	0438 3.8 / 1054 1.0	SA 1721 3.5 / 2252 1.5		16	0444 4.2 / 1109 0.5	SU 1736 3.9 / 2319 1.2
2	0520 3.7 / 1137 1.2	SU 1805 3.4 / 2336 1.6 ◖		17	0536 4.1 / 1202 0.7	M 1830 3.7
3	0607 3.6 / 1225 1.3	M 1854 3.3 ◖		18	0014 1.3 / 0634 3.9	TU 1259 1.0 / 1929 3.6
4	0030 1.8 / 0659 3.4	TU 1319 1.4 / 1947 3.3		19	0118 1.5 / 0739 3.8	W 1403 1.2 / 2035 3.5
5	0134 1.8 / 0758 3.4	W 1418 1.5 / 2047 3.3		20	0230 1.5 / 0855 3.6	TH 1516 1.4 / 2145 3.5
6	0243 1.8 / 0903 3.3	TH 1519 1.5 / 2149 3.4		21	0352 1.5 / 1013 3.6	F 1630 1.5 / 2249 3.6
7	0351 1.7 / 1010 3.4	F 1619 1.5 / 2245 3.5		22	0503 1.3 / 1122 3.7	SA 1729 1.4 / 2345 3.8
8	0450 1.5 / 1109 3.5	SA 1713 1.3 / 2333 3.7		23	0559 1.1 / 1219 3.8	SU 1817 1.4
9	0541 1.3 / 1201 3.7	SU 1801 1.2		24	0031 3.9 / 0645 1.0	M 1307 3.8 / 1857 1.3
10	0017 3.9 / 0628 1.1	M 1250 3.9 / 1846 1.1		25	0113 4.0 / 0726 0.8	TU 1347 3.9 / ● 1934 1.2
11	0100 4.0 / 0713 0.8	TU 1337 4.0 / ○ 1931 1.0		26	0149 4.1 / 0804 0.7	W 1424 3.9 / 2008 1.2
12	0142 4.2 / 0759 0.6	W 1423 4.2 / 2015 0.9		27	0224 4.1 / 0839 0.7	TH 1458 3.9 / 2040 1.2
13	0225 4.3 / 0845 0.4	TH 1510 4.2 / 2059 0.9		28	0257 4.1 / 0911 0.7	F 1531 3.8 / 2110 1.2
14	0309 4.3 / 0932 0.4	F 1557 4.1 / 2144 0.9		29	0329 4.1 / 0943 0.8	SA 1604 3.8 / 2141 1.2
15	0355 4.3 / 1020 0.4	SA 1646 4.0 / 2230 1.0		30	0403 4.0 / 1016 0.9	SU 1638 3.7 / 2213 1.3
				31	0439 3.9 / 1050 1.1	M 1716 3.6 / 2248 1.5

AUGUST

Day	Time m	Time m		Day	Time m	Time m
1	0519 3.7 / 1128 1.3	TU 1758 3.5 / 2330 1.6		16	0607 3.9 / 1223 1.2	W 1853 3.6 ◖
2	0605 3.6 / 1214 1.4	W 1848 3.4 ◖		17	0046 1.5 / 0717 3.7	TH 1330 1.6 / 2003 3.4
3	0024 1.8 / 0702 3.4	TH 1313 1.6 / 1948 3.3		18	0210 1.6 / 0843 3.5	F 1458 1.8 / 2124 3.3
4	0139 1.9 / 0812 3.3	F 1425 1.7 / 2058 3.3		19	0350 1.6 / 1014 3.5	SA 1626 1.8 / 2238 3.6
5	0305 1.8 / 0933 3.3	SA 1544 1.7 / 2209 3.4		20	0502 1.4 / 1125 3.6	SU 1724 1.7 / 2336 3.7
6	0425 1.6 / 1048 3.5	SU 1653 1.6 / 2309 3.6		21	0553 1.2 / 1216 3.7	M 1807 1.5
7	0525 1.3 / 1147 3.7	M 1747 1.3 / 2358 3.9		22	0020 3.9 / 0634 1.0	TU 1256 3.8 / 1842 1.3
8	0615 1.0 / 1237 4.0	TU 1833 1.1		23	0057 4.0 / 0709 0.8	W 1329 3.9 / ● 1915 1.2
9	0043 4.1 / 0700 0.6	W 1324 4.2 / ○ 1917 0.9		24	0130 4.1 / 0742 0.7	TH 1400 4.0 / 1945 1.1
10	0126 4.4 / 0745 0.3	TH 1408 4.3 / 1959 0.8		25	0200 4.2 / 0812 0.7	F 1428 4.0 / 2013 1.0
11	0208 4.5 / 0829 0.2	F 1451 4.4 / 2040 0.7		26	0229 4.2 / 0841 0.7	SA 1457 4.0 / 2041 1.0
12	0250 4.6 / 0913 0.1	SA 1534 4.3 / 2122 0.7		27	0258 4.2 / 0909 0.8	SU 1526 3.9 / 2108 1.1
13	0334 4.6 / 0957 0.3	SU 1618 4.2 / 2204 0.8		28	0329 4.1 / 0937 0.9	M 1557 3.8 / 2137 1.2
14	0420 4.5 / 1041 0.5	M 1704 4.0 / 2249 1.0		29	0402 4.0 / 1007 1.1	TU 1630 3.7 / 2209 1.3
15	0510 4.2 / 1129 0.9	TU 1755 3.8 / 2341 1.3		30	0439 3.8 / 1040 1.3	W 1708 3.6 / 2247 1.5
				31	0522 3.6 / 1121 1.5	TH 1755 3.5 / ◖ 2336 1.7

Chart Datum: 2·25 metres below Ordnance Datum (Newlyn)

TIME ZONE (UT)
For Summer Time add ONE hour in **non-shaded areas**

SCOTLAND – ABERDEEN   2006

LAT 57°09′N   LONG 2°05′W

TIMES AND HEIGHTS OF HIGH AND LOW WATERS

SEPTEMBER

Day	Time	m	Time	m	Time	m	Time	m
1 F	0619	3.4	1218	1.8	1858	3.3		
2 SA	0051	1.9	0737	3.3	1343	1.9	2016	3.3
3 SU	0233	1.9	0909	3.3	1522	1.9	2138	3.4
4 M	0407	1.6	1032	3.5	1638	1.7	2246	3.7
5 TU	0509	1.2	1132	3.8	1730	1.4	2337	4.0
6 W	0557	0.8	1220	4.1	1815	1.1		
7 TH	0021	4.3	0641	0.4	1303	4.4	1856 ○	0.8
8 F	0103	4.6	0724	0.2	1344	4.5	1936	0.6
9 SA	0144	4.7	0806	0.1	1424	4.5	2016	0.6
10 SU	0226	4.8	0847	0.1	1505	4.4	2056	0.6
11 M	0310	4.7	0928	0.3	1546	4.3	2137	0.7
12 TU	0354	4.5	1010	0.7	1626	4.0	2221	1.0
13 W	0447	4.2	1055	1.1	1727	3.8	2314	1.3
14 TH	0547	3.8	1148	1.5	1819 ◑	3.6		
15 F	0023	1.6	0701	3.5	1301	1.9	1934	3.4
16 SA	0158	1.7	0720	3.3	1447	2.1	2103	3.4
17 SU	0345	1.6	0852	3.4	1616	2.0	2222	3.6
18 M	0450	1.4	1013	3.6	1708	1.8	2317	3.8
19 TU	0535	1.2	1158	3.7	1746	1.6	2358	3.9
20 W	0611	1.0	1231	3.9	1819	1.4		
21 TH	0032	4.1	0642	0.9	1302	4.0	1848	1.2
22 F	0102	4.2	0712	0.8	1329	4.0	1917 ●	1.1
23 SA	0131	4.2	0740	0.7	1355	4.1	1944	1.0
24 SU	0159	4.3	0807	0.7	1422	4.1	2011	1.0
25 M	0229	4.2	0834	0.8	1450	4.1	2039	1.1
26 TU	0300	4.1	0901	1.0	1520	4.0	2107	1.2
27 W	0333	4.0	0930	1.1	1553	3.9	2139	1.3
28 TH	0410	3.8	1003	1.4	1630	3.8	2218	1.5
29 F	0455	3.6	1043	1.6	1716	3.6	2310	1.7
30 SA	0557	3.4	1144	1.9	1821 ☾	3.4		

OCTOBER

Day	Time	m	Time	m	Time	m	Time	m
1 SU	0029	1.8	0720	3.3	1319	2.0	1945	3.4
2 M	0214	1.8	0852	3.4	1503	1.9	2109	3.5
3 TU	0344	1.5	1013	3.6	1615	1.7	2218	3.8
4 W	0445	1.1	1110	4.0	1707	1.4	2311	4.1
5 TH	0533	0.7	1156	4.2	1750	1.1	2355	4.4
6 F	0617	0.4	1237	4.4	1831	0.8		
7 SA	0037	4.7	0658	0.2	1317	4.5	1911 ○	0.6
8 SU	0120	4.8	0739	0.2	1356	4.5	1951	0.6
9 M	0203	4.8	0820	0.3	1435	4.5	2032	0.6
10 TU	0248	4.7	0900	0.6	1516	4.3	2115	0.8
11 W	0336	4.4	0941	1.0	1600	4.1	2201	1.0
12 TH	0429	4.1	1025	1.4	1649	3.8	2256	1.3
13 F	0532	3.7	1118	1.8	1749	3.6		
14 SA	0005	1.5	0646	3.4	1232	2.1	1903 ◑	3.5
15 SU	0138	1.7	0813	3.3	1415	2.2	2028	3.4
16 M	0317	1.6	0943	3.4	1544	2.1	2148	3.5
17 TU	0419	1.4	1044	3.5	1636	1.9	2243	3.7
18 W	0502	1.3	1125	3.7	1714	1.6	2325	3.9
19 TH	0538	1.1	1158	3.8	1748	1.4	2359	4.0
20 F	0609	1.0	1227	4.0	1819	1.3		
21 SA	0030	4.1	0638	0.9	1255	4.1	1848	1.1
22 SU	0101	4.2	0707	0.9	1322	4.1	1916 ●	1.1
23 M	0132	4.2	0735	0.9	1351	4.2	1945	1.1
24 TU	0203	4.2	0803	1.0	1420	4.1	2015	1.1
25 W	0237	4.1	0832	1.1	1451	4.1	2047	1.1
26 TH	0313	4.0	0904	1.3	1525	4.0	2123	1.3
27 F	0354	3.9	0940	1.5	1604	3.9	2206	1.4
28 SA	0444	3.7	1026	1.7	1653	3.7	2304	1.7
29 SU	0549	3.5	1131	1.9	1758 ◐	3.6		
30 M	0021	1.6	0707	3.5	1301	2.0	1918	3.5
31 TU	0152	1.5	0829	3.5	1432	1.9	2036	3.6

NOVEMBER

Day	Time	m	Time	m	Time	m	Time	m
1 W	0312	1.3	0943	3.7	1541	1.7	2144	3.9
2 TH	0413	1.0	1041	4.0	1635	1.4	2240	4.1
3 F	0504	0.7	1127	4.2	1722	1.1	2328	4.4
4 SA	0550	0.5	1210	4.4	1806	0.9		
5 SU	0014	4.6	0633	0.5	1250	4.5	1848 ○	0.7
6 M	0059	4.7	0715	0.5	1330	4.5	1931	0.7
7 TU	0145	4.6	0756	0.7	1410	4.4	2015	0.7
8 W	0233	4.5	0837	0.9	1452	4.3	2100	0.8
9 TH	0323	4.3	0919	1.2	1536	4.1	2149	1.0
10 F	0418	4.0	1003	1.6	1624	3.9	2242	1.4
11 SA	0517	3.7	1052	1.9	1721	3.7	2343	1.5
12 SU	0625	3.5	1155	2.1	1826 ◐	3.6		
13 M	0056	1.6	0730	3.3	1315	2.2	1937	3.5
14 TU	0215	1.6	0845	3.3	1438	2.1	2051	3.5
15 W	0324	1.6	0950	3.4	1544	2.0	2153	3.6
16 TH	0415	1.4	1038	3.6	1632	1.8	2241	3.7
17 F	0456	1.3	1116	3.7	1711	1.6	2322	3.9
18 SA	0531	1.2	1149	3.9	1746	1.4	2358	4.0
19 SU	0604	1.1	1221	4.0	1820	1.3		
20 M	0033	4.1	0635	1.1	1253	4.1	1852	1.2
21 TU	0109	4.1	0707	1.1	1324	4.2	1925	1.1
22 W	0144	4.1	0740	1.1	1356	4.2	2000	1.1
23 TH	0222	4.1	0814	1.2	1431	4.2	2038	1.1
24 F	0302	4.0	0852	1.3	1508	4.1	2119	1.1
25 SA	0348	3.9	0933	1.5	1550	4.0	2207	1.2
26 SU	0440	3.8	1022	1.6	1640	3.9	2303	1.3
27 M	0541	3.7	1122	1.7	1740 ◐	3.8		
28 TU	0009	1.3	0647	3.6	1235	1.8	1848	3.8
29 W	0122	1.3	0757	3.6	1350	1.8	1958	3.8
30 TH	0233	1.2	0906	3.7	1459	1.7	2107	3.9

DECEMBER

Day	Time	m	Time	m	Time	m	Time	m
1 F	0337	1.1	1007	3.9	1600	1.5	2210	4.1
2 SA	0434	1.0	1059	4.0	1655	1.3	2305	4.2
3 SU	0526	0.9	1145	4.2	1746	1.1	2357	4.4
4 M	0613	0.9	1229	4.3	1834	0.9		
5 TU	0047	4.4	0657	0.9	1312	4.3	1921 ○	0.8
6 W	0137	4.4	0740	1.0	1354	4.3	2006	0.8
7 TH	0226	4.3	0822	1.2	1436	4.3	2052	0.8
8 F	0315	4.1	0902	1.4	1519	4.2	2137	1.0
9 SA	0404	3.9	0943	1.5	1604	4.1	2224	1.1
10 SU	0453	3.7	1025	1.7	1651	3.9	2312	1.3
11 M	0543	3.6	1112	1.9	1742	3.7		
12 TU	0005	1.4	0635	3.4	1208	2.0	1837 ◑	3.6
13 W	0104	1.6	0732	3.3	1315	2.1	1938	3.5
14 TH	0205	1.6	0834	3.3	1424	2.1	2043	3.5
15 F	0306	1.6	0935	3.4	1531	2.0	2146	3.6
16 SA	0402	1.6	1027	3.5	1628	1.8	2240	3.6
17 SU	0450	1.5	1111	3.7	1714	1.7	2327	3.8
18 M	0531	1.4	1151	3.8	1755	1.5		
19 TU	0010	3.9	0609	1.3	1228	4.0	1833	1.3
20 W	0052	4.0	0647	1.3	1304	4.1	1911	1.1
21 TH	0132	4.0	0725	1.2	1340	4.2	1951	1.0
22 F	0214	4.1	0805	1.2	1418	4.2	2033	0.9
23 SA	0257	4.1	0846	1.2	1458	4.3	2117	0.9
24 SU	0342	4.1	0928	1.3	1541	4.2	2203	0.9
25 M	0431	4.0	1014	1.4	1628	4.2	2253	0.9
26 TU	0523	3.9	1104	1.5	1720	4.1	2347	1.0
27 W	0619	3.8	1201	1.6	1818 ◑	4.0		
28 TH	0047	1.1	0719	3.7	1306	1.7	1922	3.9
29 F	0152	1.2	0825	3.7	1415	1.7	2032	3.9
30 SA	0300	1.3	0932	3.7	1527	1.6	2145	4.0
31 SU	0408	1.3	1034	3.8	1637	1.5	2252	4.0

Chart Datum: 2·25 metres below Ordnance Datum (Newlyn)

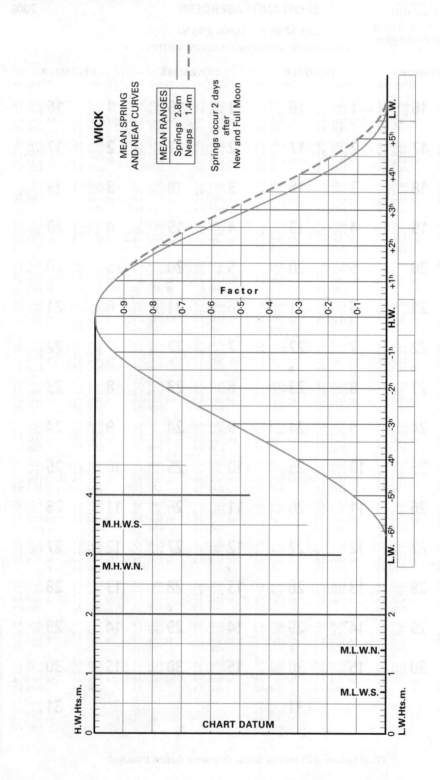

WICK

MEAN SPRING AND NEAP CURVES

MEAN RANGES	
Springs	2.8m
Neaps	1.4m

Springs occur 2 days after New and Full Moon

TIME ZONE (UT)
For Summer Time add ONE hour in **non-shaded areas**

SCOTLAND – WICK

LAT 58°26'N   LONG 3°05'W

TIMES AND HEIGHTS OF HIGH AND LOW WATERS

2006

JANUARY

Day	Time m	Day	Time m
1 SU	0533 1.0 / 1155 3.6 / 1805 0.6	16 M	0025 3.2 / 0602 1.2 / 1232 3.4 / 1838 0.8
2 M	0035 3.5 / 0619 1.0 / 1241 3.7 / 1853 0.5	17 TU	0100 3.2 / 0633 1.2 / 1304 3.4 / 1910 0.8
3 TU	0125 3.5 / 0704 1.0 / 1328 3.7 / 1944 0.5	18 W	0133 3.1 / 0703 1.2 / 1336 3.4 / 1942 0.9
4 W	0216 3.4 / 0750 1.1 / 1416 3.6 / 2036 0.6	19 TH	0205 3.0 / 0732 1.2 / 1407 3.3 / 2014 1.0
5 TH	0308 3.2 / 0838 1.2 / 1507 3.5 / 2133 0.8	20 F	0239 2.9 / 0803 1.3 / 1440 3.2 / 2049 1.1
6 F	0402 3.1 / 0930 1.3 / 1603 3.4 / 2234 0.9	21 SA	0316 2.8 / 0837 1.4 / 1518 3.1 / 2128 1.2
7 SA	0459 2.9 / 1034 1.4 / 1703 3.2 / 2339 1.1	22 SU	0359 2.8 / 0919 1.5 / 1604 2.9 / 2220 1.3
8 SU	0559 2.9 / 1149 1.5 / 1809 3.1	23 M	0453 2.7 / 1016 1.6 / 1704 2.8 / 2332 1.4
9 M	0047 1.2 / 0704 2.9 / 1309 1.5 / 1920 3.0	24 TU	0557 2.7 / 1152 1.7 / 1819 2.8
10 TU	0154 1.3 / 0810 2.9 / 1422 1.4 / 2032 3.0	25 W	0050 1.4 / 0707 2.8 / 1326 1.6 / 1939 2.8
11 W	0251 1.3 / 0908 3.1 / 1521 1.3 / 2134 3.1	26 TH	0203 1.4 / 0816 2.9 / 1439 1.4 / 2053 2.8
12 TH	0338 1.2 / 0958 3.2 / 1609 1.1 / 2225 3.1	27 F	0304 1.3 / 0916 3.1 / 1536 1.1 / 2154 3.2
13 F	0419 1.2 / 1041 3.3 / 1651 1.0 / 2310 3.2	28 SA	0355 1.1 / 1009 3.3 / 1625 0.8 / 2248 3.4
14 SA	0455 1.2 / 1121 3.4 / 1729 0.9 / ○ 2349 3.2	29 SU	0441 1.0 / 1057 3.5 / 1712 0.6 / ● 2337 3.5
15 SU	0530 1.2 / 1157 3.4 / 1804 0.9	30 M	0525 0.9 / 1144 3.7 / 1757 0.4
		31 TU	0025 3.6 / 0607 0.8 / 1229 3.8 / 1842 0.3

FEBRUARY

Day	Time m	Day	Time m
1 W	0112 3.6 / 0649 0.8 / 1314 3.8 / 1927 0.3	16 TH	0106 3.1 / 0638 0.9 / 1311 3.4 / 1911 0.7
2 TH	0157 3.5 / 0729 0.8 / 1359 3.8 / 2011 0.4	17 F	0134 3.1 / 0705 1.0 / 1339 3.3 / 1939 0.8
3 F	0241 3.3 / 0810 0.9 / 1444 3.6 / 2057 0.7	18 SA	0202 3.0 / 0733 1.0 / 1408 3.2 / 2007 0.9
4 SA	0327 3.1 / 0853 1.1 / 1533 3.4 / 2146 0.9	19 SU	0234 3.0 / 0804 1.1 / 1442 3.1 / 2040 1.1
5 SU	0416 2.9 / 0945 1.3 / 1629 3.2 / ◐ 2247 1.2	20 M	0312 2.9 / 0839 1.3 / 1524 2.9 / 2119 1.3
6 M	0513 2.8 / 1103 1.5 / 1736 2.9	21 TU	0359 2.8 / 0925 1.4 / 1619 2.8 / 2218 1.4
7 TU	0003 1.5 / 0620 2.7 / 1245 1.5 / 1857 2.8	22 W	0501 2.7 / 1043 1.6 / 1739 2.7
8 W	0132 1.6 / 0740 2.8 / 1417 1.4 / 2025 2.8	23 TH	0008 1.5 / 0621 2.7 / 1300 1.5 / 1916 2.7
9 TH	0243 1.5 / 0851 2.9 / 1518 1.2 / 2130 2.9	24 F	0145 1.5 / 0745 2.8 / 1427 1.3 / 2043 2.9
10 F	0332 1.4 / 0944 3.1 / 1603 1.1 / 2219 3.0	25 SA	0254 1.3 / 0856 3.0 / 1526 0.9 / 2145 3.1
11 SA	0410 1.3 / 1028 3.2 / 1640 0.9 / 2259 3.1	26 SU	0344 1.1 / 0952 3.3 / 1613 0.6 / 2237 3.4
12 SU	0443 1.2 / 1106 3.3 / 1713 0.8 / 2334 3.1	27 M	0428 0.9 / 1041 3.5 / 1657 0.3 / 2323 3.5
13 M	0514 1.1 / 1141 3.4 / 1744 0.7 / ○	28 TU	0508 0.7 / 1127 3.7 / 1740 0.1 / ●
14 TU	0006 3.2 / 0543 1.0 / 1213 3.4 / 1814 0.7		
15 W	0037 3.2 / 0611 1.0 / 1243 3.4 / 1843 0.7		

MARCH

Day	Time m	Day	Time m
1 W	0007 3.6 / 0547 0.6 / 1211 3.9 / 1820 0.1	16 TH	0008 3.2 / 0544 0.8 / 1216 3.4 / 1811 0.6
2 TH	0049 3.6 / 0626 0.5 / 1254 3.9 / 1901 0.2	17 F	0035 3.2 / 0611 0.8 / 1244 3.4 / 1838 0.6
3 F	0130 3.5 / 0704 0.6 / 1336 3.8 / 1940 0.4	18 SA	0102 3.2 / 0639 0.8 / 1312 3.3 / 1905 0.7
4 SA	0209 3.3 / 0742 0.7 / 1419 3.6 / 2019 0.7	19 SU	0131 3.1 / 0707 0.9 / 1342 3.2 / 1933 0.9
5 SU	0250 3.1 / 0823 0.9 / 1506 3.3 / 2100 1.0	20 M	0202 3.0 / 0738 1.0 / 1417 3.0 / 2005 1.0
6 M	0334 2.9 / 0911 1.1 / 1600 3.0 / ◐ 2151 1.4	21 TU	0238 2.9 / 0815 1.1 / 1501 2.9 / 2044 1.2
7 TU	0429 2.7 / 1030 1.4 / 1709 2.7 / 2317 1.6	22 W	0324 2.8 / 0902 1.3 / 1600 2.7 / 2143 1.5
8 W	0540 2.6 / 1228 1.4 / 1841 2.6	23 TH	0426 2.7 / 1028 1.4 / 1726 2.6 / 2350 1.6
9 TH	0111 1.7 / 0708 2.6 / 1405 1.3 / 2016 2.6	24 F	0552 2.6 / 1249 1.3 / 1909 2.6
10 F	0230 1.6 / 0828 2.8 / 1502 1.1 / 2118 2.8	25 SA	0130 1.5 / 0721 2.7 / 1410 1.0 / 2031 2.9
11 SA	0317 1.5 / 0924 2.9 / 1543 1.0 / 2201 2.9	26 SU	0236 1.2 / 0834 3.0 / 1507 0.7 / 2130 3.1
12 SU	0352 1.3 / 1006 3.1 / 1617 0.8 / 2237 3.0	27 M	0325 1.0 / 0931 3.2 / 1553 0.4 / 2218 3.3
13 M	0422 1.1 / 1043 3.2 / 1647 0.7 / 2309 3.1	28 TU	0406 0.8 / 1020 3.5 / 1635 0.2 / 2301 3.5
14 TU	0450 1.0 / 1116 3.3 / 1716 0.6 / ○ 2339 3.1	29 W	0445 0.6 / 1105 3.7 / 1715 0.1 / ● 2342 3.5
15 W	0518 0.9 / 1146 3.4 / 1745 0.6	30 TH	0524 0.5 / 1148 3.8 / 1755 0.1
		31 F	0022 3.5 / 0602 0.4 / 1231 3.8 / 1833 0.3

APRIL

Day	Time m	Day	Time m
1 SA	0101 3.4 / 0641 0.5 / 1313 3.6 / 1910 0.5	16 SU	0034 3.2 / 0616 0.7 / 1250 3.2 / 1837 0.7
2 SU	0138 3.3 / 0720 0.6 / 1356 3.4 / 1946 0.8	17 M	0104 3.2 / 0648 0.8 / 1325 3.1 / 1908 0.9
3 M	0217 3.1 / 0802 0.8 / 1443 3.1 / 2024 1.2	18 TU	0138 3.1 / 0724 0.9 / 1405 3.0 / 1945 1.1
4 TU	0259 2.9 / 0853 1.1 / 1537 2.8 / 2109 1.5	19 W	0217 3.0 / 0807 1.0 / 1454 2.8 / 2031 1.3
5 W	0352 2.7 / 1015 1.3 / 1648 2.6 / ◐ 2232 1.7	20 TH	0306 2.8 / 0905 1.1 / 1559 2.7 / 2141 1.5
6 TH	0503 2.6 / 1201 1.3 / 1817 2.4	21 F	0411 2.7 / 1052 1.2 / 1726 2.6 / 2338 1.5
7 F	0032 1.7 / 0629 2.6 / 1333 1.2 / 1948 2.5	22 SA	0534 2.7 / 1232 1.0 / 1856 2.7
8 SA	0159 1.6 / 0751 2.7 / 1429 1.1 / 2047 2.7	23 SU	0104 1.4 / 0656 2.8 / 1345 0.8 / 2009 2.9
9 SU	0246 1.4 / 0849 2.8 / 1510 0.9 / 2129 2.8	24 M	0208 1.2 / 0806 3.0 / 1440 0.6 / 2105 3.0
10 M	0321 1.3 / 0933 3.0 / 1543 0.8 / 2205 2.9	25 TU	0257 1.0 / 0904 3.2 / 1527 0.4 / 2152 3.2
11 TU	0352 1.1 / 1010 3.1 / 1614 0.7 / 2236 3.0	26 W	0339 0.8 / 0954 3.4 / 1609 0.3 / 2235 3.3
12 W	0421 0.9 / 1044 3.2 / 1643 0.6 / 2306 3.1	27 TH	0420 0.6 / 1041 3.5 / 1649 0.2 / ● 2316 3.4
13 TH	0449 0.8 / 1115 3.2 / 1712 0.6 / ○ 2335 3.2	28 F	0501 0.5 / 1126 3.6 / 1728 0.3 / 2355 3.4
14 F	0517 0.7 / 1146 3.3 / 1740 0.6	29 SA	0542 0.4 / 1210 3.5 / 1806 0.5
15 SA	0004 3.2 / 0546 0.7 / 1218 3.3 / 1807 0.6	30 SU	0033 3.4 / 0623 0.5 / 1254 3.4 / 1844 0.7

Chart Datum: 1·71 metres below Ordnance Datum (Newlyn)

TIME ZONE (UT)
For Summer Time add ONE hour in **non-shaded areas**

SCOTLAND – WICK

2006

LAT 58°26′N   LONG 3°05′W

TIMES AND HEIGHTS OF HIGH AND LOW WATERS

MAY

Day	Time m	Day	Time m
1 M	0111 3.3 / 0706 0.6 / 1338 3.2 / 1921 1.0	16 TU	0046 3.2 / 0639 0.7 / 1316 3.1 / 1856 0.9
2 TU	0150 3.1 / 0752 0.8 / 1425 2.9 / 1959 1.2	17 W	0125 3.2 / 0723 0.8 / 1402 3.0 / 1940 1.1
3 W	0233 3.0 / 0845 1.0 / 1519 2.7 / 2043 1.5	18 TH	0208 3.1 / 0815 0.8 / 1456 2.8 / 2034 1.2
4 TH	0323 2.8 / 0954 1.1 / 1622 2.5 / 2150 1.6	19 F	0300 3.0 / 0923 0.9 / 1602 2.7 / 2146 1.4
5 F	0428 2.7 / 1115 1.2 / 1736 2.4 / ◑ 2325 1.7	20 SA	0404 2.9 / 1048 0.9 / 1717 2.7 / ◐ 2313 1.4
6 SA	0542 2.6 / 1235 1.2 / 1853 2.5	21 SU	0517 2.8 / 1205 0.8 / 1830 2.7
7 SU	0054 1.6 / 0655 2.6 / 1338 1.1 / 1956 2.6	22 M	0027 1.3 / 0628 2.9 / 1313 0.7 / 1936 2.8
8 M	0155 1.5 / 0758 2.7 / 1424 1.0 / 2044 2.7	23 TU	0131 1.2 / 0734 3.0 / 1410 0.6 / 2033 3.0
9 TU	0238 1.3 / 0848 2.8 / 1502 0.9 / 2123 2.8	24 W	0226 1.0 / 0835 3.1 / 1459 0.5 / 2123 3.1
10 W	0314 1.1 / 0929 2.9 / 1536 0.8 / 2158 2.9	25 TH	0314 0.8 / 0930 3.3 / 1544 0.5 / 2209 3.2
11 TH	0347 1.0 / 1007 3.0 / 1608 0.7 / 2231 3.0	26 F	0400 0.7 / 1021 3.3 / 1625 0.6 / 2251 3.3
12 F	0419 0.9 / 1043 3.1 / 1639 0.7 / 2303 3.1	27 SA	0445 0.6 / 1109 3.3 / 1706 0.7 / ● 2332 3.3
13 SA	0452 0.8 / 1119 3.2 / 1710 0.7 / ○ 2336 3.2	28 SU	0529 0.6 / 1155 3.3 / 1746 0.8
14 SU	0525 0.7 / 1155 3.2 / 1742 0.7	29 M	0012 3.3 / 0613 0.6 / 1241 3.2 / 1825 0.9
15 M	0009 3.2 / 0600 0.7 / 1233 3.2 / 1817 0.8	30 TU	0052 3.3 / 0658 0.7 / 1325 3.0 / 1903 1.1
		31 W	0132 3.2 / 0743 0.8 / 1410 2.9 / 1941 1.2

JUNE

Day	Time m	Day	Time m
1 TH	0213 3.0 / 0830 0.9 / 1457 2.7 / 2022 1.4	16 F	0203 3.2 / 0821 0.6 / 1455 3.0 / 2031 1.1
2 F	0258 2.9 / 0922 1.0 / 1549 2.6 / 2109 1.5	17 SA	0254 3.2 / 0920 0.6 / 1553 2.9 / 2128 1.2
3 SA	0350 2.8 / 1021 1.1 / 1646 2.5 / ◑ 2212 1.5	18 SU	0351 3.1 / 1026 0.7 / 1653 2.8 / ◐ 2235 1.2
4 SU	0449 2.7 / 1124 1.1 / 1747 2.5 / 2327 1.6	19 M	0453 3.0 / 1132 0.8 / 1756 2.8 / 2345 1.3
5 M	0552 2.6 / 1226 1.1 / 1847 2.5	20 TU	0558 3.0 / 1237 0.8 / 1858 2.8
6 TU	0039 1.5 / 0653 2.7 / 1324 1.1 / 1943 2.6	21 W	0053 1.1 / 0704 3.0 / 1339 0.8 / 1959 2.9
7 W	0140 1.4 / 0751 2.7 / 1412 1.0 / 2032 2.7	22 TH	0159 1.1 / 0811 3.0 / 1435 0.9 / 2056 3.0
8 TH	0230 1.3 / 0843 2.8 / 1454 0.9 / 2115 2.9	23 F	0258 1.0 / 0914 3.1 / 1525 0.9 / 2147 3.1
9 F	0313 1.1 / 0930 2.9 / 1533 0.9 / 2155 3.0	24 SA	0351 0.9 / 1010 3.1 / 1610 0.9 / 2234 3.2
10 SA	0353 1.0 / 1014 3.0 / 1610 0.9 / 2233 3.1	25 SU	0439 0.8 / 1101 3.1 / 1652 1.0 / ● 2317 3.3
11 SU	0432 0.9 / 1057 3.1 / 1647 0.8 / ○ 2312 3.2	26 M	0524 0.7 / 1147 3.1 / 1732 1.0 / ○ 2358 3.3
12 M	0512 0.8 / 1140 3.2 / 1727 0.8 / 2351 3.3	27 TU	0607 0.6 / 1230 3.1 / 1810 1.0
13 TU	0554 0.7 / 1225 3.2 / 1808 0.9	28 W	0037 3.3 / 0647 0.7 / 1311 3.0 / 1846 1.1
14 W	0033 3.3 / 0639 0.6 / 1312 3.2 / 1852 0.9	29 TH	0116 3.2 / 0726 0.7 / 1350 2.9 / 1920 1.1
15 TH	0117 3.3 / 0728 0.6 / 1401 3.1 / 1940 1.0	30 F	0153 3.2 / 0804 0.8 / 1429 2.8 / 1954 1.2

JULY

Day	Time m	Day	Time m
1 SA	0230 3.1 / 0843 0.9 / 1509 2.7 / 2030 1.3	16 SU	0240 3.4 / 0858 0.5 / 1529 3.0 / 2059 1.0
2 SU	0310 3.0 / 0925 1.0 / 1553 2.6 / 2110 1.4	17 M	0330 3.3 / 0953 0.6 / 1622 2.9 / ◐ 2153 1.1
3 M	0354 2.8 / 1014 1.1 / 1641 2.6 / ◑ 2202 1.4	18 TU	0426 3.2 / 1054 0.8 / 1718 2.8 / 2303 1.3
4 TU	0446 2.7 / 1112 1.2 / 1736 2.5 / 2315 1.5	19 W	0529 3.0 / 1200 0.9 / 1820 2.8
5 W	0545 2.7 / 1214 1.2 / 1835 2.6	20 TH	0023 1.3 / 0639 2.9 / 1312 1.0 / 1928 2.8
6 TH	0034 1.5 / 0649 2.7 / 1316 1.2 / 1934 2.7	21 F	0147 1.3 / 0757 2.9 / 1421 1.2 / 2036 2.9
7 F	0145 1.4 / 0755 2.7 / 1413 1.2 / 2031 2.8	22 SA	0257 1.1 / 0909 2.9 / 1518 1.2 / 2134 3.0
8 SA	0244 1.3 / 0857 2.8 / 1504 1.1 / 2122 2.9	23 SU	0351 1.0 / 1007 3.0 / 1603 1.2 / 2222 3.2
9 SU	0335 1.1 / 0951 2.9 / 1550 1.0 / 2208 3.1	24 M	0436 0.8 / 1056 3.0 / 1643 1.1 / 2306 3.3
10 M	0420 0.9 / 1041 3.1 / 1634 1.0 / 2253 3.3	25 TU	0516 0.7 / 1138 3.1 / 1719 1.1 / ● 2345 3.3
11 TU	0504 0.7 / 1129 3.2 / 1717 0.9 / ○ 2337 3.4	26 W	0553 0.6 / 1216 3.1 / 1752 1.0
12 W	0549 0.5 / 1217 3.3 / 1801 0.8	27 TH	0021 3.4 / 0627 0.6 / 1251 3.1 / 1824 1.0
13 TH	0022 3.5 / 0634 0.4 / 1304 3.3 / 1844 0.8	28 F	0055 3.3 / 0700 0.6 / 1324 3.0 / 1854 1.0
14 F	0107 3.5 / 0720 0.3 / 1352 3.3 / 1928 0.8	29 SA	0127 3.3 / 0731 0.7 / 1356 3.0 / 1923 1.0
15 SA	0153 3.5 / 0808 0.4 / 1440 3.2 / 2012 0.9	30 SU	0159 3.2 / 0802 0.8 / 1428 2.9 / 1953 1.1
		31 M	0231 3.1 / 0835 0.9 / 1503 2.8 / 2025 1.2

AUGUST

Day	Time m	Day	Time m
1 TU	0306 3.0 / 0911 1.0 / 1542 2.7 / 2104 1.3	16 W	0359 3.2 / 1011 1.1 / 1640 2.8 / ◐ 2228 1.3
2 W	0348 2.8 / 0955 1.2 / 1630 2.7 / ◑ 2155 1.5	17 TH	0504 2.9 / 1125 1.3 / 1745 2.7
3 TH	0443 2.7 / 1100 1.3 / 1730 2.6 / 2324 1.6	18 F	0009 1.4 / 0623 2.8 / 1255 1.5 / 1903 2.7
4 F	0554 2.6 / 1222 1.4 / 1839 2.6	19 SA	0148 1.3 / 0756 2.7 / 1418 1.5 / 2021 2.9
5 SA	0106 1.5 / 0716 2.6 / 1340 1.4 / 1950 2.8	20 SU	0257 1.1 / 0909 2.8 / 1513 1.4 / 2122 3.0
6 SU	0225 1.3 / 0834 2.8 / 1445 1.3 / 2054 2.9	21 M	0345 1.0 / 1001 3.0 / 1554 1.3 / 2209 3.2
7 M	0322 1.1 / 0936 3.0 / 1537 1.1 / 2148 3.1	22 TU	0424 0.8 / 1043 3.1 / 1628 1.2 / 2249 3.3
8 TU	0409 0.8 / 1029 3.2 / 1612 1.0 / 2236 3.4	23 W	0458 0.7 / 1120 3.1 / 1659 1.1 / ● 2325 3.4
9 W	0452 0.5 / 1117 3.4 / 1704 0.8 / ○ 2321 3.6	24 TH	0529 0.6 / 1153 3.2 / 1728 1.0 / 2358 3.4
10 TH	0535 0.3 / 1202 3.5 / 1745 0.7	25 F	0559 0.6 / 1223 3.2 / 1757 0.9
11 F	0006 3.7 / 0618 0.2 / 1248 3.5 / 1825 0.6	26 SA	0028 3.4 / 0628 0.6 / 1253 3.1 / 1825 0.9
12 SA	0050 3.8 / 0701 0.1 / 1331 3.4 / 1905 0.7	27 SU	0058 3.4 / 0656 0.7 / 1321 3.0 / 1852 0.9
13 SU	0133 3.7 / 0744 0.3 / 1415 3.3 / 1946 0.8	28 M	0126 3.3 / 0723 0.8 / 1349 3.0 / 1920 1.0
14 M	0218 3.6 / 0827 0.5 / 1459 3.1 / 2028 0.9	29 TU	0155 3.2 / 0751 0.9 / 1419 3.0 / •1949 1.1
15 TU	0305 3.4 / 0914 0.8 / 1546 3.0 / 2117 1.1	30 W	0228 3.1 / 0822 1.1 / 1455 2.9 / 2024 1.3
		31 TH	0308 3.0 / 0858 1.3 / 1539 2.8 / ◐ 2108 1.4

Chart Datum: 1·71 metres below Ordnance Datum (Newlyn)

SCOTLAND – WICK

LAT 58°26'N LONG 3°05'W

TIMES AND HEIGHTS OF HIGH AND LOW WATERS

TIME ZONE (UT)
For Summer Time add ONE hour in **non-shaded areas**

SEPTEMBER

#	Time m	#	Time m
1	0400 2.7 / 0951 1.5 / F 1637 2.7 / 2222 1.6	16	0004 1.4 / 0615 2.7 / SA 1242 1.7 / 1839 2.8
2	0516 2.6 / 1138 1.6 / SA 1754 2.7	17	0142 1.3 / 0753 2.7 / SU 1408 1.7 / 2002 2.9
3	0043 1.5 / 0652 2.6 / SU 1320 1.5 / 1917 2.8	18	0243 1.1 / 0858 2.8 / M 1458 1.5 / 2101 3.1
4	0209 1.3 / 0819 2.8 / M 1430 1.4 / 2029 3.0	19	0326 1.0 / 0943 3.0 / TU 1534 1.3 / 2146 3.2
5	0305 1.0 / 0922 3.0 / TU 1521 1.2 / 2126 3.2	20	0400 0.8 / 1020 3.1 / W 1604 1.2 / 2224 3.3
6	0350 0.7 / 1012 3.3 / W 1603 0.9 / 2215 3.5	21	0430 0.7 / 1052 3.2 / TH 1633 1.1 / 2258 3.4
7	0432 0.4 / 1058 3.5 / TH 1643 0.8 / ○ 2300 3.7	22	0459 0.7 / 1123 3.2 / F 1701 1.0 / 2329 3.5
8	0513 0.2 / 1141 3.6 / F 1722 0.6 / 2344 3.9	23	0527 0.6 / 1151 3.3 / SA 1728 0.9 / 2358 3.5
9	0554 0.1 / 1223 3.6 / SA 1801 0.5	24	0555 0.6 / 1219 3.3 / SU 1756 0.9
10	0027 3.9 / 0634 0.1 / SU 1304 3.6 / 1839 0.6	25	0027 3.4 / 0621 0.7 / M 1246 3.2 / 1823 0.9
11	0110 3.9 / 0714 0.3 / M 1344 3.4 / 1919 0.7	26	0056 3.3 / 0647 0.8 / TU 1314 3.2 / 1851 1.0
12	0154 3.7 / 0754 0.6 / TU 1425 3.2 / 2001 0.9	27	0126 3.2 / 0715 1.0 / W 1344 3.1 / 1922 1.1
13	0241 3.4 / 0836 1.0 / W 1510 3.1 / 2051 1.1	28	0200 3.1 / 0745 1.2 / TH 1419 3.0 / 1957 1.2
14	0336 3.1 / 0927 1.4 / TH 1604 2.9 / ☽ 2210 1.3	29	0242 2.9 / 0821 1.4 / F 1503 2.9 / 2043 1.4
15	0446 2.8 / 1052 1.6 / F 1714 2.8	30	0337 2.8 / 0914 1.6 / SA 1601 2.8 / ☽ 2203 1.5

OCTOBER

#	Time m	#	Time m
1	0458 2.6 / 1113 1.7 / SU 1722 2.7	16	0114 1.3 / 0726 2.7 / M 1337 1.8 / 1927 2.9
2	0025 1.5 / 0638 2.7 / M 1300 1.6 / 1849 2.8	17	0212 1.2 / 0827 2.8 / TU 1427 1.6 / 2027 3.0
3	0145 1.2 / 0802 2.9 / TU 1408 1.4 / 2002 3.0	18	0254 1.0 / 0911 3.0 / W 1503 1.4 / 2113 3.2
4	0240 0.9 / 0901 3.1 / W 1457 1.2 / 2100 3.3	19	0327 0.9 / 0947 3.1 / TH 1534 1.3 / 2151 3.3
5	0326 0.6 / 0949 3.4 / TH 1538 0.9 / 2149 3.6	20	0357 0.8 / 1019 3.2 / F 1603 1.1 / 2226 3.4
6	0407 0.4 / 1033 3.5 / F 1618 0.7 / 2235 3.8	21	0426 0.8 / 1049 3.3 / SA 1632 1.0 / 2258 3.4
7	0447 0.2 / 1114 3.6 / SA 1657 0.6 / ○ 2319 3.9	22	0454 0.8 / 1118 3.3 / SU 1701 0.9 / ● 2329 3.4
8	0527 0.2 / 1155 3.7 / SU 1736 0.5	23	0522 0.8 / 1147 3.4 / M 1730 0.9
9	0003 3.9 / 0606 0.3 / M 1235 3.6 / 1816 0.6	24	0000 3.4 / 0549 0.9 / TU 1216 3.4 / 1759 0.9
10	0048 3.8 / 0645 0.6 / TU 1314 3.5 / 1858 0.7	25	0032 3.3 / 0617 1.0 / W 1246 3.3 / 1831 1.0
11	0133 3.6 / 0724 0.9 / W 1355 3.3 / 1943 0.9	26	0106 3.2 / 0648 1.1 / TH 1319 3.3 / 1906 1.1
12	0222 3.3 / 0805 1.2 / TH 1439 3.1 / 2038 1.1	27	0144 3.1 / 0722 1.3 / F 1356 3.2 / 1947 1.1
13	0318 3.0 / 0853 1.6 / F 1533 3.0 / 2202 1.3	28	0231 3.0 / 0804 1.4 / SA 1442 3.0 / 2040 1.3
14	0430 2.7 / 1016 1.8 / SA 1644 2.8 / ☽ 2343 1.4	29	0330 2.8 / 0904 1.6 / SU 1541 2.9 / ☽ 2212 1.4
15	0557 2.6 / 1208 1.9 / SU 1807 2.8	30	0451 2.7 / 1053 1.7 / M 1659 2.9 / 2358 1.3
		31	0619 2.8 / 1227 1.6 / TU 1820 3.0

NOVEMBER

#	Time m	#	Time m
1	0112 1.1 / 0733 3.0 / W 1334 1.4 / 1930 3.1	16	0208 1.2 / 0825 2.9 / TH 1421 1.5 / 2029 3.1
2	0210 0.8 / 0832 3.2 / TH 1426 1.2 / 2029 3.4	17	0246 1.1 / 0906 3.0 / F 1459 1.4 / 2112 3.1
3	0257 0.6 / 0921 3.4 / F 1510 1.0 / 2122 3.6	18	0320 1.0 / 0942 3.1 / SA 1533 1.3 / 2151 3.2
4	0340 0.5 / 1006 3.5 / SA 1552 0.8 / 2211 3.7	19	0352 1.0 / 1015 3.2 / SU 1606 1.1 / 2228 3.3
5	0422 0.4 / 1048 3.6 / SU 1634 0.7 / ○ 2258 3.8	20	0423 1.0 / 1047 3.3 / M 1638 1.1 / ● 2303 3.3
6	0502 0.5 / 1129 3.6 / M 1717 0.6 / 2344 3.8	21	0454 1.0 / 1119 3.4 / TU 1711 1.0 / 2339 3.3
7	0542 0.7 / 1209 3.6 / TU 1801 0.7	22	0525 1.0 / 1151 3.4 / W 1745 1.0
8	0030 3.7 / 0622 0.9 / W 1250 3.5 / 1846 0.8	23	0016 3.3 / 0558 1.1 / TH 1226 3.4 / 1822 1.0
9	0118 3.4 / 0702 1.1 / TH 1331 3.4 / 1935 0.9	24	0056 3.3 / 0634 1.2 / F 1303 3.4 / 1903 1.0
10	0207 3.2 / 0743 1.4 / F 1416 3.3 / 2031 1.1	25	0139 3.2 / 0715 1.3 / SA 1344 3.3 / 1950 1.1
11	0302 3.0 / 0829 1.6 / SA 1508 3.1 / 2140 1.3	26	0228 3.0 / 0802 1.4 / SU 1432 3.2 / 2047 1.1
12	0406 2.8 / 0931 1.8 / SU 1611 3.0 / ☽ 2258 1.3	27	0327 2.9 / 0900 1.5 / M 1528 3.1 / 2202 1.1
13	0517 2.7 / 1100 1.9 / M 1723 2.9	28	0436 2.9 / 1019 1.6 / TU 1636 3.1 / ☽ 2323 1.1
14	0016 1.3 / 0630 2.7 / TU 1229 1.8 / 1833 2.9	29	0548 2.9 / 1142 1.6 / W 1747 3.1
15	0121 1.3 / 0735 2.8 / W 1335 1.7 / 1937 3.0	30	0033 1.0 / 0656 3.0 / TH 1251 1.5 / 1854 3.2

DECEMBER

#	Time m	#	Time m
1	0135 0.9 / 0757 3.1 / F 1351 1.3 / 1958 3.3	16	0157 1.3 / 0816 2.9 / SA 1418 1.6 / 2028 3.0
2	0228 0.8 / 0851 3.2 / SA 1444 1.2 / 2057 3.4	17	0242 1.2 / 0901 3.0 / SU 1504 1.4 / 2117 3.1
3	0316 0.8 / 0940 3.4 / SU 1534 1.0 / 2152 3.5	18	0322 1.2 / 0941 3.2 / M 1545 1.3 / 2201 3.1
4	0401 0.8 / 1025 3.5 / M 1621 0.9 / 2244 3.6	19	0358 1.2 / 1019 3.3 / TU 1623 1.2 / 2243 3.1
5	0444 0.9 / 1109 3.6 / TU 1708 0.8 / ○ 2333 3.6	20	0434 1.1 / 1056 3.4 / W 1700 1.0 / ● 2324 3.3
6	0526 1.0 / 1151 3.6 / W 1755 0.8	21	0510 1.1 / 1134 3.5 / TH 1739 0.9
7	0020 3.5 / 0607 1.1 / TH 1233 3.6 / 1841 0.8	22	0006 3.3 / 0548 1.1 / F 1214 3.5 / 1820 0.8
8	0108 3.3 / 0647 1.2 / F 1315 3.5 / 1927 0.9	23	0050 3.3 / 0629 1.1 / SA 1254 3.5 / 1903 0.8
9	0154 3.2 / 0726 1.4 / SA 1358 3.4 / 2014 1.0	24	0135 3.3 / 0711 1.0 / SU 1337 3.5 / 1949 0.8
10	0241 3.0 / 0805 1.5 / SU 1443 3.2 / 2104 1.1	25	0222 3.2 / 0756 1.2 / M 1423 3.4 / 2040 0.8
11	0331 2.8 / 0848 1.6 / M 1533 3.1 / 2159 1.2	26	0314 3.1 / 0844 1.3 / TU 1513 3.4 / 2137 0.9
12	0425 2.7 / 0940 1.7 / TU 1629 3.0 / ☽ 2259 1.3	27	0410 3.0 / 0940 1.4 / W 1610 3.3 / ☽ 2242 1.0
13	0523 2.7 / 1052 1.8 / W 1730 2.9	28	0511 2.9 / 1050 1.5 / TH 1713 3.2 / 2351 1.1
14	0003 1.4 / 0623 2.7 / TH 1211 1.8 / 1831 2.9	29	0615 2.9 / 1206 1.5 / F 1821 3.0
15	0104 1.3 / 0723 2.8 / F 1321 1.7 / 1933 2.9	30	0059 1.1 / 0719 3.0 / SA 1321 1.4 / 1932 3.2
		31	0203 1.1 / 0823 1.3 / SU 1429 1.3 / 2042 3.2

Chart Datum: 1·71 metres below Ordnance Datum (Newlyn)

TIDES

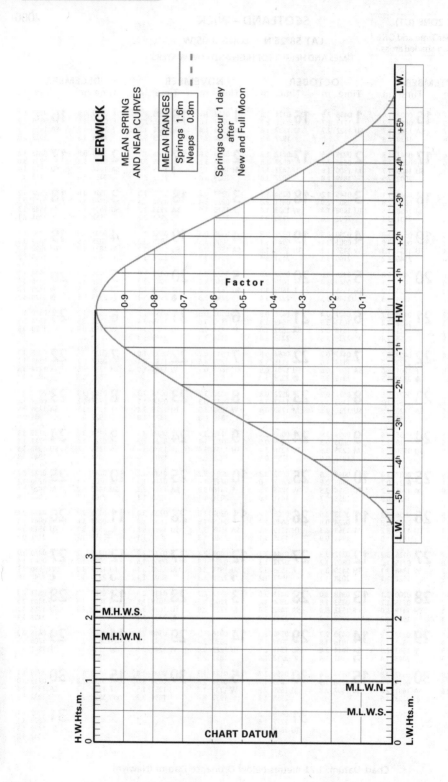

LERWICK

MEAN SPRING
AND NEAP CURVES

MEAN RANGES
Springs 1.6m
Neaps 0.8m

Springs occur 1 day
after
New and Full Moon

Factor

0·9 0·8 0·7 0·6 0·5 0·4 0·3 0·2 0·1

H.W.

L.W.

H.W.Hts.m.

M.H.W.S.
M.H.W.N.

M.L.W.N.
M.L.W.S.

CHART DATUM

L.W.Hts.m.

TIME ZONE (UT)
For Summer Time add ONE hour in **non-shaded areas**

SCOTLAND – LERWICK

LAT 60°09′N LONG 1°08′W

TIMES AND HEIGHTS OF HIGH AND LOW WATERS

2006

JANUARY

Time	m		Time	m
1 0517 / 1129 / SU 1749	0.7 / 2.3 / 0.4		**16** 0006 / 0551 / M 1208 / 1823	2.0 / 0.8 / 2.2 / 0.6
2 0015 / 0603 / M 1215 / 1836	2.2 / 0.7 / 2.3 / 0.4		**17** 0041 / 0622 / TU 1241 / 1856	2.0 / 0.8 / 2.2 / 0.6
3 0107 / 0649 / TU 1303 / 1925	2.2 / 0.7 / 2.3 / 0.4		**18** 0113 / 0652 / W 1312 / 1929	1.9 / 0.8 / 2.1 / 0.6
4 0157 / 0735 / W 1352 / 2014	2.1 / 0.8 / 2.3 / 0.4		**19** 0145 / 0722 / TH 1344 / 2003	1.9 / 0.9 / 2.0 / 0.7
5 0247 / 0823 / TH 1444 / 2107	2.0 / 0.8 / 2.2 / 0.5		**20** 0218 / 0755 / F 1420 / 2040	1.8 / 0.9 / 2.0 / 0.7
6 0338 / 0914 / F 1539 / ☽ 2206	1.9 / 0.9 / 2.1 / 0.6		**21** 0256 / 0831 / SA 1500 / 2120	1.8 / 1.0 / 1.9 / 0.8
7 0434 / 1015 / SA 1639 / 2318	1.8 / 1.0 / 2.0 / 0.8		**22** 0339 / 0916 / SU 1547 / ☾ 2210	1.7 / 1.0 / 1.8 / 0.9
8 0536 / 1136 / SU 1750	1.8 / 1.0 / 1.9		**23** 0431 / 1016 / M 1646 / 2316	1.7 / 1.1 / 1.7 / 1.0
9 0033 / 0643 / M 1300 / 1906	0.8 / 1.8 / 1.0 / 1.8		**24** 0532 / 1153 / TU 1758	1.7 / 1.1 / 1.7
10 0139 / 0747 / TU 1407 / 2016	0.9 / 1.8 / 0.9 / 1.9		**25** 0035 / 0644 / W 1318 / 1922	1.0 / 1.7 / 1.1 / 1.7
11 0234 / 0844 / W 1503 / 2117	0.9 / 1.9 / 0.8 / 1.9		**26** 0143 / 0754 / TH 1421 / 2033	1.0 / 1.8 / 0.9 / 1.8
12 0321 / 0937 / TH 1551 / 2208	0.9 / 2.0 / 0.8 / 1.9		**27** 0241 / 0852 / F 1516 / 2132	0.9 / 2.0 / 0.8 / 2.0
13 0403 / 1017 / F 1633 / 2251	0.9 / 2.1 / 0.7 / 2.0		**28** 0334 / 0943 / SA 1606 / 2226	0.8 / 2.1 / 0.6 / 2.1
14 0442 / 1056 / SA 1712 / ○ 2330	0.9 / 2.2 / 0.6 / 2.0		**29** 0423 / 1032 / SU 1653 / ◐ 2317	0.7 / 2.2 / 0.4 / 2.2
15 0518 / 1133 / SU 1749	0.9 / 2.2 / 0.6		**30** 0508 / 1119 / M 1738	0.6 / 2.3 / 0.2
			31 0005 / 0550 / TU 1205 / 1822	2.2 / 0.6 / 2.4 / 0.2

FEBRUARY

Time	m		Time	m
1 0051 / 0632 / W 1250 / 1906	2.2 / 0.5 / 2.4 / 0.2		**16** 0043 / 0625 / TH 1246 / 1856	1.9 / 0.6 / 2.1 / 0.5
2 0135 / 0714 / TH 1335 / 1950	2.1 / 0.6 / 2.3 / 0.3		**17** 0110 / 0654 / F 1314 / 1926	1.9 / 0.7 / 2.1 / 0.5
3 0219 / 0756 / F 1421 / 2036	2.0 / 0.6 / 2.2 / 0.4		**18** 0139 / 0725 / SA 1346 / 1959	1.9 / 0.7 / 2.0 / 0.6
4 0303 / 0842 / SA 1510 / 2126	1.9 / 0.7 / 2.1 / 0.6		**19** 0211 / 0758 / SU 1421 / 2034	1.8 / 0.8 / 1.9 / 0.7
5 0351 / 0936 / SU 1606 / ◐ 2227	1.8 / 0.8 / 1.9 / 0.8		**20** 0249 / 0837 / M 1505 / 2117	1.8 / 0.9 / 1.8 / 0.9
6 0447 / 1053 / M 1715 / 2355	1.7 / 1.0 / 1.7 / 1.0		**21** 0337 / 0930 / TU 1603 / 2215	1.7 / 1.0 / 1.7 / 1.0
7 0559 / 1240 / TU 1847	1.7 / 1.0 / 1.7		**22** 0439 / 1052 / W 1720 / 2351	1.6 / 1.0 / 1.6 / 1.0
8 0120 / 0722 / W 1401 / 2015	1.0 / 1.7 / 0.9 / 1.7		**23** 0556 / 1251 / TH 1900	1.6 / 0.9 / 1.6
9 0226 / 0831 / TH 1501 / 2118	1.0 / 1.8 / 0.8 / 1.7		**24** 0124 / 0725 / F 1406 / 2024	1.0 / 1.7 / 0.8 / 1.8
10 0315 / 0923 / F 1546 / 2202	1.0 / 1.9 / 0.7 / 1.8		**25** 0230 / 0834 / SA 1504 / 2124	0.9 / 1.9 / 0.6 / 1.9
11 0355 / 1005 / SA 1623 / 2239	0.9 / 2.0 / 0.6 / 1.9		**26** 0323 / 0928 / SU 1552 / 2215	0.7 / 2.0 / 0.4 / 2.0
12 0430 / 1017 / SU 1657 / 2313	0.8 / 2.2 / 0.5 / 1.9		**27** 0408 / 1017 / M 1637 / 2301	0.6 / 2.2 / 0.2 / 2.1
13 0501 / 1117 / M 1728 / ○ 2345	0.8 / 2.1 / 0.5 / 2.0		**28** 0450 / 1102 / TU 1719 / ● 2345	0.5 / 2.3 / 0.1 / 2.2
14 0531 / 1149 / TU 1758	0.7 / 2.1 / 0.4			
15 0015 / 0558 / W 1218 / 1826	1.9 / 0.7 / 2.1 / 0.4			

MARCH

Time	m		Time	m
1 0530 / 1146 / W 1800	0.4 / 2.4 / 0.0		**16** 0531 / 1150 / TH 1754	0.5 / 2.1 / 0.4
2 0026 / 0609 / TH 1229 / 1841	2.2 / 0.3 / 2.4 / 0.1		**17** 0009 / 0558 / F 1217 / 1822	1.9 / 0.5 / 2.1 / 0.4
3 0106 / 0649 / F 1312 / 1922	2.1 / 0.4 / 2.3 / 0.2		**18** 0035 / 0628 / SA 1246 / 1853	1.9 / 0.5 / 2.0 / 0.5
4 0145 / 0731 / SA 1356 / 2004	2.0 / 0.5 / 2.2 / 0.5		**19** 0103 / 0700 / SU 1318 / 1925	1.9 / 0.6 / 2.0 / 0.6
5 0225 / 0815 / SU 1443 / 2048	1.9 / 0.6 / 2.0 / 0.7		**20** 0134 / 0734 / M 1354 / 2000	1.9 / 0.7 / 1.9 / 0.7
6 0308 / 0907 / M 1537 / ◐ 2140	1.8 / 0.7 / 1.8 / 0.9		**21** 0210 / 0816 / TU 1439 / 2043	1.8 / 0.8 / 1.7 / 0.8
7 0359 / 1025 / TU 1645 / 2312	1.7 / 0.9 / 1.6 / 1.1		**22** 0256 / 0911 / W 1542 / ☾ 2144	1.7 / 0.8 / 1.6 / 1.0
8 0510 / 1223 / W 1835	1.6 / 0.9 / 1.5		**23** 0400 / 1034 / TH 1705 / 2327	1.6 / 0.9 / 1.5 / 1.0
9 0100 / 0654 / TH 1347 / 2012	1.1 / 1.6 / 0.9 / 1.6		**24** 0522 / 1232 / F 1853	1.6 / 0.8 / 1.6
10 0211 / 0811 / F 1446 / 2105	1.1 / 1.7 / 0.7 / 1.6		**25** 0110 / 0701 / SA 1348 / 2013	1.0 / 1.6 / 0.7 / 1.7
11 0259 / 0902 / SA 1527 / 2142	1.0 / 1.8 / 0.6 / 1.7		**26** 0214 / 0814 / SU 1444 / 2107	0.8 / 1.8 / 0.4 / 1.9
12 0336 / 0943 / SU 1600 / 2214	0.8 / 1.9 / 0.5 / 1.8		**27** 0304 / 0908 / M 1531 / 2154	0.7 / 2.0 / 0.2 / 2.0
13 0408 / 1019 / M 1630 / 2246	0.7 / 2.0 / 0.3 / 1.9		**28** 0347 / 0955 / TU 1614 / 2237	0.5 / 2.1 / 0.1 / 2.1
14 0437 / 1052 / TU 1659 / ○ 2316	0.6 / 2.0 / 0.4 / 1.9		**29** 0427 / 1040 / W 1655 / ● 2318	0.4 / 2.3 / 0.0 / 2.1
15 0504 / 1122 / W 1726 / 2343	0.6 / 2.1 / 0.4 / 1.9		**30** 0506 / 1123 / TH 1734 / 2356	0.3 / 2.3 / 0.0 / 2.1
			31 0546 / 1206 / F 1814	0.2 / 2.3 / 0.2

APRIL

Time	m		Time	m
1 0034 / 0626 / SA 1249 / 1853	2.1 / 0.3 / 2.2 / 0.3		**16** 0003 / 0605 / SU 1223 / 1824	2.0 / 0.5 / 2.0 / 0.5
2 0111 / 0709 / SU 1334 / 1934	2.0 / 0.4 / 2.0 / 0.6		**17** 0034 / 0641 / M 1259 / 1859	1.9 / 0.5 / 1.9 / 0.6
3 0150 / 0754 / M 1422 / 2015	1.9 / 0.5 / 1.8 / 0.8		**18** 0108 / 0720 / TU 1340 / 1938	1.9 / 0.6 / 1.8 / 0.7
4 0232 / 0849 / TU 1515 / 2104	1.8 / 0.7 / 1.6 / 1.0		**19** 0146 / 0807 / W 1433 / 2027	1.8 / 0.6 / 1.7 / 0.8
5 0321 / 1008 / W 1621 / ◐ 2230	1.7 / 0.8 / 1.5 / 1.1		**20** 0235 / 0908 / TH 1541 / 2133	1.7 / 0.7 / 1.6 / 1.0
6 0426 / 1151 / TH 1809	1.6 / 0.8 / 1.4		**21** 0342 / 1031 / F 1703 / ☾ 2313	1.6 / 0.7 / 1.5 / 1.0
7 0023 / 0612 / F 1313 / 1941	1.1 / 1.5 / 0.8 / 1.5		**22** 0504 / 1210 / SA 1838	1.6 / 0.6 / 1.6
8 0139 / 0734 / SA 1411 / 2030	1.0 / 1.6 / 0.7 / 1.6		**23** 0045 / 0635 / SU 1322 / 1948	0.9 / 1.6 / 0.5 / 1.7
9 0228 / 0827 / SU 1452 / 2106	0.9 / 1.7 / 0.6 / 1.6		**24** 0147 / 0747 / M 1418 / 2041	0.8 / 1.8 / 0.3 / 1.9
10 0305 / 0909 / M 1525 / 2139	0.8 / 1.8 / 0.5 / 1.7		**25** 0237 / 0842 / TU 1505 / 2126	0.6 / 1.9 / 0.2 / 1.9
11 0336 / 0945 / TU 1555 / 2210	0.7 / 1.9 / 0.4 / 1.8		**26** 0321 / 0931 / W 1548 / 2209	0.5 / 2.1 / 0.1 / 2.0
12 0405 / 1019 / W 1623 / 2240	0.6 / 1.9 / 0.4 / 1.9		**27** 0403 / 1017 / TH 1629 / ● 2248	0.3 / 2.1 / 0.1 / 2.0
13 0433 / 1050 / TH 1652 / ○ 2308	0.5 / 2.0 / 0.4 / 1.9		**28** 0444 / 1101 / F 1709 / 2326	0.3 / 2.2 / 0.2 / 2.1
14 0502 / 1120 / F 1721 / 2335	0.5 / 2.0 / 0.4 / 1.9		**29** 0525 / 1146 / SA 1749	0.3 / 2.1 / 0.3
15 0533 / 1150 / SA 1752	0.5 / 2.0 / 0.4		**30** 0004 / 0608 / SU 1231 / 1828	2.0 / 0.3 / 2.0 / 0.5

Chart Datum: 1·22 metres below Ordnance Datum (Local)

TIME ZONE (UT)
For Summer Time add ONE hour in **non-shaded areas**

SCOTLAND – LERWICK
LAT 60°09'N   LONG 1°08'W

2006

TIMES AND HEIGHTS OF HIGH AND LOW WATERS

MAY

Day	Time m	Time m	Time m	Time m		Day	Time m	Time m	Time m	Time m
1 M	0043 2.0	0652 0.4	1317 1.9	1909 0.7		16 TU	0014 2.0	0629 0.5	1252 1.9	1844 0.6
2 TU	0123 1.9	0741 0.5	1406 1.7	1951 0.8		17 W	0053 1.9	0715 0.5	1341 1.8	1929 0.7
3 W	0206 1.8	0836 0.6	1457 1.6	2039 1.0		18 TH	0137 1.9	0807 0.5	1438 1.7	2023 0.8
4 TH	0254 1.7	0943 0.7	1555 1.5	2148 1.1		19 F	0230 1.8	0908 0.5	1542 1.6	2127 0.9
5 F	0351 1.6	1100 0.7	1711 1.4	◐2318 1.1		20 SA	0336 1.7	1021 0.5	1652 1.6	◑2246 0.9
6 SA	0507 1.5	1213 0.7	1838 1.4			21 SU	0448 1.7	1141 0.5	1808 1.6	
7 SU	0038 1.0	0639 1.5	1315 0.7	1934 1.5		22 M	0008 0.8	0606 1.7	1251 0.4	1914 1.7
8 M	0138 0.9	0739 1.6	1402 0.6	2018 1.6		23 TU	0114 0.7	0716 1.8	1348 0.4	2008 1.7
9 TU	0222 0.8	0826 1.7	1440 0.6	2056 1.7		24 W	0208 0.6	0815 1.9	1438 0.3	2056 1.8
10 W	0257 0.7	0906 1.7	1513 0.5	2130 1.8		25 TH	0257 0.5	0908 2.0	1523 0.3	2141 1.9
11 TH	0330 0.6	0942 1.8	1545 0.5	2202 1.8		26 F	0342 0.4	0958 2.0	1606 0.4	2222 2.0
12 F	0402 0.5	1017 1.9	1617 0.4	2233 1.9		27 SA	0426 0.4	1046 2.0	1647 0.5	●2303 2.0
13 SA	0435 0.5	1052 1.9	1651 0.5	○2305 2.0		28 SU	0511 0.3	1133 2.0	1729 0.5	2343 2.0
14 SU	0511 0.5	1129 1.9	1726 0.5	2338 2.0		29 M	0556 0.4	1219 1.9	1810 0.7	
15 M	0549 0.4	1208 1.9	1804 0.6			30 TU	0023 2.0	0642 0.4	1305 1.8	1851 0.8
						31 W	0105 1.9	0729 0.5	1350 1.7	1932 0.8

JUNE

Day	Time m	Time m	Time m	Time m		Day	Time m	Time m	Time m	Time m
1 TH	0147 1.9	0817 0.6	1435 1.6	2016 0.9		16 F	0135 2.0	0802 0.4	1435 1.8	2014 0.7
2 F	0232 1.8	0909 0.6	1522 1.5	2105 1.0		17 SA	0228 1.9	0857 0.4	1530 1.7	2109 0.8
3 SA	0320 1.7	1004 0.7	1614 1.5	◐2207 1.0		18 SU	0326 1.9	0957 0.4	1628 1.6	◑2211 0.8
4 SU	0414 1.6	1103 0.7	1716 1.4	2319 1.0		19 M	0428 1.8	1105 0.5	1731 1.6	2324 0.8
5 M	0519 1.6	1203 0.7	1826 1.5			20 TU	0536 1.8	1216 0.5	1836 1.6	
6 TU	0028 0.9	0635 1.6	1258 0.7	1922 1.5		21 W	0039 0.8	0647 1.8	1320 0.6	1936 1.7
7 W	0126 0.9	0735 1.6	1346 0.7	2007 1.6		22 TH	0144 0.7	0753 1.8	1416 0.6	2030 1.8
8 TH	0213 0.8	0823 1.7	1429 0.6	2047 1.7		23 F	0240 0.6	0853 1.8	1506 0.6	2119 1.9
9 F	0254 0.7	0906 1.7	1508 0.6	2125 1.8		24 SA	0331 0.5	0949 1.9	1551 0.6	2206 1.9
10 SA	0334 0.6	0948 1.8	1547 0.6	2203 1.9		25 SU	0419 0.5	1040 1.9	1634 0.7	●2249 2.0
11 SU	0413 0.6	1030 1.9	1628 0.6	○2241 2.0		26 M	0504 0.4	1127 1.9	1716 0.7	2331 2.0
12 M	0455 0.5	1115 1.9	1709 0.6	2321 2.0		27 TU	0548 0.4	1210 1.9	1756 0.7	
13 TU	0539 0.4	1202 1.9	1753 0.6			28 W	0011 2.0	0629 0.4	1251 1.8	1834 0.7
14 W	0003 2.0	0624 0.4	1251 1.9	1837 0.6		29 TH	0050 2.0	0710 0.5	1330 1.8	1911 0.8
15 TH	0048 2.0	0712 0.4	1342 1.9	1924 0.7		30 F	0128 1.9	0749 0.5	1407 1.7	1946 0.8

JULY

Day	Time m	Time m	Time m	Time m		Day	Time m	Time m	Time m	Time m
1 SA	0206 1.9	0829 0.6	1445 1.6	2022 0.8		16 SU	0215 2.1	0835 0.3	1506 1.8	2043 0.7
2 SU	0245 1.8	0910 0.6	1525 1.6	2104 0.9		17 M	0306 2.0	0927 0.4	1556 1.7	◐2136 0.7
3 M	0329 1.7	0958 0.7	1611 1.5	◐2157 0.9		18 TU	0402 1.9	1027 0.6	1653 1.7	2244 0.8
4 TU	0418 1.6	1054 0.8	1703 1.5	2311 1.0		19 W	0507 1.8	1141 0.7	1757 1.6	
5 W	0515 1.6	1156 0.8	1805 1.5			20 TH	0012 0.8	0623 1.7	1258 0.8	1907 1.7
6 TH	0029 1.0	0626 1.6	1256 0.8	1910 1.6		21 F	0131 0.8	0742 1.7	1403 0.8	2012 1.8
7 F	0131 0.9	0737 1.6	1349 0.8	2005 1.7		22 SA	0236 0.7	0852 1.7	1458 0.8	2109 1.9
8 SA	0223 0.8	0835 1.7	1438 0.8	2053 1.8		23 SU	0330 0.6	0950 1.8	1545 0.8	2157 2.0
9 SU	0312 0.7	0926 1.8	1526 0.7	2139 1.9		24 M	0416 0.5	1037 1.8	1626 0.8	2240 2.0
10 M	0358 0.6	1016 1.9	1613 0.7	2224 2.0		25 TU	0456 0.5	1117 1.9	1704 0.7	●2320 2.1
11 TU	0444 0.4	1106 2.0	1659 0.6	○2309 2.1		26 W	0534 0.4	1154 1.9	1739 0.7	2356 2.1
12 W	0530 0.3	1155 2.0	1743 0.6	2355 2.2		27 TH	0610 0.4	1229 1.9	1812 0.7	
13 TH	0615 0.2	1243 2.0	1827 0.6			28 F	0030 2.1	0643 0.4	1302 1.8	1842 0.7
14 F	0040 2.2	0700 0.2	1311 2.0	1911 0.6		29 SA	0103 2.0	0715 0.5	1333 1.8	1912 0.7
15 SA	0127 2.2	0746 0.2	1418 1.9	1955 0.6		30 SU	0134 2.0	0748 0.5	1404 1.7	1943 0.8
						31 M	0207 1.9	0822 0.6	1438 1.7	2018 0.8

AUGUST

Day	Time m	Time m	Time m	Time m		Day	Time m	Time m	Time m	Time m
1 TU	0245 1.8	0900 0.7	1518 1.7	2100 0.9		16 W	0337 1.9	0949 0.8	1613 1.7	◑2214 0.8
2 W	0329 1.7	0945 0.8	1605 1.6	◐2154 1.0		17 TH	0442 1.8	1109 0.9	1719 1.7	
3 TH	0423 1.6	1045 0.9	1701 1.6	2323 1.0		18 F	0001 0.9	0609 1.7	1245 1.0	1844 1.7
4 F	0530 1.6	1206 1.0	1809 1.6			19 SA	0129 0.9	0746 1.7	1358 1.0	2001 1.8
5 SA	0056 1.0	0655 1.6	1318 1.0	1925 1.7		20 SU	0236 0.8	0856 1.7	1453 1.0	2100 1.9
6 SU	0201 0.9	0813 1.7	1419 0.9	2028 1.8		21 M	0325 0.7	0944 1.8	1536 0.9	2145 2.0
7 M	0256 0.7	0912 1.8	1513 0.8	2121 1.9		22 TU	0404 0.6	1023 1.9	1612 0.8	2225 2.1
8 TU	0345 0.5	1004 2.0	1601 0.7	2209 2.1		23 W	0439 0.5	1057 1.9	1644 0.7	●2300 2.1
9 W	0431 0.4	1053 2.1	1645 0.6	○2255 2.2		24 TH	0511 0.4	1129 1.9	1715 0.7	2333 2.1
10 TH	0515 0.2	1140 2.1	1727 0.5	2340 2.3		25 F	0542 0.4	1200 2.0	1744 0.6	
11 F	0558 0.1	1225 2.1	1808 0.5			26 SA	0003 2.1	0610 0.4	1228 1.9	1811 0.6
12 SA	0024 2.3	0640 0.1	1308 2.1	1849 0.5		27 SU	0032 2.1	0639 0.5	1255 1.9	1839 0.7
13 SU	0108 2.3	0722 0.2	1351 2.0	1931 0.5		28 M	0100 2.1	0709 0.5	1322 1.9	1910 0.7
14 M	0153 2.2	0807 0.3	1434 1.9	2016 0.6		29 TU	0131 2.0	0740 0.6	1353 1.8	1943 0.8
15 TU	0242 2.1	0854 0.5	1520 1.8	2107 0.7		30 W	0206 1.9	0814 0.6	1429 1.8	2021 0.9
						31 TH	0248 1.8	0854 0.7	1514 1.7	◑2112 1.0

Chart Datum: 1·22 metres below Ordnance Datum (Local)

SCOTLAND – LERWICK

2006

LAT 60°09'N LONG 1°08'W

TIMES AND HEIGHTS OF HIGH AND LOW WATERS

TIME ZONE (UT)
For Summer Time add ONE hour in **non-shaded areas**

SEPTEMBER

Day	Time	m		Day	Time	m
1 F	0343 / 0948 / 1612 / 2229	1.7 / 1.0 / 1.7 / 1.1		**16** SA	0606 / 1231 / 1824	1.6 / 1.2 / 1.7
2 SA	0455 / 1119 / 1723	1.6 / 1.1 / 1.7		**17** SU	0120 / 0748 / 1346 / 1945	0.9 / 1.6 / 1.1 / 1.8
3 SU	0031 / 0630 / 1259 / 1852	1.0 / 1.6 / 1.1 / 1.7		**18** M	0223 / 0845 / 1437 / 2039	0.8 / 1.7 / 1.0 / 1.9
4 M	0144 / 0801 / 1405 / 2007	0.9 / 1.7 / 1.0 / 1.8		**19** TU	0306 / 0923 / 1515 / 2122	0.7 / 1.8 / 0.9 / 2.0
5 TU	0240 / 0859 / 1458 / 2102	0.7 / 1.9 / 0.8 / 2.0		**20** W	0341 / 0956 / 1548 / 2159	0.6 / 1.9 / 0.8 / 2.1
6 W	0327 / 0948 / 1543 / 2150	0.5 / 2.0 / 0.7 / 2.2		**21** TH	0412 / 1027 / 1618 / 2233	0.5 / 2.0 / 0.7 / 2.1
7 TH	0411 / 1033 / 1624 / ○2234	0.3 / 2.1 / 0.5 / 2.3		**22** F	0441 / 1057 / 1646 / ●2304	0.5 / 2.0 / 0.7 / 2.2
8 F	0453 / 1117 / 1704 / 2318	0.1 / 2.2 / 0.4 / 2.4		**23** SA	0509 / 1126 / 1714 / 2333	0.5 / 2.0 / 0.6 / 2.2
9 SA	0534 / 1158 / 1744	0.1 / 2.2 / 0.4		**24** SU	0536 / 1152 / 1741	0.5 / 2.0 / 0.6
10 SU	0001 / 0614 / 1239 / 1824	2.4 / 0.1 / 2.2 / 0.4		**25** M	0000 / 0604 / 1217 / 1811	2.1 / 0.5 / 2.0 / 0.7
11 M	0045 / 0655 / 1318 / 1906	2.4 / 0.3 / 2.1 / 0.5		**26** TU	0029 / 0633 / 1245 / 1842	2.1 / 0.6 / 2.0 / 0.7
12 TU	0130 / 0738 / 1359 / 1951	2.3 / 0.5 / 2.0 / 0.6		**27** W	0100 / 0704 / 1315 / 1917	2.0 / 0.7 / 2.0 / 0.8
13 W	0219 / 0823 / 1444 / 2044	2.1 / 0.7 / 1.9 / 0.7		**28** TH	0136 / 0738 / 1350 / 1957	1.9 / 0.9 / 1.9 / 0.9
14 TH	0315 / 0915 / 1536 / ◑2158	1.9 / 1.0 / 1.8 / 0.9		**29** F	0220 / 0818 / 1434 / 2050	1.8 / 1.0 / 1.8 / 1.0
15 F	0423 / 1041 / 1644 / 2355	1.7 / 1.1 / 1.7 / 0.9		**30** SA	0320 / 0915 / 1534 / ◐2209	1.7 / 1.1 / 1.8 / 1.0

OCTOBER

Day	Time	m		Day	Time	m
1 SU	0438 / 1050 / 1652	1.6 / 1.2 / 1.7		**16** M	0052 / 0718 / 1315 / 1910	0.9 / 1.6 / 1.2 / 1.8
2 M	0008 / 0617 / 1241 / 1824	1.0 / 1.7 / 1.1 / 1.7		**17** TU	0152 / 0809 / 1406 / 2005	0.8 / 1.7 / 1.1 / 1.9
3 TU	0122 / 0744 / 1345 / 1943	0.8 / 1.8 / 1.0 / 1.9		**18** W	0234 / 0846 / 1445 / 2048	0.7 / 1.8 / 1.0 / 2.0
4 W	0217 / 0838 / 1435 / 2038	0.6 / 1.9 / 0.8 / 2.1		**19** TH	0308 / 0920 / 1518 / 2126	0.7 / 1.9 / 0.9 / 2.0
5 TH	0303 / 0924 / 1519 / 2125	0.4 / 2.1 / 0.7 / 2.2		**20** F	0338 / 0951 / 1548 / 2201	0.6 / 2.0 / 0.8 / 2.1
6 F	0346 / 1007 / 1600 / 2210	0.3 / 2.2 / 0.5 / 2.4		**21** SA	0406 / 1022 / 1616 / 2233	0.6 / 2.0 / 0.7 / 2.1
7 SA	0427 / 1048 / 1640 / ○2254	0.2 / 2.3 / 0.4 / 2.5		**22** SU	0434 / 1050 / 1645 / ●2303	0.6 / 2.1 / 0.7 / 2.2
8 SU	0508 / 1128 / 1720 / 2338	0.2 / 2.3 / 0.4 / 2.5		**23** M	0503 / 1117 / 1715 / 2333	0.6 / 2.1 / 0.7 / 2.1
9 M	0548 / 1207 / 1802	0.3 / 2.2 / 0.4		**24** TU	0533 / 1145 / 1748	0.6 / 2.1 / 0.7
10 TU	0022 / 0629 / 1246 / 1846	2.4 / 0.5 / 2.2 / 0.5		**25** W	0005 / 0604 / 1216 / 1822	2.1 / 0.7 / 2.1 / 0.7
11 W	0110 / 0711 / 1327 / 1934	2.2 / 0.7 / 2.1 / 0.6		**26** TH	0040 / 0638 / 1248 / 1901	2.1 / 0.8 / 2.1 / 0.8
12 TH	0201 / 0755 / 1413 / 2030	2.0 / 0.9 / 2.0 / 0.8		**27** F	0120 / 0715 / 1325 / 1946	2.0 / 0.9 / 2.0 / 0.9
13 F	0258 / 0848 / 1506 / 2148	1.8 / 1.1 / 1.9 / 0.9		**28** SA	0210 / 0800 / 1411 / 2043	1.9 / 1.0 / 1.9 / 0.9
14 SA	0405 / 1011 / 1612 / ◑2331	1.7 / 1.3 / 1.8 / 0.9		**29** SU	0314 / 0901 / 1514 / ◐2159	1.8 / 1.1 / 1.8 / 0.9
15 SU	0545 / 1158 / 1748	1.6 / 1.3 / 1.7		**30** M	0429 / 1028 / 1631 / 2337	1.7 / 1.2 / 1.8 / 0.9
				31 TU	0557 / 1209 / 1756	1.7 / 1.1 / 1.8

NOVEMBER

Day	Time	m		Day	Time	m
1 W	0050 / 0714 / 1315 / 1912	0.7 / 1.8 / 1.0 / 1.9		**16** TH	0147 / 0758 / 1405 / 2007	0.8 / 1.8 / 1.0 / 1.9
2 TH	0147 / 0809 / 1407 / 2010	0.6 / 2.0 / 0.9 / 2.1		**17** F	0226 / 0838 / 1443 / 2049	0.8 / 1.9 / 0.9 / 2.0
3 F	0236 / 0856 / 1452 / 2100	0.5 / 2.1 / 0.7 / 2.1		**18** SA	0259 / 0914 / 1516 / 2127	0.7 / 2.0 / 0.9 / 2.0
4 SA	0320 / 0939 / 1536 / 2147	0.4 / 2.2 / 0.6 / 2.3		**19** SU	0330 / 0947 / 1548 / 2203	0.7 / 2.0 / 0.8 / 2.1
5 SU	0402 / 1020 / 1618 / ○2233	0.4 / 2.2 / 0.5 / 2.4		**20** M	0402 / 1018 / 1621 / ●2237	0.7 / 2.1 / 0.8 / 2.1
6 M	0444 / 1100 / 1701 / 2320	0.4 / 2.3 / 0.5 / 2.4		**21** TU	0434 / 1049 / 1655 / 2313	0.7 / 2.2 / 0.7 / 2.1
7 TU	0525 / 1140 / 1746	0.5 / 2.3 / 0.5		**22** W	0508 / 1122 / 1732 / 2351	0.8 / 2.2 / 0.7 / 2.1
8 W	0007 / 0607 / 1221 / 1832	2.3 / 0.7 / 2.2 / 0.5		**23** TH	0544 / 1156 / 1812	0.8 / 2.2 / 0.7
9 TH	0057 / 0650 / 1304 / 1922	2.2 / 0.9 / 2.2 / 0.6		**24** F	0032 / 0623 / 1233 / 1855	2.1 / 0.9 / 2.2 / 0.7
10 F	0149 / 0735 / 1351 / 2018	2.0 / 1.0 / 2.1 / 0.8		**25** SA	0118 / 0705 / 1315 / 1943	2.0 / 0.9 / 2.1 / 0.7
11 SA	0242 / 0826 / 1442 / 2125	1.8 / 1.2 / 2.0 / 0.9		**26** SU	0210 / 0754 / 1403 / 2038	1.9 / 1.0 / 2.0 / 0.8
12 SU	0341 / 0930 / 1540 / ◐2241	1.7 / 1.2 / 1.9 / 0.9		**27** M	0309 / 0851 / 1503 / 2142	1.8 / 1.1 / 2.0 / 0.8
13 M	0451 / 1054 / 1652 / 2356	1.6 / 1.3 / 1.8 / 0.9		**28** TU	0414 / 0959 / 1610 / ◐2257	1.8 / 1.1 / 1.9 / 0.9
14 TU	0613 / 1215 / 1816	1.6 / 1.2 / 1.9		**29** W	0525 / 1120 / 1723	1.8 / 1.1 / 1.9
15 W	0059 / 0712 / 1319 / 1918	0.9 / 1.7 / 1.1 / 1.9		**30** TH	0012 / 0635 / 1236 / 1837	0.7 / 1.8 / 1.0 / 2.0

DECEMBER

Day	Time	m		Day	Time	m
1 F	0115 / 0735 / 1336 / 1941	0.7 / 1.9 / 0.9 / 2.1		**16** SA	0133 / 0752 / 1403 / 2010	0.9 / 1.8 / 1.0 / 1.8
2 SA	0209 / 0826 / 1429 / 2038	0.6 / 2.0 / 0.8 / 2.1		**17** SU	0217 / 0835 / 1446 / 2056	0.9 / 1.9 / 1.0 / 1.9
3 SU	0257 / 0913 / 1517 / 2130	0.6 / 2.1 / 0.7 / 2.2		**18** M	0257 / 0914 / 1525 / 2138	0.9 / 2.0 / 0.9 / 2.0
4 M	0342 / 0958 / 1604 / 2222	0.6 / 2.2 / 0.6 / 2.2		**19** TU	0335 / 0951 / 1603 / 2219	0.9 / 2.1 / 0.8 / 2.1
5 TU	0426 / 1041 / 1650 / ○2312	0.7 / 2.3 / 0.5 / 2.2		**20** W	0414 / 1028 / 1643 / ●2301	0.8 / 2.2 / 0.7 / 2.1
6 W	0509 / 1123 / 1737	0.7 / 2.3 / 0.5		**21** TH	0453 / 1106 / 1724 / 2344	0.8 / 2.2 / 0.7 / 2.1
7 TH	0001 / 0552 / 1207 / 1824	2.2 / 0.8 / 2.3 / 0.6		**22** F	0534 / 1146 / 1806	0.8 / 2.2 / 0.6
8 F	0049 / 0635 / 1250 / 1912	2.1 / 0.9 / 2.2 / 0.6		**23** SA	0029 / 0615 / 1227 / 1850	2.1 / 0.8 / 2.2 / 0.6
9 SA	0135 / 0718 / 1334 / 2000	2.0 / 1.0 / 2.1 / 0.7		**24** SU	0116 / 0659 / 1310 / 1935	2.0 / 0.8 / 2.2 / 0.5
10 SU	0221 / 0801 / 1419 / 2050	1.9 / 1.1 / 2.1 / 0.8		**25** M	0204 / 0744 / 1357 / 2024	2.0 / 0.9 / 2.2 / 0.5
11 M	0307 / 0846 / 1506 / 2142	1.8 / 1.1 / 1.9 / 0.9		**26** TU	0255 / 0832 / 1448 / 2117	1.9 / 0.9 / 2.1 / 0.6
12 TU	0355 / 0939 / 1557 / ◐2240	1.7 / 1.2 / 1.9 / 0.9		**27** W	0349 / 0926 / 1546 / ◐2217	1.8 / 1.0 / 2.0 / 0.7
13 W	0452 / 1047 / 1657 / 2341	1.6 / 1.2 / 1.8 / 0.9		**28** TH	0448 / 1031 / 1650 / 2329	1.8 / 1.0 / 2.0 / 0.7
14 TH	0559 / 1204 / 1812	1.7 / 1.2 / 1.9		**29** F	0553 / 1152 / 1803	1.8 / 1.0 / 1.9
15 F	0041 / 0702 / 1311 / 1918	0.9 / 1.7 / 1.1 / 1.8		**30** SA	0042 / 0700 / 1310 / 1917	0.8 / 1.8 / 0.9 / 1.9
				31 SU	0147 / 0801 / 1414 / 2025	0.8 / 0.9 / 0.9 / 1.0

Chart Datum: 1·22 metres below Ordnance Datum (Local)

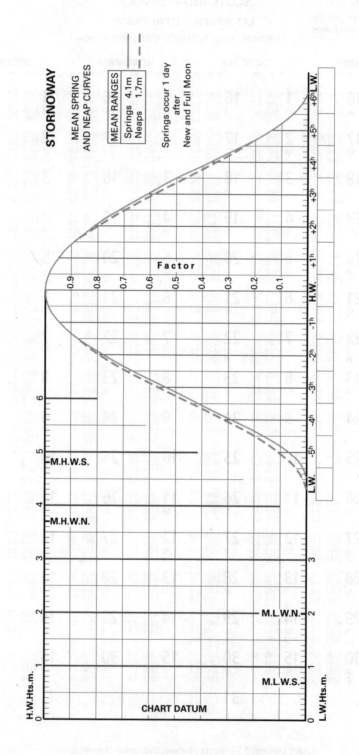

STORNOWAY

MEAN SPRING
AND NEAP CURVES

MEAN RANGES	
Springs	4.1m
Neaps	1.7m

Springs occur 1 day
after
New and Full Moon

Factor

0.9 0.8 0.7 0.6 0.5 0.4 0.3 0.2 0.1

H.W.Hts.m.

M.H.W.S.

M.H.W.N.

M.L.W.N.

M.L.W.S.

CHART DATUM

L.W.Hts.m.

L.W.

H.W.

L.W.

+6ʰ +5ʰ +4ʰ +3ʰ +2ʰ +1ʰ H.W. -1ʰ -2ʰ -3ʰ -4ʰ -5ʰ L.W.

TIME ZONE (UT)
For Summer Time add ONE hour in **non-shaded areas**

SCOTLAND – STORNOWAY

LAT 58°12'N   LONG 6°23'W

2006

TIMES AND HEIGHTS OF HIGH AND LOW WATERS

JANUARY

Time	m	Time	m
1 SU 0126 / 0724 / 1356 / 1956	1.0 / 4.9 / 0.8 / 4.6	**16** M 0159 / 0757 / 1435 / 2017	1.1 / 4.6 / 1.0 / 4.2
2 M 0211 / 0810 / 1443 / 2043	0.9 / 5.0 / 0.6 / 4.5	**17** TU 0232 / 0828 / 1508 / 2050	1.1 / 4.5 / 1.0 / 4.1
3 TU 0255 / 0857 / 1530 / 2131	0.9 / 5.0 / 0.6 / 4.4	**18** W 0305 / 0900 / 1541 / 2124	1.1 / 4.4 / 1.1 / 4.0
4 W 0340 / 0947 / 1618 / 2223	1.0 / 4.9 / 0.7 / 4.2	**19** TH 0338 / 0933 / 1615 / 2201	1.2 / 4.3 / 1.2 / 3.9
5 TH 0427 / 1042 / 1709 / 2323	1.2 / 4.7 / 0.9 / 4.0	**20** F 0413 / 1008 / 1652 / 2243	1.4 / 4.1 / 1.4 / 3.7
6 F 0520 / 1143 / 1803 ●	1.4 / 4.4 / 1.2	**21** SA 0451 / 1049 / 1734 / 2335	1.6 / 3.9 / 1.6 / 3.6
7 SA 0030 / 0620 / 1254 / 1903	3.7 / 1.7 / 4.2 / 1.4	**22** SU 0535 / 1141 / 1822 ◐	1.8 / 3.7 / 1.7
8 SU 0143 / 0729 / 1400 / 2010	3.6 / 1.8 / 4.0 / 1.6	**23** M 0036 / 0627 / 1245 / 1918	3.5 / 2.0 / 3.6 / 1.9
9 M 0256 / 0849 / 1511 / 2124	3.6 / 1.9 / 3.9 / 1.7	**24** TU 0143 / 0731 / 1357 / 2027	3.5 / 2.1 / 3.6 / 1.9
10 TU 0401 / 1005 / 1615 / 2229	3.8 / 1.8 / 3.9 / 1.6	**25** W 0252 / 0849 / 1517 / 2145	3.6 / 2.1 / 3.7 / 1.8
11 W 0454 / 1107 / 1709 / 2322	3.9 / 1.6 / 3.9 / 1.6	**26** TH 0358 / 1010 / 1630 / 2251	3.8 / 1.9 / 3.8 / 1.6
12 TH 0537 / 1200 / 1755	4.1 / 1.4 / 4.0	**27** F 0454 / 1117 / 1729 / 2346	4.2 / 1.5 / 4.1 / 1.3
13 F 0006 / 0615 / 1245 / 1835	1.4 / 4.3 / 1.3 / 4.1	**28** SA 0545 / 1213 / 1819	4.5 / 1.1 / 4.4
14 SA 0047 / 0651 / 1325 / 1911 ○	1.3 / 4.4 / 1.1 / 4.1	**29** SU 0034 / 0630 / 1302 / 1903 ●	1.0 / 4.8 / 0.7 / 4.6
15 SU 0124 / 0724 / 1401 / 1945	1.2 / 4.5 / 1.0 / 4.2	**30** M 0118 / 0714 / 1348 / 1945	0.8 / 5.1 / 0.4 / 4.7
		31 TU 0201 / 0756 / 1431 / 2026	0.6 / 5.3 / 0.2 / 4.8

FEBRUARY

Time	m	Time	m
1 W 0241 / 0837 / 1512 / 2106	0.5 / 5.3 / 0.2 / 4.6	**16** TH 0241 / 0827 / 1509 / 2047	0.8 / 4.5 / 0.8 / 4.2
2 TH 0322 / 0921 / 1554 / 2148	0.6 / 5.1 / 0.4 / 4.4	**17** F 0310 / 0853 / 1539 / 2117	0.9 / 4.4 / 0.9 / 4.1
3 F 0404 / 1007 / 1637 / 2236	0.8 / 4.8 / 0.7 / 4.1	**18** SA 0340 / 0921 / 1612 / 2149	1.1 / 4.2 / 1.1 / 3.9
4 SA 0449 / 1102 / 1724 / 2337	1.1 / 4.5 / 1.1 / 3.8	**19** SU 0413 / 0951 / 1648 / 2228	1.3 / 4.0 / 1.4 / 3.7
5 SU 0539 / 1209 / 1815 ●	1.5 / 4.1 / 1.5	**20** M 0450 / 1031 / 1729 / 2326	1.5 / 3.8 / 1.6 / 3.5
6 M 0058 / 0642 / 1331 / 1919	3.5 / 1.8 / 3.8 / 1.8	**21** TU 0536 / 1138 / 1822	1.8 / 3.6 / 1.9
7 TU 0225 / 0813 / 1453 / 2051	3.5 / 2.0 / 3.6 / 2.0	**22** W 0050 / 0637 / 1322 / 1937	3.4 / 2.0 / 3.4 / 2.0
8 W 0343 / 0958 / 1608 / 2220	3.5 / 2.0 / 3.6 / 1.9	**23** TH 0216 / 0810 / 1504 / 2121	3.5 / 2.1 / 3.6 / 2.0
9 TH 0445 / 1108 / 1707 / 2317	3.7 / 1.7 / 3.7 / 1.7	**24** F 0336 / 1000 / 1624 / 2239	3.7 / 1.8 / 3.7 / 1.7
10 F 0531 / 1158 / 1751 / 2359	4.0 / 1.5 / 3.8 / 1.5	**25** SA 0440 / 1110 / 1721 / 2334	4.1 / 1.4 / 4.1 / 1.5
11 SA 0607 / 1237 / 1825	4.2 / 1.2 / 3.9	**26** SU 0531 / 1202 / 1806	4.5 / 0.9 / 4.5
12 SU 0036 / 0638 / 1312 / 1855	1.3 / 4.4 / 1.0 / 4.1	**27** M 0020 / 0615 / 1248 / 1847	0.9 / 5.0 / 0.5 / 4.7
13 M 0111 / 0707 / 1344 / 1924 ○	1.0 / 4.5 / 0.8 / 4.2	**28** TU 0102 / 0656 / 1329 / 1924 ●	0.6 / 5.3 / 0.1 / 4.9
14 TU 0143 / 0735 / 1413 / 1951	0.9 / 4.6 / 0.7 / 4.3		
15 W 0212 / 0801 / 1441 / 2019	0.8 / 4.6 / 0.7 / 4.3		

MARCH

Time	m	Time	m
1 W 0142 / 0735 / 1409 / 2001	0.4 / 5.4 / 0.0 / 4.9	**16** TH 0146 / 0731 / 1409 / 1947	0.7 / 4.6 / 0.6 / 4.5
2 TH 0221 / 0813 / 1447 / 2037	0.3 / 5.4 / 0.0 / 4.8	**17** F 0213 / 0755 / 1436 / 2013	0.7 / 4.6 / 0.7 / 4.4
3 F 0300 / 0853 / 1526 / 2115	0.4 / 5.2 / 0.3 / 4.6	**18** SA 0241 / 0820 / 1505 / 2041	0.8 / 4.5 / 0.8 / 4.3
4 SA 0339 / 0935 / 1605 / 2155	0.6 / 4.8 / 0.7 / 4.2	**19** SU 0310 / 0847 / 1536 / 2110	0.9 / 4.3 / 1.0 / 4.1
5 SU 0421 / 1025 / 1646 / 2246	1.0 / 4.4 / 1.2 / 3.9	**20** M 0342 / 0917 / 1610 / 2146	1.1 / 4.0 / 1.3 / 3.9
6 M 0507 / 1134 / 1733 ●	1.5 / 3.9 / 1.7	**21** TU 0419 / 0958 / 1649 / 2240	1.4 / 3.8 / 1.6 / 3.7
7 TU 0016 / 0606 / 1310 / 1832	3.5 / 1.9 / 3.5 / 2.1	**22** W 0505 / 1114 / 1741 ◐	1.7 / 3.5 / 1.9
8 W 0157 / 0749 / 1439 / 2021	3.4 / 2.1 / 3.4 / 2.3	**23** TH 0021 / 0609 / 1318 / 1905	3.5 / 1.9 / 3.3 / 2.1
9 TH 0321 / 0955 / 1600 / 2209	3.5 / 2.0 / 3.4 / 2.2	**24** F 0156 / 0803 / 1500 / 2107	3.5 / 2.0 / 3.5 / 2.1
10 F 0428 / 1100 / 1658 / 2302	3.7 / 1.7 / 3.6 / 1.9	**25** SA 0317 / 0952 / 1612 / 2222	3.8 / 1.7 / 3.8 / 1.7
11 SA 0513 / 1142 / 1736 / 2341	4.0 / 1.4 / 3.8 / 1.6	**26** SU 0421 / 1054 / 1704 / 2314	4.2 / 1.2 / 4.2 / 1.3
12 SU 0547 / 1217 / 1805	4.2 / 1.2 / 4.0	**27** M 0511 / 1142 / 1746 / 2358	4.6 / 0.7 / 4.5 / 0.9
13 M 0016 / 0616 / 1248 / 1832	1.3 / 4.4 / 0.9 / 4.2	**28** TU 0554 / 1224 / 1825	5.0 / 0.4 / 4.8
14 TU 0049 / 0643 / 1316 / 1857 ○	1.0 / 4.5 / 0.8 / 4.3	**29** W 0039 / 0633 / 1305 / 1900 ●	0.6 / 5.3 / 0.1 / 5.0
15 W 0118 / 0707 / 1343 / 1922	0.8 / 4.6 / 0.7 / 4.4	**30** TH 0119 / 0711 / 1343 / 1935	0.4 / 5.4 / 0.1 / 5.0
		31 F 0158 / 0749 / 1420 / 2010	0.3 / 5.3 / 0.2 / 4.9

APRIL

Time	m	Time	m
1 SA 0237 / 0828 / 1457 / 2046	0.5 / 5.1 / 0.5 / 4.6	**16** SU 0214 / 0756 / 1435 / 2016	0.8 / 4.4 / 0.8 / 4.4
2 SU 0316 / 0910 / 1535 / 2125	0.7 / 4.7 / 0.9 / 4.3	**17** M 0247 / 0828 / 1508 / 2050	0.9 / 4.3 / 1.0 / 4.3
3 M 0358 / 0959 / 1614 / 2214	1.1 / 4.2 / 1.4 / 4.0	**18** TU 0322 / 0906 / 1544 / 2132	1.1 / 4.0 / 1.3 / 4.0
4 TU 0445 / 1110 / 1658 / 2342	1.5 / 3.8 / 1.8 / 3.7	**19** W 0403 / 1001 / 1626 / 2238	1.4 / 3.7 / 1.6 / 3.8
5 W 0545 / 1247 / 1754	1.9 / 3.4 / 2.2	**20** TH 0455 / 1135 / 1722	1.6 / 3.5 / 1.9
6 TH 0122 / 0728 / 1414 / 1943	3.5 / 2.2 / 3.3 / 2.5	**21** F 0013 / 0612 / 1317 / 1857 ◐	3.7 / 1.8 / 3.4 / 2.1
7 F 0244 / 0926 / 1534 / 2132	3.6 / 2.0 / 3.4 / 2.3	**22** SA 0138 / 0801 / 1443 / 2043	3.7 / 1.7 / 3.6 / 2.0
8 SA 0351 / 1028 / 1631 / 2229	3.7 / 1.8 / 3.6 / 2.0	**23** SU 0253 / 0927 / 1550 / 2154	4.0 / 1.4 / 3.8 / 1.7
9 SU 0439 / 1109 / 1707 / 2310	3.9 / 1.5 / 3.8 / 1.7	**24** M 0355 / 1027 / 1640 / 2246	4.3 / 1.1 / 4.2 / 1.3
10 M 0516 / 1143 / 1736 / 2345	4.1 / 1.3 / 4.0 / 1.4	**25** TU 0446 / 1114 / 1722 / 2331	4.6 / 0.7 / 4.5 / 1.0
11 TU 0546 / 1214 / 1803	4.3 / 1.0 / 4.2	**26** W 0530 / 1157 / 1800	4.9 / 0.5 / 4.7
12 W 0017 / 0612 / 1243 / 1827	1.2 / 4.4 / 0.9 / 4.4	**27** TH 0014 / 0610 / 1237 / 1835	0.8 / 5.1 / 0.4 / 4.8
13 TH 0047 / 0637 / 1309 / 1852 ○	1.0 / 4.5 / 0.8 / 4.5	**28** F 0056 / 0649 / 1316 / 1911	0.6 / 5.1 / 0.4 / 4.9
14 F 0115 / 0701 / 1336 / 1918	0.9 / 4.6 / 0.7 / 4.6	**29** SA 0137 / 0729 / 1354 / 1947	0.6 / 5.0 / 0.5 / 4.8
15 SA 0144 / 0728 / 1405 / 1946	0.8 / 4.5 / 0.7 / 4.6	**30** SU 0218 / 0810 / 1432 / 2025	0.7 / 4.7 / 0.8 / 4.6

Chart Datum: 2·71 metres below Ordnance Datum (Newlyn)

SCOTLAND – STORNOWAY

TIME ZONE (UT)
For Summer Time add ONE hour in **non-shaded areas**

LAT 58°12'N   LONG 6°23'W

TIMES AND HEIGHTS OF HIGH AND LOW WATERS

2006

MAY

Day	Time m	Time m	Time m	Time m		Day	Time m	Time m	Time m	Time m
1 M	0259 0.9	0854 4.4	1510 1.1	2107 4.4		16 TU	0233 1.0	0826 4.2	1451 1.1	2045 4.4
2 TU	0343 1.2	0946 4.0	1549 1.5	2159 4.1		17 W	0315 1.1	0916 4.0	1531 1.3	2137 4.2
3 W	0432 1.6	1051 3.7	1632 1.9	2312 3.9		18 TH	0403 1.2	1020 3.8	1619 1.6	2244 4.0
4 TH	0532 1.8	1210 3.6	1727 2.2			19 F	0503 1.4	1139 3.6	1721 1.8	
5 F	0035 3.7	0653 2.0	1328 3.3	1850 2.4		20 SA	0001 3.9	0618 1.5	1258 3.5	1844 1.9
6 SA	0150 3.7	0824 2.0	1443 3.4	2031 2.3		21 SU	0114 4.0	0737 1.4	1412 3.6	2007 1.8
7 SU	0258 3.7	0932 1.8	1544 3.5	2138 2.1		22 M	0222 4.1	0850 1.3	1518 3.8	2117 1.6
8 M	0352 3.8	1021 1.6	1627 3.7	2226 1.9		23 TU	0324 4.3	0951 1.2	1612 4.0	2214 1.4
9 TU	0434 4.0	1059 1.4	1700 4.0	2305 1.6		24 W	0418 4.4	1043 0.9	1657 4.3	2304 1.2
10 W	0509 4.1	1133 1.2	1729 4.2	2339 1.4		25 TH	0506 4.6	1129 0.8	1737 4.4	2351 1.0
11 TH	0538 4.3	1204 1.1	1756 4.4			26 F	0550 4.6	1215 0.8	1815 4.6	
12 F	0012 1.2	0606 4.4	1235 1.0	1823 4.5		27 SA	0037 0.9	0633 4.6	1254 0.8	1853 4.6
13 SA	0045 1.1	0636 4.4	1306 0.9	1854 4.6		28 SU	0122 0.9	0716 4.5	1334 0.9	1932 4.6
14 SU	0119 1.0	0709 4.4	1339 0.9	1927 4.6		29 M	0206 0.9	0800 4.4	1413 1.1	2013 4.5
15 M	0155 0.9	0745 4.3	1414 1.0	2003 4.5		30 TU	0250 1.1	0845 4.2	1453 1.3	2056 4.4
						31 W	0334 1.2	0933 4.0	1532 1.5	2143 4.2

JUNE

Day	Time m	Time m	Time m	Time m		Day	Time m	Time m	Time m	Time m
1 TH	0421 1.4	1024 3.7	1615 1.7	2237 4.0		16 F	0406 0.9	1017 4.0	1616 1.3	2232 4.4
2 F	0511 1.6	1121 3.6	1702 2.0	2337 3.9		17 SA	0500 1.0	1121 3.8	1712 1.5	2336 4.2
3 SA	0607 1.8	1224 3.4	1801 2.1			18 SU	0559 1.1	1224 3.7	1816 1.6	
4 SU	0040 3.7	0710 1.9	1332 3.4	1910 2.2		19 M	0042 4.1	0702 1.2	1333 3.7	1926 1.7
5 M	0146 3.7	0817 1.9	1440 3.5	2024 2.2		20 TU	0148 4.1	0807 1.3	1441 3.7	2037 1.7
6 TU	0248 3.7	0917 1.8	1534 3.6	2125 2.0		21 W	0253 4.1	0913 1.3	1543 3.8	2144 1.6
7 W	0340 3.8	1006 1.6	1616 3.8	2214 1.9		22 TH	0354 4.1	1014 1.3	1636 4.0	2245 1.4
8 TH	0424 3.9	1048 1.5	1650 4.0	2256 1.7		23 F	0449 4.2	1108 1.2	1721 4.2	2340 1.3
9 F	0502 4.0	1127 1.3	1724 4.2	2337 1.5		24 SA	0539 4.2	1157 1.2	1804 4.3	
10 SA	0540 4.1	1205 1.2	1759 4.4			25 SU	0030 1.2	0626 4.2	1242 1.2	1844 4.4
11 SU	0018 1.3	0619 4.2	1244 1.1	1836 4.5		26 M	0118 1.1	0709 4.2	1323 1.1	1923 4.5
12 M	0101 1.1	0701 4.3	1323 1.0	1915 4.6		27 TU	0201 1.0	0751 4.2	1402 1.1	2001 4.5
13 TU	0145 1.0	0745 4.3	1403 1.0	1957 4.6		28 W	0242 1.0	0831 4.1	1440 1.2	2039 4.5
14 W	0229 0.9	0831 4.2	1444 1.1	2043 4.6		29 TH	0321 1.1	0910 4.0	1517 1.3	2118 4.3
15 TH	0316 0.9	0921 4.1	1528 1.2	2134 4.5		30 F	0400 1.2	0950 3.9	1554 1.4	2158 4.2

JULY

Day	Time m	Time m	Time m	Time m		Day	Time m	Time m	Time m	Time m
1 SA	0439 1.3	1033 3.7	1633 1.6	2243 4.0		16 SU	0439 0.7	1046 4.1	1650 1.2	2303 4.5
2 SU	0520 1.5	1121 3.6	1717 1.8	2333 3.8		17 M	0529 0.9	1146 3.8	1743 1.4	
3 M	0605 1.6	1215 3.5	1806 2.0			18 TU	0008 4.2	0622 1.2	1254 3.7	1845 1.6
4 TU	0027 3.7	0655 1.8	1315 3.5	1902 2.1		19 W	0118 4.0	0724 1.4	1408 3.6	2001 1.8
5 W	0125 3.6	0752 1.8	1418 3.5	2005 2.1		20 TH	0231 3.9	0837 1.6	1521 3.7	2128 1.8
6 TH	0228 3.6	0856 1.8	1518 3.6	2112 2.0		21 F	0342 3.8	0956 1.7	1624 3.8	2242 1.6
7 F	0332 3.6	0959 1.8	1610 3.8	2215 1.9		22 SA	0445 3.8	1101 1.6	1716 4.0	2340 1.4
8 SA	0431 3.8	1054 1.6	1656 4.0	2311 1.7		23 SU	0538 3.9	1152 1.5	1758 4.2	
9 SU	0524 3.9	1143 1.4	1740 4.3			24 M	0029 1.2	0622 4.0	1235 1.3	1835 4.4
10 M	0002 1.4	0611 4.1	1229 1.2	1822 4.5		25 TU	0112 1.1	0700 4.1	1314 1.2	1910 4.5
11 TU	0052 1.1	0657 4.3	1312 1.0	1905 4.7		26 W	0150 0.9	0735 4.1	1349 1.1	1943 4.6
12 W	0138 0.8	0741 4.4	1355 0.9	1948 4.9		27 TH	0224 0.9	0808 4.2	1423 1.0	2014 4.6
13 TH	0223 0.6	0824 4.5	1436 0.8	2031 4.9		28 F	0257 0.9	0840 4.1	1455 1.1	2045 4.6
14 F	0307 0.5	0908 4.4	1518 0.9	2117 4.9		29 SA	0328 0.9	0912 4.1	1527 1.2	2117 4.3
15 SA	0352 0.5	0954 4.3	1602 1.0	2207 4.7		30 SU	0400 1.1	0947 3.9	1559 1.4	2151 4.1
						31 M	0435 1.3	1026 3.8	1635 1.6	2229 3.9

AUGUST

Day	Time m	Time m	Time m	Time m		Day	Time m	Time m	Time m	Time m
1 TU	0513 1.5	1113 3.6	1716 1.8	2317 3.7		16 W	0543 1.3	1220 3.7	1810 1.7	
2 W	0557 1.7	1210 3.5	1804 2.0			17 TH	0057 3.9	0643 1.8	1346 3.6	1936 2.0
3 TH	0019 3.5	0648 1.9	1314 3.5	1902 2.1		18 F	0221 3.6	0809 2.0	1509 3.6	2132 2.0
4 F	0132 3.5	0753 2.0	1424 3.5	2018 2.2		19 SA	0341 3.6	0954 2.0	1620 3.8	2247 1.7
5 SA	0256 3.5	0916 2.0	1535 3.7	2147 2.0		20 SU	0447 3.7	1058 1.8	1711 4.0	2339 1.5
6 SU	0415 3.7	1032 1.8	1634 4.0	2257 1.7		21 M	0536 3.8	1144 1.6	1749 4.3	
7 M	0514 3.9	1128 1.6	1724 4.3	2352 1.3		22 TU	0020 1.2	0611 4.0	1221 1.4	1821 4.5
8 TU	0602 4.2	1215 1.3	1809 4.7			23 W	0056 1.0	0642 4.1	1257 1.2	1850 4.6
9 W	0040 0.9	0645 4.5	1259 0.9	1850 5.0		24 TH	0128 0.9	0711 4.3	1328 1.0	1918 4.7
10 TH	0124 0.5	0725 4.7	1340 0.7	1931 5.2		25 F	0157 0.8	0739 4.3	1358 0.9	1944 4.7
11 F	0206 0.3	0804 4.8	1419 0.6	2011 5.3		26 SA	0225 0.8	0806 4.4	1427 0.9	2010 4.6
12 SA	0247 0.2	0844 4.7	1459 0.6	2052 5.2		27 SU	0252 0.8	0833 4.3	1455 1.0	2036 4.4
13 SU	0328 0.3	0925 4.6	1539 0.7	2137 5.0		28 M	0321 1.0	0903 4.2	1525 1.2	2102 4.2
14 M	0410 0.5	1010 4.3	1622 1.0	2229 4.6		29 TU	0352 1.2	0935 4.0	1557 1.4	2129 4.0
15 TU	0454 0.9	1106 4.0	1711 1.4	2336 4.2		30 W	0427 1.4	1014 3.8	1632 1.7	2203 3.8
						31 TH	0507 1.7	1111 3.6	1715 2.0	2306 3.5

Chart Datum: 2·71 metres below Ordnance Datum (Newlyn)

TIME ZONE (UT)
For Summer Time add ONE hour in **non-shaded areas**

SCOTLAND–STORNOWAY

LAT 58°12′N   LONG 6°23′W

TIMES AND HEIGHTS OF HIGH AND LOW WATERS

SEPTEMBER

Day	Time m	Time m	Day	Time m	Time m
1 F	0556 2.0	1229 3.5	**16** SA	0213 3.6	0751 2.4
	1813 2.2			1453 3.7	2135 2.1
2 SA	0102 3.4	0705 2.2	**17** SU	0337 3.6	0948 2.2
	1350 3.6	1942 2.2		1606 3.9	2241 1.8
3 SU	0244 3.5	0850 2.2	**18** M	0441 3.7	1044 2.0
	1510 3.8	2137 2.0		1655 4.1	2323 1.5
4 M	0405 3.7	1016 2.0	**19** TU	0521 3.9	1123 1.7
	1615 4.1	2246 1.6		1729 4.4	2357 1.3
5 TU	0500 4.1	1111 1.6	**20** W	0551 4.1	1158 1.5
	1706 4.5	2336 1.6		1758 4.5	
6 W	0545 4.4	1156 1.2	**21** TH	0028 1.1	0617 4.3
	1750 5.0			1231 1.2	1825 4.7
7 TH	0020 0.7	0624 4.8	**22** F	0057 0.9	0642 4.4
○	1238 0.9	1830 5.3		1301 1.1	1850 4.7
8 F	0102 0.3	0702 5.0	**23** SA	0124 0.8	0707 4.5
	1317 0.6	1909 5.5		1329 1.0	1913 4.7
9 SA	0141 0.1	0739 5.1	**24** SU	0150 0.8	0732 4.6
	1356 0.5	1947 5.5		1356 1.0	1937 4.7
10 SU	0220 0.1	0816 5.0	**25** M	0216 0.9	0758 4.5
	1435 0.5	2027 5.4		1424 1.0	2001 4.5
11 M	0259 0.3	0854 4.8	**26** TU	0245 1.0	0826 4.4
	1515 0.7	2109 5.0		1453 1.2	2027 4.4
12 TU	0339 0.7	0936 4.5	**27** W	0315 1.2	0855 4.2
	1557 1.1	2200 4.6		1525 1.4	2054 4.1
13 W	0421 1.1	1031 4.1	**28** TH	0349 1.5	0930 4.0
	1644 1.6	2311 4.1		1600 1.7	2130 3.8
14 TH	0507 1.7	1157 3.8	**29** F	0427 1.8	1025 3.8
◐	1743 1.9			1643 1.9	2241 3.6
15 F	0045 3.7	0606 2.1	**30** SA	0516 2.1	1203 3.6
	1328 3.7	1927 2.2	◑	1746 2.2	

OCTOBER

Day	Time m	Time m	Day	Time m	Time m
1 SU	0058 3.4	0634 2.4	**16** M	0311 3.6	0911 2.4
	1330 3.7	1932 2.2		1530 4.0	2208 1.9
2 M	0235 3.6	0833 2.3	**17** TU	0413 3.8	1009 2.2
	1448 3.9	2123 1.9		1621 4.2	2249 1.6
3 TU	0347 3.9	0954 2.0	**18** W	0451 4.0	1050 1.9
	1552 4.3	2225 1.5		1658 4.3	2323 1.4
4 W	0439 4.2	1046 1.6	**19** TH	0521 4.2	1126 1.6
	1643 4.7	2312 1.0		1729 4.5	2353 1.3
5 TH	0521 4.6	1130 1.2	**20** F	0547 4.4	1159 1.4
	1727 5.1	2354 0.6		1756 4.6	
6 F	0600 4.9	1212 0.9	**21** SA	0022 1.1	0612 4.5
	1807 5.4			1230 1.2	1821 4.7
7 SA	0034 0.4	0636 5.1	**22** SU	0049 1.0	0637 4.7
○	1252 0.6	1845 5.6	●	1258 1.1	1845 4.7
8 SU	0114 0.3	0712 5.2	**23** M	0116 1.0	0702 4.7
	1332 0.6	1924 5.5		1327 1.1	1910 4.6
9 M	0152 0.3	0749 5.1	**24** TU	0145 1.0	0730 4.7
	1412 0.6	2004 5.3		1358 1.1	1938 4.5
10 TU	0231 0.6	0827 4.9	**25** W	0215 1.1	0800 4.6
	1453 0.9	2048 4.9		1429 1.2	2008 4.3
11 W	0310 1.0	0911 4.6	**26** TH	0248 1.3	0834 4.4
	1536 1.2	2140 4.5		1504 1.4	2044 4.1
12 TH	0351 1.4	1007 4.3	**27** F	0323 1.5	0915 4.2
	1625 1.6	2256 4.0		1543 1.6	2134 3.8
13 F	0437 1.9	1134 4.0	**28** SA	0403 1.8	1018 4.0
	1728 2.0			1632 1.8	2307 3.6
14 SA	0027 3.7	0535 2.3	**29** SU	0456 2.1	1147 3.8
◑	1300 3.8	1911 2.3	◐	1743 2.0	
15 SU	0150 3.6	0720 2.6	**30** M	0048 3.6	0621 2.4
	1419 3.8	2106 2.1		1307 3.9	1922 2.0
			31 TU	0210 3.7	0804 2.2
				1419 4.1	2050 1.7

NOVEMBER

Day	Time m	Time m	Day	Time m	Time m
1 W	0318 4.0	0920 2.0	**16** TH	0409 3.9	1005 2.1
	1522 4.4	2153 1.4		1618 4.1	2239 1.7
2 TH	0411 4.3	1014 1.6	**17** F	0445 4.1	1047 1.8
	1615 4.7	2242 1.0		1655 4.2	2314 1.5
3 F	0455 4.6	1101 1.3	**18** SA	0515 4.3	1123 1.6
	1701 5.0	2325 0.8		1726 4.3	2346 1.3
4 SA	0534 4.8	1145 1.0	**19** SU	0543 4.5	1157 1.5
	1744 5.2			1754 4.4	
5 SU	0007 0.6	0612 5.0	**20** M	0017 1.2	0610 4.6
○	1229 0.9	1824 5.3	●	1231 1.3	1823 4.5
6 M	0048 0.6	0649 5.1	**21** TU	0048 1.2	0640 4.7
	1312 0.8	1906 5.2		1304 1.3	1854 4.5
7 TU	0128 0.7	0728 5.0	**22** W	0121 1.1	0712 4.7
	1355 0.9	1949 5.0		1340 1.2	1928 4.4
8 W	0208 0.9	0809 4.9	**23** TH	0156 1.2	0748 4.6
	1439 1.1	2036 4.7		1417 1.2	2007 4.3
9 TH	0248 1.2	0855 4.6	**24** F	0232 1.3	0827 4.4
	1525 1.3	2130 4.3		1457 1.3	2052 4.1
10 F	0330 1.6	0951 4.4	**25** SA	0311 1.5	0914 4.4
	1615 1.6	2236 4.0		1542 1.4	2149 3.9
11 SA	0415 2.0	1101 4.2	**26** SU	0355 1.7	1014 4.2
	1715 1.9	2350 3.7		1635 1.5	2302 3.8
12 SU	0511 2.3	1215 4.0	**27** M	0450 1.9	1125 4.1
◐	1832 2.1			1741 1.6	
13 M	0104 3.6	0628 2.5	**28** TU	0019 3.7	0602 2.0
	1326 3.9	1958 2.1	◑	1236 4.1	1854 1.6
14 TU	0217 3.6	0803 2.5	**29** W	0132 3.7	0722 2.0
	1434 3.9	2109 2.0		1343 4.2	2007 1.5
15 W	0321 3.7	0914 2.3	**30** TH	0239 3.9	0836 1.9
	1532 4.0	2159 1.8		1447 4.3	2112 1.4

DECEMBER

Day	Time m	Time m	Day	Time m	Time m
1 F	0337 4.1	0938 1.7	**16** SA	0403 3.9	0959 2.1
	1545 4.5	2208 1.2		1615 3.9	2232 1.7
2 SA	0427 4.3	1033 1.4	**17** SU	0442 4.0	1046 1.9
	1637 4.6	2258 1.0		1656 4.0	2313 1.6
3 SU	0512 4.5	1124 1.2	**18** M	0516 4.2	1128 1.7
	1725 4.7	2344 1.0		1734 4.1	2351 1.4
4 M	0554 4.7	1213 1.1	**19** TU	0550 4.4	1209 1.5
	1811 4.8			1811 4.2	
5 TU	0028 1.0	0635 4.8	**20** W	0029 1.3	0625 4.5
○	1301 1.0	1856 4.7		1251 1.3	1849 4.3
6 W	0111 1.0	0716 4.8	**21** TH	0107 1.2	0702 4.7
	1347 1.0	1941 4.6		1332 1.1	1929 4.3
7 TH	0153 1.1	0759 4.6	**22** F	0146 1.1	0741 4.7
	1433 1.1	2027 4.4		1413 1.0	2010 4.3
8 F	0234 1.3	0843 4.7	**23** SA	0225 1.1	0822 4.7
	1518 1.2	2114 4.2		1456 1.0	2053 4.3
9 SA	0315 1.5	0930 4.5	**24** SU	0306 1.2	0907 4.6
	1603 1.4	2204 4.0		1540 1.0	2140 4.1
10 SU	0358 1.7	1020 4.3	**25** M	0349 1.3	0956 4.5
	1652 1.6	2257 3.8		1628 1.0	2235 4.0
11 M	0444 1.9	1115 4.1	**26** TU	0438 1.4	1053 4.4
	1744 1.8	2357 3.6		1721 1.2	2337 3.8
12 TU	0538 2.2	1215 4.0	**27** W	0534 1.6	1157 4.3
◐	1842 1.9		◐	1819 1.3	
13 W	0104 3.5	0641 2.3	**28** TH	0046 3.7	0638 1.7
	1320 3.9	1947 2.0		1304 4.2	1921 1.4
14 TH	0214 3.6	0754 2.3	**29** F	0156 3.7	0749 1.8
	1426 3.8	2051 2.0		1411 4.1	2029 1.5
15 F	0315 3.7	0903 2.2	**30** SA	0304 3.8	0904 1.7
	1526 3.8	2147 1.9		1519 4.1	2137 1.5
			31 SU	0405 4.0	1014 1.6
				1621 4.2	2239 1.4

Chart Datum: 2·71 metres below Ordnance Datum (Newlyn)

TIDES

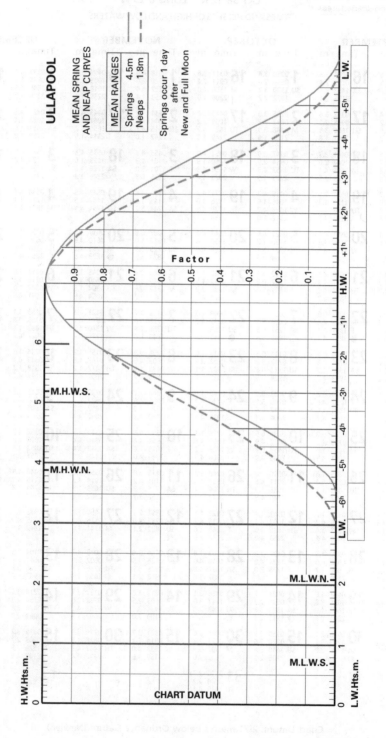

ULLAPOOL

MEAN SPRING
AND NEAP CURVES

MEAN RANGES
Springs 4.5m
Neaps 1.8m

Springs occur 1 day
after
New and Full Moon

SCOTLAND – ULLAPOOL

LAT 57°54'N   LONG 5°10'W

TIMES AND HEIGHTS OF HIGH AND LOW WATERS

TIME ZONE (UT)
For Summer Time add ONE hour in **non-shaded areas**

JANUARY

Day	Time m	Time m	Time m	Time m
1 SU	0134 1.2	0731 5.4	1401 0.9	2002 5.2
2 M	0219 1.1	0816 5.5	1448 0.9	2050 5.1
3 TU	0304 1.1	0903 5.5	1535 0.9	2140 5.0
4 W	0351 1.2	0953 5.3	1624 1.0	2233 4.8
5 TH	0439 1.4	1047 5.1	1715 1.2	2331 4.5
6 F	0532 1.7	1147 4.8	1810 1.5	
7 SA	0036 4.3	0631 1.9	1255 4.6	1909 1.7
8 SU	0147 4.2	0739 2.1	1406 4.4	2018 1.9
9 M	0301 4.2	0857 2.1	1520 4.3	2131 2.0
10 TU	0409 4.3	1013 2.1	1627 4.4	2238 1.9
11 W	0503 4.5	1116 1.9	1722 4.5	2332 1.8
12 TH	0548 4.7	1208 1.7	1809 4.6	
13 F	0017 1.7	0626 4.8	1252 1.5	1848 4.7
14 SA ○	0058 1.6	0700 5.0	1332 1.4	1923 4.8
15 SU	0134 1.5	0732 5.0	1408 1.3	1956 4.8
16 M	0208 1.5	0802 5.1	1441 1.3	2028 4.8
17 TU	0241 1.4	0831 5.0	1514 1.3	2059 4.7
18 W	0313 1.5	0901 4.9	1547 1.3	2131 4.6
19 TH	0345 1.6	0932 4.8	1620 1.5	2206 4.4
20 F	0419 1.7	1006 4.6	1654 1.6	2245 4.3
21 SA	0456 1.9	1045 4.4	1733 1.8	2334 4.1
22 SU ◑	0538 2.1	1134 4.2	1818 2.0	
23 M	0039 4.0	0631 2.3	1241 4.0	1916 2.2
24 TU	0154 3.9	0741 2.4	1405 4.0	2033 2.3
25 W	0307 4.0	0905 2.4	1526 4.0	2155 2.2
26 TH	0412 4.3	1024 2.1	1638 4.3	2300 1.9
27 F	0507 4.6	1126 1.8	1735 4.6	2353 1.6
28 SA	0554 5.0	1218 1.3	1824 4.9	
29 SU ●	0041 1.3	0637 5.3	1307 0.9	1908 5.2
30 M	0126 1.0	0720 5.6	1353 0.6	1951 5.3
31 TU	0209 0.8	0802 5.7	1437 0.4	2034 5.3

FEBRUARY

Day	Time m	Time m	Time m	Time m
1 W	0251 0.7	0845 5.7	1520 0.4	2117 5.2
2 TH	0333 0.8	0929 5.6	1602 0.6	2201 5.0
3 F	0416 1.0	1016 5.3	1645 0.9	2250 4.6
4 SA	0501 1.3	1109 4.9	1731 1.3	2347 4.3
5 SU ○	0552 1.7	1214 4.5	1822 1.7	
6 M	0100 4.1	0654 2.1	1333 4.1	1926 2.1
7 TU	0227 3.9	0822 2.3	1502 4.0	2058 2.3
8 W	0352 4.0	1004 2.3	1621 4.0	2228 2.3
9 TH	0456 4.2	1115 2.0	1720 4.2	2327 2.1
10 F	0542 4.5	1204 1.7	1803 4.4	
11 SA	0010 1.8	0617 4.7	1244 1.5	1837 4.6
12 SU	0048 1.6	0647 4.9	1319 1.3	1907 4.7
13 M ○	0121 1.4	0715 5.0	1351 1.1	1935 4.8
14 TU	0152 1.2	0741 5.1	1420 1.0	2002 4.9
15 W	0221 1.2	0806 5.1	1449 1.0	2029 4.8
16 TH	0249 1.1	0832 5.0	1517 1.0	2056 4.8
17 F	0318 1.2	0859 4.9	1545 1.1	2126 4.6
18 SA	0348 1.3	0929 4.8	1615 1.3	2159 4.5
19 SU	0421 1.5	1003 4.5	1648 1.5	2238 4.3
20 M	0458 1.8	1043 4.3	1726 1.8	2331 4.0
21 TU	0544 2.1	1140 4.0	1817 2.1	
22 W	0055 3.9	0648 2.3	1321 3.8	1936 2.4
23 TH	0229 3.9	0826 2.4	1508 3.8	2131 2.3
24 F	0349 4.1	1009 2.1	1631 4.1	2249 2.1
25 SA	0451 4.5	1116 1.6	1728 4.5	2343 1.5
26 SU	0539 4.9	1208 1.1	1812 4.9	
27 M	0028 1.1	0620 5.3	1253 0.6	1852 5.2
28 TU ●	0110 0.7	0701 5.7	1336 0.3	1931 5.4

MARCH

Day	Time m	Time m	Time m	Time m
1 W	0151 0.5	0740 5.8	1416 0.1	2009 5.4
2 TH	0230 0.4	0820 5.8	1456 0.1	2047 5.3
3 F	0310 0.5	0902 5.6	1534 0.4	2126 5.0
4 SA	0350 0.7	0946 5.2	1613 0.8	2209 4.7
5 SU	0432 1.1	1036 4.7	1654 1.3	2259 4.3
6 M ◑	0519 1.6	1141 4.2	1739 1.8	
7 TU	0014 4.0	0617 2.1	1308 3.9	1838 2.3
8 W	0154 3.8	0754 2.4	1445 3.7	2027 2.5
9 TH	0331 3.8	0958 2.3	1609 3.8	2218 2.4
10 F	0438 4.0	1104 2.0	1705 4.0	2313 2.1
11 SA	0523 4.3	1146 1.7	1744 4.3	2352 1.8
12 SU	0556 4.5	1222 1.4	1815 4.5	
13 M	0026 1.5	0623 4.7	1254 1.1	1842 4.7
14 TU ○	0057 1.2	0649 4.9	1323 0.9	1907 4.8
15 W	0126 1.1	0713 5.0	1351 0.8	1932 4.9
16 TH	0154 0.9	0737 5.1	1418 0.8	1957 4.9
17 F	0222 0.9	0802 5.0	1444 0.8	2023 4.9
18 SA	0250 1.0	0829 4.9	1512 1.0	2052 4.8
19 SU	0320 1.1	0859 4.7	1541 1.1	2123 4.6
20 M	0352 1.3	0933 4.5	1613 1.4	2201 4.4
21 TU	0430 1.6	1015 4.2	1651 1.7	2253 4.1
22 W ◑	0516 1.9	1119 3.9	1741 2.1	
23 TH	0021 3.9	0621 2.2	1314 3.7	1906 2.4
24 F	0203 3.8	0810 2.2	1459 3.8	2118 2.3
25 SA	0326 4.1	0957 1.9	1617 4.1	2233 1.9
26 SU	0424 4.5	1059 1.4	1710 4.5	2323 1.4
27 M	0516 4.9	1147 0.9	1751 4.9	
28 TU	0006 0.9	0557 5.3	1231 0.4	1829 5.2
29 W ●	0048 0.6	0637 5.6	1311 0.1	1905 5.4
30 TH	0127 0.3	0716 5.7	1350 0.1	1941 5.4
31 F	0207 0.3	0755 5.6	1428 0.2	2018 5.3

APRIL

Day	Time m	Time m	Time m	Time m
1 SA	0246 0.4	0836 5.3	1505 0.5	2055 5.0
2 SU	0326 0.7	0921 4.9	1543 0.9	2135 4.7
3 M	0408 1.2	1013 4.5	1622 1.4	2223 4.3
4 TU	0454 1.6	1121 4.0	1706 1.9	2335 3.9
5 W ◑	0554 2.0	1245 3.7	1803 2.3	
6 TH	0115 3.7	0728 2.3	1416 3.6	1949 2.6
7 F	0252 3.7	0926 2.2	1537 3.7	2144 2.4
8 SA	0402 3.9	1029 1.9	1633 3.9	2240 2.1
9 SU	0448 4.1	1112 1.6	1712 4.1	2320 1.8
10 M	0522 4.3	1147 1.3	1743 4.4	2354 1.5
11 TU	0551 4.5	1219 1.1	1810 4.6	
12 W	0025 1.2	0616 4.7	1249 0.9	1835 4.7
13 TH ○	0055 1.0	0641 4.8	1317 0.8	1901 4.9
14 F	0124 0.9	0707 4.9	1345 0.8	1927 4.9
15 SA	0153 0.9	0734 4.9	1413 0.8	1955 4.9
16 SU	0224 0.9	0804 4.8	1442 0.9	2026 4.8
17 M	0256 1.0	0839 4.6	1514 1.1	2101 4.6
18 TU	0332 1.2	0919 4.4	1550 1.4	2145 4.4
19 W	0414 1.5	1014 4.1	1632 1.7	2245 4.1
20 TH	0505 1.7	1136 3.8	1729 2.1	
21 F ◑	0014 4.0	0618 2.0	1315 3.7	1903 2.3
22 SA	0142 4.0	0803 1.9	1441 3.9	2054 2.1
23 SU	0257 4.2	0931 1.6	1551 4.1	2203 1.7
24 M	0359 4.5	1031 1.2	1643 4.5	2255 1.3
25 TU	0448 4.8	1119 0.8	1725 4.8	2340 0.9
26 W	0532 5.1	1203 0.5	1804 5.0	
27 TH	0022 0.6	0613 5.3	1244 0.3	1840 5.2
28 F	0104 0.5	0653 5.4	1324 0.3	1916 5.2
29 SA	0145 0.5	0735 5.2	1402 0.5	1953 5.1
30 SU	0226 0.6	0818 5.0	1440 0.8	2032 4.9

Chart Datum: 2·75 metres below Ordnance Datum (Newlyn)

TIDES

TIME ZONE (UT)
For Summer Time add ONE hour in **non-shaded areas**

SCOTLAND – ULLAPOOL
LAT 57°54'N   LONG 5°10'W

2006

TIMES AND HEIGHTS OF HIGH AND LOW WATERS

MAY

Time m	Time m	Time m	Time m
1 0307 0.9 / 0906 4.6 / M 1518 1.1 / 2113 4.6	**16** 0241 1.0 / 0834 4.5 / TU 1458 1.2 / 2053 4.7		
2 0350 1.2 / 1000 4.3 / TU 1558 1.5 / 2202 4.3	**17** 0323 1.2 / 0925 4.3 / W 1540 1.4 / 2145 4.5		
3 0438 1.6 / 1103 3.9 / W 1643 1.9 / 2306 4.0	**18** 0411 1.3 / 1029 4.1 / TH 1629 1.7 / 2249 4.3		
4 0536 1.9 / 1214 3.7 / TH 1738 2.2	**19** 0508 1.5 / 1143 4.0 / F 1731 1.9		
5 0028 3.8 / 0652 2.1 / F 1328 3.6 / ☾ 1900 2.4	**20** 0003 4.2 / 0619 1.6 / SA 1300 3.9 / ☽ 1852 2.0		
6 0151 3.7 / 0822 2.1 / SA 1442 3.6 / 2037 2.4	**21** 0117 4.2 / 0740 1.6 / SU 1412 4.0 / 2017 1.9		
7 0304 3.8 / 0933 1.9 / SU 1543 3.8 / 2146 2.1	**22** 0225 4.3 / 0854 1.4 / M 1519 4.2 / 2125 1.7		
8 0357 4.0 / 1023 1.7 / M 1628 4.0 / 2233 1.9	**23** 0327 4.5 / 0956 1.2 / TU 1614 4.4 / 2222 1.4		
9 0438 4.1 / 1103 1.5 / TU 1703 4.2 / 2312 1.6	**24** 0421 4.7 / 1049 1.0 / W 1700 4.6 / 2313 1.1		
10 0511 4.3 / 1138 1.3 / W 1734 4.4 / 2348 1.4	**25** 0510 4.8 / 1136 0.8 / TH 1742 4.8		
11 0541 4.5 / 1211 1.1 / TH 1803 4.6	**26** 0000 0.9 / 0555 4.9 / F 1220 0.8 / 1820 4.9		
12 0021 1.2 / 0610 4.6 / F 1243 1.0 / 1831 4.8	**27** 0046 0.8 / 0639 4.9 / SA 1302 0.8 / ● 1859 5.0		
13 0054 1.1 / 0640 4.7 / SA 1314 0.9 / ○ 1901 4.9	**28** 0130 0.8 / 0724 4.9 / SU 1342 0.9 / 1938 4.9		
14 0128 1.0 / 0714 4.7 / SU 1347 0.9 / 1934 4.9	**29** 0213 0.9 / 0809 4.7 / M 1421 1.1 / 2018 4.8		
15 0204 1.0 / 0751 4.7 / M 1421 1.0 / 2011 4.8	**30** 0255 1.0 / 0856 4.5 / TU 1501 1.3 / 2100 4.6		
	31 0339 1.2 / 0945 4.3 / W 1541 1.6 / 2144 4.4		

JUNE

Time m	Time m	Time m	Time m
1 0424 1.5 / 1036 4.0 / TH 1625 1.8 / 2235 4.2	**16** 0411 1.0 / 1026 4.4 / F 1628 1.4 / 2239 4.7		
2 0513 1.7 / 1130 3.9 / F 1713 2.0 / 2333 4.0	**17** 0505 1.1 / 1127 4.3 / SA 1724 1.6 / 2341 4.5		
3 0609 1.8 / 1230 3.7 / SA 1810 2.2 / ☽	**18** 0603 1.3 / 1231 4.1 / SU 1827 1.7 / ☾		
4 0040 3.9 / 0711 1.9 / SU 1333 3.7 / 1919 2.2	**19** 0046 4.4 / 0706 1.4 / M 1338 4.1 / 1935 1.8		
5 0147 3.8 / 0817 1.9 / M 1436 3.7 / 2030 2.2	**20** 0152 4.4 / 0813 1.4 / TU 1444 4.1 / 2046 1.7		
6 0249 3.9 / 0918 1.8 / TU 1531 3.9 / 2132 2.1	**21** 0258 4.4 / 0919 1.4 / W 1546 4.2 / 2153 1.6		
7 0341 4.0 / 1009 1.7 / W 1617 4.0 / 2223 1.9	**22** 0401 4.4 / 1021 1.4 / TH 1641 4.4 / 2253 1.5		
8 0426 4.1 / 1053 1.5 / TH 1656 4.3 / 2308 1.7	**23** 0458 4.5 / 1115 1.3 / F 1729 4.6 / 2348 1.3		
9 0506 4.3 / 1133 1.4 / F 1732 4.5 / 2349 1.5	**24** 0549 4.6 / 1204 1.3 / SA 1812 4.7		
10 0544 4.4 / 1211 1.3 / SA 1807 4.7	**25** 0037 1.2 / 0636 4.6 / SU 1249 1.2 / ● 1852 4.8		
11 0029 1.3 / 0623 4.5 / SU 1250 1.2 / ○ 1843 4.8	**26** 0123 1.1 / 0720 4.6 / M 1331 1.2 / 1930 4.9		
12 0110 1.1 / 0704 4.6 / M 1329 1.1 / 1923 4.9	**27** 0206 1.1 / 0802 4.6 / TU 1410 1.3 / 2007 4.8		
13 0152 1.0 / 0749 4.7 / TU 1409 1.1 / 2005 4.9	**28** 0247 1.1 / 0841 4.5 / W 1448 1.3 / 2044 4.7		
14 0235 0.9 / 0837 4.6 / W 1452 1.2 / 2051 4.9	**29** 0325 1.2 / 0920 4.4 / TH 1525 1.4 / 2120 4.6		
15 0321 1.0 / 0930 4.5 / TH 1538 1.3 / 2143 4.8	**30** 0404 1.3 / 0959 4.2 / F 1603 1.6 / 2158 4.4		

JULY

Time m	Time m	Time m	Time m
1 0443 1.4 / 1040 4.1 / SA 1642 1.7 / 2239 4.3	**16** 0446 0.8 / 1057 4.5 / SU 1702 1.2 / 2312 4.8		
2 0524 1.6 / 1128 3.9 / SU 1725 1.9 / 2327 4.1	**17** 0535 1.0 / 1156 4.3 / M 1755 1.5 / ☽		
3 0609 1.7 / 1223 3.8 / M 1813 2.0	**18** 0014 4.5 / 0629 1.3 / TU 1302 4.1 / 1856 1.7		
4 0026 3.9 / 0659 1.9 / TU 1326 3.8 / 1911 2.2	**19** 0123 4.3 / 0731 1.6 / W 1413 4.0 / 2010 1.9		
5 0133 3.8 / 0759 2.0 / W 1429 3.8 / 2019 2.2	**20** 0237 4.2 / 0844 1.8 / TH 1527 4.1 / 2133 1.9		
6 0239 3.8 / 0905 2.0 / TH 1528 3.9 / 2129 2.1	**21** 0353 4.1 / 1002 1.9 / F 1633 4.2 / 2248 1.8		
7 0341 3.9 / 1007 1.9 / F 1621 4.1 / 2230 2.0	**22** 0458 4.2 / 1107 1.8 / SA 1726 4.4 / 2347 1.6		
8 0438 4.0 / 1101 1.7 / SA 1707 4.3 / 2323 1.7	**23** 0551 4.3 / 1159 1.6 / SU 1809 4.6		
9 0528 4.3 / 1149 1.5 / SU 1750 4.6	**24** 0036 1.4 / 0634 4.5 / M 1243 1.5 / 1846 4.8		
10 0012 1.6 / 0615 4.5 / M 1234 1.3 / 1831 4.9	**25** 0118 1.2 / 0711 4.6 / TU 1322 1.4 / ● 1919 4.9		
11 0059 1.4 / 0700 4.7 / TU 1318 1.1 / ○ 1913 5.1	**26** 0156 1.1 / 0745 4.7 / W 1357 1.3 / 1950 4.9		
12 0144 0.9 / 0744 4.8 / W 1402 1.0 / 1956 5.2	**27** 0231 1.0 / 0817 4.7 / TH 1431 1.2 / 2020 4.9		
13 0229 0.7 / 0830 4.9 / TH 1445 0.9 / 2040 5.3	**28** 0304 1.0 / 0848 4.6 / F 1503 1.2 / 2049 4.8		
14 0314 0.6 / 0916 4.9 / F 1529 0.9 / 2127 5.2	**29** 0335 1.1 / 0919 4.5 / SA 1535 1.3 / 2119 4.7		
15 0400 0.6 / 1004 4.7 / SA 1614 1.1 / 2216 5.0	**30** 0407 1.2 / 0952 4.3 / SU 1608 1.4 / 2152 4.5		
	31 0440 1.4 / 1029 4.2 / M 1643 1.6 / 2228 4.3		

AUGUST

Time m	Time m	Time m	Time m
1 0515 1.6 / 1114 4.0 / TU 1722 1.9 / 2313 4.1	**16** 0551 1.5 / 1225 4.1 / W 1822 1.8 / ☽		
2 0556 1.8 / 1214 3.9 / W 1810 2.1 / ☾	**17** 0100 4.1 / 0650 1.9 / TH 1350 4.0 / 1944 2.1		
3 0015 3.9 / 0647 2.1 / TH 1329 3.8 / 1912 2.3	**18** 0228 3.9 / 0816 2.2 / F 1517 4.0 / 2131 2.2		
4 0142 3.7 / 0758 2.2 / F 1443 3.8 / 2037 2.3	**19** 0354 3.9 / 0958 2.2 / SA 1629 4.2 / 2252 1.9		
5 0307 3.8 / 0928 2.2 / SA 1551 4.0 / 2203 2.2	**20** 0459 4.1 / 1105 2.0 / SU 1720 4.4 / 2345 1.6		
6 0422 3.9 / 1040 2.0 / SU 1648 4.3 / 2308 1.8	**21** 0545 4.3 / 1152 1.7 / M 1759 4.6		
7 0519 4.2 / 1135 1.7 / M 1735 4.7	**22** 0026 1.4 / 0621 4.5 / TU 1231 1.5 / 1830 4.8		
8 0000 1.4 / 0606 4.6 / TU 1222 1.3 / 1817 5.0	**23** 0103 1.1 / 0652 4.7 / W 1305 1.3 / ● 1858 4.9		
9 0047 1.0 / 0648 4.9 / W 1306 1.0 / ○ 1857 5.3	**24** 0135 1.0 / 0720 4.8 / TH 1337 1.2 / 1925 5.0		
10 0131 0.6 / 0729 5.1 / TH 1348 0.7 / 1938 5.5	**25** 0205 0.9 / 0746 4.8 / F 1407 1.1 / 1950 5.0		
11 0214 0.3 / 0809 5.2 / F 1429 0.6 / 2019 5.6	**26** 0234 0.9 / 0813 4.8 / SA 1435 1.1 / 2016 5.0		
12 0256 0.2 / 0850 5.2 / SA 1510 0.6 / 2101 5.5	**27** 0302 0.9 / 0840 4.7 / SU 1504 1.1 / 2042 4.9		
13 0337 0.5 / 0933 5.0 / SU 1551 0.8 / 2147 5.3	**28** 0330 1.0 / 0908 4.6 / M 1534 1.3 / 2111 4.7		
14 0419 0.6 / 1020 4.7 / M 1635 1.0 / 2239 4.9	**29** 0359 1.2 / 0940 4.4 / TU 1606 1.5 / 2143 4.5		
15 0503 1.0 / 1115 4.4 / TU 1724 1.4 / 2342 4.5	**30** 0430 1.5 / 1018 4.2 / W 1642 1.8 / 2222 4.2		
	31 0507 1.8 / 1109 4.0 / TH 1726 2.0 / ☽ 2317 3.9		

Chart Datum: 2·75 metres below Ordnance Datum (Newlyn)

TIME ZONE (UT)
For Summer Time add ONE hour in **non-shaded areas**

SCOTLAND – ULLAPOOL

LAT 57°54'N   LONG 5°10'W

TIMES AND HEIGHTS OF HIGH AND LOW WATERS

2006

SEPTEMBER

Time m	Time m
1 F 0552 2.1 / 1233 3.8 / 1825 2.3	**16** SA 0222 3.8 / 0756 2.5 / 1504 4.0 / 2133 2.2
2 SA 0102 3.7 / 0704 2.4 / 1408 3.8 / 1959 2.4	**17** SU 0347 3.9 / 0953 2.0 / 1615 4.2 / 2242 1.9
3 SU 0249 3.7 / 0903 2.4 / 1527 4.0 / 2148 2.2	**18** M 0446 4.1 / 1051 2.1 / 1702 4.4 / 2326 1.6
4 M 0411 4.0 / 1027 2.1 / 1628 4.4 / 2255 1.7	**19** TU 0526 4.3 / 1132 1.8 / 1737 4.6
5 TU 0506 4.4 / 1120 1.7 / 1715 4.8 / 2344 1.7	**20** W 0002 1.4 / 0557 4.6 / 1207 1.5 / 1805 4.8
6 W 0549 4.8 / 1204 1.2 / 1756 5.2	**21** TH 0035 1.1 / 0624 4.7 / 1239 1.3 / 1831 5.0
7 TH 0028 0.7 / 0627 5.1 / 1246 0.8 / ○ 1835 5.6	**22** F 0105 1.0 / 0650 4.9 / 1309 1.2 / 1855 5.1
8 F 0110 0.3 / 0705 5.4 / 1326 0.5 / 1913 5.8	**23** SA 0134 0.9 / 0715 5.0 / 1337 1.1 / 1919 5.1
9 SA 0150 0.1 / 0742 5.5 / 1405 0.4 / 1953 5.8	**24** SU 0201 0.9 / 0740 5.0 / 1405 1.1 / 1944 5.1
10 SU 0230 0.1 / 0820 5.4 / 1445 0.4 / 2034 5.7	**25** M 0227 0.9 / 0805 4.9 / 1433 1.1 / 2010 4.9
11 M 0309 0.3 / 0900 5.2 / 1526 0.7 / 2118 5.3	**26** TU 0254 1.1 / 0833 4.8 / 1503 1.3 / 2039 4.8
12 TU 0348 0.7 / 0943 4.8 / 1609 1.0 / 2210 4.8	**27** W 0323 1.3 / 0903 4.6 / 1535 1.5 / 2111 4.5
13 W 0430 1.2 / 1035 4.5 / 1656 1.5 / 2318 4.3	**28** TH 0354 1.6 / 0939 4.4 / 1612 1.7 / 2152 4.2
14 TH 0516 1.7 / 1151 4.1 / 1756 2.0 ◑	**29** F 0430 1.9 / 1029 4.2 / 1656 2.0 / 2254 3.9
15 F 0047 4.0 / 0615 2.2 / 1330 3.9 / 1928 2.3	**30** SA 0517 2.2 / 1156 3.9 / 1758 2.3 ◑

OCTOBER

Time m	Time m
1 SU 0053 3.7 / 0633 2.5 / 1340 3.9 / 1941 2.4	**16** M 0319 3.9 / 0918 2.5 / 1543 4.1 / 2209 2.0
2 M 0234 3.8 / 0846 2.5 / 1500 4.1 / 2130 2.1	**17** TU 0416 4.1 / 1018 2.2 / 1630 4.3 / 2252 1.7
3 TU 0351 4.1 / 1006 2.1 / 1602 4.5 / 2232 1.6	**18** W 0455 4.3 / 1059 1.9 / 1705 4.5 / 2328 1.5
4 W 0444 4.5 / 1056 1.6 / 1649 4.9 / 2320 1.1	**19** TH 0526 4.5 / 1135 1.7 / 1734 4.7
5 TH 0525 4.9 / 1139 1.2 / 1731 5.3	**20** F 0000 1.3 / 0553 4.7 / 1207 1.2 / 1800 4.9
6 F 0002 0.6 / 0602 5.2 / 1220 0.8 / 1809 5.7	**21** SA 0031 1.1 / 0619 4.9 / 1238 1.3 / 1825 5.0
7 SA 0044 0.3 / 0638 5.5 / 1300 0.5 / ○ 1848 5.8	**22** SU 0100 1.0 / 0645 5.0 / 1307 1.2 / ● 1851 5.0
8 SU 0123 0.2 / 0715 5.6 / 1341 0.4 / 1928 5.8	**23** M 0128 1.0 / 0710 5.1 / 1337 1.2 / 1918 5.0
9 M 0202 0.3 / 0755 5.5 / 1421 0.5 / 2010 5.6	**24** TU 0155 1.1 / 0737 5.0 / 1407 1.2 / 1947 4.9
10 TU 0241 0.5 / 0831 5.2 / 1503 0.8 / 2056 5.2	**25** W 0224 1.2 / 0807 5.0 / 1439 1.3 / 2019 4.9
11 W 0320 1.0 / 0913 4.9 / 1547 1.2 / 2150 4.7	**26** TH 0255 1.4 / 0840 4.8 / 1514 1.5 / 2057 4.5
12 TH 0401 1.5 / 1004 4.5 / 1636 1.6 / 2302 4.2	**27** F 0329 1.7 / 0921 4.6 / 1554 1.7 / 2147 4.3
13 F 0447 2.0 / 1120 4.2 / 1738 2.1	**28** SA 0409 2.0 / 1017 4.3 / 1643 2.0 / 2303 4.0
14 SA 0029 3.9 / 0547 2.4 / 1301 4.0 / ◑ 1911 2.3	**29** SU 0502 2.3 / 1141 4.2 / 1749 2.3 ●
15 SU 0158 3.8 / 0727 2.7 / 1433 4.0 / 2103 2.3	**30** M 0042 3.9 / 0623 2.5 / 1311 4.1 / 1925 2.2
	31 TU 0208 4.0 / 0814 2.4 / 1426 4.3 / 2056 1.9

NOVEMBER

Time m	Time m
1 W 0319 4.2 / 0930 2.1 / 1528 4.6 / 2159 1.5	**16** TH 0413 4.2 / 1013 2.2 / 1624 4.4 / 2245 1.7
2 TH 0414 4.6 / 1024 1.7 / 1619 5.0 / 2249 1.1	**17** F 0450 4.4 / 1055 1.9 / 1659 4.5 / 2322 1.6
3 F 0458 4.9 / 1110 1.3 / 1704 5.3 / 2334 0.8	**18** SA 0522 4.6 / 1132 1.7 / 1730 4.7 / 2355 1.4
4 SA 0537 5.2 / 1154 1.0 / 1747 5.5	**19** SU 0551 4.8 / 1206 1.6 / 1759 4.8
5 SU 0016 0.6 / 0615 5.4 / 1237 0.8 / ○ 1828 5.6	**20** M 0027 1.3 / 0619 5.0 / 1240 1.4 / ● 1829 4.9
6 M 0058 0.6 / 0652 5.5 / 1320 0.7 / 1911 5.6	**21** TU 0059 1.3 / 0648 5.1 / 1313 1.3 / 1901 4.9
7 TU 0138 0.7 / 0731 5.4 / 1403 0.8 / 1956 5.3	**22** W 0131 1.3 / 0719 5.1 / 1348 1.3 / 1936 4.9
8 W 0218 0.9 / 0811 5.3 / 1447 1.0 / 2044 5.0	**23** TH 0204 1.4 / 0754 5.1 / 1424 1.4 / 2015 4.8
9 TH 0259 1.3 / 0855 5.0 / 1532 1.3 / 2139 4.6	**24** F 0239 1.5 / 0833 5.0 / 1504 1.5 / 2100 4.6
10 F 0341 1.6 / 0945 4.7 / 1622 1.7 / 2243 4.3	**25** SA 0318 1.7 / 0918 4.8 / 1548 1.6 / 2155 4.4
11 SA 0427 2.0 / 1049 4.4 / 1721 2.0 / 2354 4.0	**26** SU 0403 1.9 / 1014 4.6 / 1640 1.7 / 2302 4.3
12 SU 0523 2.4 / 1211 4.2 / 1835 2.2 ◑	**27** M 0458 2.1 / 1122 4.5 / 1742 1.9
13 M 0109 3.9 / 0639 2.6 / 1334 4.1 / 1958 2.4	**28** TU 0017 4.2 / 0608 2.2 / 1237 4.5 / ◑ 1856 1.9
14 TU 0224 3.9 / 0809 2.6 / 1448 4.1 / 2110 2.1	**29** W 0131 4.2 / 0730 2.2 / 1347 4.5 / 2012 1.8
15 W 0326 4.0 / 0922 2.4 / 1543 4.2 / 2203 1.9	**30** TH 0241 4.3 / 0845 2.1 / 1451 4.7 / 2119 1.6

DECEMBER

Time m	Time m
1 F 0341 4.5 / 0948 1.8 / 1550 4.8 / 2216 1.4	**16** SA 0407 4.2 / 1007 2.3 / 1619 4.3 / 2240 1.9
2 SA 0432 4.8 / 1043 1.5 / 1642 5.0 / 2307 1.2	**17** SU 0449 4.4 / 1056 2.1 / 1701 4.4 / 2322 1.8
3 SU 0517 5.0 / 1133 1.3 / 1731 5.2 / 2354 1.1	**18** M 0526 4.6 / 1138 1.9 / 1740 4.5
4 M 0559 5.2 / 1221 1.1 / 1818 5.2	**19** TU 0000 1.6 / 0600 4.8 / 1218 1.7 / 1816 4.7
5 TU 0039 1.0 / 0640 5.3 / 1308 1.0 / ○ 1904 5.2	**20** W 0038 1.5 / 0634 5.0 / 1258 1.5 / ● 1854 4.8
6 W 0122 1.1 / 0721 5.3 / 1353 1.0 / 1951 5.1	**21** TH 0115 1.4 / 0710 5.1 / 1337 1.3 / 1934 4.9
7 TH 0203 1.2 / 0802 5.2 / 1438 1.2 / 2037 4.9	**22** F 0153 1.4 / 0748 5.2 / 1418 1.2 / 2016 4.9
8 F 0245 1.4 / 0844 5.1 / 1523 1.3 / 2125 4.7	**23** SA 0233 1.4 / 0829 5.2 / 1500 1.2 / 2100 4.8
9 SA 0326 1.6 / 0928 4.9 / 1609 1.5 / 2213 4.4	**24** SU 0314 1.4 / 0913 5.1 / 1545 1.2 / 2148 4.7
10 SU 0409 1.9 / 1015 4.6 / 1657 1.8 / 2305 4.2	**25** M 0359 1.5 / 1002 5.0 / 1632 1.3 / 2242 4.6
11 M 0456 2.1 / 1108 4.4 / 1748 2.0	**26** TU 0447 1.7 / 1057 4.9 / 1724 1.4 / 2342 4.4
12 TU 0002 4.0 / 0547 2.3 / 1213 4.2 / ◑ 1845 2.1	**27** W 0543 1.8 / 1159 4.7 / 1822 1.6
13 W 0107 3.9 / 0650 2.4 / 1323 4.1 / 1949 2.2	**28** TH 0049 4.3 / 0646 2.0 / 1307 4.6 / 1926 1.7
14 TH 0214 3.9 / 0800 2.5 / 1431 4.1 / 2054 2.2	**29** F 0159 4.3 / 0758 2.1 / 1416 4.5 / 2036 1.8
15 F 0316 4.0 / 0909 2.4 / 1530 4.1 / 2152 2.1	**30** SA 0309 4.3 / 0913 2.0 / 1526 4.6 / 2146 1.7
	31 SU 0413 4.5 / 1023 1.6 / 1631 4.6 / 2249 1.7

TIDES

Chart Datum: 2·75 metres below Ordnance Datum (Newlyn)

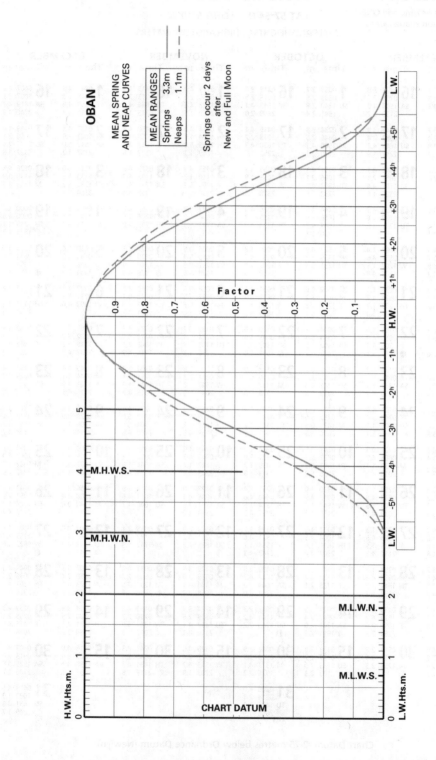

TIME ZONE (UT)
For Summer Time add ONE hour in **non-shaded areas**

SCOTLAND – OBAN
LAT 56°25'N LONG 5°29'W
TIMES AND HEIGHTS OF HIGH AND LOW WATERS

JANUARY

Day	Time m	Time m	Time m	Time m
1 SU	0517 0.7	1129 2.3	1749 0.4	
2 M	0015 2.2	0603 0.7	1215 2.3	1836 0.4
3 TU	0107 2.2	0649 0.7	1303 2.3	1925 0.4
4 W	0157 2.1	0735 0.8	1352 2.2	2014 0.4
5 TH	0247 0.8	0823 0.8	1444 2.2	2107 0.5
6 F	0338 1.9	0914 0.9	1539 2.1	◑ 2206 0.6
7 SA	0434 1.8	1015 1.0	1639 2.0	2318 0.8
8 SU	0536 1.8	1136 1.0	1750 1.9	
9 M	0033 0.8	0643 1.8	1300 1.0	1906 1.8
10 TU	0139 0.9	0747 1.8	1407 1.0	2016 1.9
11 W	0234 0.9	0844 1.9	1503 0.8	2117 1.9
12 TH	0321 0.9	0933 2.0	1551 0.8	2208 1.9
13 F	0403 0.9	1017 2.1	1633 0.7	2251 2.0
14 SA	0442 0.9	1056 2.2	1712 0.6	○ 2330 2.0
15 SU	0518 0.9	1133 2.2	1749 0.6	
16 M	0006 2.0	0551 0.8	1208 2.2	1823 0.6
17 TU	0041 2.0	0622 0.8	1241 2.2	1856 0.6
18 W	0113 1.9	0652 0.8	1312 2.1	1929 0.6
19 TH	0145 1.9	0722 0.9	1344 2.0	2003 0.7
20 F	0218 1.8	0755 0.9	1420 2.0	2040 0.7
21 SA	0256 1.8	0831 1.0	1500 1.9	2120 0.8
22 SU	0339 1.7	0916 1.0	1547 1.8	◐ 2210 0.9
23 M	0431 1.7	1016 1.1	1646 1.7	2316 1.0
24 TU	0532 1.7	1153 1.1	1758 1.7	
25 W	0035 1.0	0644 1.7	1318 1.1	1922 1.7
26 TH	0143 1.0	0754 1.8	1421 0.9	2033 1.8
27 F	0241 0.9	0852 2.0	1516 0.8	2132 2.0
28 SA	0334 0.8	0943 2.1	1606 0.8	2226 2.1
29 SU	0423 0.7	1032 2.2	1653 0.4	● 2317 2.2
30 M	0508 0.6	1119 2.3	1738 0.2	
31 TU	0005 2.2	0550 0.6	1205 2.4	1822 0.2

FEBRUARY

Day	Time m	Time m	Time m	Time m
1 W	0051 2.2	0632 0.5	1250 2.4	1906 0.2
2 TH	0135 2.1	0714 0.6	1335 2.3	1950 0.3
3 F	0219 2.0	0756 0.6	1421 2.2	2036 0.4
4 SA	0303 1.9	0842 0.7	1510 2.1	2126 0.6
5 SU	0351 1.8	0936 0.8	1606 1.9	◑ 2227 0.8
6 M	0447 1.7	1053 1.0	1715 1.7	2355 1.0
7 TU	0559 1.7	1240 1.0	1847 1.7	
8 W	0120 1.0	0722 1.7	1401 0.9	2015 1.7
9 TH	0226 1.0	0831 1.8	1501 0.8	2118 1.7
10 F	0315 1.0	0923 1.9	1546 0.7	2202 1.8
11 SA	0355 0.9	1005 2.0	1623 0.6	2239 1.9
12 SU	0430 0.8	1043 2.1	1657 0.5	2313 1.9
13 M	0501 0.8	1117 2.1	1728 0.5	○ 2345 2.0
14 TU	0531 0.7	1149 2.1	1758 0.4	
15 W	0015 1.9	0558 0.7	1218 2.1	1826 0.4
16 TH	0043 1.9	0625 0.6	1246 2.1	1856 0.5
17 F	0110 1.9	0654 0.7	1314 2.1	1926 0.5
18 SA	0139 1.9	0725 0.7	1346 2.0	1959 0.6
19 SU	0211 1.8	0758 0.8	1421 1.9	2034 0.7
20 M	0249 1.8	0837 0.9	1505 1.8	2117 0.9
21 TU	0337 1.7	0930 1.0	1603 1.7	2215 1.0
22 W	0439 1.6	1052 1.0	1720 1.6	◐ 2351 1.0
23 TH	0556 1.6	1251 1.0	1900 1.6	
24 F	0124 1.0	0725 1.7	1406 0.8	2024 1.8
25 SA	0230 0.9	0834 1.9	1504 0.6	2124 1.9
26 SU	0323 0.7	0928 2.0	1552 0.4	2215 2.0
27 M	0408 0.6	1017 2.2	1637 0.2	2301 2.1
28 TU	0450 0.5	1102 2.3	1719 0.1	● 2345 2.2

MARCH

Day	Time m	Time m	Time m	Time m
1 W	0530 0.4	1146 2.4	1800 0.0	
2 TH	0026 2.2	0609 0.3	1229 2.4	1841 0.1
3 F	0106 2.1	0649 0.4	1312 2.3	1922 0.2
4 SA	0145 2.0	0731 0.5	1356 2.2	2004 0.5
5 SU	0225 1.9	0815 0.6	1443 2.0	2048 0.7
6 M	0308 1.8	0907 0.8	1537 1.8	◑ 2140 0.9
7 TU	0359 1.7	1025 0.9	1645 1.6	2312 1.1
8 W	0510 1.6	1223 0.9	1835 1.5	
9 TH	0100 1.1	0654 1.6	1347 0.9	2012 1.6
10 F	0211 1.1	0811 1.7	1446 0.7	2105 1.7
11 SA	0259 1.0	0902 1.8	1527 0.6	2142 1.7
12 SU	0336 0.8	0943 1.9	1600 0.5	2214 1.8
13 M	0408 0.7	1019 2.0	1630 0.5	2246 1.9
14 TU	0437 0.6	1052 2.0	1659 0.4	○ 2316 1.9
15 W	0504 0.6	1122 2.1	1726 0.4	2343 1.9
16 TH	0531 0.5	1150 2.1	1754 0.4	
17 F	0009 1.9	0558 0.5	1217 2.1	1822 0.4
18 SA	0035 1.9	0628 0.5	1246 2.0	1853 0.5
19 SU	0103 1.9	0700 0.6	1318 2.0	1925 0.6
20 M	0134 1.9	0734 0.7	1354 1.9	2000 0.7
21 TU	0210 1.8	0816 0.8	1439 1.7	2043 0.8
22 W	0256 1.7	0911 0.8	1542 1.6	◐ 2144 1.0
23 TH	0400 1.6	1034 0.9	1705 1.5	2327 1.0
24 F	0522 1.6	1232 0.8	1853 1.6	
25 SA	0110 1.0	0701 1.6	1348 0.7	2013 1.7
26 SU	0214 0.8	0814 1.8	1444 0.4	2107 1.9
27 M	0304 0.7	0908 2.0	1531 0.2	2154 2.0
28 TU	0347 0.5	0955 2.1	1614 0.1	2237 2.1
29 W	0427 0.4	1040 2.3	1655 0.0	● 2318 2.1
30 TH	0506 0.3	1123 2.3	1734 0.0	2356 2.1
31 F	0546 0.2	1206 2.3	1814 0.2	

APRIL

Day	Time m	Time m	Time m	Time m
1 SA	0034 2.1	0626 0.3	1249 2.2	1853 0.3
2 SU	0111 2.0	0709 0.4	1334 2.0	1934 0.6
3 M	0150 1.9	0754 0.5	1422 1.8	2015 0.8
4 TU	0232 1.8	0849 0.7	1515 1.6	2104 1.0
5 W	0321 1.7	1008 0.8	1621 1.5	◑ 2230 1.1
6 TH	0426 1.6	1151 0.9	1809 1.4	
7 F	0023 1.1	0612 1.5	1313 0.8	1941 1.5
8 SA	0139 1.0	0734 1.6	1411 0.7	2030 1.6
9 SU	0228 0.9	0827 1.7	1452 0.6	2106 1.6
10 M	0305 0.8	0909 1.8	1525 0.5	2139 1.7
11 TU	0336 0.7	0945 1.9	1555 0.4	2210 1.8
12 W	0405 0.6	1019 1.9	1623 0.4	2240 1.9
13 TH	0433 0.5	1050 2.0	1652 0.4	○ 2308 1.9
14 F	0502 0.5	1120 2.0	1721 0.4	2335 1.9
15 SA	0533 0.5	1150 2.0	1752 0.4	
16 SU	0003 2.0	0605 0.5	1223 2.0	1824 0.5
17 M	0034 1.9	0641 0.5	1259 1.9	1859 0.6
18 TU	0108 1.9	0720 0.6	1340 1.8	1938 0.7
19 W	0146 1.8	0807 0.6	1433 1.7	2027 0.8
20 TH	0235 1.7	0908 0.7	1541 1.6	2133 1.0
21 F	0342 1.6	1031 0.7	1703 1.5	◐ 2313 1.0
22 SA	0504 1.6	1210 0.6	1838 1.6	
23 SU	0045 0.9	0635 1.6	1322 0.5	1948 1.7
24 M	0147 0.8	0747 1.8	1418 0.3	2041 1.8
25 TU	0237 0.6	0842 1.9	1505 0.2	2126 1.9
26 W	0321 0.5	0931 2.1	1548 0.1	2209 2.0
27 TH	0403 0.3	1017 2.1	1629 0.1	● 2248 2.0
28 F	0444 0.3	1101 2.2	1709 0.2	2326 2.1
29 SA	0525 0.3	1146 2.1	1749 0.3	
30 SU	0004 2.0	0608 0.3	1231 2.0	1828 0.5

Chart Datum: 2·10 metres below Ordnance Datum (Newlyn)

TIDES

SCOTLAND – OBAN 2006

TIME ZONE (UT)
For Summer Time add ONE hour in **non-shaded areas**

LAT 56°25′N   LONG 5°29′W

TIMES AND HEIGHTS OF HIGH AND LOW WATERS

MAY

Day	Time	m	Day	Time	m
1 M	0043 / 0652 / 1317 / 1909	2.0 / 0.4 / 1.9 / 0.7	**16** TU	0014 / 0629 / 1252 / 1844	2.0 / 0.5 / 1.9 / 0.6
2 TU	0123 / 0741 / 1406 / 1951	1.9 / 0.5 / 1.7 / 0.8	**17** W	0053 / 0715 / 1341 / 1929	1.9 / 0.5 / 1.8 / 0.7
3 W	0206 / 0836 / 1457 / 2039	1.8 / 0.6 / 1.6 / 1.0	**18** TH	0137 / 0807 / 1438 / 2023	1.9 / 0.5 / 1.7 / 0.8
4 TH	0254 / 0943 / 1555 / 2148	1.7 / 0.7 / 1.5 / 1.1	**19** F	0230 / 0908 / 1542 / 2127	1.8 / 0.5 / 1.6 / 0.9
5 F	0351 / 1100 / 1711 / ☽2318	1.6 / 0.7 / 1.4 / 1.1	**20** SA	0336 / 1021 / 1652 / 2246	1.7 / 0.5 / 1.6 / 0.9
6 SA	0507 / 1213 / 1838	1.5 / 0.7 / 1.4	**21** SU	0448 / 1141 / 1808	1.7 / 0.5 / 1.6
7 SU	0038 / 0639 / 1315 / 1934	1.0 / 1.5 / 0.7 / 1.5	**22** M	0008 / 0606 / 1251 / 1914	0.8 / 1.7 / 0.4 / 1.7
8 M	0138 / 0739 / 1402 / 2018	0.9 / 1.6 / 0.6 / 1.6	**23** TU	0114 / 0716 / 1348 / 2008	0.7 / 1.8 / 0.4 / 1.7
9 TU	0222 / 0826 / 1440 / 2056	0.8 / 1.7 / 0.6 / 1.7	**24** W	0208 / 0815 / 1438 / 2056	0.6 / 1.9 / 0.3 / 1.8
10 W	0257 / 0906 / 1513 / 2130	0.7 / 1.7 / 0.5 / 1.8	**25** TH	0257 / 0908 / 1523 / 2141	0.5 / 2.0 / 0.3 / 1.9
11 TH	0330 / 0942 / 1545 / 2202	0.6 / 1.8 / 0.5 / 1.8	**26** F	0342 / 0958 / 1606 / 2222	0.4 / 2.0 / 0.4 / 2.0
12 F	0402 / 1017 / 1617 / 2233	0.5 / 1.9 / 0.4 / 1.9	**27** SA	0426 / 1046 / ●1647 / 2303	0.4 / 2.0 / 0.5 / 2.0
13 SA	0435 / 1052 / 1651 / ○2305	0.5 / 1.9 / 0.5 / 2.0	**28** SU	0511 / 1133 / 1729 / 2343	0.3 / 2.0 / 0.5 / 2.0
14 SU	0511 / 1129 / 1726 / 2338	0.5 / 1.9 / 0.5 / 2.0	**29** M	0556 / 1219 / 1810	0.4 / 1.9 / 0.7
15 M	0549 / 1208 / 1804	0.4 / 1.9 / 0.6	**30** TU	0023 / 0642 / 1305 / 1851	2.0 / 0.4 / 1.8 / 0.8
			31 W	0105 / 0729 / 1350 / 1932	1.9 / 0.5 / 1.7 / 0.8

JUNE

Day	Time	m	Day	Time	m
1 TH	0147 / 0817 / 1435 / 2016	1.9 / 0.6 / 1.6 / 0.9	**16** F	0135 / 0802 / 1435 / 2014	2.0 / 0.4 / 1.8 / 0.7
2 F	0232 / 0909 / 1522 / 2105	1.8 / 0.6 / 1.5 / 1.0	**17** SA	0228 / 0857 / 1530 / 2109	1.9 / 0.4 / 1.7 / 0.8
3 SA	0320 / 1004 / 1614 / ●2207	1.7 / 0.7 / 1.5 / 1.0	**18** SU	0326 / 0957 / 1628 / ○2211	1.9 / 0.4 / 1.6 / 0.8
4 SU	0414 / 1103 / 1716 / 2319	1.6 / 0.7 / 1.4 / 1.0	**19** M	0428 / 1105 / 1731 / 2324	1.8 / 0.5 / 1.6 / 0.8
5 M	0519 / 1203 / 1826	1.6 / 0.7 / 1.5	**20** TU	0536 / 1216 / 1836	1.8 / 0.5 / 1.6
6 TU	0028 / 0635 / 1258 / 1922	0.9 / 1.6 / 0.7 / 1.5	**21** W	0039 / 0647 / 1320 / 1936	0.8 / 1.8 / 0.6 / 1.7
7 W	0126 / 0735 / 1346 / 2007	0.9 / 1.6 / 0.7 / 1.6	**22** TH	0144 / 0753 / 1416 / 2030	0.7 / 1.8 / 0.6 / 1.8
8 TH	0213 / 0823 / 1429 / 2047	0.8 / 1.7 / 0.6 / 1.7	**23** F	0240 / 0853 / 1506 / 2119	0.6 / 1.8 / 0.6 / 1.9
9 F	0254 / 0906 / 1508 / 2125	0.7 / 1.7 / 0.6 / 1.8	**24** SA	0331 / 0949 / 1551 / 2206	0.5 / 1.9 / 0.6 / 1.9
10 SA	0334 / 0948 / 1547 / 2203	0.6 / 1.8 / 0.6 / 1.9	**25** SU	0419 / 1040 / 1634 / ●2249	0.5 / 1.9 / 0.7 / 2.0
11 SU	0413 / 1030 / 1628 / ○2241	0.6 / 1.8 / 0.6 / 2.0	**26** M	0504 / 1127 / 1716 / 2331	0.4 / 1.9 / 0.7 / 2.0
12 M	0455 / 1115 / 1709 / 2321	0.5 / 1.9 / 0.6 / 2.0	**27** TU	0548 / 1210 / 1756	0.4 / 1.9 / 0.7
13 TU	0539 / 1202 / 1753	0.4 / 1.9 / 0.6	**28** W	0011 / 0629 / 1251 / 1834	2.0 / 0.4 / 1.8 / 0.7
14 W	0003 / 0624 / 1251 / 1837	2.0 / 0.4 / 1.9 / 0.6	**29** TH	0050 / 0710 / 1330 / 1911	2.0 / 0.5 / 1.8 / 0.8
15 TH	0048 / 0712 / 1342 / 1924	2.0 / 0.4 / 1.9 / 0.7	**30** F	0128 / 0749 / 1407 / 1946	1.9 / 0.5 / 1.7 / 0.8

JULY

Day	Time	m	Day	Time	m
1 SA	0206 / 0829 / 1445 / 2022	1.9 / 0.6 / 1.6 / 0.8	**16** SU	0215 / 0835 / 1506 / 2043	2.1 / 0.3 / 1.8 / 0.7
2 SU	0245 / 0910 / 1525 / 2104	1.8 / 0.6 / 1.6 / 0.9	**17** M	0306 / 0927 / 1556 / ●2136	2.0 / 0.4 / 1.7 / 0.7
3 M	0329 / 0958 / 1611 / ●2157	1.7 / 0.7 / 1.5 / 0.9	**18** TU	0402 / 1027 / 1653 / 2244	1.9 / 0.6 / 1.7 / 0.8
4 TU	0418 / 1054 / 1703 / 2311	1.6 / 0.8 / 1.5 / 1.0	**19** W	0507 / 1141 / 1757	1.8 / 0.7 / 1.6
5 W	0515 / 1156 / 1805	1.6 / 0.8 / 1.5	**20** TH	0012 / 0623 / 1258 / 1907	0.8 / 1.7 / 0.8 / 1.7
6 TH	0029 / 0626 / 1256 / 1910	1.0 / 1.6 / 0.8 / 1.6	**21** F	0131 / 0742 / 1403 / 2012	0.8 / 1.7 / 0.8 / 1.8
7 F	0131 / 0737 / 1349 / 2005	0.9 / 1.6 / 0.8 / 1.7	**22** SA	0236 / 0852 / 1458 / 2109	0.7 / 1.7 / 0.8 / 1.9
8 SA	0223 / 0835 / 1438 / 2053	0.8 / 1.7 / 0.8 / 1.8	**23** SU	0330 / 0950 / 1545 / 2157	0.6 / 1.8 / 0.8 / 2.0
9 SU	0312 / 0926 / 1526 / 2139	0.7 / 1.8 / 0.7 / 1.9	**24** M	0416 / 1037 / 1626 / 2240	0.5 / 1.8 / 0.8 / 2.0
10 M	0358 / 1016 / 1613 / 2224	0.6 / 1.9 / 0.7 / 2.0	**25** TU	0456 / 1117 / 1704 / ●2320	0.5 / 1.9 / 0.7 / 2.1
11 TU	0444 / 1106 / 1659 / ○2309	0.4 / 2.0 / 0.6 / 2.1	**26** W	0534 / 1154 / 1739 / 2356	0.4 / 1.9 / 0.7 / 2.1
12 W	0530 / 1155 / 1743 / 2355	0.3 / 2.0 / 0.6 / 2.2	**27** TH	0610 / 1229 / 1812	0.4 / 1.9 / 0.7
13 TH	0615 / 1243 / 1827	0.2 / 2.0 / 0.6	**28** F	0030 / 0643 / 1302 / 1842	2.1 / 0.4 / 1.8 / 0.7
14 F	0040 / 0700 / 1331 / 1911	2.2 / 0.2 / 2.0 / 0.6	**29** SA	0103 / 0715 / 1333 / 1912	2.0 / 0.5 / 1.8 / 0.7
15 SA	0127 / 0746 / 1418 / 1955	2.2 / 0.2 / 1.9 / 0.6	**30** SU	0134 / 0748 / 1404 / 1943	2.0 / 0.5 / 1.7 / 0.8
			31 M	0207 / 0822 / 1438 / 2018	1.9 / 0.6 / 1.7 / 0.8

AUGUST

Day	Time	m	Day	Time	m
1 TU	0245 / 0900 / 1518 / 2100	1.8 / 0.7 / 1.7 / 0.9	**16** W	0337 / 0949 / 1613 / ☽2214	1.9 / 0.8 / 1.7 / 0.8
2 W	0329 / 0945 / 1605 / ●2154	1.7 / 0.8 / 1.6 / 1.0	**17** TH	0442 / 1109 / 1719	1.8 / 0.9 / 1.7
3 TH	0423 / 1045 / 1701 / 2323	1.6 / 0.9 / 1.6 / 1.0	**18** F	0001 / 0609 / 1245 / 1844	0.9 / 1.7 / 1.0 / 1.7
4 F	0530 / 1206 / 1809	1.6 / 1.0 / 1.6	**19** SA	0129 / 0746 / 1358 / 2001	0.9 / 1.7 / 1.0 / 1.8
5 SA	0056 / 0655 / 1318 / 1925	1.0 / 1.6 / 1.0 / 1.7	**20** SU	0236 / 0856 / 1453 / 2100	0.8 / 1.7 / 1.0 / 1.9
6 SU	0201 / 0813 / 1419 / 2028	0.9 / 1.7 / 0.9 / 1.8	**21** M	0325 / 0944 / 1536 / 2145	0.7 / 1.8 / 0.9 / 2.0
7 M	0256 / 0912 / 1513 / 2121	0.7 / 1.8 / 0.8 / 1.9	**22** TU	0404 / 1023 / 1612 / 2225	0.6 / 1.9 / 0.8 / 2.1
8 TU	0345 / 1004 / 1601 / 2209	0.5 / 2.0 / 0.7 / 2.1	**23** W	0439 / 1057 / 1644 / ●2300	0.5 / 1.9 / 0.7 / 2.1
9 W	0431 / 1053 / 1645 / ○2255	0.4 / 2.1 / 0.6 / 2.2	**24** TH	0511 / 1129 / 1715 / 2333	0.4 / 1.9 / 0.7 / 2.1
10 TH	0515 / 1140 / 1727 / 2340	0.2 / 2.1 / 0.5 / 2.3	**25** F	0542 / 1200 / 1744	0.4 / 2.0 / 0.6
11 F	0558 / 1225 / 1808	0.1 / 2.1 / 0.5	**26** SA	0003 / 0610 / 1228 / 1811	2.1 / 0.4 / 1.9 / 0.6
12 SA	0024 / 0640 / 1308 / 1849	2.3 / 0.1 / 2.1 / 0.5	**27** SU	0032 / 0639 / 1255 / 1839	2.1 / 0.5 / 1.9 / 0.7
13 SU	0108 / 0722 / 1350 / 1931	2.3 / 0.2 / 2.0 / 0.5	**28** M	0100 / 0709 / 1322 / 1910	2.1 / 0.5 / 1.9 / 0.7
14 M	0153 / 0807 / 1434 / 2016	2.2 / 0.3 / 1.9 / 0.6	**29** TU	0131 / 0740 / 1353 / 1943	2.0 / 0.6 / 1.8 / 0.8
15 TU	0242 / 0854 / 1520 / 2107	2.1 / 0.5 / 1.8 / 0.7	**30** W	0206 / 0814 / 1429 / 2021	1.9 / 0.8 / 1.7 / 0.9
			31 TH	0248 / 0854 / 1514 / ☽2112	1.8 / 0.9 / 1.7 / 1.0

Chart Datum: 2·10 metres below Ordnance Datum (Newlyn)

SCOTLAND – OBAN

LAT 56°25'N LONG 5°29'W

TIMES AND HEIGHTS OF HIGH AND LOW WATERS

2006

SEPTEMBER

Day	Time	m	Time	m		Day	Time	m	Time	m
1 F	0343	1.7	0948	1.0		**16** SA	0606	1.6	1231	1.2
	1612	1.7	2229	1.1			1824	1.7		
2 SA	0455	1.6	1119	1.1		**17** SU	0120	0.9	0748	1.6
	1723	1.7					1346	1.1	1945	1.8
3 SU	0031	1.0	0630	1.6		**18** M	0223	0.8	0845	1.7
	1259	1.1	1852	1.7			1437	1.0	2039	1.9
4 M	0144	0.9	0801	1.7		**19** TU	0306	0.7	0923	1.8
	1405	1.0	2007	1.8			1515	0.9	2122	2.0
5 TU	0240	0.7	0859	1.9		**20** W	0341	0.6	0956	1.9
	1458	0.8	2102	2.0			1548	0.8	2159	2.1
6 W	0327	0.5	0948	2.0		**21** TH	0412	0.5	1027	2.0
	1543	0.7	2150	2.2			1618	0.7	2233	2.1
7 TH	0411	0.3	1033	2.1		**22** F	0441	0.5	1057	2.0
	1624	0.5	○ 2234	2.3			1646	0.7	2304	2.2
8 F	0453	0.1	1117	2.2		**23** SA	0509	0.5	1126	2.0
	1704	0.4	2318	2.4			1714	0.6	2333	2.2
9 SA	0534	0.1	1158	2.2		**24** SU	0536	0.5	1152	2.0
	1744	0.4					1741	0.6		
10 SU	0001	2.4	0614	0.1		**25** M	0000	2.1	0604	0.5
	1239	2.2	1824	0.4			1217	2.0	1811	0.7
11 M	0045	2.4	0655	0.3		**26** TU	0029	2.1	0633	0.6
	1318	2.1	1906	0.5			1245	2.0	1842	0.7
12 TU	0130	2.3	0738	0.5		**27** W	0100	2.0	0704	0.7
	1359	2.0	1951	0.6			1315	2.0	1917	0.8
13 W	0219	2.1	0823	0.7		**28** TH	0136	1.9	0738	0.9
	1444	1.9	2044	0.7			1350	1.9	1957	0.9
14 TH	0315	1.9	0915	1.0		**29** F	0220	1.8	0818	1.0
	1536	1.8	◑ 2158	0.9			1434	1.8	2050	1.0
15 F	0423	1.7	1041	1.1		**30** SA	0320	1.7	0915	1.1
	1644	1.7	2355	0.9			1534	1.8	◐ 2209	1.0

OCTOBER

Day	Time	m	Time	m		Day	Time	m	Time	m
1 SU	0438	1.6	1050	1.2		**16** M	0052	0.9	0718	1.6
	1652	1.7					1315	1.2	1910	1.8
2 M	0008	1.0	0617	1.7		**17** TU	0152	0.8	0809	1.7
	1241	1.1	1824	1.7			1406	1.1	2005	1.9
3 TU	0122	0.8	0744	1.8		**18** W	0234	0.7	0846	1.8
	1345	1.0	1943	1.9			1445	1.0	2048	2.0
4 W	0217	0.6	0838	1.9		**19** TH	0308	0.7	0920	1.9
	1435	0.8	2038	2.1			1518	0.9	2126	2.0
5 TH	0303	0.4	0924	2.1		**20** F	0338	0.6	0951	2.0
	1519	0.7	2125	2.2			1548	0.8	2201	2.1
6 F	0346	0.3	1007	2.2		**21** SA	0406	0.6	1022	2.0
	1600	0.5	2210	2.4			1616	0.7	2233	2.1
7 SA	0427	0.2	1048	2.3		**22** SU	0434	0.6	1050	2.1
	1640	0.4	○ 2254	2.5			● 1645	0.7	2303	2.2
8 SU	0508	0.2	1128	2.3		**23** M	0503	0.6	1117	2.1
	1720	0.4	2338	2.5			1715	0.7	2333	2.1
9 M	0548	0.3	1207	2.2		**24** TU	0533	0.6	1145	2.1
	1802	0.4					1748	0.7		
10 TU	0022	2.4	0629	0.5		**25** W	0005	2.1	0604	0.7
	1246	2.2	1846	0.5			1216	2.1	1822	0.7
11 W	0110	2.2	0711	0.7		**26** TH	0040	2.1	0638	0.8
	1327	2.1	1934	0.6			1248	2.1	1901	0.8
12 TH	0201	2.0	0755	0.9		**27** F	0120	2.0	0715	0.9
	1413	2.0	2030	0.8			1325	2.0	1946	0.9
13 F	0258	1.8	0848	1.1		**28** SA	0210	1.9	0800	1.0
	1506	1.9	2148	0.9			1411	1.9	2043	0.9
14 SA	0405	1.7	1011	1.3		**29** SU	0314	1.8	0901	1.1
	1612	1.8	◑ 2331	0.9			1514	1.8	◑ 2159	0.9
15 SU	0545	1.6	1158	1.3		**30** M	0429	1.7	1028	1.2
	1748	1.7					1631	1.8	2337	0.9
						31 TU	0557	1.7	1209	1.1
							1756	1.8		

NOVEMBER

Day	Time	m	Time	m		Day	Time	m	Time	m
1 W	0050	0.7	0714	1.8		**16** TH	0147	0.8	0758	1.8
	1315	1.0	1912	1.9			1405	1.0	2007	1.9
2 TH	0147	0.6	0809	2.0		**17** F	0226	0.8	0838	1.9
	1407	0.9	2010	2.1			1443	0.9	2049	2.0
3 F	0236	0.5	0856	2.1		**18** SA	0259	0.7	0914	2.0
	1452	0.7	2100	2.1			1516	0.9	2127	2.0
4 SA	0320	0.4	0939	2.2		**19** SU	0330	0.7	0947	2.0
	1536	0.6	2147	2.3			1548	0.8	2203	2.1
5 SU	0402	0.4	1020	2.2		**20** M	0402	0.7	1018	2.1
	1618	0.5	○ 2233	2.4			1621	0.8	● 2237	2.1
6 M	0444	0.4	1100	2.3		**21** TU	0434	0.7	1049	2.2
	1701	0.5	2320	2.4			1655	0.7	2313	2.1
7 TU	0525	0.5	1140	2.3		**22** W	0508	0.8	1122	2.2
	1746	0.5					1732	0.7	2351	2.1
8 W	0007	2.3	0607	0.7		**23** TH	0544	0.8	1156	2.2
	1221	2.2	1832	0.5			1812	0.7		
9 TH	0057	2.2	0650	0.9		**24** F	0032	2.1	0625	0.9
	1304	2.2	1922	0.6			1233	2.2	1855	0.7
10 F	0149	2.0	0735	1.0		**25** SA	0118	2.0	0705	0.9
	1351	2.1	2018	0.8			1315	2.1	1943	0.7
11 SA	0242	1.8	0826	1.2		**26** SU	0210	1.9	0754	1.0
	1442	2.0	2125	0.9			1403	2.0	2038	0.8
12 SU	0341	1.7	0930	1.2		**27** M	0309	1.8	0851	1.1
	1540	1.9	◑ 2241	0.9			1503	2.0	2142	0.8
13 M	0451	1.6	1054	1.3		**28** TU	0414	1.8	0959	1.1
	1652	1.8	2356	0.9			1610	1.9	◑ 2257	0.8
14 TU	0613	1.6	1215	1.2		**29** W	0525	1.8	1120	1.1
	1816	1.8					1723	1.9		
15 W	0059	0.9	0712	1.7		**30** TH	0012	0.7	0635	1.8
	1319	1.1	1918	1.8			1236	1.0	1837	2.0

DECEMBER

Day	Time	m	Time	m		Day	Time	m	Time	m
1 F	0115	0.7	0735	1.9		**16** SA	0133	0.9	0752	1.8
	1336	0.9	1941	2.1			1403	1.0	2010	1.8
2 SA	0209	0.6	0826	2.0		**17** SU	0217	0.9	0835	1.9
	1429	0.8	2038	2.1			1446	1.0	2056	1.9
3 SU	0257	0.6	0913	2.1		**18** M	0257	0.9	0914	2.0
	1517	0.7	2130	2.1			1525	0.9	2138	2.0
4 M	0342	0.6	0958	2.2		**19** TU	0335	0.9	0951	2.1
	1604	0.6	2222	2.1			1603	0.8	2219	2.0
5 TU	0426	0.7	1041	2.3		**20** W	0414	0.8	1028	2.2
	1650	0.5	○ 2312	2.2			1643	0.7	● 2301	2.1
6 W	0509	0.7	1123	2.3		**21** TH	0453	0.8	1106	2.2
	1737	0.5					1724	0.7	2344	2.1
7 TH	0001	2.2	0552	0.8		**22** F	0534	0.8	1146	2.2
	1207	2.3	1824	0.6			1806	0.6		
8 F	0049	2.1	0635	0.9		**23** SA	0029	2.1	0615	0.8
	1250	2.2	1912	0.6			1227	2.2	1850	0.6
9 SA	0135	2.0	0718	1.0		**24** SU	0116	2.0	0659	0.8
	1334	2.1	2000	0.7			1310	2.2	1935	0.5
10 SU	0221	1.9	0801	1.1		**25** M	0204	2.0	0744	0.9
	1419	2.1	2050	0.8			1357	2.2	2024	0.6
11 M	0307	1.8	0846	1.1		**26** TU	0255	1.9	0832	0.9
	1506	1.9	2142	0.9			1448	2.1	2117	0.6
12 TU	0355	1.7	0939	1.2		**27** W	0349	1.8	0926	1.0
	1557	1.9	◑ 2240	0.9			1546	2.0	2217	0.7
13 W	0452	1.6	1047	1.2		**28** TH	0448	1.8	1031	1.0
	1657	1.8	2341	0.9			1650	2.0	2329	0.7
14 TH	0559	1.7	1204	1.2		**29** F	0553	1.8	1152	1.0
	1812	1.8					1803	1.9		
15 F	0041	0.9	0702	1.7		**30** SA	0042	0.8	0700	1.8
	1311	1.1	1918	1.8			1310	0.9	1917	1.9
						31 SU	0147	0.8	0801	0.9
							1414	0.9	2025	2.0

Chart Datum: 2·10 metres below Ordnance Datum (Newlyn)

TIDES

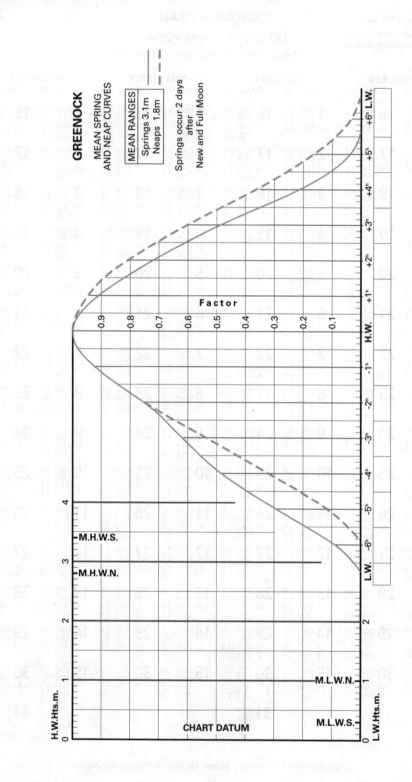

GREENOCK

MEAN SPRING
AND NEAP CURVES

MEAN RANGES
Springs 3.1m
Neaps 1.8m

Springs occur 2 days
after
New and Full Moon

TIME ZONE (UT)
For Summer Time add ONE hour in **non-shaded areas**

SCOTLAND – GREENOCK
LAT 55°57'N   LONG 4°46'W
TIMES AND HEIGHTS OF HIGH AND LOW WATERS

2006

JANUARY

Time	m	Time	m
1 0052	3.3	**16** 0155	3.1
0615	0.6	0704	0.8
SU 1317	3.6	M 1344	3.6
1849	0.3	1917	0.6
2 0144	3.3	**17** 0230	3.1
0703	0.6	0738	0.8
M 1400	3.7	TU 1418	3.6
1937	0.2	1950	0.6
3 0234	3.3	**18** 0302	3.0
0753	0.6	0813	0.8
TU 1444	3.7	W 1451	3.5
2027	0.3	2025	0.6
4 0323	3.3	**19** 0335	3.0
0843	0.7	0849	0.8
W 1529	3.7	TH 1525	3.5
2118	0.3	2101	0.6
5 0412	3.3	**20** 0409	0.8
0934	0.8	0926	0.8
TH 1616	3.7	F 1601	3.4
2213	0.4	2139	0.6
6 0501	3.2	**21** 0445	0.9
1028	0.9	1007	0.9
F 1707	3.6	SA 1639	3.3
☾ 2312	0.5	2223	0.7
7 0551	3.1	**22** 0524	2.9
1127	1.0	1054	1.0
SA 1802	3.4	SU 1721	3.2
		☽ 2314	0.8
8 0017	0.6	**23** 0608	2.8
0643	3.0	1150	1.1
SU 1233	1.1	M 1809	3.0
1904	3.2		
9 0123	0.7	**24** 0012	0.9
0742	3.0	0701	2.7
M 1345	1.1	TU 1253	1.2
2026	3.1	1907	2.9
10 0226	0.8	**25** 0115	1.0
0901	3.0	0812	2.7
TU 1456	1.0	W 1404	1.1
2149	3.1	2021	2.9
11 0324	0.8	**26** 0222	1.0
1011	3.1	0940	2.8
W 1556	0.9	TH 1517	1.0
2253	3.1	2146	2.9
12 0418	0.8	**27** 0328	0.9
1104	3.2	1045	3.0
TH 1646	0.7	F 1617	0.7
2346	3.1	2255	3.0
13 0505	0.8	**28** 0426	0.8
1149	3.4	1135	3.3
F 1730	0.6	SA 1707	0.4
		2353	3.2
14 0034	3.1	**29** 0517	0.6
0548	0.8	1220	3.5
SA 1230	3.5	SU 1752	0.2
○ 1808	0.6	●	
15 0117	3.1	**30** 0047	3.2
0627	0.8	0604	0.5
SU 1308	3.5	M 1306	3.6
1843	0.6	1837	0.0
		31 0138	3.3
		0650	0.4
		TU 1350	3.8
		1922	0.0

FEBRUARY

Time	m	Time	m
1 0226	3.3	**16** 0238	3.0
0736	0.4	0741	0.5
W 1434	3.8	TH 1427	3.4
2007	0.0	1952	0.4
2 0309	3.4	**17** 0304	3.0
0822	0.4	0814	0.5
TH 1516	3.9	F 1459	3.4
2054	0.1	2024	0.4
3 0349	3.4	**18** 0332	3.1
0908	0.5	0848	0.5
F 1558	3.8	SA 1532	3.4
2142	0.2	2100	0.4
4 0427	3.3	**19** 0402	3.0
0956	0.6	0926	0.6
SA 1641	3.6	SU 1607	3.3
2236	0.4	2140	0.5
5 0507	3.2	**20** 0435	2.9
1048	0.8	1009	0.7
SU 1725	3.4	M 1645	3.2
☾ 2338	0.7	2227	0.7
6 0550	3.1	**21** 0511	2.8
1152	1.0	1102	0.9
M 1815	3.1	TU 1728	3.0
		2325	0.9
7 0051	0.9	**22** 0558	2.7
0640	2.9	1207	1.0
TU 1317	1.1	W 1824	2.8
1919	2.8		
8 0206	1.0	**23** 0032	1.0
0746	2.8	0709	2.6
W 1441	1.1	TH 1324	1.1
2143	2.7	1942	2.7
9 0311	1.0	**24** 0148	1.1
0948	2.9	0904	2.6
TH 1546	0.9	F 1456	0.9
2252	2.9	2130	2.7
10 0407	0.9	**25** 0311	1.0
1050	3.1	1024	2.9
F 1636	0.7	SA 1602	0.6
2342	3.0	2249	2.9
11 0454	0.8	**26** 0414	0.7
1137	3.2	1117	3.2
SA 1717	0.6	SU 1651	0.2
		2346	3.1
12 0026	3.0	**27** 0503	0.5
0534	0.7	1204	3.4
SU 1218	3.4	M 1735	0.0
1753	0.5		
13 0106	3.0	**28** 0036	3.2
0610	0.6	0547	0.4
M 1255	3.4	TU 1249	3.6
○ 1825	0.4	● 1816	-0.1
14 0141	3.0		
0642	0.6		
TU 1328	3.4		
1854	0.4		
15 0212	3.0		
0711	0.6		
W 1358	3.4		
1923	0.4		

MARCH

Time	m	Time	m
1 0123	3.3	**16** 0143	3.0
0630	0.2	0640	0.4
W 1334	3.8	TH 1330	3.3
1859	-0.2	1850	0.3
2 0205	3.4	**17** 0206	3.0
0712	0.2	0708	0.4
TH 1416	3.9	F 1359	3.3
1941	-0.1	1918	0.3
3 0242	3.4	**18** 0229	3.1
0755	0.2	0740	0.3
F 1457	3.9	SA 1431	3.3
2025	0.0	1951	0.3
4 0317	3.4	**19** 0256	3.1
0837	0.3	0814	0.3
SA 1535	3.8	SU 1505	3.3
2110	0.2	2027	0.3
5 0352	3.4	**20** 0325	3.1
0921	0.4	0853	0.4
SU 1614	3.6	M 1540	3.2
2158	0.5	2108	0.4
6 0429	3.3	**21** 0356	3.0
1009	0.6	0937	0.6
M 1655	3.3	TU 1617	3.1
☾ 2255	0.8	2156	0.6
7 0510	3.1	**22** 0429	2.9
1109	0.9	1032	0.7
TU 1741	3.0	W 1700	2.9
		☽ 2254	0.9
8 0019	1.1	**23** 0513	2.7
0558	2.9	1141	0.9
W 1252	1.1	TH 1758	2.7
1839	2.6		
9 0145	1.2	**24** 0004	1.0
0659	2.6	0626	2.6
TH 1422	1.0	F 1303	0.9
2141	2.6	1926	2.6
10 0252	1.1	**25** 0126	1.1
0923	2.7	0837	2.6
F 1525	0.9	SA 1437	0.7
2241	2.7	2124	2.7
11 0348	1.0	**26** 0254	1.0
1031	3.0	1001	2.9
SA 1614	0.7	SU 1541	0.4
2326	2.9	2237	2.9
12 0434	0.8	**27** 0356	0.7
1117	3.1	1054	3.2
SU 1653	0.5	M 1628	0.1
		2329	3.1
13 0005	3.0	**28** 0444	0.4
0511	0.6	1142	3.4
M 1157	3.2	TU 1711	-0.1
1727	0.4		
14 0042	3.0	**29** 0015	3.2
0544	0.5	0525	0.3
TU 1232	3.3	W 1228	3.6
○ 1757	0.4	● 1752	-0.2
15 0114	3.0	**30** 0058	3.3
0613	0.5	0606	0.1
W 1303	3.3	TH 1312	3.7
1824	0.4	1833	-0.2
		31 0136	3.4
		0647	0.1
		F 1354	3.8
		1914	-0.1

APRIL

Time	m	Time	m
1 0211	3.4	**16** 0157	3.1
0727	0.1	0712	0.3
SA 1434	3.7	SU 1405	3.2
1956	0.1	1924	0.3
2 0246	3.5	**17** 0226	3.2
0809	0.2	0749	0.3
SU 1513	3.6	M 1441	3.2
2040	0.4	2004	0.3
3 0321	3.5	**18** 0257	3.2
0852	0.3	0831	0.2
M 1551	3.4	TU 1519	3.1
2127	0.6	2049	0.5
4 0358	3.4	**19** 0330	3.1
0938	0.6	0919	0.3
TU 1632	3.1	W 1600	3.0
2220	0.9	2140	0.7
5 0438	3.2	**20** 0406	3.0
1037	0.8	1019	0.6
W 1720	2.8	TH 1649	2.8
☾ 2342	1.2	2240	0.9
6 0527	3.0	**21** 0455	2.8
1222	1.0	1130	0.7
TH 1824	2.5	F 1757	2.6
		☽ 2350	1.0
7 0111	1.3	**22** 0617	2.7
0630	2.8	1253	0.7
F 1350	1.0	SA 1932	2.6
2114	2.5		
8 0220	1.2	**23** 0110	1.0
0814	2.7	0813	2.7
SA 1450	0.8	SU 1412	0.5
2212	2.7	2107	2.7
9 0316	1.0	**24** 0229	0.9
0956	2.9	0932	3.0
SU 1539	0.7	M 1512	0.2
2254	2.8	2213	2.9
10 0403	0.8	**25** 0331	0.7
1044	3.0	1028	3.2
M 1619	0.5	TU 1601	0.0
2332	2.9	2303	3.1
11 0441	0.6	**26** 0420	0.4
1123	3.1	1116	3.4
TU 1653	0.4	W 1645	-0.1
		2347	3.2
12 0007	3.0	**27** 0503	0.2
0513	0.5	1203	3.5
W 1158	3.1	TH 1727	-0.1
1723	0.4		
13 0040	3.0	**28** 0028	3.3
0542	0.4	0544	0.1
TH 1228	3.1	F 1248	3.6
○ 1750	0.3	1808	0.0
14 0108	3.0	**29** 0107	3.4
0609	0.4	0624	0.1
F 1257	3.2	SA 1332	3.5
1818	0.3	1850	0.1
15 0132	3.0	**30** 0143	3.4
0639	0.3	0705	0.1
SA 1329	3.2	SU 1414	3.5
1848	0.3	1934	0.3

Chart Datum: 1·62 metres below Ordnance Datum (Newlyn)

TIME ZONE (UT)
For Summer Time add ONE hour in **non-shaded areas**

SCOTLAND – GREENOCK

2006

LAT 55°57′N   LONG 4°46′W

TIMES AND HEIGHTS OF HIGH AND LOW WATERS

MAY

Time	m	Time	m
1 0219 3.5 0747 0.2 M 1454 3.4 2019 0.5		**16** 0204 3.2 0734 0.2 TU 1425 3.1 1952 0.4	
2 0256 3.5 0831 0.4 TU 1535 3.2 2107 0.7		**17** 0240 3.3 0820 0.3 W 1509 3.0 2041 0.5	
3 0334 3.4 0919 0.6 W 1619 3.0 2200 1.0		**18** 0317 3.2 0914 0.4 TH 1557 2.9 2135 0.7	
4 0415 3.2 1017 0.8 TH 1711 2.7 2305 1.2		**19** 0400 3.1 1015 0.4 F 1655 2.8 2234 0.8	
5 0504 3.0 1139 0.9 F 1815 2.6 ◐		**20** 0457 3.0 1124 0.5 SA 1805 2.7 ◑ 2339 0.9	
6 0021 1.3 0604 2.8 SA 1302 0.9 1940 2.5		**21** 0615 2.9 1236 0.5 SU 1920 2.7	
7 0131 1.2 0719 2.8 SU 1404 0.8 2113 2.6		**22** 0048 0.9 0744 2.9 M 1343 0.3 2033 2.8	
8 0231 1.1 0850 2.8 M 1454 0.7 2205 2.7		**23** 0158 0.8 0859 3.0 TU 1442 0.2 2138 2.9	
9 0322 0.9 0953 2.9 TU 1537 0.6 2248 2.8		**24** 0302 0.7 0959 3.2 W 1534 0.1 2231 3.0	
10 0404 0.7 1037 3.0 W 1614 0.5 2326 2.9		**25** 0356 0.5 1051 3.3 TH 1621 0.1 2318 3.1	
11 0439 0.6 1113 3.0 TH 1647 0.5		**26** 0443 0.3 1136 3.3 F 1706 0.2	
12 0001 3.0 0511 0.5 F 1148 3.0 1717 0.4		**27** 0001 3.1 0526 0.3 SA 1228 3.3 ● 1750 0.3	
13 0032 3.0 0542 0.4 SA 1224 3.1 ○ 1749 0.4		**28** 0042 3.3 0608 0.2 SU 1314 3.3 1834 0.4	
14 0101 3.1 0615 0.3 SU 1302 3.1 1825 0.4		**29** 0121 3.4 0650 0.2 M 1359 3.2 1919 0.5	
15 0131 3.2 0652 0.3 M 1343 3.1 1906 0.4		**30** 0200 3.5 0733 0.3 TU 1442 3.1 2006 0.6	
		31 0238 3.5 0817 0.4 W 1525 3.0 2052 0.8	

JUNE

Time	m	Time	m
1 0317 3.4 0904 0.5 TH 1610 2.9 2140 0.9		**16** 0314 3.3 0908 0.2 F 1600 3.0 2128 0.6	
2 0357 3.3 0955 0.7 F 1659 2.8 2230 1.0		**17** 0400 3.3 1005 0.2 SA 1656 2.9 2222 0.6	
3 0442 3.1 1054 0.8 SA 1752 2.7 ◑ 2325 1.1		**18** 0454 3.2 1107 0.3 SU 1753 2.9 ◑ 2319 0.7	
4 0534 3.0 1201 0.8 SU 1847 2.7		**19** 0557 3.1 1211 0.3 M 1850 2.9	
5 0026 1.1 0632 2.9 M 1305 0.8 1945 2.6		**20** 0021 0.8 0707 3.0 TU 1314 0.3 1949 2.8	
6 0129 1.1 0733 2.8 TU 1400 0.8 2049 2.7		**21** 0127 0.8 0823 3.0 W 1414 0.3 2055 2.8	
7 0228 1.0 0837 2.8 W 1448 0.7 2150 2.7		**22** 0235 0.7 0932 3.1 TH 1510 0.3 2200 2.9	
8 0319 0.9 0937 2.9 TH 1531 0.6 2240 2.8		**23** 0337 0.6 1033 3.1 F 1603 0.4 2254 3.0	
9 0403 0.7 1027 2.9 F 1611 0.6 2322 2.9		**24** 0431 0.5 1127 3.1 SA 1653 0.4 2342 3.1	
10 0443 0.6 1112 3.0 SA 1649 0.5		**25** 0518 0.4 1218 3.1 SU 1740 0.5 ●	
11 0000 3.0 0521 0.4 SU 1157 3.0 ○ 1728 0.5		**26** 0025 3.2 0601 0.3 M 1307 3.1 1825 0.6	
12 0036 3.1 0600 0.3 M 1242 3.1 1810 0.5		**27** 0106 3.3 0642 0.3 TU 1353 3.0 1909 0.6	
13 0113 3.2 0641 0.2 TU 1329 3.1 1856 0.6		**28** 0146 3.4 0722 0.4 W 1436 3.0 1951 0.6	
14 0151 3.3 0727 0.2 W 1418 3.0 1945 0.6		**29** 0223 3.4 0802 0.4 TH 1516 2.9 2032 0.7	
15 0231 3.4 0816 0.2 TH 1508 3.0 2036 0.5		**30** 0301 3.4 0842 0.5 F 1555 2.9 2112 0.7	

JULY

Time	m	Time	m
1 0338 3.3 0924 0.6 SA 1636 2.9 2153 0.8		**16** 0351 3.5 0943 0.1 SU 1636 3.1 2159 0.5	
2 0417 3.2 1009 0.6 SU 1717 2.8 2237 0.8		**17** 0438 3.4 1039 0.2 M 1722 3.1 ◐ 2252 0.6	
3 0458 3.1 1059 0.7 M 1800 2.8 ◐ 2325 0.9		**18** 0528 3.3 1141 0.4 TU 1808 3.1 2350 0.7	
4 0545 3.0 1155 0.8 TU 1845 2.7		**19** 0626 3.1 1246 0.5 W 1858 2.9	
5 0019 1.0 0636 2.9 W 1253 0.8 1936 2.7		**20** 0057 0.8 0738 2.9 TH 1352 0.6 2000 2.8	
6 0121 1.0 0735 2.8 TH 1351 0.8 2038 2.7		**21** 0215 0.9 0914 2.8 F 1456 0.7 2131 2.8	
7 0227 1.0 0842 2.8 F 1446 0.8 2150 2.7		**22** 0329 0.8 1029 2.9 SA 1554 0.7 2239 3.0	
8 0328 0.9 0949 2.8 SA 1538 0.7 2248 2.9		**23** 0427 0.6 1127 3.0 SU 1646 0.7 2330 3.1	
9 0420 0.7 1047 2.9 SU 1626 0.6 2334 3.0		**24** 0514 0.5 1218 3.0 M 1733 0.6	
10 0506 0.5 1139 3.0 M 1713 0.6		**25** 0015 3.2 0554 0.4 TU 1305 3.0 ● 1814 0.6	
11 0017 3.2 0549 0.3 TU 1231 3.1 ○ 1759 0.5		**26** 0056 3.3 0631 0.4 W 1347 3.0 1853 0.6	
12 0059 3.3 0632 0.1 W 1323 3.1 1846 0.5		**27** 0133 3.4 0705 0.4 TH 1424 2.9 1928 0.6	
13 0141 3.4 0717 0.0 TH 1414 3.1 1934 0.4		**28** 0208 3.4 0739 0.4 F 1457 2.9 2003 0.6	
14 0224 3.5 0804 0.0 F 1504 3.1 2022 0.4		**29** 0241 3.4 0812 0.4 SA 1529 2.9 2037 0.6	
15 0307 3.5 0852 0.0 SA 1551 3.1 2110 0.4		**30** 0313 3.4 0846 0.5 SU 1601 3.0 2113 0.6	
		31 0346 3.3 0923 0.6 M 1634 2.9 2151 0.7	

AUGUST

Time	m	Time	m
1 0422 3.2 1003 0.7 TU 1710 2.9 2234 0.8		**16** 0457 3.4 1105 0.6 W 1724 3.1 ◑ 2316 0.8	
2 0502 3.1 1051 0.8 W 1751 2.8 ◑ 2324 0.9		**17** 0546 3.1 1220 0.8 TH 1811 3.0	
3 0549 2.9 1148 0.9 TH 1839 2.7		**18** 0031 1.0 0649 2.8 F 1338 1.0 1909 2.8	
4 0023 1.1 0647 2.8 F 1252 1.0 1939 2.6		**19** 0207 1.0 0920 2.7 SA 1446 1.0 2109 2.8	
5 0133 1.1 0759 2.7 SA 1401 1.0 2102 2.7		**20** 0323 0.9 1033 2.8 SU 1545 0.9 2228 3.0	
6 0257 1.0 0922 2.7 SU 1511 0.9 2220 2.8		**21** 0418 0.7 1125 3.0 M 1635 0.8 2318 3.2	
7 0403 0.7 1033 2.9 M 1610 0.8 2314 3.1		**22** 0501 0.5 1210 3.1 TU 1718 0.7	
8 0452 0.4 1131 3.0 TU 1659 0.6 2359 3.3		**23** 0001 3.3 0537 0.4 W 1251 3.1 ● 1755 0.6	
9 0535 0.2 1223 3.1 W 1745 0.5 ○		**24** 0040 3.4 0610 0.4 TH 1327 3.0 1828 0.6	
10 0043 3.4 0616 0.0 TH 1314 3.2 1829 0.4		**25** 0115 3.4 0640 0.4 F 1359 3.0 1858 0.6	
11 0127 3.6 0658 -0.1 F 1402 3.2 1913 0.3		**26** 0146 3.4 0708 0.4 SA 1428 3.0 1928 0.6	
12 0210 3.7 0742 -0.1 SA 1446 3.3 1958 0.3		**27** 0214 3.4 0736 0.4 SU 1454 3.1 1959 0.6	
13 0252 3.7 0826 0.0 SU 1526 3.3 2043 0.3		**28** 0244 3.4 0806 0.5 M 1520 3.1 2033 0.6	
14 0333 3.7 0914 0.1 M 1604 3.3 2129 0.4		**29** 0316 3.4 0839 0.5 TU 1550 3.1 2109 0.6	
15 0414 3.6 1005 0.3 TU 1642 3.2 2219 0.6		**30** 0349 3.3 0916 0.6 W 1623 3.0 2150 0.8	
		31 0426 3.1 1001 0.8 TH 1700 2.9 ◑ 2239 0.9	

Chart Datum: 1·62 metres below Ordnance Datum (Newlyn)

SCOTLAND – GREENOCK — 2006
LAT 55°57'N LONG 4°46'W
TIMES AND HEIGHTS OF HIGH AND LOW WATERS

SEPTEMBER

Day	Time m	Day	Time m
1 F	0509 2.9 / 1058 1.0 / 1745 2.8 / 2341 1.1	**16** SA	0014 1.1 / 0620 2.7 / 1321 1.3 / 1835 2.9
2 SA	0606 2.7 / 1207 1.2 / 1850 2.6	**17** SU	0155 1.1 / 0926 2.7 / 1429 1.3 / 2044 2.8
3 SU	0055 1.1 / 0727 2.6 / 1326 1.2 / 2024 2.7	**18** M	0303 1.0 / 1025 2.9 / 1526 1.1 / 2208 3.1
4 M	0234 1.0 / 0908 2.7 / 1451 1.1 / 2156 2.9	**19** TU	0355 0.7 / 1109 3.1 / 1614 0.9 / 2257 3.3
5 TU	0343 0.7 / 1028 2.9 / 1553 0.9 / 2252 3.2	**20** W	0436 0.6 / 1148 3.4 / 1654 0.7 / 2338 3.4
6 W	0431 0.5 / 1122 3.1 / 1641 0.7 / 2339 3.4	**21** TH	0511 0.5 / 1223 3.2 / 1729 0.7
7 TH ○	0513 0.1 / 1210 3.2 / 1724 0.5	**22** F	0015 3.4 / 0541 0.5 / 1257 3.2 / 1758 0.6
8 F	0023 3.6 / 0553 -0.1 / 1255 3.3 / 1805 0.4	**23** SA	0048 3.4 / 0608 0.5 / 1327 3.2 / 1826 0.6
9 SA	0107 3.7 / 0633 -0.1 / 1338 3.4 / 1847 0.3	**24** SU	0116 3.4 / 0634 0.5 / 1353 3.2 / 1853 0.6
10 SU	0150 3.8 / 0714 -0.1 / 1417 3.4 / 1929 0.3	**25** M	0144 3.4 / 0700 0.5 / 1416 3.2 / 1923 0.6
11 M	0231 3.8 / 0757 0.1 / 1453 3.5 / 2013 0.3	**26** TU	0214 3.4 / 0730 0.5 / 1442 3.3 / 1957 0.6
12 TU	0310 3.8 / 0842 0.3 / 1529 3.5 / 2057 0.3	**27** W	0247 3.4 / 0804 0.6 / 1512 3.3 / 2034 0.6
13 W	0349 3.6 / 0930 0.6 / 1606 3.4 / 2145 0.7	**28** TH	0321 3.3 / 0842 0.7 / 1544 3.2 / 2117 0.8
14 TH ◑	0430 3.3 / 1028 0.9 / 1647 3.3 / 2243 0.9	**29** F	0357 3.1 / 0928 0.9 / 1618 3.1 / 2209 0.9
15 F	0517 3.0 / 1155 1.2 / 1735 3.1	**30** SA ◐	0439 2.9 / 1025 1.1 / 1701 2.9 / 2314 1.1

OCTOBER

Day	Time m	Day	Time m
1 SU	0537 2.7 / 1137 1.3 / 1809 2.8	**16** M	0123 1.2 / 0901 2.7 / 1357 1.4 / 1946 3.0
2 M	0033 1.1 / 0709 2.6 / 1302 1.4 / 1955 2.8	**17** TU	0228 1.0 / 0956 2.9 / 1454 1.3 / 2131 3.1
3 TU	0209 0.9 / 0858 2.8 / 1427 1.2 / 2128 3.0	**18** W	0319 0.9 / 1038 3.1 / 1542 1.0 / 2223 3.3
4 W	0315 0.6 / 1012 3.0 / 1529 1.0 / 2226 3.3	**19** TH	0402 0.7 / 1114 3.2 / 1623 0.9 / 2305 3.4
5 TH	0403 0.3 / 1103 3.2 / 1617 0.7 / 2314 3.5	**20** F	0437 0.6 / 1148 3.3 / 1658 0.7 / 2342 3.4
6 F	0446 0.1 / 1147 3.4 / 1700 0.5 / 2359 3.7	**21** SA	0508 0.6 / 1221 3.3 / 1728 0.7
7 SA ○	0526 0.0 / 1228 3.5 / 1740 0.4	**22** SU ●	0014 3.4 / 0535 0.6 / 1252 3.3 / 1755 0.7
8 SU	0043 3.8 / 0606 0.0 / 1308 3.5 / 1821 0.4	**23** M	0043 3.3 / 0602 0.6 / 1318 3.3 / 1823 0.6
9 M	0127 3.9 / 0647 0.1 / 1346 3.6 / 1903 0.3	**24** TU	0114 3.3 / 0630 0.6 / 1343 3.4 / 1855 0.6
10 TU	0209 3.8 / 0730 0.3 / 1422 3.7 / 1946 0.4	**25** W	0147 3.4 / 0702 0.6 / 1412 3.4 / 1930 0.4
11 W	0249 3.7 / 0814 0.5 / 1459 3.7 / 2031 0.5	**26** TH	0223 3.3 / 0740 0.7 / 1443 3.4 / 2011 0.4
12 TH	0328 3.6 / 0902 0.8 / 1537 3.6 / 2119 0.8	**27** F	0300 3.3 / 0822 0.8 / 1517 3.3 / 2057 0.8
13 F	0410 3.3 / 0959 1.2 / 1619 3.5 / 2219 1.0	**28** SA	0339 3.1 / 0911 0.9 / 1553 3.2 / 2153 0.9
14 SA ◐	0500 3.0 / 1124 1.4 / 1638 3.1 / 2353 1.2	**29** SU ◐	0425 3.0 / 1010 1.2 / 1708 3.1 / 2300 1.0
15 SU	0611 2.7 / 1250 1.5 / 1811 3.0	**30** M	0529 2.8 / 1120 1.3 / 1749 2.9
		31 TU	0018 1.0 / 0700 2.8 / 1240 1.4 / 1926 3.0

NOVEMBER

Day	Time m	Day	Time m
1 W	0137 0.8 / 0832 2.9 / 1356 1.2 / 2053 3.1	**16** TH	0234 1.0 / 0949 3.0 / 1503 1.2 / 2132 3.2
2 TH	0240 0.6 / 0942 3.1 / 1458 1.0 / 2155 3.4	**17** F	0320 0.9 / 1031 3.2 / 1548 1.0 / 2221 3.2
3 F	0332 0.3 / 1034 3.3 / 1550 0.8 / 2247 3.6	**18** SA	0359 0.8 / 1110 3.3 / 1626 0.9 / 2302 3.3
4 SA	0417 0.2 / 1119 3.4 / 1635 0.6 / 2334 3.7	**19** SU	0434 0.7 / 1146 3.3 / 1659 0.6 / 2337 3.3
5 SU ○	0500 0.2 / 1200 3.5 / 1718 0.4	**20** M ●	0505 0.7 / 1218 3.4 / 1730 0.7
6 M	0021 3.8 / 0542 0.2 / 1240 3.6 / 1759 0.4	**21** TU	0011 3.3 / 0535 0.7 / 1248 3.4 / 1802 0.7
7 TU	0106 3.8 / 0625 0.4 / 1319 3.7 / 1842 0.4	**22** W	0048 3.3 / 0607 0.7 / 1318 3.5 / 1836 0.6
8 W	0150 3.7 / 0709 0.5 / 1358 3.8 / 1926 0.5	**23** TH	0126 3.3 / 0645 0.7 / 1350 3.5 / 1915 0.6
9 TH	0232 3.6 / 0756 0.8 / 1437 3.8 / 2013 0.6	**24** F	0206 3.3 / 0727 0.8 / 1425 3.5 / 1959 0.6
10 F	0315 3.4 / 0845 1.0 / 1517 3.7 / 2103 0.8	**25** SA	0248 3.2 / 0813 0.9 / 1502 3.5 / 2048 0.7
11 SA	0400 3.2 / 0941 1.2 / 1559 3.6 / 2201 1.0	**26** SU	0333 3.1 / 0904 1.0 / 1543 3.4 / 2144 0.7
12 SU ◐	0453 3.0 / 1048 1.4 / 1648 3.4 / 2315 1.1	**27** M	0424 3.0 / 1001 1.1 / 1632 3.3 / 2247 0.7
13 M	0600 2.8 / 1202 1.5 / 1747 3.2	**28** TU ◐	0526 2.9 / 1104 1.2 / 1736 3.2 / 2355 0.7
14 TU	0035 1.2 / 0733 2.8 / 1311 1.5 / 1857 3.1	**29** W	0638 2.9 / 1213 1.2 / 1852 3.2
15 W	0140 1.1 / 0858 2.9 / 1411 1.4 / 2021 3.1	**30** TH	0103 0.6 / 0750 3.0 / 1321 1.2 / 2012 3.2

DECEMBER

Day	Time m	Day	Time m
1 F	0205 0.5 / 0900 3.1 / 1426 1.0 / 2122 3.3	**16** SA	0231 1.0 / 0934 3.0 / 1507 1.0 / 2116 3.0
2 SA	0301 0.5 / 1000 3.2 / 1524 0.8 / 2221 3.5	**17** SU	0318 1.0 / 1028 3.1 / 1554 1.0 / 2214 3.1
3 SU	0352 0.4 / 1050 3.3 / 1615 0.7 / 2313 3.5	**18** M	0400 0.9 / 1112 3.2 / 1634 0.9 / 2302 3.1
4 M	0439 0.4 / 1136 3.5 / 1702 0.6	**19** TU	0438 0.8 / 1149 3.3 / 1712 0.8 / 2345 3.2
5 TU ○	0004 3.6 / 0525 0.5 / 1219 3.6 / 1746 0.5	**20** W ●	0515 0.8 / 1224 3.4 / 1748 0.6
6 W	0053 3.5 / 0610 0.6 / 1300 3.7 / 1830 0.5	**21** TH	0028 3.2 / 0553 0.8 / 1259 3.5 / 1826 0.5
7 TH	0140 3.4 / 0657 0.7 / 1341 3.8 / 1915 0.5	**22** F	0113 3.2 / 0634 0.7 / 1335 3.5 / 1907 0.5
8 F	0225 3.4 / 0744 0.9 / 1421 3.8 / 2001 0.6	**23** SA	0158 3.2 / 0719 0.7 / 1414 3.6 / 1952 0.4
9 SA	0309 3.3 / 0831 1.0 / 1502 3.7 / 2048 0.8	**24** SU	0243 3.2 / 0806 0.7 / 1454 3.6 / 2040 0.4
10 SU	0353 3.2 / 0920 1.1 / 1544 3.6 / 2137 0.8	**25** M	0329 3.2 / 0855 0.8 / 1537 3.6 / 2131 0.4
11 M	0441 3.1 / 1010 1.2 / 1629 3.5 / 2231 1.0	**26** TU	0417 3.1 / 0946 0.8 / 1623 3.5 / 2226 0.5
12 TU ◐	0532 3.0 / 1106 1.3 / 1717 3.4 / 2333 1.1	**27** W ◐	0508 3.1 / 1041 0.9 / 1716 3.4 / 2326 0.5
13 W	0625 2.9 / 1208 1.4 / 1810 3.2	**28** TH	0601 3.0 / 1141 1.0 / 1815 3.3
14 TH	0038 1.1 / 0722 2.9 / 1312 1.4 / 1906 3.1	**29** F	0029 0.6 / 0657 3.0 / 1247 1.1 / 1923 3.2
15 F	0138 1.1 / 0827 2.9 / 1413 1.3 / 2008 3.0	**30** SA	0133 0.6 / 0804 3.0 / 1355 1.0 / 2046 3.2
		31 SU	0235 0.7 / 0922 3.0 / 1503 0.9 / 2201 3.2

Chart Datum: 1·62 metres below Ordnance Datum (Newlyn)

TIDES

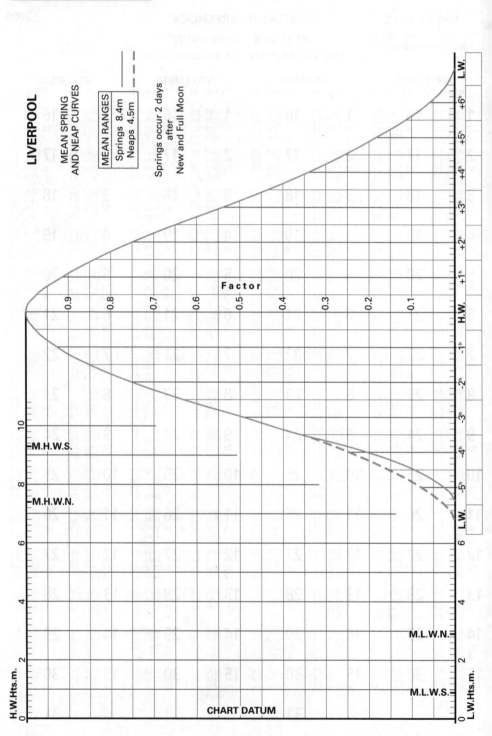

LIVERPOOL

MEAN SPRING
AND NEAP CURVES

MEAN RANGES
Springs 8.4m
Neaps 4.5m

Springs occur 2 days
after
New and Full Moon

Factor

0.9 0.8 0.7 0.6 0.5 0.4 0.3 0.2 0.1

H.W. -1ʰ -2ʰ -3ʰ -4ʰ -5ʰ L.W.

+6ʰ +5ʰ +4ʰ +3ʰ +2ʰ +1ʰ

L.W.

H.W.Hts.m.

M.H.W.S.
M.H.W.N.

CHART DATUM

L.W.Hts.m.

M.L.W.N.
M.L.W.S.

ENGLAND – LIVERPOOL (ALFRED DK)   2006

LAT 53°24′N   LONG 3°01′W

TIMES AND HEIGHTS OF HIGH AND LOW WATERS

JANUARY

Day	Time m	Time m	Time m	Time m		Day	Time m	Time m	Time m	Time m
1 SU	0613 1.4	1153 9.5	1844 1.1			16 M	0012 8.7	0640 1.9	1226 9.0	1916 1.7
2 M	0021 9.3	0700 1.3	1242 9.6	1933 1.0		17 TU	0047 8.7	0713 2.0	1300 9.0	1950 1.8
3 TU	0111 9.3	0746 1.3	1331 9.7	2021 0.9		18 W	0120 8.6	0743 2.0	1334 8.9	2020 1.9
4 W	0200 9.2	0833 1.4	1420 9.6	2108 1.1		19 TH	0154 8.5	0812 2.1	1408 8.7	2049 2.1
5 TH	0249 8.9	0920 1.7	1510 9.3	2156 1.4		20 F	0228 8.3	0845 2.1	1444 8.5	2121 2.3
6 F	0339 8.6	1008 2.0	1602 9.0	◑ 2245 1.8		21 SA	0305 8.1	0923 2.6	1522 8.3	2158 2.6
7 SA	0434 8.2	1102 2.4	1658 8.5	2341 2.2		22 SU	0346 7.8	1007 2.9	1606 7.9	◑ 2246 2.9
8 SU	0536 7.8	1204 2.7	1802 8.1			23 M	0437 7.5	1102 3.2	1702 7.6	2349 3.2
9 M	0044 2.5	0646 7.6	1317 2.9	1913 7.9		24 TU	0541 7.3	1213 3.4	1809 7.5	
10 TU	0157 2.7	0757 7.7	1434 2.8	2024 8.0		25 W	0107 3.2	0655 7.3	1333 3.2	1922 7.5
11 W	0306 2.6	0859 8.0	1541 2.5	2124 8.2		26 TH	0222 2.9	0808 7.7	1448 2.8	2035 7.9
12 TH	0402 2.4	0950 8.4	1635 2.2	2214 8.4		27 F	0327 2.5	0911 8.3	1554 2.2	2138 8.4
13 F	0447 2.2	1034 8.7	1721 1.9	2258 8.6		28 SA	0424 2.0	1005 8.9	1653 1.6	2233 8.9
14 SA	0527 2.1	1114 8.9	1802 1.8	○ 2337 8.7		29 SU	0517 1.5	1055 9.4	1747 1.0	○ 2323 9.3
15 SU	0605 2.0	1151 9.0	1841 1.7			30 M	0606 1.1	1143 9.8	1837 0.6	
						31 TU	0011 9.6	0653 0.8	1230 10.1	1924 0.3

FEBRUARY

Day	Time m	Time m	Time m	Time m		Day	Time m	Time m	Time m	Time m
1 W	0058 9.7	0737 0.7	1316 10.1	2008 0.3		16 TH	0057 8.8	0723 1.6	1310 9.0	1952 1.6
2 TH	0142 9.6	0819 0.8	1401 10.0	2049 0.5		17 F	0127 8.8	0748 1.7	1340 8.9	2017 1.7
3 F	0226 9.3	0900 1.1	1446 9.7	2130 1.0		18 SA	0157 8.7	0817 1.8	1411 8.8	2043 1.9
4 SA	0309 8.9	0941 1.5	1531 9.1	2211 1.6		19 SU	0228 8.5	0850 2.1	1444 8.5	2114 2.3
5 SU	0355 8.3	1027 2.1	1620 8.5	◑ 2258 2.3		20 M	0303 8.1	0927 2.5	1524 8.1	2152 2.7
6 M	0448 7.7	1124 2.7	1720 7.8	2357 2.9		21 TU	0348 7.5	1013 3.0	1617 7.7	2247 3.2
7 TU	0558 7.3	1237 3.1	1840 7.3			22 W	0451 7.3	1124 3.3	1729 7.3	
8 W	0112 3.3	0729 7.2	1409 3.2	2007 7.3		23 TH	0018 3.5	0613 7.1	1300 3.4	1854 7.2
9 TH	0242 3.2	0843 7.6	1534 2.8	2114 7.7		24 F	0155 3.3	0742 7.4	1430 2.9	2021 7.6
10 F	0353 2.9	0938 8.1	1630 2.3	2204 8.1		25 SA	0311 2.7	0855 8.1	1543 2.1	2128 8.3
11 SA	0441 2.5	1023 8.5	1714 1.9	2246 8.4		26 SU	0412 1.9	0951 8.9	1643 1.3	2221 9.0
12 SU	0520 2.1	1101 8.8	1752 1.7	2323 8.7		27 M	0505 1.3	1040 9.6	1734 0.6	2308 9.5
13 M	0555 1.9	1136 9.0	1826 1.5	○ 2356 8.8		28 TU	0553 0.7	1126 10.1	1821 0.1	● 2353 9.8
14 TU	0628 1.7	1208 9.1	1859 1.4							
15 W	0027 8.8	0657 1.6	1240 9.1	1927 1.5						

MARCH

Day	Time m	Time m	Time m	Time m		Day	Time m	Time m	Time m	Time m
1 W	0637 0.4	1210 10.3	1905 -0.1			16 TH	0000 8.9	0632 1.4	1213 9.0	1856 1.3
2 TH	0036 9.9	0719 0.3	1254 10.3	1945 0.0		17 F	0029 8.9	0657 1.4	1242 9.0	1919 1.3
3 F	0118 9.8	0758 0.4	1337 10.1	2023 0.3		18 SA	0057 8.9	0722 1.4	1311 8.9	1944 1.5
4 SA	0158 9.5	0836 0.7	1419 9.7	2059 0.9		19 SU	0126 8.8	0751 1.6	1341 8.8	2011 1.8
5 SU	0238 9.0	0914 1.3	1501 9.0	2135 1.7		20 M	0156 8.6	0823 1.8	1415 8.5	2041 2.2
6 M	0319 8.4	0956 2.0	1546 8.2	2218 2.5		21 TU	0231 8.3	0858 2.3	1455 8.1	2118 2.7
7 TU	0406 7.7	1050 2.6	1644 7.4	2315 3.2		22 W	0316 7.9	0945 2.8	1549 7.6	2212 3.2
8 W	0515 7.1	1207 3.3	1812 6.9			23 TH	0420 7.4	1057 3.2	1705 7.1	2346 3.5
9 TH	0036 3.7	0659 6.9	1349 3.3	1949 6.9		24 F	0548 7.1	1240 3.2	1841 7.1	
10 F	0219 3.6	0821 7.3	1520 2.9	2055 7.4		25 SA	0132 3.3	0723 7.5	1415 2.7	2009 7.6
11 SA	0337 3.1	0916 7.9	1613 2.3	2144 7.9		26 SU	0253 2.6	0836 8.2	1528 1.8	2112 8.4
12 SU	0424 2.5	1000 8.4	1653 1.8	2223 8.4		27 M	0354 1.8	0931 9.0	1624 1.0	2202 9.1
13 M	0501 2.0	1038 8.8	1728 1.5	2258 8.7		28 TU	0445 1.1	1019 9.7	1713 0.4	2246 9.6
14 TU	0535 1.7	1112 9.0	1800 1.3	○ 2330 8.8		29 W	0531 0.5	1104 10.1	1758 0.0	● 2329 9.8
15 W	0606 1.5	1143 9.0	1830 1.3			30 TH	0615 0.2	1147 10.2	1839 -0.1	
						31 F	0010 9.9	0655 0.2	1230 10.1	1917 0.1

APRIL

Day	Time m	Time m	Time m	Time m		Day	Time m	Time m	Time m	Time m
1 SA	0051 9.7	0734 0.4	1311 9.8	1953 0.6		16 SU	0027 8.9	0658 1.3	1244 8.9	1916 1.5
2 SU	0130 9.4	0812 0.8	1352 9.3	2027 1.2		17 M	0059 8.8	0731 1.5	1319 8.7	1947 1.7
3 M	0208 8.9	0849 1.4	1433 8.7	2101 1.9		18 TU	0134 8.7	0806 1.7	1357 8.5	2021 2.1
4 TU	0248 8.3	0931 2.1	1518 7.9	2142 2.7		19 W	0214 8.4	0846 2.1	1443 8.1	2103 2.6
5 W	0333 7.7	1025 2.8	1615 7.2	◑ 2239 3.4		20 TH	0304 8.0	0938 2.5	1540 7.6	2203 3.1
6 TH	0440 7.1	1141 3.2	1744 6.7			21 F	0410 7.5	1053 2.9	1657 7.2	◑ 2332 3.3
7 F	0001 3.8	0623 6.9	1316 3.3	1916 6.8		22 SA	0535 7.4	1225 2.8	1828 7.3	
8 SA	0140 3.7	0743 7.2	1441 2.9	2021 7.2		23 SU	0107 3.0	0701 7.7	1352 2.3	1947 7.8
9 SU	0259 3.2	0841 7.7	1536 2.3	2109 7.8		24 M	0226 2.4	0809 8.4	1502 1.6	2046 8.5
10 M	0349 2.6	0926 8.2	1617 1.9	2149 8.2		25 TU	0327 1.7	0905 9.0	1558 1.0	2136 9.0
11 TU	0428 2.1	1005 8.5	1652 1.6	2225 8.6		26 W	0419 1.1	0954 9.5	1646 0.5	2221 9.4
12 W	0502 1.8	1040 8.8	1724 1.4	2257 8.8		27 TH	0505 0.7	1039 9.8	1730 0.3	● 2303 9.6
13 TH	0532 1.5	1112 8.9	1753 1.3	○ 2328 8.9		28 F	0549 0.5	1123 9.8	1810 0.4	2344 9.6
14 F	0600 1.4	1142 8.9	1820 1.2	2357 8.9		29 SA	0631 0.5	1206 9.7	1848 0.6	
15 SA	0628 1.3	1212 8.9	1847 1.3			30 SU	0024 9.4	0711 0.7	1248 9.4	1923 1.0

Chart Datum: 4·93 metres below Ordnance Datum (Newlyn)

TIDES

TIME ZONE (UT)
For Summer Time add ONE hour in **non-shaded areas**

ENGLAND – LIVERPOOL (ALFRED DK) 2006

LAT 53°24'N LONG 3°01'W

TIMES AND HEIGHTS OF HIGH AND LOW WATERS

MAY

Time	m		Time	m
1 0103	9.1	**16** 0040	8.9
0750	1.1	0718	1.5
M 1329	8.9	TU 1305	8.7
1957	1.6	1933	1.7
2 0143	8.7	**17** 0122	8.7
0830	1.6	0800	1.6
TU 1411	8.4	W 1350	8.5
2033	2.2	2014	2.1
3 0223	8.3	**18** 0209	8.5
0913	2.1	0847	1.9
W 1456	7.8	TH 1440	8.2
2114	2.8	2103	2.4
4 0309	7.8	**19** 0303	8.3
1005	2.6	0944	2.1
TH 1550	7.2	F 1539	7.8
2207	3.3	2204	2.7
5 0410	7.3	**20** 0406	8.0
1110	3.0	1050	2.3
F 1705	6.8	SA 1648	7.6
☽ 2319	3.6	☽ 2317	2.8
6 0536	7.1	**21** 0519	7.9
1224	3.1	1204	2.3
SA 1826	6.8	SU 1805	7.6
7 0038	3.6	**22** 0034	2.7
0652	7.2	0631	8.1
SU 1337	2.9	M 1319	2.0
1931	7.1	1915	7.9
8 0154	3.3	**23** 0149	2.3
0752	7.5	0737	8.4
M 1438	2.6	TU 1428	1.7
2024	7.6	2015	8.3
9 0253	2.8	**24** 0254	1.9
0842	7.9	0836	8.8
TU 1525	2.2	W 1527	1.3
2107	8.0	2108	8.7
10 0338	2.4	**25** 0350	1.4
0924	8.2	0928	9.1
W 1604	1.8	TH 1617	1.1
2146	8.4	2155	9.0
11 0415	2.0	**26** 0439	1.1
1002	8.5	1017	9.3
TH 1639	1.6	F 1702	1.0
2221	8.6	2240	9.2
12 0450	1.7	**27** 0526	1.0
1036	8.6	1103	9.3
F 1712	1.4	SA 1742	1.0
2254	8.8	● 2322	9.2
13 0525	1.5	**28** 0610	1.0
1111	8.7	1147	9.1
SA 1746	1.4	SU 1821	1.2
○ 2327	8.9		
14 0602	1.4	**29** 0002	9.1
1146	8.8	0652	1.2
SU 1821	1.4	M 1230	8.9
		1858	1.5
15 0002	8.9	**30** 0043	8.9
0639	1.4	0734	1.4
M 1224	8.8	TU 1312	8.6
1856	1.5	1934	1.9
		31 0123	8.6
		0815	1.7
		W 1353	8.3
		2011	2.3

JUNE

Time	m		Time	m
1 0205	8.4	**16** 0206	9.0
0858	2.1	0851	1.4
TH 1436	7.9	F 1437	8.6
2051	2.9	2102	1.9
2 0249	8.0	**17** 0258	8.8
0943	2.4	0942	1.5
F 1522	7.5	SA 1531	8.3
2137	3.0	2155	2.1
3 0338	7.7	**18** 0354	8.6
1032	2.7	1036	1.7
SA 1616	7.2	SU 1628	8.1
○ 2232	3.3	☽ 2254	2.3
4 0437	7.4	**19** 0454	8.5
1127	2.8	1134	1.9
SU 1720	7.1	M 1732	7.9
2334	3.3	2358	2.4
5 0544	7.3	**20** 0558	8.3
1224	2.9	1238	2.0
M 1827	7.1	TU 1839	7.9
6 0037	3.3	**21** 0108	2.4
0648	7.4	0703	8.3
TU 1323	2.8	W 1348	2.1
1926	7.3	1944	8.0
7 0138	3.0	**22** 0219	2.3
0745	7.6	0808	8.4
W 1419	2.5	TH 1454	2.0
2018	7.7	2043	8.3
8 0235	2.7	**23** 0324	2.0
0835	7.8	0908	8.5
TH 1510	2.2	F 1551	1.8
2103	8.1	2136	8.5
9 0326	2.3	**24** 0420	1.7
0919	8.1	1001	8.6
F 1556	1.9	SA 1639	1.7
2144	8.4	2223	8.7
10 0413	2.0	**25** 0510	1.6
1002	8.4	1050	8.7
SA 1639	1.7	SU 1722	1.7
2223	8.7	● 2307	8.8
11 0458	1.7	**26** 0556	1.5
1044	8.6	1135	8.7
SU 1720	1.6	M 1803	1.7
○ 2303	8.8	2348	8.9
12 0542	1.5	**27** 0641	1.5
1127	8.7	1217	8.6
M 1802	1.5	TU 1841	1.8
2345	9.0		
13 0628	1.4	**28** 0028	8.8
1211	8.8	0722	1.6
TU 1844	1.5	W 1257	8.5
		1918	2.0
14 0029	9.0	**29** 0107	8.7
0714	1.3	0802	1.7
W 1259	8.8	TH 1335	8.3
1927	1.6	1954	2.2
15 0116	9.0	**30** 0146	8.6
0802	1.3	0839	1.9
TH 1347	8.7	F 1412	8.2
2013	1.8	2028	2.4

JULY

Time	m		Time	m
1 0224	8.4	**16** 0243	9.4
0915	2.1	0927	1.0
SA 1451	8.0	SU 1511	8.8
2104	2.6	2137	1.6
2 0305	8.1	**17** 0332	9.1
0951	2.3	1012	1.3
SU 1531	7.7	M 1600	8.5
2145	2.8	☽ 2226	2.0
3 0348	7.9	**18** 0424	8.7
1032	2.6	1102	1.8
M 1617	7.5	TU 1655	8.0
☽ 2235	3.0	2323	2.4
4 0437	7.6	**19** 0523	8.2
1117	2.9	1159	2.3
TU 1711	7.3	W 1759	7.7
2333	3.2		
5 0533	7.4	**20** 0031	2.7
1220	2.9	0631	7.9
W 1814	7.2	TH 1308	2.6
		1914	7.6
6 0039	3.2	**21** 0152	2.7
0635	7.4	0747	7.8
TH 1323	2.9	F 1425	2.7
1919	7.4	2025	7.8
7 0145	3.0	**22** 0310	2.5
0739	7.5	0856	7.9
F 1425	2.7	SA 1534	2.5
2019	7.7	2125	8.1
8 0248	2.7	**23** 0413	2.2
0839	7.8	0954	8.2
SA 1522	2.4	SU 1628	2.3
2111	8.2	2214	8.5
9 0345	2.2	**24** 0505	1.9
0934	8.1	1043	8.4
SU 1614	2.0	M 1713	2.1
2159	8.6	2258	8.7
10 0439	1.8	**25** 0550	1.6
1025	8.5	1126	8.5
M 1703	1.7	TU 1753	1.9
2246	8.9	● 2337	8.9
11 0531	1.5	**26** 0631	1.5
1114	8.7	1204	8.6
TU 1750	1.5	W 1830	1.9
○ 2332	9.2		
12 0622	1.2	**27** 0014	8.9
1203	8.9	0708	1.5
W 1837	1.3	TH 1239	8.6
		1904	1.9
13 0019	9.4	**28** 0048	8.9
0710	0.9	0742	1.6
TH 1251	9.1	F 1312	8.5
1922	1.2	1934	1.9
14 0107	9.5	**29** 0122	8.8
0758	0.8	0813	1.7
F 1338	9.1	SA 1344	8.5
2007	1.2	2002	2.0
15 0155	9.5	**30** 0155	8.7
0843	0.8	0840	1.8
SA 1424	9.0	SU 1417	8.3
2051	1.4	2030	2.2
		31 0229	8.5
		0908	2.1
		M 1451	8.1
		2104	2.4

AUGUST

Time	m		Time	m
1 0305	8.2	**16** 0352	8.6
0941	2.4	1028	2.0
TU 1528	7.9	W 1618	8.0
2145	2.7	☽ 2251	2.5
2 0346	7.9	**17** 0449	7.9
1023	2.7	1123	2.7
W 1613	7.5	TH 1722	7.4
☽ 2236	3.1		
3 0437	7.5	**18** 0004	3.0
1120	3.1	0605	7.3
TH 1710	7.3	F 1237	3.2
2345	3.4	1851	7.2
4 0540	7.3	**19** 0139	3.1
1234	3.3	0737	7.2
F 1822	7.2	SA 1410	3.3
		2014	7.5
5 0106	3.3	**20** 0310	2.8
0653	7.2	0850	7.6
SA 1350	3.1	SU 1531	2.9
1940	7.4	2115	8.0
6 0221	3.0	**21** 0411	2.3
0810	7.5	0944	8.0
SU 1458	2.7	M 1623	2.5
2047	8.0	2203	8.5
7 0328	2.4	**22** 0457	1.8
0917	8.0	1029	8.4
M 1557	2.2	TU 1704	2.1
2142	8.6	2243	8.8
8 0427	1.8	**23** 0537	1.5
1012	8.5	1108	8.6
TU 1650	1.7	W 1740	1.9
2231	9.1	● 2320	9.0
9 0521	1.2	**24** 0612	1.4
1102	9.0	1143	8.7
W 1740	1.3	TH 1814	1.7
○ 2318	9.6	2353	9.1
10 0611	0.7	**25** 0645	1.3
1148	9.3	1214	8.7
TH 1826	0.9	F 1844	1.7
11 0004	9.9	**26** 0023	9.0
0658	0.4	0714	1.4
F 1234	9.5	SA 1244	8.7
1910	0.8	1909	1.7
12 0050	10.0	**27** 0053	8.9
0742	0.3	0739	1.5
SA 1318	9.5	SU 1313	8.7
1952	0.7	1933	1.7
13 0134	10.0	**28** 0122	8.8
0823	0.4	0803	1.7
SU 1401	9.4	M 1342	8.6
2032	0.9	1959	1.9
14 0219	9.7	**29** 0153	8.6
0903	0.7	0828	1.9
M 1444	9.1	TU 1412	8.4
2113	1.3	2030	2.1
15 0304	9.1	**30** 0225	8.4
0943	1.3	0857	2.2
TU 1528	8.6	W 1445	8.1
2157	1.9	2105	2.5
		31 0303	8.0
		0933	2.8
		TH 1527	7.7
		☽ 2149	3.0

Chart Datum: 4·93 metres below Ordnance Datum (Newlyn)

TIME ZONE (UT)
For Summer Time add ONE hour in **non-shaded areas**

LAT 53°24'N   LONG 3°01'W

TIMES AND HEIGHTS OF HIGH AND LOW WATERS

SEPTEMBER

Time m	Time m
1 0353 7.5 / 1023 3.3 / F 1623 7.3 / 2257 3.5	**16** 0550 7.0 / 1212 3.6 / SA 1833 7.0
2 0500 7.1 / 1150 3.6 / SA 1740 7.1	**17** 0133 3.3 / 0726 7.0 / SU 1400 3.6 / 1956 7.4
3 0035 3.5 / 0624 7.0 / SU 1324 3.4 / 1911 7.3	**18** 0259 2.8 / 0833 7.4 / M 1517 3.1 / 2054 8.0
4 0203 3.1 / 0755 7.4 / M 1440 2.9 / 2029 8.0	**19** 0353 2.2 / 0924 8.0 / TU 1605 2.5 / 2140 8.5
5 0314 2.3 / 0904 8.0 / TU 1542 2.2 / 2125 8.7	**20** 0435 1.7 / 1005 8.4 / W 1643 2.1 / 2219 8.9
6 0414 1.5 / 0957 8.7 / W 1635 1.5 / 2213 9.4	**21** 0511 1.4 / 1041 8.7 / TH 1717 1.8 / 2254 9.0
7 0505 0.8 / 1043 9.3 / TH 1723 1.0 / ○ 2258 9.9	**22** 0543 1.3 / 1114 8.8 / F 1748 1.6 / ● 2325 9.1
8 0552 0.3 / 1127 9.6 / F 1808 0.6 / 2342 10.2	**23** 0613 1.3 / 1144 8.9 / SA 1815 1.5 / 2354 9.0
9 0637 0.0 / 1210 9.8 / SA 1850 0.4	**24** 0639 1.4 / 1211 8.9 / SU 1839 1.5
10 0025 10.3 / 0718 0.1 / SU 1252 9.7 / 1930 0.5	**25** 0021 9.0 / 0702 1.5 / M 1239 8.8 / 1904 1.6
11 0109 10.1 / 0757 0.3 / M 1333 9.5 / 2009 0.7	**26** 0050 8.9 / 0727 1.7 / TU 1308 8.7 / 1932 1.8
12 0152 9.7 / 0834 0.8 / TU 1414 9.1 / 2048 1.3	**27** 0120 8.7 / 0754 1.9 / W 1338 8.5 / 2003 2.0
13 0236 9.1 / 0911 1.5 / W 1456 8.5 / 2131 1.9	**28** 0153 8.4 / 0823 2.3 / TH 1412 8.3 / 2037 2.5
14 0323 8.3 / 0955 2.4 / TH 1544 7.9 / ◑ 2226 2.7	**29** 0233 8.0 / 0858 2.8 / F 1455 7.9 / 2120 2.9
15 0421 7.5 / 1052 3.1 / F 1651 7.3 / 2345 3.2	**30** 0324 7.5 / 0947 3.3 / SA 1553 7.4 / ◑ 2228 3.4

OCTOBER

Time m	Time m
1 0435 7.1 / 1117 3.7 / SU 1714 7.1	**16** 0104 3.2 / 0656 6.9 / M 1325 3.7 / 1921 7.4
2 0013 3.4 / 0606 7.0 / M 1300 3.5 / 1848 7.4	**17** 0224 2.8 / 0801 7.4 / TU 1440 3.2 / 2020 7.9
3 0144 2.9 / 0739 7.5 / TU 1419 2.9 / 2005 8.1	**18** 0318 2.3 / 0850 7.9 / W 1530 2.7 / 2106 8.3
4 0255 2.1 / 0844 8.2 / W 1521 2.1 / 2101 8.9	**19** 0359 1.9 / 0931 8.3 / TH 1610 2.2 / 2146 8.7
5 0353 1.3 / 0933 8.9 / TH 1613 1.4 / 2149 9.6	**20** 0435 1.6 / 1008 8.7 / F 1644 1.9 / 2222 8.9
6 0442 0.6 / 1018 9.5 / F 1700 0.8 / 2234 10.1	**21** 0506 1.5 / 1041 8.8 / SA 1714 1.7 / 2253 9.0
7 0527 0.2 / 1101 9.8 / SA 1744 0.5 / ○ 2317 10.3	**22** 0534 1.4 / 1111 8.9 / SU 1742 1.6 / ● 2322 9.0
8 0610 0.1 / 1143 9.9 / SU 1826 0.4	**23** 0601 1.4 / 1139 8.9 / M 1810 1.5 / 2351 8.9
9 0000 10.2 / 0649 0.2 / M 1224 9.8 / 1907 0.5	**24** 0629 1.5 / 1208 8.9 / TU 1840 1.6
10 0044 9.9 / 0727 0.6 / TU 1305 9.5 / 1946 0.8	**25** 0022 8.8 / 0658 1.7 / W 1240 8.8 / 1911 1.8
11 0127 9.4 / 0804 1.2 / W 1346 9.0 / 2027 1.4	**26** 0056 8.7 / 0729 2.0 / TH 1314 8.7 / 1945 2.0
12 0210 8.8 / 0842 1.9 / TH 1428 8.5 / 2112 2.1	**27** 0134 8.4 / 0802 2.3 / F 1353 8.4 / 2023 2.4
13 0258 8.1 / 0926 2.7 / F 1516 7.9 / 2208 2.8	**28** 0217 8.1 / 0841 2.8 / SA 1440 8.1 / 2111 2.8
14 0358 7.3 / 1024 3.4 / SA 1624 7.3 / ◑ 2327 3.2	**29** 0311 7.6 / 0936 3.2 / SU 1540 7.7 / ◑ 2222 3.1
15 0528 6.9 / 1145 3.8 / SU 1802 7.1	**30** 0421 7.3 / 1058 3.5 / M 1656 7.5 / 2352 3.1
	31 0548 7.2 / 1229 3.3 / TU 1820 7.7

NOVEMBER

Time m	Time m
1 0115 2.6 / 0711 7.7 / W 1346 2.8 / 1933 8.3	**16** 0222 2.7 / 0806 7.6 / TH 1435 3.0 / 2023 8.0
2 0226 2.0 / 0814 8.3 / TH 1451 2.1 / 2031 8.9	**17** 0310 2.3 / 0851 8.1 / F 1522 2.6 / 2107 8.3
3 0324 1.3 / 0905 8.9 / F 1545 1.5 / 2122 9.5	**18** 0349 2.0 / 0930 8.4 / SA 1601 2.2 / 2145 8.5
4 0414 0.8 / 0951 9.4 / SA 1634 1.0 / 2209 9.9	**19** 0423 1.8 / 1006 8.7 / SU 1636 2.0 / 2220 8.7
5 0500 0.5 / 1035 9.7 / SU 1720 0.7 / ○ 2254 10.0	**20** 0456 1.7 / 1039 8.8 / M 1710 1.8 / ● 2253 8.8
6 0542 0.5 / 1118 9.7 / M 1804 0.6 / 2338 9.9	**21** 0529 1.6 / 1112 8.9 / TU 1745 1.7 / 2327 8.8
7 0622 0.7 / 1200 9.6 / TU 1847 0.8	**22** 0603 1.6 / 1145 9.0 / W 1822 1.7
8 0022 9.6 / 0701 1.1 / W 1242 9.3 / 1929 1.1	**23** 0003 8.8 / 0638 1.8 / TH 1222 8.9 / 1859 1.8
9 0106 9.1 / 0740 1.6 / TH 1324 9.0 / 2012 1.6	**24** 0042 8.7 / 0715 2.0 / F 1301 8.8 / 1940 1.9
10 0151 8.6 / 0820 2.2 / F 1407 8.5 / 2059 2.1	**25** 0125 8.5 / 0755 2.2 / SA 1345 8.7 / 2024 2.1
11 0239 8.0 / 0904 2.8 / SA 1455 8.1 / 2153 2.6	**26** 0212 8.3 / 0839 2.5 / SU 1435 8.5 / 2115 2.3
12 0334 7.4 / 0958 3.3 / SU 1554 7.6 / ◑ 2257 3.0	**27** 0305 8.0 / 0933 2.8 / M 1531 8.3 / 2216 2.5
13 0447 7.0 / 1105 3.6 / M 1713 7.3	**28** 0408 7.7 / 1039 3.0 / TU 1636 8.1 / ◑ 2324 2.5
14 0009 3.1 / 0606 7.0 / TU 1221 3.7 / 1829 7.4	**29** 0519 7.6 / 1151 2.9 / W 1746 8.2
15 0121 3.0 / 0712 7.2 / W 1335 3.4 / 1932 7.6	**30** 0036 2.4 / 0632 7.8 / TH 1304 2.7 / 1855 8.4

DECEMBER

Time m	Time m
1 0147 2.1 / 0739 8.2 / F 1414 2.3 / 1959 8.7	**16** 0202 2.8 / 0801 7.6 / SA 1419 3.0 / 2018 7.8
2 0251 1.7 / 0836 8.6 / SA 1516 1.9 / 2056 9.1	**17** 0255 2.6 / 0850 8.0 / SU 1513 2.7 / 2106 8.1
3 0346 1.4 / 0927 9.0 / SU 1610 1.5 / 2148 9.3	**18** 0342 2.3 / 0932 8.3 / M 1600 2.3 / 2149 8.3
4 0435 1.2 / 1014 9.3 / M 1700 1.2 / 2237 9.4	**19** 0425 2.0 / 1012 8.6 / TU 1644 2.0 / 2229 8.6
5 0519 1.1 / 1059 9.4 / TU 1747 1.1 / ○ 2323 9.4	**20** 0506 1.8 / 1051 8.9 / W 1728 1.8 / ● 2310 8.7
6 0602 1.2 / 1143 9.4 / W 1833 1.2	**21** 0546 1.7 / 1130 9.0 / TH 1812 1.7 / 2352 8.7
7 0008 9.2 / 0642 1.5 / TH 1226 9.2 / 1918 1.4	**22** 0628 1.7 / 1211 9.1 / F 1856 1.6
8 0053 8.9 / 0723 1.8 / F 1308 9.0 / 2002 1.6	**23** 0035 8.9 / 0709 1.7 / SA 1255 9.2 / 1940 1.5
9 0136 8.6 / 0804 2.2 / SA 1351 8.7 / 2047 2.0	**24** 0120 8.8 / 0752 1.8 / SU 1340 9.2 / 2026 1.5
10 0219 8.2 / 0846 2.6 / SU 1435 8.4 / 2132 2.3	**25** 0206 8.7 / 0837 1.9 / M 1428 9.1 / 2111 1.6
11 0305 7.8 / 0930 2.9 / M 1521 8.1 / 2219 2.6	**26** 0255 8.6 / 0923 2.1 / TU 1517 8.9 / 2200 1.8
12 0355 7.5 / 1019 3.2 / TU 1614 7.8 / ◑ 2310 2.9	**27** 0347 8.3 / 1015 2.3 / W 1611 8.7 / ◑ 2253 2.1
13 0454 7.2 / 1115 3.4 / W 1715 7.5	**28** 0445 8.0 / 1113 2.6 / TH 1711 8.5 / 2354 2.3
14 0005 3.0 / 0600 7.2 / TH 1216 3.5 / 1820 7.4	**29** 0551 7.9 / 1220 2.7 / F 1817 8.3
15 0104 3.0 / 0705 7.3 / F 1319 3.3 / 1923 7.6	**30** 0102 2.4 / 0701 7.9 / SA 1336 2.7 / 1927 8.3
	31 0216 2.3 / 0810 8.1 / SU 1450 2.4 / 2036 8.4

TIDES

Chart Datum: 4·93 metres below Ordnance Datum (Newlyn)

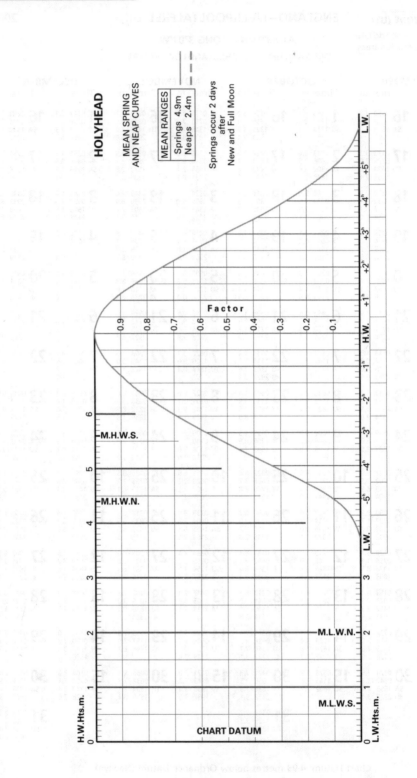

HOLYHEAD

MEAN SPRING
AND NEAP CURVES

MEAN RANGES
Springs 4.9m
Neaps 2.4m

Springs occur 2 days
after
New and Full Moon

TIME ZONE (UT)
For Summer Time add ONE hour in **non-shaded areas**

WALES – HOLYHEAD
LAT 53°19'N   LONG 4°37'W
TIMES AND HEIGHTS OF HIGH AND LOW WATERS

2006

JANUARY

Time	m		Time	m
1 SU 0440	1.0		**16** M 0516	1.3
1054	5.8		1130	5.5
1709	0.8		1747	1.1
2324	5.5		2352	5.1
2 M 0527	0.9		**17** TU 0548	1.3
1140	5.9		1202	5.4
1757	0.7		1820	1.2
3 TU 0012	5.5		**18** W 0025	5.1
0614	1.0		0621	1.4
1228	5.9		1235	5.4
1847	0.7		1853	1.2
4 W 0103	5.4		**19** TH 0058	5.0
0703	1.1		0655	1.5
1318	5.8		1309	5.2
1938	0.8		1927	1.4
5 TH 0155	5.2		**20** F 0133	4.9
0754	1.3		0730	1.6
1409	5.6		1344	5.1
2032	1.0		2004	1.5
6 F 0250	5.0		**21** SA 0211	4.7
0849	1.5		0809	1.8
1505	5.4		1423	4.9
◖ 2131	1.2		2045	1.7
7 SA 0351	4.8		**22** SU 0254	4.6
0951	1.7		0854	2.0
1607	5.2		1507	4.7
2234	1.5		◖ 2133	1.9
8 SU 0459	4.6		**23** M 0348	4.4
1059	1.8		0950	2.2
1716	5.0		1605	4.5
2341	1.7		2235	2.0
9 M 0609	4.6		**24** TU 0458	4.3
1210	1.9		1101	2.3
1829	4.9		1722	4.4
			2349	2.1
10 TU 0047	1.8		**25** W 0616	4.4
0715	4.7		1221	2.2
1320	1.8		1845	4.5
1937	4.9			
11 W 0150	1.7		**26** TH 0101	1.9
0813	4.9		0725	4.6
1422	1.7		1332	1.9
2036	4.9		1955	4.7
12 TH 0243	1.7		**27** F 0204	1.7
0902	5.1		0823	5.0
1515	1.5		1432	1.5
2125	5.0		2052	5.0
13 F 0329	1.5		**28** SA 0258	1.4
0944	5.3		0912	5.3
1559	1.3		1525	1.1
2208	5.1		2142	5.3
14 SA 0408	1.4		**29** SU 0345	1.1
1022	5.4		0958	5.6
1638	1.2		1612	0.7
○ 2245	5.1		● 2228	5.5
15 SU 0443	1.4		**30** M 0430	0.8
1057	5.4		1042	5.9
1714	1.2		1658	0.4
2320	5.1		2313	5.7
			31 TU 0514	0.6
			1126	6.1
			1743	0.3
			2358	5.7

FEBRUARY

Time	m		Time	m
1 W 0558	0.6		**16** TH 0555	1.0
1211	6.1		1208	5.4
1829	0.3		1821	1.0
2 TH 0042	5.6		**17** F 0027	5.2
0642	0.6		0624	1.1
1257	6.0		1239	5.4
1914	0.5		1851	1.1
3 F 0128	5.4		**18** SA 0058	5.1
0728	0.8		0656	1.2
1344	5.8		1310	5.2
2001	0.8		1922	1.3
4 SA 0214	5.1		**19** SU 0131	4.9
0817	1.1		0730	1.4
1433	5.5		1343	5.0
2052	1.2		1957	1.5
5 SU 0306	4.8		**20** M 0208	4.7
0912	1.5		0810	1.7
1529	5.1		1422	4.8
◖ 2150	1.6		2040	1.7
6 M 0408	4.6		**21** TU 0253	4.5
1020	1.9		0901	1.9
1638	4.7		1513	4.5
2301	2.0		2139	2.0
7 TU 0527	4.4		**22** W 0358	4.3
1142	2.1		1014	2.2
1805	4.5		1634	4.3
			2304	2.2
8 W 0021	2.1		**23** TH 0532	4.3
0653	4.5		1149	2.2
1307	2.0		1822	4.3
1932	4.5			
9 TH 0139	2.1		**24** F 0037	2.1
0804	4.7		0700	4.5
1418	1.8		1315	1.8
2037	4.6		1944	4.6
10 F 0238	1.9		**25** SA 0149	1.8
0856	4.9		0805	4.9
1510	1.5		1419	1.4
2123	4.8		2043	5.0
11 SA 0322	1.6		**26** SU 0244	1.3
0936	5.1		0856	5.3
1550	1.3		1511	0.9
2200	5.0		2130	5.3
12 SU 0357	1.4		**27** M 0331	0.9
1010	5.3		0941	5.7
1624	1.1		1556	0.4
2231	5.1		2213	5.6
13 M 0428	1.2		**28** TU 0413	0.6
1040	5.4		1024	6.0
1654	1.0		1639	0.1
2300	5.2		● 2254	5.8
14 TU 0457	1.1			
1109	5.5			
1723	0.9			
2328	5.2			
15 W 0525	1.0			
1138	5.5			
1752	0.9			
2357	5.2			

MARCH

Time	m		Time	m
1 W 0454	0.3		**16** TH 0458	0.9
1106	6.2		1110	5.5
1721	0.0		1720	0.8
2335	5.8		2327	5.3
2 TH 0535	0.3		**17** F 0526	0.9
1149	6.2		1139	5.4
1803	0.1		1748	0.9
			2356	5.3
3 F 0016	5.7		**18** SA 0556	0.9
0617	0.4		1209	5.4
1233	6.1		1817	1.0
1845	0.4			
4 SA 0058	5.5		**19** SU 0026	5.2
0700	0.6		0626	1.1
1317	5.8		1240	5.2
1928	0.8		1847	1.2
5 SU 0140	5.2		**20** M 0059	5.1
0746	1.0		0700	1.3
1403	5.3		1314	5.0
2014	1.3		1923	1.4
6 M 0226	4.9		**21** TU 0135	4.9
0839	1.4		0741	1.5
1456	4.9		1354	4.8
◖ 2108	1.8		2006	1.7
7 TU 0323	4.5		**22** W 0221	4.6
0947	1.9		0834	1.8
1606	4.4		1449	4.5
2221	2.2		◖ 2108	2.0
8 W 0445	4.3		**23** TH 0327	4.4
1118	2.1		0951	2.0
1748	4.2		1617	4.2
2356	2.4		2240	2.3
9 TH 0629	4.3		**24** F 0504	4.3
1252	2.1		1132	2.0
1926	4.3		1811	4.3
10 F 0123	2.3		**25** SA 0018	2.1
0747	4.5		0637	4.5
1404	1.8		1258	1.6
2027	4.5		1931	4.6
11 SA 0223	2.0		**26** SU 0131	1.7
0838	4.8		0743	4.9
1452	1.5		1400	1.2
2108	4.7		2026	5.0
12 SU 0304	1.7		**27** M 0224	1.2
0915	5.0		0834	5.4
1528	1.2		1450	0.7
2139	4.9		2110	5.3
13 M 0336	1.4		**28** TU 0309	0.8
0946	5.2		0918	5.7
1559	1.0		1533	0.3
2207	5.1		2150	5.6
14 TU 0404	1.2		**29** W 0350	0.5
1014	5.4		1001	6.0
1626	0.9		1615	0.1
○ 2232	5.2		● 2230	5.8
15 W 0431	1.0		**30** TH 0430	0.3
1042	5.4		1043	6.1
1653	0.8		1655	0.1
2259	5.3		2309	5.8
			31 F 0511	0.2
			1125	6.1
			1736	0.2
			2349	5.7

APRIL

Time	m		Time	m
1 SA 0553	0.3		**16** SU 0530	0.9
1208	5.9		1143	5.3
1817	0.5		1749	1.0
2 SU 0029	5.5		**17** M 0000	5.3
0636	0.6		0604	1.0
1253	5.6		1218	5.2
1858	0.9		1823	1.2
3 M 0111	5.2		**18** TU 0037	5.2
0723	1.0		0643	1.2
1339	5.1		1257	5.0
1943	1.4		1903	1.4
4 TU 0155	4.9		**19** W 0117	5.0
0815	1.5		0729	1.4
1431	4.7		1344	4.7
2034	1.9		1952	1.7
5 W 0249	4.6		**20** TH 0209	4.8
0922	1.9		0828	1.7
1541	4.2		1447	4.4
◖ 2144	2.3		2059	2.0
6 TH 0405	4.3		**21** F 0318	4.5
1050	2.1		0948	1.8
1721	4.0		1618	4.3
2320	2.5		◖ 2228	2.1
7 F 0547	4.2		**22** SA 0447	4.5
1220	2.0		1117	1.7
1856	4.2		1756	4.4
			2355	2.0
8 SA 0048	2.4		**23** SU 0610	4.7
0708	4.4		1233	1.4
1329	1.8		1907	4.7
1955	4.4			
9 SU 0149	2.1		**24** M 0102	1.6
0801	4.7		0714	5.0
1417	1.5		1333	1.0
2035	4.7		2000	5.0
10 M 0230	1.7		**25** TU 0156	1.2
0840	4.9		0806	5.4
1453	1.3		1423	0.7
2106	4.9		2044	5.3
11 TU 0303	1.4		**26** W 0242	0.9
0912	5.1		0852	5.7
1524	1.1		1507	0.4
2134	5.0		2125	5.5
12 W 0331	1.2		**27** TH 0325	0.6
0941	5.2		0936	5.8
1552	0.9		1549	0.3
2200	5.2		● 2204	5.6
13 TH 0359	1.0		**28** F 0407	0.4
1010	5.3		1020	5.9
1619	0.8		1630	0.4
○ 2228	5.3		2245	5.7
14 F 0428	0.9		**29** SA 0450	0.4
1040	5.4		1104	5.8
1648	0.8		1711	0.5
2257	5.3		2325	5.6
15 SA 0458	0.9		**30** SU 0534	0.6
1111	5.4		1149	5.6
1717	0.9		1752	0.8
2328	5.3			

Chart Datum: 3·05 metres below Ordnance Datum (Newlyn)

TIME ZONE (UT)
For Summer Time add ONE hour in **non-shaded areas**

WALES – HOLYHEAD

LAT 53°19'N   LONG 4°37'W

TIMES AND HEIGHTS OF HIGH AND LOW WATERS

2006

MAY

Time m	Time m
1 M 0007 5.4 / 0618 0.8 / 1234 5.3 / 1834 1.2	**16** TU 0552 1.0 / 1206 5.1 / 1810 1.2
2 TU 0049 5.2 / 0706 1.1 / 1253 4.9 / 1918 1.6	**17** W 0024 5.2 / 0636 1.1 / 1253 4.9 / 1856 1.4
3 W 0133 5.0 / 0757 1.5 / 1411 4.6 / 2008 1.9	**18** TH 0111 5.1 / 0729 1.3 / 1346 4.8 / 1950 1.6
4 TH 0224 4.7 / 0858 1.8 / 1515 4.3 / 2109 2.3	**19** F 0206 5.0 / 0830 1.4 / 1451 4.6 / 2056 1.8
5 F 0328 4.4 / 1012 2.0 / 1635 4.1 / ☽ 2229 2.4	**20** SA 0312 4.8 / 0941 1.5 / 1609 4.5 / ☽ 2211 1.9
6 SA 0448 4.3 / 1128 2.0 / 1757 4.1 / 2350 2.4	**21** SU 0426 4.8 / 1055 1.4 / 1727 4.5 / 2324 1.8
7 SU 0606 4.4 / 1234 1.8 / 1901 4.3	**22** M 0538 4.9 / 1203 1.2 / 1834 4.7
8 M 0053 2.2 / 0706 4.5 / 1326 1.6 / 1947 4.5	**23** TU 0029 1.6 / 0641 5.1 / 1303 1.0 / 1929 4.9
9 TU 0141 1.9 / 0751 4.7 / 1407 1.4 / 2023 4.7	**24** W 0126 1.3 / 0737 5.3 / 1355 0.9 / 2017 5.1
10 W 0220 1.6 / 0829 4.9 / 1442 1.2 / 2055 4.9	**25** TH 0216 1.0 / 0828 5.4 / 1442 0.8 / 2101 5.3
11 TH 0253 1.4 / 0904 5.0 / 1514 1.1 / 2126 5.1	**26** F 0304 0.9 / 0916 5.5 / 1527 0.7 / 2143 5.4
12 F 0326 1.2 / 0937 5.2 / 1546 1.0 / 2157 5.2	**27** SA 0350 0.8 / 1003 5.5 / 1610 0.8 / ● 2226 5.5
13 SA 0359 1.1 / 1011 5.2 / 1618 1.0 / ○ 2230 5.3	**28** SU 0436 0.7 / 1049 5.4 / 1652 0.9 / 2308 5.5
14 SU 0434 1.0 / 1047 5.2 / 1652 1.0 / 2305 5.3	**29** M 0521 0.8 / 1134 5.3 / 1734 1.1 / 2350 5.4
15 M 0511 1.0 / 1125 5.2 / 1729 1.1 / 2343 5.3	**30** TU 0607 1.0 / 1219 5.1 / 1816 1.3
	31 W 0031 5.2 / 0652 1.2 / 1304 4.8 / 1858 1.6

JUNE

Time m	Time m
1 TH 0114 5.0 / 0739 1.4 / 1350 4.6 / 1943 1.8	**16** F 0106 5.4 / 0726 0.9 / 1343 5.0 / 1944 1.3
2 F 0159 4.8 / 0829 1.6 / 1441 4.4 / 2034 2.0	**17** SA 0159 5.3 / 0821 1.0 / 1440 4.8 / 2041 1.5
3 SA 0250 4.6 / 0924 1.7 / 1539 4.2 / ◐ 2132 2.2	**18** SU 0256 5.2 / 0922 1.1 / 1544 4.7 / ◐ 2144 1.6
4 SU 0349 4.5 / 1025 1.8 / 1643 4.2 / 2237 2.3	**19** M 0359 5.1 / 1025 1.2 / 1651 4.6 / 2250 1.6
5 M 0454 4.4 / 1127 1.8 / 1747 4.2 / 2343 2.2	**20** TU 0504 5.0 / 1130 1.3 / 1757 4.7 / 2356 1.6
6 TU 0557 4.4 / 1223 1.8 / 1844 4.4	**21** W 0610 5.0 / 1232 1.3 / 1859 4.8
7 W 0040 2.0 / 0653 4.5 / 1313 1.6 / 1932 4.6	**22** TH 0058 1.5 / 0713 5.0 / 1330 1.3 / 1954 4.9
8 TH 0130 1.8 / 0743 4.7 / 1357 1.5 / 2014 4.8	**23** F 0158 1.3 / 0811 5.1 / 1424 1.2 / 2044 5.1
9 F 0214 1.6 / 0827 4.8 / 1437 1.4 / 2053 4.9	**24** SA 0253 1.2 / 0905 5.1 / 1513 1.2 / 2130 5.2
10 SA 0255 1.4 / 0908 5.0 / 1516 1.4 / 2130 5.1	**25** SU 0343 1.1 / 0954 5.2 / 1558 1.2 / ● 2214 5.3
11 SU 0336 1.2 / 0949 5.1 / 1555 1.1 / ○ 2208 5.3	**26** M 0430 1.0 / 1040 5.1 / 1640 1.2 / 2256 5.4
12 M 0417 1.1 / 1031 5.1 / 1635 1.1 / 2249 5.4	**27** TU 0513 1.0 / 1123 5.1 / 1720 1.2 / 2336 5.3
13 TU 0500 0.9 / 1114 5.2 / 1718 1.1 / 2331 5.4	**28** W 0554 1.0 / 1204 5.0 / 1759 1.3
14 W 0545 0.9 / 1200 5.2 / 1803 1.1	**29** TH 0014 5.3 / 0634 1.1 / 1243 4.9 / 1836 1.4
15 TH 0017 5.4 / 0634 0.9 / 1250 5.1 / 1851 1.2	**30** F 0052 5.2 / 0713 1.2 / 1321 4.8 / 1915 1.6

JULY

Time m	Time m
1 SA 0130 5.0 / 0753 1.4 / 1401 4.6 / 1956 1.7	**16** SU 0140 5.6 / 0800 0.7 / 1416 5.1 / 2016 1.2
2 SU 0210 4.9 / 0835 1.5 / 1444 4.5 / 2040 1.9	**17** M 0231 5.5 / 0853 0.9 / 1510 4.9 / ◐ 2112 1.4
3 M 0255 4.7 / 0922 1.7 / 1534 4.4 / ◐ 2130 2.1	**18** TU 0327 5.2 / 0951 1.2 / 1611 4.7 / 2215 1.6
4 TU 0346 4.5 / 1014 1.8 / 1631 4.3 / 2229 2.2	**19** W 0432 5.0 / 1056 1.5 / 1720 4.6 / 2327 1.7
5 W 0446 4.4 / 1114 1.9 / 1736 4.3 / 2334 2.2	**20** TH 0544 4.8 / 1205 1.7 / 1833 4.6
6 TH 0552 4.4 / 1215 1.9 / 1839 4.4	**21** F 0041 1.7 / 0700 4.7 / 1314 1.7 / 1940 4.7
7 F 0039 2.1 / 0657 4.5 / 1314 1.8 / 1935 4.6	**22** SA 0152 1.6 / 0809 4.8 / 1416 1.6 / 2038 4.9
8 SA 0138 1.9 / 0756 4.6 / 1406 1.6 / 2024 4.8	**23** SU 0252 1.4 / 0906 4.9 / 1509 1.5 / 2125 5.1
9 SU 0231 1.6 / 0847 4.8 / 1454 1.4 / 2109 5.1	**24** M 0342 1.2 / 0953 5.0 / 1552 1.4 / 2207 5.3
10 M 0319 1.3 / 0934 5.0 / 1539 1.2 / 2152 5.3	**25** TU 0424 1.1 / 1033 5.0 / 1630 1.3 / ● 2244 5.4
11 TU 0405 1.0 / 1020 5.2 / 1623 1.0 / ○ 2235 5.5	**26** W 0501 1.0 / 1108 5.1 / 1704 1.2 / 2318 5.4
12 W 0450 0.8 / 1105 5.3 / 1707 0.9 / 2319 5.7	**27** TH 0535 1.0 / 1142 5.1 / 1737 1.2 / 2351 5.4
13 TH 0536 0.6 / 1151 5.4 / 1752 0.8	**28** F 0608 1.0 / 1214 5.0 / 1810 1.2
14 F 0005 5.7 / 0622 0.5 / 1238 5.3 / 1838 0.9	**29** SA 0024 5.3 / 0640 1.1 / 1247 5.0 / 1842 1.3
15 SA 0052 5.7 / 0710 0.6 / 1326 5.2 / 1925 1.0	**30** SU 0057 5.2 / 0714 1.2 / 1319 4.9 / 1917 1.5
	31 M 0131 5.1 / 0748 1.4 / 1356 4.7 / 1954 1.6

AUGUST

Time m	Time m
1 TU 0207 4.9 / 0826 1.6 / 1436 4.6 / 2036 1.9	**16** W 0257 5.2 / 0915 1.4 / 1532 4.7 / ◐ 2145 1.7
2 W 0248 4.7 / 0911 1.8 / 1524 4.4 / ◐ 2127 2.1	**17** TH 0403 4.8 / 1023 1.8 / 1648 4.5 / 2306 1.9
3 TH 0340 4.5 / 1007 2.0 / 1628 4.3 / 2234 2.2	**18** F 0529 4.5 / 1145 2.1 / 1817 4.5
4 F 0453 4.3 / 1119 2.1 / 1747 4.3 / 2355 2.2	**19** SA 0034 2.0 / 0701 4.5 / 1307 2.1 / 1935 4.7
5 SA 0619 4.3 / 1236 2.1 / 1902 4.5	**20** SU 0152 1.8 / 0814 4.6 / 1414 1.9 / 2033 4.9
6 SU 0111 2.0 / 0735 4.5 / 1343 1.9 / 2002 4.8	**21** M 0249 1.5 / 0906 4.8 / 1502 1.7 / 2117 5.1
7 M 0213 1.6 / 0834 4.8 / 1437 1.5 / 2052 5.1	**22** TU 0332 1.3 / 0944 5.0 / 1540 1.5 / 2153 5.3
8 TU 0305 1.2 / 0923 5.1 / 1524 1.2 / 2136 5.4	**23** W 0408 1.1 / 1016 5.1 / 1612 1.3 / 2224 5.4
9 W 0351 0.8 / 1007 5.3 / 1608 0.9 / ○ 2219 5.7	**24** TH 0439 1.0 / 1045 5.2 / 1642 1.1 / 2254 5.5
10 TH 0435 0.5 / 1050 5.5 / 1650 0.7 / 2302 6.0	**25** F 0508 0.9 / 1113 5.2 / 1710 1.1 / 2323 5.5
11 F 0518 0.3 / 1132 5.6 / 1732 0.5 / 2345 6.1	**26** SA 0536 0.9 / 1142 5.2 / 1739 1.1 / 2352 5.4
12 SA 0602 0.2 / 1215 5.6 / 1816 0.6	**27** SU 0605 1.0 / 1211 5.2 / 1809 1.2
13 SU 0029 6.0 / 0645 0.3 / 1300 5.5 / 1900 0.7	**28** M 0022 5.3 / 0634 1.1 / 1242 5.1 / 1840 1.3
14 M 0115 5.9 / 0731 0.6 / 1345 5.2 / 1947 1.0	**29** TU 0053 5.2 / 0705 1.3 / 1315 4.9 / 1913 1.5
15 TU 0203 5.6 / 0820 1.0 / 1434 5.0 / 2040 1.3	**30** W 0126 5.0 / 0739 1.5 / 1350 4.8 / 1952 1.8
	31 TH 0203 4.8 / 0819 1.6 / 1434 4.6 / ◑ 2041 2.0

Chart Datum: 3·05 metres below Ordnance Datum (Newlyn)

TIME ZONE (UT)
For Summer Time add ONE hour in **non-shaded areas**

WALES – HOLYHEAD

LAT 53°19'N   LONG 4°37'W

TIMES AND HEIGHTS OF HIGH AND LOW WATERS

SEPTEMBER

Day	Time m	Time m	Time m	Time m		Day	Time m	Time m	Time m	Time m
1 F	0252 4.5	0914 2.1	1534 4.4	2150 2.3		**16** SA	0522 4.3	1127 2.4	1801 4.5	
2 SA	0407 4.2	1034 2.3	1704 4.3	2323 2.3		**17** SU	0026 2.1	0700 4.4	1256 2.3	1922 4.7
3 SU	0556 4.2	1209 2.3	1835 4.5			**18** M	0141 1.8	0806 4.6	1400 2.1	2017 4.9
4 M	0051 2.0	0722 4.5	1324 2.0	1941 4.8		**19** TU	0232 1.5	0850 4.8	1443 1.8	2056 5.2
5 TU	0156 1.5	0820 4.9	1420 1.5	2032 5.3		**20** W	0310 1.3	0922 5.0	1517 1.5	2128 5.3
6 W	0247 1.0	0906 5.2	1505 1.1	2115 5.6		**21** TH	0341 1.1	0950 5.1	1546 1.3	2156 5.4
7 TH	0331 0.6	0947 5.5	1547 0.7	○2157 6.0		**22** F	0409 1.0	1016 5.3	1613 1.1	●2224 5.5
8 F	0412 0.3	1027 5.7	1627 0.5	2238 6.2		**23** SA	0436 0.9	1042 5.3	1640 1.1	2252 5.5
9 SA	0453 0.1	1107 5.8	1708 0.4	2321 6.3		**24** SU	0503 0.9	1109 5.3	1708 1.1	2320 5.5
10 SU	0535 0.1	1148 5.8	1750 0.4			**25** M	0530 1.0	1138 5.3	1738 1.1	2350 5.4
11 M	0004 6.2	0617 0.4	1231 5.6	1833 0.6		**26** TU	0559 1.2	1208 5.2	1809 1.3	
12 TU	0050 5.9	0701 0.7	1314 5.4	1920 1.0		**27** W	0021 5.2	0629 1.3	1241 5.1	1842 1.5
13 W	0137 5.5	0748 1.2	1402 5.1	2014 1.4		**28** TH	0055 5.0	0703 1.6	1317 4.9	1922 1.7
14 TH	0231 5.0	0842 1.7	1459 4.7	☽2122 1.8		**29** F	0133 4.8	0744 1.9	1401 4.7	2013 2.0
15 F	0342 4.6	0954 2.2	1620 4.5	2252 2.1		**30** SA	0226 4.5	0842 2.2	1503 4.5	◑2127 2.2

OCTOBER

Day	Time m	Time m	Time m	Time m		Day	Time m	Time m	Time m	Time m
1 SU	0348 4.2	1008 2.4	1635 4.4	2304 2.2		**16** M	0635 4.4	1224 2.5	1847 4.7	
2 M	0542 4.3	1147 2.3	1808 4.6			**17** TU	0107 1.9	0735 4.6	1326 2.2	1942 4.9
3 TU	0030 1.9	0703 4.6	1301 2.0	1915 5.0		**18** W	0158 1.6	0817 4.8	1411 1.9	2022 5.1
4 W	0133 1.4	0759 5.0	1355 1.5	2005 5.4		**19** TH	0236 1.4	0849 5.0	1445 1.6	2054 5.2
5 TH	0222 0.9	0843 5.4	1440 1.1	2050 5.8		**20** F	0307 1.2	0917 5.2	1514 1.4	2124 5.4
6 F	0305 0.5	0923 5.6	1521 0.7	2131 6.1		**21** SA	0335 1.1	0944 5.3	1542 1.3	2152 5.5
7 SA	0346 0.3	1001 5.8	1602 0.5	○2214 6.3		**22** SU	0403 1.1	1011 5.4	1611 1.2	●2222 5.5
8 SU	0427 0.2	1041 5.9	1643 0.4	2257 6.3		**23** M	0430 1.1	1039 5.4	1641 1.2	2252 5.4
9 M	0508 0.3	1122 5.9	1726 0.5	2341 6.1		**24** TU	0500 1.1	1110 5.4	1712 1.2	2324 5.4
10 TU	0550 0.6	1204 5.7	1811 0.7			**25** W	0530 1.3	1142 5.4	1746 1.3	2358 5.2
11 W	0027 5.8	0634 1.0	1248 5.5	1900 1.1		**26** TH	0604 1.4	1217 5.3	1824 1.5	
12 TH	0116 5.3	0721 1.5	1336 5.1	1955 1.5		**27** F	0036 5.0	0641 1.7	1257 5.1	1908 1.7
13 F	0212 4.9	0815 2.0	1433 4.8	2104 1.9		**28** SA	0121 4.8	0728 1.9	1346 4.9	2004 1.9
14 SA	0325 4.4	0926 2.4	1551 4.6	☽2231 2.1		**29** SU	0220 4.5	0829 2.2	1450 4.7	◑2117 2.0
15 SU	0503 4.3	1058 2.6	1727 4.5	2358 2.1		**30** M	0342 4.4	0951 2.3	1613 4.7	2243 2.0
						31 TU	0520 4.5	1118 2.2	1736 4.8	

NOVEMBER

Day	Time m	Time m	Time m	Time m		Day	Time m	Time m	Time m	Time m
1 W	0000 1.7	0633 4.7	1229 1.9	1841 5.1		**16** TH	0108 1.8	0730 4.7	1323 2.1	1935 4.9
2 TH	0102 1.3	0729 5.1	1324 1.5	1935 5.5		**17** F	0151 1.6	0808 4.9	1404 1.9	2014 5.0
3 F	0152 0.9	0815 5.4	1412 1.1	2022 5.8		**18** SA	0228 1.5	0841 5.1	1440 1.7	2050 5.2
4 SA	0238 0.7	0856 5.6	1456 0.8	2107 6.0		**19** SU	0300 1.4	0912 5.2	1513 1.5	2123 5.3
5 SU	0321 0.5	0937 5.8	1539 0.7	○2152 6.1		**20** M	0332 1.3	0943 5.3	1546 1.4	○2157 5.3
6 M	0403 0.5	1018 5.9	1624 0.6	2237 6.0		**21** TU	0403 1.2	1015 5.4	1620 1.3	2231 5.3
7 TU	0446 0.7	1101 5.8	1709 0.7	2324 5.8		**22** W	0436 1.3	1049 5.5	1656 1.3	2307 5.3
8 W	0529 0.9	1144 5.7	1757 0.9			**23** TH	0512 1.3	1125 5.5	1734 1.3	2346 5.2
9 TH	0012 5.5	0613 1.3	1229 5.5	1846 1.2		**24** F	0550 1.4	1204 5.4	1817 1.4	
10 F	0102 5.2	0700 1.6	1317 5.2	1941 1.5		**25** SA	0029 5.1	0632 1.6	1248 5.3	1904 1.5
11 SA	0156 4.8	0751 2.0	1410 5.0	2043 1.8		**26** SU	0119 4.9	0722 1.8	1339 5.2	2000 1.6
12 SU	0300 4.5	0853 2.3	1515 4.7	◑2154 2.0		**27** M	0217 4.7	0820 2.0	1438 5.0	2104 1.7
13 M	0418 4.3	1009 2.5	1631 4.6	2308 2.1		**28** TU	0326 4.6	0929 2.1	1546 5.0	◑2215 1.6
14 TU	0537 4.3	1127 2.5	1746 4.6			**29** W	0444 4.6	1042 2.0	1658 5.0	2324 1.5
15 W	0014 2.0	0642 4.5	1233 2.3	1847 4.7		**30** TH	0555 4.8	1151 1.8	1805 5.2	

DECEMBER

Day	Time m	Time m	Time m	Time m		Day	Time m	Time m	Time m	Time m
1 F	0027 1.3	0655 5.0	1251 1.6	1904 5.4		**16** SA	0058 1.9	0718 4.6	1317 2.1	1930 4.7
2 SA	0123 1.1	0747 5.2	1346 1.3	1958 5.6		**17** SU	0145 1.8	0803 4.8	1404 1.9	2017 4.9
3 SU	0213 1.0	0834 5.4	1436 1.1	2049 5.7		**18** M	0227 1.7	0843 5.0	1446 1.7	2059 5.0
4 M	0301 0.9	0919 5.6	1525 1.0	2138 5.7		**19** TU	0306 1.5	0920 5.2	1526 1.5	2139 5.1
5 TU	0346 0.9	1003 5.7	1613 0.9	○2226 5.7		**20** W	0343 1.4	0957 5.3	1606 1.3	●2218 5.2
6 W	0431 1.0	1047 5.7	1701 0.9	2314 5.5		**21** TH	0421 1.3	1034 5.5	1646 1.2	2258 5.3
7 TH	0515 1.2	1131 5.7	1748 1.0			**22** F	0500 1.2	1113 5.6	1727 1.1	2340 5.3
8 F	0001 5.3	0558 1.4	1215 5.5	1835 1.2		**23** SA	0542 1.2	1155 5.6	1811 1.0	
9 SA	0047 5.1	0642 1.6	1259 5.4	1922 1.4		**24** SU	0024 5.2	0625 1.3	1240 5.6	1857 1.1
10 SU	0134 4.9	0727 1.8	1344 5.1	2012 1.6		**25** M	0112 5.1	0712 1.4	1327 5.5	1947 1.1
11 M	0223 4.6	0815 2.1	1433 4.9	2105 1.8		**26** TU	0202 5.0	0803 1.5	1418 5.4	2041 1.2
12 TU	0317 4.5	0910 2.3	1528 4.7	◑2203 2.0		**27** W	0258 4.9	0900 1.7	1515 5.3	◑2141 1.4
13 W	0419 4.3	1012 2.4	1630 4.6	2305 2.0		**28** TH	0401 4.7	1003 1.8	1619 5.2	2245 1.5
14 TH	0524 4.3	1119 2.4	1735 4.6			**29** F	0511 4.7	1112 1.8	1728 5.1	2352 1.5
15 F	0004 2.0	0625 4.4	1222 2.3	1836 4.6		**30** SA	0620 4.8	1221 1.8	1837 5.1	
						31 SU	0056 1.5	0723 4.9	1327 1.6	1943 5.2

TIDES

Chart Datum: 3·05 metres below Ordnance Datum (Newlyn)

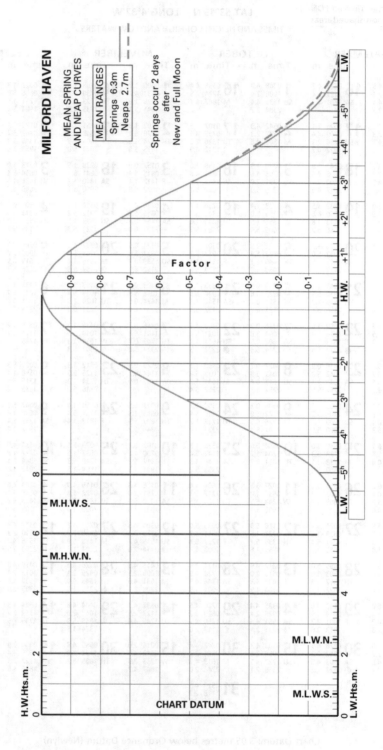

MILFORD HAVEN

MEAN SPRING
AND NEAP CURVES

MEAN RANGES
Springs 6.3m
Neaps 2.7m

Springs occur 2 days
after
New and Full Moon

Factor

0·9 0·8 0·7 0·6 0·5 0·4 0·3 0·2 0·1

H.W.

−1ʰ −2ʰ −3ʰ −4ʰ −5ʰ L.W.

L.W. +5ʰ +4ʰ +3ʰ +2ʰ +1ʰ H.W.

H.W.Hts.m.

M.H.W.S.

M.H.W.N.

M.L.W.N.

M.L.W.S.

CHART DATUM

L.W.Hts.m.

TIME ZONE (UT)
For Summer Time add ONE hour in **non-shaded areas**

WALES – MILFORD HAVEN

LAT 51°42′N LONG 5°03′W

TIMES AND HEIGHTS OF HIGH AND LOW WATERS

2006

JANUARY

Time	m	Time	m
1 0046	1.0	**16** 0119	1.4
0649	7.0	0725	6.6
SU 1313	0.8	M 1345	1.3
1915	6.9	1944	6.4
2 0132	0.9	**17** 0152	1.3
0736	7.2	0757	6.6
M 1401	0.7	TU 1416	1.3
2003	6.9	2016	6.3
3 0219	0.9	**18** 0223	1.4
0825	7.2	0829	6.5
TU 1449	0.8	W 1447	1.4
2050	6.8	2048	6.2
4 0306	1.0	**19** 0254	1.5
0913	7.0	0901	6.3
W 1537	0.9	TH 1517	1.6
2139	6.6	2119	6.0
5 0354	1.2	**20** 0326	1.7
1003	6.8	0933	6.2
TH 1627	1.2	F 1550	1.7
2228	6.3	2153	5.8
6 0445	1.5	**21** 0400	1.9
1055	6.5	1008	5.9
F 1720	1.5	SA 1625	2.0
◐ 2321	6.0	2230	5.6
7 0541	1.8	**22** 0439	2.1
1151	6.2	1049	5.6
SA 1817	1.8	SU 1707	2.2
		◔ 2315	5.3
8 0020	5.7	**23** 0527	2.4
0644	2.1	1139	5.4
SU 1254	5.9	M 1802	2.5
1922	2.1		
9 0129	5.5	**24** 0015	5.2
0756	2.2	0634	2.6
M 1403	5.7	TU 1247	5.2
2033	2.2	1920	2.6
10 0240	5.5	**25** 0134	5.1
0910	2.2	0802	2.6
TU 1513	5.7	W 1410	5.3
2139	2.1	2047	2.4
11 0347	5.7	**26** 0255	5.4
1014	2.0	0923	2.3
W 1617	5.8	TH 1528	5.6
2236	1.9	2158	2.1
12 0444	6.0	**27** 0403	5.9
1108	1.8	1029	1.8
TH 1710	6.0	F 1633	6.0
2324	1.7	2257	1.6
13 0532	6.2	**28** 0500	6.4
1154	1.6	1125	1.3
F 1755	6.2	SA 1729	6.5
		2348	1.2
14 0006	1.5	**29** 0552	6.9
0613	6.4	1216	0.8
SA 1235	1.4	SU 1819	6.8
○ 1834	6.3	●	
15 0044	1.4	**30** 0036	0.8
0650	6.5	0639	7.2
SU 1311	1.4	M 1304	0.5
1911	6.4	1906	7.1
		31 0123	0.5
		0726	7.5
		TU 1350	0.3
		1951	7.2

FEBRUARY

Time	m	Time	m
1 0207	0.4	**16** 0200	1.0
0811	7.5	0804	6.7
W 1434	0.3	TH 1420	1.1
2034	7.2	2020	6.5
2 0250	0.5	**17** 0228	1.1
0855	7.4	0832	6.6
TH 1517	0.5	F 1447	1.2
2117	6.9	2048	6.4
3 0332	0.7	**18** 0257	1.3
0939	7.1	0901	6.4
F 1559	0.8	SA 1515	1.4
2159	6.6	2116	6.2
4 0414	1.1	**19** 0326	1.5
1023	6.7	0931	6.2
SA 1641	1.3	SU 1545	1.7
2243	6.1	2148	5.9
5 0500	1.6	**20** 0359	1.8
1111	6.1	1005	5.9
SU 1729	1.9	M 1618	2.0
◐ 2333	5.7	2227	5.6
6 0554	2.1	**21** 0439	2.2
1208	5.6	1049	5.5
M 1829	2.3	TU 1704	2.3
		2320	5.2
7 0039	5.3	**22** 0538	2.5
0710	2.3	1153	5.2
TU 1323	5.2	W 1817	2.6
1952	2.6		
8 0207	5.1	**23** 0043	5.0
0847	2.6	0717	2.6
W 1452	5.2	TH 1332	5.0
2121	2.5	2014	2.6
9 0333	5.3	**24** 0226	5.2
1006	2.3	0902	2.3
TH 1609	5.4	F 1511	5.3
2226	2.2	2142	2.2
10 0436	5.7	**25** 0347	5.7
1103	1.9	1015	1.7
F 1702	5.8	SA 1622	5.9
2315	1.8	2244	1.6
11 0522	6.1	**26** 0447	6.4
1146	1.6	1112	1.1
SA 1744	6.1	SU 1717	6.5
2355	1.5	2335	1.0
12 0601	6.4	**27** 0538	7.0
1222	1.3	1202	0.5
SU 1820	6.3	M 1804	7.0
13 0030	1.3	**28** 0022	0.5
0634	6.6	0623	7.4
M 1255	1.2	TU 1248	0.1
○ 1853	6.5	● 1848	7.3
14 0102	1.1		
0706	6.7		
TU 1324	1.1		
1923	6.5		
15 0131	1.1		
0735	6.7		
W 1353	1.0		
1952	6.5		

MARCH

Time	m	Time	m
1 0106	0.2	**16** 0105	0.9
0707	7.7	0707	6.8
W 1331	0.0	TH 1324	0.9
1930	7.4	1922	6.7
2 0147	0.1	**17** 0133	0.9
0750	7.7	0735	6.8
TH 1411	0.0	F 1351	0.9
2010	7.4	1950	6.7
3 0227	0.2	**18** 0201	0.9
0831	7.5	0802	6.7
F 1450	0.3	SA 1418	1.0
2049	7.1	2017	6.5
4 0305	0.5	**19** 0229	1.1
0911	7.1	0830	6.5
SA 1527	0.8	SU 1445	1.2
2127	6.7	2046	6.3
5 0343	1.0	**20** 0259	1.3
0950	6.6	0901	6.3
SU 1604	1.3	M 1514	1.5
2206	6.2	2117	6.1
6 0423	1.6	**21** 0331	1.7
1033	6.0	0935	5.9
M 1645	1.9	TU 1547	1.9
◐ 2251	5.6	2156	5.7
7 0512	2.2	**22** 0412	2.0
1125	5.3	1020	5.5
TU 1739	2.5	W 1633	2.3
2353	5.1	◔ 2251	5.3
8 0628	2.7	**23** 0514	2.4
1245	4.8	1128	5.1
W 1912	2.9	TH 1750	2.6
9 0136	4.9	**24** 0018	5.1
0829	2.8	0659	2.6
TH 1435	4.8	F 1314	4.9
2102	2.7	1956	2.6
10 0317	5.1	**25** 0208	5.2
0954	2.4	0846	2.2
F 1555	5.2	SA 1457	5.3
2211	2.3	2124	2.1
11 0418	5.6	**26** 0329	5.8
1046	1.9	0958	1.6
SA 1645	5.7	SU 1605	6.0
2257	1.9	2225	1.4
12 0501	6.0	**27** 0427	6.5
1125	1.6	1053	0.9
SU 1723	6.0	M 1657	6.6
2333	1.5	2315	0.9
13 0537	6.4	**28** 0516	7.1
1158	1.3	1140	0.4
M 1756	6.3	TU 1742	7.1
14 0006	1.2	**29** 0000	0.4
0609	6.6	0601	7.5
TU 1228	1.0	W 1224	0.0
○ 1826	6.5	● 1824	7.3
15 0036	1.0	**30** 0042	0.1
0639	6.7	0643	7.7
W 1257	0.9	TH 1305	0.0
1855	6.6	1904	7.4
		31 0123	0.1
		0724	7.6
		F 1344	0.1
		1943	7.3

APRIL

Time	m	Time	m
1 0201	0.3	**16** 0135	0.9
0804	7.4	0735	6.7
SA 1421	0.4	SU 1351	1.0
2020	7.1	1951	6.6
2 0239	0.6	**17** 0207	1.1
0843	6.9	0806	6.5
SU 1457	0.9	M 1422	1.2
2057	6.6	2023	6.4
3 0316	1.1	**18** 0240	1.3
0921	6.4	0841	6.2
M 1533	1.5	TU 1455	1.5
2136	6.1	2100	6.1
4 0356	1.7	**19** 0319	1.6
1003	5.8	0921	5.9
TU 1611	2.0	W 1534	1.9
2220	5.6	2145	5.8
5 0443	2.3	**20** 0407	2.0
1054	5.2	1013	5.5
W 1702	2.6	TH 1628	2.2
◐ 2320	5.1	◐ 2246	5.5
6 0558	2.7	**21** 0516	2.2
1211	4.7	1127	5.2
TH 1833	2.9	F 1750	2.5
		◔	
7 0100	4.9	**22** 0013	5.3
0755	2.8	0654	2.3
F 1403	4.7	SA 1305	5.1
2026	2.8	1938	2.4
8 0240	5.1	**23** 0148	5.5
0919	2.4	0823	1.9
SA 1521	5.1	SU 1433	5.5
2136	2.4	2057	1.9
9 0342	5.5	**24** 0302	6.0
1010	2.0	0931	1.4
SU 1611	5.5	M 1537	6.0
2222	2.0	2157	1.4
10 0426	5.9	**25** 0359	6.5
1050	1.6	1025	0.9
M 1649	5.9	TU 1629	6.5
2300	1.6	2248	0.9
11 0503	6.2	**26** 0449	7.0
1123	1.3	1113	0.6
TU 1722	6.2	W 1715	6.9
2333	1.3	2333	0.6
12 0535	6.5	**27** 0535	7.2
1154	1.1	1156	0.4
W 1753	6.5	TH 1757	7.1
		●	
13 0004	1.1	**28** 0016	0.4
0605	6.6	0618	7.3
TH 1224	1.0	F 1238	0.4
○ 1822	6.6	1837	7.2
14 0035	0.9	**29** 0058	0.4
0635	6.7	0659	7.2
F 1252	0.9	SA 1317	0.5
1851	6.7	1917	7.1
15 0105	0.9	**30** 0138	0.6
0705	6.7	0740	7.0
SA 1322	0.9	SU 1355	0.8
1920	6.7	1956	6.9

Chart Datum: 3·71 metres below Ordnance Datum (Newlyn)

TIDES

TIME ZONE (UT)
For Summer Time add ONE hour in **non-shaded areas**

WALES – MILFORD HAVEN

2006

LAT 51°42'N   LONG 5°03'W

TIMES AND HEIGHTS OF HIGH AND LOW WATERS

MAY

Day	Time m	Time m	Day	Time m	Time m
1 M	0217 0.9 / 0819 6.6	1432 1.2 / 2034 6.5	**16** TU	0152 1.1 / 0752 6.4	1408 1.3 / 2011 6.5
2 TU	0256 1.3 / 0859 6.1	1509 1.6 / 2114 6.1	**17** W	0233 1.3 / 0834 6.2	1449 1.5 / 2055 6.3
3 W	0337 1.8 / 0942 5.6	1549 2.1 / 2159 5.6	**18** TH	0319 1.5 / 0922 5.9	1536 1.8 / 2148 6.0
4 TH	0425 2.2 / 1031 5.2	1638 2.5 / 2255 5.3	**19** F	0413 1.7 / 1019 5.6	1634 2.0 / 2251 5.8
5 F	0530 2.5 / 1137 4.8	1752 2.8 ◐	**20** SA	0520 1.9 / 1127 5.4	1749 2.1
6 SA	0012 5.0 / 0656 2.6	1307 4.8 / 1923 2.8	**21** SU	0004 5.7 / 0638 1.9	1245 5.4 / 1911 2.1
7 SU	0141 5.1 / 0817 2.5	1424 5.0 / 2038 2.5	**22** M	0120 5.8 / 0752 1.7	1359 5.6 / 2023 1.8
8 M	0247 5.4 / 0916 2.2	1520 5.3 / 2132 2.1	**23** TU	0228 6.1 / 0857 1.5	1503 6.0 / 2124 1.5
9 TU	0337 5.7 / 1001 1.8	1603 5.7 / 2215 1.8	**24** W	0328 6.4 / 0953 1.2	1557 6.3 / 2218 1.2
10 W	0418 6.0 / 1040 1.6	1641 6.0 / 2253 1.5	**25** TH	0421 6.6 / 1044 1.0	1647 6.6 / 2307 1.0
11 TH	0455 6.2 / 1115 1.3	1715 6.3 / 2328 1.3	**26** F	0510 6.8 / 1130 0.9	1732 6.7 / 2353 0.9
12 F	0529 6.4 / 1148 1.2	1748 6.5	**27** SA	0556 6.8 / 1213 0.9	1816 6.8 ●
13 SA	0003 1.1 / 0603 6.5	1222 1.1 / 1821 6.6 ○	**28** SU	0037 0.9 / 0639 6.7	1255 1.0 / 1857 6.8
14 SU	0038 1.1 / 0638 6.6	1256 1.1 / 1856 6.7	**29** M	0120 1.0 / 0722 6.6	1335 1.1 / 1938 6.6
15 M	0115 1.1 / 0714 6.5	1331 1.1 / 1932 6.6	**30** TU	0202 1.2 / 0803 6.3	1414 1.4 / 2018 6.4
			31 W	0242 1.4 / 0843 6.0	1452 1.7 / 2059 6.1

JUNE

Day	Time m	Time m	Day	Time m	Time m
1 TH	0323 1.7 / 0925 5.7	1532 2.0 / 2141 5.8	**16** F	0320 1.1 / 0923 6.2	1537 1.4 / 2148 6.4
2 F	0406 2.0 / 1009 5.4	1615 2.2 / 2228 5.5	**17** SA	0412 1.3 / 1016 6.0	1631 1.6 / 2243 6.3
3 SA	0455 2.2 / 1059 5.2	1709 2.4 / 2323 5.3 ◐	**18** SU	0509 1.5 / 1113 5.8	1731 1.7 / 2343 6.1 ◑
4 SU	0554 2.4 / 1159 5.0	1814 2.5	**19** M	0611 1.6 / 1214 5.7	1837 1.8
5 M	0027 5.2 / 0659 2.4	1309 5.0 / 1922 2.4	**20** TU	0047 6.0 / 0715 1.7	1321 5.7 / 1944 1.8
6 TU	0135 5.3 / 0803 2.3	1414 5.2 / 2025 2.3	**21** W	0153 6.0 / 0820 1.7	1427 5.8 / 2051 1.8
7 W	0235 5.4 / 0900 2.1	1508 5.4 / 2120 2.1	**22** TH	0256 6.0 / 0922 1.6	1528 5.9 / 2153 1.6
8 TH	0326 5.6 / 0949 1.9	1554 5.7 / 2208 1.8	**23** F	0356 6.1 / 1019 1.5	1625 6.1 / 2248 1.5
9 F	0412 5.9 / 1033 1.7	1636 6.0 / 2252 1.6	**24** SA	0452 6.2 / 1114 1.4	1716 6.3 / 2339 1.3
10 SA	0454 6.1 / 1115 1.4	1717 6.3 / 2335 1.4	**25** SU	0542 6.3 / 1157 1.3	1803 6.5 ●
11 SU	0536 6.3 / 1156 1.3	1757 6.5 ○	**26** M	0026 1.3 / 0628 6.3	1240 1.3 / 1846 6.5
12 M	0017 1.2 / 0618 6.4	1237 1.2 / 1839 6.6	**27** TU	0109 1.2 / 0710 6.3	1321 1.3 / 1926 6.5
13 TU	0101 1.1 / 0701 6.5	1319 1.1 / 1922 6.7	**28** W	0149 1.3 / 0750 6.2	1359 1.4 / 2005 6.4
14 W	0145 1.0 / 0746 6.5	1403 1.2 / 2008 6.7	**29** TH	0227 1.4 / 0827 6.1	1435 1.5 / 2042 6.3
15 TH	0231 1.0 / 0833 6.4	1448 1.3 / 2056 6.6	**30** F	0303 1.5 / 0904 5.9	1510 1.7 / 2118 6.1

JULY

Day	Time m	Time m	Day	Time m	Time m
1 SA	0338 1.7 / 0940 5.7	1546 1.8 / 2156 5.9	**16** SU	0356 0.9 / 1002 6.4	1613 1.1 / 2222 6.7
2 SU	0415 1.9 / 1019 5.5	1625 2.0 / 2236 5.7	**17** M	0444 1.2 / 1046 6.1	1703 1.4 / 2314 6.3 ◑
3 M	0457 2.1 / 1102 5.3	1711 2.2 / 2322 5.5 ◑	**18** TU	0536 1.5 / 1139 5.8	1759 1.8
4 TU	0546 2.3 / 1152 5.2	1807 2.4	**19** W	0011 6.0 / 0634 1.9	1242 5.6 / 1906 2.0
5 W	0016 5.3 / 0646 2.4	1254 5.1 / 1913 2.5	**20** TH	0118 5.7 / 0744 2.1	1354 5.4 / 2024 2.2
6 TH	0121 5.2 / 0752 2.4	1403 5.2 / 2022 2.4	**21** F	0231 5.5 / 0859 2.1	1508 5.5 / 2139 2.1
7 F	0230 5.3 / 0858 2.2	1507 5.4 / 2126 2.2	**22** SA	0343 5.6 / 1006 2.0	1615 5.8 / 2242 1.8
8 SA	0332 5.5 / 0957 2.0	1603 5.8 / 2223 1.9	**23** SU	0446 5.8 / 1101 1.8	1710 6.1 / 2334 1.6
9 SU	0427 5.8 / 1049 1.7	1653 6.1 / 2315 1.5	**24** M	0536 6.0 / 1149 1.6	1756 6.3
10 M	0517 6.2 / 1137 1.4	1741 6.5 ●	**25** TU	0019 1.4 / 0619 6.2	1229 1.4 / 1835 6.5 ●
11 TU	0003 1.2 / 0605 6.4	1224 1.1 / 1827 6.8 ○	**26** W	0058 1.3 / 0657 6.3	1306 1.3 / 1912 6.6
12 W	0051 0.9 / 0653 6.6	1310 0.9 / 1914 7.0	**27** TH	0133 1.2 / 0732 6.3	1340 1.2 / 1945 6.6
13 TH	0138 0.7 / 0739 6.7	1355 0.8 / 2000 7.1	**28** F	0205 1.2 / 0804 6.3	1412 1.3 / 2018 6.5
14 F	0224 0.6 / 0825 6.8	1441 0.8 / 2047 7.0	**29** SA	0236 1.3 / 0836 6.2	1443 1.4 / 2049 6.4
15 SA	0310 0.7 / 0911 6.6	1526 0.9 / 2134 6.9	**30** SU	0305 1.4 / 0906 6.1	1513 1.5 / 2120 6.2
			31 M	0335 1.6 / 0938 5.9	1545 1.7 / 2153 6.0

AUGUST

Day	Time m	Time m	Day	Time m	Time m
1 TU	0408 1.8 / 1012 5.6	1620 2.0 / 2229 5.7	**16** W	0458 1.7 / 1102 5.8	1722 1.9 / 2335 5.7 ◑
2 W	0445 2.1 / 1053 5.4	1703 2.3 / 2313 5.4 ◑	**17** TH	0554 2.2 / 1203 5.4	1832 2.4
3 TH	0533 2.4 / 1145 5.1	1802 2.6	**18** F	0045 5.3 / 0712 2.5	1328 5.2 / 2010 2.5
4 F	0013 5.1 / 0642 2.6	1259 5.0 / 1927 2.6	**19** SA	0217 5.1 / 0847 2.5	1501 5.3 / 2139 2.3
5 SA	0135 5.1 / 0813 2.6	1426 5.2 / 2054 2.4	**20** SU	0342 5.3 / 1002 2.2	1612 5.7 / 2242 2.0
6 SU	0301 5.3 / 0931 2.2	1538 5.6 / 2204 2.0	**21** M	0441 5.7 / 1055 1.9	1702 6.1 / 2328 1.6
7 M	0409 5.7 / 1032 1.8	1637 6.1 / 2300 1.5	**22** TU	0526 6.1 / 1137 1.6	1742 6.4
8 TU	0505 6.2 / 1123 1.3	1727 6.6 / 2351 1.0	**23** W	0005 1.3 / 0603 6.3	1213 1.3 / 1817 6.6 ●
9 W	0554 6.6 / 1211 0.9	1815 7.0 ○	**24** TH	0038 1.2 / 0636 6.5	1245 1.2 / 1849 6.6
10 TH	0038 0.6 / 0640 6.9	1256 0.6 / 1900 7.3	**25** F	0108 1.1 / 0707 6.5	1315 1.1 / 1919 6.7
11 F	0123 0.3 / 0724 7.1	1340 0.4 / 1944 7.5	**26** SA	0137 1.0 / 0736 6.6	1344 1.1 / 1948 6.7
12 SA	0207 0.2 / 0807 7.2	1423 0.4 / 2028 7.4	**27** SU	0204 1.1 / 0804 6.5	1412 1.1 / 2016 6.6
13 SU	0250 0.4 / 0849 7.0	1505 0.6 / 2111 7.2	**28** M	0231 1.2 / 0831 6.4	1440 1.3 / 2044 6.4
14 M	0331 0.7 / 0931 6.7	1546 0.9 / 2155 6.8	**29** TU	0258 1.4 / 0859 6.2	1509 1.6 / 2113 6.2
15 TU	0413 1.1 / 1014 6.3	1630 1.4 / 2241 6.3	**30** W	0326 1.7 / 0929 5.9	1540 1.9 / 2145 5.8
			31 TH	0358 2.1 / 1005 5.6	1617 2.4 / 2225 5.5 ◐

Chart Datum: 3·71 metres below Ordnance Datum (Newlyn)

WALES – MILFORD HAVEN

LAT 51°42'N   LONG 5°03'W

TIMES AND HEIGHTS OF HIGH AND LOW WATERS

2006

SEPTEMBER

Day	Time m	Time m	Time m	Time m		Day	Time m	Time m	Time m	Time m
1 F	0439 2.4	1053 5.3	1711 2.6	2323 5.1		**16** SA	0019 5.0	0648 2.9	1309 5.0	2006 2.8
2 SA	0544 2.7	1209 5.0	1844 2.8			**17** SU	0209 4.9	0839 2.8	1453 5.2	2134 2.4
3 SU	0055 4.9	0741 2.8	1356 5.1	2034 2.5		**18** M	0334 5.3	0951 2.4	1557 5.7	2228 2.0
4 M	0243 5.1	0924 2.4	1521 5.6	2149 2.0		**19** TU	0425 5.7	1038 1.9	1642 6.1	2307 1.6
5 TU	0356 5.7	1016 1.8	1620 6.2	2245 1.3		**20** W	0504 6.1	1115 1.6	1719 6.5	2340 1.3
6 W	0450 6.3	1107 1.2	1710 6.9	2334 0.8		**21** TH	0538 6.4	1147 1.3	1751 6.7	
7 TH ○	0536 6.9	1153 0.7	1756 7.4			**22** F	0010 1.1	0608 6.6	1218 1.1	1821 6.8
8 F	0018 0.3	0620 7.2	1237 0.4	1839 7.7		**23** SA	0038 1.0	0637 6.7	1246 1.0	1849 6.8
9 SA	0102 0.1	0701 7.4	1319 0.2	1922 7.8		**24** SU	0105 1.0	0704 6.7	1314 1.0	1917 6.8
10 SU	0143 0.1	0742 7.4	1359 0.3	2003 7.6		**25** M	0132 1.1	0731 6.7	1342 1.1	1944 6.7
11 M	0223 0.3	0822 7.2	1439 0.5	2044 7.3		**26** TU	0159 1.2	0758 6.6	1410 1.3	2011 6.5
12 TU	0302 0.7	0902 6.8	1519 1.0	2126 6.8		**27** W	0226 1.4	0826 6.4	1439 1.5	2040 6.3
13 W	0341 1.3	0942 6.1	1601 1.6	2210 6.1		**28** TH	0254 1.7	0857 6.1	1511 1.9	2113 5.9
14 TH ☽	0423 1.9	1029 5.8	1651 2.2	2302 5.5		**29** F	0325 2.1	0933 5.7	1550 2.3	2155 5.5
15 F	0517 2.5	1130 5.3	1808 2.7			**30** SA ☽	0408 2.5	1024 5.4	1647 2.6	2257 5.1

OCTOBER

Day	Time m	Time m	Time m	Time m		Day	Time m	Time m	Time m	Time m
1 SU	0517 2.8	1145 5.1	1827 2.8			**16** M	0142 4.9	0809 2.9	1420 5.3	2102 2.5
2 M	0037 4.9	0722 2.8	1335 5.2	2017 2.5		**17** TU	0302 5.2	0918 2.5	1524 5.7	2154 2.1
3 TU	0226 5.2	0854 2.4	1459 5.8	2128 1.8		**18** W	0353 5.7	1005 2.1	1608 6.1	2233 1.7
4 W	0335 5.9	0955 1.7	1558 6.4	2223 1.2		**19** TH	0431 6.1	1042 1.7	1645 6.4	2306 1.5
5 TH	0427 6.5	1044 1.1	1646 7.0	2310 0.7		**20** F	0505 6.4	1115 1.4	1718 6.6	2337 1.3
6 F	0512 7.0	1129 0.6	1732 7.5	2354 0.3		**21** SA	0536 6.6	1146 1.3	1749 6.7	
7 SA ○	0555 7.4	1212 0.3	1815 7.7			**22** SU ●	0006 1.2	0605 6.7	1217 1.2	1818 6.8
8 SU	0036 0.2	0636 7.5	1254 0.3	1857 7.7		**23** M	0035 1.1	0633 6.8	1246 1.1	1847 6.8
9 M	0117 0.3	0716 7.5	1335 0.4	1938 7.5		**24** TU	0103 1.2	0702 6.7	1316 1.2	1916 6.7
10 TU	0156 0.5	0756 7.2	1415 0.7	2019 7.1		**25** W	0132 1.3	0732 6.7	1348 1.4	1947 6.5
11 W	0235 1.0	0835 6.8	1456 1.2	2100 6.6		**26** TH	0202 1.5	0804 6.5	1421 1.6	2020 6.3
12 TH	0314 1.5	0917 6.3	1539 1.8	2145 5.9		**27** F	0234 1.8	0838 6.2	1457 1.9	2058 5.9
13 F	0356 2.1	1004 5.8	1630 2.3	2239 5.3		**28** SA	0312 2.1	0921 5.9	1543 2.2	2146 5.6
14 SA	0450 2.7	1106 5.3	1750 2.8	2356 4.9		**29** SU ☽	0401 2.4	1017 5.6	1646 2.5	2254 5.2
15 SU	0622 3.0	1242 5.1	1942 2.8			**30** M	0514 2.7	1138 5.4	1818 2.5	
						31 TU	0025 5.2	0700 2.6	1311 5.5	1950 2.6

NOVEMBER

Day	Time m	Time m	Time m	Time m		Day	Time m	Time m	Time m	Time m
1 W	0157 5.4	0823 2.2	1428 6.0	2058 1.7		**16** TH	0302 5.4	0916 2.3	1521 5.8	2147 2.0
2 TH	0304 6.0	0925 1.7	1528 6.5	2154 1.3		**17** F	0348 5.8	1000 2.0	1603 6.1	2226 1.8
3 F	0358 6.5	1017 1.2	1619 7.0	2243 0.9		**18** SA	0426 6.1	1038 1.7	1641 6.3	2301 1.6
4 SA	0445 6.9	1104 0.8	1706 7.3	2328 0.6		**19** SU	0501 6.3	1114 1.5	1716 6.5	2334 1.4
5 SU ○	0529 7.2	1149 0.6	1751 7.4			**20** M ●	0534 6.5	1148 1.4	1749 6.6	
6 M	0011 0.5	0611 7.3	1232 0.6	1834 7.4		**21** TU	0006 1.3	0607 6.7	1223 1.3	1823 6.6
7 TU	0053 0.6	0653 7.3	1315 0.7	1917 7.2		**22** W	0040 1.3	0640 6.7	1258 1.3	1857 6.6
8 W	0134 0.9	0735 7.1	1358 1.0	2000 6.8		**23** TH	0114 1.4	0715 6.7	1335 1.4	1934 6.5
9 TH	0214 1.2	0817 6.7	1440 1.4	2043 6.4		**24** F	0150 1.5	0752 6.6	1413 1.5	2013 6.3
10 F	0255 1.7	0900 6.3	1525 1.8	2128 5.9		**25** SA	0228 1.7	0834 6.4	1456 1.7	2057 6.1
11 SA	0338 2.2	0947 5.9	1616 2.3	2220 5.4		**26** SU	0312 1.9	0922 6.2	1546 1.9	2149 5.8
12 SU	0429 2.6	1044 5.5	1721 2.6	2323 5.1		**27** M	0404 2.1	1019 6.0	1646 2.0	2251 5.6
13 M	0541 2.8	1157 5.3	1844 2.7			**28** TU ☽	0509 2.3	1126 5.8	1758 2.1	
14 TU	0045 5.0	0707 2.9	1321 5.3	2002 2.6		**29** W	0002 5.5	0628 2.3	1239 5.9	1913 2.0
15 W	0204 5.1	0821 2.6	1429 5.5	2101 2.3		**30** TH	0118 5.6	0744 2.1	1350 6.1	2021 1.8

DECEMBER

Day	Time m	Time m	Time m	Time m		Day	Time m	Time m	Time m	Time m
1 F	0226 5.9	0850 1.8	1454 6.3	2122 1.5		**16** SA	0252 5.4	0906 2.4	1513 5.6	2138 2.2
2 SA	0325 6.2	0948 1.5	1551 6.6	2216 1.3		**17** SU	0343 5.7	0958 2.1	1602 5.8	2224 2.0
3 SU	0418 6.6	1041 1.2	1643 6.8	2305 1.1		**18** M	0427 6.0	1043 1.9	1645 6.1	2305 1.7
4 M	0508 6.8	1130 1.1	1733 6.9	2352 1.0		**19** TU	0508 6.3	1125 1.7	1726 6.3	2345 1.5
5 TU ○	0555 6.9	1217 1.0	1820 6.9			**20** W ●	0547 6.5	1206 1.4	1807 6.4	
6 W	0036 1.0	0639 7.0	1303 1.0	1905 6.8		**21** TH	0024 1.4	0626 6.7	1247 1.3	1847 6.5
7 TH	0119 1.1	0723 6.9	1347 1.2	1949 6.6		**22** F	0103 1.3	0706 6.8	1328 1.2	1928 6.6
8 F	0201 1.4	0805 6.7	1430 1.4	2031 6.3		**23** SA	0144 1.3	0748 6.8	1411 1.2	2011 6.5
9 SA	0241 1.6	0848 6.4	1513 1.7	2113 6.0		**24** SU	0226 1.3	0833 6.8	1455 1.2	2057 6.4
10 SU	0322 1.9	0930 6.1	1556 2.0	2156 5.7		**25** M	0310 1.4	0919 6.6	1542 1.3	2144 6.3
11 M	0404 2.2	1015 5.8	1642 2.3	2243 5.4		**26** TU	0358 1.6	1009 6.5	1632 1.5	2235 6.0
12 TU ☽	0453 2.5	1106 5.6	1736 2.5	2338 5.2		**27** W ☽	0450 1.8	1104 6.3	1728 1.7	2332 5.8
13 W	0552 2.6	1204 5.4	1838 2.6			**28** TH	0551 1.9	1204 6.1	1831 1.9	
14 TH	0043 5.1	0659 2.7	1312 5.3	1943 2.5		**29** F	0036 5.7	0659 2.1	1311 6.0	1939 2.0
15 F	0153 5.2	0806 2.6	1417 5.4	2045 2.4		**30** SA	0146 5.7	0812 2.1	1420 5.9	2049 1.9
						31 SU	0255 5.8	0923 1.9	1527 6.0	2154 1.8

Chart Datum: 3·71 metres below Ordnance Datum (Newlyn)

TIDES

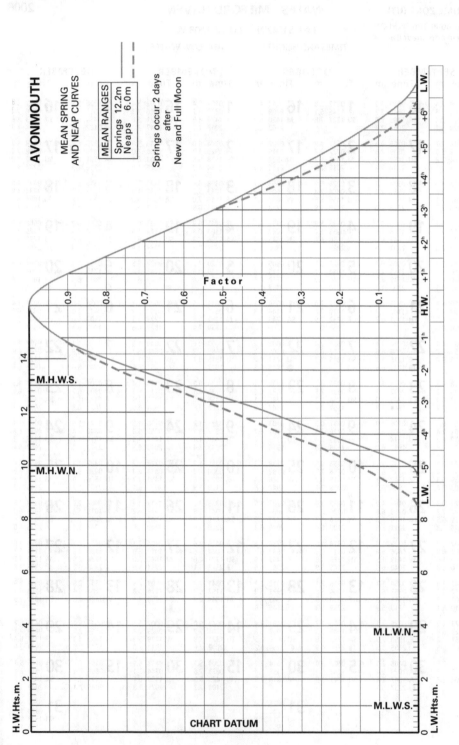

AVONMOUTH

MEAN SPRING
AND NEAP CURVES

MEAN RANGES
Springs 12.2m
Neaps 6.0m

Springs occur 2 days
after
New and Full Moon

Factor

0.9 0.8 0.7 0.6 0.5 0.4 0.3 0.2 0.1

H.W.Hts.m.

M.H.W.S.

M.H.W.N.

M.L.W.N.

M.L.W.S.

CHART DATUM

L.W.Hts.m.

L.W.

H.W.

L.W.

ENGLAND – AVONMOUTH

LAT 51°30′N   LONG 2°44′W

TIMES AND HEIGHTS OF HIGH AND LOW WATERS

2006

JANUARY

Day				
1 SU	0212 1.7	0749 13.2	1439 1.4	2017 13.0
2 M	0301 1.5	0837 13.3	1529 1.3	2105 13.1
3 TU	0347 1.5	0924 13.3	1614 1.3	2151 13.0
4 W	0429 1.6	1010 13.1	1657 1.6	2235 12.7
5 TH	0509 1.8	1056 12.8	1737 1.6	2320 12.2
6 F ◐	0548 2.1	1144 12.2	1817 2.1	
7 SA	0008 11.6	0630 2.6	1219 11.6	1902 2.6
8 SU	0103 11.0	0720 3.1	1343 11.0	1956 3.1
9 M	0211 10.5	0826 3.6	1453 10.7	2107 3.5
10 TU	0323 10.4	0951 3.7	1600 10.9	2225 3.4
11 W	0428 10.7	1103 3.3	1701 11.0	2330 3.0
12 TH	0525 11.2	1202 2.8	1756 11.4	
13 F	0024 2.5	0615 11.7	1254 2.4	1844 11.8
14 SA ○	0115 2.1	0701 12.1	1344 2.1	1929 12.0
15 SU	0202 2.0	0743 12.3	1429 2.1	2010 12.1
16 M	0244 1.9	0822 12.3	1510 2.2	2046 12.0
17 TU	0321 2.1	0857 12.2	1542 2.4	2118 11.8
18 W	0349 2.3	0928 12.0	1607 2.5	2147 11.7
19 TH	0411 2.4	0957 11.8	1628 2.6	2215 11.4
20 F	0435 2.4	1025 11.5	1652 2.6	2243 11.2
21 SA	0504 2.5	1056 11.3	1724 2.7	2317 10.9
22 SU ◑	0540 2.8	1135 10.9	1802 3.0	
23 M	0000 10.5	0623 3.3	1225 10.4	1849 3.5
24 TU	0056 10.1	0721 3.7	1331 10.1	1956 3.9
25 W	0211 9.8	0847 4.0	1454 10.0	2133 3.9
26 TH	0343 10.2	1019 3.6	1620 10.5	2300 3.3
27 F	0458 11.0	1134 2.8	1729 11.4	
28 SA	0008 2.6	0557 12.0	1238 2.1	1826 12.3
29 SU ●	0109 1.9	0650 12.9	1339 1.5	1919 13.0
30 M	0207 1.4	0740 13.5	1435 1.0	2008 13.5
31 TU	0259 1.0	0828 13.9	1525 0.6	2054 13.7

FEBRUARY

Day				
1 W	0344 0.8	0913 14.1	1608 0.5	2137 13.8
2 TH	0423 0.8	0955 14.0	1645 0.6	2217 13.5
3 F	0456 1.0	1035 13.5	1716 1.1	2254 12.9
4 SA	0525 1.5	1115 12.8	1745 1.7	2332 12.1
5 SU ◐	0553 2.2	1156 11.8	1816 2.4	
6 M	0013 11.1	0627 2.9	1247 10.7	1856 3.3
7 TU	0107 10.2	0716 3.8	1402 9.9	1955 4.0
8 W	0237 9.6	0836 4.4	1531 9.7	2138 4.3
9 TH	0401 9.8	1039 4.1	1643 10.1	2306 3.7
10 F	0508 10.5	1145 3.3	1742 10.8	
11 SA	0006 2.9	0602 11.3	1239 2.6	1831 11.5
12 SU	0058 2.2	0648 12.0	1328 2.0	1915 12.0
13 M ○	0146 1.8	0728 12.4	1414 1.8	1953 12.3
14 TU	0230 1.6	0805 12.6	1456 1.8	2027 12.3
15 W	0309 1.7	0838 12.5	1531 1.9	2057 12.2
16 TH	0340 1.9	0907 12.3	1556 2.2	2124 12.1
17 F	0359 2.1	0933 12.2	1610 2.3	2148 11.9
18 SA	0414 2.1	0958 12.0	1625 2.4	2213 11.8
19 SU	0436 2.1	1026 11.8	1650 2.3	2243 11.5
20 M	0506 2.3	1100 11.4	1722 2.6	2321 11.0
21 TU ◑	0542 2.8	1145 10.7	1802 3.1	
22 W	0011 10.3	0631 3.5	1246 10.0	1859 3.9
23 TH	0123 9.7	0749 4.1	1412 9.6	2039 4.3
24 F	0308 9.7	0952 3.9	1601 10.1	2243 3.7
25 SA	0442 10.7	1123 2.9	1719 11.2	2359 2.7
26 SU	0546 11.9	1230 1.9	1816 12.4	
27 M	0100 1.7	0638 13.1	1330 1.1	1906 13.3
28 TU ●	0156 1.0	0726 13.9	1423 0.5	1952 13.9

MARCH

Day				
1 W	0246 0.5	0811 14.4	1510 0.1	2035 14.2
2 TH	0329 0.2	0853 14.5	1550 0.0	2115 14.2
3 F	0405 0.3	0933 14.3	1622 0.4	2151 13.8
4 SA	0433 0.8	1009 13.7	1647 1.0	2224 13.1
5 SU	0455 1.4	1043 12.8	1708 1.7	2256 12.2
6 M ◐	0516 2.1	1118 11.6	1734 2.5	2330 11.1
7 TU	0546 2.9	1158 10.3	1809 3.4	
8 W	0014 9.9	0628 3.9	1307 9.2	1904 4.4
9 TH	0150 9.0	0744 4.7	1507 8.9	2050 4.8
10 F	0339 9.3	1024 4.4	1623 9.6	2247 4.0
11 SA	0447 10.2	1127 3.4	1722 10.6	2345 3.0
12 SU	0541 11.2	1217 2.4	1809 11.5	
13 M	0034 2.1	0624 12.0	1304 1.8	1849 12.1
14 TU ○	0122 1.6	0703 12.5	1349 1.5	1925 12.4
15 W	0206 1.4	0738 12.6	1430 1.5	1958 12.5
16 TH	0245 1.5	0810 12.6	1506 1.7	2028 12.4
17 F	0317 1.7	0839 12.4	1532 2.0	2055 12.3
18 SA	0338 1.9	0905 12.3	1545 2.2	2119 12.2
19 SU	0351 2.0	0930 12.2	1557 2.1	2145 12.0
20 M	0410 1.9	0959 12.0	1621 2.1	2216 11.7
21 TU	0439 2.1	1035 11.5	1651 2.4	2254 11.2
22 W ◑	0514 2.6	1119 10.8	1730 3.0	2344 10.4
23 TH	0601 3.3	1220 9.9	1826 3.9	
24 F	0056 9.6	0718 4.1	1352 9.4	2008 4.4
25 SA	0252 9.7	0940 3.9	1551 10.0	2233 3.6
26 SU	0426 10.8	1110 2.7	1704 11.3	2343 2.4
27 M	0528 12.1	1213 1.6	1758 12.6	
28 TU	0040 1.4	0618 13.2	1308 0.8	1845 13.5
29 W ●	0133 0.7	0704 14.0	1359 0.2	1928 14.1
30 TH	0221 0.3	0748 14.4	1444 0.0	2009 14.3
31 F	0303 0.2	0828 14.4	1522 0.2	2048 14.1

APRIL

Day				
1 SA	0339 0.4	0907 14.0	1553 0.6	2123 13.6
2 SU	0406 1.0	0942 13.3	1616 1.3	2155 12.9
3 M	0425 1.6	1015 12.3	1635 1.9	2225 11.9
4 TU	0445 2.3	1047 11.2	1700 2.7	2256 10.8
5 W ◐	0514 3.0	1124 10.0	1734 3.5	2337 9.7
6 TH	0557 4.0	1226 8.9	1828 4.5	
7 F	0114 8.9	0714 4.7	1438 8.7	2012 4.9
8 SA	0309 9.2	0948 4.5	1551 9.4	2215 4.1
9 SU	0414 10.0	1055 3.4	1648 10.4	2313 3.0
10 M	0506 11.0	1144 2.5	1734 11.3	
11 TU	0002 2.2	0549 11.8	1230 1.9	1814 12.0
12 W	0048 1.7	0628 12.2	1314 1.6	1850 12.3
13 TH ○	0132 1.5	0704 12.4	1356 1.6	1924 12.5
14 F	0212 1.5	0737 12.5	1432 1.7	1955 12.5
15 SA	0246 1.7	0810 12.4	1501 1.9	2024 12.4
16 SU	0311 1.8	0838 12.3	1519 2.1	2052 12.3
17 M	0330 1.9	0908 12.2	1537 2.0	2123 12.1
18 TU	0353 1.9	0944 12.0	1602 2.1	2158 11.8
19 W	0423 2.1	1021 11.5	1635 2.4	2240 11.2
20 TH ◑	0502 2.6	1109 10.7	1717 3.0	2333 10.5
21 F	0554 3.3	1212 10.0	1817 3.8	
22 SA	0049 9.9	0720 3.8	1346 9.7	2015 4.1
23 SU	0240 10.1	0922 3.4	1528 10.4	2207 3.3
24 M	0401 11.1	1041 2.4	1637 11.5	2313 2.2
25 TU	0501 12.2	1142 1.5	1731 12.5	
26 W	0010 1.4	0552 13.1	1237 0.9	1817 13.3
27 TH ●	0102 0.8	0638 13.7	1327 0.5	1900 13.7
28 F	0149 0.6	0721 13.9	1412 0.4	1941 13.8
29 SA	0233 0.6	0803 13.7	1451 0.7	2020 13.6
30 SU	0310 0.9	0842 13.3	1524 1.1	2056 13.1

Chart Datum: 6·50 metres below Ordnance Datum (Newlyn)

TIDES

TIME ZONE (UT)
For Summer Time add ONE hour in **non-shaded areas**

ENGLAND – AVONMOUTH

LAT 51°30′N   LONG 2°44′W

TIMES AND HEIGHTS OF HIGH AND LOW WATERS

2006

MAY

Day	Time m	Time m		Day	Time m	Time m
1 M	0340 1.4 / 0919 12.6	1549 1.7 / 2130 12.4		**16** TU	0317 1.8 / 0855 12.2	1527 2.0 / 2112 12.2
2 TU	0402 2.0 / 0954 11.8	1611 2.2 / 2202 11.6		**17** W	0349 1.9 / 0936 12.0	1559 2.2 / 2153 11.9
3 W	0425 2.5 / 1027 10.9	1638 2.8 / 2235 10.7		**18** TH	0425 2.1 / 1020 11.5	1637 2.5 / 2239 11.4
4 TH	0457 3.1 / 1105 10.0	1713 3.5 / 2318 9.9		**19** F	0509 2.5 / 1111 11.0	1724 2.9 / 2335 10.9
5 F ◐	0541 3.8 / 1202 9.2	1806 4.2		**20** SA ◐	0607 2.9 / 1212 10.6	1828 3.4
6 SA	0036 9.2 / 0649 4.3	1343 8.9 / 1929 4.5		**21** SU	0048 10.6 / 0724 3.1	1331 10.4 / 2001 3.5
7 SU	0221 9.3 / 0817 4.3	1501 9.4 / 2102 4.1		**22** M	0214 10.7 / 0847 2.8	1453 10.7 / 2127 3.0
8 M	0326 9.9 / 0946 3.7	1559 10.1 / 2219 3.4		**23** TU	0326 11.3 / 1001 2.4	1600 11.4 / 2235 2.4
9 TU	0419 10.6 / 1052 3.0	1648 10.9 / 2315 2.6		**24** W	0428 11.9 / 1104 1.9	1657 12.1 / 2334 1.8
10 W	0505 11.3 / 1143 2.4	1731 11.5		**25** TH	0522 12.5 / 1201 1.5	1747 12.6
11 TH	0004 2.1 / 0547 11.8	1231 2.0 / 1810 12.0		**26** F	0028 1.4 / 0610 12.9	1253 1.2 / 1833 12.9
12 F	0050 1.8 / 0626 12.1	1314 1.9 / 1848 12.3		**27** SA ●	0118 1.2 / 0656 13.0	1340 1.2 / 1916 13.0
13 SA ○	0132 1.7 / 0704 12.3	1354 1.8 / 1924 12.4		**28** SU	0204 1.3 / 0741 12.8	1423 1.3 / 1957 12.9
14 SU	0211 1.7 / 0741 12.3	1429 1.9 / 1959 12.5		**29** M	0246 1.5 / 0823 12.5	1501 1.6 / 2037 12.5
15 M	0246 1.7 / 0818 12.3	1459 1.9 / 2034 12.4		**30** TU	0322 1.9 / 0903 12.0	1532 2.0 / 2114 12.0
				31 W	0351 2.3 / 0941 11.5	1559 2.4 / 2150 11.5

JUNE

Day	Time m	Time m		Day	Time m	Time m
1 TH	0418 2.7 / 1016 10.9	1627 2.8 / 2226 10.9		**16** F	0437 1.8 / 1022 12.1	1650 2.1 / 2241 12.1
2 F	0449 3.0 / 1053 10.4	1702 3.1 / 2306 10.4		**17** SA	0522 1.9 / 1110 11.8	1735 2.3 / 2333 11.8
3 SA ◐	0530 3.3 / 1137 9.9	1747 3.5 / 2357 9.9		**18** SU ◐	0611 2.1 / 1202 11.4	1827 2.6
4 SU	0621 3.6 / 1233 9.6	1845 3.8		**19** M	0032 11.4 / 0705 2.3	1303 11.1 / 1928 2.8
5 M	0105 9.7 / 0722 3.7	1343 9.5 / 1953 3.8		**20** TU	0139 11.2 / 0806 2.5	1411 10.9 / 2039 3.0
6 TU	0216 9.8 / 0827 3.6	1450 9.8 / 2103 3.6		**21** W	0248 11.2 / 0914 2.7	1519 11.0 / 2153 2.9
7 W	0317 10.2 / 0935 3.3	1550 10.4 / 2211 3.2		**22** TH	0353 11.3 / 1024 2.6	1623 11.3 / 2300 2.6
8 TH	0412 10.7 / 1042 3.0	1643 11.0 / 2312 2.7		**23** F	0453 11.6 / 1127 2.4	1719 11.7 / 2359 2.2
9 F	0503 11.2 / 1141 2.5	1731 11.5		**24** SA	0547 11.8 / 1223 2.1	1810 12.0
10 SA	0006 2.2 / 0550 11.7	1233 2.2 / 1815 12.0		**25** SU ●	0052 2.0 / 0637 12.0	1315 1.9 / 1857 12.3
11 SU ○	0055 1.9 / 0635 12.0	1320 1.9 / 1858 12.4		**26** M	0143 1.9 / 0725 12.1	1403 1.8 / 1942 12.3
12 M	0142 1.7 / 0720 12.2	1405 1.8 / 1941 12.5		**27** TU	0230 1.9 / 0810 12.0	1447 1.9 / 2024 12.2
13 TU	0228 1.6 / 0805 12.4	1447 1.8 / 2024 12.6		**28** W	0313 2.1 / 0852 11.8	1524 2.1 / 2103 12.0
14 W	0312 1.6 / 0850 12.4	1528 1.9 / 2109 12.5		**29** TH	0348 2.3 / 0930 11.6	1555 2.3 / 2139 11.7
15 TH	0355 1.7 / 0936 12.3	1608 2.0 / 2154 12.4		**30** F	0416 2.5 / 1003 11.3	1622 2.5 / 2212 11.4

JULY

Day	Time m	Time m		Day	Time m	Time m
1 SA	0442 2.7 / 1034 11.0	1650 2.7 / 2245 11.0		**16** SU	0518 1.2 / 1056 12.6	1729 1.7 / 2317 12.6
2 SU ◐	0512 2.8 / 1107 10.7	1724 2.8 / 2321 10.7		**17** M	0555 1.5 / 1140 12.1	1807 2.1
3 M ◐	0548 2.9 / 1145 10.4	1804 3.1		**18** TU	0004 12.0 / 0634 2.0	1228 11.5 / 1849 2.6
4 TU	0003 10.4 / 0631 3.1	1233 10.1 / 1854 3.4		**19** W	0101 11.3 / 0720 2.7	1327 10.8 / 1944 3.2
5 W	0058 10.1 / 0725 3.4	1332 9.9 / 1958 3.7		**20** TH	0209 10.7 / 0821 3.2	1439 10.4 / 2107 3.7
6 TH	0204 10.0 / 0830 3.6	1443 10.0 / 2112 3.6		**21** F	0323 10.4 / 0945 3.5	1553 10.4 / 2233 3.5
7 F	0315 10.2 / 0946 3.4	1554 10.4 / 2226 3.2		**22** SA	0431 10.6 / 1101 3.2	1659 10.8 / 2339 3.0
8 SA	0421 10.7 / 1058 3.0	1656 11.0 / 2330 2.6		**23** SU	0533 11.0 / 1203 2.7	1756 11.4
9 SU	0521 11.3 / 1200 2.5	1751 11.7		**24** M	0036 2.5 / 0626 11.5	1258 2.3 / 1845 11.9
10 M	0028 2.1 / 0614 11.8	1256 2.1 / 1840 12.3		**25** TU ●	0129 2.1 / 0714 11.8	1349 1.9 / 1930 12.3
11 TU ○	0124 1.8 / 0706 12.3	1351 1.8 / 1929 12.8		**26** W	0218 1.9 / 0758 12.0	1436 1.8 / 2012 12.4
12 W	0219 1.5 / 0756 12.6	1443 1.6 / 2017 13.1		**27** TH	0303 1.9 / 0838 12.1	1516 1.8 / 2049 12.3
13 TH	0311 1.3 / 0844 12.8	1531 1.5 / 2103 13.2		**28** F	0340 2.0 / 0912 11.9	1549 2.0 / 2121 12.1
14 F	0358 1.1 / 0930 13.0	1614 1.4 / 2148 13.2		**29** SA	0409 2.2 / 0941 11.7	1613 2.2 / 2150 11.9
15 SA	0440 1.1 / 1014 12.9	1653 1.4 / 2232 13.0		**30** SU	0428 2.4 / 1008 11.5	1632 2.3 / 2216 11.6
				31 M	0447 2.5 / 1034 11.3	1655 2.4 / 2244 11.3

AUGUST

Day	Time m	Time m		Day	Time m	Time m
1 TU	0512 2.5 / 1104 11.0	1725 2.7 / 2316 10.9		**16** W ◐	0557 2.2 / 1150 11.4	1807 2.8
2 W ◐	0545 2.8 / 1140 10.5	1803 3.1 / 2359 10.4		**17** TH	0019 10.9 / 0633 3.1	1241 10.4 / 1851 3.7
3 TH	0627 3.3 / 1230 10.0	1855 3.7		**18** F	0130 9.9 / 0727 3.9	1405 9.6 / 2010 4.5
4 F	0059 9.9 / 0726 3.8	1339 9.7 / 2015 4.0		**19** SA	0303 9.5 / 0912 4.4	1535 9.7 / 2222 4.2
5 SA	0221 9.7 / 0855 4.0	1511 9.8 / 2149 3.8		**20** SU	0419 9.9 / 1047 3.8	1647 10.4 / 2329 3.3
6 SU	0350 10.1 / 1027 3.6	1631 10.6 / 2307 3.0		**21** M	0522 10.7 / 1149 2.9	1744 11.3
7 M	0503 10.9 / 1140 2.8	1734 11.6		**22** TU	0023 2.5 / 0613 11.5	1242 2.2 / 1832 12.1
8 TU	0013 2.2 / 0602 11.8	1244 2.2 / 1827 12.5		**23** W ●	0112 1.9 / 0658 12.1	1331 1.7 / 1914 12.6
9 W ○	0115 1.6 / 0654 12.6	1343 1.7 / 1917 13.2		**24** TH	0159 1.5 / 0738 12.4	1416 1.4 / 1951 12.7
10 TH	0212 1.1 / 0744 13.1	1437 1.2 / 2004 13.7		**25** F	0243 1.5 / 0814 12.4	1457 1.5 / 2025 12.7
11 F	0304 0.7 / 0831 13.5	1525 0.9 / 2049 14.0		**26** SA	0320 1.7 / 0845 12.3	1531 1.7 / 2055 12.4
12 SA	0349 0.5 / 0914 13.6	1606 0.8 / 2132 13.9		**27** SU	0349 2.0 / 0912 12.1	1555 2.1 / 2121 12.2
13 SU	0428 0.6 / 0955 13.5	1640 1.0 / 2212 13.6		**28** M	0406 2.3 / 0936 11.8	1608 2.3 / 2144 11.9
14 M	0500 0.9 / 1033 13.1	1709 1.4 / 2251 13.0		**29** TU	0416 2.4 / 0959 11.6	1624 2.4 / 2208 11.6
15 TU	0528 1.5 / 1110 12.4	1736 2.0 / 2332 12.0		**30** W	0434 2.5 / 1025 11.3	1649 2.5 / 2238 11.2
				31 TH ◑	0502 2.7 / 1059 10.8	1721 3.0 / 2318 10.6

Chart Datum: 6·50 metres below Ordnance Datum (Newlyn)

ENGLAND – AVONMOUTH

LAT 51°30′N   LONG 2°44′W

TIMES AND HEIGHTS OF HIGH AND LOW WATERS

TIME ZONE (UT)
For Summer Time add ONE hour in **non-shaded areas**

SEPTEMBER

Time m	Time m
1 0538 3.2 / 1145 10.2 / F 1803 3.6	**16** 0054 9.2 / 0643 4.5 / SA 1345 9.1 / 1928 5.0
2 0014 9.8 / 0629 3.9 / SA 1252 9.5 / 1914 4.3	**17** 0250 9.0 / 0858 4.6 / SU 1521 9.4 / 2215 4.5
3 0139 9.3 / 0800 4.5 / SU 1439 9.5 / 2124 4.2	**18** 0404 9.6 / 1034 4.0 / M 1628 10.3 / 2313 3.3
4 0333 9.7 / 1010 4.0 / M 1616 10.4 / 2258 3.2	**19** 0502 10.6 / 1129 2.9 / TU 1722 11.4
5 0451 10.9 / 1131 2.9 / TU 1720 11.7	**20** 0000 2.3 / 0550 11.6 / W 1218 2.0 / 1807 12.2
6 0005 2.1 / 0549 12.0 / W 1233 2.0 / 1812 12.8	**21** 0046 1.6 / 0631 12.3 / TH 1304 1.5 / 1846 12.7
7 0103 1.3 / 0639 13.0 / TH 1329 1.3 / O 1859 13.7	**22** 0131 1.3 / 0708 12.6 / F 1348 1.3 / ● 1922 12.9
8 0157 0.7 / 0725 13.7 / F 1420 0.8 / 1945 14.3	**23** 0213 1.3 / 0741 12.6 / SA 1428 1.4 / 1954 12.8
9 0245 0.3 / 0809 14.0 / SA 1506 0.5 / 2028 14.4	**24** 0250 1.6 / 0812 12.5 / SU 1503 1.7 / 2023 12.5
10 0328 0.2 / 0850 14.1 / SU 1545 0.5 / 2108 14.3	**25** 0319 2.0 / 0839 12.2 / M 1527 2.1 / 2049 12.3
11 0404 0.5 / 0928 13.8 / M 1617 0.9 / 2147 13.8	**26** 0336 2.3 / 0903 12.0 / TU 1540 2.3 / 2112 12.0
12 0432 1.1 / 1004 13.2 / TU 1641 1.6 / 2223 12.9	**27** 0344 2.4 / 0926 11.8 / W 1555 2.4 / 2138 11.8
13 0454 1.8 / 1038 12.3 / W 1702 2.3 / 2259 11.7	**28** 0403 2.4 / 0954 11.5 / TH 1619 2.5 / 2210 11.3
14 0518 2.6 / 1114 11.2 / TH 1729 3.1 / ◐ 2341 10.4	**29** 0431 2.6 / 1030 11.0 / F 1651 2.9 / 2251 10.6
15 0551 3.5 / 1200 10.0 / F 1810 4.1	**30** 0506 3.2 / 1117 10.3 / SA 1733 3.6 / ◑ 2348 9.8

OCTOBER

Time m	Time m
1 0555 4.0 / 1225 9.5 / SU 1841 4.4	**16** 0226 8.9 / 0808 5.1 / M 1455 9.4 / 2145 4.6
2 0115 9.2 / 0722 4.7 / M 1420 9.5 / 2108 4.3	**17** 0333 9.6 / 1004 4.1 / TU 1556 10.3 / 2241 3.5
3 0320 9.8 / 0959 4.1 / TU 1558 10.6 / 2243 3.1	**18** 0428 10.5 / 1057 3.1 / W 1648 11.2 / 2327 2.5
4 0434 11.0 / 1114 2.8 / W 1659 11.9 / 2345 2.0	**19** 0515 11.5 / 1144 2.2 / TH 1732 12.0
5 0529 12.3 / 1211 1.8 / TH 1750 13.1	**20** 0012 1.9 / 0555 12.1 / F 1229 1.7 / 1811 12.5
6 0039 1.1 / 0616 13.3 / F 1304 1.1 / 1836 13.9	**21** 0055 1.5 / 0632 12.5 / SA 1312 1.5 / 1847 12.7
7 0130 0.5 / 0700 13.9 / SA 1353 0.7 / O 1920 14.4	**22** 0136 1.5 / 0706 12.6 / SU 1352 1.5 / ● 1920 12.7
8 0217 0.3 / 0742 14.2 / SU 1438 0.5 / 2002 14.4	**23** 0213 1.7 / 0737 12.5 / M 1428 1.8 / 1952 12.5
9 0259 0.4 / 0820 14.1 / M 1517 0.7 / 2043 14.1	**24** 0244 2.0 / 0807 12.4 / TU 1456 2.0 / 2021 12.3
10 0334 0.8 / 0900 13.7 / TU 1549 1.2 / 2121 13.5	**25** 0306 2.3 / 0834 12.2 / W 1516 2.2 / 2049 12.1
11 0401 1.4 / 0936 13.0 / W 1614 1.8 / 2158 12.5	**26** 0321 2.4 / 0903 12.0 / TH 1536 2.4 / 2119 11.8
12 0423 2.1 / 1010 12.0 / TH 1635 2.6 / 2233 11.3	**27** 0344 2.5 / 0936 11.6 / F 1604 2.5 / 2156 11.4
13 0447 2.9 / 1046 10.9 / F 1703 3.4 / 2313 10.1	**28** 0414 2.7 / 1015 11.1 / SA 1639 2.9 / 2240 10.8
14 0521 3.8 / 1131 9.8 / SA 1744 4.3	**29** 0453 3.2 / 1105 10.5 / SU 1726 3.5 / ◐ 2338 10.0
15 0025 9.0 / 0613 4.7 / SU 1325 9.1 / 1903 5.1	**30** 0546 3.9 / 1214 9.9 / M 1838 4.1
	31 0101 9.6 / 0713 4.4 / TU 1358 10.0 / 2039 3.9

NOVEMBER

Time m	Time m
1 0250 10.1 / 0925 3.9 / W 1527 10.8 / 2208 3.0	**16** 0342 10.2 / 1001 3.6 / TH 1603 10.8 / 2237 3.2
2 0403 11.1 / 1040 2.8 / TH 1630 11.9 / 2312 2.1	**17** 0431 10.9 / 1057 2.9 / F 1649 11.4 / 2326 2.6
3 0500 12.2 / 1139 1.9 / F 1722 12.9	**18** 0515 11.6 / 1145 2.3 / SA 1732 11.9
4 0007 1.3 / 0548 13.1 / SA 1232 1.3 / 1810 13.6	**19** 0012 2.1 / 0554 12.1 / SU 1230 2.0 / 1811 12.2
5 0058 0.8 / 0632 13.6 / SU 1321 0.9 / O 1855 14.0	**20** 0055 1.9 / 0631 12.3 / M 1312 1.8 / ● 1848 12.4
6 0145 0.7 / 0715 13.8 / M 1407 0.9 / 1938 13.9	**21** 0135 1.9 / 0707 12.5 / TU 1352 1.9 / 1924 12.4
7 0228 0.8 / 0756 13.7 / TU 1449 1.1 / 2020 13.6	**22** 0211 2.0 / 0742 12.4 / W 1428 2.0 / 2000 12.3
8 0305 1.2 / 0836 13.3 / W 1525 1.5 / 2101 12.9	**23** 0242 2.1 / 0816 12.3 / TH 1500 2.1 / 2036 12.2
9 0337 1.7 / 0915 12.7 / TH 1554 2.1 / 2140 12.1	**24** 0310 2.3 / 0852 12.2 / F 1531 2.3 / 2114 11.9
10 0403 2.4 / 0952 11.9 / F 1620 2.8 / 2218 11.2	**25** 0340 2.4 / 0931 11.9 / SA 1605 2.4 / 2155 11.6
11 0430 3.0 / 1030 11.0 / SA 1650 3.4 / 2259 10.2	**26** 0415 2.6 / 1014 11.6 / SU 1645 2.7 / 2241 11.2
12 0505 3.7 / 1116 10.1 / SU 1733 4.0 / ◐ 2356 9.4	**27** 0457 3.0 / 1105 11.1 / M 1735 3.1 / 2336 10.8
13 0555 4.3 / 1235 9.5 / M 1836 4.5	**28** 0551 3.4 / 1207 10.8 / TU 1840 3.3 / ◐
14 0133 9.1 / 0709 4.6 / TU 1408 9.6 / 2002 4.5	**29** 0043 10.4 / 0703 3.7 / W 1325 10.7 / 1959 3.3
15 0246 9.5 / 0843 4.4 / W 1510 10.1 / 2137 4.0	**30** 0205 10.5 / 0835 3.5 / TH 1446 11.0 / 2120 3.0

DECEMBER

Time m	Time m
1 0322 11.0 / 0955 3.1 / F 1553 11.6 / 2231 2.5	**16** 0331 10.1 / 0943 3.6 / SA 1556 10.5 / 2220 3.4
2 0425 11.7 / 1102 2.9 / SA 1652 12.3 / 2332 2.0	**17** 0427 10.7 / 1050 3.1 / SU 1648 11.0 / 2322 2.9
3 0519 12.3 / 1159 1.9 / SU 1744 12.8	**18** 0516 11.3 / 1145 2.6 / M 1736 11.5
4 0026 1.6 / 0607 12.9 / M 1252 1.6 / 1832 13.1	**19** 0014 2.4 / 0600 11.9 / TU 1235 2.2 / 1820 11.9
5 0116 1.4 / 0653 13.1 / TU 1341 1.5 / O 1919 13.1	**20** 0101 2.1 / 0642 12.3 / W 1322 2.0 / ● 1904 12.2
6 0203 1.4 / 0737 13.1 / W 1428 1.6 / 2004 12.9	**21** 0146 2.0 / 0724 12.5 / TH 1408 1.9 / 1947 12.4
7 0245 1.6 / 0820 12.9 / TH 1510 1.9 / 2048 12.5	**22** 0228 2.0 / 0806 12.6 / F 1453 1.9 / 2030 12.4
8 0323 2.0 / 0902 12.5 / F 1546 2.3 / 2129 12.0	**23** 0309 2.0 / 0848 12.6 / SA 1535 1.9 / 2113 12.4
9 0354 2.4 / 0941 12.0 / SA 1616 2.7 / 2208 11.4	**24** 0347 2.1 / 0931 12.5 / SU 1615 2.0 / 2156 12.3
10 0423 2.8 / 1020 11.4 / SU 1645 3.1 / 2245 10.8	**25** 0425 2.2 / 1014 12.4 / M 1655 2.1 / 2239 12.1
11 0455 3.1 / 1059 10.8 / M 1721 3.4 / 2324 10.3	**26** 0505 2.3 / 1100 12.1 / TU 1737 2.2 / 2325 11.7
12 0535 3.5 / 1145 10.3 / TU 1804 3.6 / ◑	**27** 0549 2.6 / 1150 11.8 / W 1824 2.5
13 0013 9.8 / 0638 2.9 / W 1244 10.0 / 1857 3.9	**28** 0016 11.3 / 0638 2.9 / TH 1250 11.3 / 1917 2.8
14 0117 9.6 / 0724 4.0 / TH 1353 9.9 / 1959 3.9	**29** 0118 10.9 / 0740 3.2 / F 1400 11.0 / 2024 3.1
15 0228 9.7 / 0832 3.9 / F 1458 10.1 / 2108 3.8	**30** 0233 10.7 / 0902 3.4 / SA 1514 11.0 / 2146 3.2
	31 0348 10.9 / 1025 3.3 / SU 1623 11.2 / 2259 2.9

Chart Datum: 6·50 metres below Ordnance Datum (Newlyn)

TIDES

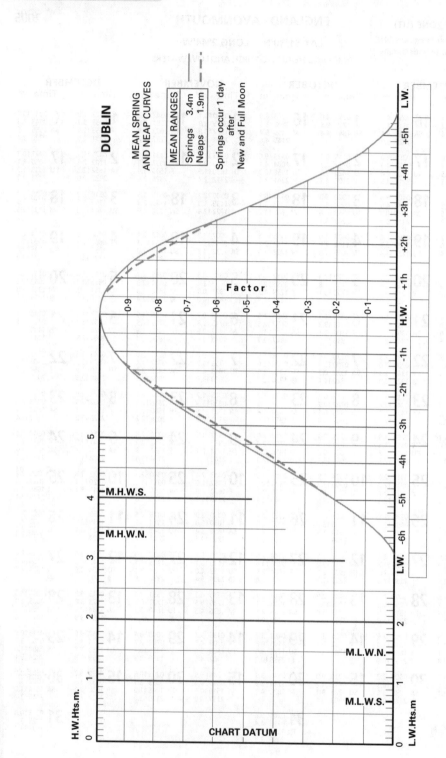

DUBLIN

MEAN SPRING
AND NEAP CURVES

MEAN RANGES	
Springs	3.4m
Neaps	1.9m

Springs occur 1 day
after
New and Full Moon

IRELAND – DUBLIN (NORTH WALL)   2006

LAT 53°21'N   LONG 6°13'W

TIMES AND HEIGHTS OF HIGH AND LOW WATERS

TIME ZONE (UT)
For Summer Time add ONE hour in **non-shaded areas**

JANUARY

Day	Times & heights (m)	Day	Times & heights (m)
1 SU	0526 0.8 · 1203 4.2 · 1755 0.6	16 M	0034 3.7 · 0612 1.1 · 1246 4.0 · 1844 0.9
2 M	0040 4.0 · 0610 0.8 · 1250 4.3 · 1843 0.5	17 TU	0106 3.6 · 0643 1.1 · 1319 4.0 · 1918 0.9
3 TU	0131 4.0 · 0658 0.8 · 1340 4.3 · 1935 0.5	18 W	0140 3.6 · 0715 1.1 · 1354 3.9 · 1952 0.9
4 W	0223 3.9 · 0749 0.9 · 1433 4.2 · 2030 0.6	19 TH	0216 3.6 · 0749 1.1 · 1432 3.8 · 2027 1.0
5 TH	0319 3.8 · 0845 1.1 · 1528 4.2 · 2128 0.7	20 F	0255 3.5 · 0826 1.2 · 1512 3.7 · 2104 1.0
6 F	0417 3.7 · 0945 1.2 · 1626 4.0 · ◑ 2227 0.9	21 SA	0338 3.4 · 0908 1.3 · 1555 3.6 · 2146 1.2
7 SA	0520 3.6 · 1048 1.3 · 1729 3.9 · 2331 1.0	22 SU	0426 3.4 · 0955 1.5 · 1644 3.5 · 2235 1.3
8 SU	0625 3.6 · 1155 1.4 · 1837 3.8	23 M	0520 3.3 · 1051 1.6 · 1740 3.4 · 2335 1.4
9 M	0039 1.2 · 0731 3.6 · 1306 1.4 · 1947 3.7	24 TU	0625 3.2 · 1202 1.6 · 1849 3.3
10 TU	0149 1.3 · 0834 3.6 · 1416 1.4 · 2054 3.6	25 W	0046 1.5 · 0735 3.3 · 1318 1.6 · 2005 3.3
11 W	0254 1.3 · 0932 3.7 · 1518 1.3 · 2156 3.6	26 TH	0156 1.4 · 0838 3.5 · 1425 1.4 · 2112 3.5
12 TH	0347 1.3 · 1023 3.8 · 1611 1.1 · 2248 3.7	27 F	0256 1.3 · 0933 3.7 · 1523 1.1 · 2207 3.7
13 F	0430 1.2 · 1107 3.9 · 1655 1.0 · 2329 3.7	28 SA	0347 1.0 · 1021 3.9 · 1613 0.7 · 2256 3.9
14 SA	0508 1.1 · 1143 4.0 · 1734 0.9 · ○	29 SU	0432 0.8 · 1106 4.2 · 1659 0.5 · ● 2342 4.0
15 SU	0003 3.7 · 0541 1.1 · 1215 4.0 · 1810 0.9	30 M	0515 0.7 · 1150 4.3 · 1744 0.3
		31 TU	0026 4.1 · 0557 0.6 · 1235 4.4 · 1828 0.2

FEBRUARY

Day	Times & heights (m)	Day	Times & heights (m)
1 W	0112 4.1 · 0640 0.5 · 1321 4.4 · 1915 0.2	16 TH	0106 3.7 · 0643 0.8 · 1323 3.9 · 1912 0.7
2 TH	0158 4.0 · 0726 0.6 · 1409 4.3 · 2004 0.4	17 F	0138 3.7 · 0713 0.9 · 1358 3.8 · 1943 0.8
3 F	0247 3.9 · 0816 0.8 · 1459 4.2 · 2055 0.6	18 SA	0214 3.6 · 0747 0.9 · 1436 3.8 · 2019 0.9
4 SA	0338 3.7 · 0911 0.9 · 1553 4.0 · 2149 0.9	19 SU	0254 3.6 · 0826 1.0 · 1517 3.6 · 2059 1.0
5 SU	0436 3.6 · 1010 1.2 · 1654 3.8 · ◑ 2248 1.2	20 M	0338 3.5 · 0909 1.2 · 1603 3.5 · 2145 1.2
6 M	0542 3.4 · 1117 1.4 · 1806 3.5 · 2356 1.4	21 TU	0429 3.3 · 1001 1.4 · 1658 3.3 · 2242 1.4
7 TU	0654 3.4 · 1234 1.5 · 1924 3.4	22 W	0532 3.2 · 1111 1.5 · 1811 3.2
8 W	0121 1.6 · 0805 3.4 · 1401 1.5 · 2040 3.4	23 TH	0002 1.6 · 0653 3.2 · 1247 1.5 · 1943 3.2
9 TH	0242 1.5 · 0912 3.5 · 1512 1.3 · 2149 3.4	24 F	0132 1.5 · 0812 3.3 · 1409 1.3 · 2058 3.4
10 F	0338 1.4 · 1008 3.7 · 1603 1.1 · 2241 3.5	25 SA	0243 1.3 · 0914 3.6 · 1512 0.9 · 2155 3.7
11 SA	0419 1.3 · 1053 3.8 · 1643 1.0 · 2319 3.6	26 SU	0336 1.0 · 1005 3.9 · 1602 0.5 · 2243 3.9
12 SU	0454 1.1 · 1128 3.9 · 1718 0.8 · 2348 3.6	27 M	0420 0.7 · 1050 4.2 · 1646 0.2 · 2326 4.0
13 M	0524 1.0 · 1156 3.9 · 1749 0.8 · ○	28 TU	0500 0.5 · 1132 4.3 · 1727 0.1 · ●
14 TU	0012 3.6 · 0552 0.9 · 1224 3.9 · 1818 0.7		
15 W	0038 3.6 · 0618 0.8 · 1252 3.9 · 1845 0.7		

MARCH

Day	Times & heights (m)	Day	Times & heights (m)
1 W	0007 4.1 · 0538 0.3 · 1215 4.4 · 1808 0.0	16 TH	0007 3.7 · 0548 0.7 · 1223 3.9 · 1809 0.6
2 TH	0047 4.1 · 0619 0.3 · 1258 4.4 · 1851 0.1	17 F	0032 3.7 · 0612 0.7 · 1253 3.9 · 1835 0.6
3 F	0128 4.0 · 0702 0.4 · 1343 4.3 · 1935 0.3	18 SA	0104 3.8 · 0641 0.7 · 1328 3.8 · 1907 0.7
4 SA	0212 3.9 · 0749 0.5 · 1431 4.1 · 2022 0.6	19 SU	0140 3.7 · 0716 0.7 · 1407 3.7 · 1943 0.8
5 SU	0259 3.7 · 0841 0.8 · 1523 3.9 · 2113 0.9	20 M	0221 3.7 · 0755 0.9 · 1449 3.6 · 2025 1.0
6 M	0351 3.5 · 0940 1.0 · 1623 3.6 · ◑ 2208 1.3	21 TU	0305 3.5 · 0841 1.0 · 1537 3.5 · 2114 1.2
7 TU	0456 3.4 · 1046 1.3 · 1738 3.3 · 2314 1.6	22 W	0356 3.4 · 0938 1.2 · 1635 3.3 · ◐ 2215 1.4
8 W	0616 3.3 · 1205 1.4 · 1901 3.2	23 TH	0500 3.2 · 1054 1.4 · 1754 3.1 · 2341 1.6
9 TH	0045 1.7 · 0734 3.3 · 1344 1.4 · 2025 3.2	24 F	0623 3.2 · 1231 1.3 · 1929 3.2
10 F	0223 1.7 · 0848 3.4 · 1455 1.2 · 2136 3.3	25 SA	0113 1.5 · 0748 3.3 · 1355 1.1 · 2043 3.4
11 SA	0319 1.5 · 0947 3.6 · 1543 1.0 · 2224 3.4	26 SU	0225 1.2 · 0853 3.6 · 1457 0.7 · 2140 3.7
12 SU	0359 1.2 · 1030 3.7 · 1620 0.9 · 2258 3.5	27 M	0318 0.9 · 0945 3.9 · 1545 0.4 · 2226 3.9
13 M	0431 1.1 · 1104 3.8 · 1651 0.7 · 2323 3.6	28 TU	0401 0.6 · 1031 4.1 · 1627 0.1 · 2306 4.0
14 TU	0500 0.9 · 1132 3.9 · 1720 0.7 · ○ 2345 3.6	29 W	0440 0.4 · 1113 4.3 · 1707 0.0 · ● 2344 4.0
15 W	0526 0.8 · 1157 3.9 · 1746 0.6	30 TH	0519 0.3 · 1155 4.3 · 1747 0.0
		31 F	0022 4.0 · 0559 0.2 · 1238 4.3 · 1827 0.2

APRIL

Day	Times & heights (m)	Day	Times & heights (m)
1 SA	0101 4.0 · 0641 0.3 · 1322 4.2 · 1909 0.4	16 SU	0035 3.8 · 0614 0.7 · 1304 3.8 · 1838 0.7
2 SU	0142 3.9 · 0728 0.5 · 1409 4.0 · 1953 0.7	17 M	0113 3.8 · 0652 0.7 · 1345 3.7 · 1918 0.9
3 M	0227 3.7 · 0820 0.7 · 1501 3.7 · 2042 1.0	18 TU	0156 3.7 · 0737 0.8 · 1432 3.6 · 2004 1.0
4 TU	0317 3.6 · 0918 0.9 · 1600 3.4 · 2137 1.4	19 W	0244 3.6 · 0830 1.0 · 1525 3.4 · 2059 1.2
5 W	0419 3.4 · 1023 1.2 · 1714 3.2 · ◑ 2241 1.6	20 TH	0339 3.5 · 0935 1.1 · 1628 3.3 · 2207 1.4
6 TH	0540 3.3 · 1137 1.3 · 1835 3.1	21 F	0444 3.4 · 1054 1.2 · 1747 3.2 · ◐ 2328 1.5
7 F	0001 1.8 · 0659 3.3 · 1309 1.3 · 1956 3.1	22 SA	0604 3.4 · 1218 1.1 · 1910 3.3
8 SA	0143 1.7 · 0812 3.4 · 1420 1.2 · 2104 3.2	23 SU	0049 1.4 · 0721 3.5 · 1332 0.9 · 2019 3.5
9 SU	0244 1.5 · 0911 3.5 · 1508 1.0 · 2149 3.4	24 M	0157 1.2 · 0826 3.7 · 1432 0.6 · 2116 3.7
10 M	0326 1.3 · 0956 3.6 · 1546 0.8 · 2222 3.5	25 TU	0251 0.9 · 0921 3.9 · 1522 0.4 · 2203 3.8
11 TU	0359 1.1 · 1031 3.7 · 1617 0.7 · 2250 3.6	26 W	0337 0.7 · 1010 4.1 · 1606 0.2 · 2245 3.9
12 W	0428 0.9 · 1102 3.8 · 1645 0.7 · 2314 3.6	27 TH	0419 0.5 · 1055 4.2 · 1647 0.2 · ● 2323 4.0
13 TH	0454 0.8 · 1128 3.8 · 1710 0.6 · ○ 2335 3.7	28 F	0501 0.4 · 1138 4.2 · 1727 0.3
14 F	0518 0.7 · 1155 3.8 · 1735 0.6	29 SA	0000 4.0 · 0542 0.4 · 1222 4.1 · 1806 0.4
15 SA	0001 3.8 · 0543 0.7 · 1226 3.8 · 1803 0.7	30 SU	0039 3.9 · 0626 0.4 · 1307 4.0 · 1847 0.6

Chart Datum: 0·20 metres above Ordnance Datum (Dublin)

TIDES

TIME ZONE (UT)
For Summer Time add ONE hour in **non-shaded areas**

IRELAND – DUBLIN (NORTH WALL)   2006

LAT 53°21'N   LONG 6°13'W

TIMES AND HEIGHTS OF HIGH AND LOW WATERS

MAY

Day	Time	m	Day	Time	m
1 M	0120 / 0714 / 1354 / 1931	3.9 / 0.6 / 3.8 / 0.9	**16** TU	0054 / 0639 / 1333 / 1902	3.9 / 0.8 / 3.7 / 0.9
2 TU	0205 / 0805 / 1445 / 2019	3.8 / 0.7 / 3.6 / 1.1	**17** W	0141 / 0730 / 1424 / 1953	3.8 / 0.8 / 3.6 / 1.1
3 W	0255 / 0902 / 1541 / 2112	3.6 / 0.9 / 3.4 / 1.4	**18** TH	0232 / 0829 / 1520 / 2052	3.8 / 0.9 / 3.5 / 1.2
4 TH	0353 / 1002 / 1647 / 2213	3.5 / 1.1 / 3.2 / 1.6	**19** F	0330 / 0935 / 1623 / 2158	3.7 / 0.9 / 3.5 / 1.3
5 F	0504 / 1107 / 1759 / ☽2321	3.4 / 1.2 / 3.1 / 1.7	**20** SA	0434 / 1046 / 1733 / ☽2308	3.6 / 0.9 / 3.4 / 1.4
6 SA	0619 / 1219 / 1909	3.3 / 1.2 / 3.1	**21** SU	0543 / 1157 / 1844	3.6 / 0.9 / 3.5
7 SU	0037 / 0726 / 1327 / 2010	1.7 / 3.4 / 1.2 / 3.2	**22** M	0018 / 0653 / 1303 / 1949	1.3 / 3.7 / 0.8 / 3.6
8 M	0148 / 0824 / 1421 / 2059	1.5 / 3.4 / 1.1 / 3.3	**23** TU	0123 / 0757 / 1403 / 2047	1.2 / 3.8 / 0.7 / 3.7
9 TU	0238 / 0912 / 1502 / 2138	1.4 / 3.5 / 1.0 / 3.5	**24** W	0220 / 0856 / 1456 / 2138	1.0 / 3.9 / 0.6 / 3.8
10 W	0317 / 0952 / 1537 / 2210	1.2 / 3.6 / 0.9 / 3.6	**25** TH	0313 / 0951 / 1545 / 2224	0.9 / 4.0 / 0.6 / 3.8
11 TH	0350 / 1026 / 1607 / 2238	1.0 / 3.7 / 0.8 / 3.7	**26** F	0401 / 1041 / 1629 / 2306	0.7 / 4.0 / 0.6 / 3.9
12 F	0419 / 1057 / 1635 / 2304	0.9 / 3.7 / 0.8 / 3.8	**27** SA	0447 / 1127 / 1711 / ●2345	0.7 / 4.0 / 0.6 / 3.9
13 SA	0447 / 1129 / 1705 / ○2335	0.8 / 3.7 / 0.8 / 3.8	**28** SU	0532 / 1211 / 1751	0.6 / 3.9 / 0.7
14 SU	0519 / 1205 / 1739	0.8 / 3.6 / 0.8	**29** M	0023 / 0616 / 1255 / 1830	3.9 / 0.6 / 3.8 / 0.9
15 M	0012 / 0555 / 1247 / 1817	3.9 / 0.7 / 3.8 / 0.8	**30** TU	0104 / 0703 / 1339 / 1912	3.9 / 0.7 / 3.7 / 1.0
			31 W	0147 / 0752 / 1426 / 1957	3.8 / 0.8 / 3.6 / 1.2

JUNE

Day	Time	m	Day	Time	m
1 TH	0234 / 0843 / 1516 / 2047	3.7 / 0.9 / 3.4 / 1.3	**16** F	0221 / 0822 / 1509 / 2038	4.0 / 0.7 / 3.7 / 1.1
2 F	0325 / 0936 / 1611 / 2141	3.6 / 1.0 / 3.3 / 1.5	**17** SA	0317 / 0923 / 1607 / 2138	4.0 / 0.7 / 3.6 / 1.1
3 SA	0423 / 1032 / 1711 / ☽2240	3.5 / 1.1 / 3.2 / 1.6	**18** SU	0416 / 1025 / 1709 / ☽2240	3.9 / 0.8 / 3.6 / 1.2
4 SU	0527 / 1129 / 1814 / 2341	3.4 / 1.2 / 3.2 / 1.6	**19** M	0519 / 1128 / 1813 / 2344	3.8 / 0.8 / 3.6 / 1.2
5 M	0632 / 1226 / 1912	3.4 / 1.2 / 3.2	**20** TU	0624 / 1231 / 1917	3.8 / 0.9 / 3.6
6 TU	0042 / 0730 / 1321 / 2003	1.6 / 3.4 / 1.2 / 3.3	**21** W	0049 / 0731 / 1334 / 2018	1.2 / 3.8 / 0.9 / 3.6
7 W	0138 / 0822 / 1409 / 2049	1.5 / 3.4 / 1.1 / 3.4	**22** TH	0153 / 0835 / 1433 / 2115	1.2 / 3.8 / 0.9 / 3.7
8 TH	0226 / 0908 / 1451 / 2128	1.4 / 3.5 / 1.1 / 3.5	**23** F	0253 / 0936 / 1528 / 2207	1.1 / 3.8 / 0.9 / 3.8
9 F	0307 / 0950 / 1529 / 2203	1.2 / 3.6 / 1.0 / 3.7	**24** SA	0349 / 1031 / 1616 / 2253	1.0 / 3.8 / 1.0 / 3.8
10 SA	0344 / 1029 / 1605 / 2238	1.1 / 3.7 / 0.9 / 3.8	**25** SU	0439 / 1120 / 1659 / ●2333	0.9 / 3.8 / 1.0 / 3.9
11 SU	0421 / 1109 / 1642 / ○2315	1.0 / 3.7 / 0.9 / 3.9	**26** M	0525 / 1202 / 1738	0.8 / 3.8 / 1.0
12 M	0501 / 1150 / 1721 / 2355	0.8 / 3.8 / 0.9 / 4.0	**27** TU	0010 / 0608 / 1241 / 1815	3.9 / 0.8 / 3.7 / 1.0
13 TU	0544 / 1235 / 1804	0.8 / 3.8 / 0.9	**28** W	0047 / 0650 / 1320 / 1852	3.9 / 0.8 / 3.6 / 1.1
14 W	0040 / 0631 / 1323 / 1850	4.0 / 0.7 / 3.8 / 0.9	**29** TH	0126 / 0733 / 1400 / 1931	3.9 / 0.8 / 3.5 / 1.1
15 TH	0129 / 0724 / 1415 / 1942	4.0 / 0.7 / 3.8 / 1.0	**30** F	0206 / 0816 / 1442 / 2013	3.8 / 0.9 / 3.5 / 1.2

JULY

Day	Time	m	Day	Time	m
1 SA	0249 / 0901 / 1526 / 2059	3.8 / 1.0 / 3.4 / 1.3	**16** SU	0254 / 0858 / 1540 / 2109	4.2 / 0.6 / 3.8 / 1.0
2 SU	0335 / 0948 / 1613 / 2148	3.6 / 1.1 / 3.3 / 1.4	**17** M	0349 / 0956 / 1636 / ☽2208	4.1 / 0.7 / 3.7 / 1.1
3 M	0425 / 1036 / 1705 / 2242	3.5 / 1.2 / 3.2 / 1.5	**18** TU	0449 / 1055 / 1739 / 2310	3.9 / 0.9 / 3.6 / 1.2
4 TU	0520 / 1127 / 1802 / 2339	3.4 / 1.3 / 3.2 / 1.6	**19** W	0556 / 1158 / 1846	3.8 / 1.1 / 3.5
5 W	0623 / 1221 / 1902	3.3 / 1.3 / 3.2	**20** TH	0019 / 0709 / 1307 / 1953	1.3 / 3.7 / 1.2 / 3.5
6 TH	0038 / 0726 / 1315 / 1958	1.6 / 3.3 / 1.4 / 3.3	**21** F	0133 / 0821 / 1416 / 2057	1.4 / 3.6 / 1.3 / 3.6
7 F	0135 / 0826 / 1408 / 2049	1.5 / 3.4 / 1.3 / 3.5	**22** SA	0244 / 0928 / 1517 / 2154	1.3 / 3.6 / 1.3 / 3.7
8 SA	0229 / 0919 / 1457 / 2134	1.4 / 3.5 / 1.2 / 3.6	**23** SU	0346 / 1027 / 1607 / 2243	1.2 / 3.6 / 1.2 / 3.8
9 SU	0318 / 1008 / 1542 / 2217	1.2 / 3.6 / 1.1 / 3.8	**24** M	0435 / 1115 / 1649 / 2323	1.0 / 3.7 / 1.1 / 3.9
10 M	0404 / 1053 / 1625 / 2259	1.0 / 3.7 / 1.0 / 4.0	**25** TU	0517 / 1153 / 1724 / ●2355	0.9 / 3.7 / 1.1 / 3.9
11 TU	0448 / 1137 / 1707 / ○2341	0.8 / 3.8 / 0.8 / 4.1	**26** W	0555 / 1224 / 1757	0.8 / 3.6 / 1.0
12 W	0533 / 1222 / 1750	0.6 / 3.9 / 0.8	**27** TH	0026 / 0630 / 1254 / 1828	4.0 / 0.8 / 3.6 / 1.0
13 TH	0025 / 0620 / 1308 / 1834	4.2 / 0.5 / 3.9 / 0.7	**28** F	0059 / 0705 / 1327 / 1901	3.9 / 0.8 / 3.6 / 1.0
14 F	0112 / 0709 / 1356 / 1922	4.2 / 0.4 / 3.9 / 0.8	**29** SA	0134 / 0740 / 1402 / 1934	3.9 / 0.8 / 3.6 / 1.0
15 SA	0201 / 0802 / 1447 / 2014	4.2 / 0.5 / 3.8 / 0.9	**30** SU	0211 / 0816 / 1439 / 2011	3.8 / 0.9 / 3.5 / 1.1
			31 M	0251 / 0853 / 1519 / 2050	3.7 / 1.0 / 3.5 / 1.2

AUGUST

Day	Time	m	Day	Time	m
1 TU	0334 / 0934 / 1604 / 2135	3.6 / 1.1 / 3.4 / 1.4	**16** W	0417 / 1019 / 1701 / ☽2240	3.8 / 1.1 / 3.5 / 1.3
2 W	0422 / 1021 / 1654 / ☽2227	3.5 / 1.3 / 3.3 / 1.5	**17** TH	0530 / 1124 / 1815 / 2354	3.6 / 1.3 / 3.4 / 1.4
3 TH	0519 / 1118 / 1756 / 2334	3.3 / 1.4 / 3.2 / 1.6	**18** F	0653 / 1241 / 1930	3.4 / 1.5 / 3.4
4 F	0632 / 1226 / 1909	3.2 / 1.5 / 3.2	**19** SA	0122 / 0813 / 1405 / 2041	1.5 / 3.5 / 1.5 / 3.6
5 SA	0052 / 0752 / 1334 / 2016	1.6 / 3.3 / 1.5 / 3.4	**20** SU	0243 / 0926 / 1509 / 2142	1.3 / 3.5 / 1.5 / 3.7
6 SU	0203 / 0858 / 1435 / 2112	1.5 / 3.4 / 1.4 / 3.6	**21** M	0341 / 1022 / 1555 / 2231	1.1 / 3.6 / 1.3 / 3.9
7 M	0302 / 0952 / 1527 / 2159	1.2 / 3.6 / 1.2 / 3.8	**22** TU	0424 / 1106 / 1633 / 2308	1.0 / 3.6 / 1.2 / 3.9
8 TU	0352 / 1039 / 1611 / 2242	0.9 / 3.8 / 0.9 / 4.1	**23** W	0500 / 1138 / 1705 / ●2337	0.8 / 3.6 / 1.0 / 4.0
9 W	0436 / 1122 / 1652 / ○2323	0.6 / 3.9 / 0.7 / 4.3	**24** TH	0533 / 1202 / 1735	0.8 / 3.6 / 0.9
10 TH	0519 / 1204 / 1732	0.3 / 4.0 / 0.6	**25** F	0002 / 0602 / 1226 / 1802	4.0 / 0.7 / 3.7 / 0.9
11 F	0005 / 0602 / 1246 / 1813	4.4 / 0.2 / 4.1 / 0.5	**26** SA	0030 / 0631 / 1253 / 1828	4.0 / 0.7 / 3.7 / 0.9
12 SA	0049 / 0647 / 1330 / 1858	4.4 / 0.2 / 4.0 / 0.5	**27** SU	0101 / 0658 / 1324 / 1857	3.9 / 0.8 / 3.7 / 0.9
13 SU	0135 / 0735 / 1417 / 1945	4.4 / 0.3 / 3.9 / 0.7	**28** M	0135 / 0728 / 1359 / 1930	3.9 / 0.9 / 3.7 / 1.0
14 M	0224 / 0826 / 1506 / 2038	4.3 / 0.5 / 3.8 / 0.8	**29** TU	0214 / 0802 / 1438 / 2008	3.8 / 0.9 / 3.6 / 1.1
15 TU	0318 / 0921 / 1559 / 2136	4.1 / 0.8 / 3.7 / 1.1	**30** W	0255 / 0842 / 1521 / 2050	3.7 / 1.1 / 3.5 / 1.3
			31 TH	0341 / 0928 / 1609 / ☽2141	3.5 / 1.3 / 3.4 / 1.4

Chart Datum: 0·20 metres above Ordnance Datum (Dublin)

IRELAND – DUBLIN (NORTH WALL)

2006

LAT 53°21′N   LONG 6°13′W

TIMES AND HEIGHTS OF HIGH AND LOW WATERS

SEPTEMBER

Day	Time m	Time m	Time m	Time m		Day	Time m	Time m	Time m	Time m
1 F	0437 3.3	1026 1.5	1708 3.2	2248 1.6		**16** SA	0638 3.3	1215 1.7	1906 3.4	
2 SA	0553 3.1	1146 1.7	1827 3.2			**17** SU	0112 1.5	0805 3.3	1348 1.7	2021 3.6
3 SU	0023 1.6	0730 3.2	1311 1.6	1948 3.3		**18** M	0230 1.3	0916 3.4	1450 1.5	2123 3.7
4 M	0147 1.4	0842 3.4	1420 1.4	2050 3.6		**19** TU	0322 1.1	1007 3.6	1534 1.3	2210 3.9
5 TU	0250 1.1	0937 3.6	1512 1.1	2139 3.9		**20** W	0402 0.9	1045 3.6	1609 1.1	2245 4.0
6 W	0338 0.7	1022 3.9	1554 0.8	2223 4.2		**21** TH	0435 0.8	1113 3.7	1641 1.0	2313 4.0
7 TH	0420 0.3	1103 4.0	1633 0.6	O 2303 4.4		**22** F	0504 0.7	1135 3.7	1709 1.0	● 2338 4.0
8 F	0500 0.1	1142 4.1	1712 0.4	2343 4.5		**23** SA	0531 0.7	1157 3.7	1735 0.8	
9 SA	0540 0.0	1221 4.1	1751 0.3			**24** SU	0003 4.0	0556 0.7	1222 3.8	1758 0.8
10 SU	0024 4.5	0621 0.1	1302 4.1	1833 0.4		**25** M	0032 3.9	0620 0.8	1251 3.8	1826 0.9
11 M	0109 4.4	0706 0.3	1345 4.0	1919 0.5		**26** TU	0106 3.9	0649 0.9	1326 3.8	1858 0.9
12 TU	0157 4.2	0754 0.6	1432 3.9	2011 0.8		**27** W	0144 3.8	0724 1.0	1406 3.7	1937 1.1
13 W	0250 4.0	0846 0.9	1524 3.7	2110 1.0		**28** TH	0226 3.6	0805 1.2	1449 3.6	2021 1.2
14 TH	0351 3.7	0945 1.3	1627 3.5	◑ 2216 1.3		**29** F	0314 3.5	0853 1.4	1539 3.5	2115 1.4
15 F	0509 3.4	1052 1.5	1745 3.4	2334 1.5		**30** SA	0413 3.3	0956 1.6	1638 3.3	◐ 2229 1.5

OCTOBER

Day	Time m	Time m	Time m	Time m		Day	Time m	Time m	Time m	Time m
1 SU	0533 3.1	1122 1.7	1756 3.3			**16** M	0042 1.4	0739 3.3	1313 1.8	1948 3.6
2 M	0005 1.5	0709 3.2	1249 1.7	1918 3.4		**17** TU	0158 1.3	0847 3.4	1417 1.6	2049 3.7
3 TU	0129 1.3	0822 3.4	1358 1.4	2023 3.7		**18** W	0250 1.1	0935 3.6	1503 1.4	2136 3.8
4 W	0230 0.9	0916 3.7	1449 1.1	2115 4.0		**19** TH	0330 0.9	1011 3.7	1540 1.2	2214 3.9
5 TH	0318 0.5	1001 3.9	1532 0.8	2200 4.2		**20** F	0403 0.8	1039 3.7	1612 1.0	2245 3.9
6 F	0400 0.3	1041 4.1	1612 0.5	2241 4.4		**21** SA	0433 0.8	1105 3.8	1642 1.0	2312 3.9
7 SA	0439 0.1	1119 4.2	1651 0.4	O 2322 4.5		**22** SU	0459 0.8	1129 3.8	1708 0.9	● 2339 3.9
8 SU	0518 0.1	1157 4.2	1731 0.3			**23** M	0523 0.8	1153 3.9	1733 0.9	
9 M	0004 4.5	0558 0.2	1237 4.1	1813 0.4		**24** TU	0008 3.9	0549 0.9	1224 3.9	1801 0.9
10 TU	0050 4.3	0640 0.4	1320 4.1	1900 0.6		**25** W	0043 3.8	0620 0.9	1300 3.9	1836 1.0
11 W	0138 4.1	0726 0.8	1406 3.9	1952 0.8		**26** TH	0123 3.8	0657 1.1	1341 3.8	1918 1.1
12 TH	0232 3.9	0818 1.1	1458 3.8	2052 1.0		**27** F	0208 3.6	0741 1.2	1428 3.7	2007 1.2
13 F	0334 3.6	0916 1.4	1600 3.6	2157 1.2		**28** SA	0300 3.5	0834 1.4	1520 3.6	2107 1.3
14 SA	0452 3.3	1023 1.7	1716 3.5	◑ 2312 1.4		**29** SU	0402 3.4	0941 1.6	1630 3.5	◐ 2221 1.4
15 SU	0616 3.2	1142 1.8	1835 3.5			**30** M	0519 3.3	1101 1.7	1731 3.5	2344 1.3
						31 TU	0641 3.4	1219 1.6	1845 3.6	

NOVEMBER

Day	Time m	Time m	Time m	Time m		Day	Time m	Time m	Time m	Time m
1 W	0059 1.1	0750 3.5	1326 1.4	1950 3.8		**16** TH	0204 1.2	0845 3.5	1422 1.5	2052 3.7
2 TH	0201 0.8	0847 3.7	1420 1.1	2045 4.0		**17** F	0250 1.1	0926 3.6	1505 1.4	2135 3.7
3 F	0252 0.6	0934 3.9	1507 0.9	2135 4.2		**18** SA	0327 1.0	1001 3.7	1541 1.2	2213 3.8
4 SA	0337 0.4	1017 4.1	1551 0.7	2222 4.3		**19** SU	0359 1.0	1033 3.8	1613 1.1	2246 3.8
5 SU	0419 0.3	1058 4.2	1634 0.5	O 2307 4.3		**20** M	0427 1.0	1101 3.9	1643 1.1	● 2317 3.8
6 M	0500 0.4	1138 4.2	1717 0.5	2351 4.3		**21** TU	0455 1.0	1129 3.9	1712 1.0	2350 3.8
7 TU	0540 0.5	1218 4.2	1801 0.5			**22** W	0525 1.0	1202 4.0	1745 1.0	
8 W	0038 4.2	0622 0.7	1302 4.1	1849 0.6		**23** TH	0027 3.8	0600 1.0	1241 4.0	1823 1.0
9 TH	0127 4.0	0707 0.9	1348 4.0	1940 0.6		**24** F	0110 3.8	0640 1.1	1324 3.9	1909 1.0
10 F	0220 3.8	0756 1.2	1439 3.9	2037 1.0		**25** SA	0158 3.7	0727 1.2	1413 3.9	2001 1.0
11 SA	0320 3.5	0852 1.5	1537 3.7	2137 1.1		**26** SU	0251 3.6	0822 1.4	1505 3.8	2100 1.1
12 SU	0427 3.4	0954 1.7	1644 3.6	◑ 2242 1.3		**27** M	0351 3.5	0924 1.5	1603 3.8	2205 1.1
13 M	0540 3.3	1102 1.8	1754 3.5	2354 1.3		**28** TU	0457 3.5	1033 1.5	1705 3.8	◐ 2315 1.1
14 TU	0651 3.3	1217 1.8	1902 3.5			**29** W	0606 3.5	1142 1.5	1810 3.8	
15 W	0106 1.3	0755 3.4	1328 1.7	2001 3.6		**30** TH	0024 1.0	0712 3.6	1248 1.4	1914 3.9

DECEMBER

Day	Time m	Time m	Time m	Time m		Day	Time m	Time m	Time m	Time m
1 F	0127 0.9	0812 3.7	1348 1.2	2016 4.0		**16** SA	0157 1.4	0837 3.5	1420 1.6	2053 3.5
2 SA	0225 0.8	0907 3.9	1443 1.1	2114 4.0		**17** SU	0244 1.3	0921 3.6	1506 1.4	2139 3.6
3 SU	0316 0.7	0956 4.0	1534 0.9	2208 4.1		**18** M	0324 1.2	1000 3.7	1545 1.3	2220 3.7
4 M	0403 0.7	1042 4.1	1623 0.8	2258 4.1		**19** TU	0359 1.2	1035 3.8	1621 1.2	2259 3.7
5 TU	0447 0.7	1125 4.1	1709 0.7	O 2345 4.1		**20** W	0433 1.1	1109 3.9	1656 1.1	● 2336 3.8
6 W	0529 0.8	1207 4.1	1755 0.7			**21** TH	0509 1.0	1145 4.0	1733 1.0	
7 TH	0031 4.0	0609 0.9	1249 4.1	1841 0.7		**22** F	0016 3.8	0546 1.0	1226 4.1	1814 0.8
8 F	0117 3.9	0651 1.0	1333 4.1	1929 0.8		**23** SA	0059 3.8	0628 1.0	1309 4.1	1859 0.8
9 SA	0205 3.7	0736 1.2	1420 4.0	2018 0.9		**24** SU	0146 3.8	0713 1.0	1357 4.1	1949 0.7
10 SU	0256 3.6	0825 1.4	1510 3.9	2110 1.0		**25** M	0236 3.8	0804 1.1	1447 4.1	2042 0.8
11 M	0351 3.4	0919 1.5	1604 3.7	2204 1.2		**26** TU	0330 3.7	0859 1.2	1540 4.0	2139 0.8
12 TU	0450 3.3	1018 1.6	1703 3.6	◑ 2301 1.3		**27** W	0427 3.7	0959 1.3	1636 4.0	◑ 2240 0.9
13 W	0553 3.3	1120 1.7	1805 3.5			**28** TH	0529 3.6	1103 1.3	1737 3.9	2345 1.0
14 TH	0001 1.4	0652 3.3	1225 1.7	1906 3.5		**29** F	0635 3.6	1210 1.4	1843 3.8	
15 F	0102 1.4	0748 3.4	1326 1.7	2002 3.5		**30** SA	0052 1.1	0740 3.6	1319 1.3	1952 3.8
						31 SU	0200 1.1	0843 3.7	1425 1.3	2100 3.8

TIDES

Chart Datum: 0·20 metres above Ordnance Datum (Dublin)

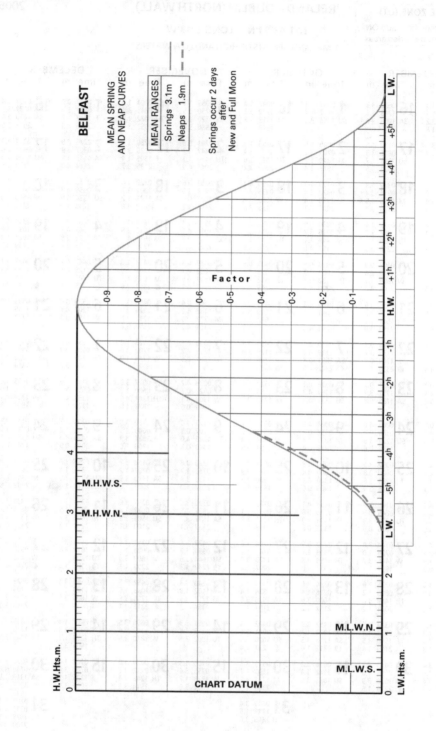

BELFAST

MEAN SPRING
AND NEAP CURVES

MEAN RANGES	
Springs	3.1m
Neaps	1.9m

Springs occur 2 days
after
New and Full Moon

Factor

NORTHERN IRELAND – BELFAST

LAT 54°36'N   LONG 5°55'W

TIMES AND HEIGHTS OF HIGH AND LOW WATERS

TIME ZONE (UT)
For Summer Time add ONE hour in **non-shaded areas**

JANUARY

#	Day	Time m				#	Day	Time m			
1	SU	0520 0.7	1140 3.6	1755 0.5		16	M	0008 3.1	0602 0.9	1222 3.6	1823 0.7
2	M	0009 3.4	0606 0.7	1225 3.6	1841 0.4	17	TU	0042 3.0	0634 0.9	1257 3.6	1855 0.7
3	TU	0100 3.3	0653 0.7	1312 3.7	1929 0.4	18	W	0116 3.0	0708 0.9	1332 3.5	1928 0.7
4	W	0152 3.3	0742 0.8	1402 3.6	2021 0.4	19	TH	0152 3.0	0744 0.9	1407 3.5	2005 0.7
5	TH	0248 3.2	0834 0.8	1456 3.6	2117 0.5	20	F	0230 3.0	0822 0.9	1443 3.4	2044 0.7
6	F	0345 3.1	0928 0.9	1554 3.5	2217 0.6	21	SA	0310 3.0	0904 1.0	1522 3.3	2127 0.8
7	SA	0443 3.1	1028 0.9	1655 3.4	2322 0.7	22	SU	0355 2.9	0950 1.1	1608 3.2	2217 0.9
8	SU	0542 3.0	1134 1.0	1800 3.3		23	M	0445 2.9	1045 1.2	1704 3.1	2316 1.0
9	M	0029 0.8	0644 3.0	1245 1.1	1908 3.2	24	TU	0544 2.8	1156 1.3	1811 3.0	
10	TU	0132 0.9	0747 3.1	1353 1.0	2017 3.2	25	W	0028 1.1	0649 2.8	1322 1.2	1920 3.0
11	W	0231 0.9	0846 3.2	1456 1.0	2117 3.2	26	TH	0145 1.0	0758 2.9	1430 1.1	2028 3.0
12	TH	0324 0.9	0940 3.3	1552 0.9	2209 3.2	27	F	0247 0.9	0902 3.1	1526 0.8	2129 3.2
13	F	0411 0.9	1026 3.4	1639 0.8	2254 3.2	28	SA	0339 0.8	0955 3.3	1615 0.6	2221 3.3
14	SA	0453 0.9	1108 3.5	1718 0.7	○ 2333 3.1	29	SU	0426 0.7	1041 3.4	1700 0.4	● 2309 3.3
15	SU	0529 0.9	1146 3.6	1752 0.7		30	M	0510 0.6	1126 3.6	1744 0.2	2356 3.3
						31	TU	0554 0.5	1211 3.7	1828 0.2	

FEBRUARY

#	Day	Time m				#	Day	Time m			
1	W	0044 3.3	0637 0.5	1259 3.7	1912 0.2	16	TH	0046 3.0	0640 0.7	1300 3.4	1857 0.6
2	TH	0133 3.3	0723 0.5	1347 3.7	1959 0.2	17	F	0112 3.0	0712 0.7	1330 3.4	1929 0.6
3	F	0223 3.2	0809 0.5	1437 3.7	2047 0.3	18	SA	0143 3.0	0747 0.7	1403 3.4	2005 0.6
4	SA	0313 3.2	0858 0.6	1528 3.5	2141 0.5	19	SU	0219 3.0	0825 0.8	1441 3.3	2045 0.7
5	SU	0403 3.1	0951 0.8	1622 3.3	☽ 2242 0.8	20	M	0259 3.0	0907 0.9	1526 3.2	2132 0.9
6	M	0457 3.0	1056 0.9	1723 3.1	2355 1.0	21	TU	0347 2.9	0959 1.1	1623 3.0	2228 1.0
7	TU	0601 2.9	1216 1.1	1840 2.9		22	W	0449 2.8	1107 1.2	1737 2.9	2342 1.2
8	W	0108 1.1	0718 2.9	1336 1.1	2006 2.9	23	TH	0607 2.7	1303 1.2	1853 2.8	
9	TH	0215 1.1	0829 3.0	1449 1.0	2111 2.9	24	F	0129 1.1	0726 2.8	1416 1.0	2009 2.9
10	F	0313 1.0	0926 3.2	1548 0.8	2202 3.0	25	SA	0235 1.0	0839 3.0	1512 0.7	2115 3.1
11	SA	0400 0.9	1013 3.3	1631 0.7	2243 3.0	26	SU	0327 0.8	0935 3.2	1601 0.4	2206 3.3
12	SU	0439 0.8	1053 3.4	1705 0.6	2319 3.0	27	M	0412 0.6	1022 3.4	1645 0.2	2252 3.3
13	M	0511 0.8	1129 3.5	1732 0.6	○ 2351 3.0	28	TU	0454 0.5	1107 3.6	1726 0.1	● 2337 3.3
14	TU	0540 0.8	1202 3.5	1758 0.6							
15	W	0020 3.0	0609 0.7	1232 3.5	1827 0.6						

MARCH

#	Day	Time m				#	Day	Time m			
1	W	0536 0.4	1152 3.7	1808 0.0		16	TH	0543 0.6	1159 3.4	1757 0.5	
2	TH	0022 3.3	0616 0.3	1240 3.7	1849 0.1	17	F	0009 3.0	0612 0.6	1224 3.4	1825 0.5
3	F	0109 3.3	0659 0.3	1327 3.7	1931 0.2	18	SA	0034 3.1	0642 0.6	1254 3.4	1856 0.5
4	SA	0155 3.3	0742 0.4	1415 3.6	2016 0.4	19	SU	0105 3.2	0716 0.6	1330 3.4	1932 0.6
5	SU	0240 3.3	0828 0.5	1503 3.4	2104 0.6	20	M	0142 3.2	0753 0.7	1411 3.3	2013 0.7
6	M	0326 3.2	0919 0.7	1554 3.2	2201 0.9	21	TU	0222 3.1	0837 0.8	1459 3.1	2100 0.9
7	TU	0417 3.0	1022 0.9	1653 2.9	2320 1.1	22	W	0311 3.0	0930 1.0	1601 3.0	☽ 2157 1.1
8	W	0518 2.9	1152 1.0	1818 2.7		23	TH	0413 2.8	1041 1.1	1718 2.8	2312 1.3
9	TH	0042 1.2	0646 2.8	1317 1.0	1957 2.7	24	F	0537 2.7	1248 1.1	1836 2.7	
10	F	0154 1.2	0808 2.9	1435 0.9	2058 2.8	25	SA	0111 1.2	0701 2.8	1358 0.8	1954 2.9
11	SA	0255 1.1	0905 3.1	1531 0.7	2145 2.9	26	SU	0217 1.0	0815 3.0	1453 0.5	2057 3.1
12	SU	0342 0.9	0950 3.2	1610 0.6	2223 3.0	27	M	0308 0.8	0912 3.3	1540 0.2	2146 3.2
13	M	0418 0.8	1029 3.3	1639 0.6	2256 3.0	28	TU	0352 0.6	0959 3.5	1623 0.1	2230 3.3
14	TU	0447 0.7	1104 3.4	1703 0.5	○ 2326 3.0	29	W	0434 0.4	1045 3.6	1703 0.0	● 2314 3.4
15	W	0514 0.7	1134 3.4	1729 0.5	2350 3.0	30	TH	0514 0.4	1131 3.7	1743 0.1	2359 3.4
						31	F	0554 0.3	1218 3.7	1824 0.2	

APRIL

#	Day	Time m				#	Day	Time m			
1	SA	0043 3.4	0635 0.3	1306 3.6	1905 0.3	16	SU	0005 3.2	0617 0.6	1227 3.3	1829 0.6
2	SU	0128 3.4	0718 0.4	1353 3.5	1948 0.5	17	M	0040 3.3	0653 0.6	1307 3.3	1907 0.7
3	M	0211 3.4	0804 0.5	1440 3.3	2035 0.8	18	TU	0119 3.3	0733 0.7	1353 3.2	1950 0.8
4	TU	0256 3.3	0855 0.6	1530 3.0	2130 1.0	19	W	0202 3.2	0819 0.8	1447 3.1	2041 0.9
5	W	0344 3.1	0959 0.8	1627 2.8	☽ 2245 1.2	20	TH	0254 3.1	0917 0.9	1554 2.9	2142 1.1
6	TH	0441 2.9	1126 1.0	1753 2.6		21	F	0358 2.9	1037 1.0	1707 2.8	☽ 2259 1.2
7	F	0007 1.3	0600 2.8	1246 1.0	1934 2.6	22	SA	0518 2.9	1224 0.9	1823 2.8	
8	SA	0119 1.3	0733 2.9	1359 0.9	2031 2.7	23	SU	0039 1.2	0641 3.0	1332 0.6	1935 2.9
9	SU	0221 1.1	0832 3.0	1454 0.7	2115 2.8	24	M	0147 1.0	0751 3.1	1426 0.4	2032 3.1
10	M	0309 1.0	0918 3.1	1532 0.6	2152 2.9	25	TU	0240 0.9	0847 3.3	1513 0.2	2121 3.2
11	TU	0346 0.8	0956 3.2	1601 0.6	2223 3.0	26	W	0327 0.6	0937 3.5	1557 0.2	2206 3.3
12	W	0416 0.7	1029 3.2	1629 0.5	2251 3.0	27	TH	0410 0.5	1024 3.6	1638 0.2	2251 3.4
13	TH	0446 0.7	1058 3.3	1657 0.6	○ 2315 3.1	28	F	0452 0.4	1111 3.6	1719 0.3	2335 3.4
14	F	0516 0.7	1124 3.3	1726 0.6	2337 3.1	29	SA	0534 0.4	1157 3.5	1801 0.4	
15	SA	0546 0.6	1152 3.3	1756 0.6		30	SU	0019 3.5	0617 0.4	1245 3.4	1843 0.6

Chart Datum: 2·01 metres below Ordnance Datum (Belfast)

TIDES

NORTHERN IRELAND – BELFAST

2006

TIME ZONE (UT)
For Summer Time add ONE hour in **non-shaded areas**

LAT 54°36'N   LONG 5°55'W

TIMES AND HEIGHTS OF HIGH AND LOW WATERS

MAY

Day	Time m	Time m	Day	Time m	Time m
1 M	0103 3.5 / 0701 0.5	1331 3.3 / 1928 0.7	**16** TU	0024 3.4 / 0640 0.6	1255 3.3 / 1853 0.8
2 TU	0146 3.4 / 0748 0.5	1418 3.1 / 2015 0.9	**17** W	0107 3.4 / 0724 0.6	1345 3.2 / 1940 0.9
3 W	0230 3.4 / 0839 0.7	1507 2.9 / 2109 1.1	**18** TH	0153 3.3 / 0814 0.7	1442 3.1 / 2034 1.0
4 TH	0317 3.2 / 0941 0.8	1602 2.7 / 2214 1.2	**19** F	0246 3.2 / 0916 0.7	1547 2.9 / 2135 1.1
5 F	0410 3.1 / 1053 0.9	1709 2.6 / ◑2324 1.3	**20** SA	0349 3.1 / 1031 0.7	1656 2.9 / ◑2245 1.1
6 SA	0513 2.9 / 1202 0.9	1844 2.6	**21** SU	0502 3.1 / 1151 0.7	1804 2.9
7 SU	0029 1.3 / 0628 2.9	1305 0.9 / 1944 2.7	**22** M	0000 1.1 / 0617 3.1	1257 0.6 / 1908 3.0
8 M	0128 1.2 / 0737 2.9	1357 0.8 / 2029 2.8	**23** TU	0108 1.0 / 0724 3.3	1353 0.4 / 2004 3.1
9 TU	0219 1.1 / 0829 3.0	1440 0.7 / 2106 2.9	**24** W	0206 0.8 / 0822 3.4	1444 0.4 / 2054 3.2
10 W	0303 0.9 / 0910 3.1	1517 0.7 / 2140 3.0	**25** TH	0259 0.7 / 0915 3.4	1530 0.4 / 2142 3.3
11 TH	0340 0.9 / 0947 3.2	1551 0.6 / 2211 3.1	**26** F	0348 0.6 / 1005 3.5	1615 0.4 / 2229 3.4
12 F	0415 0.8 / 1022 3.2	1624 0.6 / 2242 3.2	**27** SA	0435 0.6 / 1053 3.5	●1700 0.5 / ●2314 3.5
13 SA	0450 0.7 / 1055 3.3	1657 0.6 / ○2313 3.2	**28** SU	0521 0.5 / 1140 3.4	1744 0.7 / 2358 3.5
14 SU	0524 0.7 / 1131 3.3	1732 0.7 / 2347 3.3	**29** M	0606 0.5 / 1225 3.3	1828 0.8
15 M	0601 0.6 / 1211 3.3	1811 0.7	**30** TU	0041 3.5 / 0650 0.6	1310 3.2 / 1912 0.9
			31 W	0124 3.5 / 0734 0.6	1355 3.0 / 1957 1.0

JUNE

Day	Time m	Time m	Day	Time m	Time m
1 TH	0207 3.4 / 0821 0.7	1442 2.9 / 2044 1.1	**16** F	0145 3.4 / 0810 0.5	1433 3.1 / 2026 0.9
2 F	0252 3.3 / 0912 0.8	1532 2.8 / 2135 1.1	**17** SA	0237 3.4 / 0906 0.5	1533 3.0 / 2122 0.9
3 SA	0340 3.2 / 1007 0.8	1626 2.7 / ◑2231 1.2	**18** SU	0335 3.3 / 1009 0.5	1635 3.0 / ◑2222 0.9
4 SU	0433 3.1 / 1106 0.9	1722 2.7 / 2329 1.2	**19** M	0440 3.3 / 1116 0.6	1736 3.0 / 2326 0.9
5 M	0530 3.0 / 1203 0.9	1820 2.7	**20** TU	0548 3.3 / 1221 0.6	1836 3.0
6 TU	0027 1.2 / 0628 3.0	1257 0.9 / 1914 2.8	**21** W	0032 0.9 / 0655 3.3	1322 0.6 / 1933 3.1
7 W	0123 1.2 / 0726 3.0	1346 0.8 / 2004 2.9	**22** TH	0137 0.9 / 0759 3.3	1418 0.6 / 2029 3.2
8 TH	0215 1.1 / 0819 3.0	1432 0.8 / 2051 3.0	**23** F	0238 0.8 / 0858 3.3	1511 0.6 / 2122 3.3
9 F	0302 1.0 / 0908 3.1	1514 0.7 / 2134 3.1	**24** SA	0335 0.7 / 0952 3.3	1600 0.7 / 2211 3.4
10 SA	0346 0.9 / 0952 3.2	1555 0.7 / 2215 3.2	**25** SU	0427 0.7 / 1042 3.3	1646 0.8 / ●2257 3.5
11 SU	0428 0.9 / 1034 3.3	1635 0.7 / ○2254 3.3	**26** M	0514 0.6 / 1127 3.2	1730 0.8 / 2340 3.5
12 M	0509 0.7 / 1116 3.3	1716 0.7 / 2332 3.4	**27** TU	0558 0.6 / 1209 3.1	1812 0.9
13 TU	0550 0.6 / 1159 3.3	1759 0.8	**28** W	0021 3.5 / 0637 0.6	1250 3.0 / 1851 0.9
14 W	0013 3.4 / 0633 0.5	1246 3.3 / 1845 0.8	**29** TH	0102 3.5 / 0715 0.7	1331 3.0 / 1930 1.0
15 TH	0057 3.4 / 0719 0.5	1337 3.2 / 1933 0.8	**30** F	0143 3.5 / 0752 0.7	1413 2.9 / 2009 1.0

JULY

Day	Time m	Time m	Day	Time m	Time m
1 SA	0224 3.4 / 0830 0.7	1458 2.9 / 2050 1.0	**16** SU	0221 3.6 / 0844 0.3	1509 3.1 / 2057 0.7
2 SU	0307 3.3 / 0913 0.8	1545 2.8 / 2134 1.1	**17** M	0315 3.5 / 0938 0.4	1604 3.1 / ◑2151 0.8
3 M	0352 3.2 / 0959 0.8	1633 2.8 / ◑2223 1.1	**18** TU	0413 3.4 / 1040 0.6	1701 3.0 / 2252 0.9
4 TU	0441 3.1 / 1051 0.9	1723 2.8 / 2319 1.2	**19** W	0516 3.3 / 1148 0.7	1800 3.0
5 W	0534 3.0 / 1149 0.9	1816 2.8	**20** TH	0002 1.0 / 0625 3.1	1257 0.8 / 1903 3.0
6 TH	0023 1.2 / 0632 3.0	1252 1.0 / 1911 2.9	**21** F	0117 1.0 / 0741 3.1	1401 0.9 / 2008 3.1
7 F	0131 1.2 / 0734 3.0	1352 0.9 / 2007 3.0	**22** SA	0227 0.9 / 0850 3.1	1458 0.9 / 2107 3.2
8 SA	0231 1.1 / 0834 3.0	1445 0.9 / 2102 3.1	**23** SU	0331 0.8 / 0947 3.1	1550 0.9 / 2159 3.3
9 SU	0324 0.9 / 0929 3.1	1534 0.8 / 2150 3.2	**24** M	0424 0.7 / 1035 3.1	1635 0.9 / 2244 3.4
10 M	0412 0.7 / 1017 3.2	1619 0.7 / 2233 3.3	**25** TU	0508 0.6 / 1117 3.1	1715 0.9 / ●2324 3.5
11 TU	0456 0.6 / 1102 3.3	1703 0.7 / ○2315 3.4	**26** W	0545 0.6 / 1154 3.0	1751 0.9
12 W	0539 0.4 / 1146 3.3	1747 0.7 / 2357 3.5	**27** TH	0002 3.5 / 0616 0.6	1229 3.0 / 1823 0.9
13 TH	0622 0.3 / 1232 3.3	1832 0.7	**28** F	0038 3.5 / 0645 0.7	1303 2.9 / 1855 0.9
14 F	0042 3.6 / 0706 0.3	1322 3.2 / 1918 0.7	**29** SA	0114 3.5 / 0715 0.7	1338 2.9 / 1930 0.9
15 SA	0130 3.6 / 0753 0.3	1415 3.2 / 2007 0.7	**30** SU	0150 3.4 / 0748 0.7	1416 3.0 / 2007 0.9
			31 M	0226 3.4 / 0825 0.7	1457 3.0 / 2047 0.9

AUGUST

Day	Time m	Time m	Day	Time m	Time m
1 TU	0304 3.3 / 0905 0.8	1540 2.9 / 2131 1.0	**16** W	0346 3.4 / 1000 0.7	1623 3.1 / ◑2218 0.9
2 W	0347 3.2 / 0951 0.9	1627 2.9 / ◑2221 1.1	**17** TH	0447 3.2 / 1114 1.0	1724 3.0 / 2338 1.0
3 TH	0440 3.0 / 1046 1.0	1722 2.9 / 2326 1.2	**18** F	0601 2.9 / 1235 1.1	1837 3.0
4 F	0545 2.9 / 1155 1.1	1823 2.8	**19** SA	0104 1.1 / 0734 2.8	1347 1.1 / 1954 3.0
5 SA	0056 1.2 / 0655 2.9	1321 1.1 / 1928 2.9	**20** SU	0224 1.0 / 0847 2.9	1449 1.1 / 2055 3.2
6 SU	0210 1.1 / 0806 2.9	1426 1.0 / 2032 3.0	**21** M	0329 0.8 / 0941 3.0	1540 1.0 / 2145 3.3
7 M	0307 0.9 / 0909 3.1	1519 0.9 / 2125 3.2	**22** TU	0418 0.7 / 1024 3.0	1622 0.9 / 2227 3.4
8 TU	0357 0.6 / 1000 3.2	1605 0.7 / 2211 3.4	**23** W	0455 0.6 / 1101 3.0	1656 0.9 / ●2305 3.5
9 W	0441 0.4 / 1045 3.3	1647 0.6 / ○2253 3.5	**24** TH	0523 0.6 / 1134 3.0	1725 0.9 / 2339 3.5
10 TH	0523 0.2 / 1128 3.3	1729 0.6 / 2337 3.6	**25** F	0547 0.6 / 1203 3.0	1753 0.9
11 F	0604 0.2 / 1212 3.3	1811 0.5	**26** SA	0009 3.4 / 0611 0.7	1230 3.0 / 1822 0.8
12 SA	0023 3.7 / 0645 0.1	1300 3.3 / 1855 0.5	**27** SU	0039 3.4 / 0639 0.7	1257 3.0 / 1853 0.8
13 SU	0111 3.7 / 0728 0.2	1349 3.3 / 1940 0.6	**28** M	0109 3.4 / 0709 0.7	1328 3.1 / 1928 0.8
14 M	0201 3.6 / 0814 0.3	1439 3.2 / 2027 0.6	**29** TU	0142 3.4 / 0743 0.7	1403 3.1 / 2006 0.9
15 TU	0252 3.5 / 0904 0.5	1530 3.2 / 2119 0.7	**30** W	0219 3.3 / 0821 0.8	1443 3.1 / 2048 0.9
			31 TH	0301 3.2 / 0906 0.9	1529 3.0 / ◑2137 1.1

Chart Datum: 2·01 metres below Ordnance Datum (Belfast)

NORTHERN IRELAND – BELFAST

LAT 54°36′N   LONG 5°55′W

TIMES AND HEIGHTS OF HIGH AND LOW WATERS

2006

SEPTEMBER

Day	Time m	Day	Time m
1 F	0355 3.0 / 0959 1.1 / 1629 2.9 / 2240 1.3	**16** SA	0543 2.8 / 1213 1.3 / 1810 3.0
2 SA	0509 2.8 / 1106 1.2 / 1742 2.8	**17** SU	0049 1.1 / 0730 2.7 / 1329 1.3 / 1935 3.0
3 SU	0032 1.3 / 0626 2.8 / 1257 1.3 / 1856 2.9	**18** M	0213 1.0 / 0835 2.8 / 1433 1.2 / 2036 3.2
4 M	0152 1.1 / 0743 2.9 / 1409 1.1 / 2004 3.0	**19** TU	0314 0.8 / 0924 2.9 / 1523 1.0 / 2124 3.3
5 TU	0249 0.8 / 0851 3.0 / 1501 0.9 / 2100 3.3	**20** W	0357 0.7 / 1003 3.0 / 1601 0.9 / 2204 3.4
6 W	0338 0.5 / 0941 3.2 / 1546 0.7 / 2147 3.5	**21** TH	0429 0.6 / 1037 3.1 / 1631 0.9 / 2240 3.4
7 TH	0420 0.3 / 1023 3.3 / 1627 0.6 / ○ 2231 3.6	**22** F	0452 0.6 / 1107 3.1 / 1657 0.8 / 2311 3.4
8 F	0500 0.2 / 1106 3.4 / 1706 0.5 / 2315 3.7	**23** SA	0513 0.7 / 1133 3.1 / 1723 0.8 / 2337 3.4
9 SA	0539 0.1 / 1149 3.4 / 1746 0.5	**24** SU	0538 0.7 / 1154 3.1 / 1752 0.8
10 SU	0002 3.7 / 0618 0.1 / 1235 3.4 / 1828 0.5	**25** M	0002 3.4 / 0604 0.7 / 1218 3.2 / 1822 0.8
11 M	0051 3.7 / 0700 0.3 / 1322 3.4 / 1912 0.6	**26** TU	0032 3.4 / 0634 0.7 / 1248 3.3 / 1855 0.8
12 TU	0140 3.6 / 0744 0.4 / 1409 3.4 / 1959 0.6	**27** W	0106 3.4 / 0708 0.7 / 1323 3.3 / 1933 0.9
13 W	0231 3.5 / 0831 0.7 / 1458 3.3 / 2050 0.7	**28** TH	0146 3.3 / 0748 0.8 / 1403 3.2 / 2016 1.0
14 TH	0324 3.3 / 0926 0.9 / 1550 3.2 / ☽ 2150 0.9	**29** F	0231 3.2 / 0833 1.0 / 1449 3.1 / 2106 1.1
15 F	0423 3.0 / 1040 1.2 / 1651 3.0 / 2318 1.1	**30** SA	0330 3.0 / 0928 1.2 / 1549 3.0 / ☽ 2212 1.2

OCTOBER

Day	Time m	Day	Time m
1 SU	0448 2.8 / 1037 1.4 / 1709 2.9	**16** M	0019 1.1 / 0707 2.7 / 1255 1.4 / 1902 3.0
2 M	0008 1.2 / 0606 2.8 / 1228 1.4 / 1829 2.9	**17** TU	0136 1.0 / 0808 2.8 / 1359 1.3 / 2004 3.1
3 TU	0128 1.0 / 0722 2.9 / 1345 1.2 / 1939 3.1	**18** W	0236 0.9 / 0854 2.9 / 1450 1.1 / 2053 3.3
4 W	0224 0.7 / 0827 3.1 / 1437 1.0 / 2036 3.3	**19** TH	0318 0.8 / 0932 3.0 / 1529 1.0 / 2133 3.3
5 TH	0311 0.5 / 0916 3.3 / 1521 0.8 / 2124 3.5	**20** F	0348 0.7 / 1006 3.1 / 1559 0.9 / 2208 3.4
6 F	0353 0.3 / 1000 3.4 / 1601 0.6 / 2210 3.7	**21** SA	0413 0.7 / 1035 3.2 / 1627 0.9 / 2239 3.4
7 SA	0433 0.2 / 1043 3.5 / 1641 0.5 / ○ 2255 3.8	**22** SU	0439 0.8 / 1101 3.2 / 1656 0.9 / ● 2307 3.4
8 SU	0512 0.2 / 1126 3.5 / 1722 0.5 / 2343 3.8	**23** M	0506 0.8 / 1125 3.3 / 1726 0.8 / 2335 3.4
9 M	0552 0.3 / 1211 3.5 / 1804 0.5	**24** TU	0535 0.8 / 1151 3.4 / 1758 0.8
10 TU	0032 3.7 / 0634 0.5 / 1258 3.5 / 1849 0.5	**25** W	0007 3.4 / 0607 0.8 / 1223 3.4 / 1832 0.8
11 W	0122 3.6 / 0719 0.6 / 1344 3.5 / 1937 0.6	**26** TH	0045 3.4 / 0643 0.9 / 1300 3.4 / 1911 0.9
12 TH	0212 3.4 / 0807 0.9 / 1431 3.4 / 2029 0.8	**27** F	0127 3.3 / 0725 1.0 / 1342 3.3 / 1956 1.0
13 F	0305 3.2 / 0902 1.1 / 1522 3.3 / 2132 0.9	**28** SA	0217 3.2 / 0813 1.1 / 1430 3.2 / 2050 1.1
14 SA	0404 2.9 / 1015 1.3 / 1621 3.1 / ☽ 2256 1.1	**29** SU	0320 3.0 / 0911 1.2 / 1529 3.1 / ☽ 2159 1.1
15 SU	0526 2.7 / 1141 1.4 / 1736 3.0	**30** M	0433 2.9 / 1020 1.4 / 1644 3.0 / 2333 1.1
		31 TU	0547 2.9 / 1146 1.4 / 1803 3.1

NOVEMBER

Day	Time m	Day	Time m
1 W	0052 0.9 / 0658 3.0 / 1306 1.2 / 1912 3.2	**16** TH	0135 1.0 / 0810 2.9 / 1359 1.2 / 2007 3.1
2 TH	0150 0.7 / 0759 3.1 / 1402 1.0 / 2011 3.4	**17** F	0221 0.9 / 0850 3.0 / 1444 1.1 / 2052 3.2
3 F	0239 0.5 / 0849 3.3 / 1450 0.8 / 2102 3.6	**18** SA	0259 0.9 / 0927 3.1 / 1523 1.0 / 2132 3.3
4 SA	0323 0.4 / 0936 3.4 / 1535 0.7 / 2151 3.7	**19** SU	0334 0.9 / 1001 3.2 / 1558 1.0 / 2209 3.3
5 SU	0405 0.4 / 1021 3.5 / 1618 0.6 / ○ 2239 3.7	**20** M	0407 0.9 / 1034 3.3 / 1633 0.9 / ● 2244 3.4
6 M	0447 0.4 / 1106 3.6 / 1702 0.5 / 2327 3.7	**21** TU	0440 0.9 / 1106 3.4 / 1707 0.9 / 2318 3.4
7 TU	0530 0.6 / 1151 3.6 / 1747 0.5	**22** W	0514 0.9 / 1137 3.5 / 1743 0.8 / 2354 3.4
8 W	0016 3.6 / 0615 0.7 / 1237 3.7 / 1833 0.6	**23** TH	0551 0.9 / 1210 3.5 / 1821 0.8
9 TH	0105 3.5 / 0701 0.9 / 1323 3.6 / 1922 0.6	**24** F	0034 3.4 / 0630 0.9 / 1248 3.5 / 1902 0.8
10 F	0155 3.3 / 0751 1.0 / 1409 3.5 / 2015 0.8	**25** SA	0119 3.3 / 0714 1.0 / 1331 3.4 / 1948 0.8
11 SA	0246 3.1 / 0846 1.2 / 1458 3.4 / 2116 0.9	**26** SU	0210 3.2 / 0804 1.1 / 1419 3.4 / 2042 0.9
12 SU	0343 2.9 / 0950 1.3 / 1552 3.3 / 2226 1.0	**27** M	0309 3.1 / 0900 1.2 / 1515 3.3 / ☽ 2146 0.9
13 M	0450 2.7 / 1100 1.4 / 1655 3.1 / 2335 1.1	**28** TU	0415 3.0 / 1002 1.2 / 1620 3.2 / ☽ 2259 0.9
14 TU	0617 2.7 / 1206 1.4 / 1806 3.1	**29** W	0523 3.0 / 1111 1.2 / 1733 3.2
15 W	0039 1.0 / 0721 2.8 / 1306 1.3 / 1913 3.1	**30** TH	0009 0.8 / 0628 3.0 / 1222 1.1 / 1842 3.3

DECEMBER

Day	Time m	Day	Time m
1 F	0111 0.7 / 0728 3.2 / 1325 1.0 / 1944 3.4	**16** SA	0125 1.0 / 0752 2.9 / 1357 1.2 / 2004 3.1
2 SA	0206 0.6 / 0822 3.3 / 1422 0.9 / 2041 3.5	**17** SU	0214 1.0 / 0844 3.1 / 1447 1.1 / 2057 3.1
3 SU	0256 0.6 / 0914 3.4 / 1514 0.8 / 2135 3.6	**18** M	0259 1.0 / 0930 3.2 / 1532 1.0 / 2144 3.2
4 M	0345 0.6 / 1003 3.5 / 1604 0.7 / 2226 3.6	**19** TU	0342 0.9 / 1012 3.3 / 1614 0.9 / 2226 3.3
5 TU	0431 0.7 / 1050 3.6 / 1653 0.6 / ○ 2316 3.5	**20** W	0422 0.9 / 1050 3.4 / 1654 0.8 / ● 2306 3.3
6 W	0518 0.8 / 1136 3.7 / 1740 0.6	**21** TH	0502 0.9 / 1126 3.5 / 1734 0.7 / 2344 3.3
7 TH	0004 3.4 / 0603 0.9 / 1222 3.7 / 1826 0.6	**22** F	0542 0.8 / 1200 3.5 / 1814 0.7
8 F	0051 3.3 / 0649 1.0 / 1306 3.7 / 1912 0.6	**23** SA	0024 3.3 / 0622 0.8 / 1238 3.6 / 1855 0.6
9 SA	0138 3.2 / 0736 1.1 / 1350 3.6 / 2000 0.7	**24** SU	0109 3.3 / 0706 0.9 / 1320 3.6 / 1941 0.6
10 SU	0225 3.0 / 0823 1.1 / 1436 3.5 / 2050 0.8	**25** M	0158 3.2 / 0753 0.9 / 1407 3.5 / 2030 0.6
11 M	0315 2.9 / 0913 1.2 / 1524 3.4 / 2142 0.9	**26** TU	0251 3.1 / 0843 0.9 / 1458 3.5 / 2125 0.6
12 TU	0406 2.8 / 1006 1.3 / 1615 3.3 / ☽ 2238 1.0	**27** W	0349 3.1 / 0937 1.0 / 1556 3.4 / 2225 0.7
13 W	0501 2.8 / 1103 1.3 / 1710 3.2 / 2335 1.0	**28** TH	0449 3.0 / 1037 1.0 / 1700 3.4 / 2331 0.7
14 TH	0558 2.8 / 1203 1.3 / 1807 3.1	**29** F	0551 3.0 / 1144 1.1 / 1809 3.3
15 F	0031 1.1 / 0656 2.8 / 1302 1.3 / 1906 3.0	**30** SA	0038 0.8 / 0654 3.1 / 1256 1.0 / 1918 3.3
		31 SU	0142 0.8 / 0757 3.2 / 1403 1.0 / 2025 3.3

Chart Datum: 2·01 metres below Ordnance Datum (Belfast)

TIDES

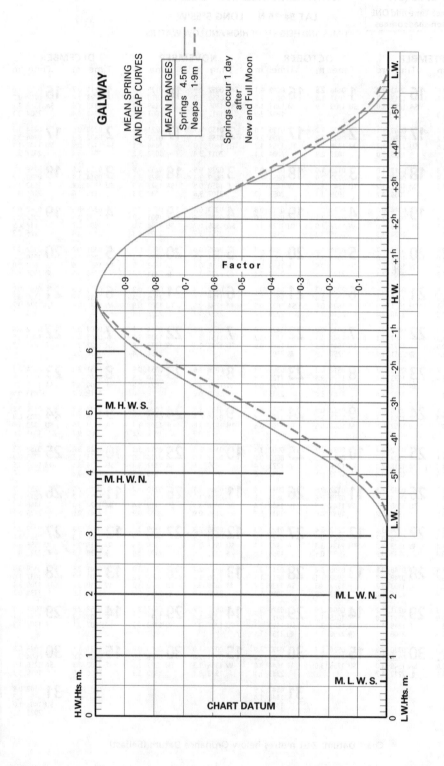

GALWAY

MEAN SPRING
AND NEAP CURVES

MEAN RANGES	
Springs	4.5m
Neaps	1.9m

Springs occur 1 day
after
New and Full Moon

Factor

0·9 0·8 0·7 0·6 0·5 0·4 0·3 0·2 0·1

L.W. +5h +4h +3h +2h +1h H.W. -1h -2h -3h -4h -5h L.W.

M. H. W. S.

M. H. W. N.

M. L. W. N.

M. L. W. S.

H.W.Hts. m.

L.W.Hts. m.

CHART DATUM

TIME ZONE (UT)
For Summer Time add ONE hour in **non-shaded areas**

IRELAND – GALWAY

LAT 53°16'N   LONG 9°03'W

TIMES AND HEIGHTS OF HIGH AND LOW WATERS

JANUARY

Time	m		Time	m
1 SU	0539 1141 1810 2358	5.1 0.5 5.0 0.8	**16** M	0622 1219 1845	4.7 0.9 4.6
2 M	0627 1225 1857	5.2 0.4 5.0	**17** TU	0025 0658 1253 1922	1.2 4.7 0.9 4.5
3 TU	0044 0713 1311 1944	0.8 5.2 0.4 4.9	**18** W	0100 0734 1327 1959	1.2 4.7 1.0 4.4
4 W	0131 0801 1356 2034	1.1 5.1 0.6 4.7	**19** TH	0136 0808 1400 2036	1.3 4.6 1.1 4.3
5 TH	0219 0852 1444 2130	1.2 4.9 0.9 4.5	**20** F	0212 0841 1435 2115	1.5 4.4 1.3 4.2
6 F	0313 0948 1538 2231	1.4 4.6 1.2 4.3	**21** SA	0250 0915 1513 2157	1.7 4.2 1.5 4.0
7 SA	0417 1050 1642 2336	1.7 4.4 1.5 4.2	**22** SU	0334 0957 1556 2246	1.9 4.1 1.7 3.9
8 SU	0532 1155 1800	1.8 4.2 1.7	**23** M	0426 1048 1650 2340	2.0 3.9 1.8 3.8
9 M	0042 0647 1305 1921	4.1 1.8 4.1 1.8	**24** TU	0532 1149 1801	2.1 3.8 2.0
10 TU	0150 0754 1413 2023	4.2 1.7 4.2 1.7	**25** W	0044 0701 1304 1940	3.9 2.1 3.8 1.9
11 W	0249 0851 1512 2112	4.3 1.6 4.3 1.6	**26** TH	0156 0818 1430 2046	4.0 2.0 4.0 1.7
12 TH	0339 0939 1602 2154	4.4 1.4 4.4 1.5	**27** F	0300 0915 1534 2137	4.4 1.4 4.3 1.3
13 F	0423 1023 1646 2233	4.6 1.3 4.4 1.4	**28** SA	0353 1004 1626 2223	4.6 0.9 4.6 1.0
14 SA	0504 1105 1728 2312	4.6 1.1 4.5 1.3	**29** SU	0442 1049 1713 2307	4.9 0.5 4.9 0.7
15 SU	0544 1143 1807 2349	4.7 1.0 4.5 1.2	**30** M	0530 1132 1759 2350	5.2 0.2 5.0 0.4
			31 TU	0616 1214 1843	5.3 0.0 5.1

FEBRUARY

Time	m		Time	m
1 W	0032 0700 1255 1926	0.4 5.4 0.0 5.1	**16** TH	0036 0712 1257 1931	0.8 4.7 0.7 4.6
2 TH	0115 0744 1336 2010	0.5 5.2 0.2 4.9	**17** F	0108 0741 1327 2001	0.9 4.6 0.8 4.5
3 F	0158 0829 1418 2057	0.7 5.0 0.6 4.6	**18** SA	0139 0807 1357 2030	1.1 4.5 1.0 4.3
4 SA	0244 0918 1504 2150	1.0 4.7 1.0 4.3	**19** SU	0213 0833 1431 2102	1.3 4.3 1.3 4.1
5 SU	0338 1013 1557 2252	1.4 4.3 1.5 4.0	**20** M	0252 0910 1511 2150	1.6 4.1 1.6 3.9
6 M	0446 1118 1707	1.8 4.0 1.9	**21** TU	0340 1006 1602 2253	1.8 3.9 1.9 3.8
7 TU	0004 0609 1235 1845	3.8 1.9 3.7 2.1	**22** W	0441 1117 1709	2.0 3.7 2.1
8 W	0128 0736 1401 2012	3.8 1.9 3.7 2.0	**23** TH	0004 0616 1238 1928	3.7 2.1 3.6 2.1
9 TH	0241 0847 1508 2106	3.9 1.8 3.9 1.8	**24** F	0129 0808 1423 2039	3.8 1.8 3.8 1.7
10 F	0333 0936 1556 2145	4.2 1.6 4.1 1.5	**25** SA	0248 0906 1528 2127	4.2 1.3 4.2 1.2
11 SA	0416 1014 1637 2221	4.4 1.4 4.3 1.3	**26** SU	0343 0952 1615 2210	4.5 0.8 4.6 0.8
12 SU	0455 1050 1715 2256	4.5 1.0 4.5 1.1	**27** M	0430 1034 1659 2251	5.0 0.3 5.0 0.4
13 M	0532 1124 1751 2330	4.7 0.8 4.7 0.9	**28** TU	0515 1114 1741 2332	5.3 0.0 5.2 0.2
14 TU	0607 1156 1826	4.8 0.7 4.7			
15 W	0004 0640 1227 1859	0.8 4.8 0.6 4.7			

MARCH

Time	m		Time	m
1 W	0559 1154 1823	5.4 -0.2 5.3	**16** TH	0616 1157 1831	4.8 0.6 4.8
2 TH	0012 0641 1233 1903	0.1 5.5 -0.1 5.2	**17** F	0008 0645 1225 1859	0.7 4.8 0.6 4.7
3 F	0053 0722 1311 1942	0.2 5.3 0.1 5.0	**18** SA	0038 0712 1253 1926	0.8 4.7 0.8 4.6
4 SA	0134 0804 1350 2023	0.4 5.0 0.5 4.7	**19** SU	0109 0737 1323 1951	0.9 4.5 1.0 4.4
5 SU	0216 0847 1431 2107	0.8 4.6 1.1 4.3	**20** M	0143 0804 1358 2020	1.1 4.3 1.3 4.2
6 M	0306 0937 1519 2203	1.3 4.2 1.6 3.9	**21** TU	0223 0841 1439 2107	1.4 4.1 1.6 4.0
7 TU	0412 1042 1628 2324	1.7 3.7 2.1 3.6	**22** W	0311 0941 1531 2221	1.7 3.8 1.9 3.8
8 W	0540 1210 1814	2.0 3.5 2.2	**23** TH	0414 1101 1643 2339	1.9 3.6 2.2 3.7
9 TH	0110 0714 1352 1958	3.6 2.0 3.6 2.1	**24** F	0603 1227 1918	2.0 3.6 2.1
10 F	0226 0843 1456 2055	3.8 1.7 3.8 1.8	**25** SA	0109 0750 1414 2020	3.8 1.6 3.9 1.7
11 SA	0316 0923 1539 2127	4.0 1.4 4.1 1.5	**26** SU	0231 0845 1511 2107	4.2 1.1 4.3 1.2
12 SU	0357 0953 1617 2159	4.3 1.1 4.3 1.2	**27** M	0324 0930 1555 2149	4.7 0.7 4.8 0.7
13 M	0434 1024 1652 2232	4.5 0.9 4.5 0.9	**28** TU	0409 1011 1636 2229	5.0 0.3 5.1 0.3
14 TU	0509 1056 1726 2305	4.7 0.7 4.7 0.7	**29** W	0453 1050 1717 2310	5.3 0.0 5.3 0.1
15 W	0543 1127 1759 2337	4.8 0.6 4.8 0.7	**30** TH	0536 1129 1757 2350	5.5 0.0 5.3 0.1
			31 F	0618 1207 1836	5.4 0.1 5.3

APRIL

Time	m		Time	m
1 SA	0030 0659 1246 1914	0.2 5.3 0.3 5.0	**16** SU	0009 0645 1222 1855	0.8 4.7 0.9 4.7
2 SU	0111 0740 1324 1953	0.5 4.9 0.7 4.7	**17** M	0043 0716 1256 1925	0.9 4.5 1.1 4.5
3 M	0154 0822 1403 2035	0.9 4.5 1.2 4.3	**18** TU	0122 0751 1334 2002	1.1 4.3 1.4 4.3
4 TU	0242 0911 1449 2127	1.3 4.1 1.7 3.9	**19** W	0205 0835 1419 2053	1.3 4.1 1.7 4.1
5 W	0349 1015 1601 2245	1.7 3.7 2.2 3.6	**20** TH	0257 0938 1515 2207	1.6 3.9 2.0 3.9
6 TH	0516 1147 1745	1.9 3.5 2.3	**21** F	0404 1054 1636 2325	1.8 3.7 2.2 3.9
7 F	0042 0637 1327 1910	3.6 1.9 3.5 2.2	**22** SA	0555 1216 1850	1.8 3.8 2.0
8 SA	0157 0758 1429 2016	3.7 1.7 3.8 1.9	**23** SU	0048 0719 1345 1951	4.1 1.5 4.1 1.6
9 SU	0247 0845 1511 2054	4.0 1.4 4.1 1.6	**24** M	0202 0815 1443 2040	4.4 1.1 4.5 1.1
10 M	0328 0918 1548 2128	4.2 1.2 4.4 1.2	**25** TU	0257 0902 1528 2123	4.7 0.7 4.8 0.8
11 TU	0404 0950 1622 2202	4.4 0.9 4.6 1.0	**26** W	0344 0944 1609 2205	5.1 0.5 5.1 0.5
12 W	0439 1023 1655 2236	4.6 0.8 4.7 0.8	**27** TH	0428 1025 1650 2246	5.2 0.3 5.2 0.3
13 TH	0513 1054 1726 2308	4.7 0.7 4.8 0.7	**28** F	0512 1104 1730 2328	5.3 0.3 5.3 0.3
14 F	0545 1124 1757 2338	4.7 0.7 4.8 0.7	**29** SA	0556 1143 1810	5.2 0.5 5.2
15 SA	0615 1152 1826	4.7 0.8 4.8	**30** SU	0010 0638 1222 1850	0.4 5.1 0.6 5.0

Chart Datum: 0·20 metres above Ordnance Datum (Dublin)

TIDES

TIDES

TIME ZONE (UT)
For Summer Time add ONE hour in **non-shaded areas**

IRELAND – GALWAY

LAT 53°16′N   LONG 9°03′W

TIMES AND HEIGHTS OF HIGH AND LOW WATERS

2006

MAY

Day	Time m	Time m	Time m	Time m
1 M	0053 0.7	0720 4.8	1301	1930 4.7
2 TU	0137 1.0	0804 4.4	1342 1.4	2014 4.4
3 W	0227 1.3	0852 4.1	1429 1.8	2105 4.0
4 TH	0329 1.6	0952 3.8	1537 2.1	2213 3.8
5 F	0445 1.8	1109 3.6	1707 2.3	◐ 2350 3.7
6 SA	0553 1.8	1233 3.6	1819 2.2	
7 SU	0107 3.7	0654 1.7	1342 3.8	1920 2.0
8 M	0204 3.9	0749 1.6	1431 4.0	2010 1.7
9 TU	0249 4.1	0834 1.4	1509 4.3	2051 1.4
10 W	0327 4.2	0912 1.2	1544 4.5	2128 1.2
11 TH	0403 4.4	0947 1.1	1617 4.6	2203 1.0
12 F	0437 4.5	1020 1.0	1649 4.7	2237 0.9
13 SA	0511 4.6	1052 0.9	1724 4.8	○ 2311 0.8
14 SU	0546 4.6	1124 0.9	1756 4.8	2347 0.8
15 M	0624 4.6	1159 1.0	1833 4.8	
16 TU	0026 0.9	0702 4.5	1239 1.1	1912 4.7
17 W	0109 1.0	0745 4.4	1322 1.3	1956 4.5
18 TH	0157 1.1	0834 4.2	1411 1.6	2051 4.3
19 F	0251 1.3	0934 4.1	1510 1.8	2158 4.2
20 SA	0357 1.5	1042 4.0	1631 1.9	2310 4.2
21 SU	0522 1.5	1154 4.0	1812 1.8	
22 M	0021 4.3	0641 1.4	1307 4.2	1917 1.5
23 TU	0129 4.5	0742 1.2	1409 4.5	2011 1.2
24 W	0228 4.7	0834 1.0	1459 4.8	2059 1.0
25 TH	0318 4.9	0919 0.8	1543 4.9	2143 0.8
26 F	0405 5.0	1001 0.8	1625 5.0	2226 0.7
27 SA	0451 5.0	1042 0.8	1707 5.0	● 2310 0.7
28 SU	0536 4.9	1123 0.9	1749 5.0	2355 0.7
29 M	0621 4.8	1203 1.1	1832 4.8	
30 TU	0039 0.9	0704 4.6	1244 1.3	1914 4.7
31 W	0124 1.0	0748 4.4	1326 1.5	1958 4.4

JUNE

Day	Time m	Time m	Time m	Time m
1 TH	0210 1.2	0834 4.1	1411 1.7	2045 4.2
2 F	0301 1.4	0925 3.9	1504 1.9	2140 4.0
3 SA	0359 1.6	1023 3.8	1611 2.1	◐ 2242 3.8
4 SU	0459 1.7	1123 3.7	1722 2.1	2345 3.8
5 M	0557 1.7	1225 3.8	1824 2.0	
6 TU	0050 3.8	0651 1.7	1326 3.9	1920 1.9
7 W	0150 3.8	0744 1.6	1417 4.1	2010 1.7
8 TH	0239 4.0	0830 1.5	1459 4.2	2054 1.5
9 F	0321 4.1	0912 1.4	1537 4.4	2134 1.2
10 SA	0401 4.3	0950 1.2	1613 4.6	2212 1.1
11 SU	0442 4.4	1027 1.1	1652 4.7	○ 2252 0.9
12 M	0524 4.5	1106 1.0	1734 4.8	2334 0.8
13 TU	0608 4.6	1147 1.0	1817 4.9	
14 W	0018 0.7	0652 4.6	1231 1.0	1902 4.8
15 TH	0103 0.7	0737 4.6	1317 1.1	1949 4.7
16 F	0150 0.8	0826 4.5	1405 1.3	2042 4.6
17 SA	0241 0.9	0920 4.3	1500 1.5	2142 4.5
18 SU	0338 1.1	1021 4.2	1606 1.6	◑ 2247 4.4
19 M	0444 1.3	1124 4.2	1726 1.7	2352 4.3
20 TU	0556 1.4	1230 4.2	1842 1.6	
21 W	0057 4.4	0706 1.4	1336 4.3	1945 1.4
22 TH	0201 4.4	0807 1.3	1434 4.5	2039 1.2
23 F	0257 4.5	0858 1.3	1524 4.6	2127 1.1
24 SA	0349 4.6	0943 1.2	1609 4.7	2213 1.0
25 SU	0437 4.6	1026 1.2	1653 4.8	● 2259 0.9
26 M	0524 4.6	1108 1.2	1736 4.8	2344 0.9
27 TU	0608 4.6	1149 1.2	1819 4.7	
28 W	0026 0.9	0650 4.5	1229 1.2	1900 4.6
29 TH	0106 0.9	0724 4.4	1307 1.3	1941 4.5
30 F	0145 1.0	0813 4.3	1347 1.4	2022 4.4

JULY

Day	Time m	Time m	Time m	Time m
1 SA	0225 1.2	0855 4.2	1428 1.6	2105 4.2
2 SU	0308 1.4	0939 4.0	1514 1.8	2151 4.0
3 M	0355 1.5	1026 3.9	1608 1.9	◐ 2238 3.9
4 TU	0446 1.7	1114 3.8	1712 2.0	2328 3.8
5 W	0543 1.8	1206 3.8	1821 2.0	
6 TH	0024 3.7	0645 1.9	1306 3.9	1926 1.9
7 F	0134 3.7	0748 1.8	1408 4.0	2023 1.7
8 SA	0241 3.9	0843 1.6	1501 4.2	2112 1.4
9 SU	0334 4.1	0930 1.4	1547 4.5	2158 1.1
10 M	0423 4.3	1014 1.2	1633 4.7	2242 0.8
11 TU	0510 4.5	1057 1.0	1719 4.9	○ 2326 0.5
12 W	0556 4.7	1141 0.8	1805 5.0	
13 TH	0009 0.4	0640 4.8	1224 0.7	1850 5.0
14 F	0053 0.3	0724 4.8	1307 0.7	1936 5.0
15 SA	0136 0.4	0809 4.7	1351 0.8	2024 4.8
16 SU	0221 0.6	0857 4.5	1439 1.1	2118 4.6
17 M	0310 0.9	0950 4.4	1534 1.4	◐ 2218 4.4
18 TU	0406 1.2	1050 4.2	1642 1.6	2321 4.2
19 W	0512 1.5	1154 4.0	1804 1.7	
20 TH	0028 4.1	0629 1.7	1307 4.0	1923 1.7
21 F	0141 4.0	0744 1.7	1418 4.1	2029 1.5
22 SA	0247 4.1	0843 1.6	1515 4.3	2121 1.3
23 SU	0341 4.2	0931 1.5	1603 4.5	2206 1.1
24 M	0429 4.3	1014 1.4	1646 4.6	2248 0.9
25 TU	0513 4.4	1054 1.2	1727 4.7	● 2328 0.8
26 W	0554 4.5	1132 1.1	1806 4.7	
27 TH	0005 0.7	0633 4.5	1209 1.0	1843 4.7
28 F	0041 0.7	0710 4.5	1224 0.7	1919 4.6
29 SA	0114 0.8	0746 4.5	1318 1.1	1954 4.5
30 SU	0148 0.9	0822 4.4	1353 1.3	2028 4.3
31 M	0222 1.1	0858 4.2	1429 1.5	2103 4.1

AUGUST

Day	Time m	Time m	Time m	Time m
1 TU	0259 1.4	0934 4.1	1508 1.7	2145 3.9
2 W	0339 1.7	1017 3.9	1557 1.9	◐ 2235 3.8
3 TH	0427 1.9	1107 3.8	1701 2.1	2334 3.6
4 F	0532 2.0	1206 3.8	1844 2.1	
5 SA	0043 3.6	0714 2.0	1319 3.8	2005 1.8
6 SU	0213 3.7	0827 1.8	1436 4.1	2101 1.4
7 M	0321 4.0	0918 1.5	1532 4.4	2147 1.0
8 TU	0411 4.3	1003 1.1	1619 4.7	2229 0.6
9 W	0456 4.6	1045 0.8	1705 5.0	○ 2311 0.2
10 TH	0540 4.9	1126 0.5	1750 5.2	2352 0.0
11 F	0623 5.0	1207 0.3	1834 5.3	
12 SA	0032 0.0	0704 5.1	1248 0.3	1916 5.2
13 SU	0113 0.1	0745 5.0	1329 0.5	2000 5.0
14 M	0155 0.4	0827 4.7	1413 0.8	2048 4.7
15 TU	0239 0.8	0913 4.4	1502 1.2	2143 4.3
16 W	0330 1.3	1009 4.1	1604 1.6	◑ 2250 4.0
17 TH	0435 1.8	1117 3.9	1732 1.9	
18 F	0005 3.8	0601 2.0	1246 3.8	1913 1.8
19 SA	0131 3.8	0729 2.0	1411 3.9	2033 1.9
20 SU	0243 3.9	0833 1.8	1509 4.2	2120 1.4
21 M	0334 4.1	0919 1.5	1553 4.4	2156 1.1
22 TU	0417 4.3	0958 1.3	1633 4.6	2230 0.9
23 W	0456 4.5	1034 1.1	1710 4.7	● 2304 0.7
24 TH	0533 4.6	1109 0.9	1746 4.8	2337 0.6
25 F	0609 4.7	1143 0.8	1821 4.8	
26 SA	0009 0.6	0643 4.7	1216 0.8	1853 4.8
27 SU	0040 0.7	0716 4.6	1247 0.9	1923 4.6
28 M	0111 0.9	0747 4.5	1318 1.1	1951 4.5
29 TU	0141 1.1	0816 4.3	1350 1.3	2019 4.2
30 W	0213 1.4	0846 4.2	1426 1.6	2056 4.0
31 TH	0251 1.7	0926 4.0	1510 1.9	◑ 2153 3.7

Chart Datum: 0·20 metres above Ordnance Datum (Dublin)

TIME ZONE (UT)
For Summer Time add ONE hour in **non-shaded areas**

IRELAND – GALWAY

LAT 53°16'N   LONG 9°03'W

TIMES AND HEIGHTS OF HIGH AND LOW WATERS

SEPTEMBER
Time m   Time m

1 0338 2.0 / 1022 3.8 / F 1608 2.1 / 2302 3.6
16 0545 2.3 / 1231 3.7 / SA 1909 2.0

2 0441 2.2 / 1128 3.7 / SA 1755 2.2
17 0123 3.7 / 0712 2.2 / SU 1358 3.9 / 2033 1.7

3 0017 3.5 / 0703 2.2 / SU 1245 3.8 / 1952 1.9
18 0231 3.9 / 0817 1.9 / M 1452 4.2 / 2109 1.4

4 0202 3.7 / 0813 1.9 / M 1419 4.1 / 2045 1.4
19 0316 4.2 / 0858 1.6 / TU 1533 4.4 / 2134 1.1

5 0309 4.1 / 0902 1.4 / TU 1517 4.5 / 2128 0.9
20 0354 4.5 / 0934 1.3 / W 1611 4.7 / 2203 0.9

6 0354 4.5 / 0944 1.0 / W 1603 4.9 / 2209 0.4
21 0430 4.6 / 1008 1.1 / TH 1646 4.8 / 2234 0.7

7 0435 4.9 / 1025 0.6 / TH 1646 5.2 / ○ 2248 0.1
22 0506 4.8 / 1042 0.9 / F 1720 4.9 / ● 2305 0.7

8 0517 5.1 / 1105 0.3 / F 1729 5.5 / 2328 -0.1
23 0540 4.8 / 1115 0.8 / SA 1753 4.9 / 2336 0.7

9 0558 5.3 / 1145 0.1 / SA 1811 5.5
24 0612 4.8 / 1145 0.8 / SU 1823 4.8

10 0007 -0.1 / 0637 5.3 / SU 1225 0.2 / 1852 5.4
25 0005 0.8 / 0643 4.8 / M 1215 0.9 / 1851 4.7

11 0047 0.1 / 0716 5.1 / M 1305 0.4 / 1934 5.1
26 0034 1.0 / 0712 4.7 / TU 1245 1.1 / 1917 4.5

12 0127 0.5 / 0756 4.9 / TU 1347 0.8 / 2018 4.8
27 0104 1.2 / 0739 4.5 / W 1318 1.3 / 1945 4.3

13 0209 1.0 / 0838 4.5 / W 1433 1.2 / 2111 4.3
28 0137 1.5 / 0808 4.3 / TH 1356 1.6 / 2022 4.1

14 0258 1.6 / 0928 4.1 / TH 1534 1.7 / ◑ 2220 3.9
29 0217 1.8 / 0847 4.1 / F 1441 1.9 / 2124 3.8

15 0406 2.0 / 1040 3.8 / F 1709 2.0 / 2349 3.7
30 0306 2.2 / 0950 3.9 / SA 1539 2.1 / ◑ 2242 3.6

OCTOBER
Time m   Time m

1 0415 2.4 / 1103 3.8 / SU 1717 2.2
16 0059 3.8 / 0640 2.3 / M 1327 3.9 / 2000 1.8

2 0001 3.6 / 0648 2.3 / M 1221 3.9 / 1927 1.8
17 0203 4.0 / 0742 2.0 / TU 1422 4.2 / 2035 1.5

3 0142 3.9 / 0749 1.9 / TU 1353 4.2 / 2019 1.3
18 0247 4.3 / 0827 1.7 / W 1505 4.4 / 2101 1.3

4 0244 4.3 / 0837 1.4 / W 1453 4.7 / 2102 0.9
19 0325 4.5 / 0904 1.4 / TH 1542 4.6 / 2131 1.1

5 0327 4.8 / 0919 1.0 / TH 1539 5.1 / 2143 0.5
20 0400 4.7 / 0939 1.2 / F 1617 4.7 / 2202 1.0

6 0408 5.1 / 1000 0.6 / F 1622 5.4 / 2222 0.2
21 0433 4.8 / 1013 1.0 / SA 1650 4.8 / 2233 0.9

7 0448 5.3 / 1040 0.4 / SA 1704 5.6 / ○ 2301 0.1
22 0506 4.9 / 1045 1.0 / SU 1721 4.8 / ● 2302 1.0

8 0529 5.4 / 1121 0.2 / SU 1747 5.6 / 2340 0.1
23 0538 4.9 / 1116 1.0 / M 1752 4.8 / 2331 1.0

9 0609 5.4 / 1201 0.3 / M 1829 5.4
24 0609 4.8 / 1146 1.0 / TU 1822 4.7

10 0020 0.4 / 0649 5.3 / TU 1243 0.5 / 1911 5.2
25 0000 1.2 / 0640 4.8 / W 1219 1.1 / 1854 4.6

11 0101 0.8 / 0729 5.0 / W 1325 0.9 / 1956 4.7
26 0034 1.4 / 0712 4.6 / TH 1256 1.3 / 1929 4.4

12 0144 1.3 / 0812 4.6 / TH 1412 1.3 / 2048 4.3
27 0113 1.6 / 0746 4.5 / F 1337 1.5 / 2013 4.2

13 0233 1.8 / 0901 4.2 / F 1513 1.8 / 2157 3.9
28 0156 1.9 / 0831 4.3 / SA 1425 1.7 / 2114 4.0

14 0345 2.2 / 1011 3.9 / SA 1645 2.1 / ◑ 2329 3.7
29 0250 2.2 / 0933 4.1 / SU 1526 1.9 / ◑ 2228 3.8

15 0522 2.4 / 1204 3.8 / SU 1827 2.0
30 0404 2.4 / 1044 4.1 / M 1654 2.0 / 2344 3.9

31 0614 2.2 / 1158 4.2 / TU 1849 1.7

NOVEMBER
Time m   Time m

1 0103 4.2 / 0716 1.9 / W 1316 4.4 / 1946 1.4
16 0206 4.2 / 0745 1.9 / TH 1425 4.2 / 2019 1.6

2 0208 4.5 / 0807 1.5 / TH 1421 4.8 / 2033 1.0
17 0247 4.4 / 0829 1.7 / F 1507 4.4 / 2055 1.4

3 0256 4.9 / 0853 1.1 / F 1511 5.1 / 2115 0.7
18 0324 4.6 / 0908 1.5 / SA 1543 4.5 / 2129 1.3

4 0339 5.2 / 0935 0.7 / SA 1556 5.4 / 2156 0.5
19 0358 4.7 / 0944 1.3 / SU 1617 4.6 / 2201 1.2

5 0420 5.4 / 1017 0.5 / SU 1641 5.5 / ○ 2236 0.5
20 0431 4.8 / 1019 1.2 / M 1650 4.7 / ● 2233 1.2

6 0502 5.4 / 1059 0.5 / M 1725 5.5 / 2316 0.6
21 0504 4.9 / 1052 1.1 / TU 1724 4.7 / 2305 1.2

7 0545 5.4 / 1142 0.5 / TU 1810 5.3 / 2358 0.8
22 0540 4.9 / 1126 1.1 / W 1801 4.7 / 2339 1.3

8 0627 5.2 / 1226 0.7 / W 1854 5.0
23 0617 4.9 / 1204 1.1 / TH 1840 4.6

9 0040 1.1 / 0710 5.0 / TH 1311 1.0 / 1940 4.7
24 0018 1.4 / 0655 4.8 / F 1245 1.2 / 1921 4.5

10 0125 1.5 / 0754 4.7 / F 1358 1.4 / 2031 4.3
25 0101 1.6 / 0737 4.7 / SA 1329 1.3 / 2008 4.4

11 0215 1.9 / 0844 4.3 / SA 1455 1.7 / 2134 4.0
26 0148 1.8 / 0823 4.5 / SU 1418 1.4 / 2105 4.2

12 0320 2.2 / 0946 4.1 / SU 1608 1.9 / ◐ 2252 3.8
27 0243 2.0 / 0920 4.4 / M 1515 1.6 / 2210 4.1

13 0442 2.3 / 1110 3.9 / M 1728 2.0 / ◐ 2318 4.2
28 0351 2.1 / 1025 4.4 / TU 1625 1.7

14 0009 3.9 / 0553 2.3 / TU 1231 3.9 / 1838 1.9
29 0521 2.0 / 1132 4.4 / W 1752 1.6

15 0115 4.0 / 0653 2.1 / W 1335 4.0 / 1935 1.8
30 0026 4.3 / 0637 1.8 / TH 1241 4.5 / 1906 1.5

DECEMBER
Time m   Time m

1 0131 4.6 / 0736 1.6 / F 1348 4.7 / 2003 1.2
16 0156 4.1 / 0749 2.0 / SA 1418 4.0 / 2015 1.8

2 0226 4.8 / 0828 1.3 / SA 1445 4.9 / 2051 1.1
17 0242 4.3 / 0837 1.8 / SU 1505 4.1 / 2058 1.6

3 0314 5.0 / 0915 1.1 / SU 1535 5.1 / 2134 1.0
18 0323 4.4 / 0920 1.6 / M 1546 4.3 / 2137 1.5

4 0359 5.2 / 1000 0.9 / M 1622 5.1 / 2217 0.9
19 0401 4.6 / 1000 1.4 / TU 1625 4.4 / 2214 1.4

5 0443 5.2 / 1045 0.8 / TU 1709 5.1 / ○ 2300 1.0
20 0439 4.7 / 1039 1.2 / W 1705 4.6 / ● 2252 1.3

6 0528 5.2 / 1130 0.8 / W 1756 5.0 / 2343 1.1
21 0520 4.8 / 1119 1.0 / TH 1747 4.7 / 2332 1.2

7 0613 5.1 / 1215 0.9 / TH 1842 4.9
22 0602 4.9 / 1159 0.9 / F 1830 4.7

8 0027 1.3 / 0657 4.9 / F 1300 1.0 / 1927 4.6
23 0013 1.2 / 0644 5.0 / SA 1241 0.8 / 1913 4.7

9 0111 1.5 / 0741 4.7 / SA 1344 1.2 / 2015 4.4
24 0057 1.2 / 0728 4.9 / SU 1323 0.8 / 1958 4.6

10 0156 1.7 / 0827 4.5 / SU 1430 1.4 / 2106 4.2
25 0142 1.3 / 0813 4.8 / M 1408 0.9 / 2048 4.5

11 0247 1.9 / 0916 4.3 / M 1522 1.7 / 2204 4.0
26 0231 1.5 / 0903 4.7 / TU 1458 1.1 / 2145 4.4

12 0346 2.1 / 1012 4.1 / TU 1621 1.8 / ◐ 2304 3.9
27 0327 1.7 / 1001 4.6 / W 1554 1.3 / ◐ 2247 4.3

13 0452 2.2 / 1110 3.9 / W 1725 1.9
28 0434 1.8 / 1103 4.5 / TH 1659 1.5 / 2351 4.3

14 0003 3.9 / 0555 2.2 / TH 1213 3.9 / 1827 1.9
29 0550 1.8 / 1209 4.4 / F 1817 1.6

15 0102 4.0 / 0654 2.1 / F 1319 3.9 / 1925 1.9
30 0057 4.3 / 0704 1.7 / SA 1319 4.4 / 1933 1.6

31 0202 4.5 / 0808 1.6 / SU 1426 4.5 / 2033 1.5

Chart Datum: 0·20 metres above Ordnance Datum (Dublin)

TIDES

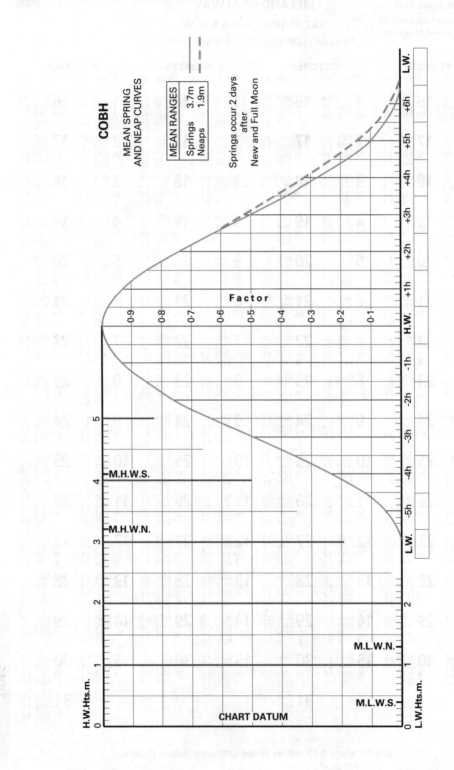

COBH

MEAN SPRING
AND NEAP CURVES

MEAN RANGES	
Springs	3.7m
Neaps	1.9m

Springs occur 2 days
after
New and Full Moon

<table>
<tr><td colspan="2">TIME ZONE (UT)
For Summer Time add ONE hour in non-shaded areas</td><td colspan="4">IRELAND – COBH
LAT 51°51′N   LONG 8°18′W
TIMES AND HEIGHTS OF HIGH AND LOW WATERS</td><td colspan="2">2006</td></tr>
</table>

JANUARY

Day	Time	m	Time	m	Time	m	Time	m
1 SU	0009	0.6	0604	4.2	1234	0.6	1824	4.1
2 M	0054	0.5	0652	4.2	1319	0.6	1910	4.1
3 TU	0140	0.5	0739	4.2	1406	0.5	1957	4.0
4 W	0228	0.5	0828	4.1	1454	0.6	2046	3.9
5 TH	0318	0.6	0918	4.0	1544	0.8	2135	3.8
6 F ◑	0410	0.7	1009	3.9	1636	0.9	2227	3.7
7 SA	0506	0.9	1103	3.7	1734	1.0	2324	3.5
8 SU	0607	1.0	1203	3.6	1837	1.2		
9 M	0028	3.5	0714	1.1	1309	3.5	1944	1.2
10 TU	0134	3.4	0823	1.1	1415	3.5	2051	1.2
11 W	0246	3.5	0929	1.1	1517	3.6	2153	1.1
12 TH	0348	3.7	1027	1.0	1612	3.7	2245	1.0
13 F	0440	3.8	1115	0.9	1659	3.8	2329	0.8
14 SA ○	0524	3.9	1155	0.9	1740	3.9		
15 SU	0005	0.8	0602	4.0	1229	0.8	1815	3.9
16 M	0038	0.8	0637	4.0	1300	0.9	1848	3.9
17 TU	0109	0.8	0710	4.0	1331	0.9	1919	3.8
18 W	0139	0.8	0743	3.9	1403	1.0	1952	3.8
19 TH	0212	0.9	0816	3.8	1437	1.0	2026	3.7
20 F	0248	1.0	0851	3.8	1514	1.1	2104	3.7
21 SA	0327	1.1	0929	3.7	1554	1.2	2145	3.6
22 SU ◐	0411	1.2	1012	3.6	1640	1.4	2240	3.5
23 M	0504	1.3	1103	3.5	1739	1.5	2331	3.4
24 TU	0611	1.4	1205	3.4	1853	1.5		
25 W	0041	3.4	0726	1.4	1317	3.4	2007	1.4
26 TH	0156	3.4	0840	1.3	1431	3.4	2116	1.2
27 F	0309	3.6	0948	1.1	1540	3.6	2217	0.9
28 SA	0412	3.8	1047	0.8	1638	3.8	2310	0.6
29 SU ●	0506	4.1	1137	0.5	1728	4.0	2357	0.4
30 M	0554	4.2	1223	0.3	1814	4.1		
31 TU	0041	0.3	0639	4.3	1307	0.3	1857	4.2

FEBRUARY

Day	Time	m	Time	m	Time	m	Time	m
1 W	0126	0.2	0723	4.3	1350	0.3	1941	4.1
2 TH	0210	0.2	0807	4.2	1433	0.4	2024	4.1
3 F	0254	0.4	0852	4.1	1517	0.5	2107	3.9
4 SA	0340	0.5	0936	3.9	1601	0.7	2152	3.7
5 SU ◑	0427	0.8	1023	3.7	1650	1.0	2240	3.5
6 M	0522	1.0	1116	3.4	1747	1.2	2340	3.3
7 TU	0627	1.2	1224	3.2	1859	1.4		
8 W	0059	3.2	0747	1.3	1345	3.2	2022	1.4
9 TH	0225	3.3	0912	1.3	1500	3.3	2141	1.2
10 F	0334	3.4	1018	1.1	1559	3.5	2238	1.0
11 SA	0427	3.7	1106	0.7	1646	3.7	2320	0.8
12 SU	0509	3.9	1143	0.4	1726	3.8	2354	0.7
13 M ○	0546	4.0	1214	0.7	1800	3.9		
14 TU	0022	0.6	0619	4.0	1241	0.7	1830	3.9
15 W	0047	0.6	0649	4.0	1307	0.7	1859	3.9
16 TH	0113	0.7	0717	4.0	1334	0.8	1927	3.9
17 F	0142	0.7	0745	3.9	1405	0.8	1956	3.8
18 SA	0215	0.8	0815	3.8	1437	0.9	2028	3.8
19 SU	0250	0.9	0848	3.8	1511	1.1	2103	3.7
20 M ◐	0329	1.1	0927	3.6	1549	1.2	2146	3.6
21 TU	0416	1.3	1014	3.5	1640	1.4	2242	3.4
22 W	0521	1.5	1118	3.3	1800	1.5	2357	3.2
23 TH	0647	1.5	1239	3.1	1933	1.5		
24 F	0126	3.3	0814	1.3	1408	3.2	2053	1.2
25 SA	0251	3.5	0930	1.0	1526	3.5	2159	0.9
26 SU	0357	3.8	1030	0.7	1625	3.8	2253	0.5
27 M	0449	4.1	1120	0.3	1713	4.0	2339	0.2
28 TU ●	0536	4.3	1204	0.1	1756	4.2		

MARCH

Day	Time	m	Time	m	Time	m	Time	m
1 W	0022	0.0	0618	4.4	1246	0.0	1837	4.3
2 TH	0104	0.0	0700	4.4	1327	0.1	1917	4.2
3 F	0146	0.1	0741	4.3	1407	0.2	1957	4.1
4 SA	0227	0.2	0821	4.1	1447	0.4	2036	4.0
5 SU	0310	0.4	0902	3.9	1529	0.6	2117	3.7
6 M ◑	0354	0.7	0945	3.6	1613	0.9	2202	3.5
7 TU	0445	1.0	1034	3.3	1707	1.2	2259	3.2
8 W	0549	1.3	1142	3.0	1820	1.4		
9 TH	0027	3.0	0713	1.4	1320	2.9	1955	1.4
10 F	0207	3.1	0854	1.3	1443	3.1	2125	1.2
11 SA	0316	3.3	1000	1.0	1541	3.4	2221	0.9
12 SU	0406	3.6	1046	0.6	1626	3.6	2301	0.7
13 M	0447	3.8	1121	0.7	1704	3.8	2333	0.6
14 TU ○	0522	3.9	1150	0.6	1733	4.2		
15 W	0554	4.0	1214	0.6	1806	3.9		
16 TH	0020	0.5	0621	4.0	1238	0.6	1832	3.9
17 F	0044	0.6	0646	3.9	1305	0.6	1859	3.9
18 SA	0113	0.6	0712	3.9	1334	0.7	1926	3.9
19 SU	0145	0.7	0742	3.8	1405	0.8	1957	3.8
20 M	0220	0.8	0815	3.8	1439	1.0	2032	3.7
21 TU	0300	1.0	0854	3.6	1518	1.1	2115	3.6
22 W ◐	0349	1.2	0943	3.4	1611	1.3	2212	3.4
23 TH	0455	1.3	1050	3.2	1731	1.4	2331	3.2
24 F	0622	1.4	1216	3.0	1906	1.4		
25 SA	0106	3.2	0751	1.2	1351	3.2	2029	1.1
26 SU	0233	3.5	0907	0.9	1507	3.5	2136	0.7
27 M	0336	3.8	1007	0.5	1603	3.8	2230	0.4
28 TU	0427	4.1	1057	0.2	1650	4.1	2317	0.1
29 W ●	0512	4.3	1141	0.1	1733	4.2	2358	0.0
30 TH	0000	0.0	0554	4.3	1222	0.0	1813	4.3
31 F	0042	0.0	0635	4.3	1302	0.0	1852	4.2

APRIL

Day	Time	m	Time	m	Time	m	Time	m
1 SA	0122	0.0	0714	4.2	1342	0.2	1931	4.1
2 SU	0203	0.2	0753	4.0	1422	0.4	2009	3.9
3 M	0245	0.5	0833	3.8	1503	0.6	2049	3.7
4 TU	0329	0.8	0914	3.5	1547	0.9	2134	3.4
5 W ◑	0419	1.1	1002	3.2	1641	1.2	2230	3.1
6 TH	0522	1.3	1108	2.9	1753	1.4	2359	2.9
7 F	0643	1.4	1250	2.8	1924	1.4		
8 SA	0139	3.0	0816	1.3	1413	3.0	2048	1.2
9 SU	0244	3.2	0922	1.1	1510	3.3	2144	0.9
10 M	0333	3.5	1008	0.8	1554	3.5	2225	0.7
11 TU	0414	3.7	1044	0.7	1632	3.7	2257	0.6
12 W	0450	3.8	1114	0.6	1705	3.8	2324	0.6
13 TH ○	0521	3.9	1141	0.6	1735	3.9	2348	0.6
14 F	0549	3.9	1208	0.6	1803	3.9		
15 SA	0015	0.6	0619	3.9	1237	0.6	1831	3.9
16 SU	0047	0.6	0644	3.8	1309	0.7	1902	3.9
17 M	0122	0.7	0717	3.8	1344	0.8	1936	3.8
18 TU	0201	0.8	0755	3.7	1422	0.9	2016	3.7
19 W	0246	0.9	0840	3.6	1508	1.0	2104	3.6
20 TH	0340	1.1	0933	3.4	1607	1.2	2204	3.4
21 F ◐	0447	1.2	1041	3.2	1723	1.3	2321	3.3
22 SA	0607	1.2	1203	3.1	1848	1.2		
23 SU	0050	3.3	0729	1.1	1329	3.3	2004	0.9
24 M	0208	3.6	0840	0.8	1439	3.5	2108	0.6
25 TU	0308	3.8	0938	0.5	1535	3.8	2203	0.4
26 W	0400	4.0	1028	0.3	1624	4.0	2252	0.2
27 TH ●	0447	4.2	1115	0.2	1708	4.1	2337	0.1
28 F	0530	4.2	1158	0.1	1750	4.2		
29 SA	0020	0.1	0611	4.1	1240	0.2	1830	4.1
30 SU	0102	0.2	0651	4.0	1321	0.3	1909	4.0

Chart Datum: 0·13 metres above Ordnance Datum (Dublin)

TIME ZONE (UT)
For Summer Time add ONE hour in **non-shaded areas**

IRELAND – COBH 2006

LAT 51°51′N LONG 8°18′W

TIMES AND HEIGHTS OF HIGH AND LOW WATERS

MAY

Day	Time m	Time m	Day	Time m	Time m
1 M	0143 0.4 / 0730 3.9	1402 0.5 / 1948 3.9	16 TU	0110 0.7 / 0704 3.8	1335 0.7 / 1927 3.8
2 TU	0225 0.6 / 0809 3.7	1444 0.7 / 2029 3.6	17 W	0154 0.7 / 0748 3.8	1420 0.8 / 2013 3.8
3 W	0309 0.8 / 0851 3.4	1529 0.9 / 2114 3.4	18 TH	0243 0.8 / 0837 3.6	1511 0.9 / 2105 3.7
4 TH	0358 1.1 / 0938 3.2	1622 1.1 / 2208 3.2	19 F	0339 0.9 / 0933 3.5	1609 1.0 / 2205 3.5
5 F	0457 1.3 / 1038 3.0	1726 1.3 / 2322 3.0	20 SA	0442 1.0 / 1036 3.3	1715 1.0 / 2313 3.5
6 SA	0607 1.3 / 1159 2.9	1841 1.3	21 SU	0552 1.0 / 1147 3.3	1827 1.0
7 SU	0049 3.1 / 0720 1.3	1321 3.0 / 1950 1.2	22 M	0027 3.5 / 0703 0.9	1259 3.4 / 1937 0.8
8 M	0156 3.2 / 0822 1.1	1420 3.2 / 2046 1.0	23 TU	0137 3.6 / 0809 0.8	1405 3.6 / 2039 0.6
9 TU	0247 3.4 / 0911 1.0	1507 3.4 / 2131 0.9	24 W	0237 3.8 / 0908 0.6	1503 3.8 / 2136 0.5
10 W	0330 3.6 / 0953 0.8	1548 3.6 / 2209 0.8	25 TH	0331 3.9 / 1002 0.5	1556 3.9 / 2228 0.4
11 TH	0408 3.7 / 1031 0.7	1626 3.7 / 2244 0.7	26 F	0421 4.0 / 1052 0.4	1645 4.0 / 2317 0.4
12 F	0443 3.8 / 1105 0.7	1701 3.8 / 2317 0.6	27 SA	0509 4.0 / 1138 0.4	1730 4.0
13 SA	0516 3.8 / 1140 0.6	1736 3.9 / 2352 0.6	28 SU	0002 0.4 / 0552 3.9	1222 0.4 / 1812 4.0
14 SU	0550 3.8 / 1216 0.6	1810 3.9	29 M	0045 0.5 / 0633 3.9	1304 0.5 / 1853 3.9
15 M	0029 0.6 / 0625 3.8	1254 0.7 / 1847 3.9	30 TU	0126 0.6 / 0712 3.7	1345 0.6 / 1932 3.8
			31 W	0207 0.7 / 0751 3.6	1426 0.8 / 2013 3.6

JUNE

Day	Time m	Time m	Day	Time m	Time m
1 TH	0249 0.9 / 0832 3.5	1510 0.9 / 2056 3.5	16 F	0240 0.6 / 0835 3.7	1507 0.7 / 2103 3.8
2 F	0335 1.1 / 0916 3.3	1557 1.1 / 2144 3.3	17 SA	0332 0.7 / 0928 3.6	1600 0.7 / 2157 3.7
3 SA	0425 1.2 / 1006 3.2	1649 1.2 / 2238 3.2	18 SU	0428 0.8 / 1023 3.6	1657 0.8 / 2255 3.7
4 SU	0522 1.3 / 1103 3.1	1748 1.2 / 2341 3.2	19 M	0528 0.8 / 1122 3.5	1800 0.8 / 2357 3.6
5 M	0622 1.3 / 1208 3.2	1848 1.2	20 TU	0631 0.9 / 1224 3.5	1905 0.8
6 TU	0046 3.2 / 0719 1.2	1311 3.2 / 1943 1.1	21 W	0101 3.6 / 0735 0.9	1329 3.5 / 2008 0.8
7 W	0144 3.3 / 0812 1.1	1407 3.4 / 2034 1.0	22 TH	0204 3.6 / 0837 0.8	1431 3.6 / 2110 0.8
8 TH	0234 3.4 / 0901 1.0	1457 3.5 / 2122 0.9	23 F	0304 3.6 / 0937 0.8	1531 3.7 / 2209 0.7
9 F	0321 3.6 / 0949 0.9	1544 3.6 / 2208 0.8	24 SA	0400 3.7 / 1033 0.7	1627 3.8 / 2302 0.7
10 SA	0405 3.7 / 1035 0.8	1629 3.7 / 2253 0.7	25 SU	0451 3.8 / 1123 0.6	1716 3.9 / 2348 0.6
11 SU	0449 3.7 / 1119 0.7	1713 3.8 / 2336 0.7	26 M	0537 3.8 / 1208 0.6	1800 3.9
12 M	0531 3.8 / 1202 0.6	1756 3.9	27 TU	0030 0.6 / 0618 3.8	1249 0.6 / 1839 3.9
13 TU	0019 0.6 / 0614 3.8	1246 0.6 / 1839 3.9	28 W	0109 0.7 / 0657 3.7	1327 0.7 / 1917 3.8
14 W	0104 0.6 / 0658 3.8	1330 0.6 / 1924 3.9	29 TH	0146 0.8 / 0734 3.7	1404 0.8 / 1955 3.7
15 TH	0150 0.6 / 0745 3.8	1417 0.6 / 2012 3.9	30 F	0224 0.9 / 0811 3.6	1442 0.9 / 2033 3.6

JULY

Day	Time m	Time m	Day	Time m	Time m
1 SA	0302 1.0 / 0850 3.5	1520 1.0 / 2113 3.5	16 SU	0314 0.5 / 0910 3.8	1539 0.5 / 2136 3.9
2 SU	0344 1.1 / 0931 3.4	1602 1.0 / 2155 3.5	17 M	0402 0.6 / 0958 3.7	1629 0.6 / 2226 3.7
3 M	0429 1.2 / 1016 3.4	1648 1.1 / 2241 3.4	18 TU	0454 0.8 / 1050 3.6	1724 0.8 / 2321 3.6
4 TU	0519 1.2 / 1106 3.3	1741 1.2 / 2333 3.3	19 W	0552 0.9 / 1147 3.5	1827 0.9
5 W	0616 1.3 / 1203 3.3	1841 1.2	20 TH	0024 3.4 / 0658 1.1	1254 3.4 / 1936 1.0
6 TH	0032 3.3 / 0716 1.3	1306 3.3 / 1941 1.2	21 F	0133 3.4 / 0809 1.1	1406 3.4 / 2049 1.0
7 F	0135 3.4 / 0816 1.2	1408 3.4 / 2041 1.1	22 SA	0242 3.4 / 0920 1.0	1516 3.5 / 2157 0.9
8 SA	0236 3.4 / 0915 1.1	1508 3.5 / 2139 1.0	23 SU	0345 3.5 / 1023 0.9	1616 3.6 / 2253 0.8
9 SU	0334 3.5 / 1011 0.9	1605 3.7 / 2234 0.8	24 M	0439 3.6 / 1105 0.8	1705 3.8 / 2339 0.7
10 M	0429 3.7 / 1102 0.7	1656 3.8 / 2323 0.6	25 TU	0524 3.7 / 1156 0.7	1747 3.9
11 TU	0518 3.8 / 1149 0.6	1744 4.0	26 W	0017 0.7 / 0603 3.8	1233 0.6 / 1824 3.9
12 W	0009 0.5 / 0604 3.9	1235 0.5 / 1829 4.1	27 TH	0050 0.7 / 0639 3.8	1305 0.6 / 1858 3.9
13 TH	0055 0.4 / 0650 3.9	1319 0.4 / 1914 4.1	28 F	0121 0.7 / 0712 3.8	1335 0.7 / 1931 3.8
14 F	0140 0.4 / 0736 3.9	1404 0.4 / 2000 4.1	29 SA	0151 0.8 / 0744 3.7	1406 0.8 / 2003 3.8
15 SA	0226 0.4 / 0822 3.9	1451 0.4 / 2048 4.0	30 SU	0224 0.9 / 0818 3.7	1438 0.9 / 2036 3.7
			31 M	0259 1.0 / 0853 3.6	1513 1.0 / 2111 3.6

AUGUST

Day	Time m	Time m	Day	Time m	Time m
1 TU	0336 1.1 / 0931 3.5	1552 1.1 / 2150 3.5	16 W	0419 0.8 / 1015 3.6	1648 0.9 / 2243 3.5
2 W	0419 1.2 / 1015 3.4	1639 1.2 / 2236 3.4	17 TH	0514 1.0 / 1111 3.4	1750 1.1 / 2347 3.2
3 TH	0511 1.3 / 1107 3.3	1738 1.3 / 2333 3.3	18 F	0623 1.2 / 1225 3.2	1908 1.3
4 F	0620 1.4 / 1213 3.3	1852 1.4	19 SA	0109 3.1 / 0747 1.3	1354 3.2 / 2038 1.2
5 SA	0043 3.2 / 0736 1.4	1328 3.3 / 2007 1.3	20 SU	0231 3.2 / 0913 1.1	1508 3.4 / 2152 1.1
6 SU	0200 3.3 / 0847 1.2	1442 3.4 / 2116 1.1	21 M	0335 3.4 / 1018 0.9	1605 3.6 / 2245 0.9
7 M	0313 3.4 / 0950 1.0	1547 3.7 / 2216 0.8	22 TU	0426 3.6 / 1104 0.7	1650 3.8 / 2326 0.7
8 TU	0413 3.7 / 1044 0.7	1640 3.9 / 2308 0.5	23 W	0508 3.8 / 1142 0.6	1729 3.9 / 2359 0.6
9 W	0503 3.9 / 1132 0.4	1728 4.1 / 2354 0.3	24 TH	0544 3.8 / 1212 0.6	1803 4.0
10 TH	0549 4.0 / 1216 0.3	1812 4.2	25 F	0026 0.6 / 0616 3.9	1238 0.6 / 1833 3.9
11 F	0037 0.2 / 0632 4.1	1300 0.2 / 1855 4.2	26 SA	0051 0.7 / 0645 3.8	1302 0.6 / 1901 3.9
12 SA	0120 0.2 / 0715 4.1	1343 0.2 / 1938 4.2	27 SU	0116 0.7 / 0713 3.8	1328 0.7 / 1928 3.8
13 SU	0203 0.3 / 0759 4.0	1426 0.2 / 2022 4.1	28 M	0145 0.8 / 0742 3.8	1358 0.8 / 1957 3.8
14 M	0247 0.4 / 0842 3.9	1511 0.4 / 2106 3.9	29 TU	0217 0.9 / 0814 3.7	1431 0.9 / 2028 3.7
15 TU	0331 0.6 / 0927 3.8	1557 0.6 / 2152 3.7	30 W	0252 1.0 / 0848 3.6	1508 1.1 / 2105 3.6
			31 TH	0330 1.2 / 0929 3.5	1552 1.2 / 2149 3.5

Chart Datum: 0·13 metres above Ordnance Datum (Dublin)

IRELAND – COBH

2006

LAT 51°51′N   LONG 8°18′W

TIMES AND HEIGHTS OF HIGH AND LOW WATERS

SEPTEMBER

Day	Time	m	Day	Time	m
1 F	0419 / 1021 / 1651 / 2248	1.4 / 3.3 / 1.4 / 3.3	**16** SA	0557 / 1206 / 1847	1.3 / 3.1 / 1.4
2 SA	0531 / 1131 / 1812	1.5 / 3.2 / 1.5	**17** SU	0053 / 0734 / 1346 / 2030	3.0 / 1.4 / 3.1 / 1.3
3 SU	0005 / 0701 / 1258 / 1939	3.1 / 1.5 / 3.2 / 1.4	**18** M	0219 / 0904 / 1455 / 2138	3.1 / 1.2 / 3.4 / 1.1
4 M	0134 / 0822 / 1423 / 2055	3.2 / 1.3 / 3.4 / 1.1	**19** TU	0319 / 1001 / 1546 / 2225	3.0 / 0.9 / 3.6 / 0.9
5 TU	0255 / 0928 / 1529 / 2156	3.4 / 0.9 / 3.7 / 0.8	**20** W	0405 / 1043 / 1627 / 2302	3.6 / 0.7 / 3.8 / 0.7
6 W	0354 / 1023 / 1621 / 2247	3.7 / 0.6 / 4.0 / 0.5	**21** TH	0444 / 1117 / 1703 / 2332	3.8 / 0.6 / 4.0 / 0.6
7 TH	0443 / 1110 / 1706 / ○ 2332	4.0 / 0.3 / 4.2 / 0.2	**22** F	0518 / 1144 / 1735 / 2356	3.9 / 0.6 / 4.0 / 0.6
8 F	0527 / 1153 / 1749	4.2 / 0.1 / 4.3	**23** SA	0548 / 1206 / 1804	3.9 / 0.6 / 4.0
9 SA	0013 / 0608 / 1236 / 1831	0.1 / 4.2 / 0.0 / 4.4	**24** SU	0017 / 0615 / 1228 / 1828	0.7 / 3.9 / 0.7 / 3.9
10 SU	0055 / 0650 / 1317 / 1912	0.1 / 4.2 / 0.1 / 4.3	**25** M	0043 / 0641 / 1254 / 1853	0.7 / 3.9 / 0.7 / 3.9
11 M	0136 / 0731 / 1400 / 1953	0.2 / 4.1 / 0.2 / 4.1	**26** TU	0111 / 0709 / 1324 / 1921	0.8 / 3.8 / 0.8 / 3.9
12 TU	0219 / 0813 / 1443 / 2035	0.4 / 4.0 / 0.4 / 3.9	**27** W	0143 / 0739 / 1358 / 1953	0.9 / 3.8 / 0.9 / 3.8
13 W	0302 / 0856 / 1529 / 2119	0.6 / 3.8 / 0.7 / 3.7	**28** TH	0217 / 0814 / 1437 / 2030	1.0 / 3.7 / 1.0 / 3.7
14 TH	0350 / 0943 / 1619 / ☽ 2209	0.9 / 3.5 / 1.0 / 3.4	**29** F	0257 / 0856 / 1523 / 2117	1.2 / 3.6 / 1.3 / 3.5
15 F	0445 / 1041 / 1722 / 2315	1.1 / 3.3 / 1.3 / 3.1	**30** SA	0350 / 0952 / 1625 / ☽ 2219	1.4 / 3.4 / 1.4 / 3.3

OCTOBER

Day	Time	m	Day	Time	m
1 SU	0505 / 1105 / 1747 / 2340	1.5 / 3.2 / 1.5 / 3.1	**16** M	0027 / 0711 / 1321 / 1959	3.0 / 1.4 / 3.1 / 1.4
2 M	0636 / 1236 / 1916	1.5 / 3.2 / 1.4	**17** TU	0152 / 0832 / 1426 / 2102	3.1 / 1.2 / 3.4 / 1.2
3 TU	0112 / 0757 / 1402 / 2031	3.2 / 1.2 / 3.5 / 1.1	**18** W	0249 / 0926 / 1514 / 2148	3.4 / 1.0 / 3.6 / 1.0
4 W	0232 / 0903 / 1505 / 2131	3.5 / 0.9 / 3.8 / 0.7	**19** TH	0334 / 1007 / 1555 / 2225	3.6 / 0.8 / 3.8 / 0.8
5 TH	0329 / 0957 / 1556 / 2222	3.8 / 0.6 / 4.1 / 0.4	**20** F	0412 / 1041 / 1631 / 2256	3.8 / 0.7 / 3.9 / 0.7
6 F	0417 / 1045 / 1642 / 2307	4.1 / 0.3 / 4.3 / 0.2	**21** SA	0446 / 1109 / 1703 / 2321	3.9 / 0.7 / 4.0 / 0.7
7 SA	0502 / 1130 / 1725 / ○ 2349	4.3 / 0.1 / 4.4 / 0.1	**22** SU	0517 / 1133 / 1732 / ● 2346	3.9 / 0.7 / 4.0 / 0.7
8 SU	0544 / 1212 / 1806	4.3 / 0.1 / 4.4	**23** M	0545 / 1158 / 1758	4.0 / 0.7 / 4.0
9 M	0031 / 0625 / 1255 / 1847	0.2 / 4.3 / 0.1 / 4.3	**24** TU	0014 / 0613 / 1228 / 1824	0.8 / 3.9 / 0.8 / 3.9
10 TU	0113 / 0706 / 1338 / 1928	0.3 / 4.2 / 0.3 / 4.1	**25** W	0046 / 0644 / 1301 / 1855	0.8 / 3.9 / 0.9 / 3.9
11 W	0155 / 0748 / 1421 / 2009	0.4 / 4.0 / 0.5 / 3.9	**26** TH	0120 / 0717 / 1339 / 1930	0.9 / 3.9 / 1.0 / 3.8
12 TH	0240 / 0832 / 1507 / 2053	0.7 / 3.8 / 0.8 / 3.6	**27** F	0158 / 0756 / 1421 / 2012	1.0 / 3.8 / 1.1 / 3.7
13 F	0328 / 0920 / 1559 / 2142	1.0 / 3.5 / 1.1 / 3.3	**28** SA	0244 / 0843 / 1512 / 2103	1.2 / 3.6 / 1.3 / 3.5
14 SA	0425 / 1020 / 1702 / ☽ 2248	1.2 / 3.2 / 1.4 / 3.0	**29** SU	0341 / 0941 / 1615 / ☽ 2207	1.3 / 3.5 / 1.4 / 3.3
15 SU	0538 / 1147 / 1826	1.4 / 3.1 / 1.5	**30** M	0453 / 1053 / 1731 / 2324	1.4 / 3.4 / 1.4 / 3.3
			31 TU	0614 / 1215 / 1852	1.3 / 3.4 / 1.4

NOVEMBER

Day	Time	m	Day	Time	m
1 W	0047 / 0730 / 1333 / 2004	3.4 / 1.1 / 3.6 / 1.0	**16** TH	0200 / 0831 / 1428 / 2055	3.3 / 1.2 / 3.5 / 1.2
2 TH	0201 / 0835 / 1435 / 2103	3.6 / 0.8 / 3.9 / 0.8	**17** F	0248 / 0917 / 1512 / 2137	3.5 / 1.0 / 3.7 / 1.0
3 F	0259 / 0931 / 1528 / 2155	3.9 / 0.6 / 4.1 / 0.5	**18** SA	0330 / 0956 / 1552 / 2214	3.7 / 0.9 / 3.8 / 0.9
4 SA	0350 / 1021 / 1616 / 2243	4.1 / 0.4 / 4.2 / 0.4	**19** SU	0409 / 1031 / 1628 / 2248	3.8 / 0.9 / 3.9 / 0.9
5 SU	0438 / 1109 / 1702 / ○ 2328	4.2 / 0.3 / 4.3 / 0.3	**20** M	0445 / 1104 / 1701 / ● 2322	3.9 / 0.8 / 3.9 / 0.8
6 M	0522 / 1154 / 1745	4.3 / 0.3 / 4.3	**21** TU	0520 / 1138 / 1733 / 2356	4.0 / 0.8 / 4.0 / 0.8
7 TU	0012 / 0605 / 1238 / 1827	0.3 / 4.3 / 0.4 / 4.2	**22** W	0554 / 1213 / 1806	4.0 / 0.8 / 3.9
8 W	0055 / 0648 / 1322 / 1908	0.4 / 4.2 / 0.5 / 4.0	**23** TH	0032 / 0630 / 1251 / 1842	0.8 / 4.0 / 0.9 / 3.9
9 TH	0138 / 0731 / 1406 / 1949	0.6 / 4.0 / 0.7 / 3.8	**24** F	0111 / 0708 / 1332 / 1922	0.9 / 3.9 / 0.9 / 3.8
10 F	0223 / 0815 / 1452 / 2033	0.8 / 3.8 / 1.0 / 3.6	**25** SA	0153 / 0751 / 1418 / 2007	1.0 / 3.9 / 1.0 / 3.7
11 SA	0311 / 0903 / 1542 / 2121	1.0 / 3.6 / 1.2 / 3.4	**26** SU	0242 / 0841 / 1509 / 2059	1.1 / 3.8 / 1.1 / 3.6
12 SU	0406 / 1000 / 1640 / ☽ 2219	1.2 / 3.3 / 1.4 / 3.2	**27** M	0337 / 0937 / 1607 / 2159	1.1 / 3.7 / 1.2 / 3.5
13 M	0511 / 1110 / 1750 / 2336	1.4 / 3.2 / 1.5 / 3.1	**28** TU	0440 / 1040 / 1712 / ☽ 2305	1.2 / 3.6 / 1.2 / 3.5
14 TU	0626 / 1230 / 1904	1.4 / 3.2 / 1.4	**29** W	0548 / 1149 / 1823	1.2 / 3.6 / 1.2
15 W	0058 / 0736 / 1337 / 2006	3.1 / 1.3 / 3.3 / 1.3	**30** TH	0016 / 0659 / 1258 / 1931	3.5 / 1.1 / 3.7 / 1.1

DECEMBER

Day	Time	m	Day	Time	m
1 F	0125 / 0804 / 1401 / 2033	3.7 / 0.9 / 3.8 / 0.9	**16** SA	0147 / 0819 / 1419 / 2046	3.4 / 1.3 / 3.5 / 1.2
2 SA	0227 / 0904 / 1459 / 2130	3.8 / 0.8 / 4.0 / 0.8	**17** SU	0241 / 0910 / 1508 / 2135	3.5 / 1.2 / 3.6 / 1.1
3 SU	0324 / 1000 / 1553 / 2223	4.0 / 0.7 / 4.0 / 0.6	**18** M	0331 / 0957 / 1555 / 2221	3.7 / 1.0 / 3.7 / 1.0
4 M	0417 / 1052 / 1643 / 2312	4.1 / 0.6 / 4.1 / 0.6	**19** TU	0417 / 1042 / 1638 / 2303	3.8 / 1.0 / 3.8 / 0.9
5 TU	0507 / 1141 / 1730 / ○ 2358	4.2 / 0.5 / 4.1 / 0.6	**20** W	0501 / 1125 / 1718 / ● 2344	3.9 / 0.9 / 3.9 / 0.8
6 W	0553 / 1226 / 1813	4.2 / 0.6 / 4.1	**21** TH	0542 / 1205 / 1757	4.0 / 0.8 / 3.9
7 TH	0041 / 0636 / 1310 / 1854	0.6 / 4.1 / 0.7 / 4.0	**22** F	0024 / 0623 / 1247 / 1837	0.7 / 4.1 / 0.8 / 4.0
8 F	0124 / 0719 / 1352 / 1934	0.7 / 4.0 / 0.8 / 3.8	**23** SA	0105 / 0704 / 1329 / 1919	0.7 / 4.1 / 0.8 / 3.9
9 SA	0207 / 0801 / 1435 / 2015	0.8 / 3.9 / 0.9 / 3.7	**24** SU	0148 / 0748 / 1413 / 2004	0.7 / 4.0 / 0.8 / 3.9
10 SU	0251 / 0846 / 1520 / 2058	1.0 / 3.7 / 1.2 / 3.5	**25** M	0235 / 0835 / 1500 / 2052	0.8 / 4.0 / 0.9 / 3.8
11 M	0338 / 0933 / 1607 / 2145	1.1 / 3.5 / 1.3 / 3.4	**26** TU	0324 / 0925 / 1550 / 2143	0.9 / 3.9 / 1.0 / 3.7
12 TU	0430 / 1024 / 1701 / ☽ 2238	1.3 / 3.4 / 1.4 / 3.3	**27** W	0417 / 1018 / 1645 / 2238	0.9 / 3.8 / 1.0 / 3.6
13 W	0527 / 1121 / 1759 / 2339	1.3 / 3.3 / 1.4 / 3.3	**28** TH	0516 / 1116 / 1745 / 2338	1.0 / 3.7 / 1.1 / 3.6
14 TH	0628 / 1224 / 1859	1.4 / 3.3 / 1.4	**29** F	0621 / 1219 / 1852	1.1 / 3.7 / 1.2
15 F	0045 / 0725 / 1325 / 1955	3.3 / 1.3 / 3.4 / 1.4	**30** SA	0044 / 0729 / 1326 / 2000	3.6 / 1.1 / 3.6 / 1.1
			31 SU	0154 / 0839 / 1432 / 2107	3.6 / 1.2 / 3.7 / 1.1

Chart Datum: 0·13 metres above Ordnance Datum (Dublin)

TIDES

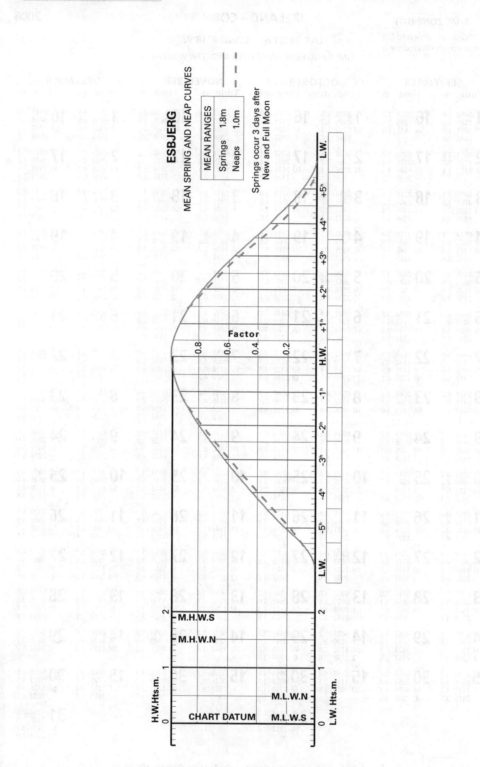

ESBJERG

MEAN SPRING AND NEAP CURVES

MEAN RANGES	
Springs	1.8m
Neaps	1.0m

Springs occur 3 days after
New and Full Moon

TIME ZONE -0100
(Danish Standard Time)
Subtract 1 hour for UT
For Danish Summer Time add
ONE hour in **non-shaded areas**

DENMARK – ESBJERG

LAT 55°28'N   LONG 8°26'E

TIMES AND HEIGHTS OF HIGH AND LOW WATERS

JANUARY

Time m	Time m
1 SU 0325 1.7 / 0922 0.0 / 1558 1.6 / 2138 0.2	**16** M 0400 1.7 / 1007 0.1 / 1626 1.5 / 2208 0.2
2 M 0410 1.8 / 1009 0.0 / 1645 1.6 / 2222 0.1	**17** TU 0433 1.7 / 1042 0.1 / 1655 1.4 / 2239 0.2
3 TU 0454 1.8 / 1057 0.0 / 1732 1.6 / 2308 0.1	**18** W 0500 1.7 / 1112 0.1 / 1721 1.4 / 2311 0.2
4 W 0538 1.8 / 1144 -0.1 / 1818 1.5 / 2354 0.1	**19** TH 0526 1.7 / 1215 0.1 / 1748 1.4 / 2344 0.1
5 TH 0624 1.8 / 1233 0.0 / 1906 1.5	**20** F 0555 1.7 / 1215 0.1 / 1820 1.4 ◑ 2012 1.4
6 F 0042 0.1 / 0715 1.8 / 1324 0.0 ◑ 1957 1.5	**21** SA 0021 0.1 / 0630 1.7 / 1253 0.1 / 1858 1.5
7 SA 0133 0.1 / 0809 1.8 / 1418 0.1 / 2053 1.5	**22** SU 0102 0.1 / 0713 1.7 / 1335 0.1 ◐ 1944 1.5
8 SU 0229 0.2 / 0911 1.8 / 1518 0.1 / 2153 1.5	**23** M 0148 0.1 / 0803 1.6 / 1422 0.2 / 2037 1.4
9 M 0331 0.2 / 1017 1.7 / 1622 0.2 / 2256 1.5	**24** TU 0241 0.2 / 0900 1.6 / 1518 0.2 / 2140 1.4
10 TU 0441 0.2 / 1124 1.7 / 1727 0.2 / 2358 1.5	**25** W 0342 0.2 / 1011 1.5 / 1622 0.3 / 2254 1.4
11 W 0551 0.2 / 1230 1.7 / 1829 0.2	**26** TH 0455 0.3 / 1133 1.5 / 1736 0.3
12 TH 0057 1.6 / 0656 0.1 / 1329 1.6 / 1924 0.2	**27** F 0012 1.4 / 0613 0.2 / 1251 1.5 / 1846 0.2
13 F 0150 1.7 / 0753 0.1 / 1423 1.6 / 2012 0.2	**28** SA 0119 1.5 / 0722 0.1 / 1357 1.5 / 1945 0.2
14 SA 0239 1.7 / 0843 0.1 / 1510 1.5 ○ 2055 0.2	**29** SU 0218 1.6 / 0819 0.0 / 1455 1.5 / 2036 0.1
15 SU 0322 1.7 / 0928 0.1 / 1551 1.5 / 2133 0.2	**30** M 0309 1.7 / 0910 -0.1 / 1546 1.6 / 2123 0.0
	31 TU 0356 1.8 / 0957 -0.2 / 1632 1.6 / 2207 0.0

FEBRUARY

Time m	Time m
1 W 0440 1.8 / 1042 -0.2 / 1715 1.5 / 2251 -0.1	**16** TH 0440 1.6 / 1045 0.0 / 1658 1.4 / 2247 0.0
2 TH 0523 1.8 / 1126 -0.2 / 1756 1.4 / 2334 -0.1	**17** F 0504 1.6 / 1113 0.0 / 1722 1.4 / 2318 0.0
3 F 0607 1.8 / 1210 -0.2 / 1838 1.5	**18** SA 0530 1.6 / 1144 0.0 / 1749 1.4 / 2353 -0.1
4 SA 0019 -0.1 / 0653 1.8 / 1256 -0.1 / 1923 1.5	**19** SU 0602 1.6 / 1219 0.0 / 1823 1.4
5 SU 0106 -0.1 / 0743 1.7 / 1345 0.0 ◐ 2012 1.4	**20** M 0032 -0.1 / 0641 1.6 / 1259 0.0 / 1903 1.4
6 M 0158 0.0 / 0839 1.6 / 1439 0.1 / 2109 1.4	**21** TU 0115 0.0 / 0728 1.5 / 1344 0.0 / 1952 1.4
7 TU 0258 0.1 / 0946 1.5 / 1542 0.2 / 2215 1.4	**22** W 0206 0.0 / 0824 1.5 / 1437 0.1 / 2051 1.4
8 W 0412 0.1 / 1058 1.5 / 1657 0.3 / 2326 1.4	**23** TH 0306 0.1 / 0936 1.4 / 1542 0.2 / 2206 1.3
9 TH 0534 0.1 / 1208 1.4 / 1809 0.2	**24** F 0424 0.2 / 1109 1.3 / 1704 0.3 / 2339 1.3
10 F 0031 1.5 / 0645 0.1 / 1311 1.4 / 1907 0.2	**25** SA 0554 0.1 / 1234 1.3 / 1824 0.2
11 SA 0130 1.6 / 0742 0.0 / 1406 1.4 / 1956 0.1	**26** SU 0055 1.4 / 0707 0.0 / 1342 1.4 / 1926 0.1
12 SU 0221 1.6 / 0830 0.0 / 1453 1.4 / 2039 0.1	**27** M 0157 1.6 / 0803 -0.1 / 1438 1.4 / 2017 0.0
13 M 0305 1.6 / 0912 0.0 / 1533 1.4 ○ 2115 0.1	**28** TU 0249 1.7 / 0852 -0.3 / 1527 1.5 ● 2103 -0.1
14 TU 0342 1.6 / 0948 0.0 / 1606 1.4 / 2148 0.0	
15 W 0414 1.6 / 1018 0.0 / 1633 1.4 / 2218 0.0	

MARCH

Time m	Time m
1 W 0336 1.7 / 0936 -0.3 / 1609 1.5 / 2146 -0.2	**16** TH 0348 1.6 / 0948 -0.1 / 1608 1.4 / 2151 -0.1
2 TH 0420 1.8 / 1019 -0.3 / 1649 1.5 / 2229 -0.3	**17** F 0415 1.5 / 1015 -0.1 / 1633 1.4 / 2221 -0.1
3 F 0502 1.8 / 1100 -0.3 / 1727 1.5 / 2311 -0.3	**18** SA 0440 1.5 / 1042 -0.1 / 1657 1.4 / 2253 -0.2
4 SA 0544 1.7 / 1142 -0.2 / 1806 1.5 / 2354 -0.3	**19** SU 0507 1.5 / 1114 -0.1 / 1723 1.4 / 2327 -0.2
5 SU 0627 1.7 / 1224 -0.1 / 1845 1.4	**20** M 0539 1.5 / 1149 -0.1 / 1754 1.4
6 M 0039 -0.2 / 0714 1.6 / 1309 0.0 ◐ 1930 1.4	**21** TU 0007 -0.2 / 0617 1.5 / 1229 -0.1 / 1833 1.4
7 TU 0129 -0.1 / 0808 1.4 / 1359 0.1 / 2024 1.3	**22** W 0051 -0.1 / 0704 1.4 / 1315 0.0 ◐ 1920 1.3
8 W 0227 0.0 / 0914 1.3 / 1500 0.2 / 2133 1.3	**23** TH 0142 -0.1 / 0802 1.3 / 1408 0.1 / 2018 1.3
9 TH 0346 0.1 / 1030 1.3 / 1624 0.3 / 2251 1.3	**24** F 0245 0.0 / 0918 1.2 / 1515 0.2 / 2136 1.3
10 F 0519 0.1 / 1143 1.3 / 1744 0.2	**25** SA 0409 0.1 / 1057 1.2 / 1641 0.2 / 2314 1.3
11 SA 0003 1.4 / 0628 0.0 / 1246 1.3 / 1844 0.2	**26** SU 0539 0.0 / 1218 1.2 / 1801 0.1
12 SU 0103 1.5 / 0722 -0.1 / 1340 1.3 / 1933 0.1	**27** M 0031 1.4 / 0647 -0.1 / 1321 1.3 / 1903 0.0
13 M 0155 1.5 / 0808 -0.1 / 1427 1.4 / 2015 0.0	**28** TU 0133 1.5 / 0741 -0.3 / 1415 1.4 / 1953 -0.1
14 TU 0239 1.6 / 0846 -0.1 / 1506 1.4 ○ 2051 -0.1	**29** W 0226 1.6 / 0828 -0.4 / 1501 1.4 ● 2039 -0.3
15 W 0317 1.6 / 0919 -0.1 / 1539 1.4 / 2122 -0.1	**30** TH 0313 1.7 / 0912 -0.4 / 1542 1.6 / 2123 -0.4
	31 F 0357 1.7 / 0954 -0.4 / 1621 1.5 / 2206 -0.4

APRIL

Time m	Time m
1 SA 0439 1.7 / 1033 -0.3 / 1657 1.5 / 2247 -0.4	**16** SU 0418 1.4 / 1015 -0.2 / 1634 1.4 / 2230 -0.2
2 SU 0519 1.6 / 1113 -0.2 / 1733 1.4 / 2330 -0.3	**17** M 0449 1.4 / 1048 -0.2 / 1702 1.4 / 2307 -0.2
3 M 0600 1.5 / 1154 -0.1 / 1811 1.4	**18** TU 0523 1.4 / 1134 -0.1 / 1734 1.4 / 2348 -0.2
4 TU 0014 -0.2 / 0645 1.4 / 1236 0.0 / 1853 1.4	**19** W 0603 1.3 / 1207 -0.1 / 1813 1.4
5 W 0103 -0.1 / 0736 1.3 / 1322 0.0 ◐ 1943 1.3	**20** TH 0036 -0.2 / 0653 1.3 / 1254 0.0 / 1902 1.4
6 TH 0201 0.0 / 0839 1.2 / 1419 0.2 / 2051 1.3	**21** F 0130 -0.1 / 0755 1.2 / 1350 0.1 ◐ 2003 1.3
7 F 0321 0.1 / 0957 1.1 / 1540 0.3 / 2212 1.3	**22** SA 0236 0.0 / 0915 1.1 / 1458 0.2 / 2124 1.3
8 SA 0453 0.1 / 1109 1.1 / 1708 0.2 / 2325 1.3	**23** SU 0357 0.0 / 1042 1.1 / 1619 0.2 / 2252 1.4
9 SU 0600 0.0 / 1212 1.2 / 1810 0.1	**24** M 0518 -0.1 / 1155 1.2 / 1733 0.1
10 M 0027 1.4 / 0651 -0.1 / 1306 1.3 / 1900 0.0	**25** TU 0006 1.4 / 0621 -0.2 / 1255 1.3 / 1834 -0.1
11 TU 0120 1.4 / 0735 -0.1 / 1352 1.3 / 1942 -0.1	**26** W 0106 1.5 / 0715 -0.3 / 1347 1.4 / 1927 -0.2
12 W 0205 1.5 / 0812 -0.2 / 1433 1.4 / 2019 -0.1	**27** TH 0200 1.6 / 0802 -0.4 / 1433 1.4 ● 2015 -0.3
13 TH 0244 1.5 / 0845 -0.2 / 1509 1.4 ○ 2052 -0.1	**28** F 0249 1.6 / 0846 -0.4 / 1515 1.4 / 2100 -0.4
14 F 0318 1.5 / 0915 -0.2 / 1539 1.4 ● 2124 -0.1	**29** SA 0335 1.6 / 0927 -0.3 / 1554 1.5 / 2144 -0.4
15 SA 0349 1.5 / 0944 -0.2 / 1607 1.4 / 2156 -0.2	**30** SU 0417 1.5 / 1008 -0.3 / 1631 1.4 / 2227 -0.4

TIDES

Chart Datum: 0·69 metres below Dansk Normal Null

TIME ZONE -0100
(Danish Standard Time)
Subtract 1 hour for UT
For Danish Summer Time add
ONE hour in **non-shaded areas**

DENMARK – ESBJERG
LAT 55°28′N   LONG 8°26′E
TIMES AND HEIGHTS OF HIGH AND LOW WATERS
2006

MAY

Date	Day	Time	m	Time	m	Time	m	Time	m
1	M	0457	1.4	1047	-0.2	1706	1.4	2310	-0.3
2	TU	0538	1.3	1126	-0.1	1742	1.4	2354	-0.2
3	W	0619	1.2	1206	0.0	1822	1.4		
4	TH	0042	-0.1	0706	1.1	1250	0.1	1909	1.3
5	F ◗	0137	0.0	0803	1.1	1342	0.2	2009	1.3
6	SA	0245	0.1	0911	1.0	1448	0.2	2121	1.3
7	SU	0406	0.1	1021	1.1	1609	0.2	2235	1.3
8	M	0514	0.0	1125	1.1	1719	0.1	2339	1.3
9	TU	0607	0.0	1221	1.2	1815	0.1		
10	W	0034	1.4	0652	-0.1	1310	1.3	1901	0.0
11	TH	0124	1.6	0732	-0.1	1355	1.3	1942	-0.1
12	F	0207	1.4	0808	-0.2	1435	1.4	2020	-0.1
13	SA ○	0248	1.4	0842	-0.2	1511	1.4	2057	-0.2
14	SU	0325	1.4	0915	-0.2	1545	1.4	2133	-0.2
15	M	0401	1.4	0951	-0.2	1617	1.4	2212	-0.2
16	TU	0438	1.3	1028	-0.1	1649	1.4	2254	-0.2
17	W	0518	1.3	1109	-0.1	1725	1.4	2338	-0.2
18	TH	0602	1.3	1154	-0.1	1807	1.4		
19	F	0028	-0.2	0654	1.2	1242	0.0	1858	1.4
20	SA ◐	0124	-0.2	0756	1.2	1339	0.0	2000	1.4
21	SU	0227	-0.1	0906	1.1	1442	0.1	2112	1.4
22	M	0339	-0.1	1019	1.2	1553	0.1	2229	1.4
23	TU	0448	-0.1	1126	1.2	1703	0.0	2339	1.5
24	W	0551	-0.2	1225	1.3	1805	-0.1		
25	TH	0041	1.5	0646	-0.2	1318	1.4	1901	-0.2
26	F	0137	1.6	0736	-0.3	1406	1.4	1953	-0.3
27	SA ●	0229	1.5	0822	-0.2	1451	1.4	2042	-0.3
28	SU	0316	1.5	0906	-0.2	1533	1.5	2127	-0.3
29	M	0400	1.4	0946	-0.1	1611	1.5	2212	-0.3
30	TU	0442	1.3	1026	-0.1	1648	1.5	2256	-0.2
31	W	0520	1.2	1104	0.0	1724	1.4	2339	-0.1

JUNE

Date	Day	Time	m	Time	m	Time	m	Time	m
1	TH	0558	1.2	1143	0.0	1800	1.4		
2	F	0024	0.0	0638	1.1	1224	0.1	1842	1.4
3	SA ◗	0110	0.0	0723	1.1	1309	0.1	1930	1.4
4	SU	0201	0.1	0816	1.1	1400	0.2	2026	1.4
5	M	0259	0.1	0918	1.1	1500	0.2	2130	1.3
6	TU	0401	0.1	1023	1.1	1607	0.2	2236	1.3
7	W	0502	0.0	1124	1.2	1712	0.1	2339	1.4
8	TH	0557	0.0	1221	1.3	1811	0.1		
9	F	0036	1.4	0645	0.0	1313	1.3	1903	0.0
10	SA	0130	1.4	0730	0.0	1400	1.4	1949	0.0
11	SU ○	0219	1.4	0812	0.0	1445	1.4	2033	-0.1
12	M	0305	1.4	0852	0.0	1525	1.4	2117	-0.1
13	TU	0349	1.4	0933	-0.1	1604	1.5	2200	-0.2
14	W	0433	1.3	1015	-0.1	1642	1.5	2245	-0.2
15	TH	0517	1.3	1058	-0.1	1723	1.5	2332	-0.2
16	F	0603	1.3	1143	-0.1	1806	1.5		
17	SA	0021	-0.2	0651	1.3	1231	0.0	1856	1.4
18	SU ◑	0113	-0.2	0745	1.2	1324	0.0	1951	1.6
19	M	0209	-0.1	0844	1.2	1421	0.0	2054	1.5
20	TU	0311	0.1	0947	1.2	1523	0.0	2203	1.5
21	W	0415	-0.1	1051	1.3	1630	0.0	2311	1.5
22	TH	0519	-0.1	1152	1.3	1736	0.0		
23	F	0017	1.5	0619	-0.1	1250	1.4	1839	-0.1
24	SA	0118	1.5	0713	-0.1	1343	1.4	1937	-0.1
25	SU ●	0213	1.5	0803	-0.1	1433	1.5	2030	-0.2
26	M	0303	1.4	0849	0.0	1518	1.5	2118	-0.2
27	TU	0349	1.4	0931	0.0	1559	1.5	2203	-0.1
28	W	0430	1.3	1010	0.0	1636	1.5	2245	-0.1
29	TH	0505	1.3	1048	0.0	1709	1.5	2324	0.0
30	F	0537	1.2	1123	0.0	1742	1.5		

JULY

Date	Day	Time	m	Time	m	Time	m	Time	m
1	SA	0000	0.0	0609	1.2	1159	0.1	1815	1.5
2	SU	0038	0.0	0644	1.2	1238	0.1	1853	1.5
3	M ◗	0117	0.1	0724	1.2	1320	0.1	1937	1.5
4	TU	0200	0.1	0814	1.2	1408	0.1	2029	1.5
5	W	0249	0.1	0911	1.3	1502	0.2	2128	1.4
6	TH	0345	0.1	1015	1.3	1604	0.2	2236	1.4
7	F	0448	0.2	1124	1.3	1713	0.2	2348	1.4
8	SA	0553	0.1	1228	1.3	1822	0.2		
9	SU	0054	1.4	0653	0.1	1327	1.4	1923	0.1
10	M	0154	1.4	0745	0.1	1419	1.5	2016	0.0
11	TU ○	0249	1.4	0833	0.0	1507	1.5	2104	-0.1
12	W	0339	1.4	0918	0.1	1551	1.6	2150	-0.1
13	TH	0424	1.4	1002	0.0	1633	1.6	2235	-0.2
14	F	0509	1.4	1045	-0.1	1715	1.7	2320	-0.1
15	SA	0551	1.4	1130	-0.1	1758	1.7		
16	SU	0006	-0.2	0636	1.4	1215	-0.1	1844	1.7
17	M ◑	0054	-0.2	0722	1.4	1303	-0.1	1934	1.7
18	TU	0144	-0.1	0812	1.4	1354	0.0	2031	1.7
19	W	0238	0.0	0909	1.3	1452	0.0	2135	1.6
20	TH	0339	0.1	1013	1.3	1559	0.1	2246	1.5
21	F	0447	0.1	1121	1.4	1713	0.1	2357	1.5
22	SA	0555	0.2	1225	1.4	1826	0.0		
23	SU	0103	1.5	0657	0.1	1324	1.5	1929	0.0
24	M	0201	1.5	0750	0.1	1418	1.6	2023	-0.1
25	TU ●	0253	1.5	0836	0.1	1506	1.6	2110	-0.1
26	W	0337	1.4	0918	0.1	1547	1.6	2152	0.0
27	TH	0415	1.4	0955	0.1	1622	1.6	2229	0.0
28	F	0447	1.4	1029	0.1	1653	1.6	2302	0.0
29	SA	0515	1.4	1100	0.1	1720	1.6	2332	0.1
30	SU	0540	1.4	1133	0.0	1747	1.6		
31	M	0003	0.1	0607	1.4	1206	0.0	1818	1.6

AUGUST

Date	Day	Time	m	Time	m	Time	m	Time	m
1	TU	0036	0.1	0641	1.4	1245	0.1	1857	1.6
2	W	0114	0.1	0722	1.4	1327	0.1	1942	1.6
3	TH	0157	0.1	0812	1.4	1415	0.2	2036	1.5
4	F	0248	0.2	0910	1.4	1513	0.2	2142	1.5
5	SA	0349	0.3	1021	1.4	1624	0.3	2303	1.4
6	SU	0504	0.3	1142	1.4	1747	0.3		
7	M	0025	1.4	0621	0.3	1254	1.5	1901	0.2
8	TU	0134	1.5	0724	0.2	1354	1.6	1959	0.0
9	W ○	0232	1.5	0815	0.1	1447	1.7	2049	-0.1
10	TH	0323	1.6	0901	0.0	1533	1.8	2134	-0.2
11	F	0408	1.6	0945	0.0	1617	1.8	2218	-0.2
12	SA	0450	1.6	1027	-0.1	1659	1.9	2300	-0.2
13	SU	0530	1.6	1109	-0.1	1741	1.9	2343	-0.2
14	M	0610	1.6	1153	-0.1	1824	1.9		
15	TU	0027	-0.1	0651	1.5	1239	-0.1	1912	1.8
16	W ◑	0113	0.0	0737	1.5	1327	0.0	2005	1.7
17	TH	0203	0.1	0830	1.5	1424	0.1	2109	1.6
18	F	0303	0.3	0936	1.4	1532	0.2	2224	1.5
19	SA	0415	0.4	1050	1.5	1658	0.2	2339	1.5
20	SU	0536	0.4	1202	1.5	1818	0.2		
21	M	0048	1.5	0641	0.3	1306	1.6	1919	0.1
22	TU	0146	1.5	0734	0.2	1401	1.7	2010	0.0
23	W ●	0236	1.5	0820	0.2	1448	1.7	2054	0.0
24	TH	0318	1.5	0900	0.2	1529	1.8	2132	0.0
25	F	0354	1.5	0935	0.1	1603	1.8	2205	0.1
26	SA	0423	1.5	1006	0.1	1631	1.7	2233	0.1
27	SU	0448	1.5	1036	0.1	1656	1.7	2300	0.1
28	M	0511	1.5	1105	0.1	1720	1.7	2328	0.1
29	TU	0535	1.5	1137	0.1	1748	1.7		
30	W	0000	0.1	0605	1.6	1213	0.1	1823	1.7
31	TH ◗	0036	0.1	0642	1.6	1254	0.1	1906	1.7

Chart Datum: 0·69 metres below Dansk Normal Null

TIME ZONE –0100
(Danish Standard Time)
Subtract 1 hour for UT
For Danish Summer Time add
ONE hour in **non-shaded areas**

DENMARK – ESBJERG

LAT 55°28′N   LONG 8°26′E

TIMES AND HEIGHTS OF HIGH AND LOW WATERS

2006

SEPTEMBER

Time m	Time m
1 0118 0.2 / 0728 1.6 / F 1341 0.2 / 1959 1.6	**16** 0227 0.4 / 0900 1.6 / SA 1512 0.3 / 2202 1.5
2 0208 0.3 / 0823 1.5 / SA 1437 0.3 / 2104 1.5	**17** 0345 0.5 / 0900 1.6 / SU 1646 0.3 / 2319 1.5
3 0308 0.4 / 0931 1.5 / SU 1550 0.3 / 2232 1.4	**18** 0512 0.5 / 1136 1.6 / M 1803 0.3
4 0426 0.4 / 1100 1.5 / M 1721 0.3	**19** 0025 1.5 / 0619 0.4 / TU 1241 1.7 / 1900 0.2
5 0003 1.5 / 0552 0.4 / TU 1224 1.6 / 1840 0.2	**20** 0122 1.6 / 0711 0.3 / W 1336 1.8 / 1948 0.1
6 0113 1.5 / 0659 0.3 / W 1328 1.7 / 1938 0.1	**21** 0210 1.6 / 0756 0.2 / TH 1423 1.8 / 2029 0.1
7 0210 1.6 / 0752 0.2 / TH 1422 1.8 / ○ 2027 –0.1	**22** 0251 1.7 / 0835 0.2 / F 1503 1.8 / ● 2104 0.1
8 0300 1.7 / 0839 0.1 / F 1510 1.9 / 2112 –0.1	**23** 0326 1.7 / 0909 0.2 / SA 1536 1.8 / 2135 0.1
9 0344 1.7 / 0922 0.0 / SA 1554 2.0 / 2154 –0.2	**24** 0356 1.7 / 0939 0.1 / SU 1605 1.8 / 2202 0.2
10 0424 1.7 / 1004 –0.1 / SU 1637 2.0 / 2235 –0.1	**25** 0421 1.7 / 1009 0.1 / M 1630 1.8 / 2228 0.2
11 0502 1.7 / 1047 –0.1 / M 1718 2.0 / 2316 –0.1	**26** 0444 1.7 / 1039 0.1 / TU 1654 1.8 / 2257 0.2
12 0540 1.7 / 1130 –0.1 / TU 1801 1.9 / 2358 0.0	**27** 0508 1.7 / 1111 0.1 / W 1723 1.7 / 2330 0.2
13 0619 1.7 / 1214 0.0 / W 1848 1.8	**28** 0536 1.7 / 1148 0.1 / TH 1757 1.7
14 0042 0.2 / 0702 1.6 / TH 1303 0.1 / ◑ 1939 1.7	**29** 0006 0.2 / 0612 1.7 / F 1229 0.2 / 1841 1.7
15 0130 0.3 / 0754 1.6 / F 1359 0.2 / 2044 1.6	**30** 0049 0.3 / 0656 1.7 / SA 1318 0.2 / ◐ 1935 1.6

OCTOBER

Time m	Time m
1 0139 0.4 / 0751 1.6 / SU 1415 0.3 / 2043 1.5	**16** 0310 0.6 / 0946 1.6 / M 1623 0.4 / 2248 1.5
2 0241 0.5 / 0859 1.6 / M 1530 0.4 / 2213 1.5	**17** 0436 0.6 / 1101 1.7 / TU 1734 0.3 / 2351 1.5
3 0359 0.5 / 1028 1.6 / TU 1700 0.3 / 2340 1.5	**18** 0545 0.5 / 1206 1.7 / W 1829 0.3
4 0524 0.5 / 1153 1.7 / W 1814 0.2	**19** 0047 1.6 / 0639 0.4 / TH 1300 1.8 / 1915 0.2
5 0048 1.6 / 0630 0.3 / TH 1259 1.8 / 1911 0.1	**20** 0135 1.7 / 0724 0.3 / F 1348 1.8 / 1956 0.2
6 0143 1.7 / 0724 0.2 / F 1355 1.9 / 2000 0.1	**21** 0217 1.7 / 0804 0.2 / SA 1430 1.8 / 2031 0.2
7 0232 1.8 / 0812 0.1 / SA 1445 2.0 / ○ 2045 –0.1	**22** 0254 1.7 / 0839 0.2 / SU 1506 1.8 / ● 2102 0.2
8 0315 1.8 / 0857 0.1 / SU 1530 2.0 / 2127 –0.1	**23** 0327 1.7 / 0912 0.2 / M 1538 1.8 / 2130 0.2
9 0356 1.8 / 0941 –0.1 / M 1614 1.9 / 2209 0.0	**24** 0355 1.7 / 0942 0.2 / TU 1607 1.8 / 2159 0.2
10 0434 1.8 / 1024 –0.1 / TU 1657 1.9 / 2250 0.1	**25** 0421 1.7 / 1015 0.2 / W 1636 1.7 / 2230 0.2
11 0512 1.8 / 1108 0.0 / W 1739 1.8 / 2330 0.2	**26** 0448 1.7 / 1050 0.2 / TH 1706 1.7 / 2306 0.2
12 0550 1.8 / 1153 0.0 / TH 1824 1.7	**27** 0517 1.7 / 1129 0.2 / F 1744 1.7 / 2345 0.3
13 0014 0.3 / 0632 1.7 / F 1242 0.2 / 1916 1.6	**28** 0553 1.8 / 1213 0.2 / SA 1829 1.6
14 0100 0.4 / 0722 1.7 / SA 1339 0.3 / ◑ 2018 1.5	**29** 0030 0.3 / 0638 1.8 / SU 1304 0.2 / ◑ 1924 1.6
15 0156 0.5 / 0827 1.6 / SU 1453 0.4 / 2134 1.4	**30** 0121 0.4 / 0733 1.7 / M 1404 0.3 / 2033 1.5
	31 0223 0.5 / 0841 1.7 / TU 1517 0.3 / 2156 1.5

NOVEMBER

Time m	Time m
1 0336 0.5 / 1003 1.7 / W 1635 0.3 / 2312 1.5	**16** 0454 0.5 / 1118 1.7 / TH 1745 0.3
2 0452 0.4 / 1123 1.8 / TH 1743 0.2	**17** 0000 1.6 / 0554 0.4 / F 1215 1.8 / 1834 0.3
3 0017 1.6 / 0558 0.3 / F 1229 1.9 / 1841 0.1	**18** 0051 1.6 / 0645 0.4 / SA 1306 1.8 / 1917 0.3
4 0113 1.7 / 0655 0.2 / SA 1327 1.9 / 1932 0.0	**19** 0138 1.7 / 0729 0.3 / SU 1353 1.8 / 1954 0.2
5 0203 1.8 / 0746 0.1 / SU 1420 2.0 / ○ 2018 0.0	**20** 0220 1.7 / 0808 0.3 / M 1434 1.8 / ● 2029 0.2
6 0248 1.8 / 0834 0.0 / M 1508 2.0 / 2102 0.1	**21** 0257 1.7 / 0845 0.2 / TU 1512 1.7 / 2102 0.2
7 0330 1.8 / 0920 0.0 / TU 1554 1.9 / 2145 0.1	**22** 0332 1.8 / 0921 0.2 / W 1548 1.7 / 2136 0.3
8 0409 1.8 / 1006 0.0 / W 1638 1.8 / 2226 0.2	**23** 0403 1.8 / 0957 0.2 / TH 1624 1.7 / 2211 0.3
9 0448 1.8 / 1051 0.1 / TH 1721 1.7 / 2307 0.3	**24** 0435 1.8 / 1036 0.2 / F 1700 1.6 / 2249 0.3
10 0527 1.8 / 1137 0.1 / F 1806 1.6 / 2350 0.4	**25** 0508 1.8 / 1119 0.2 / SA 1741 1.6 / 2331 0.3
11 0609 1.8 / 1227 0.2 / SA 1854 1.5	**26** 0546 1.8 / 1205 0.2 / SU 1827 1.6
12 0035 0.4 / 0657 1.7 / SU 1321 0.3 / ◐ 1950 1.5	**27** 0018 0.3 / 0632 1.8 / M 1257 0.2 / 1921 1.5
13 0127 0.5 / 0754 1.7 / M 1546 0.3 / 2054 1.4	**28** 0109 0.3 / 0725 1.8 / TU 1354 0.3 / ◑ 2023 1.5
14 0229 0.6 / 0903 1.7 / TU 1540 0.4 / 2201 1.4	**29** 0207 0.4 / 0829 1.8 / W 1457 0.2 / 2132 1.5
15 0343 0.6 / 1014 1.7 / W 1648 0.4 / 2304 1.5	**30** 0312 0.4 / 0941 1.8 / TH 1605 0.2 / 2240 1.5

DECEMBER

Time m	Time m
1 0420 0.3 / 1053 1.8 / F 1710 0.2 / 2344 1.6	**16** 0451 0.4 / 1120 1.6 / SA 1738 0.4
2 0526 0.3 / 1200 1.8 / SA 1810 0.2	**17** 0001 1.5 / 0554 0.4 / SU 1218 1.6 / 1829 0.3
3 0042 1.6 / 0627 0.2 / SU 1303 1.9 / 1904 0.1	**18** 0054 1.6 / 0648 0.4 / M 1313 1.6 / 1915 0.3
4 0135 1.7 / 0724 0.1 / M 1359 1.9 / 1954 0.1	**19** 0144 1.6 / 0737 0.3 / TU 1404 1.6 / 1958 0.3
5 0224 1.8 / 0816 0.1 / TU 1451 1.8 / ○ 2041 0.1	**20** 0230 1.7 / 0821 0.2 / W 1451 1.6 / ● 2038 0.2
6 0309 1.8 / 0906 0.0 / W 1540 1.7 / 2125 0.2	**21** 0311 1.7 / 0904 0.2 / TH 1534 1.6 / 2117 0.2
7 0353 1.8 / 0954 0.1 / TH 1625 1.7 / 2208 0.2	**22** 0349 1.7 / 0945 0.1 / F 1616 1.6 / 2157 0.2
8 0433 1.8 / 1039 0.1 / F 1708 1.6 / 2249 0.3	**23** 0426 1.8 / 1027 0.1 / SA 1657 1.6 / 2238 0.2
9 0513 1.8 / 1125 0.2 / SA 1749 1.5 / 2330 0.3	**24** 0503 1.8 / 1111 0.0 / SU 1739 1.6 / 2321 0.2
10 0552 1.8 / 1211 0.2 / SU 1830 1.5	**25** 0543 1.8 / 1156 0.0 / M 1823 1.5
11 0012 0.4 / 0634 1.8 / M 1257 0.3 / 1914 1.4	**26** 0006 0.2 / 0627 1.8 / TU 1245 0.0 / 1910 1.5
12 0057 0.4 / 0721 1.7 / TU 1347 0.3 / ◐ 2004 1.4	**27** 0054 0.2 / 0717 1.8 / W 1336 0.1 / ◐ 2003 1.5
13 0147 0.4 / 0813 1.7 / W 1441 0.4 / 2100 1.4	**28** 0147 0.2 / 0813 1.8 / TH 1431 0.1 / 2100 1.5
14 0242 0.4 / 0913 1.7 / TH 1539 0.4 / 2201 1.4	**29** 0244 0.2 / 0916 1.8 / F 1532 0.2 / 2204 1.5
15 0345 0.5 / 1017 1.6 / F 1640 0.4 / 2303 1.5	**30** 0347 0.2 / 1026 1.7 / SA 1636 0.2 / 2309 1.5
	31 0456 0.2 / 1137 1.7 / SU 1741 0.2

Chart Datum: 0·69 metres below Dansk Normal Null

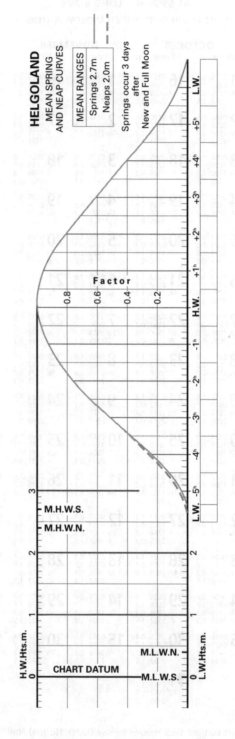

HELGOLAND
MEAN SPRING
AND NEAP CURVES

MEAN RANGES
Springs 2.7m
Neaps 2.0m

Springs occur 3 days
after
New and Full Moon

Factor
0.8
0.6
0.4
0.2

L.W.   +5ʰ   +4ʰ   +3ʰ   +2ʰ   +1ʰ   H.W.   -1ʰ   -2ʰ   -3ʰ   -4ʰ   -5ʰ   L.W.

3
M.H.W.S.
M.H.W.N.
2
1
H.W.Hts.m.
0   CHART DATUM

2
1
L.W.Hts.m.
0   M.L.W.N.
M.L.W.S.

TIME ZONE -0100 (German Standard Time) **Subtract 1 hour for UT**	GERMANY – HELGOLAND	2006
For German Summer Time add ONE hour in **non-shaded areas**	LAT 54°11'N LONG 7°53'E TIMES AND HEIGHTS OF HIGH AND LOW WATERS	

JANUARY

Day	Time m	Day	Time m
1 SU	0005 3.2 / 0701 0.5 / 1237 3.1 / 1918 0.7	**16** M	0057 3.3 / 0746 0.6 / 1320 3.0 / 1950 0.7
2 M	0055 3.3 / 0753 0.5 / 1332 3.1 / 2010 0.6	**17** TU	0133 3.3 / 0821 0.6 / 1353 3.0 / 2023 0.6
3 TU	0144 3.3 / 0845 0.6 / 1422 3.0 / 2056 0.6	**18** W	0205 3.3 / 0853 0.6 / 1425 2.9 / 2053 0.6
4 W	0231 3.4 / 0931 0.6 / 1507 3.0 / 2138 0.6	**19** TH	0235 3.2 / 0922 0.5 / 1456 2.9 / 2124 0.6
5 TH	0316 3.3 / 1017 0.4 / 1551 2.9 / 2222 0.6	**20** F	0305 3.1 / 0952 0.5 / 1529 2.9 / 2157 0.6
6 F	0405 3.3 / 1105 0.5 / 1640 2.9 / ☽ 2310 0.7	**21** SA	0336 3.1 / 1023 0.6 / 1603 2.8 / 2229 0.7
7 SA	0457 3.2 / 1154 0.6 / 1733 2.8	**22** SU	0408 3.0 / 1052 0.7 / 1637 2.8 / 2303 0.8
8 SU	0003 0.7 / 0554 3.1 / 1247 0.7 / 1831 2.8	**23** M	0446 3.0 / 1129 0.8 / 1719 2.7 / 2352 0.9
9 M	0106 0.8 / 0658 3.0 / 1350 0.8 / 1936 2.8	**24** TU	0540 2.9 / 1226 0.9 / 1819 2.7
10 TU	0220 0.8 / 0810 2.9 / 1501 0.8 / 2047 2.8	**25** W	0102 1.0 / 0653 2.8 / 1341 0.9 / 1934 2.8
11 W	0336 0.7 / 0922 2.9 / 1608 0.8 / 2153 2.9	**26** TH	0225 0.9 / 0816 2.9 / 1502 0.9 / 2052 2.9
12 TH	0443 0.7 / 1026 2.9 / 1706 0.8 / 2250 3.0	**27** F	0346 0.8 / 0933 2.9 / 1615 0.8 / 2202 3.0
13 F	0539 0.7 / 1121 3.0 / 1756 0.8 / 2338 3.2	**28** SA	0458 0.7 / 1039 3.0 / 1721 0.7 / 2304 3.1
14 SA	0627 0.7 / 1207 3.0 / 1839 0.8 / ○	**29** SU	0602 0.5 / 1137 3.1 / 1819 0.6 / ● 2357 3.2
15 SU	0020 3.2 / 0708 0.6 / 1246 3.0 / 1915 0.7	**30** M	0657 0.4 / 1231 3.1 / 1912 0.5
		31 TU	0046 3.3 / 0748 0.3 / 1322 3.0 / 2001 0.4

FEBRUARY

Day	Time m	Day	Time m
1 W	0133 3.4 / 0837 0.2 / 1410 3.0 / 2046 0.4	**16** TH	0144 3.2 / 0829 0.4 / 1358 3.0 / 2034 0.4
2 TH	0219 3.4 / 0921 0.2 / 1452 3.0 / 2125 0.4	**17** F	0211 3.1 / 0855 0.4 / 1427 2.9 / 2102 0.4
3 F	0302 3.4 / 1000 0.3 / 1531 3.0 / 2203 0.4	**18** SA	0238 3.1 / 0923 0.4 / 1458 2.9 / 2133 0.4
4 SA	0345 3.3 / 1039 0.5 / 1611 3.0 / 2244 0.5	**19** SU	0307 3.0 / 0951 0.4 / 1528 2.9 / 2201 0.5
5 SU	0429 3.2 / 1118 0.6 / 1654 2.9 / ☽ 2328 0.6	**20** M	0334 3.0 / 1013 0.5 / 1554 2.8 / 2225 0.5
6 M	0517 3.1 / 1200 0.7 / 1743 2.8	**21** TU	0402 2.9 / 1039 0.6 / 1626 2.7 / 2302 0.7
7 TU	0023 0.7 / 0616 3.0 / 1258 0.8 / 1848 2.7	**22** W	0448 2.8 / 1128 0.8 / 1722 2.6
8 W	0138 0.8 / 0731 2.7 / 1417 0.9 / 2009 2.8	**23** TH	0011 0.8 / 0604 2.6 / 1249 0.9 / 1847 2.7
9 TH	0307 0.9 / 0857 2.7 / 1541 0.9 / 2131 2.9	**24** F	0146 0.8 / 0740 2.7 / 1426 0.9 / 2021 2.8
10 F	0428 0.7 / 1013 2.8 / 1651 0.8 / 2238 3.0	**25** SA	0323 0.7 / 0914 2.8 / 1556 0.8 / 2145 3.0
11 SA	0530 0.6 / 1112 2.9 / 1744 0.6 / 2327 3.1	**26** SU	0446 0.5 / 1030 2.9 / 1710 0.6 / 2251 3.1
12 SU	0617 0.6 / 1156 3.0 / 1827 0.5	**27** M	0553 0.3 / 1129 3.0 / 1811 0.5 / 2344 3.2
13 M	0007 3.2 / 0656 0.5 / 1232 3.0 / ○ 1904 0.6	**28** TU	0647 0.2 / 1219 3.0 / 1900 0.3 / ●
14 TU	0042 3.2 / 0731 0.5 / 1303 3.0 / 1936 0.5		
15 W	0115 3.2 / 0802 0.5 / 1331 3.0 / 2006 0.4		

MARCH

Day	Time m	Day	Time m
1 W	0030 3.3 / 0735 0.1 / 1304 3.0 / 1945 0.2	**16** TH	0048 3.1 / 0733 0.3 / 1304 3.0 / 1943 0.3
2 TH	0114 3.3 / 0818 0.1 / 1348 3.0 / 2026 0.2	**17** F	0117 3.1 / 0800 0.3 / 1329 3.0 / 2009 0.3
3 F	0158 3.4 / 0858 0.2 / 1427 3.0 / 2105 0.2	**18** SA	0142 3.1 / 0826 0.3 / 1356 2.9 / 2038 0.2
4 SA	0240 3.3 / 0934 0.3 / 1504 3.0 / 2141 0.3	**19** SU	0209 3.0 / 0853 0.3 / 1425 2.9 / 2108 0.2
5 SU	0319 3.2 / 1007 0.4 / 1539 3.0 / 2219 0.4	**20** M	0238 3.0 / 0920 0.3 / 1455 2.9 / 2136 0.3
6 M	0359 3.1 / 1040 0.6 / 1617 2.9 / ☽ 2258 0.5	**21** TU	0308 2.9 / 0944 0.4 / 1523 2.8 / 2202 0.3
7 TU	0443 2.9 / 1119 0.7 / 1702 2.8 / 2349 0.6	**22** W	0340 2.8 / 1011 0.5 / 1558 2.7 / ☽ 2240 0.5
8 W	0539 2.7 / 1214 0.8 / 1806 2.7	**23** TH	0426 2.6 / 1101 0.7 / 1655 2.6 / 2348 0.6
9 TH	0102 0.7 / 0656 2.5 / 1336 0.9 / 1932 2.7	**24** F	0543 2.5 / 1225 0.8 / 1822 2.7
10 F	0236 0.9 / 0828 2.5 / 1511 0.9 / 2104 2.8	**25** SA	0127 0.6 / 0721 2.5 / 1408 0.9 / 2000 2.8
11 SA	0407 0.7 / 0953 2.6 / 1631 0.8 / 2218 2.9	**26** SU	0309 0.5 / 0858 2.7 / 1542 0.7 / 2126 3.0
12 SU	0514 0.6 / 1054 2.8 / 1727 0.7 / 2307 3.0	**27** M	0431 0.3 / 1014 2.8 / 1654 0.5 / 2231 3.1
13 M	0558 0.5 / 1134 2.9 / 1807 0.6 / 2343 3.1	**28** TU	0535 0.2 / 1111 2.9 / 1752 0.3 / 2323 3.2
14 TU	0633 0.4 / 1207 2.9 / 1843 0.5 / ○	**29** W	0627 0.0 / 1158 2.9 / 1840 0.1 / ●
15 W	0016 3.1 / 0705 0.3 / 1237 2.9 / 1915 0.4	**30** TH	0009 3.2 / 0713 0.0 / 1240 2.9 / 1923 0.1
		31 F	0052 3.3 / 0752 0.1 / 1319 3.0 / 2002 0.1

APRIL

Day	Time m	Day	Time m
1 SA	0133 3.3 / 0829 0.2 / 1357 3.0 / 2041 0.2	**16** SU	0112 3.1 / 0756 0.3 / 1325 3.0 / 2012 0.2
2 SU	0214 3.2 / 0903 0.3 / 1433 3.0 / 2119 0.2	**17** M	0142 3.0 / 0826 0.3 / 1357 2.9 / 2045 0.2
3 M	0254 3.1 / 0935 0.4 / 1510 3.0 / 2156 0.3	**18** TU	0216 2.9 / 0856 0.3 / 1431 2.9 / 2120 0.2
4 TU	0334 2.9 / 1008 0.5 / 1548 2.9 / 2236 0.4	**19** W	0255 2.8 / 0929 0.4 / 1508 2.9 / 2157 0.3
5 W	0418 2.7 / 1047 0.6 / 1633 2.8 / ☽ 2324 0.5	**20** TH	0337 2.7 / 1007 0.5 / 1552 2.8 / 2243 0.3
6 TH	0512 2.6 / 1141 0.8 / 1733 2.7	**21** F	0429 2.6 / 1101 0.6 / 1651 2.7 / ☽ 2350 0.4
7 F	0030 0.6 / 0624 2.4 / 1257 0.9 / 1853 2.7	**22** SA	0541 2.5 / 1220 0.7 / 1811 2.8
8 SA	0158 0.7 / 0751 2.4 / 1431 0.9 / 2023 2.8	**23** SU	0120 0.4 / 0710 2.5 / 1354 0.7 / 1941 2.9
9 SU	0330 0.6 / 0916 2.5 / 1555 0.7 / 2139 2.9	**24** M	0253 0.4 / 0838 2.6 / 1521 0.6 / 2101 3.0
10 M	0439 0.5 / 1019 2.7 / 1653 0.6 / 2231 3.0	**25** TU	0408 0.2 / 0949 2.7 / 1628 0.4 / 2203 3.1
11 TU	0523 0.4 / 1059 2.8 / 1733 0.5 / 2308 3.0	**26** W	0507 0.1 / 1043 2.8 / 1723 0.2 / 2255 3.1
12 W	0556 0.3 / 1131 2.9 / 1809 0.4 / 2342 3.0	**27** TH	0558 0.1 / 1130 2.9 / 1814 0.1 / ● 2345 3.1
13 TH	0628 0.3 / 1202 3.0 / 1843 0.3 / ○	**28** F	0644 0.1 / 1213 3.0 / 1859 0.1
14 F	0015 3.1 / 0659 0.3 / 1231 3.0 / 1913 0.3	**29** SA	0029 3.1 / 0724 0.1 / 1251 3.0 / 1939 0.1
15 SA	0044 3.1 / 0727 0.3 / 1258 3.0 / 1942 0.3	**30** SU	0109 3.1 / 0759 0.2 / 1328 3.1 / 2019 0.2

Chart Datum: 1·68 metres below Normal Null (German reference level)

TIME ZONE -0100
(German Standard Time)
Subtract 1 hour for UT
For German Summer Time add
ONE hour in **non-shaded areas**

GERMANY–HELGOLAND 2006

LAT 54°11'N   LONG 7°53'E

TIMES AND HEIGHTS OF HIGH AND LOW WATERS

MAY

#	Time m	#	Time m
1	0150 3.1 / 0833 0.3 / M 1406 3.1 / 2059 0.2	16	0124 3.0 / 0806 0.4 / TU 1339 3.0 / 2033 0.2
2	0232 2.9 / 0909 0.4 / TU 1446 3.0 / 2139 0.2	17	0207 2.9 / 0845 0.4 / W 1421 3.0 / 2115 0.2
3	0315 2.8 / 0945 0.5 / W 1528 3.0 / 2219 0.3	18	0253 2.8 / 0926 0.4 / TH 1505 3.0 / 2202 0.2
4	0400 2.7 / 1025 0.6 / TH 1612 2.9 / 2305 0.5	19	0342 2.7 / 1013 0.5 / F 1555 3.0 / 2255 0.3
5	0450 2.6 / 1113 0.7 / F 1705 2.9 / ◐	20	0437 2.6 / 1109 0.5 / SA 1654 2.9 / ◑ 2357 0.3
6	0001 0.6 / 0550 2.5 / SA 1218 0.8 / 1811 2.8	21	0542 2.6 / 1217 0.6 / SU 1803 2.9
7	0113 0.6 / 0703 2.4 / SU 1337 0.8 / 1928 2.8	22	0110 0.3 / 0656 2.6 / M 1335 0.6 / 1919 3.0
8	0233 0.6 / 0820 2.5 / M 1458 0.7 / 2041 2.8	23	0228 0.3 / 0810 2.7 / TU 1451 0.5 / 2032 3.0
9	0342 0.5 / 0925 2.7 / TU 1600 0.6 / 2139 2.9	24	0336 0.2 / 0915 2.7 / W 1556 0.4 / 2133 3.0
10	0432 0.4 / 1010 2.8 / W 1646 0.5 / 2222 3.0	25	0433 0.2 / 1010 2.8 / TH 1652 0.3 / 2228 3.0
11	0510 0.4 / 1046 2.9 / TH 1726 0.5 / 2301 3.0	26	0525 0.2 / 1100 2.9 / F 1747 0.2 / 2321 3.0
12	0546 0.4 / 1121 3.0 / F 1805 0.4 / 2337 3.1	27	0615 0.2 / 1147 3.0 / SA 1837 0.2 ●
13	0621 0.4 / 1155 3.0 / SA 1841 0.4 / ○	28	0010 3.0 / 0657 0.3 / SU 1228 3.1 / 1920 0.2
14	0011 3.1 / 0654 0.4 / SU 1226 3.1 / 1915 0.4	29	0053 3.0 / 0734 0.4 / M 1307 3.1 / 2001 0.2
15	0045 3.1 / 0729 0.4 / M 1301 3.1 / 1952 0.3	30	0134 3.0 / 0811 0.4 / TU 1347 3.1 / 2043 0.3
		31	0217 2.9 / 0849 0.4 / W 1429 3.1 / 2124 0.3

JUNE

#	Time m	#	Time m
1	0300 2.8 / 0927 0.5 / TH 1510 3.1 / 2204 0.4	16	0252 2.9 / 0926 0.4 / F 1502 3.2 / 2204 0.2
2	0342 2.7 / 1005 0.6 / F 1552 3.1 / 2245 0.5	17	0341 2.8 / 1013 0.5 / SA 1552 3.1 / 2256 0.3
3	0425 2.6 / 1047 0.6 / SA 1636 3.0 / ◐ 2330 0.6	18	0434 2.7 / 1106 0.5 / SU 1648 3.1 / ◑ 2352 0.3
4	0513 2.6 / 1137 0.7 / SU 1726 2.9	19	0532 2.7 / 1203 0.5 / M 1749 3.1
5	0022 0.6 / 0609 2.6 / M 1237 0.8 / 1825 2.9	20	0050 0.4 / 0632 2.7 / TU 1307 0.5 / 1853 3.1
6	0124 0.6 / 0713 2.6 / TU 1347 0.8 / 1932 2.9	21	0154 0.4 / 0735 2.7 / W 1416 0.5 / 2000 3.0
7	0230 0.6 / 0816 2.7 / W 1454 0.7 / 2036 2.9	22	0259 0.4 / 0838 2.8 / TH 1524 0.5 / 2105 3.0
8	0328 0.5 / 0911 2.8 / TH 1550 0.7 / 2130 3.0	23	0400 0.4 / 0938 2.9 / F 1627 0.4 / 2206 3.0
9	0417 0.5 / 0956 2.9 / F 1639 0.6 / 2217 3.0	24	0456 0.4 / 1035 3.0 / SA 1726 0.4 / 2304 3.0
10	0502 0.5 / 1038 2.9 / SA 1727 0.6 / 2301 3.1	25	0550 0.5 / 1127 3.1 / SU 1820 0.4 / ● 2357 3.0
11	0545 0.5 / 1120 3.1 / SU 1812 0.5 / ○ 2343 3.1	26	0637 0.5 / 1213 3.1 / M 1906 0.4
12	0627 0.5 / 1202 3.1 / M 1856 0.5	27	0042 3.0 / 0718 0.5 / TU 1254 3.2 / 1948 0.4
13	0027 3.1 / 0711 0.5 / TU 1246 3.2 / 1942 0.4	28	0123 2.9 / 0756 0.5 / W 1334 3.2 / 2030 0.4
14	0116 3.1 / 0758 0.5 / W 1332 3.2 / 2030 0.3	29	0202 2.9 / 0834 0.5 / TH 1414 3.2 / 2108 0.4
15	0205 3.0 / 0843 0.4 / TH 1417 3.2 / 2116 0.2	30	0241 2.9 / 0909 0.5 / F 1451 3.2 / 2144 0.4

JULY

#	Time m	#	Time m
1	0317 2.8 / 0943 0.5 / SA 1526 3.2 / 2218 0.5	16	0327 2.9 / 1001 0.4 / SU 1540 3.3 / 2242 0.3
2	0354 2.8 / 1019 0.6 / SU 1603 3.1 / 2254 0.6	17	0415 2.9 / 1048 0.5 / M 1631 3.3 / ◐ 2329 0.4
3	0432 2.8 / 1057 0.7 / M 1642 3.0 / ◐ 2331 0.6	18	0506 2.8 / 1138 0.5 / TU 1724 3.2
4	0514 2.7 / 1140 0.7 / TU 1725 2.9	19	0017 0.5 / 0558 2.8 / W 1233 0.6 / 1822 3.1
5	0015 0.7 / 0603 2.7 / W 1235 0.8 / 1821 2.9	20	0112 0.6 / 0656 2.8 / TH 1341 0.6 / 1929 3.0
6	0113 0.7 / 0702 2.7 / TH 1342 0.8 / 1927 2.9	21	0220 0.7 / 0805 2.8 / F 1458 0.6 / 2043 2.9
7	0218 0.7 / 0805 2.8 / F 1450 0.8 / 2035 2.9	22	0333 0.7 / 0916 3.0 / SA 1613 0.6 / 2155 2.9
8	0322 0.7 / 0905 2.9 / SA 1554 0.7 / 2137 3.0	23	0439 0.7 / 1021 3.0 / SU 1716 0.5 / 2256 2.9
9	0420 0.7 / 1002 3.0 / SU 1655 0.7 / 2234 3.0	24	0535 0.7 / 1116 3.1 / M 1809 0.5 / 2348 3.0
10	0516 0.7 / 1056 3.1 / M 1752 0.6 / 2326 3.1	25	0624 0.7 / 1203 3.2 / TU 1856 0.5 ●
11	0610 0.6 / 1147 3.2 / TU 1845 0.5 / ○	26	0032 3.0 / 0705 0.6 / W 1244 3.3 / 1937 0.5
12	0018 3.1 / 0701 0.6 / W 1236 3.3 / 1936 0.4	27	0110 3.0 / 0742 0.6 / TH 1321 3.3 / 2014 0.5
13	0110 3.1 / 0752 0.5 / TH 1334 3.3 / 2026 0.3	28	0144 3.0 / 0817 0.5 / F 1355 3.3 / 2047 0.5
14	0159 3.0 / 0837 0.4 / F 1410 3.3 / 2111 0.2	29	0215 3.0 / 0847 0.5 / SA 1426 3.2 / 2115 0.5
15	0243 2.9 / 0918 0.4 / SA 1453 3.3 / 2155 0.2	30	0246 2.9 / 0916 0.5 / SU 1456 3.2 / 2144 0.5
		31	0318 2.9 / 0948 0.6 / M 1528 3.1 / 2215 0.6

AUGUST

#	Time m	#	Time m
1	0352 2.9 / 1020 0.6 / TU 1600 3.1 / 2243 0.6	16	0430 3.0 / 1107 0.6 / W 1653 3.2 / ◑ 2337 0.7
2	0424 2.9 / 1051 0.7 / W 1633 3.0 / ◐ 2314 0.7	17	0519 2.9 / 1159 0.7 / TH 1749 3.0
3	0500 2.8 / 1131 0.8 / TH 1717 2.9	18	0030 0.9 / 0618 2.9 / F 1309 0.8 / 1900 2.9
4	0001 0.8 / 0552 2.7 / F 1234 0.9 / 1823 2.8	19	0144 0.9 / 0736 2.8 / SA 1436 0.8 / 2026 2.8
5	0110 0.9 / 0703 2.7 / SA 1356 0.9 / 1945 2.8	20	0311 1.0 / 0900 2.9 / SU 1603 0.7 / 2148 2.8
6	0231 0.9 / 0822 2.8 / SU 1519 0.8 / 2107 2.9	21	0428 0.9 / 1014 3.1 / M 1711 0.7 / 2252 2.9
7	0349 0.8 / 0936 3.0 / M 1634 0.7 / 2217 3.0	22	0526 0.8 / 1108 3.2 / TU 1801 0.6 / 2338 3.0
8	0458 0.8 / 1040 3.1 / TU 1739 0.6 / 2316 3.1	23	0610 0.7 / 1149 3.3 / W 1841 0.6 ●
9	0559 0.7 / 1135 3.3 / W 1835 0.5 / ○	24	0016 3.0 / 0649 0.7 / TH 1226 3.3 / 1917 0.5
10	0009 3.1 / 0652 0.6 / TH 1224 3.3 / 1926 0.4	25	0049 3.0 / 0724 0.6 / F 1300 3.3 / 1949 0.5
11	0058 3.1 / 0740 0.5 / F 1310 3.4 / 2012 0.3	26	0118 3.0 / 0754 0.5 / SA 1330 3.3 / 2017 0.5
12	0144 3.1 / 0823 0.4 / SA 1354 3.5 / 2056 0.3	27	0145 3.0 / 0821 0.5 / SU 1357 3.2 / 2042 0.5
13	0225 3.0 / 0902 0.4 / SU 1437 3.4 / 2135 0.3	28	0212 3.0 / 0848 0.5 / M 1423 3.2 / 2108 0.5
14	0304 3.0 / 0940 0.4 / M 1520 3.4 / 2214 0.5	29	0241 3.0 / 0916 0.5 / TU 1452 3.1 / 2135 0.5
15	0345 3.0 / 1022 0.5 / TU 1605 3.3 / 2255 0.6	30	0311 3.0 / 0946 0.6 / W 1521 3.1 / 2200 0.7
		31	0340 2.9 / 1011 0.7 / TH 1551 3.0 / ◑ 2225 0.8

Chart Datum: 1·68 metres below Normal Null (German reference level)

TIME ZONE -0100
(German Standard Time)
Subtract 1 hour for UT
For German Summer Time add
ONE hour in **non-shaded areas**

LAT 54°11′N   LONG 7°53′E

TIMES AND HEIGHTS OF HIGH AND LOW WATERS

SEPTEMBER

Time	m		Time	m
1 0410	2.8	**16** 0545	2.9
1044	0.8	1240	0.8
F 1631	2.8	SA 1834	2.6
2306	0.9		
2 0459	2.7	**17** 0110	1.1
1145	0.9	0707	2.8
SA 1738	2.7	SU 1411	0.9
		2004	2.6
3 0019	1.0	**18** 0245	1.1
0617	2.7	0840	2.9
SU 1315	0.9	M 1546	0.8
1910	2.7	2132	2.7
4 0155	1.0	**19** 0411	1.0
0751	2.8	0958	3.1
M 1454	0.8	TU 1658	0.7
2045	2.8	2238	2.9
5 0327	0.9	**20** 0510	0.8
0917	3.0	1051	3.2
TU 1618	0.7	W 1743	0.6
2203	2.9	2318	3.0
6 0443	0.8	**21** 0549	0.7
1024	3.2	1126	3.2
W 1725	0.5	TH 1815	0.6
2304	3.0	2349	3.0
7 0544	0.7	**22** 0623	0.7
1118	3.3	1158	3.2
TH 1819	0.4	F 1846	0.5
○ 2353	3.1	●	
8 0635	0.5	**23** 0019	3.1
1204	3.4	0656	0.6
F 1906	0.3	SA 1231	3.2
		1916	0.4
9 0038	3.1	**24** 0048	3.1
0719	0.4	0726	0.5
SA 1248	3.4	SU 1301	3.2
1949	0.3	1942	0.5
10 0120	3.1	**25** 0113	3.1
0800	0.4	0752	0.5
SU 1331	3.5	M 1326	3.2
2030	0.4	2008	0.5
11 0159	3.1	**26** 0138	3.1
0840	0.4	0819	0.5
M 1414	3.4	TU 1351	3.1
2107	0.5	2033	0.5
12 0236	3.2	**27** 0206	3.0
0917	0.4	0847	0.5
TU 1455	3.3	W 1419	3.1
2142	0.6	2059	0.6
13 0314	3.1	**28** 0235	3.0
0957	0.5	0916	0.6
W 1537	3.2	TH 1450	3.0
2218	0.7	2125	0.7
14 0355	3.1	**29** 0306	3.0
1039	0.6	0944	0.6
TH 1624	3.0	F 1524	2.9
◑ 2259	0.9	2153	0.8
15 0443	3.0	**30** 0341	2.9
1130	0.7	1020	0.7
F 1720	2.8	SA 1608	2.7
2353	1.0	◐ 2237	0.9

OCTOBER

Time	m		Time	m
1 0432	2.8	**16** 0035	1.1
1120	0.8	0633	2.9
SU 1716	2.6	M 1337	0.9
2352	1.1	1930	2.5
2 0550	2.8	**17** 0205	1.1
1251	0.8	0802	2.9
M 1849	2.6	TU 1508	0.9
		2056	2.6
3 0130	1.1	**18** 0332	1.0
0726	2.9	0922	3.0
TU 1433	0.8	W 1622	0.8
2025	2.7	2204	2.8
4 0307	1.0	**19** 0435	0.9
0854	3.0	1017	3.1
W 1559	0.6	TH 1708	0.6
2144	2.8	2245	2.9
5 0422	0.8	**20** 0515	0.8
1002	3.2	1052	3.2
TH 1703	0.4	F 1738	0.6
2243	3.0	2315	3.0
6 0521	0.6	**21** 0548	0.7
1053	3.3	1124	3.2
F 1754	0.3	SA 1808	0.6
2330	3.0	2344	3.1
7 0610	0.5	**22** 0622	0.6
1140	3.4	1157	3.2
SA 1840	0.3	SU 1838	0.6
○		●	
8 0012	3.1	**23** 0014	3.1
0655	0.4	0654	0.6
SU 1224	3.4	M 1229	3.2
1921	0.3	1907	0.6
9 0052	3.2	**24** 0041	3.1
0736	0.4	0722	0.6
M 1306	3.4	TU 1256	3.2
1959	0.4	1935	0.6
10 0131	3.2	**25** 0108	3.1
0816	0.4	0752	0.6
TU 1349	3.4	W 1325	3.1
2037	0.5	2004	0.6
11 0209	3.2	**26** 0138	3.1
0856	0.4	0824	0.5
W 1432	3.2	TH 1356	3.0
2112	0.6	2034	0.7
12 0247	3.2	**27** 0211	3.1
0936	0.5	0857	0.6
TH 1515	3.0	F 1433	3.0
2149	0.7	2105	0.7
13 0328	3.1	**28** 0247	3.0
1018	0.6	0933	0.6
F 1602	2.9	SA 1514	2.9
2230	0.9	2142	0.8
14 0415	3.0	**29** 0329	3.0
1108	0.7	1016	0.7
SA 1656	2.7	SU 1603	2.7
◑ 2322	1.0	◑ 2231	0.9
15 0515	2.9	**30** 0423	2.9
1212	0.9	1115	0.7
SU 1805	2.6	M 1709	2.6
		2341	1.0
		31 0535	2.9
		1236	0.7
		TU 1832	2.6

NOVEMBER

Time	m		Time	m
1 0110	1.0	**16** 0230	1.1
0701	3.0	0821	3.0
W 1409	0.7	TH 1520	0.8
2000	2.7	2106	2.8
2 0239	0.9	**17** 0338	1.0
0825	3.1	0923	3.0
TH 1530	0.6	F 1614	0.8
2115	2.8	2157	2.9
3 0352	0.7	**18** 0427	0.9
0931	3.2	1008	3.1
F 1631	0.4	SA 1652	0.7
2212	2.9	2232	3.0
4 0449	0.6	**19** 0506	0.8
1025	3.2	1046	3.2
SA 1723	0.4	SU 1727	0.7
2300	3.0	2305	3.1
5 0542	0.5	**20** 0545	0.7
1114	3.3	1122	3.2
SU 1810	0.4	M 1801	0.7
○ 2345	3.1	● 2338	3.2
6 0630	0.4	**21** 0622	0.7
1201	3.3	1157	3.2
M 1853	0.4	TU 1835	0.7
7 0026	3.2	**22** 0011	3.2
0713	0.4	0657	0.6
TU 1245	3.3	W 1231	3.2
1931	0.5	1909	0.7
8 0106	3.2	**23** 0045	3.2
0755	0.5	0733	0.6
W 1329	3.2	TH 1308	3.1
2010	0.6	1946	0.7
9 0146	3.2	**24** 0122	3.2
0839	0.5	0812	0.6
TH 1414	3.1	F 1348	3.0
2049	0.7	2023	0.7
10 0228	3.2	**25** 0201	3.2
0921	0.5	0852	0.5
F 1500	2.9	SA 1429	3.0
2128	0.7	2101	0.7
11 0310	3.1	**26** 0241	3.1
1003	0.6	0933	0.5
SA 1546	2.8	SU 1513	2.9
2208	0.8	2142	0.8
12 0354	3.1	**27** 0325	3.1
1049	0.6	1020	0.6
SU 1635	2.7	M 1603	2.8
◐ 2256	0.9	2232	0.8
13 0446	3.0	**28** 0418	3.1
1143	0.8	1115	0.6
M 1732	2.6	TU 1702	2.7
2355	1.0	◐ 2332	0.9
14 0551	2.9	**29** 0521	3.0
1250	0.9	1221	0.6
TU 1841	2.6	W 1811	2.7
15 0110	1.1	**30** 0044	0.9
0706	2.9	0634	3.1
W 1407	0.9	TH 1337	0.7
1958	2.6	1926	2.7

DECEMBER

Time	m		Time	m
1 0202	0.9	**16** 0225	1.1
0750	3.1	0814	3.0
F 1451	0.6	SA 1504	0.9
2036	2.8	2052	2.9
2 0314	0.7	**17** 0328	1.0
0858	3.2	0914	3.0
SA 1554	0.5	SU 1558	0.9
2136	2.9	2142	3.0
3 0417	0.6	**18** 0421	0.9
0957	3.2	1005	3.1
SU 1650	0.5	M 1644	0.8
2230	3.0	2225	3.1
4 0515	0.5	**19** 0510	0.8
1052	3.2	1049	3.1
M 1743	0.5	TU 1727	0.8
2320	3.1	2307	3.2
5 0609	0.5	**20** 0556	0.8
1145	3.2	1131	3.1
TU 1830	0.5	W 1809	0.8
○		● 2349	3.2
6 0006	3.2	**21** 0640	0.7
0657	0.5	1214	3.1
W 1232	3.1	TH 1852	0.7
1911	0.6		
7 0048	3.3	**22** 0031	3.2
0741	0.5	0724	0.6
TH 1316	3.1	F 1300	3.1
1951	0.7	1938	0.7
8 0131	3.3	**23** 0114	3.3
0826	0.5	0809	0.5
F 1401	3.0	SA 1346	3.1
2033	0.7	2021	0.7
9 0214	3.3	**24** 0156	3.3
0909	0.5	0852	0.4
SA 1446	2.9	SU 1428	3.0
2112	0.7	2100	0.6
10 0255	3.2	**25** 0237	3.3
0949	0.6	0933	0.4
SU 1528	2.8	M 1509	2.9
2150	0.7	2140	0.6
11 0334	3.2	**26** 0320	3.2
1028	0.6	1019	0.5
M 1609	2.8	TU 1555	2.9
2229	0.8	2226	0.7
12 0416	3.1	**27** 0410	3.2
1109	0.7	1107	0.5
TU 1653	2.7	W 1647	2.8
◑ 2314	0.9	◑ 2316	0.7
13 0504	3.0	**28** 0504	3.2
1156	0.8	1159	0.6
W 1745	2.7	TH 1743	2.8
14 0008	1.0	**29** 0013	0.8
0600	2.9	0604	3.1
TH 1254	0.9	F 1259	0.7
1845	2.7	1845	2.8
15 0114	1.1	**30** 0122	0.8
0706	2.9	0712	3.1
F 1400	0.9	SA 1407	0.8
1951	2.8	1953	2.8
		31 0237	0.8
		0825	3.1
		SU 1518	0.7
		2102	2.9

Chart Datum: 1·68 metres below Normal Null (German reference level)

TIDES

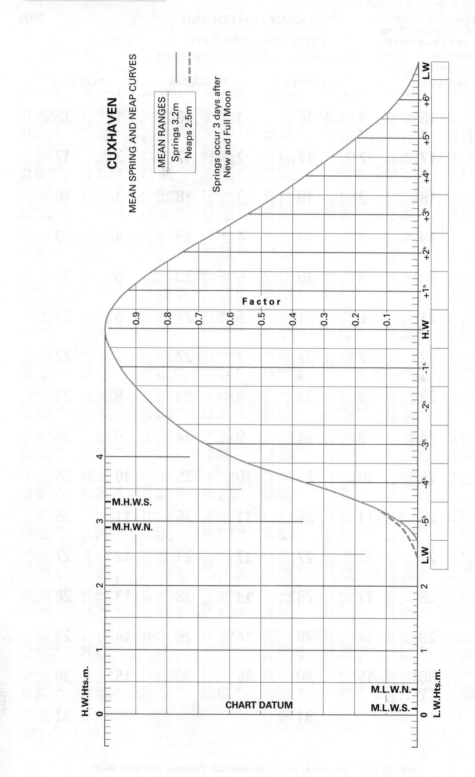

CUXHAVEN
MEAN SPRING AND NEAP CURVES

MEAN RANGES
Springs 3.2m
Neaps 2.5m

Springs occur 3 days after
New and Full Moon

GERMANY – CUXHAVEN

LAT 53°52'N   LONG 8°43'E

TIMES AND HEIGHTS OF HIGH AND LOW WATERS

JANUARY

Day	Time m	Time m	Time m	Time m
1 SU	0120 3.8	0824 0.6	1355 3.7	2045 0.7
16 M	0208 3.9	0910 0.6	1434 3.6	2118 0.7
2 M	0210 3.9	0918 0.5	1449 3.7	2137 0.6
17 TU	0243 3.9	0946 0.6	1507 3.6	2151 0.6
3 TU	0259 4.0	1010 0.4	1539 3.6	2223 0.6
18 W	0315 3.9	1018 0.6	1540 3.5	2220 0.5
4 W	0345 4.0	1056 0.4	1625 3.6	2303 0.6
19 TH	0346 3.8	1046 0.5	1612 3.4	2248 0.6
5 TH	0429 4.0	1139 0.4	1711 3.5	2345 0.7
20 F	0417 3.7	1114 0.5	1645 3.4	2319 0.6
6 F	0516 3.9	1226 0.6	1759 3.4 ◐	
21 SA	0450 3.7	1144 0.6	1718 3.4	2349 0.7
7 SA	0032 0.7	0608 3.9	1314 0.6	1849 3.4
22 SU	0522 3.6	1212 0.7	1752 3.3 ◑	
8 SU	0124 0.8	0704 3.7	1405 0.7	1944 3.3
23 M	0019 0.8	0559 3.5	1245 0.8	1834 3.3
9 M	0224 0.8	0809 3.6	1508 0.8	2049 3.3
24 TU	0104 1.0	0652 3.4	1339 0.9	1935 3.2
10 TU	0337 0.8	0922 3.5	1619 0.8	2159 3.3
25 W	0212 1.0	0804 3.4	1455 1.0	2049 3.3
11 W	0454 0.8	1035 3.4	1729 0.8	2306 3.4
26 TH	0335 1.0	0925 3.4	1618 0.9	2206 3.4
12 TH	0604 0.7	1141 3.5	1830 0.8	
27 F	0459 0.8	1043 3.5	1737 0.9	2315 3.6
13 F	0004 3.6	0702 0.7	1236 3.5	1923 0.8
28 SA	0616 0.7	1153 3.6	1846 0.8	
14 SA	0052 3.7	0751 0.7	1321 3.6	○ 2006 0.8
29 SU	0016 3.8	0722 0.5	1253 3.7	● 1945 0.6
15 SU	0132 3.8	0832 0.6	1359 3.6	2043 0.7
30 M	0110 3.9	0819 0.4	1348 3.7	2039 0.5
31 TU	0200 4.0	0912 0.3	1440 3.7	2129 0.4

FEBRUARY

Day	Time m	Time m	Time m	Time m
1 W	0248 4.0	1002 0.3	1527 3.6	2214 0.4
16 TH	0254 3.8	0954 0.4	1513 3.6	2159 0.4
2 TH	0332 4.1	1046 0.3	1609 3.6	2252 0.4
17 F	0321 3.8	1019 0.4	1542 3.5	2225 0.4
3 F	0414 4.0	1125 0.4	1648 3.6	2329 0.5
18 SA	0349 3.7	1046 0.4	1613 3.4	2254 0.4
4 SA	0455 4.0	1203 0.5	1729 3.5	
19 SU	0420 3.7	1113 0.4	1643 3.4	2320 0.5
5 SU	0007 0.6	0539 3.9	1240 0.6	◑ 1809 3.5
20 M	0448 3.6	1134 0.5	1709 3.4	2340 0.6
6 M	0047 0.7	0627 3.7	1319 0.7	1856 3.3
21 TU	0516 3.5	1156 0.6	1741 3.2	
7 TU	0137 0.7	0726 3.4	1413 0.8	1959 3.3
22 W	0012 0.7	0601 3.3	1239 0.8	1837 3.2
8 W	0248 0.8	0843 3.2	1530 0.9	2120 3.3
23 TH	0115 0.8	0715 3.2	1358 0.9	2000 3.2
9 TH	0417 0.8	1009 3.2	1656 0.9	2242 3.4
24 F	0250 0.8	0850 3.2	1539 0.9	2132 3.4
10 F	0543 0.7	1127 3.3	1812 0.8	2349 3.6
25 SA	0432 0.7	1023 3.4	1716 0.8	2255 3.6
11 SA	0650 0.5	1226 3.4	1909 0.8	
26 SU	0601 0.5	1141 3.5	1834 0.7	
12 SU	0039 3.7	0738 0.6	1310 3.5	1953 0.7
27 M	0001 3.7	0712 0.3	1244 3.6	1936 0.5
13 M	0118 3.8	0818 0.6	1345 3.6	2030 0.6
28 TU	0056 3.9	0809 0.2	1336 3.6	● 2026 0.3
14 TU	0153 3.9	0854 0.5	1417 3.6	2103 0.5
15 W	0225 3.9	0926 0.5	1446 3.6	2133 0.4

MARCH

Day	Time m	Time m	Time m	Time m
1 W	0144 3.9	0857 0.1	1422 3.6	2110 0.2
16 TH	0158 3.8	0856 0.3	1417 3.6	2107 0.3
2 TH	0229 4.0	0943 0.1	1505 3.6	2152 0.2
17 F	0226 3.8	0923 0.3	1443 3.6	2133 0.3
3 F	0312 4.1	1024 0.2	1543 3.7	2231 0.3
18 SA	0252 3.7	0949 0.3	1510 3.6	2159 0.2
4 SA	0352 4.0	1059 0.3	1619 3.7	2306 0.3
19 SU	0320 3.6	1015 0.3	1539 3.5	2226 0.2
5 SU	0431 3.9	1132 0.4	1655 3.6	2339 0.4
20 M	0351 3.6	1041 0.3	1610 3.4	2253 0.3
6 M	0511 3.7	1202 0.6	1731 3.5 ●	
21 TU	0422 3.5	1104 0.4	1638 3.4	2316 0.4
7 TU	0013 0.5	0555 3.5	1235 0.7	1814 3.3
22 W	0453 3.4	1128 0.5	1712 3.3	◑ 2348 0.5
8 W	0056 0.6	0650 3.2	1325 0.8	1917 3.2
23 TH	0539 3.2	1211 0.7	1808 3.2	
9 TH	0205 0.7	0808 3.0	1444 0.9	2042 3.2
24 F	0052 0.6	0655 3.1	1331 0.8	1933 3.2
10 F	0340 0.8	0941 3.1	1621 0.9	2213 3.4
25 SA	0229 0.6	0833 3.1	1517 0.9	2110 3.4
11 SA	0517 0.7	1107 3.2	1748 0.8	2327 3.5
26 SU	0416 0.5	1009 3.3	1657 0.7	2235 3.6
12 SU	0630 0.5	1209 3.4	1848 0.7	
27 M	0545 0.3	1126 3.4	1815 0.5	2341 3.7
13 M	0018 3.7	0717 0.5	1249 3.5	1931 0.6
28 TU	0653 0.2	1225 3.5	1915 0.3	
14 TU	0055 3.8	0752 0.4	1321 3.5	○ 2006 0.5
29 W	0035 3.8	0747 0.1	1314 3.5	● 2004 0.1
15 W	0128 3.8	0825 0.3	1350 3.6	2038 0.4
30 TH	0123 3.9	0834 0.0	1358 3.6	2046 0.1
31 F	0207 3.9	0915 0.1	1437 3.7	2126 0.1

APRIL

Day	Time m	Time m	Time m	Time m
1 SA	0248 4.0	0953 0.2	1513 3.7	2204 0.2
16 SU	0223 3.7	0917 0.3	1438 3.6	2132 0.2
2 SU	0327 3.9	1027 0.3	1548 3.7	2240 0.2
17 M	0254 3.6	0945 0.3	1510 3.6	2202 0.2
3 M	0406 3.7	1059 0.4	1623 3.6	2313 0.3
18 TU	0330 3.5	1015 0.3	1545 3.5	2235 0.2
4 TU	0446 3.5	1129 0.5	1700 3.5	2347 0.4
19 W	0408 3.4	1046 0.3	1623 3.5	2310 0.3
5 W	0530 3.3	1203 0.6	1743 3.4 ○	
20 TH	0450 3.3	1122 0.5	1706 3.4	◐ 2352 0.3
6 TH	0029 0.5	0624 3.1	1249 0.8	1842 3.3
21 F	0543 3.2	1212 0.6	1804 3.3 ◑	
7 F	0131 0.6	0736 2.9	1402 0.9	2003 3.3
22 SA	0055 0.4	0656 3.1	1328 0.7	1923 3.3
8 SA	0259 0.7	0904 3.0	1537 0.9	2134 3.4
23 SU	0224 0.4	0825 3.1	1503 0.7	2052 3.5
9 SU	0436 0.6	1030 3.1	1707 0.8	2250 3.5
24 M	0400 0.4	0952 3.2	1634 0.6	2211 3.6
10 M	0552 0.5	1133 3.3	1811 0.6	2342 3.6
25 TU	0521 0.2	1102 3.3	1746 0.4	2314 3.7
11 TU	0640 0.3	1213 3.4	1854 0.5	
26 W	0623 0.1	1157 3.4	1844 0.2	
12 W	0019 3.7	0714 0.3	1244 3.5	1930 0.4
27 TH	0008 3.8	0717 0.0	1246 3.5	● 1935 0.1
13 TH	0052 3.7	0747 0.3	1315 3.6	○ 2005 0.3
28 F	0058 3.8	0805 0.1	1330 3.7	2021 0.1
14 F	0125 3.7	0819 0.3	1344 3.6	2035 0.3
29 SA	0144 3.8	0846 0.1	1409 3.7	2100 0.1
15 SA	0154 3.8	0848 0.2	1411 3.6	2103 0.3
30 SU	0225 3.8	0922 0.3	1445 3.7	2137 0.1

Chart Datum: 1·66 metres below Normal Null (German reference level)

TIDES

TIME ZONE -0100
(German Standard Time)
Subtract 1 hour for UT
For German Summer Time add
ONE hour in **non-shaded areas**

GERMANY–CUXHAVEN

LAT 53°52'N   LONG 8°43'E

2006

TIMES AND HEIGHTS OF HIGH AND LOW WATERS

MAY

Day	Time m	Day	Time m
1 M	0305 3.7 / 0957 0.3 / 1521 3.7 / 2216 0.2	**16** TU	0238 3.7 / 0925 0.4 / 1452 3.7 / 2149 0.3
2 TU	0346 3.5 / 1031 0.4 / 1559 3.6 / 2253 0.2	**17** W	0321 3.5 / 1003 0.4 / 1534 3.7 / 2231 0.2
3 W	0428 3.4 / 1104 0.5 / 1638 3.6 / 2330 0.3	**18** TH	0408 3.4 / 1043 0.4 / 1619 3.6 / 2315 0.3
4 TH	0512 3.2 / 1140 0.6 / 1721 3.5	**19** F	0458 3.3 / 1127 0.5 / 1709 3.6
5 F	0012 0.5 / 0602 3.1 / 1224 0.7 / ◑ 1814 3.4	**20** SA	0005 0.3 / 0553 3.2 / 1222 0.6 / 1807 3.5
6 SA	0105 0.6 / 0703 3.0 / 1324 0.8 / 1921 3.3	**21** SU	0105 0.3 / 0659 3.2 / 1328 0.6 / 1916 3.5
7 SU	0216 0.6 / 0817 3.0 / 1444 0.8 / 2040 3.4	**22** M	0219 0.3 / 0813 3.2 / 1446 0.6 / 2032 3.6
8 M	0338 0.6 / 0935 3.1 / 1608 0.7 / 2154 3.4	**23** TU	0339 0.3 / 0926 3.3 / 1605 0.5 / 2143 3.7
9 TU	0453 0.5 / 1038 3.3 / 1715 0.6 / 2250 3.5	**24** W	0450 0.2 / 1030 3.3 / 1712 0.4 / 2245 3.7
10 W	0546 0.3 / 1124 3.4 / 1804 0.5 / 2333 3.6	**25** TH	0549 0.2 / 1124 3.4 / 1811 0.3 / 2341 3.7
11 TH	0626 0.3 / 1200 3.5 / 1845 0.5	**26** F	0643 0.2 / 1216 3.5 / 1907 0.2
12 F	0011 3.7 / 0704 0.4 / 1235 3.6 / 1925 0.4	**27** SA	0036 3.7 / 0735 0.2 / 1303 3.6 / ● 1957 0.2
13 SA	0048 3.7 / 0740 0.4 / 1309 3.7 / ○ 2000 0.4	**28** SU	0125 3.7 / 0819 0.3 / 1345 3.7 / 2039 0.2
14 SU	0123 3.8 / 0814 0.3 / 1341 3.7 / 2034 0.4	**29** M	0208 3.7 / 0857 0.4 / 1423 3.8 / 2118 0.2
15 M	0158 3.7 / 0848 0.4 / 1414 3.7 / 2110 0.3	**30** TU	0249 3.6 / 0934 0.4 / 1501 3.8 / 2159 0.3
		31 W	0330 3.5 / 1011 0.4 / 1541 3.7 / 2239 0.3

JUNE

Day	Time m	Day	Time m
1 TH	0412 3.4 / 1046 0.5 / 1620 3.7 / 2318 0.4	**16** F	0409 3.5 / 1044 0.4 / 1617 3.8 / 2320 0.3
2 F	0455 3.3 / 1122 0.6 / 1701 3.7 / 2357 0.5	**17** SA	0459 3.4 / 1130 0.5 / 1707 3.8
3 SA	0539 3.2 / 1202 0.7 / 1746 3.6 ◐	**18** SU	0010 0.3 / 0553 3.4 / 1222 0.5 / ◑ 1802 3.8
4 SU	0039 0.5 / 0628 3.1 / 1248 0.7 / 1838 3.5	**19** M	0105 0.3 / 0649 3.3 / 1320 0.6 / 1901 3.7
5 M	0129 0.6 / 0724 3.1 / 1347 0.8 / 1939 3.4	**20** TU	0203 0.4 / 0749 3.3 / 1423 0.6 / 2006 3.7
6 TU	0231 0.6 / 0827 3.2 / 1456 0.8 / 2046 3.5	**21** W	0308 0.4 / 0852 3.3 / 1531 0.6 / 2113 3.7
7 W	0339 0.6 / 0931 3.3 / 1605 0.8 / 2148 3.5	**22** TH	0414 0.4 / 0955 3.4 / 1640 0.6 / 2219 3.6
8 TH	0441 0.5 / 1026 3.4 / 1704 0.7 / 2241 3.6	**23** F	0516 0.4 / 1055 3.5 / 1744 0.4 / 2321 3.6
9 F	0533 0.5 / 1112 3.5 / 1756 0.6 / 2329 3.7	**24** SA	0615 0.4 / 1151 3.6 / 1845 0.4
10 SA	0619 0.5 / 1155 3.6 / 1844 0.5	**25** SU	0020 3.6 / 0711 0.5 / 1243 3.7 / ● 1940 0.4
11 SU	0014 3.7 / 0703 0.5 / 1237 3.7 / ○ 1929 0.5	**26** M	0113 3.6 / 0800 0.5 / 1329 3.8 / 2027 0.4
12 M	0058 3.8 / 0746 0.5 / 1317 3.8 / 2013 0.5	**27** TU	0157 3.6 / 0841 0.5 / 1409 3.9 / 2108 0.4
13 TU	0144 3.8 / 0830 0.5 / 1400 3.9 / 2100 0.4	**28** W	0238 3.6 / 0919 0.5 / 1448 3.9 / 2148 0.4
14 W	0232 3.7 / 0917 0.5 / 1445 3.9 / 2148 0.3	**29** TH	0317 3.5 / 0957 0.5 / 1526 3.9 / 2227 0.4
15 TH	0321 3.6 / 1002 0.5 / 1531 3.9 / 2233 0.3	**30** F	0356 3.5 / 1030 0.5 / 1602 3.8 / 2301 0.4

JULY

Day	Time m	Day	Time m
1 SA	0433 3.4 / 1102 0.6 / 1638 3.8 / 2335 0.5	**16** SU	0447 3.5 / 1122 0.5 / 1654 4.0
2 SU	0510 3.4 / 1137 0.6 / 1715 3.7	**17** M	0000 0.4 / 0535 3.5 / 1209 0.5 / ◑ 1744 3.9
3 M	0009 0.6 / 0549 3.3 / 1213 0.7 / ◐ 1755 3.6	**18** TU	0047 0.5 / 0624 3.5 / 1259 0.6 / 1837 3.8
4 TU	0045 0.6 / 0630 3.3 / 1253 0.8 / 1840 3.5	**19** W	0134 0.6 / 0714 3.4 / 1352 0.7 / 1935 3.7
5 W	0127 0.7 / 0719 3.3 / 1345 0.9 / 1937 3.5	**20** TH	0228 0.7 / 0812 3.4 / 1456 0.7 / 2043 3.6
6 TH	0223 0.7 / 0818 3.3 / 1450 0.9 / 2042 3.5	**21** F	0335 0.7 / 0921 3.4 / 1611 0.7 / 2159 3.5
7 F	0330 0.7 / 0922 3.4 / 1600 0.8 / 2148 3.6	**22** SA	0449 0.7 / 1033 3.5 / 1728 0.6 / 2311 3.5
8 SA	0437 0.7 / 1024 3.5 / 1707 0.7 / 2250 3.6	**23** SU	0557 0.7 / 1138 3.6 / 1834 0.6
9 SU	0538 0.7 / 1120 3.6 / 1810 0.6 / 2348 3.7	**24** M	0013 3.6 / 0657 0.7 / 1232 3.8 / 1930 0.6
10 M	0636 0.7 / 1212 3.8 / 1909 0.6	**25** TU	0105 3.6 / 0747 0.7 / 1318 3.9 / ● 2017 0.5
11 TU	0043 3.8 / 0731 0.7 / 1303 3.9 / ○ 2003 0.5	**26** W	0148 3.6 / 0829 0.7 / 1358 3.9 / 2058 0.5
12 W	0137 3.8 / 0823 0.6 / 1352 4.0 / 2056 0.4	**27** TH	0226 3.6 / 0907 0.6 / 1435 4.0 / 2135 0.5
13 TH	0229 3.8 / 0914 0.6 / 1448 4.1 / 2146 0.4	**28** F	0300 3.6 / 0942 0.5 / 1509 4.0 / 2208 0.5
14 F	0318 3.7 / 1000 0.5 / 1524 4.1 / 2232 0.3	**29** SA	0333 3.6 / 1011 0.5 / 1539 3.9 / 2236 0.5
15 SA	0402 3.6 / 1040 0.4 / 1608 4.0 / 2314 0.4	**30** SU	0403 3.5 / 1038 0.5 / 1610 3.8 / 2304 0.5
		31 M	0436 3.5 / 1108 0.6 / 1643 3.8 / 2335 0.6

AUGUST

Day	Time m	Day	Time m
1 TU	0509 3.5 / 1139 0.7 / 1715 3.7	**16** W	0017 0.7 / 0549 3.6 / 1229 0.7 / ◑ 1807 3.8
2 W	0003 0.7 / 0541 3.4 / 1207 0.8 / ◐ 1749 3.6	**17** TH	0057 0.8 / 0635 3.5 / 1316 0.7 / 1903 3.6
3 TH	0030 0.8 / 0617 3.4 / 1243 0.8 / 1834 3.5	**18** F	0146 0.9 / 0733 3.4 / 1420 0.8 / 2016 3.4
4 F	0113 0.9 / 0710 3.3 / 1341 0.9 / 1939 3.4	**19** SA	0257 1.0 / 0851 3.3 / 1546 0.9 / 2142 3.3
5 SA	0221 0.9 / 0822 3.3 / 1501 0.9 / 2100 3.4	**20** SU	0425 1.0 / 1016 3.5 / 1716 0.8 / 2305 3.4
6 SU	0345 0.9 / 0940 3.4 / 1628 0.8 / 2221 3.5	**21** M	0547 0.9 / 1130 3.5 / 1830 0.7
7 M	0507 0.9 / 1053 3.6 / 1748 0.7 / 2332 3.6	**22** TU	0010 3.5 / 0649 0.8 / 1224 3.8 / 1922 0.6
8 TU	0620 0.8 / 1156 3.8 / 1857 0.6	**23** W	0057 3.6 / 0735 0.8 / 1305 3.9 / ● 2003 0.6
9 W	0034 3.7 / 0723 0.7 / 1250 4.0 / 1956 0.5	**24** TH	0133 3.7 / 0814 0.7 / 1341 3.9 / 2040 0.6
10 TH	0129 3.8 / 0817 0.6 / 1340 4.1 / 2048 0.4	**25** F	0206 3.7 / 0849 0.6 / 1415 3.9 / 2113 0.5
11 F	0219 3.8 / 0905 0.5 / 1426 4.1 / 2136 0.3	**26** SA	0236 3.7 / 0921 0.5 / 1445 3.9 / 2142 0.5
12 SA	0304 3.8 / 0949 0.4 / 1510 4.2 / 2219 0.3	**27** SU	0303 3.7 / 0947 0.5 / 1511 3.9 / 2206 0.5
13 SU	0345 3.7 / 1027 0.4 / 1552 4.2 / 2258 0.4	**28** M	0330 3.6 / 1012 0.5 / 1538 3.8 / 2230 0.5
14 M	0424 3.7 / 1105 0.4 / 1633 4.1 / 2337 0.5	**29** TU	0358 3.6 / 1038 0.5 / 1608 3.8 / 2257 0.5
15 TU	0506 3.7 / 1146 0.6 / 1719 4.0	**30** W	0429 3.5 / 1105 0.7 / 1638 3.7 / 2322 0.7
		31 TH	0457 3.7 / 1129 0.7 / 1707 3.7 / ◐ 2345 0.8

Chart Datum: 1·66 metres below Normal Null (German reference level)

TIME ZONE -0100
(German Standard Time)
Subtract 1 hour for UT
For German Summer Time add
ONE hour in **non-shaded areas**

LAT 53°52′N LONG 8°43′E

TIMES AND HEIGHTS OF HIGH AND LOW WATERS

SEPTEMBER

Time	m		Time	m
1 0528	3.4	**16**	0108	1.0
1157	0.8		0659	3.4
F 1747	3.4	SA	1348	0.9
			1949	3.2
2 0021	0.9	**17**	0222	1.1
0617	3.3		0821	3.4
SA 1251	0.9	SU	1518	0.9
1854	3.2		2121	3.1
3 0130	1.0	**18**	0357	1.1
0734	3.3		0954	3.4
SU 1420	0.9	M	1658	0.9
2025	3.2		2251	3.3
4 0308	1.1	**19**	0529	1.0
0907	3.4		1113	0.9
M 1601	0.8	TU	1817	0.7
2200	3.3		2357	3.4
5 0446	1.0	**20**	0634	0.9
1032	3.6		1207	3.8
TU 1733	0.7	W	1905	0.6
2320	3.5			
6 0607	0.8	**21**	0038	3.6
1139	3.8		0715	0.8
W 1845	0.5	TH	1243	3.9
			1938	0.6
7 0022	3.6	**22**	0107	3.7
0711	0.7		0750	0.7
TH 1244	4.0	F	1314	3.9
○ 1942	0.4		2010	0.5
8 0114	3.7	**23**	0136	3.7
0802	0.5		0823	0.6
F 1321	4.1	SA	1346	3.9
2031	0.3		2042	0.5
9 0159	3.7	**24**	0204	3.7
0847	0.4		0853	0.5
SA 1405	4.2	SU	1415	3.9
2115	0.3		2109	0.5
10 0241	3.8	**25**	0230	3.7
0928	0.4		0919	0.5
SU 1448	4.2	M	1440	3.8
2156	0.4		2134	0.5
11 0319	3.8	**26**	0255	3.7
1007	0.4		0944	0.5
M 1529	4.2	TU	1507	3.8
2233	0.5		2157	0.6
12 0356	3.8	**27**	0323	3.6
1044	0.5		1009	0.5
TU 1610	4.0	W	1536	3.7
2307	0.6		2222	0.6
13 0434	3.8	**28**	0353	3.6
1120	0.5		1035	0.6
W 1652	3.8	TH	1607	3.6
2342	0.8		2248	0.7
14 0514	3.7	**29**	0423	3.5
1159	0.7		1102	0.7
TH 1739	3.6	F	1641	3.5
◐			2314	0.8
15 0020	0.9	**30**	0457	3.5
0559	3.5		1134	0.8
F 1244	0.8	SA	1723	3.3
1835	3.4	◑	2354	1.0

OCTOBER

Time	m		Time	m
1 0547	3.3	**16**	0146	1.1
1229	0.8		0745	3.4
SU 1831	3.1	M	1444	0.9
			2047	3.0
2 0104	1.1	**17**	0317	1.2
0705	3.3		0915	3.4
M 1358	0.9	TU	1619	0.9
2004	3.1		2215	3.2
3 0244	1.1	**18**	0450	1.1
0840	3.4		1036	3.6
TU 1542	0.8	W	1740	0.8
2141	3.3		2322	3.4
4 0426	1.0	**19**	0558	0.9
1009	3.6		1132	3.7
W 1715	0.6	TH	1830	0.6
2301	3.4			
5 0547	0.8	**20**	0003	3.5
1116	3.8		0641	0.6
TH 1824	0.4	F	1208	3.8
			1901	0.6
6 0001	3.6	**21**	0031	3.6
0648	0.6		0715	0.7
F 1209	3.9	SA	1239	3.8
1919	0.3		1932	0.6
7 0050	3.6	**22**	0059	3.7
0738	0.5		0749	0.6
SA 1256	4.0	SU	1311	3.8
○ 2006	0.3	●	2004	0.6
8 0133	3.7	**23**	0129	3.7
0822	0.4		0821	0.6
SU 1341	4.1	M	1342	3.8
2048	0.4		2035	0.6
9 0213	3.8	**24**	0157	3.7
0903	0.4		0849	0.6
M 1424	4.1	TU	1410	3.8
2128	0.5		2102	0.6
10 0251	3.9	**25**	0224	3.7
0943	0.5		0917	0.6
TU 1506	4.0	W	1440	3.7
2205	0.6		2129	0.6
11 0328	3.9	**26**	0254	3.7
1022	0.5		0946	0.5
W 1548	3.9	TH	1514	3.6
2239	0.7		2157	0.6
12 0406	3.8	**27**	0327	3.6
1058	0.5		1017	0.6
TH 1631	3.6	F	1551	3.5
2313	0.8		2227	0.7
13 0445	3.6	**28**	0403	3.6
1135	0.6		1051	0.7
F 1717	3.4	SA	1631	3.4
2351	0.9		2302	0.9
14 0530	3.5	**29**	0444	3.6
1220	0.8		1131	0.7
SA 1811	3.2	SU	1719	3.3
◑		◑	2348	1.0
15 0038	1.0	**30**	0536	3.5
0628	3.4		1227	0.7
SU 1320	0.9	M	1824	3.1
1921	3.0			
		31	0056	1.0
			0648	3.4
		TU	1347	0.8
			1948	3.1

NOVEMBER

Time	m		Time	m
1 0225	1.1	**16**	0346	1.1
0815	3.5		0935	3.5
W 1521	0.7	TH	1636	0.9
2116	3.2		2222	3.3
2 0358	1.0	**17**	0459	1.0
0938	3.7		1036	3.6
TH 1647	0.6	F	1735	0.7
2231	3.4		2311	3.5
3 0515	0.8	**18**	0551	0.9
1046	3.8		1122	3.7
F 1754	0.4	SA	1815	0.7
2329	3.5		2347	3.6
4 0616	0.6	**19**	0632	0.8
1140	3.9		1159	3.7
SA 1848	0.4	SU	1851	0.7
5 0019	3.6	**20**	0020	3.7
0709	0.5		0711	0.7
SU 1230	3.9	M	1235	3.8
○ 1937	0.4	●	1927	0.7
6 0104	3.7	**21**	0054	3.7
0757	0.4		0747	0.7
M 1318	3.9	TU	1311	3.8
2021	0.4		2001	0.7
7 0146	3.8	**22**	0127	3.8
0840	0.4		0822	0.6
TU 1403	3.9	W	1346	3.7
2100	0.5		2036	0.7
8 0225	3.8	**23**	0200	3.8
0920	0.5		0858	0.6
W 1446	3.8	TH	1424	3.7
2139	0.6		2112	0.7
9 0304	3.8	**24**	0237	3.8
1002	0.5		0936	0.6
TH 1530	3.7	F	1505	3.6
2217	0.7		2148	0.7
10 0344	3.8	**25**	0316	3.8
1043	0.5		1013	0.6
F 1614	3.5	SA	1547	3.5
2253	0.7		2223	0.7
11 0425	3.7	**26**	0356	3.7
1121	0.6		1053	0.6
SA 1659	3.3	SU	1631	3.4
2330	0.8		2302	0.8
12 0508	3.6	**27**	0440	3.7
1203	0.7		1137	0.6
SU 1749	3.2	M	1721	3.3
◐			2350	0.9
13 0013	1.0	**28**	0531	3.6
0559	3.5		1230	0.6
M 1254	0.8	TU	1819	3.2
1848	3.1	◐		
14 0109	1.1	**29**	0050	0.9
0702	3.4		0634	3.6
TU 1400	0.9	W	1336	0.7
1958	3.0		1928	3.2
15 0223	1.1	**30**	0202	0.9
0818	3.4		0746	3.6
W 1519	0.9	TH	1453	0.7
2114	3.1		2041	3.3

DECEMBER

Time	m		Time	m
1 0322	0.9	**16**	0341	1.1
0902	3.7		0926	3.6
F 1610	0.6	SA	1622	0.9
2151	3.4		2205	3.4
2 0437	0.8	**17**	0447	1.0
1010	3.7		1025	3.6
SA 1716	0.6	SU	1719	0.8
2252	3.5		2256	3.5
3 0541	0.6	**18**	0542	0.9
1111	3.7		1116	3.7
SU 1814	0.5	M	1807	0.8
2347	3.6		2341	3.6
4 0640	0.5	**19**	0632	0.8
1208	3.7		1202	3.7
M 1909	0.5	TU	1852	0.8
5 0038	3.7	**20**	0023	3.7
0735	0.5		0719	0.7
TU 1301	3.7	W	1246	3.7
○ 1958	0.5	●	1935	0.8
6 0124	3.8	**21**	0104	3.8
0822	0.5		0802	0.7
W 1348	3.7	TH	1331	3.7
2040	0.6		2018	0.7
7 0205	3.8	**22**	0146	3.8
0905	0.5		0847	0.6
TH 1432	3.7	F	1417	3.7
2120	0.7		2104	0.7
8 0246	3.9	**23**	0229	3.9
0949	0.6		0933	0.6
F 1516	3.6	SA	1503	3.7
2201	0.7		2147	0.7
9 0328	3.9	**24**	0311	3.9
1032	0.6		1016	0.5
SA 1600	3.5	SU	1545	3.6
2239	0.7		2225	0.6
10 0408	3.8	**25**	0351	3.9
1110	0.5		1055	0.4
SU 1642	3.3	M	1628	3.5
2313	0.7		2302	0.7
11 0447	3.7	**26**	0434	3.9
1146	0.6		1138	0.5
M 1724	3.2	TU	1715	3.4
2350	0.8		2346	0.7
12 0528	3.6	**27**	0522	3.8
1225	0.7		1226	0.6
TU 1809	3.2	W	1805	3.4
◐		◐		
13 0031	0.9	**28**	0038	0.8
0616	3.5		0615	3.8
W 1310	0.8	TH	1318	0.6
1900	3.1		1859	3.3
14 0123	1.0	**29**	0135	0.8
0713	3.5		0714	3.7
TH 1407	0.9	F	1417	0.7
2000	3.2		2000	3.3
15 0229	1.1	**30**	0242	0.8
0819	3.5		0823	3.7
F 1514	1.0	SA	1526	0.8
2105	3.3		2107	3.4
		31	0357	0.8
			0937	3.6
		SU	1638	0.7
			2216	3.4

Chart Datum: 1·66 metres below Normal Null (German reference level)

TIDES

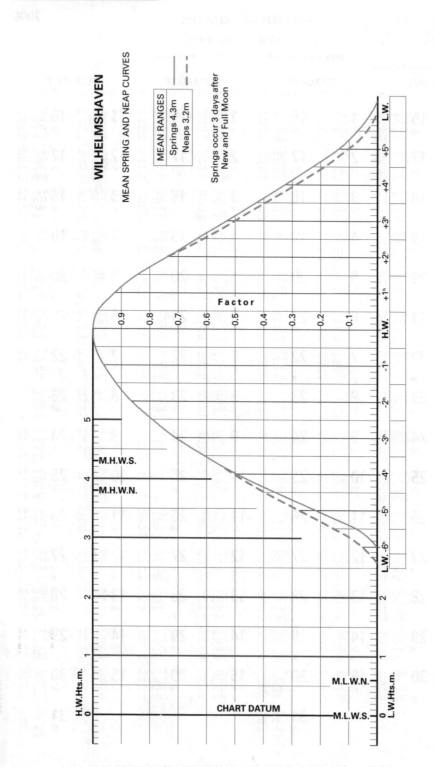

WILHELMSHAVEN

MEAN SPRING AND NEAP CURVES

MEAN RANGES
Springs 4.3m
Neaps 3.2m

Springs occur 3 days after
New and Full Moon

Factor

0.9 0.8 0.7 0.6 0.5 0.4 0.3 0.2 0.1

H.W. -1ʰ -2ʰ -3ʰ -4ʰ -5ʰ L.W. -6ʰ

+1ʰ +2ʰ +3ʰ +4ʰ +5ʰ L.W.

H.W.Hts.m.

M.H.W.S.
M.H.W.N.

CHART DATUM

M.L.W.N.
M.L.W.S.

L.W.Hts.m.

GERMANY – WILHELMSHAVEN 2006

LAT 53°31'N LONG 8°09'E

TIMES AND HEIGHTS OF HIGH AND LOW WATERS

TIME ZONE –0100
(German Standard Time)
Subtract 1 hour for UT
For German Summer Time add
ONE hour in **non-shaded areas**

JANUARY

Day	Times (Time m)	Day	Times (Time m)
1 SU	0105 4.8 / 0730 0.6 / 1342 4.6 / 1955 0.8	**16** M	0154 4.8 / 0818 0.7 / 1420 4.5 / 2028 0.8
2 M	0156 4.9 / 0824 0.6 / 1437 4.6 / 2047 0.7	**17** TU	0230 4.9 / 0854 0.7 / 1454 4.5 / 2101 0.7
3 TU	0246 4.9 / 0916 0.4 / 1528 4.5 / 2132 0.7	**18** W	0304 4.8 / 0927 0.7 / 1526 4.4 / 2129 0.6
4 W	0333 4.9 / 1002 0.4 / 1614 4.5 / 2210 0.6	**19** TH	0334 4.8 / 0954 0.6 / 1558 4.4 / 2157 0.7
5 TH	0419 4.9 / 1046 0.4 / 1659 4.4 / 2251 0.7	**20** F	0405 4.7 / 1023 0.6 / 1630 4.3 / 2227 0.7
6 F ◐	0506 4.9 / 1132 0.6 / 1745 4.3 / 2336 0.8	**21** SA	0437 4.6 / 1053 0.7 / 1701 4.3 / 2257 0.8
7 SA	0556 4.8 / 1219 0.7 / 1833 4.2	**22** SU ◑	0508 4.5 / 1121 0.8 / 1732 4.2 / 2328 1.0
8 SU	0026 0.9 / 0650 4.6 / 1304 0.8 / 1927 4.2	**23** M	0542 4.4 / 1154 0.9 / 1812 4.1
9 M	0125 0.9 / 0754 4.5 / 1410 0.9 / 2031 4.2	**24** TU	0011 1.1 / 0633 4.3 / 1246 1.1 / 1912 4.1
10 TU	0236 1.0 / 0906 4.4 / 1519 1.0 / 2142 4.3	**25** W	0117 1.3 / 0744 4.3 / 1358 1.2 / 2028 4.2
11 W	0353 0.9 / 1020 4.4 / 1629 1.0 / 2248 4.4	**26** TH	0238 1.2 / 0906 4.4 / 1519 1.1 / 2146 4.3
12 TH	0504 0.9 / 1125 4.4 / 1732 0.9 / 2346 4.5	**27** F	0401 1.0 / 1026 4.4 / 1639 1.0 / 2257 4.5
13 F	0605 0.8 / 1219 4.5 / 1827 0.9	**28** SA	0517 0.9 / 1138 4.5 / 1751 0.9
14 SA ○	0035 4.7 / 0657 0.8 / 1305 4.5 / 1912 0.9	**29** SU ●	0000 4.7 / 0624 0.7 / 1241 4.6 / 1853 0.7
15 SU	0116 4.8 / 0739 0.8 / 1344 4.5 / 1951 0.9	**30** M	0056 4.8 / 0723 0.5 / 1339 4.6 / 1948 0.6
		31 TU	0148 4.9 / 0817 0.3 / 1432 4.6 / 2038 0.5

FEBRUARY

Day	Times (Time m)	Day	Times (Time m)
1 W	0238 5.0 / 0909 0.3 / 1520 4.5 / 2122 0.4	**16** TH	0246 4.8 / 0903 0.5 / 1504 4.5 / 2109 0.4
2 TH	0324 5.0 / 0954 0.2 / 1602 4.5 / 2159 0.4	**17** F	0313 4.7 / 0928 0.4 / 1532 4.4 / 2134 0.4
3 F	0407 5.0 / 1033 0.3 / 1640 4.5 / 2235 0.5	**18** SA	0341 4.7 / 0955 0.4 / 1601 4.4 / 2202 0.5
4 SA	0448 4.9 / 1111 0.5 / 1717 4.4 / 2312 0.6	**19** SU	0411 4.6 / 1022 0.5 / 1629 4.3 / 2228 0.6
5 SU ◑	0530 4.8 / 1147 0.7 / 1755 4.4 / 2351 0.7	**20** M	0436 4.5 / 1045 0.6 / 1652 4.3 / 2249 0.7
6 M	0615 4.6 / 1226 0.8 / 1840 4.2	**21** TU	0502 4.4 / 1105 0.7 / 1721 4.1 / 2319 0.8
7 TU	0039 0.8 / 0712 4.3 / 1317 1.0 / 1942 4.2	**22** W	0544 4.2 / 1145 1.0 / 1816 4.0
8 W	0148 1.0 / 0828 4.3 / 1431 1.2 / 2102 4.2	**23** TH	0019 1.0 / 0657 4.1 / 1301 1.2 / 1940 4.1
9 TH	0317 1.0 / 0954 4.3 / 1556 1.1 / 2224 4.3	**24** F	0151 1.1 / 0833 4.1 / 1439 1.2 / 2114 4.2
10 F	0444 0.9 / 1111 4.2 / 1713 1.0 / 2332 4.5	**25** SA	0331 0.9 / 1009 4.2 / 1616 1.0 / 2239 4.5
11 SA	0553 0.8 / 1209 4.4 / 1813 0.9	**26** SU	0501 0.7 / 1130 4.4 / 1738 0.8 / 2348 4.7
12 SU	0023 4.7 / 0645 0.7 / 1254 4.5 / 1859 0.9	**27** M	0613 0.5 / 1235 4.5 / 1842 0.6
13 M	0105 4.8 / 0726 0.7 / 1332 4.5 / 1938 0.7 ○	**28** TU ●	0046 4.8 / 0712 0.3 / 1330 4.5 / 1934 0.4
14 TU	0142 4.8 / 0802 0.6 / 1406 4.6 / 2013 0.6		
15 W	0216 4.8 / 0835 0.5 / 1436 4.6 / 2043 0.5		

MARCH

Day	Times (Time m)	Day	Times (Time m)
1 W	0137 4.9 / 0803 0.1 / 1418 4.5 / 2020 0.3	**16** TH	0152 4.7 / 0805 0.3 / 1411 4.5 / 2017 0.4
2 TH	0224 5.0 / 0850 0.1 / 1501 4.6 / 2102 0.2	**17** F	0221 4.7 / 0833 0.3 / 1437 4.5 / 2043 0.3
3 F	0308 5.0 / 0932 0.2 / 1539 4.6 / 2139 0.3	**18** SA	0248 4.7 / 0858 0.3 / 1503 4.5 / 2108 0.3
4 SA	0348 5.0 / 1009 0.3 / 1613 4.6 / 2213 0.3	**19** SU	0315 4.6 / 0924 0.3 / 1531 4.4 / 2134 0.3
5 SU	0426 4.8 / 1041 0.4 / 1645 4.5 / 2245 0.4	**20** M	0345 4.5 / 0950 0.4 / 1559 4.4 / 2200 0.4
6 M ◑	0503 4.7 / 1111 0.6 / 1718 4.4 / 2319 0.6	**21** TU	0413 4.5 / 1014 0.5 / 1625 4.3 / 2224 0.4
7 TU	0544 4.4 / 1143 0.8 / 1759 4.3	**22** W	0441 4.3 / 1036 0.6 / 1656 4.2 / 2255 0.6
8 W	0000 0.7 / 0637 4.1 / 1231 1.0 / 1900 4.1	**23** TH	0525 4.1 / 1117 0.8 / 1752 4.1 / 2355 0.8
9 TH	0106 0.9 / 0754 3.9 / 1347 1.2 / 2025 4.1	**24** F	0639 4.0 / 1234 1.1 / 1917 4.1
10 F	0241 1.0 / 0926 3.9 / 1522 1.2 / 2158 4.3	**25** SA	0129 0.8 / 0819 4.0 / 1418 1.1 / 2056 4.3
11 SA	0419 0.9 / 1052 4.1 / 1649 1.0 / 2314 4.4	**26** SU	0314 0.7 / 0957 4.1 / 1558 1.0 / 2223 4.5
12 SU	0534 0.7 / 1154 4.3 / 1752 0.8	**27** M	0445 0.5 / 1118 4.3 / 1718 0.7 / 2332 4.7
13 M	0006 4.6 / 0623 0.6 / 1235 4.4 / 1837 0.7	**28** TU	0555 0.3 / 1220 4.4 / 1820 0.4
14 TU ○	0044 4.7 / 0700 0.5 / 1310 4.5 / 1914 0.6	**29** W ●	0029 4.8 / 0651 0.1 / 1312 4.5 / 1911 0.2
15 W	0119 4.7 / 0734 0.4 / 1343 4.5 / 1947 0.4	**30** TH	0121 4.9 / 0740 0.0 / 1356 4.5 / 1955 0.1
		31 F	0206 4.9 / 0823 0.0 / 1435 4.6 / 2036 0.1

APRIL

Day	Times (Time m)	Day	Times (Time m)
1 SA	0247 4.9 / 0902 0.2 / 1510 4.6 / 2113 0.2	**16** SU	0220 4.7 / 0827 0.5 / 1434 4.6 / 2041 0.3
2 SU	0326 4.8 / 0937 0.3 / 1543 4.6 / 2147 0.2	**17** M	0251 4.6 / 0855 0.3 / 1504 4.5 / 2110 0.2
3 M	0403 4.6 / 1007 0.4 / 1615 4.5 / 2219 0.3	**18** TU	0325 4.5 / 0925 0.3 / 1537 4.4 / 2142 0.3
4 TU	0440 4.4 / 1037 0.5 / 1649 4.4 / 2253 0.4	**19** W	0401 4.4 / 0956 0.5 / 1613 4.4 / 2216 0.3
5 W ◑	0521 4.2 / 1110 0.7 / 1730 4.3 / 2334 0.6	**20** TH	0441 4.2 / 1031 0.6 / 1654 4.3 / 2257 0.4
6 TH	0611 4.0 / 1156 0.9 / 1828 4.2	**21** F ◐	0531 4.1 / 1119 0.7 / 1752 4.2 / 2359 0.5
7 F	0035 0.8 / 0722 3.8 / 1307 1.1 / 1949 4.1	**22** SA	0643 4.0 / 1231 0.9 / 1912 4.2
8 SA	0202 0.9 / 0851 3.8 / 1440 1.1 / 2121 4.2	**23** SU	0126 0.6 / 0813 4.0 / 1405 0.9 / 2043 4.4
9 SU	0339 0.8 / 1017 4.0 / 1610 0.9 / 2239 4.4	**24** M	0301 0.5 / 0943 4.1 / 1536 0.8 / 2204 4.6
10 M	0456 0.6 / 1121 4.2 / 1715 0.7 / 2333 4.5	**25** TU	0423 0.3 / 1056 4.2 / 1649 0.5 / 2310 4.7
11 TU	0545 0.4 / 1203 4.3 / 1800 0.6	**26** W	0527 0.1 / 1154 4.3 / 1749 0.3
12 W	0011 4.6 / 0621 0.4 / 1237 4.5 / 1837 0.5	**27** TH ●	0006 4.8 / 0622 0.1 / 1244 4.4 / 1842 0.2
13 TH ○	0046 4.6 / 0656 0.3 / 1310 4.5 / 1913 0.4	**28** F	0059 4.8 / 0711 0.1 / 1329 4.5 / 1929 0.1
14 F	0119 4.7 / 0729 0.3 / 1340 4.6 / 1945 0.3	**29** SA	0145 4.8 / 0754 0.1 / 1407 4.6 / 2009 0.1
15 SA	0150 4.7 / 0759 0.3 / 1407 4.6 / 2013 0.3	**30** SU	0225 4.8 / 0830 0.2 / 1441 4.7 / 2046 0.2

Chart Datum: 2·26 metres below Normal Null (German reference level)

TIDES

TIME ZONE -0100
(German Standard Time)
Subtract 1 hour for UT
For German Summer Time add
ONE hour in **non-shaded areas**

GERMANY–WILHELMSHAVEN

LAT 53°31'N   LONG 8°09'E

TIMES AND HEIGHTS OF HIGH AND LOW WATERS

2006

MAY

Time	m	Time	m	Time	m	Time	m
1 M	0303 4.6 / 0905 0.3 / 1515 4.6 / 2123 0.2		**16** TU	0234 4.6 / 0837 0.5 / 1447 4.6 / 2058 0.3				
2 TU	0342 4.5 / 0938 0.4 / 1551 4.5 / 2159 0.3		**17** W	0316 4.5 / 0914 0.4 / 1528 4.6 / 2138 0.2				
3 W	0422 4.3 / 1012 0.5 / 1629 4.5 / 2236 0.4		**18** TH	0401 4.3 / 0953 0.5 / 1612 4.5 / 2222 0.3				
4 TH	0503 4.1 / 1048 0.7 / 1710 4.4 / 2319 0.5		**19** F	0449 4.2 / 1038 0.6 / 1701 4.5 / 2311 0.3				
5 F ◐	0550 4.0 / 1132 0.8 / 1802 4.3		**20** SA	0544 4.1 / 1129 0.7 / 1759 4.4				
6 SA	0011 0.7 / 0650 3.8 / 1231 0.9 / 1909 4.2		**21** SU	0011 0.4 / 0648 4.0 / 1233 0.7 / 1908 4.4				
7 SU	0121 0.7 / 0804 3.8 / 1349 1.0 / 2028 4.2		**22** M	0124 0.4 / 0802 4.1 / 1350 0.7 / 2025 4.5				
8 M	0243 0.7 / 0922 4.0 / 1512 0.9 / 2144 4.3		**23** TU	0243 0.4 / 0917 4.1 / 1508 0.6 / 2139 4.6				
9 TU	0358 0.6 / 1028 4.1 / 1620 0.7 / 2242 4.4		**24** W	0354 0.3 / 1023 4.3 / 1615 0.5 / 2243 4.7				
10 W	0453 0.4 / 1115 4.3 / 1710 0.6 / 2325 4.5		**25** TH	0454 0.2 / 1120 4.4 / 1715 0.3 / 2340 4.7				
11 TH	0535 0.4 / 1153 4.4 / 1754 0.5		**26** F	0549 0.2 / 1212 4.5 / 1813 0.3				
12 F	0004 4.6 / 0614 0.4 / 1230 4.6 / 1834 0.5		**27** SA ●	0034 4.7 / 0642 0.3 / 1300 4.6 / 1905 0.2				
13 SA ○	0042 4.6 / 0652 0.4 / 1304 4.6 / 1911 0.4		**28** SU	0124 4.7 / 0727 0.3 / 1341 4.7 / 1948 0.2				
14 SU	0118 4.7 / 0726 0.3 / 1336 4.6 / 1945 0.4		**29** M	0206 4.6 / 0805 0.4 / 1417 4.7 / 2027 0.2				
15 M	0154 4.7 / 0800 0.4 / 1410 4.6 / 2020 0.3		**30** TU	0245 4.5 / 0842 0.4 / 1455 4.7 / 2107 0.3				
			31 W	0326 4.4 / 0919 0.5 / 1533 4.7 / 2147 0.3				

JUNE

Time	m	Time	m
1 TH	0406 4.3 / 0956 0.5 / 1612 4.6 / 2226 0.4	**16** F	0404 4.4 / 0956 0.5 / 1611 4.7 / 2228 0.2
2 F	0446 4.2 / 1032 0.6 / 1652 4.6 / 2306 0.5	**17** SA	0453 4.3 / 1040 0.5 / 1701 4.7 / 2319 0.3
3 SA ◐	0528 4.1 / 1112 0.7 / 1736 4.5 / 2348 0.6	**18** SU ◐	0545 4.2 / 1131 0.6 / 1756 4.7
4 SU	0614 4.0 / 1157 0.8 / 1827 4.4	**19** M	0013 0.3 / 0639 4.2 / 1226 0.6 / 1855 4.6
5 M	0038 0.7 / 0710 4.0 / 1255 0.9 / 1927 4.3	**20** TU	0111 0.4 / 0738 4.2 / 1328 0.6 / 1959 4.6
6 TU	0140 0.7 / 0814 4.0 / 1404 0.9 / 2034 4.3	**21** W	0215 0.5 / 0841 4.2 / 1436 0.6 / 2107 4.6
7 W	0249 0.7 / 0919 4.2 / 1513 0.9 / 2137 4.4	**22** TH	0320 0.5 / 0945 4.3 / 1544 0.6 / 2214 4.6
8 TH	0351 0.6 / 1015 4.3 / 1613 0.8 / 2232 4.5	**23** F	0422 0.5 / 1046 4.4 / 1648 0.6 / 2317 4.5
9 F	0443 0.5 / 1103 4.4 / 1706 0.7 / 2320 4.6	**24** SA	0522 0.5 / 1143 4.5 / 1751 0.4
10 SA	0531 0.5 / 1147 4.5 / 1755 0.6	**25** SU ●	0015 4.6 / 0619 0.5 / 1236 4.6 / 1849 0.4
11 SU ○	0007 4.6 / 0616 0.5 / 1230 4.6 / 1840 0.6	**26** M	0107 4.6 / 0709 0.5 / 1322 4.7 / 1936 0.4
12 M	0052 4.7 / 0659 0.5 / 1311 4.7 / 1924 0.5	**27** TU	0152 4.5 / 0751 0.6 / 1402 4.8 / 2018 0.4
13 TU	0138 4.7 / 0744 0.5 / 1354 4.8 / 2010 0.4	**28** W	0232 4.5 / 0830 0.6 / 1441 4.8 / 2059 0.4
14 W	0227 4.6 / 0831 0.5 / 1440 4.8 / 2058 0.5	**29** TH	0311 4.4 / 0908 0.5 / 1519 4.8 / 2138 0.4
15 TH	0316 4.5 / 0915 0.5 / 1525 4.8 / 2143 0.2	**30** F	0348 4.4 / 0943 0.5 / 1555 4.8 / 2212 0.4

JULY

Time	m	Time	m
1 SA	0424 4.3 / 1015 0.6 / 1630 4.7 / 2246 0.5	**16** SU	0442 4.4 / 1032 0.4 / 1650 4.9 / 2311 0.3
2 SU ◐	0459 4.2 / 1049 0.7 / 1707 4.6 / 2321 0.6	**17** M	0527 4.4 / 1118 0.5 / 1739 4.8 / 2358 0.4
3 M	0536 4.2 / 1125 0.7 / 1744 4.5 / 2357 0.7	**18** TU	0613 4.3 / 1206 0.6 / 1830 4.7
4 TU	0616 4.1 / 1205 0.8 / 1828 4.4	**19** W	0045 0.6 / 0701 4.3 / 1258 0.7 / 1926 4.6
5 W	0040 0.8 / 0703 4.1 / 1256 1.0 / 1922 4.4	**20** TH	0138 0.7 / 0758 4.3 / 1401 0.7 / 2034 4.5
6 TH	0136 0.8 / 0803 4.2 / 1401 1.0 / 2027 4.4	**21** F	0243 0.8 / 0907 4.3 / 1516 0.7 / 2150 4.4
7 F	0241 0.9 / 0908 4.2 / 1510 1.0 / 2135 4.4	**22** SA	0355 0.8 / 1020 4.4 / 1632 0.7 / 2302 4.4
8 SA	0346 0.8 / 1011 4.3 / 1617 0.8 / 2239 4.5	**23** SU	0505 0.8 / 1125 4.6 / 1741 0.6
9 SU	0448 0.8 / 1108 4.5 / 1720 0.7 / 2339 4.6	**24** M	0004 4.5 / 0606 0.8 / 1221 4.7 / 1840 0.6
10 M	0548 0.7 / 1203 4.7 / 1818 0.7	**25** TU	0055 4.5 / 0658 0.8 / 1308 4.8 / 1929 0.6
11 TU ○	0035 4.6 / 0644 0.7 / 1254 4.8 / 1913 0.5	**26** W	0139 4.5 / 0742 0.7 / 1350 4.9 / 2010 0.5
12 W	0130 4.7 / 0736 0.6 / 1344 4.9 / 2006 0.4	**27** TH	0218 4.5 / 0821 0.6 / 1427 4.9 / 2048 0.5
13 TH	0223 4.7 / 0829 0.5 / 1433 5.0 / 2058 0.3	**28** F	0253 4.5 / 0856 0.6 / 1502 4.9 / 2122 0.5
14 F	0313 4.6 / 0914 0.5 / 1519 5.0 / 2144 0.2	**29** SA	0325 4.5 / 0926 0.5 / 1532 4.9 / 2150 0.5
15 SA	0359 4.5 / 0953 0.4 / 1604 4.9 / 2226 0.2	**30** SU	0355 4.4 / 0952 0.5 / 1602 4.8 / 2217 0.5
		31 M	0426 4.4 / 1022 0.6 / 1634 4.7 / 2248 0.6

AUGUST

Time	m	Time	m
1 TU	0456 4.4 / 1052 0.7 / 1704 4.6 / 2317 0.7	**16** W ◐	0537 4.5 / 1138 0.7 / 1758 4.7
2 W ◐	0525 4.3 / 1121 0.8 / 1735 4.5 / 2345 0.8	**17** TH	0009 0.8 / 0620 4.4 / 1223 0.8 / 1851 4.5
3 TH	0559 4.2 / 1156 1.0 / 1817 4.4	**18** F	0056 1.0 / 0716 4.3 / 1325 0.9 / 2002 4.3
4 F	0026 1.0 / 0650 4.1 / 1253 1.1 / 1921 4.3	**19** SA	0205 1.1 / 0833 4.3 / 1450 1.0 / 2129 4.2
5 SA	0132 1.1 / 0803 4.1 / 1410 1.1 / 2043 4.2	**20** SU	0331 1.1 / 0959 4.4 / 1621 0.9 / 2252 4.3
6 SU	0253 1.1 / 0924 4.2 / 1548 0.9 / 2206 4.3	**21** M	0453 1.0 / 1114 4.6 / 1737 0.8 / 2357 4.4
7 M	0415 1.0 / 1039 4.4 / 1655 0.8 / 2320 4.5	**22** TU	0558 0.9 / 1210 4.7 / 1833 0.7
8 TU	0530 0.9 / 1143 4.7 / 1805 0.7	**23** W ●	0044 4.5 / 0647 0.8 / 1254 4.8 / 1916 0.6
9 W ○	0025 4.6 / 0635 0.8 / 1240 4.9 / 1905 0.5	**24** TH	0122 4.6 / 0728 0.7 / 1332 4.9 / 1953 0.5
10 TH	0122 4.7 / 0730 0.6 / 1332 5.0 / 1959 0.4	**25** F	0157 4.6 / 0804 0.6 / 1407 4.9 / 2026 0.5
11 F	0213 4.7 / 0819 0.5 / 1420 5.1 / 2049 0.2	**26** SA	0228 4.6 / 0836 0.5 / 1438 4.9 / 2056 0.5
12 SA	0300 4.7 / 0903 0.4 / 1505 5.1 / 2133 0.2	**27** SU	0256 4.6 / 0902 0.5 / 1504 4.8 / 2120 0.5
13 SU	0342 4.6 / 0941 0.3 / 1548 5.1 / 2212 0.2	**28** M	0322 4.6 / 0925 0.5 / 1531 4.8 / 2144 0.5
14 M	0420 4.6 / 1016 0.4 / 1630 5.0 / 2250 0.4	**29** TU	0349 4.5 / 0951 0.6 / 1559 4.7 / 2211 0.6
15 TU	0458 4.5 / 1056 0.5 / 1713 4.9 / 2330 0.6	**30** W	0416 4.4 / 1019 0.7 / 1626 4.6 / 2236 0.7
		31 TH ◐	0441 4.4 / 1043 0.8 / 1652 4.5 / 2258 0.8

Chart Datum: 2·26 metres below Normal Null (German reference level)

GERMANY – WILHELMSHAVEN

2006

LAT 53°31′N LONG 8°09′E

TIMES AND HEIGHTS OF HIGH AND LOW WATERS

TIME ZONE -0100
(German Standard Time)
Subtract 1 hour for UT
For German Summer Time add
ONE hour in **non-shaded areas**

SEPTEMBER

Day	Time m	Time m	Time m	Time m	Day	Time m	Time m	Time m	Time m
1 F	0508 4.2	1110 0.9	1729 4.3	2332 1.0	16 SA	0017 1.1	0639 4.3	1252 1.0	1932 4.0
2 SA	0555 4.1	1201 1.0	1833 4.1		17 SU	0128 1.3	0800 4.2	1422 1.1	2104 4.0
3 SU	0038 1.2	0713 4.1	1326 1.1	2005 4.1	18 M	0302 1.3	0934 4.2	1602 1.1	2234 4.1
4 M	0213 1.3	0848 4.2	1506 1.0	2142 4.2	19 TU	0434 1.2	1056 4.5	1723 0.8	2341 4.3
5 TU	0351 1.1	1015 4.4	1637 0.8	2306 4.4	20 W	0542 1.0	1152 4.7	1814 0.7	
6 W	0514 1.0	1125 4.7	1751 0.6		21 TH	0023 4.5	0626 0.8	1230 4.8	1849 0.6
7 TH ○	0012 4.5	0621 0.8	1223 4.9	1851 0.4	22 F	0055 4.5	0702 0.7	1304 4.8	1922 0.6
8 F	0107 4.6	0714 0.6	1314 5.0	1942 0.3	23 SA	0126 4.6	0736 0.6	1337 4.8	1954 0.5
9 SA	0154 4.7	0800 0.4	1401 5.1	2028 0.2	24 SU	0156 4.6	0807 0.5	1407 4.8	2022 0.5
10 SU	0237 4.7	0842 0.4	1444 5.1	2111 0.3	25 M	0222 4.6	0833 0.5	1433 4.8	2047 0.5
11 M	0315 4.7	0920 0.4	1525 5.1	2148 0.4	26 TU	0246 4.6	0856 0.5	1458 4.7	2110 0.5
12 TU	0350 4.7	0955 0.4	1605 4.9	2222 0.5	27 W	0312 4.5	0921 0.5	1526 4.6	2134 0.6
13 W	0425 4.7	1030 0.5	1645 4.7	2255 0.7	28 TH	0340 4.5	0947 0.6	1554 4.5	2200 0.7
14 TH ◔	0500 4.5	1107 0.7	1727 4.5	2331 0.9	29 F	0406 4.4	1013 0.7	1624 4.4	2225 0.9
15 F	0542 4.4	1150 0.8	1820 4.2		30 SA ◑	0437 4.3	1044 0.8	1705 4.2	2302 1.1

OCTOBER

Day	Time m	Time m	Time m	Time m	Day	Time m	Time m	Time m	Time m
1 SU	0526 4.2	1136 1.0	1810 4.0		16 M	0052 1.3	0725 4.2	1346 1.1	2027 3.9
2 M	0010 1.3	0644 4.1	1301 1.1	1943 4.0	17 TU	0221 1.4	0855 4.3	1522 1.1	2155 4.0
3 TU	0147 1.4	0821 4.3	1444 1.0	2122 4.1	18 W	0353 1.3	1018 4.5	1644 0.9	2304 4.2
4 W	0328 1.2	0951 4.5	1617 0.7	2246 4.3	19 TH	0504 1.0	1116 4.6	1736 0.7	2347 4.4
5 TH	0451 0.9	1102 4.7	1729 0.5	2349 4.4	20 F	0549 0.8	1153 4.7	1810 0.6	
6 F	0555 0.7	1159 4.9	1826 0.4		21 SA	0017 4.5	0624 0.6	1226 4.7	1842 0.6
7 SA ○	0041 4.6	0648 0.5	1250 5.0	1916 0.3	22 SU ●	0047 4.6	0700 0.5	1300 4.7	1916 0.6
8 SU	0127 4.6	0734 0.4	1337 5.0	2001 0.3	23 M	0118 4.6	0733 0.6	1332 4.7	1946 0.6
9 M	0207 4.7	0815 0.4	1419 5.0	2041 0.4	24 TU	0146 4.6	0802 0.6	1401 4.7	2014 0.6
10 TU	0244 4.8	0855 0.4	1500 5.0	2118 0.5	25 W	0213 4.6	0829 0.6	1430 4.6	2041 0.6
11 W	0319 4.8	0932 0.4	1541 4.8	2152 0.6	26 TH	0242 4.6	0856 0.6	1502 4.6	2108 0.7
12 TH	0355 4.7	1006 0.5	1621 4.5	2224 0.8	27 F	0314 4.6	0927 0.6	1536 4.4	2138 0.8
13 F	0431 4.6	1042 0.6	1704 4.3	2259 1.0	28 SA	0348 4.5	1000 0.7	1614 4.3	2212 0.9
14 SA ◔	0513 4.4	1125 0.8	1754 4.1	2345 1.2	29 SU ◑	0426 4.4	1039 0.8	1701 4.1	2255 1.1
15 SU	0609 4.3	1224 1.0	1901 3.9		30 M	0517 4.3	1133 0.9	1805 4.0	2359 1.2
					31 TU	0629 4.3	1250 0.9	1928 4.0	

NOVEMBER

Day	Time m	Time m	Time m	Time m	Day	Time m	Time m	Time m	Time m
1 W	0127 1.3	0757 4.4	1423 0.9	2057 4.1	16 TH	0249 1.3	0916 4.4	1540 1.0	2202 4.2
2 TH	0259 1.2	0922 4.6	1549 0.7	2215 4.2	17 F	0402 1.2	1018 4.5	1640 0.9	2253 4.4
3 F	0417 0.9	1032 4.7	1657 0.5	2316 4.4	18 SA	0456 1.0	1104 4.6	1723 0.8	2330 4.5
4 SA	0520 0.7	1130 4.8	1753 0.4		19 SU	0540 0.9	1143 4.6	1800 0.8	
5 SU ○	0008 4.5	0615 0.6	1223 4.9	1845 0.4	20 M ●	0005 4.6	0620 0.9	1221 4.7	1837 0.8
6 M	0055 4.6	0705 0.5	1312 4.9	1931 0.4	21 TU	0040 4.6	0658 0.8	1258 4.7	1912 0.7
7 TU	0137 4.7	0749 0.4	1356 4.8	2011 0.5	22 W	0113 4.7	0732 0.7	1334 4.7	1946 0.7
8 W	0215 4.8	0830 0.5	1438 4.7	2049 0.7	23 TH	0147 4.7	0807 0.7	1412 4.6	2023 0.8
9 TH	0252 4.8	0910 0.5	1520 4.6	2126 0.7	24 F	0223 4.7	0844 0.6	1452 4.5	2058 0.8
10 F	0331 4.6	0948 0.5	1603 4.4	2201 0.8	25 SA	0302 4.7	0922 0.6	1533 4.4	2133 0.8
11 SA	0410 4.6	1026 0.6	1645 4.2	2238 0.9	26 SU	0341 4.6	1001 0.6	1616 4.3	2211 0.9
12 SU ◔	0451 4.5	1108 0.8	1731 4.0	2320 1.1	27 M	0425 4.6	1044 0.7	1704 4.2	2257 1.0
13 M	0541 4.4	1158 0.9	1827 3.9		28 TU ◑	0516 4.5	1137 0.7	1749 4.1	2353 1.1
14 TU	0015 1.2	0643 4.3	1302 1.1	1936 3.9	29 W	0618 4.5	1241 0.8	1909 4.1	
15 W	0127 1.3	0759 4.3	1421 1.1	2053 4.0	30 TH	0104 1.1	0730 4.5	1356 0.8	2023 4.1

DECEMBER

Day	Time m	Time m	Time m	Time m	Day	Time m	Time m	Time m	Time m
1 F	0223 1.1	0846 4.6	1511 0.8	2134 4.2	16 SA	0245 1.3	0906 4.4	1528 1.1	2144 4.3
2 SA	0337 0.9	0956 4.7	1618 0.7	2236 4.4	17 SU	0352 1.3	1005 4.5	1626 1.0	2236 4.4
3 SU	0442 0.8	1059 4.8	1718 0.6	2333 4.5	18 M	0449 1.1	1057 4.6	1715 0.9	2322 4.5
4 M	0544 0.6	1157 4.7	1814 0.6		19 TU	0539 1.0	1145 4.6	1801 0.9	
5 TU ○	0025 4.6	0640 0.6	1251 4.7	1904 0.6	20 W	0006 4.7	0626 0.9	1231 4.6	1845 0.8
6 W	0111 4.7	0729 0.5	1338 4.7	1947 0.7	21 TH	0048 4.7	0710 0.8	1317 4.6	1929 0.8
7 TH	0152 4.8	0812 0.6	1421 4.6	2028 0.7	22 F	0131 4.8	0755 0.7	1404 4.6	2015 0.8
8 F	0233 4.8	0855 0.6	1504 4.5	2108 0.8	23 SA	0214 4.8	0841 0.6	1450 4.5	2058 0.8
9 SA	0314 4.8	0938 0.6	1547 4.4	2146 0.8	24 SU	0257 4.8	0924 0.5	1533 4.5	2134 0.7
10 SU	0354 4.8	1016 0.6	1627 4.2	2221 0.8	25 M	0338 4.8	1003 0.5	1615 4.4	2211 0.7
11 M	0432 4.7	1052 0.7	1706 4.1	2257 0.9	26 TU	0422 4.8	1046 0.5	1701 4.3	2253 0.8
12 TU ◔	0513 4.6	1131 0.8	1749 4.0	2338 1.0	27 W	0510 4.7	1133 0.6	1749 4.2	2342 0.9
13 W	0559 4.4	1216 0.9	1838 4.0		28 TH	0602 4.7	1224 0.7	1842 4.2	
14 TH	0029 1.2	0655 4.3	1312 1.1	1938 4.0	29 F	0037 0.9	0700 4.6	1322 0.8	1942 4.2
15 F	0134 1.3	0759 4.3	1420 1.2	2043 4.2	30 SA	0142 1.0	0807 4.6	1428 0.9	2049 4.3
					31 SU	0256 1.2	0921 4.6	1538 0.9	2159 4.3

Chart Datum: 2·26 metres below Normal Null (German reference level)

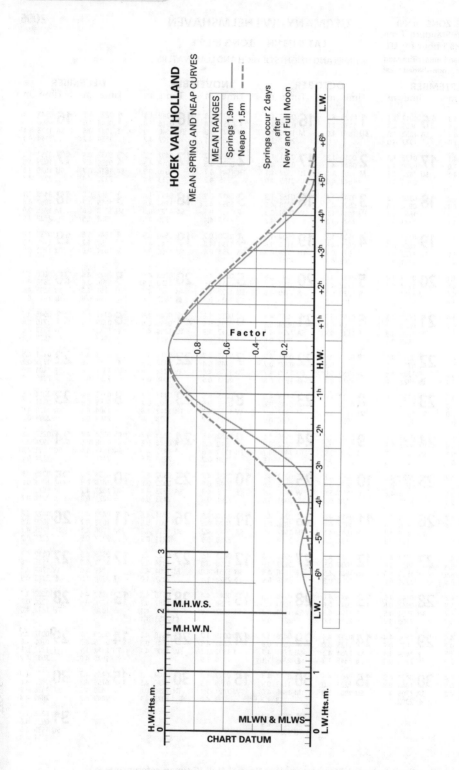

HOEK VAN HOLLAND

MEAN SPRING AND NEAP CURVES

MEAN RANGES
Springs 1.9m
Neaps 1.5m

Springs occur 2 days after
New and Full Moon

TIME ZONE −0100
(Dutch Standard Time)
Subtract 1 hour for UT
For Dutch Summer Time add
ONE hour in **non-shaded areas**

NETHERLANDS – HOEK VAN HOLLAND

LAT 51°59′N   LONG 4°07′E

TIMES AND HEIGHTS OF HIGH AND LOW WATERS

2006

Note - Double LWs often occur. The predictions are for the lower LW which is usually the first.

JANUARY

Day	Time m	Time m	Time m	Time m		Day	Time m	Time m	Time m	Time m
1 SU	0315 2.1	0830 0.2	1531 2.3	2325 0.4		16 M	0414 1.9	0904 0.2	1614 2.1	
2 M	0359 0.1	0910 0.1	1615 2.3			17 TU	0020 0.5	0445 1.9	0939 0.1	1655 2.1
3 TU	0015 0.4	0445 2.0	0956 0.1	1706 2.3		18 W	0037 0.5	0516 1.9	1015 0.1	1729 2.1
4 W	0106 0.4	0535 1.9	1046 0.0	1755 2.3		19 TH	0040 0.5	0545 1.9	1106 0.1	1806 2.1
5 TH	0135 0.5	0625 1.9	1131 0.0	1844 2.2		20 F	0107 0.4	0615 1.9	1140 0.1	1846 2.0
6 F	0224 0.5	0726 1.9	1234 0.0	1949 2.1		21 SA	0140 0.4	0656 1.9	1214 0.1	1915 2.0
7 SA	0324 0.5	0820 1.9	1334 0.1	2056 2.0		22 SU	0150 0.4	0735 1.8	1314 0.1	1959 1.9
8 SU	0255 0.5	0914 1.8	1455 0.1	2154 1.9		23 M	0230 0.4	0830 1.8	1405 0.1	2116 1.9
9 M	0550 0.5	1030 1.8	1554 0.2	2316 1.9		24 TU	0315 0.4	0947 1.7	1520 0.2	2226 1.8
10 TU	0650 0.5	1136 1.8	1715 0.3			25 W	0405 0.4	1050 1.7	1630 0.3	2325 1.8
11 W	0020 1.9	0757 0.4	1235 1.9	2010 0.3		26 TH	0524 0.4	1154 1.8	1744 0.3	
12 TH	0120 1.9	0920 0.4	1336 2.0	2155 0.4		27 F	0025 1.8	0620 0.4	1255 1.9	1825 0.4
13 F	0215 1.9	1016 0.3	1425 2.0	2240 0.4		28 SA	0125 1.8	0655 0.3	1345 2.1	1920 0.4
14 SA	0254 1.9	1050 0.3	1505 2.1	2307 0.5		29 SU	0215 1.9	0736 0.2	1435 2.2	2245 0.4
15 SU	0345 1.9	0840 0.2	1545 2.1	2355 0.5		30 M	0301 2.0	0805 0.1	1518 2.3	2326 0.4
						31 TU	0348 2.0	0845 0.0	1600 2.3	

FEBRUARY

Day	Time m	Time m	Time m	Time m		Day	Time m	Time m	Time m	Time m
1 W	0005 0.4	0428 2.0	0929 0.0	1647 2.3		16 TH	0000 0.4	0449 2.0	0946 0.1	1706 2.1
2 TH	0034 0.4	0516 2.0	1016 0.0	1736 2.3		17 F	0030 0.4	0514 2.0	1020 0.1	1732 2.1
3 F	0136 0.4	0558 2.0	1110 0.0	1825 2.2		18 SA	0106 0.4	0545 2.0	1055 0.1	1759 2.1
4 SA	0210 0.4	0649 2.0	1204 0.0	1915 2.1		19 SU	0130 0.4	0615 2.0	1129 0.0	1831 2.1
5 SU	0200 0.5	0745 2.0	1330 0.0	2015 1.9		20 M	0000 0.3	0649 2.0	1215 0.0	1915 2.0
6 M	0220 0.4	0834 1.9	1440 0.1	2125 1.8		21 TU	0040 0.3	0735 1.9	1330 0.1	2005 1.9
7 TU	0326 0.4	0950 1.8	1544 0.2	2250 1.7		22 W	0225 0.3	0835 1.8	1445 0.2	2125 1.7
8 W	0425 0.4	1116 1.7	1705 0.3			23 TH	0314 0.3	1004 1.7	1605 0.3	2256 1.6
9 TH	0010 1.7	0540 0.4	1230 1.8	1830 0.4		24 F	0450 0.3	1136 1.7	1725 0.3	
10 F	0104 1.7	0904 0.3	1335 1.9	2150 0.3		25 SA	0016 1.6	0550 0.3	1239 1.9	2040 0.3
11 SA	0204 1.8	1000 0.2	1414 2.0	2225 0.4		26 SU	0111 1.7	0629 0.2	1336 2.0	2135 0.3
12 SU	0249 1.9	1034 0.2	1453 2.0	2255 0.4		27 M	0205 1.8	0710 0.1	1419 2.2	2215 0.4
13 M	0325 1.9	1115 0.2	1530 2.1	2327 0.4		28 TU	0240 1.9	0745 0.0	1458 2.3	2306 0.4
14 TU	0355 1.9	0845 0.2	1555 2.1							
15 W	0005 0.4	0426 2.0	0915 0.1	1636 2.1						

MARCH

Day	Time m	Time m	Time m	Time m		Day	Time m	Time m	Time m	Time m
1 W	0325 2.0	0826 0.0	1540 2.3	2339 0.4		16 TH	0349 2.0	0839 0.1	1559 2.1	2330 0.3
2 TH	0409 2.1	0905 -0.1	1625 2.3			17 F	0419 2.0	1144 0.1	1629 2.1	2359 0.3
3 F	0036 0.4	0448 2.1	0949 -0.1	1707 2.2		18 SA	0445 2.0	1224 0.1	1657 2.1	2205 0.3
4 SA	0115 0.4	0536 2.1	1039 0.0	1755 2.1		19 SU	0510 2.0	1015 0.1	1725 2.1	2240 0.3
5 SU	0205 0.4	0615 2.1	1144 0.0	1845 2.0		20 M	0545 2.1	1056 0.1	1805 2.0	2316 0.2
6 M	0020 0.3	0705 2.0	1315 0.1	1940 1.8		21 TU	0619 2.1	1133 0.1	1841 2.0	2353 0.1
7 TU	0134 0.3	0759 1.9	1430 0.1	2045 1.6		22 W	0701 2.0	1320 0.1	1935 1.8	
8 W	0250 0.3	0903 1.7	1546 0.2	2225 1.5		23 TH	0130 0.2	0759 1.9	1444 0.2	2044 1.6
9 TH	0405 0.3	1055 1.6	1650 0.3	2344 1.5		24 F	0306 0.2	0934 1.7	1600 0.3	2224 1.5
10 F	0505 0.3	1214 1.7	1810 0.4			25 SA	0416 0.2	1126 1.7	1800 0.3	2355 1.5
11 SA	0056 1.6	0604 0.2	1314 1.9	2115 0.3		26 SU	0505 0.2	1223 1.9	2015 0.3	
12 SU	0145 1.7	0934 0.2	1406 2.0	2210 0.3		27 M	0056 1.6	0600 0.1	1316 2.1	2124 0.3
13 M	0225 1.8	1025 0.1	1436 2.0	2235 0.3		28 TU	0139 1.8	0635 0.1	1358 2.2	2155 0.3
14 TU	0250 1.9	1050 0.2	1459 2.1	2316 0.3		29 W	0218 1.9	0715 0.1	1437 2.2	2234 0.3
15 W	0325 1.9	0819 0.2	1529 2.1	2320 0.4		30 TH	0301 2.0	0800 0.1	1518 2.3	2320 0.3
						31 F	0340 2.1	0839 0.0	1602 2.2	

APRIL

Day	Time m	Time m	Time m	Time m		Day	Time m	Time m	Time m	Time m
1 SA	0016 0.3	0425 2.1	0926 0.0	1646 2.1		16 SU	0415 2.1	1204 0.1	1629 2.1	2145 0.2
2 SU	0101 0.3	0505 2.2	1324 0.0	1728 2.0		17 M	0446 2.1	0955 0.2	1702 2.0	2215 0.2
3 M	0140 0.2	0545 2.1	1410 0.1	1816 1.8		18 TU	0522 2.1	1035 0.2	1739 2.0	2254 0.1
4 TU	0215 0.2	0635 2.0	1334 0.1	1906 1.7		19 W	0558 2.1	1130 0.2	1826 1.9	2349 0.1
5 W	0100 0.2	0723 1.9	1420 0.1	1955 1.5		20 TH	0645 2.0	1400 0.2	1915 1.7	
6 TH	0230 0.2	0846 1.7	1530 0.3	2140 1.3		21 F	0126 0.1	0743 1.9	1435 0.3	2034 1.5
7 F	0345 0.2	1024 1.6	1625 0.3	2315 1.4		22 SA	0224 0.1	0935 1.8	1554 0.3	2205 1.4
8 SA	0444 0.2	1156 1.7	1740 0.3			23 SU	0335 0.1	1100 1.8	1840 0.3	2325 1.5
9 SU	0026 1.5	0535 0.2	1246 1.8	2017 0.3		24 M	0434 0.1	1206 2.0	1955 0.3	
10 M	0105 1.7	0624 0.2	1325 1.9	2115 0.2		25 TU	0030 1.6	0525 0.1	1249 2.1	2100 0.3
11 TU	0144 1.8	0930 0.1	1355 2.0	2155 0.2		26 W	0116 1.8	0615 0.0	1336 2.2	2125 0.3
12 W	0219 1.8	0950 0.2	1430 2.1	2225 0.3		27 TH	0156 1.9	0656 0.0	1416 2.2	2204 0.3
13 TH	0245 1.9	1020 0.2	1456 2.1	2300 0.3		28 F	0236 2.0	0738 0.0	1457 2.2	2306 0.3
14 F	0315 2.0	1054 0.1	1525 2.1	2307 0.3		29 SA	0319 2.1	0826 0.1	1541 2.1	2355 0.2
15 SA	0345 2.0	1124 0.1	1559 2.1	2356 0.2		30 SU	0401 2.2	1214 0.1	1625 2.0	

Chart Datum: 0·84 metres below NAP Datum

TIME ZONE –0100
(Dutch Standard Time)
Subtract 1 hour for UT
For Dutch Summer Time add
ONE hour in **non-shaded areas**

NETHERLANDS – HOEK VAN HOLLAND

LAT 51°59′N   LONG 4°07′E

TIMES AND HEIGHTS OF HIGH AND LOW WATERS

2006

Note - Double LWs often occur. The predictions are for the lower LW which is usually the first.

MAY

Day	Time m	Day	Time m
1 M	0045 0.2 / 0445 2.1 / 1255 0.1 / 1709 1.9	**16** TU	0426 2.1 / 1236 0.2 / 1645 1.9 / 2206 0.1
2 TU	0126 0.1 / 0530 2.1 / 1356 0.2 / 1751 1.8	**17** W	0506 2.1 / 1255 0.2 / 1725 1.8 / 2244 0.1
3 W	0200 0.1 / 0615 2.0 / 1407 0.2 / 1835 1.6	**18** TH	0548 2.1 / 1335 0.2 / 1815 1.7 / 2344 0.0
4 TH	0030 0.1 / 0710 1.9 / 1410 0.3 / 1929 1.5	**19** F	0639 2.0 / 1420 0.3 / 1915 1.6
5 F	0200 0.1 / 0805 1.7 / 1510 0.3 / ◑2046 1.4	**20** SA	0054 0.0 / 0743 1.9 / 1520 0.3 / ◐2041 1.5
6 SA	0315 0.1 / 0924 1.6 / 1554 0.3 / 2225 1.3	**21** SU	0155 0.0 / 0921 1.9 / 1654 0.3 / 2143 1.5
7 SU	0420 0.1 / 1105 1.7 / 1654 0.3 / 2335 1.4	**22** M	0316 0.1 / 1025 1.9 / 1820 0.3 / 2300 1.6
8 M	0509 0.1 / 1154 1.8 / 1800 0.3	**23** TU	0404 0.0 / 1135 2.0 / 1940 0.3 / 2355 1.7
9 TU	0030 1.6 / 0559 0.1 / 1246 1.9 / 2030 0.2	**24** W	0750 0.0 / 1225 2.1 / 2035 0.3
10 W	0105 1.7 / 0720 0.1 / 1320 2.0 / 2126 0.2	**25** TH	0050 1.8 / 0556 0.1 / 1311 2.1 / 2104 0.3
11 TH	0134 1.8 / 0900 0.2 / 1349 2.0 / 2205 0.2	**26** F	0131 1.9 / 0645 0.1 / 1357 2.1 / 2135 0.3
12 F	0209 1.9 / 0955 0.2 / 1421 2.1 / 2240 0.2	**27** SA	0217 2.0 / 0723 0.2 / 1445 2.0 / ●2240 0.3
13 SA	0241 2.0 / 1025 0.2 / 1458 2.1 / ○2255 0.2	**28** SU	0301 2.1 / 1100 0.2 / 1525 1.9 / 2336 0.2
14 SU	0315 2.0 / 1114 0.2 / 1531 2.1 / 2340 0.2	**29** M	0345 2.1 / 1206 0.2 / 1615 1.9
15 M	0350 2.1 / 1145 0.2 / 1607 2.0 / 2125 0.2	**30** TU	0020 0.1 / 0429 2.1 / 1256 0.3 / 1659 1.8
		31 W	0105 0.1 / 0516 2.1 / 1335 0.3 / 1734 1.7

JUNE

Day	Time m	Day	Time m
1 TH	0140 0.1 / 0559 2.0 / 1410 0.3 / 1826 1.7	**16** F	0541 2.1 / 1346 0.3 / 1816 1.7 / 2330 0.0
2 F	0000 0.0 / 0644 1.9 / 1400 0.4 / 1916 1.6	**17** SA	0636 2.1 / 1346 0.3 / 1916 1.7
3 SA	0110 0.0 / 0746 1.8 / 1440 0.4 / ◐2000 1.5	**18** SU	0024 0.0 / 0739 2.0 / 1520 0.4 / ◐2020 1.7
4 SU	0237 0.0 / 0835 1.7 / 1525 0.3 / 2055 1.5	**19** M	0125 0.0 / 0856 2.0 / 1620 0.4 / 2114 1.7
5 M	0355 0.1 / 0956 1.7 / 1615 0.3 / 2210 1.5	**20** TU	0234 0.0 / 0953 2.0 / 1750 0.4 / 2226 1.7
6 TU	0434 0.1 / 1106 1.8 / 1705 0.3 / 2325 1.5	**21** W	0335 0.0 / 1105 2.0 / 1847 0.4 / 2325 1.8
7 W	0525 0.1 / 1156 1.8 / 1755 0.3	**22** TH	0444 0.1 / 1159 2.0 / 1950 0.3
8 TH	0016 1.6 / 0630 0.2 / 1236 1.9 / 1844 0.3	**23** F	0026 1.8 / 0550 0.1 / 1255 2.0 / 2040 0.3
9 F	0055 1.8 / 0820 0.2 / 1316 2.0 / 2117 0.2	**24** SA	0116 1.9 / 0635 0.2 / 1349 1.9 / 1914 0.3
10 SA	0135 1.9 / 0920 0.2 / 1356 2.0 / 2216 0.2	**25** SU	0205 2.0 / 0735 0.3 / 1439 1.9 / ●1945 0.2
11 SU	0208 2.0 / 0729 0.3 / 1429 2.0 / ○2245 0.2	**26** M	0248 2.0 / 1054 0.3 / 1523 1.9 / 2030 0.2
12 M	0249 2.0 / 1100 0.3 / 1509 2.0 / 2029 0.2	**27** TU	0335 2.1 / 1150 0.4 / 1615 1.8 / 2103 0.1
13 TU	0328 2.1 / 1125 0.3 / 1556 1.9 / 2104 0.1	**28** W	0419 2.1 / 1235 0.4 / 1644 1.8 / 2145 0.1
14 W	0411 2.1 / 1205 0.3 / 1636 1.9 / 2149 0.1	**29** TH	0459 2.1 / 1315 0.4 / 1725 1.8 / 2229 0.0
15 TH	0452 2.1 / 1255 0.3 / 1721 1.8 / 2235 0.0	**30** F	0546 2.0 / 1347 0.4 / 1754 1.8 / 2314 0.0

JULY

Day	Time m	Day	Time m
1 SA	0626 2.0 / 1350 0.4 / 1840 1.7	**16** SU	0618 2.2 / 1416 0.4 / 1844 1.8 / 2354 0.0
2 SU	0004 0.0 / 0705 1.9 / 1410 0.4 / 1926 1.7 ◐	**17** M	0714 2.1 / 1450 0.4 / 1950 1.8 ◐
3 M	0110 0.0 / 0756 1.9 / 1450 0.4 / ◐2010 1.7	**18** TU	0104 0.0 / 0820 2.0 / 1520 0.4 / 2051 1.8
4 TU	0210 0.1 / 0845 1.8 / 1534 0.3 / 2116 1.6	**19** W	0214 0.0 / 0926 1.9 / 1530 0.4 / 2150 1.8
5 W	0244 0.1 / 0946 1.8 / 1620 0.3 / 2210 1.6	**20** TH	0330 0.1 / 1036 1.9 / 1615 0.4 / 2300 1.8
6 TH	0420 0.2 / 1045 1.8 / 1720 0.3 / 2315 1.6	**21** F	0440 0.2 / 1146 1.8 / 1740 0.4
7 F	0530 0.2 / 1146 1.8 / 1807 0.3	**22** SA	0005 1.8 / 0544 0.3 / 1244 1.8 / 1815 0.3
8 SA	0009 1.7 / 0610 0.3 / 1234 1.8 / 1844 0.3	**23** SU	0104 1.9 / 0650 0.3 / 1343 1.8 / 2146 0.3
9 SU	0101 1.8 / 0635 0.2 / 1330 1.9 / 1905 0.3	**24** M	0205 2.0 / 1024 0.4 / 1435 1.9 / 1935 0.2
10 M	0144 1.9 / 0719 0.3 / 1411 1.9 / 1935 0.2	**25** TU	0244 2.0 / 1055 0.4 / 1525 1.9 / ●2015 0.2
11 TU	0231 2.1 / 0755 0.4 / 1455 1.9 / ○2005 0.2	**26** W	0324 2.1 / 1146 0.5 / 1559 1.9 / 2050 0.1
12 W	0318 2.2 / 1126 0.4 / 1546 1.9 / 2050 0.1	**27** TH	0405 2.1 / 1205 0.5 / 1646 1.9 / 2126 0.1
13 TH	0355 2.2 / 1144 0.4 / 1628 1.9 / 2129 0.0	**28** F	0445 2.1 / 1255 0.5 / 1705 1.9 / 2154 0.1
14 F	0445 2.2 / 1234 0.4 / 1715 1.9 / 2211 0.0	**29** SA	0520 2.1 / 1335 0.5 / 1735 1.9 / 2234 0.1
15 SA	0528 2.2 / 1325 0.4 / 1758 1.8 / 2306 0.0	**30** SU	0556 2.1 / 1317 0.5 / 1805 1.9 / 2325 0.1
		31 M	0636 2.0 / 1337 0.4 / 1839 1.9

AUGUST

Day	Time m	Day	Time m
1 TU	0005 0.1 / 0705 2.0 / 1400 0.4 / 1913 1.8	**16** W	0045 0.1 / 0746 2.0 / 1410 0.5 / ◐2005 1.9
2 W	0055 0.1 / 0746 1.9 / 1405 0.4 / ◐2016 1.8	**17** TH	0205 0.1 / 0850 1.9 / 1450 0.4 / 2116 1.8
3 TH	0200 0.2 / 0840 1.8 / 1500 0.4 / 2104 1.7	**18** F	0326 0.2 / 1005 1.9 / 1604 0.4 / 2224 1.8
4 F	0306 0.2 / 0945 1.8 / 1600 0.4 / 2226 1.7	**19** SA	0424 0.3 / 1124 1.7 / 1714 0.4 / 2353 1.8
5 SA	0405 0.3 / 1106 1.7 / 1740 0.4 / 2346 1.7	**20** SU	0550 0.4 / 1246 1.7 / 1755 0.3
6 SU	0540 0.3 / 1210 1.7 / 1817 0.3	**21** M	0115 1.9 / 0925 0.4 / 1334 1.8 / 2135 0.3
7 M	0045 1.8 / 0625 0.4 / 1310 1.8 / 1856 0.3	**22** TU	0205 2.0 / 1024 0.4 / 1430 1.9 / 2214 0.2
8 TU	0128 2.0 / 0716 0.4 / 1355 1.9 / 1915 0.2	**23** W	0239 2.1 / 1100 0.5 / 1503 1.9 / ●1955 0.2
9 W	0215 2.1 / 1017 0.4 / 1446 1.9 / ○1949 0.1	**24** TH	0316 2.1 / 1120 0.5 / 1534 2.0 / 2024 0.2
10 TH	0257 2.3 / 1106 0.5 / 1526 2.0 / 2026 0.1	**25** F	0341 2.2 / 1150 0.5 / 1604 2.0 / 2055 0.2
11 F	0346 2.3 / 1146 0.5 / 1607 2.0 / 2106 0.0	**26** SA	0415 2.2 / 1226 0.5 / 1636 2.0 / 2125 0.2
12 SA	0426 2.3 / 1225 0.5 / 1648 2.0 / 2145 0.0	**27** SU	0445 2.2 / 1230 0.5 / 1705 2.0 / 2159 0.2
13 SU	0508 2.3 / 1316 0.5 / 1736 2.0 / 2235 0.0	**28** M	0515 2.1 / 1245 0.5 / 1735 2.0 / 2235 0.2
14 M	0558 2.2 / 1356 0.5 / 1819 2.0 / 2335 0.0	**29** TU	0545 2.1 / 1325 0.4 / 1754 2.0 / 2316 0.2
15 TU	0648 2.1 / 1420 0.5 / 1909 2.0	**30** W	0615 2.1 / 1134 0.4 / 1829 2.0 / 2349 0.2
		31 TH	0649 2.0 / 1215 0.4 / 1905 2.0 ◑

Chart Datum: 0·84 metres below NAP Datum

TIME ZONE -0100
(Dutch Standard Time)
Subtract 1 hour for UT
For Dutch Summer Time add
ONE hour in **non-shaded areas**

NETHERLANDS – HOEK VAN HOLLAND

2006

LAT 51°59'N   LONG 4°07'E

TIMES AND HEIGHTS OF HIGH AND LOW WATERS

Note - Double LWs often
occur. The predictions are
for the lower LW which is
usually the first.

SEPTEMBER

Time m	Time m
1 0045 0.2 / 0736 1.9 / F 1347 0.4 / 1953 1.9	**16** 0316 0.3 / 0945 1.6 / SA 1535 0.4 / 2226 1.8
2 0230 0.3 / 0834 1.8 / SA 1506 0.4 / 2130 1.7	**17** 0430 0.4 / 1120 1.6 / SU 1644 0.4 / 2345 1.8
3 0350 0.4 / 1025 1.6 / SU 1630 0.4 / 2304 1.7	**18** 0650 0.5 / 1225 1.7 / M 1735 0.3
4 0520 0.4 / 1145 1.6 / M 1735 0.4	**19** 0055 2.0 / 0857 0.4 / TU 1319 1.8 / 2105 0.3
5 0019 1.9 / 0650 0.4 / TU 1244 1.8 / 1809 0.3	**20** 0134 2.1 / 0955 0.4 / W 1405 1.9 / 2155 0.2
6 0116 2.1 / 0920 0.4 / W 1334 1.9 / 1845 0.2	**21** 0213 2.2 / 1015 0.4 / TH 1434 2.0 / 2240 0.3
7 0155 2.2 / 0955 0.5 / TH 1418 2.0 / ○ 1921 0.1	**22** 0245 2.2 / 1045 0.5 / F 1509 2.0 / ● 2005 0.3
8 0236 2.3 / 1040 0.5 / F 1501 2.1 / 1959 0.0	**23** 0316 2.2 / 1114 0.5 / SA 1535 2.1 / 2025 0.3
9 0317 2.4 / 1120 0.5 / SA 1542 2.1 / 2039 0.0	**24** 0346 2.2 / 1134 0.5 / SU 1605 2.1 / 2055 0.2
10 0401 2.4 / 1154 0.5 / SU 1625 2.2 / 2121 0.0	**25** 0416 2.2 / 0920 0.5 / M 1628 2.1 / 2125 0.3
11 0446 2.2 / 1235 0.5 / M 1705 2.2 / 2209 0.1	**26** 0441 2.2 / 0944 0.5 / TU 1659 2.1 / 2154 0.3
12 0527 2.2 / 1325 0.5 / TU 1750 2.2 / 2305 0.2	**27** 0511 2.2 / 1026 0.4 / W 1728 2.1 / 2225 0.3
13 0616 2.1 / 1125 0.5 / W 1835 2.1	**28** 0546 2.1 / 1055 0.3 / TH 1800 2.2 / 2315 0.3
14 0050 0.2 / 0705 1.9 / TH 1300 0.4 / ◑ 1930 2.0	**29** 0620 2.1 / 1135 0.3 / F 1838 2.1
15 0155 0.3 / 0816 1.7 / F 1426 0.4 / 2046 1.9	**30** 0004 0.3 / 0706 2.0 / SA 1240 0.3 / ◑ 1925 2.0

OCTOBER

Time m	Time m
1 0205 0.4 / 0805 1.7 / SU 1425 0.3 / 2044 1.8	**16** 0420 0.5 / 1056 1.5 / M 1624 0.3 / 2336 1.9
2 0325 0.5 / 0956 1.6 / M 1540 0.4 / 2235 1.8	**17** 0620 0.5 / 1155 1.7 / TU 1719 0.3
3 0520 0.5 / 1115 1.6 / TU 1650 0.3	**18** 0026 2.0 / 0757 0.5 / W 1249 1.8 / 1810 0.3
4 0000 2.0 / 0750 0.5 / W 1230 1.7 / 1734 0.3	**19** 0104 2.1 / 0905 0.4 / TH 1329 1.9 / 2107 0.3
5 0049 2.2 / 0906 0.4 / TH 1315 1.9 / 1815 0.2	**20** 0145 2.2 / 0945 0.4 / F 1405 2.0 / 2144 0.3
6 0135 2.3 / 0935 0.5 / F 1356 2.0 / 1855 0.1	**21** 0211 2.2 / 1026 0.4 / SA 1436 2.0 / 2200 0.3
7 0216 2.4 / 1005 0.5 / SA 1436 2.2 / ○ 1935 0.1	**22** 0246 2.2 / 1050 0.5 / SU 1506 2.1 / ● 1954 0.3
8 0255 2.4 / 0759 0.5 / SU 1517 2.2 / 2015 0.1	**23** 0316 2.2 / 0830 0.5 / M 1529 2.2 / 2024 0.3
9 0335 2.4 / 0839 0.5 / M 1557 2.3 / 2059 0.1	**24** 0341 2.2 / 0855 0.4 / TU 1559 2.2 / 2054 0.3
10 0419 2.3 / 0926 0.4 / TU 1641 2.3 / 2148 0.2	**25** 0415 2.2 / 0925 0.4 / W 1628 2.2 / 2135 0.3
11 0505 2.2 / 1009 0.4 / W 1725 2.3 / 2245 0.3	**26** 0446 2.2 / 0953 0.3 / TH 1702 2.2 / 2216 0.4
12 0555 2.0 / 1105 0.4 / TH 1807 2.2	**27** 0519 2.1 / 1035 0.3 / F 1736 2.2 / 2255 0.4
13 0057 0.4 / 0635 1.9 / F 1215 0.3 / 1859 2.1	**28** 0559 2.0 / 1115 0.2 / SA 1819 2.1
14 0150 0.5 / 0745 1.7 / SA 1340 0.3 / ◑ 2005 1.9	**29** 0050 0.4 / 0645 1.9 / SU 1236 0.2 / ◑ 1912 2.1
15 0254 0.5 / 0910 1.5 / SU 1520 0.3 / 2144 1.8	**30** 0220 0.5 / 0755 1.7 / M 1350 0.3 / 2034 1.9
	31 0330 0.5 / 0936 1.6 / TU 1500 0.3 / 2226 1.9

NOVEMBER

Time m	Time m
1 0550 0.5 / 1043 1.6 / W 1605 0.3 / 2325 2.1	**16** 0700 0.5 / 1216 1.7 / TH 1734 0.3
2 0734 0.5 / 1156 1.8 / TH 1700 0.2	**17** 0030 2.0 / 0816 0.4 / F 1244 1.8 / 1910 0.3
3 0025 2.2 / 0825 0.5 / F 1246 1.9 / 1745 0.2	**18** 0105 2.1 / 0900 0.4 / SA 1325 1.9 / 2040 0.3
4 0108 2.3 / 0905 0.5 / SA 1330 2.1 / 1829 0.1	**19** 0140 2.1 / 0945 0.4 / SU 1355 2.0 / 2117 0.3
5 0148 2.3 / 0950 0.5 / SU 1411 2.2 / ○ 1915 0.1	**20** 0209 2.2 / 1020 0.4 / M 1425 2.1 / ● 2216 0.4
6 0235 2.3 / 0734 0.5 / M 1456 2.3 / 2000 0.2	**21** 0246 2.2 / 1055 0.4 / TU 1459 2.2 / 2016 0.4
7 0317 2.3 / 0819 0.4 / TU 1535 2.3 / 2041 0.3	**22** 0318 2.1 / 0834 0.4 / W 1535 2.2 / 2045 0.4
8 0405 2.2 / 0906 0.4 / W 1622 2.3	**23** 0351 2.2 / 0905 0.3 / TH 1609 2.2 / 2125 0.4
9 0046 0.4 / 0449 2.1 / TH 0949 0.3 / 1705 2.3	**24** 0427 2.1 / 0945 0.3 / F 1648 2.2 / 2205 0.4
10 0130 0.4 / 0535 1.9 / F 1050 0.3 / 1756 2.2	**25** 0508 2.0 / 1025 0.2 / SA 1725 2.2
11 0210 0.5 / 0626 1.8 / SA 1155 0.2 / 1846 2.1	**26** 0105 0.5 / 0552 1.9 / SU 1115 0.2 / 1808 2.2
12 0115 0.5 / 0715 1.7 / SU 1255 0.2 / ◑ 1950 1.9	**27** 0206 0.5 / 0645 1.8 / M 1204 0.1 / 1909 2.1
13 0230 0.5 / 0814 1.6 / M 1440 0.3 / 2105 1.8	**28** 0240 0.5 / 0756 1.7 / TU 1319 0.1 / ◑ 2023 2.0
14 0340 0.6 / 0945 1.5 / TU 1555 0.3 / 2234 1.8	**29** 0350 0.6 / 0910 1.7 / W 1425 0.2 / 2145 2.0
15 0447 0.5 / 1115 1.6 / W 1645 0.3 / 2346 1.9	**30** 0527 0.6 / 1015 1.7 / TH 1523 0.2 / 2255 2.1

DECEMBER

Time m	Time m
1 0704 0.5 / 1119 1.8 / F 1625 0.2 / 2356 2.1	**16** 0535 0.5 / 1155 1.7 / SA 1820 0.3
2 0757 0.5 / 1215 1.9 / SA 1725 0.2	**17** 0026 1.9 / 0720 0.4 / SU 1234 1.8 / 1940 0.3
3 0046 2.2 / 0835 0.5 / SU 1308 2.0 / 1815 0.2	**18** 0106 2.0 / 0857 0.4 / M 1326 1.9 / 2054 0.4
4 0135 2.2 / 0917 0.5 / M 1351 2.1 / 1905 0.3	**19** 0145 2.0 / 0950 0.4 / TU 1359 2.0 / 2140 0.4
5 0218 2.2 / 0729 0.4 / TU 1435 2.2 / ○ 1956 0.3	**20** 0219 2.1 / 1036 0.4 / W 1435 2.1 / ● 1955 0.4
6 0306 2.1 / 0816 0.4 / W 1525 2.3 / 2034 0.4	**21** 0300 2.1 / 0815 0.3 / TH 1515 2.2 / 2035 0.4
7 0355 2.0 / 0900 0.3 / TH 1606 2.3	**22** 0335 2.1 / 0856 0.3 / F 1555 2.2 / 2335 0.3
8 0025 0.4 / 0439 2.0 / F 0939 0.2 / 1655 2.2	**23** 0419 2.0 / 0929 0.2 / SA 1635 2.2
9 0105 0.5 / 0523 1.9 / SA 1024 0.2 / 1739 2.2	**24** 0025 0.4 / 0458 2.0 / SU 1015 0.1 / 1717 2.2
10 0145 0.5 / 0604 1.9 / SU 1130 0.1 / 1825 2.1	**25** 0110 0.4 / 0545 1.9 / M 1100 0.1 / 1806 2.2
11 0246 0.5 / 0649 1.8 / M 1224 0.1 / 1919 2.0	**26** 0155 0.5 / 0635 1.8 / TU 1149 0.0 / 1905 2.1
12 0150 0.5 / 0740 1.7 / TU 1330 0.2 / ◑ 2015 1.9	**27** 0225 0.5 / 0725 1.7 / W 1243 0.1 / ◑ 2005 2.1
13 0250 0.5 / 0835 1.7 / W 1457 0.2 / 2120 1.8	**28** 0320 0.5 / 0840 1.8 / TH 1354 0.1 / 2116 2.0
14 0354 0.5 / 0934 1.6 / TH 1614 0.2 / 2224 1.8	**29** 0330 0.6 / 0945 1.8 / F 1505 0.1 / 2225 2.0
15 0450 0.5 / 1106 1.6 / F 1705 0.3 / 2345 1.9	**30** 0405 0.6 / 1045 1.8 / SA 1604 0.2 / 2336 2.0
	31 0710 0.5 / 1144 1.9 / SU 1726 0.2

Chart Datum: 0·84 metres below NAP Datum

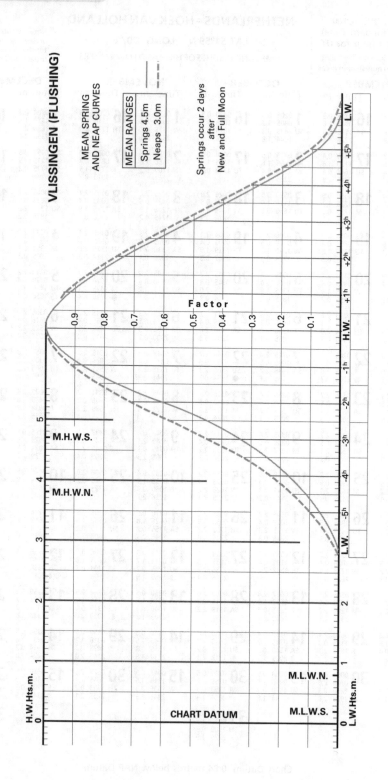

VLISSINGEN (FLUSHING)

MEAN SPRING
AND NEAP CURVES

MEAN RANGES
Springs 4.5m
Neaps 3.0m

Springs occur 2 days
after
New and Full Moon

NETHERLANDS – VLISSINGEN

LAT 51°27'N   LONG 3°36'E

TIMES AND HEIGHTS OF HIGH AND LOW WATERS

2006

JANUARY

Time	m	Time	m
1 0226	4.7	**16** 0320	4.4
0856	0.3	0935	0.4
SU 1445	4.9	M 1535	4.6
2109	0.5	2135	0.7
2 0313	4.7	**17** 0352	4.5
0939	0.2	1010	0.4
M 1532	4.9	TU 1608	4.6
2156	0.5	2216	0.7
3 0357	4.7	**18** 0421	4.5
1030	0.1	1046	0.4
TU 1619	4.9	W 1642	4.5
2245	0.6	2247	0.7
4 0445	4.6	**19** 0455	4.4
1119	0.1	1121	0.4
W 1709	4.8	TH 1716	4.5
2332	0.6	2318	0.7
5 0536	4.5	**20** 0530	4.4
1210	0.1	1150	0.4
TH 1805	4.7	F 1748	4.4
		2350	0.8
6 0026	0.7	**21** 0601	4.3
0629	4.4	1214	0.5
F 1306	0.2	SA 1825	4.3
◐ 1901	4.5		
7 0116	0.8	**22** 0028	0.8
0726	4.3	0642	4.2
SA 1356	0.3	SU 1254	0.5
2008	4.3	○ 1916	4.1
8 0216	1.0	**23** 0110	0.9
0830	4.1	0729	4.0
SU 1500	0.5	M 1350	0.7
2116	4.1	2016	4.0
9 0326	1.0	**24** 0203	1.0
0935	4.0	0842	3.9
M 1605	0.7	TU 1455	0.8
2226	4.1	2127	3.9
10 0456	1.0	**25** 0325	1.1
1045	4.0	0956	3.8
TU 1726	0.7	W 1626	0.9
2336	4.1	2236	3.9
11 0555	0.9	**26** 0450	1.0
1156	4.1	1110	4.0
W 1826	0.7	TH 1730	0.8
		. 2341	4.0
12 0029	4.2	**27** 0606	0.8
0644	0.7	1209	4.2
TH 1248	4.3	F 1832	0.7
1909	0.7		
13 0121	4.3	**28** 0039	4.3
0738	0.6	0706	0.6
F 1341	4.4	SA 1306	4.3
1956	0.6	1926	0.5
14 0205	4.4	**29** 0129	4.5
0819	0.5	0756	0.3
SA 1427	4.5	SU 1349	4.5
○ 2030	0.7	● 2016	0.5
15 0246	4.4	**30** 0216	4.6
0858	0.4	0846	0.1
SU 1458	4.5	M 1435	4.9
2106	0.7	2058	0.4
		31 0256	4.8
		0930	0.0
		TU 1516	5.0
		2143	0.4

FEBRUARY

Time	m	Time	m
1 0342	4.8	**16** 0356	4.6
1016	-0.1	1020	0.2
W 1605	5.1	TH 1612	4.7
2228	0.4	2220	0.5
2 0425	4.8	**17** 0426	4.6
1101	-0.1	1050	0.2
TH 1649	5.0	F 1646	4.6
2316	0.5	2251	0.5
3 0513	4.8	**18** 0456	4.6
1145	-0.1	1115	0.3
F 1737	4.8	SA 1712	4.5
2358	0.5	2316	0.5
4 0559	4.7	**19** 0525	4.5
1232	0.1	1146	0.3
SA 1828	4.6	SU 1741	4.5
		2345	0.4
5 0046	0.6	**20** 0555	4.4
0652	4.5	1226	0.4
SU 1320	0.3	M 1821	4.4
◐ 1928	4.3		
6 0136	0.8	**21** 0031	0.6
0752	4.2	0639	4.3
M 1416	0.6	TU 1306	0.6
2036	3.9	1916	4.0
7 0234	1.0	**22** 0126	0.8
0859	3.9	0739	4.0
TU 1523	0.8	W 1404	0.8
2155	3.7	2029	3.8
8 0410	1.0	**23** 0234	1.0
1026	3.8	0919	3.8
W 1655	0.9	TH 1535	0.9
2315	3.8	2202	3.7
9 0536	1.0	**24** 0426	1.0
1148	3.9	1041	3.8
TH 1805	0.9	F 1710	0.9
		2325	3.8
10 0022	3.9	**25** 0546	0.8
0640	0.6	1156	4.1
F 1244	4.2	SA 1815	0.7
1854	0.8		
11 0111	4.1	**26** 0026	4.1
0730	0.6	0650	0.5
SA 1336	4.4	SU 1248	4.5
1939	0.7	1909	0.5
12 0156	4.3	**27** 0115	4.4
0810	0.5	0746	0.2
SU 1416	4.5	M 1335	4.8
2016	0.7	1955	0.4
13 0230	4.4	**28** 0157	4.7
0842	0.4	0831	0.0
M 1445	4.5	TU 1416	5.0
○ 2046	0.7	● 2042	0.3
14 0258	4.5		
0916	0.3		
TU 1511	4.6		
2118	0.6		
15 0326	4.6		
0948	0.2		
W 1546	4.7		
2148	0.5		

MARCH

Time	m	Time	m
1 0236	4.8	**16** 0255	4.6
0916	-0.2	0920	0.2
W 1459	5.1	TH 1516	4.7
2126	0.3	2126	0.4
2 0318	5.0	**17** 0326	4.7
0955	-0.2	0952	0.1
TH 1542	5.1	F 1541	4.7
2207	0.3	2156	0.4
3 0402	5.0	**18** 0356	4.7
1040	-0.2	1022	0.2
F 1626	5.0	SA 1612	4.7
2248	0.3	2226	0.4
4 0446	4.9	**19** 0423	4.7
1120	-0.1	1051	0.2
SA 1711	4.8	SU 1640	4.6
2328	0.4	2250	0.4
5 0527	4.8	**20** 0456	4.7
1159	0.1	1121	0.3
SU 1756	4.5	M 1716	4.5
		2326	0.4
6 0016	0.5	**21** 0527	4.6
0618	4.5	1150	0.4
M 1245	0.4	TU 1751	4.4
◐ 1850	4.1		
7 0106	0.7	**22** 0006	0.5
0716	4.2	0612	4.4
TU 1335	0.7	W 1235	0.6
1955	3.7	◐ 1841	4.0
8 0210	0.9	**23** 0100	0.6
0836	3.8	0705	4.0
W 1455	1.0	TH 1346	0.8
2126	3.4	2000	3.7
9 0340	1.0	**24** 0227	0.8
1005	3.6	0850	3.8
TH 1636	1.1	F 1514	1.0
2256	3.5	2146	3.5
10 0517	1.0	**25** 0354	0.9
1129	3.8	1026	3.8
F 1750	1.0	SA 1644	0.9
		2306	3.7
11 0006	3.8	**26** 0530	0.6
0620	0.7	1139	4.2
SA 1229	4.1	SU 1806	0.7
1845	0.8		
12 0056	4.0	**27** 0006	4.1
0710	0.5	0631	0.3
SU 1315	4.3	M 1231	4.5
1926	0.7	1855	0.5
13 0136	4.2	**28** 0051	4.4
0746	0.4	0726	0.1
M 1348	4.5	TU 1313	4.8
1956	0.6	1940	0.4
14 0201	4.4	**29** 0132	4.7
0820	0.3	0808	-0.1
TU 1418	4.6	W 1355	5.0
○ 2022	0.6	● 2022	0.3
15 0227	4.5	**30** 0213	4.9
0850	0.2	0852	-0.2
W 1445	4.7	TH 1436	5.1
2052	0.5	2102	0.2
		31 0255	5.0
		0933	-0.2
		F 1518	5.0
		2143	0.2

APRIL

Time	m	Time	m
1 0335	5.0	**16** 0325	4.7
1011	-0.1	0952	0.2
SA 1600	4.9	SU 1540	4.7
2226	0.2	2200	0.3
2 0418	4.9	**17** 0355	4.7
1052	0.0	1026	0.3
SU 1645	4.7	M 1615	4.6
2305	0.3	2232	0.3
3 0503	4.8	**18** 0432	4.7
1129	0.3	1101	0.4
M 1727	4.4	TU 1651	4.5
2346	0.4	2316	0.3
4 0547	4.5	**19** 0510	4.6
1216	0.5	1136	0.5
TU 1816	4.0	W 1732	4.3
		2356	0.4
5 0036	0.6	**20** 0556	4.4
0639	4.1	1225	0.7
W 1306	0.8	TH 1828	4.0
◐ 1916	3.6		
6 0145	0.8	**21** 0056	0.6
0806	3.7	0706	4.0
TH 1415	1.1	F 1336	0.9
2034	3.3	◐ 1956	3.7
7 0304	0.9	**22** 0226	0.7
0933	3.5	0846	3.9
F 1555	1.1	SA 1515	1.0
2226	3.4	2120	3.6
8 0425	0.9	**23** 0345	0.6
1059	3.7	1006	4.0
SA 1716	1.0	SU 1636	0.9
2329	3.6	2235	3.8
9 0546	0.7	**24** 0516	0.5
1200	4.0	1116	4.3
SU 1804	0.9	M 1739	0.7
		2338	4.1
10 0020	3.9	**25** 0616	0.2
0638	0.5	1206	4.5
M 1239	4.3	TU 1836	0.5
1850	0.7		
11 0058	4.2	**26** 0026	4.4
0715	0.4	0702	0.1
TU 1316	4.6	W 1251	4.8
1926	0.6	1918	0.4
12 0128	4.3	**27** 0106	4.6
0748	0.3	0746	0.0
W 1346	4.6	TH 1332	4.9
1955	0.5	○ 2000	0.3
13 0156	4.5	**28** 0149	4.8
0818	0.2	0828	-0.1
TH 1411	4.7	F 1415	4.9
○ 2026	0.4	2042	0.2
14 0226	4.6	**29** 0233	4.9
0848	0.2	0908	0.0
F 1439	4.7	SA 1456	4.8
2059	0.3	2125	0.2
15 0253	4.7	**30** 0315	4.9
0922	0.2	0951	0.1
SA 1510	4.8	SU 1541	4.7
2128	0.3	2206	0.2

TIDES

Chart Datum: 2·32 metres below NAP Datum

TIME ZONE -0100
(Dutch Standard Time)
Subtract 1 hour for UT
For Dutch Summer Time add
ONE hour in **non-shaded areas**

NETHERLANDS – VLISSINGEN

LAT 51°27′N   LONG 3°36′E

TIMES AND HEIGHTS OF HIGH AND LOW WATERS

2006

MAY

#	Time m	Time m	Time m	Time m		#	Time m	Time m	Time m	Time m
1 M	0357 4.8	1028 0.3	1622 4.5	2246 0.3		**16** TU	0335 4.7	1005 0.4	1600 4.5	2226 0.3
2 TU	0440 4.6	1106 0.5	1708 4.2	2330 0.4		**17** W	0416 4.7	1049 0.5	1642 4.4	2306 0.3
3 W	0529 4.4	1145 0.7	1756 4.0			**18** TH	0502 4.6	1130 0.6	1729 4.2	2355 0.3
4 TH	0020 0.5	0619 4.1	1234 0.9	1845 3.7		**19** F	0555 4.4	1226 0.7	1830 4.0	
5 F	0126 0.7	0731 3.8	1350 1.1	◐ 1950 3.4		**20** SA	0100 0.4	0708 4.2	1329 0.8	◐ 1945 3.8
6 SA	0236 0.8	0845 3.6	1505 1.1	2135 3.4		**21** SU	0209 0.4	0825 4.1	1443 0.9	2055 3.8
7 SU	0334 0.8	1015 3.7	1616 1.0	2246 3.6		**22** M	0336 0.4	0940 4.2	1606 0.9	2208 3.9
8 M	0450 0.7	1116 3.9	1715 0.9	2332 3.8		**23** TU	0446 0.4	1048 4.3	1715 0.8	2306 4.1
9 TU	0556 0.6	1156 4.1	1805 0.7			**24** W	0546 0.2	1141 4.5	1811 0.6	
10 W	0011 4.0	0636 0.4	1235 4.3	1846 0.6		**25** TH	0000 4.4	0636 0.2	1227 4.6	1855 0.5
11 TH	0048 4.2	0706 0.4	1306 4.5	1920 0.6		**26** F	0047 4.5	0726 0.1	1316 4.7	1939 0.3
12 F	0115 4.4	0739 0.3	1337 4.6	1956 0.4		**27** SA	0130 4.7	0806 0.1	1359 4.7	● 2026 0.3
13 SA	0151 4.6	0816 0.3	1408 4.7	○ 2028 0.4		**28** SU	0215 4.7	0845 0.2	1442 4.6	2111 0.2
14 SU	0225 4.7	0849 0.3	1445 4.7	2106 0.3		**29** M	0259 4.7	0928 0.3	1527 4.5	2149 0.2
15 M	0301 4.7	0926 0.3	1519 4.6	2142 0.3		**30** TU	0346 4.7	1005 0.5	1611 4.4	2235 0.3
						31 W	0431 4.5	1045 0.6	1656 4.2	2315 0.4

JUNE

#	Time m	Time m	Time m	Time m		#	Time m	Time m	Time m	Time m
1 TH	0516 4.4	1128 0.8	1735 4.0			**16** F	0457 4.6	1125 0.6	1726 4.3	
2 F	0006 0.5	0606 4.2	1209 0.9	1814 3.9		**17** SA	0006 0.2	0551 4.5	1215 0.7	1825 4.2
3 SA	0056 0.5	0651 4.0	1303 1.0	◐ 1909 3.7		**18** SU	0055 0.2	0658 4.4	1320 0.8	◑ 1926 4.1
4 SU	0156 0.6	0755 3.8	1415 1.1	2009 3.6		**19** M	0201 0.2	0806 4.3	1420 0.8	2025 4.0
5 M	0250 0.7	0854 3.8	1520 1.0	2126 3.6		**20** TU	0300 0.3	0910 4.2	1525 0.9	2131 4.1
6 TU	0350 0.7	1016 3.8	1615 1.0	2230 3.7		**21** W	0416 0.4	1015 4.3	1635 0.8	2236 4.1
7 W	0456 0.6	1105 4.0	1715 0.9	2319 3.9		**22** TH	0521 0.4	1116 4.3	1746 0.7	2338 4.3
8 TH	0540 0.6	1151 4.2	1806 0.7			**23** F	0616 0.4	1211 4.4	1838 0.6	
9 F	0006 4.1	0625 0.5	1228 4.3	1846 0.6		**24** SA	0028 4.4	0702 0.4	1302 4.4	1925 0.4
10 SA	0046 4.3	0708 0.4	1308 4.5	1922 0.5		**25** SU	0121 4.5	0748 0.4	1351 4.5	● 2016 0.4
11 SU	0122 4.5	0749 0.4	1346 4.6	○ 2006 0.4		**26** M	0208 4.6	0830 0.5	1435 4.5	2056 0.3
12 M	0202 4.6	0826 0.4	1426 4.6	2046 0.3		**27** TU	0257 4.6	0910 0.6	1521 4.4	2140 0.3
13 TU	0242 4.7	0908 0.4	1507 4.6	2132 0.3		**28** W	0336 4.6	0945 0.7	1559 4.4	2220 0.3
14 W	0325 4.7	0949 0.5	1548 4.5	2215 0.2		**29** TH	0415 4.5	1025 0.7	1638 4.3	2300 0.3
15 TH	0407 4.7	1035 0.5	1636 4.4	2310 0.2		**30** F	0456 4.4	1102 0.8	1716 4.2	2335 0.4

JULY

#	Time m	Time m	Time m	Time m		#	Time m	Time m	Time m	Time m
1 SA	0538 4.3	1145 0.8	1751 4.2			**16** SU	0537 4.7	1159 0.6	1801 4.5	
2 SU	0020 0.4	0620 4.2	1226 0.9	1835 4.0		**17** M	0035 0.1	0631 4.6	1256 0.7	◑ 1858 4.4
3 M	0059 0.5	0706 4.1	1305 1.0	1926 3.9		**18** TU	0130 0.2	0736 4.4	1346 0.8	1956 4.2
4 TU	0143 0.6	0801 3.9	1416 1.0	2015 3.8		**19** W	0225 0.3	0835 4.2	1450 0.9	2106 4.1
5 W	0245 0.7	0856 3.9	1516 1.0	2126 3.7		**20** TH	0324 0.5	0946 4.1	1606 0.9	2209 4.1
6 TH	0346 0.7	0955 3.9	1615 1.0	2225 3.8		**21** F	0450 0.6	1055 4.1	1726 0.8	2326 4.1
7 F	0445 0.7	1055 4.0	1716 0.9	2326 4.0		**22** SA	0555 0.6	1206 4.2	1826 0.7	
8 SA	0546 0.7	1156 4.1	1810 0.8			**23** SU	0025 4.3	0650 0.6	1259 4.3	1915 0.5
9 SU	0016 4.2	0635 0.6	1246 4.3	1900 0.6		**24** M	0125 4.4	0738 0.6	1346 4.4	2001 0.4
10 M	0101 4.4	0719 0.5	1325 4.4	1951 0.5		**25** TU	0209 4.5	0815 0.7	1429 4.4	● 2046 0.4
11 TU	0145 4.6	0808 0.5	1411 4.5	○ 2036 0.3		**26** W	0249 4.6	0855 0.7	1505 4.5	2126 0.3
12 W	0231 4.7	0855 0.5	1455 4.6	2125 0.2		**27** TH	0326 4.6	0928 0.7	1542 4.5	2159 0.3
13 TH	0313 4.8	0940 0.5	1537 4.6	2216 0.1		**28** F	0356 4.6	0959 0.7	1615 4.5	2238 0.3
14 F	0359 4.9	1025 0.5	1625 4.6	2306 0.0		**29** SA	0431 4.6	1035 0.7	1648 4.5	2310 0.3
15 SA	0445 4.8	1115 0.6	1711 4.5	2350 0.0		**30** SU	0508 4.5	1110 0.7	1718 4.4	2339 0.4
						31 M	0539 4.4	1139 0.8	1751 4.3	

AUGUST

#	Time m	Time m	Time m	Time m		#	Time m	Time m	Time m	Time m
1 TU	0016 0.5	0615 4.3	1215 0.8	1830 4.2		**16** W	0055 0.3	0700 4.4	1316 0.8	◑ 1915 4.3
2 W	0050 0.6	0656 4.1	1255 0.9	◑ 1915 4.0		**17** TH	0145 0.5	0759 4.1	1416 0.9	2025 4.1
3 TH	0130 0.7	0745 4.0	1346 1.0	2021 3.8		**18** F	0300 0.8	0915 3.9	1535 1.0	2150 3.9
4 F	0236 0.8	0856 3.8	1454 1.1	2136 3.7		**19** SA	0425 0.9	1042 3.8	1705 0.9	2315 4.0
5 SA	0356 0.9	1010 3.8	1636 1.1	2248 3.8		**20** SU	0545 0.9	1156 4.0	1816 0.8	
6 SU	0504 0.9	1122 3.9	1745 0.9	2356 4.1		**21** M	0025 4.2	0645 0.8	1248 4.2	1916 0.6
7 M	0615 0.8	1221 4.2	1846 0.7			**22** TU	0115 4.5	0725 0.7	1338 4.4	1955 0.4
8 TU	0048 4.4	0706 0.6	1311 4.4	1936 0.4		**23** W	0158 4.6	0806 0.7	1415 4.5	● 2029 0.4
9 W	0132 4.7	0752 0.5	1356 4.6	○ 2021 0.2		**24** TH	0229 4.6	0836 0.7	1442 4.6	2106 0.3
10 TH	0216 4.9	0838 0.5	1436 4.7	2110 0.0		**25** F	0258 4.7	0906 0.7	1516 4.6	2135 0.3
11 F	0256 5.0	0926 0.5	1519 4.8	2156 -0.1		**26** SA	0328 4.7	0936 0.7	1545 4.7	2208 0.3
12 SA	0340 5.0	1008 0.5	1602 4.8	2242 -0.1		**27** SU	0401 4.7	1008 0.7	1616 4.7	2241 0.3
13 SU	0425 5.0	1056 0.5	1645 4.8	2327 -0.1		**28** M	0432 4.6	1036 0.7	1646 4.6	2306 0.4
14 M	0512 4.9	1136 0.6	1732 4.7			**29** TU	0459 4.5	1106 0.7	1712 4.5	2330 0.5
15 TU	0009 0.1	0601 4.7	1220 0.6	1821 4.6		**30** W	0527 4.4	1129 0.7	1738 4.4	
						31 TH	0000 0.6	0601 4.3	1205 0.8	◐ 1818 4.3

Chart Datum: 2·32 metres below NAP Datum

TIME ZONE -0100
(Dutch Standard Time)
Subtract 1 hour for UT
For Dutch Summer Time add
ONE hour in **non-shaded areas**

NETHERLANDS – VLISSINGEN

2006

LAT 51°27'N   LONG 3°36'E

TIMES AND HEIGHTS OF HIGH AND LOW WATERS

SEPTEMBER

Day	Time m	Time m	Time m	Time m		Day	Time m	Time m	Time m	Time m
1 F	0046 0.7	0645 4.1	1256 0.9	1905 4.0		16 SA	0230 1.0	0850 3.6	1516 1.1	2136 3.8
2 SA	0134 0.9	0755 3.8	1406 1.1	2047 3.7		17 SU	0405 1.1	1025 3.6	1656 1.1	2305 3.9
3 SU	0316 1.1	0930 3.7	1555 1.1	2221 3.8		18 M	0536 1.1	1140 3.9	1800 0.8	
4 M	0446 1.1	1100 3.8	1714 0.9	2336 4.1		19 TU	0016 4.2	0624 0.9	1236 4.2	1856 0.6
5 TU	0555 0.9	1206 4.1	1826 0.6			20 W	0055 4.5	0715 0.8	1316 4.4	1936 0.4
6 W	0029 4.5	0650 0.7	1251 4.4	1920 0.3		21 TH	0136 4.6	0739 0.7	1348 4.5	2006 0.4
7 TH	0115 4.8	0735 0.5	1336 4.7	○ 2006 0.1		22 F	0205 4.7	0810 0.7	1416 4.6	2036 0.4
8 F	0155 5.0	0818 0.5	1416 4.9	2050 0.0		23 SA	0231 4.7	0838 0.6	1442 4.7	2105 0.3
9 SA	0236 5.1	0902 0.4	1456 5.0	2132 -0.1		24 SU	0257 4.8	0905 0.6	1512 4.8	2136 0.3
10 SU	0316 5.2	0946 0.4	1536 5.1	2215 -0.1		25 M	0327 4.8	0941 0.6	1542 4.8	2206 0.4
11 M	0358 5.1	1027 0.4	1619 5.0	2258 0.0		26 TU	0357 4.7	1006 0.6	1607 4.7	2230 0.5
12 TU	0443 4.9	1106 0.5	1703 4.9	2340 0.2		27 W	0426 4.6	1032 0.6	1637 4.6	2256 0.5
13 W	0529 4.6	1149 0.6	1748 4.7			28 TH	0453 4.6	1106 0.6	1707 4.6	2325 0.6
14 TH	0022 0.4	0626 4.3	1240 0.8	◑ 1846 4.3		29 F	0527 4.4	1146 0.7	1747 4.5	
15 F	0116 0.7	0725 3.9	1345 1.0	2000 4.0		30 SA	0016 0.8	0611 4.2	1230 0.8	◐ 1836 4.2

OCTOBER

Day	Time m	Time m	Time m	Time m		Day	Time m	Time m	Time m	Time m
1 SU	0116 1.0	0715 3.8	1346 1.0	2005 3.8		16 M	0335 1.3	1001 3.5	1616 1.0	2235 3.9
2 M	0246 1.2	0906 3.6	1524 1.0	2149 3.8		17 TU	0506 1.2	1110 3.8	1736 0.8	2335 4.2
3 TU	0426 1.1	1024 3.7	1706 0.8	2309 4.2		18 W	0600 1.0	1159 4.1	1815 0.6	
4 W	0536 1.0	1135 4.1	1806 0.5			19 TH	0021 4.4	0640 0.8	1239 4.3	1905 0.5
5 TH	0005 4.5	0630 0.7	1227 4.4	1858 0.3		20 F	0059 4.6	0716 0.8	1311 4.5	1936 0.4
6 F	0049 4.9	0716 0.6	1306 4.7	1946 0.1		21 SA	0129 4.6	0740 0.7	1342 4.6	2005 0.4
7 SA	0131 5.1	0757 0.5	1348 5.0	○ 2026 0.0		22 SU	0157 4.7	0810 0.6	1407 4.7	● 2032 0.4
8 SU	0212 5.2	0838 0.4	1429 5.1	2108 0.0		23 M	0226 4.8	0840 0.6	1437 4.8	2102 0.4
9 M	0253 5.1	0920 0.4	1511 5.1	2148 0.0		24 TU	0256 4.8	0916 0.6	1510 4.8	2136 0.5
10 TU	0336 5.0	1006 0.4	1555 5.1	2230 0.2		25 W	0327 4.7	0940 0.6	1539 4.8	2206 0.5
11 W	0419 4.8	1046 0.5	1637 4.9	2309 0.4		26 TH	0357 4.7	1015 0.6	1613 4.7	2236 0.6
12 TH	0506 4.5	1128 0.6	1725 4.6	2356 0.7		27 F	0432 4.6	1049 0.6	1647 4.7	2305 0.7
13 F	0555 4.2	1221 0.7	1815 4.3			28 SA	0510 4.4	1125 0.6	1730 4.5	2356 0.9
14 SA	0045 1.0	0656 3.8	1326 0.9	◑ 1924 3.9		29 SU	0555 4.1	1226 0.7	◐ 1825 4.2	
15 SU	0154 1.2	0815 3.5	1444 1.0	2103 3.7		30 M	0056 1.1	0711 3.8	1336 0.9	1956 4.0
						31 TU	0213 1.2	0840 3.7	1505 0.9	2126 4.0

NOVEMBER

Day	Time m	Time m	Time m	Time m		Day	Time m	Time m	Time m	Time m
1 W	0356 1.2	1000 3.8	1637 0.7	2246 4.2		16 TH	0454 1.1	1116 3.9	1736 0.7	2339 4.2
2 TH	0516 1.0	1106 4.1	1735 0.5	2338 4.6		17 F	0556 1.0	1158 4.1	1826 0.6	
3 F	0606 0.8	1157 4.4	1836 0.3			18 SA	0019 4.4	0629 0.8	1236 4.3	1855 0.6
4 SA	0026 4.8	0650 0.6	1240 4.7	1918 0.2		19 SU	0055 4.5	0706 0.8	1305 4.4	1926 0.5
5 SU	0106 5.0	0736 0.5	1325 4.9	○ 2006 0.1		20 M	0126 4.6	0735 0.7	1337 4.6	● 2000 0.5
6 M	0151 5.0	0819 0.4	1406 5.0	2045 0.1		21 TU	0157 4.7	0812 0.6	1412 4.7	2036 0.5
7 TU	0235 5.0	0900 0.3	1450 5.1	2125 0.2		22 W	0228 4.7	0845 0.6	1443 4.7	2106 0.5
8 W	0316 4.9	0943 0.4	1535 5.0	2206 0.4		23 TH	0306 4.7	0922 0.5	1517 4.8	2139 0.6
9 TH	0400 4.7	1028 0.4	1617 4.8	2245 0.6		24 F	0338 4.6	1006 0.5	1557 4.7	2221 0.6
10 F	0446 4.4	1109 0.5	1710 4.6	2331 0.8		25 SA	0420 4.5	1039 0.5	1637 4.7	2300 0.7
11 SA	0535 4.2	1154 0.7	1806 4.3			26 SU	0505 4.4	1136 0.5	1725 4.5	2350 0.9
12 SU	0016 1.0	0625 3.9	1300 0.8	◑ 1905 4.0		27 M	0555 4.2	1225 0.6	1825 4.3	
13 M	0120 1.2	0736 3.7	1410 0.9	2025 3.8		28 TU	0045 1.0	0659 4.0	1335 0.6	◐ 1939 4.2
14 TU	0240 1.3	0907 3.5	1515 0.9	2156 3.8		29 W	0155 1.1	0815 3.9	1446 0.6	2056 4.2
15 W	0355 1.3	1020 3.7	1636 0.9	2256 4.0		30 TH	0325 1.1	0926 3.9	1555 0.6	2208 4.3

DECEMBER

Day	Time m	Time m	Time m	Time m		Day	Time m	Time m	Time m	Time m
1 F	0430 1.0	1029 4.1	1716 0.5	2306 4.4		16 SA	0455 1.1	1106 3.9	1726 0.8	2336 4.1
2 SA	0536 0.9	1128 4.4	1806 0.4	2358 4.6		17 SU	0546 1.0	1148 4.0	1816 0.8	
3 SU	0628 0.7	1217 4.6	1859 0.3			18 M	0016 4.2	0636 0.9	1229 4.2	1849 0.7
4 M	0050 4.7	0713 0.6	1305 4.7	1942 0.3		19 TU	0056 4.4	0716 0.8	1309 4.4	1930 0.6
5 TU	0136 4.7	0759 0.4	1352 4.8	○ 2023 0.3		20 W	0131 4.5	0750 0.6		● 2005 0.6
6 W	0221 4.7	0845 0.4	1437 4.9	2106 0.4		21 TH	0208 4.6	0830 0.5	1427 4.7	2048 0.6
7 TH	0305 4.7	0930 0.3	1525 4.8	2148 0.6		22 F	0249 4.6	0916 0.4	1507 4.8	2131 0.6
8 F	0350 4.6	1011 0.4	1609 4.7	2225 0.7		23 SA	0329 4.6	0958 0.3	1547 4.8	2209 0.6
9 SA	0435 4.4	1055 0.4	1658 4.6	2305 0.8		24 SU	0412 4.5	1042 0.3	1630 4.7	2256 0.7
10 SU	0519 4.3	1146 0.5	1746 4.4	2350 1.0		25 M	0457 4.5	1129 0.3	1721 4.7	2346 0.8
11 M	0606 4.1	1230 0.6	1836 4.2			26 TU	0545 4.3	1222 0.3	1815 4.5	
12 TU	0040 1.1	0649 3.9	1326 0.7	◑ 1925 4.0		27 W	0036 0.9	0646 4.2	1318 0.4	◑ 1918 4.4
13 W	0135 1.2	0745 3.8	1426 0.8	2029 3.8		28 TH	0135 0.9	0745 4.1	1416 0.5	2025 4.3
14 TH	0245 1.2	0856 3.7	1519 0.9	2145 3.8		29 F	0236 1.0	0852 4.1	1520 0.5	2136 4.2
15 F	0350 1.2	1006 3.7	1626 0.9	2245 3.9		30 SA	0346 1.0	0958 4.1	1630 0.6	2240 4.2
						31 SU	0500 1.0	1102 4.2	1746 0.6	2340 4.3

Chart Datum: 2·32 metres below NAP Datum

TIDES

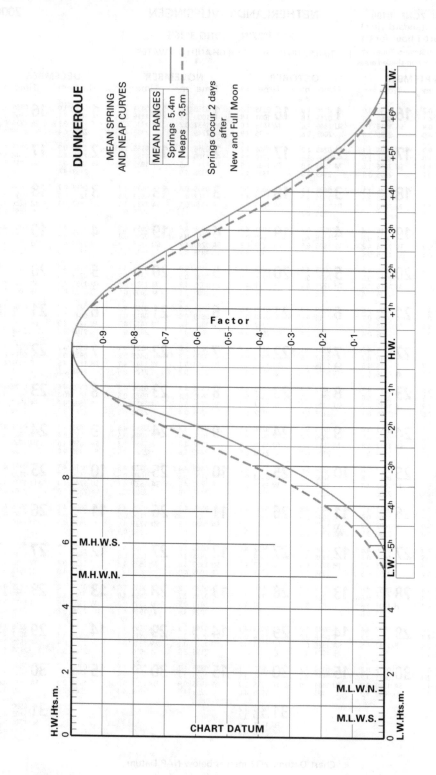

DUNKERQUE

MEAN SPRING
AND NEAP CURVES

MEAN RANGES
Springs 5.4m
Neaps 3.5m

Springs occur 2 days
after
New and Full Moon

Factor

0·9 0·8 0·7 0·6 0·5 0·4 0·3 0·2 0·1

L.W. +6ʰ +5ʰ +4ʰ +3ʰ +2ʰ +1ʰ H.W. -1ʰ -2ʰ -3ʰ -4ʰ -5ʰ L.W.

M.H.W.S.
M.H.W.N.

M.L.W.N.
M.L.W.S.

H.W.Hts.m.

L.W.Hts.m.

CHART DATUM

TIME ZONE −0100
(French Standard Time)
Subtract 1 hour for UT
For French Summer Time add
ONE hour in **non-shaded areas**

FRANCE – DUNKERQUE

LAT 51°03′N   LONG 2°22′E

TIMES AND HEIGHTS OF HIGH AND LOW WATERS

2006

JANUARY

Day	Time	m	Time	m	Time	m	Time	m
1 SU	0107	5.9	0806	0.7	1330	6.0	2027	0.8
2 M	0153	5.9	0855	0.6	1419	6.1	2115	0.8
3 TU	0240	5.9	0943	0.6	1509	6.0	2203	0.8
4 W	0327	5.8	1032	0.6	1559	5.9	2251	1.0
5 TH	0416	5.7	1121	0.7	1652	5.7	2340	1.1
6 F ◐	0506	5.6	1214	0.8	1748	5.5		
7 SA	0037	1.3	0602	5.4	1311	1.0	1851	5.3
8 SU	0137	1.5	0707	5.2	1414	1.2	2000	5.1
9 M	0242	1.6	0819	5.1	1520	1.3	2109	5.0
10 TU	0350	1.6	0928	5.1	1632	1.3	2214	5.1
11 W	0502	1.5	1032	5.2	1738	1.3	2315	5.2
12 TH	0603	1.3	1130	5.3	1830	1.2		
13 F	0005	5.3	0651	1.1	1220	5.5	1913	1.1
14 SA ○	0044	5.5	0733	1.0	1302	5.6	1951	1.1
15 SU	0122	5.6	0811	0.9	1340	5.7	2027	1.1
16 M	0156	5.6	0846	0.8	1415	5.7	2100	1.0
17 TU	0227	5.7	0920	0.8	1447	5.7	2132	1.1
18 W	0258	5.6	0952	0.8	1518	5.6	2203	1.1
19 TH	0330	5.6	1023	0.9	1551	5.5	2234	1.2
20 F	0403	5.5	1054	1.0	1625	5.4	2305	1.3
21 SA	0437	5.4	1128	1.1	1703	5.3	2341	1.4
22 SU ◑	0515	5.2	1208	1.2	1748	5.1		
23 M	0025	1.6	0606	5.0	1256	1.4	1845	4.9
24 TU	0120	1.8	0710	4.9	1402	1.6	1952	4.8
25 W	0237	1.9	0822	4.8	1524	1.6	2108	4.8
26 TH	0400	1.8	0941	4.9	1638	1.5	2224	5.0
27 F	0513	1.5	1051	5.2	1744	1.2	2325	5.3
28 SA	0617	1.1	1147	5.6	1842	1.0		
29 SU ●	0012	5.6	0710	0.8	1236	5.9	1932	0.8
30 M	0057	5.8	0759	0.5	1323	6.1	2018	0.6
31 TU	0142	6.0	0845	0.3	1409	6.2	2103	0.6

FEBRUARY

Day	Time	m	Time	m	Time	m	Time	m
1 W	0225	6.1	0931	0.2	1455	6.2	2147	0.6
2 TH	0308	6.1	1016	0.2	1541	6.1	2230	0.7
3 F	0351	6.0	1100	0.4	1626	5.9	2313	0.9
4 SA	0437	5.6	1145	0.6	1713	5.6	2358	1.1
5 SU ◐	0526	5.6	1234	0.9	1806	5.3		
6 M	0052	1.4	0625	5.3	1331	1.3	1912	4.9
7 TU	0155	1.6	0738	4.9	1440	1.6	2031	4.7
8 W	0312	1.8	0902	4.8	1606	1.7	2154	4.7
9 TH	0444	1.7	1022	4.9	1725	1.5	2306	4.9
10 F	0552	1.4	1128	5.1	1819	1.3	2358	5.1
11 SA	0641	1.1	1215	5.4	1901	1.2		
12 SU	0034	5.4	0720	0.9	1252	5.6	1936	1.0
13 M ○	0108	5.6	0755	0.7	1326	5.7	2008	0.9
14 TU	0138	5.7	0827	0.7	1356	5.8	2038	0.9
15 W	0205	5.8	0857	0.6	1424	5.8	2108	0.9
16 TH	0232	5.8	0927	0.6	1451	5.8	2137	0.9
17 F	0300	5.8	0955	0.6	1518	5.7	2204	0.9
18 SA	0326	5.7	1023	0.7	1545	5.6	2232	1.0
19 SU	0351	5.6	1053	0.8	1612	5.5	2302	1.1
20 M	0423	5.5	1127	1.0	1647	5.3	2339	1.3
21 TU	0506	5.3	1210	1.3	1739	5.0		
22 W	0030	1.6	0611	4.9	1310	1.6	1900	4.7
23 TH	0144	1.8	0740	4.7	1440	1.7	2035	4.6
24 F	0323	1.8	0919	4.8	1612	1.6	2208	4.8
25 SA	0455	1.5	1040	5.2	1732	1.3	2312	5.2
26 SU	0605	1.0	1137	5.6	1831	0.9		
27 M	0002	5.6	0658	0.6	1224	6.0	1918	0.7
28 TU ●	0041	5.9	0744	0.3	1308	6.2	2001	0.5

MARCH

Day	Time	m	Time	m	Time	m	Time	m
1 W	0122	6.1	0828	0.1	1350	6.3	2043	0.5
2 TH	0203	6.2	0911	0.1	1432	6.2	2124	0.5
3 F	0243	6.2	0952	0.1	1514	6.1	2204	0.6
4 SA	0324	6.1	1033	0.3	1555	5.9	2243	0.7
5 SU	0407	5.9	1113	0.6	1638	5.6	2324	1.0
6 M ◐	0453	5.6	1156	1.0	1727	5.2		
7 TU	0012	1.3	0549	5.2	1249	1.5	1829	4.8
8 W	0113	1.7	0704	4.8	1401	1.8	1956	4.4
9 TH	0237	1.9	0840	4.5	1540	1.9	2133	4.4
10 F	0422	1.8	1009	4.7	1704	1.7	2246	4.7
11 SA	0533	1.4	1112	5.0	1758	1.4	2336	5.1
12 SU	0621	1.1	1156	5.3	1839	1.1		
13 M	0011	5.4	0658	0.8	1230	5.5	1912	1.0
14 TU ○	0043	5.6	0729	0.7	1301	5.7	1941	0.9
15 W	0112	5.7	0758	0.6	1330	5.8	2009	0.8
16 TH	0137	5.8	0828	0.5	1355	5.8	2038	0.7
17 F	0202	5.8	0857	0.5	1419	5.8	2107	0.7
18 SA	0227	5.8	0925	0.4	1444	5.8	2135	0.8
19 SU	0252	5.8	0953	0.7	1509	5.7	2203	0.9
20 M	0318	5.8	1022	0.8	1537	5.6	2233	1.0
21 TU	0351	5.6	1056	1.0	1612	5.3	2311	1.2
22 W ◑	0435	5.3	1140	1.3	1702	5.0		
23 TH	0002	1.5	0541	5.0	1243	1.6	1833	4.6
24 F	0121	1.7	0722	4.7	1417	1.8	2017	4.5
25 SA	0303	1.7	0907	4.8	1556	1.6	2151	4.8
26 SU	0438	1.3	1025	5.2	1714	1.2	2253	5.2
27 M	0546	0.9	1120	5.7	1810	0.8	2341	5.6
28 TU	0638	0.5	1205	6.0	1856	0.6		
29 W ●	0017	5.9	0723	0.3	1246	6.1	1938	0.5
30 TH	0057	6.1	0805	0.2	1325	6.2	2018	0.5
31 F	0136	6.2	0846	0.2	1405	6.2	2057	0.5

APRIL

Day	Time	m	Time	m	Time	m	Time	m
1 SA	0217	6.2	0925	0.3	1445	6.0	2137	0.5
2 SU	0258	6.1	1005	0.5	1526	5.8	2216	0.7
3 M	0341	5.9	1043	0.8	1609	5.5	2256	0.9
4 TU	0427	5.6	1124	1.2	1656	5.1	2341	1.3
5 W ◐	0522	5.1	1215	1.6	1756	4.7		
6 TH	0040	1.6	0634	4.7	1325	1.9	1920	4.4
7 F	0202	1.8	0811	4.4	1504	2.0	2058	4.4
8 SA	0344	1.8	0939	4.6	1627	1.8	2208	4.6
9 SU	0456	1.4	1038	4.9	1724	1.4	2258	5.0
10 M	0545	1.1	1121	5.3	1805	1.2	2337	5.3
11 TU	0622	0.9	1157	5.5	1838	1.0		
12 W	0009	5.5	0653	0.7	1229	5.6	1907	0.9
13 TH ○	0039	5.6	0723	0.7	1257	5.7	1936	0.8
14 F	0104	5.7	0754	0.6	1321	5.8	2007	0.7
15 SA	0130	5.8	0826	0.6	1346	5.8	2038	0.7
16 SU	0157	5.8	0857	0.6	1414	5.8	2110	0.7
17 M	0226	5.8	0928	0.7	1444	5.7	2142	0.8
18 TU	0259	5.7	1001	0.9	1517	5.5	2217	0.9
19 W	0338	5.6	1040	1.1	1559	5.3	2259	1.1
20 TH	0430	5.3	1129	1.3	1703	4.9	2355	1.4
21 F ◑	0548	5.0	1238	1.6	1832	4.6		
22 SA	0117	1.5	0716	4.8	1408	1.7	2002	4.6
23 SU	0251	1.5	0850	5.0	1536	1.5	2127	4.9
24 M	0415	1.1	1002	5.3	1647	1.1	2226	5.3
25 TU	0520	0.7	1055	5.7	1743	0.9	2314	5.6
26 W	0612	0.5	1139	5.9	1829	0.7	2355	5.9
27 TH ●	0657	0.4	1220	6.0	1912	0.6		
28 F	0031	6.0	0739	0.3	1259	6.0	1953	0.6
29 SA	0112	6.1	0820	0.4	1340	5.9	2033	0.6
30 SU	0154	6.1	0900	0.5	1421	5.9	2114	0.6

Chart Datum: 2·69 metres below IGN Datum

TIME ZONE −0100
(French Standard Time)
Subtract 1 hour for UT
For French Summer Time add ONE hour in **non-shaded areas**

FRANCE–DUNKERQUE 2006

LAT 51°03′N LONG 2°22′E

TIMES AND HEIGHTS OF HIGH AND LOW WATERS

MAY

Day	Time	m	Time	m	Time	m	Time	m
1 M	0238	6.0	0940	0.7	1505	5.7	2154	0.7
2 TU	0323	5.8	1019	1.0	1549	5.4	2236	0.9
3 W	0410	5.5	1101	1.3	1636	5.1	2321	1.2
4 TH	0503	5.1	1148	1.6	1731	4.8		
5 F	0015	1.5	0605	4.7	1250	1.9	◐1838	4.5
6 SA	0124	1.7	0724	4.5	1412	1.9	2005	4.4
7 SU	0248	1.7	0849	4.6	1531	1.8	2116	4.6
8 M	0359	1.4	0949	4.9	1630	1.5	2209	4.9
9 TU	0453	1.2	1036	5.1	1717	1.3	2252	5.2
10 W	0535	1.0	1116	5.3	1755	1.1	2330	5.4
11 TH	0612	0.9	1150	5.5	1829	1.0		
12 F	0003	5.5	0646	0.8	1220	5.6	1902	0.9
13 SA	0030	5.6	0722	0.8	1249	5.7	○1937	0.8
14 SU	0101	5.7	0758	0.7	1320	5.7	2014	0.8
15 M	0135	5.8	0835	0.8	1355	5.7	2052	0.8
16 TU	0213	5.8	0902	1.1	1435	5.6	2131	0.8
17 W	0256	5.7	0953	0.9	1520	5.5	2213	0.9
18 TH	0346	5.5	1038	1.1	1614	5.3	2302	1.0
19 F	0445	5.4	1132	1.3	1717	5.0		
20 SA	0000	1.2	0551	5.2	1238	1.5	◐1823	4.9
21 SU	0115	1.2	0702	5.1	1355	1.5	1938	4.9
22 M	0234	1.1	0823	5.2	1509	1.3	2054	5.1
23 TU	0346	1.0	0931	5.4	1615	1.2	2154	5.3
24 W	0449	0.8	1026	5.6	1712	1.0	2244	5.5
25 TH	0544	0.7	1113	5.7	1802	0.9	2329	5.7
26 F	0632	0.6	1157	5.8	1848	0.8		
27 SA	0009	5.8	0717	0.7	1239	5.8	●1933	0.7
28 SU	0055	5.9	0800	0.7	1323	5.8	2016	0.7
29 M	0141	5.9	0841	0.8	1408	5.7	2058	0.7
30 TU	0227	5.8	0922	0.9	1453	5.6	2140	0.8
31 W	0312	5.6	1002	1.1	1537	5.4	2221	0.9

JUNE

Day	Time	m	Time	m	Time	m	Time	m
1 TH	0357	5.4	1042	1.3	1619	5.2	2303	1.1
2 F	0443	5.2	1125	1.5	1704	5.0	2348	1.3
3 SA	0532	5.0	1213	1.7	1754	4.8	◐	
4 SU	0042	1.4	0628	4.8	1312	1.8	1854	4.7
5 M	0144	1.5	0732	4.7	1422	1.7	2003	4.7
6 TU	0251	1.4	0840	4.8	1526	1.6	2107	4.8
7 W	0351	1.3	0937	4.9	1620	1.5	2200	5.0
8 TH	0443	1.2	1025	5.1	1708	1.3	2246	5.2
9 F	0529	1.1	1108	5.3	1752	1.2	2328	5.3
10 SA	0612	1.0	1146	5.4	1833	1.1		
11 SU	0004	5.5	0654	0.9	1224	5.5	○1914	0.9
12 M	0042	5.7	0737	0.9	1303	5.6	1957	0.8
13 TU	0124	5.8	0821	0.8	1347	5.7	2041	0.7
14 W	0209	5.8	0906	0.8	1434	5.7	2127	0.7
15 TH	0258	5.8	0952	0.9	1523	5.6	2215	0.7
16 F	0348	5.7	1041	1.0	1614	5.5	2304	0.8
17 SA	0442	5.6	1131	1.1	1706	5.4	2358	0.8
18 SU	0538	5.5	1228	1.2	1802	5.3	◑	
19 M	0102	0.9	0640	5.4	1331	1.3	1905	5.2
20 TU	0208	0.9	0749	5.3	1436	1.3	2015	5.2
21 W	0314	1.0	0857	5.3	1540	1.3	2120	5.3
22 TH	0419	1.0	0958	5.3	1643	1.2	2219	5.4
23 F	0520	1.0	1054	5.4	1742	1.1	2314	5.5
24 SA	0616	1.0	1108	5.5	1835	1.0		
25 SU	0004	5.6	0704	1.0	1235	5.5	●1922	0.9
26 M	0050	5.7	0748	1.0	1320	5.6	2006	0.8
27 TU	0136	5.7	0829	1.0	1402	5.6	2048	0.7
28 W	0219	5.7	0908	1.0	1442	5.6	2128	0.7
29 TH	0300	5.6	0946	1.1	1520	5.5	2206	0.8
30 F	0338	5.5	1022	1.2	1555	5.4	2242	0.9

JULY

Day	Time	m	Time	m	Time	m	Time	m
1 SA	0416	5.4	1058	1.3	1632	5.3	2319	1.0
2 SU	0456	5.2	1135	1.4	1712	5.1	2358	1.1 ◑
3 M	0540	5.1	1217	1.5	1758	5.0		
4 TU	0044	1.3	0629	5.0	1307	1.6	1850	4.9
5 W	0140	1.4	0724	4.9	1411	1.7	1950	4.8
6 TH	0245	1.5	0825	4.8	1520	1.7	2056	4.8
7 F	0350	1.4	0929	4.9	1621	1.6	2201	5.0
8 SA	0449	1.4	1029	5.0	1718	1.4	2257	5.2
9 SU	0544	1.2	1121	5.2	1811	1.2	2347	5.4
10 M	0636	1.1	1209	5.4	1900	1.0		
11 TU	0029	5.7	0724	0.9	1253	5.6	○1947	0.8
12 W	0115	5.8	0812	0.8	1338	5.7	2034	0.6
13 TH	0201	6.0	0858	0.8	1424	5.8	2120	0.5
14 F	0248	6.0	0944	0.7	1510	5.8	2207	0.4
15 SA	0336	6.0	1030	0.8	1555	5.8	2253	0.5
16 SU	0424	5.9	1116	0.9	1642	5.7	2341	0.6
17 M	0515	5.7	1204	1.1	1731	5.6	◑	
18 TU	0037	0.7	0610	5.5	1258	1.2	1829	5.4
19 W	0137	1.0	0713	5.3	1400	1.4	1936	5.2
20 TH	0242	1.2	0823	5.1	1508	1.5	2051	5.1
21 F	0353	1.3	0936	5.0	1622	1.4	2205	5.1
22 SA	0508	1.3	1045	5.1	1733	1.3	2311	5.3
23 SU	0609	1.2	1145	5.2	1828	1.1		
24 M	0005	5.4	0657	1.1	1233	5.4	1915	0.9
25 TU	0048	5.6	0739	1.1	1313	5.5	●1956	0.7
26 W	0129	5.7	0816	1.0	1349	5.6	2034	0.7
27 TH	0206	5.7	0851	1.0	1423	5.7	2110	0.7
28 F	0240	5.7	0924	1.0	1454	5.7	2143	0.7
29 SA	0312	5.7	0956	1.1	1524	5.6	2215	0.8
30 SU	0344	5.6	1026	1.1	1555	5.5	2245	0.9
31 M	0417	5.5	1056	1.2	1628	5.4	2317	1.0

AUGUST

Day	Time	m	Time	m	Time	m	Time	m
1 TU	0451	5.3	1129	1.3	1705	5.2	2352	1.2
2 W	0532	5.1	1207	1.5	1750	5.0	◑	
3 TH	0037	1.4	0623	4.9	1257	1.7	1849	4.8
4 F	0136	1.6	0727	4.7	1409	1.9	2001	4.7
5 SA	0256	1.7	0842	4.7	1535	1.8	2123	4.8
6 SU	0414	1.6	1001	4.8	1650	1.6	2236	5.0
7 M	0525	1.4	1105	5.1	1755	1.3	2333	5.4
8 TU	0624	1.1	1156	5.4	1849	0.9		
9 W	0017	5.8	0713	0.9	1240	5.7	○1935	0.6
10 TH	0101	6.0	0759	0.7	1322	5.9	2020	0.4
11 F	0145	6.2	0842	0.6	1403	6.0	2104	0.3
12 SA	0229	6.2	0925	0.6	1444	6.0	2148	0.2
13 SU	0313	6.1	1008	0.7	1526	6.0	2231	0.3
14 M	0358	6.0	1050	0.8	1610	5.9	2315	0.5
15 TU	0445	5.8	1134	1.0	1657	5.7		
16 W	0002	0.8	0538	5.5	1223	1.3	◑1754	5.4
17 TH	0101	1.2	0639	5.1	1325	1.5	1904	5.1
18 F	0211	1.5	0755	4.8	1441	1.7	2031	4.9
19 SA	0335	1.7	0921	4.7	1611	1.6	2200	4.9
20 SU	0501	1.6	1041	4.9	1726	1.4	2310	5.2
21 M	0601	1.4	1140	5.2	1819	1.1		
22 TU	0001	5.4	0645	1.2	1222	5.4	1902	0.8
23 W	0037	5.6	0722	1.1	1256	5.6	●1939	0.7
24 TH	0112	5.8	0755	1.0	1326	5.7	2013	0.6
25 F	0143	5.8	0828	0.9	1356	5.8	2044	0.6
26 SA	0212	5.8	0856	0.9	1422	5.8	2113	0.6
27 SU	0239	5.8	0925	1.0	1448	5.8	2142	0.7
28 M	0305	5.8	0952	1.0	1515	5.7	2210	0.8
29 TU	0332	5.7	1018	1.1	1541	5.6	2237	1.0
30 W	0358	5.5	1047	1.2	1608	5.4	2309	1.2
31 TH	0429	5.4	1122	1.4	1643	5.4	◑2348	1.4

Chart Datum: 2·69 metres below IGN Datum

UTDEC

TIME ZONE -0100
(French Standard Time)
Subtract 1 hour for UT
For French Summer Time add
ONE hour in **non-shaded areas**

FRANCE – DUNKERQUE

LAT 51°03'N   LONG 2°22'E

TIMES AND HEIGHTS OF HIGH AND LOW WATERS

SEPTEMBER

Time m	Time m
1 F 0515 5.0 / 1207 1.7 / 1740 4.9	**16** SA 0141 1.9 / 0729 4.6 / 1418 1.9 / 2016 4.7
2 SA 0045 1.7 / 0633 4.7 / 1315 1.9 / 1919 4.6	**17** SU 0320 2.0 / 0906 4.6 / 1556 1.8 / 2151 4.8
3 SU 0210 1.9 / 0807 4.5 / 1455 2.0 / 2057 4.7	**18** M 0446 1.8 / 1025 4.9 / 1709 1.4 / 2256 5.2
4 M 0346 1.8 / 0940 4.7 / 1628 1.7 / 2219 5.1	**19** TU 0542 1.4 / 1119 5.2 / 1800 1.0 / 2342 5.5
5 TU 0509 1.5 / 1048 5.1 / 1739 1.2 / 2317 5.5	**20** W 0624 1.2 / 1157 5.5 / 1840 0.8
6 W 0609 1.1 / 1138 5.5 / 1832 0.8	**21** TH 0015 5.7 / 0658 1.1 / 1228 5.7 / 1914 0.7
7 TH ○ 0003 5.9 / 0656 0.8 / 1219 5.8 / 1917 0.5	**22** F ● 0046 5.8 / 0727 1.0 / 1257 5.8 / 1943 0.7
8 F 0041 6.2 / 0738 0.7 / 1257 6.1 / 2000 0.3	**23** SA 0113 5.9 / 0755 0.9 / 1324 5.9 / 2011 0.7
9 SA 0122 6.3 / 0819 0.6 / 1335 6.2 / 2041 0.2	**24** SU 0138 5.9 / 0823 0.9 / 1348 5.9 / 2040 0.7
10 SU 0203 6.3 / 0900 0.6 / 1414 6.2 / 2123 0.2	**25** M 0202 5.9 / 0852 0.9 / 1412 5.9 / 2108 0.8
11 M 0245 6.2 / 0941 0.7 / 1455 6.2 / 2204 0.4	**26** TU 0227 5.9 / 0919 1.0 / 1437 5.8 / 2136 0.9
12 TU 0328 6.0 / 1021 0.8 / 1538 6.0 / 2246 0.7	**27** W 0252 5.8 / 0946 1.1 / 1502 5.7 / 2204 1.0
13 W 0414 5.8 / 1103 1.0 / 1626 5.8 / 2331 1.0	**28** TH 0319 5.6 / 1015 1.2 / 1530 5.6 / 2235 1.2
14 TH ◑ 0505 5.4 / 1151 1.3 / 1724 5.4	**29** F 0351 5.4 / 1051 1.4 / 1606 5.3 / 2315 1.5
15 F 0027 1.5 / 0607 5.0 / 1252 1.7 / 1838 4.9	**30** SA ◑ 0436 5.1 / 1138 1.7 / 1700 4.9

OCTOBER

Time m	Time m
1 SU 0015 1.8 / 0556 4.7 / 1249 1.9 / 1857 4.6	**16** M 0249 2.1 / 0836 4.5 / 1525 1.9 / 2121 4.8
2 M 0143 2.0 / 0742 4.5 / 1428 1.9 / 2036 4.7	**17** TU 0411 1.9 / 0948 4.8 / 1636 1.5 / 2222 5.1
3 TU 0324 1.9 / 0917 4.8 / 1604 1.6 / 2158 5.2	**18** W 0508 1.6 / 1040 5.1 / 1709 1.1 / 2306 5.4
4 W 0447 1.5 / 1025 5.2 / 1715 1.1 / 2255 5.7	**19** TH 0550 1.3 / 1119 5.4 / 1807 0.9 / 2342 5.6
5 TH 0545 1.1 / 1112 5.6 / 1808 0.7 / 2340 6.0	**20** F 0624 1.1 / 1153 5.6 / 1840 0.8
6 F 0631 0.8 / 1151 5.9 / 1853 0.4	**21** SA 0012 5.8 / 0653 1.1 / 1224 5.8 / 1908 0.8
7 SA ○ 0016 6.2 / 0713 0.7 / 1228 6.2 / 1935 0.3	**22** SU ● 0039 5.8 / 0721 1.0 / 1251 5.8 / 1937 0.8
8 SU 0056 6.3 / 0753 0.7 / 1306 6.3 / 2016 0.4	**23** M 0104 5.9 / 0751 1.0 / 1315 5.9 / 2007 0.8
9 M 0136 6.3 / 0834 0.6 / 1346 6.3 / 2057 0.4	**24** TU 0129 5.9 / 0822 1.0 / 1341 5.9 / 2038 0.9
10 TU 0218 6.2 / 0914 0.7 / 1429 6.2 / 2138 0.6	**25** W 0157 5.9 / 0852 1.0 / 1409 5.9 / 2109 1.0
11 W 0301 6.0 / 0955 0.8 / 1514 6.0 / 2219 0.9	**26** TH 0226 5.8 / 0923 1.1 / 1440 5.8 / 2140 1.1
12 TH 0347 5.7 / 1038 1.1 / 1604 5.7 / 2303 1.3	**27** F 0258 5.6 / 0956 1.2 / 1514 5.6 / 2216 1.3
13 F 0438 5.3 / 1126 1.4 / 1702 5.3 / 2355 1.7	**28** SA 0336 5.4 / 1036 1.4 / 1557 5.3 / 2301 1.6
14 SA ◑ 0539 4.9 / 1225 1.7 / 1816 4.9	**29** SU ◑ 0428 5.1 / 1128 1.6 / 1709 5.0
15 SU 0110 2.1 / 0659 4.6 / 1350 1.9 / 1953 4.6	**30** M 0002 1.8 / 0551 4.8 / 1239 1.7 / 1843 4.8
	31 TU 0127 1.9 / 0717 4.7 / 1408 1.7 / 2011 4.9

NOVEMBER

Time m	Time m
1 W 0258 1.8 / 0844 4.9 / 1535 1.4 / 2129 5.3	**16** TH 0413 1.8 / 0949 5.0 / 1636 1.4 / 2219 5.2
2 TH 0415 1.5 / 0951 5.3 / 1644 1.0 / 2226 5.7	**17** F 0502 1.5 / 1035 5.2 / 1721 1.2 / 2259 5.4
3 F 0514 1.1 / 1040 5.6 / 1739 0.7 / 2313 6.0	**18** SA 0541 1.3 / 1114 5.5 / 1759 1.1 / 2335 5.6
4 SA 0603 0.9 / 1121 5.9 / 1826 0.5 / 2355 6.1	**19** SU 0616 1.2 / 1149 5.6 / 1832 1.0
5 SU ○ 0647 0.8 / 1201 6.1 / 1910 0.5	**20** M ● 0005 5.7 / 0649 1.1 / 1219 5.7 / 1905 1.0
6 M 0031 6.2 / 0729 0.8 / 1242 6.2 / 1953 0.5	**21** TU 0034 5.7 / 0723 1.1 / 1248 5.8 / 1939 1.0
7 TU 0113 6.2 / 0811 0.7 / 1325 6.2 / 2035 0.6	**22** W 0104 5.8 / 0759 1.0 / 1320 5.8 / 2015 1.0
8 W 0157 6.0 / 0853 0.8 / 1411 6.1 / 2117 0.8	**23** TH 0138 5.8 / 0835 1.0 / 1355 5.8 / 2052 1.0
9 TH 0242 5.9 / 0936 0.9 / 1459 5.9 / 2159 1.1	**24** F 0215 5.8 / 0912 1.0 / 1435 5.8 / 2130 1.1
10 F 0328 5.6 / 1020 1.1 / 1550 5.6 / 2243 1.4	**25** SA 0255 5.6 / 0952 1.1 / 1519 5.6 / 2212 1.3
11 SA 0418 5.3 / 1107 1.3 / 1646 5.3 / 2332 1.7	**26** SU 0340 5.4 / 1037 1.2 / 1612 5.4 / 2300 1.5
12 SU ◐ 0512 5.0 / 1200 1.6 / 1748 4.9	**27** M 0435 5.2 / 1129 1.3 / 1715 5.2 / 2356 1.6
13 M 0033 2.0 / 0616 4.7 / 1309 1.8 / 1908 4.7	**28** TU 0538 5.1 / 1232 1.4 / 1822 5.1
14 TU 0153 2.1 / 0740 4.6 / 1430 1.8 / 2030 4.7	**29** W 0108 1.7 / 0646 5.0 / 1345 1.4 / 1937 5.1
15 W 0311 2.0 / 0854 4.7 / 1540 1.6 / 2131 4.9	**30** TH 0224 1.6 / 0800 5.1 / 1501 1.2 / 2052 5.3

DECEMBER

Time m	Time m
1 F 0336 1.5 / 0909 5.3 / 1609 1.0 / 2153 5.5	**16** SA 0359 1.8 / 0939 5.0 / 1624 1.5 / 2210 5.0
2 SA 0439 1.3 / 1006 5.5 / 1709 0.9 / 2246 5.7	**17** SU 0452 1.6 / 1030 5.1 / 1714 1.3 / 2256 5.2
3 SU 0535 1.1 / 1056 5.8 / 1803 0.8 / 2334 5.8	**18** M 0539 1.4 / 1115 5.3 / 1758 1.2 / 2337 5.4
4 M 0625 1.0 / 1143 5.9 / 1851 0.7	**19** TU 0621 1.3 / 1154 5.5 / 1839 1.0
5 TU ○ 0015 5.9 / 0712 0.9 / 1229 6.0 / 1937 0.8	**20** W 0012 5.5 / 0702 1.1 / 1231 5.6 / 1920 1.1
6 W 0101 5.9 / 0757 0.8 / 1317 6.0 / 2021 0.9	**21** TH 0049 5.7 / 0744 1.0 / 1309 5.8 / 2001 0.9
7 TH 0146 5.9 / 0842 0.8 / 1405 6.0 / 2104 1.0	**22** F 0128 5.8 / 0826 0.9 / 1350 5.9 / 2044 0.8
8 F 0231 5.8 / 0925 0.8 / 1453 5.8 / 2145 1.2	**23** SA 0209 5.8 / 0908 0.8 / 1433 5.9 / 2127 1.0
9 SA 0315 5.6 / 1008 1.0 / 1540 5.6 / 2226 1.4	**24** SU 0252 5.7 / 0952 0.8 / 1519 5.8 / 2210 1.1
10 SU 0358 5.4 / 1050 1.1 / 1625 5.4 / 2308 1.6	**25** M 0336 5.6 / 1037 0.9 / 1607 5.7 / 2255 1.2
11 M 0442 5.2 / 1133 1.3 / 1712 5.1 / 2353 1.7	**26** TU 0423 5.5 / 1124 0.9 / 1658 5.6 / 2343 1.3
12 TU ◐ 0529 5.0 / 1222 1.5 / 1805 4.9	**27** W 0515 5.4 / 1217 1.0 / 1755 5.4
13 W 0047 1.9 / 0625 4.8 / 1320 1.6 / 1909 4.8	**28** TH 0041 1.4 / 0613 5.3 / 1317 1.1 / 1900 5.3
14 TH 0152 1.9 / 0731 4.8 / 1426 1.6 / 2019 4.8	**29** F 0146 1.5 / 0718 5.2 / 1426 1.2 / 2011 5.2
15 F 0300 1.9 / 0840 4.8 / 1528 1.6 / 2119 4.9	**30** SA 0256 1.5 / 0830 5.2 / 1535 1.2 / 2122 5.2
	31 SU 0406 1.5 / 0939 5.3 / 1643 1.1 / 2226 5.3

Chart Datum: 2·69 metres below IGN Datum

TIDES

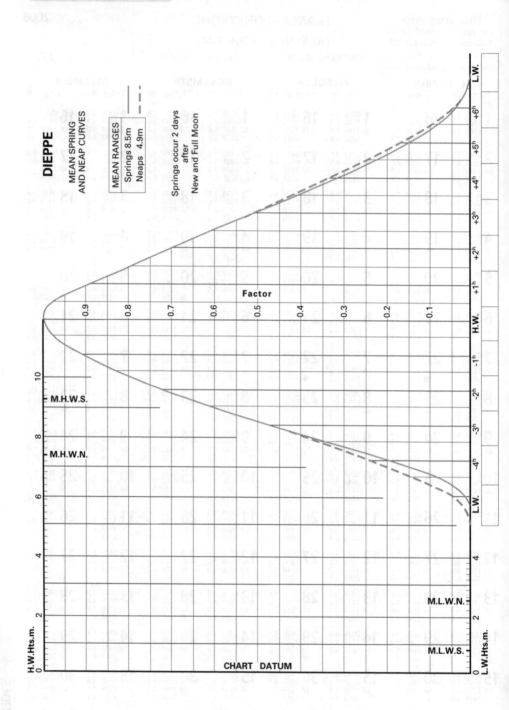

DIEPPE

MEAN SPRING
AND NEAP CURVES

MEAN RANGES
Springs 8.5m
Neaps 4.9m

Springs occur 2 days
after
New and Full Moon

Factor

0.9 0.8 0.7 0.6 0.5 0.4 0.3 0.2 0.1

M.H.W.S.

M.H.W.N.

M.L.W.N.

M.L.W.S.

H.W.Hts.m.

L.W.Hts.m.

CHART DATUM

L.W.

H.W.

TIME ZONE -0100
(French Standard Time)
Subtract 1 hour for UT
For French Summer Time add
ONE hour in **non-shaded areas**

FRANCE – DIEPPE

LAT 49°56′N   LONG 1°05′E

TIMES AND HEIGHTS OF HIGH AND LOW WATERS

JANUARY

#	Day	Time	m	Time	m	#	Day	Time	m	Time	m
1	SU	0005 / 1224	8.9 / 9.2	0658 / 1926	1.3 / 0.9	16	M	0046 / 1257	8.6 / 8.7	0732 / 1954	1.5 / 1.3
2	M	0054 / 1312	9.1 / 9.3	0749 / 2016	1.2 / 0.8	17	TU	0120 / 1331	8.6 / 8.7	0807 / 2027	1.5 / 1.3
3	TU	0142 / 1401	9.1 / 9.2	0838 / 2105	1.1 / 0.8	18	W	0153 / 1404	8.6 / 8.6	0837 / 2057	1.6 / 1.5
4	W	0231 / 1449	9.0 / 9.1	0926 / 2152	1.2 / 0.9	19	TH	0225 / 1436	8.3 / 8.4	0906 / 2124	1.7 / 1.6
5	TH	0319 / 1538	8.8 / 8.8	1014 / 2238	1.4 / 1.2	20	F	0255 / 1507	8.3 / 8.2	0935 / 2153	1.9 / 1.8
6	F	0408 / 1629	8.5 / 8.4	1102 / 2325	1.7 / 1.6	21	SA	0327 / 1540	8.1 / 7.9	1009 / 2226	2.1 / 2.1
7	SA	0500 / 1725	8.2 / 8.0	1153	2.0	22	SU	0403 / 1620	7.8 / 7.6	1048 / 2307	2.4 / 2.4
8	SU	0016 / 1253	2.0 / 2.3	0559 / 1829	7.8 / 7.6	23	M	0447 / 1710	7.5 / 7.2	1136 / 2359	2.6 / 2.7
9	M	0117 / 1402	2.3 / 2.4	0709 / 1941	7.6 / 7.5	24	TU	0546 / 1820	7.2 / 6.9	1238	2.8
10	TU	0229 / 1514	2.5 / 2.3	0821 / 2053	7.6 / 7.5	25	W	0108 / 1356	2.9 / 2.8	0708 / 1948	7.1 / 7.0
11	W	0341 / 1619	2.4 / 2.1	0927 / 2155	7.8 / 7.8	26	TH	0235 / 1520	2.8 / 2.5	0831 / 2104	7.4 / 7.4
12	TH	0441 / 1713	2.2 / 1.8	1021 / 2247	8.1 / 8.1	27	F	0355 / 1629	2.4 / 1.9	0937 / 2207	7.9 / 8.0
13	F	0531 / 1759	2.0 / 1.6	1107 / 2331	8.3 / 8.3	28	SA	0459 / 1730	1.9 / 1.4	1035 / 2303	8.4 / 8.6
14	SA	0615 / 1840	1.8 / 1.4	1147	8.5	29	SU	0558 / 1828	1.4 / 0.9	1127 / ● 2354	8.9 / 9.0
15	SU	0010 / 1223	8.5 / 8.6	0655 / 1918	1.6 / 1.3	30	M	0654 / 1922	1.0 / 0.6	1217	9.3
						31	TU	0047 / 1304	9.4 / 9.6	0747 / 2011	0.8 / 0.3

FEBRUARY

#	Day	Time	m	Time	m	#	Day	Time	m	Time	m
1	W	0132 / 1350	9.5 / 9.7	0834 / 2056	0.6 / 0.3	16	TH	0129 / 1340	8.9 / 8.9	0816 / 2033	1.2 / 1.1
2	TH	0216 / 1433	9.5 / 9.5	0917 / 2137	0.7 / 0.5	17	F	0157 / 1408	8.8 / 8.8	0842 / 2058	1.3 / 1.2
3	F	0258 / 1516	9.3 / 9.2	0956 / 2215	0.9 / 0.9	18	SA	0224 / 1436	8.7 / 8.6	0908 / 2123	1.4 / 1.5
4	SA	0339 / 1559	8.9 / 8.7	1034 / 2252	1.3 / 1.4	19	SU	0252 / 1506	8.5 / 8.3	0936 / 2150	1.6 / 1.8
5	SU	0421 / 1646	8.3 / 8.0	1115 / (2334	1.8 / 2.0	20	M	0323 / 1540	8.2 / 7.9	1008 / 2224	2.0 / 2.2
6	M	0511 / 1745	7.7 / 7.3	1205	2.4	21	TU	0359 / 1624	7.7 / 7.4	1050 / 2311	2.4 / 2.6
7	TU	0027 / 1315	2.7 / 2.8	0620 / 1905	7.2 / 6.9	22	W	0451 / 1728	7.3 / 6.9	1149	2.8
8	W	0146 / 1444	3.0 / 2.8	0751 / 2037	7.0 / 6.9	23	TH	0019 / 1311	3.0 / 3.0	0614 / 1910	6.9 / 6.7
9	TH	0318 / 1604	2.9 / 2.5	0915 / 2149	7.2 / 7.4	24	F	0159 / 1452	3.1 / 2.6	0803 / 2046	7.0 / 7.2
10	F	0432 / 1704	2.5 / 2.0	1014 / 2240	7.7 / 7.9	25	SA	0335 / 1611	2.5 / 1.9	0922 / 2156	7.7 / 7.9
11	SA	0525 / 1751	2.1 / 1.6	1058 / 2320	8.1 / 8.3	26	SU	0446 / 1717	1.8 / 1.3	1023 / 2252	8.4 / 8.7
12	SU	0607 / 1830	1.7 / 1.4	1135 / 2355	8.5 / 8.6	27	M	0548 / 1817	1.2 / 0.7	1116 / 2341	9.1 / 9.2
13	M	0644 / 1905	1.5 / 1.2	1208 / O	8.7	28	TU	0644 / 1909	0.8 / 0.3	1203 / ●	9.6
14	TU	0028 / 1239	8.7 / 8.9	0717 / 1937	1.4 / 1.1						
15	W	0059 / 1310	8.8 / 8.9	0748 / 2006	1.2 / 1.0						

MARCH

#	Day	Time	m	Time	m	#	Day	Time	m	Time	m
1	W	0030 / 1248	9.6 / 9.8	0733 / 1955	0.4 / 0.0	16	TH	0031 / 1243	9.0 / 9.0	0721 / 1939	1.0 / 0.9
2	TH	0112 / 1330	9.7 / 9.9	0817 / 2036	0.3 / 0.1	17	F	0059 / 1312	9.0 / 9.0	0749 / 2005	1.0 / 1.0
3	F	0152 / 1410	9.7 / 9.7	0856 / 2113	0.4 / 0.4	18	SA	0127 / 1340	9.0 / 9.0	0816 / 2031	1.1 / 1.1
4	SA	0230 / 1449	9.4 / 9.3	0930 / 2146	0.7 / 0.8	19	SU	0154 / 1408	8.9 / 8.8	0843 / 2056	1.2 / 1.3
5	SU	0307 / 1528	9.0 / 8.7	1003 / 2217	1.2 / 1.5	20	M	0223 / 1439	8.7 / 8.5	0910 / 2122	1.5 / 1.7
6	M	0344 / 1610	8.3 / 7.9	1039 / 2254	1.8 / 2.2	21	TU	0253 / 1514	8.3 / 8.0	0940 / 2155	1.8 / 2.1
7	TU	0427 / 1704	7.6 / 7.1	1125 / 2345	2.5 / 2.9	22	W	0330 / 1559	7.9 / 7.5	1022 / (2244	2.2 / 2.6
8	W	0533 / 1832	6.8 / 6.5	1233	3.0	23	TH	0422 / 1705	7.3 / 6.9	1122 / 2355	2.7 / 3.1
9	TH	0110 / 1413	3.4 / 3.1	0723 / 2023	6.5 / 6.6	24	F	0550 / 1854	6.8 / 6.7	1249	2.9
10	F	0259 / 1545	3.2 / 2.7	0901 / 2134	6.9 / 7.2	25	SA	0142 / 1435	3.1 / 2.5	0746 / 2032	7.0 / 7.3
11	SA	0417 / 1646	2.6 / 2.1	0957 / 2220	7.5 / 7.8	26	SU	0320 / 1555	2.4 / 1.8	0906 / 2140	7.7 / 8.1
12	SU	0507 / 1730	2.0 / 1.6	1038 / 2257	8.0 / 8.3	27	M	0430 / 1700	1.7 / 1.1	1006 / 2233	8.5 / 8.8
13	M	0546 / 1807	1.6 / 1.3	1112 / 2330	8.5 / 8.6	28	TU	0530 / 1757	1.1 / 0.6	1056 / 2319	9.2 / 9.3
14	TU	0620 / 1840	1.3 / 1.1	1144 / O	8.7	29	W	0623 / 1847	0.6 / 0.3	1142 / ●	9.6
15	W	0000 / 1214	8.8 / 8.9	0710 / 1910	0.4 / 1.0	30	TH	0003 / 1225	9.6 / 9.8	0710 / 1930	0.4 / 0.2
						31	F	0047 / 1305	9.7 / 9.8	0752 / 2010	0.4 / 0.3

APRIL

#	Day	Time	m	Time	m	#	Day	Time	m	Time	m
1	SA	0125 / 1344	9.6 / 9.6	0829 / 2044	0.5 / 0.6	16	SU	0058 / 1314	9.0 / 8.9	0751 / 2005	1.1 / 1.2
2	SU	0201 / 1422	9.3 / 9.1	0902 / 2115	0.8 / 1.1	17	M	0128 / 1347	8.9 / 8.8	0821 / 2034	1.2 / 1.4
3	M	0237 / 1500	8.8 / 8.5	0934 / 2146	1.3 / 1.7	18	TU	0201 / 1422	8.7 / 8.5	0853 / 2107	1.4 / 1.7
4	TU	0313 / 1541	8.2 / 7.8	1009 / 2223	1.9 / 2.4	19	W	0236 / 1502	8.3 / 8.0	0928 / 2146	1.7 / 2.2
5	W	0355 / 1634	7.5 / 7.0	1053 / (2314	2.5 / 3.0	20	TH	0318 / 1552	7.8 / 7.5	1014 / 2239	2.1 / 2.6
6	TH	0458 / 1759	6.7 / 6.5	1159	3.1	21	F	0417 / 1704	7.3 / 7.0	1117 / (2352	2.5 / 2.9
7	F	0039 / 1335	3.4 / 3.2	0642 / 1947	6.4 / 6.5	22	SA	0548 / 1845	7.0 / 7.0	1243	2.6
8	SA	0221 / 1503	3.2 / 2.8	0823 / 2058	6.7 / 7.1	23	SU	0132 / 1418	2.7 / 2.2	0727 / 2009	7.3 / 7.6
9	SU	0336 / 1604	2.7 / 2.2	0921 / 2144	7.3 / 7.7	24	M	0258 / 1531	2.2 / 1.6	0841 / 2113	7.9 / 8.2
10	M	0427 / 1650	2.1 / 1.7	1003 / 2222	7.9 / 8.2	25	TU	0404 / 1634	1.5 / 1.1	0940 / 2206	8.5 / 8.8
11	TU	0508 / 1729	1.7 / 1.4	1038 / 2255	8.3 / 8.6	26	W	0503 / 1729	1.1 / 0.7	1031 / 2252	9.0 / 9.2
12	W	0544 / 1804	1.4 / 1.2	1111 / 2327	8.6 / 8.8	27	TH	0555 / 1818	0.8 / 0.6	1117 / ● 2336	9.3 / 9.4
13	TH	0618 / 1837	1.2 / 1.1	1143 / O 2358	8.8 / 8.9	28	F	0642 / 1901	0.7 / 0.6	1200	9.5
14	F	0650 / 1907	1.1 / 1.0	1213	8.9	29	SA	0019 / 1240	9.4 / 9.4	0723 / 1940	0.7 / 0.7
15	SA	0028 / 1244	9.0 / 9.0	0721 / 1936	1.1 / 1.1	30	SU	0057 / 1320	9.3 / 9.2	0801 / 2015	0.8 / 1.0

Chart Datum: 4·45 metres below IGN Datum

TIDES

TIME ZONE -0100
(French Standard Time)
Subtract 1 hour for UT
For French Summer Time add
ONE hour in **non-shaded areas**

FRANCE – DIEPPE   2006

LAT 49°56′N   LONG 1°05′E

TIMES AND HEIGHTS OF HIGH AND LOW WATERS

MAY

Day	Time m	Time m	Time m	Time m		Day	Time m	Time m	Time m	Time m
1 M	0135 9.1	0836 1.0	1359 8.8	2049 1.4		16 TU	0109 8.8	0806 1.2	1333 8.7	2022 1.5
2 TU	0212 8.6	0910 1.4	1439 8.3	2123 1.9		17 W	0148 8.7	0845 1.3	1414 8.5	2102 1.7
3 W	0251 8.1	0947 1.9	1521 7.7	2202 2.4		18 TH	0231 8.3	0928 1.6	1501 8.1	2148 2.0
4 TH	0334 7.5	1030 2.4	1613 7.2	2252 2.9		19 F	0321 8.0	1019 1.9	1557 7.7	2244 2.3
5 F ●	0433 6.9	1129 2.8	1721 6.7			20 SA ◗	0424 7.6	1121 2.1	1707 7.5	2353 2.4
6 SA	0002 3.2	0552 6.6	1246 3.0	1843 6.7		21 SU	0541 7.5	1235 2.1	1824 7.5	
7 SU	0125 3.1	0715 6.7	1401 2.8	1956 7.0		22 M	0114 2.3	0659 7.6	1352 1.9	1936 7.8
8 M	0234 2.7	0715 7.1	1504 2.4	2051 7.5		23 TU	0227 2.0	0809 8.0	1500 1.6	2040 8.2
9 TU	0330 2.3	0912 7.6	1555 2.0	2135 7.9		24 W	0332 1.6	0910 8.4	1601 1.3	2135 8.6
10 W	0417 1.9	0954 8.0	1640 1.7	2213 8.3		25 TH	0431 1.3	1004 8.7	1657 1.2	2225 8.8
11 TH	0500 1.6	1033 8.3	1722 1.4	2249 8.6		26 F	0524 1.2	1052 8.9	1747 1.1	2310 9.0
12 F	0539 1.4	1109 8.5	1759 1.3	2324 8.7		27 SA ●	0612 1.1	1137 9.0	1831 1.1	2353 9.0
13 SA ○	0617 1.3	1144 8.7	1835 1.3	2358 8.8		28 SU	0656 1.0	1220 8.9	1912 1.2	
14 SU	0653 1.2	1218 8.8	1910 1.3			29 M	0035 8.9	0737 1.1	1301 8.8	1951 1.3
15 M	0033 8.9	0729 1.1	1254 8.8	1945 1.3		30 TU	0115 8.8	0816 1.2	1342 8.6	2029 1.5
						31 W	0155 8.5	0854 1.5	1423 8.3	2107 1.9

JUNE

Day	Time m	Time m	Time m	Time m		Day	Time m	Time m	Time m	Time m
1 TH	0235 8.1	0931 1.8	1505 7.9	2146 2.2		16 F	0233 8.6	0933 1.2	1504 8.5	2153 1.6
2 F	0318 7.7	1010 2.2	1551 7.5	2229 2.5		17 SA	0324 8.4	1023 1.4	1556 8.3	2246 1.8
3 SA ◗	0405 7.3	1056 2.5	1641 7.2	2320 2.8		18 SU ◗	0419 8.2	1117 1.6	1653 8.1	2343 1.9
4 SU	0501 7.0	1151 2.7	1739 7.1			19 M	0520 8.0	1215 1.7	1754 8.0	
5 M	0019 2.8	0604 6.9	1252 2.7	1842 7.1		20 TU	0045 2.0	0625 7.9	1318 1.8	1859 7.9
6 TU	0122 2.6	0710 7.0	1354 2.6	1944 7.3		21 W	0151 2.0	0734 7.9	1424 1.8	2005 8.0
7 W	0223 2.5	0811 7.3	1454 2.3	2040 7.6		22 TH	0258 1.9	0841 8.0	1529 1.8	2107 8.2
8 TH	0320 2.2	0905 7.6	1548 2.1	2128 7.9		23 F	0402 1.7	0941 8.2	1629 1.7	2203 8.3
9 F	0412 2.0	0953 7.9	1638 1.8	2212 8.2		24 SA	0459 1.6	1035 8.3	1722 1.6	2253 8.5
10 SA	0500 1.7	1036 8.2	1724 1.7	2253 8.5		25 SU ●	0550 1.4	1124 8.5	1810 1.5	2338 8.6
11 SU ○	0546 1.5	1118 8.4	1807 1.5	2333 8.6		26 M	0637 1.3	1208 8.6	1853 1.5	
12 M	0630 1.3	1200 8.6	1850 1.4			27 TU	0022 8.6	0720 1.3	1250 8.6	1935 1.5
13 TU	0016 8.8	0714 1.2	1242 8.7	1933 1.3		28 W	0102 8.6	0801 1.3	1329 8.6	2014 1.5
14 W	0059 8.8	0759 1.1	1327 8.8	2018 1.4		29 TH	0141 8.5	0839 1.4	1407 8.5	2051 1.7
15 TH	0145 8.8	0845 1.1	1414 8.7	2104 1.5		30 F	0219 8.3	0914 1.6	1445 8.3	2126 1.9

JULY

Day	Time m	Time m	Time m	Time m		Day	Time m	Time m	Time m	Time m
1 SA	0256 8.1	0947 1.8	1522 8.0	2200 2.1		16 SU	0313 9.0	1015 0.9	1539 8.8	2234 1.3
2 SU ◗	0332 7.8	1020 2.0	1559 7.8	2236 2.3		17 M ◗	0400 8.7	1058 1.2	1626 8.5	2320 1.6
3 M ◗	0411 7.6	1059 2.3	1641 7.5	2319 2.5		18 TU	0450 8.3	1144 1.6	1719 8.1	
4 TU	0457 7.3	1144 2.5	1730 7.3			19 W	0012 1.9	0549 7.8	1239 2.0	1821 7.8
5 W	0011 2.7	0552 7.1	1239 2.7	1830 7.2		20 TH	0115 2.2	0700 7.5	1347 2.3	1934 7.6
6 TH	0111 2.7	0701 7.0	1344 2.7	1939 7.2		21 F	0229 2.3	0819 7.4	1503 2.4	2048 7.6
7 F	0220 2.6	0813 7.2	1455 2.6	2043 7.5		22 SA	0342 2.2	0931 7.6	1612 2.2	2153 7.9
8 SA	0328 2.3	0915 7.5	1559 2.3	2138 7.8		23 SU	0446 1.9	1030 8.0	1710 1.9	2247 8.2
9 SU	0427 2.0	1009 7.9	1655 1.9	2229 8.2		24 M	0541 1.6	1119 8.3	1800 1.7	2332 8.4
10 M	0522 1.6	1059 8.3	1747 1.6	2316 8.5		25 TU ●	0628 1.4	1201 8.5	1844 1.5	
11 TU ○	0615 1.3	1148 8.6	1838 1.4			26 W	0013 8.6	0709 1.3	1238 8.7	1922 1.4
12 W	0004 8.8	0707 1.1	1235 8.9	1928 1.2		27 TH	0049 8.7	0747 1.2	1312 8.7	1958 1.4
13 TH	0054 9.0	0758 0.8	1322 9.1	2017 1.0		28 F	0123 8.7	0821 1.2	1345 8.7	2031 1.4
14 F	0141 9.1	0846 0.7	1408 9.1	2104 1.0		29 SA	0156 8.7	0850 1.3	1417 8.6	2100 1.5
15 SA	0227 9.1	0931 0.7	1454 9.0	2149 1.1		30 SU	0227 8.5	0917 1.5	1448 8.4	2127 1.7
						31 M	0256 8.3	0943 1.7	1517 8.2	2156 1.9

AUGUST

Day	Time m	Time m	Time m	Time m		Day	Time m	Time m	Time m	Time m
1 TU	0327 8.0	1013 2.0	1549 7.9	2230 2.2		16 W	0418 8.3	1110 1.8	1642 8.1	2338 2.1
2 W	0402 7.6	1050 2.3	1627 7.5	2313 2.5		17 TH	0514 7.6	1202 2.4	1744 7.4	
3 TH	0447 7.2	1137 2.7	1717 7.2			18 F	0041 2.6	0631 7.0	1316 2.9	1909 7.1
4 F	0009 2.8	0550 6.9	1240 3.0	1831 6.9		19 SA	0208 2.8	0809 7.0	1448 2.9	2041 7.3
5 SA	0123 2.9	0720 6.8	1405 3.0	2001 7.0		20 SU	0335 2.5	0930 7.4	1607 2.5	2150 7.7
6 SU	0250 2.7	0845 7.2	1529 2.6	2113 7.5		21 M	0444 2.0	1025 7.9	1707 2.0	2239 8.2
7 M	0404 2.2	0951 7.7	1634 2.1	2211 8.1		22 TU	0535 1.6	1108 8.4	1753 1.6	2320 8.5
8 TU	0506 1.7	1046 8.3	1732 1.6	2304 8.6		23 W ●	0617 1.4	1144 8.7	1831 1.4	2355 8.7
9 W ○	0604 1.2	1136 8.8	1827 1.2	2352 9.1		24 TH	0652 1.2	1217 8.8	1904 1.3	
10 TH	0700 0.8	1223 9.2	1919 0.9			25 F	0027 8.9	0725 1.1	1247 8.9	1935 1.2
11 F	0042 9.4	0750 0.5	1308 9.5	2007 0.6		26 SA	0057 8.9	0754 1.1	1316 8.9	2003 1.3
12 SA	0127 9.6	0835 0.3	1351 9.5	2051 0.6		27 SU	0127 8.9	0821 1.2	1345 8.9	2029 1.4
13 SU	0210 9.5	0915 0.4	1434 9.4	2132 0.7		28 M	0154 8.8	0844 1.5	1412 8.7	2054 1.5
14 M	0251 9.3	0953 0.7	1514 9.1	2211 1.1		29 TU	0221 8.6	0908 1.6	1438 8.5	2120 1.7
15 TU	0333 8.9	1030 1.2	1555 8.7	2251 1.5		30 W	0249 8.2	0933 1.9	1506 8.2	2150 2.1
						31 TH ◗	0321 7.9	1004 2.3	1541 7.7	2228 2.5

Chart Datum: 4·45 metres below IGN Datum

FRANCE – DIEPPE

LAT 49°56'N   LONG 1°05'E

TIMES AND HEIGHTS OF HIGH AND LOW WATERS

2006

SEPTEMBER

Day	Time	m	Time	m	Day	Time	m	Time	m
1 F	0402	7.4	1047	2.8	16 SA	0012	2.9	0609	6.7
	1627	7.2	2321	2.9		1252	3.3	1850	6.7
2 SA	0501	6.8	1152	3.2	17 SU	0150	3.1	0801	6.8
	1739	6.7				1437	3.1	2032	7.0
3 SU	0038	3.2	0640	6.6	18 M	0324	2.7	0916	7.4
	1329	3.3	1930	6.8		1555	2.5	2134	7.6
4 M	0224	2.9	0825	7.0	19 TU	0428	2.1	1005	8.0
	1508	2.8	2054	7.4		1648	1.9	2219	8.2
5 TU	0347	2.2	0935	7.8	20 W	0513	1.6	1044	8.5
	1617	2.0	2155	8.2		1729	1.5	2255	8.6
6 W	0451	1.5	1030	8.5	21 TH	0551	1.3	1117	8.8
	1716	1.4	2247	8.9		1804	1.3	2328	8.8
7 TH	0549	0.9	1118	9.1	22 F	0623	1.2	1147	9.0
	1811	0.9	O 2334	9.4		1835	1.2	(2358	9.0
8 F	0643	0.5	1203	9.5	23 SA	0654	1.1	1216	9.0
	1902	0.6				1905	1.2		
9 SA	0022	9.7	0730	0.3	24 SU	0027	9.0	0722	1.1
	1246	9.8	1948	0.4		1244	9.0	1932	1.2
10 SU	0105	9.8	0812	0.3	25 M	0055	9.0	0748	1.2
	1327	9.8	2030	0.5		1311	9.0	1959	1.3
11 M	0146	9.7	0850	0.5	26 TU	0122	8.9	0812	1.4
	1406	9.6	2108	0.7		1338	8.9	2024	1.4
12 TU	0225	9.4	0925	0.9	27 W	0150	8.7	0836	1.6
	1445	9.2	2144	1.1		1405	8.6	2050	1.7
13 W	0305	8.8	0958	1.4	28 TH	0219	8.4	0901	2.0
	1524	8.6	2221	1.7		1434	8.3	2120	2.0
14 TH	0348	8.1	1037	2.1	29 F	0252	8.0	0931	2.4
	1609	7.9	(2306	2.3		1509	7.8	2158	2.4
15 F	0442	7.3	1129	2.8	30 SA	0333	7.4	1016	2.9
	1711	7.1				1557	7.2	(2252	2.9

OCTOBER

Day	Time	m	Time	m	Day	Time	m	Time	m
1 SU	0435	6.9	1125	3.3	16 M	0119	3.2	0727	6.7
	1713	6.7				1404	3.2	1956	6.9
2 M	0012	3.2	0621	6.6	17 TU	0246	2.8	0841	7.3
	1308	3.3	1908	6.8		1517	2.7	2100	7.4
3 TU	0204	2.9	0805	7.2	18 W	0347	2.3	0929	7.9
	1448	2.7	2032	7.5		1609	2.1	2144	8.0
4 W	0327	2.1	0912	8.0	19 TH	0433	1.8	1007	8.3
	1556	1.9	2132	8.3		1650	1.7	2221	8.4
5 TH	0429	1.4	1006	8.8	20 F	0511	1.5	1041	8.7
	1654	1.4	2223	9.0		1726	1.5	2254	8.7
6 F	0526	0.9	1053	9.3	21 SA	0546	1.3	1112	8.9
	1748	0.8	2310	9.5		1800	1.3	2325	8.8
7 SA	0617	0.5	1137	9.7	22 SU	0618	1.3	1142	9.0
	1837	0.5	O 2354	9.8		1832	1.3	● 2355	8.9
8 SU	0703	0.4	1219	9.8	23 M	0648	1.3	1212	9.0
	1922	0.5				1902	1.3		
9 M	0039	9.8	0744	0.5	24 TU	0025	8.9	0716	1.4
	1259	9.7	2003	0.6		1240	9.0	1931	1.3
10 TU	0120	9.6	0821	0.7	25 W	0055	8.8	0744	1.5
	1338	9.5	2041	0.8		1309	8.9	2000	1.4
11 W	0200	9.2	0856	1.2	26 TH	0126	8.7	0813	1.7
	1417	9.1	2117	1.3		1340	8.7	2031	1.7
12 TH	0240	8.7	0930	1.8	27 F	0200	8.4	0843	2.0
	1457	8.5	2155	1.9		1414	8.3	2105	2.0
13 F	0324	7.9	1010	2.4	28 SA	0237	8.0	0919	2.4
	1542	7.7	2240	2.5		1455	7.9	2147	2.4
14 SA	0419	7.2	1104	3.1	29 SU	0323	7.5	1008	2.8
	1645	7.0	(2344	3.0		1547	7.3	(2243	2.7
15 SU	0543	6.7	1227	3.4	30 M	0430	7.1	1118	3.1
	1820	6.6				1705	7.0	2359	2.9
					31 TU	0607	7.0	1252	3.1
						1843	7.1		

NOVEMBER

Day	Time	m	Time	m	Day	Time	m	Time	m
1 W	0139	2.6	0734	7.5	16 TH	0246	2.6	0834	7.5
	1421	2.5	2000	7.7		1512	2.5	2053	7.6
2 TH	0257	2.0	0841	8.1	17 F	0339	2.2	0920	8.0
	1528	1.8	2102	8.4		1601	2.1	2136	8.0
3 F	0400	1.4	0936	8.8	18 SA	0425	1.9	0959	8.3
	1626	1.3	2155	9.0		1644	1.8	2215	8.3
4 SA	0456	1.0	1024	9.2	19 SU	0505	1.7	1035	8.6
	1720	0.9	2243	9.3		1723	1.6	2251	8.5
5 SU	0546	0.8	1110	9.5	20 M	0542	1.6	1110	8.7
	1810	0.7	O 2329	9.5		1800	1.5	● 2326	8.6
6 M	0633	0.8	1152	9.6	21 TU	0617	1.5	1143	8.8
	1856	0.7				1835	1.4		
7 TU	0015	9.5	0715	0.9	22 W	0000	8.7	0651	1.5
	1234	9.5	1938	0.8		1216	8.9	1909	1.4
8 W	0058	9.3	0754	1.1	23 TH	0035	8.7	0725	1.6
	1314	9.3	2017	1.0		1250	8.8	1945	1.4
9 TH	0139	9.0	0831	1.5	24 F	0112	8.7	0800	1.7
	1355	8.9	2056	1.4		1327	8.7	2022	1.7
10 F	0222	8.5	0909	1.9	25 SA	0151	8.5	0838	1.9
	1437	8.4	2135	1.9		1407	8.4	2103	1.8
11 SA	0307	7.9	0950	2.4	26 SU	0235	8.2	0921	2.2
	1523	7.8	2219	2.4		1453	8.1	2149	2.0
12 SU	0359	7.4	1042	2.9	27 M	0326	7.8	1012	2.5
	1620	7.2	(2315	2.9		1548	7.7	2243	2.3
13 M	0505	7.0	1150	3.2	28 TU	0428	7.6	1115	2.6
	1732	6.8				1656	7.5	(2348	2.4
14 TU	0027	3.1	0622	6.9	29 W	0542	7.5	1229	2.6
	1307	3.2	1850	6.8		1811	7.6		
15 W	0142	3.0	0736	7.1	30 TH	0104	2.3	0656	7.7
	1415	2.9	2000	7.1		1345	2.3	1923	7.8

DECEMBER

Day	Time	m	Time	m	Day	Time	m	Time	m
1 F	0218	2.0	0804	8.1	16 SA	0232	2.7	0822	7.4
	1454	1.9	2028	8.2		1504	2.6	2046	7.4
2 SA	0324	1.7	0904	8.5	17 SU	0332	2.5	0914	7.5
	1556	1.5	2127	8.6		1559	2.3	2136	7.7
3 SU	0424	1.4	0957	8.8	18 M	0424	2.2	1000	8.1
	1653	1.3	2220	8.8		1648	2.0	2220	8.1
4 M	0517	1.3	1046	9.1	19 TU	0510	2.0	1041	8.4
	1745	1.1	2309	9.0		1732	1.7	2302	8.3
5 TU	0606	1.2	1132	9.2	20 W	0552	1.8	1121	8.6
	1833	1.0	2355	9.1		1814	1.5	● 2342	8.5
6 W	0651	1.2	1216	9.2	21 TH	0632	1.6	1200	8.8
	1917	1.0				1856	1.3		
7 TH	0042	9.0	0734	1.3	22 F	0024	8.7	0714	1.5
	1258	9.0	2000	1.1		1240	8.9	1938	1.2
8 F	0126	8.8	0815	1.5	23 SA	0106	8.8	0756	1.5
	1340	8.8	2040	1.4		1323	8.9	2021	1.2
9 SA	0208	8.5	0855	1.8	24 SU	0150	8.8	0840	1.5
	1422	8.5	2119	1.7		1407	8.8	2106	1.3
10 SU	0251	8.2	0934	2.2	25 M	0236	8.6	0925	1.7
	1505	8.1	2159	2.1		1453	8.6	2151	1.4
11 M	0335	7.8	1015	2.5	26 TU	0323	8.4	1012	1.8
	1551	7.6	2240	2.4		1542	8.4	2238	1.6
12 TU	0422	7.5	1102	2.8	27 W	0413	8.2	1103	2.0
	1641	7.3	(2328	2.7		1636	8.3	(2329	1.8
13 W	0515	7.2	1157	2.9	28 TH	0510	8.0	1200	2.2
	1738	7.0				1736	7.9		
14 TH	0023	2.9	0616	7.1	29 F	0026	2.1	0614	7.9
	1258	3.0	1842	7.0		1305	2.2	1844	7.8
15 F	0126	2.9	0722	7.2	30 SA	0134	2.2	0725	7.8
	1402	2.8	1947	7.1		1418	2.2	1956	7.8
					31 SU	0248	2.2	0835	8.0
						1529	2.0	2105	8.0

Chart Datum: 4·45 metres below IGN Datum

TIDES

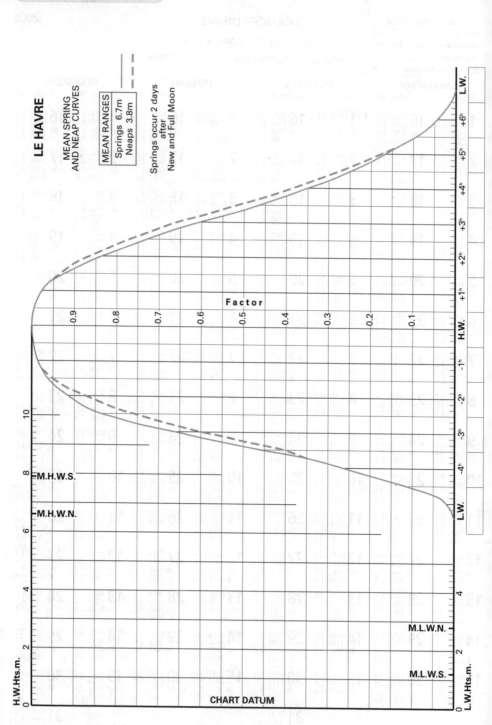

LE HAVRE

MEAN SPRING
AND NEAP CURVES

MEAN RANGES
Springs 6.7m
Neaps 3.8m

Springs occur 2 days
after
New and Full Moon

Factor

0.9 0.8 0.7 0.6 0.5 0.4 0.3 0.2 0.1

L.W.

+6ʰ +5ʰ +4ʰ +3ʰ +2ʰ +1ʰ H.W. -1ʰ -2ʰ -3ʰ -4ʰ L.W.

10

M.H.W.S.
M.H.W.N.

8
6
4
2

M.L.W.N.
M.L.W.S.

H.W.Hts.m.

CHART DATUM

L.W.Hts.m.

FRANCE – LE HAVRE

2006

LAT 49°29′N   LONG 0°07′E

TIMES AND HEIGHTS OF HIGH AND LOW WATERS

JANUARY

Time	m	Time	m
1 SU	0609 1.6 / 1122 7.9 / 1838 1.2 / 2354 7.7	**16** M	0640 1.9 / 1156 7.6 / 1903 1.6
2 M	0700 1.5 / 1209 7.9 / 1928 1.1	**17** TU	0023 7.4 / 0715 1.9 / 1229 7.5 / 1936 1.7
3 TU	0043 7.8 / 0750 1.5 / 1258 7.9 / 2017 1.2	**18** W	0055 7.4 / 0748 2.0 / 1301 7.5 / 2006 1.8
4 W	0132 7.7 / 0838 1.6 / 1347 7.7 / 2103 1.3	**19** TH	0127 7.3 / 0817 2.1 / 1332 7.4 / 2034 2.0
5 TH	0222 7.5 / 0923 1.8 / 1437 7.6 / 2147 1.6	**20** F	0158 7.2 / 0846 2.3 / 1403 7.2 / 2102 2.2
6 F	0313 7.3 / 1009 2.1 / 1529 7.3 / ◑ 2232 1.9	**21** SA	0230 7.0 / 0916 2.5 / 1438 7.0 / 2133 2.4
7 SA	0407 7.1 / 1059 2.4 / 1628 7.1 / 2323 2.3	**22** SU	0307 6.9 / 0952 2.7 / 1519 6.8 / ◑ 2212 2.7
8 SU	0508 6.9 / 1156 2.6 / 1734 6.8	**23** M	0352 6.7 / 1039 3.0 / 1611 6.5 / 2304 3.0
9 M	0024 2.6 / 0616 6.8 / 1307 2.8 / 1850 6.7	**24** TU	0452 6.5 / 1139 3.2 / 1722 6.4
10 TU	0138 2.8 / 0730 6.9 / 1422 2.7 / 2005 6.8	**25** W	0012 3.2 / 0615 6.5 / 1257 3.2 / 1855 6.4
11 W	0249 2.7 / 0832 7.0 / 1527 2.5 / 2106 7.0	**26** TH	0142 3.1 / 0734 6.6 / 1428 2.8 / 2012 6.6
12 TH	0349 2.6 / 0925 7.2 / 1622 2.2 / 2156 7.2	**27** F	0305 2.7 / 0839 7.0 / 1540 2.3 / 2115 7.0
13 F	0439 2.4 / 1009 7.3 / 1708 2.0 / 2239 7.3	**28** SA	0410 2.2 / 0935 7.4 / 1642 1.8 / 2209 7.4
14 SA	0523 2.2 / 1050 7.5 / 1749 1.8 / ○ 2316 7.4	**29** SU	0510 1.8 / 1025 7.7 / 1741 1.3 / ● 2258 7.7
15 SU	0603 2.0 / 1123 7.5 / 1827 1.7 / 2350 7.5	**30** M	0607 1.4 / 1114 8.0 / 1836 0.9 / 2346 7.9
		31 TU	0658 1.1 / 1200 8.1 / 1924 0.7

FEBRUARY

Time	m	Time	m
1 W	0032 8.0 / 0745 1.0 / 1246 8.2 / 2008 0.6	**16** TH	0028 7.6 / 0726 1.6 / 1236 7.7 / 1942 1.5
2 TH	0116 8.0 / 0826 1.0 / 1331 8.1 / 2048 0.8	**17** F	0058 7.5 / 0752 1.7 / 1304 7.6 / 2007 1.6
3 F	0200 7.8 / 0905 1.3 / 1414 7.8 / 2124 1.3	**18** SA	0126 7.4 / 0818 1.8 / 1333 7.5 / 2033 1.8
4 SA	0242 7.5 / 0942 1.7 / 1457 7.5 / 2200 1.8	**19** SU	0154 7.3 / 0846 2.1 / 1404 7.2 / 2059 2.2
5 SU	0325 7.2 / 1021 2.2 / 1546 7.0 / ◑ 2239 2.4	**20** M	0225 7.1 / 0916 2.4 / 1438 7.0 / 2130 2.5
6 M	0416 6.8 / 1109 2.7 / 1649 6.6 / 2332 3.0	**21** TU	0302 6.8 / 0954 2.7 / 1524 6.6 / 2214 3.0
7 TU	0526 6.5 / 1218 3.1 / 1818 6.3	**22** W	0355 6.5 / 1050 3.1 / 1634 6.3 / 2323 3.3
8 W	0052 3.3 / 0703 6.4 / 1350 3.1 / 1953 6.4	**23** TH	0524 6.3 / 1213 3.2 / 1825 6.2
9 TH	0224 3.2 / 0820 6.6 / 1510 2.8 / 2059 6.6	**24** F	0108 3.3 / 0709 6.4 / 1403 2.9 / 1957 6.5
10 F	0339 2.9 / 0916 6.8 / 1616 2.4 / 2147 6.9	**25** SA	0247 2.8 / 0824 6.8 / 1524 2.3 / 2104 7.0
11 SA	0436 2.5 / 0958 7.1 / 1703 2.1 / 2226 7.2	**26** SU	0358 2.2 / 0923 7.3 / 1632 1.6 / 2157 7.5
12 SU	0518 2.1 / 1034 7.4 / 1741 1.8 / 2258 7.4	**27** M	0502 1.6 / 1013 7.8 / 1732 1.0 / 2244 7.9
13 M	0554 1.9 / 1105 7.5 / 1815 1.5 / ○ 2328 7.5	**28** TU	0557 1.1 / 1059 8.1 / 1824 0.6 / ● 2328 8.1
14 TU	0628 1.7 / 1135 7.6 / 1847 1.5 / 2358 7.6		
15 W	0658 1.6 / 1206 7.7 / 1916 1.4		

MARCH

Time	m	Time	m
1 W	0645 0.7 / 1143 8.3 / 1908 0.4	**16** TH	0633 1.4 / 1139 7.7 / 1848 1.3 / 2358 7.7
2 TH	0011 8.2 / 0727 0.6 / 1226 8.3 / 1948 0.4	**17** F	0659 1.4 / 1208 7.7 / 1914 1.3
3 F	0053 8.1 / 0805 0.8 / 1308 8.2 / 2023 0.7	**18** SA	0027 7.7 / 0725 1.5 / 1238 7.7 / 1940 1.5
4 SA	0132 7.9 / 0840 1.1 / 1348 7.9 / 2055 1.2	**19** SU	0055 7.6 / 0753 1.6 / 1307 7.5 / 2006 1.7
5 SU	0209 7.6 / 0912 1.6 / 1428 7.4 / 2126 1.9	**20** M	0124 7.4 / 0821 1.8 / 1339 7.3 / 2033 2.1
6 M	0246 7.2 / 0945 2.2 / 1511 6.9 / ◑ 2159 2.6	**21** TU	0154 7.2 / 0851 2.2 / 1414 7.0 / 2102 2.5
7 TU	0331 6.7 / 1027 2.8 / 1611 6.4 / 2247 3.2	**22** W	0230 6.9 / 0928 2.6 / 1502 6.5 / ◑ 2147 3.0
8 W	0439 6.3 / 1134 3.3 / 1751 6.0	**23** TH	0327 6.5 / 1024 3.0 / 1618 6.2 / 2259 3.3
9 TH	0011 3.6 / 0635 6.1 / 1317 3.4 / 1937 6.1	**24** F	0504 6.2 / 1152 3.2 / 1815 6.2
10 F	0203 3.5 / 0803 6.3 / 1452 3.0 / 2044 6.5	**25** SA	0055 3.3 / 0653 6.4 / 1347 2.8 / 1943 6.6
11 SA	0327 3.0 / 0858 6.6 / 1558 2.5 / 2128 6.9	**26** SU	0232 2.7 / 0807 6.9 / 1507 2.1 / 2053 7.2
12 SU	0420 2.4 / 0937 7.0 / 1642 2.0 / 2202 7.2	**27** M	0342 2.0 / 0904 7.4 / 1613 1.5 / 2139 7.6
13 M	0458 2.0 / 1009 7.3 / 1718 1.7 / 2231 7.4	**28** TU	0444 1.4 / 0952 7.8 / 1711 0.9 / 2221 7.9
14 TU	0533 1.7 / 1039 7.5 / 1751 1.4 / ○ 2259 7.6	**29** W	0536 0.9 / 1037 8.1 / 1800 0.6 / ● 2304 8.1
15 W	0604 1.5 / 1108 7.7 / 1821 1.3 / 2329 7.6	**30** TH	0622 0.7 / 1120 8.2 / 1843 0.5 / 2345 8.2
		31 F	0702 0.6 / 1203 8.2 / 1920 0.6

APRIL

Time	m	Time	m
1 SA	0025 8.1 / 0739 0.8 / 1244 8.1 / 1955 1.0	**16** SU	0700 1.4 / 1214 7.6 / 1914 1.5
2 SU	0103 7.9 / 0812 1.1 / 1323 7.7 / 2025 1.5	**17** M	0029 7.6 / 0732 1.5 / 1249 7.4 / 1945 1.8
3 M	0139 7.5 / 0843 1.6 / 1403 7.3 / 2054 2.1	**18** TU	0103 7.4 / 0804 1.7 / 1327 7.2 / 2016 2.1
4 TU	0216 7.1 / 0915 2.2 / 1446 6.8 / 2126 2.7	**19** W	0140 7.2 / 0838 2.0 / 1410 6.9 / 2052 2.5
5 W	0259 6.7 / 0955 2.8 / 1546 6.3 / ◑ 2216 3.3	**20** TH	0225 6.8 / 0919 2.4 / 1504 6.6 / 2142 2.9
6 TH	0406 6.2 / 1101 3.3 / 1721 6.0 / 2342 3.7	**21** F	0326 6.5 / 1018 2.8 / 1622 6.3 / ◑ 2259 3.2
7 F	0551 6.0 / 1239 3.3 / 1900 6.1	**22** SA	0500 6.4 / 1149 2.9 / 1804 6.4
8 SA	0125 3.5 / 0724 6.1 / 1404 3.0 / 2009 6.4	**23** SU	0046 3.0 / 0632 6.6 / 1327 2.5 / 1920 6.8
9 SU	0241 3.0 / 0823 6.5 / 1508 2.5 / 2053 6.8	**24** M	0208 2.5 / 0741 7.0 / 1440 2.2 / 2026 7.3
10 M	0336 2.5 / 0902 6.9 / 1558 2.1 / 2126 7.1	**25** TU	0315 1.9 / 0838 7.4 / 1544 1.5 / 2111 7.6
11 TU	0419 2.0 / 0937 7.2 / 1640 1.8 / 2156 7.4	**26** W	0415 1.4 / 0927 7.7 / 1641 1.1 / 2155 7.9
12 W	0457 1.7 / 1006 7.4 / 1716 1.5 / 2226 7.6	**27** TH	0508 1.1 / 1013 7.9 / 1730 0.9 / ● 2238 8.0
13 TH	0531 1.6 / 1038 7.6 / 1748 1.4 / ○ 2257 7.6	**28** F	0554 0.9 / 1057 8.0 / 1813 0.9 / 2319 8.0
14 F	0601 1.5 / 1110 7.7 / 1816 1.4 / 2328 7.7	**29** SA	0635 0.9 / 1140 8.0 / 1851 1.1 / 2359 7.9
15 SA	0630 1.4 / 1142 7.7 / 1844 1.4 / 2358 7.7	**30** SU	0712 1.0 / 1222 7.8 / 1926 1.3

Chart Datum: 4·38 metres below IGN Datum

TIDES

TIME ZONE -0100
(French Standard Time)
Subtract 1 hour for UT
For French Summer Time add
ONE hour in **non-shaded areas**

FRANCE – LE HAVRE 2006

LAT 49°29'N   LONG 0°07'E

TIMES AND HEIGHTS OF HIGH AND LOW WATERS

MAY

Day	Time	m		Day	Time	m
1 M	0037 / 0746 / 1304 / 1958	7.7 / 1.3 / 7.5 / 1.8		**16** TU	0010 / 0716 / 1237 / 1931	7.6 / 1.5 / 7.4 / 1.8
2 TU	0115 / 0820 / 1345 / 2030	7.4 / 1.7 / 7.2 / 2.2		**17** W	0050 / 0754 / 1321 / 2009	7.4 / 1.6 / 7.2 / 2.1
3 W	0154 / 0853 / 1430 / 2106	7.1 / 2.2 / 6.8 / 2.7		**18** TH	0135 / 0835 / 1409 / 2053	7.3 / 1.9 / 7.0 / 2.4
4 TH	0239 / 0935 / 1526 / 2156	6.7 / 2.7 / 6.4 / 3.2		**19** F	0226 / 0922 / 1507 / 2150	7.0 / 2.2 / 6.8 / 2.7
5 F	0338 / 1035 / 1641 / (2311	6.3 / 3.2 / 6.1 / 3.4		**20** SA	0328 / 1024 / 1620 /) 2304	6.8 / 2.4 / 6.7 / 2.8
6 SA	0501 / 1153 / 1801	6.1 / 3.2 / 6.2		**21** SU	0447 / 1141 / 1740	6.7 / 2.4 / 6.8
7 SU	0033 / 0625 / 1306 / 1908	3.4 / 6.2 / 3.0 / 6.4		**22** M	0024 / 0603 / 1257 / 1847	2.6 / 6.8 / 2.2 / 7.0
8 M	0141 / 0729 / 1408 / 2000	3.0 / 6.4 / 2.7 / 6.7		**23** TU	0136 / 0709 / 1406 / 1947	2.3 / 7.1 / 2.0 / 7.3
9 TU	0238 / 0818 / 1502 / 2040	2.6 / 6.7 / 2.3 / 7.0		**24** W	0241 / 0808 / 1509 / 2041	2.0 / 7.3 / 1.7 / 7.5
10 W	0328 / 0855 / 1550 / 2116	2.3 / 7.0 / 2.0 / 7.3		**25** TH	0342 / 0902 / 1606 / 2129	1.7 / 7.5 / 1.5 / 7.7
11 TH	0413 / 0930 / 1632 / 2150	2.0 / 7.2 / 1.8 / 7.5		**26** F	0437 / 0952 / 1658 / 2214	1.5 / 7.6 / 1.5 / 7.7
12 F	0451 / 1006 / 1708 / 2224	1.8 / 7.4 / 1.7 / 7.5		**27** SA	0525 / 1039 / 1743 / ● 2257	1.3 / 7.7 / 1.5 / 7.7
13 SA	0527 / 1042 / 1743 / ○ 2258	1.6 / 7.5 / 1.6 / 7.6		**28** SU	0608 / 1124 / 1823 / 2338	1.3 / 7.7 / 1.5 / 7.7
14 SU	0602 / 1118 / 1818 / 2333	1.5 / 7.5 / 1.6 / 7.6		**29** M	0648 / 1207 / 1901	1.4 / 7.6 / 1.7
15 M	0638 / 1156 / 1854	1.4 / 7.5 / 1.7		**30** TU	0018 / 0725 / 1249 / 1937	7.6 / 1.5 / 7.4 / 2.0
				31 W	0058 / 0801 / 1331 / 2014	7.4 / 1.8 / 7.2 / 2.3

JUNE

Day	Time	m		Day	Time	m
1 TH	0138 / 0838 / 1414 / 2053	7.1 / 2.1 / 6.9 / 2.6		**16** F	0132 / 0841 / 1408 / 2103	7.5 / 1.5 / 7.3 / 2.0
2 F	0220 / 0918 / 1500 / 2137	6.8 / 2.4 / 6.6 / 2.9		**17** SA	0223 / 0930 / 1502 / 2155	7.3 / 1.7 / 7.2 / 2.2
3 SA	0308 / 1005 / 1554 / ○ 2231	6.6 / 2.7 / 6.5 / 3.1		**18** SU	0319 / 1023 / 1602 /) 2252	7.2 / 1.9 / 7.1 / 2.3
4 SU	0405 / 1100 / 1656 / 2331	6.3 / 2.9 / 6.4 / 3.1		**19** M	0422 / 1120 / 1706 / 2353	7.0 / 2.1 / 7.0 / 2.4
5 M	0512 / 1159 / 1758	6.3 / 2.9 / 6.5		**20** TU	0529 / 1222 / 1810	7.0 / 2.2 / 7.0
6 TU	0032 / 0616 / 1259 / 1856	3.1 / 6.4 / 2.8 / 6.6		**21** W	0100 / 0636 / 1329 / 1914	2.3 / 7.0 / 2.2 / 7.1
7 W	0131 / 0714 / 1358 / 1947	2.9 / 6.5 / 2.7 / 6.8		**22** TH	0208 / 0742 / 1435 / 2016	2.2 / 7.1 / 2.2 / 7.2
8 TH	0229 / 0806 / 1454 / 2032	2.6 / 6.7 / 2.4 / 7.0		**23** F	0312 / 0845 / 1536 / 2111	2.1 / 7.2 / 2.1 / 7.4
9 F	0322 / 0853 / 1544 / 2114	2.3 / 7.0 / 2.2 / 7.2		**24** SA	0410 / 0940 / 1630 / 2200	1.9 / 7.3 / 2.0 / 7.5
10 SA	0410 / 0936 / 1631 / 2155	2.1 / 7.1 / 2.0 / 7.4		**25** SU	0501 / 1029 / 1718 / ● 2244	1.7 / 7.4 / 1.9 / 7.5
11 SU	0455 / 1019 / 1714 / ○ 2234	1.8 / 7.3 / 1.9 / 7.5		**26** M	0547 / 1114 / 1802 / 2325	1.6 / 7.5 / 1.9 / 7.5
12 M	0539 / 1101 / 1758 / 2315	1.6 / 7.4 / 1.8 / 7.6		**27** TU	0629 / 1156 / 1843	1.6 / 7.4 / 1.9
13 TU	0624 / 1144 / 1842 / 2358	1.5 / 7.5 / 1.7 / 7.6		**28** W	0004 / 0709 / 1235 / 1922	7.5 / 1.6 / 7.4 / 2.0
14 W	0708 / 1230 / 1928	1.4 / 7.5 / 1.7		**29** TH	0042 / 0746 / 1313 / 2000	7.4 / 1.7 / 7.3 / 2.1
15 TH	0044 / 0754 / 1317 / 2014	7.6 / 1.4 / 7.4 / 1.8		**30** F	0119 / 0822 / 1350 / 2035	7.3 / 1.9 / 7.1 / 2.2

JULY

Day	Time	m		Day	Time	m
1 SA	0156 / 0856 / 1427 / 2110	7.1 / 2.1 / 7.0 / 2.5		**16** SU	0211 / 0923 / 1444 / 2143	7.7 / 1.3 / 7.5 / 1.7
2 SU	0232 / 0929 / 1505 / 2146	6.9 / 2.3 / 6.8 / 2.7		**17** M	0259 / 1004 / 1532 /) 2227	7.5 / 1.6 / 7.3 / 2.0
3 M	0311 / 1005 / 1547 / ○ 2227	6.7 / 2.6 / 6.7 / 2.9		**18** TU	0351 / 1049 / 1626 / 2318	7.2 / 2.0 / 7.1 / 2.3
4 TU	0357 / 1049 / 1638 / 2317	6.6 / 2.8 / 6.6 / 3.0		**19** W	0452 / 1143 / 1730	6.9 / 2.4 / 6.9
5 W	0454 / 1142 / 1741	6.4 / 2.9 / 6.5		**20** TH	0022 / 0605 / 1251 / 1844	2.6 / 6.7 / 2.7 / 6.8
6 TH	0016 / 0604 / 1246 / 1847	3.1 / 6.4 / 3.0 / 6.6		**21** F	0139 / 0726 / 1408 / 2001	2.6 / 6.7 / 2.7 / 6.9
7 F	0124 / 0715 / 1358 / 1948	3.0 / 6.5 / 2.9 / 6.7		**22** SA	0250 / 0839 / 1516 / 2102	2.5 / 6.9 / 2.6 / 7.1
8 SA	0235 / 0818 / 1505 / 2042	2.7 / 6.7 / 2.6 / 7.0		**23** SU	0353 / 0936 / 1615 / 2152	2.2 / 7.1 / 2.4 / 7.3
9 SU	0337 / 0912 / 1602 / 2131	2.3 / 6.9 / 2.3 / 7.2		**24** M	0450 / 1023 / 1708 / 2235	2.0 / 7.3 / 2.2 / 7.4
10 M	0431 / 1002 / 1655 / 2218	2.0 / 7.2 / 2.0 / 7.5		**25** TU	0538 / 1104 / 1752 / ● 2313	1.8 / 7.4 / 2.0 / 7.5
11 TU	0524 / 1050 / 1748 / ○ 2304	1.6 / 7.4 / 1.8 / 7.6		**26** W	0618 / 1140 / 1831 / 2347	1.6 / 7.5 / 1.9 / 7.6
12 W	0617 / 1136 / 1840 / 2350	1.3 / 7.6 / 1.6 / 7.8		**27** TH	0655 / 1214 / 1907	1.5 / 7.5 / 1.8
13 TH	0708 / 1223 / 1929	1.1 / 7.7 / 1.4		**28** F	0020 / 0728 / 1247 / 1940	7.6 / 1.5 / 7.5 / 1.8
14 F	0037 / 0756 / 1310 / 2016	7.8 / 1.0 / 7.7 / 1.4		**29** SA	0053 / 0758 / 1319 / 2010	7.5 / 1.6 / 7.4 / 1.9
15 SA	0124 / 0841 / 1357 / 2100	7.8 / 1.1 / 7.6 / 1.5		**30** SU	0125 / 0826 / 1350 / 2037	7.4 / 1.8 / 7.3 / 2.1
				31 M	0155 / 0851 / 1420 / 2104	7.2 / 2.0 / 7.1 / 2.3

AUGUST

Day	Time	m		Day	Time	m
1 TU	0226 / 0918 / 1452 / 2136	7.1 / 2.3 / 6.9 / 2.6		**16** W	0319 / 1015 / 1547 /) 2244	7.2 / 2.1 / 7.0 / 2.5
2 W	0302 / 0952 / 1531 / ○ 2216	6.8 / 2.6 / 6.7 / 2.9		**17** TH	0418 / 1105 / 1651 / 2348	6.8 / 2.7 / 6.7 / 2.9
3 TH	0349 / 1037 / 1624 / 2311	6.5 / 3.0 / 6.5 / 3.1		**18** F	0542 / 1219 / 1822	6.4 / 3.2 / 6.5
4 F	0453 / 1140 / 1741	6.3 / 3.3 / 6.4		**19** SA	0118 / 0723 / 1353 / 1954	3.0 / 6.4 / 3.2 / 6.6
5 SA	0025 / 0626 / 1309 / 1909	3.2 / 6.2 / 3.3 / 6.4		**20** SU	0241 / 0837 / 1512 / 2056	2.8 / 6.7 / 2.9 / 6.9
6 SU	0159 / 0752 / 1438 / 2019	3.0 / 6.4 / 2.9 / 6.8		**21** M	0352 / 0930 / 1618 / 2142	2.3 / 7.0 / 2.5 / 7.2
7 M	0314 / 0856 / 1544 / 2115	2.5 / 6.8 / 2.4 / 7.2		**22** TU	0448 / 1011 / 1705 / 2219	2.0 / 7.3 / 2.1 / 7.4
8 TU	0415 / 0950 / 1644 / 2205	1.9 / 7.2 / 2.0 / 7.5		**23** W	0528 / 1045 / 1741 / ● 2253	1.7 / 7.5 / 1.9 / 7.6
9 W	0514 / 1037 / 1741 / ○ 2251	1.5 / 7.6 / 1.6 / 7.8		**24** TH	0602 / 1116 / 1814 / 2323	1.5 / 7.6 / 1.7 / 7.7
10 TH	0610 / 1123 / 1834 / 2337	1.1 / 7.8 / 1.2 / 8.0		**25** F	0633 / 1146 / 1845 / 2353	1.4 / 7.6 / 1.6 / 7.7
11 F	0659 / 1208 / 1920	0.8 / 8.0 / 1.0		**26** SA	0702 / 1215 / 1913	1.4 / 7.6 / 1.6
12 SA	0022 / 0744 / 1252 / 2002	8.1 / 0.6 / 8.0 / 1.0		**27** SU	0023 / 0729 / 1245 / 1939	7.7 / 1.5 / 7.5 / 1.7
13 SU	0106 / 0824 / 1335 / 2042	8.1 / 0.7 / 7.9 / 1.1		**28** M	0052 / 0753 / 1313 / 2004	7.6 / 1.7 / 7.5 / 1.9
14 M	0149 / 0901 / 1417 / 2119	7.9 / 1.1 / 7.7 / 1.5		**29** TU	0119 / 0817 / 1340 / 2030	7.4 / 1.9 / 7.3 / 2.1
15 TU	0233 / 0937 / 1459 / 2158	7.6 / 1.5 / 7.4 / 2.0		**30** W	0148 / 0842 / 1409 / 2059	7.2 / 2.2 / 7.1 / 2.4
				31 TH	0221 / 0911 / 1444 /) 2134	7.0 / 2.6 / 6.8 / 2.8

Chart Datum: 4·38 metres below IGN Datum

FRANCE – LE HAVRE

LAT 49°29′N   LONG 0°07′E

TIMES AND HEIGHTS OF HIGH AND LOW WATERS

2006

SEPTEMBER

	Time	m		Time	m
1 F	0305 0951 1533 2224	6.5 3.0 6.5 3.2	**16** SA	0529 1154 1807	6.2 3.6 6.2
2 SA	0410 1052 1653 2341	6.2 3.4 6.2 3.4	**17** SU	0101 1218 1344 1941	3.3 3.6 3.4 6.4
3 SU	0556 1233 1843	6.1 3.5 6.3	**18** M	0231 0825 1505 2040	2.9 6.6 2.9 6.8
4 M	0136 0735 1421 2001	3.2 6.4 3.1 6.7	**19** TU	0337 0912 1601 2122	2.4 7.0 2.4 7.1
5 TU	0258 0841 1530 2059	2.5 6.9 2.4 7.2	**20** W	0423 0947 1641 2155	2.0 7.3 2.0 7.4
6 W	0401 0933 1610 2148	1.8 7.4 1.8 7.7	**21** TH	0500 1017 1715 2226	1.7 7.5 1.6 7.6
7 TH ○	0500 1018 1726 2233	1.2 7.8 1.3 8.0	**22** F	0532 1045 1746 2253	1.5 7.7 1.6 7.8
8 F	0553 1102 1816 2317	0.8 8.0 0.9 8.2	**23** SA	0603 1113 1816 2322	1.4 7.7 1.6 7.8
9 SA	0640 1145 1900	0.6 8.2 0.8	**24** SU	0631 1142 1843 2352	1.4 7.7 1.6 7.7
10 SU	0000 0721 1227 1940	8.3 0.5 8.2 0.8	**25** M	0656 1210 1908	1.5 7.7 1.7
11 M	0043 0759 1308 2017	8.2 0.7 8.0 1.1	**26** TU	0020 0721 1237 1935	7.6 1.7 7.6 1.8
12 TU	0125 0834 1347 2053	8.0 1.2 7.7 1.5	**27** W	0048 0747 1305 2002	7.5 1.9 7.4 2.0
13 W	0207 0907 1427 2128	7.6 1.8 7.4 2.1	**28** TH	0119 0813 1334 2032	7.2 2.3 7.2 2.4
14 TH ◑	0252 0943 1512 2211	7.1 2.5 6.9 2.7	**29** F	0154 0842 1410 2106	6.9 2.7 6.9 2.7
15 F	0351 1031 1618 2317	6.5 3.1 6.4 3.2	**30** SA ◐	0241 0923 1504 2156	6.5 3.1 6.4 3.1

OCTOBER

	Time	m		Time	m
1 SU	0351 1027 1630 2316	6.2 3.5 6.2 3.4	**16** M	0030 0643 1313 1906	3.3 6.2 3.5 6.3
2 M	0543 1218 1823	6.1 3.6 6.3	**17** TU	0151 0753 1424 2007	3.0 6.6 3.0 6.7
3 TU	0117 0715 1403 1938	3.1 6.5 3.0 6.8	**18** W	0251 0838 1516 2048	2.6 7.0 2.5 7.0
4 W	0237 0818 1509 2035	2.4 7.1 2.2 7.4	**19** TH	0338 0912 1559 2121	2.2 7.3 2.1 7.3
5 TH	0338 0908 1608 2123	1.7 7.6 1.6 7.8	**20** F	0419 0941 1637 2152	1.9 7.5 1.9 7.5
6 F	0435 0953 1701 2208	1.2 7.9 1.2 8.1	**21** SA	0456 1010 1712 2222	1.7 7.7 1.7 7.7
7 SA ○	0526 1035 1750 2252	0.8 8.2 0.8 8.3	**22** SU ●	0528 1039 1743 2252	1.6 7.7 1.7 7.7
8 SU	0612 1118 1834 2336	0.7 8.2 0.8 8.3	**23** M	0557 1109 1812 2323	1.6 7.7 1.7 7.7
9 M	0654 1159 1914	0.7 8.2 0.9	**24** TU	0625 1138 1840 2354	1.7 7.7 1.7 7.6
10 TU	0019 0732 1240 1951	8.2 1.0 8.0 1.2	**25** W	0654 1208 1911	1.8 7.6 1.8
11 W	0101 0806 1319 2027	7.9 1.5 7.7 1.6	**26** TH	0027 0724 1240 1943	7.4 2.0 7.5 2.0
12 TH	0144 0840 1359 2102	7.4 2.1 7.3 2.2	**27** F	0103 0755 1316 2016	7.2 2.4 7.2 2.3
13 F	0231 0915 1445 2145	6.9 2.7 6.8 2.8	**28** SA	0145 0829 1400 2054	6.9 2.7 6.9 2.6
14 SA ◑	0332 1005 1552 2251	6.4 3.3 6.4 3.3	**29** SU ◐	0237 0914 1457 2147	6.6 3.1 6.6 2.9
15 SU	0506 1131 1734	6.2 3.7 6.1	**30** M	0346 1021 1618 2307	6.4 3.4 6.4 3.1
			31 TU	0526 1204 1756	6.4 3.3 6.5

NOVEMBER

	Time	m		Time	m
1 W	0050 0646 1333 1907	2.8 6.8 2.8 6.9	**16** TH	0151 0744 1421 2000	2.8 6.8 2.8 6.8
2 TH	0206 0747 1440 2005	2.3 7.2 2.2 7.4	**17** F	0246 0825 1512 2043	2.5 7.1 2.5 7.1
3 F	0308 0838 1539 2056	1.7 7.6 1.7 7.8	**18** SA	0333 0900 1556 2116	2.2 7.3 2.2 7.3
4 SA	0405 0925 1633 2144	1.3 8.0 1.3 8.0	**19** SU	0415 0934 1635 2151	2.1 7.5 2.0 7.4
5 SU ○	0457 1009 1723 2230	1.1 8.1 1.1 8.1	**20** M ●	0452 1008 1711 2226	2.0 7.6 1.9 7.5
6 M	0543 1052 1808 2315	1.0 8.1 1.0 8.1	**21** TU	0526 1041 1744 2301	1.9 7.6 1.8 7.5
7 TU	0626 1134 1849	1.1 8.0 1.1	**22** W	0559 1114 1819 2336	1.9 7.7 1.7 7.5
8 W	0000 0705 1216 1928	8.0 1.4 7.9 1.4	**23** TH	0633 1148 1855	1.9 7.6 1.7
9 TH	0044 0742 1257 2005	7.7 1.8 7.6 1.7	**24** F	0014 0710 1226 1932	7.4 2.1 7.5 1.9
10 F	0129 0818 1339 2043	7.4 2.3 7.3 2.2	**25** SA	0056 0747 1309 2011	7.3 2.3 7.3 2.1
11 SA	0216 0857 1426 2126	7.0 2.8 6.9 2.7	**26** SU	0142 0829 1357 2055	7.1 2.5 7.1 2.3
12 SU ◑	0312 0947 1525 2224	6.6 3.2 6.6 3.1	**27** M	0234 0918 1452 2149	6.9 2.8 6.9 2.5
13 M	0424 1056 1643 2337	6.3 3.5 6.3 3.2	**28** TU	0338 1023 1601 2257	6.8 2.9 6.9 2.6
14 TU	0541 1215 1806	6.3 3.5 6.3	**29** W	0455 1138 1720	6.8 2.9 6.8
15 W	0049 0650 1323 1909	3.1 6.5 3.2 6.5	**30** TH	0013 0607 1253 1830	2.6 6.9 2.7 7.0

DECEMBER

	Time	m		Time	m
1 F	0125 0710 1403 1932	2.3 7.2 2.3 7.3	**16** SA	0138 0729 1412 1951	3.0 6.7 3.0 6.6
2 SA	0233 0806 1507 2030	2.0 7.5 2.0 7.5	**17** SU	0240 0817 1510 2040	2.8 7.1 2.7 6.9
3 SU	0333 0858 1605 2124	1.8 7.7 1.7 7.7	**18** M	0333 0900 1558 2124	2.6 7.2 2.4 7.1
4 M	0428 0947 1658 2214	1.6 7.9 1.5 7.8	**19** TU	0418 0940 1642 2205	2.3 7.4 2.1 7.3
5 TU ○	0518 1033 1745 2302	1.5 7.9 1.4 7.8	**20** W ●	0500 1019 1723 2245	2.1 7.5 1.9 7.4
6 W	0603 1117 1829 2348	1.6 7.9 1.4 7.8	**21** TH	0541 1058 1805 2326	2.0 7.6 1.7 7.5
7 TH	0644 1200 1910	1.7 7.8 1.5	**22** F	0623 1138 1848	1.9 7.7 1.6
8 F	0032 0724 1242 1949	7.6 1.9 7.6 1.7	**23** SA	0008 0707 1220 1932	7.5 1.9 7.7 1.5
9 SA	0115 0803 1324 2028	7.4 2.2 7.4 2.0	**24** SU	0051 0751 1305 2016	7.5 1.9 7.6 1.6
10 SU	0158 0843 1406 2107	7.1 2.5 7.1 2.3	**25** M	0138 0836 1352 2100	7.4 2.0 7.5 1.8
11 M	0243 0925 1451 2150	6.9 2.7 6.8 2.7	**26** TU	0226 0925 1441 2146	7.3 2.2 7.3 2.0
12 TU ◑	0333 1012 1544 2238	6.7 3.1 6.5 2.9	**27** W ◑	0319 1011 1537 2237	7.2 2.4 7.2 2.2
13 W	0431 1105 1646 2333	6.5 3.2 6.4 3.1	**28** TH	0418 1107 1640 2334	7.0 2.5 7.0 2.4
14 TH	0533 1204 1751	6.5 3.3 6.4	**29** F	0524 1211 1751	7.0 2.6 6.9
15 F	0033 0634 1307 1854	3.1 6.6 3.2 6.5	**30** SA	0041 0632 1325 1903	2.5 7.0 2.6 7.0
			31 SU	0157 0739 1440 2013	2.5 7.0 2.4 7.1

Chart Datum: 4·38 metres below IGN Datum

TIDES

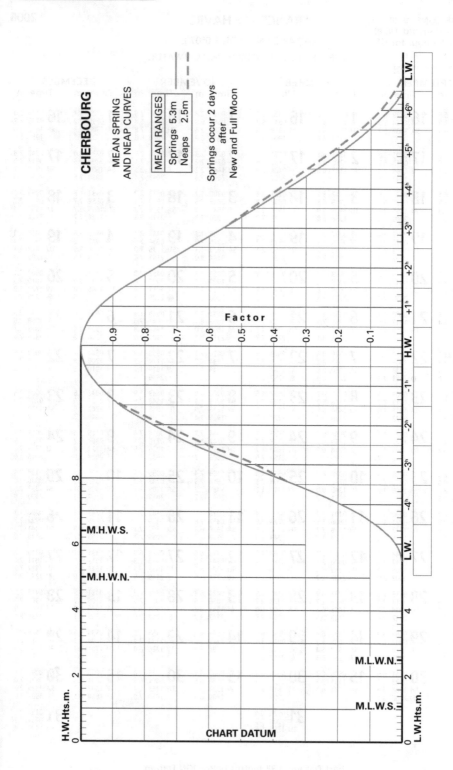

<table>
<tr><td colspan="3">

TIME ZONE -0100
(French Standard Time)
Subtract 1 hour for UT
For French Summer Time add
ONE hour in **non-shaded areas**

</td><td colspan="3">

FRANCE – CHERBOURG

LAT 49°39′N   LONG 1°38′W

TIMES AND HEIGHTS OF HIGH AND LOW WATERS

</td><td>**2006**</td></tr>
</table>

JANUARY		FEBRUARY		MARCH		APRIL	
Time m	Time m	Time m	Time m	Time m	Time m	Time m	Time m
1 0353 1.4 / 0926 6.4 / SU 1619 1.1 / 2157 6.2	**16** 0430 1.8 / 1000 6.1 / M 1652 1.5 / 2226 5.9	**1** 0519 0.9 / 1053 6.8 / W 1742 0.6 / 2321 6.5	**16** 0512 1.5 / 1041 6.2 / TH 1729 1.3 / 2301 5.9	**1** 0418 0.7 / 0953 6.9 / W 1640 0.3 / 2218 6.7	**16** 0417 1.3 / 0948 6.2 / TH 1632 1.1 / 2205 6.1	**1** 0515 0.7 / 1050 6.6 / SA 1731 0.8 / 2306 6.4	**16** 0446 1.2 / 1017 6.1 / SU 1659 1.3 / 2232 6.1
2 0441 1.4 / 1013 6.5 / M 1707 1.0 / 2245 6.3	**17** 0503 1.7 / 1033 6.0 / TU 1724 1.5 / 2258 5.8	**2** 0603 1.0 / 1137 6.8 / TH 1825 0.7	**17** 0539 1.5 / 1108 6.1 / F 1755 1.4 / 2328 5.8	**2** 0500 0.6 / 1036 6.9 / TH 1721 0.4 / 2258 6.7	**17** 0444 1.3 / 1014 6.2 / F 1659 1.2 / 2231 6.1	**2** 0552 1.0 / 1126 6.2 / SU 1806 1.3 / 2338 6.1	**17** 0517 1.3 / 1049 5.9 / M 1730 1.5 / 2303 5.9
3 0529 1.4 / 1101 6.5 / TU 1755 1.0 / 2334 6.2	**18** 0535 1.8 / 1104 6.0 / W 1755 1.6 / 2329 5.7	**3** 0003 6.3 / 0645 1.2 / F 1218 6.4 / 1907 1.1	**18** 0607 1.6 / 1135 5.9 / SA 1822 1.6 / 2354 5.7	**3** 0540 0.7 / 1115 6.8 / F 1800 0.6 / 2335 6.4	**18** 0511 1.3 / 1041 6.1 / SA 1725 1.3 / 2257 6.0	**3** 0629 1.5 / 1201 5.8 / M 1842 1.9	**18** 0550 1.5 / 1123 5.7 / TU 1804 1.8 / 2337 5.7
4 0617 1.5 / 1150 6.3 / W 1843 1.1	**19** 0606 1.9 / 1135 5.8 / TH 1825 1.7	**4** 0042 6.0 / 0728 1.6 / SA 1300 6.0 / 1949 1.6	**19** 0636 1.8 / 1202 5.6 / SU 1852 1.9	**4** 0619 1.0 / 1152 6.4 / SA 1837 1.1	**19** 0539 1.4 / 1108 6.0 / SU 1752 1.5 / 2323 5.9	**4** 0011 5.6 / 0707 2.0 / TU 1240 5.2 / 1921 2.4	**19** 0629 1.8 / 1202 5.4 / W 1845 2.2
5 0022 6.0 / 0706 1.7 / TH 1239 6.1 / 1932 1.4	**20** 0000 5.6 / 0637 2.0 / F 1206 5.6 / 1856 1.9	**5** 0123 5.6 / 0814 2.0 / SU 1345 5.5 / ☽ 2036 2.1	**20** 0022 5.5 / 0711 2.1 / M 1234 5.4 / 1927 2.2	**5** 0010 6.1 / 0657 1.4 / SU 1228 5.9 / 1914 1.7	**20** 0609 1.6 / 1135 5.7 / M 1822 1.8 / 2351 5.6	**5** 0051 5.2 / 0755 2.4 / W 1334 4.7 / ☽ 2015 2.9	**20** 0019 5.4 / 0718 2.1 / TH 1254 5.0 / 1941 2.6
6 0112 5.7 / 0758 1.9 / F 1330 5.8 / ☽ 2024 1.7	**21** 0032 5.4 / 0711 2.2 / SA 1239 5.4 / 1930 2.1	**6** 0212 5.2 / 0910 2.4 / M 1443 5.0 / 2135 2.6	**21** 0058 5.2 / 0754 2.4 / TU 1317 5.0 / 2014 2.5	**6** 0043 5.6 / 0737 2.0 / M 1308 5.4 / ☽ 1954 2.3	**21** 0643 1.9 / 1207 5.4 / TU 1858 2.2	**6** 0154 4.7 / 0907 2.8 / TH 1518 4.4 / 2150 3.2	**21** 0120 5.0 / 0825 2.4 / F 1415 4.7 / ☾ 2104 2.8
7 0205 5.5 / 0854 2.2 / SA 1426 5.5 / 2121 2.0	**22** 0108 5.2 / 0751 2.4 / SU 1319 5.2 / ☾ 2011 2.4	**7** 0321 4.9 / 1027 2.7 / TU 1611 4.7 / 2259 2.8	**22** 0152 4.9 / 0855 2.7 / W 1426 4.7 / 2128 2.8	**7** 0125 5.2 / 0826 2.5 / TU 1402 4.8 / 2048 2.8	**22** 0025 5.3 / 0727 2.2 / W 1251 5.0 / ☾ 1947 2.6	**7** 0348 4.5 / 1054 2.8 / F 1712 4.5 / 2337 3.0	**22** 0252 4.8 / 0956 2.4 / SA 1607 4.8 / 2243 2.7
8 0305 5.3 / 0958 2.4 / SU 1532 5.3 / 2227 2.3	**23** 0154 5.0 / 0841 2.6 / M 1411 5.0 / 2106 2.6	**8** 0453 4.8 / 1158 2.7 / W 1749 4.7	**23** 0321 4.7 / 1026 2.8 / TH 1622 4.6 / 2312 2.8	**8** 0230 4.7 / 0943 2.8 / W 1543 4.5 / 2223 3.1	**23** 0120 5.0 / 0829 2.6 / TH 1405 4.7 / 2104 2.9	**8** 0523 4.7 / 1217 2.6 / SA 1815 4.9	**23** 0434 5.0 / 1126 2.1 / SU 1728 5.2
9 0414 5.2 / 1110 2.5 / M 1646 5.1 / 2338 2.4	**24** 0256 4.9 / 0948 2.7 / TU 1523 4.8 / 2220 2.7	**9** 0031 2.8 / 0616 5.0 / TH 1314 2.4 / 1902 5.0	**24** 0512 4.9 / 1205 2.5 / F 1802 5.0	**9** 0424 4.6 / 1134 2.8 / TH 1744 4.6	**24** 0255 4.7 / 1004 2.7 / F 1615 4.6 / 2256 2.8	**9** 0048 2.6 / 0622 5.0 / SU 1311 2.2 / 1856 5.2	**24** 0003 2.2 / 0546 5.4 / M 1234 1.7 / 1826 5.6
10 0525 5.2 / 1222 2.4 / TU 1759 5.2	**25** 0416 4.9 / 1110 2.7 / W 1652 4.8 / 2345 2.6	**10** 0138 2.5 / 0716 5.3 / F 1409 2.1 / 1951 5.4	**25** 0046 2.4 / 0629 5.3 / SA 1319 1.9 / 1907 5.4	**10** 0017 3.0 / 0601 4.8 / F 1257 2.5 / 1851 4.9	**25** 0455 4.9 / 1147 2.4 / SA 1752 5.0	**10** 0134 2.2 / 0705 5.4 / M 1353 1.8 / 1931 5.6	**25** 0107 1.7 / 0643 5.9 / TU 1331 1.2 / 1916 6.0
11 0047 2.4 / 0629 5.4 / W 1324 2.2 / 1903 5.4	**26** 0537 5.1 / 1228 2.4 / TH 1813 5.1	**11** 0228 2.2 / 0801 5.6 / SA 1452 1.8 / 2030 5.8	**26** 0151 1.9 / 0727 5.8 / SU 1417 1.4 / 2001 5.9	**11** 0125 2.6 / 0700 5.2 / SA 1351 2.1 / 1933 5.3	**26** 0031 2.4 / 0612 5.3 / SU 1301 1.8 / 1852 5.5	**11** 0212 1.9 / 0742 5.7 / TU 1429 1.6 / 2004 5.8	**26** 0159 1.3 / 0734 6.3 / W 1421 0.9 / 2001 6.3
12 0145 2.2 / 0723 5.6 / TH 1416 2.0 / 1956 5.5	**27** 0101 2.3 / 0643 5.5 / F 1333 2.0 / 1916 5.5	**12** 0308 1.9 / 0839 5.9 / SU 1529 1.5 / 2104 5.8	**27** 0245 1.4 / 0819 6.3 / M 1509 0.9 / 2050 6.3	**12** 0211 2.2 / 0741 5.5 / SU 1431 1.8 / 2007 5.6	**27** 0133 1.8 / 0710 5.9 / M 1358 1.2 / 1942 6.0	**12** 0245 1.6 / 0816 5.9 / W 1501 1.4 / 2036 6.0	**27** 0247 1.0 / 0822 6.5 / TH 1506 0.8 / ● 2045 6.5
13 0233 2.1 / 0809 5.8 / F 1501 1.8 / 2040 5.7	**28** 0202 1.9 / 0739 5.9 / SA 1430 1.5 / 2011 5.9	**13** 0342 1.7 / 0913 6.0 / M 1602 1.4 / ○ 2136 5.9	**28** 0333 1.0 / 0908 6.7 / TU 1556 0.5 / ● 2136 6.6	**13** 0247 1.8 / 0816 5.8 / M 1506 1.5 / 2039 5.9	**28** 0225 1.3 / 0800 6.4 / TU 1447 0.8 / 2029 6.4	**13** 0315 1.4 / 0848 6.1 / TH 1531 1.3 / ○ 2106 6.1	**28** 0331 0.9 / 0906 6.6 / F 1548 0.8 / 2125 6.5
14 0316 1.9 / 0849 5.9 / SA 1541 1.6 / ○ 2118 5.8	**29** 0256 1.6 / 0830 6.2 / SU 1522 1.1 / ● 2102 6.2	**14** 0414 1.5 / 0944 6.2 / TU 1633 1.3 / 2206 6.0		**14** 0319 1.6 / 0849 6.0 / TU 1537 1.3 / ○ 2109 6.0	**29** 0312 0.9 / 0847 6.7 / W 1533 0.5 / ● 2112 6.6	**14** 0345 1.3 / 0918 6.1 / F 1600 1.2 / 2135 6.2	**29** 0412 0.8 / 0948 6.5 / SA 1627 0.9 / 2203 6.4
15 0354 1.8 / 0920 6.0 / SU 1617 1.5 / 2153 5.9	**30** 0346 1.2 / 0920 6.5 / M 1611 0.8 / 2151 6.4	**15** 0444 1.5 / 1013 6.2 / W 1702 1.2 / 2234 6.0		**15** 0349 1.4 / 0919 6.2 / W 1605 1.2 / 2138 6.1	**30** 0355 0.7 / 0931 6.8 / TH 1615 0.4 / 2153 6.7	**15** 0416 1.2 / 0947 6.2 / SA 1629 1.2 / 2203 6.2	**30** 0451 1.0 / 1027 6.3 / SU 1705 1.2 / 2238 6.2
	31 0434 1.0 / 1007 6.7 / TU 1658 0.6 / 2237 6.5				**31** 0436 0.6 / 1012 6.8 / F 1654 0.5 / 2231 6.6		

Chart Datum: 3·29 metres below IGN Datum

FRANCE – CHERBOURG

TIME ZONE -0100
(French Standard Time)
Subtract 1 hour for UT
For French Summer Time add
ONE hour in **non-shaded areas**

LAT 49°39'N   LONG 1°38'W

TIMES AND HEIGHTS OF HIGH AND LOW WATERS

2006

MAY

Time m	Time m
1 0529 1.2 / 1104 6.0 / M 1741 1.6 / 2313 6.0	**16** 0503 1.3 / 1039 5.9 / TU 1717 1.6 / 2253 6.0
2 0607 1.5 / 1143 5.6 / TU 1819 2.0 / 2350 5.6	**17** 0543 1.5 / 1121 5.7 / W 1758 1.9 / 2336 5.8
3 0647 1.9 / 1225 5.2 / W 1901 2.4	**18** 0628 1.6 / 1208 5.4 / TH 1848 2.1
4 0033 5.2 / 0734 2.3 / TH 1318 4.8 / 1955 2.8	**19** 0025 5.5 / 0722 1.9 / F 1305 5.2 / 1949 2.4
5 0132 4.8 / 0837 2.6 / F 1439 4.6 / ☽ 2112 3.0	**20** 0127 5.3 / 0827 2.0 / SA 1418 5.0 / 2103 2.5
6 0259 4.6 / 0959 2.7 / SA 1609 4.6 / 2239 2.9	**21** 0243 5.2 / 0942 2.0 / SU 1542 5.1 / 2222 2.4
7 0422 4.7 / 1116 2.5 / SU 1715 4.8 / 2347 2.7	**22** 0403 5.3 / 1056 1.9 / M 1653 5.3 / 2332 2.1
8 0525 4.9 / 1215 2.3 / M 1804 5.1	**23** 0512 5.5 / 1202 1.7 / TU 1752 5.6
9 0041 2.4 / 0614 5.2 / TU 1302 2.0 / 1845 5.4	**24** 0036 1.8 / 0612 5.8 / W 1300 1.4 / 1845 5.9
10 0124 2.1 / 0657 5.5 / W 1343 1.8 / 1922 5.7	**25** 0131 1.5 / 0707 6.0 / TH 1352 1.3 / 1933 6.1
11 0203 1.8 / 0737 5.7 / TH 1419 1.6 / 1958 5.9	**26** 0222 1.3 / 0758 6.1 / F 1440 1.2 / 2019 6.2
12 0239 1.6 / 0814 5.8 / F 1454 1.5 / 2032 6.0	**27** 0308 1.2 / 0845 6.1 / SA 1524 1.3 / ● 2101 6.2
13 0314 1.4 / 0849 6.0 / SA 1528 1.4 / ○ 2105 6.1	**28** 0352 1.2 / 0929 6.1 / SU 1605 1.4 / 2141 6.2
14 0350 1.3 / 0924 6.0 / SU 1604 1.4 / 2139 6.1	**29** 0433 1.2 / 1010 6.0 / M 1645 1.6 / 2219 6.1
15 0426 1.3 / 1000 6.0 / M 1639 1.5 / 2214 6.1	**30** 0512 1.4 / 1050 5.8 / TU 1724 1.8 / 2257 5.9
	31 0552 1.6 / 1130 5.6 / W 1804 2.0 / 2337 5.7

JUNE

Time m	Time m
1 0632 1.8 / 1212 5.3 / TH 1846 2.3	**16** 0630 1.3 / 1210 5.7 / F 1851 1.8
2 0020 5.4 / 0715 2.1 / F 1258 5.1 / 1933 2.5	**17** 0026 5.9 / 0722 1.5 / SA 1303 5.6 / 1947 2.0
3 0108 5.1 / 0804 2.3 / SA 1353 4.9 / ☽ 2029 2.7	**18** 0121 5.7 / 0817 1.6 / SU 1402 5.4 / ☽ 2047 2.1
4 0205 4.9 / 0901 2.4 / SU 1455 4.8 / 2132 2.8	**19** 0222 5.5 / 0918 1.8 / M 1506 5.3 / 2152 2.2
5 0308 4.8 / 1004 2.5 / M 1600 4.8 / 2237 2.7	**20** 0327 5.4 / 1022 1.9 / TU 1612 5.3 / 2259 2.1
6 0412 4.8 / 1106 2.4 / TU 1658 5.0 / 2337 2.5	**21** 0436 5.4 / 1128 1.9 / W 1717 5.4
7 0511 5.0 / 1202 2.3 / W 1750 5.2	**22** 0005 2.0 / 0543 5.5 / TH 1231 1.8 / 1817 5.6
8 0031 2.3 / 0605 5.2 / TH 1252 2.1 / 1836 5.4	**23** 0108 1.9 / 0646 5.6 / F 1328 1.8 / 1911 5.8
9 0119 2.1 / 0655 5.4 / F 1338 1.9 / 1920 5.7	**24** 0203 1.7 / 0743 5.7 / SA 1421 1.7 / 2001 5.9
10 0204 1.8 / 0741 5.6 / SA 1421 1.7 / 2001 5.9	**25** 0253 1.5 / 0834 5.8 / SU 1508 1.7 / ● 2046 6.0
11 0247 1.6 / 0825 5.8 / SU 1503 1.6 / ○ 2041 6.0	**26** 0339 1.4 / 0919 5.8 / M 1552 1.7 / 2128 6.0
12 0330 1.4 / 0907 5.9 / M 1546 1.5 / 2122 6.1	**27** 0421 1.4 / 1000 5.8 / TU 1632 1.7 / 2207 6.0
13 0413 1.3 / 0950 5.9 / TU 1629 1.5 / 2204 6.1	**28** 0500 1.4 / 1038 5.8 / W 1711 1.8 / 2245 5.9
14 0457 1.2 / 1034 5.9 / W 1713 1.6 / 2249 6.1	**29** 0538 1.5 / 1115 5.7 / TH 1749 1.9 / 2323 5.8
15 0542 1.2 / 1121 5.8 / TH 1800 1.7 / 2336 6.0	**30** 0614 1.6 / 1152 5.5 / F 1826 2.0

JULY

Time m	Time m
1 0000 5.6 / 0650 1.8 / SA 1229 5.4 / 1903 2.2	**16** 0016 6.2 / 0707 1.1 / SU 1247 5.9 / 1929 1.6
2 0036 5.4 / 0727 2.0 / SU 1307 5.2 / 1943 2.4	**17** 0103 6.0 / 0755 1.4 / M 1333 5.7 / ☽ 2020 1.8
3 0115 5.2 / 0807 2.2 / M 1349 5.0 / ☽ 2029 2.5	**18** 0153 5.7 / 0846 1.7 / TU 1425 5.4 / 2118 2.1
4 0200 5.0 / 0854 2.4 / TU 1440 4.9 / 2124 2.7	**19** 0251 5.4 / 0945 2.1 / W 1529 5.2 / 2226 2.3
5 0255 4.9 / 0951 2.5 / W 1540 4.9 / 2228 2.7	**20** 0403 5.1 / 1055 2.3 / TH 1644 5.2 / 2340 2.3
6 0401 4.8 / 1057 2.5 / TH 1647 5.0 / 2335 2.6	**21** 0523 5.1 / 1209 2.3 / F 1757 5.3
7 0512 4.9 / 1203 2.4 / F 1751 5.2	**22** 0054 2.2 / 0638 5.2 / SA 1316 2.3 / 1901 5.5
8 0039 2.3 / 0619 5.1 / SA 1302 2.2 / 1847 5.4	**23** 0155 2.0 / 0740 5.4 / SU 1413 2.1 / 1954 5.7
9 0135 2.0 / 0717 5.4 / SU 1356 2.0 / 1937 5.7	**24** 0246 1.7 / 0830 5.6 / M 1501 1.9 / 2039 5.9
10 0226 1.7 / 0808 5.6 / M 1446 1.8 / 2025 5.9	**25** 0330 1.5 / 0911 5.8 / TU 1543 1.8 / ● 2118 6.0
11 0316 1.4 / 0856 5.9 / TU 1534 1.5 / ○ 2111 6.2	**26** 0409 1.4 / 0948 5.9 / W 1620 1.7 / 2154 6.1
12 0403 1.2 / 0943 6.0 / W 1621 1.4 / 2157 6.3	**27** 0445 1.3 / 1021 5.9 / TH 1655 1.6 / 2228 6.1
13 0450 1.0 / 1030 6.1 / TH 1708 1.3 / 2243 6.4	**28** 0518 1.3 / 1054 5.9 / F 1727 1.7 / 2300 6.0
14 0536 0.9 / 1116 6.2 / F 1755 1.3 / 2330 6.4	**29** 0549 1.4 / 1124 5.8 / SA 1758 1.7 / 2331 5.9
15 0622 0.9 / 1201 6.1 / SA 1841 1.4	**30** 0618 1.6 / 1154 5.6 / SU 1828 1.9
	31 0000 5.7 / 0647 1.6 / M 1223 5.5 / 1859 2.1

AUGUST

Time m	Time m
1 0030 5.5 / 0718 2.0 / TU 1254 5.3 / 1935 2.3	**16** 0121 5.7 / 0810 1.9 / W 1344 5.4 / ☽ 2043 2.2
2 0104 5.2 / 0754 2.3 / W 1333 5.1 / ☽ 2019 2.6	**17** 0216 5.2 / 0907 2.4 / TH 1445 5.1 / 2155 2.6
3 0150 4.9 / 0842 2.6 / TH 1426 4.9 / 2121 2.8	**18** 0337 4.8 / 1027 2.8 / F 1618 4.9 / 2326 2.6
4 0254 4.7 / 0951 2.8 / F 1542 4.8 / 2242 2.8	**19** 0520 4.8 / 1200 2.8 / SA 1751 5.0
5 0425 4.7 / 1120 2.8 / SA 1713 4.9	**20** 0049 2.4 / 0643 5.0 / SU 1313 2.5 / 1858 5.3
6 0005 2.5 / 0555 4.9 / SU 1237 2.5 / 1824 5.2	**21** 0150 2.1 / 0737 5.4 / M 1408 2.2 / 1947 5.6
7 0115 2.1 / 0702 5.3 / M 1339 2.1 / 1921 5.6	**22** 0236 1.8 / 0819 5.7 / TU 1451 1.9 / 2026 5.9
8 0211 1.7 / 0756 5.7 / TU 1433 1.7 / 2011 6.0	**23** 0315 1.5 / 0854 5.9 / W 1527 1.7 / ● 2101 6.1
9 0302 1.3 / 0845 6.0 / W 1522 1.4 / ○ 2059 6.4	**24** 0350 1.4 / 0926 6.0 / TH 1600 1.5 / 2133 6.2
10 0350 0.9 / 0932 6.3 / TH 1609 1.1 / 2145 6.6	**25** 0421 1.3 / 0956 6.0 / F 1630 1.5 / 2203 6.2
11 0436 0.6 / 1017 6.5 / F 1654 0.9 / 2230 6.7	**26** 0450 1.3 / 1024 6.0 / SA 1658 1.5 / 2230 6.2
12 0520 0.6 / 1100 6.5 / SA 1738 0.9 / 2314 6.7	**27** 0517 1.3 / 1050 6.0 / SU 1725 1.6 / 2257 6.0
13 0602 0.6 / 1141 6.4 / SU 1820 1.1 / 2356 6.5	**28** 0542 1.5 / 1115 5.9 / M 1752 1.7 / 2322 5.9
14 0643 0.9 / 1220 6.2 / M 1903 1.4	**29** 0608 1.7 / 1140 5.7 / TU 1819 1.9 / 2348 5.6
15 0037 6.1 / 0725 1.4 / TU 1259 5.8 / 1949 1.8	**30** 0635 1.7 / 1207 5.5 / W 1851 2.0
	31 0017 5.3 / 0707 2.3 / TH 1239 5.2 / ☽ 1930 2.5

Chart Datum: 3·29 metres below IGN Datum

TIME ZONE -0100
(French Standard Time)
Subtract 1 hour for UT
For French Summer Time add ONE hour in **non-shaded areas**

LAT 49°39'N   LONG 1°38'W

TIMES AND HEIGHTS OF HIGH AND LOW WATERS

SEPTEMBER

Time	m		Time	m
1 F 0057 / 0750 / 1326 / 2027	5.0 / 2.6 / 4.9 / 2.8	**16** SA	0322 / 1007 / 1559 / 2314	4.6 / 3.1 / 4.7 / 2.8
2 SA 0202 / 0858 / 1448 / 2157	4.7 / 3.0 / 4.7 / 2.9	**17** SU	0524 / 1153 / 1743	4.7 / 3.0 / 4.9
3 SU 0354 / 1047 / 1646 / 2340	4.5 / 3.0 / 4.8 / 2.7	**18** M	0038 / 0634 / 1302 / 1843	2.5 / 5.0 / 2.6 / 5.3
4 M 0543 / 1220 / 1807	4.8 / 2.7 / 5.2	**19** TU	0131 / 0717 / 1349 / 1925	2.1 / 5.4 / 2.2 / 5.6
5 TU 0057 / 0648 / 1324 / 1904	2.1 / 5.3 / 2.1 / 5.7	**20** W	0213 / 0752 / 1427 / 2000	1.8 / 5.7 / 1.9 / 5.9
6 W 0154 / 0740 / 1416 / 1953	1.6 / 5.8 / 1.6 / 6.2	**21** TH	0248 / 0824 / 1501 / 2033	1.5 / 6.0 / 1.6 / 6.1
7 TH 0243 / 0827 / 1504 / 2040 ○	1.1 / 6.2 / 1.2 / 6.6	**22** F	0320 / 0855 / 1531 / 2103	1.4 / 6.1 / 1.5 / 6.2
8 F 0330 / 0911 / 1549 / 2125	0.7 / 6.5 / 0.9 / 6.9	**23** SA	0349 / 0924 / 1559 / 2132	1.3 / 6.2 / 1.4 / 6.3
9 SA 0414 / 0954 / 1632 / 2209	0.5 / 6.7 / 0.7 / 7.0	**24** SU	0416 / 0950 / 1626 / 2158	1.3 / 6.1 / 1.4 / 6.2
10 SU 0455 / 1035 / 1714 / 2251	0.5 / 6.7 / 0.7 / 6.9	**25** M	0443 / 1014 / 1653 / 2223	1.4 / 6.1 / 1.5 / 6.1
11 M 0535 / 1113 / 1754 / 2330	0.7 / 6.5 / 1.0 / 6.6	**26** TU	0508 / 1038 / 1720 / 2248	1.5 / 6.0 / 1.6 / 5.9
12 TU 0614 / 1148 / 1834	1.1 / 6.2 / 1.4	**27** W	0534 / 1103 / 1748 / 2315	1.7 / 5.9 / 1.8 / 5.7
13 W 0009 / 0652 / 1224 / 1917	6.1 / 1.6 / 5.8 / 1.9	**28** TH	0601 / 1130 / 1819 / 2346	2.0 / 5.6 / 2.1 / 5.4
14 TH 0050 / 0735 / 1305 / 2009 ◐	5.5 / 2.2 / 5.4 / 2.4	**29** F	0634 / 1202 / 1859	2.3 / 5.3 / 2.4
15 F 0145 / 0831 / 1407 / 2127	5.0 / 2.8 / 4.9 / 2.8	**30** SA	0027 / 0719 / 1250 / 1957 ◑	5.0 / 2.7 / 5.0 / 2.7

OCTOBER

Time	m		Time	m
1 SU 0137 / 0831 / 1419 / 2130	4.7 / 3.1 / 4.7 / 2.9	**16** M	0454 / 1123 / 1706	4.7 / 3.1 / 4.8
2 M 0342 / 1027 / 1624 / 2318	4.6 / 3.1 / 4.8 / 2.6	**17** TU	0000 / 0558 / 1227 / 1805	2.6 / 5.0 / 2.7 / 5.2
3 TU 0526 / 1200 / 1744	4.9 / 2.6 / 5.3	**18** W	0054 / 0639 / 1313 / 1847	2.2 / 5.4 / 2.3 / 5.5
4 W 0035 / 0626 / 1302 / 1840	2.0 / 5.5 / 2.1 / 5.8	**19** TH	0136 / 0714 / 1352 / 1923	1.9 / 5.7 / 2.0 / 5.8
5 TH 0129 / 0715 / 1353 / 1929	1.5 / 6.0 / 1.5 / 6.3	**20** F	0211 / 0747 / 1426 / 1957	1.7 / 5.9 / 1.8 / 6.0
6 F 0218 / 0800 / 1440 / 2015	1.0 / 6.4 / 1.1 / 6.7	**21** SA	0244 / 0818 / 1457 / 2029	1.5 / 6.1 / 1.6 / 6.1
7 SA 0304 / 0844 / 1524 / 2100 ○	0.7 / 6.7 / 0.8 / 6.9	**22** SU	0313 / 0848 / 1526 / 2059 ●	1.5 / 6.2 / 1.5 / 6.0
8 SU 0347 / 0925 / 1607 / 2143	0.6 / 6.8 / 0.7 / 6.9	**23** M	0342 / 0915 / 1556 / 2127	1.4 / 6.2 / 1.5 / 6.2
9 M 0428 / 1005 / 1648 / 2225	0.6 / 6.7 / 0.8 / 6.8	**24** TU	0411 / 0942 / 1625 / 2155	1.5 / 6.2 / 1.5 / 6.1
10 TU 0507 / 1042 / 1728 / 2304	0.9 / 6.5 / 1.1 / 6.4	**25** W	0440 / 1009 / 1655 / 2225	1.6 / 6.1 / 1.6 / 5.9
11 W 0545 / 1117 / 1808 / 2344	1.4 / 6.2 / 1.5 / 5.9	**26** TH	0509 / 1039 / 1727 / 2258	1.8 / 5.9 / 1.8 / 5.7
12 TH 0624 / 1154 / 1850	1.9 / 5.8 / 2.0	**27** F	0540 / 1112 / 1803 / 2336	2.1 / 5.7 / 2.0 / 5.4
13 F 0026 / 0706 / 1236 / 1941	5.4 / 2.5 / 5.3 / 2.5	**28** SA	0619 / 1151 / 1847	2.4 / 5.4 / 2.3
14 SA 0124 / 0803 / 1339 / 2057 ◑	4.9 / 3.0 / 4.9 / 2.9	**29** SU	0024 / 0710 / 1247 / 1949 ◑	5.1 / 2.7 / 5.1 / 2.6
15 SU 0303 / 0941 / 1528 / 2243	4.6 / 3.2 / 4.7 / 2.9	**30** M	0138 / 0825 / 1411 / 2115	4.8 / 3.0 / 4.9 / 2.7
		31 TU	0324 / 1006 / 1554 / 2248	4.8 / 2.9 / 5.0 / 2.4

NOVEMBER

Time	m		Time	m
1 W 0453 / 1130 / 1710	5.1 / 2.5 / 5.4	**16** TH	0545 / 1223 / 1755	5.2 / 2.5 / 5.3
2 TH 0000 / 0558 / 1232 / 1808	2.0 / 5.6 / 2.0 / 5.9	**17** F	0047 / 0627 / 1307 / 1839	2.2 / 5.5 / 2.2 / 5.5
3 F 0059 / 0643 / 1325 / 1859	1.5 / 6.0 / 1.6 / 6.4	**18** SA	0128 / 0705 / 1346 / 1918	2.0 / 5.7 / 2.0 / 5.7
4 SA 0149 / 0730 / 1413 / 1948	1.1 / 6.4 / 1.2 / 6.6	**19** SU	0204 / 0740 / 1422 / 1955	1.8 / 5.9 / 1.8 / 5.9
5 SU 0236 / 0814 / 1500 / 2035 ●	0.9 / 6.6 / 1.0 / 6.7	**20** M	0239 / 0813 / 1456 / 2030	1.7 / 6.1 / 1.6 / 6.0
6 M 0320 / 0857 / 1544 / 2119	0.9 / 6.7 / 0.9 / 6.7	**21** TU	0312 / 0845 / 1530 / 2104	1.7 / 6.1 / 1.5 / 6.0
7 TU 0403 / 0937 / 1626 / 2202	1.0 / 6.6 / 1.0 / 6.5	**22** W	0346 / 0917 / 1605 / 2138	1.7 / 6.2 / 1.5 / 6.0
8 W 0443 / 1015 / 1707 / 2244	1.3 / 6.4 / 1.2 / 6.2	**23** TH	0421 / 0951 / 1641 / 2214	1.7 / 6.1 / 1.6 / 5.9
9 TH 0522 / 1053 / 1748 / 2326	1.7 / 6.2 / 1.6 / 5.8	**24** F	0456 / 1028 / 1719 / 2254	1.9 / 6.0 / 1.7 / 5.8
10 F 0603 / 1133 / 1831	2.1 / 5.8 / 2.0	**25** SA	0534 / 1109 / 1800 / 2339	2.0 / 5.9 / 1.8 / 5.5
11 SA 0010 / 0647 / 1218 / 1920	5.4 / 2.5 / 5.4 / 2.4	**26** SU	0619 / 1155 / 1849	2.2 / 5.6 / 2.0
12 SU 0105 / 0741 / 1316 / 2022 ◐	5.0 / 2.9 / 5.0 / 2.7	**27** M	0030 / 0713 / 1250 / 1947	5.3 / 2.5 / 5.4 / 2.2
13 M 0221 / 0856 / 1436 / 2143	4.8 / 3.1 / 4.8 / 2.8	**28** TU	0135 / 0820 / 1358 / 2057 ◐	5.1 / 2.6 / 5.3 / 2.3
14 TU 0346 / 1021 / 1559 / 2258	4.7 / 3.0 / 4.8 / 2.7	**29** W	0253 / 0937 / 1517 / 2212	5.1 / 2.6 / 5.3 / 2.2
15 W 0454 / 1130 / 1704 / 2357	4.9 / 2.8 / 5.0 / 2.5	**30** TH	0409 / 1052 / 1630 / 2322	5.3 / 2.4 / 5.5 / 2.0

DECEMBER

Time	m		Time	m
1 F 0514 / 1158 / 1734	5.5 / 2.1 / 5.7	**16** SA	0530 / 1214 / 1747	5.1 / 2.6 / 5.1
2 SA 0026 / 0610 / 1257 / 1831	1.7 / 5.8 / 1.8 / 6.0	**17** SU	0039 / 0619 / 1304 / 1839	2.4 / 5.4 / 2.3 / 5.3
3 SU 0122 / 0701 / 1350 / 1925	1.5 / 6.1 / 1.5 / 6.2	**18** M	0126 / 0704 / 1349 / 1925	2.2 / 5.6 / 2.1 / 5.6
4 M 0212 / 0750 / 1440 / 2016	1.4 / 6.3 / 1.3 / 6.3	**19** TU	0208 / 0745 / 1431 / 2008	2.0 / 5.8 / 1.8 / 5.8
5 TU 0300 / 0835 / 1527 / 2104 ○	1.4 / 6.4 / 1.2 / 6.3	**20** W	0249 / 0824 / 1512 / 2048	1.9 / 6.0 / 1.6 / 5.9
6 W 0344 / 0918 / 1611 / 2148	1.4 / 6.4 / 1.2 / 6.2	**21** TH	0330 / 0903 / 1553 / 2128	1.7 / 6.1 / 1.5 / 6.0
7 TH 0427 / 0959 / 1653 / 2231	1.6 / 6.3 / 1.3 / 6.0	**22** F	0411 / 0942 / 1634 / 2209	1.7 / 6.2 / 1.4 / 6.0
8 F 0508 / 1040 / 1735 / 2313	1.8 / 6.1 / 1.5 / 5.8	**23** SA	0452 / 1024 / 1717 / 2253	1.7 / 6.2 / 1.3 / 6.2
9 SA 0549 / 1121 / 1816 / 2355	2.0 / 5.9 / 1.8 / 5.5	**24** SU	0535 / 1108 / 1801 / 2338	1.7 / 6.2 / 1.4 / 5.9
10 SU 0631 / 1203 / 1858	2.3 / 5.6 / 2.1	**25** M	0621 / 1154 / 1847	1.8 / 6.0 / 1.5
11 M 0040 / 0715 / 1249 / 1944	5.3 / 2.5 / 5.3 / 2.3	**26** TU	0026 / 0709 / 1243 / 1936	5.7 / 2.0 / 5.9 / 1.7
12 TU 0130 / 0806 / 1340 / 2036 ◐	5.0 / 2.7 / 5.1 / 2.5	**27** W	0118 / 0803 / 1337 / 2031 ◐	5.5 / 2.1 / 5.7 / 1.9
13 W 0228 / 0904 / 1440 / 2136	4.9 / 2.9 / 4.9 / 2.7	**28** TH	0216 / 0903 / 1438 / 2133	5.4 / 2.3 / 5.5 / 2.0
14 TH 0331 / 1010 / 1544 / 2241	4.9 / 2.9 / 4.9 / 2.7	**29** F	0321 / 1011 / 1548 / 2241	5.3 / 2.3 / 5.4 / 2.1
15 F 0433 / 1116 / 1648 / 2343	5.0 / 2.8 / 4.9 / 2.6	**30** SA	0432 / 1124 / 1702 / 2352	5.4 / 2.3 / 5.4 / 2.1
		31 SU	0540 / 1233 / 1811	5.5 / 2.1 / 5.5

Chart Datum: 3·29 metres below IGN Datum

TIDES

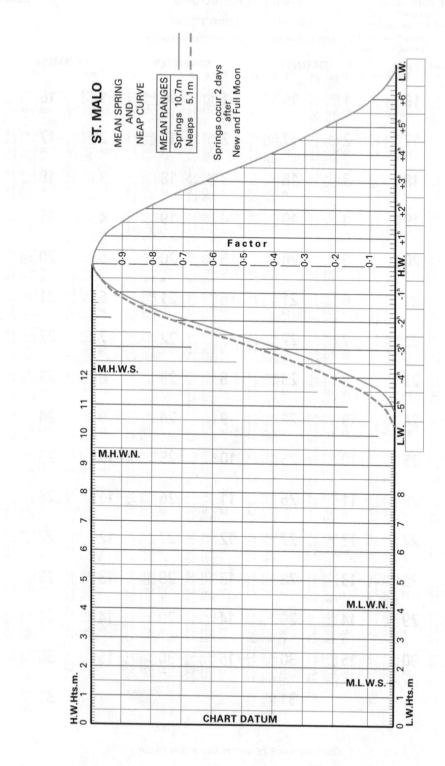

ST. MALO

MEAN SPRING
AND
NEAP CURVE

MEAN RANGES
Springs 10.7m
Neaps 5.1m

Springs occur 2 days
after
New and Full Moon

FRANCE – ST MALO

LAT 48°38'N   LONG 2°02'W

TIMES AND HEIGHTS OF HIGH AND LOW WATERS

TIME ZONE -0100
(French Standard Time)
Subtract 1 hour for UT
For French Summer Time add
ONE hour in **non-shaded areas**

JANUARY

Day	Time	m	Time	m	Time	m	Time	m
1 SU	0218	2.0	0746	12.0	1446	1.6	2014	11.8
2 M	0308	1.8	0833	12.2	1536	1.5	2101	11.9
3 TU	0356	1.8	0921	12.2	1624	1.5	2148	11.7
4 W	0443	2.0	1008	11.9	1712	1.8	2234	11.3
5 TH	0529	2.4	1056	11.5	1758	2.2	2321	10.8
6 F	0616	2.9	1145	10.9	1846	2.8		
7 SA	0012	10.2	0706	3.4	1239	10.3	1937	3.4
8 SU	0111	9.7	0804	3.8	1344	9.7	2037	3.8
9 M	0220	9.4	0912	4.0	1459	9.5	2144	3.9
10 TU	0335	9.5	1025	3.9	1613	9.6	2252	3.8
11 W	0443	9.8	1131	3.6	1717	9.9	2353	3.5
12 TH	0539	10.3	1227	3.2	1810	10.3		
13 F	0047	3.2	0626	10.7	1315	2.8	1855	10.6
14 SA	0131	2.9	0706	11.0	1357	2.4	1934	10.8
15 SU	0211	2.6	0743	11.2	1435	2.4	2009	11.0
16 M	0248	2.5	0818	11.3	1511	2.3	2042	11.0
17 TU	0322	2.5	0851	11.3	1545	2.3	2114	10.9
18 W	0354	2.6	0922	11.2	1615	2.5	2144	10.7
19 TH	0425	2.8	0952	10.9	1644	2.8	2213	10.4
20 F	0454	3.1	1021	10.5	1713	3.1	2242	10.1
21 SA	0524	3.4	1052	10.1	1744	3.5	2313	9.6
22 SU	0559	3.9	1127	9.6	1821	3.9	2352	9.2
23 M	0643	4.3	1214	9.2	1909	4.3		
24 TU	0051	8.8	0744	4.5	1325	8.8	2018	4.6
25 W	0219	8.7	0906	4.5	1458	8.8	2146	4.4
26 TH	0348	9.1	1032	4.0	1621	9.3	2307	3.9
27 F	0459	9.9	1144	3.3	1730	10.1		
28 SA	0018	3.1	0559	10.8	1248	2.4	1828	10.9
29 SU	0119	2.3	0652	11.6	1347	1.7	1921	11.6
30 M	0215	1.7	0741	12.3	1442	1.1	2009	12.1
31 TU	0306	1.2	0828	12.7	1532	0.7	2054	12.4

FEBRUARY

Day	Time	m	Time	m	Time	m	Time	m
1 W	0353	1.0	0913	12.8	1618	0.6	2137	12.4
2 TH	0436	1.1	0955	12.6	1700	0.9	2217	12.0
3 F	0515	1.5	1036	12.1	1739	1.6	2256	11.4
4 SA	0553	2.2	1116	11.3	1816	2.4	2335	10.6
5 SU	0631	3.1	1159	10.3	1855	3.3		
6 M	0021	9.8	0716	3.9	1251	9.4	1945	4.1
7 TU	0122	9.1	0821	4.5	1412	9.1	2056	4.7
8 W	0255	8.8	0949	4.6	1554	8.7	2223	4.6
9 TH	0427	9.1	1113	4.2	1710	9.2	2339	4.1
10 F	0529	9.7	1215	3.4	1803	9.9		
11 SA	0037	3.5	0616	10.4	1305	3.0	1844	10.4
12 SU	0122	2.9	0654	10.9	1346	2.5	1920	10.9
13 M	0201	2.5	0729	11.3	1423	2.2	1953	11.2
14 TU	0236	2.2	0801	11.5	1457	2.0	2023	11.3
15 W	0307	2.0	0832	11.6	1527	1.9	2053	11.4
16 TH	0336	2.0	0901	11.6	1554	1.9	2120	11.3
17 F	0403	2.1	0927	11.4	1620	2.1	2145	11.1
18 SA	0429	2.4	0953	11.1	1644	2.5	2210	10.7
19 SU	0455	2.8	1019	10.7	1710	3.0	2235	10.2
20 M	0523	3.3	1048	10.1	1739	3.6	2305	9.7
21 TU	0559	3.9	1125	9.5	1818	4.2	2348	9.1
22 W	0652	4.4	1223	8.8	1920	4.7		
23 TH	0111	8.6	0815	4.7	1413	8.4	2101	4.8
24 F	0318	8.7	1004	4.3	1606	8.9	2246	4.2
25 SA	0445	9.6	1129	3.4	1721	9.9		
26 SU	0003	3.2	0548	10.7	1238	2.3	1818	11.0
27 M	0110	2.1	0641	11.8	1337	1.3	1908	11.9
28 TU	0204	1.2	0729	12.6	1430	0.6	1954	12.5

MARCH

Day	Time	m	Time	m	Time	m	Time	m
1 W	0253	0.6	0813	13.1	1517	0.2	2036	12.8
2 TH	0337	0.4	0855	13.2	1559	0.2	2115	12.8
3 F	0416	0.6	0934	12.9	1637	0.6	2152	12.4
4 SA	0451	1.2	1010	12.3	1710	1.4	2226	11.7
5 SU	0523	2.0	1045	11.3	1740	2.5	2259	10.8
6 M	0554	3.0	1121	10.2	1811	3.5	2336	9.9
7 TU	0630	4.0	1206	9.2	1853	4.5		
8 W	0030	8.9	0730	4.8	1327	8.3	2008	5.2
9 TH	0217	8.3	0915	5.1	1539	8.2	2200	5.0
10 F	0409	8.7	1056	4.6	1656	8.9	2323	4.4
11 SA	0511	9.4	1158	3.8	1744	9.7		
12 SU	0019	3.6	0554	10.2	1244	3.1	1821	10.4
13 M	0101	2.9	0631	10.8	1323	2.5	1854	11.0
14 TU	0138	2.4	0704	11.3	1358	2.1	1926	11.3
15 W	0211	2.0	0736	11.6	1430	1.8	1956	11.6
16 TH	0242	1.8	0806	11.8	1500	1.7	2025	11.7
17 F	0310	1.7	0834	11.9	1526	1.7	2051	11.7
18 SA	0337	1.8	0901	11.7	1551	1.9	2116	11.5
19 SU	0403	2.1	0926	11.4	1616	2.3	2140	11.1
20 M	0429	2.5	0952	11.0	1641	2.8	2206	10.7
21 TU	0457	3.1	1021	10.4	1709	3.5	2236	10.1
22 W	0532	3.7	1058	9.6	1748	4.2	2319	9.3
23 TH	0625	4.3	1157	8.8	1851	4.8		
24 F	0045	8.7	0750	4.7	1400	8.4	2040	5.0
25 SA	0302	8.8	0947	4.6	1554	9.0	2232	4.2
26 SU	0428	9.7	1115	3.3	1704	10.1	2346	3.1
27 M	0529	10.9	1221	2.2	1759	11.2		
28 TU	0051	2.0	0621	12.0	1318	1.2	1847	12.1
29 W	0144	1.1	0708	12.7	1408	0.6	1930	12.7
30 TH	0231	0.6	0751	13.1	1453	0.3	2011	12.9
31 F	0313	0.5	0831	13.1	1532	0.4	2048	12.8

APRIL

Day	Time	m	Time	m	Time	m	Time	m
1 SA	0350	0.8	0908	12.8	1606	1.0	2123	12.4
2 SU	0423	1.4	0943	12.1	1637	1.8	2155	11.7
3 M	0452	2.2	1017	11.1	1704	2.8	2227	10.9
4 TU	0521	3.1	1051	10.1	1733	3.8	2303	9.9
5 W	0555	4.1	1134	9.0	1813	4.7	2352	8.9
6 TH	0650	4.9	1252	8.2	1927	5.4		
7 F	0138	8.3	0833	5.2	1504	8.2	2126	5.4
8 SA	0331	8.6	1019	4.8	1621	8.8	2248	4.6
9 SU	0434	9.3	1121	4.0	1708	9.6	2340	3.8
10 M	0518	10.0	1205	3.3	1745	10.3		
11 TU	0023	3.1	0555	10.6	1245	2.7	1819	10.9
12 W	0101	2.6	0630	11.2	1321	2.3	1852	11.3
13 TH	0136	2.2	0704	11.5	1355	2.0	1923	11.6
14 F	0209	1.9	0736	11.8	1426	1.8	1953	11.8
15 SA	0240	1.8	0805	11.8	1456	1.8	2021	11.8
16 SU	0311	1.8	0834	11.8	1524	2.0	2049	11.7
17 M	0341	2.0	0903	11.5	1553	2.3	2117	11.4
18 TU	0411	2.4	0934	11.1	1622	2.9	2148	10.9
19 W	0444	3.0	1010	10.4	1655	3.5	2226	10.3
20 TH	0524	3.6	1055	9.7	1740	4.2	2319	9.5
21 F	0621	4.2	1206	9.0	1850	4.7		
22 SA	0056	9.0	0748	4.4	1358	8.8	2036	4.7
23 SU	0244	9.3	0931	4.0	1531	9.4	2211	4.0
24 M	0402	10.1	1051	3.1	1638	10.3	2320	3.0
25 TU	0502	11.0	1154	2.2	1731	11.2		
26 W	0023	2.1	0554	11.8	1249	1.5	1819	11.9
27 TH	0115	1.5	0641	12.4	1339	1.1	1902	12.4
28 F	0202	1.1	0724	12.6	1422	1.0	1942	12.5
29 SA	0244	1.1	0805	12.5	1500	1.2	2019	12.4
30 SU	0320	1.3	0842	12.2	1534	1.6	2055	12.1

Chart Datum: 6·29 metres below IGN Datum

TIDES

FRANCE – ST MALO 2006

TIME ZONE -0100
(French Standard Time)
Subtract 1 hour for UT
For French Summer Time add
ONE hour in **non-shaded areas**

LAT 48°38'N   LONG 2°02'W

TIMES AND HEIGHTS OF HIGH AND LOW WATERS

MAY

Time m	Time m
1 M 0354 1.8 / 0919 11.6 / 1605 2.3 / 2129 11.5	**16** TU 0324 2.1 / 0849 11.4 / 1538 2.5 / 2104 11.5
2 TU 0425 2.5 / 0954 10.8 / 1635 3.0 / 2204 10.8	**17** W 0402 2.4 / 0929 11.1 / 1615 2.9 / 2145 11.1
3 W 0456 3.2 / 1031 10.0 / 1708 3.9 / 2242 10.0	**18** TH 0443 2.8 / 1014 10.6 / 1658 3.4 / 2233 10.5
4 TH 0533 4.0 / 1116 9.2 / 1750 4.6 / 2333 9.2	**19** F 0531 3.3 / 1109 10.0 / 1751 3.9 / 2335 10.0
5 F 0624 4.7 / 1223 8.5 / 1855 5.2 ●	**20** SA 0631 3.7 / 1219 9.5 / 1900 4.2 ○
6 SA 0053 8.6 / 0743 5.0 / 1401 8.4 / 2028 5.2	**21** SU 0056 9.7 / 0747 3.8 / 1340 9.5 / 2024 4.1
7 SU 0227 8.6 / 0913 4.8 / 1521 8.8 / 2148 4.8	**22** M 0217 9.8 / 0907 3.6 / 1457 9.8 / 2141 3.7
8 M 0336 9.1 / 1021 4.3 / 1615 9.4 / 2245 4.1	**23** TU 0329 10.3 / 1018 3.1 / 1603 10.4 / 2248 3.0
9 TU 0427 9.7 / 1112 3.6 / 1658 10.0 / 2331 3.5	**24** W 0430 10.8 / 1121 2.5 / 1659 11.0 / 2347 2.5
10 W 0510 10.3 / 1156 3.1 / 1736 10.6	**25** TH 0525 11.3 / 1217 2.1 / 1749 11.4
11 TH 0015 3.0 / 0550 10.8 / 1237 2.7 / 1813 11.1	**26** F 0044 2.1 / 0615 11.6 / 1307 1.9 / 1835 11.8
12 F 0055 2.5 / 0627 11.2 / 1316 2.4 / 1848 11.4	**27** SA 0132 1.9 / 0700 11.7 / 1351 1.9 / 1917 11.9 ●
13 SA 0134 2.2 / 0703 11.5 / 1352 2.2 / 1922 11.6 ○	**28** SU 0215 1.8 / 0743 11.7 / 1431 2.0 / 1956 11.9
14 SU 0211 2.1 / 0738 11.6 / 1427 2.1 / 1955 11.7	**29** M 0254 1.9 / 0823 11.5 / 1507 2.2 / 2034 11.7
15 M 0248 2.0 / 0813 11.6 / 1502 2.2 / 2028 11.7	**30** TU 0331 2.2 / 0902 11.1 / 1542 2.6 / 2111 11.3
	31 W 0406 2.6 / 0940 10.7 / 1617 3.1 / 2149 10.8

JUNE

Time m	Time m
1 TH 0441 3.1 / 1019 10.1 / 1653 3.6 / 2229 10.2	**16** F 0450 2.3 / 1020 11.0 / 1707 2.8 / 2240 11.2
2 F 0519 3.7 / 1101 9.6 / 1734 4.2 / 2314 9.7	**17** SA 0540 2.6 / 1112 10.7 / 1759 3.1 / 2334 10.8
3 SA 0602 4.1 / 1150 9.1 / 1824 4.6 ○	**18** SU 0633 2.9 / 1208 10.3 / 1856 3.4 ○
4 SU 0007 9.2 / 0656 4.5 / 1250 8.8 / 1925 4.8	**19** M 0037 10.4 / 0731 3.2 / 1310 10.0 / 1959 3.6
5 M 0112 9.0 / 0800 4.6 / 1359 8.8 / 2033 4.7	**20** TU 0142 10.2 / 0835 3.3 / 1417 9.9 / 2107 3.6
6 TU 0220 9.0 / 0906 4.4 / 1505 9.1 / 2137 4.4	**21** W 0251 10.2 / 0941 3.3 / 1525 10.1 / 2214 3.4
7 W 0322 9.3 / 1008 4.1 / 1600 9.5 / 2234 3.9	**22** TH 0358 10.3 / 1045 3.2 / 1629 10.4 / 2317 3.1
8 TH 0417 9.8 / 1103 3.6 / 1649 10.1 / 2326 3.5	**23** F 0500 10.5 / 1146 2.9 / 1726 10.8
9 F 0506 10.2 / 1153 3.2 / 1733 10.6	**24** SA 0017 2.8 / 0556 10.8 / 1240 2.7 / 1816 11.1
10 SA 0016 3.0 / 0552 10.7 / 1239 2.8 / 1816 11.0	**25** SU 0109 2.6 / 0646 10.9 / 1328 2.6 / 1901 11.3 ●
11 SU 0102 2.6 / 0636 11.0 / 1324 2.6 / 1856 11.4 ○	**26** M 0155 2.4 / 0731 11.0 / 1411 2.6 / 1943 11.4
12 M 0148 2.3 / 0718 11.3 / 1407 2.4 / 1937 11.6	**27** TU 0237 2.3 / 0813 11.1 / 1451 2.6 / 2022 11.4
13 TU 0232 2.1 / 0801 11.4 / 1450 2.3 / 2018 11.7	**28** W 0316 2.4 / 0851 11.0 / 1529 2.6 / 2059 11.3
14 W 0317 2.0 / 0845 11.4 / 1534 2.4 / 2102 11.7	**29** TH 0353 2.5 / 0928 10.8 / 1605 2.8 / 2136 11.0
15 TH 0403 2.1 / 0931 11.3 / 1619 2.5 / 2149 11.5	**30** F 0428 2.8 / 1003 10.5 / 1640 3.1 / 2211 10.7

JULY

Time m	Time m
1 SA 0502 3.1 / 1038 10.2 / 1714 3.5 / 2246 10.3	**16** SU 0535 1.8 / 1058 11.4 / 1751 2.3 / 2318 11.5
2 SU 0536 3.5 / 1113 9.8 / 1750 3.9 / 2324 9.8	**17** M 0619 2.3 / 1144 10.9 / 1837 2.9 ●
3 M 0613 3.8 / 1152 9.4 / 1832 4.2 ●	**18** TU 0006 10.8 / 0705 2.9 / 1234 10.3 / 1929 3.4
4 TU 0007 9.4 / 0656 4.1 / 1241 9.1 / 1923 4.5	**19** W 0105 10.2 / 0758 3.5 / 1334 9.8 / 2031 3.9
5 W 0104 9.1 / 0750 4.4 / 1344 8.9 / 2025 4.6	**20** TH 0213 9.7 / 0902 3.9 / 1448 9.6 / 2143 4.0
6 TH 0212 9.0 / 0857 4.4 / 1456 9.1 / 2135 4.4	**21** F 0333 9.5 / 1015 3.9 / 1607 9.7 / 2256 3.8
7 F 0322 9.2 / 1008 4.2 / 1602 9.4 / 2242 4.0	**22** SA 0448 9.8 / 1125 3.7 / 1714 10.2
8 SA 0426 9.6 / 1113 3.8 / 1700 10.0 / 2341 3.4	**23** SU 0001 3.4 / 0550 10.2 / 1225 3.4 / 1808 10.6
9 SU 0524 10.1 / 1210 3.3 / 1752 10.6	**24** M 0058 3.0 / 0640 10.6 / 1316 3.0 / 1854 11.0
10 M 0039 2.9 / 0617 10.6 / 1304 2.8 / 1841 11.2	**25** TU 0145 2.6 / 0723 10.9 / 1401 2.7 / 1934 11.3 ●
11 TU 0133 2.4 / 0708 11.1 / 1356 2.4 / 1928 11.7 ○	**26** W 0227 2.4 / 0801 11.1 / 1440 2.5 / 2010 11.5
12 W 0225 1.9 / 0756 11.5 / 1446 2.1 / 2014 12.0	**27** TH 0305 2.3 / 0836 11.2 / 1517 2.4 / 2043 11.5
13 TH 0316 1.6 / 0843 11.8 / 1535 1.8 / 2100 12.2	**28** F 0339 2.2 / 0908 11.2 / 1550 2.4 / 2115 11.4
14 F 0405 1.4 / 0929 11.9 / 1622 1.8 / 2146 12.2	**29** SA 0410 2.3 / 0939 11.0 / 1619 2.6 / 2146 11.2
15 SA 0451 1.5 / 1014 11.7 / 1707 1.9 / 2232 11.9	**30** SU 0437 2.6 / 1007 10.7 / 1647 2.9 / 2214 10.8
	31 M 0504 2.9 / 1035 10.4 / 1715 3.3 / 2243 10.3

AUGUST

Time m	Time m
1 TU 0531 3.4 / 1104 9.9 / 1746 3.8 / 2314 9.8	**16** W 0631 3.1 / 1156 10.3 / 1854 3.6 ○
2 W 0603 3.8 / 1138 9.4 / 1824 4.3 / 2354 9.3 ◑	**17** TH 0026 9.9 / 0717 4.0 / 1251 9.5 / 1953 4.4
3 TH 0645 4.3 / 1226 9.0 / 1917 4.7	**18** F 0139 9.1 / 0825 4.6 / 1416 9.0 / 2119 4.6
4 F 0057 8.8 / 0744 4.7 / 1345 8.7 / 2034 4.9	**19** SA 0321 8.9 / 0955 4.7 / 1558 9.2 / 2246 4.3
5 SA 0229 8.7 / 0912 4.8 / 1521 8.9 / 2204 4.5	**20** SU 0446 9.3 / 1117 4.3 / 1709 9.8 / 2355 3.6
6 SU 0357 9.1 / 1042 4.4 / 1637 9.6 / 2319 3.8	**21** M 0544 10.0 / 1218 3.6 / 1759 10.5
7 M 0508 9.8 / 1152 3.6 / 1737 10.4	**22** TU 0050 3.0 / 0629 10.6 / 1306 3.0 / 1840 11.1
8 TU 0025 2.9 / 0606 10.6 / 1252 2.8 / 1830 11.3	**23** W 0133 2.6 / 0706 11.0 / 1347 2.6 / 1916 11.5 ●
9 W 0124 2.1 / 0659 11.3 / 1348 2.1 / 1919 12.0 ○	**24** TH 0211 2.2 / 0740 11.3 / 1423 2.3 / 1949 11.5
10 TH 0219 1.5 / 0747 12.0 / 1440 1.5 / 2005 12.6	**25** F 0245 2.1 / 0811 11.5 / 1456 2.1 / 2020 11.8
11 F 0309 1.0 / 0832 12.4 / 1528 1.1 / 2049 12.9	**26** SA 0315 2.0 / 0841 11.5 / 1525 2.1 / 2048 11.8
12 SA 0355 0.8 / 0915 12.5 / 1612 1.0 / 2131 12.9	**27** SU 0342 2.1 / 0908 11.4 / 1551 2.1 / 2115 11.6
13 SU 0437 0.9 / 0955 12.2 / 1652 1.3 / 2212 12.5	**28** M 0406 2.3 / 0933 11.2 / 1616 2.5 / 2140 11.2
14 M 0516 1.4 / 1034 11.9 / 1731 1.9 / 2252 11.8	**29** TU 0429 2.7 / 0956 10.8 / 1640 3.0 / 2204 10.7
15 TU 0553 2.1 / 1113 11.2 / 1810 2.7 / 2334 10.9	**30** W 0452 3.1 / 1020 10.4 / 1706 3.5 / 2230 10.2
	31 TH 0518 3.7 / 1047 9.9 / 1739 4.1 / 2303 9.5 ◐

Chart Datum: 6·29 metres below IGN Datum

TIME ZONE -0100
(French Standard Time)
Subtract 1 hour for UT
For French Summer Time add
ONE hour in **non-shaded areas**

FRANCE – ST MALO

LAT 48°38′N   LONG 2°02′W

TIMES AND HEIGHTS OF HIGH AND LOW WATERS

SEPTEMBER

#	Time m	#	Time m
1	0554 4.4 / 1124 9.2 / F 1826 4.7 / 2353 8.8	**16**	0109 8.6 / 0748 5.3 / SA 1352 8.6 / 2057 5.2
2	0649 5.0 / 1233 8.6 / SA 1942 5.1	**17**	0315 8.5 / 0943 5.3 / SU 1547 8.9 / 2238 4.6
3	0144 8.4 / 0824 5.2 / SU 1451 8.6 / 2135 4.9	**18**	0436 9.2 / 1107 4.5 / M 1653 9.7 / 2340 3.8
4	0341 8.8 / 1022 4.7 / M 1620 9.4 / 2302 3.9	**19**	0526 10.0 / 1201 3.6 / TU 1738 10.5
5	0455 9.7 / 1138 3.7 / TU 1722 10.5	**20**	0028 3.1 / 0605 10.7 / W 1243 3.0 / 1815 11.1
6	0010 2.8 / 0552 10.8 / W 1239 2.6 / 1814 11.6	**21**	0107 2.6 / 0638 11.2 / TH 1321 2.5 / 1849 11.5
7	0110 1.8 / 0642 11.7 / TH 1333 1.7 / ○ 1902 12.5	**22**	0142 2.2 / 0710 11.5 / F 1355 2.2 / ● 1920 11.8
8	0203 1.0 / 0728 12.4 / F 1424 1.0 / 1946 13.1	**23**	0214 2.0 / 0740 11.7 / SA 1426 2.0 / 1950 11.9
9	0251 0.6 / 0811 12.8 / SA 1510 0.7 / 2029 13.3	**24**	0242 2.0 / 0808 11.8 / SU 1454 2.0 / 2017 11.9
10	0334 0.5 / 0851 12.9 / SU 1551 0.7 / 2109 13.2	**25**	0308 2.0 / 0834 11.7 / M 1520 2.2 / 2043 11.7
11	0413 0.8 / 0929 12.6 / M 1629 1.2 / 2147 12.6	**26**	0332 2.2 / 0858 11.5 / TU 1544 2.4 / 2107 11.4
12	0448 1.5 / 1005 12.0 / TU 1704 2.0 / 2223 11.7	**27**	0356 2.6 / 0921 11.2 / W 1610 2.8 / 2132 11.0
13	0520 2.4 / 1040 11.2 / W 1738 2.9 / 2301 10.7	**28**	0419 3.1 / 0944 10.7 / TH 1636 3.4 / 2158 10.4
14	0553 3.5 / 1118 10.3 / TH 1817 3.9 / ◑ 2347 9.5	**29**	0444 3.7 / 1012 10.1 / F 1709 4.0 / 2231 9.7
15	0635 4.5 / 1211 9.3 / F 1915 4.8	**30**	0520 4.4 / 1050 9.4 / SA 1756 4.7 / ◑ 2322 8.8

OCTOBER

#	Time m	#	Time m
1	0617 5.1 / 1200 8.7 / SU 1913 5.1	**16**	0245 8.4 / 0912 5.5 / M 1513 8.8 / 2205 4.9
2	0124 8.4 / 0759 5.4 / M 1429 8.7 / 2113 4.8	**17**	0403 9.0 / 1034 4.7 / TU 1618 9.5 / 2305 4.1
3	0324 8.9 / 1003 4.7 / TU 1558 9.5 / 2243 3.8	**18**	0451 9.8 / 1125 3.9 / W 1703 10.2 / 2349 3.4
4	0434 10.0 / 1117 3.5 / W 1659 10.7 / 2347 2.7	**19**	0528 10.5 / 1206 3.2 / TH 1740 10.8
5	0529 11.1 / 1216 2.4 / TH 1750 11.8	**20**	0029 2.8 / 0602 11.0 / F 1243 2.7 / 1814 11.3
6	0047 1.6 / 0617 12.0 / F 1310 1.5 / 1837 12.6	**21**	0104 2.4 / 0634 11.4 / SA 1318 2.4 / 1846 11.6
7	0138 1.0 / 0702 12.6 / SA 1359 0.9 / ○ 1922 13.1	**22**	0136 2.2 / 0705 11.7 / SU 1350 2.2 / ● 1917 11.8
8	0224 0.6 / 0744 12.9 / SU 1444 0.7 / 2003 13.2	**23**	0207 2.1 / 0734 11.8 / M 1421 2.2 / 1946 11.8
9	0306 0.7 / 0823 12.9 / M 1525 0.9 / 2043 13.0	**24**	0235 2.2 / 0801 11.8 / TU 1450 2.2 / 2014 11.7
10	0343 1.1 / 0900 12.6 / TU 1602 1.4 / 2120 12.3	**25**	0303 2.4 / 0827 11.6 / W 1519 2.4 / 2041 11.4
11	0416 1.9 / 0935 12.0 / W 1636 2.2 / 2156 11.4	**26**	0330 2.7 / 0854 11.4 / TH 1549 2.8 / 2110 11.0
12	0447 2.8 / 1010 11.1 / TH 1709 3.2 / 2234 10.4	**27**	0357 3.2 / 0924 11.0 / F 1620 3.3 / 2143 10.5
13	0519 3.9 / 1048 10.2 / F 1746 4.1 / 2320 9.3	**28**	0428 3.7 / 0959 10.4 / SA 1658 3.8 / 2224 9.8
14	0600 4.8 / 1140 9.2 / SA 1841 5.0 / ◑	**29**	0510 4.4 / 1045 9.6 / SU 1749 4.6 / ◑ 2325 9.0
15	0042 8.5 / 0713 5.5 / SU 1322 8.6 / ◑ 2023 5.3	**30**	0612 4.9 / 1206 9.0 / M 1906 4.7
		31	0115 8.7 / 0750 5.0 / TU 1402 9.1 / 2049 4.5

NOVEMBER

#	Time m	#	Time m
1	0254 9.2 / 0934 4.4 / W 1526 9.8 / 2213 3.6	**16**	0358 9.4 / 1029 4.3 / TH 1612 9.6 / 2256 3.9
2	0403 10.1 / 1047 3.4 / TH 1628 10.8 / 2317 2.7	**17**	0442 10.0 / 1116 3.7 / F 1655 10.2 / 2339 3.3
3	0459 11.0 / 1147 2.5 / F 1721 11.6	**18**	0520 10.5 / 1158 3.2 / SA 1734 10.7
4	0017 1.9 / 0548 11.8 / SA 1241 1.8 / 1810 12.3	**19**	0021 2.9 / 0556 11.0 / SU 1238 2.8 / 1811 11.1
5	0108 1.3 / 0633 12.4 / SU 1331 1.3 / ○ 1856 12.6	**20**	0058 2.6 / 0631 11.3 / M 1315 2.5 / ● 1846 11.3
6	0154 1.2 / 0716 12.6 / M 1417 1.2 / 1939 12.7	**21**	0134 2.5 / 0704 11.5 / TU 1351 2.4 / 1920 11.5
7	0236 1.3 / 0756 12.6 / TU 1458 1.3 / 2019 12.4	**22**	0208 2.4 / 0735 11.6 / W 1426 2.3 / 1953 11.5
8	0314 1.7 / 0834 12.3 / W 1536 1.8 / 2058 11.8	**23**	0241 2.5 / 0807 11.6 / TH 1502 2.4 / 2027 11.3
9	0348 2.3 / 0911 11.8 / TH 1611 2.4 / 2137 11.1	**24**	0315 2.7 / 0842 11.5 / F 1539 2.6 / 2104 11.0
10	0421 3.1 / 0948 11.0 / F 1647 3.2 / 2217 10.2	**25**	0351 3.0 / 0920 11.1 / SA 1618 2.9 / 2145 10.6
11	0456 3.9 / 1029 10.2 / SA 1725 4.0 / 2303 9.4	**26**	0430 3.5 / 1004 10.7 / SU 1703 3.4 / 2234 10.1
12	0539 4.6 / 1120 9.4 / SU 1815 4.7 / ○	**27**	0518 3.9 / 1058 10.1 / M 1756 3.8 / 2334 9.6
13	0007 8.7 / 0640 5.2 / M 1235 8.8 / 1928 5.1	**28**	0619 4.3 / 1207 9.7 / TU 1903 4.0 / ◑
14	0140 8.5 / 0807 5.3 / TU 1408 8.7 / 2056 5.0	**29**	0052 9.4 / 0736 4.4 / W 1328 9.4 / 2020 3.9
15	0301 8.8 / 0930 4.9 / W 1520 9.1 / 2204 4.5	**30**	0213 9.5 / 0857 4.1 / TH 1445 10.0 / 2135 3.5

DECEMBER

#	Time m	#	Time m
1	0324 10.0 / 1010 3.5 / F 1553 10.5 / 2242 2.9	**16**	0342 9.2 / 1015 4.3 / SA 1601 9.4 / 2244 4.0
2	0425 10.7 / 1114 2.9 / SA 1652 11.1 / 2342 2.4	**17**	0434 9.8 / 1110 3.8 / SU 1652 9.9 / 2336 3.6
3	0519 11.3 / 1212 2.3 / SU 1745 11.5	**18**	0519 10.3 / 1200 3.3 / M 1738 10.4
4	0038 2.1 / 0609 11.7 / M 1305 1.9 / 1835 11.8	**19**	0024 3.2 / 0601 10.8 / TU 1245 2.9 / 1821 10.8
5	0127 1.9 / 0654 12.0 / TU 1353 1.8 / ○ 1921 11.8	**20**	0107 2.8 / 0641 11.2 / W 1329 2.5 / ● 1902 11.1
6	0149 2.6 / 0737 12.0 / W 1437 1.8 / 2005 11.7	**21**	0149 2.6 / 0720 11.5 / TH 1412 2.3 / 1943 11.3
7	0252 2.1 / 0818 11.9 / TH 1517 2.0 / 2046 11.4	**22**	0231 2.4 / 0800 11.7 / F 1456 2.1 / 2024 11.4
8	0330 2.5 / 0857 11.6 / F 1556 2.4 / 2126 11.0	**23**	0313 2.4 / 0841 11.7 / SA 1540 2.1 / 2106 11.3
9	0407 2.9 / 0937 11.1 / SA 1633 2.9 / 2205 10.4	**24**	0356 2.5 / 0924 11.6 / SU 1624 2.2 / 2150 11.1
10	0443 3.4 / 1016 10.5 / SU 1711 3.5 / 2246 9.9	**25**	0440 2.7 / 1009 11.3 / M 1710 2.5 / 2236 10.8
11	0522 4.0 / 1058 9.9 / M 1751 4.0 / 2330 9.3	**26**	0526 3.0 / 1058 10.9 / TU 1758 2.8 / 2326 10.4
12	0607 4.4 / 1145 9.4 / TU 1837 4.2 / ○	**27**	0616 3.3 / 1151 10.5 / W 1850 3.2
13	0023 8.9 / 0701 4.7 / W 1242 9.0 / 1933 4.6	**28**	0023 10.0 / 0712 3.6 / TH 1251 10.1 / 1948 3.5
14	0129 8.8 / 0805 4.8 / TH 1353 8.9 / 2039 4.6	**29**	0128 9.7 / 0818 3.8 / F 1401 9.7 / 2054 3.6
15	0241 8.9 / 0913 4.7 / F 1502 9.0 / 2145 4.4	**30**	0241 9.7 / 0931 3.8 / SA 1516 9.9 / 2205 3.5
		31	0353 10.0 / 1043 3.4 / SU 1628 10.2 / 2313 3.2

TIDES

Chart Datum: 6·29 metres below IGN Datum

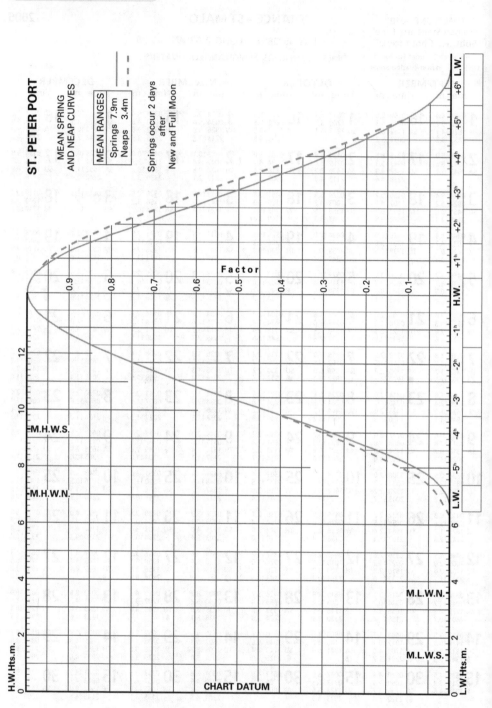

ST. PETER PORT

MEAN SPRING
AND NEAP CURVES

MEAN RANGES
Springs 7.9m
Neaps 3.4m

Springs occur 2 days
after
New and Full Moon

CHANNEL ISLES – ST PETER PORT

LAT 49°27′N   LONG 2°31′W

TIMES AND HEIGHTS OF HIGH AND LOW WATERS

2006

JANUARY

Day				
1	0110 1.7	0708 9.2	SU 1411 1.3	1937 9.0
2	0157 1.5	0756 9.4	M 1427 1.2	2024 9.1
3	0244 1.5	0842 9.4	TU 1514 1.2	2110 9.0
4	0330 1.6	0929 9.2	W 1600 1.4	2156 8.7
5	0416 1.9	1016 8.9	TH 1647 1.8	2244 8.4
6	0504 2.3	1106 8.4	F 1736 2.2	☾ 2335 7.9
7	0558 2.8	1202 7.9	SA 1831 2.7	
8	0034 7.5	0701 3.2	SU 1307 7.5	1935 3.1
9	0144 7.3	0818 3.4	M 1421 7.3	2049 3.3
10	0259 7.3	0933 3.3	TU 1537 7.3	2158 3.2
11	0403 7.5	1036 3.0	W 1634 7.5	2256 3.0
12	0457 7.9	1129 2.7	TH 1727 7.8	2345 2.7
13	0544 8.2	1215 2.4	F 1813 8.1	
14	0029 2.5	0626 8.5	SA 1258 2.2	○ 1854 8.3
15	0109 2.3	0705 8.6	SU 1336 2.0	1932 8.4
16	0145 2.2	0741 8.7	M 1411 2.0	2007 8.4
17	0218 2.1	0815 8.7	TU 1443 2.0	2039 8.3
18	0249 2.2	0846 8.5	W 1513 2.2	2109 8.2
19	0318 2.4	0917 8.3	TH 1542 2.4	2138 7.9
20	0348 2.7	0947 8.0	F 1610 2.7	2208 7.7
21	0419 3.0	1020 7.7	SA 1641 3.0	2241 7.4
22	0455 3.3	1059 7.4	SU 1720 3.3	◐ 2324 7.1
23	0543 3.6	1149 7.1	M 1812 3.6	
24	0022 6.9	0650 3.8	TU 1257 6.9	1925 3.7
25	0142 6.9	0819 3.7	W 1424 6.9	2055 3.6
26	0310 7.2	0941 3.3	TH 1545 7.3	2212 3.2
27	0420 7.7	1049 2.7	F 1653 7.8	2315 2.6
28	0519 8.3	1148 2.0	SA 1751 8.4	
29	0012 2.0	0612 9.0	SU 1243 1.4	● 1843 8.9
30	0104 1.4	0702 9.5	M 1333 0.9	1931 9.3
31	0151 1.0	0748 9.9	TU 1419 0.5	2015 9.6

FEBRUARY

Day				
1	0236 0.8	0832 10.0	W 1502 0.5	2057 9.6
2	0317 0.8	0914 9.8	TH 1543 0.7	2137 9.3
3	0357 1.2	0955 9.4	F 1622 1.2	2216 8.8
4	0437 1.8	1036 8.7	SA 1701 1.9	2257 8.1
5	0518 2.5	1121 7.9	SU 1744 2.7	◑ 2343 7.5
6	0609 3.2	1216 7.2	M 1838 3.4	
7	0045 6.9	0720 3.7	TU 1337 6.7	1957 3.9
8	0220 6.7	0907 3.9	W 1516 6.6	2138 3.9
9	0349 6.9	1028 3.5	TH 1627 7.0	2247 3.5
10	0448 7.4	1122 3.0	F 1719 7.4	2336 3.0
11	0534 7.9	1206 2.5	SA 1802 7.9	
12	0018 2.5	0614 8.4	SU 1245 2.1	1840 8.3
13	0056 2.1	0651 8.7	M 1321 1.8	○ 1915 8.6
14	0130 1.8	0725 8.9	TU 1353 1.6	1947 8.7
15	0200 1.7	0756 8.9	W 1422 1.6	2017 8.7
16	0229 1.7	0825 8.9	TH 1449 1.7	2044 8.6
17	0255 1.9	0852 8.7	F 1514 1.9	2109 8.3
18	0321 2.1	0919 8.4	SA 1538 2.2	2134 8.1
19	0347 2.5	0946 8.1	SU 1604 2.6	2202 7.8
20	0417 2.8	1019 7.7	M 1636 3.0	2238 7.4
21	0456 3.3	1103 7.2	TU 1720 3.5	2329 7.0
22	0556 3.7	1208 6.8	W 1830 3.8	
23	0049 6.7	0734 3.8	TH 1348 6.6	2021 3.9
24	0242 6.9	0922 3.4	F 1533 7.0	2157 3.3
25	0408 7.5	1038 2.7	SA 1645 7.7	2305 2.6
26	0509 8.4	1138 1.8	SU 1741 8.5	
27	0001 1.7	0600 9.1	M 1230 1.0	1830 9.2
28	0050 1.0	0647 9.8	TU 1317 0.4	● 1914 9.7

MARCH

Day				
1	0136 0.5	0731 10.2	W 1400 0.1	1956 9.9
2	0217 0.3	0813 10.3	TH 1440 0.1	2035 9.9
3	0256 0.4	0852 10.0	F 1518 0.4	2111 9.6
4	0332 0.8	0929 9.5	SA 1552 1.1	2146 9.0
5	0407 1.5	1005 8.7	SU 1626 1.9	2220 8.2
6	0442 2.4	1042 7.8	M 1702 2.9	◑ 2257 7.4
7	0524 3.3	1129 6.9	TU 1748 3.7	2348 6.7
8	0631 4.0	1250 6.2	W 1907 4.3	
9	0134 6.3	0844 4.2	TH 1504 6.2	2121 4.2
10	0333 6.6	1016 3.7	F 1614 6.7	2232 3.7
11	0431 7.2	1105 3.1	SA 1701 7.3	2318 3.0
12	0514 7.8	1145 2.5	SU 1739 7.9	2356 2.4
13	0552 8.3	1220 2.0	M 1815 8.4	
14	0031 2.0	0626 8.7	TU 1254 1.7	○ 1848 8.7
15	0104 1.6	0659 9.0	W 1325 1.4	1920 8.9
16	0134 1.4	0730 9.1	TH 1354 1.4	1949 8.9
17	0202 1.4	0759 9.0	F 1419 1.5	2015 8.8
18	0229 1.6	0825 8.8	SA 1444 1.7	2040 8.6
19	0254 1.8	0851 8.6	SU 1508 2.0	2105 8.3
20	0320 2.2	0919 8.2	M 1534 2.4	2132 8.0
21	0349 2.6	0951 7.8	TU 1605 2.9	2208 7.6
22	0428 3.1	1036 7.2	W 1650 3.5	◐ 2300 7.1
23	0530 3.6	1145 6.7	TH 1804 3.9	
24	0025 6.7	0717 3.8	F 1334 6.6	2006 3.9
25	0225 6.9	0909 3.3	SA 1523 7.1	2144 3.3
26	0352 7.6	1022 2.4	SU 1630 7.9	2248 2.4
27	0450 8.5	1118 1.6	M 1721 8.7	2340 1.5
28	0540 9.2	1207 0.8	TU 1807 9.3	
29	0028 0.8	0625 9.8	W 1252 0.3	● 1850 9.8
30	0112 0.4	0708 10.1	TH 1334 0.1	1930 10.0
31	0153 0.2	0748 10.1	F 1413 0.2	2008 9.9

APRIL

Day				
1	0231 0.4	0827 9.8	SA 1449 0.6	2043 9.5
2	0306 0.9	0903 9.2	SU 1523 1.3	2116 8.9
3	0339 1.6	0937 8.6	M 1555 2.2	2148 8.2
4	0413 2.5	1013 7.6	TU 1628 3.0	2223 7.4
5	0453 3.3	1057 6.7	W 1711 3.8	◑ 2311 6.7
6	0559 4.0	1215 6.2	TH 1830 4.4	○
7	0046 6.3	0756 4.2	F 1431 6.2	2038 4.3
8	0255 6.5	0939 3.7	SA 1541 6.7	2157 3.8
9	0356 7.0	1029 3.1	SU 1627 7.3	2243 3.1
10	0440 7.6	1109 2.6	M 1705 7.8	2322 2.5
11	0518 8.1	1144 2.1	TU 1741 8.3	2357 2.0
12	0553 8.5	1218 1.7	W 1815 8.6	
13	0030 1.7	0627 8.8	TH 1250 1.5	○ 1847 8.9
14	0102 1.5	0659 8.9	F 1320 1.4	1917 8.9
15	0132 1.4	0729 8.9	SA 1349 1.5	1945 8.9
16	0202 1.5	0759 8.8	SU 1416 1.7	2013 8.7
17	0231 1.7	0828 8.6	M 1444 2.0	2042 8.5
18	0300 2.1	0900 8.2	TU 1514 2.4	2115 8.1
19	0335 2.5	0939 7.8	W 1551 2.9	2156 7.7
20	0420 3.0	1030 7.2	TH 1643 3.4	2255 7.2
21	0529 3.4	1144 6.8	F 1802 3.8	◐
22	0020 7.0	0712 3.4	SA 1235 6.8	1953 3.7
23	0203 7.2	0847 3.0	SU 1458 7.3	2119 3.0
24	0323 7.8	0954 2.2	M 1601 8.0	2221 2.3
25	0421 8.5	1049 1.6	TU 1652 8.7	2313 1.6
26	0512 9.1	1138 1.0	W 1738 9.0	
27	0000 1.0	0558 9.5	TH 1224 0.7	● 1821 9.5
28	0045 0.6	0642 9.7	F 1306 0.6	1902 9.6
29	0127 0.7	0724 9.6	SA 1346 0.8	1941 9.4
30	0206 0.9	0803 9.3	SU 1423 1.2	2017 9.2

Chart Datum: 5·06 metres below Ordnance Datum (Local)

TIDES

CHANNEL ISLES – ST PETER PORT — 2006

LAT 49°27'N   LONG 2°31'W

TIMES AND HEIGHTS OF HIGH AND LOW WATERS

TIME ZONE (UT)
For Summer Time add ONE hour in **non-shaded areas**

MAY

Day				
1 M	0243 1.3	0840 8.8	1458 1.8	2052 8.7
2 TU	0318 1.9	0917 8.2	1531 2.4	2126 8.1
3 W	0354 2.6	0955 7.5	1606 3.1	2203 7.5
4 TH	0437 3.2	1041 6.9	1651 3.7	2251 6.9
5 F ◑	0538 3.7	1148 6.4	1800 4.1	
6 SA	0005 6.5	0700 3.9	1322 6.3	1927 4.2
7 SU	0143 6.5	0828 3.7	1442 6.6	2052 3.8
8 M	0257 6.9	0932 3.3	1536 7.1	2150 3.3
9 TU	0349 7.3	1018 2.8	1619 7.6	2234 2.8
10 W	0432 7.8	1058 2.4	1658 8.0	2313 2.3
11 TH	0512 8.1	1135 2.1	1735 8.4	2350 2.0
12 F	0548 8.4	1211 1.8	1811 8.6	
13 SA ○	0027 1.7	0626 8.6	1246 1.7	1845 8.8
14 SU	0103 1.6	0702 8.7	1321 1.7	1919 8.8
15 M	0139 1.6	0737 8.7	1355 1.8	1953 8.8
16 TU	0215 1.7	0814 8.5	1430 2.1	2029 8.6
17 W	0253 2.0	0854 8.2	1508 2.4	2110 8.3
18 TH	0335 2.3	0940 7.9	1553 2.8	2159 8.0
19 F	0428 2.7	1036 7.5	1650 3.1	2259 7.6
20 SA ◑	0536 2.9	1143 7.3	1803 3.3	
21 SU	0012 7.5	0655 2.9	1303 7.3	1928 3.2
22 M	0133 7.6	0813 2.7	1421 7.5	2045 2.9
23 TU	0247 7.9	0920 2.3	1525 8.0	2149 2.4
24 W	0348 8.3	1017 1.9	1619 8.4	2243 1.9
25 TH	0443 8.6	1108 1.6	1709 8.8	2333 1.6
26 F	0532 8.9	1156 1.4	1755 9.0	
27 SA ●	0020 1.4	0619 9.0	1241 1.4	1838 9.1
28 SU	0105 1.3	0703 8.9	1324 1.5	1919 9.0
29 M	0147 1.4	0746 8.7	1403 1.7	1958 8.8
30 TU	0227 1.7	0826 8.4	1441 2.1	2035 8.5
31 W	0305 2.1	0904 8.0	1517 2.5	2111 8.1

JUNE

Day				
1 TH	0343 2.5	0943 7.6	1553 3.0	2150 7.7
2 F	0424 3.0	1026 7.2	1635 3.4	2233 7.3
3 SA ◑	0512 3.3	1115 6.9	1726 3.7	2325 7.0
4 SU	0610 3.6	1216 6.7	1828 3.8	
5 M	0030 6.8	0712 3.6	1323 6.7	1934 3.8
6 TU	0140 6.8	0815 3.5	1426 6.9	2038 3.5
7 W	0244 7.0	0912 3.2	1521 7.2	2135 3.2
8 TH	0338 7.4	1004 2.9	1609 7.6	2225 2.8
9 F	0427 7.7	1050 2.6	1654 8.0	2311 2.4
10 SA	0513 8.0	1134 2.3	1737 8.3	2356 2.1
11 SU ○	0557 8.3	1218 2.1	1818 8.6	
12 M	0040 1.8	0641 8.5	1301 1.9	1900 8.8
13 TU	0124 1.7	0725 8.6	1344 1.9	1942 8.9
14 W	0209 1.6	0809 8.6	1427 1.9	2026 8.8
15 TH	0254 1.7	0855 8.5	1512 2.0	2111 8.7
16 F	0341 1.8	0942 8.3	1559 2.2	2200 8.5
17 SA	0432 2.0	1033 8.1	1651 2.5	2253 8.2
18 SU ◑	0527 2.3	1129 7.8	1749 2.7	2352 8.0
19 M	0628 2.5	1231 7.6	1854 2.9	
20 TU	0058 7.8	0734 2.6	1339 7.6	2006 2.9
21 W	0209 7.7	0842 2.6	1447 7.7	2115 2.7
22 TH	0317 7.8	0945 2.5	1549 7.9	2217 2.5
23 F	0418 8.0	1043 2.3	1644 8.2	2313 2.2
24 SA	0514 8.2	1135 2.2	1735 8.4	
25 SU ●	0004 2.0	0604 8.3	1224 2.1	1821 8.6
26 M	0051 1.9	0651 8.4	1309 2.0	1905 8.7
27 TU	0135 1.8	0735 8.4	1350 2.1	1945 8.7
28 W	0215 1.9	0815 8.3	1428 2.2	2023 8.5
29 TH	0253 2.0	0852 8.2	1504 2.4	2058 8.3
30 F	0328 2.3	0927 7.9	1537 2.6	2132 8.0

JULY

Day				
1 SA	0403 2.6	1002 7.6	1611 2.9	2207 7.7
2 SU	0438 2.9	1038 7.4	1648 3.2	2245 7.4
3 M	0517 3.2	1118 7.1	1730 3.4	2329 7.1
4 TU	0603 3.4	1207 6.9	1823 3.6	
5 W	0023 6.9	0700 3.6	1307 6.8	1928 3.7
6 TH	0130 6.9	0805 3.6	1416 6.9	2037 3.5
7 F	0241 7.0	0911 3.4	1520 7.2	2141 3.2
8 SA	0346 7.3	1011 3.1	1618 7.6	2240 2.8
9 SU	0444 7.7	1107 2.7	1711 8.1	2334 2.3
10 M	0538 8.1	1159 2.3	1801 8.5	
11 TU ○	0026 1.9	0629 8.4	1250 1.9	1849 8.9
12 W	0117 1.5	0718 8.8	1338 1.6	1936 9.2
13 TH	0205 1.2	0805 9.0	1424 1.4	2021 9.4
14 F	0251 1.1	0850 9.0	1509 1.4	2106 9.3
15 SA	0336 1.1	0934 8.9	1552 1.5	2150 9.1
16 SU	0420 1.4	1018 8.7	1636 1.9	2236 8.7
17 M ◑	0505 1.8	1104 8.3	1723 2.4	2325 8.2
18 TU	0555 2.3	1156 7.8	1817 2.8	
19 W	0022 7.7	0652 2.8	1258 7.4	1923 3.2
20 TH	0133 7.3	0803 3.2	1412 7.2	2046 3.3
21 F	0254 7.2	0921 3.3	1528 7.3	2203 3.2
22 SA	0407 7.3	1029 3.1	1632 7.6	2305 2.8
23 SU	0507 7.6	1126 2.8	1726 8.0	2357 2.4
24 M	0558 8.0	1215 2.5	1812 8.3	
25 TU ●	0043 2.1	0642 8.2	1259 2.2	1854 8.6
26 W	0124 1.9	0722 8.4	1338 2.0	1932 8.8
27 TH	0202 1.8	0759 8.5	1413 1.9	2007 8.8
28 F	0235 1.8	0832 8.5	1445 2.0	2038 8.7
29 SA	0305 1.9	0903 8.3	1514 2.2	2108 8.4
30 SU	0333 2.2	0931 8.1	1541 2.4	2136 8.2
31 M	0400 2.5	0959 7.8	1609 2.7	2206 7.8

AUGUST

Day				
1 TU	0427 2.9	1028 7.5	1640 3.1	2239 7.5
2 W	0500 3.3	1104 7.2	1720 3.5	2321 7.1
3 TH	0545 3.6	1154 6.9	1817 3.7	
4 F	0021 6.8	0653 3.8	1307 6.7	1940 3.8
5 SA	0147 6.7	0825 3.8	1438 6.9	2109 3.6
6 SU	0317 7.0	0945 3.5	1554 7.4	2221 3.0
7 M	0428 7.5	1050 2.9	1656 8.0	2322 2.3
8 TU	0527 8.1	1148 2.3	1749 8.6	
9 W ○	0016 1.7	0619 8.7	1240 1.6	1838 9.2
10 TH	0107 1.1	0707 9.2	1328 1.1	1924 9.7
11 F	0153 0.6	0752 9.5	1412 0.8	2008 9.9
12 SA	0237 0.5	0834 9.6	1454 0.8	2050 9.9
13 SU	0317 0.6	0914 9.5	1534 1.0	2130 9.6
14 M	0357 1.0	0953 9.1	1613 1.5	2210 9.0
15 TU	0436 1.5	1033 8.5	1653 2.2	2253 8.2
16 W ◑	0518 2.5	1118 7.8	1739 2.9	2344 7.4
17 TH	0611 3.3	1216 7.1	1844 3.6	
18 F	0059 6.8	0728 3.8	1344 6.8	2029 3.9
19 SA	0248 6.6	0912 3.9	1522 6.9	2204 3.4
20 SU	0408 7.0	1027 3.5	1628 7.4	2303 3.1
21 M	0502 7.5	1120 3.0	1717 7.9	2349 2.6
22 TU	0546 8.0	1203 2.5	1758 8.4	
23 W ●	0029 2.1	0624 8.4	1242 2.1	1836 8.8
24 TH	0105 1.8	0700 8.7	1318 1.8	1911 9.0
25 F	0138 1.6	0734 8.8	1349 1.7	1943 9.0
26 SA	0208 1.6	0804 8.8	1418 1.7	2012 9.0
27 SU	0235 1.7	0831 8.7	1444 1.8	2038 8.8
28 M	0259 1.9	0856 8.4	1509 2.1	2104 8.5
29 TU	0322 2.3	0920 8.1	1533 2.5	2129 8.1
30 W	0345 2.7	0945 7.8	1600 2.9	2157 7.7
31 TH ◑	0413 3.1	1017 7.4	1633 3.4	2235 7.2

Chart Datum: 5·06 metres below Ordnance Datum (Local)

TIME ZONE (UT)
For Summer Time add ONE hour in **non-shaded areas**

LAT 49°27′N   LONG 2°31′W

TIMES AND HEIGHTS OF HIGH AND LOW WATERS

SEPTEMBER

Day	Time	m		Day	Time	m
1 F	0452 1102 1724 2333	3.6 7.0 3.8 6.8		**16** SA	0030 0658 1321 2023	6.4 4.3 6.5 4.2
2 SA	0557 1217 1855	4.1 6.7 4.1		**17** SU	0246 0907 1512 2157	6.4 4.2 6.8 3.8
3 SU	0109 0752 1409 2050	6.5 4.1 6.8 3.8		**18** M	0357 1016 1612 2247	6.9 3.7 7.3 3.1
4 M	0304 0930 1540 2209	6.9 3.7 7.4 3.0		**19** TU	0444 1101 1656 2327	7.5 3.0 7.9 2.6
5 TU	0419 1038 1642 2309	7.6 2.9 8.2 2.2		**20** W	0522 1140 1734	8.1 2.5 8.4
6 W	0514 1134 1734	8.3 2.1 8.9		**21** TH	0002 0557 1216 1809	2.1 8.5 2.0 8.8
7 TH ○	0001 0602 1223 1820	1.4 9.0 1.3 9.6		**22** F ●	0036 0630 1249 1842	1.7 8.9 1.7 9.1
8 F	0048 0647 1309 1905	0.7 9.6 0.7 10.1		**23** SA	0107 0702 1319 1913	1.5 9.0 1.6 9.2
9 SA	0132 0729 1352 1947	0.3 9.9 0.4 10.3		**24** SU ●	0135 0731 1347 1941	1.5 9.0 1.6 9.1
10 SU	0213 0810 1432 2027	0.2 10.0 0.5 10.1		**25** M	0201 0758 1413 2008	1.7 8.9 1.7 8.9
11 M	0252 0848 1510 2105	0.5 9.7 0.8 9.7		**26** TU	0225 0822 1438 2033	1.9 8.7 2.0 8.6
12 TU	0329 0924 1546 2143	1.1 9.2 1.5 9.0		**27** W	0248 0846 1503 2058	2.3 8.4 2.4 8.2
13 W	0404 1001 1623 2221	1.9 8.5 2.3 8.1		**28** TH	0312 0912 1529 2127	2.7 8.0 2.9 7.8
14 TH ◐	0443 1041 1706 2309	2.8 7.7 3.2 7.2		**29** F	0340 0944 1603 2206	3.2 7.6 3.3 7.3
15 F	0532 1136 1812	3.7 6.9 4.0		**30** SA ◑	0419 1031 1657 2309	3.7 7.1 3.8 6.8

OCTOBER

Day	Time	m		Day	Time	m
1 SU	0529 1153 1833	4.2 6.7 4.1		**16** M	0217 0837 1439 2123	6.4 4.4 6.7 3.9
2 M	0053 0735 1350 2035	6.5 4.2 6.9 3.7		**17** TU	0325 0944 1538 2212	6.9 3.8 7.2 3.3
3 TU	0252 0915 1521 2151	7.0 3.6 7.5 2.9		**18** W	0411 1028 1622 2252	7.5 3.2 7.8 2.7
4 W	0400 1019 1620 2247	7.8 2.7 8.4 2.0		**19** TH	0448 1106 1700 2327	8.0 2.6 8.3 2.3
5 TH	0452 1111 1710 2336	8.6 1.9 9.1 1.2		**20** F	0523 1141 1735	8.5 2.2 8.6
6 F	0538 1159 1756	9.3 1.2 9.7		**21** SA	0000 0555 1214 1808	2.0 8.8 1.9 8.9
7 SA ○	0022 0621 1244 1840	0.7 9.8 0.7 10.1		**22** SU ●	0031 0627 1245 1840	1.8 9.0 1.7 9.0
8 SU	0106 0702 1327 1922	0.4 10.0 0.5 10.2		**23** M	0101 0657 1315 1911	1.7 9.0 1.7 9.0
9 M	0147 0742 1407 2002	0.4 10.0 0.6 10.0		**24** TU	0128 0726 1344 1940	1.8 8.9 1.8 8.8
10 TU	0225 0820 1445 2041	0.8 9.7 1.0 9.5		**25** W	0156 0753 1413 2008	2.0 8.8 2.1 8.6
11 W	0301 0857 1522 2118	1.4 9.2 1.7 8.7		**26** TH	0223 0821 1441 2038	2.3 8.5 2.4 8.3
12 TH	0337 0933 1559 2157	2.2 8.4 2.5 7.9		**27** F	0251 0852 1513 2113	2.7 8.2 2.8 7.9
13 F	0414 1013 1643 2244	3.1 7.7 3.3 7.4		**28** SA	0325 0930 1554 2159	3.2 7.8 3.2 7.4
14 SA ◐	0504 1107 1751	3.9 6.9 4.0		**29** SU ◑	0411 1025 1654 2306	3.7 7.3 3.6 7.0
15 SU	0006 0630 1249 1950	6.4 4.5 6.5 4.3		**30** M	0524 1145 1826	4.0 7.0 3.8
				31 TU	0039 0715 1324 2007	6.8 4.0 7.2 3.4

NOVEMBER

Day	Time	m		Day	Time	m
1 W	0220 0846 1448 2120	7.2 3.4 7.7 2.7		**16** TH	0321 0939 1533 2203	7.2 3.5 7.4 3.1
2 TH	0328 0950 1549 2217	7.9 2.7 8.4 2.0		**17** F	0403 1022 1616 2243	7.7 3.0 7.8 2.7
3 F	0421 1043 1641 2307	8.6 2.0 9.0 1.4		**18** SA	0441 1100 1655 2319	8.1 2.6 8.2 2.4
4 SA	0508 1132 1729 2354	9.2 1.4 9.5 1.1		**19** SU	0518 1136 1732 2353	8.4 2.3 8.4 2.2
5 SU ○	0553 1218 1815	9.6 1.0 9.7		**20** M ●	0553 1211 1809	8.7 2.1 8.6
6 M	0039 0636 1303 1859	0.9 9.8 0.9 9.7		**21** TU	0027 0626 1247 1844	2.1 8.8 2.0 8.7
7 TU	0122 0717 1345 1941	1.0 9.7 1.0 9.5		**22** W	0101 0700 1322 1918	2.0 8.8 2.0 8.7
8 W	0202 0757 1426 2022	1.3 9.4 1.4 9.0		**23** TH	0135 0733 1357 1954	2.1 8.8 2.1 8.5
9 TH	0240 0836 1505 2101	1.8 9.0 1.9 8.4		**24** F	0209 0808 1433 2031	2.3 8.6 2.3 8.3
10 F	0318 0914 1546 2142	2.5 8.4 2.6 7.8		**25** SA	0245 0847 1513 2113	2.6 8.4 2.5 8.0
11 SA	0357 0955 1631 2230	3.2 7.8 3.2 7.1		**26** SU	0326 0932 1600 2203	2.9 8.1 2.8 7.7
12 SU ◐	0445 1047 1729 2335	3.8 7.2 3.8 6.7		**27** M	0417 1027 1658 2303	3.3 7.8 3.1 7.4
13 M	0554 1200 1847	4.2 6.8 4.0		**28** TU ◑	0522 1134 1809	3.5 7.6 3.2
14 TU	0106 0722 1331 2013	6.5 4.4 6.7 3.9		**29** W	0015 0643 1250 1927	7.3 3.5 7.6 3.1
15 W	0226 0844 1442 2117	6.8 4.0 7.0 3.6		**30** TH	0136 0805 1407 2040	7.5 3.3 7.8 2.7

DECEMBER

Day	Time	m		Day	Time	m
1 F	0248 0915 1513 2143	7.9 2.8 8.2 2.4		**16** SA	0304 0920 1521 2146	7.1 3.5 7.2 3.3
2 SA	0347 1014 1612 2239	8.3 2.3 8.5 2.0		**17** SU	0354 1012 1612 2235	7.5 3.2 7.6 3.0
3 SU	0440 1107 1705 2329	8.7 1.9 8.8 1.7		**18** M	0439 1058 1658 2319	7.9 2.8 7.9 2.7
4 M	0529 1157 1755	9.0 1.6 9.0		**19** TU	0522 1142 1742	8.2 2.5 8.2
5 TU ○	0017 0615 1245 1842	1.6 9.2 1.5 9.0		**20** W ●	0001 0602 1226 1825	2.4 8.5 2.2 8.4
6 W	0103 0659 1331 1928	1.6 9.3 1.5 8.9		**21** TH	0043 0643 1309 1907	2.2 8.7 2.0 8.6
7 TH	0146 0742 1414 2011	1.8 9.1 1.7 8.7		**22** F	0124 0723 1351 1949	2.1 8.9 1.8 8.6
8 F	0227 0823 1456 2052	2.1 8.9 2.0 8.4		**23** SA	0205 0805 1434 2031	2.0 8.9 1.8 8.6
9 SA	0306 0902 1536 2131	2.4 8.5 2.4 8.0		**24** SU	0247 0848 1517 2114	2.1 8.9 1.9 8.5
10 SU	0345 0942 1616 2212	2.9 8.1 2.8 7.5		**25** M	0330 0933 1602 2200	2.3 8.7 2.1 8.3
11 M	0425 1024 1659 2257	3.3 7.6 3.2 7.1		**26** TU	0417 1021 1650 2249	2.5 8.4 2.3 8.0
12 TU	0512 1112 1749 2351	3.7 7.2 3.6 6.9		**27** W ◑	0508 1114 1743 2345	2.8 8.1 2.6 7.7
13 W	0608 1211 1847	3.9 7.0 3.8		**28** TH	0608 1215 1844	3.0 7.9 2.8
14 TH	0056 0714 1319 1949	6.8 4.0 6.9 3.8		**29** F	0050 0718 1325 1954	7.6 3.2 7.7 2.9
15 F	0204 0820 1424 2051	6.9 3.8 7.0 3.6		**30** SA	0204 0837 1439 2109	7.5 3.1 7.7 2.9
				31 SU	0316 0949 1549 2215	7.7 2.9 7.8 2.7

Chart Datum: 5·06 metres below Ordnance Datum (Local)

TIDES

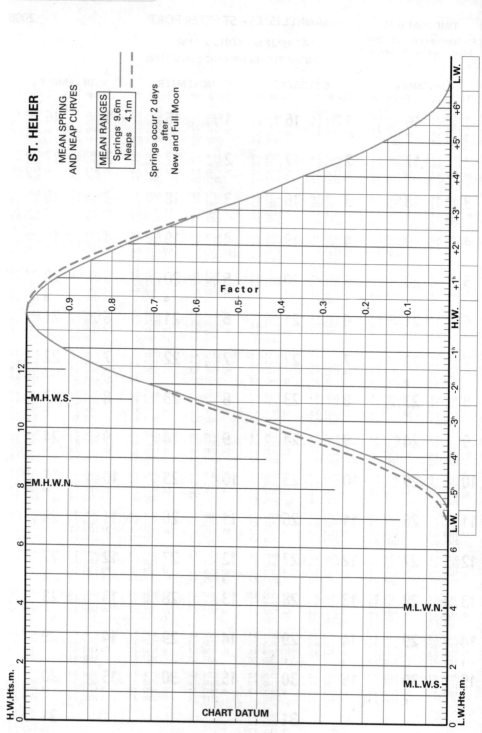

ST. HELIER

MEAN SPRING
AND NEAP CURVES

MEAN RANGES
Springs 9.6m
Neaps 4.1m

Springs occur 2 days
after
New and Full Moon

Factor

0.9 0.8 0.7 0.6 0.5 0.4 0.3 0.2 0.1

M.H.W.S.

M.H.W.N.

H.W.Hts.m.

CHART DATUM

M.L.W.N.

M.L.W.S.

L.W.Hts.m.

TIME ZONE (UT)
For Summer Time add ONE hour in **non-shaded areas**

CHANNEL ISLES – ST HELIER
LAT 49°11'N   LONG 2°07'W
TIMES AND HEIGHTS OF HIGH AND LOW WATERS

JANUARY

Time m	Time m
1 0122 1.8 / 0703 10.9 / SU 1349 1.4 / 1932 10.7	**16** 0153 2.3 / 0734 10.2 / M 1416 2.2 / 1959 9.9
2 0210 1.6 / 0751 11.1 / M 1438 1.3 / 2019 10.8	**17** 0225 2.3 / 0806 10.2 / TU 1447 2.2 / 2030 9.8
3 0257 1.6 / 0838 11.1 / TU 1526 1.3 / 2106 10.6	**18** 0255 2.4 / 0837 10.1 / W 1517 2.3 / 2100 9.7
4 0343 1.7 / 0925 10.9 / W 1612 1.5 / 2152 10.3	**19** 0325 2.5 / 0907 9.9 / TH 1546 2.5 / 2129 9.4
5 0429 2.0 / 1011 10.5 / TH 1659 1.9 / 2238 9.9	**20** 0355 2.8 / 0937 9.5 / F 1615 2.8 / 2159 9.1
6 0516 2.5 / 1059 9.9 / F 1747 2.4 / ☽ 2327 9.3	**21** 0427 3.1 / 1009 9.1 / SA 1646 3.2 / 2232 8.7
7 0607 2.9 / 1151 9.3 / SA 1839 2.9	**22** 0502 3.6 / 1045 8.7 / SU 1723 3.7 / ☾ 2312 8.3
8 0022 8.9 / 0705 3.4 / SU 1254 8.8 / 1939 3.4	**23** 0548 4.0 / 1133 8.2 / M 1813 4.1
9 0129 8.6 / 0814 3.6 / M 1406 8.5 / 2049 3.6	**24** 0011 8.0 / 0652 4.2 / TU 1242 7.9 / 1928 4.3
10 0242 8.5 / 0927 3.6 / TU 1524 8.5 / 2158 3.5	**25** 0133 7.9 / 0818 4.2 / W 1411 8.0 / 2100 4.1
11 0352 8.8 / 1036 3.3 / W 1628 8.8 / 2301 3.2	**26** 0259 8.3 / 0943 3.7 / TH 1535 8.5 / 2220 3.5
12 0450 9.2 / 1135 3.0 / TH 1722 9.2 / 2354 2.9	**27** 0412 9.0 / 1054 2.9 / F 1645 9.2 / 2325 2.8
13 0539 9.6 / 1223 2.6 / F 1809 9.5	**28** 0513 9.8 / 1155 2.1 / SA 1744 10.0
14 0038 2.6 / 0621 9.9 / SA 1306 2.1 / ○ 1849 9.7	**29** 0022 2.0 / 0607 10.6 / SU 1252 1.4 / ● 1837 10.6
15 0118 2.4 / 0659 10.1 / SU 1343 2.2 / 1925 9.9	**30** 0116 1.5 / 0657 11.2 / M 1344 0.9 / 1925 11.1
	31 0205 1.0 / 0743 11.6 / TU 1432 0.6 / 2010 11.3

FEBRUARY

Time m	Time m
1 0250 0.8 / 0828 11.7 / W 1516 0.5 / 2052 11.3	**16** 0237 1.8 / 0816 10.5 / TH 1456 1.8 / 2035 10.2
2 0332 0.9 / 0910 11.6 / TH 1557 0.6 / 2132 11.0	**17** 0304 1.9 / 0843 10.3 / F 1522 2.0 / 2100 10.0
3 0412 1.3 / 0950 11.1 / F 1636 1.3 / 2211 10.4	**18** 0331 2.1 / 0909 10.0 / SA 1547 2.3 / 2126 9.7
4 0450 1.9 / 1029 10.3 / SA 1713 2.1 / 2249 9.7	**19** 0358 2.6 / 0935 9.6 / SU 1612 2.8 / 2151 9.2
5 0529 2.7 / 1111 9.4 / SU 1752 3.0 / ☽ 2333 8.9	**20** 0427 3.1 / 1004 9.1 / M 1639 3.3 / 2223 8.7
6 0615 3.4 / 1201 8.5 / M 1843 3.8	**21** 0502 3.6 / 1043 8.5 / TU 1718 3.9 / 2310 8.2
7 0031 8.2 / 0720 4.1 / TU 1317 7.8 / 1959 4.3	**22** 0557 4.1 / 1146 7.9 / W 1827 4.4
8 0159 7.8 / 0854 4.2 / W 1459 7.7 / 2134 4.2	**23** 0033 7.7 / 0729 4.4 / TH 1330 7.6 / 2021 4.4
9 0333 8.1 / 1024 3.9 / TH 1620 8.2 / 2251 3.7	**24** 0230 7.9 / 0917 3.9 / F 1522 8.1 / 2201 3.7
10 0440 8.6 / 1128 3.2 / F 1716 8.8 / 2346 3.1	**25** 0359 8.8 / 1039 2.9 / SA 1637 9.1 / 2312 2.7
11 0529 9.3 / 1215 2.7 / SA 1759 9.3	**26** 0502 9.8 / 1143 1.9 / SU 1734 10.1
12 0029 2.6 / 0610 9.7 / SU 1255 2.3 / 1836 9.8	**27** 0011 1.8 / 0555 10.8 / M 1240 1.1 / 1824 10.9
13 0106 2.3 / 0645 10.1 / M 1330 2.0 / ○ 1909 10.0	**28** 0103 1.0 / 0643 11.5 / TU 1330 0.4 / ● 1909 11.5
14 0139 2.0 / 0717 10.3 / TU 1401 1.8 / 1939 10.2	
15 0209 1.9 / 0747 10.5 / W 1429 1.7 / 2007 10.2	

MARCH

Time m	Time m
1 0150 0.5 / 0727 12.0 / W 1415 0.1 / 1950 11.8	**16** 0145 1.6 / 0721 10.6 / TH 1403 1.5 / 1939 10.5
2 0233 0.3 / 0808 12.1 / TH 1456 0.1 / 2030 11.7	**17** 0213 1.5 / 0749 10.6 / F 1430 1.5 / 2006 10.5
3 0312 0.5 / 0847 11.8 / F 1533 0.5 / 2106 11.3	**18** 0240 1.6 / 0816 10.5 / SA 1455 1.7 / 2031 10.3
4 0348 0.9 / 0924 11.2 / SA 1606 1.2 / 2140 10.6	**19** 0307 1.8 / 0842 10.2 / SU 1520 2.1 / 2055 10.0
5 0421 1.7 / 0958 10.2 / SU 1637 2.2 / 2212 9.7	**20** 0334 2.3 / 0908 9.8 / M 1545 2.6 / 2121 9.5
6 0453 2.6 / 1034 9.2 / M 1709 3.1 / ☽ 2249 8.8	**21** 0402 2.8 / 0937 9.2 / TU 1612 3.2 / 2152 9.0
7 0530 3.6 / 1118 8.2 / TU 1751 4.1 / 2340 7.9	**22** 0437 3.4 / 1016 8.5 / W 1652 3.8 / ☾ 2239 8.3
8 0630 4.3 / 1235 7.3 / W 1910 4.7	**23** 0533 4.0 / 1121 7.9 / TH 1804 4.4
9 0121 7.4 / 0825 4.6 / TH 1445 7.3 / 2114 4.7	**24** 0008 7.8 / 0708 4.2 / F 1319 7.6 / 2002 4.4
10 0317 7.7 / 1012 4.1 / F 1607 7.9 / 2238 3.9	**25** 0218 8.0 / 0900 3.7 / SA 1512 8.2 / 2145 3.6
11 0424 8.4 / 1112 3.3 / SA 1658 8.7 / 2328 3.2	**26** 0344 8.9 / 1022 2.7 / SU 1621 9.3 / 2254 2.5
12 0510 9.1 / 1154 2.6 / SU 1737 9.4	**27** 0444 10.0 / 1124 1.7 / M 1715 10.3 / 2350 1.6
13 0008 2.5 / 0548 9.7 / M 1231 2.1 / 1811 9.8	**28** 0535 10.9 / 1217 0.9 / TU 1802 11.1
14 0043 2.1 / 0621 10.1 / TU 1304 1.8 / ○ 1843 10.2	**29** 0040 0.9 / 0621 11.6 / W 1306 0.4 / ● 1845 11.6
15 0115 1.8 / 0652 10.4 / W 1335 1.6 / 1912 10.4	**30** 0126 0.4 / 0704 11.9 / TH 1349 0.2 / 1925 11.7
	31 0208 0.3 / 0744 11.9 / F 1428 0.3 / 2002 11.6

APRIL

Time m	Time m
1 0246 0.6 / 0822 11.5 / SA 1504 0.8 / 2037 11.2	**16** 0216 1.6 / 0749 10.5 / SU 1430 1.8 / 2004 10.4
2 0320 1.1 / 0857 10.8 / SU 1536 1.5 / 2109 10.5	**17** 0245 1.8 / 0819 10.2 / M 1457 2.1 / 2033 10.1
3 0352 1.9 / 0930 9.9 / M 1605 2.4 / 2141 9.6	**18** 0315 2.2 / 0850 9.8 / TU 1527 2.6 / 2104 9.7
4 0423 2.8 / 1005 8.9 / TU 1635 3.4 / 2215 8.7	**19** 0349 2.7 / 0926 9.2 / W 1602 3.1 / 2142 9.1
5 0459 3.7 / 1048 7.9 / W 1715 4.2 / ☽ 2305 7.7	**20** 0432 3.2 / 1014 8.5 / TH 1650 3.7 / 2239 8.4
6 0557 4.4 / 1209 7.2 / TH 1832 4.9	**21** 0534 3.7 / 1129 8.0 / F 1807 4.1 / ☽
7 0048 7.3 / 0748 4.7 / F 1416 7.2 / 2039 4.8	**22** 0013 8.0 / 0704 3.8 / SA 1317 7.9 / 1950 4.0
8 0244 7.6 / 0935 4.2 / SA 1533 7.9 / 2202 4.1	**23** 0201 8.4 / 0840 3.3 / SU 1449 8.6 / 2119 3.3
9 0350 8.3 / 1034 3.4 / SU 1623 8.6 / 2251 3.3	**24** 0318 9.2 / 0955 2.5 / M 1554 9.4 / 2226 2.4
10 0435 9.0 / 1116 2.8 / M 1702 9.2 / 2331 2.7	**25** 0417 10.0 / 1055 1.7 / TU 1647 10.2 / 2321 1.7
11 0514 9.5 / 1153 2.3 / TU 1737 9.7	**26** 0508 10.7 / 1148 1.1 / W 1734 10.8
12 0007 2.2 / 0547 10.0 / W 1228 1.9 / 1808 10.1	**27** 0011 1.1 / 0554 11.2 / TH 1236 0.8 / ● 1816 11.2
13 0042 1.8 / 0619 10.3 / TH 1301 1.7 / ○ 1839 10.3	**28** 0058 0.9 / 0637 11.4 / F 1320 0.8 / 1857 11.3
14 0114 1.6 / 0650 10.5 / F 1332 1.6 / 1908 10.5	**29** 0140 0.8 / 0718 11.3 / SA 1359 0.9 / 1935 11.2
15 0146 1.5 / 0720 10.5 / SA 1401 1.6 / 1936 10.5	**30** 0219 1.1 / 0757 10.9 / SU 1435 1.4 / 2010 10.8

Chart Datum: 5·88 metres below Ordnance Datum (Local)

TIDES

TIME ZONE (UT)

For Summer Time add ONE hour in **non-shaded areas**

CHANNEL ISLES – ST HELIER

LAT 49°11'N   LONG 2°07'W

TIMES AND HEIGHTS OF HIGH AND LOW WATERS

2006

MAY

Time	m		Time	m
1 0255	1.5	**16** 0229	1.8
0834	10.3		0806	10.1
M 1508	2.0	TU 1443	2.2
2044	10.2		2022	10.2
2 0329	2.2	**17** 0306	2.1
0910	9.5		0846	9.8
TU 1540	2.7	W 1521	2.5
2118	9.5		2103	9.8
3 0403	2.9	**18** 0348	2.4
0947	8.7		0932	9.3
W 1614	3.5	TH 1605	2.9
2155	8.7		2152	9.3
4 0441	3.6	**19** 0438	2.8
1033	8.0		1028	8.8
TH 1656	4.2	F 1659	3.3
2246	8.0		2253	8.9
5 0535	4.2	**20** 0540	3.1
1143	7.5		1137	8.5
F 1801	4.6	SA 1809	3.6
◐		◐	
6 0007	7.6	**21** 0009	8.7
0656	4.4		0654	3.2
SA 1320	7.4	SU 1257	8.3
1935	4.6		1929	3.5
7 0145	7.6	**22** 0131	8.8
0828	4.2		0811	2.9
SU 1436	7.8	M 1413	8.8
2059	4.2		2045	3.1
8 0255	8.1	**23** 0242	9.3
0933	3.7		0920	2.5
M 1531	8.3	TU 1518	9.4
2156	3.6		2151	2.6
9 0346	8.6	**24** 0344	9.7
1022	3.1		1020	2.1
TU 1615	8.9	W 1613	9.9
2242	3.0		2249	2.1
10 0428	9.1	**25** 0438	10.1
1105	2.7		1115	1.8
W 1653	9.4	TH 1703	10.3
2323	2.5		2342	1.7
11 0506	9.6	**26** 0528	10.4
1144	2.3		1205	1.6
TH 1729	9.8	F 1749	10.6
12 0002	2.2	**27** 0031	1.6
0542	9.9		0614	10.5
F 1223	2.0	SA 1252	1.6
1802	10.1		1832	10.7
13 0041	1.9	**28** 0116	1.5
0617	10.2		0657	10.5
SA 1300	1.9	SU 1334	1.7
○ 1836	10.3		1912	10.6
14 0118	1.7	**29** 0158	1.7
0653	10.3		0739	10.2
SU 1335	1.8	M 1412	2.0
1910	10.4		1950	10.4
15 0154	1.7	**30** 0237	1.9
0729	10.3		0818	9.9
M 1409	1.9	TU 1449	2.3
1945	10.4		2027	10.0
		31 0313	2.4
			0857	9.4
		W 1524	2.8
			2104	9.5

JUNE

Time	m		Time	m
1 0349	2.8	**16** 0353	1.9
0935	8.9		0938	9.8
TH 1559	3.3	F 1610	2.4
2142	9.0		2157	10.0
2 0427	3.3	**17** 0442	2.1
1017	8.4		1029	9.5
F 1639	3.7	SA 1702	2.6
2226	8.5		2250	9.7
3 0511	3.7	**18** 0536	2.4
1107	8.0		1124	9.2
SA 1728	4.1	SU 1758	2.9
◑ 2321	8.1	◑ 2349	9.4
4 0604	4.0	**19** 0634	2.6
1210	7.8		1224	9.0
SU 1829	4.2	M 1900	3.1
5 0029	7.9	**20** 0053	9.1
0708	4.0		0736	2.8
M 1321	7.8	TU 1330	8.9
1938	4.2		2007	3.1
6 0141	8.0	**21** 0202	9.0
0816	3.9		0841	2.8
TU 1424	8.1	W 1437	9.0
2046	3.9		2115	3.0
7 0242	8.2	**22** 0309	9.1
0917	3.6		0946	2.8
W 1517	8.5	TH 1540	9.3
2144	3.5		2219	2.7
8 0334	8.6	**23** 0412	9.3
1011	3.2		1047	2.6
TH 1604	8.9	F 1637	9.6
2235	3.0		2319	2.5
9 0421	9.0	**24** 0508	9.5
1100	2.8		1142	2.4
F 1647	9.4	SA 1729	9.8
2324	2.6			
10 0506	9.4	**25** 0013	2.3
1146	2.5		0559	9.7
SA 1729	9.8	SU 1233	2.3
		● 1815	10.1
11 0010	2.2	**26** 0102	2.1
0549	9.8		0645	9.9
SU 1231	2.2	M 1318	2.2
○ 1810	10.1		1858	10.2
12 0055	1.9	**27** 0146	2.0
0633	10.0		0727	9.9
M 1314	2.0	TU 1359	2.3
1853	10.4		1938	10.1
13 0138	1.8	**28** 0225	2.1
0718	10.2		0806	9.8
TU 1357	2.0	W 1436	2.4
1936	10.5		2015	10.0
14 0222	1.7	**29** 0301	2.3
0803	10.2		0843	9.6
W 1439	2.0	TH 1510	2.6
2021	10.4		2050	9.7
15 0306	1.7	**30** 0334	2.5
0850	10.1		0917	9.3
TH 1523	2.1	F 1543	2.8
2108	10.3		2124	9.4

JULY

Time	m		Time	m
1 0407	2.8	**16** 0434	1.4
0951	9.0		1013	10.2
SA 1616	3.1	SU 1650	1.9
2159	9.1		2232	10.3
2 0440	3.1	**17** 0517	1.9
1028	8.6		1058	9.8
SU 1652	3.4	M 1736	2.4
2238	8.7	◐ 2319	9.7
3 0518	3.4	**18** 0604	2.4
1109	8.3		1147	9.2
M 1735	3.7	TU 1826	2.9
◑ 2322	8.3			
4 0602	3.7	**19** 0013	9.1
1159	8.0		0656	3.0
TU 1827	4.0	W 1245	8.7
			1928	3.4
5 0018	8.0	**20** 0120	8.6
0657	3.9		0802	3.5
W 1302	7.9	TH 1357	8.5
1931	4.1		2042	3.6
6 0125	7.9	**21** 0240	8.4
0804	4.0		0917	3.6
TH 1410	8.0	F 1514	8.6
2042	3.9		2200	3.4
7 0235	8.1	**22** 0357	8.5
0915	3.8		1030	3.4
F 1514	8.4	SA 1623	8.9
2150	3.5		2310	3.1
8 0339	8.5	**23** 0501	8.9
1020	3.4		1132	3.0
SA 1611	8.9	SU 1719	9.4
2250	3.0			
9 0437	9.0	**24** 0007	2.6
1117	2.9		0552	9.3
SU 1704	9.5	M 1225	2.6
2346	2.4		1806	9.8
10 0531	9.6	**25** 0055	2.3
1211	2.4		0636	9.7
M 1755	10.1	TU 1308	2.4
		● 1847	10.0
11 0038	1.9	**26** 0136	2.1
0622	10.0		0715	9.9
TU 1302	2.0	W 1347	2.2
○ 1843	10.5		1924	10.2
12 0130	1.5	**27** 0212	2.0
0712	10.4		0750	10.0
W 1350	1.7	TH 1420	2.2
1931	10.9		1958	10.2
13 0218	1.3	**28** 0243	2.0
0759	10.6		0822	9.9
TH 1437	1.5	F 1451	2.2
2017	11.0		2029	10.2
14 0305	1.1	**29** 0312	2.1
0845	10.7		0851	9.8
F 1522	1.5	SA 1519	2.3
2103	11.0		2059	10.0
15 0350	1.1	**30** 0340	2.3
0929	10.6		0920	9.6
SA 1606	1.6	SU 1548	2.5
2147	10.8		2128	9.7
		31 0407	2.6
			0948	9.3
		M 1617	2.9
			2157	9.3

AUGUST

Time	m		Time	m
1 0436	3.0	**16** 0529	2.6
1018	8.8		1107	9.2
TU 1650	3.3	W 1751	3.1
2229	8.8	◑ 2334	8.8
2 0508	3.5	**17** 0615	3.5
1053	8.4		1200	8.4
W 1730	3.8	TH 1850	3.9
◑ 2310	8.3			
3 0550	4.0	**18** 0042	8.0
1142	8.0		0725	4.2
TH 1825	4.2	F 1322	7.9
			2019	4.2
4 0010	7.8	**19** 0226	7.7
0654	4.3		0901	4.3
F 1258	7.8	SA 1504	8.0
1944	4.3		2157	3.9
5 0137	7.7	**20** 0357	8.1
0824	4.3		1027	3.8
SA 1430	8.0	SU 1619	8.6
2112	4.0		2308	3.3
6 0309	8.1	**21** 0457	8.6
0950	3.8		1127	3.2
SU 1547	8.6	M 1712	9.3
2227	3.3		2359	2.7
7 0421	8.8	**22** 0542	9.4
1058	3.1		1213	2.6
M 1649	9.4	TU 1754	9.9
2329	2.5			
8 0521	9.6	**23** 0041	2.2
1157	2.3		0620	9.8
TU 1743	10.2	W 1253	2.2
		● 1830	10.2
9 0026	1.7	**24** 0117	1.9
0613	10.3		0654	10.1
W 1251	1.7	TH 1327	2.0
○ 1833	10.9		1903	10.4
10 0119	1.1	**25** 0149	1.8
0701	10.9		0725	10.3
TH 1340	1.2	F 1357	1.9
1919	11.5		1934	10.5
11 0208	0.7	**26** 0217	1.7
0746	11.3		0754	10.3
F 1426	0.9	SA 1425	1.8
2004	11.7		2002	10.5
12 0253	0.5	**27** 0243	1.8
0828	11.4		0821	10.3
SA 1509	0.8	SU 1451	1.9
2046	11.7		2029	10.4
13 0334	0.6	**28** 0309	2.0
0909	11.2		0846	10.1
SU 1549	1.0	M 1518	2.2
2127	11.3		2055	10.1
14 0413	1.0	**29** 0333	2.3
0948	10.7		0910	9.6
M 1628	1.6	TU 1545	2.6
2206	10.6		2120	9.6
15 0450	1.8	**30** 0358	2.8
1026	10.0		0934	9.2
TU 1707	2.3	W 1612	3.1
2247	9.7		2146	9.1
		31 0424	3.4
			1002	8.7
		TH 1645	3.7
		◑ 2219	8.5

Chart Datum: 5·88 metres below Ordnance Datum (Local)

TIME ZONE (UT)
For Summer Time add ONE hour in **non-shaded areas**

LAT 49°11′N   LONG 2°07′W

TIMES AND HEIGHTS OF HIGH AND LOW WATERS

SEPTEMBER

Time m	Time m
1 F 0459 4.0 / 1042 8.2 / 1735 4.2 / 2313 7.8	**16** SA 0015 7.5 / 0654 4.7 / 1258 7.5 / 2008 4.6
2 SA 0600 4.5 / 1156 7.7 / 1901 4.5	**17** SU 0226 7.4 / 0854 4.7 / 1459 7.8 / 2153 4.1
3 SU 0055 7.5 / 0747 4.6 / 1402 7.7 / 2047 4.2	**18** M 0349 8.0 / 1018 4.0 / 1606 8.6 / 2253 3.3
4 M 0256 7.9 / 0931 4.0 / 1534 8.5 / 2210 3.3	**19** TU 0440 8.8 / 1109 3.2 / 1652 9.3 / 2336 2.7
5 TU 0411 8.9 / 1043 3.1 / 1636 9.6 / 2314 2.3	**20** W 0519 9.5 / 1150 2.6 / 1730 9.9
6 W 0507 9.9 / 1141 2.1 / 1728 10.6	**21** TH 0013 2.2 / 0553 10.0 / 1225 2.1 / 1804 10.3
7 TH 0009 1.4 / 0556 10.7 / 1233 1.3 / 1815 11.4 ○	**22** F 0047 1.9 / 0625 10.3 / 1257 1.9 / 1835 10.5
8 F 0101 0.7 / 0641 11.4 / 1321 0.8 / 1900 11.9	**23** SA 0117 1.7 / 0654 10.5 / 1327 1.8 / 1904 10.7
9 SA 0147 0.3 / 0724 11.7 / 1406 0.5 / 1942 12.1	**24** SU 0145 1.7 / 0722 10.5 / 1355 1.7 / 1932 10.7
10 SU 0230 0.3 / 0804 11.9 / 1447 0.5 / 2023 11.9	**25** M 0211 1.7 / 0748 10.5 / 1422 1.8 / 1958 10.5
11 M 0309 0.5 / 0842 11.4 / 1525 0.9 / 2101 11.4	**26** TU 0237 1.9 / 0813 10.3 / 1449 2.1 / 2023 10.2
12 TU 0345 1.1 / 0918 10.8 / 1601 1.6 / 2138 10.5	**27** W 0302 2.3 / 0836 10.0 / 1516 2.5 / 2048 9.8
13 W 0419 2.0 / 0953 10.0 / 1637 2.5 / 2215 9.4	**28** TH 0326 2.8 / 0900 9.5 / 1543 3.0 / 2115 9.2
14 TH 0454 3.1 / 1030 9.1 / 1717 3.5 ◑ / 2259 8.4	**29** F 0353 3.4 / 0928 9.0 / 1617 3.6 / 2150 8.5
15 F 0538 4.0 / 1121 8.1 / 1818 4.3	**30** SA 0429 4.0 / 1009 8.3 / 1708 4.2 / 2247 7.9 ◐

OCTOBER

Time m	Time m
1 SU 0535 4.6 / 1128 7.7 / 1839 4.5	**16** M 0200 7.4 / 0827 4.8 / 1429 7.8 / 2121 4.2
2 M 0041 7.5 / 0727 4.2 / 1346 7.8 / 2028 4.1	**17** TU 0317 8.0 / 0945 4.1 / 1533 8.4 / 2217 3.5
3 TU 0243 8.1 / 0912 4.0 / 1516 8.7 / 2150 3.1	**18** W 0405 8.7 / 1034 3.4 / 1619 9.1 / 2259 2.9
4 W 0352 9.1 / 1022 2.9 / 1615 9.8 / 2251 2.1	**19** TH 0444 9.4 / 1113 2.8 / 1656 9.7 / 2335 2.4
5 TH 0445 10.1 / 1117 2.0 / 1706 10.8 / 2345 1.3	**20** F 0519 9.9 / 1148 2.3 / 1730 10.1
6 F 0532 10.9 / 1208 1.2 / 1752 11.5	**21** SA 0008 2.1 / 0550 10.2 / 1221 2.0 / 1802 10.4
7 SA 0034 0.7 / 0616 11.5 / 1255 0.8 / 1835 11.9 ○	**22** SU 0040 1.9 / 0620 10.4 / 1253 1.9 / 1832 10.5
8 SU 0120 0.5 / 0657 11.8 / 1339 0.6 / 1917 12.0	**23** M 0111 1.8 / 0649 10.5 / 1325 1.8 / 1901 10.5
9 M 0202 0.5 / 0737 11.7 / 1420 0.7 / 1957 11.7	**24** TU 0141 1.9 / 0717 10.5 / 1355 1.9 / 1930 10.4
10 TU 0240 0.9 / 0814 11.4 / 1459 1.2 / 2035 11.1	**25** W 0209 2.1 / 0744 10.4 / 1424 2.1 / 1959 10.2
11 W 0316 1.6 / 0849 10.7 / 1535 1.9 / 2112 10.2	**26** TH 0237 2.4 / 0812 10.1 / 1454 2.5 / 2028 9.8
12 TH 0350 2.5 / 0924 9.9 / 1611 2.8 / 2150 9.1	**27** F 0305 2.9 / 0841 9.7 / 1527 3.0 / 2102 9.2
13 F 0425 3.4 / 1001 8.9 / 1652 3.7 / 2236 8.1	**28** SA 0338 3.4 / 0917 9.2 / 1607 3.5 / 2145 8.6
14 SA 0510 4.3 / 1053 8.1 / 1756 4.5 / 2356 7.4 ◐	**29** SU 0423 3.9 / 1007 8.6 / 1704 3.9 / 2251 8.1 ◑
15 SU 0629 4.9 / 1233 7.5 / 1946 4.7	**30** M 0532 4.4 / 1130 8.1 / 1829 4.1
	31 TU 0033 7.9 / 0710 4.4 / 1321 8.2 / 2004 3.8

NOVEMBER

Time m	Time m
1 W 0213 8.4 / 0843 3.8 / 1444 9.0 / 2120 3.0	**16** TH 0313 8.4 / 0940 3.8 / 1529 8.7 / 2207 3.4
2 TH 0321 9.2 / 0951 2.9 / 1545 9.8 / 2221 2.2	**17** F 0358 8.9 / 1025 3.3 / 1613 9.2 / 2248 2.9
3 F 0415 10.1 / 1048 2.1 / 1637 10.6 / 2315 1.5	**18** SA 0437 9.4 / 1106 2.8 / 1651 9.6 / 2327 2.6
4 SA 0504 10.7 / 1139 1.5 / 1725 11.2	**19** SU 0513 9.8 / 1144 2.4 / 1727 9.9
5 SU 0004 1.1 / 0548 11.2 / 1228 1.2 / 1810 11.4 ○	**20** M 0004 2.3 / 0546 10.1 / 1222 2.2 / 1801 10.1
6 M 0051 1.0 / 0630 11.4 / 1313 1.1 / 1854 11.4	**21** TU 0040 2.2 / 0619 10.3 / 1258 2.0 / 1835 10.2
7 TU 0134 1.1 / 0711 11.4 / 1356 1.2 / 1935 11.1	**22** W 0115 2.1 / 0652 10.4 / 1333 2.0 / 1910 10.2
8 W 0214 1.5 / 0750 11.0 / 1436 1.6 / 2016 10.6	**23** TH 0148 2.2 / 0726 10.4 / 1408 2.1 / 1946 10.1
9 TH 0252 2.0 / 0827 10.5 / 1515 2.2 / 2055 9.8	**24** F 0222 2.4 / 0801 10.2 / 1444 2.3 / 2024 9.8
10 F 0328 2.8 / 0905 9.8 / 1554 2.9 / 2136 9.0	**25** SA 0258 2.7 / 0839 9.9 / 1523 2.6 / 2106 9.5
11 SA 0406 3.5 / 0945 9.0 / 1637 3.7 / 2222 8.3	**26** SU 0338 3.1 / 0924 9.5 / 1609 3.0 / 2156 9.0
12 SU 0451 4.2 / 1035 8.3 / 1732 4.3 / 2328 7.7 ◑	**27** M 0427 3.4 / 1018 9.1 / 1706 3.3 / 2257 8.7
13 M 0555 4.7 / 1149 7.8 / 1852 4.5	**28** TU 0530 3.7 / 1126 8.8 / 1814 3.5 ◐
14 TU 0057 7.6 / 0723 4.7 / 1324 7.8 / 2015 4.3	**29** W 0010 8.5 / 0645 3.8 / 1245 8.8 / 1930 3.4
15 W 0216 7.9 / 0843 4.4 / 1436 8.2 / 2119 3.9	**30** TH 0129 8.7 / 0804 3.5 / 1401 9.0 / 2042 3.0

DECEMBER

Time m	Time m
1 F 0240 9.1 / 0914 3.1 / 1508 9.5 / 2146 2.6	**16** SA 0300 8.3 / 0927 3.9 / 1519 8.4 / 2156 3.6
2 SA 0340 9.6 / 1015 2.5 / 1607 10.0 / 2243 2.2	**17** SU 0351 8.7 / 1021 3.4 / 1609 8.8 / 2246 3.2
3 SU 0434 10.1 / 1112 2.1 / 1701 10.4 / 2337 1.9	**18** M 0435 9.2 / 1109 3.0 / 1654 9.2 / 2331 2.8
4 M 0524 10.5 / 1204 1.8 / 1750 10.6	**19** TU 0516 9.6 / 1154 2.9 / 1737 9.6
5 TU 0027 1.8 / 0609 10.8 / 1256 1.7 / 1837 10.6	**20** W 0015 2.5 / 0556 10.0 / 1238 2.2 / 1818 9.9 ●
6 W 0113 1.8 / 0653 10.8 / 1340 1.7 / 1922 10.5	**21** TH 0057 2.3 / 0637 10.3 / 1320 2.0 / 1900 10.1
7 TH 0156 2.0 / 0735 10.7 / 1423 1.9 / 2004 10.2	**22** F 0137 2.2 / 0717 10.5 / 1401 1.9 / 1942 10.2
8 F 0237 2.3 / 0815 10.4 / 1503 2.3 / 2045 9.8	**23** SA 0217 2.1 / 0759 10.5 / 1443 1.9 / 2025 10.2
9 SA 0315 2.7 / 0853 9.9 / 1542 2.7 / 2124 9.3	**24** SU 0258 2.2 / 0843 10.5 / 1526 2.0 / 2110 10.1
10 SU 0352 3.2 / 0932 9.4 / 1620 3.2 / 2204 8.8	**25** M 0341 2.3 / 0928 10.3 / 1611 2.2 / 2156 9.8
11 M 0430 3.6 / 1013 8.9 / 1701 3.7 / 2249 8.3	**26** TU 0427 2.6 / 1015 10.0 / 1659 2.4 / 2245 9.5
12 TU 0514 4.0 / 1101 8.4 / 1749 4.0 / 2343 8.0 ◑	**27** W 0518 2.9 / 1107 9.6 / 1751 2.8 / 2339 9.1
13 W 0609 4.3 / 1202 8.1 / 1848 4.2	**28** TH 0615 3.2 / 1206 9.2 / 1851 3.1
14 TH 0051 7.9 / 0715 4.4 / 1314 8.0 / 1955 4.2	**29** F 0041 8.8 / 0720 3.4 / 1314 8.9 / 1958 3.2
15 F 0200 8.0 / 0825 4.2 / 1422 8.1 / 2059 4.0	**30** SA 0152 8.8 / 0833 3.4 / 1428 8.9 / 2109 3.2
	31 SU 0304 9.0 / 0946 3.2 / 1541 9.1 / 2217 3.0

Chart Datum: 5·88 metres below Ordnance Datum (Local)

TIDES

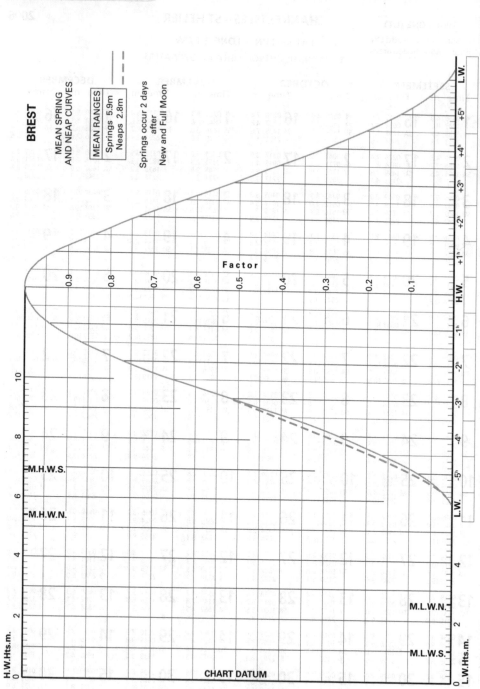

BREST

MEAN SPRING
AND NEAP CURVES

MEAN RANGES	
Springs 5.9m	
Neaps 2.8m	

Springs occur 2 days
after
New and Full Moon

TIME ZONE –0100
(French Standard Time)
Subtract 1 hour for UT
For French Summer Time add
ONE hour in **non-shaded areas**

FRANCE – BREST

LAT 48°23'N   LONG 4°30'W

TIMES AND HEIGHTS OF HIGH AND LOW WATERS

JANUARY

Time	m	Time	m
1 0535	7.0	**16** 0008	1.7
1158	1.0	0607	6.5
SU 1759	6.8	M 1233	1.6
		1827	6.3
2 0020	1.2	**17** 0042	1.7
0622	7.1	0640	6.5
M 1246	0.9	TU 1305	1.6
1847	6.8	1859	6.2
3 0108	1.2	**18** 0114	1.7
0711	7.1	0711	6.4
TU 1334	1.0	W 1337	1.7
1935	6.7	1930	6.1
4 0157	1.3	**19** 0146	1.9
0759	6.9	0743	6.3
W 1424	1.2	TH 1409	1.9
2024	6.4	2002	5.9
5 0247	1.5	**20** 0219	2.0
0850	6.7	0814	6.1
TH 1514	1.4	F 1441	2.1
2114	6.2	2035	5.8
6 0339	1.8	**21** 0254	2.2
0942	6.3	0849	5.8
F 1608	1.8	SA 1518	2.3
◑ 2209	5.9	2114	5.5
7 0436	2.1	**22** 0336	2.5
1040	6.0	0930	5.6
SA 1706	2.1	SU 1602	2.6
2310	5.6	◑ 2202	5.3
8 0539	2.3	**23** 0427	2.7
1144	5.7	1024	5.3
SU 1810	2.4	M 1657	2.8
		2306	5.2
9 0023	5.5	**24** 0531	2.8
0648	2.5	1136	5.2
M 1256	5.6	TU 1808	2.8
1919	2.4		
10 0135	5.6	**25** 0028	5.2
0800	2.4	0648	2.8
TU 1406	5.6	W 1259	5.2
2026	2.4	1927	2.7
11 0239	5.7	**26** 0145	5.5
0903	2.2	0805	2.5
W 1507	5.8	TH 1417	5.5
2123	2.2	2038	2.4
12 0333	6.0	**27** 0252	5.9
0957	2.0	0911	2.1
TH 1557	5.9	F 1520	5.9
2212	2.0	2137	2.0
13 0418	6.2	**28** 0348	6.3
1042	1.8	1008	1.6
F 1641	6.1	SA 1614	6.4
2254	1.9	2230	1.5
14 0458	6.4	**29** 0439	6.8
1122	1.7	1059	1.1
SA 1719	6.2	SU 1704	6.7
○ 2332	1.7	● 2319	1.1
15 0534	6.5	**30** 0526	7.2
1159	1.6	1148	0.7
SU 1754	6.3	M 1750	7.0
		31 0007	0.8
		0613	7.4
		TU 1234	0.5
		1835	7.1

FEBRUARY

Time	m	Time	m
1 0056	0.7	**16** 0049	1.4
0657	7.5	0645	6.7
W 1320	0.5	TH 1308	1.4
1918	7.1	1901	6.4
2 0141	0.8	**17** 0117	1.5
0741	7.3	0713	6.5
TH 1404	0.8	F 1336	1.6
2001	6.8	1929	6.3
3 0225	1.1	**18** 0147	1.7
0824	7.0	0741	6.4
F 1449	1.2	SA 1405	1.8
2043	6.4	1958	6.1
4 0311	1.5	**19** 0219	1.9
0909	6.5	0811	6.1
SA 1534	1.7	SU 1437	2.1
2129	6.0	2031	5.8
5 0400	2.0	**20** 0257	2.2
0958	5.9	0847	5.8
SU 1625	2.2	M 1517	2.4
◐ 2222	5.6	2112	5.5
6 0458	2.4	**21** 0343	2.5
1058	5.4	0934	5.4
M 1725	2.6	TU 1607	2.7
2331	5.2	2210	5.2
7 0610	2.7	**22** 0444	2.8
1219	5.1	1044	5.1
TU 1842	2.9	W 1717	3.0
		2334	5.1
8 0107	5.2	**23** 0607	2.9
0738	2.8	1224	5.0
W 1352	5.1	TH 1851	2.9
2008	2.8		
9 0230	5.4	**24** 0119	5.3
0854	2.5	0742	2.6
TH 1502	5.4	F 1401	5.3
2114	2.5	2019	2.5
10 0326	5.7	**25** 0237	5.8
0949	2.2	0857	2.1
F 1551	5.7	SA 1509	5.9
2202	2.2	2124	2.0
11 0409	6.0	**26** 0335	6.4
1032	1.9	0954	1.4
SA 1630	6.0	SU 1602	6.4
2242	1.9	2216	1.4
12 0445	6.3	**27** 0425	7.0
1108	1.6	1045	0.8
SU 1705	6.2	M 1649	6.9
2317	1.7	2304	0.9
13 0518	6.5	**28** 0511	7.4
1141	1.5	1131	0.4
M 1736	6.4	TU 1733	7.3
○ 2349	1.5	● 2350	0.5
14 0548	6.6		
1211	1.4		
TU 1805	6.5		
15 0020	1.4		
0617	6.7		
W 1240	1.3		
1833	6.5		

MARCH

Time	m	Time	m
1 0555	7.7	**16** 0549	6.8
1216	0.3	1211	1.2
W 1815	7.4	TH 1804	6.7
2 0036	0.4	**17** 0021	1.3
0636	7.7	0616	6.8
TH 1258	0.3	F 1238	1.3
1855	7.3	1831	6.7
3 0118	0.6	**18** 0049	1.3
0716	7.4	0643	6.7
F 1339	0.7	SA 1305	1.4
1933	7.0	1858	6.5
4 0200	0.9	**19** 0119	1.5
0756	7.0	0712	6.5
SA 1419	1.2	SU 1334	1.6
2011	6.4	1928	6.3
5 0242	1.4	**20** 0152	1.7
0835	6.4	0743	6.2
SU 1501	1.7	M 1407	1.9
2051	6.1	2001	6.0
6 0327	2.0	**21** 0230	2.0
0919	5.8	0819	5.8
M 1547	2.4	TU 1447	2.3
2139	5.5	2042	5.7
7 0422	2.5	**22** 0317	2.4
1017	5.2	0907	5.4
TU 1646	2.9	W 1539	2.7
2248	5.1	◑ 2141	5.3
8 0535	2.9	**23** 0420	2.7
1147	4.8	1022	5.0
W 1808	3.1	TH 1652	3.0
		2311	5.1
9 0040	4.9	**24** 0547	2.8
0717	3.0	1211	5.0
TH 1341	4.9	F 1832	2.9
1951	3.0		
10 0215	5.2	**25** 0103	5.3
0839	2.6	0726	2.5
F 1449	5.3	SA 1348	5.4
2058	2.6	2003	2.5
11 0309	5.6	**26** 0219	5.9
0930	2.2	0840	1.9
SA 1533	5.7	SU 1452	6.0
2143	2.2	2106	1.8
12 0349	6.0	**27** 0315	6.5
1010	1.9	0935	1.3
SU 1608	6.0	M 1542	6.6
2220	1.9	2157	1.2
13 0422	6.3	**28** 0404	7.1
1043	1.6	1024	0.7
M 1640	6.3	TU 1627	7.0
2252	1.6	2244	0.7
14 0452	6.5	**29** 0449	7.4
1114	1.4	1109	0.4
TU 1709	6.5	W 1710	7.3
○ 2322	1.4	● 2328	0.5
15 0521	6.7	**30** 0531	7.6
1143	1.3	1152	0.3
W 1736	6.6	TH 1750	7.4
2351	1.3		
		31 0012	0.4
		0611	7.5
		F 1232	0.5
		1828	7.3

APRIL

Time	m	Time	m
1 0054	0.6	**16** 0023	1.3
0650	7.3	0618	6.6
SA 1312	0.8	SU 1239	1.4
1905	7.0	1833	6.6
2 0134	1.0	**17** 0056	1.4
0728	6.8	0650	6.4
SU 1351	1.3	M 1311	1.7
1942	6.5	1906	6.4
3 0215	1.5	**18** 0133	1.7
0807	6.2	0725	6.1
M 1431	1.9	TU 1349	1.9
2021	6.0	1944	6.1
4 0300	2.1	**19** 0216	2.0
0851	5.6	0808	5.8
TU 1517	2.5	W 1433	2.3
2109	5.5	2032	5.7
5 0354	2.6	**20** 0308	2.3
0949	5.1	0904	5.4
W 1614	2.9	TH 1530	2.6
◐ 2217	5.1	2138	5.4
6 0505	3.0	**21** 0414	2.5
1117	4.8	1024	5.1
TH 1734	3.2	F 1646	2.8
2358	4.9	◑ 2306	5.3
7 0642	3.0	**22** 0540	2.6
1306	4.8	1203	5.2
F 1914	3.1	SA 1819	2.7
8 0137	5.1	**23** 0043	5.6
0804	2.7	0707	2.6
SA 1414	5.2	SU 1325	5.5
2022	2.7	1939	2.3
9 0232	5.5	**24** 0153	6.0
0855	2.3	0815	1.8
SU 1458	5.6	M 1425	6.1
2108	2.3	2040	1.7
10 0312	5.8	**25** 0249	6.5
0934	2.0	0910	1.3
M 1533	5.9	TU 1516	6.5
2145	1.9	2132	1.2
11 0347	6.2	**26** 0338	6.9
1008	1.7	0958	0.9
TU 1605	6.2	W 1601	6.9
2218	1.7	2219	0.9
12 0418	6.4	**27** 0424	7.2
1039	1.5	1044	0.7
W 1635	6.5	TH 1644	7.1
2250	1.4	2304	0.7
13 0449	6.6	**28** 0506	7.3
1110	1.3	1126	0.7
TH 1705	6.6	F 1724	7.2
○ 2321	1.3	2347	0.7
14 0518	6.7	**29** 0547	7.1
1139	1.3	1207	0.9
F 1734	6.7	SA 1803	7.0
2352	1.3		
15 0548	6.7	**30** 0031	0.9
1209	1.3	0627	6.9
SA 1803	6.7	SU 1247	1.2
		1841	6.8

Chart Datum: 3·64 metres below IGN Datum

TIDES

TIME ZONE -0100
(French Standard Time)
Subtract 1 hour for UT
For French Summer Time add
ONE hour in **non-shaded areas**

FRANCE – BREST 2006

LAT 48°23'N   LONG 4°30'W

TIMES AND HEIGHTS OF HIGH AND LOW WATERS

MAY

Day	Time m
1 SU	0414 2.3 · 1026 5.3 · 1646 2.6 · 2303 5.5
2 M	0536 2.4 · 1157 5.3 · 1813 2.6
3 TU	0033 5.7 · 0658 2.2 · 1316 5.6 · 1930 2.2
4 W	0143 6.0 · 0806 1.8 · 1417 6.0 · 2031 1.8
5 TH	0239 6.3 · 0901 1.5 · 1506 6.3 · ◐2122 1.5
6 F	0327 6.6 · 0948 1.2 · 1549 6.6 · 2208 1.2
7 SA	0410 6.8 · 1030 1.1 · 1629 6.7 · 2249 1.1
8 SU	0449 6.8 · 1108 1.1 · 1705 6.8 · 2328 1.1
9 M	0525 6.8 · 1144 1.3 · 1739 6.7
10 TU	0005 1.3 · 0600 6.6 · 1219 1.4 · 1813 6.6
11 W	0042 1.5 · 0634 6.3 · 1253 1.7 · 1847 6.4
12 TH	0118 1.7 · 0710 6.0 · 1329 2.0 · 1922 6.1
13 F	0156 2.0 · 0747 5.7 · 1406 2.3 · ○2000 5.7
14 SA	0237 2.4 · 0830 5.3 · 1449 2.6 · 2046 5.4
15 SU	0325 2.7 · 0923 5.0 · 1541 2.9 · 2145 5.2
16 M	0424 2.8 · 1033 4.9 · 1647 3.0 · 2259 5.0
17 TU	0535 2.9 · 1151 4.9 · 1801 2.9
18 W	0016 5.2 · 0646 2.7 · 1258 5.2 · 1908 2.7
19 TH	0119 5.4 · 0745 2.4 · 1352 5.5 · 2003 2.4
20 F	0210 5.7 · 0833 2.1 · 1437 5.9 · ◑2050 2.0
21 SA	0255 6.1 · 0917 1.7 · 1519 6.2 · 2134 1.6
22 SU	0337 6.4 · 0958 1.5 · 1559 6.5 · 2216 1.4
23 M	0418 6.6 · 1039 1.3 · 1639 6.8 · 2258 1.2
24 TU	0500 6.7 · 1121 1.2 · 1719 6.9 · 2341 1.0
25 W	0543 6.8 · 1204 1.2 · 1802 6.9
26 TH	0030 1.1 · 0628 6.7 · 1249 1.3 · 1849 6.8
27 F	0118 1.2 · 0718 6.4 · 1338 1.5 · ●1940 6.6
28 SA	0210 1.4 · 0812 6.1 · 1431 1.8 · 2036 6.3
29 SU	0308 1.7 · 0912 5.8 · 1531 2.1 · 2140 6.0
30 M	0411 1.9 · 1020 5.6 · 1638 2.3 · 2248 5.9
31 TU	0519 2.0 · 1132 5.5 · 1749 2.3 · 2358 5.8

JUNE

Day	Time m
1 W	0628 2.0 · 1240 5.6 · 1857 2.2
2 TH	0108 5.9 · 0732 1.9 · 1342 5.8 · 1959 2.0
3 F	0207 6.1 · 0829 1.8 · 1435 6.0 · ◑2054 1.8
4 SA	0258 6.2 · 0919 1.7 · 1521 6.2 · 2142 1.6
5 SU	0344 6.3 · 1003 1.6 · 1604 6.3 · 2226 1.6
6 M	0426 6.3 · 1044 1.6 · 1642 6.4 · 2307 1.5
7 TU	0504 6.3 · 1122 1.6 · 1719 6.4 · 2345 1.6
8 W	0542 6.2 · 1158 1.7 · 1755 6.4
9 TH	0024 1.7 · 0618 6.1 · 1234 1.8 · 1831 6.4
10 F	0101 1.8 · 0655 6.0 · 1310 2.0 · 1907 6.1
11 SA	0138 2.0 · 0732 5.7 · 1347 2.2 · ○1945 5.9
12 SU	0216 2.1 · 0811 5.5 · 1426 2.4 · 2026 5.7
13 M	0257 2.3 · 0855 5.3 · 1510 2.5 · 2111 5.5
14 TU	0344 2.5 · 0946 5.2 · 1601 2.7 · 2205 5.4
15 W	0437 2.6 · 1046 5.1 · 1659 2.7 · 2306 5.3
16 TH	0538 2.6 · 1149 5.2 · 1802 2.6
17 F	0011 5.4 · 0641 2.5 · 1251 5.4 · 1905 2.5
18 SA	0114 5.6 · 0740 2.3 · 1347 5.7 · ◑2002 2.2
19 SU	0210 5.8 · 0834 2.0 · 1439 6.0 · 2056 1.9
20 M	0303 6.1 · 0925 1.7 · 1529 6.3 · 2148 1.6
21 TU	0354 6.3 · 1014 1.5 · 1617 6.6 · 2238 1.3
22 W	0444 6.5 · 1103 1.3 · 1705 6.8 · 2328 1.1
23 TH	0534 6.7 · 1152 1.2 · 1755 6.9
24 F	0022 0.9 · 0624 6.7 · 1242 1.2 · 1845 6.9
25 SA	0113 0.9 · 0715 6.6 · 1333 1.3 · ●1936 6.9
26 SU	0205 1.1 · 0807 6.3 · 1425 1.4 · 2029 6.7
27 M	0258 1.3 · 0900 6.1 · 1519 1.7 · 2123 6.4
28 TU	0352 1.6 · 0955 5.9 · 1615 1.9 · 2219 6.1
29 W	0449 1.9 · 1053 5.7 · 1715 2.1 · 2319 5.8
30 TH	0549 2.1 · 1156 5.5 · 1818 2.2

JULY

Day	Time m
1 F	0026 5.7 · 0651 2.2 · 1301 5.5 · 1923 2.3
2 SA	0131 5.6 · 0754 2.3 · 1403 5.6 · 2026 2.2
3 SU	0232 5.7 · 0852 2.2 · 1458 5.8 · ◑2121 2.1
4 M	0325 5.8 · 0942 2.1 · 1546 6.0 · 2210 1.9
5 TU	0411 5.9 · 1026 2.0 · 1628 6.1 · 2253 1.8
6 W	0451 6.0 · 1106 1.9 · 1706 6.2 · 2332 1.7
7 TH	0529 6.1 · 1143 1.8 · 1742 6.3
8 F	0009 1.7 · 0604 6.1 · 1218 1.8 · 1817 6.3
9 SA	0044 1.7 · 0639 6.0 · 1252 1.8 · 1851 6.3
10 SU	0118 1.7 · 0713 6.0 · 1326 1.9 · 1925 6.2
11 M	0152 1.8 · 0747 5.9 · 1401 2.0 · ○1959 6.0
12 TU	0226 2.0 · 0822 5.7 · 1437 2.1 · 2035 5.9
13 W	0304 2.1 · 0901 5.6 · 1518 2.3 · 2117 5.7
14 TH	0347 2.3 · 0948 5.4 · 1606 2.5 · 2206 5.5
15 F	0438 2.5 · 1044 5.3 · 1702 2.6 · 2306 5.4
16 SA	0539 2.5 · 1150 5.3 · 1808 2.6
17 SU	0018 5.4 · 0648 2.5 · 1300 5.5 · ◑1919 2.4
18 M	0132 5.5 · 0757 2.3 · 1407 5.7 · 2027 2.1
19 TU	0240 5.8 · 0900 2.0 · 1508 6.1 · 2129 1.7
20 W	0341 6.2 · 0958 1.6 · 1604 6.5 · 2225 1.3
21 TH	0436 6.5 · 1052 1.3 · 1657 6.9 · 2318 0.9
22 F	0527 6.7 · 1143 1.0 · 1747 7.1
23 SA	0011 0.7 · 0616 6.9 · 1232 0.9 · 1835 7.3
24 SU	0102 0.6 · 0703 6.9 · 1320 0.9 · 1922 7.2
25 M	0149 0.7 · 0748 6.7 · 1407 1.1 · ●2008 7.0
26 TU	0235 1.0 · 0833 6.4 · 1454 1.4 · 2054 6.6
27 W	0322 1.4 · 0919 6.1 · 1543 1.7 · 2142 6.2
28 TH	0410 1.9 · 1008 5.7 · 1636 2.1 · 2235 5.7
29 F	0504 2.3 · 1106 5.4 · 1736 2.5 · 2338 5.3
30 SA	0607 2.6 · 1218 5.2 · 1847 2.7
31 SU	0058 5.2 · 0721 2.7 · 1337 5.3 · 2003 2.6

AUGUST

Day	Time m
1 M	0215 5.3 · 0832 2.6 · 1444 5.5 · 2108 2.4
2 TU	0315 5.5 · 0928 2.4 · 1535 5.8 · ◑2158 2.1
3 W	0401 5.7 · 1013 2.1 · 1617 6.0 · 2240 1.9
4 TH	0439 5.9 · 1051 1.9 · 1653 6.2 · 2316 1.7
5 F	0513 6.1 · 1126 1.8 · 1726 6.4 · 2350 1.6
6 SA	0546 6.2 · 1158 1.6 · 1757 6.5
7 SU	0022 1.5 · 0616 6.3 · 1230 1.6 · 1828 6.5
8 M	0053 1.5 · 0647 6.3 · 1301 1.6 · 1858 6.5
9 TU	0123 1.5 · 0717 6.2 · 1332 1.7 · 1928 6.4
10 W	0154 1.7 · 0748 6.1 · 1405 1.8 · 2000 6.2
11 TH	0227 1.9 · 0821 5.9 · 1441 2.0 · 2036 5.9
12 F	0305 2.1 · 0901 5.7 · 1524 2.3 · 2118 5.7
13 SA	0351 2.4 · 0952 5.4 · 1617 2.5 · 2215 5.4
14 SU	0451 2.6 · 1100 5.3 · 1725 2.7 · 2332 5.2
15 M	0608 2.7 · 1225 5.3 · 1848 2.6
16 TU	0110 5.3 · 0734 2.6 · 1349 5.6 · ◐2011 2.3
17 W	0231 5.7 · 0848 2.2 · 1458 6.1 · 2119 1.7
18 TH	0334 6.2 · 0948 1.6 · 1554 6.6 · 2216 1.2
19 F	0427 6.6 · 1041 1.2 · 1645 7.1 · 2307 0.7
20 SA	0514 7.0 · 1129 0.8 · 1733 7.4 · 2354 0.5
21 SU	0559 7.2 · 1215 0.6 · 1817 7.5
22 M	0042 0.4 · 0641 7.1 · 1259 0.7 · 1859 7.4
23 TU	0124 0.6 · 0720 7.0 · 1342 0.9 · ●1940 7.1
24 W	0205 1.0 · 0759 6.6 · 1424 1.3 · 2019 6.7
25 TH	0246 1.5 · 0837 6.2 · 1507 1.8 · 2100 6.1
26 F	0329 2.1 · 0920 5.7 · 1555 2.3 · 2148 5.5
27 SA	0418 2.6 · 1015 5.3 · 1654 2.8 · 2253 5.1
28 SU	0523 3.0 · 1136 5.0 · 1813 3.0
29 M	0031 4.9 · 0652 3.1 · 1317 5.0 · 1947 2.9
30 TU	0206 5.0 · 0817 2.9 · 1432 5.4 · 2055 2.5
31 W	0303 5.3 · 0913 2.5 · 1520 5.7 · ◑2141 2.2

Chart Datum: 3·64 metres below IGN Datum

TIME ZONE -0100
(French Standard Time)
Subtract 1 hour for UT
For French Summer Time add
ONE hour in non-shaded areas

FRANCE – BREST

LAT 48°23'N   LONG 4°30'W

TIMES AND HEIGHTS OF HIGH AND LOW WATERS

SEPTEMBER

Time m	Time m
1 0345 2.8 / 0946 5.2 / F 1618 2.9 / 2215 5.0	**16** 0548 3.1 / 1213 5.1 / SA 1848 2.9
2 0452 3.0 / 1109 5.0 / SA 1737 3.0 / 2353 4.9	**17** 0117 5.0 / 0726 3.0 / SU 1348 5.3 / 2013 2.6
3 0625 3.1 / 1250 5.1 / SU 1913 2.8	**18** 0228 5.4 / 0836 2.6 / M 1446 5.7 / 2108 2.2
4 0140 5.2 / 0756 2.7 / M 1409 5.6 / 2030 2.3	**19** 0314 5.8 / 0924 2.2 / TU 1528 6.1 / 2149 1.8
5 0247 5.7 / 0900 2.1 / TU 1507 6.2 / 2127 1.7	**20** 0351 6.1 / 1002 1.8 / W 1604 6.4 / 2225 1.6
6 0338 6.3 / 0951 1.6 / W 1556 6.8 / 2216 1.1	**21** 0423 6.3 / 1036 1.6 / TH 1635 6.6 / 2257 1.4
7 0424 6.8 / 1038 1.0 / TH 1642 7.3 / ○ 2302 0.6	**22** 0452 6.5 / 1106 1.5 / F 1704 6.7 / ● 2326 1.3
8 0507 7.2 / 1123 0.7 / F 1725 7.6 / 2346 0.4	**23** 0520 6.6 / 1135 1.4 / SA 1731 6.8 / 2354 1.3
9 0549 7.3 / 1207 0.5 / SA 1807 7.7	**24** 0547 6.7 / 1203 1.4 / SU 1758 6.7
10 0032 0.4 / 0629 7.3 / SU 1250 0.5 / 1849 7.5	**25** 0021 1.4 / 0614 6.6 / M 1231 1.5 / 1825 6.6
11 0114 0.6 / 0708 7.1 / M 1333 0.8 / 1929 7.2	**26** 0048 1.6 / 0640 6.5 / TU 1300 1.7 / 1852 6.4
12 0155 1.1 / 0748 6.7 / TU 1416 1.3 / 2011 6.6	**27** 0116 1.8 / 0708 6.3 / W 1331 1.9 / 1921 6.1
13 0238 1.6 / 0830 6.2 / W 1504 1.8 / 2057 6.0	**28** 0147 2.1 / 0740 6.0 / TH 1407 2.2 / 1955 5.8
14 0326 2.2 / 0920 5.7 / TH 1559 2.4 / ◑ 2156 5.4	**29** 0225 2.5 / 0819 5.6 / F 1452 2.6 / 2040 5.3
15 0426 2.8 / 1031 5.2 / F 1711 2.8 / 2322 4.9	**30** 0315 2.8 / 0916 5.3 / SA 1552 2.9 / ◑ 2150 5.0

OCTOBER

Time m	Time m
1 0426 3.1 / 1045 5.1 / SU 1714 3.0 / 2337 4.9	**16** 0047 5.0 / 0655 3.0 / M 1315 5.3 / 1942 2.7
2 0604 3.1 / 1230 5.2 / M 1854 2.7	**17** 0155 5.3 / 0803 2.7 / TU 1412 5.6 / 2034 2.3
3 0122 5.3 / 0735 2.7 / TU 1347 5.8 / 2009 2.2	**18** 0240 5.7 / 0850 2.3 / W 1454 6.0 / 2115 2.0
4 0225 5.9 / 0838 2.0 / W 1443 6.4 / 2104 1.5	**19** 0316 6.0 / 0928 2.0 / TH 1529 6.3 / 2150 1.7
5 0315 6.5 / 0929 1.4 / TH 1532 7.0 / 2152 1.0	**20** 0348 6.3 / 1002 1.7 / F 1601 6.5 / 2222 1.6
6 0400 7.0 / 1015 0.9 / F 1618 7.4 / 2238 0.6	**21** 0418 6.5 / 1034 1.6 / SA 1631 6.6 / 2252 1.5
7 0442 7.3 / 1100 0.6 / SA 1701 7.6 / ○ 2321 0.4	**22** 0448 6.6 / 1104 1.5 / SU 1701 6.7 / ● 2322 1.5
8 0523 7.4 / 1143 0.5 / SU 1743 7.6	**23** 0516 6.7 / 1135 1.5 / M 1730 6.6 / 2351 1.5
9 0004 0.5 / 0603 7.4 / M 1226 0.6 / 1824 7.4	**24** 0545 6.7 / 1205 1.5 / TU 1759 6.6
10 0048 0.8 / 0642 7.1 / TU 1309 1.0 / 1905 7.0	**25** 0020 1.7 / 0614 6.6 / W 1236 1.7 / 1829 6.4
11 0129 1.3 / 0722 6.7 / W 1353 1.4 / 1947 6.4	**26** 0051 1.9 / 0646 6.4 / TH 1311 1.9 / 1902 6.1
12 0212 1.9 / 0804 6.2 / TH 1441 2.0 / 2034 5.8	**27** 0127 2.1 / 0722 6.1 / F 1351 2.2 / 1942 5.8
13 0300 2.4 / 0856 5.7 / F 1534 2.5 / 2135 5.2	**28** 0209 2.4 / 0807 5.8 / SA 1440 2.5 / 2033 5.4
14 0400 2.9 / 1008 5.2 / SA 1648 2.9 / ◑ 2301 4.9	**29** 0303 2.8 / 0909 5.5 / SU 1541 2.7 / 2146 5.1
15 0521 3.2 / 1146 5.1 / SU 1821 3.0	**30** 0414 3.0 / 1033 5.3 / M 1700 2.8 / 2322 5.1
	31 0544 2.9 / 1204 5.5 / TU 1827 2.5

NOVEMBER

Time m	Time m
1 0052 5.5 / 0706 2.5 / W 1316 5.9 / 1938 2.0	**16** 0149 5.5 / 0801 2.6 / TH 1406 5.7 / 2029 2.3
2 0155 6.0 / 0809 2.0 / TH 1414 6.4 / 2035 1.5	**17** 0232 5.8 / 0845 2.3 / F 1447 5.9 / 2109 2.1
3 0246 6.5 / 0902 1.5 / F 1505 6.9 / 2125 1.1	**18** 0309 6.1 / 0924 2.0 / SA 1524 6.2 / 2145 1.9
4 0333 6.9 / 0950 1.1 / SA 1552 7.2 / 2212 0.8	**19** 0344 6.3 / 1000 1.8 / SU 1559 6.3 / 2219 1.7
5 0417 7.2 / 1037 0.8 / SU 1637 7.4 / ○ 2257 0.8	**20** 0417 6.5 / 1036 1.7 / M 1633 6.4 / ● 2253 1.7
6 0459 7.3 / 1122 0.8 / M 1721 7.3 / 2340 0.9	**21** 0450 6.6 / 1110 1.6 / TU 1707 6.5 / 2326 1.7
7 0540 7.2 / 1206 0.9 / TU 1803 7.1	**22** 0524 6.6 / 1146 1.6 / W 1741 6.4
8 0025 1.2 / 0621 7.0 / W 1250 1.2 / 1846 6.7	**23** 0001 1.7 / 0559 6.6 / TH 1223 1.6 / 1817 6.3
9 0108 1.6 / 0703 6.6 / TH 1335 1.6 / 1930 6.2	**24** 0039 1.8 / 0637 6.5 / F 1302 1.8 / 1857 6.1
10 0151 2.0 / 0747 6.2 / F 1423 2.0 / 2017 5.8	**25** 0119 2.0 / 0719 6.3 / SA 1346 1.9 / 1942 5.8
11 0239 2.4 / 0838 5.8 / SA 1515 2.4 / 2113 5.3	**26** 0206 2.2 / 0808 6.0 / SU 1436 2.1 / 2036 5.7
12 0334 2.8 / 0939 5.4 / SU 1616 2.8 / ◐ 2223 5.1	**27** 0259 2.4 / 0907 5.8 / M 1534 2.3 / 2140 5.5
13 0440 3.0 / 1054 5.2 / M 1729 2.9 / 2343 5.0	**28** 0403 2.6 / 1016 5.7 / TU 1641 2.4 / ◐ 2254 5.4
14 0556 3.0 / 1212 5.2 / TU 1843 2.8	**29** 0517 2.6 / 1129 5.8 / W 1754 2.4
15 0056 5.2 / 0706 2.8 / W 1316 5.4 / 1943 2.6	**30** 0010 5.6 / 0630 2.4 / TH 1239 6.0 / 1902 2.0

DECEMBER

Time m	Time m
1 0118 5.9 / 0736 2.1 / F 1342 6.3 / 2003 1.8	**16** 0137 5.4 / 0752 2.6 / SA 1357 5.5 / 2022 2.5
2 0215 6.3 / 0834 1.7 / SA 1439 6.5 / 2059 1.6	**17** 0227 5.7 / 0843 2.4 / SU 1446 5.7 / 2107 2.3
3 0307 6.6 / 0928 1.4 / SU 1531 6.7 / 2149 1.3	**18** 0311 6.0 / 0929 2.2 / M 1530 5.9 / 2150 2.0
4 0356 6.8 / 1018 1.2 / M 1619 6.8 / 2237 1.3	**19** 0352 6.2 / 1011 1.9 / TU 1611 6.1 / 2230 1.9
5 0442 6.9 / 1106 1.1 / TU 1706 6.8 / ○ 2323 1.3	**20** 0431 6.4 / 1052 1.7 / W 1651 6.3 / ● 2309 1.7
6 0526 6.9 / 1152 1.2 / W 1751 6.6	**21** 0511 6.6 / 1133 1.5 / TH 1731 6.4 / 2349 1.6
7 0008 1.4 / 0609 6.8 / TH 1237 1.3 / 1834 6.5	**22** 0551 6.7 / 1215 1.4 / F 1813 6.4
8 0052 1.6 / 0651 6.6 / F 1321 1.6 / 1917 6.3	**23** 0033 1.6 / 0634 6.7 / SA 1257 1.4 / 1855 6.4
9 0134 1.9 / 0733 6.3 / SA 1404 1.9 / 2000 5.9	**24** 0116 1.6 / 0718 6.6 / SU 1342 1.4 / 1941 6.3
10 0217 2.2 / 0817 6.0 / SU 1449 2.2 / 2045 5.6	**25** 0202 1.7 / 0805 6.5 / M 1429 1.6 / 2028 6.1
11 0302 2.5 / 0903 5.7 / M 1536 2.5 / 2134 5.4	**26** 0251 1.9 / 0855 6.3 / TU 1520 1.8 / 2121 5.9
12 0352 2.7 / 0954 5.5 / TU 1628 2.7 / 2231 5.2	**27** 0345 2.1 / 0950 6.1 / W 1615 2.0 / 2219 5.8
13 0448 2.9 / 1054 5.3 / W 1726 2.8 / 2334 5.1	**28** 0445 2.2 / 1051 6.0 / TH 1717 2.1 / 2325 5.7
14 0550 2.9 / 1158 5.2 / TH 1829 2.8	**29** 0552 2.3 / 1159 5.8 / F 1824 2.2
15 0040 5.2 / 0654 2.8 / F 1301 5.3 / 1929 2.7	**30** 0039 5.7 / 0702 2.3 / SA 1310 5.9 / 1932 2.2
	31 0148 5.9 / 0811 2.2 / SU 1418 6.0 / 2037 2.0

TIDES

Chart Datum: 3·64 metres below IGN Datum

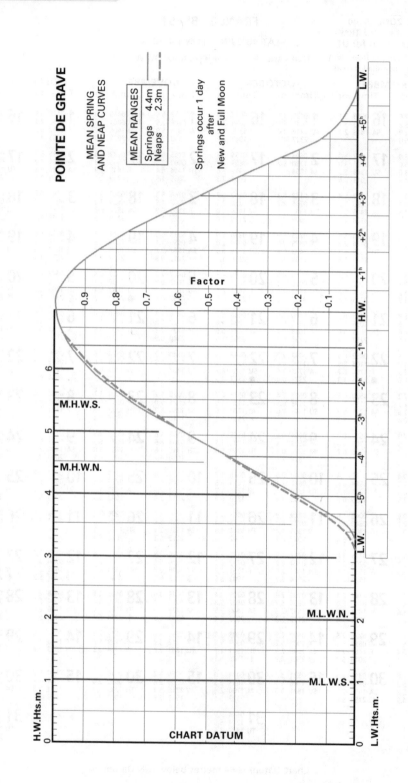

FRANCE – POINTE DE GRAVE

LAT 45°34′N   LONG 1°04′W

TIMES AND HEIGHTS OF HIGH AND LOW WATERS

2006

JANUARY

Time m	Time m
1 SU 0542 5.5 / 1149 1.1 / 1812 5.4	**16** M 0611 5.2 / 1223 1.4 / 1833 5.0
2 M 0007 1.3 / 0630 5.6 / 1238 1.1 / 1900 5.3	**17** TU 0029 1.5 / 0642 5.2 / 1256 1.5 / 1903 4.9
3 TU 0057 1.3 / 0720 5.6 / 1326 1.1 / 1950 5.2	**18** W 0102 1.6 / 0713 5.1 / 1328 1.5 / 1933 4.8
4 W 0145 1.3 / 0810 5.5 / 1413 1.2 / 2041 5.1	**19** TH 0135 1.6 / 0744 5.0 / 1401 1.6 / 2006 4.7
5 TH 0234 1.4 / 0903 5.3 / 1502 1.4 / 2135 4.8	**20** F 0209 1.7 / 0818 4.9 / 1435 1.7 / 2042 4.6
6 F 0326 1.6 / 0959 5.1 / 1554 1.6 / ◐ 2236 4.6	**21** SA 0246 1.8 / 0856 4.7 / 1512 1.9 / 2125 4.4
7 SA 0423 1.8 / 1102 4.9 / 1653 1.8 / 2345 4.5	**22** SU 0328 2.0 / 0942 4.5 / 1556 2.1 / ◐ 2222 4.3
8 SU 0528 1.9 / 1212 4.7 / 1758 2.0	**23** M 0420 2.1 / 1043 4.3 / 1653 2.2 / 2335 4.2
9 M 0057 4.5 / 0638 2.0 / 1324 4.6 / 1908 2.0	**24** TU 0526 2.2 / 1204 4.3 / 1807 2.3
10 TU 0202 4.6 / 0747 2.0 / 1430 4.7 / 2014 2.0	**25** W 0055 4.3 / 0642 2.2 / 1328 4.3 / 1922 2.2
11 W 0258 4.7 / 0850 1.9 / 1526 4.7 / 2110 1.9	**26** TH 0204 4.5 / 0754 2.0 / 1438 4.6 / 2028 2.0
12 TH 0346 4.9 / 0944 1.7 / 1613 4.8 / 2158 1.7	**27** F 0303 4.8 / 0859 1.8 / 1537 4.9 / 2126 1.7
13 F 0427 5.0 / 1031 1.6 / 1653 4.9 / 2241 1.6	**28** SA 0356 5.2 / 0957 1.4 / 1629 5.2 / 2220 1.4
14 SA 0504 5.1 / 1112 1.5 / 1728 5.0 / ○ 2319 1.6	**29** SU 0446 5.5 / 1051 1.1 / 1717 5.4 / ● 2310 1.2
15 SU 0539 5.2 / 1149 1.5 / 1801 5.0 / 2355 1.5	**30** M 0534 5.7 / 1141 0.9 / 1803 5.5 / 2358 1.0
	31 TU 0620 5.9 / 1228 0.8 / 1848 5.6

FEBRUARY

Time m	Time m
1 W 0046 0.9 / 0706 5.9 / 1312 0.8 / 1931 5.5	**16** TH 0039 1.3 / 0645 5.3 / 1301 1.3 / 1902 5.1
2 TH 0130 1.0 / 0751 5.7 / 1355 0.8 / 2014 5.3	**17** F 0108 1.3 / 0713 5.2 / 1329 1.4 / 1930 5.0
3 F 0214 1.1 / 0835 5.5 / 1437 1.2 / 2058 5.0	**18** SA 0137 1.4 / 0742 5.0 / 1357 1.5 / 2000 4.8
4 SA 0259 1.3 / 0922 5.1 / 1522 1.5 / 2147 4.7	**19** SU 0209 1.4 / 0814 4.8 / 1429 1.7 / 2035 4.6
5 SU 0350 1.6 / 1016 4.8 / 1613 1.8 / ◐ 2252 4.4	**20** M 0246 1.7 / 0853 4.6 / 1507 1.9 / 2122 4.4
6 M 0450 2.0 / 1130 4.4 / 1717 2.2	**21** TU 0332 2.0 / 0948 4.3 / 1557 2.2 / 2232 4.2
7 TU 0018 4.3 / 0606 2.2 / 1300 4.3 / 1837 2.3	**22** W 0435 2.2 / 1115 4.1 / 1712 2.4
8 W 0143 4.3 / 0729 2.2 / 1421 4.3 / 1957 2.3	**23** TH 0012 4.2 / 0602 2.3 / 1303 4.1 / 1847 2.4
9 TH 0249 4.5 / 0840 2.0 / 1522 4.5 / 2100 2.1	**24** F 0141 4.4 / 0731 2.1 / 1425 4.5 / 2009 2.1
10 F 0340 4.7 / 0935 1.8 / 1607 4.7 / 2149 1.8	**25** SA 0248 4.8 / 0845 1.7 / 1526 4.9 / 2113 1.7
11 SA 0419 4.9 / 1020 1.6 / 1643 4.9 / 2229 1.6	**26** SU 0344 5.2 / 0945 1.3 / 1617 5.2 / 2207 1.3
12 SU 0452 5.1 / 1058 1.5 / 1713 5.0 / 2305 1.5	**27** M 0433 5.6 / 1037 1.0 / 1702 5.5 / 2255 1.0
13 M 0522 5.2 / 1132 1.4 / 1742 5.1 / ○ 2338 1.4	**28** TU 0518 5.9 / 1124 0.7 / 1745 5.7 / ● 2341 0.8
14 TU 0551 5.3 / 1203 1.3 / 1809 5.1	
15 W 0009 1.3 / 0618 5.3 / 1222 1.3 / 1836 5.0	

MARCH

Time m	Time m
1 W 0602 6.0 / 1208 0.6 / 1826 5.7	**16** TH 0550 5.3 / 1203 1.2 / 1805 5.2
2 TH 0027 0.7 / 0644 6.0 / 1249 0.7 / 1906 5.6	**17** F 0011 1.2 / 0617 5.3 / 1230 1.2 / 1832 5.2
3 F 0109 0.8 / 0725 5.8 / 1329 0.8 / 1944 5.4	**18** SA 0040 1.2 / 0644 5.2 / 1257 1.3 / 1859 5.1
4 SA 0149 0.9 / 0805 5.5 / 1408 1.1 / 2021 5.1	**19** SU 0109 1.3 / 0712 5.1 / 1325 1.4 / 1929 5.0
5 SU 0231 1.2 / 0845 5.0 / 1449 1.5 / 2100 4.7	**20** M 0141 1.4 / 0744 4.9 / 1357 1.6 / 2003 4.8
6 M 0317 1.6 / 0933 4.6 / 1536 1.9 / ◐ 2155 4.4	**21** TU 0217 1.6 / 0823 4.6 / 1435 1.8 / 2049 4.5
7 TU 0414 2.0 / 1047 4.2 / 1638 2.3 / 2335 4.2	**22** W 0303 1.8 / 0921 4.3 / 1525 2.1 / ◐ 2200 4.3
8 W 0534 2.3 / 1239 4.1 / 1806 2.5	**23** TH 0406 2.1 / 1057 4.1 / 1641 2.4 / 2343 4.2
9 TH 0119 4.2 / 0709 2.3 / 1407 4.2 / 1938 2.4	**24** F 0540 2.2 / 1250 4.2 / 1825 2.4
10 F 0232 4.4 / 0824 2.0 / 1506 4.4 / 2042 2.2	**25** SA 0121 4.5 / 0716 2.0 / 1408 4.5 / 1951 2.1
11 SA 0322 4.7 / 0916 1.9 / 1547 4.7 / 2129 1.9	**26** SU 0229 4.9 / 0829 1.6 / 1507 4.9 / 2054 1.7
12 SU 0358 4.9 / 0957 1.6 / 1619 4.9 / 2207 1.6	**27** M 0324 5.3 / 0926 1.2 / 1556 5.3 / 2146 1.3
13 M 0429 5.1 / 1032 1.4 / 1647 5.0 / 2241 1.5	**28** TU 0412 5.6 / 1015 0.9 / 1640 5.5 / 2234 0.9
14 TU 0457 5.2 / 1104 1.3 / 1713 5.1 / ○ 2312 1.3	**29** W 0456 5.9 / 1100 0.7 / 1720 5.7 / ● 2318 0.7
15 W 0524 5.3 / 1134 1.2 / 1740 5.2 / 2342 1.2	**30** TH 0538 5.9 / 1142 0.7 / 1800 5.7
	31 F 0001 0.7 / 0619 5.9 / 1222 0.7 / 1838 5.6

APRIL

Time m	Time m
1 SA 0044 0.8 / 0658 5.6 / 1301 1.0 / 1914 5.4	**16** SU 0014 1.2 / 0620 5.2 / 1229 1.3 / 1836 5.2
2 SU 0123 1.0 / 0736 5.3 / 1338 1.3 / 1950 5.1	**17** M 0046 1.2 / 0652 5.0 / 1300 1.4 / 1909 5.0
3 M 0204 1.3 / 0815 4.9 / 1418 1.6 / 2027 4.8	**18** TU 0121 1.4 / 0729 4.8 / 1336 1.6 / 1950 4.9
4 TU 0248 1.7 / 0901 4.5 / 1503 2.0 / 2119 4.4	**19** W 0201 1.5 / 0815 4.6 / 1418 1.8 / 2042 4.6
5 W 0343 2.1 / 1013 4.1 / 1604 2.4 / ◐ 2248 4.2	**20** TH 0251 1.8 / 0922 4.3 / 1514 2.1 / 2156 4.5
6 TH 0500 2.4 / 1205 4.0 / 1729 2.6	**21** F 0358 2.0 / 1056 4.2 / 1633 2.3 / ◐ 2328 4.4
7 F 0037 4.2 / 0635 2.4 / 1332 4.1 / 1901 2.5	**22** SA 0528 2.0 / 1233 4.3 / 1806 2.2
8 SA 0153 4.3 / 0750 2.2 / 1430 4.4 / 2007 2.2	**23** SU 0057 4.7 / 0654 1.8 / 1344 4.6 / 1924 1.9
9 SU 0245 4.6 / 0842 1.9 / 1511 4.6 / 2053 2.0	**24** M 0203 5.0 / 0803 1.5 / 1441 5.0 / 2027 1.6
10 M 0324 4.8 / 0922 1.7 / 1543 4.8 / 2132 1.7	**25** TU 0259 5.3 / 0859 1.2 / 1530 5.2 / 2120 1.2
11 TU 0356 5.0 / 0957 1.5 / 1612 5.0 / 2207 1.5	**26** W 0348 5.5 / 0948 1.0 / 1613 5.4 / 2208 1.0
12 W 0425 5.1 / 1030 1.4 / 1640 5.1 / 2240 1.4	**27** TH 0432 5.7 / 1033 0.9 / 1654 5.5 / 2254 0.9
13 TH 0453 5.2 / 1101 1.3 / 1708 5.2 / ○ 2311 1.3	**28** F 0515 5.7 / 1115 0.9 / 1734 5.5 / 2337 0.8
14 F 0521 5.3 / 1131 1.2 / 1736 5.3 / 2342 1.2	**29** SA 0556 5.6 / 1155 1.0 / 1813 5.5
15 SA 0550 5.3 / 1200 1.2 / 1805 5.2	**30** SU 0020 0.9 / 0636 5.4 / 1234 1.2 / 1851 5.3

TIDES

Chart Datum: 2·83 metres below IGN Datum

TIME ZONE -0100
(French Standard Time)
Subtract 1 hour for UT
For French Summer Time add
ONE hour in **non-shaded areas**

FRANCE – POINTE DE GRAVE

LAT 45°34'N   LONG 1°04'W

TIMES AND HEIGHTS OF HIGH AND LOW WATERS

2006

MAY

Time	m		Time	m
1 M	0100 0715 1312 1929	1.1 5.1 1.4 5.1	**16** TU	0031 0645 1246 1903	1.3 5.0 1.5 5.1
2 TU	0141 0755 1352 2010	1.4 4.8 1.7 4.8	**17** W	0112 0730 1327 1951	1.3 4.8 1.6 5.0
3 W	0225 0842 1438 2059	1.7 4.5 2.0 4.5	**18** TH	0157 0823 1415 2048	1.5 4.6 1.8 4.8
4 TH	0317 0944 1534 2207	2.0 4.2 2.3 4.3	**19** F	0251 0929 1515 2155	1.6 4.5 2.0 4.7
5 F ☽	0423 1111 1646 2333	2.2 4.1 2.4 4.2	**20** SA ☽	0357 1038 1627 2311	1.8 4.4 2.0 4.7
6 SA	0542 1233 1804	2.3 4.1 2.4	**21** SU	0512 1207 1743	1.8 4.5 2.0
7 SU	0051 0655 1334 1911	4.3 2.2 4.3 2.3	**22** M	0027 0625 1314 1853	4.8 1.7 4.7 1.8
8 M	0150 0751 1420 2004	4.5 2.0 4.5 2.1	**23** TU	0133 0731 1412 1956	5.0 1.5 4.9 1.6
9 TU	0236 0836 1458 2047	4.6 1.8 4.7 1.8	**24** W	0231 0829 1503 2052	5.1 1.3 5.1 1.3
10 W	0314 0915 1532 2126	4.8 1.6 4.9 1.6	**25** TH	0323 0920 1549 2143	5.2 1.2 5.2 1.2
11 TH	0349 0951 1604 2204	5.0 1.5 5.0 1.5	**26** F	0411 1007 1632 2231	5.3 1.2 5.3 1.1
12 F	0422 1025 1637 2240	5.1 1.4 5.1 1.4	**27** SA	0456 1051 1714 2317	5.3 1.2 5.3 1.1
13 SA ○	0455 1100 1710 2316	5.1 1.3 5.2 1.3	**28** SU	0539 1133 1755	5.2 1.2 5.3
14 SU	0529 1134 1745 2352	5.1 1.3 5.2 1.2	**29** M	0000 0620 1213 1835	1.2 5.1 1.4 5.2
15 M	0606 1209 1822	5.1 1.4 5.2	**30** TU	0043 0701 1252 1915	1.3 4.9 1.5 5.0
			31 W	0123 0741 1332 1955	1.5 4.7 1.7 4.9

JUNE

Time	m		Time	m
1 TH	0206 0823 1416 2039	1.6 4.5 1.9 4.7	**16** F	0159 0825 1416 2046	1.3 4.8 1.5 5.1
2 F	0252 0912 1505 2129	1.8 4.3 2.1 4.5	**17** SA	0250 0922 1511 2144	1.4 4.7 1.6 5.0
3 SA ☽	0343 1011 1600 2228	2.0 4.2 2.2 4.4	**18** SU ☽	0346 1025 1610 2247	1.5 4.6 1.7 4.9
4 SU	0443 1118 1702 2334	2.1 4.2 2.3 4.3	**19** M	0447 1133 1714 2354	1.6 4.2 1.7 4.8
5 M	0546 1223 1805	2.1 4.2 2.2	**20** TU	0551 1241 1821	1.6 4.6 1.7
6 TU	0039 0647 1320 1903	4.3 2.1 4.3 2.1	**21** W	0102 0657 1343 1927	4.8 1.6 4.7 1.6
7 W	0137 0741 1408 1956	4.4 1.9 4.5 2.0	**22** TH	0206 0800 1440 2029	4.9 1.6 4.8 1.5
8 TH	0226 0828 1451 2043	4.6 1.8 4.7 1.8	**23** F	0305 0857 1531 2125	4.9 1.5 4.9 1.4
9 F	0311 0911 1531 2128	4.7 1.7 4.9 1.6	**24** SA	0357 0948 1618 2217	4.9 1.4 5.0 1.3
10 SA	0353 0953 1610 2211	4.8 1.5 5.0 1.5	**25** SU ●	0445 1035 1702 2304	4.9 1.4 5.1 1.3
11 SU ○	0434 1034 1650 2255	4.9 1.4 5.1 1.3	**26** M	0529 1118 1743 2348	5.0 1.4 5.1 1.3
12 M	0516 1115 1732 2338	5.0 1.4 5.2 1.2	**27** TU	0609 1159 1822	4.9 1.4 5.1
13 TU	0600 1157 1816	5.0 1.4 5.2	**28** W	0030 0646 1237 1858	1.3 4.9 1.5 5.0
14 W	0025 0645 1240 1903	1.2 5.0 1.4 5.2	**29** TH	0108 0722 1314 1934	1.4 4.8 1.6 4.9
15 TH	0111 0733 1327 1953	1.2 4.9 1.5 5.0	**30** F	0145 0757 1352 2010	1.5 4.6 1.7 4.8

JULY

Time	m		Time	m
1 SA	0223 0834 1432 2049	1.6 4.5 1.8 4.7	**16** SU	0236 0900 1454 2123	1.1 4.9 1.3 5.1
2 SU	0303 0917 1515 2133	1.8 4.4 1.9 4.5	**17** M ◑	0324 0953 1546 2218	1.3 4.7 1.5 4.9
3 M ☽	0347 1007 1603 2224	1.9 4.3 2.0 4.3	**18** TU	0416 1055 1645 2322	1.5 4.5 1.7 4.7
4 TU	0438 1107 1659 2324	2.0 4.2 2.1 4.2	**19** W	0517 1208 1752	1.7 4.4 1.8
5 W	0537 1212 1801	2.1 4.2 2.2	**20** TH	0036 0626 1322 1905	1.6 4.5 1.9 4.8
6 TH	0031 0641 1315 1904	4.4 2.1 4.3 2.1	**21** F	0151 0739 1429 2016	4.5 1.9 4.6 1.8
7 F	0138 0741 1411 2003	4.3 2.0 4.5 2.0	**22** SA	0258 0844 1525 2117	4.6 1.8 4.7 1.6
8 SA	0237 0836 1502 2058	4.4 1.9 4.7 1.8	**23** SU	0354 0939 1613 2210	4.6 1.7 4.9 1.5
9 SU	0331 0926 1550 2149	4.6 1.7 4.9 1.5	**24** M	0440 1026 1653 2255	4.8 1.5 5.1 1.4
10 M	0420 1014 1636 2239	4.8 1.5 5.1 1.3	**25** TU ●	0519 1108 1730 2336	4.9 1.4 5.1 1.3
11 TU ○	0507 1102 1722 2328	5.0 1.3 5.3 1.1	**26** W	0553 1145 1803	4.9 1.4 5.1
12 W	0554 1149 1809	5.1 1.2 5.4	**27** TH	0013 0625 1219 1835	1.3 4.9 1.4 5.1
13 TH	0019 0640 1235 1856	1.0 5.2 1.2 5.5	**28** F	0047 0654 1252 1905	1.3 4.9 1.4 5.0
14 F	0105 0726 1320 1943	1.0 5.2 1.1 5.4	**29** SA	0119 0724 1324 1935	1.4 4.8 1.5 4.9
15 SA	0150 0812 1406 2032	1.0 5.0 1.2 5.3	**30** SU	0150 0754 1357 2006	1.5 4.7 1.6 4.8
			31 M	0222 0828 1431 2041	1.6 4.5 1.7 4.6

AUGUST

Time	m		Time	m
1 TU	0256 0907 1509 2123	1.7 4.4 1.9 4.4	**16** W ◑	0344 1015 1615 2254	1.6 4.5 1.7 4.4
2 W ◑	0335 0956 1555 2217	1.9 4.2 2.0 4.2	**17** TH	0443 1139 1726	2.0 4.3 1.9
3 TH	0426 1103 1657 2329	2.1 4.1 2.2 4.1	**18** F	0021 0600 1310 1852	4.2 2.2 4.3 2.1
4 F	0537 1223 1815	2.3 4.1 2.2	**19** SA	0148 0726 1424 2011	4.3 2.2 4.5 2.0
5 SA	0056 0657 1338 1930	4.1 2.2 4.3 2.1	**20** SU	0258 0837 1521 2112	4.4 2.0 4.7 1.7
6 SU	0213 0806 1440 2035	4.3 2.0 4.6 1.8	**21** M	0349 0930 1604 2159	4.6 1.8 4.9 1.5
7 M	0315 0906 1533 2133	4.6 1.8 4.9 1.5	**22** TU	0427 1013 1639 2239	4.8 1.6 5.1 1.4
8 TU	0407 0959 1622 2226	4.9 1.5 5.2 1.2	**23** W ●	0459 1050 1709 2315	4.9 1.4 5.2 1.3
9 W ○	0455 1049 1709 2315	5.1 1.2 5.5 1.0	**24** TH	0528 1124 1737 2348	5.0 1.3 5.2 1.3
10 TH	0540 1135 1754	5.3 1.0 5.7	**25** F	0555 1155 1804	5.0 1.3 5.2
11 F	0001 0623 1220 1839	0.8 5.4 0.9 5.7	**26** SA	0019 0621 1224 1831	1.3 5.0 1.3 5.1
12 SA	0048 0706 1304 1923	0.7 5.4 0.9 5.7	**27** SU	0047 0647 1253 1857	1.3 5.0 1.4 5.0
13 SU	0130 0748 1347 2008	0.8 5.2 1.0 5.5	**28** M	0114 0714 1321 1925	1.4 4.9 1.4 4.9
14 M	0212 0830 1430 2055	1.0 5.0 1.1 5.2	**29** TU	0141 0743 1351 1955	1.5 4.7 1.5 4.7
15 TU	0255 0917 1518 2147	1.3 4.7 1.4 4.8	**30** W	0211 0815 1425 2030	1.7 4.5 1.7 4.4
			31 TH ☽	0246 0858 1506 2121	1.9 4.3 2.0 4.2

Chart Datum: 2·83 metres below IGN Datum

FRANCE – POINTE DE GRAVE

LAT 45°34'N   LONG 1°04'W

TIMES AND HEIGHTS OF HIGH AND LOW WATERS

SEPTEMBER

Time m	Time m
1 0332 2.1 / 1004 4.1 / F 1603 2.2 / 2242 4.0	**16** 0013 4.1 / 0538 2.4 / SA 1257 4.3 / 1841 2.3
2 0441 2.4 / 1140 4.1 / SA 1730 2.3	**17** 0141 4.2 / 0712 2.4 / SU 1411 4.5 / 2000 2.1
3 0031 4.0 / 0619 2.4 / SU 1312 4.3 / 1905 2.2	**18** 0244 4.4 / 0820 2.1 / M 1504 4.7 / 2054 1.8
4 0156 4.3 / 0743 2.1 / M 1420 4.6 / 2018 1.8	**19** 0328 4.6 / 0909 1.8 / TU 1543 4.9 / 2136 1.6
5 0258 4.6 / 0847 1.8 / TU 1515 5.0 / 2116 1.5	**20** 0401 4.8 / 0949 1.6 / W 1613 5.1 / 2213 1.4
6 0349 5.0 / 0941 1.4 / W 1603 5.4 / 2207 1.1	**21** 0429 5.0 / 1024 1.5 / TH 1640 5.2 / 2246 1.3
7 0434 5.3 / 1029 1.1 / TH 1648 5.7 / ○ 2254 0.8	**22** 0455 5.1 / 1056 1.3 / F 1706 5.2 / ○ 2316 1.3
8 0517 5.5 / 1115 0.8 / F 1732 5.9 / 2338 0.7	**23** 0520 5.1 / 1125 1.3 / SA 1732 5.3 / 2345 1.3
9 0558 5.6 / 1159 0.7 / SA 1815 5.9	**24** 0546 5.1 / 1154 1.3 / SU 1758 5.2
10 0024 0.7 / 0639 5.5 / SU 1241 0.7 / 1858 5.8	**25** 0013 1.3 / 0612 5.1 / M 1222 1.3 / 1823 5.1
11 0104 0.8 / 0718 5.4 / M 1322 0.9 / 1941 5.5	**26** 0039 1.4 / 0639 5.0 / TU 1250 1.4 / 1850 5.0
12 0144 1.1 / 0758 5.1 / TU 1405 1.2 / 2026 5.1	**27** 0106 1.5 / 0707 4.9 / W 1320 1.5 / 1920 4.7
13 0225 1.4 / 0840 4.8 / W 1451 1.5 / 2118 4.6	**28** 0137 1.7 / 0739 4.7 / TH 1354 1.7 / 1955 4.5
14 0312 1.8 / 0938 4.4 / TH 1547 1.9 / ◑ 2231 4.3	**29** 0213 1.9 / 0822 4.5 / F 1436 2.0 / 2048 4.2
15 0412 2.2 / 1115 4.2 / F 1703 2.2	**30** 0300 2.2 / 0930 4.2 / SA 1533 2.2 / ◐ 2221 4.0

OCTOBER

Time m	Time m
1 0410 2.4 / 1112 4.2 / SU 1702 2.4	**16** 0113 4.2 / 0639 2.5 / M 1338 4.5 / 1930 2.2
2 0015 4.1 / 0552 2.4 / M 1247 4.4 / 1843 2.2	**17** 0210 4.4 / 0746 2.2 / TU 1430 4.7 / 2022 2.0
3 0136 4.4 / 0718 2.2 / TU 1356 4.8 / 1956 1.8	**18** 0251 4.6 / 0835 2.0 / W 1508 4.9 / 2103 1.7
4 0234 4.8 / 0822 1.8 / W 1451 5.2 / 2052 1.4	**19** 0323 4.8 / 0914 1.8 / TH 1539 5.0 / 2138 1.6
5 0323 5.1 / 0915 1.4 / TH 1539 5.6 / 2141 1.1	**20** 0352 5.0 / 0950 1.6 / F 1607 5.1 / 2211 1.5
6 0408 5.4 / 1004 1.0 / F 1624 5.8 / 2227 0.8	**21** 0419 5.1 / 1022 1.5 / SA 1634 5.2 / 2242 1.4
7 0449 5.6 / 1050 0.8 / SA 1708 5.9 / ○ 2311 0.7	**22** 0447 5.2 / 1054 1.4 / SU 1702 5.2 / ● 2311 1.4
8 0530 5.6 / 1134 0.7 / SU 1750 5.9 / 2353 0.8	**23** 0515 5.2 / 1124 1.4 / M 1730 5.2 / 2340 1.4
9 0610 5.6 / 1217 0.8 / M 1833 5.7	**24** 0543 5.2 / 1155 1.4 / TU 1758 5.1
10 0036 1.0 / 0650 5.4 / TU 1258 1.0 / 1916 5.4	**25** 0010 1.5 / 0613 5.1 / W 1226 1.4 / 1828 5.0
11 0116 1.3 / 0730 5.1 / W 1341 1.3 / 2001 5.0	**26** 0041 1.6 / 0645 5.0 / TH 1259 1.6 / 1902 4.8
12 0158 1.6 / 0814 4.8 / TH 1427 1.7 / 2054 4.5	**27** 0115 1.8 / 0723 4.8 / F 1337 1.7 / 1945 4.5
13 0245 2.0 / 0912 4.5 / F 1522 2.1 / 2211 4.3	**28** 0155 2.0 / 0813 4.6 / SA 1422 2.0 / 2046 4.3
14 0345 2.4 / 1046 4.3 / SA 1637 2.4 / ◑ 2350 4.1	**29** 0247 2.2 / 0924 4.5 / SU 1522 2.2 / ◐ 2216 4.2
15 0508 2.5 / 1225 4.3 / SU 1812 2.4	**30** 0359 2.4 / 1054 4.4 / M 1647 2.2 / 2352 4.3
	31 0529 2.3 / 1219 4.6 / TU 1814 2.1

NOVEMBER

Time m	Time m
1 0108 4.6 / 0647 2.1 / W 1327 4.9 / 1924 1.8	**16** 0202 4.5 / 0746 2.2 / TH 1421 4.7 / 2019 2.0
2 0206 4.9 / 0751 1.7 / TH 1424 5.3 / 2022 1.4	**17** 0240 4.7 / 0831 2.0 / F 1459 4.9 / 2058 1.8
3 0255 5.2 / 0847 1.4 / F 1514 5.5 / 2112 1.2	**18** 0314 4.9 / 0910 1.8 / SA 1533 5.0 / 2134 1.7
4 0340 5.4 / 0938 1.1 / SA 1601 5.7 / 2159 1.0	**19** 0346 5.0 / 0948 1.7 / SU 1605 5.1 / 2208 1.6
5 0423 5.5 / 1025 1.0 / SU 1645 5.8 / ○ 2244 1.0	**20** 0418 5.1 / 1024 1.6 / M 1638 5.1 / ● 2241 1.5
6 0505 5.6 / 1111 0.9 / M 1730 5.7 / 2328 1.0	**21** 0451 5.2 / 1059 1.5 / TU 1710 5.1 / 2315 1.5
7 0547 5.5 / 1155 1.0 / TU 1814 5.5	**22** 0524 5.2 / 1135 1.5 / W 1745 5.1 / 2349 1.6
8 0011 1.2 / 0630 5.4 / W 1238 1.2 / 1858 5.2	**23** 0600 5.2 / 1212 1.5 / TH 1821 5.0
9 0053 1.5 / 0713 5.2 / TH 1322 1.4 / 1944 4.9	**24** 0026 1.6 / 0639 5.1 / F 1250 1.5 / 1902 4.8
10 0136 1.7 / 0758 4.9 / F 1407 1.7 / 2035 4.6	**25** 0106 1.7 / 0724 5.0 / SA 1332 1.7 / 1951 4.7
11 0223 2.0 / 0851 4.7 / SA 1500 2.0 / 2140 4.3	**26** 0151 1.9 / 0816 4.7 / SU 1421 1.8 / 2050 4.5
12 0319 2.3 / 1000 4.5 / SU 1603 2.3 / ◑ 2300 4.2	**27** 0245 2.0 / 0919 4.8 / M 1519 1.9 / 2203 4.4
13 0427 2.5 / 1123 4.4 / M 1720 2.4	**28** 0350 2.1 / 1032 4.7 / TU 1628 2.0 / ◐ 2321 4.5
14 0016 4.2 / 0543 2.5 / TU 1237 4.4 / 1834 2.3	**29** 0502 2.1 / 1146 4.8 / W 1740 1.9
15 0116 4.4 / 0651 2.4 / W 1336 4.5 / 1933 2.1	**30** 0034 4.6 / 0613 2.0 / TH 1254 5.0 / 1848 1.8

DECEMBER

Time m	Time m
1 0135 4.8 / 0719 1.8 / F 1356 5.1 / 1949 1.6	**16** 0152 4.5 / 0740 2.2 / SA 1415 4.6 / 2013 2.1
2 0229 5.0 / 0819 1.5 / SA 1451 5.3 / 2045 1.4	**17** 0237 4.7 / 0830 2.0 / SU 1501 4.7 / 2057 1.9
3 0318 5.2 / 0914 1.4 / SU 1542 5.4 / 2136 1.3	**18** 0317 4.9 / 0915 1.9 / M 1542 4.8 / 2138 1.8
4 0404 5.4 / 1006 1.2 / M 1631 5.4 / 2223 1.3	**19** 0356 5.0 / 0959 1.7 / TU 1621 4.9 / 2218 1.7
5 0450 5.4 / 1055 1.2 / TU 1717 5.4 / ○ 2309 1.3	**20** 0434 5.2 / 1041 1.6 / W 1700 5.0 / ● 2257 1.6
6 0534 5.4 / 1141 1.2 / W 1802 5.3 / 2353 1.4	**21** 0514 5.3 / 1123 1.4 / TH 1739 5.1 / 2338 1.5
7 0618 5.4 / 1225 1.3 / TH 1846 5.1	**22** 0555 5.3 / 1205 1.4 / F 1821 5.1
8 0037 1.5 / 0700 5.2 / F 1308 1.5 / 1929 4.9	**23** 0021 1.5 / 0638 5.3 / SA 1248 1.4 / 1904 5.0
9 0119 1.7 / 0742 5.1 / SA 1351 1.7 / 2012 4.7	**24** 0104 1.5 / 0723 5.2 / SU 1332 1.4 / 1950 5.0
10 0203 1.9 / 0824 4.9 / SU 1436 1.9 / 2058 4.5	**25** 0150 1.6 / 0812 5.2 / M 1418 1.5 / 2041 4.8
11 0250 2.1 / 0912 4.7 / M 1524 2.1 / 2151 4.3	**26** 0239 1.7 / 0905 5.1 / TU 1508 1.6 / 2138 4.7
12 0342 2.2 / 1008 4.5 / TU 1620 2.2 / ◑ 2255 4.3	**27** 0333 1.8 / 1004 5.0 / W 1603 1.7 / 2243 4.6
13 0440 2.3 / 1113 4.4 / W 1722 2.3	**28** 0433 1.8 / 1111 4.9 / TH 1704 1.8 / 2354 4.6
14 0001 4.3 / 0542 2.4 / TH 1221 4.4 / 1826 2.3	**29** 0539 1.9 / 1222 4.8 / F 1811 1.9
15 0101 4.4 / 0644 2.3 / F 1323 4.4 / 1924 2.2	**30** 0105 4.7 / 0649 1.9 / SA 1332 4.8 / 1920 2.0
	31 0208 4.8 / 0757 1.8 / SU 1437 4.9 / 2024 1.8

TIDES

Chart Datum: 2·83 metres below IGN Datum

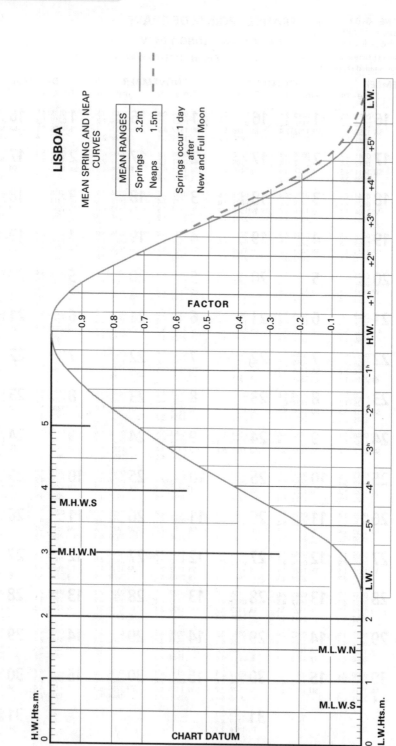

PORTUGAL – LISBOA   2006

LAT 38°43'N   LONG 9°07'W

TIMES AND HEIGHTS OF HIGH AND LOW WATERS

JANUARY

Day	Time	m	Time	m	Time	m	Time	m
1 SU	0350	3.8	0946	0.4	1620	3.6	2201	0.6
2 M	0438	3.9	1034	0.4	1708	3.6	2248	0.6
3 TU	0527	3.9	1122	0.4	1756	3.5	2336	0.7
4 W	0615	3.8	1211	0.6	1846	3.4		
5 TH	0026	0.8	0705	3.7	1302	0.7	1937	3.3
6 F ☽	0119	0.9	0800	3.5	1357	0.9	2034	3.1
7 SA	0219	1.1	0900	3.3	1458	1.1	2138	3.0
8 SU	0327	1.2	1008	3.1	1606	1.2	2247	3.0
9 M	0441	1.2	1118	3.0	1715	1.2	2353	3.1
10 TU	0554	1.2	1224	3.0	1818	1.2		
11 W	0053	3.2	0656	1.1	1323	3.1	1912	1.1
12 TH	0145	3.3	0748	0.9	1414	3.2	1958	1.0
13 F	0232	3.4	0832	0.9	1458	3.2	2038	0.9
14 SA ○	0313	3.5	0910	0.8	1536	3.3	2114	0.9
15 SU	0349	3.5	0945	0.8	1611	3.3	2148	0.9
16 M	0421	3.5	1016	0.7	1642	3.3	2220	0.9
17 TU	0452	3.5	1048	0.8	1712	3.3	2252	0.9
18 W	0522	3.5	1119	0.8	1743	3.2	2324	0.9
19 TH	0554	3.4	1153	0.9	1816	3.1	2359	1.0
20 F	0629	3.3	1229	1.0	1853	3.0		
21 SA	0037	1.1	0708	3.1	1309	1.1	1937	2.9
22 SU	0122	1.3	0755	3.0	1358	1.3	2031	2.8
23 M	0219	1.4	0854	2.8	1501	1.4	2139	2.8
24 TU	0333	1.4	1008	2.8	1615	1.4	2253	2.8
25 W	0454	1.4	1125	2.8	1728	1.3		
26 TH	0002	3.0	0606	1.2	1236	3.0	1832	1.1
27 F	0104	3.2	0707	0.9	1338	3.2	1928	0.9
28 SA	0200	3.5	0801	0.7	1432	3.4	2018	0.7
29 SU ●	0252	3.8	0850	0.4	1522	3.6	2106	0.5
30 M	0341	4.0	0937	0.3	1609	3.8	2152	0.4
31 TU	0427	4.1	1022	0.3	1654	3.8	2236	0.3

FEBRUARY

Day	Time	m	Time	m	Time	m	Time	m
1 W	0512	4.1	1105	0.2	1737	3.8	2319	0.4
2 TH	0556	4.0	1148	0.4	1820	3.6		
3 F	0002	0.5	0640	3.8	1232	0.6	1905	3.4
4 SA	0048	0.7	0727	3.5	1318	0.9	1953	3.2
5 SU ☽	0141	1.0	0821	3.2	1412	1.1	2052	3.0
6 M	0246	1.2	0928	2.9	1520	1.4	2207	2.9
7 TU	0411	1.4	1052	2.8	1646	1.4	2330	2.9
8 W	0545	1.3	1214	2.8	1806	1.4		
9 TH	0042	3.0	0655	1.2	1318	2.9	1906	1.3
10 F	0137	3.2	0744	1.0	1406	3.1	1950	1.1
11 SA	0220	3.3	0822	0.9	1445	3.2	2027	1.0
12 SU	0257	3.5	0855	0.8	1519	3.3	2059	0.9
13 M ○	0330	3.5	0924	0.7	1549	3.4	2129	0.8
14 TU	0400	3.6	0953	0.6	1618	3.4	2159	0.7
15 W	0429	3.6	1022	0.6	1646	3.4	2228	0.7
16 TH	0458	3.6	1051	0.7	1716	3.4	2258	0.7
17 F	0528	3.5	1120	0.8	1746	3.3	2328	0.8
18 SA	0559	3.4	1151	0.9	1818	3.2		
19 SU	0001	1.0	0633	3.3	1224	1.0	1854	3.1
20 M	0039	1.1	0712	3.1	1303	1.2	1940	2.9
21 TU	0128	1.3	0803	2.9	1359	1.4	2043	2.8
22 W	0241	1.5	0920	2.7	1523	1.5	2208	2.8
23 TH	0420	1.5	1058	2.8	1659	1.4	2338	3.0
24 F	0549	1.2	1224	3.0	1817	1.2		
25 SA	0050	3.3	0656	0.9	1328	3.3	1916	0.9
26 SU	0148	3.6	0749	0.6	1420	3.6	2006	0.6
27 M	0238	3.9	0836	0.3	1507	3.8	2052	0.4
28 TU ●	0325	4.1	0920	0.2	1551	4.0	2134	0.3

MARCH

Day	Time	m	Time	m	Time	m	Time	m
1 W	0408	4.3	1001	0.1	1632	4.0	2215	0.2
2 TH	0451	4.2	1041	0.2	1712	4.0	2256	0.3
3 F	0532	4.1	1120	0.4	1752	3.8	2337	0.4
4 SA	0613	3.8	1200	0.6	1832	3.6		
5 SU	0020	0.7	0656	3.5	1242	0.9	1916	3.3
6 M	0109	1.0	0745	3.1	1330	1.3	2011	3.0
7 TU	0213	1.4	0852	2.8	1438	1.6	2129	2.8
8 W	0350	1.5	1032	2.6	1621	1.7	2309	2.8
9 TH	0536	1.5	1206	2.7	1754	1.6		
10 F	0026	3.0	0641	1.3	1305	2.9	1851	1.4
11 SA	0118	3.2	0724	1.1	1347	3.1	1931	1.2
12 SU	0158	3.4	0758	0.9	1421	3.3	2004	1.0
13 M	0232	3.5	0828	0.8	1452	3.4	2035	0.9
14 TU ○	0303	3.7	0857	0.7	1521	3.5	2104	0.8
15 W	0333	3.7	0925	0.6	1550	3.6	2133	0.7
16 TH	0403	3.8	0953	0.6	1619	3.6	2202	0.7
17 F	0432	3.7	1021	0.7	1648	3.6	2231	0.7
18 SA	0502	3.6	1049	0.8	1718	3.5	2301	0.8
19 SU	0533	3.5	1118	0.9	1749	3.4	2333	0.9
20 M	0606	3.3	1150	1.0	1825	3.3		
21 TU	0011	1.1	0645	3.1	1229	1.2	1909	3.1
22 W ☾	0102	1.3	0737	2.9	1325	1.5	2012	3.0
23 TH	0218	1.5	0859	2.8	1457	1.6	2145	2.9
24 F	0405	1.5	1049	2.8	1644	1.5	2322	3.1
25 SA	0536	1.2	1213	3.1	1802	1.3		
26 SU	0034	3.4	0639	0.9	1312	3.4	1859	0.9
27 M	0129	3.8	0730	0.6	1401	3.7	1947	0.6
28 TU	0218	4.0	0814	0.4	1445	4.0	2030	0.4
29 W ●	0303	4.2	0856	0.3	1526	4.1	2112	0.3
30 TH	0345	4.3	0936	0.2	1607	4.1	2152	0.3
31 F	0427	4.2	1014	0.3	1646	4.0	2232	0.4

APRIL

Day	Time	m	Time	m	Time	m	Time	m
1 SA	0507	4.0	1052	0.5	1725	3.9	2313	0.6
2 SU	0548	3.7	1130	0.8	1804	3.6	2356	0.9
3 M	0630	3.4	1210	1.1	1846	3.4		
4 TU	0045	1.2	0718	3.0	1257	1.4	1937	3.1
5 W ☾	0149	1.5	0823	2.8	1404	1.7	2052	2.9
6 TH	0325	1.6	1006	2.6	1549	1.8	2235	2.9
7 F ☽	0502	1.6	1137	2.8	1720	1.7	2352	3.0
8 SA	0604	1.4	1233	3.0	1817	1.5		
9 SU	0043	3.2	0647	1.2	1313	3.2	1857	1.3
10 M	0123	3.4	0722	1.0	1346	3.4	1932	1.1
11 TU	0157	3.5	0754	0.9	1418	3.5	2004	0.9
12 W	0230	3.7	0824	0.8	1449	3.6	2034	0.8
13 TH ○	0302	3.7	0854	0.7	1519	3.7	2105	0.8
14 F	0334	3.8	0923	0.7	1550	3.7	2136	0.8
15 SA	0406	3.7	0952	0.8	1621	3.7	2207	0.8
16 SU	0438	3.6	1022	0.8	1654	3.6	2240	0.9
17 M	0512	3.5	1053	0.9	1729	3.5	2316	1.0
18 TU	0549	3.3	1129	1.1	1808	3.4	2359	1.1
19 W	0634	3.2	1214	1.3	1857	3.3		
20 TH	0056	1.3	0734	3.0	1318	1.5	2005	3.1
21 F ☾	0217	1.4	0901	2.9	1450	1.6	2135	3.1
22 SA	0353	1.4	1038	3.0	1626	1.5	2303	3.3
23 SU	0513	1.2	1151	3.2	1738	1.3		
24 M	0010	3.5	0614	0.9	1247	3.5	1834	1.0
25 TU	0104	3.8	0703	0.7	1334	3.8	1922	0.7
26 W	0153	4.0	0748	0.5	1418	3.9	2006	0.5
27 TH	0238	4.1	0829	0.4	1500	4.0	2048	0.4
28 F	0321	4.1	0909	0.5	1542	4.0	2130	0.4
29 SA	0404	4.0	0948	0.6	1622	4.0	2212	0.6
30 SU	0446	3.8	1027	0.8	1702	3.8	2254	0.8

TIDES

TIME ZONE (UT)
For Summer Time add ONE hour in **non-shaded areas**

PORTUGAL – LISBOA

LAT 38°43′N   LONG 9°07′W

TIMES AND HEIGHTS OF HIGH AND LOW WATERS

2006

MAY

Day	Time	m	Time	m	Day	Time	m	Time	m
1 M	0527 1105 1742 2338	3.5 1.0 3.6 1.0			16 TU	0500 1039 1718 2310	3.5 1.0 3.6 0.9		
2 TU	0609 1146 1823	3.3 1.3 3.4			17 W	0544 1122 1804	3.3 1.1 3.5		
3 W	0026 0656 1232 1910	1.2 3.0 1.5 3.2			18 TH	0000 0636 1214 1858	1.0 3.2 1.3 3.4		
4 TH	0125 0754 1333 2011	1.5 2.8 1.7 3.0			19 F	0100 0739 1320 2004	1.2 3.1 1.4 3.3		
5 F	0241 0916 1457 ☽2135	1.6 2.7 1.8 2.9			20 SA	0213 0855 1439 ☽2120	1.2 3.0 1.4 3.3		
6 SA	0401 1039 1620 2253	1.6 2.8 1.7 3.0			21 SU	0331 1012 1558 2235	1.2 3.1 1.4 3.4		
7 SU	0506 1140 1723 2351	1.5 2.9 1.6 3.1			22 M	0441 1119 1706 2340	1.1 3.3 1.2 3.5		
8 M	0556 1225 1811	1.3 3.1 1.4			23 TU	0541 1216 1804	0.9 3.5 1.0		
9 TU	0036 0638 1304 1851	3.3 1.1 3.3 1.2			24 W	0036 0633 1306 1855	3.7 0.8 3.6 0.8		
10 W	0116 0714 1339 1928	3.4 1.0 3.5 1.1			25 TH	0127 0720 1352 1943	3.8 0.7 3.8 0.7		
11 TH	0153 0748 1413 2002	3.5 0.9 3.6 0.9			26 F	0215 0804 1437 2029	3.8 0.7 3.8 0.6		
12 F	0229 0820 1448 2037	3.6 0.9 3.6 0.9			27 SA	0301 0846 1521 ●2114	3.8 0.7 3.8 0.6		
13 SA	0305 0853 1522 ○2111	3.6 0.8 3.7 0.8			28 SU	0346 0927 1604 2158	3.7 0.8 3.8 0.7		
14 SU	0341 0926 1558 2148	3.6 0.8 3.7 0.8			29 M	0430 1007 1645 2241	3.5 0.9 3.7 0.9		
15 M	0419 1001 1636 2226	3.5 0.9 3.7 0.9			30 TU	0512 1046 1724 2323	3.3 1.0 3.5 1.0		
					31 W	0552 1126 1803	3.2 1.2 3.4		

JUNE

Day	Time	m	Time	m	Day	Time	m	Time	m
1 TH	0007 0633 1209 1843	1.1 3.0 1.4 3.2			16 F	0635 1213 1854	3.3 1.0 3.6		
2 F	0054 0719 1259 1930	1.3 2.9 1.5 3.1			17 SA	0054 0730 1311 1951	0.9 3.2 1.1 3.5		
3 SA	0149 0814 1400 ☽2028	1.4 2.8 1.6 3.0			18 SU	0154 0832 1414 ☽2054	1.0 3.2 1.2 3.4		
4 SU	0251 0921 1509 2136	1.4 2.8 1.6 3.0			19 M	0258 0937 1522 2201	1.0 3.2 1.2 3.3		
5 M	0356 1028 1616 2243	1.4 2.9 1.6 3.0			20 TU	0403 1042 1630 2307	1.1 3.2 1.2 3.3		
6 TU	0455 1126 1714 2340	1.3 3.0 1.5 3.1			21 W	0506 1143 1735	1.0 3.3 1.1		
7 W	0546 1214 1805	1.2 3.1 1.3			22 TH	0008 0604 1239 1835	3.4 1.0 3.4 1.0		
8 TH	0029 0630 1257 1849	3.2 1.1 3.3 1.2			23 F	0106 0657 1332 1929	3.4 0.9 3.5 0.9		
9 F	0114 0710 1337 1931	3.3 1.0 3.4 1.0			24 SA	0159 0746 1421 2019	3.4 0.9 3.6 0.8		
10 SA	0156 0748 1418 2011	3.4 0.9 3.5 0.9			25 SU	0249 0831 1508 ●2105	3.4 0.9 3.7 0.8		
11 SU	0239 0827 1459 ○2053	3.4 0.9 3.6 0.8			26 M	0335 0913 1551 2147	3.4 0.9 3.6 0.8		
12 M	0322 0906 1542 2135	3.5 0.8 3.7 0.8			27 TU	0417 0953 1631 2227	3.3 0.9 3.6 0.8		
13 TU	0407 0948 1626 2220	3.5 0.8 3.7 0.8			28 W	0456 1030 1707 2304	3.3 1.0 3.5 0.9		
14 W	0454 1033 1713 2308	3.5 0.9 3.7 0.7			29 TH	0531 1106 1741 2340	3.2 1.1 3.4 1.0		
15 TH	0543 1121 1802 2359	3.4 0.9 3.7 0.8			30 F	0605 1143 1814	3.1 1.1 3.3		

JULY

Day	Time	m	Time	m	Day	Time	m	Time	m
1 SA	0018 0641 1223 1851	1.1 3.0 1.2 3.2			16 SU	0034 0708 1249 1928	0.6 3.4 0.8 3.6		
2 SU	0059 0722 1308 1935	1.2 3.0 1.3 3.1			17 M	0124 0800 1343 ☽2024	0.8 3.3 1.0 3.4		
3 M	0148 0812 1401 ☽2028	1.3 2.9 1.4 3.0			18 TU	0220 0859 1446 2127	1.0 3.2 1.1 3.3		
4 TU	0244 0912 1504 2131	1.3 2.8 1.5 2.9			19 W	0324 1005 1558 2237	1.1 3.1 1.2 3.1		
5 W	0346 1017 1611 2237	1.4 2.8 1.5 2.9			20 TH	0434 1115 1715 2349	1.2 3.1 1.2 3.1		
6 TH	0448 1119 1715 2339	1.4 2.9 1.4 3.0			21 F	0544 1222 1826	1.2 3.2 1.1		
7 F	0544 1214 1812	1.3 3.1 1.3			22 SA	0055 0645 1321 1926	3.1 1.1 3.4 1.0		
8 SA	0036 0634 1304 1904	3.0 1.2 3.2 1.1			23 SU	0152 0737 1412 2015	3.2 1.1 3.5 0.9		
9 SU	0129 0722 1353 1953	3.2 1.0 3.4 0.9			24 M	0241 0822 1457 2056	3.3 1.0 3.6 0.8		
10 M	0221 0808 1442 2040	3.3 0.9 3.6 0.8			25 TU	0323 0901 1537 ●2133	3.3 0.9 3.6 0.8		
11 TU	0310 0854 1530 ○2127	3.4 0.8 3.8 0.6			26 W	0400 0936 1612 2206	3.3 0.9 3.6 0.8		
12 W	0359 0940 1617 2213	3.5 0.7 3.9 0.5			27 TH	0433 1009 1643 2237	3.3 0.9 3.6 0.8		
13 TH	0446 1026 1704 2259	3.6 0.6 3.9 0.5			28 F	0503 1041 1713 2309	3.3 0.9 3.6 0.8		
14 F	0533 1112 1751 2346	3.6 0.6 3.9 0.5			29 SA	0533 1114 1744 2341	3.3 0.9 3.5 0.9		
15 SA	0620 1159 1839	3.5 0.7 3.8			30 SU	0604 1147 1816	3.2 1.0 3.4		
					31 M	0015 0639 1223 1852	1.0 3.1 1.1 3.2		

AUGUST

Day	Time	m	Time	m	Day	Time	m	Time	m
1 TU	0053 0719 1305 1935	1.1 3.0 1.3 3.1			16 W	0143 0822 1414 ☽2056	1.1 3.2 1.2 3.1		
2 W	0137 0808 1356 ●2028	1.3 2.9 1.5 2.9			17 TH	0247 0932 1535 ●2216	1.3 3.1 1.4 2.9		
3 TH	0234 0910 1505 2136	1.4 2.8 1.5 2.8			18 F	0410 1056 1710 2342	1.5 3.0 1.4 2.9		
4 F	0346 1023 1627 2254	1.5 2.8 1.5 2.8			19 SA	0536 1213 1828	1.5 3.2 1.3		
5 SA	0501 1135 1743	1.5 3.0 1.4			20 SU	0053 0642 1313 1923	3.0 1.3 3.3 1.1		
6 SU	0009 0607 1239 1845	2.9 1.3 3.2 1.1			21 M	0146 0730 1401 2004	3.2 1.2 3.5 1.0		
7 M	0113 0704 1337 1939	3.1 1.1 3.5 0.9			22 TU	0227 0809 1440 2038	3.3 1.0 3.6 0.9		
8 TU	0208 0755 1428 2028	3.4 0.9 3.7 0.6			23 W	0303 0843 1515 ○2109	3.4 0.9 3.7 0.8		
9 W	0258 0842 1517 ○2113	3.6 0.6 3.9 0.4			24 TH	0335 0914 1546 2138	3.5 0.8 3.7 0.7		
10 TH	0345 0927 1603 2157	3.8 0.5 4.1 0.3			25 F	0404 0944 1615 2207	3.5 0.8 3.7 0.7		
11 F	0429 1011 1648 2240	3.8 0.4 4.2 0.3			26 SA	0432 1013 1644 2236	3.5 0.8 3.7 0.8		
12 SA	0513 1054 1731 2323	3.8 0.4 4.1 0.4			27 SU	0501 1043 1713 2305	3.5 0.8 3.6 0.8		
13 SU	0555 1137 1815	3.8 0.5 4.0			28 M	0530 1113 1743 2335	3.4 0.9 3.5 1.0		
14 M	0006 0639 1222 1901	0.6 3.6 0.7 3.7			29 TU	0602 1145 1816	3.3 1.1 3.3		
15 TU	0051 0727 1313 1953	0.8 3.4 0.9 3.4			30 W	0006 0637 1220 1853	1.1 3.2 1.3 3.1		
					31 TH	0043 0719 1306 ☽1941	1.3 3.0 1.4 2.9		

TIME ZONE (UT)
For Summer Time add ONE hour in **non-shaded areas**

PORTUGAL – LISBOA

LAT 38°43'N   LONG 9°07'W

TIMES AND HEIGHTS OF HIGH AND LOW WATERS

SEPTEMBER

Day	Time m	Day	Time m
1 F	0133 1.5 / 0818 2.9 / 1414 1.6 / 2050 2.8	**16** SA	0355 1.7 / 1041 3.0 / 1709 1.5 / 2338 2.9
2 SA	0252 1.6 / 0938 2.9 / 1552 1.6 / 2225 2.8	**17** SU	0529 1.6 / 1201 3.2 / 1818 1.4
3 SU	0431 1.6 / 1108 3.0 / 1724 1.4 / 2355 3.0	**18** M	0042 3.1 / 0629 1.5 / 1257 3.3 / 1904 1.2
4 M	0550 1.4 / 1223 3.3 / 1831 1.1	**19** TU	0127 3.3 / 0712 1.3 / 1339 3.5 / 1939 1.0
5 TU	0101 3.3 / 0650 1.1 / 1321 3.6 / 1924 0.8	**20** W	0203 3.4 / 0746 1.1 / 1414 3.7 / 2010 0.9
6 W	0153 3.5 / 0740 0.8 / 1411 3.9 / 2010 0.5	**21** TH	0234 3.6 / 0817 0.9 / 1446 3.8 / 2039 0.8
7 TH	0240 3.8 / 0825 0.6 / 1458 4.2 / ○ 2053 0.3	**22** F	0304 3.7 / 0847 0.9 / 1516 3.8 / 2108 0.8
8 F	0324 4.0 / 0908 0.4 / 1542 4.3 / 2135 0.3	**23** SA	0333 3.7 / 0916 0.8 / 1545 3.8 / 2136 0.7
9 SA	0406 4.1 / 0949 0.3 / 1625 4.3 / 2216 0.3	**24** SU	0401 3.7 / 0945 0.8 / 1614 3.8 / 2204 0.8
10 SU	0447 4.1 / 1030 0.3 / 1707 4.2 / 2256 0.4	**25** M	0430 3.7 / 1014 0.9 / 1644 3.7 / 2231 0.9
11 M	0528 4.0 / 1112 0.5 / 1750 4.0 / 2336 0.6	**26** TU	0459 3.6 / 1043 0.9 / 1714 3.5 / 2259 1.0
12 TU	0610 3.8 / 1156 0.7 / 1835 3.7	**27** W	0530 3.5 / 1114 1.1 / 1746 3.4 / 2329 1.2
13 W	0019 1.0 / 0656 3.5 / 1246 1.0 / 1925 3.3	**28** TH	0604 3.3 / 1150 1.3 / 1823 3.2
14 TH	0109 1.3 / 0750 3.3 / 1350 1.4 / ◑ 2031 3.1	**29** F	0646 3.2 / 1236 1.5 / 1912 3.0
15 F	0216 1.6 / 0906 3.0 / 1523 1.5 / 2204 2.8	**30** SA	0056 1.6 / 0745 3.0 / 1348 1.6 / ◑ 2027 2.8

OCTOBER

Day	Time m	Day	Time m
1 SU	0221 1.7 / 0912 3.0 / 1533 1.6 / 2214 2.8	**16** M	0500 1.7 / 1130 3.1 / 1745 1.5
2 M	0411 1.7 / 1050 3.1 / 1707 1.4 / 2342 3.1	**17** TU	0012 3.1 / 0557 1.6 / 1224 3.3 / 1829 1.3
3 TU	0533 1.4 / 1204 3.4 / 1811 1.1	**18** W	0054 3.3 / 0639 1.4 / 1305 3.5 / 1904 1.1
4 W	0043 3.4 / 0630 1.1 / 1300 3.8 / 1902 0.8	**19** TH	0128 3.5 / 0714 1.2 / 1340 3.6 / 1936 1.0
5 TH	0132 3.7 / 0718 0.8 / 1349 4.0 / 1946 0.5	**20** F	0200 3.6 / 0746 1.0 / 1413 3.7 / 2007 0.9
6 F	0216 4.0 / 0802 0.6 / 1434 4.3 / 2029 0.4	**21** SA	0231 3.7 / 0817 0.9 / 1444 3.8 / 2036 0.8
7 SA	0259 4.1 / 0845 0.4 / 1518 4.3 / ○ 2109 0.3	**22** SU	0301 3.7 / 0848 0.9 / 1515 3.8 / ● 2105 0.8
8 SU	0340 4.2 / 0926 0.3 / 1601 4.3 / 2149 0.4	**23** M	0331 3.7 / 0918 0.9 / 1546 3.7 / 2134 0.9
9 M	0421 4.2 / 1008 0.4 / 1643 4.2 / 2229 0.6	**24** TU	0402 3.7 / 0949 0.9 / 1618 3.6 / 2203 0.9
10 TU	0502 4.0 / 1020 0.6 / 1727 3.9 / 2309 0.8	**25** W	0434 3.6 / 1020 1.0 / 1651 3.5 / 2233 1.1
11 W	0544 3.8 / 1135 0.8 / 1812 3.6 / 2352 1.1	**26** TH	0507 3.5 / 1055 1.1 / 1727 3.3 / 2306 1.2
12 TH	0630 3.5 / 1226 1.1 / 1903 3.2	**27** F	0545 3.4 / 1135 1.2 / 1809 3.2 / 2347 1.4
13 F	0041 1.5 / 0724 3.3 / 1332 1.5 / 2010 2.9	**28** SA	0631 3.3 / 1227 1.4 / 1904 3.0
14 SA	0149 1.7 / 0839 3.1 / 1506 1.6 / ◑ 2145 2.8	**29** SU	0044 1.6 / 0733 3.2 / 1341 1.5 / ◑ 2022 2.9
15 SU	0330 1.8 / 1014 3.0 / 1641 1.6 / 2313 2.9	**30** M	0210 1.7 / 0858 3.1 / 1515 1.5 / 2159 3.0
		31 TU	0348 1.6 / 1027 3.2 / 1639 1.3 / 2317 3.2

NOVEMBER

Day	Time m	Day	Time m
1 W	0505 1.4 / 1138 3.5 / 1742 1.1	**16** TH	0007 3.1 / 0554 1.4 / 1220 3.3 / 1821 1.2
2 TH	0016 3.5 / 0603 1.1 / 1234 3.8 / 1834 0.8	**17** F	0047 3.3 / 0636 1.3 / 1300 3.4 / 1859 1.1
3 F	0105 3.7 / 0652 0.8 / 1323 4.0 / 1920 0.6	**18** SA	0123 3.4 / 0713 1.1 / 1337 3.5 / 1933 1.0
4 SA	0150 3.9 / 0738 0.6 / 1410 4.1 / 2003 0.5	**19** SU	0157 3.5 / 0748 1.0 / 1412 3.6 / 2005 0.9
5 SU	0233 4.1 / 0822 0.5 / 1455 4.2 / ○ 2044 0.5	**20** M	0231 3.6 / 0822 0.9 / 1447 3.6 / ● 2037 0.9
6 M	0316 4.1 / 0906 0.4 / 1539 4.1 / 2125 0.6	**21** TU	0305 3.6 / 0856 0.9 / 1523 3.5 / 2109 0.9
7 TU	0359 4.1 / 0949 0.5 / 1624 3.9 / 2206 0.7	**22** W	0339 3.7 / 0930 0.9 / 1559 3.5 / 2142 0.9
8 W	0442 3.9 / 1034 0.7 / 1709 3.7 / 2248 0.9	**23** TH	0416 3.6 / 1007 0.9 / 1638 3.4 / 2218 1.0
9 TH	0525 3.8 / 1120 0.9 / 1755 3.4 / 2330 1.2	**24** F	0455 3.6 / 1047 1.0 / 1720 3.3 / 2258 1.1
10 F	0610 3.5 / 1211 1.1 / 1844 3.1	**25** SA	0538 3.5 / 1133 1.1 / 1807 3.2 / 2345 1.2
11 SA	0018 1.4 / 0700 3.2 / 1310 1.4 / 1944 2.9	**26** SU	0628 3.4 / 1227 1.2 / 1904 3.1
12 SU	0119 1.6 / 0802 3.1 / 1422 1.5 / ◐ 2059 2.8	**27** M	0043 1.4 / 0728 3.3 / 1333 1.3 / 2013 3.0
13 M	0238 1.8 / 0919 3.0 / 1540 1.6 / 2217 2.8	**28** TU	0155 1.4 / 0839 3.2 / 1448 1.3 / ◐ 2130 3.0
14 TU	0359 1.7 / 1034 3.0 / 1647 1.5 / 2320 3.0	**29** W	0315 1.4 / 0955 3.3 / 1602 1.2 / 2242 3.2
15 W	0504 1.6 / 1133 3.1 / 1739 1.3	**30** TH	0428 1.3 / 1104 3.4 / 1707 1.0 / 2342 3.3

DECEMBER

Day	Time m	Day	Time m
1 F	0531 1.1 / 1204 3.6 / 1803 0.9	**16** SA	0550 1.4 / 1215 3.1 / 1817 1.2
2 SA	0036 3.5 / 0626 0.9 / 1258 3.7 / 1853 0.7	**17** SU	0043 3.2 / 0638 1.2 / 1301 3.2 / 1858 1.1
3 SU	0125 3.7 / 0717 0.7 / 1348 3.8 / 1940 0.7	**18** M	0124 3.3 / 0720 1.1 / 1343 3.3 / 1937 1.0
4 M	0212 3.8 / 0806 0.6 / 1437 3.8 / 2025 0.6	**19** TU	0204 3.4 / 0800 1.0 / 1425 3.3 / 2014 0.9
5 TU	0258 3.9 / 0853 0.6 / 1525 3.7 / ○ 2108 0.7	**20** W	0243 3.5 / 0839 0.9 / 1506 3.3 / ● 2051 0.9
6 W	0344 3.9 / 0939 0.6 / 1611 3.6 / 2151 0.8	**21** TH	0324 3.6 / 0919 0.8 / 1549 3.4 / 2131 0.8
7 TH	0428 3.8 / 1024 0.7 / 1656 3.5 / 2232 0.9	**22** F	0406 3.7 / 1001 0.7 / 1632 3.4 / 2212 0.8
8 F	0511 3.7 / 1108 0.8 / 1739 3.3 / 2314 1.1	**23** SA	0450 3.7 / 1044 0.7 / 1717 3.4 / 2256 0.8
9 SA	0552 3.5 / 1152 1.0 / 1822 3.1 / 2356 1.2	**24** SU	0535 3.6 / 1130 0.7 / 1804 3.3 / 2343 0.9
10 SU	0633 3.3 / 1237 1.2 / 1906 3.0	**25** M	0623 3.6 / 1219 0.8 / 1855 3.2
11 M	0043 1.4 / 0718 3.1 / 1328 1.3 / 1956 2.8	**26** TU	0034 1.0 / 0715 3.5 / 1313 0.9 / 1950 3.2
12 TU	0138 1.5 / 0810 3.0 / 1425 1.4 / ◐ 2056 2.8	**27** W	0132 1.1 / 0813 3.3 / 1413 1.0 / ◐ 2053 3.1
13 W	0242 1.6 / 0914 2.9 / 1530 1.4 / 2204 2.8	**28** TH	0236 1.2 / 0918 3.3 / 1519 1.1 / 2200 3.1
14 TH	0351 1.6 / 1022 2.9 / 1633 1.4 / 2306 2.9	**29** F	0347 1.2 / 1028 3.2 / 1627 1.1 / 2307 3.2
15 F	0455 1.5 / 1123 3.0 / 1729 1.3 / 2358 3.0	**30** SA	0458 1.1 / 1135 3.3 / 1733 1.0
		31 SU	0009 3.3 / 0605 1.0 / 1238 3.3 / 1832 0.9

TIDES

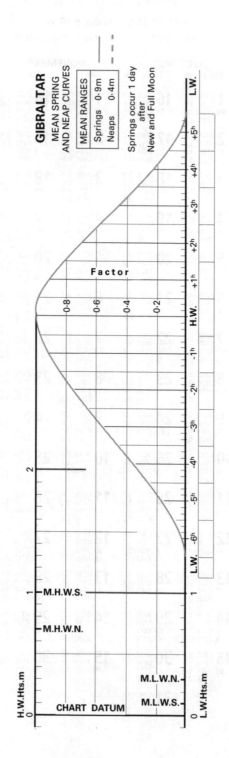

GIBRALTAR

TIME ZONE -0100
(Gibraltar Standard Time)
Subtract 1 hour for UT
For Gibraltar Summer Time add
ONE hour in **non-shaded areas**

LAT 36°08'N   LONG 5°21'W

TIMES AND HEIGHTS OF HIGH AND LOW WATERS

2006

JANUARY

Day	Time	m		Day	Time	m
1 SU	0346 / 0921 / 1607 / 2154	1.0 / 0.1 / 1.0 / 0.0		**16** M	0428 / 1001 / 1638 / 2221	0.8 / 0.1 / 0.8 / 0.1
2 M	0433 / 1008 / 1654 / 2239	1.0 / 0.1 / 1.0 / 0.1		**17** TU	0459 / 1035 / 1711 / 2251	0.8 / 0.1 / 0.8 / 0.1
3 TU	0519 / 1057 / 1743 / 2325	1.0 / 0.1 / 0.9 / 0.1		**18** W	0529 / 1108 / 1743 / 2321	0.8 / 0.2 / 0.8 / 0.1
4 W	0607 / 1149 / 1833 / 2351	1.0 / 0.1 / 0.9 / 0.2		**19** TH	0601 / 1142 / 1817	0.8 / 0.2 / 0.8
5 TH	0014 / 0659 / 1246 / 1927	0.1 / 0.9 / 0.2 / 0.8		**20** F	0635 / 1218 / 1854	0.8 / 0.2 / 0.7
6 F	0110 / 0756 / 1348 / 2026 ◑	0.2 / 0.9 / 0.2 / 0.8		**21** SA	0024 / 0714 / 1301 / 1937	0.2 / 0.7 / 0.2 / 0.7
7 SA	0212 / 0856 / 1456 / 2131	0.2 / 0.8 / 0.2 / 0.7		**22** SU	0104 / 0802 / 1354 / 2029 ◐	0.3 / 0.7 / 0.3 / 0.6
8 SU	0322 / 1002 / 1612 / 2246	0.3 / 0.8 / 0.2 / 0.7		**23** M	0158 / 0900 / 1504 / 2133	0.3 / 0.7 / 0.3 / 0.6
9 M	0441 / 1112 / 1731	0.3 / 0.8 / 0.2		**24** TU	0319 / 1010 / 1634 / 2253	0.3 / 0.7 / 0.3 / 0.6
10 TU	0000 / 0550 / 1216 / 1832	0.7 / 0.3 / 0.8 / 0.2		**25** W	0459 / 1128 / 1752	0.3 / 0.7 / 0.2
11 W	0102 / 0644 / 1311 / 1920	0.8 / 0.2 / 0.8 / 0.2		**26** TH	0011 / 0607 / 1234 / 1847	0.7 / 0.2 / 0.8 / 0.1
12 TH	0154 / 0729 / 1359 / 2001	0.8 / 0.2 / 0.8 / 0.1		**27** F	0112 / 0659 / 1331 / 1935	0.8 / 0.2 / 0.8 / 0.1
13 F	0238 / 0809 / 1444 / 2040	0.8 / 0.2 / 0.8 / 0.1		**28** SA	0204 / 0746 / 1423 / 2021	0.8 / 0.1 / 0.9 / 0.1
14 SA	0319 / 0848 / 1525 / 2115 ○	0.8 / 0.2 / 0.8 / 0.1		**29** SU	0252 / 0833 / 1513 / 2106 ●	0.9 / 0.1 / 0.9 / 0.0
15 SU	0355 / 0925 / 1603 / 2149	0.8 / 0.1 / 0.8 / 0.1		**30** M	0339 / 0919 / 1600 / 2149	1.0 / 0.0 / 1.0 / 0.0
				31 TU	0423 / 1005 / 1646 / 2230	1.0 / 0.0 / 1.0 / 0.0

FEBRUARY

Day	Time	m		Day	Time	m
1 W	0507 / 1049 / 1731 / 2311	1.0 / 0.0 / 1.0 / 0.0		**16** TH	0501 / 1043 / 1717 / 2254	0.9 / 0.1 / 0.8 / 0.1
2 TH	0551 / 1134 / 1817 / 2352	1.0 / 0.0 / 0.9 / 0.0		**17** F	0529 / 1111 / 1747 / 2319	0.8 / 0.1 / 0.8 / 0.1
3 F	0637 / 1220 / 1906	1.0 / 0.1 / 0.9		**18** SA	0559 / 1141 / 1820 / 2347	0.8 / 0.1 / 0.8 / 0.2
4 SA	0036 / 0727 / 1311 / 1958	0.1 / 0.9 / 0.2 / 0.8		**19** SU	0633 / 1215 / 1900	0.8 / 0.2 / 0.7
5 SU	0127 / 0821 / 1410 / 2056 ◑	0.2 / 0.8 / 0.2 / 0.7		**20** M	0019 / 0716 / 1259 / 1950	0.2 / 0.7 / 0.2 / 0.7
6 M	0231 / 0924 / 1531 / 2210	0.3 / 0.7 / 0.3 / 0.6		**21** TU	0102 / 0813 / 1405 / 2053	0.3 / 0.7 / 0.3 / 0.6
7 TU	0406 / 1043 / 1725 / 2344	0.3 / 0.7 / 0.3 / 0.6		**22** W	0214 / 0926 / 1601 / 2218	0.3 / 0.6 / 0.3 / 0.6
8 W	0545 / 1207 / 1835	0.3 / 0.7 / 0.2		**23** TH	0435 / 1102 / 1744 / 2353	0.3 / 0.7 / 0.2 / 0.6
9 TH	0100 / 0644 / 1311 / 1921	0.7 / 0.2 / 0.7 / 0.2		**24** F	0602 / 1223 / 1842	0.2 / 0.7 / 0.1
10 F	0154 / 0655 / 1359 / 1958	0.7 / 0.2 / 0.8 / 0.1		**25** SA	0100 / 0655 / 1323 / 1928	0.7 / 0.2 / 0.8 / 0.1
11 SA	0235 / 0804 / 1440 / 2032	0.8 / 0.1 / 0.8 / 0.0		**26** SU	0153 / 0741 / 1414 / 2011	0.8 / 0.1 / 0.9 / 0.0
12 SU	0309 / 0839 / 1516 / 2103	0.8 / 0.1 / 0.8 / 0.1		**27** M	0239 / 0826 / 1501 / 2053	0.9 / 0.0 / 0.9 / -0.1
13 M	0340 / 0912 / 1548 / 2133 ○	0.8 / 0.1 / 0.8 / 0.1		**28** TU	0323 / 0909 / 1546 / 2133 ●	1.0 / -0.1 / 1.0 / -0.1
14 TU	0408 / 0944 / 1619 / 2201	0.9 / 0.1 / 0.9 / 0.1				
15 W	0435 / 1014 / 1648 / 2228	0.9 / 0.1 / 0.9 / 0.1				

MARCH

Day	Time	m		Day	Time	m
1 W	0406 / 0951 / 1630 / 2212	1.0 / -0.1 / 1.0 / -0.1		**16** TH	0404 / 0947 / 1621 / 2159	0.9 / 0.0 / 0.9 / 0.1
2 TH	0447 / 1032 / 1713 / 2249	1.0 / -0.1 / 1.0 / 0.0		**17** F	0431 / 1015 / 1650 / 2225	0.9 / 0.1 / 0.9 / 0.1
3 F	0529 / 1112 / 1756 / 2326	1.0 / 0.0 / 0.9 / 0.0		**18** SA	0459 / 1043 / 1721 / 2251	0.9 / 0.1 / 0.9 / 0.1
4 SA	0612 / 1152 / 1842	0.9 / 0.0 / 0.9		**19** SU	0530 / 1113 / 1755 / 2319	0.8 / 0.1 / 0.8 / 0.2
5 SU	0005 / 0657 / 1235 / 1931	0.1 / 0.9 / 0.1 / 0.8		**20** M	0605 / 1145 / 1836 / 2352	0.8 / 0.2 / 0.8 / 0.2
6 M	0049 / 0745 / 1326 / 2027 ◑	0.2 / 0.8 / 0.2 / 0.7		**21** TU	0648 / 1227 / 1928	0.7 / 0.2 / 0.7
7 TU	0147 / 0850 / 1447 / 2139	0.3 / 0.7 / 0.3 / 0.6		**22** W	0036 / 0745 / 1334 / 2033 ◐	0.3 / 0.7 / 0.3 / 0.6
8 W	0333 / 1014 / 1715 / 2325	0.3 / 0.6 / 0.3 / 0.6		**23** TH	0154 / 0903 / 1549 / 2158	0.3 / 0.6 / 0.3 / 0.6
9 TH	0540 / 1158 / 1824	0.3 / 0.6 / 0.3		**24** F	0427 / 1046 / 1728 / 2334	0.3 / 0.6 / 0.2 / 0.7
10 F	0048 / 0635 / 1303 / 1904	0.7 / 0.3 / 0.7 / 0.2		**25** SA	0551 / 1211 / 1824	0.2 / 0.7 / 0.1
11 SA	0136 / 0713 / 1346 / 1937	0.7 / 0.2 / 0.7 / 0.1		**26** SU	0041 / 0642 / 1309 / 1908	0.8 / 0.1 / 0.8 / 0.1
12 SU	0212 / 0746 / 1421 / 2007	0.8 / 0.1 / 0.8 / 0.1		**27** M	0132 / 0726 / 1357 / 1949	0.9 / 0.0 / 0.9 / 0.0
13 M	0243 / 0817 / 1453 / 2036	0.8 / 0.1 / 0.8 / 0.1		**28** TU	0216 / 0809 / 1442 / 2029	0.9 / 0.0 / 0.9 / 0.0
14 TU	0311 / 0848 / 1523 / 2105 ○	0.9 / 0.1 / 0.9 / 0.1		**29** W	0259 / 0850 / 1526 / 2108	1.0 / -0.1 / 1.0 / -0.1
15 W	0338 / 0918 / 1552 / 2132	0.9 / 0.1 / 0.9 / 0.1		**30** TH	0341 / 0931 / 1608 / 2146	1.0 / -0.1 / 1.0 / 0.0
				31 F	0423 / 1009 / 1651 / 2222	1.0 / -0.1 / 1.0 / 0.0

APRIL

Day	Time	m		Day	Time	m
1 SA	0503 / 1047 / 1733 / 2259	1.0 / 0.0 / 0.9 / 0.1		**16** SU	0433 / 1019 / 1659 / 2226	0.9 / 0.1 / 0.9 / 0.2
2 SU	0545 / 1124 / 1818 / 2337	0.9 / 0.1 / 0.8 / 0.1		**17** M	0508 / 1051 / 1737 / 2259	0.9 / 0.1 / 0.8 / 0.2
3 M	0630 / 1203 / 1907	0.8 / 0.2 / 0.8		**18** TU	0546 / 1127 / 1822 / 2338	0.8 / 0.2 / 0.8 / 0.2
4 TU	0019 / 0720 / 1251 / 2003	0.2 / 0.7 / 0.3 / 0.7		**19** W	0633 / 1214 / 1917	0.8 / 0.2 / 0.7
5 W	0117 / 0821 / 1409 / 2112 ◑	0.3 / 0.7 / 0.3 / 0.6		**20** TH	0031 / 0734 / 1331 / 2023	0.3 / 0.7 / 0.3 / 0.7
6 TH	0300 / 0942 / 1626 / 2244	0.4 / 0.6 / 0.3 / 0.6		**21** F	0203 / 0852 / 1530 / 2142 ◐	0.3 / 0.7 / 0.3 / 0.7
7 F	0506 / 1125 / 1742	0.3 / 0.6 / 0.3		**22** SA	0404 / 1026 / 1654 / 2307	0.3 / 0.7 / 0.2 / 0.7
8 SA	0006 / 0603 / 1231 / 1824	0.7 / 0.3 / 0.7 / 0.3		**23** SU	0524 / 1147 / 1751	0.2 / 0.7 / 0.2
9 SU	0056 / 0641 / 1313 / 1858	0.7 / 0.2 / 0.7 / 0.2		**24** M	0011 / 0617 / 1245 / 1836	0.8 / 0.1 / 0.8 / 0.1
10 M	0131 / 0713 / 1347 / 1929	0.8 / 0.2 / 0.8 / 0.2		**25** TU	0102 / 0702 / 1332 / 1918	0.9 / 0.1 / 0.9 / 0.1
11 TU	0202 / 0745 / 1419 / 1959	0.8 / 0.1 / 0.8 / 0.1		**26** W	0147 / 0745 / 1417 / 1958	1.0 / 0.0 / 0.9 / 0.0
12 W	0232 / 0816 / 1450 / 2028	0.9 / 0.1 / 0.9 / 0.1		**27** TH	0231 / 0826 / 1501 / 2038 ●	1.0 / 0.0 / 1.0 / 0.0
13 TH	0301 / 0847 / 1521 / 2058	0.9 / 0.1 / 0.9 / 0.1		**28** F	0314 / 0907 / 1544 / 2118	1.0 / 0.0 / 1.0 / 0.0
14 F	0331 / 0918 / 1552 / 2127 ○	0.9 / 0.1 / 0.9 / 0.1		**29** SA	0356 / 0946 / 1628 / 2156	1.0 / 0.0 / 0.9 / 0.1
15 SA	0401 / 0948 / 1625 / 2156	0.9 / 0.1 / 0.9 / 0.1		**30** SU	0438 / 1024 / 1711 / 2235	0.9 / 0.1 / 0.9 / 0.1

Chart Datum: 0·25 metres below Alicante Datum (Mean Sea Level, Alicante)

TIDES

TIME ZONE -0100
(Gibraltar Standard Time)
Subtract 1 hour for UT
For Gibraltar Summer Time add
ONE hour in **non-shaded areas**

GIBRALTAR

2006

LAT 36°08'N   LONG 5°21'W

TIMES AND HEIGHTS OF HIGH AND LOW WATERS

MAY

Time m	Time m
1 M 0521 0.9 / 1101 0.1 / 1757 0.8 / 2315 0.2	**16** TU 0453 0.9 / 1038 0.2 / 1725 0.9 / 2249 0.3
2 TU 0606 0.8 / 1141 0.2 / 1847 0.8 / 2359 0.3	**17** W 0537 0.8 / 1121 0.2 / 1812 0.8 / 2336 0.3
3 W 0658 0.7 / 1228 0.3 / 1942 0.7	**18** TH 0627 0.8 / 1213 0.2 / 1908 0.8
4 TH 0057 0.3 / 0756 0.7 / 1339 0.3 / 2043 0.7	**19** F 0037 0.3 / 0728 0.8 / 1328 0.3 / 2010 0.8
5 F 0221 0.4 / 0905 0.6 / 1514 0.3 / ◔ 2152 0.7	**20** SA 0159 0.3 / 0839 0.7 / 1453 0.3 / ◑ 2119 0.8
6 SA 0356 0.3 / 1023 0.6 / 1633 0.3 / 2302 0.7	**21** SU 0326 0.3 / 0957 0.7 / 1607 0.2 / 2231 0.8
7 SU 0507 0.3 / 1134 0.7 / 1727 0.3 / 2357 0.7	**22** M 0442 0.2 / 1113 0.8 / 1709 0.2 / 2336 0.8
8 M 0554 0.3 / 1224 0.7 / 1809 0.3	**23** TU 0545 0.2 / 1214 0.8 / 1802 0.2
9 TU 0038 0.8 / 0632 0.2 / 1304 0.8 / 1844 0.2	**24** W 0029 0.9 / 0635 0.1 / 1305 0.9 / 1847 0.1
10 W 0114 0.8 / 0707 0.2 / 1339 0.8 / 1917 0.2	**25** TH 0117 0.9 / 0721 0.1 / 1352 0.9 / 1931 0.1
11 TH 0148 0.9 / 0741 0.1 / 1413 0.9 / 1949 0.2	**26** F 0203 0.9 / 0805 0.1 / 1438 0.9 / 2013 0.1
12 F 0222 0.9 / 0815 0.1 / 1448 0.9 / 2022 0.2	**27** SA 0248 0.9 / 0847 0.1 / 1524 0.9 / ● 2055 0.1
13 SA 0257 0.9 / 0849 0.1 / 1524 0.9 / ○ 2056 0.2	**28** SU 0333 0.9 / 0928 0.1 / 1609 0.9 / 2137 0.1
14 SU 0334 0.9 / 0924 0.1 / 1602 0.9 / 2131 0.2	**29** M 0418 0.9 / 1007 0.1 / 1654 0.9 / 2218 0.2
15 M 0412 0.9 / 1000 0.1 / 1642 0.9 / 2208 0.2	**30** TU 0502 0.8 / 1046 0.1 / 1739 0.8 / 2300 0.2
	31 W 0548 0.8 / 1125 0.2 / 1825 0.8 / 2344 0.2

JUNE

Time m	Time m
1 TH 0635 0.8 / 1210 0.2 / 1915 0.8	**16** F 0621 0.9 / 1207 0.2 / 1854 0.9
2 F 0035 0.3 / 0727 0.7 / 1304 0.3 / 2005 0.7	**17** SA 0031 0.2 / 0717 0.8 / 1306 0.2 / 1950 0.9
3 SA 0136 0.3 / 0821 0.7 / 1408 0.3 / ◑ 2057 0.7	**18** SU 0137 0.2 / 0819 0.8 / 1411 0.2 / ◑ 2050 0.9
4 SU 0243 0.3 / 0919 0.7 / 1514 0.3 / 2152 0.7	**19** M 0246 0.2 / 0925 0.8 / 1518 0.2 / 2153 0.8
5 M 0350 0.3 / 1022 0.7 / 1616 0.3 / 2247 0.7	**20** TU 0358 0.2 / 1036 0.8 / 1626 0.2 / 2259 0.8
6 TU 0452 0.3 / 1123 0.7 / 1711 0.3 / 2339 0.8	**21** W 0512 0.2 / 1144 0.8 / 1730 0.2 / 2359 0.9
7 W 0545 0.3 / 1213 0.7 / 1757 0.3	**22** TH 0615 0.2 / 1243 0.8 / 1826 0.2
8 TH 0024 0.8 / 0628 0.2 / 1257 0.8 / 1837 0.3	**23** F 0053 0.9 / 0707 0.1 / 1335 0.8 / 1914 0.2
9 F 0105 0.8 / 0708 0.2 / 1338 0.8 / 1915 0.2	**24** SA 0144 0.9 / 0753 0.1 / 1425 0.9 / 1959 0.2
10 SA 0147 0.9 / 0747 0.2 / 1419 0.9 / 1953 0.2	**25** SU 0233 0.9 / 0836 0.1 / 1512 0.9 / ● 2043 0.2
11 SU 0229 0.9 / 0826 0.1 / 1501 0.9 / ○ 2033 0.2	**26** M 0320 0.9 / 0917 0.1 / 1557 0.9 / 2125 0.2
12 M 0313 0.9 / 0906 0.1 / 1545 0.9 / 2115 0.2	**27** TU 0404 0.9 / 0955 0.1 / 1639 0.9 / 2205 0.2
13 TU 0358 0.9 / 0948 0.1 / 1629 0.9 / 2159 0.2	**28** W 0447 0.8 / 1031 0.1 / 1718 0.9 / 2245 0.2
14 W 0443 0.9 / 1031 0.1 / 1714 0.9 / 2245 0.2	**29** TH 0527 0.8 / 1106 0.2 / 1757 0.8 / 2324 0.2
15 TH 0530 0.9 / 1116 0.1 / 1801 0.9 / 2335 0.2	**30** F 0607 0.8 / 1142 0.2 / 1836 0.8

JULY

Time m	Time m
1 SA 0004 0.2 / 0648 0.8 / 1221 0.2 / 1915 0.8	**16** SU 0013 0.1 / 0658 0.9 / 1236 0.2 / 1923 1.0
2 SU 0048 0.3 / 0731 0.7 / 1304 0.3 / 1957 0.8	**17** M 0107 0.2 / 0754 0.9 / 1330 0.2 / ◑ 2018 0.9
3 M 0137 0.3 / 0818 0.7 / 1353 0.3 / ◔ 2042 0.7	**18** TU 0207 0.2 / 0854 0.8 / 1433 0.3 / 2117 0.9
4 TU 0232 0.3 / 0910 0.7 / 1451 0.3 / 2133 0.7	**19** W 0317 0.3 / 1003 0.8 / 1547 0.3 / 2225 0.8
5 W 0335 0.3 / 1011 0.7 / 1558 0.3 / 2232 0.7	**20** TH 0447 0.3 / 1121 0.8 / 1710 0.3 / 2337 0.8
6 TH 0447 0.3 / 1118 0.7 / 1707 0.3 / 2333 0.8	**21** F 0609 0.2 / 1232 0.8 / 1817 0.3
7 F 0552 0.3 / 1218 0.7 / 1804 0.3	**22** SA 0042 0.8 / 0704 0.2 / 1331 0.8 / 1909 0.2
8 SA 0028 0.8 / 0642 0.2 / 1310 0.8 / 1850 0.3	**23** SU 0138 0.8 / 0748 0.2 / 1421 0.8 / 1953 0.2
9 SU 0120 0.8 / 0727 0.2 / 1358 0.8 / 1935 0.2	**24** M 0227 0.9 / 0828 0.1 / 1505 0.9 / 2034 0.2
10 M 0210 0.9 / 0810 0.1 / 1444 0.9 / 2019 0.2	**25** TU 0311 0.9 / 0904 0.1 / 1543 0.9 / ● 2112 0.2
11 TU 0259 0.9 / 0853 0.1 / 1530 1.0 / ○ 2105 0.1	**26** W 0350 0.9 / 0937 0.1 / 1619 0.9 / 2148 0.1
12 W 0347 1.0 / 0937 0.1 / 1615 1.0 / 2151 0.1	**27** TH 0426 0.9 / 1009 0.1 / 1651 0.9 / 2222 0.1
13 TH 0433 1.0 / 1020 0.1 / 1700 1.0 / 2237 0.1	**28** F 0500 0.9 / 1039 0.1 / 1721 0.9 / 2256 0.2
14 F 0519 1.0 / 1103 0.1 / 1745 1.0 / 2324 0.1	**29** SA 0532 0.9 / 1108 0.2 / 1751 0.9 / 2328 0.2
15 SA 0607 0.9 / 1148 0.1 / 1832 1.0	**30** SU 0605 0.8 / 1137 0.2 / 1822 0.8
	31 M 0002 0.2 / 0639 0.8 / 1209 0.2 / 1855 0.8

AUGUST

Time m	Time m
1 TU 0039 0.2 / 0720 0.7 / 1244 0.3 / 1936 0.8	**16** W 0128 0.3 / 0825 0.8 / 1350 0.3 / ◑ 2043 0.8
2 W 0123 0.3 / 0809 0.7 / 1330 0.3 / ◔ 2026 0.7	**17** TH 0238 0.3 / 0935 0.8 / 1513 0.4 / 2154 0.8
3 TH 0222 0.3 / 0910 0.7 / 1439 0.4 / 2128 0.7	**18** F 0436 0.4 / 1107 0.7 / 1703 0.4 / 2325 0.8
4 F 0348 0.3 / 1026 0.7 / 1619 0.4 / 2245 0.7	**19** SA 0609 0.3 / 1230 0.8 / 1816 0.3
5 SA 0525 0.3 / 1146 0.7 / 1742 0.3	**20** SU 0042 0.8 / 0659 0.3 / 1328 0.8 / 1903 0.3
6 SU 0002 0.8 / 0626 0.2 / 1250 0.8 / 1837 0.3	**21** M 0136 0.8 / 0736 0.2 / 1411 0.9 / 1941 0.2
7 M 0103 0.8 / 0713 0.2 / 1341 0.9 / 1923 0.2	**22** TU 0218 0.9 / 0809 0.2 / 1447 0.9 / 2016 0.2
8 TU 0156 0.9 / 0756 0.1 / 1428 1.0 / 2008 0.1	**23** W 0254 0.9 / 0839 0.2 / 1520 0.9 / ● 2050 0.2
9 W 0246 1.0 / 0838 0.1 / 1513 1.0 / ○ 2053 0.1	**24** TH 0327 0.9 / 0909 0.1 / 1549 1.0 / 2122 0.1
10 TH 0332 1.0 / 0920 0.0 / 1557 1.1 / 2138 0.0	**25** F 0358 0.9 / 0938 0.1 / 1616 1.0 / 2153 0.1
11 F 0418 1.1 / 1001 0.0 / 1640 1.1 / 2222 0.0	**26** SA 0427 0.9 / 1005 0.1 / 1642 1.0 / 2223 0.1
12 SA 0502 1.1 / 1041 0.0 / 1723 1.1 / 2305 0.1	**27** SU 0455 0.9 / 1032 0.2 / 1708 0.9 / 2252 0.2
13 SU 0547 1.0 / 1122 0.1 / 1807 1.1 / 2348 0.1	**28** M 0524 0.9 / 1058 0.2 / 1736 0.9 / 2321 0.2
14 M 0635 1.0 / 1204 0.1 / 1854 1.0	**29** TU 0555 0.9 / 1126 0.2 / 1807 0.9 / 2352 0.2
15 TU 0035 0.2 / 0726 0.9 / 1252 0.2 / 1944 0.9	**30** W 0634 0.8 / 1156 0.3 / 1845 0.8
	31 TH 0030 0.3 / 0723 0.8 / 1236 0.4 / ◔ 1935 0.8

Chart Datum: 0·25 metres below Alicante Datum (Mean Sea Level, Alicante)

TIME ZONE -0100
(Gibraltar Standard Time)
Subtract 1 hour for UT
For Gibraltar Summer Time add
ONE hour in **non-shaded areas**

GIBRALTAR

2006

LAT 36°08'N   LONG 5°21'W

TIMES AND HEIGHTS OF HIGH AND LOW WATERS

SEPTEMBER

Day	Time m	Time m	Time m	Time m	Day	Time m	Time m	Time m	Time m
1 F	0125 0.3	0827 0.7	1341 0.4	2042 0.7	**16** SA	0426 0.4	1051 0.7	1656 0.4	2318 0.7
2 SA	0308 0.4	0947 0.7	1551 0.4	2210 0.7	**17** SU	0555 0.4	1218 0.8	1803 0.4	
3 SU	0510 0.3	1121 0.7	1729 0.4	2344 0.8	**18** M	0035 0.8	0637 0.3	1308 0.9	1843 0.3
4 M	0612 0.3	1231 0.8	1824 0.3		**19** TU	0121 0.8	0709 0.3	1345 0.9	1916 0.3
5 TU	0050 0.9	0656 0.2	1323 0.9	1909 0.2	**20** W	0156 0.9	0738 0.2	1416 1.0	1948 0.2
6 W	0142 0.9	0736 0.1	1408 1.0	1952 0.2	**21** TH	0227 0.9	0806 0.2	1445 1.0	2019 0.2
7 TH	0228 1.0	0816 0.1	1451 1.1	O 2035 0.1	**22** F	0256 0.9	0834 0.2	1512 1.0	2050 0.1
8 F	0313 1.1	0856 0.0	1534 1.2	2118 0.0	**23** SA	0324 1.0	0903 0.2	1538 1.0	2120 0.1
9 SA	0357 1.1	0936 0.0	1615 1.2	2159 0.0	**24** SU	0352 1.0	0930 0.2	1605 1.0	2150 0.1
10 SU	0439 1.1	1014 0.0	1657 1.1	2239 0.0	**25** M	0420 1.0	0957 0.2	1632 1.0	2218 0.2
11 M	0523 1.1	1053 0.1	1739 1.1	2319 0.1	**26** TU	0450 1.0	1024 0.2	1701 1.0	2247 0.2
12 TU	0608 1.0	1132 0.2	1823 1.0		**27** W	0523 0.9	1053 0.3	1733 0.9	2318 0.3
13 W	0001 0.2	0658 0.9	1216 0.3	1912 0.9	**28** TH	0602 0.9	1125 0.3	1812 0.9	2354 0.3
14 TH	0049 0.3	0756 0.8	1312 0.4	◑ 2011 0.8	**29** F	0653 0.8	1205 0.4	1905 0.8	
15 F	0200 0.4	0910 0.8	1446 0.5	2129 0.7	**30** SA	0048 0.4	0759 0.8	1316 0.4	◐ 2016 0.8

OCTOBER

Day	Time m	Time m	Time m	Time m	Day	Time m	Time m	Time m	Time m
1 SU	0252 0.4	0921 0.7	1539 0.4	2148 0.7	**16** M	0511 0.4	1139 0.8	1727 0.4	
2 M	0450 0.4	1056 0.8	1710 0.4	2328 0.8	**17** TU	0005 0.8	0557 0.4	1230 0.9	1808 0.3
3 TU	0548 0.3	1207 0.9	1804 0.3		**18** W	0049 0.8	0630 0.3	1306 0.9	1842 0.3
4 W	0032 0.9	0632 0.2	1258 1.0	1848 0.2	**19** TH	0123 0.9	0701 0.3	1337 1.0	1914 0.2
5 TH	0121 1.0	0711 0.1	1342 1.1	1930 0.1	**20** F	0153 0.9	0730 0.2	1405 1.0	1946 0.2
6 F	0206 1.0	0750 0.1	1424 1.1	2011 0.0	**21** SA	0222 1.0	0800 0.2	1434 1.0	2011 0.0
7 SA	0249 1.1	0828 0.1	1506 1.2	O 2052 0.0	**22** SU	0251 1.0	0829 0.2	1503 1.0	● 2049 0.2
8 SU	0332 1.1	0907 0.1	1548 1.2	2133 0.0	**23** M	0320 1.0	0858 0.2	1533 1.0	2120 0.2
9 M	0414 1.1	0946 0.1	1630 1.1	2212 0.1	**24** TU	0351 1.0	0928 0.2	1604 1.0	2151 0.2
10 TU	0457 1.0	1025 0.1	1712 1.1	2251 0.2	**25** W	0425 1.0	0958 0.3	1637 1.0	2222 0.2
11 W	0542 1.0	1104 0.2	1756 1.0	2330 0.2	**26** TH	0501 0.9	1030 0.3	1713 0.9	2255 0.3
12 TH	0631 0.9	1148 0.3	1846 0.9		**27** F	0543 0.9	1107 0.3	1756 0.9	2335 0.3
13 F	0016 0.3	0730 0.8	1245 0.4	1946 0.8	**28** SA	0635 0.8	1154 0.4	1851 0.8	
14 SA	0125 0.3	0843 0.8	1423 0.5	◑ 2103 0.7	**29** SU	0034 0.4	0739 0.8	1315 0.4	● 2001 0.8
15 SU	0340 0.5	1016 0.8	1621 0.5	2247 0.7	**30** M	0233 0.4	0857 0.8	1515 0.4	2128 0.8
					31 TU	0413 0.4	1023 0.8	1638 0.3	2300 0.8

NOVEMBER

Day	Time m	Time m	Time m	Time m	Day	Time m	Time m	Time m	Time m
1 W	0514 0.3	1134 0.9	1735 0.3		**16** TH	0002 0.8	0547 0.3	1219 0.9	1804 0.3
2 TH	0006 0.9	0601 0.2	1227 1.0	1822 0.2	**17** F	0043 0.8	0624 0.3	1254 0.9	1841 0.2
3 F	0056 1.0	0643 0.2	1313 1.0	1905 0.1	**18** SA	0117 0.9	0657 0.3	1327 0.9	1916 0.2
4 SA	0141 1.0	0723 0.1	1356 1.1	1947 0.1	**19** SU	0149 0.9	0729 0.2	1400 1.0	1950 0.2
5 SU	0225 1.0	0802 0.1	1439 1.1	O 2029 0.0	**20** M	0222 0.9	0801 0.2	1433 1.0	● 2023 0.2
6 M	0308 1.1	0842 0.1	1523 1.1	2110 0.1	**21** TU	0256 1.0	0833 0.2	1509 1.0	2058 0.2
7 TU	0352 1.0	0923 0.1	1606 1.1	2150 0.1	**22** W	0332 1.0	0906 0.2	1546 1.0	2132 0.2
8 W	0436 1.0	1003 0.2	1650 1.0	2230 0.2	**23** TH	0409 1.0	0941 0.2	1624 0.9	2208 0.2
9 TH	0521 0.9	1045 0.2	1736 0.9	2310 0.2	**24** F	0449 0.9	1019 0.3	1706 0.9	2247 0.2
10 F	0610 0.9	1131 0.3	1826 0.8	2356 0.3	**25** SA	0533 0.9	1103 0.3	1751 0.9	2332 0.3
11 SA	0706 0.9	1229 0.4	1924 0.8		**26** SU	0624 0.9	1156 0.3	1845 0.8	
12 SU	0059 0.4	0812 0.8	1351 0.4	● 2031 0.7	**27** M	0031 0.3	0723 0.8	1311 0.4	1948 0.8
13 M	0235 0.4	0924 0.8	1521 0.4	2148 0.7	**28** TU	0156 0.3	0831 0.8	1439 0.3	◑ 2101 0.8
14 TU	0402 0.4	1037 0.8	1631 0.4	2306 0.7	**29** W	0321 0.3	0944 0.8	1556 0.3	2221 0.8
15 W	0502 0.4	1135 0.8	1723 0.4		**30** TH	0430 0.3	1055 0.9	1701 0.2	2333 0.8

DECEMBER

Day	Time m	Time m	Time m	Time m	Day	Time m	Time m	Time m	Time m
1 F	0528 0.2	1155 0.9	1757 0.2		**16** SA	0546 0.3	1210 0.8	1811 0.3	
2 SA	0030 0.9	0617 0.2	1246 1.0	1846 0.1	**17** SU	0041 0.8	0628 0.3	1253 0.8	1852 0.2
3 SU	0120 0.9	0702 0.1	1333 1.0	1931 0.1	**18** M	0122 0.8	0705 0.3	1333 0.9	1930 0.2
4 M	0207 1.0	0745 0.1	1419 1.0	2015 0.1	**19** TU	0201 0.9	0741 0.2	1413 0.9	2008 0.2
5 TU	0253 1.0	0828 0.1	1506 1.0	O 2058 0.1	**20** W	0241 0.9	0817 0.2	1455 0.9	● 2046 0.1
6 W	0339 1.0	0910 0.1	1552 1.0	2140 0.1	**21** TH	0321 0.9	0855 0.2	1537 0.9	2125 0.1
7 TH	0423 0.9	0953 0.2	1638 0.9	2220 0.1	**22** F	0401 0.9	0935 0.2	1619 0.9	2204 0.1
8 F	0508 0.9	1036 0.2	1723 0.9	2300 0.1	**23** SA	0443 1.0	1018 0.2	1703 0.9	2245 0.1
9 SA	0553 0.9	1121 0.2	1810 0.8	2343 0.2	**24** SU	0526 0.9	1103 0.2	1748 0.9	2330 0.2
10 SU	0642 0.8	1211 0.3	1900 0.8		**25** M	0613 0.9	1154 0.2	1837 0.9	
11 M	0031 0.3	0734 0.8	1311 0.3	1952 0.7	**26** TU	0020 0.2	0705 0.9	1254 0.2	1932 0.8
12 TU	0132 0.3	0829 0.8	1417 0.3	◑ 2048 0.7	**27** W	0120 0.2	0804 0.9	1401 0.2	◑ 2034 0.8
13 W	0241 0.4	0926 0.7	1523 0.3	2149 0.7	**28** TH	0229 0.3	0908 0.8	1513 0.2	2143 0.8
14 TH	0351 0.4	1026 0.8	1627 0.3	2256 0.7	**29** F	0343 0.3	1017 0.8	1629 0.2	2300 0.8
15 F	0455 0.3	1122 0.8	1724 0.3	2355 0.7	**30** SA	0458 0.2	1126 0.8	1741 0.2	
					31 SU	0011 0.8	0601 0.2	1227 0.9	1840 0.1

Chart Datum: 0·25 metres below Alicante Datum (Mean Sea Level, Alicante)

TIDES

INDEX